microsoft® office 2007 brief

A Professional Approach

microsoft® office 2007 brief

A Professional Approach

OFFICE 2007

Deborah Hinkle
Kathleen Stewart
Pat R. Graves
Amie Mayhall
Jon Juarez
John Carter

Higher Education

Boston Burr Ridge, IL Dubuque, IA New York San Francisco St. Louis
Bangkok Bogotá Caracas Kuala Lumpur Lisbon London Madrid Mexico City
Milan Montreal New Delhi Santiago Seoul Singapore Sydney Taipei Toronto

MICROSOFT OFFICE 2007 BRIEF: A PROFESSIONAL APPROACH
Published by McGraw-Hill, a business unit of The McGraw-Hill Companies, Inc., 1221 Avenue of the Americas, New York, NY, 10020.

Some ancillaries, including electronic and print components, may not be available to customers outside the United States.

This book is printed on acid-free paper.

1 2 3 4 5 6 7 8 9 0 QPD/QPD 0 9

ISBN 978-0-07-351926-5 (student edition)
MHID 0-07-351926-X (student edition)
ISBN 978-0-07-729185-3 (sample entity)
MHID 0-07-729185-9 (sample entity)

Vice president/Editor in chief: *Elizabeth Haefele*
Vice president/Director of marketing: *John E. Biernat*
Senior sponsoring editor: *Scott Davidson*
Editorial coordinator: *Alan Palmer*
Marketing manager: *Tiffany Wendt*
Lead media producer: *Damian Moshak*
Director, Editing/Design/Production: *Jess Ann Kosic*
Lead project manager: *Rick Hecker*
Senior production supervisor: *Janean A. Utley*
Designer: *Marianna Kinigakis*
Media developmental editor: *William Mulford*
Media project manager: *Mark A. S. Dierker*
Designer: *Marianna Kinigakis*
Typeface: *10.5/13 New Astor*
Compositor: *Aptara, Inc.*
Printer: *Quebecor World Dubuque Inc.*

Library of Congress Cataloging-in-Publication Data

Microsoft Office brief 2007 : a professional approach : Office 2007 / Deborah Hinkle . . . [et al.].
p. cm.
Includes index.
ISBN-13: 978-0-07-351926-5 (student edition : alk. paper)
ISBN-10: 0-07-351926-X (student edition : alk. paper)
ISBN-13: 978-0-07-729185-3 (annotated instructor edition : alk. paper)
ISBN-10: 0-07-729185-9 (annotated instructor edition : alk. paper)
1. Microsoft Office. 2. Business—Computer programs. I. Hinkle, Deborah A.
HF5548.4.M525M524998 2010
005.5—dc22

2008044937

The Internet addresses listed in the text were accurate at the time of publication. The inclusion of a Web site does not indicate an endorsement by the authors or McGraw-Hill, and McGraw-Hill does not guarantee the accuracy of the information presented at these sites.

www.mhhe.com

contents

WORD

Unit 1 *Basic Skills*

Unit 2 *Paragraph Formatting, Tabs, and Advanced Editing*

Unit 3 *Page Formatting*

EXCEL

Unit 1 *Introduction to Excel*

Unit 2 *Working with Formulas and Functions*

Unit 3 *Enhancing Worksheet Appearance*

POWERPOINT

Unit 1 Basic Skills

Unit 2 Presentation Illustration

ACCESS

Unit 1 Understanding Access Databases

Unit 2 Designing and Managing Database Objects

preface

Microsoft Office 2007 Brief: A Professional Approach is written to help you master Microsoft Office. The text takes you step by step through the Office features that you are likely to use in both your personal and business life. In this brief edition, the lesson review materials have been relocated to the Professional Approach Web site in an effort to conserve paper and create a more streamlined text. You can find a full list of these online review materials below.

Case Studies

Learning the features of each application is one component of the text, and applying what you learn is another component. A case study was created for each application to offer the opportunity to learn in a realistic business context. Take the time to read the case studies. All the documents for this course relate to one of the case studies.

Organization of the Text

The text includes ten units, and each unit is divided into lessons. There are thirty-seven lessons, each self-contained but building on previously learned procedures. This building-block approach, together with the case studies and the following features, enables you to maximize the learning process.

Features of the Text

- Objectives are listed for each lesson.
- The estimated time required to complete each lesson up to the Lesson Summary section is stated.
- Within a lesson, each heading corresponds to an objective.
- Easy-to-follow exercises emphasize learning by doing.
- Key terms are italicized and defined as they are encountered.
- Extensive graphics display screen contents.
- Ribbon commands and keyboard keys are shown in the text when used.
- Large buttons in the margins provide easy-to-see references.
- Lessons contain important notes, useful tips, and helpful reviews.
- The Lesson Summary reviews the important concepts taught in the lesson.
- The Command Summary lists the commands taught in the lesson.

Professional Approach Web Site

Visit the Professional Approach Web site at www.mhhe.com/pas07brief to access a wealth of additional materials, including:

- Concept Reviews
- True/False Questions
- Short Answer Questions
- Critical Thinking Questions
- Skill Reviews

- Lesson Applications
- On Your Own Exercises
- Unit Applications
- Excel Lessons 10 and 11
- Appendices
- Glossary

Conventions Used in the Text

This text uses a number of conventions to help you learn the program and save your work.

- Text to be keyed appears either in red or as a separate figure.
- Filenames appear in **boldface**.
- Options that you choose from tabs and dialog boxes, but that aren't buttons, appear in green; for example, "Choose Print from the Office menu."
- You're asked to save each document with your initials followed by the exercise name. For example, an exercise might end with this instruction: "Save the document as ***[your initials]*****5-12**." Documents are saved in folders for each lesson.

Screen Differences

As you practice each concept, illustrations of the screens help you follow the instructions. Don't worry if your screen is different from the illustration. These differences are due to variations in system and computer configurations.

microsoft® office word® brief

A Professional Approach

WORD 2007

Deborah Hinkle

There is more to learning a word processing program like Microsoft Word than simply pressing keys. You need to know how to use Word in a real-world situation. That is why all the lessons in this book relate to everyday business tasks.

As you work through the lessons, imagine yourself working as an intern for Campbell's Confections, a fictional candy store and chocolate factory located in Grove City, Pennsylvania.

Campbell's Confections

It was 1950. Harry Truman was president. Shopping malls and supermarkets were appearing in suburban areas. And Campbell's Confections began doing business.

Based in Grove City, Pennsylvania, Campbell's Confections started as a small family-owned business. Originally, Campbell's Confections was a candy store, with a few display cases in the front of the building and a kitchen in the back to create chocolates and to try new recipes. The store was an immediate success, and word traveled quickly about the rich, smooth, creamy chocolates made by Campbell's Confections. Today, the store includes several display cases for chocolates and hard candies and special displays for greeting cards and gifts. The factory is located in a separate building on Monroe Street and offers tours for visitors.

Within a few years of opening the first store, the company expanded, and Campbell's Confections opened candy stores in Mercer, New Castle, and

Meadville. Today there are 24 stores in three states—Pennsylvania, Ohio, and West Virginia.

The goal of Campbell's Confections is to offer "quality chocolate," and the company has grown from selling chocolate in retail stores exclusively to adding wholesale and fund-raising divisions. E-commerce has been the latest venture with Internet sales increasing monthly.

Currently, Thomas Campbell is the president-owner, and Lynn Tanguay is the vice president.

To understand the organization of Campbell's Confections, take a look at Figure CS-1. Notice each of the specialty areas and management divisions.

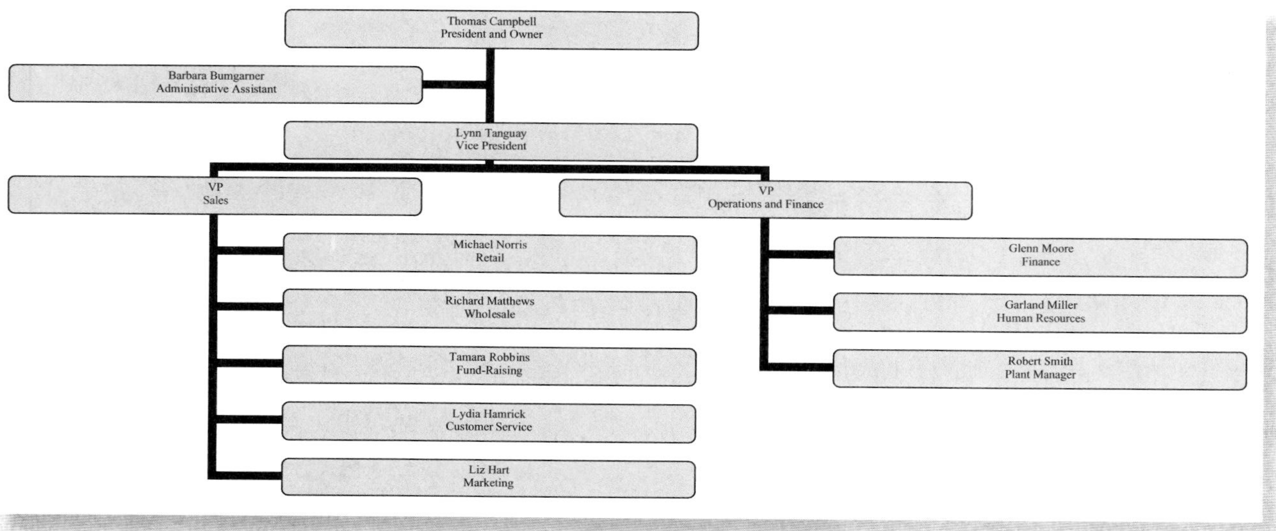

All the documents you will use in this text relate to Campbell's Confections. As you work through the documents in the text, take the time to notice the following:

- How the employees interact and how they respond to customers' queries.
- The format and tone of the business correspondence.
- References to The Gregg Reference Manual, a standard reference manual for business writing and correspondence.
- The content of the correspondence (and its relation to Campbell's Confections).

As you use this text and become experienced with Microsoft Word, you will also gain experience in creating, editing, and formatting the type of documents that are generated in a real-life business environment.

unit 1

BASIC SKILLS

Lesson 1

Creating a Document

OBJECTIVES

After completing this lesson, you will be able to:

1. Start Word.
2. Identify parts of the Word Screen.
3. Key text into a document.
4. Edit text.
5. Name and save a document.
6. Print a document.
7. Close a document and exit Word.

MCAS OBJECTIVES

In this lesson:
WW 07 6.1.1

Estimated Time: 1 hour

Microsoft Word is a versatile, easy-to-use word processing program that helps you create letters, memos, reports, and other types of documents. This lesson begins with an overview of the Word screen. Then you learn how to create, edit, name, save, print, and close a document.

Starting Word

There are several ways to start Word, depending on your system setup and personal preferences. For example, you can use the Start button on the Windows taskbar or double-click a Word shortcut icon that might be on your desktop.

NOTE

Windows provides many ways to start applications. If you have problems, ask your instructor for help.

Figure 1-1
Starting Word from the Windows taskbar

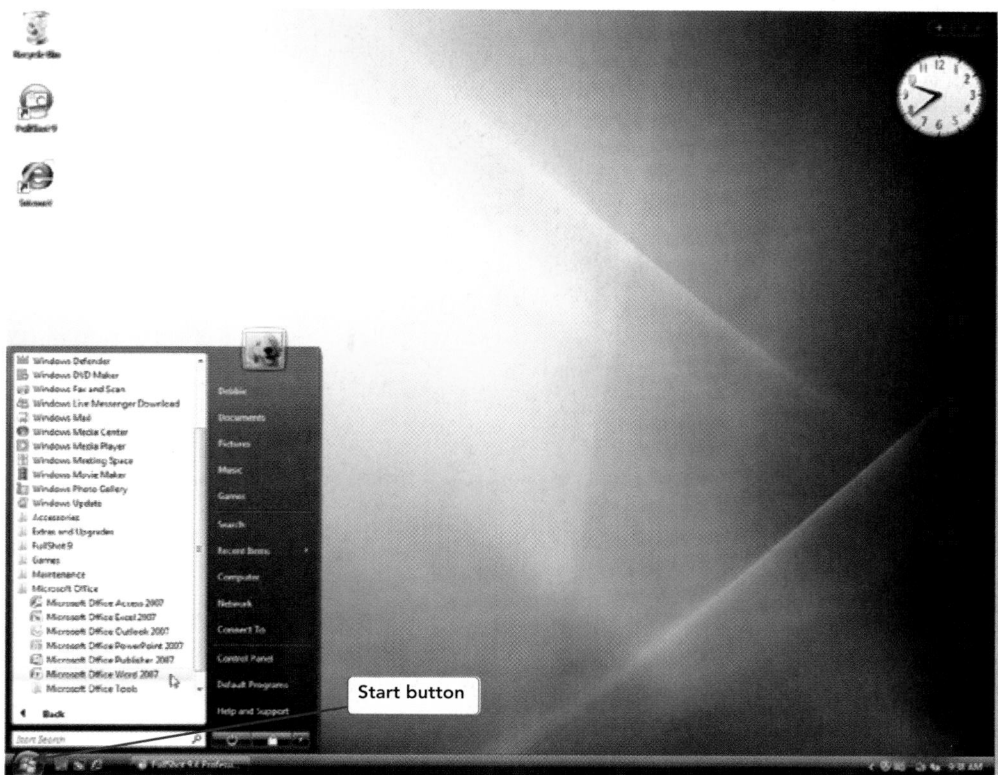

NOTE

Your screen will differ from the screen shown in Figure 1-1 depending on the programs installed on your computer.

Exercise 1-1 START WORD

1. Turn on your computer. Windows loads.
2. Click the Start button on the Windows taskbar and point to **All Programs**.

3. On the All Programs menu, click **Microsoft Office**, and then click **Microsoft Office Word 2007**. In a few seconds, the program is loaded and the Word screen appears.

NOTE

The document displays in Print Layout view. The Print Layout button appears in the lower right corner of your screen.

Figure 1-2
Word screen

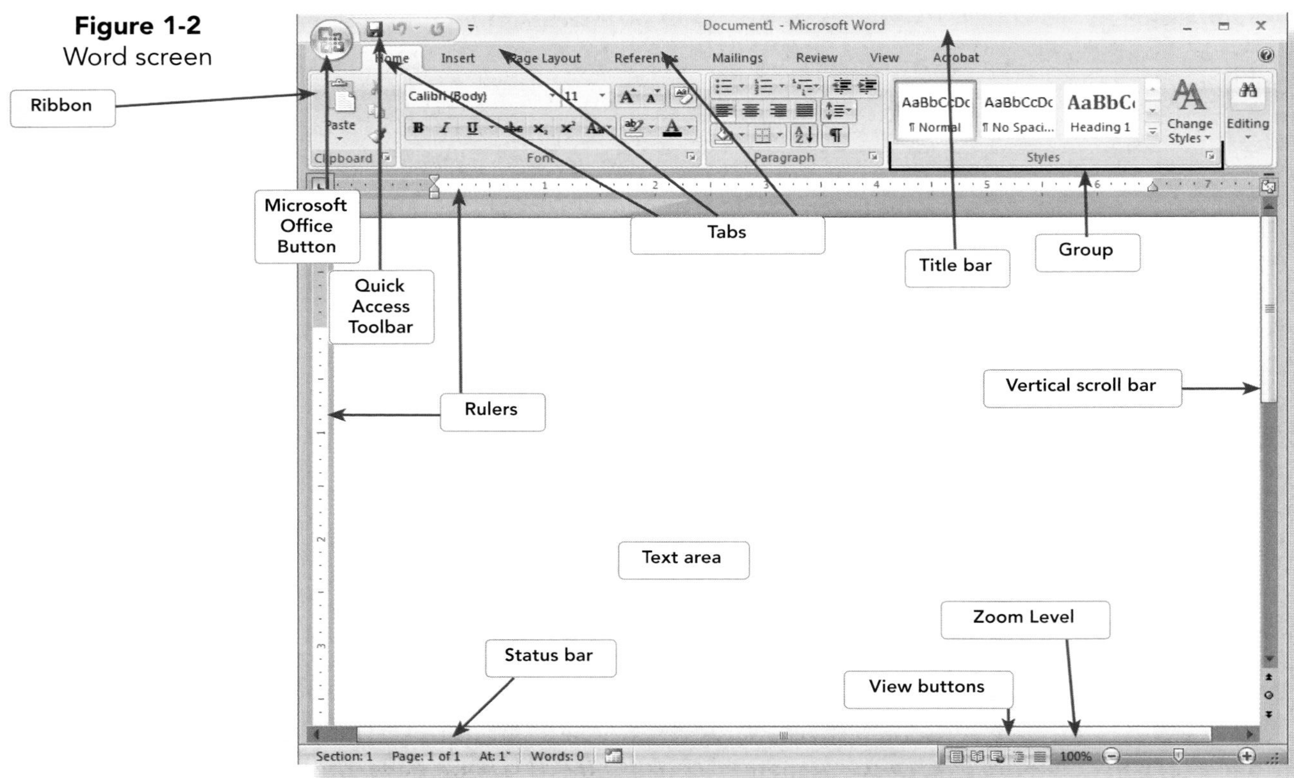

TABLE 1-1 Parts of the Word Screen

Part of Screen	Purpose
Microsoft Office Button	Displays the File menu, recently opened documents, and a command button to access Word Options.
Quick Access Toolbar	Displays icons for save, undo, and repeat. The Quick Access Toolbar can be customized, and the Quick Access Toolbar commands are available for all tabs on the Ribbon.
Title bar	Displays the name of the current document. The opening Word screen is always named "Document1."
Ribbon	Displays contextual tabs. Tabs contain groups of related commands. Commands can be buttons, menus, or drop-down list boxes.
Ruler	Shows placement of margins, indents, and tabs. The horizontal and vertical rulers display in Print Layout view.
Text area	Displays the text and graphics in the document.
Scroll bars	Used with the mouse to move right or left and up or down within a document.
Status bar	Displays the page number and page count of the document, the document view buttons, and the zoom control. It also displays the current mode of operation. The status bar can be customized.

Identifying Parts of the Word Screen

To become familiar with Word, start by identifying the parts of the screen you will work with extensively, such as the Microsoft Office Button, the Quick Access Toolbar, and the Ribbon. As you practice using Word commands, you will see *ScreenTips* to help you identify screen elements such as buttons and commands.

Exercise 1-2 IDENTIFY THE MICROSOFT OFFICE BUTTON AND THE QUICK ACCESS TOOLBAR

The *Microsoft Office Button* displays the File menu which lists the commands to create, open, save, and print a document. Recently opened documents also appear when the File menu displays. The *Quick Access Toolbar* contains frequently used commands and is positioned to the right of the Microsoft Office Button and above the Ribbon by default. The commands on the Quick Access Toolbar are available for all tabs in the Ribbon.

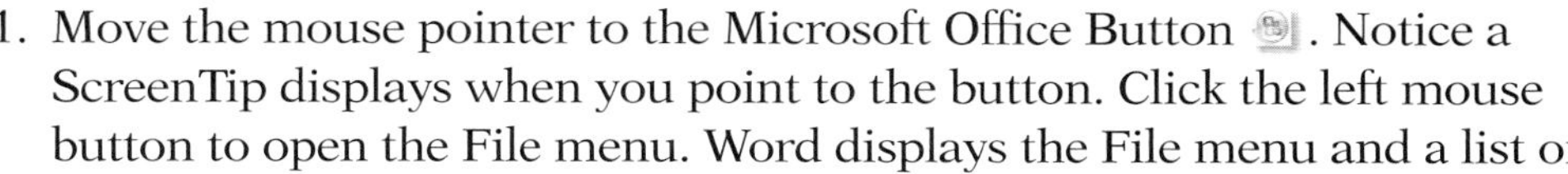

1. Move the mouse pointer to the Microsoft Office Button. Notice a ScreenTip displays when you point to the button. Click the left mouse button to open the File menu. Word displays the File menu and a list of documents recently opened. The Word default setting is to show up to 17 documents in Recent Documents.

NOTE

You can also close the File menu by pressing Esc or click the Microsoft Office Button.

2. Click the text area to close the File menu.
3. Move the mouse pointer to the right of the Microsoft Office Button and point to the **Save** button. A ScreenTip and a keyboard shortcut to save a document display.

4. Point to the commands to the right of the Save command. Notice each command includes descriptive text and a keyboard shortcut. The Save, Undo, and Repeat commands are located in the Quick Access Toolbar by default. The Quick Access Toolbar contains commands you will use frequently and displays for each tab on the Ribbon.

TIP

Commands may appear in more than one location. For example, you can save a document by choosing **Save** from the File menu, by clicking the **Save** command on the Quick Access Toolbar, or by pressing Ctrl+S.

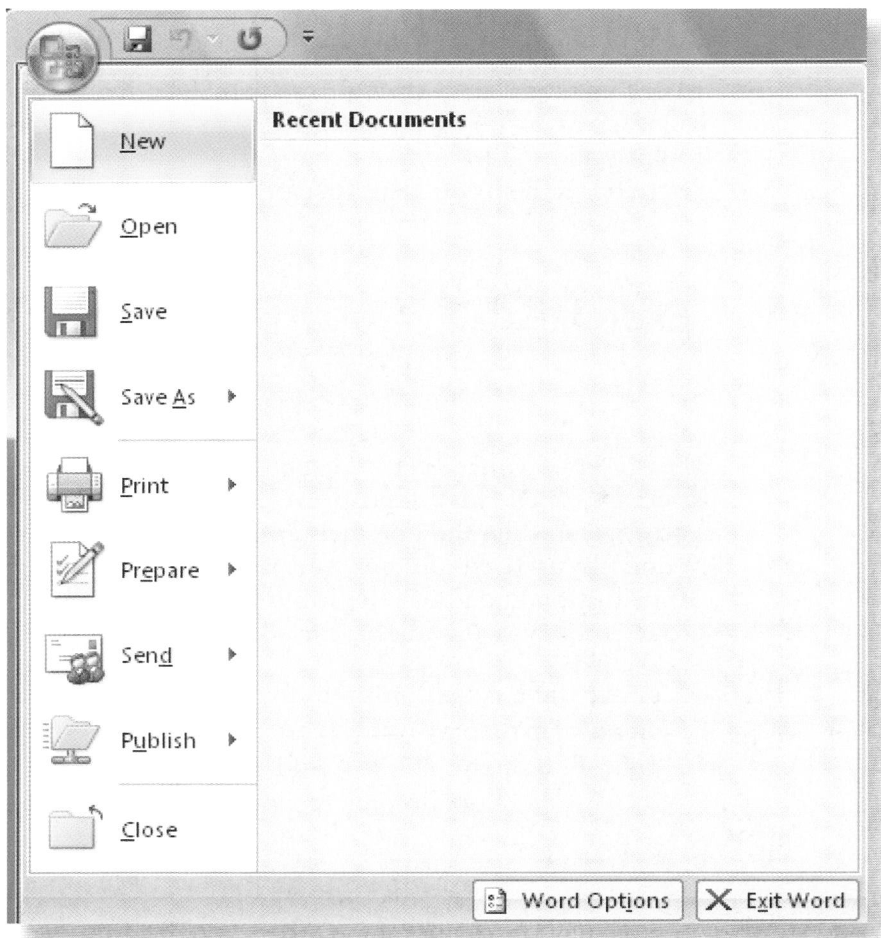

Figure 1-3 Displaying Microsoft Office Button commands

Exercise 1-3 IDENTIFY RIBBON COMMANDS

When you start Word, the Ribbon appears with the Home tab selected. The Ribbon consists of seven tabs by default. Each tab contains a group of related commands, and the number of commands for each tab varies. A command can be one of several formats. The most popular formats include buttons and drop-down lists. You can access Ribbon commands by using the mouse or Access Keys. Access Keys display badges or Key Tips. *Key Tips* are lettered or numbered squares that access or execute commands.

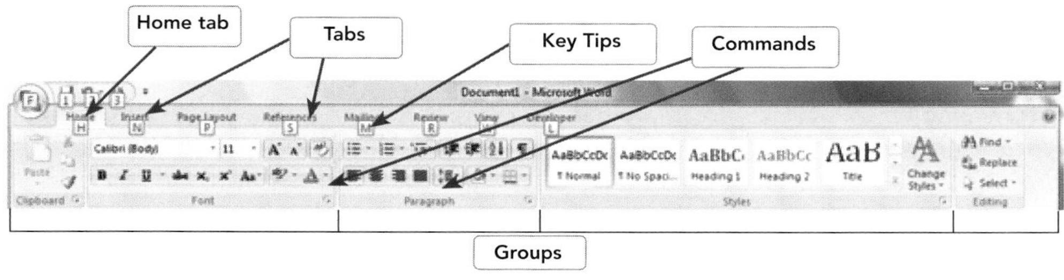

Figure 1-4 Ribbon

1. Move the mouse pointer to the **Insert** tab on the Ribbon and click **Insert**. Notice the change in the number and types of groups displayed. When you point to a Ribbon tab, the name of the tab is highlighted but not active. Click the Ribbon tab to display the commands.
2. Click the **Page Layout** tab. There are five groups of commands on the Page Layout tab.

Figure 1-5
Displaying the Page Layout tab

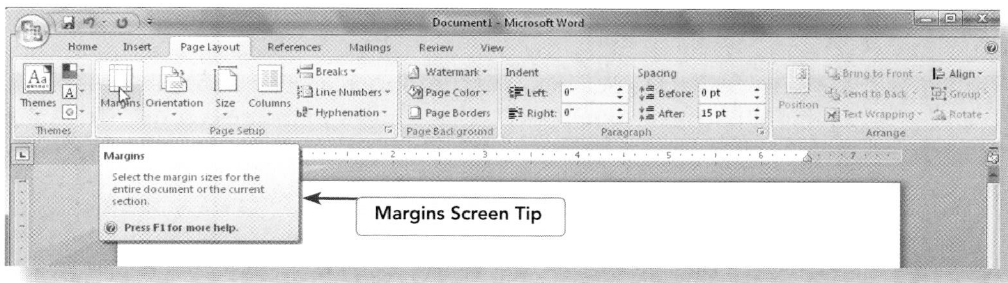

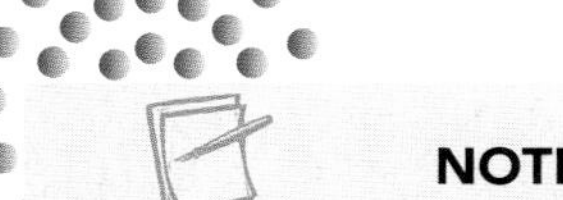

NOTE

Any Ribbon command with a light gray icon is currently not available. However, you can still identify the button by pointing to it with the mouse.

3. Click the **Page Layout** tab if necessary, and point to the **Margins** command. Read the ScreenTip.
4. Click the **Home** tab. Notice the groups and buttons available for formatting and editing.
5. Double-click the **Home** tab. The Ribbon is minimized.
6. Double-click the **Home** tab to restore the Ribbon.
7. Press the Alt key. Small lettered or numbered squares, called badges, appear on the Microsoft Office Button, Quick Access Toolbar, and Ribbon. The letters and numbers represent Key Tips and are used to execute a command.
8. Press the letter P on the keyboard to select the **Page Layout** tab.
9. Press the letter M on the keyboard to display the **Margins** gallery. Press Esc to close the gallery.

TIP

The keyboard shortcut to minimize the Ribbon is Ctrl+F1. To restore the Ribbon, press Ctrl+F1.

NOTE

The Quick Access Toolbar Key Tips are executed immediately.

TABLE 1-2 Ribbon Access Keys

Keystroke	Purpose
Alt	Select the active tab of the Ribbon and display badges for Key Tips. Press Alt a second time to cancel the access keys.
Alt, ← or →	Select the active tab of the Ribbon and move to the next or previous tab.
Alt, ↓ or ↑	Select the active tab of the Ribbon and move to the next or previous item on the Ribbon.
Alt, Tab	Select the active tab of the Ribbon and move to the first command of the first group. Each time you press Tab you move to the next command of the group. When you reach the last command of the group, press Tab to move to the next group of commands.
Alt, Shift+Tab	Rotate through Ribbon commands in the reverse direction.
Alt, Alt	Display Key Tips if they disappear.

Exercise 1-4 IDENTIFY COMMANDS

Use the Ribbon to locate and execute commands to format and edit your document. Commands also control the appearance of the Word screen.

1. Activate the **Home** tab.
2. Locate the Paragraph group and click the Show/Hide ¶ button ¶. This button is used to show or hide formatting marks on the screen. You can see special formatting for spaces, paragraph marks, and tab characters. The command toggles between show and hide.

NOTE

Drag the slider to the right to zoom in, and drag the slider to the left to zoom out. You can also use Ctrl+the wheel on your mouse to zoom in and zoom out. The View tab on the Ribbon contains Zoom commands.

3. Locate the vertical scroll bar and click the View Ruler button. Notice the rulers disappear from the Word screen. Click the View Ruler button again to display the rulers.
4. Locate the Zoom button on the status bar.

5. Click the Zoom button and click **200%**. Click **OK**. The text area is magnified, and you see a portion of the page.

6. Point to and drag the Zoom slider to 100%. The document returns to normal display.

Keying Text

When keying text, you will notice various shapes and symbols in the text area. For example:

- The *insertion point* is the vertical blinking line that marks the position of the next character to be entered.

- The mouse pointer takes the shape of an *I-beam* when it is in the text area. It changes into an arrow when you point to a command on the Quick Access Toolbar or the Ribbon.

- The *paragraph mark* ¶ indicates the end of a paragraph. The paragraph mark displays when Show/Hide ¶ is selected.

Exercise 1-5 KEY TEXT AND MOVE THE INSERTION POINT

1. Before you begin, make sure the Show/Hide ¶ button on the Home tab Paragraph group is selected. When this feature is "turned on," you can see paragraph marks and spacing between words and sentences more easily.
2. Key the words **Campbell's Confections** (don't worry about keying mistakes now—you can correct them later). Notice how the insertion point and paragraph mark move as you key text. Notice also how a space between words is indicated by a dot.

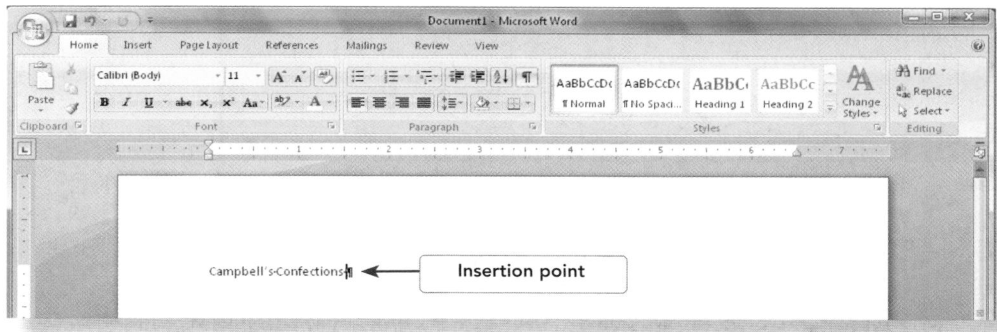

Figure 1-6 The insertion point marks the place where you begin keying.

NOTE

The documents you create in this course relate to the case study about Campbell's Confections, a fictional candy store and chocolate factory (see the Case Study in the frontmatter).

3. Move the insertion point to the left of the word "Campbell's" by positioning the I-beam and clicking the left mouse button.
4. Move the insertion point back to the right of "Confections" to continue keying.

Exercise 1-6 WRAP TEXT AND CORRECT SPELLING

As you key more text, you will notice Word performs several tasks automatically. For example, Word does the following by default:

- Wraps text from the end of one line to the beginning of the next line.
- Alerts you to spelling and grammatical errors.

- Corrects common misspellings, such as “teh” for “the” and “adn” for “and.”
- Suggests the completed word when you key the current date, day, or month.

TIP

The Proofing Errors icon at the left side of the status bar displays an “x” instead of a checkmark when it detects an error. When the error is corrected, the “x” is replaced with a checkmark.

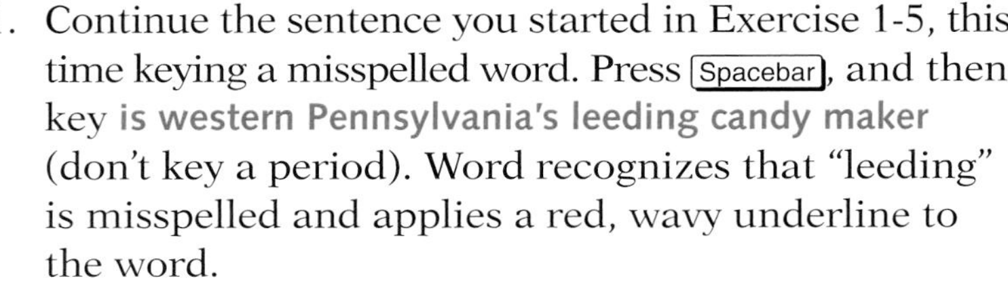

1. Continue the sentence you started in Exercise 1-5, this time keying a misspelled word. Press Spacebar, and then key **is western Pennsylvania’s leeding candy maker** (don’t key a period). Word recognizes that “leeding” is misspelled and applies a red, wavy underline to the word.

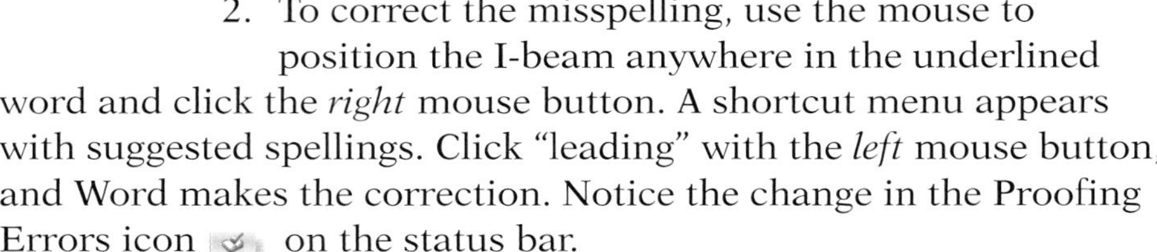

2. To correct the misspelling, use the mouse to position the I-beam anywhere in the underlined word and click the *right* mouse button. A shortcut menu appears with suggested spellings. Click “leading” with the *left* mouse button, and Word makes the correction. Notice the change in the Proofing Errors icon on the status bar.

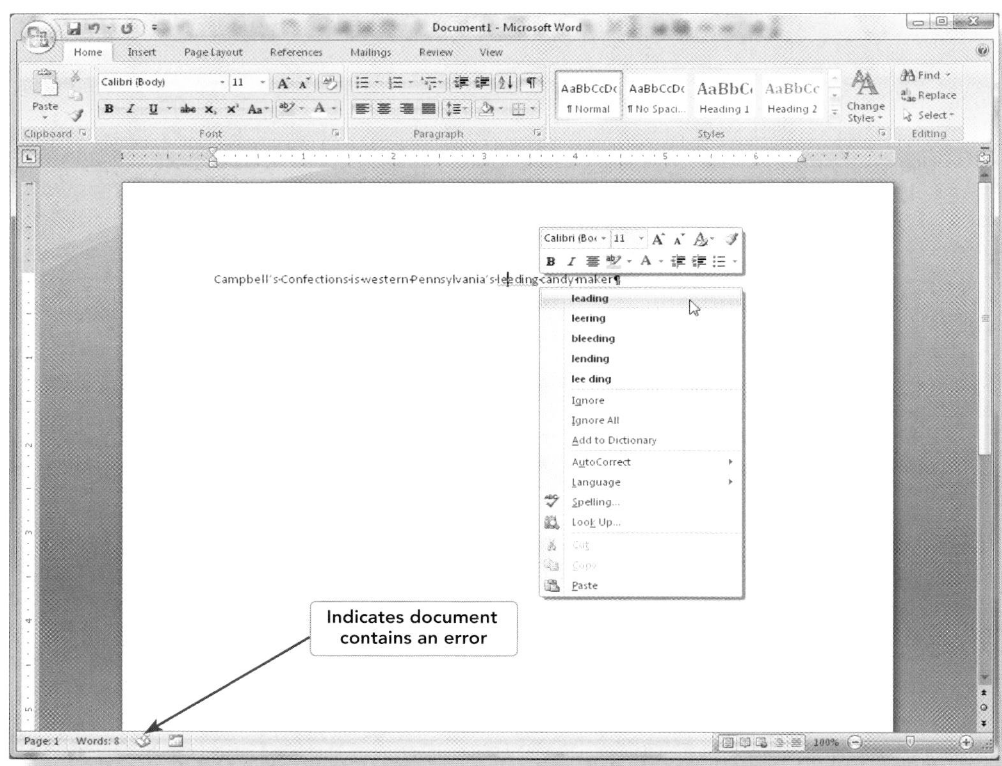

Figure 1-7
Choose the correct spelling from the shortcut menu.

3. Move the insertion point to the right of “maker,” and press Spacebar. Continue the sentence with another misspelled word by keying **adn**, and press Spacebar. Notice that “adn” is automatically corrected to “and” when you press Spacebar.

4. Complete the sentence by keying **is located in Grove City on Main Street.**
5. Verify that the insertion point is to the immediate right of the period following Street, and then press the Spacebar once. Key the following text:

   It is a family-owned business with several stores located in western Pennsylvania, eastern Ohio, and northern West Virginia.

   Notice how the text automatically wraps from the end of the line to the beginning of the next line.

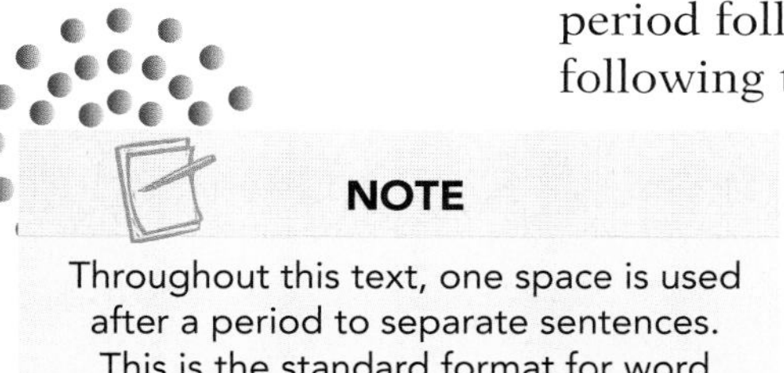

NOTE

Throughout this text, one space is used after a period to separate sentences. This is the standard format for word processing and desktop publishing.

6. Press Enter once to start a new paragraph.
7. Key the second paragraph shown in Figure 1-8. When you key the first four letters of "Monday" in the first sentence, Word suggests the completed word in a small box. Press Enter to insert the suggested word, and then press Spacebar before you key the next word. Follow the same procedure for "Saturday."

NOTE

When Word suggests a completed word as you key text, you can ignore the suggested word and continue keying or insert it by pressing Enter.

Figure 1-8

```
For more information about Campbell's Confections, visit one
of our stores Monday through Saturday, or visit our Web site
anytime. Our sales associates will be happy to help you.
```

Basic Text Editing

The keyboard offers many options for basic text editing. For example, you can press Backspace to delete a single character or Ctrl+Delete to delete an entire word.

TABLE 1-3 Basic Text Editing

Key	Result
Backspace	Deletes the character to the left of the insertion point.
Ctrl+Backspace	Deletes the word to the left of the insertion point.
Delete	Deletes the character to the right of the insertion point.
Ctrl+Delete	Deletes the word to the right of the insertion point.

Exercise 1-7 DELETE TEXT

1. Move the insertion point to the right of the word "It" in the second sentence of the first paragraph. (Use the mouse to position the I-beam, and click the left mouse button.)
2. Press Backspace twice to delete both characters and key **Campbell's Confections**.
3. Move the insertion point to the left of "one" in the second paragraph.
4. Press Delete three times and key **any**.

NOTE

When keyboard combinations (such as Ctrl+Backspace) are shown in this text, hold down the first key as you press the second key. Release the second key, and then release the first key. An example of the entire sequence is this: Hold down Ctrl, press Backspace, release Backspace, and release Ctrl. With practice, this sequence becomes easy.

5. Move the insertion point to the left of the word "information" in the second paragraph.
6. Hold down Ctrl and press Backspace. The word "more" is deleted.
7. Move the insertion point to the right of "Grove City" in the first sentence of the first paragraph.
8. Hold down Ctrl and press Delete to delete the word "on." Press Ctrl+Delete two more times to delete the words "Main Street."

Exercise 1-8 INSERT TEXT

When editing a document, you can insert text or key over existing text. When you insert text, Word is in regular *Insert mode*, and you simply click to position the insertion point and key the text to be inserted. To key over existing text, you switch to *Overtype mode*. The Overtype feature is turned off by default.

1. In the first sentence of the first paragraph, move the insertion point to the left of the "G" in "Grove City." Key **downtown**, and press Spacebar once to leave a space between the two words.
2. Move the insertion point to the beginning of the document, to the left of "Campbell's."
3. Click the **Microsoft Office Button**, and click the Word Options button Word Options.

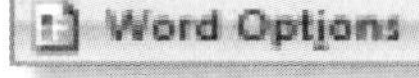

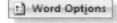

4. Click **Advanced**. Locate **Editing options**, and click to select **Use overtype mode**. Click **OK**.
5. Press Caps Lock. When you key text in Caps Lock mode, the keyed text appears in all uppercase letters.

TIP

Always remember to turn off Overtype mode as soon as you are done editing to avoid accidentally keying over text.

6. Key **campbell's confections** over the old text. Repeat the process for "Campbell's Confections" in the second sentence.

7. Press [Caps Lock] to turn off Caps Lock mode. Click the **Microsoft Office Button**, and click the Word Options button [Word Options]. Click **Advanced**, locate **Editing options**, and click to deselect **Use overtype mode**. Click **OK**.

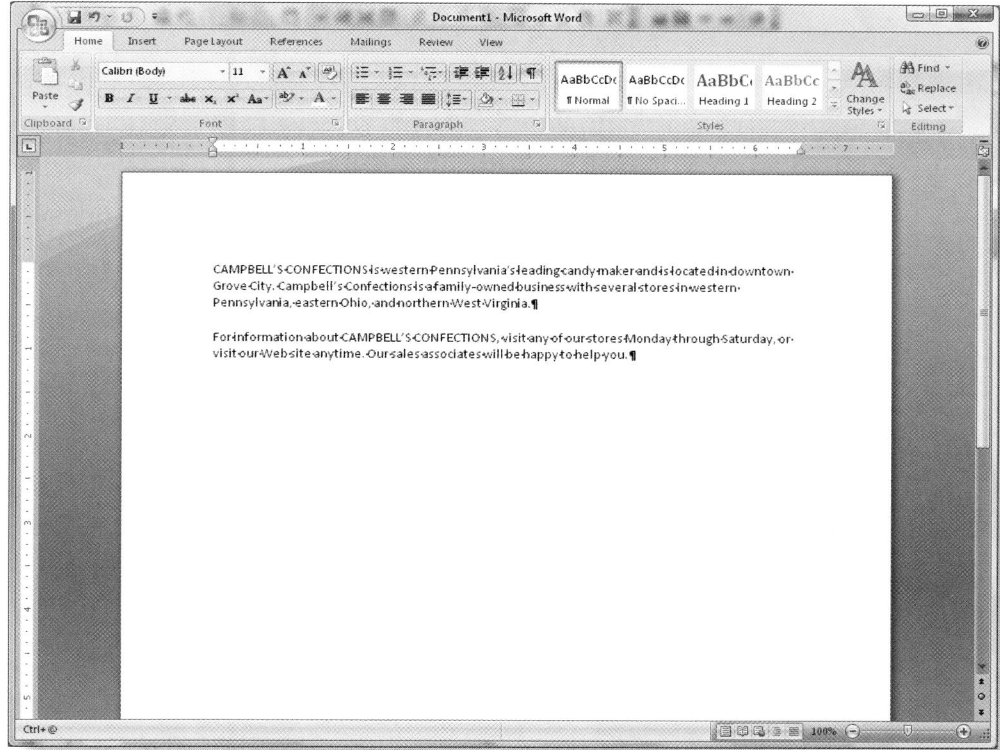

Figure 1-9
Edited document

Exercise 1-9 COMBINE AND SPLIT PARAGRAPHS

1. At the end of the first paragraph, position the insertion point to the left of the paragraph mark (after the period following "West Virginia").

2. Press [Delete]. The two paragraphs are now combined, or merged, into one.

3. Press [Spacebar] once to insert a space between the sentences.

4. With the insertion point to the left of "For" in the combined paragraph, press [Enter] to split the paragraph.

Naming and Saving a Document

Your document, called "Document1," is stored in your computer's temporary memory. Until you name and save the document, the data can be lost if you have a power failure or a computer hardware problem. It is always good practice to save your work frequently.

The first step in saving a document for future use is to assign a *file name*. Study the following rules about naming documents:

- File names can be up to 255 characters long, including the drive letter and the folder name. The following characters cannot be used in a file name: **/ \ > < * ? ": |**
- File names can include uppercase letters, lowercase letters, or a combination of both. They can also include spaces. For example, a file can be named "Business Plan."
- Throughout this course, document file names will consist of *[your initials]* (which might be your initials or the identifier your instructor asks you to use, such as **rst**), followed by the number of the exercise, such as **4-1**. The file name would, therefore, be **rst4-1**.

You can use either the Save command or the Save As command to save a document. Here are some guidelines about saving documents:

- Use Save As when you name and save a document the first time.
- Use Save As when you save an existing document under a new name. Save As creates an entirely new file and leaves the original document unchanged.
- Use Save to update an existing document.
- Before you save a new document, decide where you want to save it. Word saves documents in the current drive and folder unless you specify otherwise. For example, to save a document to a floppy disk or a jump drive, you need to change the drive to A: or E:, whichever is appropriate for your computer.

NOTE

Your instructor will advise you on the proper drive and folder to use for this course.

Exercise 1-10 NAME AND SAVE A DOCUMENT

1. Click the **Microsoft Office Button** to open the **File** menu and click **Save As**. The Save As dialog box appears.
2. In the File name text box, a suggested filename is highlighted. Replace this file name by keying *[your initials]*1-10.

NOTE

The default document type is Word Document (.docx). You can specify other file types such as RTF (Rich Text Format, which is a format used to exchange text documents between applications and operating systems) and TXT (Plain Text, which contains no formatting). To change the file type, simply click the down arrow beside the Save as type text box.

3. Drag the scroll box in the Navigation pane, and choose the appropriate drive for your data disk—Removable Disk (F:), for example. Make sure you have a formatted disk in the drive.
4. Click Save. Your document is named and saved for future use.

Figure 1-10
Save As dialog box

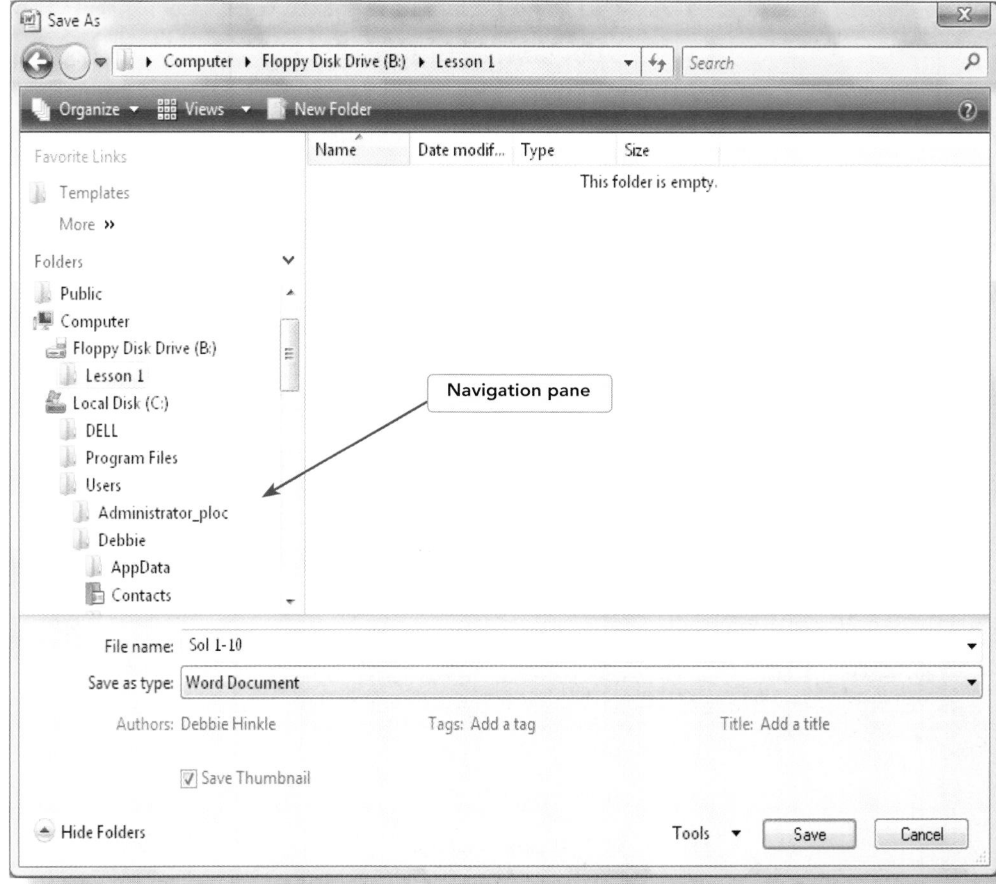

Printing a Document

After you create a document, printing it is easy. You can use any of the following methods:

- Choose Print from the File menu.
- Press Ctrl+P.

The Print option and the keyboard shortcut open the Print dialog box, where you can select printing options. Clicking Quick Print sends the document directly to the printer, using Word's default settings.

Exercise 1-11 PRINT A DOCUMENT

1. Click the Microsoft Office Button to open the File menu. Click **Print**, then click **Print** from the submenu to open the Print dialog box. The dialog box displays Word's default settings and shows your designated printer.

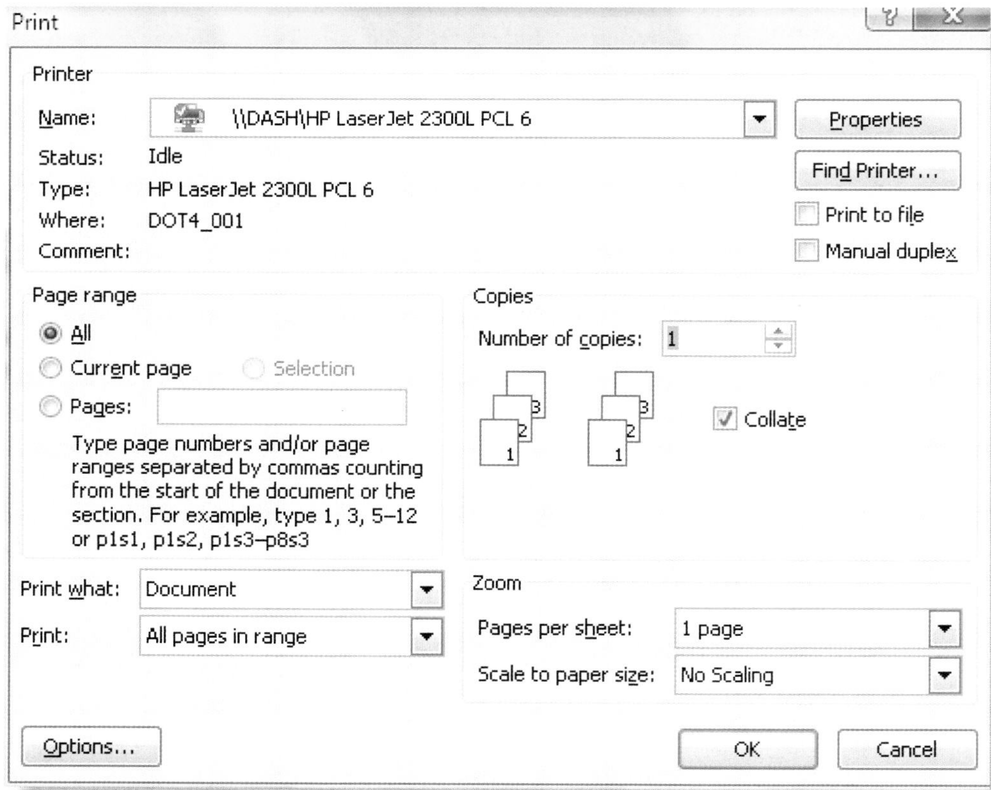

Figure 1-11
Print dialog box

2. Click **OK** or press Enter to accept the settings.

Closing a Document and Exiting Word

When you finish working on a document and save it, you can close it and open another document or you can exit Word.

The easiest ways to close a document and exit Word include using the following:

- The Close button in the upper right corner of the window.
- The Close command from the File menu.
- Keyboard shortcuts: Ctrl+W closes a document and Alt+F4 exits Word.

NOTE

When no document is open, the document window is blue. If you want to create a new document, choose New from the File menu, and click Blank Document. Click the Create button . The keyboard shortcut to create a new document is Ctrl+N.

Exercise 1-12 CLOSE A DOCUMENT AND EXIT WORD

1. Click the **Microsoft Office Button**, and choose **Close** from the File menu to close the document.
2. Click the Close button in the upper right corner of the screen to exit Word and display the Windows desktop.

Using Online Help

Online Help is available to you as you work in Word. Click the Help button or press F1 to open the Word Help window. You can click a Word Help link or key a word or phrase in the Search box.

FIND OUT MORE ABOUT USING HELP:

1. Start Word.
2. Locate the Help button in the upper right corner of the screen. Click the button to open the Word Help window.

Figure 1-12
Using the Word Help window

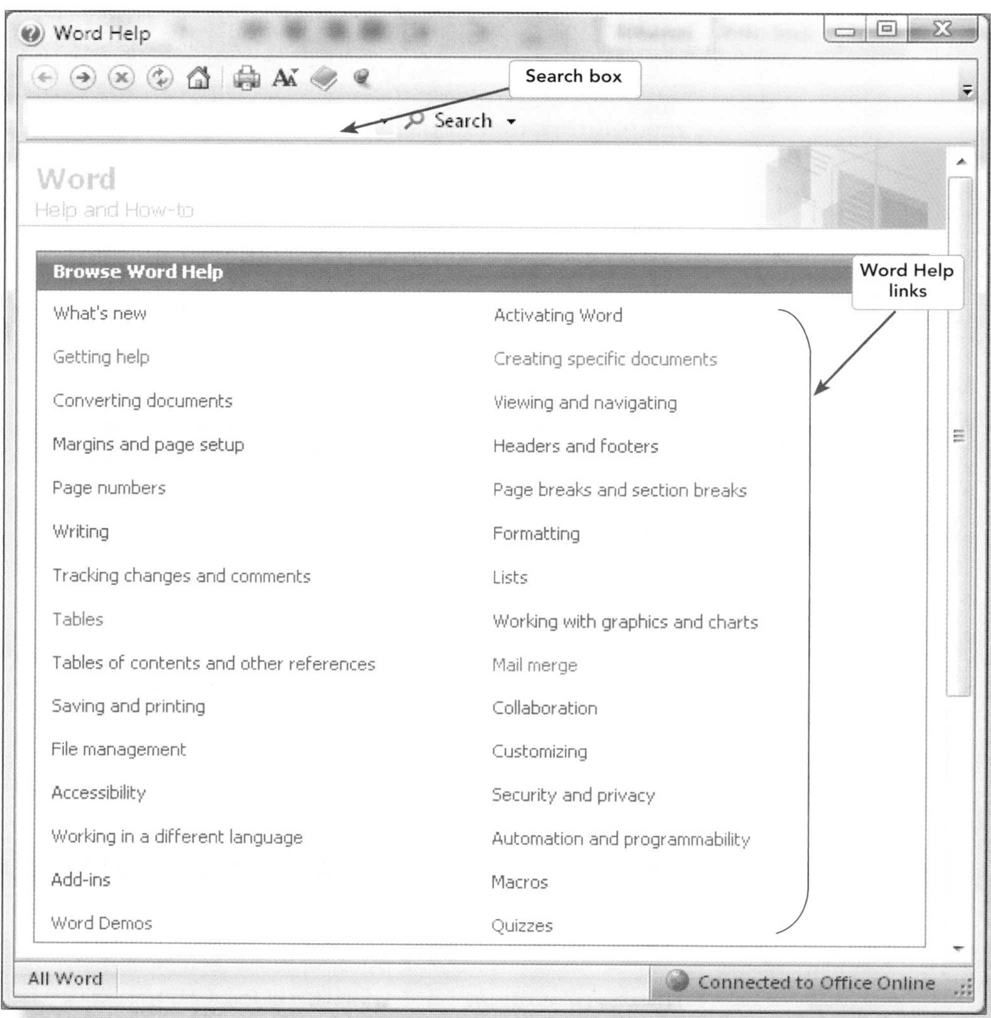

3. Locate and click the link **Getting help**.
4. Review the list of topics.
5. Click a topic and review the information.

6. Click the Back button to return to the list of categories.
7. Close Help by clicking the Word Help window's Close button .

Lesson 1 Summary

- To start Microsoft Word, click the Start button on the Windows taskbar, point to All Programs, click Microsoft Office, and click Microsoft Office Word 2007.
- The Microsoft Office Button is located in the upper left corner of the Word screen. Click the button to open the File menu.
- The title bar is at the top of the Word screen and displays the current document name.
- The Quick Access Toolbar displays icons for Save, Undo, and Repeat.
- The Ribbon contains tabs which include groups of related commands. Commands can be buttons, menus, or drop-down list boxes.
- Click a tab name to display related groups of commands. The number of groups and commands varies for each tab.
- Identify a command by name by pointing to it with the mouse. Word displays a ScreenTip with the button name.
- The horizontal ruler appears below the Ribbon.
- Scroll bars appear as blue shaded bars to the right and bottom of the text area. They are used to view different portions of a document.
- The status bar is a blue shaded bar below the horizontal scroll bar. It displays the page number and page count of the document, the document view buttons, and the zoom control. It also displays the current mode of operation. Right-click the status bar to customize it.
- The blinking vertical line is called the insertion point. It marks the position of the next character to be keyed.
- The mouse pointer displays on the screen as an I-beam when it is in the text area and as an arrow when you point to a command outside the text area.
- When the Show/Hide ¶ button ¶ is turned on, a paragraph mark symbol appears at the end of every paragraph. A dot between words represents a space.
- Word automatically wraps text to the next line as you key text. Press Enter to start a new paragraph or to insert a blank line.
- Word flags spelling errors as you key text by inserting a red, wavy line under the misspelled word. To correct the spelling, point to the underlined word, click the right mouse button, and choose the correct spelling.
- Word automatically corrects commonly misspelled words for you as you key text. Word can automatically complete a word for you, such as the name of a month or day. Word suggests the completed word, and you press Enter to insert it.
- Delete a single character by using Backspace or Delete. Ctrl+Backspace deletes the word to the left of the insertion point. Ctrl+Delete deletes the word to the right of the insertion point.

- To insert text, click to position the insertion point and key the text.
- To enter text over existing text, turn on Overtype mode by clicking the Microsoft Office Button. Click **Word Options**, and click **Advanced**. Click to select **Use overtype mode**. Click **OK**.
- Insert one space between words and between sentences.
- Document names, or file names, can contain 255 characters, including the drive letter and folder name, and can contain spaces. The following characters cannot be used in a file name: **/ \ > <* ? " : |**
- Save a new document by using the Save As command and giving the document a file name. Use the Save command to update an existing document.
- To start a new blank document, click the Microsoft Office Button. Click **New**, click **Blank document**, and click **Create**.
- To use Word Help, click the Microsoft Office Word Help button or press F1.

LESSON 1		Command Summary	
Feature	**Button**	**Command**	**Keyboard**
Save As		**File menu, Save As**	F12
Print		**File menu, Print**	Ctrl+P
Close a document		**File menu, Close**	F14 to F4
Exit Word	X	**File menu, Exit Word**	Alt+F4

NOTE

Word provides many ways to accomplish a particular task. As you become more familiar with Word, you will find the methods you prefer.

Lesson 2

Selecting and Editing

OBJECTIVES

After completing this lesson, you will be able to:

1. Open an existing document.
2. Enter formatting characters.
3. Move within a document.
4. Undo and Redo actions.
5. Repeat actions.
6. Select text.
7. Save a revised document.
8. Work with document properties.

MCAS OBJECTIVES

In this lesson:
WW 07 1.3.3
WW 07 6.1.1
WW 07 6.1.2

Estimated Time: 1 1/4 hours

To edit documents efficiently, you need to learn to select text and move quickly within a document. In this lesson you learn those skills, as well as how to open and save an existing document.

Opening an Existing Document

Instead of creating a new document, you start this lesson by opening an existing document. There are several ways to open a document:

- Choose **Open** from the File menu.
- Press Ctrl+O.
- Use the document links in the **Recent Documents** file listing.

TIP

The keyboard shortcut to open the File menu is Alt+F.

NOTE

Click **Folders** to open and close the Folders list.

Exercise 2-1 OPEN AN EXISTING FILE

1. Click the **Microsoft Office Button** to open the File menu. The file names listed under **Recent Documents** are the files opened from this computer. If the file you want is listed, you can click its name to open it from this list. The Recent Documents section displays up to 17 documents.
2. Click **Open** to display the Open dialog box. You are going to open a student file named **Campbell-1**.
3. Locate the appropriate drive and folder according to your instructor's directions.

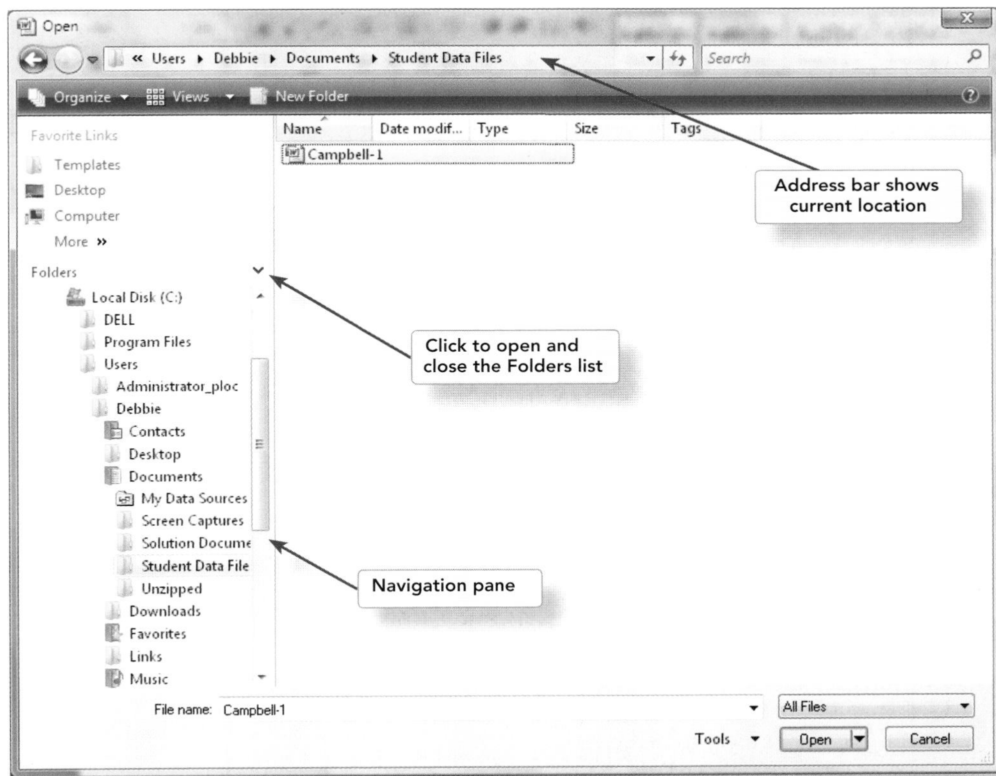

Figure 2-1
Files listed in the Open dialog box

4. After you locate the student files, click the arrow next to the Views button in the Open dialog box to display a menu of view options.
5. Choose **List** to list all files by file name.

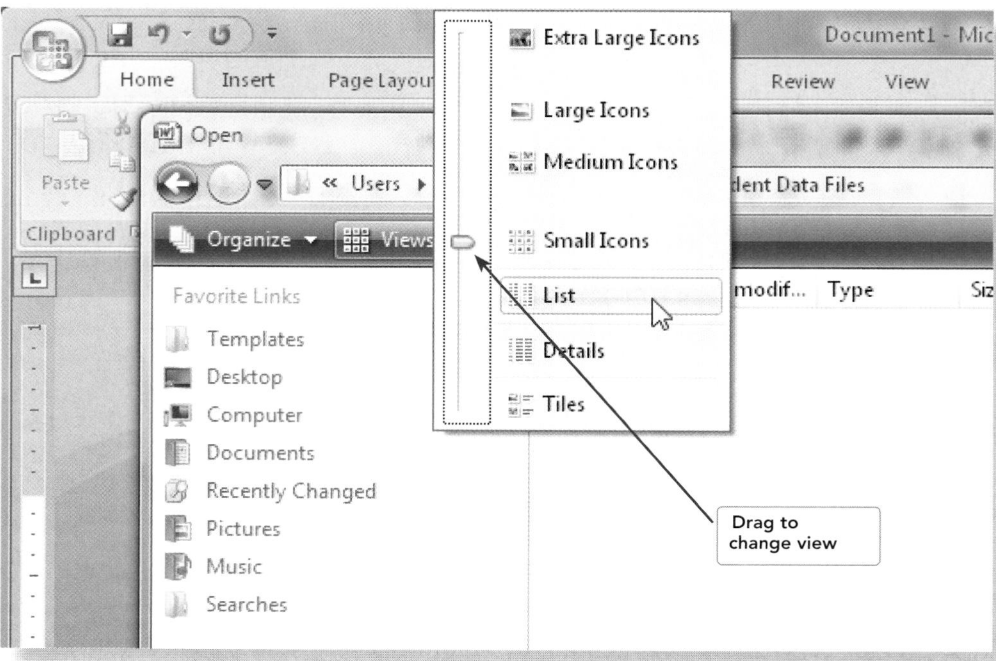

Figure 2-2
Views menu in the Open dialog box

NOTE

Documents created in earlier versions of Word display Compatibility Mode in the Title bar when opened. Compatibility Mode enables you to open, edit, and save documents that were created using earlier versions of Word. New features in Office Word 2007 are not available in Compatibility Mode. To check for features not supported by earlier versions of the Word program, click the Microsoft Office Button, and click the arrow beside **Prepare**. Click **Run Compatibility Checker**. To convert a document created in an earlier version of Word to Office Word 2007, click the Microsoft Office Button, and click **Convert**. Click **OK**.

6. From the list of file names, locate **Campbell-1** and click it once to select it.
7. Click **Open**.

You can also double-click a file name to open a file.

TABLE 2-1 Open Dialog Box Buttons

Button	Name	Purpose
Debbie ▸ Documents ▸	Address bar	Navigates to a different folder.
	Back button	Works with the Address bar, and returns to most recent previous location.
	Forward button	Works with the Address bar, and returns to location already opened.
Search	Search box	Looks for a file or subfolder.
Organize	Organize	Opens a menu of file functions, such as cutting a file, copying a file, pasting a file, deleting a file, or renaming a file. Includes the Layout option to display the Navigation pane, Details pane, and the Preview pane.
Views	Views	Opens a menu of view options for displaying drives, folders, files, and their icons.
New Folder	New Folder	Creates a new folder to organize your files.

Exercise 2-2 CREATE A NEW FOLDER

Document files are typically stored in folders that are part of a hierarchal structure similar to a family tree. At the top of the tree is a disk drive letter (such as C: or A:) that represents your computer, network, floppy drive, jump drive, or CD-ROM drive. Under the disk drive letter, you can create folders to organize your files. These folders can also contain additional folders.

Here is a scenario: You store your files on the C: drive of your office computer. You create a folder on this drive named "Word Documents." Within this folder you create folders named "Letters," "Memos," and "Reports," each containing different types of documents.

For this course, you will create a new folder for each lesson and store your completed exercise documents in these folders.

1. Click the **Microsoft Office Button** and choose **Save As**. You are going to save **Campbell-1** under a new file name, in a new folder that will contain all the files you save in this lesson.
2. Choose the appropriate drive and folder location from the **Navigation pane**. (For example, to save your files to a jump drive, insert a jump

drive in the USB port, and make sure the **Address bar** indicates the appropriate drive).

3. Click the Create New Folder button [New Folder]. A New Folder icon appears in the File list section.

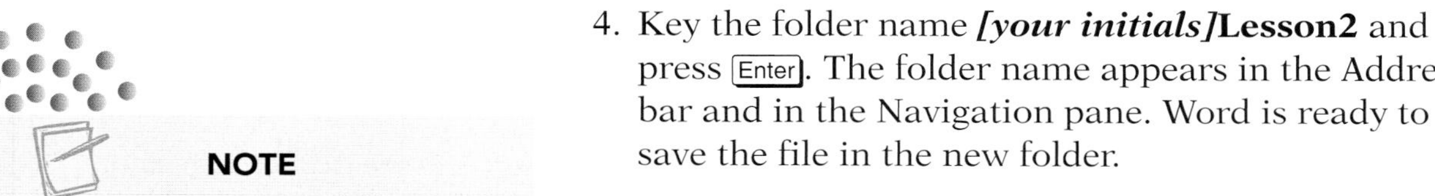

4. Key the folder name ***[your initials]*Lesson2** and press Enter. The folder name appears in the Address bar and in the Navigation pane. Word is ready to save the file in the new folder.
5. Locate the **File name** box, and make sure the file's original name (**Campbell-1**) is selected. If not, double-click it.
6. Key the file name ***[your initials]*2-2** and click **Save**.

NOTE

To rename a folder, locate the folder to rename and right-click the folder. Click Rename on the shortcut menu, key the new name, and press Enter.

Formatting Characters

The Show/Hide ¶ button [¶] on the Home tab shows or hides paragraph marks and other *formatting marks*. These characters appear on the screen, but not in the printed document. Formatting marks are included as part of words, sentences, and paragraphs in a document. Here are some examples:

- A word includes the space character that follows it.
- A sentence includes the end-of-sentence punctuation and at least one space.
- A paragraph is any amount of text followed by a paragraph mark.

The document you opened contains two additional formatting characters: *tab characters,* which you use to indent text, and *line-break characters,* which you use to start a new line within the same paragraph. Line-break characters are useful when you want to create a paragraph of short lines, such as an address, and keep the lines together as a single paragraph.

Another formatting character is a *nonbreaking space,* which you use to prevent two words from being divided between two lines. For example, you can insert a nonbreaking space between "Mr." and "Smith" to keep the name "Mr. Smith" undivided on one line.

TABLE 2-2 Formatting Characters

Character	To Insert, Press
Tab (→)	Tab
Space (·)	Spacebar
Nonbreaking space (°)	Ctrl + Shift + Spacebar
Paragraph mark (¶)	Enter
Line-break character (↵)	Shift + Enter

Exercise 2-3 ENTER FORMATTING CHARACTERS

1. Click the Show/Hide ¶ button ¶ if the formatting characters in the document are hidden.
2. Move the insertion point to the end of the document (after "family recipes.").
3. Press Enter to begin a new paragraph, and key **Campbell's Confections has been a member in good standing of the NCA for over 50** (do not press Spacebar).
4. Insert a nonbreaking space after "50" by pressing Ctrl + Shift + Spacebar. Then key **years.** (including the period). Word now treats "50 years" as a single unit.

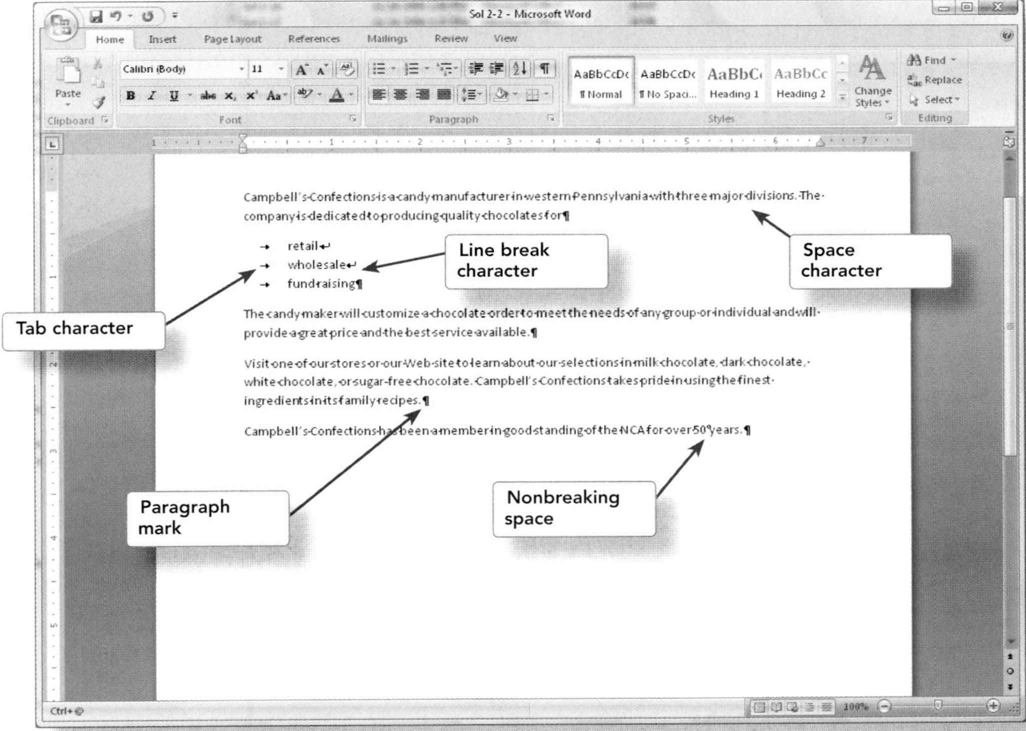

Figure 2-3
Formatting characters

NOTE

A smart tag may appear in the address. Word applies *smart tags* (nonprinting, purple dotted underlines) to address text.

5. Press Enter and key the following text as one paragraph at the end of the document, pressing Shift+Enter at the end of the first and second lines instead of Enter.

   Campbell's Confections
   25 Main Street
   Grove City, PA 16127

6. Click the Show/Hide ¶ button ¶ to hide the formatting characters, and click it again to redisplay them.

Moving within a Document

You already know how to move around a short document by positioning the I-beam pointer with the mouse and clicking. This is the easiest way to move around a document that displays in the document window. If a document is too long or wide to view in the window, you need to use different methods to navigate within a document.

Word offers two additional methods for moving within a document:

- *Using the keyboard:* You can press certain keys on the keyboard to move the insertion point. The arrow keys, for example, move the insertion point up or down one line or to the left or right one character. Key combinations quickly move the insertion point to specified locations in the document.

NOTE

Scrolling through a document does not move the insertion point. It moves only the portion of the document you are viewing in the document window. When you use the keyboard to move within a document, the insertion point always moves to the new location.

- *Using the scroll bars:* Use the vertical scroll bar at the right edge of the document window to move through a document. The position of the scroll box indicates your approximate location in the document, which is particularly helpful in long documents. To view and move through a document that is wider than the document window, use the horizontal scroll bar at the bottom of the document window.

Exercise 2-4 USE THE KEYBOARD TO MOVE THE INSERTION POINT

1. Press Ctrl+Home to move to the beginning of the document. Press End to move to the end of the first line.

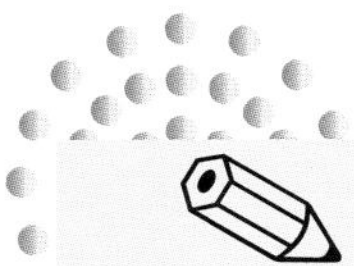

TIP

Word remembers the last three locations in the document where you edited or keyed text. You can press Shift+F5 to return the insertion point to these locations. For example, when you open a document you worked on earlier, press Shift+F5 to return to the place where you were last working before you saved and closed the document.

2. Press Ctrl+↓ several times to move the insertion point down one paragraph at a time. Notice how the text with the line-break characters is treated as a single paragraph.
3. When you reach the end of the document, press PageUp until you return to the beginning of the document.

TABLE 2-3 Keys to Move the Insertion Point

To Move	Press
One word to the left	Ctrl+←
One word to the right	Ctrl+→
Beginning of the line	Home
End of the line	End
One paragraph up	Ctrl+↑
One paragraph down	Ctrl+↓
Previous page	Ctrl+PageUp
Next page	Ctrl+PageDown
Up one window	PageUp
Down one window	PageDown
Top of the window	Alt+Ctrl+PageUp
Bottom of the window	Alt+Ctrl+PageDown
Beginning of the document	Ctrl+Home
End of the document	Ctrl+End

Exercise 2-5 SCROLL THROUGH A DOCUMENT

Using the mouse and the scroll bars, you can scroll up, down, left, and right. You can also set the Previous and Next buttons on the vertical scroll bar to scroll through a document by a specific object, such as tables or headings. For example, these buttons let you jump from one heading to the next, going forward or backward.

1. Locate the vertical scroll bar, and click below the scroll box to move down one window.

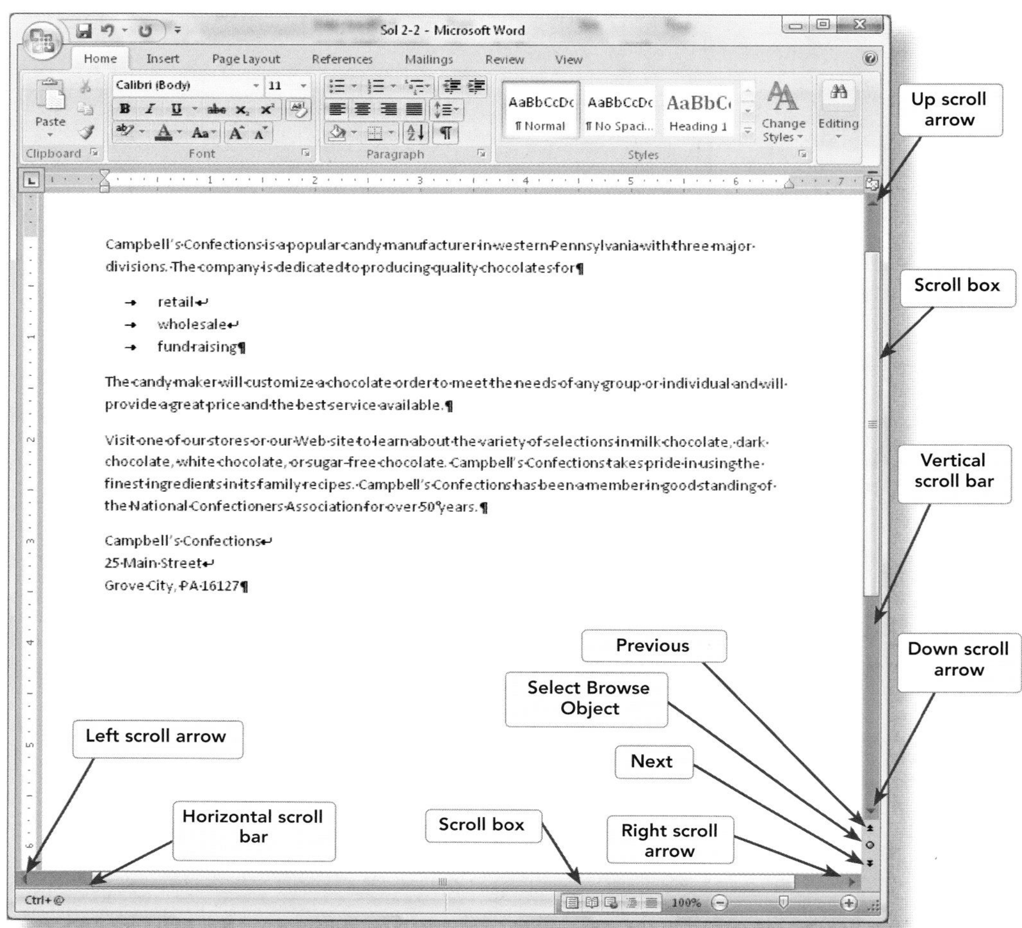

Figure 2-4
Using the scroll bars

NOTE

The horizontal scroll bar does not display if the document window is wide enough to display the document text. To display the horizontal bar, size the window by dragging the resize handle (located in the lower right corner) to the left. When you resize the document window, the appearance of the Ribbon changes.

TIP

The keyboard shortcut to display the Select Browse Object menu is Ctrl+Alt+Home.

2. Drag the scroll box to the top of the scroll bar.
3. Click the down scroll arrow on the scroll bar three times. The document moves three lines.
4. Click the right scroll arrow on the horizontal scroll bar once, and then click the left scroll arrow once to return to the correct horizontal position.
5. Click the up scroll arrow on the vertical scroll bar three times to bring the document back into full view.
   Notice that as you scroll through the document, the insertion point remains at the top of the document.
6. Click the Select Browse Object button, located toward the bottom of the vertical scroll bar. A menu of icons appears.

7. Move the pointer over each icon to identify it. These browse options become significant as your documents become more complex. Click the Browse by Page icon.

TABLE 2-4 Scrolling through a Document

To Move	Do This
Up one line	Click the up scroll arrow.
Down one line	Click the down scroll arrow.
Up one window	Click the scroll bar above the scroll box.
Down one window	Click the scroll bar below the scroll box.
To any relative position	Drag the scroll box up or down.
To the right	Click the right scroll arrow.
To the left	Click the left scroll arrow.
Into the left margin	Hold down Shift and click the left scroll arrow.
Up or down one page	Click Select Browse Object, click Browse by Page, and then click next or previous.

TIP

If you are using a mouse with a wheel, additional navigating options are available. For example, you can roll the wheel forward or backward instead of using the vertical scroll bars, hold down the wheel and drag in any direction to pan the document, or hold down Ctrl as you roll the wheel to change the magnification.

Undo and Redo Commands

Word remembers the changes you make in a document and lets you undo or redo these changes. For example, if you accidentally delete text, you can use the Undo command to reverse the action and restore the text. If you change your mind and decide to keep the deletion, you can use the Redo command to reverse the canceled action.

There are two ways to undo or redo an action:

- Click the Undo button or the Redo button on the Quick Access Toolbar.
- Press Ctrl+Z to undo or Ctrl+Y to redo.

Exercise 2-6 UNDO AND REDO ACTIONS

1. Delete the first word in the document, "Campbell's," by moving the insertion point to the right of the space after the word and pressing Ctrl+Backspace. (Remember that a word includes the space that follows it.)

2. Click the Undo button to restore the word.
3. Move the insertion point to the left of the word "candy" in the first paragraph.
4. Key **mid-size** and press Spacebar once. The text now reads "mid-size candy manufacturer."
5. Press Ctrl+Z. The word "mid-size" is deleted.

6. Click the Redo button to restore the word "mid-size."
7. Click the down arrow to the right of the Undo button. Word displays a drop-down list of the last few actions, with the most recent action at the top. You can use this feature to choose several actions to undo rather than just the last action. Click the down arrow again to close the list.
8. Click the Undo button.

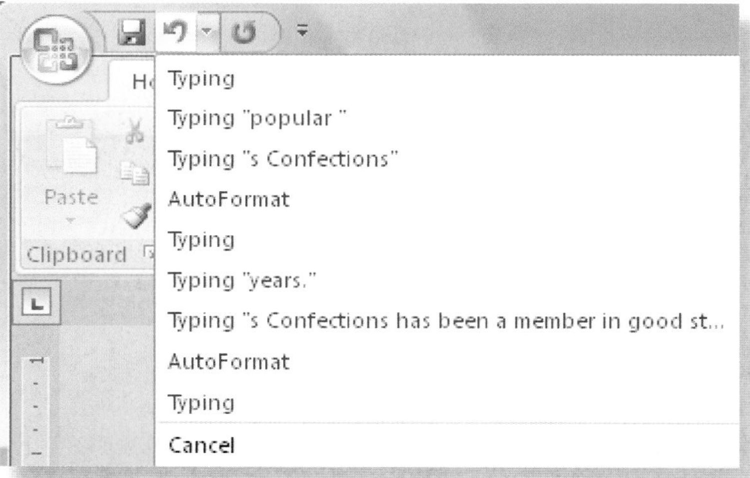

Figure 2-5
Undo Drop-Down list

Repeat Command

Suppose you key text you want to add to other areas of a document. Instead of rekeying the same text, you can use the Repeat command to duplicate the text.

To use the Repeat command:

- Press Ctrl+Y or
- Press F4.

Exercise 2-7 REPEAT ACTIONS

1. In the first paragraph position the insertion point to the left of the word "candy."

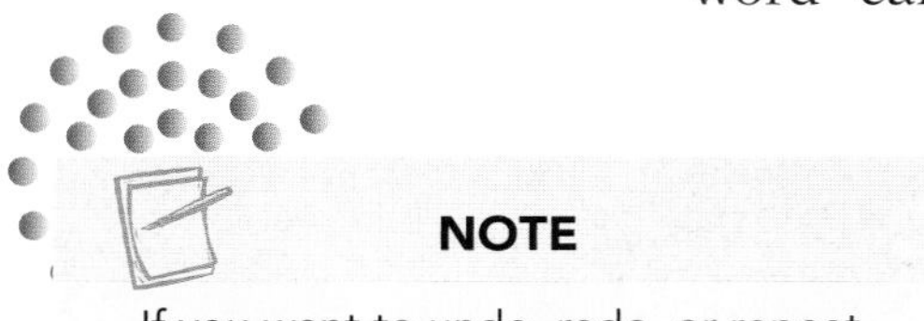

NOTE

If you want to undo, redo, or repeat your last action, do so before you press another key.

2. Key **popular** and press Spacebar once. The sentence now begins "Campbell's Confections is a popular candy."
3. Move the insertion point to the left of the word "selections" in the paragraph that begins "Visit one of our."
4. Press F4 and the word "popular" is repeated.

Selecting Text

Selecting text is a basic technique that makes revising documents easy. When you select text, that area of the document is called the *selection*, and it appears as a highlighted block of text. A selection can be a character, group of characters, word, sentence, paragraph, or the whole document. In this lesson, you delete and replace selected text. Future lessons show you how to format, move, copy, delete, and print selected text.

You can select text several ways, depending on the size of the area you want to select.

TABLE 2-5 Mouse Selection

To	Use the Mouse to Select
A series of characters	Click and drag, or click one end of the text block, and then hold down Shift and click the other end.
A word	Double-click the word.
A sentence	Press Ctrl and click anywhere in the sentence.
A line of text	Move the pointer to the left of the line until it changes to a right-pointing arrow, and then click. To select multiple lines, drag up or down.
A paragraph	Move the pointer to the left of the paragraph and double-click. To select multiple paragraphs, drag up or down.
The entire document	Move the pointer to the left of any document text until it changes to a right-pointing arrow, and then triple-click (or hold down Ctrl and click).

Exercise 2-8 SELECT TEXT WITH THE MOUSE

1. Select the first word of the document by double-clicking it. Notice that the space following the word is also selected.

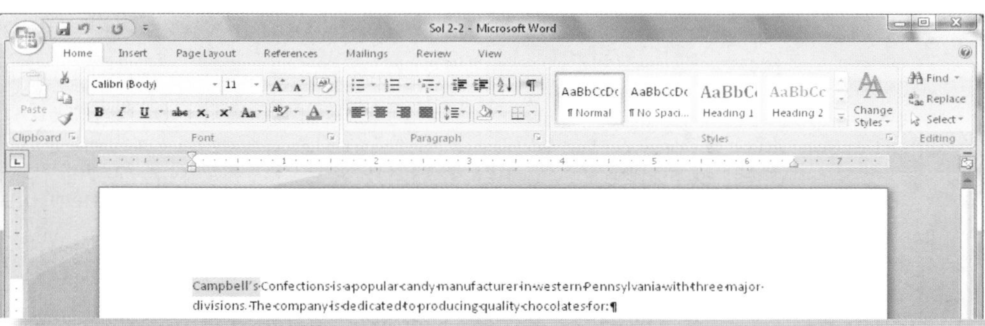

Figure 2-6
Selecting a word

NOTE

When text is selected, a Mini toolbar appears with formatting options.

2. Cancel the selection by clicking anywhere in the document. Selected text remains highlighted until you cancel the selection.
3. Select the first sentence by holding down Ctrl and clicking anywhere within the sentence. Notice that the period and space following the sentence are part of the selection. Cancel the selection.
4. Locate the paragraph that begins "Visit one of our."
5. To select the text "milk chocolate," click to the left of "milk." Hold down the left mouse button and slowly drag through the text, including the comma and space after "chocolate." Release the mouse button. Cancel the selection.

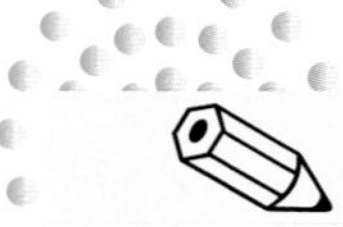

TIP

When selecting more than one word, you can click anywhere within the first word, and then drag to select additional text. Word will "smart-select" the entire first word.

6. To select the entire paragraph by dragging the mouse, click to position the insertion point to the left of "Visit." Hold down the mouse button, and then drag across and down until all the text and the paragraph mark are selected. Cancel the selection.
7. Select the same paragraph by moving the pointer into the blank area to the left of the text "Visit." (This is the margin area.) When the I-beam pointer changes to a right-pointing arrow, double-click. Notice that the first click selects the first line and the second click selects the paragraph, including the paragraph mark. Cancel the selection.

TIP

You can also triple-click within a paragraph to select it.

Figure 2-7
Selecting text

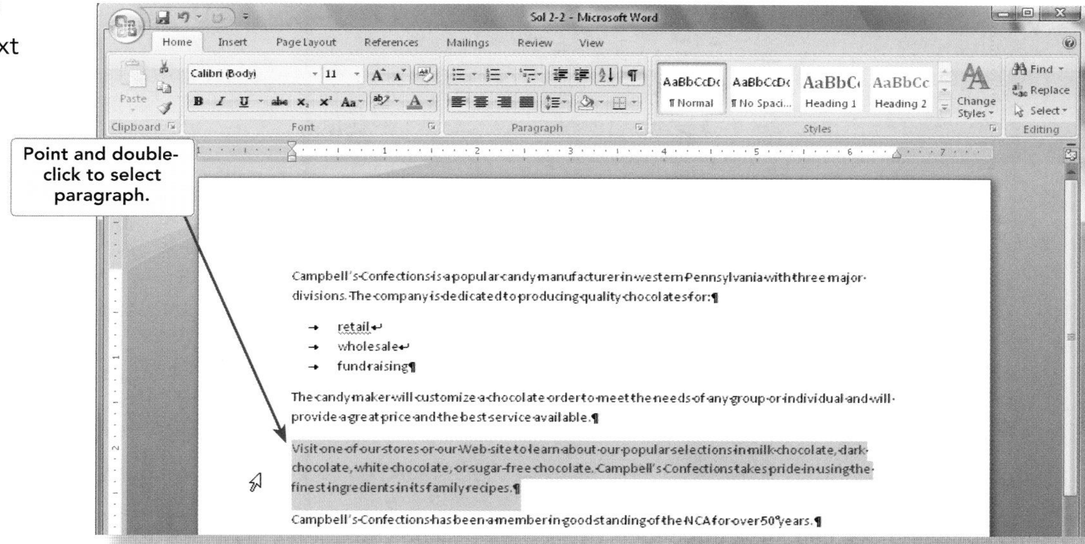

Exercise 2-9 SELECT NONCONTIGUOUS TEXT

In the previous exercise, you learned how to select *contiguous text,* where the selected characters, words, sentences, or paragraphs follow one another. But sometimes you would like to select *noncontiguous text,* such as the first and last items in a list or the third and fifth word in a paragraph. In Word, you can select noncontiguous text by using Ctrl and the mouse.

1. Select the first line of the list ("retail").
2. Press Ctrl and select the third line of the list ("fundraising"). With these two separate lines selected, you can delete, format, or move them without affecting the rest of the list.
3. Cancel the selection and go to the paragraph that begins "Visit one of our."
4. In the paragraph that begins "Visit one of our," double-click the word "our" before "Web site." With the word now selected, hold down Ctrl as you double-click the word "popular" in the same sentence and "finest" in the next sentence. (See Figure 2-8.) All three words are highlighted.

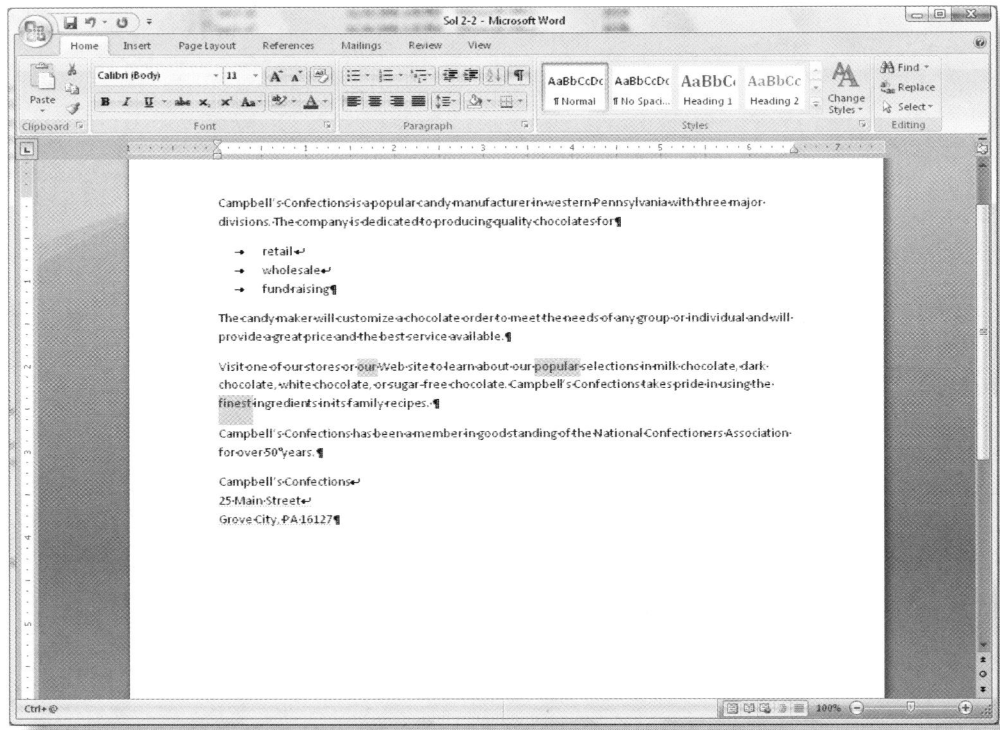

Figure 2-8 Selecting noncontiguous words

5. Cancel the selection.

Exercise 2-10 ADJUST A SELECTION USING THE MOUSE AND THE KEYBOARD

1. Select the paragraph beginning "Visit one of our."
2. Hold down Shift and press ← until the last sentence is no longer highlighted. Release Shift.
3. Increase the selection to include the last sentence by holding down Shift and pressing End and then pressing ↓. Release Shift.
4. Increase the selection to include all the text below it by holding down Shift and clicking at the end of the document (after the Zip Code).
5. Select the entire document by pressing Ctrl+A. Cancel the selection.

TABLE 2-6 Keyboard Selection

To Select	Press
One character to the right	Shift+→
One character to the left	Shift+←
One word to the right	Ctrl+Shift+→
One word to the left	Ctrl+Shift+←
To the end of a line	Shift+End
To the beginning of a line	Shift+Home
One line up	Shift+↑
One line down	Shift+↓
One window down	Shift+Page Down
One window up	Shift+Page Up
To the end of a document	Ctrl+Shift+End
To the beginning of a document	Ctrl+Shift+Home
An entire document	Ctrl+A

Exercise 2-11 EDIT TEXT BY REPLACING A SELECTION

You can edit a document by selecting text and deleting or replacing the selection.

NOTE

Although keying over selected text is an excellent editing feature, it sometimes leads to accidental deletions. Remember, when text is selected in a document (or even in a dialog box) and you begin keying text, Word deletes all the selected text with your first keystroke. If you key text without realizing a portion of the document is selected, use the Undo command to restore the text.

1. Locate the paragraph that begins "Visit one of our," select the words "our popular" using the Shift+click method: Click to the left of the word "our," hold down Shift, and click to the right of the word "popular."
2. Key **the variety of** to replace the selected text.
3. Locate the paragraph that begins "Campbell's Confections has been," select "NCA" and key **National Confectioners Association**. Notice that, unlike using Overtype mode, when you key over selected text, the new text can be longer or shorter than the selection.

Saving a Revised Document

You have already used the Save As command to rename the document you loaded at the beginning of this lesson. Now that you have made additional revisions, you can save a final version of the document by using the Save command. The document is saved with all the changes, replacing the old file with the revised file.

NOTE

If you wanted to save the current document with a different file name, you would use the **Save As** command.

Exercise 2-12 SAVE A REVISED DOCUMENT

1. Click the Save button on the Quick Access Toolbar. This action does not open the Save As dialog box.

2. Open the **File** menu and point to the arrow beside **Print**. Click **Quick Print** to print the document.

Exercise 2-13 CHECK WORD'S AUTORECOVER SETTINGS

Word's *AutoRecover* feature can automatically save open documents at an interval you specify. However, this is not the same as saving a file yourself, as you did in the preceding exercise. AutoRecover's purpose is to save open documents "in the background," so a recently saved version is always on disk. Then if the power fails or your system crashes, the AutoRecover version of the document opens automatically the next time you launch Word. In other words, AutoRecover ensures you always have a recently saved version of your document.

Even with AutoRecover working, you need to manually save a document (by using the Save command) before closing it. AutoRecover documents are not always available; if you save and close your file normally, the AutoRecover version is deleted when you exit Word. Still, it is a good idea to make sure AutoRecover is working on your system and to set it to save recovery files frequently.

1. Open the **File** menu and click **Word Options** to open the Word Options dialog box.
2. Click **Save** in the left pane.
3. Make sure the **Save AutoRecover information every** box is checked. If it is not checked, click the box.
4. Click the up or down arrow buttons to set the **minutes** to 5. Click **OK**.

Figure 2-9
Setting AutoRecover options

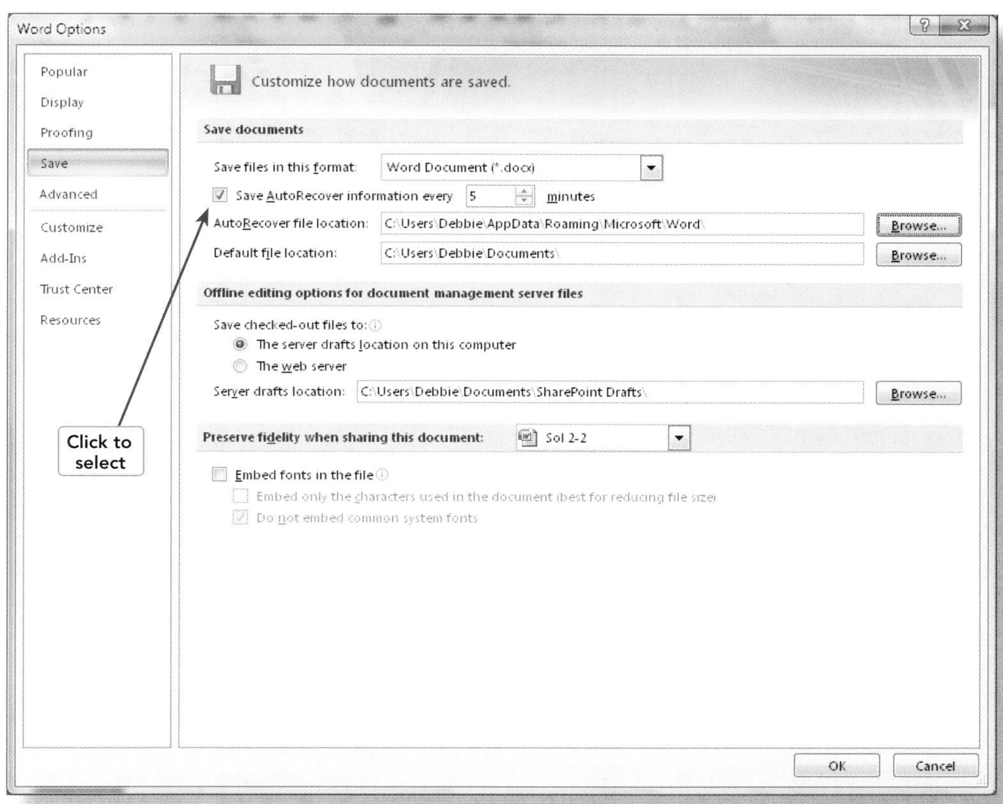

Working with Document Properties

Information that describes your document is called a *property*. Word automatically saves your document with certain properties, such as the file name, the date created, and the file size. You can add other properties to a document, such as the title, subject, author's name, and keywords. This information can help you organize and identify documents.

NOTE

You can also search for documents based on document properties by using the Search feature.

Exercise 2-14 REVIEW AND EDIT DOCUMENT PROPERTIES

1. With the file ***[your initials]*2-2** still open, open the **File** menu and click **Prepare**. Click **Properties**. The Document Information panel opens above your document.

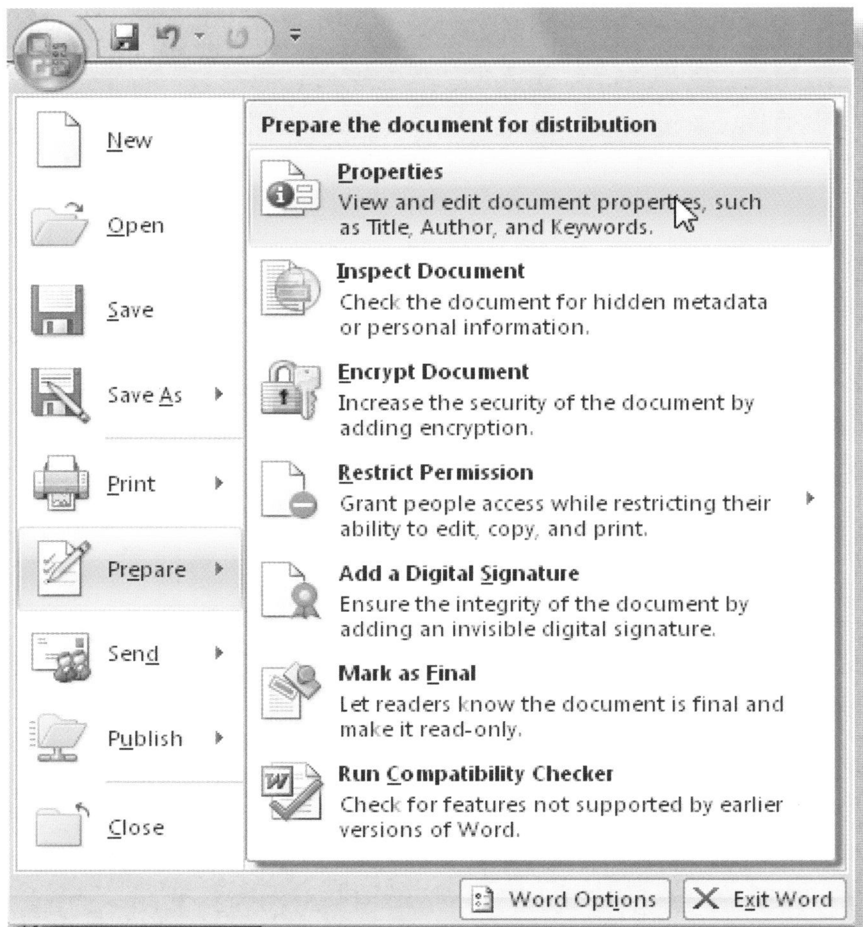

Figure 2-10 Displaying document properties

2. Notice the document properties displayed in the Document Information Panel.

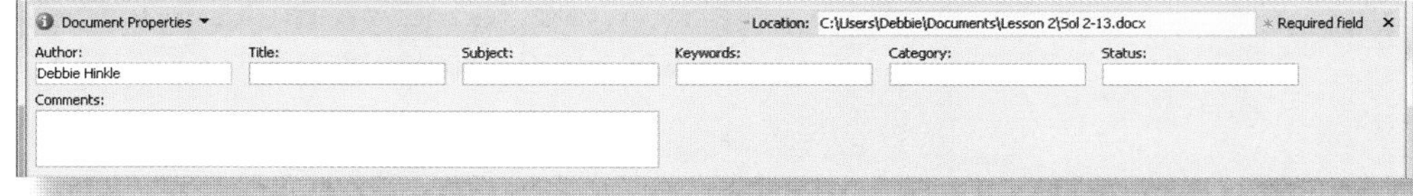

Figure 2-11 Document Information Panel

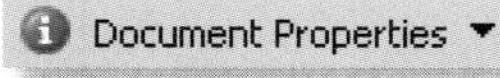

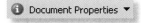

3. Click the Property Views and Options button [Document Properties]. Click **Advanced Properties**. Click the **General** tab. This tab displays basic information about the file, such as file name, file type, location, size, and creation date.

4. Click the **Statistics** tab. This tab shows the exact breakdown of the document in number of paragraphs, lines, words, and characters.

5. Click the **Summary** tab. Here you can enter specific document property information or change existing information.
6. Edit the title to read **Campbell's Confections** and key ***[your name]*** as the author. Click **OK**.

7. Click the Document Information Panel Close button to close the Document Information Panel.

Figure 2-12
Entering Summary information

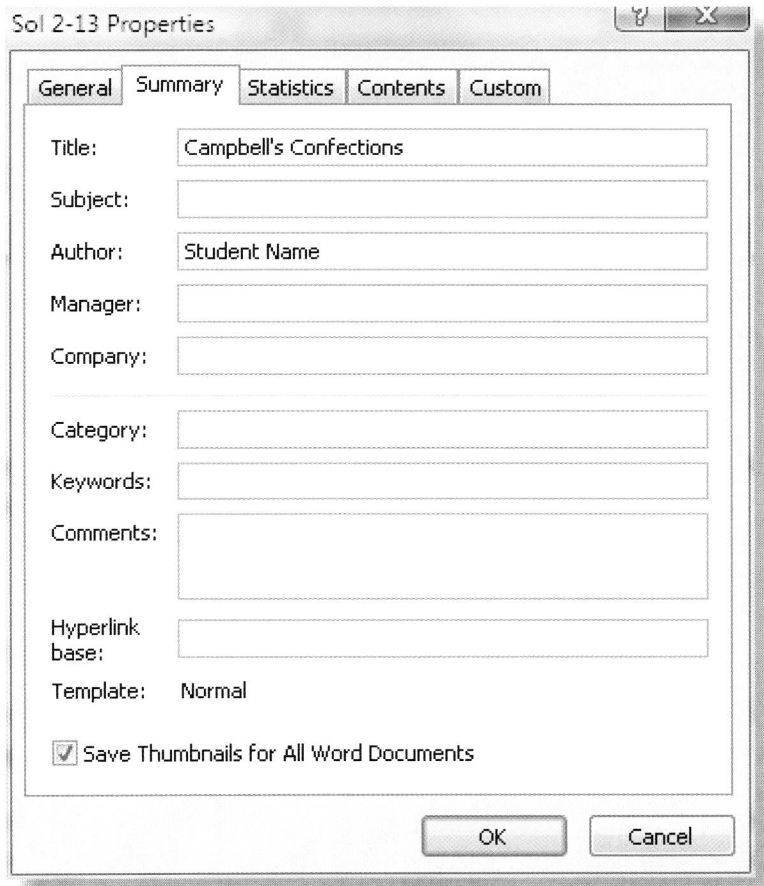

8. Save the document, and submit your work.

Lesson 2 Summary

- Use the Open dialog box to open an existing file. Use the Views button in the dialog box to change the way files are listed.
- Create folders to organize your files. You can do this in the Save As dialog box, using the New Folder button. Rename folders by locating and selecting the folder. Right-click the folder name and choose **Rename** from the shortcut menu.
- Formatting characters—such as blank spaces or paragraph marks—appear on-screen, but not in the printed document. Insert a line-break character to start a new line within the same paragraph. Insert a nonbreaking space between two words to make sure they appear on the same line.
- Use the Show/Hide ¶ button ¶ to turn the display of formatting characters on and off.
- When a document is larger than the document window, use the keyboard or the vertical scroll bar to view different parts of the document. Keyboard methods for moving within a document also move the insertion point.
- Keyboard techniques for moving within a document include single keys (such as PageUp and Home) and keyboard combinations (such as Ctrl+↑). See Table 2-3.
- Scrolling techniques for moving within a document include clicking the up or down scroll arrows on the vertical scroll bar or dragging the scroll box. Scrolling does not move the insertion point. See Table 2-4.
- If you make a change in a document that you want to reverse, use the Undo command. Use the Redo command to reverse the results of an Undo command.
- If you perform an action, such as keying text in a document, and you want to repeat that action elsewhere in the document, use the Repeat command.
- Selecting text is a basic technique for revising documents. A selection is a highlighted block of text you can format, move, copy, delete, or print.
- There are many different techniques for selecting text, using the mouse, the keyboard, or a combination of both. Mouse techniques involve dragging or clicking. See Table 2-5. Keyboard techniques are listed in Table 2-6.
- You can select any amount of contiguous text (characters, words, sentences, or paragraphs that follow one another) or noncontiguous text (such as words that appear in different parts of a document). Use Ctrl along with the mouse to select noncontiguous blocks of text.
- When text is selected, Word replaces it with any new text you key, or it deletes the selection if you press Delete.
- Use the Save command to save any revisions you make to a document.

- Word's AutoRecover feature periodically saves open documents in the background so you can recover a file in the event of a power failure or system crash.
- Document properties are details about a file that help identify it. Properties include the file name, file size, and date created, which Word updates automatically. Other properties you can add or change include title, subject, author's name, and keywords. View or add properties for an open document by using the **Properties** command (File menu, Prepare).

LESSON 2		Command Summary	
Feature	**Button**	**Command**	**Keyboard**
Open		File menu, Open	Ctrl+O or Ctrl+F12
Undo		Quick Access Toolbar	Ctrl+Z or Alt + Backspace
Redo		Quick Access Toolbar	Ctrl+Y or Alt+Shift+Backspace
Repeat			Ctrl+Y or F4
Select entire document			Ctrl+A
Save		File menu, Save	Ctrl+S or Shift+F12

Lesson 3

Formatting Characters

OBJECTIVES

MCAS OBJECTIVES

In this lesson:
WW 07 2.1.1
WW 07 2.1.3
WW 07 3.3.3

After completing this lesson, you will be able to:

1. Work with fonts.
2. Apply basic character formatting.
3. Work with the Font dialog box.
4. Repeat and copy character formats.
5. Change case and highlight text.
6. Create a drop cap.
7. Automatically format text and numbers.

Estimated Time: 1 hour

Every document is based on a theme. A *theme* is a set of formatting instructions for the entire document. Themes include fonts, colors, and effects.

Character formatting is used to emphasize text. You can change character formatting by making text bold or italic, for example, or by changing the style of the type. Word also provides special features to copy formats, highlight text, and automatically format text and numbers.

Working with Fonts

A *font* is a type design applied to an entire set of characters, including all letters of the alphabet, numerals, punctuation marks, and other keyboard symbols. Every theme defines two fonts—one for headings and one for body text.

Figure 3-1
Examples of fonts

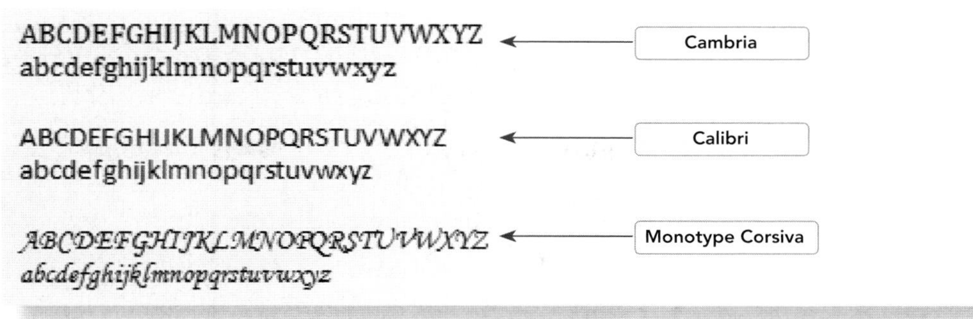

NOTE

The default theme fonts are Calibri, a sans serif font, and Cambria, a serif font. The default font size is 11.

Calibri is an example of a plain font; Cambria is more ornate; and Monotype Corsiva is an example of a more stylized font. Calibri is a *sans serif* font because it has no decorative lines, or serifs, projecting from its characters. Cambria is a *serif* font because it has decorative lines. Fonts are available in a variety of sizes, measured in *points*. There are 72 points to an inch. Like other character formatting, you can use different fonts and font sizes in the same document.

Figure 3-2
Examples of different point sizes

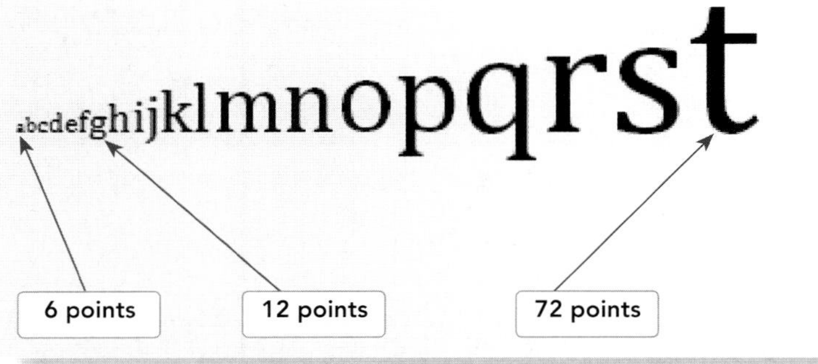

Exercise 3-1 CHANGE FONTS AND FONT SIZES USING THE RIBBON

The easiest way to choose fonts and font sizes is to use the Ribbon. The Home tab includes the Font group that contains frequently used formatting commands.

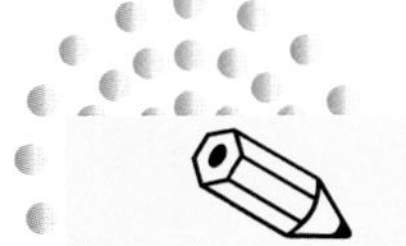

TIP

Press Ctrl+Shift+* to display formatting characters. (Do not use the asterisk on the numeric keypad.)

1. Open the file **Music**.
2. Click the Show/Hide ¶ button to display paragraph marks and space characters if they are not already showing.

3. Move to the beginning of the document and select the first line, which begins “Attention.” (Remember, you can press Ctrl+Home to move to the beginning of a document.)

Calibri (Body)

4. Click the down arrow next to the Font box Calibri (Body) on the Ribbon to open the Font drop-down list. Fonts are listed alphabetically by name and are displayed graphically.

Figure 3-3
Choosing a font

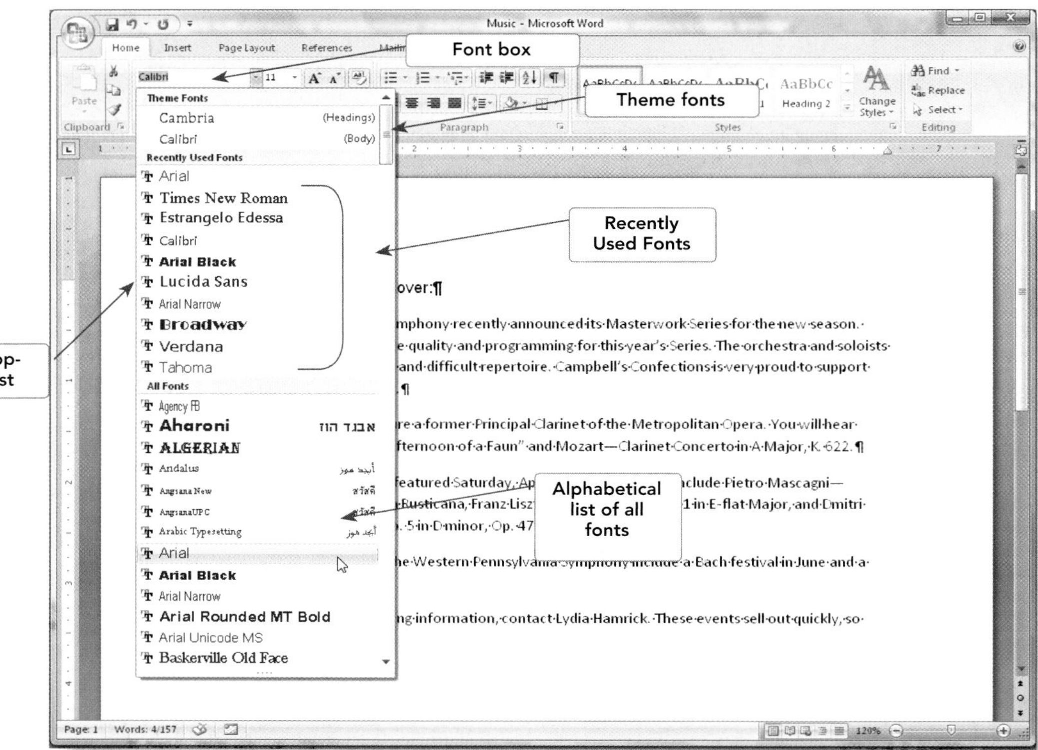

NOTE

The fonts you used most recently appear below the Theme Fonts. Shaded divider lines separate the Theme Fonts, Recently Used Fonts, and the list of All Fonts.

11

5. Using ↓ or the scroll box on the font list’s scroll bar, choose Arial.

6. Click the down arrow to open the Font Size drop-down list 11 and choose 16 points. Now the first line stands out as a headline.

Figure 3-4
Choosing a font size

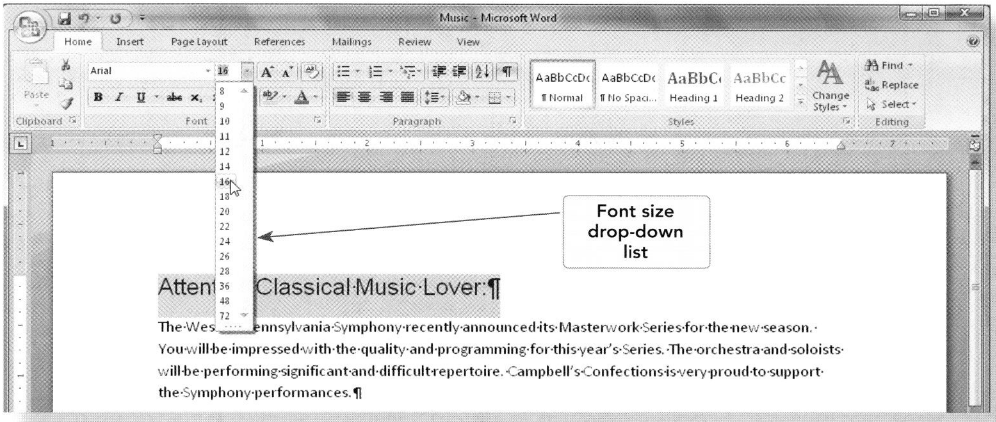

Exercise 3-2 CHANGE FONT SIZE USING KEYBOARD SHORTCUTS

If you prefer keyboard shortcuts, you can press Ctrl+Shift+> to increase the font size or Ctrl+Shift+< to decrease the font size.

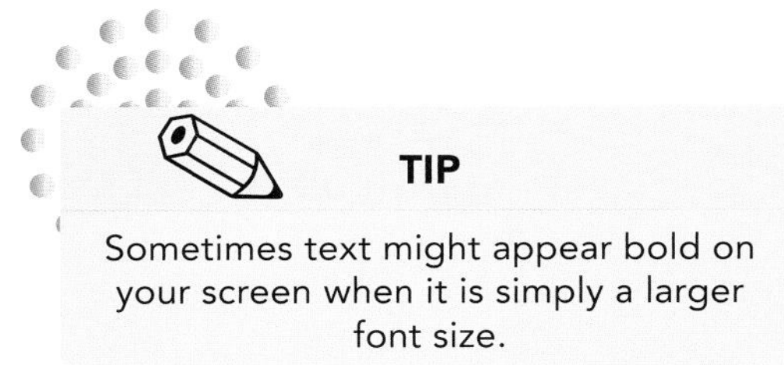

TIP

Sometimes text might appear bold on your screen when it is simply a larger font size.

1. Move the insertion point to the end of the paragraph that begins "For reservations," and press Enter to start a new paragraph.
2. Press Ctrl+Shift+> and key **Call Lydia at 555-2025**. The new sentence appears in 12-point type.
3. Press Enter to begin another paragraph. Press Ctrl+Shift+< to reduce the font size to 11 points and key **Credit card payments are accepted.**

Basic Character Formatting

The basic font styles or character formats are bold, italic, and underline. Text can have one or more character formats.

TABLE 3-1 Character Formatting

Attribute	Example
Normal	This is a sample.
Bold	**This is a sample.**
Italic	*This is a sample.*
Underline	<u>This is a sample.</u>
Bold and italic	***This is a sample.***

The simplest ways to apply basic character formatting are to use:

- Commands on the Ribbon
- Keyboard shortcuts
- Commands on the Mini toolbar

You can apply character formatting to existing text, including existing text that is noncontiguous. You can also turn on a character format before you key new text and turn it off after you enter the text. For example, you can click the Bold button, key a few words in bold, click the button again to turn off the format, and continue keying regular text.

Exercise 3-3 APPLY BASIC CHARACTER FORMATTING USING THE RIBBON

1. Select "Mozart—Clarinet Concerto in A Major, K. 622" (not including the period).
2. Click the Bold button on the Ribbon to format the text bold. (The Bold command is located in the Font group.)

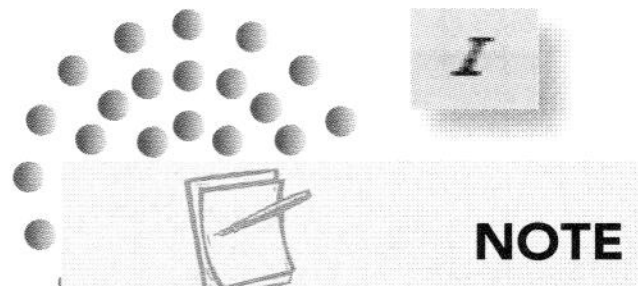

NOTE

The Home tab on the Ribbon displays by default. If the Home tab is not the active tab, click the Home tab to make it active and to display the Font group commands.

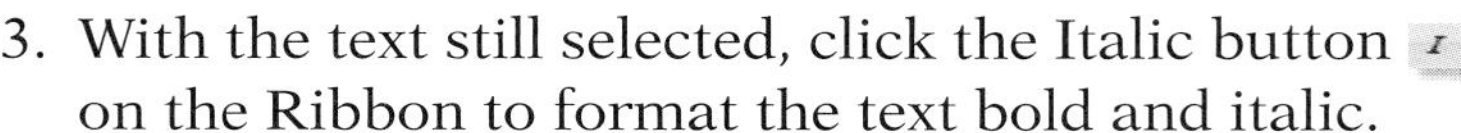

3. With the text still selected, click the Italic button on the Ribbon to format the text bold and italic.

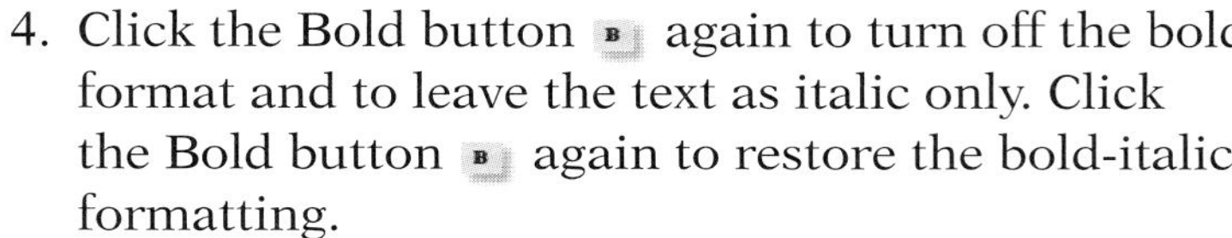

4. Click the Bold button again to turn off the bold format and to leave the text as italic only. Click the Bold button again to restore the bold-italic formatting.

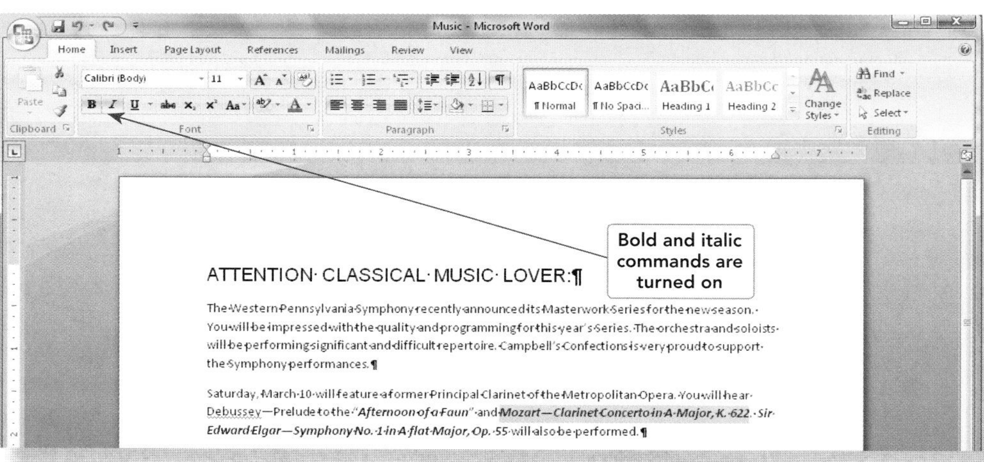

Figure 3-5
Using the Ribbon to apply character formatting

5. Move the insertion point to the end of the same paragraph and press Spacebar once.

6. Click the Bold button and the Italic button, and key **Sir Edward Elgar—Symphony No. 1 in A-flat Major, Op. 55** in bold italic.

NOTE

When text is selected, a Mini toolbar appears with character and paragraph formatting commands.

7. Click both buttons to turn off the formatting, press Spacebar, and complete the sentence by keying **will also be performed.**
8. Select the bold italic text "Mozart—Clarinet Concerto in A Major, K. 622" again.
9. Press Ctrl and select the bold italic text "**Sir Edward Elgar—Symphony No. 1 in A-flat Major, Op. 55**" as well.

10. Click the Underline button on the Ribbon to underline the noncontiguous selections.

11. Click the Undo button to remove the underlines.
12. Select the first line in the document.

13. Click the Change Case button and click **UPPERCASE**.

Exercise 3-4 APPLY AND REMOVE BASIC CHARACTER FORMATTING USING KEYBOARD SHORTCUTS

If you prefer to keep your hands on the keyboard instead of using the mouse, you can use keyboard shortcuts to turn basic character formatting on and off. You can press Ctrl+B for bold, Ctrl+I for italic, and Ctrl+U for underline. To remove character formatting from selected text, press Ctrl+Spacebar.

1. Select the text "Afternoon of a Faun."
2. Press Ctrl+B to format the selected text bold and press Ctrl+I to add italic.
3. Move the insertion point to the end of the document, and press Enter to start a new paragraph.
4. Press Caps Lock, press Ctrl+B to turn on the bold option, and key **jazz fans note:** in bold capital letters.
5. Press Caps Lock to turn it off, press Spacebar, and continue keying in bold:

   The first annual Jazz Festival, featuring some of the world's greatest musicians, will be held next May.

6. Select the bold-italic text "Afternoon of a Faun" again and press Ctrl+Spacebar to remove the formatting.
7. Click the Undo button to restore the bold-italic formatting.

Exercise 3-5 APPLY AND REMOVE BASIC CHARACTER FORMATTING USING THE MINI TOOLBAR

The Mini toolbar appears when you select text in a document. You can click any of the buttons to apply or remove character formatting from the selected text.

1. Select the first line of text. Notice the Mini toolbar displays.

Figure 3-6
Mini toolbar

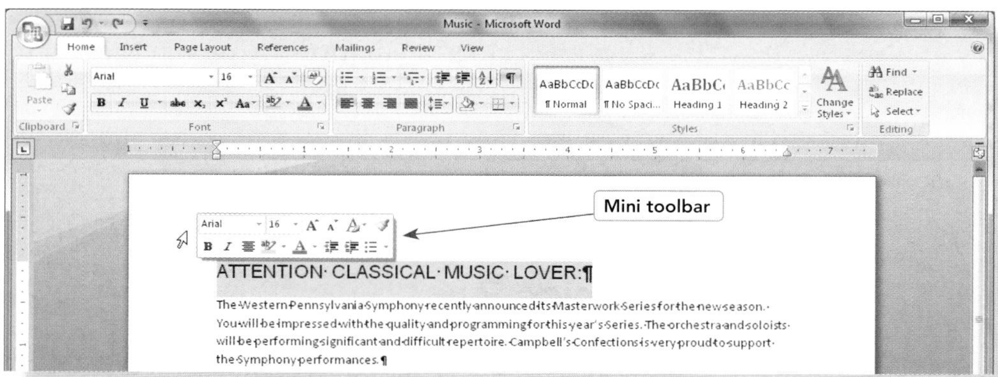

2. Click the drop-down arrow beside the Font Color button and click **Blue**.

3. Click the Grow Font button, and notice the change in the font size. Click the Shrink Font button.

Using the Font Dialog Box

The Font dialog box offers a wider variety of options than those available on the Ribbon. You can conveniently choose several options at one time.

There are several ways to open the Font dialog box:

- Click the Font Dialog Box Launcher.
- Right-click (use the right mouse button) selected text to display a *shortcut menu,* and then choose **Font**. A shortcut menu shows a list of commands relevant to a particular item you click.
- Keyboard shortcuts.

Figure 3-7
Shortcut menu

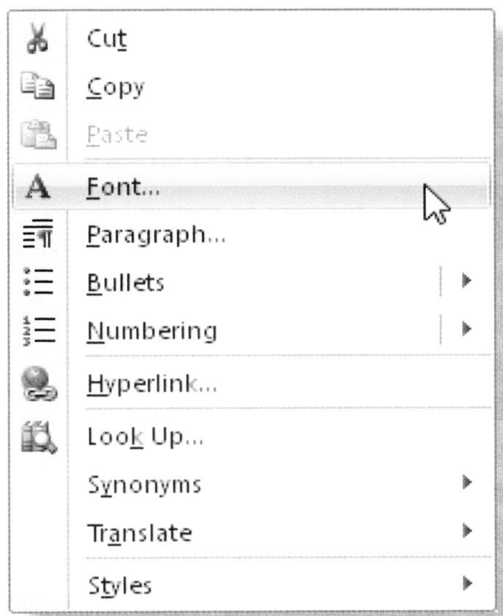

Exercise 3-6 CHOOSE FONTS AND FONT STYLES USING THE FONT DIALOG BOX

1. Select the first line of text, which is currently 16-point Arial and blue.
2. Click the arrow in the lower right corner of the Font group on the Ribbon. The Font dialog box displays.

Figure 3-8
Font Dialog Box Launcher

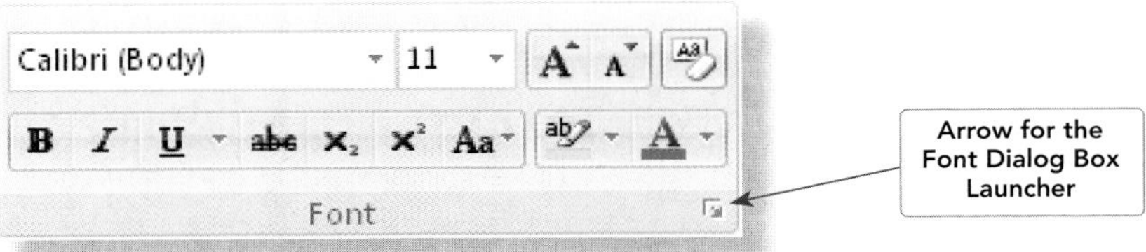

NOTE

Font availability varies, depending on the type of printer you are using and the installed software. Ask your instructor to recommend a substitute font if the specified one is unavailable.

3. Choose **Monotype Corsiva** from the **Font** list, **Bold Italic** from the **Font style** list, and **18** from the **Size** list. Look at your choices in the **Preview** box and click **OK**.

Figure 3-9
Using the Font dialog box

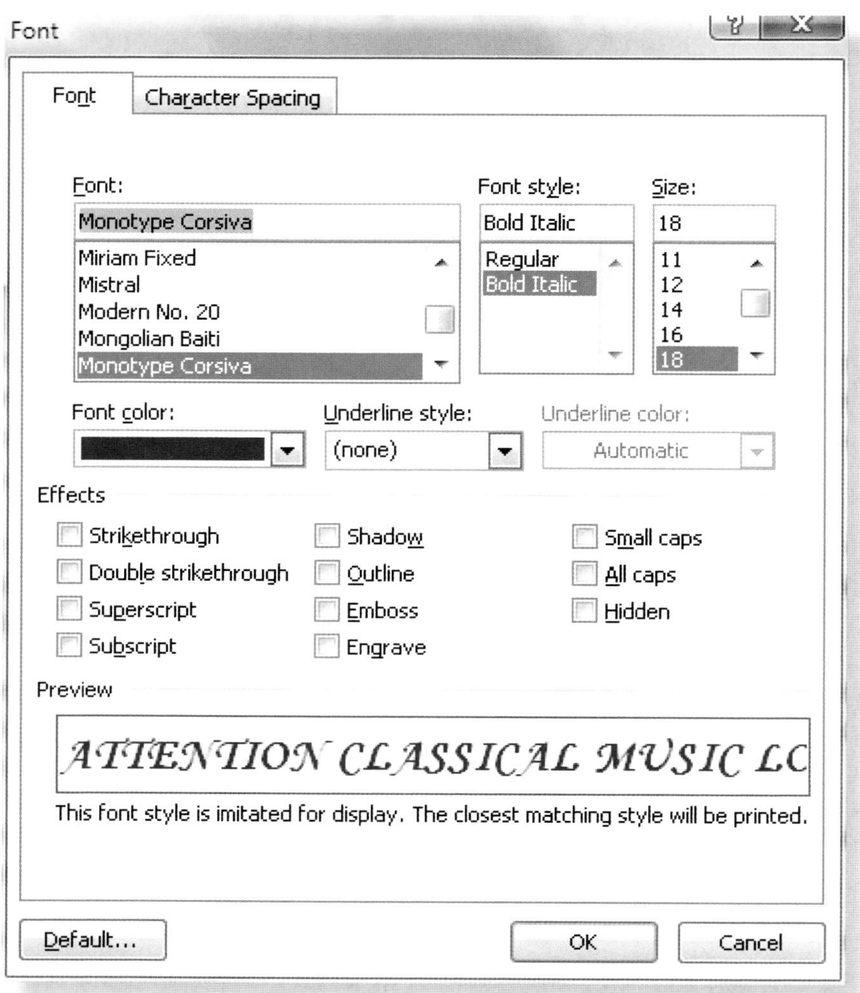

Exercise 3-7 APPLY UNDERLINE OPTIONS AND CHARACTER EFFECTS

In addition to choosing font, font size, and font style, you can choose font color, a variety of underlining options, and special character effects from the Font dialog box.

TIP

Press Ctrl+Shift+F to open the Font dialog box with the Font box active. Press Ctrl+Shift+P to open the Font dialog with the Size box active.

1. Select the text "JAZZ FANS NOTE" in the last paragraph (do not select the colon).
2. Press Ctrl+D to open the Font dialog box.

3. Click the down arrow to open the **Underline style** drop-down list. Drag the scroll box down to see all the available underline styles. Choose one of the dotted line styles.
4. Click the down arrow next to the Font color box and choose "Green." (Each color is identified by name when you point to it.) Both the text and the underline are now green in the **Preview** box.

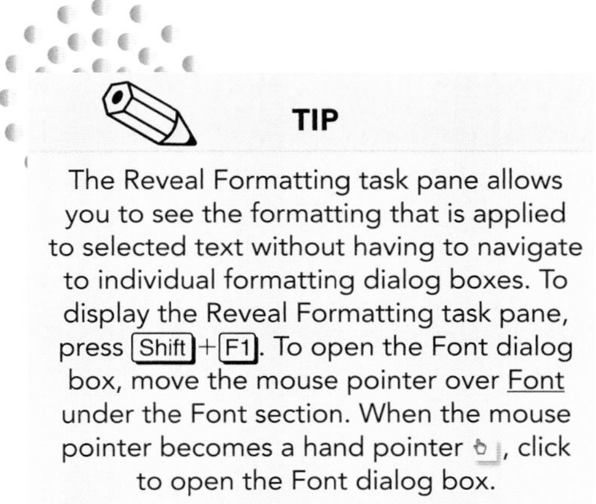

TIP

The Reveal Formatting task pane allows you to see the formatting that is applied to selected text without having to navigate to individual formatting dialog boxes. To display the Reveal Formatting task pane, press Shift+F1. To open the Font dialog box, move the mouse pointer over Font under the Font section. When the mouse pointer becomes a hand pointer, click to open the Font dialog box.

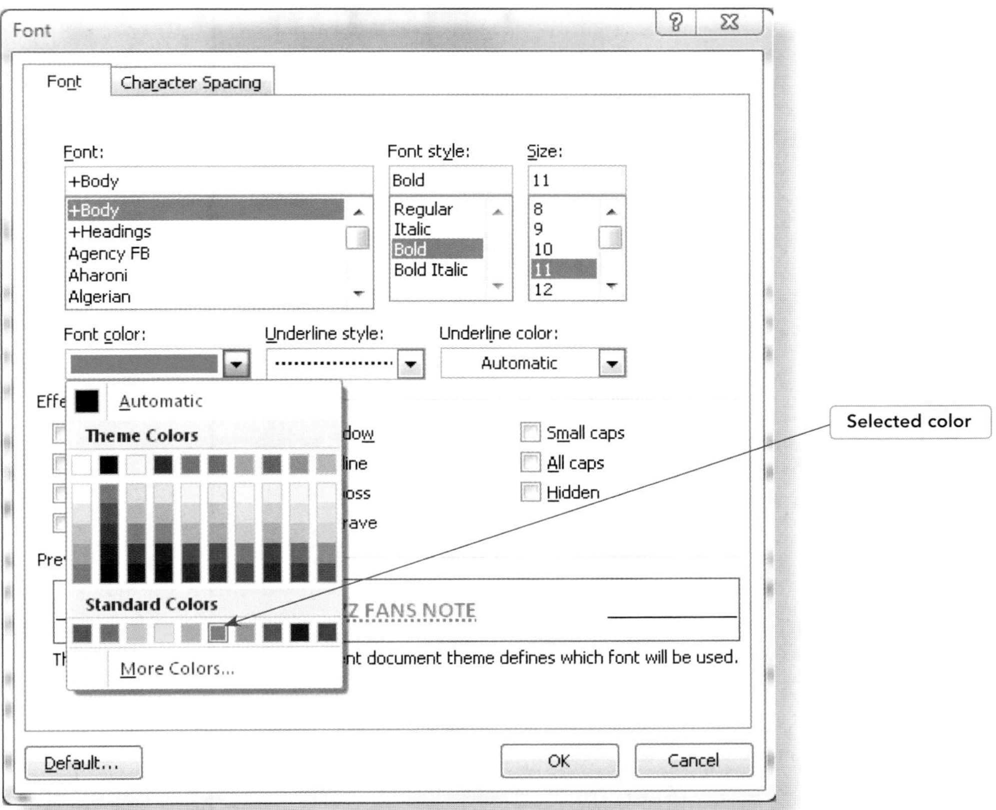

Figure 3-10 Font color options in the Font dialog box

5. Click the down arrow next to the **Underline color** box and choose **Red**.

6. Click **OK**. The text is green with a red dotted underline.
7. Select the sentence after the green, dotted-underlined text "JAZZ FANS NOTE:"
8. Move the mouse pointer to the Ribbon and click the Clear Formatting button .

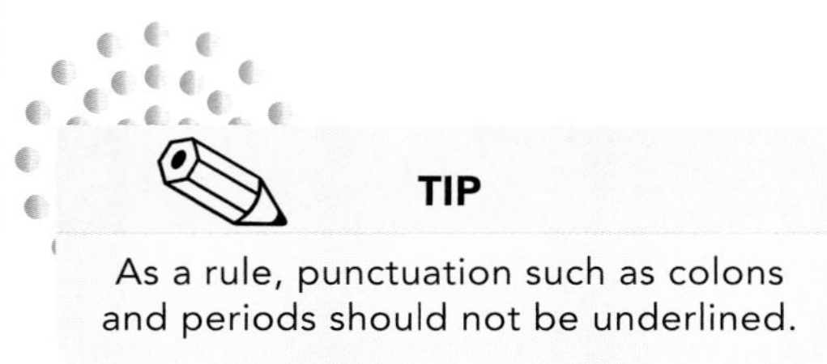

TIP

As a rule, punctuation such as colons and periods should not be underlined.

9. In the same sentence, select the text "Jazz Festival."
10. Click the selected text with the right mouse button, and from the shortcut menu, choose **Font** to open the Font dialog box. Under **Effects**, click the **Small caps** check box and click **OK**. The text that was formerly lowercase now appears in small capital letters.
11. Select the sentence that begins "Call Lydia."

12. Click the Strikethrough button on the Ribbon. The text appears with a horizontal line running through it.

TABLE 3-2 Font Effects in the Font Dialog Box

Effect	Description and Example
Strikethrough	Applies a ~~horizontal line~~.
Double strikethrough	Applies a ~~double horizontal line~~.
Superscript	Raises text above other characters on the same line.
Subscript	Places text below other characters on the same line.
Shadow	Applies a **shadow**.
Outline	Displays the inner and outer border of text.
Emboss	Makes text appear raised off the page.
Engrave	Makes text appear imprinted on the page.
Small Caps	Makes lowercase text SMALL CAPS.
All Caps	Makes all text UPPERCASE.
Hidden	Hidden text does not print and appears on-screen only if Word's Display options are set to display hidden text. See **File menu, Word Options**.

13. Click the Undo button to undo the strikethrough effect.

Exercise 3-8 USE KEYBOARD SHORTCUTS FOR UNDERLINE OPTIONS AND FONT EFFECTS

Word provides keyboard shortcuts for some underlining options and font effects as an alternative to using the Ribbon or opening the Font dialog box.

REVIEW

Remember that Ctrl+U turns on and off standard underlining.

1. Start a new sentence at the end of the last paragraph by keying **To beat the heat, bring plenty of H2O.**
2. Select the "2" in H2O.
3. Press Ctrl+= to make it subscript.
4. Select the green, dotted-underlined text "JAZZ FANS NOTE." Press Ctrl+Shift+W to change the dotted underlining to words-only underlining.

TABLE 3-3 Keyboard Shortcuts for Underlining and Character Effects

Keyboard Shortcut	Action
Ctrl+Shift+W	Turn on or off words-only underlining.
Ctrl+Shift+D	Turn on or off double underlining.
Ctrl+Shift+=	Turn on or off superscript.
Ctrl+=	Turn on or off subscript.
Ctrl+Shift+K	Turn on or off small capitals.
Ctrl+Shift+A	Turn on or off all capitals.
Ctrl+Shift+H	Turn on or off hidden text.

Exercise 3-9 CHANGE CHARACTER SPACING

The **Character Spacing** tab in the Font dialog box offers options for changing the space between characters or the position of text in relation to the baseline. Character spacing can be expanded or condensed horizontally, as well as raised or lowered vertically.

1. Select the first line of text, which begins "Attention."
2. Open the **Font** dialog box and click the **Character Spacing** tab.
3. Click the down arrow to open the **Scale** drop-down list. Click **150%** and notice the change in the **Preview** box. Change the scale back to **100%**.

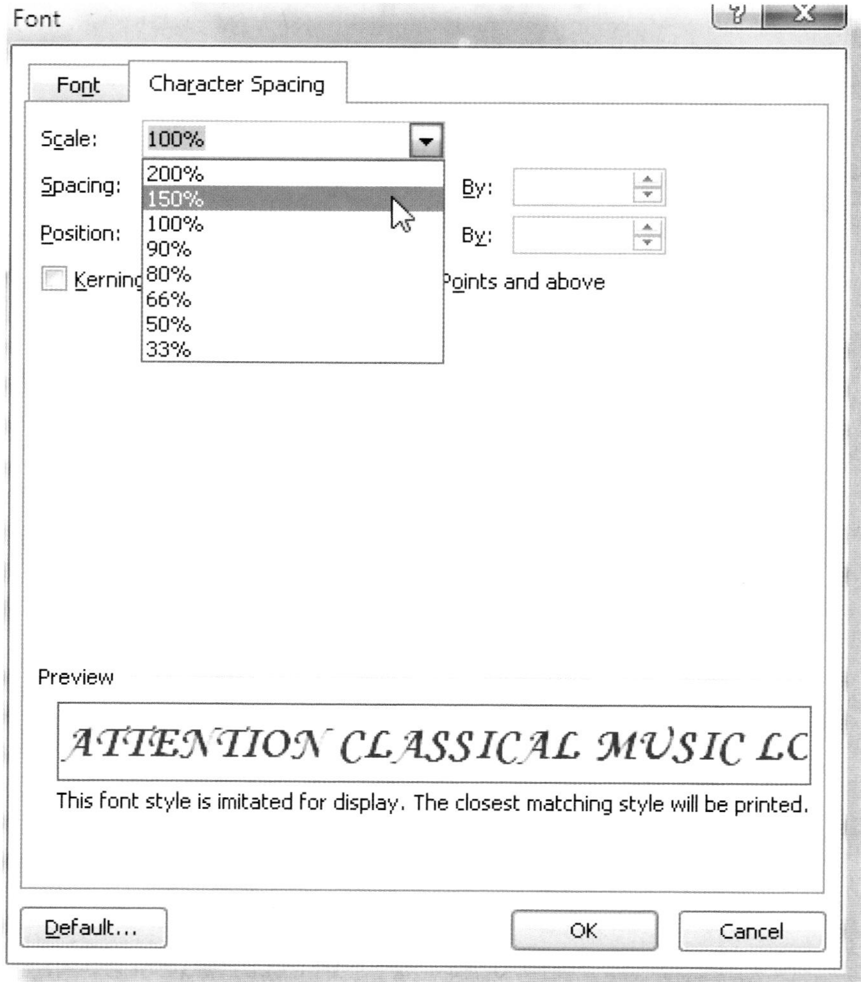

Figure 3-11
Character Spacing tab

TIP

You can increase the space between characters even more by increasing the number in the **By** box (click the arrows or key a specific number). Experiment with the **Spacing** and **Scale** options on your own to see how they change the appearance of text.

4. Click the down arrow to display the **Spacing** options. Click **Expanded**, and then click **OK**. The text appears with more space between each character.
5. In the Save As dialog box, create a new folder for your Lesson 3 files and save the document as ***[your initials]*3-9**.

NOTE

Remember to use this folder for all the exercise documents you create in this lesson.

Repeating and Copying Formatting

You can use F4 or Ctrl+Y to repeat character formatting. You can also copy character formatting with a special tool on the Ribbon—the Format Painter button .

Exercise 3-10 REPEAT CHARACTER FORMATTING

Before trying to repeat character formatting, keep in mind that you must use the Repeat command immediately after applying the format. In addition, the Repeat command repeats only the last character format applied. (If you apply multiple character formats from the Font dialog box, the Repeat command applies all formatting.)

1. Select "Intermezzo" and click the Italic button to italicize the text.
2. Select "Piano Concerto No. 1 in E-flat Major" and press F4 to repeat your last action (turning on Italic format).
3. Select the sentence that begins "Call Lydia."
4. Open the **Font** dialog box. Click the **Font** tab, if it is not already displayed, and choose another font, such as Impact. Select the font size **12 points**, and change the font color to **red**. Click **OK**. The text appears with the new formatting.
5. Select the text "JAZZ FANS NOTE:" (including the colon) and press F4. Word repeats all the formatting you chose in the Font dialog box. If you apply each character format separately, using the Ribbon, the Repeat command applies only the last format you chose.

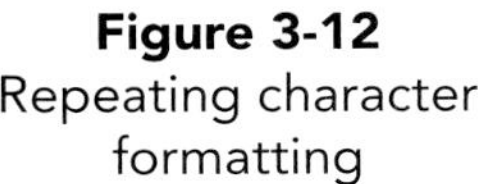

Figure 3-12 Repeating character formatting

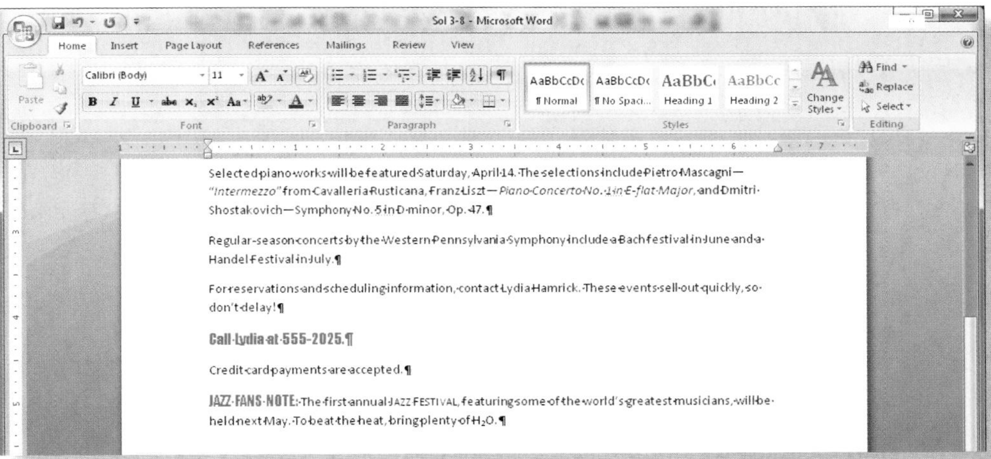

Exercise 3-11 COPY CHARACTER FORMATTING

The Format Painter button makes it easy to copy a character format. This is particularly helpful when you copy text with multiple formats, such as bold-italic small caps.

To use Format Painter to copy character formatting, first select the text with the formatting you want to copy, and then click the Format Painter button. The mouse pointer changes to a paintbrush with an I-beam pointer. Use this pointer to select the text to which you want to apply the copied formatting.

1. In the paragraph that begins "The Western," select "Masterwork Series" and click the Underline button.

2. With the text still selected, click the Format Painter button on the Ribbon. When you move the pointer back into the text area, notice the new shape of the pointer.
3. Use the paintbrush pointer to select "Series" in the next sentence. This copies the underlining to the selected text, and the pointer returns to its normal shape.
4. Select the small caps words "JAZZ FESTIVAL" in the last paragraph.
5. Double-click the Format Painter button. Double-clicking lets you copy formatting repeatedly.
6. Scroll to the top of the document. Notice that the paintbrush pointer becomes an arrow when you move out of the text area to use the scroll bars.
7. Select the sentence that begins "The Western." The small caps formatting is applied to the sentence, and the pointer remains the paintbrush pointer.
8. Scroll down to the line that begins "Call Lydia" and select the sentence. The paintbrush pointer copies the new formatting over the old formatting.
9. Press Esc or click the Format Painter button to stop copying and to restore the normal pointer.

Changing Case and Highlighting Text

You have used Caps Lock to change case, and you have seen the **Small Caps** and **All Caps** options in the Font dialog box. You can also change the case of characters by using keyboard shortcuts and the Change Case command on the Ribbon.

Exercise 3-12 CHANGE CASE

1. Select the sentence that begins “Credit card payments.” Press Shift+F3. This keyboard shortcut changes case. Now the text appears in all uppercase letters.
2. With the sentence still selected, press Shift+F3 again. Now the sentence appears in all lowercase letters.
3. Press Shift+F3 again and the original case (sentence case) is restored.

4. Select the first line of the document, and click the Change Case button on the Ribbon.
5. Click **Capitalize Each Word**. This option changes the first letter of each word to uppercase, the common format for titles.
6. Click anywhere in the document to deselect the text.

Exercise 3-13 HIGHLIGHT TEXT

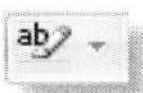

To emphasize parts of a document, you can mark text with a color highlighter by using the Highlight button on the Ribbon, Font group. As with the Format Painter button, when you click the Highlight button, the pointer changes shape. You then use the highlight pointer to select the text you want to highlight. In addition, you can choose from several highlighting colors.

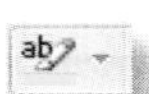

1. Make sure no text is selected. On the Ribbon, click the down arrow next to the Highlight button to display the color choices. Click **Yellow** to choose it as the highlight color. This turns on the Highlight button, and the color indicator box on the button is now yellow.

Figure 3-13
Choosing a highlight color

2. Move the highlight pointer into the text area.

3. Drag the pointer over the phone number in the paragraph that begins "CALL LYDIA."
4. Press [Esc] to turn off the highlighter and restore the normal pointer.
5. Select the first line of text, which begins "Attention."
6. Click the Highlight button to highlight the selection. This is another way to use the highlighter—by selecting the text and then clicking the Highlight button.
7. Select the first line of text again. Remove the highlight by clicking the down arrow to display the highlight color choices and choosing **No Color**.
8. Select the remaining highlighted text and click the Highlight button. Because "None" was last chosen (as shown in the color indicator box on the button), this action removes the highlight from the selected text.

NOTE

You can use highlighting to mark text as you work on a document or to point out text for others opening the same document later. It might not work as well for printed documents because the colors might print too dark. You can use the shading feature to emphasize text in a printed document.

Creating a Drop Cap

One way to call attention to a paragraph is to use a dropped capital letter, or a *drop cap*. A drop cap is a large letter that appears below the text baseline. It is usually applied to the first letter in the first word of a paragraph.

Exercise 3-14 CREATE A DROP CAP

1. Place the insertion point at the beginning of the paragraph that begins "The Western."

2. Click the **Insert** tab on the Ribbon, and click the Drop Cap button. Click **Dropped**.
3. Undo the drop cap.
4. Click the Drop Cap down arrow and click **Drop Cap Options**. The Drop Cap dialog box opens.

Figure 3-14
Drop Cap dialog box

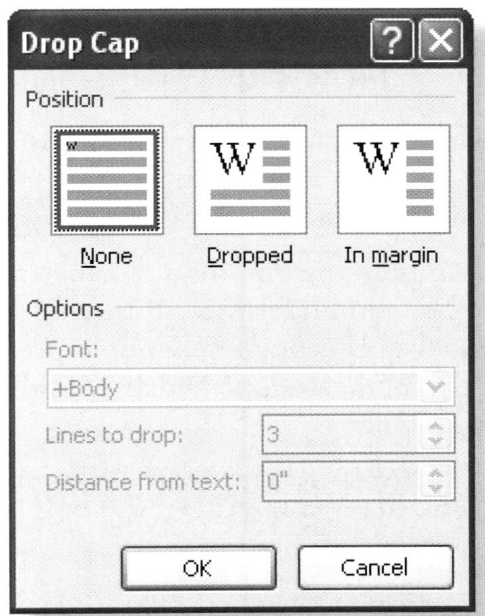

5. Under **Position**, click **Dropped**. This option is used to wrap the paragraph around the letter.
6. Click **OK**. Click within the document to deselect the "T" of "The," which is the height of three lines.

NOTE

Style manuals in general do not recommend superscript ordinals. To turn off the Ordinals and Fractions AutoFormat, open the Word Options dialog box, click Proofing, and click AutoCorrect Options to open the AutoCorrect dialog box. Click the AutoFormat tab, and click to deselect **Ordinals** and **Fractions** in the Replace section.

Word's AutoFormat Features

Word has several features that automatically change formatting as you key text or numbers. One of these *AutoFormat* features converts ordinal numbers and fractions into a more readable format, as shown in Table 3-4.

Another AutoFormat feature changes an Internet address into a hyperlink as you key the text. Clicking on the hyperlink takes you to another location, such as an HTML page on the Internet (assuming you are logged onto the Internet).

TABLE 3-4 Automatic Formatting of Ordinal Numbers and Fractions

Keyed Text	Format Change
1st	1st
2nd	2nd
1/2	$^{1}/_{2}$
1/4	$^{1}/_{4}$

Exercise 3-15 FORMAT ORDINAL NUMBERS AND FRACTIONS AUTOMATICALLY

1. In the paragraph that begins "Call Lydia," move the pointer to the immediate right of "2025" and key **or send an e-mail message to lydiahamrick@campbellsconfections.biz**. Press End.
2. Press Spacebar to initiate the automatic formatting. The e-mail address is now blue and underlined. If this were a real e-mail address, any reader of this document could press Ctrl and click the text to send an e-mail message to Lydia (providing the reader had an e-mail program installed).

Figure 3-15
Formatting hyperlink text

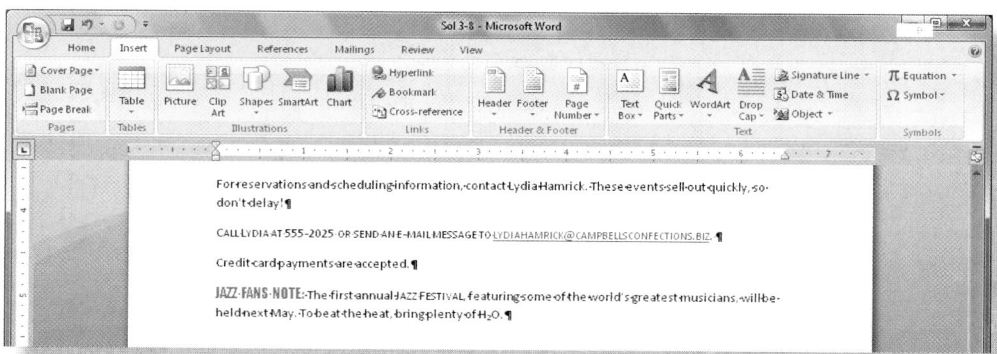

3. Move to the end of the paragraph that begins "Credit card payments." Add a new sentence by keying **Matinee performances are 1/2 price**. Notice that Word automatically converts the numbers and the slash into a fraction.
4. Save the document as ***[your initials]*3-15** in your Lesson 3 folder.
5. Submit your work and close the document.

Lesson 3 Summary

- A font is a type design applied to an entire set of characters, including all the letters of the alphabet, numerals, punctuation marks, and other keyboard symbols.
- A font can be serif (with decorative lines) or sans serif (with no decorative lines).
- Fonts are available in a variety of sizes, which are measured in points. There are 72 points to an inch.
- You can use the Ribbon to change fonts and font sizes.
- Keyboard shortcuts can also be used to change font sizes: Ctrl+Shift+> increases the text size and Ctrl+Shift+< decreases the text size.

- Use the Ribbon, Home tab, Font group to apply basic character formatting (for example, bold, italic, and/or underline) to selected contiguous (text that is together) or noncontiguous text (text that is not together).
- Use keyboard shortcuts to apply and remove basic character formatting.
- Use the Mini toolbar to apply character formatting to selected text.
- The Font dialog box can be used to change fonts, font sizes, and font styles. The Font dialog box also has settings for underline styles, font and underline colors, effects such as small caps and shadow (see Table 3-2), and character spacing.
- A hyperlink often appears as blue underlined text you click to open a software feature (such as a dialog box or a Help topic) or to go to an e-mail or a Web address.
- Keyboard shortcuts are available for some underline styles and font effects (see Table 3-3).
- A shortcut menu shows a list of commands relevant to a particular item. To display a shortcut menu, point to the item and right-click the mouse.
- Use F4 or Ctrl+Y to repeat character formatting.
- Use the Format Painter command to copy character formatting. Double-click the button to apply formatting to more than one selection.
- To change the case of selected characters, use the keyboard shortcut Shift+F3 or the Change Case command on the Ribbon, Home tab.
- Use the Highlight command to apply a color highlight to selected text you want to emphasize on-screen.
- Use **Drop Cap** from the Insert tab to create a dropped cap. A drop cap is a large letter that appears below the text baseline. It is usually applied to the first letter in the first word of a paragraph.
- Take advantage of Word's automatic formatting of ordinal numbers and fractions as you key text. An ordinal number is a number that indicates an order (for example, 1st, 3rd, or 107th).

LESSON 3 **Command Summary**

Feature	Button	Command	Keyboard
Bold	B	**Home** tab, **Font** group	Ctrl+B
Italic	I	**Home** tab, **Font** group	Ctrl+I
Underline	U	**Home** tab, **Font** group	Ctrl+U
Remove character formatting		**Home** tab, **Font** group	Ctrl+Spacebar
Increase font size	A	**Home** tab, **Font** group	Ctrl+Shift+>
Decrease font size	A	**Home** tab, **Font** group	Ctrl+Shift+<
Change case	Aa	**Home** tab, **Font** group	Shift+F3
Font color	A	**Home** tab, **Font** group	
Text Highlight Color		**Home** tab, **Font** group	

Lesson 4

Writing tools

OBJECTIVES

MCAS OBJECTIVES

In this lesson:
WW 07 1.4.1
WW 07 1.4.2
WW 07 4.1.1
WW 07 4.1.2

After completing this lesson, you will be able to:

1. Use AutoComplete, AutoCorrect, and Smart Tags.
2. Work with Building Blocks.
3. Insert the date and time as a field.
4. Check spelling and grammar.
5. Use the Thesaurus and Research task pane.

Estimated Time: 1 hour

Word provides several automated features that save you time when keying frequently used text and correcting common keying errors. Word also provides important writing and research tools: a spelling and grammar checker, a thesaurus, and access to research services. These tools help you create professional-looking documents.

Using AutoComplete, AutoCorrect, and Smart Tags

By now, you might be familiar with three of Word's automatic features, though you might not know their formal names:

- *AutoComplete* suggests the completed word when you key the first four or more letters of a day, month, or date. If you key "Janu," for example, Word displays a ScreenTip suggesting the word "January," which you can insert by pressing Enter. Continue keying if you do not want the word inserted.
- *AutoCorrect* corrects commonly misspelled words as you key text. If you key "teh" instead of "the," for example, Word automatically changes the spelling to "the." You can create AutoCorrect entries for text you frequently use, and you can control AutoCorrect options.

NOTE

You cannot turn off AutoComplete.

- *Smart tags* help you save time by performing actions in Word for which you would normally open other programs (such as Outlook). Word recognizes names, dates, addresses, and telephone numbers, as well as user-defined data types through the use of smart tags, which appear as purple dotted lines.

Exercise 4-1 PRACTICE AUTOCOMPLETE AND AUTOCORRECT

1. Open a new document. Open the **File** menu, and click **Word Options**. Click **Proofing**, and click **AutoCorrect Options** to open the AutoCorrect dialog box. Notice the available AutoCorrect options.
2. Scroll down the list of entries and notice the words that Word corrects automatically (assuming the **Replace text as you type** option is checked).

Figure 4-1
AutoCorrect dialog box

3. Click **Cancel** to close the dialog box. Click **Cancel** to close the Word Options dialog box.
4. Key **i am testing teh AutoCorrect feature.** Press Spacebar. Word corrects the "i" and "teh" automatically.
5. Try keying another incorrect sentence. Using the exact spelling and case as shown, key **TOdya is.** AutoCorrect corrects the spelling and capitalization of "Today."
6. Key today's date, beginning with the month, and then press Spacebar. When you see the AutoComplete ScreenTip that suggests the current date, press Enter.
7. Key a period at the end of the sentence.

NOTE

AutoCorrect corrects your text only after you complete a word by either pressing Spacebar or keying punctuation, such as a period or comma.

TABLE 4-1 AutoCorrect Options

Options	Description
Correct TWo INitial Capitals	Corrects words keyed accidentally with two initial capital letters, such as "WOrd" or "THis."
Capitalize first letter of sentences	Corrects any word at the beginning of a sentence that is not keyed with a capital letter.
Capitalize first letter of table cells	Corrects any word at the beginning of a table cell that is not keyed with a capital letter.
Capitalize names of days	Corrects a day spelled without an initial capital letter.
Correct accidental usage of cAPS LOCK key	If you press Caps Lock accidentally and then key "tODAY," AutoCorrect changes the word to "Today" and turns off Caps Lock.
Replace text as you type	Makes all corrections automatically.

Exercise 4-2 CREATE AN AUTOCORRECT ENTRY

You can create AutoCorrect entries for words you often misspell. You can also use AutoCorrect to create shortcuts for text you use repeatedly, such as names or phrases. Here are some examples of these types of AutoCorrect entries:

- "asap" for "as soon as possible"
- Your initials to be replaced with your full name, such as **"jh"** for **"Janet Holcomb"**
- "cc" for "Campbell's Confections"

1. Click the Microsoft Office Button, and click **Word Options**. Click **Proofing**.
2. Open the AutoCorrect dialog box by clicking **AutoCorrect Options**. Click the AutoCorrect tab if necessary. In the **Replace** box, key **fyi**.
3. In the **With** box, key **For your information**.
4. Click the **Add** button to move the entry into the alphabetized list. Click **OK** to close the AutoCorrect dialog box. Click **OK** to close the Word Options dialog box.
5. Start a new paragraph in the current document, and key **fyi, this really works**. Word spells out the entry, just as you specified in the AutoCorrect dialog box.

Exercise 4-3 CONTROL AUTOCORRECT OPTIONS

Sometimes you might not want text to be corrected. You can undo a correction or turn AutoCorrect options on or off by clicking the AutoCorrect Options button and making a selection.

1. Move the I-beam over the word "For" until a small blue box appears beneath it.

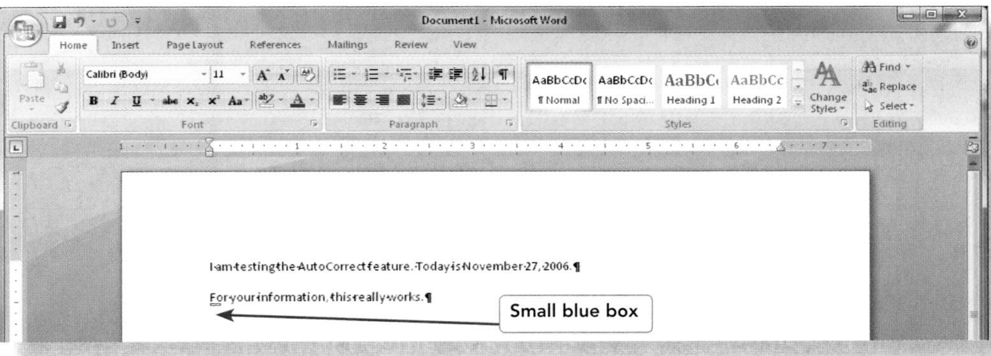

Figure 4-2
Controlling AutoCorrect options

2. Drag the I-beam down over the small blue box until your mouse becomes a pointer and the box turns into the AutoCorrect Options button.
3. Click the button and choose **Change back to "fyi"** from the menu list.

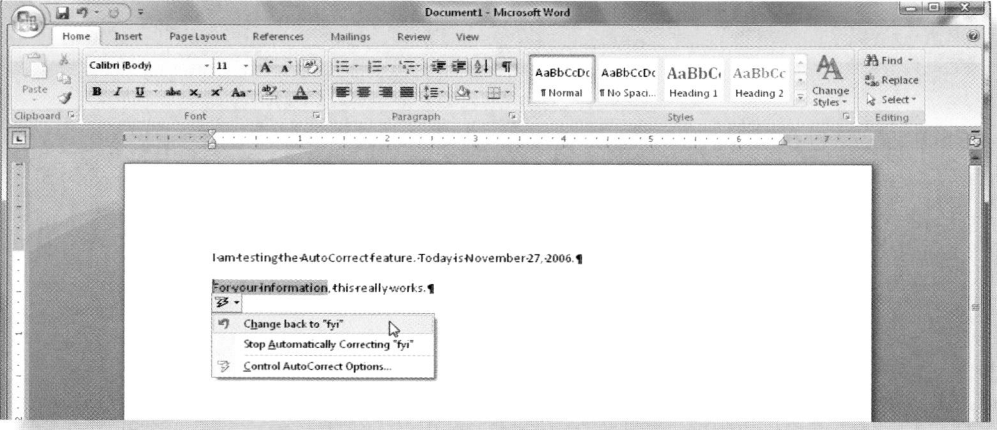

Figure 4-3 Undoing automatic corrections

4. Click the AutoCorrect Options button again, and choose **Redo AutoCorrect** from the menu list. The words "For your information" are restored.
5. Click the button again and choose **Control AutoCorrect Options**. The AutoCorrect dialog box opens.
6. Position the insertion point in the Replace text box, and key **fyi**. The AutoCorrect entry displays and is highlighted. Click **Delete**, and then click **OK**.

Exercise 4-4 CREATE AN AUTOCORRECT EXCEPTION

Another way to keep Word from correcting text you do not want corrected is to create an AutoCorrect exception. For example, you might have a company name that uses nonstandard capitalization such as "tuesday's child." In such a case, you can use the AutoCorrect Exceptions dialog box to prevent Word from making automatic changes.

1. In a new paragraph, key the following on two separate lines:

   The ABCs of chocolate:
   ABsolute is a must.

   Notice that AutoCorrect automatically makes the "B" in "ABsolute" lowercase.
2. Open the AutoCorrect dialog box and click **Exceptions**. The AutoCorrect Exceptions dialog box displays.
3. Click the **INitial CAps** tab.

4. Key the exception **ABsolute** in the **Don't Correct** text box. Click **Add**. The entry is now in the list of exceptions.

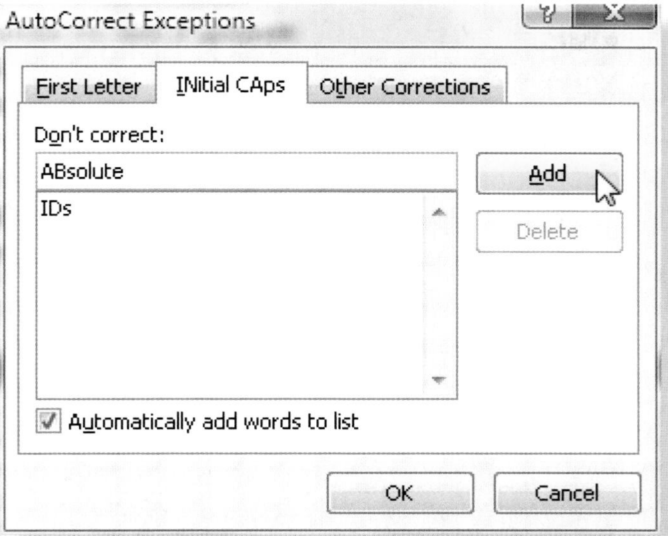

Figure 4-4
AutoCorrect Exceptions dialog box

NOTE

Notice when you select "Absolute," the small blue box appears beneath the corrected word.

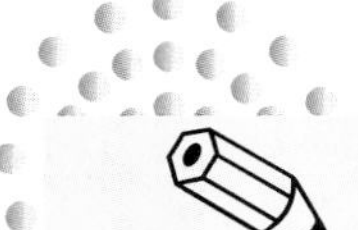

TIP

Another good example of an AutoCorrect exception is the use of lowercase initials, which are sometimes entered at the bottom of a business letter as reference initials. In this case, you would not want Word to capitalize the first letter.

5. Click **OK**, to close the AutoCorrect Exceptions dialog box, and then click **OK** again to close the AutoCorrect dialog box. Click **OK** to close the Word Options dialog box if necessary.
6. Select "Absolute" and then key **ABsolute Comfort**.
7. Delete the exception: Open the AutoCorrect dialog box, click **Exceptions**, select "ABsolute" from the list, and click **Delete.** Click **OK** to close the AutoCorrect Exceptions dialog box, click **OK** to close the AutoCorrect dialog box, and then click **OK** again to close the Word Options dialog box if necessary.

Exercise 4-5 USE SMART TAGS

Just as Word recognizes an e-mail or Web address and automatically creates a hyperlink, it also recognizes names, dates, addresses, and telephone numbers, as well as user-defined data types through the use of smart tags. You can use this feature to perform actions in Word for which you would normally open other programs, such as Microsoft Outlook. Purple dotted lines beneath text in your document indicate smart tags.

1. Open the **File** menu, and click **Word Options**. Click **Proofing**, and click **AutoCorrect Options**.

2. Click the **Smart Tags** tab, and click the **Label text with smart tags** check box if it is not selected.

3. Under **Recognizers**, select **Address (English)** and **Date (Smart tag lists)**. Deselect all other **Recognizers**.

4. Click **OK** to close the AutoCorrect dialog box. Click **OK** to close the Word Options dialog box.

5. Position the insertion point at the end of the document, and press Enter twice and key:

   Campbells Confections
   25 Main Street
   Grove City, PA 16127

6. Notice that Word recognizes the text as an address and applies a smart tag indicator (the purple dotted underline).

7. Move the I-beam over the street address, and then move your pointer over the Smart Tag Actions button.

8. Click the button to see the list of actions.

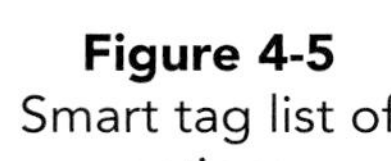

Figure 4-5
Smart tag list of actions

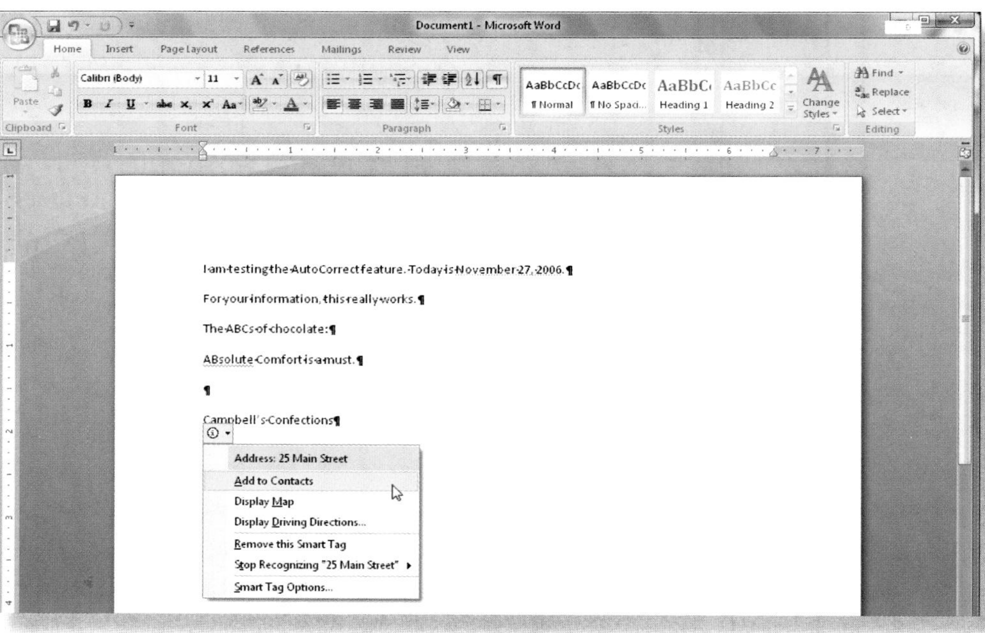

NOTE

Microsoft Outlook is a program included in the Microsoft Office suite. If it is not set up on your machine, just close the dialog box when it asks you to configure it, or ask your instructor for help. If Outlook does launch, the **Add to Contacts** option lets you record information about individuals and businesses. All this is done from within Word through the use of the smart tag.

9. Choose **Add to Contacts**. Microsoft Outlook launches, and an Untitled-Contact dialog box opens. You can add the name and address as well as telephone numbers to the listing.
10. Look over the dialog box contents, and close the dialog box. Click **No** when you are asked if you want to save the changes.
11. Close the document without saving.

Working with AutoText and Building Blocks

NOTE

You can also create AutoText entries for nontext items such as graphics and tables.

AutoText is another feature you can use to insert text automatically. This feature is extremely versatile. You can use it to create AutoText entries for text you use repeatedly (the AutoText entry can even include the text formatting). The text for which you create an AutoText entry can be a phrase, a sentence, paragraphs, logos, and so on.

After you create an entry, you can insert it with just a few keystrokes.

Exercise 4-6 CREATE AN AUTOTEXT ENTRY

To create an AutoText entry, you key the text that you want to save and select it, or you select text that already exists in a document. When you select the text to be used for an AutoText entry, be sure to include the appropriate spaces, blank lines, and paragraph marks.

1. Open the file **Letter - 1**.
2. Press Ctrl+A to select the document.
3. Click the **Insert tab** on the Ribbon.
4. Locate the **Text** group, and click **Quick Parts**. Click **Save Selection to Quick Part Gallery**. The Create New Building Block dialog box displays.

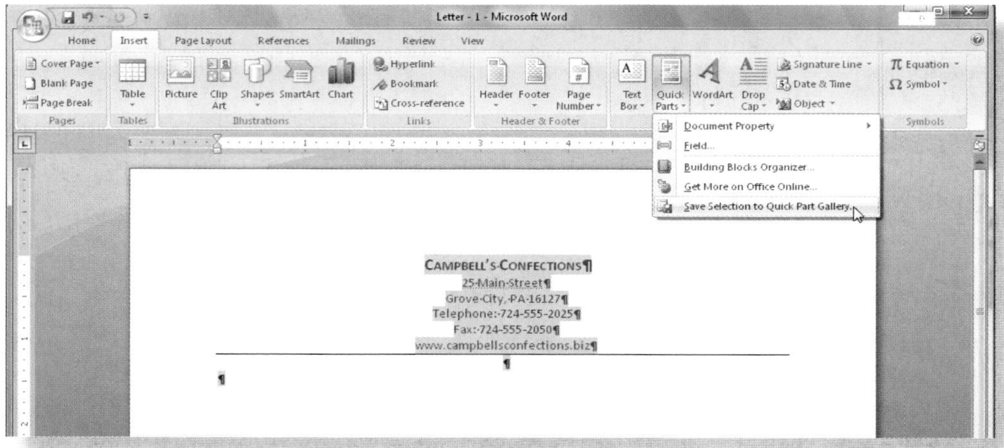

Figure 4-6
Quick Parts menu

5. Key **[your initials]Letterhead** in the **Name** box. Each AutoText entry must have a unique name.
6. Select **AutoText** from the **Gallery** drop-down list box.
7. Select **General** from the **Category** drop-down list box.
8. Key **Grove City** in the **Description** text box.
9. Select **Building Blocks** from the **Save in** drop-down list.
10. Select **Insert content only** from the Options drop-down list. Click **OK**.
11. Press Ctrl+End to move to the end of the document. Key the text in Figure 4-7.

NOTE

You can choose to insert AutoText entries as a separate paragraph by choosing **Insert content in its own paragraph**. Choose **Insert content in its own page** if you want the AutoText entry to appear on a new page.

Figure 4-7

```
Sincerely,

Thomas Campbell
President
[your initials]
```

12. Select the text you just keyed, and press Alt+F3 to open the Create New Building Block dialog box.
13. Key or select the following information in the Create New Building Block dialog box.

Name:	**[your initials]Closing**
Gallery:	**AutoText**
Category:	**General**
Description:	**Closing**
Save in:	**Building Blocks**
Options:	**Insert content only**

14. Click **OK** to close the Create New Building Block dialog box.
15. Close the document, and do not save the changes.

Exercise 4-7 INSERT AUTOTEXT ENTRIES

To insert an AutoText entry, position the insertion point and open the Building Blocks Organizer. When the Building Blocks Organizer dialog box opens, click one of the column headings to sort the lists. Click the **Name** heading to sort the text alphabetically by name. Click the **Gallery** heading to display the lists by gallery type. AutoText entries will appear at the top of the Gallery listing. If you have an AutoText entry that is unique or short, you can key the first three letters of the entry name and press F3 to insert the entry.

1. Create a new document.
2. Click the **Insert** tab and locate the **Text** group. Click **Quick Parts** and click **Building Blocks Organizer**. The Building Blocks Organizer dialog box displays.

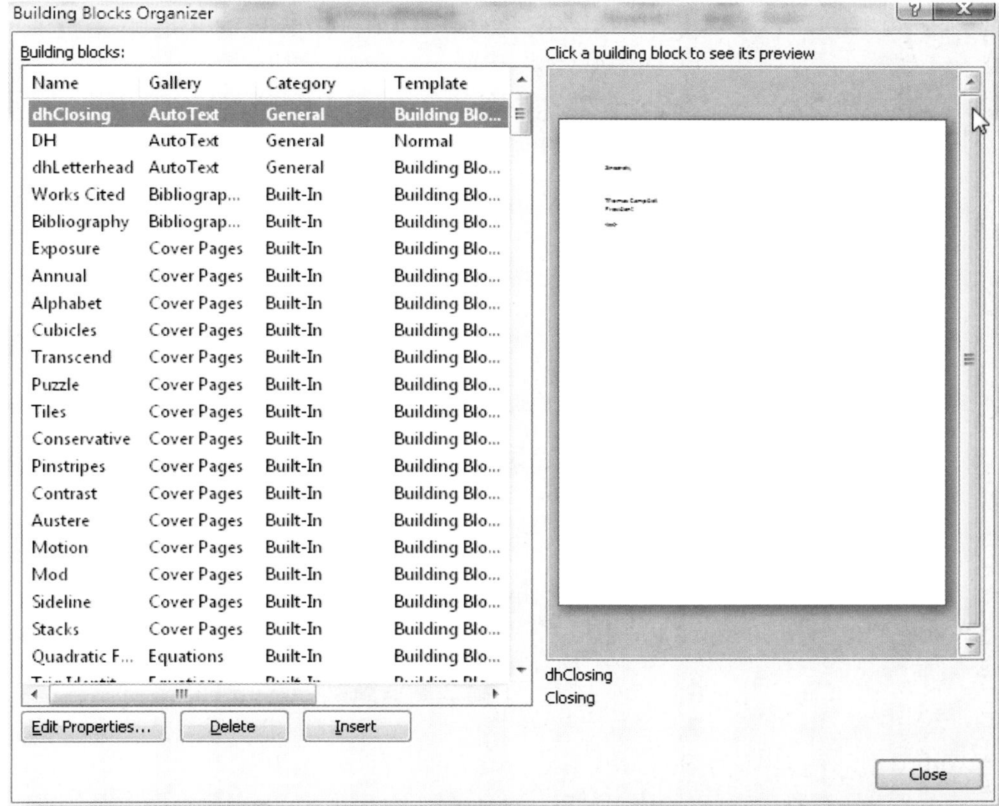

Figure 4-8 Building Blocks Organizer dialog box

3. Click the **Gallery** heading, and the list sorts by gallery type.
4. Click the **Name** heading, and the list is sorted alphabetically by name.
5. Click the **Gallery** heading, and locate "[your initials]Letterhead" AutoText entry.
6. Click the ***[your initials]*Letterhead** entry, and click **Insert**. The letterhead information is automatically inserted.
7. Click [Undo button] to remove the AutoText entry.
8. Key **[your initials]Letterhead** and press F3 to insert the Autotext entry using the keyboard shortcut.
9. Key **[your initials]Closing** and press F3 to insert the Closing AutoText entry.

NOTE

Review your letter and verify that it follows correct business letter format.

Exercise 4-8 EDIT AND DELETE AUTOTEXT ENTRIES

After you create an AutoText entry, it may need to be edited. If you no longer use an entry, you can delete it.

1. Position the insertion point to the right of "Telephone:" in the letterhead, and key the telephone number **724-555-2025**.
2. Select the letterhead text beginning with "Campbell's Confections" and ending with the left aligned paragraph mark.
3. Press Alt+F3 to open the Create New Building Block dialog box.
4. Key **[your initials]Letterhead** in the **Name** box, and select **AutoText** from the **Gallery** drop-down list. Click **OK**.
5. Click **Yes** to redefine the AutoText entry. The entry now includes the telephone number.
6. To test the change, delete all the document text. Key **[your initials]Letterhead** and press F3 to insert the letterhead AutoText.
7. Click the **Insert** tab on the Ribbon, and click the **Quick Parts** command. Click **Building Blocks Organizer** to open the Building Blocks Organizer dialog box.
8. Click the **Gallery** column heading to sort the entries in the list by Gallery type.
9. Click the entry for "[your initials]Letterhead." Click **Delete** to remove the AutoText entry from the Gallery. Click **No**. Click **Close** to return to your document.

Inserting the Date and Time

You have seen that when you begin keying a month, AutoComplete displays the suggested date, and you press Enter to insert the date as regular text. You can also insert the date or time in a document as a field. A *field* is a hidden code that tells Word to insert specific text that might need to be updated automatically, such as a date or page number. If you insert the date or time in a document as a field, Word automatically updates it each time you print the document.

There are two ways to insert the date or time as a field:

- Click the **Insert** tab on the Ribbon, and click the **Date and Time** command. Select the desired format from the Date and Time dialog box.
- Press Alt+Shift+D to insert the date, and Alt+Shift+T to insert the time.

Exercise 4-9 INSERT THE DATE AND TIME

You can enter date and time fields that can be updated automatically. You can also choose not to update these fields automatically.

1. Move the insertion point to the end of the current document.
2. Press Alt+Shift+D to enter the default date field.
3. Click the Undo button.
4. Click the **Insert** tab on the Ribbon, and click the **Date and Time** command to open the Date and Time dialog box.

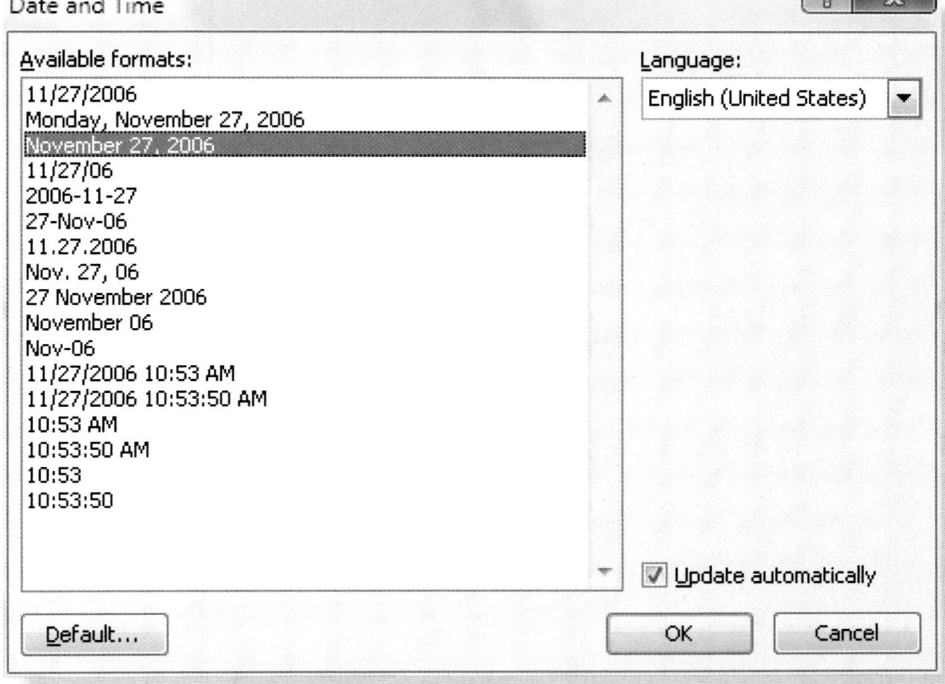

Figure 4-9
Date and Time dialog box

NOTE

You can also use this dialog box to insert the date and time in a particular text format without inserting it as an updatable field.

TIP

Although printing updates a field, you can also update a field on-screen by clicking the field and pressing F9.

5. Scroll the list of available time and date formats, and choose the third format in the list (the standard date format for business documents).
6. Check the **Update automatically** check box so the date is automatically updated each time you print the document. Click **OK**.
7. Move the insertion point after the date field, and press Spacebar twice.
8. Press Alt+Shift+T to insert the time as a field.
9. Save the document as ***[your initials]*4-9** in your Lesson 4 folder.
10. Submit your work, and close the document.

TIP

Remember that the **Update automatically** option will change the date in your document. If you are sending correspondence, do not choose this option because the date in the letter will then always reflect the current date, not the date on which you wrote the letter.

Checking Spelling and Grammar

Correct spelling and grammar are essential to good writing. As you have seen, Word checks your spelling and grammar as you key text and flags errors with these on-screen indicators:

- A red, wavy line appears under misspelled words.
- A green, wavy line appears under possible grammatical errors.
- A blue, wavy line appears under possible formatting inconsistencies.
- The Proofing Errors icon on the status bar contains an "X."

TABLE 4-2 Spelling and Grammar Status

Icon	Indicates
	Word is checking for errors as you key text.
	The document has errors.
	The document has no errors.

Exercise 4-10 SPELL- AND GRAMMAR-CHECK ERRORS INDIVIDUALLY

NOTE

If no green, wavy lines appear in your document, open the **File** menu, and click **Word Options**. Click **Proofing** in the left pane. Click the **Check grammar with spelling** check box, and click **OK**.

TIP

Word's spelling and grammar tools are not foolproof. For example, it cannot correct a word that is correctly spelled but incorrectly keyed, such as "sue" instead of "use." It might also apply a green wavy line to a type of grammatical usage, such as the passive voice, which might not be preferred, but is not incorrect.

You can right-click text marked as either a spelling or a grammar error and choose a suggested correction from a shortcut menu.

1. Open the file **Milk Chocolate - 2**. This document has several errors, indicated by the red and green wavy lines.
2. At the top of the document, press Enter and move the insertion point to the first paragraph mark. Notice that the Proofing Errors indicator on the status bar now contains an "X."
3. Using 14-point bold type, key a misspelled word by keying the title **Mlk Chocolate**. When you finish, "Mlk" is marked as misspelled.
4. Right-click the misspelled word, and choose "Milk" from the spelling shortcut menu.
5. Right-click the grammatical error "It contain" in the second sentence. Choose "contains" from the shortcut menu.

Exercise 4-11 SPELL- AND GRAMMAR-CHECK AN ENTIRE DOCUMENT

Instead of checking words or sentences individually, you can check an entire document. This is the best way to correct spelling and grammar errors in a long document. Use one of these methods:

- Click the Spelling and Grammar button on the Review tab of the Ribbon.
- Press F7.

1. Position the insertion point at the beginning of the document and click the **Review** tab of the Ribbon. Click the Spelling and Grammar button. Word locates the first misspelling, "choclate."

Figure 4-10
Checking spelling

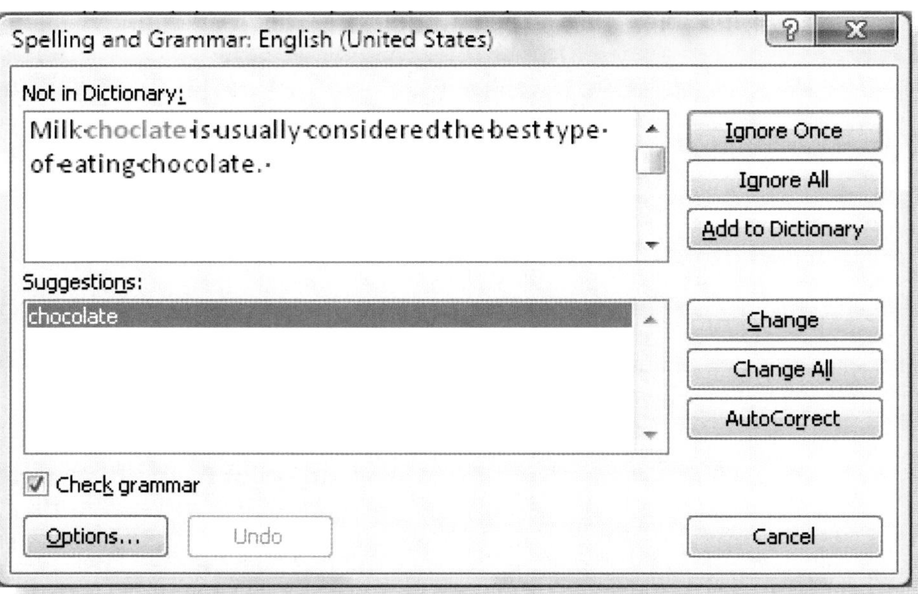

TIP

To check spelling without also checking grammar, click the **Check grammar** check box to clear it.

2. Click **Change** to correct the spelling to the first suggested spelling, "chocolate." Next, Word finds a word choice error, "hole."
3. Click **Change** to correct the word choice. Next, Word finds two words that should be separated by a space.
4. Click **Change** to correct the spacing. Next word finds a repeated word, "of."
5. Click **Delete** to delete the repeated word. Next Word finds a grammatical error—"it" is not capitalized.
6. Click **Change** to correct the capitalization in the document.

7. Click **OK** when the check is complete. Notice there are no more wavy lines in the document, and the Proofing Errors indicator shows a check mark.
8. Read the paragraph, and check for errors that were not found by the Spelling & Grammar checker.
9. Locate "10 per cent" in the second sentence. Delete the space between "per" and "cent."
10. Locate the sentence that begins "It is mild," and change "type" to "**types**."
11. Locate the sentence that begins "It used," and change it to read "**It is used**."

TABLE 4-3 Dialog Box Options When Checking Spelling and Grammar

Option	Description
Ignore Once	Skips the word.
Ignore All	Skips all occurrences of the word in the document.
Add to Dictionary	Adds the word to the default dictionary file in Word. You can also create your own dictionary and add words to it.
Change	Changes the word to the entry in the **Change To** box or to the word you choose from the **Suggestions** list.
Change All	Same as **Change**, but changes the word throughout the document.
AutoCorrect	Adds the word to the list of corrections Word makes automatically.
Options	Lets you change the Spelling and Grammar options in Word.
Undo	Changes back the most recent correction made.
Cancel	Discontinues the checking operation.

NOTE

You can create or add a custom dictionary for technical and specialized vocabulary. Open the **File** menu, click **Word Options**, and click **Proofing**. Click **Custom Dictionaries**, click **New**, and key a name for the custom dictionary. To add a custom dictionary that you purchased, follow the steps listed above, except choose Add instead of New. Locate the folder and double-click the dictionary file.

Using the Thesaurus and Research Task Pane

The *thesaurus* is a tool that can improve your writing. Use the thesaurus to look up a *synonym* (a word with a similar meaning) for a selected word to add variety or interest to a document. You can look up synonyms for any of these words to get additional word choices. The thesaurus sometimes displays *antonyms* (words with the opposite meaning) and related words.

After selecting a word to change, you can start the thesaurus in one of three ways:

- Click the **Review** tab, and click **Thesaurus**.
- Press Shift+F7.
- Right-click the word and choose **Synonyms** from the shortcut menu.

Exercise 4-12 USE THE THESAURUS

1. Select the word "best" in the first paragraph, or place the insertion point in the word.
2. Press Shift+F7. The Research task pane appears with a list of synonyms for "best."

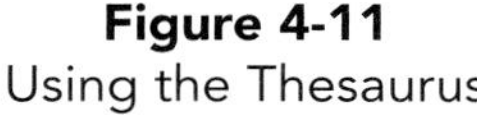

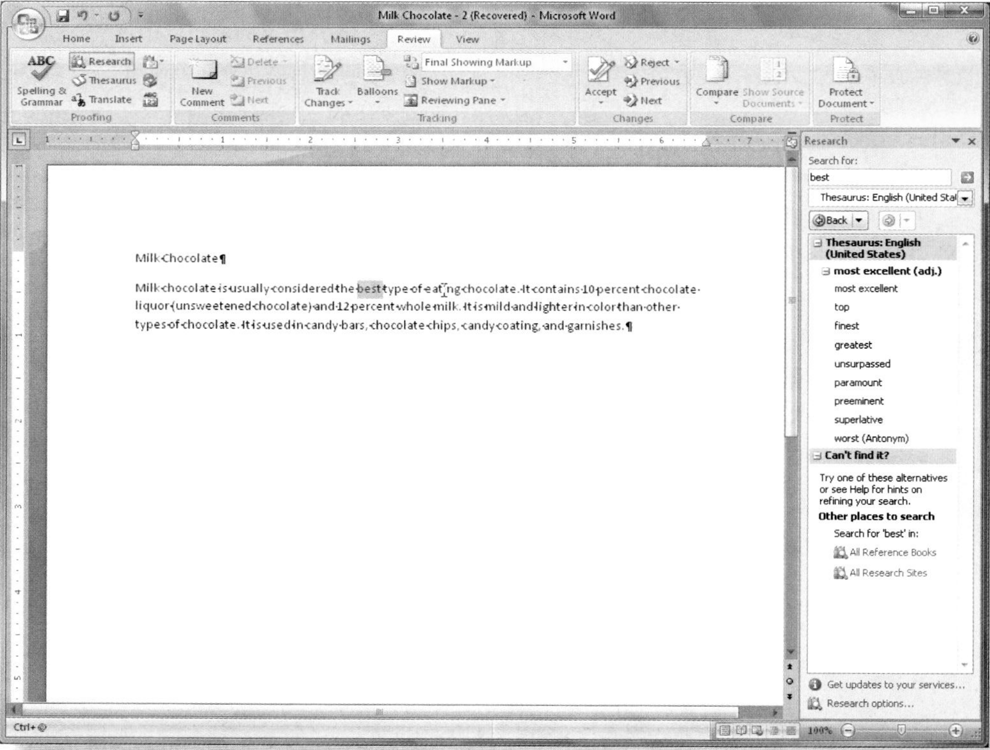

Figure 4-11
Using the Thesaurus

3. Point to the word "finest" and click the drop-down arrow. Click **Look Up**. A list of additional synonyms appears for "finest" in the task pane.

4. Go back to the word "finest" by clicking the Previous Search button .
5. Point to "finest," click the down arrow, and choose **Insert**. Word replaces "best" with "finest" and returns to the document.
6. Save the document as ***[your initials]*4-12** in your Lesson 4 folder.
7. Submit the document, but do not close it.

Exercise 4-13 USE REFERENCES

If you are connected to the Internet, you can access several research sources, such as a dictionary, an encyclopedia, and research sites such as MSN. From the Review tab on the Ribbon, you can click the Research button ; right-click a word and click **Look Up** in the shortcut menu; or press Alt and click a word to open the Research task pane.

1. Press Alt and click the word "chocolate" in the first sentence.

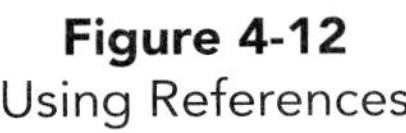

Figure 4-12
Using References

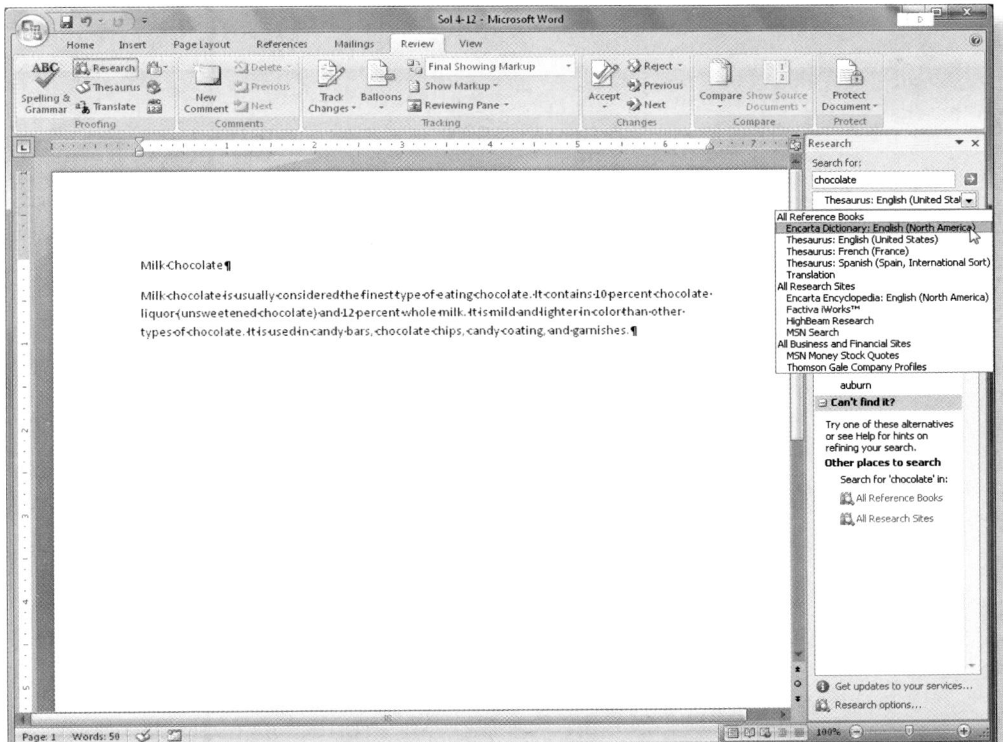

NOTE

Click Research options at the bottom of the Research task pane to open the Research Options dialog box.

TIP

Click the Translation Tool Tip button on the Ribbon to turn on or turn off a translation ScreenTip. Select a language to turn on the Translation ScreenTip. Click **Turn Off Translation ScreenTip** to turn off the ScreenTip.

2. Click the drop-down arrow beside the All Reference Books box and choose ***Encarta Dictionary***. The task pane indicates the part of speech, syllabication, and several definitions for "chocolate."
3. Click the drop-down arrow beside the All Reference Books box, and choose Translation.
4. Choose **English** in the From box and **French (France)** in the To box. The bilingual dictionary displays the French word for chocolate—chocolat.
5. Close the document.

Lesson 4 Summary

- The AutoComplete feature suggests the completed word when you key the first four or more letters of a day, month, or date.
- The AutoCorrect feature corrects some misspelled words and capitalization errors for you automatically as you key text.
- Use the AutoCorrect dialog box to create entries for words you often misspell and the AutoCorrect Options button to control AutoCorrect options.
- Use the AutoCorrect Exceptions dialog box to create an AutoCorrect exception so Word will not correct it.
- Use smart tags to perform Microsoft Outlook functions, such as creating entries in Outlook's contact list.
- AutoText is another versatile feature you can use to insert text automatically. You create AutoText entries for text you use repeatedly, including text formatting.
- Use the Building Blocks Organizer to edit and delete AutoText entries.
- Insert the date and time in a document as an automatically updated field, which is a hidden code that tells Word to insert specific information—in this case, the date and/or time. Use the Date and Time dialog box to choose different date and time formats.
- Use the spelling and grammar checker to correct misspelled words in your document as well as poor grammar usage. Check errors individually or throughout your entire document.

- Use the thesaurus to look up synonyms (words with similar meaning) or sometimes antonyms (words with the opposite meaning) for a selected word to add variety and interest to your document.
- Use the Research task pane to look up words or phrases in a dictionary, to research topics in an encyclopedia, or to access bilingual dictionaries for translations. You can also access research sites such as MSN.

LESSON 4		**Command Summary**	
Feature	**Button**	**Command**	**Keyboard**
Create AutoText entry	Quick Parts	Insert tab, **Text** group, **Quick Parts**, **Save Selection to Quick Part Gallery**	Alt+F3
Insert Date	Date & Time	Insert tab, **Text** group, **Date & Time**	Alt+Shift+D
Insert Time	Date & Time	Insert tab, **Text** group, **Date & Time**	Alt+Shift+T
Check spelling and grammar	Spelling & Grammar	Review tab, **Proofing** group, **Spelling & Grammar**	F7
Thesaurus	Thesaurus	Review tab, **Proofing** group, **Thesaurus**	Shift+F7
Research	Research	Review tab, **Proofing** group, **Research**	Alt+Click

unit 2

PARAGRAPH FORMATTING, TABS, AND ADVANCED EDITING

Lesson 5

Formatting Paragraphs

OBJECTIVES

After completing this lesson, you will be able to:

1. Align paragraphs.
2. Change line spacing.
3. Change paragraph spacing.
4. Set paragraph indents.
5. Apply borders and shading.
6. Repeat and copy paragraph formats.
7. Create bulleted and numbered lists.
8. Insert symbols and special characters.

MCAS OBJECTIVES

In this lesson:
WW 07 1.1.5
WW 07 2.1.4
WW 07 4.2.2
WW 07 4.2.3
WW 07 4.2.1

Estimated Time: 1 1/2 hours

In Microsoft Word, a *paragraph* is a unique block of information. Paragraph formatting controls the appearance of individual paragraphs within a document. For example, you can change the space between paragraphs or change the space between lines. For emphasis, you can indent paragraphs, number them, or add borders and shading.

A paragraph is always followed by a *paragraph mark*. All the formatting for a paragraph is stored in the paragraph mark. Each time you press Enter, you copy the formatting instructions in the current paragraph to a new paragraph. You can copy paragraph formats to existing paragraphs and view formats in the Reveal Formatting task pane.

Paragraph Alignment

Paragraph alignment determines how the edges of a paragraph appear horizontally. There are four ways to align text in a paragraph, as shown in Figure 5-1.

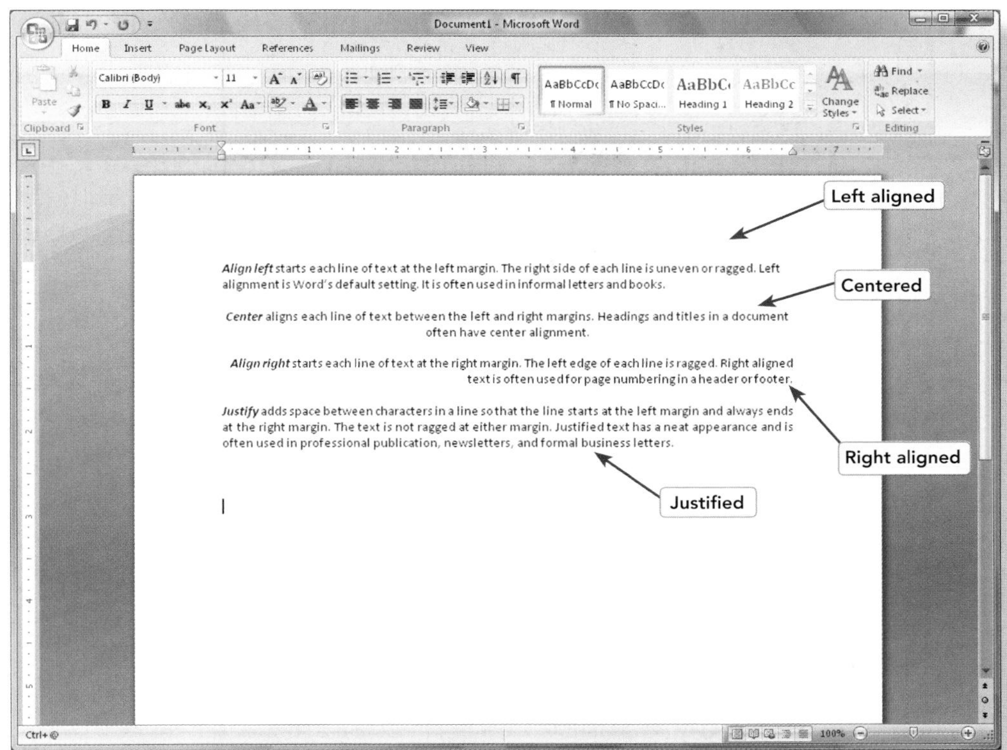

Figure 5-1
Paragraph alignment options

Exercise 5-1 CHANGE PARAGRAPH ALIGNMENT

The easiest way to change paragraph alignment is to use the alignment buttons on the Ribbon, Home tab, Paragraph group. You can also use keyboard shortcuts: Ctrl+L left align; Ctrl+E center; Ctrl+R right align; Ctrl+J justify.

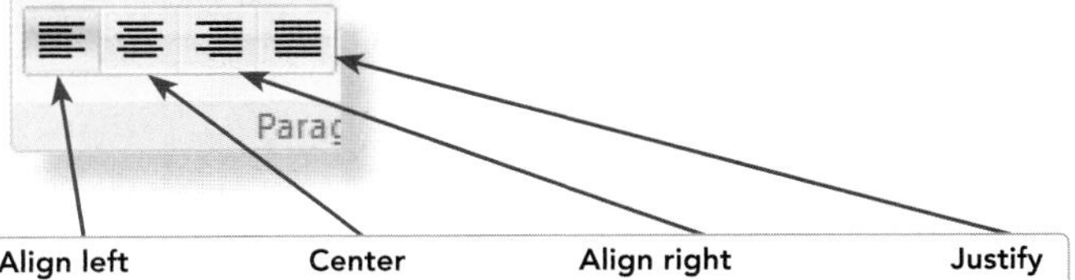

Figure 5-2
Alignment buttons on the Ribbon

NOTE

The documents you create in this course relate to the case study about Campbell's Confections, a fictional candy store and chocolate factory (see Case Study in the frontmatter of the book).

1. Open the file **Corporate Gifts**. Click the Show/Hide ¶ button to display paragraph marks if they are turned off.

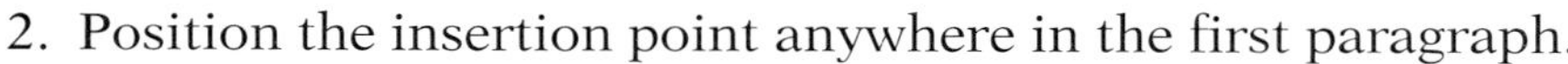

2. Position the insertion point anywhere in the first paragraph.

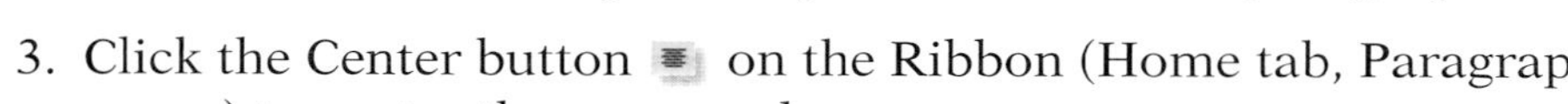

3. Click the Center button on the Ribbon (Home tab, Paragraph group) to center the paragraph.

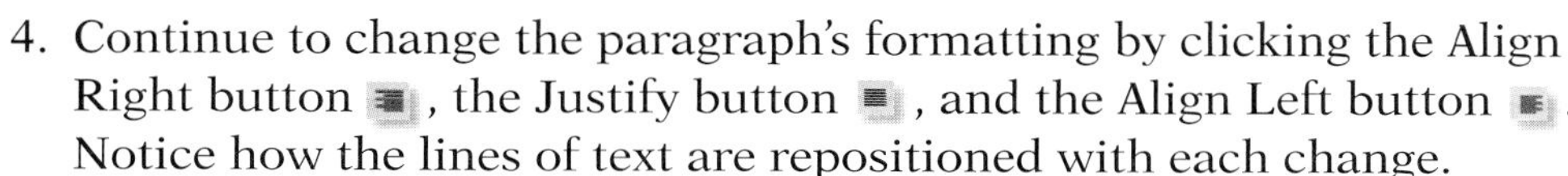

4. Continue to change the paragraph's formatting by clicking the Align Right button, the Justify button, and the Align Left button. Notice how the lines of text are repositioned with each change.

5. Position the insertion point in the second paragraph and press Ctrl+E to center the paragraph.

6. Use the keyboard shortcut Ctrl+R to right-align the third paragraph.

7. Press Ctrl+J to justify the fourth paragraph.

NOTE

When applying paragraph formatting, you do not have to select the paragraph—you just need to have the insertion point within the paragraph or just before the paragraph mark.

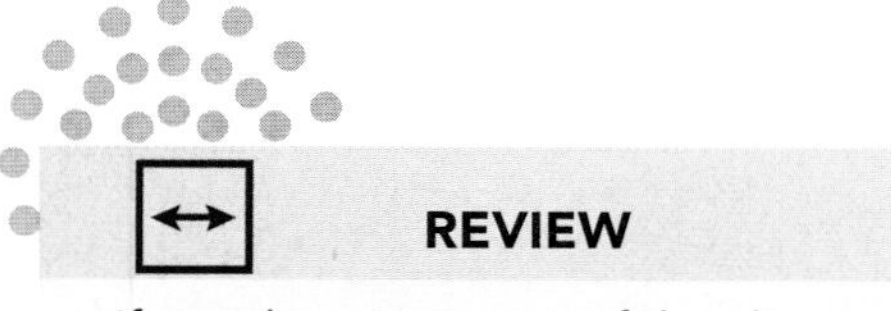

REVIEW

If you do not see one of the alignment buttons, check the Ribbon to verify that the Home tab is active.

TIP

To change the alignment of multiple paragraphs, select them, and then apply the alignment.

Exercise 5-2 USE CLICK AND TYPE TO INSERT TEXT

You can use *Click and Type* to insert text or graphics in any blank area of a document. This feature enables you to position the insertion point anywhere in the document without pressing Enter repeatedly. Word automatically inserts the paragraph marks before that point and also inserts a tab.

1. Open the file **Factory**, and leave the Corporate Gifts document open.
2. Click the Microsoft Office Button and click Word Options. Click Advanced in the left pane, and click Enable click and type if it is not already selected. Click OK.
3. Press Ctrl+End to move to the end of the document.
4. Position the I-beam about five lines below the last line of text, in the center of the page. The I-beam is now the Click and Type pointer, which includes tiny lines that show right or center alignment.

Figure 5-3
Using Click and Type

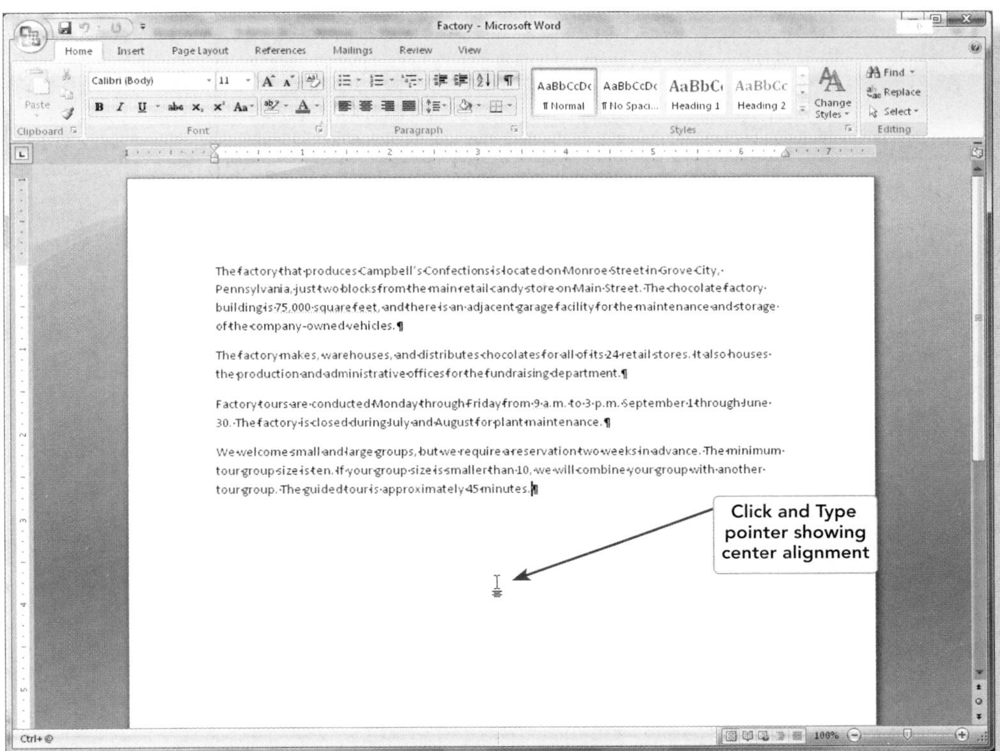

5. Move the I-beam back and forth until it shows center alignment. Double-click, and key **Visit us at www.campbellsconfections.biz**. The text is centered, and paragraph marks are inserted before it.
6. Save the document as ***[your initials]*5-2** in your Lesson 5 folder.
7. Submit your work, and close the document.

Line Spacing

Line space is the amount of vertical space between lines of text in a paragraph. Line spacing is typically based on the height of the characters, but you can change it to a specific value. For example, some paragraphs might be single-spaced and some double-spaced. The default line spacing is Multiple 1.15.

Exercise 5-3 CHANGE LINE SPACING

You can apply the most common types of line spacing by using keyboard shortcuts: single space, Ctrl+1; 1.5-line space, Ctrl+5; double space, Ctrl+2. Additional spacing options, as well as other paragraph formatting options, are available in the Paragraph dialog box or from the Line Spacing button .

1. Position the insertion point in the first paragraph of the Corporate Gifts document.
2. Press Ctrl+2 to double-space the paragraph.
3. With the insertion point in the same paragraph, press Ctrl+5 to change the spacing to 1.5 lines. Press Ctrl+1 to restore the paragraph to single spacing.

4. With the insertion point in the same paragraph, click the down arrow to the right of the Line Spacing button on the Ribbon, Home tab, Paragraph group, and choose **2.0** to change the line spacing to double. Choose **1.0** to restore the paragraph to single spacing.
5. Right-click the first paragraph and choose **Paragraph** from the shortcut menu. (You can also open the Paragraph dialog box by clicking the **Dialog Box Launcher** in the right corner of the Paragraph group.)
6. Click the down arrow to open the **Line spacing** drop-down list, and choose **Double**. The change is reflected in the **Preview** box.

Figure 5-4
Line-spacing options in the Paragraph dialog box

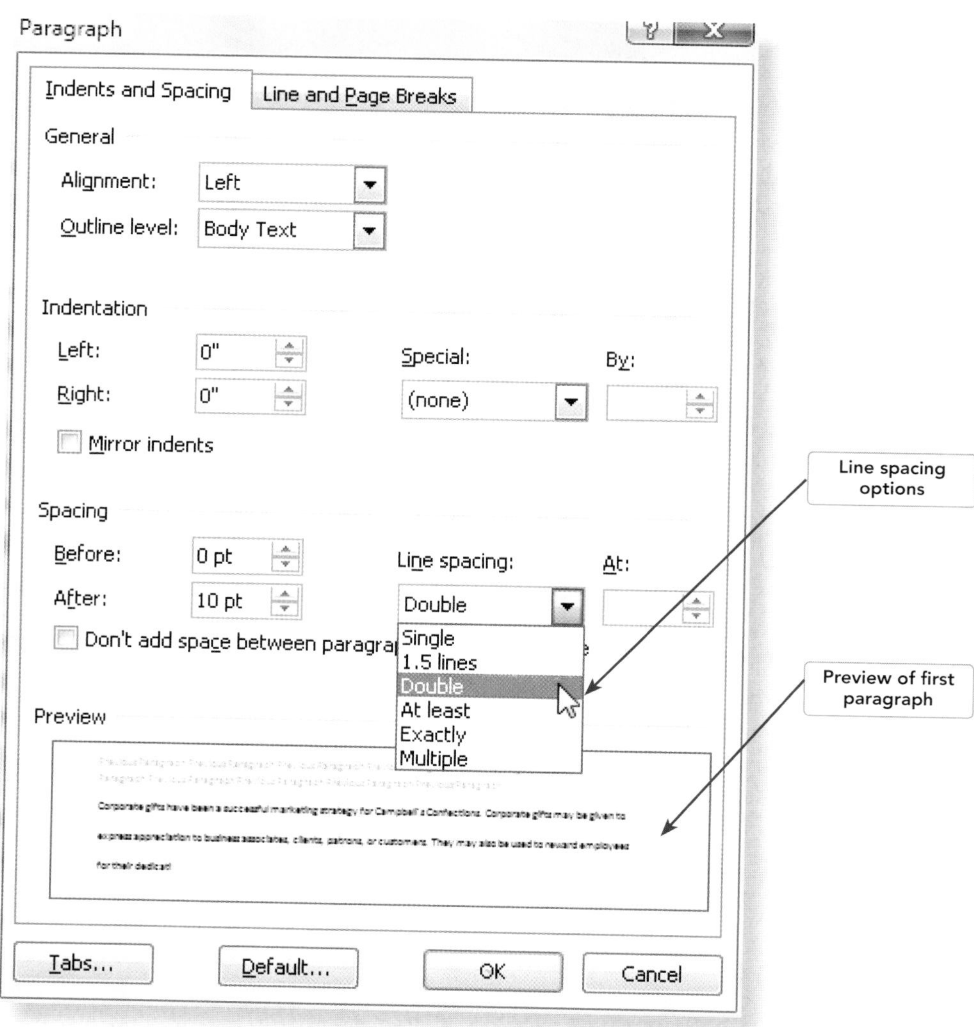

7. With the dialog box still open, choose **Single** from the **Line spacing** drop-down list. The **Preview** box shows the change.
8. Choose **Multiple** from the **Line spacing** drop-down list. In the **At** box, key **1.25**. (Select the text that appears in the box and key over it.) Press Tab to see the change displayed in the **Preview** box.
9. Click **OK**. Word adds an extra quarter-line space between lines in the paragraph.

Figure 5-5
Examples of line spacing

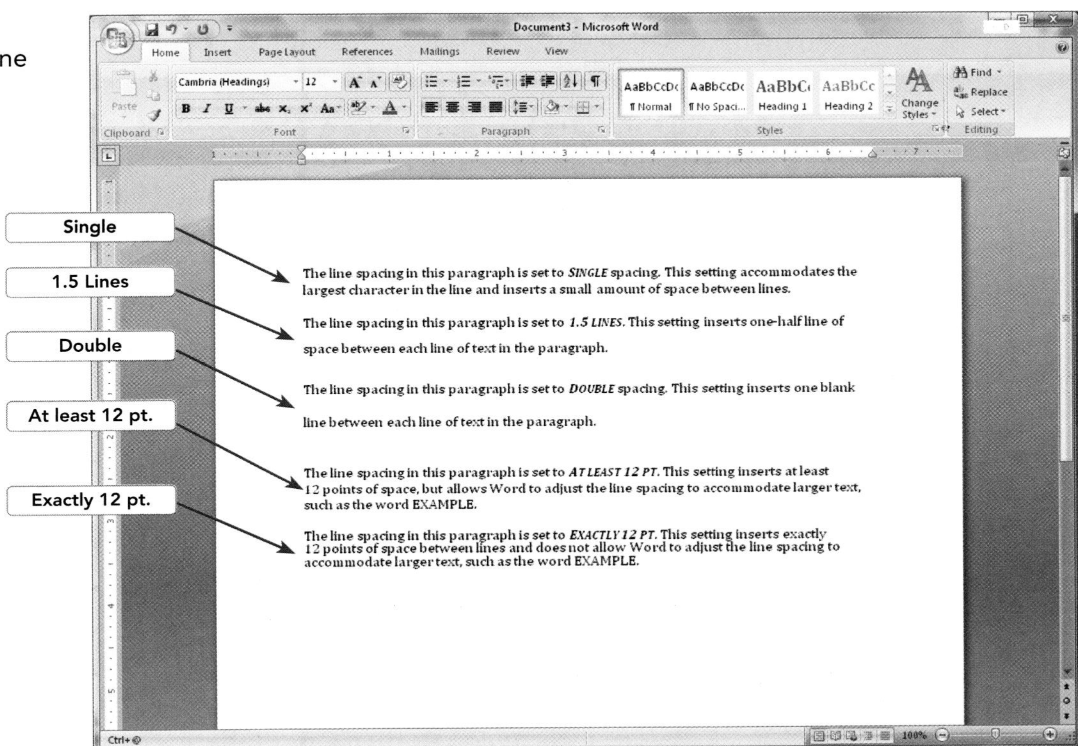

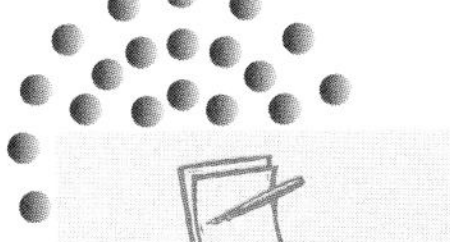

NOTE

The **At Least** option applies minimum line spacing that Word can adjust to accommodate larger font sizes. The **Exactly** option applies fixed line spacing that Word does not adjust. This option makes all lines evenly spaced. The **Multiple** option increases or decreases line spacing by the percentage you specify. For example, setting line spacing to a multiple of 1.25 increases the space by 25 percent, and setting line spacing to a multiple of 0.8 decreases the space by 20 percent.

Paragraph Spacing

In addition to changing spacing between lines of text, you can change *paragraph space*. Paragraph space is the amount of space above or below a paragraph. Instead of pressing Enter multiple times to increase space between paragraphs, you can use the Paragraph dialog box to set a specific amount of space before or after paragraphs.

Paragraph spacing is set in points. If a document has 12-point text, one line space equals 12 points. Likewise, one-half line space equals 6 points, and two line spaces equal 24 points. By default, **Paragraph Spacing** is **Before**: 0 points and **After**: 10 points.

Exercise 5-4 CHANGE THE SPACE BETWEEN PARAGRAPHS

1. Press Ctrl+Home to move the insertion point to the beginning of the document. Select the whole document by pressing Ctrl+A. Press Ctrl+L to left-align all paragraphs.
2. Use the keyboard shortcut Ctrl+1 to change the entire document to single spacing.
3. Deselect the text and position the insertion point at the beginning of the document.
4. Click the Bold button to turn on bold, key **CORPORATE GIFTS** in all capitals, and press Enter.
5. Move the insertion point into the heading you just keyed. Although this heading includes only two words, it is also a paragraph. Any text followed by a paragraph mark is considered a paragraph.
6. Open the Paragraph dialog box. You use the text boxes labeled **Before** and **After** to choose an amount of space for Word to insert before or after a paragraph.
7. Set the **Before** text box to 72 points (select the "0" and key **72**). Because 72 points equal 1 inch, this adds to the existing 1-inch top margin and places the title 2 inches from the top of the page.

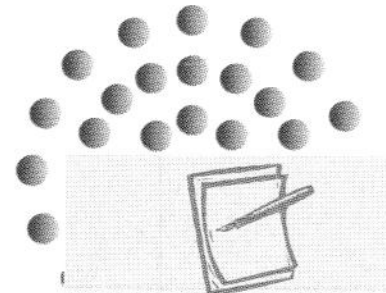

NOTE

Most business documents start 2 inches from the top of the page. You can set this standard by using paragraph formatting, as done here, or by changing margin settings.

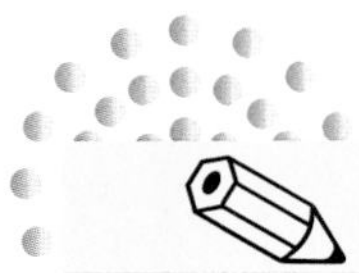

TIP

Word provides these keyboard shortcuts for paragraph spacing: Ctrl+0 adds 12 points of space before a paragraph; Ctrl+Shift+0 removes space before a paragraph; Ctrl+Shift+N removes all paragraph and character formatting, restoring the text to default formatting.

8. Press Tab, set the **After** text box to **24** points, and click **OK**. The heading now starts at 2 inches and is followed by two line spaces.
9. Right-click the **Status bar** and click **Vertical Page Position**. Deselect the shortcut menu. The status bar displays **At 2"** on the left side.
10. Click the Center button to center the heading.

Paragraph Indents

An *indent* increases the distance between the sides of a paragraph and the two side margins (left and right). Indented paragraphs appear to have different margin settings. Word provides a variety of indents to emphasize paragraphs in a document, as shown in Figure 5-6.

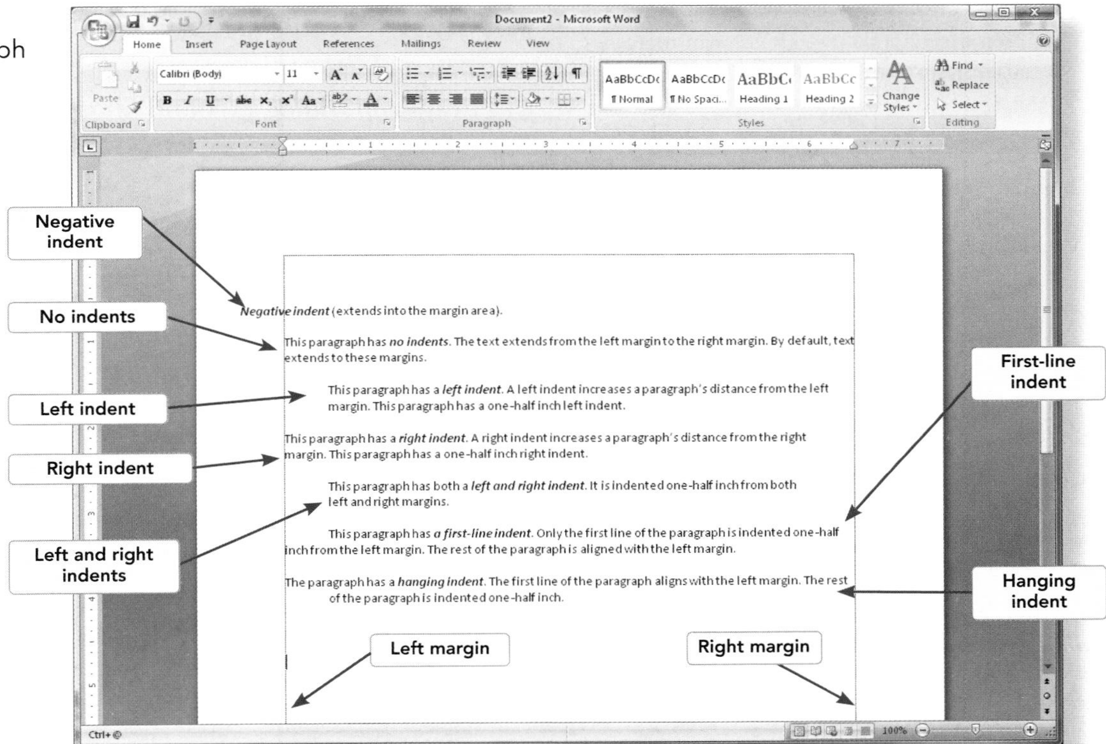

Figure 5-6
Types of paragraph indents

To set paragraph indents, you can use one of these methods:

- Indent buttons on the Ribbon, Home tab, Paragraph group
- Paragraph dialog box
- Keyboard
- Ruler

Exercise 5-5 SET INDENTS BY USING INDENT BUTTONS AND THE PARAGRAPH DIALOG BOX

1. Select the paragraph that begins "Our line" through the end of the document.

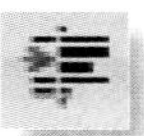

2. Click the Increase Indent button on the Ribbon. The selected text is indented 0.5 inch from the left side.
3. Click the Increase Indent button again. Now the text is indented 1 inch.

4. Click the Decrease Indent button twice to return the text to the left margin.

NOTE

To set a *negative indent*, which extends a paragraph into the left or right margin areas, enter a negative number in the **Left** or **Right** text boxes. Any indent that occurs between the left and right margins is known as a *positive indent*.

5. With the text still selected, open the Paragraph dialog box by clicking the Paragraph Dialog Box Launcher arrow .
6. Under **Indentation**, change the **Left** setting to **0.75** inch and the **Right** setting to **0.75** inch.
7. Click to open the **Special** drop-down list in the Paragraph dialog box and choose **First line**. Word sets the **By** box to 0.5″ by default. Notice the change in the Preview box.

Figure 5-7
Setting indents

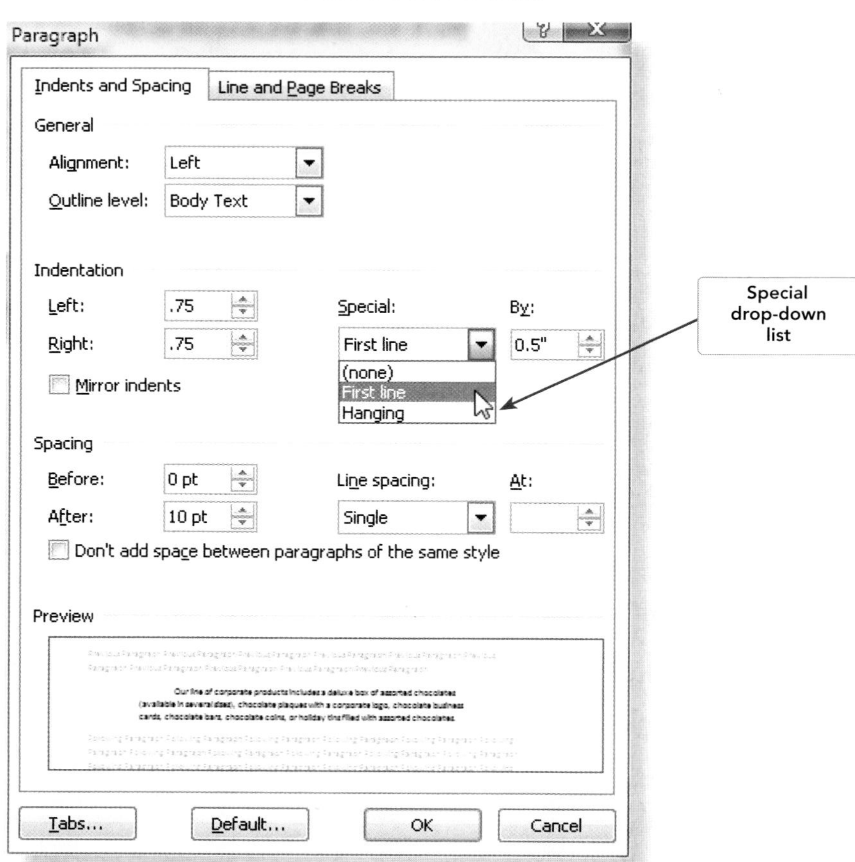

TIP

Word provides these keyboard shortcuts to set indents: Ctrl+M increases an indent; Ctrl+Shift+M decreases an indent; Ctrl+T creates a hanging indent; Ctrl+Shift+T removes a hanging indent.

8. Click **OK**. Now each paragraph is indented from the left and right margins by 0.75 inch, and the first line of each paragraph is indented another 0.5 inch.

Exercise 5-6 SET INDENTS BY USING THE RULER

You can set indents by dragging the *indent markers* that appear at the left and right of the horizontal ruler. There are four indent markers:

- The *first-line indent marker* is the top triangle on the left side of the ruler. Drag it to the right to indent the first line of a paragraph.
- The *hanging indent marker* is the bottom triangle. Drag it to the right to indent the remaining lines in a paragraph.
- The *left indent marker* is the small rectangle. Drag it to move the first-line indent marker and hanging indent marker at the same time.
- The *right indent marker* is the triangle at the right side of the ruler, at the right margin. Drag it to the left to create a right indent.

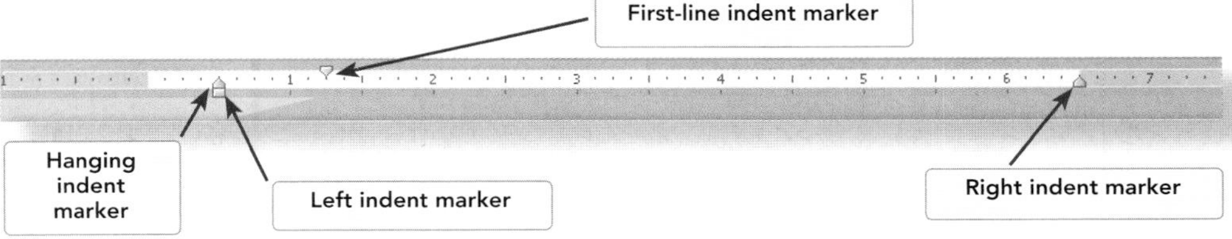

Figure 5-8
Indent markers on the ruler

1. Make sure the horizontal ruler is displayed. If it is not, click the **View Ruler button** or open the **Word Options** dialog box and click **Advanced** in the left pane and scroll to **Display**.
2. Position the insertion point in the first paragraph below the title.
3. Point to the first-line indent marker on the ruler. A ScreenTip appears when you are pointing to the correct marker.
4. Drag the first-line indent marker 0.5 inch to the right. The first line of the paragraph is indented by 0.5 inch.
5. Press Shift+F1 to display the **Reveal Formatting** task pane. Locate the Paragraph section, and notice the settings under **Indentation**.
6. Drag the first-line indent marker back to the zero position. Point to the hanging indent marker, and drag it 0.5 inch to the right. The lines below the first line are indented 0.5 inch, creating a hanging indent.

NOTE

To make sure you are pointing to the correct indent marker, check the ScreenTip identifier before you drag the marker.

7. Drag the hanging indent marker back to the zero position. Drag the left indent marker (the small rectangle) 1 inch to the right. The entire paragraph is indented by 1 inch.
8. Select the first two paragraphs below the title, and press Ctrl+Shift+N to remove all formatting from the paragraphs. Notice that the line spacing and spacing after return to the default settings.
9. Position the insertion point in the second paragraph, which begins "Our line," and re-create the indents by using the ruler:
   - Drag the left indent marker 0.75 inch to the right to indent the entire paragraph.
   - Drag the first-line indent marker to the 1.25-inch mark on the ruler.
   - Drag the right indent marker 0.75 to the left (to the 5.75-inch mark on the ruler). Now the paragraph is indented like the paragraphs below it.
10. Select all the indented paragraphs, and drag the first-line indent marker to the 1-inch mark on the ruler. Now the opening line of each paragraph is indented only 0.25 inch.

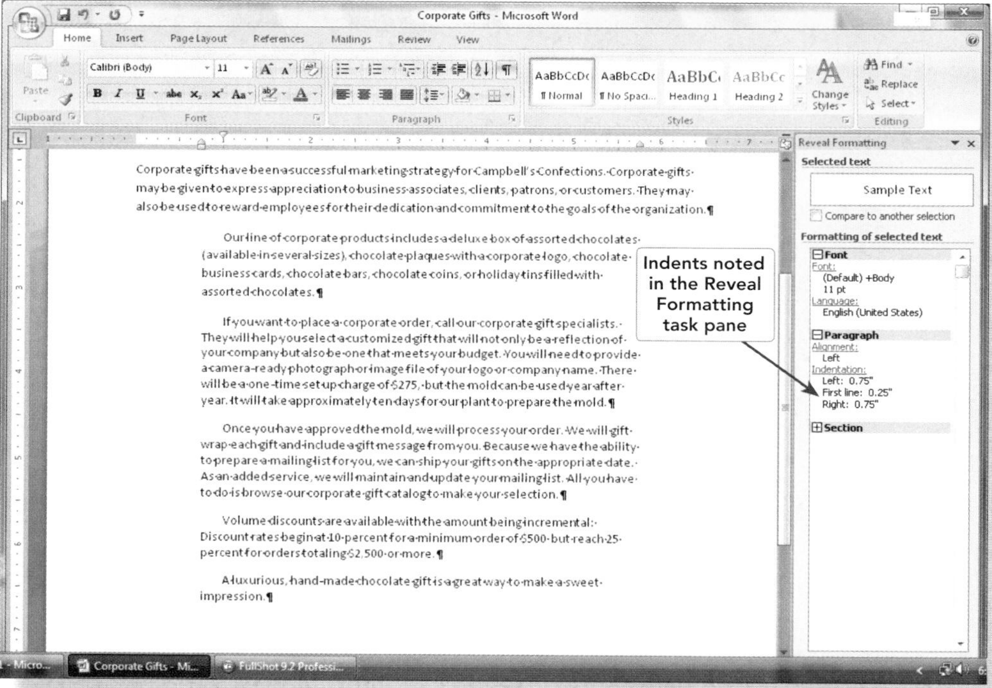

Figure 5-9
Document with indented text

11. Save the document as ***[your initials]*5-6** in a new folder for Lesson 5.
12. Submit the document, but do not close it.

Borders and Shading

To add visual interest to paragraphs or to an entire page, you can add a *border*—a line, box, or pattern—around text, a graphic, or a page. In addition, you can use *shading* to fill in the background behind the text of a paragraph. Shading can appear as a shade of gray, as a pattern, or as a color. Borders can appear in a variety of line styles and colors.

This lesson explains how to use the Borders and Shading dialog box to set border and shading options, and how to use the Borders command on the Ribbon (which applies the most recently selected border style). The Borders button ScreenTip will change to display the most recently selected border style.

Exercise 5-7 ADD BORDERS TO PARAGRAPHS

1. With the file ***[your initials]*5-6** open, go to the end of the document. Press Enter to start a new paragraph, and press Ctrl+Q to remove the paragraph formatting carried over from the previous paragraph.
2. Key the text shown in Figure 5-10.

Figure 5-10

```
Let Campbell's Confections help you with your marketing
strategy and your employees' recognition plan! We can
provide you with a unique and personalized gift that will
create a lasting impression. Call us today at 724-555-2025
for more information.
```

3. Make sure the insertion point is to the left of the current paragraph mark or within the paragraph.
4. Click the down arrow beside the Borders button and click **Borders and Shading** at the bottom of the drop-down list. The Borders and Shading dialog box appears. Click the **Borders** tab if it is not displayed.

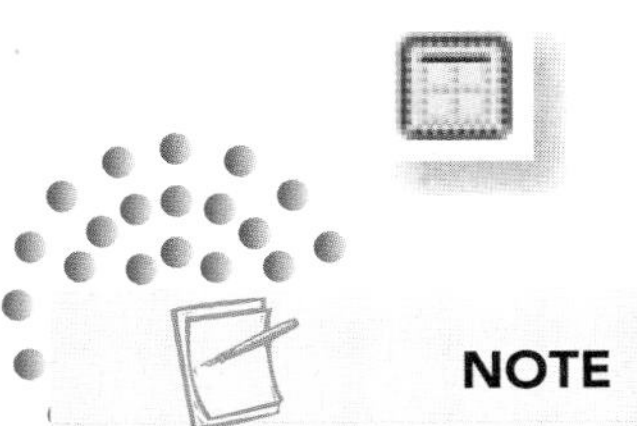

NOTE

The appearance of the Borders button and the Screen Tip change according to the most recently selected border style.

5. Under Setting, click the **Box** option. The **Preview** box shows the Box setting. Each button around the **Preview** box indicates a selected border.
6. Scroll to view the options in the **Style** box. Choose the first border style (the solid line).
7. Open the **Color** drop-down list and choose Green. (ScreenTips identify colors by name.)
8. Open the **Width** drop-down list and choose **2 1/4 pt**.

9. Click the top line of the box border in the **Preview** box. The top line is deleted, and the corresponding button is no longer selected. Click the Top Border button or the top border area in the diagram to restore the top line border.

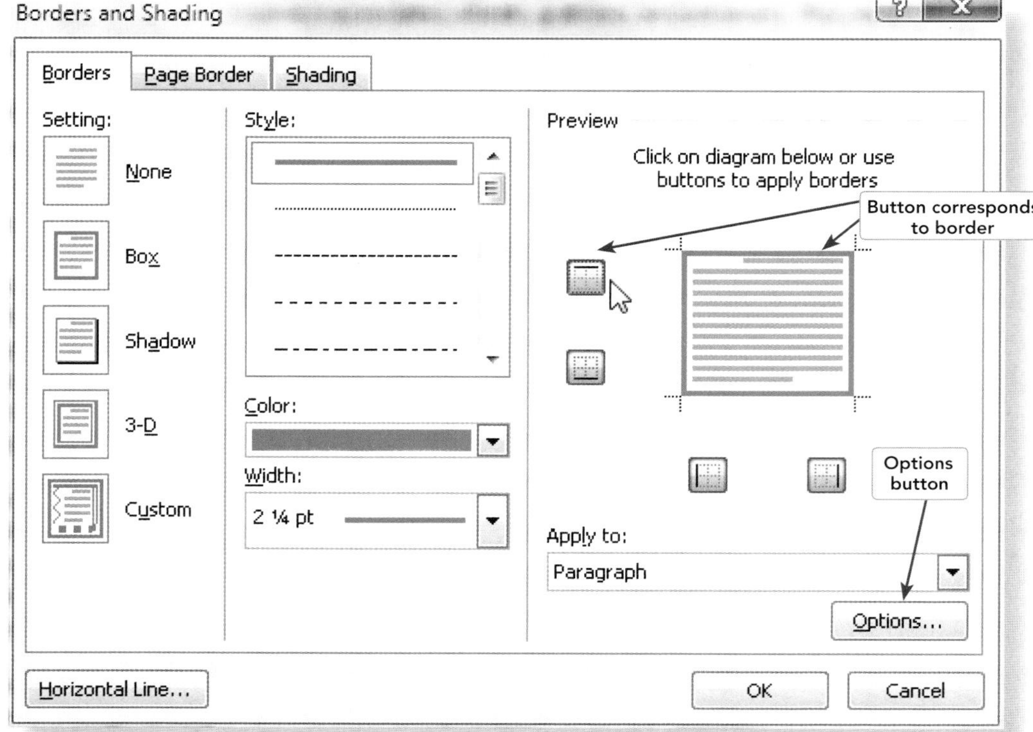

Figure 5-11 Borders and Shading dialog box

10. Click the **Options** button. In the Border and Shading Options dialog box, change the **Top**, **Bottom**, **Left**, and **Right** settings to **5 pt** to increase the space between the text and the border. Click **OK**.
11. Change the **Setting** from **Box** to **Shadow**. This setting applies a black shadow to the green border. Notice that the **Apply to** box is set to **Paragraph**. Click **OK**. The shadow border is applied to the paragraph.
12. Click anywhere within the title "CORPORATE GIFTS."

13. Click the down arrow next to the Borders button on the Ribbon. A drop-down menu of border options appears.

Figure 5-12
Border options on the Ribbon

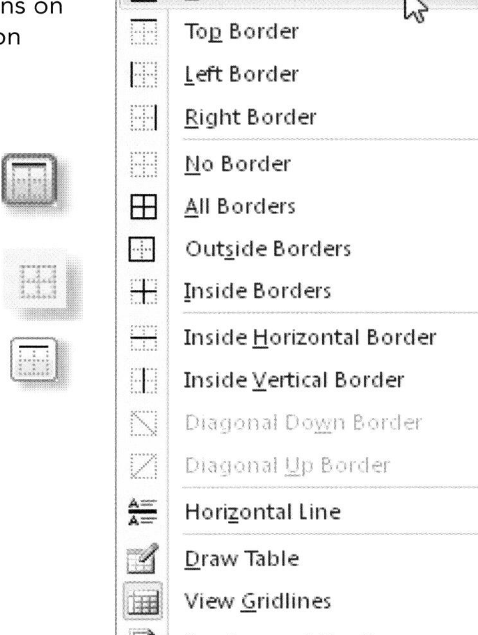

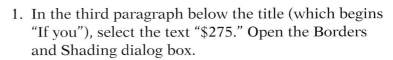

14. Click **Bottom Border**. A bottom border with the options previously set in the Borders and Shading dialog box is applied to the title.
15. Click the down arrow next to the Borders button. Click the **No Border** button to delete the border.
16. Reapply the bottom border, and click the Top Border button to add a top border as well.
17. Open the Paragraph dialog box, and change the left and right indents to **.5"**. Notice the border is indented from the left and right margins.

NOTE

Borders and shading, when applied to a paragraph, extend from the left margin to the right margin or if indents are set, from the left indent to the right indent.

Exercise 5-8 APPLY BORDERS TO SELECTED TEXT AND A PAGE

In addition to paragraphs, you can apply borders to selected text or to an entire page. When you apply a border to a page, you can choose whether to place the border on every page, the current page, the first page, or all but the first page in a document.

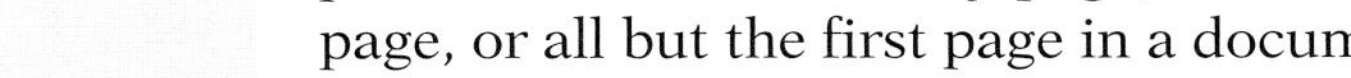

NOTE

When the **Apply to** box indicates **Text**, the borders are applied only to the selected text and not to the paragraph. If you include a paragraph mark in your selection, the borders are applied to all lines of the paragraph unless you change the **Apply to** setting to **Text**. It is important to notice the **Apply to** setting when applying borders and shading, or you might not get the results you intended.

1. In the third paragraph below the title (which begins "If you"), select the text "$275." Open the Borders and Shading dialog box.
2. From the **Style** box, scroll to the fifth line style from the bottom. Word automatically applies this style as the **Box** setting.
3. Change the **Color** to **Blue**. Notice that the **Apply to** box indicates **Text**.

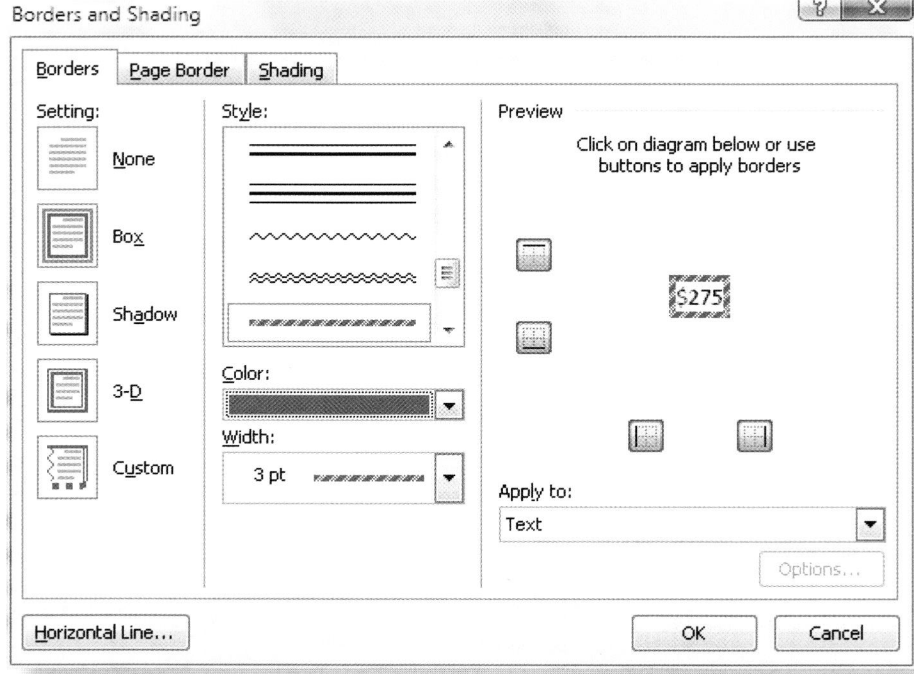

Figure 5-13 Applying borders to selected text

4. Click the **Page Border** tab. Choose the third-to-last line style (a band of three shades of gray), and click the **3-D** setting. The width should be **3 pt**.

5. Click **OK**. Notice the text border added to "$275" and the page border. Deselect the text so you can see the border color.

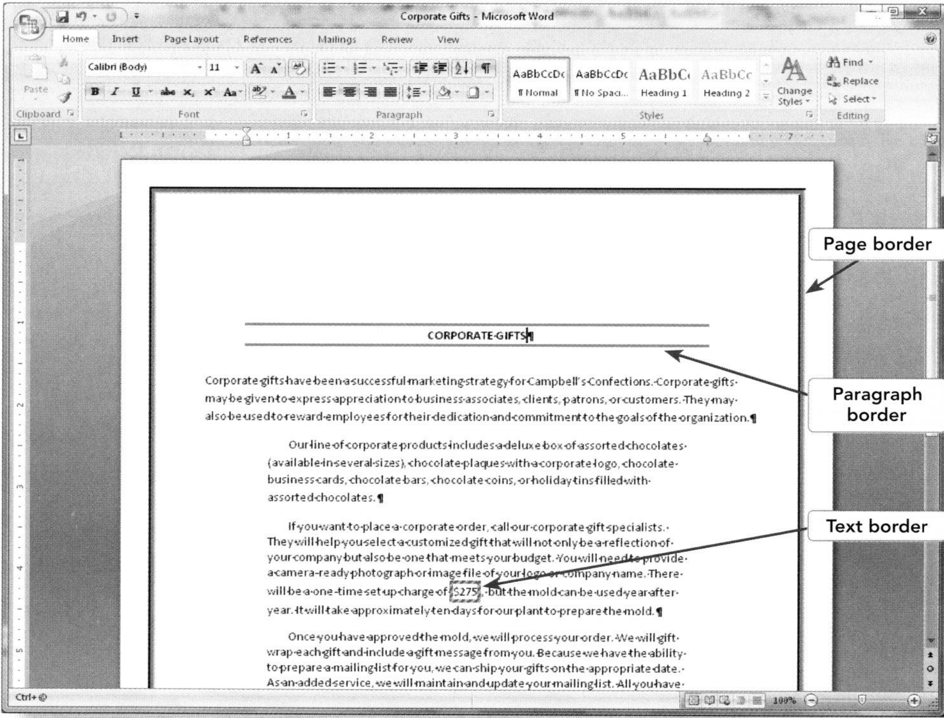

Figure 5-14 Document with border formatting

6. Save the document as ***[your initials]*****5-8** in your Lesson 5 folder. Print the document. Leave it open.

Exercise 5-9 ADD A HORIZONTAL LINE

Word provides special horizontal lines to divide or decorate a page. These lines are actually picture files (or "clips") in the shape of horizontal lines that are normally used when creating Web pages.

1. Position the insertion point anywhere in the last paragraph and open the Borders and Shading dialog box. Click the **Borders** tab.
2. Click **None** to remove the shadowed border. Click **OK**.
3. Position the insertion point at the beginning of the last paragraph.
4. Open the Borders and Shading dialog box. Click **Horizontal Line** at the bottom of the dialog box.
5. In the Horizontal Line dialog box, click the second box in the second row. Click **OK**. The line is inserted in the document.

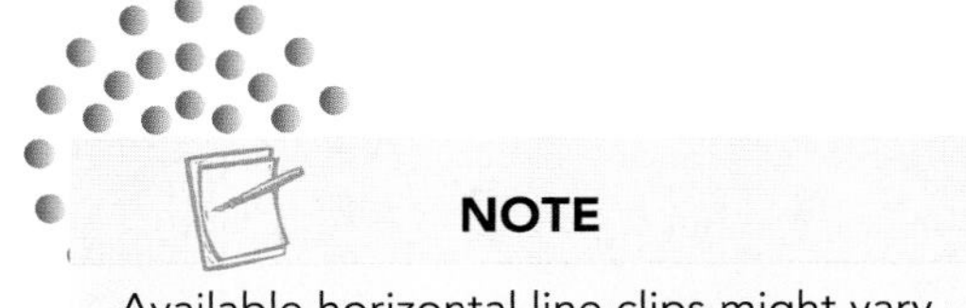

NOTE

Available horizontal line clips might vary, depending on which files are installed on your computer. Check with your instructor if the specified line is not available.

Figure 5-15
Inserting a horizontal line

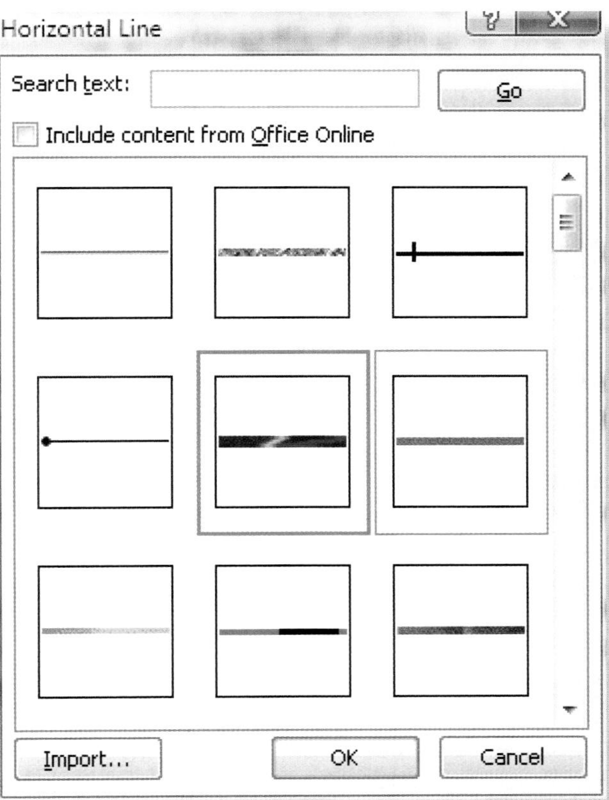

Exercise 5-10 APPLY SHADING TO A PARAGRAPH

1. Click anywhere in the last paragraph, and open the **Borders and Shading** dialog box.
2. Click the **Shading** tab.
3. Click the down arrow in the **Fill** box. Notice that you can apply Theme colors or Standard colors. Click the second gray color in the first column.

NOTE

You can click the Shading button to apply a fill color.

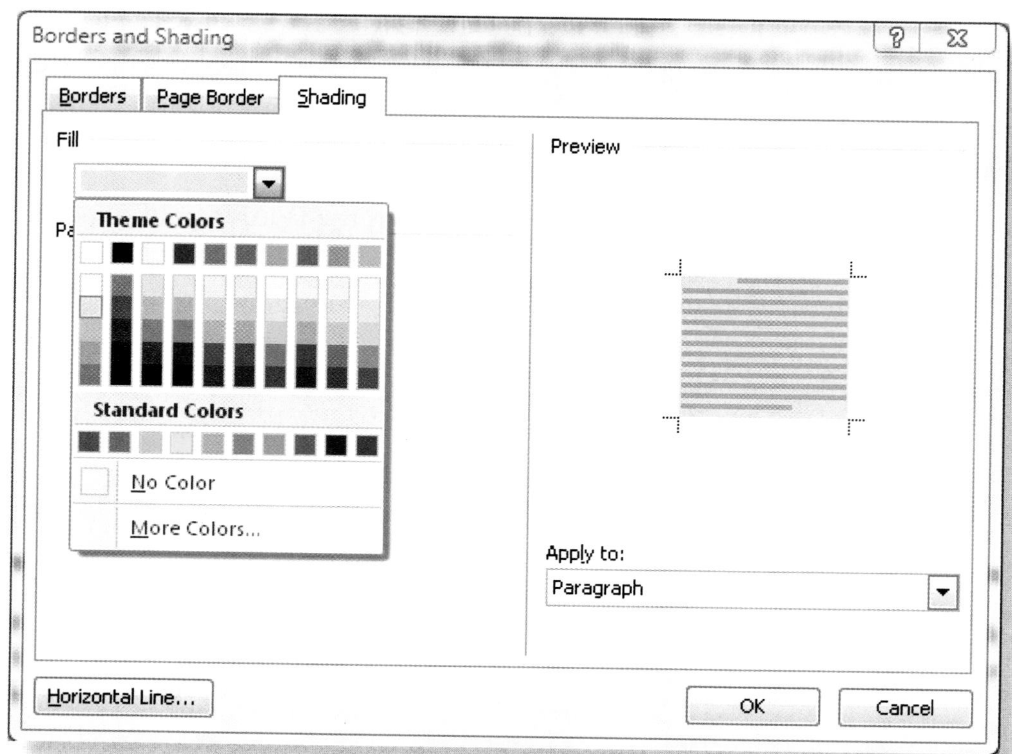

Figure 5-16
Shading options in the Borders and Shading dialog box

4. Open the **Style** drop-down list to view other shading options. Close the **Style** drop-down list without choosing a style.
5. Click **OK** to apply the gray shading to the paragraph.
6. With the insertion point still in the last paragraph, remove the gray shading by clicking the Shading button on the Ribbon. Click **No Color**.
7. Click the Undo button to restore the shading.

NOTE

Shading can affect the readability of text, especially when you use dark colors or patterns. It's a good idea to choose a larger type size and bold text when you use shading.

TIP

To remove all formatting from a paragraph (including borders, indents, and character formatting), click the Clear Formatting button in the Font group.

Exercise 5-11 APPLY BORDERS AUTOMATICALLY

Word provides an AutoFormat feature to apply bottom borders. Instead of using the Borders command or the Borders and Shading dialog box, you can key a series of characters and Word automatically applies a border.

1. Press Ctrl+N to create a new document and leave the current document open.
2. Key --- (three consecutive hyphens) and press Enter. Word applies a bottom border. Press Enter two times.
3. Key === (three consecutive equal signs) and press Enter. Word applies a double-line bottom border. Press Enter two times.
4. Key ___ (three consecutive underscores) and press Enter. Word applies a thick bottom border.
5. Close the document without saving.

TIP

If you do not want to format borders automatically, click the AutoCorrect Options button displayed after you key a series of characters and choose **Stop Automatically Creating Border Lines.**

TABLE 5-1 AutoFormatting Borders

You Key	Word Applies
Three or more hyphens (-) and press Enter	A thin bottom border
Three or more underscores (_) and press Enter	A thick bottom border
Three or more equal signs (=) and press Enter	A double-line bottom border

Repeating and Copying Formats

You can quickly repeat, copy, or remove paragraph formatting. For example, use F4 or Ctrl+Y to repeat paragraph formatting and the Format Painter button to copy paragraph formatting.

Exercise 5-12 REPEAT, COPY, AND REMOVE PARAGRAPH FORMATS

NOTE

You can click in a paragraph when repeating, copying, or removing formatting. You do not have to select the entire paragraph.

1. Click anywhere in the first paragraph under the title (which begins "Corporate Gifts"), and change the paragraph alignment to justified.
2. Select the rest of the indented paragraphs, starting with the paragraph that begins "Our line" through the paragraph that begins "A luxurious." Press F4 to repeat the formatting.

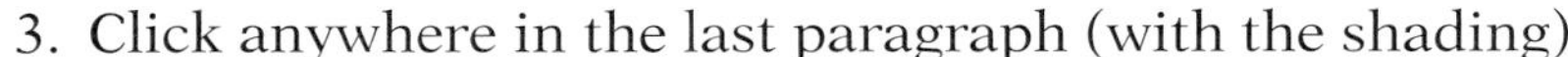

3. Click anywhere in the last paragraph (with the shading).

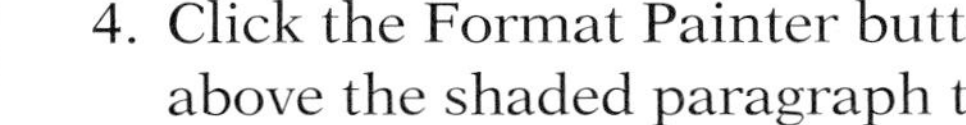

4. Click the Format Painter button; then click within the paragraph above the shaded paragraph to copy the formatting.

5. Click the Undo button to undo the paragraph formatting.
6. Click anywhere in the shaded paragraph. Click the Clear Formatting button on the Ribbon to remove the formatting.
7. Click the Undo button to restore the formatting.
8. Click just before the paragraph mark for the horizontal line you inserted above the last paragraph. Open the **Paragraph** dialog box, add 24 points of spacing before the paragraph, and click **OK**.
9. Save the document as ***[your initials]*5-12** in your Lesson 5 folder.
10. Submit and close the document.

Bulleted and Numbered Lists

Bulleted lists and *numbered lists* are types of hanging indents you can use to organize important details in a document. In a bulleted list, a bullet (•) precedes each paragraph. In a numbered list, a sequential number or letter precedes each paragraph. When you add or delete an item in a numbered list, Word automatically renumbers the list.

To create bulleted lists or numbered lists, use the Bullets command or the Numbering command on the Ribbon (which applies the most recently selected bullet or numbering style).

Exercise 5-13 CREATE A BULLETED LIST

1. Open the file **Memo - 1**. This document is a one-page memo. Key the current date in the memo date line.
2. Locate and select the four lines of text beginning with "Monday" and ending with "Thursday."

3. Click the Bullets button on the Ribbon, Home tab, Paragraph group. Word applies the bullet style that was most recently chosen in the Bullets list.

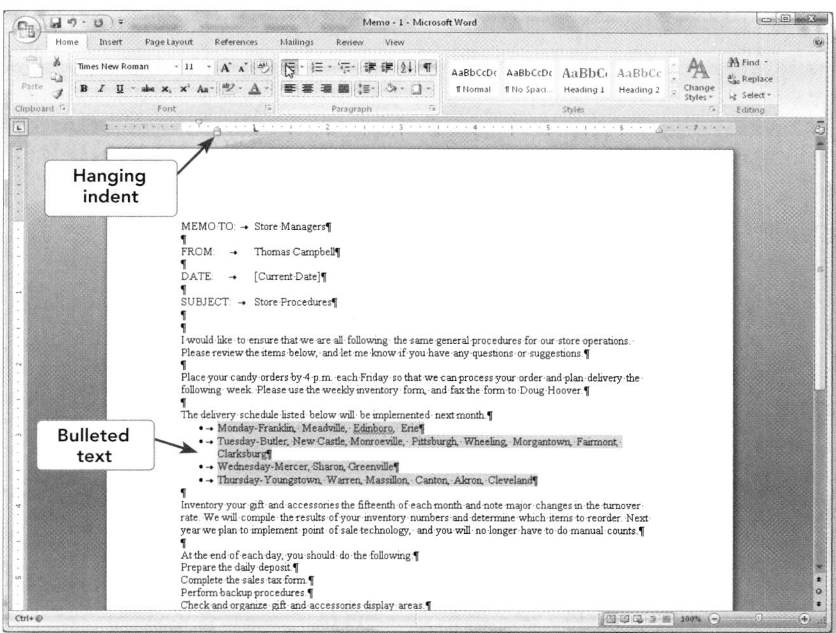

Figure 5-17
Bulleted list

NOTE

When you create bulleted or numbered lists, Word automatically sets a 0.25-inch hanging indent.

4. With the list still selected, click the down arrow beside the **Bullets** button, and click one of the bullet shapes listed in the **Bullet Library**. The list is formatted with a different bullet shape. Deselect the list.

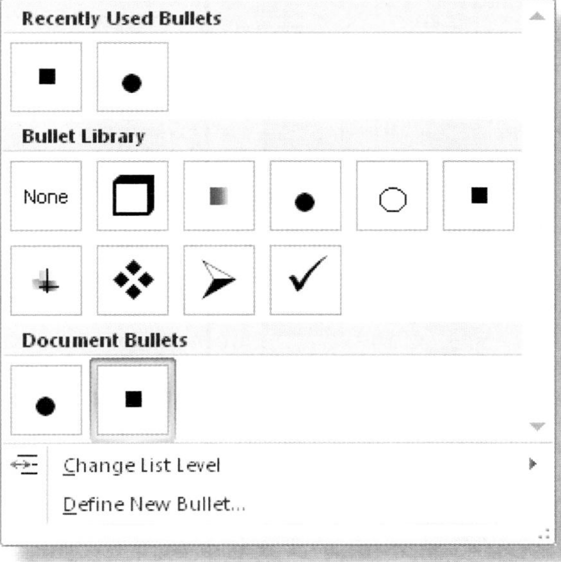

Figure 5-18
Bullet options

5. Click the first bullet in the bulleted list you just created to select all bullets.

6. Right-click the selected bullets, and click **Adjust List Indents** from the shortcut menu.

7. Change the **Bullet position** text box value to **.4**. Change the **Text indent** to **.65**. Click **OK**.

Exercise 5-14 CREATE A NUMBERED LIST

1. Select the last four paragraphs in the document, from "First Quarter" to "Fourth Quarter."

2. Click the Numbering button to format the list with the style that was most recently chosen from the Numbering list.
3. With the list still selected, click the down arrow beside the Numbering button. Click the Roman numeral format. Word reformats the list with Roman numerals.

Exercise 5-15 CHANGE A BULLETED OR NUMBERED LIST

Word's bulleting and numbering feature is very flexible. When a list is bulleted or numbered, you can change it in several ways. You can:

- Convert bullets to numbers or numbers to bullets in a list.
- Add or remove items in a bulleted or numbered list, and Word renumbers the list automatically.
- Interrupt a bulleted or numbered list to create several shorter lists.
- Customize the list formatting by changing the symbol used for bullets or changing the alignment and spacing of the bullets and numbers.
- Turn off bullets or numbering for part of a list or the entire list.

NOTE

When you select a bulleted or numbered list by dragging over the text, the list is highlighted but the bullets or numbers are not. You can select a list by clicking a bullet or number.

1. Select the bulleted list that starts with "Monday."
2. Click the down arrow beside the Numbering button.
3. Choose a numbered format that starts with "1" to convert the bullets to numbers.
4. Select and delete the line that begins "Wednesday." Word renumbers the list automatically.
5. Press Ctrl+Z to undo.
6. Place the insertion point at the end of the last item in the numbered list, after "Cleveland."
7. Press Enter and key **Friday-Emergency deliveries**. The formatting is carried to the new line.
8. Place the insertion point at the end of the fourth item (after "Cleveland.") and press Enter.
9. Key in italic ***When absolutely necessary:***

TIP

To change the shape, size, and color of a bullet, click the down arrow on the Bullets button and click **Define New Bullet**. Click the **Symbol** button to choose a new shape. Click the **Font** button to change size and color. Click the drop-down arrow of the **Alignment** box to change the bullet alignment. If you click the **Picture** button, you can insert a picture bullet—a decorative bullet often used in Web pages. You can format numbers or bullets of a list in a format different from the text of the list.

NOTE

After you format a list with bullets or numbering, each time you press Enter the format carries forward to the next paragraph. Pressing Enter twice turns off the format.

10. Click within the italic text, and click the Numbering button on the Ribbon to turn off numbering for this item. The list continues with the following paragraph.
11. Select and right-click the numbered text below the italic text (the numbered item that begins "Friday").
12. Click the **Set Numbering Value** option to open the Set Numbering Value dialog box. Select, if necessary, **Start new list** so the list does not continue the numbering. Change the **Set value to** box to **1**. Click **OK**. The new list starts with "1."
13. Insert a blank line above the italic text (click to the left of "*When*" and press Enter).
14. Select the list beginning with "At the" through "Check and organize."
15. Click the down arrow beside the Bullets button and click **Define New Bullet**.
16. Click **Symbol**, and change the **Font** to **Wingdings**. Scroll to locate and select the small, solid black square (▪). Click **OK** to close the Symbol dialog box, and click **OK** to close the Define New Bullet dialog box.

Exercise 5-16 CREATE LISTS AUTOMATICALLY

Word provides an AutoFormat feature to create bulleted and numbered lists as you type. When this feature is selected, you can enter a few keystrokes, key your list, and Word inserts the numbers and bullets automatically.

1. Press Ctrl+End to move to the end of the document.
2. Key the following: **Create a list of all equipment and fixtures in the store. Provide the following:**
3. Press Enter. Key * and press Spacebar.
4. Key **Description/Model number** and press Enter. Word automatically formats your text as a bulleted list.
5. Key the following text to complete the list, pressing Enter at the end of each line except the last line:

   Serial number
   Date acquired
   Purchase price
   Location
   Inventory number

TABLE 5-2 AutoFormatting Numbered and Bulleted Lists

You Key	Word Creates
A number; a period, closing parenthesis, or hyphen; a space or tab; and text. Example, **1.**, **1**), or **1**-Press Enter.	A numbered list
An asterisk (*) or hyphen (-); a space or tab; and text. Press Enter.	A bulleted list

Exercise 5-17 CREATE A MULTILEVEL LIST

A *multilevel list* has indented subparagraphs. For example, your list can start with item number "1)," followed by another level of indented items numbered "a)," "b)," and "c)." An outline numbered list can have up to nine levels and is often used for technical or legal documents. The Multilevel List command is located on the Ribbon, Home tab, Paragraph group.

1. Go to the end of the document and press Enter four times.

2. Click the arrow beside the Multilevel List button. Notice the outline numbering styles available in the List Library.

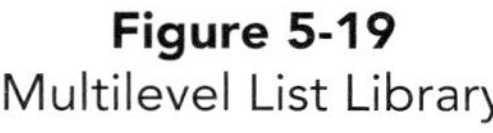

Figure 5-19
Multilevel List Library

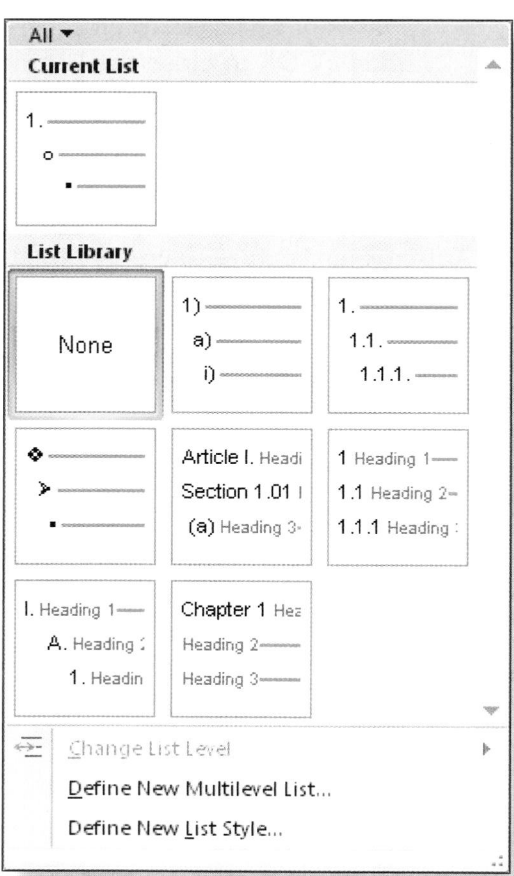

3. Click the outline numbering style that begins with "**I.**" Notice the uppercase Roman numeral in the text.

4. Key **January** and press Enter.

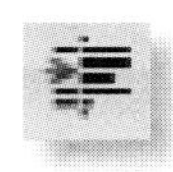

5. Click the Increase Indent button (or press Tab), and key **A.** Spacebar **Prepare memo to employees regarding changes to W-4 forms.**

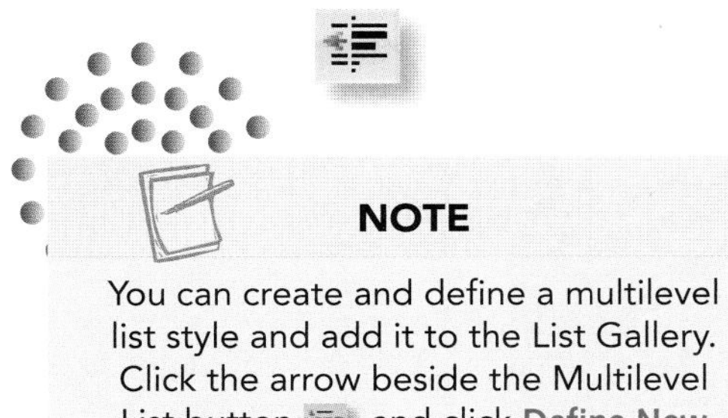

NOTE

You can create and define a multilevel list style and add it to the List Gallery. Click the arrow beside the Multilevel List button and click **Define New Multilevel List**. Enter the text and format for each level. Click **OK**.

6. Press Enter and key **B.** Spacebar **Prepare and mail W-2 forms to employees**. The numbered list now has two indented subparagraphs. Press Enter. Key **C.** Spacebar **Prepare and mail 1099 forms.** Press Enter.

7. With the insertion point at the beginning of a new line, click the Decrease Indent button (or press Shift+Tab) to position the insertion point at the left margin. You can now add a second first-level paragraph to your list.

8. Key **II. February**.

Symbols and Special Characters

The fonts you use with Word include *special characters* that do not appear on your keyboard, such as those used in foreign languages (for example, ç, Ö, and Ω). There are additional fonts, such as *Wingdings* and *Symbol* that consist entirely of special characters.

To insert symbols and special characters in your documents, click the **Insert** tab on the Ribbon, locate the **Symbols** group, and click the **Symbol** command.

Exercise 5-18 INSERT SYMBOLS

1. Scroll toward the beginning of the document. Position the insertion point to the immediate left of the paragraph that begins "*When absolutely*."

2. Click the **Insert** tab. Locate the **Symbols** group, and click the arrow beside the Symbol button. Click **More Symbols**. The Symbol dialog box appears.

3. Make sure the **Symbols** tab is displayed and choose **(normal text)** from the **Font** drop-down list box.

4. Scroll through the grid of available symbol characters for normal text, and notice that the grid contains diacritical marks that you can use for foreign languages. You will also see the symbol for cents (¢) and degrees (°).

5. Click the arrow to open the **Font** drop-down list box and choose **Symbol**. Review the available symbol characters.

6. Change the font to **Wingdings**. The characters included in the Wingdings font appear in the grid.

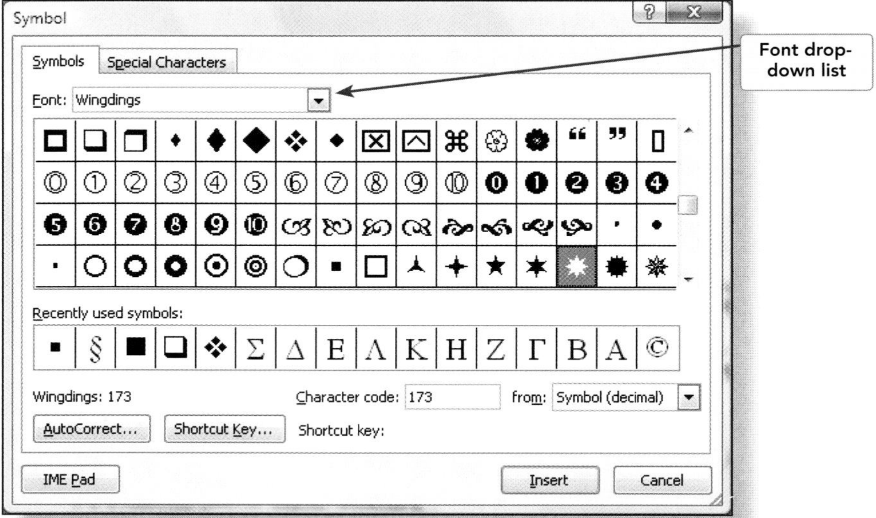

Figure 5-20
Symbol dialog box

TIP

Notice the recently used symbols shown at the bottom of the Symbol dialog box. Word displays the 16 most recently used symbols.

7. Scroll down several rows until you see symbols similar to an asterisk (*). Click one of the symbols.
8. Click **Insert**, and then click **Close**. The symbol appears in the document.
9. Select the list with Roman numerals beginning with "I. First Quarter" through "IV. Fourth Quarter."

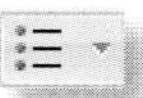

10. Click the Home tab and click the arrow beside the Bullets button.
11. Click **Define New Bullet** and click **Picture**. Click one of the picture bullets, and click **OK**, and then click **OK** again. The Roman numerals are replaced with your chosen picture bullet.

TIP

You can assign shortcut keys or AutoCorrect to a symbol by clicking **Shortcut Key** or **AutoCorrect** in the Symbol dialog box. You can also press Alt and key the numeric code (using the numeric keypad, if you have one) for a character. For example, if you change the font of the document to Wingdings and press Alt+0040, you will insert the character for a Wingdings telephone. Remember to change the Wingdings font back to your normal font after inserting a special character.

Exercise 5-19 INSERT SPECIAL CHARACTERS

You can use the Symbol dialog box and shortcut keys to insert characters such as an en dash, an em dash, or SmartQuotes. An *en dash* is a dash slightly wider than a hyphen. An *em dash,* which is twice as wide as an en dash, is used in sentences where you would normally insert two hyphens. *Smart quotes* are quotation marks that open a quote curled in one direction (“) and close a quote curled in the opposite direction (”).

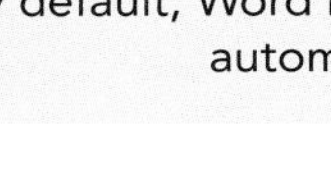

NOTE

By default, Word inserts smart quotes automatically.

1. Make sure nonprinting characters are displayed in the document. If they are not, click the Show/Hide ¶ button ¶.
2. On page 1, locate the paragraph that begins “1. Monday.” Position the insertion point to the immediate right of “Monday.” Press Delete to remove the hyphen.

3. Click the **Insert** tab, and click the arrow beside the Symbol button. Click **More Symbols**, and click the **Special Characters** tab.
4. Choose **Em Dash** from the list of characters. (Notice the keyboard shortcut listed for the character.) Click **Insert**, and then click **Close**. The em dash replaces the hyphen.
5. Select the hyphen immediately following “Tuesday.” Press Alt+Ctrl+- (the minus sign on the numeric keypad). An em dash is inserted. (If you don’t have a numeric keypad, press F4 to repeat the character.)
6. Insert em dashes after “Wednesday,” “Thursday,” and “Friday.”

Exercise 5-20 CREATE SYMBOLS AUTOMATICALLY

You can use Word’s AutoCorrect feature to create symbols as you type. Just enter a few keystrokes, and Word converts them into a symbol.

NOTE

To review the symbols AutoCorrect can enter automatically, open the **Word Options** dialog box, and click **Proofing**. Click **AutoCorrect Options**, and click the AutoCorrect tab.

1. Scroll to the “SUBJECT” line, and click to the left of “Store.”
2. Key < = = and notice that Word automatically creates an arrow (←).
3. Position the insertion point to the right of “Procedures.” Key = = >. Word creates another pointing to the right.
4. Format the first line of the memo with 72 points of paragraph spacing before it. This starts the first line two inches from the top of the page.
5. Save the document as ***[your initials]*5-20** in your Lesson 5 folder.
6. Submit and close the document.

Lesson 5 Summary

- A paragraph is any amount of text followed by a paragraph mark.
- Paragraph alignment determines how the edges of a paragraph appear horizontally. Paragraphs can be left-aligned, centered, right-aligned, or justified.
- The Click and Type feature enables you to insert text in any blank area of a document by simply positioning the insertion point and double-clicking.
- Line space is the amount of vertical space between lines of text in a paragraph. Lines can be single-spaced, 1.5-line spaced, double-spaced, or set to a specific value.
- Paragraph space is the amount of space above or below a paragraph. Paragraph space is set in points—12 points of space equals one line space for 12-point text. Change the space between paragraphs by using the Before and After options in the Paragraph dialog box or by using the Ctrl+0, Ctrl+Shift+0 keyboard shortcuts to add or remove 12 points before a paragraph.
- A left indent or right indent increases a paragraph's distance from the left or right margin. A first-line indent indents only the first line of a paragraph. A hanging indent indents the second and subsequent lines of a paragraph.
- To set indents by using the horizontal ruler, drag the left indent marker (small rectangle), the first-line indent marker (top triangle), or the hanging indent marker (bottom triangle), which are all on the left end of the ruler, or drag the right indent marker (triangle) on the right end of the ruler.
- A border is a line or box added to selected text, a paragraph, or a page. Shading fills in the background of selected text or paragraphs. Borders and shading can appear in a variety of styles and colors.
- In addition to regular borders, Word provides special decorative horizontal lines that are available from the Borders and Shading dialog box.
- The AutoFormat feature enables you to create a border automatically. Key three or more hyphens -, underscores _, or equal signs =, and press Enter. See Table 5-1.
- Repeat paragraph formats by pressing F4 or Ctrl+Y. Copy paragraph formats by using the Format Painter command. Remove paragraph formats by pressing Ctrl+Q or choosing the **Clear Formatting** command from the Ribbon, Home tab, Font group.
- Format a list of items as a bulleted or numbered list. In a bulleted list, each item is indented and preceded by a bullet character or other symbol. In a numbered list, each item is indented and preceded by a sequential number or letter.
- Remove a bullet or number from an item in a list by clicking the Bullets command or the Numbering command on the Ribbon. Press Enter in the middle of the list to add another bulleted or numbered item automatically. Press Enter twice in a list to turn off bullets or numbering.

- Change the bullet symbol or the numbering type by clicking the arrow beside the Bullets command to display the Bullet Library or the arrow beside the Numbering command to open the Numbering Library.
- The AutoFormat feature enables you to create a bulleted or numbered list automatically. See Table 5-2.
- Create a multilevel list by clicking the Multilevel List command. A multilevel list has indented subparagraphs, such as paragraph "1)" followed by indented paragraph "a)" followed by indented paragraph "i)." To increase the level of numbering for each line item, click the Increase Indent command or press Tab. To decrease the level of numbering, click the Decrease Indent command or press Shift+Tab.
- Insert symbols, such as foreign characters, by clicking the Insert tab and clicking the Symbol command. Wingdings is an example of a font that contains all symbols.
- Insert special characters, such as an em dash (—), by using the Special Characters tab in the Symbol dialog box.
- Create symbols automatically as you type by keying AutoCorrect shortcuts, such as keying (c) to produce the ©.

LESSON 5		Command Summary	
Feature	**Button**	**Command**	**Keyboard**
Left-align text		Home tab, **Paragraph** group	Ctrl+L
Center text		Home tab, **Paragraph** group	Ctrl+E
Right-align text		Home tab, **Paragraph** group	Ctrl+R
Justify text		Home tab, **Paragraph** group	Ctrl+J
Single space		Home tab, **Paragraph** group	Ctrl+1
Double space		Home tab, **Paragraph** group	Ctrl+2
1.5-line space		Home tab, **Paragraph** group	Ctrl+5
Borders and Shading		Home tab, **Paragraph** group	
Remove paragraph formatting		Home tab, **Paragraph** group	Ctrl+Q
Restore text to Normal formatting		Home tab, **Font** group	Ctrl+Shift+N
Increase indent		Home tab, **Paragraph** group	Ctrl+M
Decrease indent		Home tab, **Paragraph** group	Ctrl+Shift+M
Hanging indent		Home tab, **Paragraph** group	Ctrl+T
Bulleted list		Home tab, **Paragraph** group	
Numbered list		Home tab, **Paragraph** group	
Symbols and special characters	Symbol	Insert tab, **Symbols** group	

Lesson 6

Tabs and Tabbed Columns

OBJECTIVES

After completing this lesson, you will be able to:

1. Set tabs.
2. Set leader tabs.
3. Clear tabs.
4. Adjust tab settings.
5. Create tabbed columns.
6. Sort paragraphs and tabbed columns.

MCAS OBJECTIVES

In this lesson:
WW 07 2.1.5
WW 07 4.2.2

Estimated Time: 1 hour

A *tab* is a paragraph-formatting feature used to align text. When you press Tab, Word inserts a tab character and moves the insertion point to the position of the tab setting, called the *tab stop*. You can set custom tabs or use Word's default tab settings.

As with other paragraph-formatting features, tab settings are stored in the paragraph mark at the end of a paragraph. Each time you press Enter, the tab settings are copied to the next paragraph. You can set tabs before you key text or for existing text.

Setting Tabs

Word's default tabs are left-aligned and set every half inch from the left margin. These tabs are indicated at the bottom of the horizontal ruler by tiny tick marks.

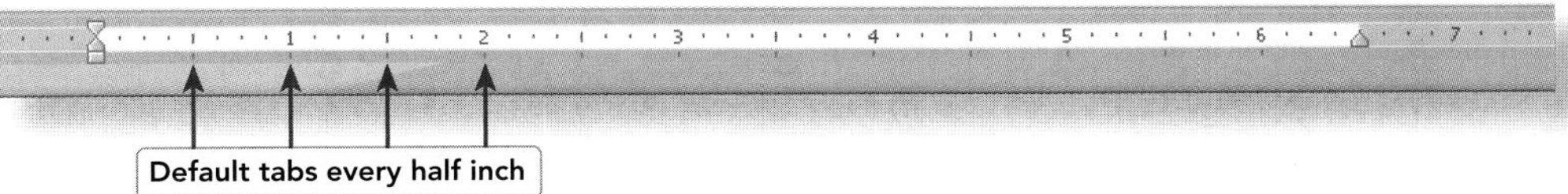

Figure 6-1
Default tabs

If you don't want to use the half-inch default tab settings, you have two choices:

- Change the distance between the default tab stops.
- Create custom tabs.

The four most common types of custom tabs are left-aligned, centered, right-aligned, and decimal-aligned. Custom tab settings are indicated by *tab markers* on the horizontal ruler. Additional custom tab options, such as leader tabs and bar tabs, are discussed in the section "Setting Leader Tabs" and in the exercise "Insert Bar Tabs."

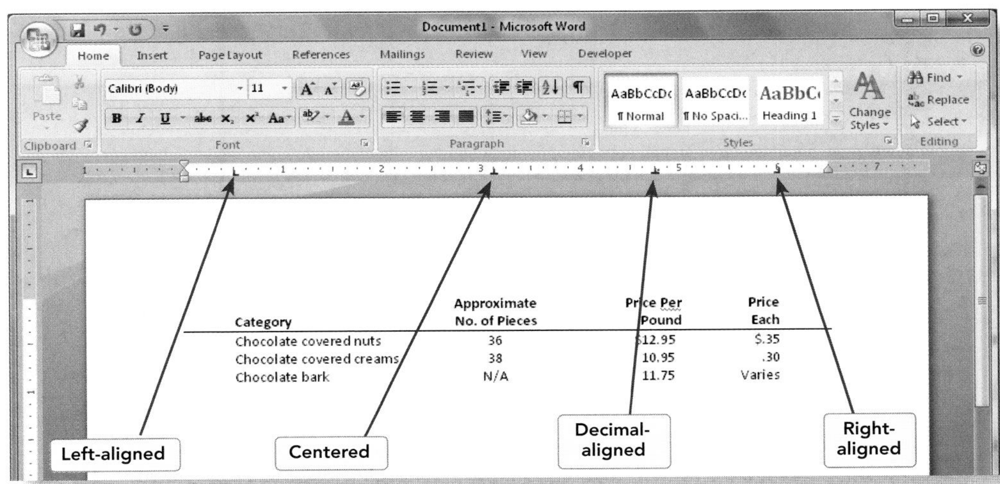

Figure 6-2
Types of tabs

TABLE 6-1 Types of Tabs

Ruler Symbol	Type of Tab	Description
	Left-aligned	The left edge of the text aligns with the tab stop.
	Centered	The text is centered at the tab stop.
	Right-aligned	The right edge of the text aligns with the tab stop.
	Decimal-aligned	The decimal point aligns with the tab stop. Use this option for columns of numbers.
	Bar	Inserts a vertical line at the tab stop. Use to create a divider line between columns.

There are two ways to set tabs:

- Use the Tabs dialog box.
- Use the ruler.

Exercise 6-1 SET TABS BY USING THE TABS DIALOG BOX

1. Open the file **Memo - 2**.

2. Click the View Ruler button to display the horizontal ruler, if necessary.

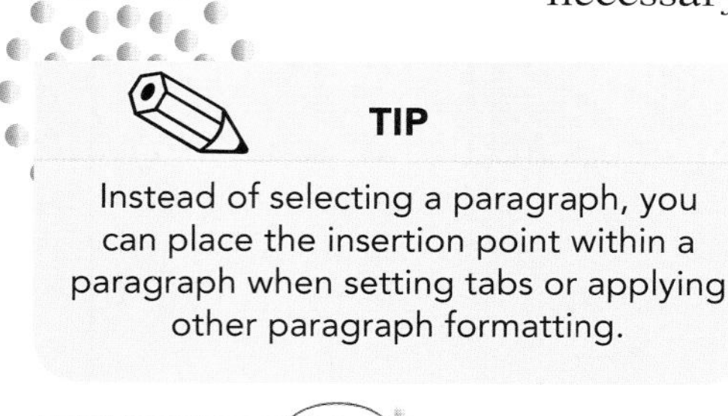

TIP

Instead of selecting a paragraph, you can place the insertion point within a paragraph when setting tabs or applying other paragraph formatting.

3. Select the text near the end of the document that begins "Item New Price" through the end of the document.

4. Click the **Home** tab, and locate the **Paragraph** group. Click the **Paragraph Dialog Box Launcher**. Click **Tabs**. The Tabs dialog box appears. Notice that the **Default tab stops** text box is set to 0.5 inch.

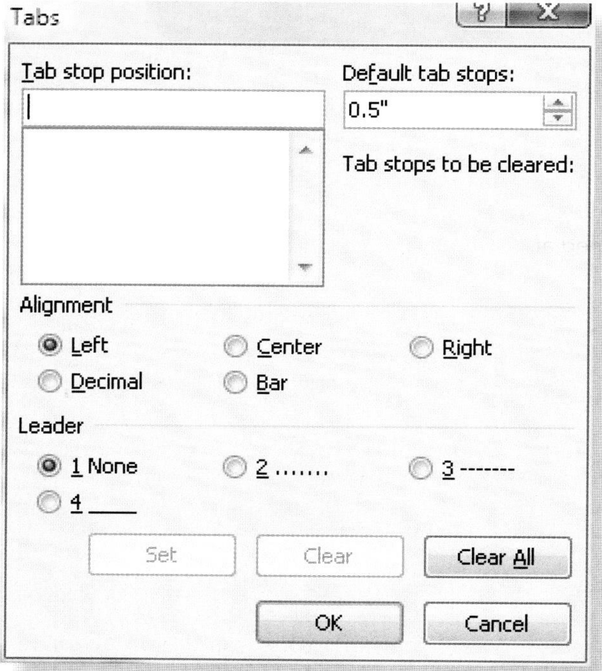

Figure 6-3
Tabs dialog box

5. Key **.25** in the **Tab stop position** text box. The alignment is already set to **Left**, by default.

6. Click **OK**. The ruler displays a left tab marker, the symbol used to indicate the type and location of a tab stop on the ruler.

7. Move the insertion point to the left of the first word on the first line of the selected text, "Item."

8. Press Tab. The first line of the group is now indented 0.25 inch. This produces the same effect as creating a first-line indent.

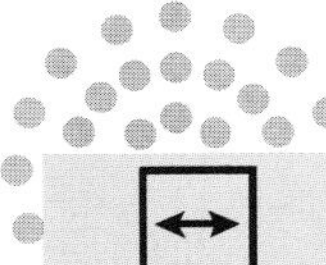

REVIEW

Tabs are nonprinting characters that can be displayed or hidden. Remember, to display or hide nonprinting characters, click the Show/Hide ¶ button.

NOTE

When you set a custom tab, Word clears all default tabs to the left of the new tab marker.

NOTE

The column heading "New Price" does not contain a decimal, but is aligned at the decimal point. You will adjust the tab for this heading later in this lesson.

9. Press Tab at the beginning of each of the lines that you formatted with the .25-inch left tab ("1.25 oz.," "1 lb.," "1 lb.," "4 oz.," and "4 oz.").
10. Select the same six lines of text ("Item" through "2.25") at the end of the document. Notice that there are tab characters between some of the words and that the text is crowded and difficult to read. The text is aligned at the default tab settings (every .5").
11. Open the Tabs dialog box by double clicking the tab marker at .25 on the ruler. Key **3.0** in the **Tab stop position** text box.
12. Under **Alignment**, choose **Decimal**. Click **Set**. Notice that the tab setting appears below the **Tab stop position** text box. The setting is automatically selected so that another tab setting can be keyed.
13. Click **OK**. The column headings "Item" and "New Price," along with the text below the headings, are now aligned at the tab stops.

Exercise 6-2 SET TABS BY USING THE RULER

Setting tabs by using the ruler is an easy two-step process: Click the Tab Alignment button on the left of the ruler to choose the type of tab alignment, and then click the position on the ruler to set the tab.

1. Go to the end of the document, and press Enter if necessary to begin a new paragraph.
2. Key **Category** at the left margin.
3. Click the **Tab Alignment** button on the horizontal ruler until it shows center alignment. Each time you click the button, the alignment changes.

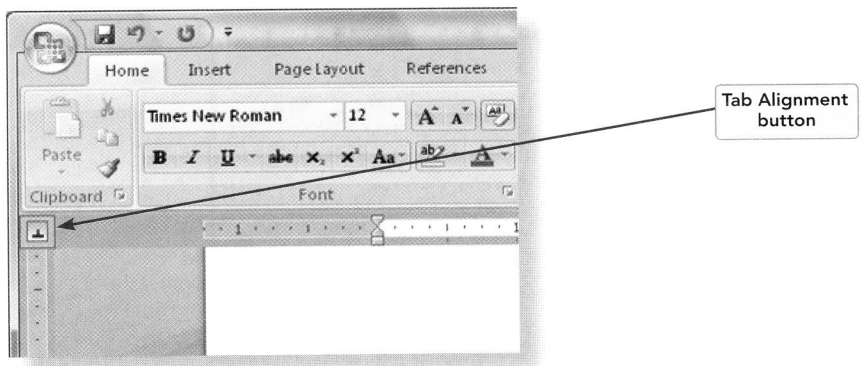

Figure 6-4
Tab Alignment button on the ruler

TIP

When choosing tab settings for information in a document, keep in mind that left-aligned text and right- or decimal-aligned numbers are easier to read.

TIP

As you toggle through the Tab Alignment button symbols, notice the appearance of the first-line indent symbol and the hanging indent symbol. You can display one of these symbols, and then just click the ruler to the desired indent position instead of using the point and drag method.

4. Click the ruler at 3.25, and a center tab marker displays.
5. Press Tab, and key **No. of Pieces**.
6. Click the **Tab Alignment** button on the horizontal ruler until it shows right alignment, and then click the ruler at 5.5.
7. Press Tab, and key **Price/Pound**.
8. Press Enter to start a new line. The tab settings will carry forward to the new line.
9. Key **Chocolate-covered nuts**, press Tab, key **36**, press Tab, and key **$12.95**.
10. Press Enter and key **Chocolate-covered creams**, press Tab, key **38**, press Tab, and key **10.95**. Press Enter.

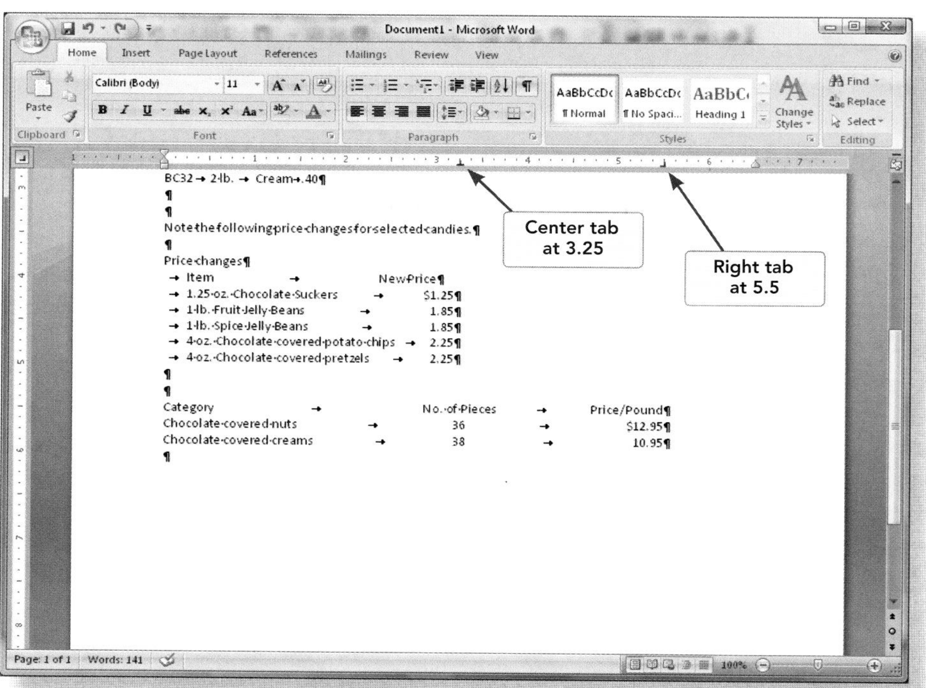

Figure 6-5
Document with tabbed text

TIP

You can copy tab settings from one paragraph to another. Click in the paragraph whose tab settings you want to copy. Click the Format Painter button. Click in the paragraph to which you are copying the tab settings.

Setting Leader Tabs

You can set tabs with *leader characters,* patterns of dots or dashes that lead the reader's eye from one tabbed column to the next. Leaders may be found in a table of contents, in which dotted lines fill the space between the headings on the left and the page numbers on the right.

Word offers three leader patterns: dotted line, dashed line, and solid line.

Figure 6-6
Leader patterns

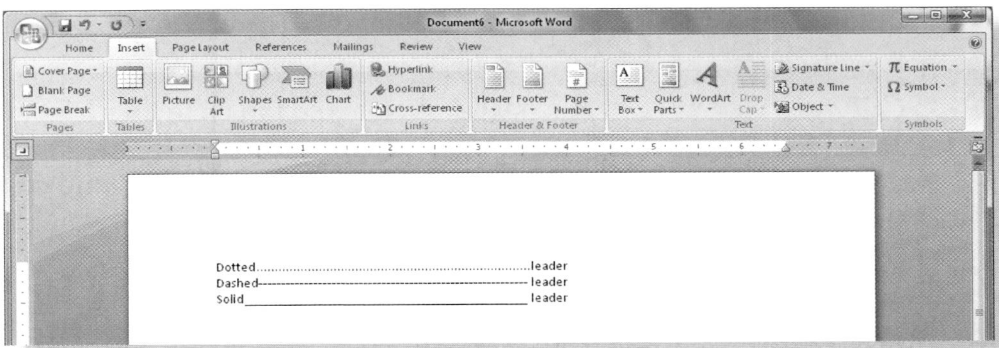

Exercise 6-3 SET LEADER TABS

1. Select the two columns of text under the headings "Item" and "New Price." The prices are aligned at a 3-inch decimal tab.
2. Open the **Tabs** dialog box. The tab settings for the selected text are displayed in the **Tab stop position** box with the **.25**-inch tab highlighted.
3. Click to select **3″** and under **Leader**, click the second leader pattern (the dotted line).
4. Click **Set** and click **OK**. A dotted-line leader fills the space to the left of the 3-inch tab setting.
5. Select the heading "Price Changes" and apply bold, small caps formatting. Select the headings "Item" and "New Price" and apply bold and italic.

NOTE

Leader patterns always fill the space to the left of a leader tab setting.

Clearing Tabs

You can clear custom tabs all at once or individually. When you clear custom tabs, Word restores the default tab stops to the left of the custom tab stop.

There are three ways to clear a tab:

- Use the Tabs dialog box.
- Use the ruler.
- Press Ctrl+Q.

Exercise 6-4 CLEAR A TAB BY USING THE TABS DIALOG BOX AND THE KEYBOARD

1. Select the six lines of text under the heading "Price Changes."
2. Open the Tabs dialog box. The 0.25-inch tab is highlighted in the **Tab stop position** box.
3. Click **Clear** and click **OK**. Word clears the 0.25-inch custom tab, and the text moves to the right to align at the tab at 3.0. (The text moves because each line is preceded by a tab character (→).

NOTE

Remember, to remove tabs from text, you must delete the tab characters.

4. Delete the tab character (→) at the beginning of each line. The text in the first column moves to the left margin, and the second column is aligned at the tab setting.
5. Select the six lines of text under the heading "Price Changes" once again.
6. Press Ctrl+Q. The remaining tab setting is deleted, and the text is no longer aligned.

7. Click the Undo button to restore the 3-inch custom tab.
8. Save the document as ***[your initials]*6-4** in your Lesson 6 folder.

Exercise 6-5 CLEAR A TAB BY USING THE RULER

1. Position the insertion point at the beginning of the line of text with the heading "Category."
2. Position the pointer on the 5.5-inch right-aligned tab marker on the ruler.

NOTE

When clearing or adjusting tabs by using the ruler, watch for the ScreenTip to correctly identify the item to which you are pointing. If no ScreenTip appears, you might inadvertently add another tab marker.

3. When the ScreenTip "Right Tab" appears, drag the tab marker down and off the ruler. The custom tab is cleared, and the heading "Price/Pound" moves to a default tab stop.
4. Undo the last action to restore the tab setting.
5. Select the headings "Category," "No. of Pieces," and "Price/Pound," and apply bold, small caps formatting.

Adjusting Tab Settings

You can adjust tabs inserted in a document by using either the Tabs dialog box or the ruler. Tabs can be adjusted only after you select the text to which they have been applied.

Exercise 6-6 ADJUST TAB SETTINGS

1. Select the line with the headings "Item" and "New Price." The second heading is not aligned with the text below.
2. Point to the tab marker at 3 inches on the ruler.
3. Drag the tab marker to the right until the heading aligns with the text below.
4. Select the last three lines of text in the document ("Category" through "10.95").
5. Open the Tabs dialog box.
6. Click to select the tab setting **5.5** in the **Tab stop position** box.
7. Change the tab alignment setting by clicking **Left**. Click **OK**. Notice the change in the alignment of the heading and the text below.
8. Click the Undo button .

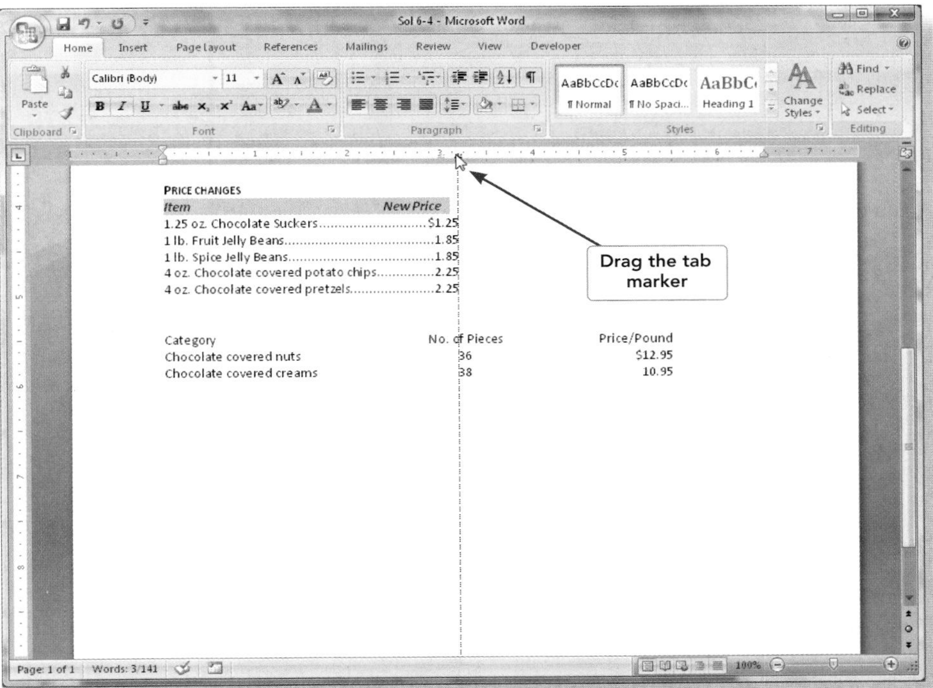

Figure 6-7
Using the ruler to adjust a tab setting

NOTE

When you change tab settings with the ruler, be careful to drag the tab marker only to the right or to the left. If you drag the tab marker up or down, you might clear it from the ruler. If you inadvertently clear a tab marker, undo your action to restore the tab.

9. With the text still selected, drag the 5.5-inch tab marker to 6.5 inches on the ruler. The text is now aligned at the right margin.

Creating Tabbed Columns

As you have seen in these practice documents, you can use tabs to present information in columns.

When you format a table using tabbed columns, follow these general rules based on *The Gregg Reference Manual*. Follow these rules for existing text or text to be keyed.

- The table should be centered horizontally within the margins.
- Columns within the table should be between six and ten spaces apart.
- The width of the table should not exceed the width of the document's body text.
- At least one blank line should separate the top and bottom of the table from the body text of the document.

Exercise 6-7 SET TABBED COLUMNS

1. Position the insertion point at the end of the document and press Enter twice.
2. Press Ctrl+Q to remove the tab settings from the paragraph mark; then key the text shown in Figure 6-8. Use single spacing.

Figure 6-8

```
The following stores offer a complete line of gifts and
accessories in addition to our fine chocolates. Other
stores offer a limited selection of gifts and accessories
due to space limitations.
```

3. Press Enter twice.
4. Study Figure 6-9 to determine the longest item in each column. (Pennsylvania is the longest item in the first column. Youngstown is the longest item in the second column, and West Virginia is the longest item in the third column.)

Figure 6-9

Pennsylvania	Ohio	West Virginia
Grove City	Akron	Clarksburg
Pittsburgh	Canton	Fairmont
Erie	Cleveland	Morgantown
Monroeville	Youngstown	Wheeling

5. Create a guide line that contains the longest item in each column by keying the following with 10 spaces between each group of words:

Pennsylvania Youngstown West Virginia

6. Click the Center button on the Ribbon to center the line.
7. Scroll down until the guide line is below the ruler.

8. Change the Tab Alignment button to left alignment. Using the I-beam as a guide, click the ruler to set a left-aligned tab at the beginning of each group of words.

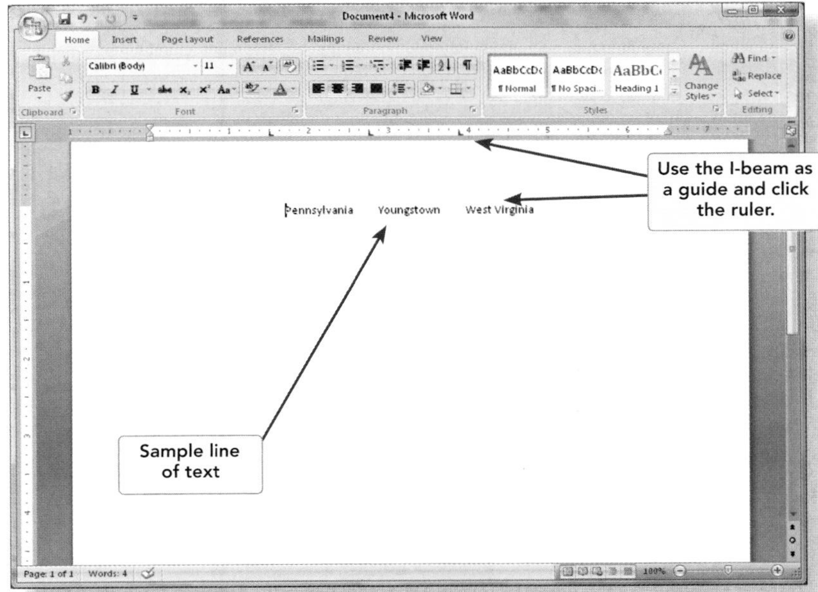

Figure 6-10
Guide line for centering tabbed columns

9. Delete the text in the guide line up to the paragraph mark. Do not delete the paragraph mark, which is now storing your left-aligned tab settings.

10. Click the Align Left button to left-align the insertion point.
11. Key the table text as shown in Figure 6-9, pressing Tab before each item and single-spacing each line. Underline each column heading.
12. Select the text near the top of the document beginning with "Item No." and ending with the line that begins "BC32."

13. Change the tab alignment button to left alignment and click the ruler at 2.5.

14. Change the tab alignment button to right alignment and click the ruler at 5.5.

15. Select the text if necessary, and click the Increase Indent button two times to move the text away from the left margin.
16. Drag the left tab marker (right or left) to position the middle column an equal distance from the first and third columns.
17. Bold and center the heading "Standard-Size Boxes." Format the title with all caps and 12 points spacing after. Apply bold and italic formatting to the column headings.

Exercise 6-8 SELECT A TABBED COLUMN

After text is formatted in tabbed columns, you can select columns individually by selecting a vertical block of text. Selecting tabbed text can be helpful for formatting or deleting text. You use Alt to select a vertical block of text.

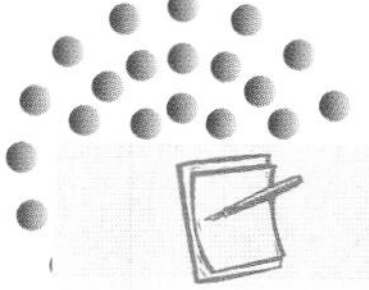

NOTE

If you do not press Alt when trying to select text vertically, you will select the entire first line of text, rather than just the column header for the column you are selecting.

1. Hold down Alt and position the I-beam to the immediate left of "Ohio."
2. Drag across the heading, and then down until the heading and all four cities are selected. Do not select the tab characters to the right of the column.

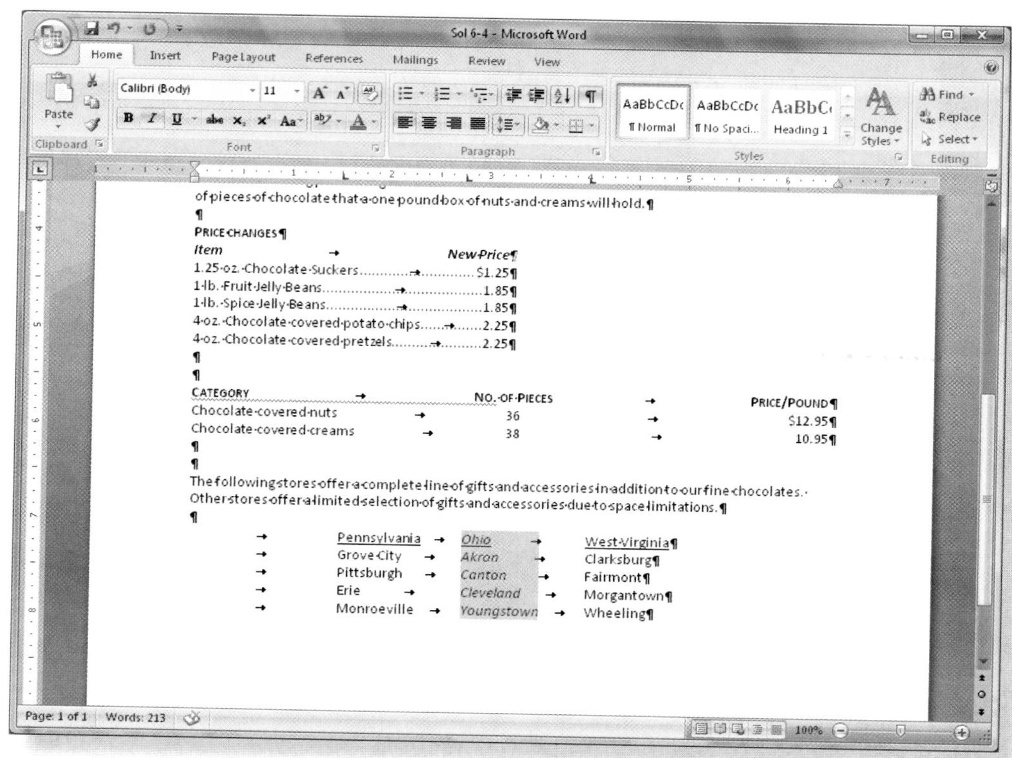

Figure 6-11 Selecting text vertically

3. Press Delete to delete the column.
4. Undo the deletion.
5. Select the column again, this time selecting only the names under the column head "Ohio."

6. Click the Italic button to format the text.

Exercise 6-9 INSERT BAR TABS

Bar tabs are used to make tabbed columns look more like a table with gridlines. A bar tab inserts a vertical line at a fixed position, creating a border between columns. You can set bar tabs by using the ruler or the Tabs dialog box.

1. At the bottom of the document, select the four lines of tabbed text below the headings "Pennsylvania," "Ohio," and "West Virginia."
2. Open the **Tabs** dialog box. Key **2.5** in the text box, click **Bar**, and click **OK**. The vertical bar is placed between the first and second columns. Do not deselect the tabbed text.

3. To set bar tabs by using the ruler, click the Tab Alignment button until it changes to a bar tab. Click the ruler at 3.75 inches. The bar tab markers appear as short vertical lines on the ruler.
4. Adjust the bar tab markers on the ruler to make them more evenly spaced, as needed.

5. Deselect the tabbed text. Click the Show/Hide ¶ button to view the document without nonprinting characters. The bar tabs act as dividing borders between the columns.

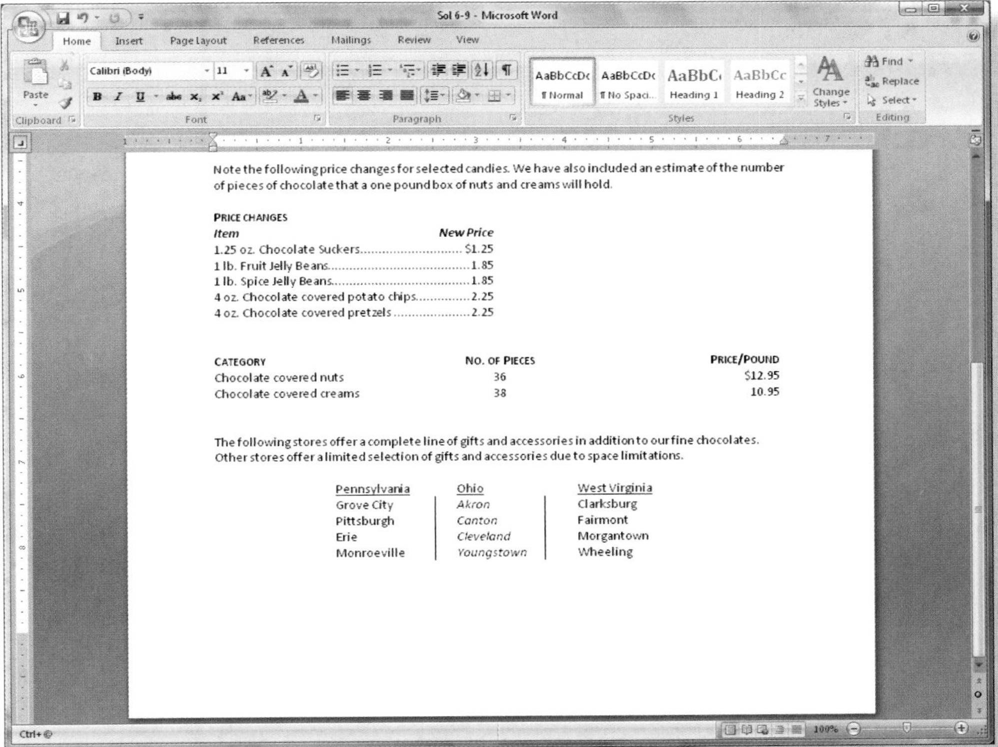

Figure 6-12
Tabbed text with bar tabs

6. Position the insertion point in the line that contains "Grove City."
7. Point to the 3.75-inch bar tab on the ruler, and drag it off the ruler. The vertical line in the table disappears.
8. Undo the deletion to restore the bar tab.
9. Save the document as ***[your initials]*****6-9** in your Lesson 6 folder.
10. Submit the document.

Sorting Paragraphs and Tabbed Columns

Sorting is the process of reordering text alphabetically or numerically. You can sort to rearrange text in ascending order (from lowest to highest, such as 0–9 or A–Z) or descending order (from highest to lowest, such as 9–0 or Z–A).

You can sort any group of paragraphs, from a single-column list to a multiple-column table, such as one created by tabbed columns. When sorting a tabbed table, you can sort by any of the columns.

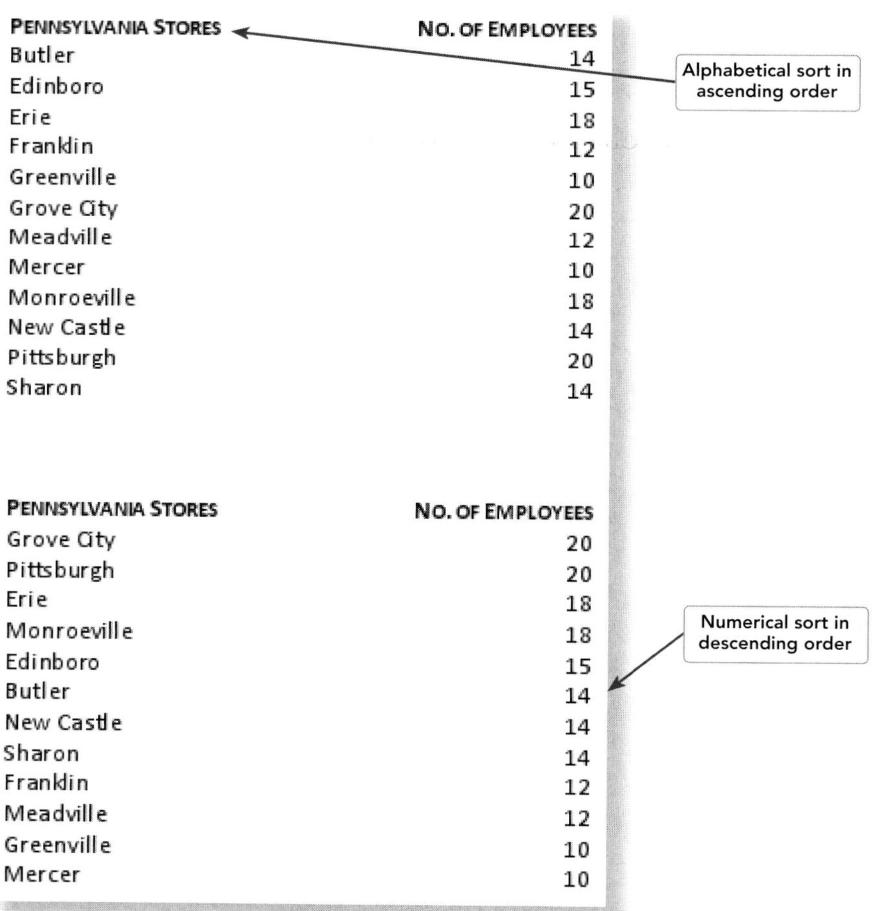

PENNSYLVANIA STORES	NO. OF EMPLOYEES
Butler	14
Edinboro	15
Erie	18
Franklin	12
Greenville	10
Grove City	20
Meadville	12
Mercer	10
Monroeville	18
New Castle	14
Pittsburgh	20
Sharon	14

PENNSYLVANIA STORES	NO. OF EMPLOYEES
Grove City	20
Pittsburgh	20
Erie	18
Monroeville	18
Edinboro	15
Butler	14
New Castle	14
Sharon	14
Franklin	12
Meadville	12
Greenville	10
Mercer	10

Figure 6-13
Sorting paragraphs and tables

Exercise 6-10 SORT TABBED TABLES

1. Select the headings "Pennsylvania," "Ohio," and "West Virginia" and the four lines of text below the headings.

2. Click the Sort button on the Ribbon, Paragraph group.
3. Open the **Sort by** drop-down list to view the other sort options. Field numbers represent each of the columns. Open the **Type** drop-down list. Notice that the type options include **Text**, **Number**, and **Date**.
4. Click **Descending** to change the sort order and click the **Header row** option to select it. Click **OK**. The text in the first column is sorted alphabetically in descending order.
5. Press Ctrl+Z to undo the sort. Do not deselect the text.

6. Click the Sort button to open the Sort Text dialog box.
7. Click **Header row** at the bottom of the dialog box. This option indicates that the selection includes column headings, which should not be sorted with the text.
8. Open the **Sort by** drop-down list. Now you can sort by the table's column headings instead of by field numbers.
9. Choose **Ohio** from the drop-down list. Click **Descending** and click **OK**.

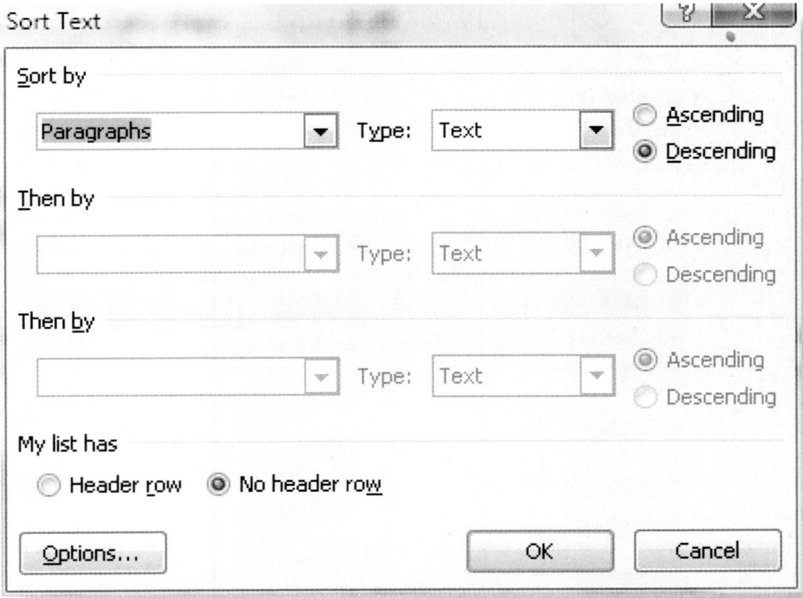

Figure 6-14 Sorting options in the Sort Text dialog box

10. Save the document as ***[your initials]*6-10** in your Lesson 6 folder.
11. Submit and close the document.

Lesson 6 Summary

- Tabs are a paragraph-formatting feature used to align text. When you press Tab, Word inserts a tab character and moves the insertion position to the tab setting, called the tab stop.
- Word's default tabs are left-aligned and set every half-inch from the left margin, as indicated at the bottom of the horizontal ruler.
- The four most common types of custom tabs are left-aligned, centered, right-aligned, and decimal-aligned. Custom tab settings are indicated on the horizontal ruler by tab markers.
- Set tabs by using the Tabs dialog box or the ruler. To use the ruler, click the Tab Alignment button on the left of the ruler to choose the type of tab alignment, and then click the position on the ruler to set the tab. See Table 6-1.
- A leader tab uses a series of dots, dashes, or solid underlines to fill the empty space to the left of a tab stop. Use the Tabs dialog box to set a leader tab.
- Clear custom tabs all at once or individually. To clear a tab, use the Tabs dialog box, or the ruler, or press Ctrl+Q.
- To adjust tab settings, position the insertion point in the tabbed text (or select the text), and then either open the Tabs dialog box or drag the tab markers on the ruler.
- Use tabs to present information in columns. Tabbed columns are a side-by-side vertical list of information.
- To select a tabbed column (for formatting or deleting the text), hold down Alt and drag the I-beam over the text.
- Use bar tabs to format tabbed columns similar to a table with gridlines. A bar tab inserts a vertical line at a fixed position, creating a border between columns. You can set bar tabs by using the ruler or the Tabs dialog box.
- Sorting is the process of reordering text alphabetically or numerically. You can sort to rearrange text in ascending order (from lowest to highest, such as 0–9 or A–Z) or descending order (from highest to lowest, such as 9–0 or Z–A).

LESSON 6		Command Summary	
Feature	**Button**	**Command**	**Keyboard**
Left tab		**Home** tab, **Paragraph** group	
Center tab		**Home** tab, **Paragraph** group	
Right tab		**Home** tab, **Paragraph** group	
Decimal tab		**Home** tab, **Paragraph** group	
Bar tab		**Home** tab, **Paragraph** group	
Leader tabs		**Home** tab, **Paragraph** group	
Clear tabs		**Home** tab, **Paragraph** group	Ctrl+Q
Sort text		**Home** tab, **Paragraph** group	

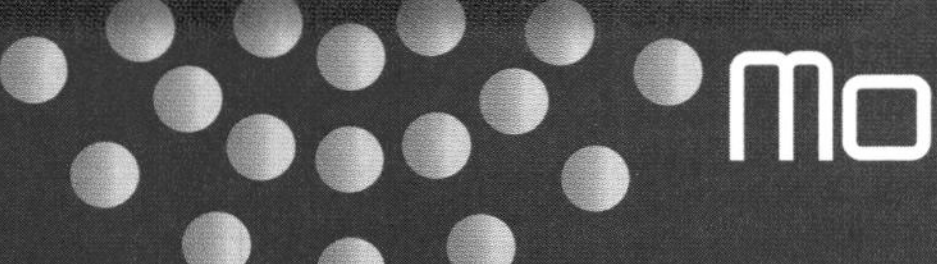

Lesson 7

Move and Copy

OBJECTIVES

After completing this lesson, you will be able to:

1. Use the Office Clipboard.
2. Move text by using cut and paste.
3. Move text by dragging.
4. Copy text by using copy and paste.
5. Copy text by dragging.
6. Work with multiple document windows.
7. Move and copy text among windows.

MCAS OBJECTIVES

In this lesson:
WW 07 2.2.1
WW 07 5.1.2

Estimated Time: 1 hour

One of the most useful features of word processing is the capability to move or copy a block of text from one part of a document to another or from one document window to another, without rekeying the text. In Word, you can move and copy text quickly by using the Cut, Copy, and Paste commands or the drag-and-drop editing feature.

Using the Office Clipboard

Perhaps the most important tool for moving and copying text is the *Clipboard,* which is a temporary storage area. Here's how it works: Cut or copy text from your document and store it on the Clipboard. Then move to a different location in your document and insert the Clipboard's contents using the Paste command.

There are two types of clipboards:

- The system Clipboard stores one item at a time. Each time you store a new item on this Clipboard, it replaces the previous item. This Clipboard is available to many software applications on your system.
- The Office Clipboard can store 24 items, which are displayed on the Clipboard task pane. The Office Clipboard lets you collect multiple items without erasing previous items. You can store items from all Office applications.

Exercise 7-1 DISPLAY THE CLIPBOARD TASK PANE

1. Click the **Home** tab. The **Clipboard** group contains a Dialog Box Launcher arrow to open the Clipboard task pane.
2. Click the **Clipboard Dialog Box Launcher** arrow. The Clipboard task pane opens. At the top of the task pane, notice the Paste All and Clear All buttons. At the bottom of the screen, at the right end of the taskbar, notice the Clipboard icon, indicating that the Office Clipboard is in use.

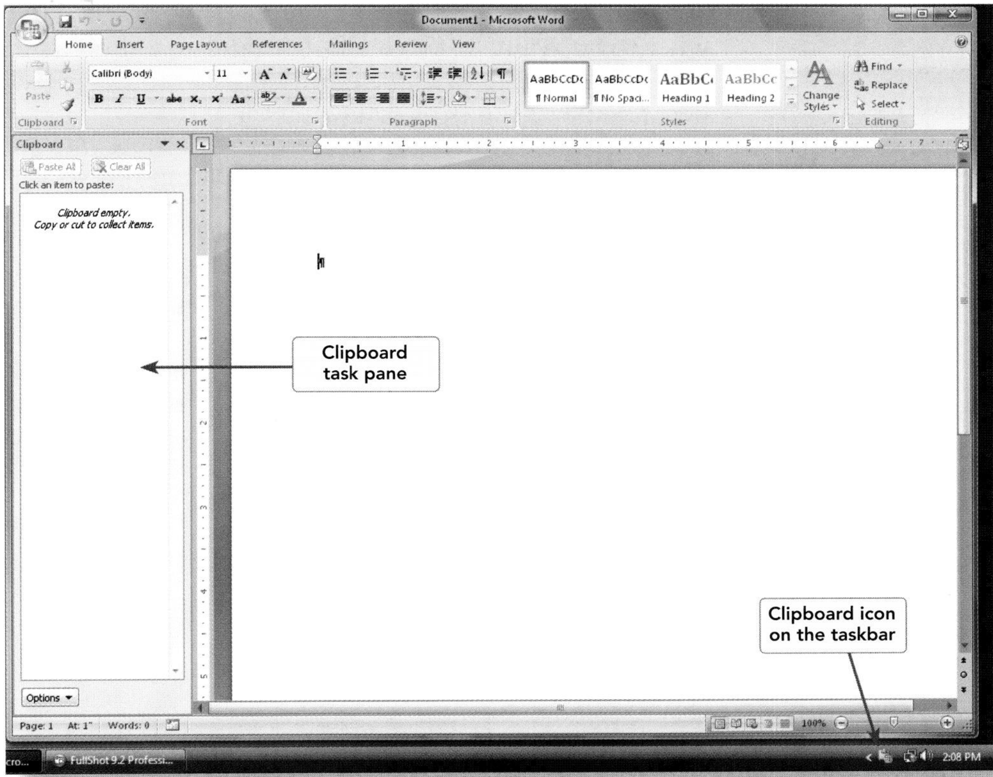

Figure 7-1
Clipboard task pane

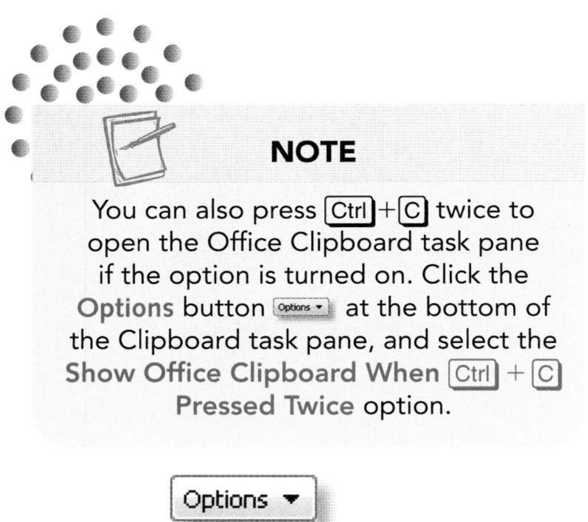

NOTE

You can also press Ctrl+C twice to open the Office Clipboard task pane if the option is turned on. Click the **Options** button at the bottom of the Clipboard task pane, and select the **Show Office Clipboard When Ctrl + C Pressed Twice** option.

3. If the Office Clipboard contains items from previous use, click the Clear All button to empty the Clipboard.
4. Click the **Options** button at the bottom of the task pane. Notice the options available for using the Office Clipboard.
5. Click outside the task pane, making sure not to choose any of the options in the list.

NOTE

If the option **Show Office Clipboard Automatically** is selected, the Clipboard task pane will open automatically when you copy twice in a row without pasting.

Moving Text by Using Cut and Paste

To move text by using the *cut-and-paste* method, start by highlighting the text you want to move and using the Cut command. Then move to the location where you want to place the text and use the Paste command. When you use cut and paste to move paragraphs, you can preserve the correct spacing between paragraphs by following these rules:

- Include the blank line below the paragraph you are moving as part of the selection.
- When you paste the selection, click to the left of the first line of text following the place where your paragraph will go—not on the blank line above it.

There are multiple ways to cut and paste text. The most commonly used methods are:

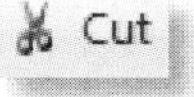

- Use the Cut and Paste buttons on the Ribbon, Home tab.
- Use the shortcut menu.
- Use the keyboard shortcuts Ctrl+X to cut and Ctrl+V to paste.
- Use the Clipboard task pane.

Exercise 7-2 USE THE RIBBON TO CUT AND PASTE

1. Open the file **Festival Memo**. Display the Clipboard task pane if necessary.
2. Key the current year in the date line of the memo heading.
3. Select the text "Strawberry Days" in the subject line of the memo.

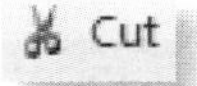

4. Click the **Home** tab, and click the Cut button to remove the text from the document and place it on the Clipboard. Notice the Clipboard item in the task pane.
5. Position the insertion point to the left of "Art" in the Subject line to indicate where you want to insert the text.
6. Click the Paste button to insert "Strawberry Days" in its new location. The Paste Options button appears below the pasted text, and the Clipboard item remains in the task pane.

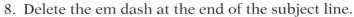

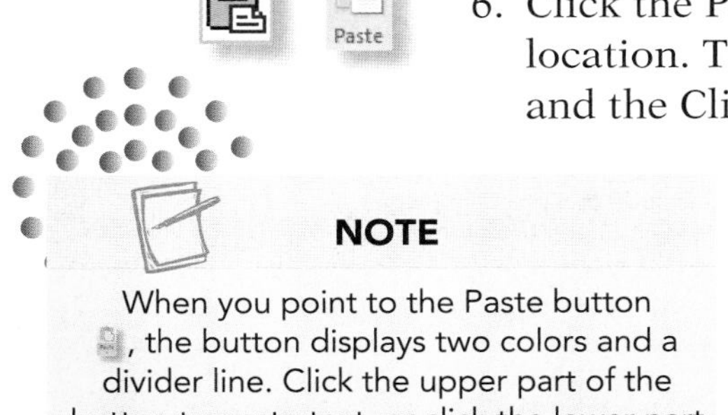

NOTE
When you point to the Paste button, the button displays two colors and a divider line. Click the upper part of the button to paste text, or click the lower part of the button to display a list of options.

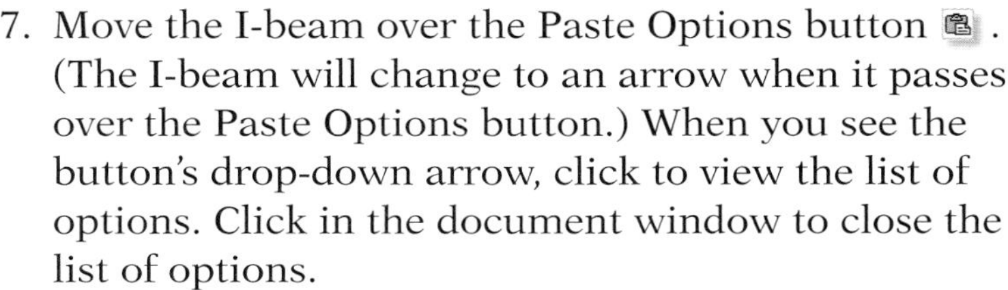

7. Move the I-beam over the Paste Options button. (The I-beam will change to an arrow when it passes over the Paste Options button.) When you see the button's drop-down arrow, click to view the list of options. Click in the document window to close the list of options.
8. Delete the em dash at the end of the subject line.

NOTE
The Paste Options button is available to make sure the text you paste has the type of formatting you want.

Exercise 7-3 USE THE SHORTCUT MENU TO CUT AND PASTE

1. Select the paragraph near the bottom of the document that begins "All hotels are." Include the paragraph mark on the blank line following the paragraph.

Figure 7-2
Using the shortcut menu to cut

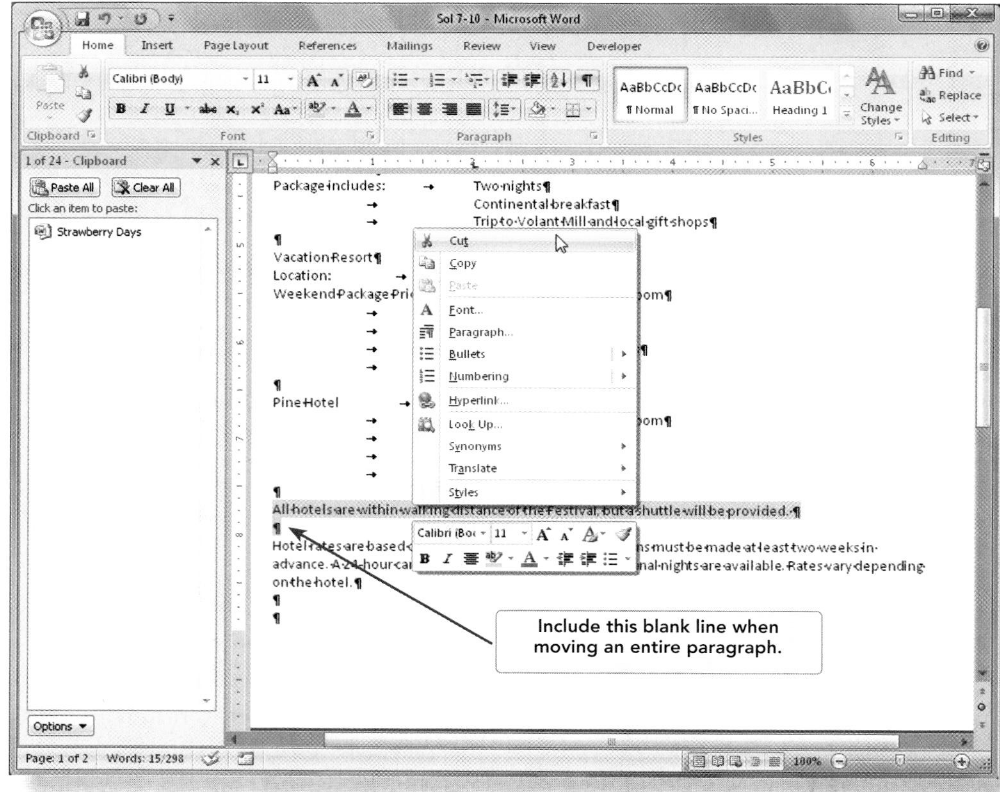

2. Point to the selected text and right-click to display the shortcut menu.
3. Click **Cut**. The item is added to the Clipboard task pane.

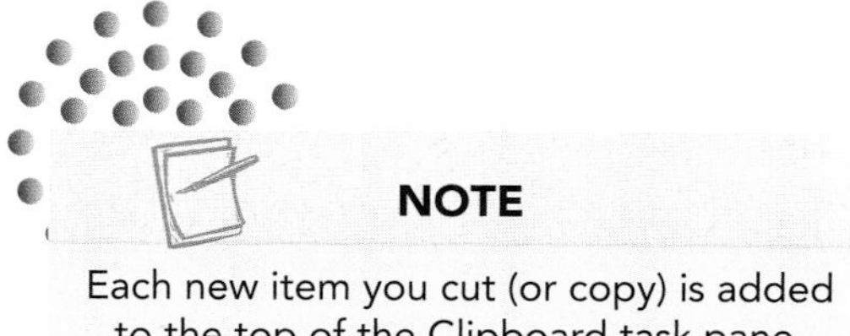

NOTE
Each new item you cut (or copy) is added to the top of the Clipboard task pane.

4. Position the I-beam to the left of the paragraph that begins “Several special.” Right-click and choose **Paste** from the shortcut menu. The paragraph moves to its new location, and the Paste Options button appears below the pasted text.

Figure 7-3
Using the shortcut menu to paste

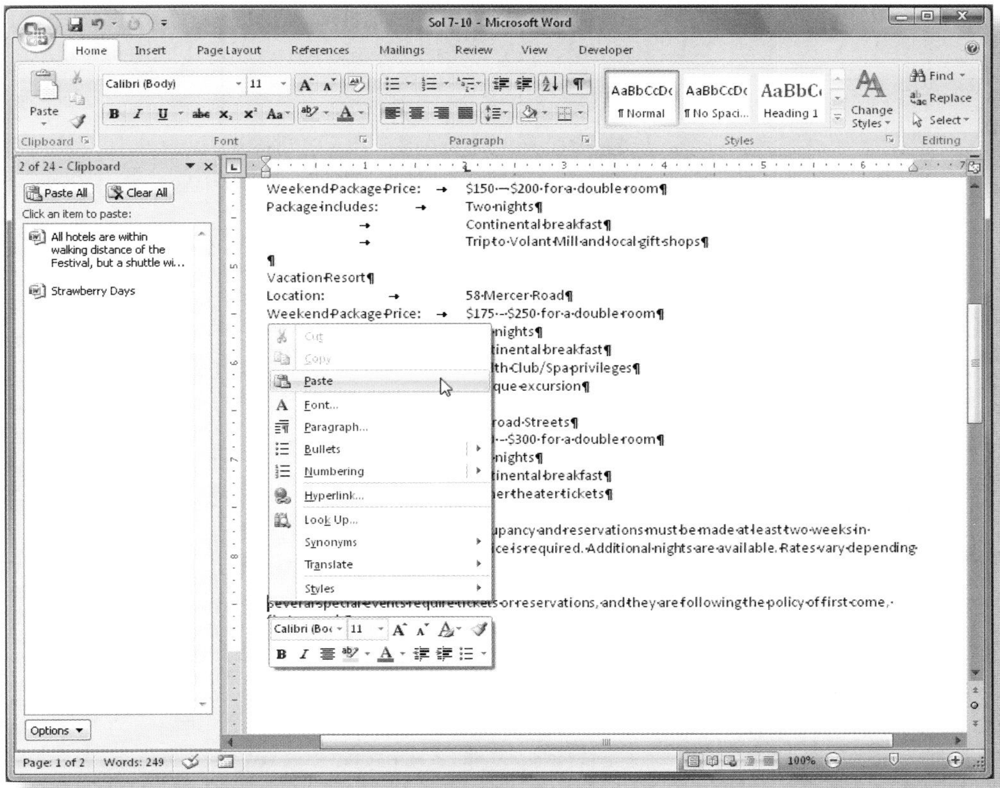

Exercise 7-4 USE KEYBOARD SHORTCUTS TO CUT AND PASTE

If you prefer using the keyboard, you can press Ctrl+X to cut text and Ctrl+V to paste text. You can also use Ctrl+Z to undo an action. The location of these shortcut keys is designed to make it easy for you to move your mouse with your right hand while you press command keys with your left hand.

1. Select the paragraph that begins "Several special." Press Ctrl+X to cut the text. A new item appears in the task pane.
2. Position the insertion point just before the paragraph that begins "Please refer." Press Ctrl+V to paste the text.
3. Press Ctrl+Z to undo the paste. Press Ctrl+Y. (Remember, you can also click the Undo button to undo actions.) Notice that the Clipboard item remains in the task pane.

Exercise 7-5 USE THE OFFICE CLIPBOARD TO PASTE

Each time you cut text in the previous exercises, a new item was added to the Office Clipboard. You can paste that item directly from the task pane.

1. Select all the information that goes with the "Pine Hotel," including the title "Pine Hotel" and the blank line that follows the hotel information.
2. Cut this text, using the Cut button on the Ribbon. The text is stored as a new item at the top of the Clipboard task pane.
3. Position the insertion point to the left of the paragraph that begins "Wolf Creek Hotel."
4. Click the task pane item for the Pine Hotel text that you just cut. (Do not click the drop-down arrow.) This pastes the text at the location of the insertion point.
5. Press Ctrl+Z to undo the paste. Press Ctrl+Z again to undo the cut. The Clipboard item remains in the task pane.
6. Point to this Clipboard item in the task pane, and click the drop-down arrow that appears to its right.
7. Choose **Delete** from the list to delete the item from the Clipboard.

NOTE

Choosing the Paste option from the drop-down list pastes that item, just like clicking directly on the item. The Paste All button on the Clipboard task pane is used to copy all Office Clipboard items to the location of the insertion point.

Moving Text by Dragging

You can also move selected text to a new location by using the *drag-and-drop* method. Text is not transferred to the Clipboard when you use drag and drop.

Exercise 7-6 USE DRAG AND DROP TO MOVE TEXT

1. Select all the information related to "Vacation Resort," including the title "Vacation Resort' and the blank line below the information.
2. Point to the selected text. Notice that the I-beam changes to a left-pointing arrow.

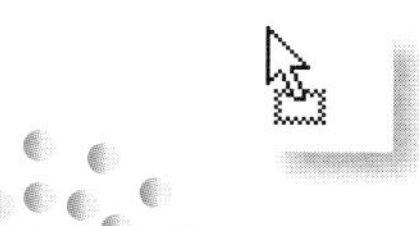

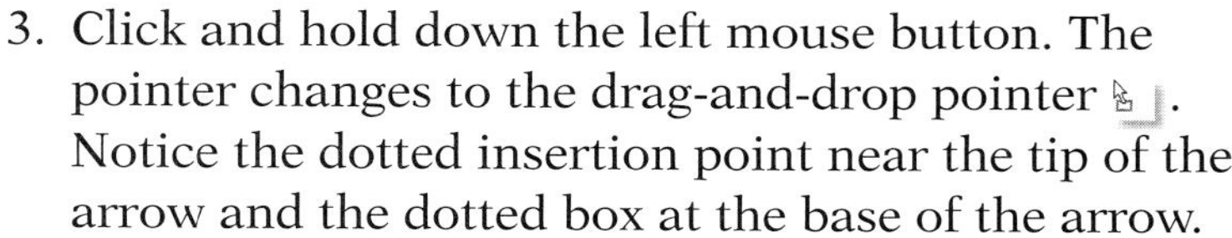

3. Click and hold down the left mouse button. The pointer changes to the drag-and-drop pointer. Notice the dotted insertion point near the tip of the arrow and the dotted box at the base of the arrow.
4. Drag the pointer until the dotted insertion point is positioned to the left of the line beginning "Wolf Creek Hotel." Release the mouse button. The paragraph moves to its new location and the Paste Options button appears.

TIP

Use cut and paste to move text over long distances—for example, onto another page. Use drag and drop to move text short distances where you can see both the selected text and the destination on the screen at the same time.

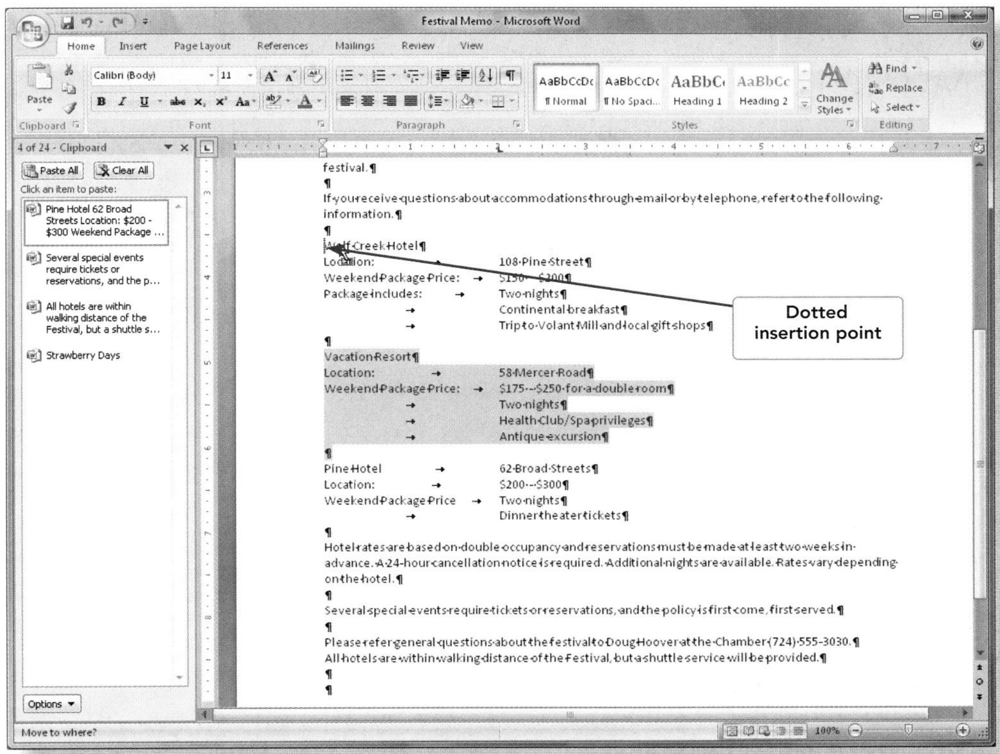

Figure 7-4
Drag-and-drop pointer

Copying Text by Using Copy and Paste

Copying and pasting text is similar to cutting and pasting text. Instead of removing the text from the document and storing it on the Clipboard, you place a copy of the text on the Clipboard.

There are several ways to copy and paste text. The most common methods are:

- Use the Copy and Paste buttons on the Ribbon, Home tab.
- Use the shortcut menu.
- Use keyboard shortcuts Ctrl+C to copy and Ctrl+V to paste.
- Use the Clipboard task pane.

Exercise 7-7 USE COPY AND PASTE

1. Under "Wolf Creek Hotel," select the entire line that contains the text "Continental breakfast." Include the tab character to the left of the text and the paragraph mark to the right of the text. Click the Show/Hide button to display formatting characters. (The selected text should begin at the left margin and end with the paragraph mark.)

2. Click the Copy button on the Ribbon to transfer a copy of the text to the Clipboard. Notice that the selected text remains in its original position in the document.
3. Position the insertion point to the left of the paragraph that begins with a tab character and includes "Health Club/Spa privileges" in the text under "Vacation Resort."
4. Right-click and choose **Paste** from the shortcut menu. A copy of the paragraph is added to the "Vacation Resort" package description, and the Paste Options button appears.
5. Point to the Paste Options button. When you see the down arrow, click the button. Notice that the same options are available when you copy and paste text. Click in the document window to close the list of options and keep the source formatting.
6. Position the insertion point to the left of the paragraph that begins "Dinner theater tickets." Press Ctrl+V to paste the text into the "Pine Hotel" package description.

Exercise 7-8 USE THE OFFICE CLIPBOARD TO PASTE COPIED TEXT

A new item is added to the Office Clipboard each time you copy text. You can click this item to paste the text into the document.

1. Under "Vacation Resort," select the text "for a double room." Include the space character to the left of the text and the paragraph mark to the right of the text.
2. Press Ctrl+C to copy this text.
3. Position the insertion point to the right of the text that begins "$150–$200."
4. Click the Clipboard that contains the text "for a double room." The Clipboard content is pasted into the document at the location of the insertion point. If necessary, delete the blank line.

NOTE

You can store up to 24 cut or copied items on the Office Clipboard. When the Clipboard is full and you cut or copy text, the bottom Clipboard item is deleted and the new item is added to the top of the task pane.

Copying Text by Dragging

To copy text by using the drag-and-drop method, press Ctrl while dragging the text. Remember, drag and drop does not store text on a Clipboard.

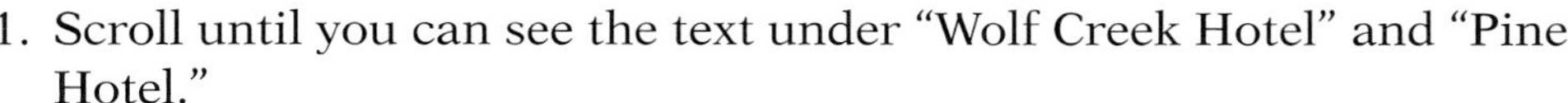

Exercise 7-9 USE DRAG AND DROP TO COPY TEXT

1. Scroll until you can see the text under "Wolf Creek Hotel" and "Pine Hotel."

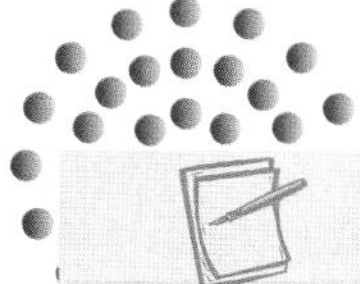

NOTE

You may already have noticed that when you delete, cut, move, or paste text, Word automatically adjusts the spacing between words. For example, if you cut a word at the end of a sentence, Word automatically deletes the leftover space. If you paste a word between two other words, Word automatically adds the needed space as part of its Smart Cut-and-Paste feature. The Smart Cut-and Paste feature is turned on by default.

2. Select the text under the Wolf Creek Hotel beginning with "for a double room." Include the paragraph mark.
3. While pressing Ctrl, drag the selected text to the immediate right of the text "$200–$300" in the "Pine Hotel" section. The plus (+) sign attached to the drag-and-drop pointer indicates the text is being copied rather than moved.
4. The text is copied, and a space is automatically inserted between "$300" and "for."

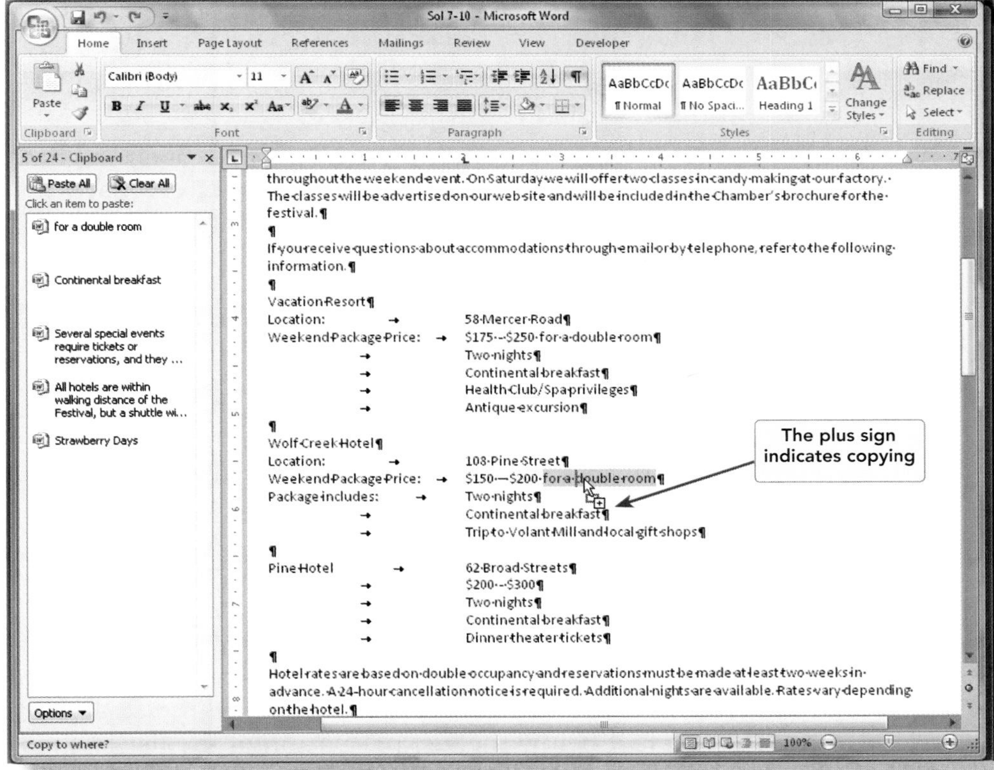

Figure 7-5
Copying with the drag-and-drop pointer

5. Move to the top of the document, and change the spacing before to 72 points, and insert your reference initials at the end of the document.

TIP

Dragging is not effective over long distances within a document. Try these alternative methods: To cut, select the text, hold down Ctrl, scroll as needed, and right-click where you want to paste the text. To copy, select the text, hold down Ctrl and Shift, scroll as needed, and right-click where you want to paste the text.

6. Open the **File** menu, and click the arrow beside **Print**. Click **Print Preview** to switch to Print Preview. Display both pages of the document by clicking **Two Pages**.
7. Locate and click the Shrink One Page button. The document is reduced to a one-page document.
8. Close Print Preview.
9. Save the document as ***[your initials]*7-9** in a new folder for Lesson 7.

10. Click the Clear All button on the Office Clipboard to clear all items. Click the Close button on the task pane to close the Office Clipboard.
11. Submit and close the document.

Working with Multiple Document Windows

In Word, you can work with several open document windows. Working with multiple windows makes it easy to compare different parts of the same document or to move or copy text from one document to another.

Exercise 7-10 SPLIT A DOCUMENT INTO PANES

Splitting a document divides it into two areas separated by a horizontal line called the *split bar*. Each of the resulting two areas, called *panes,* has its own scroll bar.

To split a screen, click the View tab and click the Split button or use the split box at the top of the vertical scroll bar.

1. Open the file **Fund2**.

2. Click the **View** tab and click the Split button. A gray bar appears along with the split pointer.

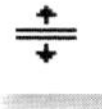

3. Move your mouse up or down (without clicking) until the gray bar is just below the last paragraph of the list of candy bars.

Figure 7-6
Splitting a document into two panes

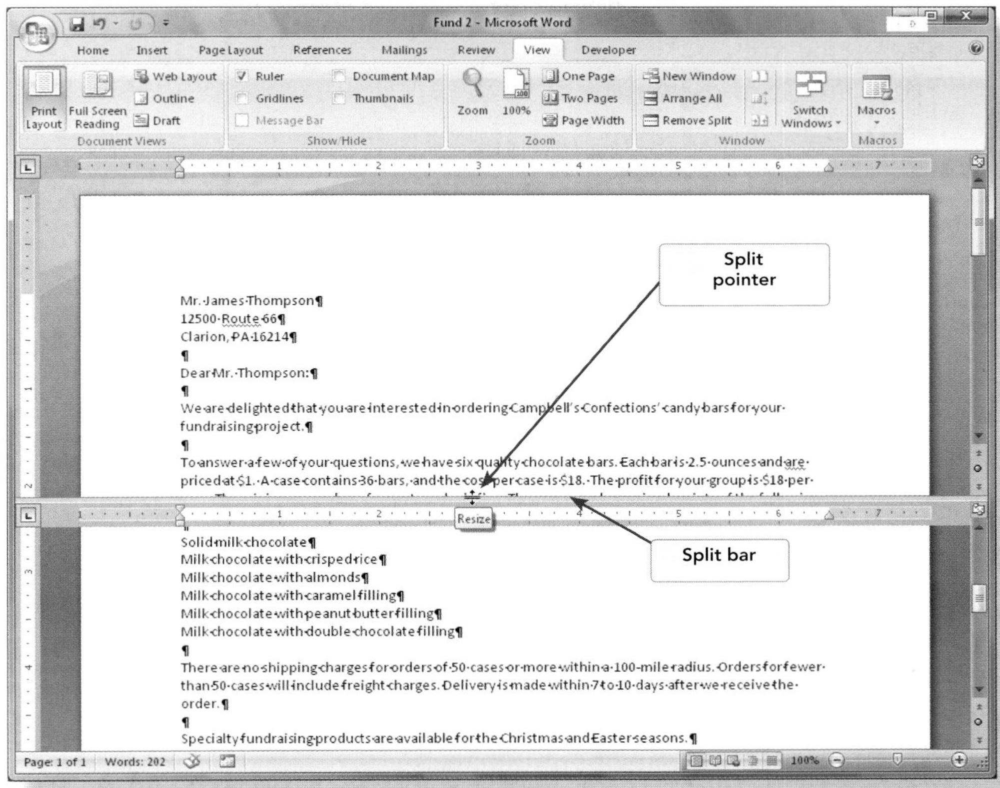

TIP

To see more of each document, you can hide the rulers by clicking the View Ruler button on the vertical scroll bar.

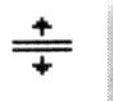

4. Click the left mouse button to set the split. The document divides into two panes, each with its own ruler and scroll bar.

5. To change the split position, move the mouse pointer over the split bar (between the top and bottom panes) until you see the split pointer and a ScreenTip that says "Resize." Then drag the bar above the list.

6. To remove the split bar, move the mouse pointer over it. When you see the split pointer, double-click. The split bar is removed.

7. Position the pointer over the *split box*—the thin gray rectangle at the top of the vertical scroll bar. (Refer to Figure 7–7 on the next page.)

Remove Split

8. When you see the split pointer, double-click. Once again the document is split into two panes. (You can also remove the split bar by choosing Remove Split from the View tab.)

Figure 7-7
Double-click the split box to create two window panes.

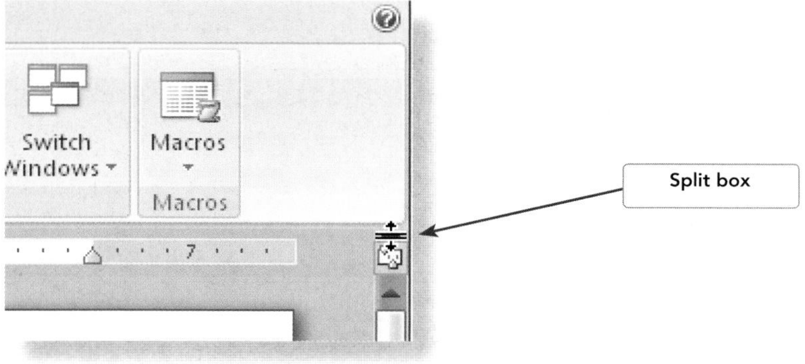

Exercise 7-11 MOVE BETWEEN PANES TO EDIT TEXT

After you split a document, you can scroll each pane separately and easily move from pane to pane to edit separate areas of the document. To switch panes, click the insertion point in the pane you want to edit.

1. Click in the top pane.
2. With the insertion point in the top pane, click the insertion point in the bottom pane.
3. Use the scroll bar in the bottom pane to scroll to the top of the document. Both panes should now show the inside address.

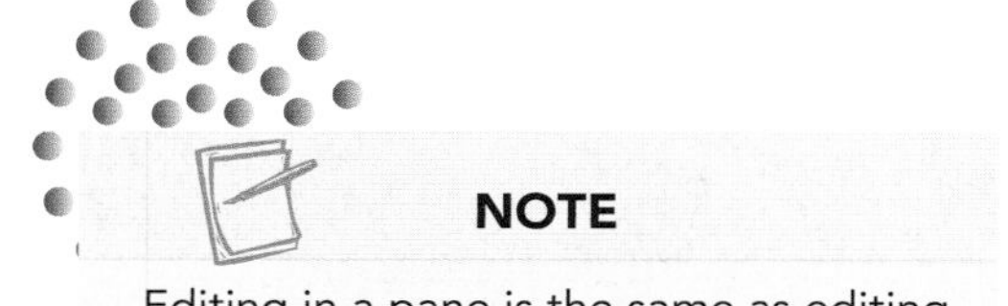

NOTE

Editing in a pane is the same as editing in a single window. It is important to understand that the changes you make to one pane affect the entire document.

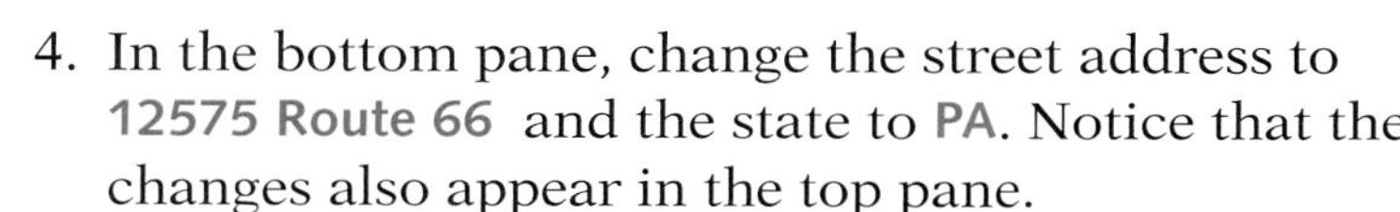

4. In the bottom pane, change the street address to **12575 Route 66** and the state to **PA**. Notice that the changes also appear in the top pane.

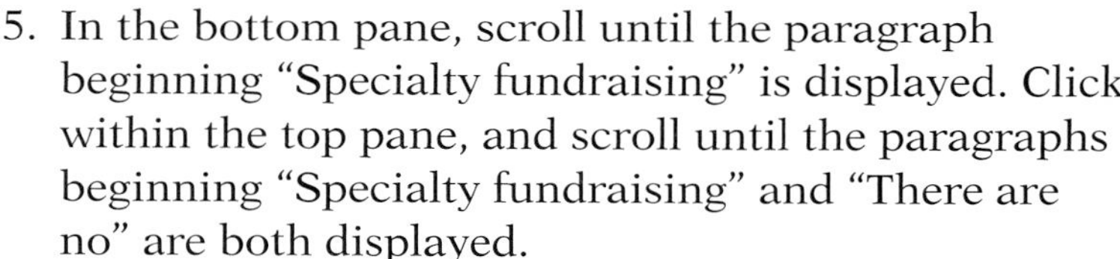

5. In the bottom pane, scroll until the paragraph beginning "Specialty fundraising" is displayed. Click within the top pane, and scroll until the paragraphs beginning "Specialty fundraising" and "There are no" are both displayed.

6. Go back to the bottom pane. Select the paragraph beginning "Specialty fundraising," and click the Cut button. (Remember to include the blank line after the paragraph when selecting it.)

7. Move to the top pane, position the insertion point to the left of "There are no," and click the Paste button. The paragraph is moved from one part of the document to another.
8. Drag the split bar to the top of the screen. This is another way to remove the split bar. The document is again displayed in one pane.

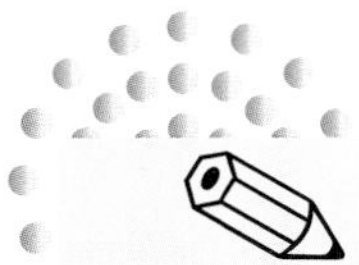

TIP

See Appendix B, "Standard Forms for Business Documents," for standard business letter formatting. See Appendix B online at www.mhhe.com/pas07brief.

9. Apply the correct letter formatting to the document by adding the date and your reference initials. Use the correct spacing between all letter elements, and place 72 points spacing before the date.
10. Save the document as ***[your initials]*****7-11** in your Lesson 7 folder.
11. Submit and close the document.

Exercise 7-12 OPEN MULTIPLE DOCUMENTS

In addition to working with window panes, you can work with more than one document file at the same time. This is useful if you keyed text in one document that you want to use in a second document.

NOTE

Noncontiguous files are files that are not listed consecutively. You can open several noncontiguous files at the same time if you keep Ctrl pressed while selecting additional files.

1. Display the Open dialog box. Simultaneously open the noncontiguous files **Bittersweet** and **Milk Chocolate**. To do this, click **Bittersweet** once, press Ctrl, and click **Milk Chocolate** once. With both files selected, click **Open**.
2. Click the **View** tab. Click the Switch Windows button, and notice that the two open files are listed at the bottom of this menu. The active file has a check next to it. Switch documents by clicking the file that is not active.
3. Press Ctrl+F6 to switch back.
4. Look at the taskbar at the bottom of your screen. Notice the two buttons that contain the names of your open documents. The highlighted button shows that it is the active document. Click the **Bittersweet** button to activate that document.

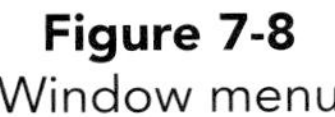

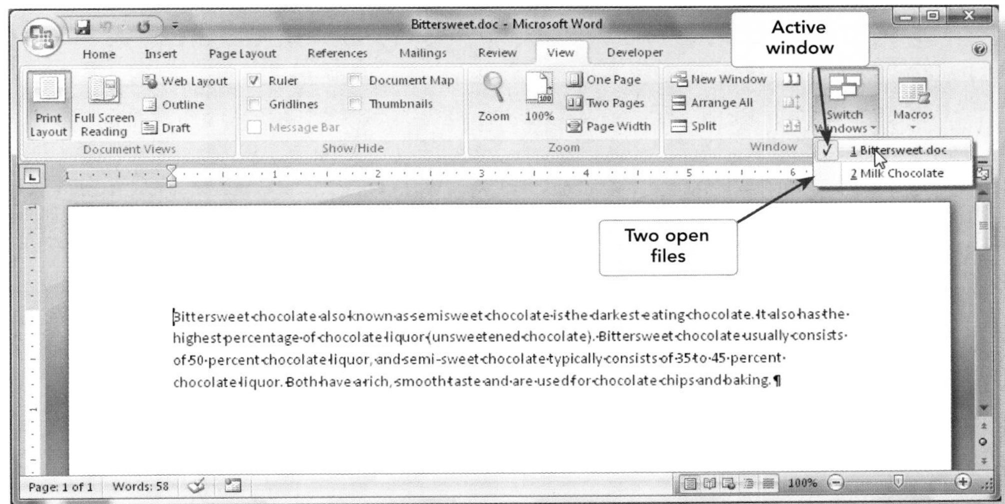

Figure 7-8
Window menu

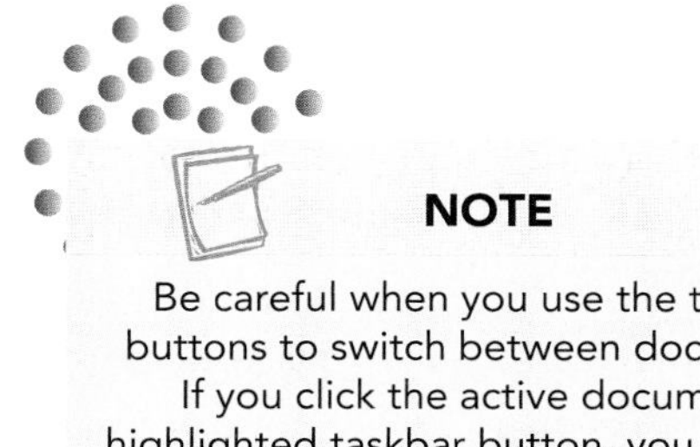

NOTE

Be careful when you use the taskbar buttons to switch between documents. If you click the active document's highlighted taskbar button, you minimize that document. You can restore a minimized document by clicking its taskbar button.

5. Click the **View** tab, if necessary. Click the Arrange All button to view both documents at the same time. The two documents appear one below the other.

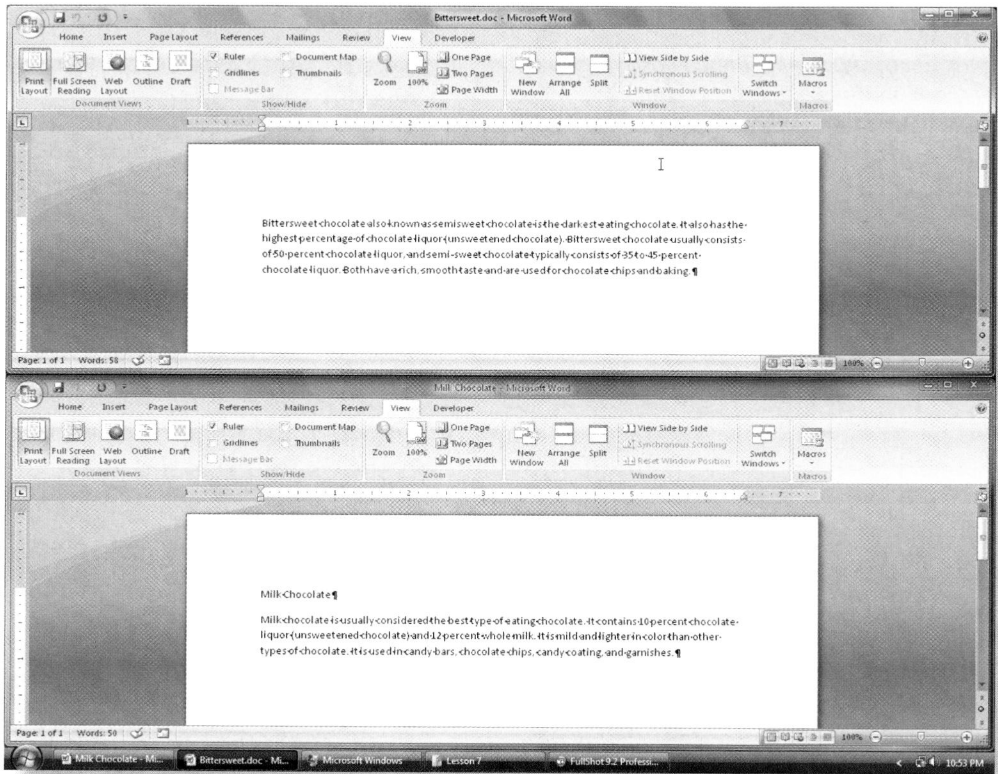

Figure 7-9
Two documents displayed on one screen

6. Press Ctrl+F6 to switch between documents. Press Ctrl+F6 again. Notice that the active window—the one containing the insertion point—has a highlighted title bar.

7. Close the **Bittersweet** and **Milk Chocolate** documents.

8. Click the Maximize button to maximize the Word window.
9. Simultaneously open three files, **Bittersweet**, **Chocolate - 2**, and **Milk Chocolate**, by accessing the **Open** dialog box. Select the first file, **Bittersweet**, and then press Ctrl and select the other two files. Click **Open**.
10. Choose **Arrange All** from the **Window** group on the View tab to display all three documents simultaneously.

Exercise 7-13 REARRANGE AND RESIZE DOCUMENT WINDOWS

You can rearrange the open documents in Word by using basic Windows techniques for minimizing, maximizing, restoring, and sizing windows.

1. Click the **Bittersweet** title bar, and drag this document's window to the top of the screen. Click the Maximize button for **Milk Chocolate**. Click the Close button for **Chocolate - 2**.
2. Minimize the **Milk Chocolate** window by clicking its Minimize button . The document disappears from view. The **Milk Chocolate** button is on the taskbar, indicating that Word is still running.
3. Restore the **Milk Chocolate** document for viewing by clicking its taskbar button. Click the Restore Down button to resize the window.
4. Drag a corner of the window's border diagonally down and to the right a few inches to make the window a different size.
5. Click the Maximize button in the **Milk Chocolate** window to return the window to full screen.
6. Click the Close button for **Milk Chocolate**. Close the **Bittersweet** document.

Moving and Copying Text among Windows

When you want to copy or move text from one document to another, you can work with either multiple (smaller) document windows or full-size document windows. Either way, you can use cut and paste or copy and paste. If you work with multiple windows, you can also use drag and drop. To use this technique, you must display both documents at the same time.

Exercise 7-14 COPY TEXT FROM ONE DOCUMENT TO ANOTHER BY USING COPY AND PASTE

When moving or copying text from one document into another, the Paste command pastes text in the format of the document from which it was cut or copied. To control the formatting of pasted text, you can use the Paste Options button or the Paste Special function. In this exercise, you will use the Paste Special function to paste text without formatting.

1. Open the files **Bittersweet**, **Chocolate - 2**, and **Milk Chocolate**. Click the **Bittersweet** button on the taskbar to make it the active document.

2. In **Bittersweet**, select the entire document and change the font to 12-point Arial. Click the Copy button .
3. Switch to the **Chocolate - 2** document.

4. Click the insertion point at the beginning of the paragraph that begins "Sweet or." Click the Paste button to insert the text copied from **Bittersweet**. Notice the format of the new text does not match the format of the current document.
5. Click the Undo button to remove the new text.
6. Click the **Home** tab, and click the lower part of the Paste button . Click **Paste Special** and select **Unformatted Text**. Click **OK**. Now the format of the new text matches the format of the current document. Press Enter if necessary.
7. Click the **View** tab, and click the Switch Windows button to activate **Bittersweet** again. Close this document without saving it.

TIP

You can insert an entire file into the current document by using the **Insert** tab. Move the insertion point to the place in the document where you want to insert the file. Then from the **Insert** tab, click the Object button . Click **Text from File** and double-click the filename. The text from the entire file is inserted at the insertion point.

Exercise 7-15 MOVE TEXT FROM ONE DOCUMENT TO ANOTHER BY USING DRAG AND DROP

1. Arrange the two open documents (**Milk Chocolate** and **Chocolate - 2**), so they are both displayed.
2. Switch to the **Milk Chocolate** document, and select the paragraph below the title.
3. Drag the selected paragraph to the **Chocolate - 2** document, and position the insertion point in front of the paragraph that begins "Sweet or."

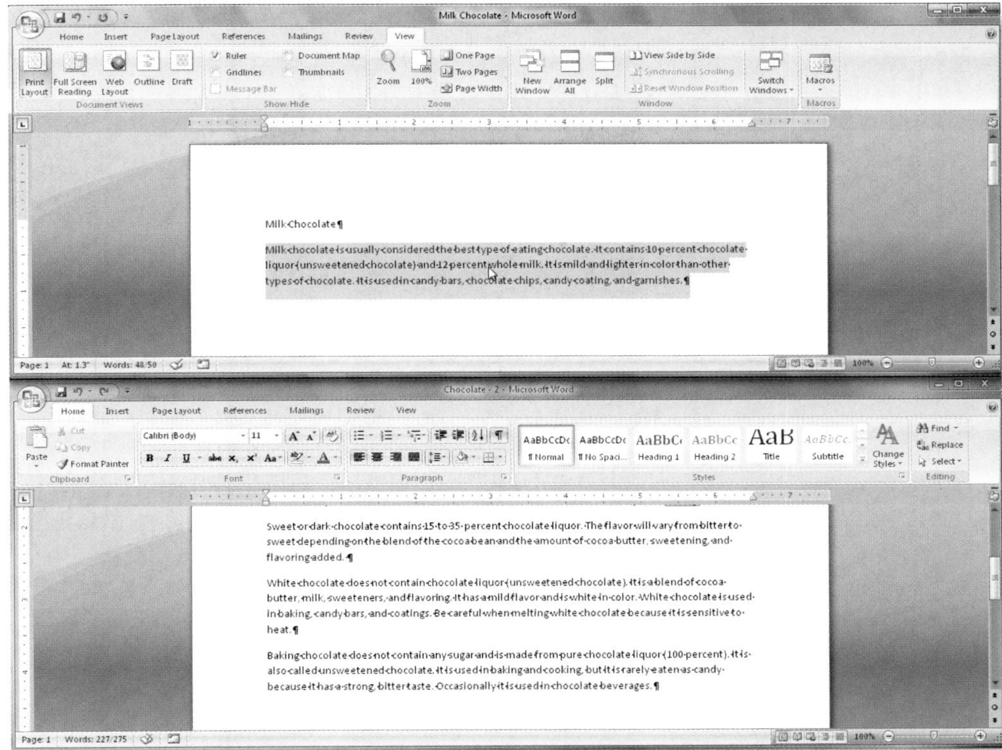

Figure 7-10 Dragging a paragraph between document windows

4. Close the **Milk Chocolate** document without saving.
5. Maximize the **Chocolate - 2** document. Correct the spacing between paragraphs (if you have extra paragraph marks, for example).
6. At the top of the document, add the title TYPES OF CHOCOLATE, formatted as 14-point bold and centered. Add 72 points spacing before and 24 points spacing after the title.
7. Save the document as ***[your initials]*7-15** in your Lesson 7 folder; then print and close it.

Lesson 7 Summary

- The most important tool for moving and copying text is the Clipboard, which is a temporary storage space.
- When you display the Clipboard task pane, you are activating the Office Clipboard, which can store up to 24 cut or copied items. With the Clipboard task pane open, cut or copied text appears as a new item in the task pane.
- You move text by cutting and pasting—cut the text from one location and paste it to another.

- Copy and paste is similar to cut and paste, but instead of removing the text from the document, you place a copy of it on the Clipboard.
- There are many methods for cutting, copying, and pasting text. Use commands on the Ribbon, keyboard shortcuts, or the shortcut menu. Use the Clipboard task pane to paste stored text items.
- Use the Paste Options button to control the formatting of pasted text.
- You can use the drag-and-drop method to copy or move text from one location to another in a document or between documents.
- Split a document into panes to compare different parts of the document or to cut or copy text from one part of the document to another. Use the View tab or the split box above the vertical scroll bar to split a document.
- Open multiple documents and arrange them to fit on one screen to move or copy text from one document to another.

LESSON 7 — Command Summary

Feature	Button	Command	Keyboard
Open Office Clipboard	Clipboard	Home tab, **Clipboard** group	Ctrl+C twice
Cut	Cut	Home tab, **Clipboard** group	Ctrl+X
Copy	Copy	Home tab, **Clipboard** group	Ctrl+C
Paste	Paste	Home tab, **Clipboard** group	Ctrl+V
Split a document	Split	View tab, **Window** group	
Arrange multiple windows	Arrange All	View tab, **Window** group	
Next window		View tab, **Switch Windows**, *[filename]*	Ctrl+F6
Previous window		View tab, **Switch Windows**, *[filename]*	Ctrl+Shift+F6

Lesson 8

Find and Replace

OBJECTIVES

After completing this lesson, you will be able to:

1. Find text.
2. Find and replace text.
3. Find and replace special characters.
4. Find and replace formatting.

MCAS OBJECTIVES

In this lesson:
WW 07 2.2.2
WW 07 5.1.1

Estimated Time: 1¼ hours

When you create documents, especially long documents, you often need to review or change text. In Word, you can do this quickly by using the Find and Replace commands.

The *Find* command locates specified text and formatting in a document. The *Replace* command finds the text and formatting and replaces it automatically with a specified alternative.

Finding Text

Instead of scrolling through a document, you can use the Find command to locate text or to move quickly to a specific document location.

Two ways to use Find are:

- Ribbon, Home tab, Editing group, Find command.
- Press Ctrl+F.

You can use the Find command to locate whole words, words that sound alike, font and paragraph formatting, and special characters. You can search an entire document or only selected text and specify the direction of the search. In the following exercise, you use Find to locate all occurrences of the word "Campbell."

Exercise 8-1 FIND TEXT

NOTE

The width of the Word window affects the appearance of the Ribbon buttons. The Editing group may or may not display the Find and Replace buttons. If the buttons do not appear, click the Editing button.

1. Open the file **Stevenson - 1**.
2. Click the **Home** tab, and locate the **Editing** group. Click the Find button to open the Find and Replace dialog box. The **Find** tab is selected by default.
3. Delete any text in the **Find what** text box and key **Campbell**.

4. Click the **More** button, if it is displayed, to expand the dialog box.

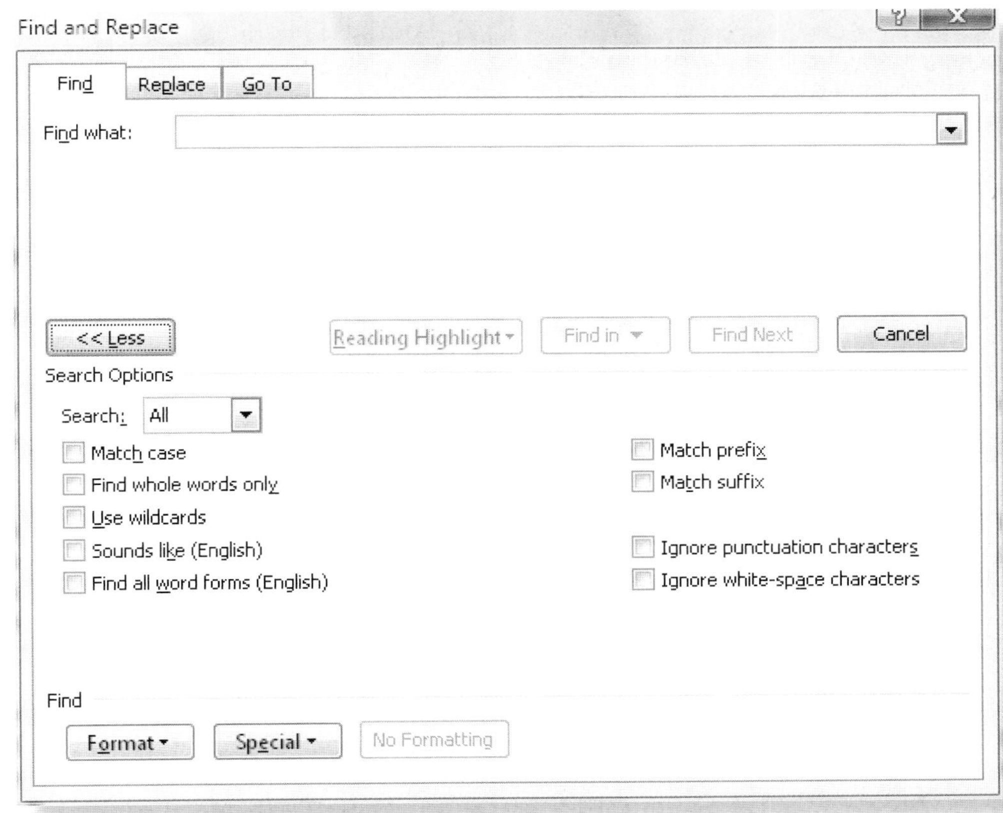

Figure 8-1
Expanded Find and Replace dialog box

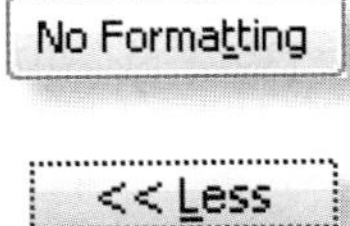

5. Click the **No Formatting** button (if it is active) to remove any formatting from previous searches. Then click the **Less** button. The dialog box should look like the one in Figure 8-2.

Word 2007

Figure 8-2 Using the Find feature

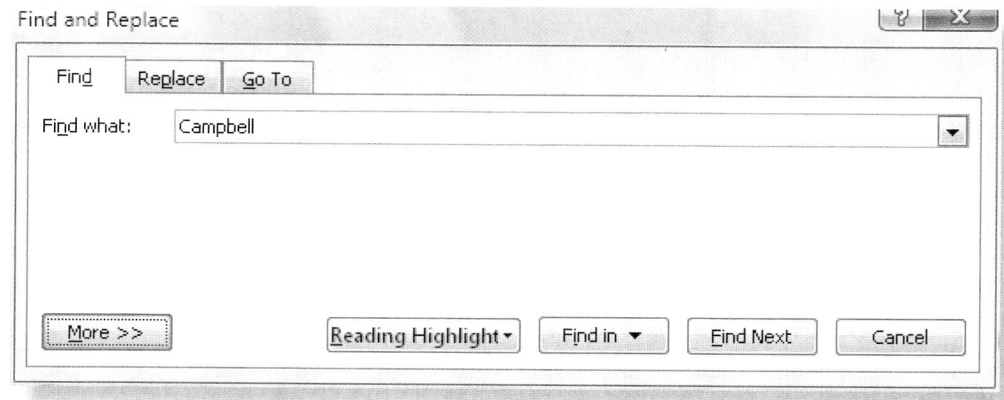

NOTE

To see more of the document text during a search, drag the Find and Replace dialog box by its title bar to the bottom right corner of the screen.

6. Click the Find Next button. Notice that the first occurrence of "Campbell" found in the document is capitalized and italicized.
7. Continue clicking **Find Next** until you reach the end of the document. Notice that Word locates "Campbell" as a word and as text embedded in "Campbell's."
8. Click **OK** in the dialog box that says Word finished searching the document.
9. Click **Cancel** to close the Find and Replace dialog box.
10. Place the insertion point at the beginning of the paragraph that begins "Thank you." Press Ctrl+F to open the Find and Replace dialog box.

Reading Highlight

11. Key **Campbell's Confections** in the **Find what** text box. Click the Reading Highlight button and click **Highlight All**. The document highlights every occurrence of the text.
12. Click the Reading Highlight button and click **Clear Highlighting**. Close the dialog box.

Exercise 8-2 FIND TEXT BY USING THE MATCH CASE OPTION

The Find command includes options for locating words or phrases that meet certain criteria. One of these options is Match case, which locates text that matches the case of text keyed in the Find what text box. The next exercise demonstrates how the Match case option narrows the search when using the Find command.

1. Move to the end of the document by pressing Ctrl+End. Position the insertion point to the right of "Hamrick" in the closing.
2. Locate the **Editing** group, and click the Find button. Click the More button to display an expanded dialog box that contains Search Options.

3. Key **confections** in the **Find what** text box.
4. Click the **Match case** check box to select this option. Choose **Up** from the **Search:** drop-down list to reverse the search direction. Notice the **Options** that appear below the **Find what** text box.

Figure 8-3
Choosing Search Options

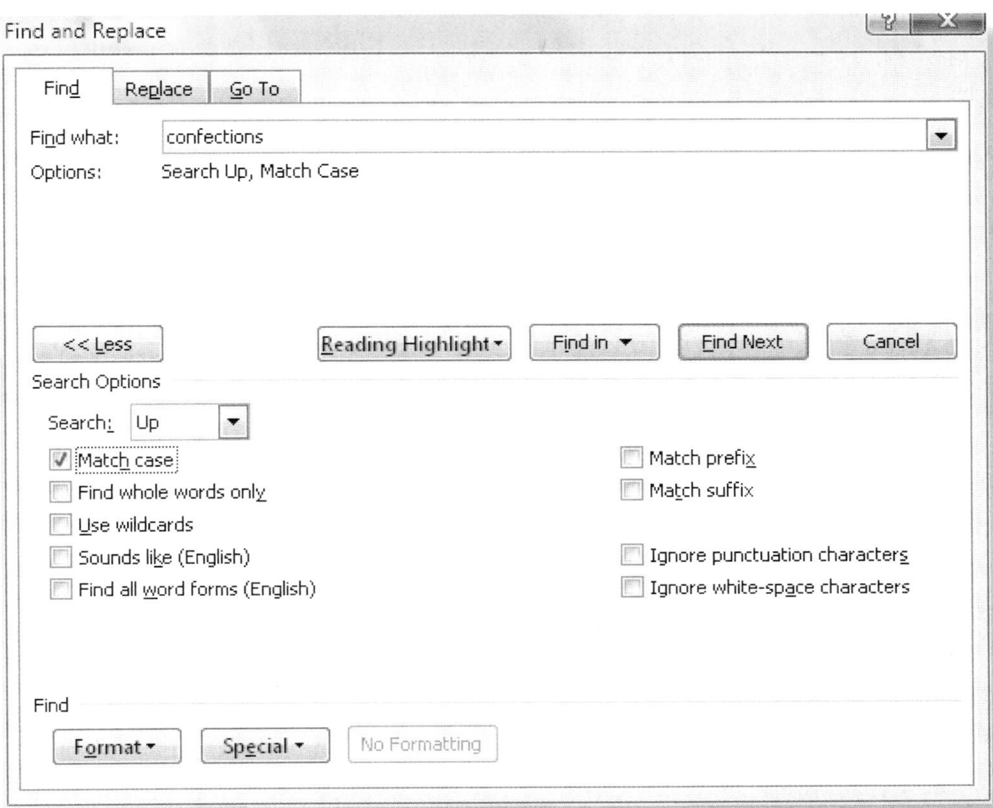

NOTE

The dialog box that appears when you end the search process is determined by the search direction and the position of the insertion point when you begin the search. When Word searches through the entire document, the dialog box tells you Word is finished searching, and the insertion point returns to its original position. When you search from a point other than the top or bottom of the document and choose Up or Down as your search direction, Word asks if you want to continue the search. If you choose not to continue, the insertion point remains at the last occurrence found.

5. Click the Less button to collapse the dialog box. Click the Find Next button to begin the search. (If the dialog box is in your way, drag it to a preferred location.) Word ignores all occurrences of the word that do not match the search criteria ("confections").
6. Click **Find Next**. Word reaches the beginning of the document with no other matches found. Notice how the **Match case** option narrows the search.
7. Click **No** in the dialog box that asks if you want to continue searching.
8. Click **Cancel** to close the Find and Replace dialog box.

Exercise 8-3 FIND TEXT BY USING THE FIND WHOLE WORDS ONLY OPTION

The **Find whole words only** option is another way to narrow the search criteria. Word locates separate words, but not characters embedded in other words.

1. Move the insertion point to the beginning of the document. Press Ctrl+F to open the Find and Replace dialog box with the **Find** tab selected. Click **More** to expand the dialog box. Click **Match case** to clear the option.
2. Key **or** in the Find what text box. Click the down arrow next to the **Find what** text box, and notice that the previous entries are listed. The last seven entries of the **Find what** text box are displayed in this list. Click the arrow to close the list. Change the **Search:** drop-down list to **Down**.
3. Click the Find Next button Find Next and notice that "for" is highlighted. Click the Find Next button Find Next. "Factory" is highlighted because it contains the characters "or."
4. Click **Find whole words only** to select it. Click and choose **Down** from the **Search:** drop-down list.
5. Click **Less**, and then click **Find Next** to begin the search. Word locates the word "or," but not other word forms, such as "factory."
6. Click **Find Next** two times. Click **No** to end the search.
7. Click **Cancel** to close the Find and Replace dialog box.

Exercise 8-4 FIND TEXT BY USING THE WILDCARD OPTION

You can use the Use wildcards option to search for text strings using special search operators. A *wildcard* is a symbol that stands for missing or unknown text. For example, the Any Character wildcard "^?" finds any character. Using the "^?" wildcard, a search for "b^?te" would find both "bite" and "byte." The question mark is replaced by a character that follows "b" and precedes "te."

TIP

Press Esc to cancel a search. You can also interrupt a search by clicking outside the Find and Replace dialog box, editing the document text, and then clicking the dialog box to reactivate it.

1. Position the insertion point at the beginning of the document. Open the Find and Replace dialog box with the **Find** tab displayed.
2. Display the expanded dialog box, and click **Use wildcards** to select this option.
3. Select the text in the **Find what** text box and key **ca**.

4. Click the **Special** button Special and choose **Any Character** from the list. The "?" is inserted.

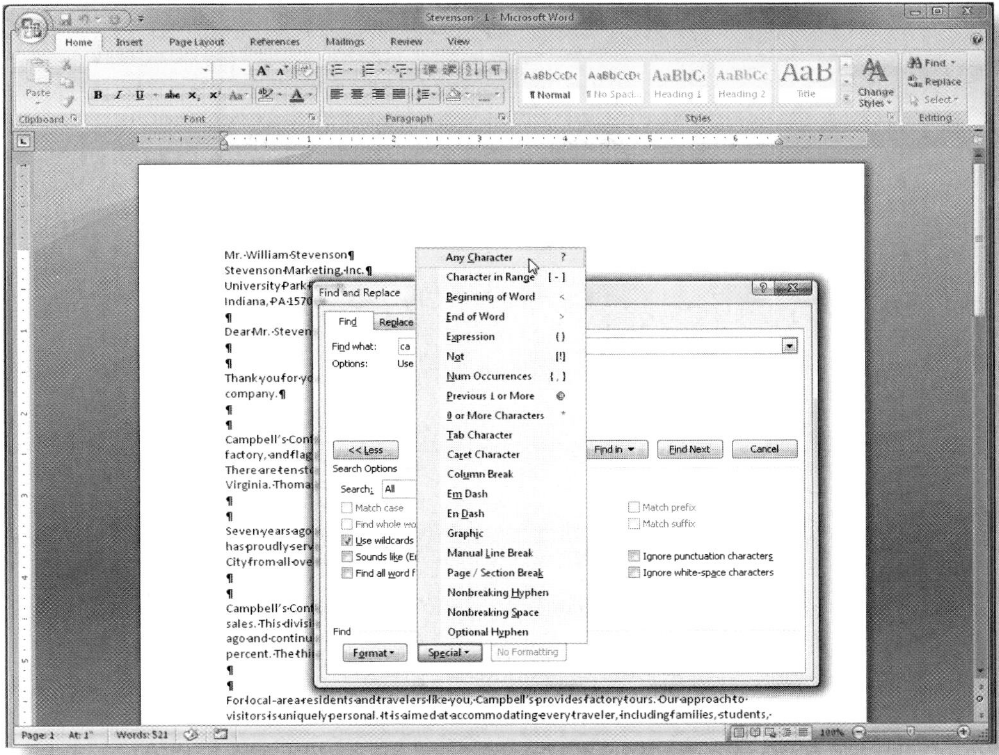

Figure 8-4
Choosing a Special search operator

TIP

After you initiate a Find by using the Find and Replace dialog box, you can close the dialog box and use the Next Find/Go To button and Previous Find/Go To button located at the bottom of the vertical scroll bar to continue the search without having the dialog box in your way. (See Figure 8-5.)

5. Choose **All** from the **Search:** drop-down list, if it is not already selected. Then click **Less**.
6. Click **Find Next**. The first occurrence appears in the word "candy."
7. Continue clicking **Find Next** and notice all the occurrences of "ca?" in the document.
8. Click **OK** in the dialog box that says Word finished searching the document.
9. Click **Cancel** to close the Find and Replace dialog box.

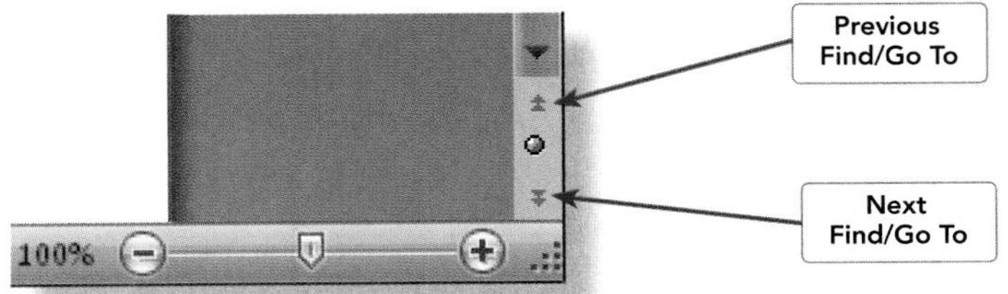

Figure 8-5
Finding text without the Find and Replace dialog box

Exercise 8-5 FIND FORMATTED TEXT

In addition to locating words and phrases, the Find command can search for text that is formatted. The formatting can include character formatting, such as bold and italic, and paragraph formatting, such as alignment and line spacing.

1. Position the insertion point at the beginning of the document. Press Ctrl+F.
2. Key **Campbell's Confections** in the **Find what** text box. Expand the dialog box and choose **All** from the **Search:** drop-down list. Click any checked search options to clear them.
3. Click the **Format** button and choose **Font**.

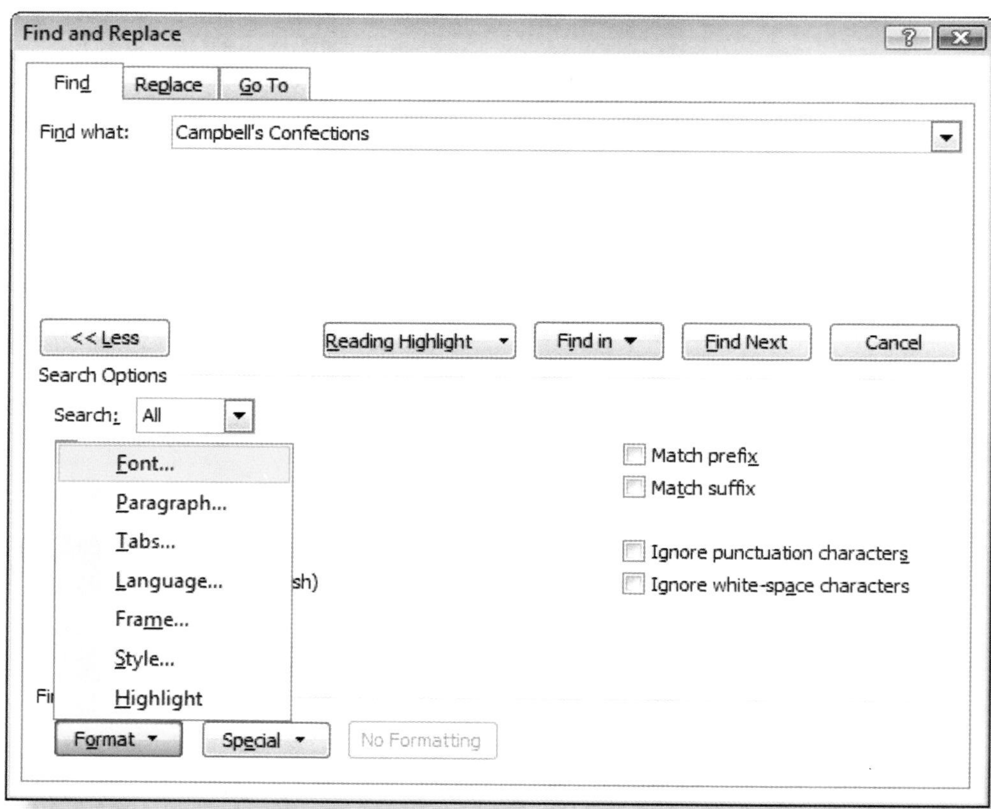

Figure 8-6
Format options

4. In the Find Font dialog box, choose **Italic** from the Font style list and click **OK**. Italic now appears below the Find what text box.
5. Click **Less**, and then click **Find Next**. Word locates *"Campbell's Confections."*
6. Click **Cancel** to close the Find and Replace dialog box.

Finding and Replacing Text

The Replace command searches for specified text or formatting and replaces it with your specified alternative. You can replace all instances of text or formatting at once, or you can find and confirm each replacement.

Two ways to replace text are:

- Ribbon, Home tab, Editing group, Replace command.
- Press Ctrl+H.

Exercise 8-6 REPLACE TEXT BY USING FIND NEXT

1. Position the insertion point at the beginning of the document, locate the **Editing** group, and click the Replace button. The **Replace** tab is now selected in the dialog box.
2. Key **traveler** in the **Find what** text box. Expand the dialog box and click the **No Formatting** button to remove formatting from previous searches. Make sure no options under **Search:** are selected.
3. Press Tab to move to the **Replace with** text box, and key **visitor**. Click the **No Formatting** button if it is active.

Figure 8-7
Replacing text

Find and Replace

Find | Replace | Go To

Find what: traveler

Replace with: visitor

<< Less | Replace | Replace All | Find Next | Cancel

Search Options

Search: All

- Match case
- Find whole words only
- Use wildcards
- Sounds like (English)
- Find all word forms (English)
- Match prefix
- Match suffix
- Ignore punctuation characters
- Ignore white-space characters

Replace

Format ▾ | Special ▾ | No Formatting

NOTE

Remember, pressing Tab in a dialog box moves the insertion point from one text box to another and highlights existing text. Pressing Enter executes the dialog box command.

4. Adjust the position and size (click **Less**) of the dialog box so you can see the document text. Click **Find Next**. Click **Replace** to replace the first occurrence of "traveler" with "visitor."
5. Continue to click **Replace** until Word reaches the end of the document.
6. Click **OK** when Word finishes searching the document.
7. Close the Find and Replace dialog box.

Exercise 8-7 REPLACE TEXT BY USING REPLACE ALL

The **Replace All** option replaces all occurrences of text or formatting in a document without confirmation.

1. Move the insertion point to the beginning of the document and press Ctrl+H to open the Find and Replace dialog box with the **Replace** tab selected.

NOTE

After replacing text or formatting, you can always undo the action. If you used **Replace All**, all changes are reversed at once. If you used **Replace**, only the last change is reversed, but you can undo the last several changes individually by selecting them from the Undo drop-down list.

2. Key **Campbell's Confections** in the **Find what** text box. Press Tab and key **CAMPBELL'S CONFECTIONS** in the **Replace with** text box.
3. Expand the dialog box, clear the **Match case** check box if necessary, and click **Replace All**. Word will indicate the number of replacements made.
4. Click **OK** and close the Find and Replace dialog box. "Campbell's Confections" now appears as "CAMPBELL'S CONFECTIONS" throughout the document.

5. Click the Undo button to undo the Replace All command.

Exercise 8-8 DELETE TEXT WITH REPLACE

You can also use the Replace command to delete text automatically. Key the text to be deleted in the **Find what** text box and leave the **Replace with** text box blank. You can find and delete text with confirmation by using the **Find Next** option or without confirmation by using the **Replace All** option.

1. Position the insertion point at the beginning of the document, and open the Find and Replace dialog box with the **Replace** tab selected.
2. Key **Campbell's** in the **Find what** text box and press Spacebar once. The space character is not visible in the text box.

3. Press Tab to move to the **Replace with** text box, and press Delete to remove the previous entry.

4. Click the Replace All button Replace All.
5. Click **OK**, and close the dialog box. The word "Campbell's" followed by a space is deleted from the company name throughout the document. If the word "Campbell's" was followed by a punctuation mark, the word would not be deleted.
6. Click the Undo button.
7. Save the document as ***[your initials]*****8-8** in a new folder for Lesson 8. Leave the document open for the next exercise.

TIP

The last option in the Find and Replace dialog box is **Find all word forms**. Use this option to find different forms of words, and replace the various word forms with comparable forms. For example, if you key "walk" in the **Find what** text box and key "jump" in the **Replace with** text box, Word replaces "walk" with "jump" and "walked" with "jumped." Use **Replace**, rather than **Replace All**, when you choose this option to verify each replacement and ensure that correct word forms are used.

Finding and Replacing Special Characters

The Find and Replace features can search for characters other than ordinary text. Special characters include paragraph marks and tab characters. Special characters are represented by codes that you can key or choose from the Special drop-down list.

Exercise 8-9 FIND AND REPLACE SPECIAL CHARACTERS

1. Click the Show/Hide ¶ button ¶ to display special characters in the document if they are not showing.
2. Position the insertion point at the top of the document. Open the Find and Replace dialog box with the **Replace** tab selected. Expand the dialog box, if it is not already. Delete the text that appears in the **Find what** text box.
3. Click the **Special** button, and choose **Paragraph Mark**. A code (^p) is inserted in the **Find what** text box. Add two additional paragraph mark codes in the **Find what** text box, to search for three consecutive paragraph marks in the document. (Use the **Special** drop-down list or key **^p^p**.)
4. Move to the **Replace with** text box, and insert two paragraph mark codes.
5. Clear any **Search Options** check boxes, and click **Less**.

6. Click **Find Next**. Word locates the extra paragraph mark after the salutation of the letter.

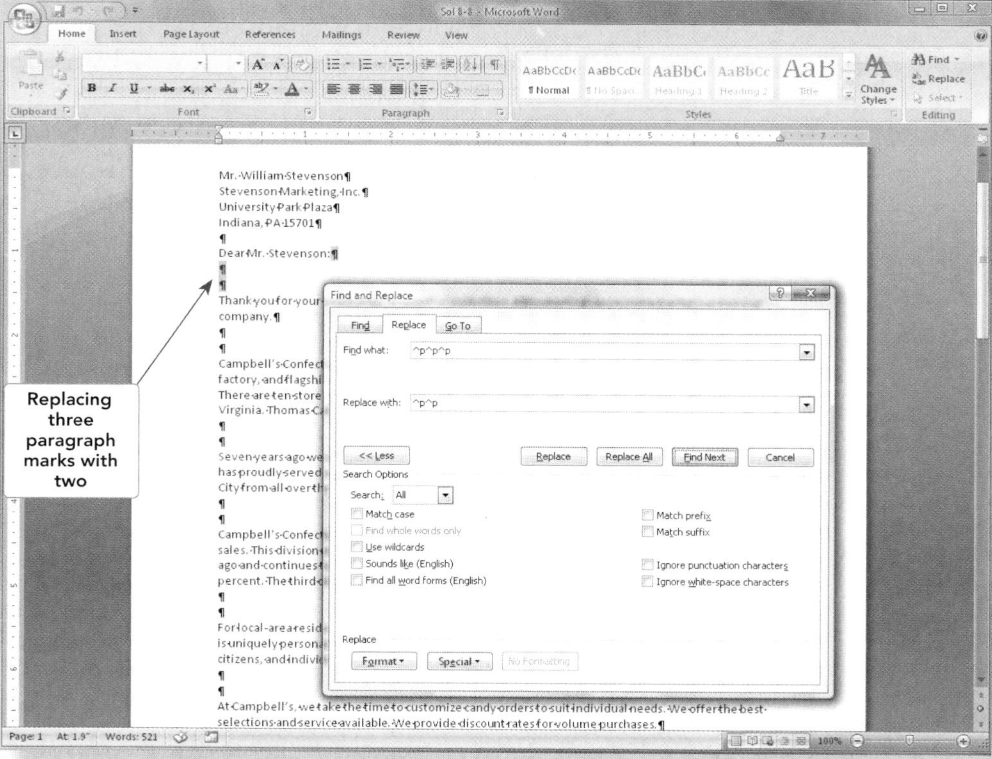

Figure 8-8
Replacing special characters

7. Click **Replace**. Notice the elimination of the extra paragraph mark. Continue to click **Replace** for each paragraph mark until you reach the paragraph marks just after "Sincerely."

8. Close the Find and Replace dialog box. The document paragraphs are now correctly spaced.

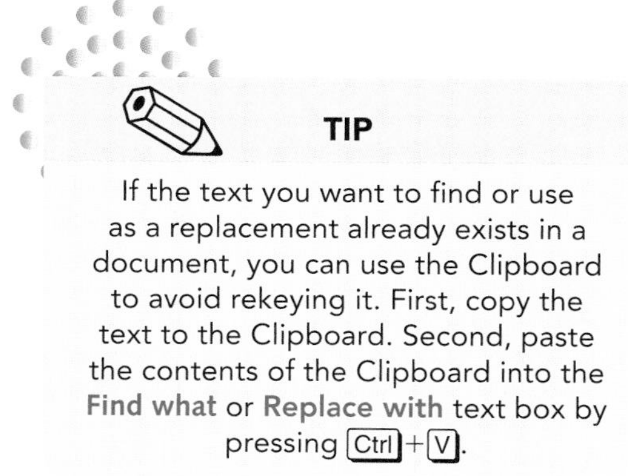

TIP

If the text you want to find or use as a replacement already exists in a document, you can use the Clipboard to avoid rekeying it. First, copy the text to the Clipboard. Second, paste the contents of the Clipboard into the **Find what** or **Replace with** text box by pressing Ctrl+V.

TABLE 8-1 Find and Replace Special Characters

Find or Replace	Special Character Code to Key
Paragraph mark (¶)	^p (must be lowercase)
Tab character →	^t (must be lowercase)
Any character (Find only)	^?
Any digit (Find only)	^#
Any letter (Find only)	^$
Column break	^n
Clipboard contents (Replace only)	^c
Em dash	^+
En dash	^=
Field (Find only)	^d
Footnote mark (Find only)	^f
Graphic (Find only)	^g
Manual line break	^l
Manual page break	^m
Nonbreaking hyphen	^~
Nonbreaking space	^s
Section break (Find only)	^b
White space (Find only)	^w

Finding and Replacing Formatting

Format ▾

Word can search for and replace both character and paragraph formatting. You can specify character or paragraph formatting by clicking the Format button Format ▾ in the Find and Replace dialog box or using keyboard shortcuts.

Exercise 8-10 FIND AND REPLACE CHARACTER FORMATTING

1. Position the insertion point at the top of the document, and open the Find and Replace dialog box with the **Replace** tab selected. Expand the dialog box.

2. Key **Campbell's Confections** in the **Find what** text box. Press Tab and delete the text in the **Replace with** text box.
3. Click the **Format** button, and choose **Font**. Choose **Bold** for **Font style**, and click **Small caps**. Click **OK**.
4. Click **Replace All**.
5. Click **OK** when Word finishes searching the document, and close the dialog box. "Campbell's Confections" appears bold and in small caps throughout the document.
6. Reopen the Find and Replace dialog box with the **Replace** tab selected.
7. Highlight the text in the **Find what** text box, if it is not already. Click the **Format** button, and choose **Font**. Choose **Bold** and **Small caps** and click **OK**.
8. Press Tab to move the insertion point to the **Replace with** text box. Click the No Formatting button No Formatting to clear existing formatting.
9. Click the **Format** button Format and choose **Font**. Choose the **Not Bold** style, deselect **Small caps**, and click **OK**.
10. Press Ctrl+I (the keyboard shortcut for italic text). Now the format for the **Replace with** text box is "**Not Bold, Not Small caps, Not All caps, Italic.**"
11. Click **Replace All**.
12. Click **OK**, and close the Find and Replace dialog box. "Campbell's Confections" is now italic, and not bold, throughout the document.

No Formatting

Exercise 8-11 FIND AND REPLACE PARAGRAPH FORMATTING

1. Position the insertion point at the end of the first paragraph that begins "Thank you." Open the Find and Replace dialog box with the **Replace** tab selected.
2. In the **Find what** text box, insert two paragraph mark special characters (use the **Special** list or key **^p^p**). Clear existing formatting.
3. Move to the **Replace with** text box, enter two paragraph mark special characters, and clear existing formatting.
4. Click the **Format** button, and choose **Paragraph**. Click the **Indents and Spacing** tab if it is not active. Deselect **Mirror indents** if necessary.

5. Choose **First Line** from the **Special** drop-down list. If "0.5" is not the measurement displayed in the **By** text box, select the text in the **By** box and key **0.5**. Click **OK**.
6. Click **Find Next**, and Word highlights the paragraph marks after "company." Click **Replace** to format that paragraph.
7. Click **Replace** seven more times (through the paragraph ending "enclosed brochure").
8. Close the Find and Replace dialog box. Scroll through the document to view the paragraph formatting changes. All these paragraphs should now have a 0.5-inch first-line indent.
9. Position the insertion point at the top of the document. Open the Find and Replace dialog box with the **Replace** tab selected.
10. Delete the text in the **Find what** text box, and set the text box to look for a 0.5-inch first-line indent. Deselect **Mirror indents** if necessary.

Figure 8-9
Defining paragraph formatting

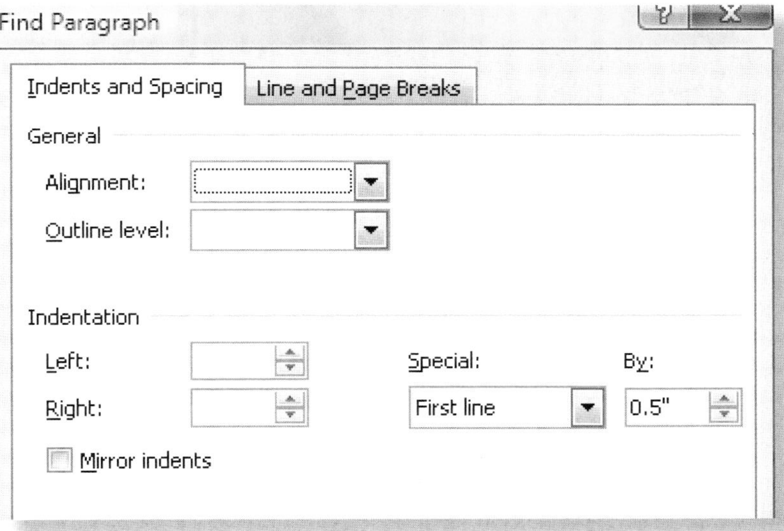

11. Delete the text in the **Replace with** text box, clear the formatting, and replace with 0.25-inch left and right indents and no first-line indent (choose **(none)** from the **Special** drop-down list in the Replace Paragraph dialog box).

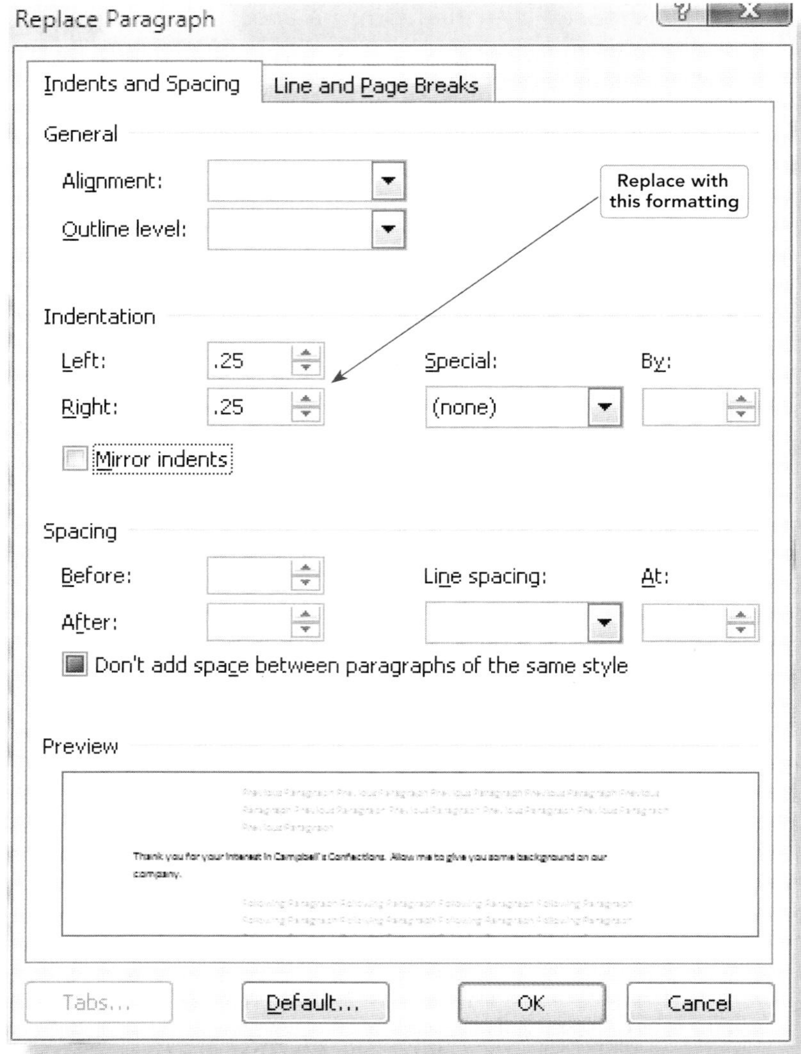

Figure 8-10
Replacing paragraph formatting

12. Click **Replace All**, and click **OK**. Close the dialog box.
13. Scroll through the document to observe the replacement of first-line indented paragraphs with 0.25-inch left- and right-indented paragraphs.
14. Enter the date at the top of the document, with 72 points spacing before and three blank lines after it. Replace "xx" with your reference initials.
15. Save the document as ***[your initials]*8-11** in your Lesson 8 folder.
16. Submit and close the document.

TABLE 8-2 Find and Replace Formatting Guidelines

Guideline	Procedure
Find specific text with specific formatting.	Key the text in the **Find what** text box and specify its formatting (choose **Font** or **Paragraph** from the **Format** drop-down list or use a keyboard shortcut).
Find specific formatting.	Delete text in the **Find what** text box, and specify formatting.
Replace specific text but not its formatting.	Key the text in the **Find what** text box. Click the **No Formatting** button to clear existing formatting. Key the replacement text in the **Replace with** text box, and clear existing formatting.
Replace specific text and its formatting.	Key the text in the **Find what** text box and specify its formatting. Key the replacement text in the **Replace with** text box, and specify the replacement formatting.
Replace only formatting for specific text.	Key the text in the **Find what** text box, and specify its formatting. Delete any text in the **Replace with** text box and specify the replacement formatting.
Replace only formatting.	Delete any text in the **Find what** text box, and specify formatting. Delete any text in the **Replace with** text box, and specify the replacement formatting.

Lesson 8 Summary

- The Find command locates specified text and formatting in a document. The Replace command finds text and formatting and replaces it automatically with specified alternatives.
- Use the Find command to locate whole words, words that sound alike, font and paragraph formatting, and special characters. Using the Find command, you can search an entire document or selected text. You can also specify the direction of the search.
- Use the Match case option to locate text that matches the case of document text. Example: When searching for "Confections," Word would not find "confections."
- When you want to locate whole words and not parts of a word, use the Find whole words only option. Example: When searching for the

whole word "can," Word would find only "can," but not "candy" or "candidate."

- Use the Use wildcards option to search for text strings by using special search operators. A wildcard is a symbol that stands for missing or unknown text. Example: A search for "b^?yte" would find "bite" and "byte." See Table 8-1.
- Use the Sounds like option to find a word that sounds similar to the search text but is spelled differently or to find a word you do not know how to spell. When you find the word, you can stop the search process and edit your document.
- Use the Find command to search for formatted text. The formatting can include character formatting, such as bold and italic, and paragraph formatting, such as alignment and line spacing. Use the Replace command to replace the formatting. See Table 8-2.
- Use the Replace command to search for all instances of text or formatting at once or to find and confirm each replacement.
- Use the Replace command to delete text automatically. Key the text to be deleted in the Find what text box and leave the Replace with text box blank.

LESSON 8		Command Summary	
Feature	**Button**	**Command**	**Keyboard**
Find	Find	Home tab, Editing group	Ctrl+F
Replace	Replace	Home tab, Editing group	Ctrl+H

unit 3

PAGE FORMATTING

Lesson 9

Margins and Print Options

OBJECTIVES

After completing this lesson, you will be able to:

1. Change margins.
2. Preview a document.
3. Change paper size and orientation.
4. Print envelopes and labels.
5. Choose print options.

MCAS OBJECTIVES

In this lesson:

WW 07 1.2.1

WW 07 4.5.3

Estimated Time: 1 1/2 hours

In a Word document, text is keyed and printed within the boundaries of the document's margins. *Margins* are the spaces between the edges of the text and the edges of the paper. Adjusting the margins can significantly change the appearance of a document.

Word offers many useful printing features: changing the orientation (the direction, either horizontal or vertical, in which a document is printed), selecting paper size, and printing envelopes and labels.

Changing Margins

By default, a document's margin settings are:

- Top margin: 1 inch
- Bottom margin: 1 inch
- Left margin: 1 inch
- Right margin: 1 inch

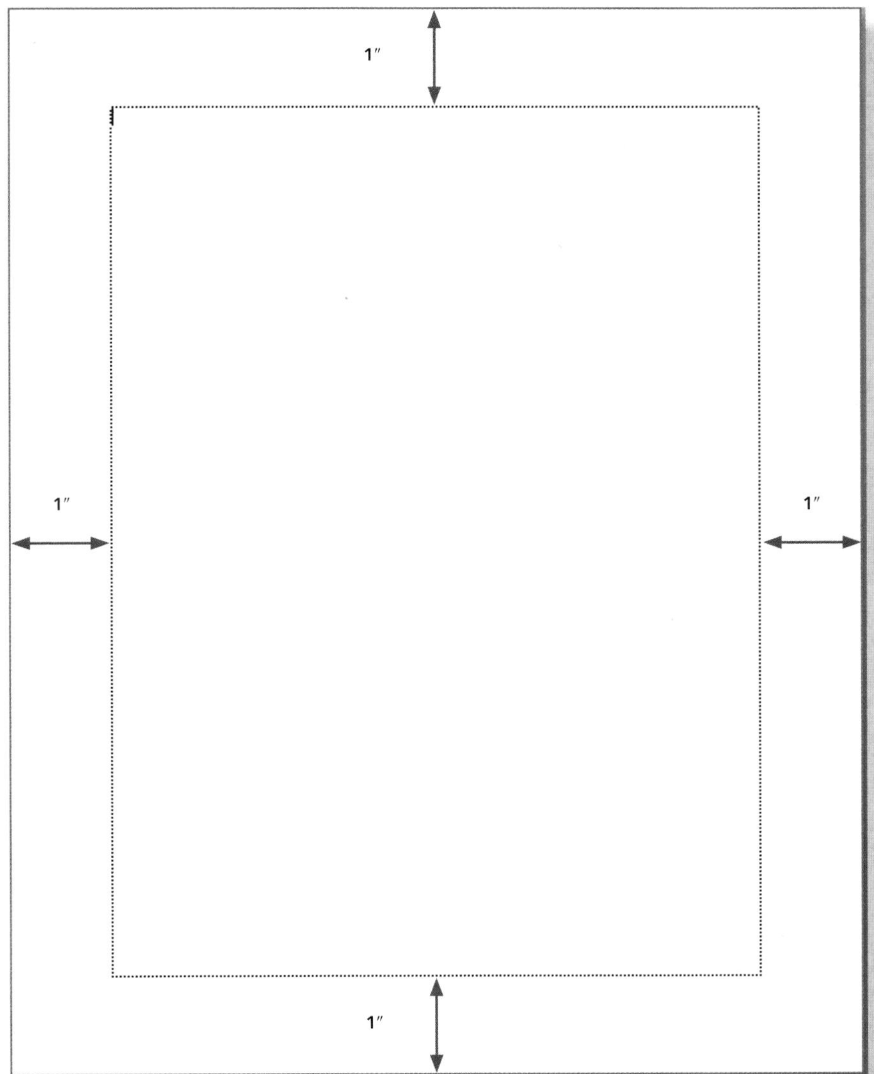

Figure 9-1
Default margin settings

Using standard-size paper (8.5 by 11 inches) and Word's default margin settings, you have $6^1/2$ by 9 inches on the page for your text. To increase or decrease this workspace, you can change margins by using the Page Setup dialog box or the rulers or Print Preview.

To set margins, you can use one of these methods:

- Change settings in the Page Setup dialog box.
- Drag margins using the horizontal and vertical rulers.
- Drag margins in Print Preview.

Figure 9-2
Actual workspace using default margin settings and standard-size paper

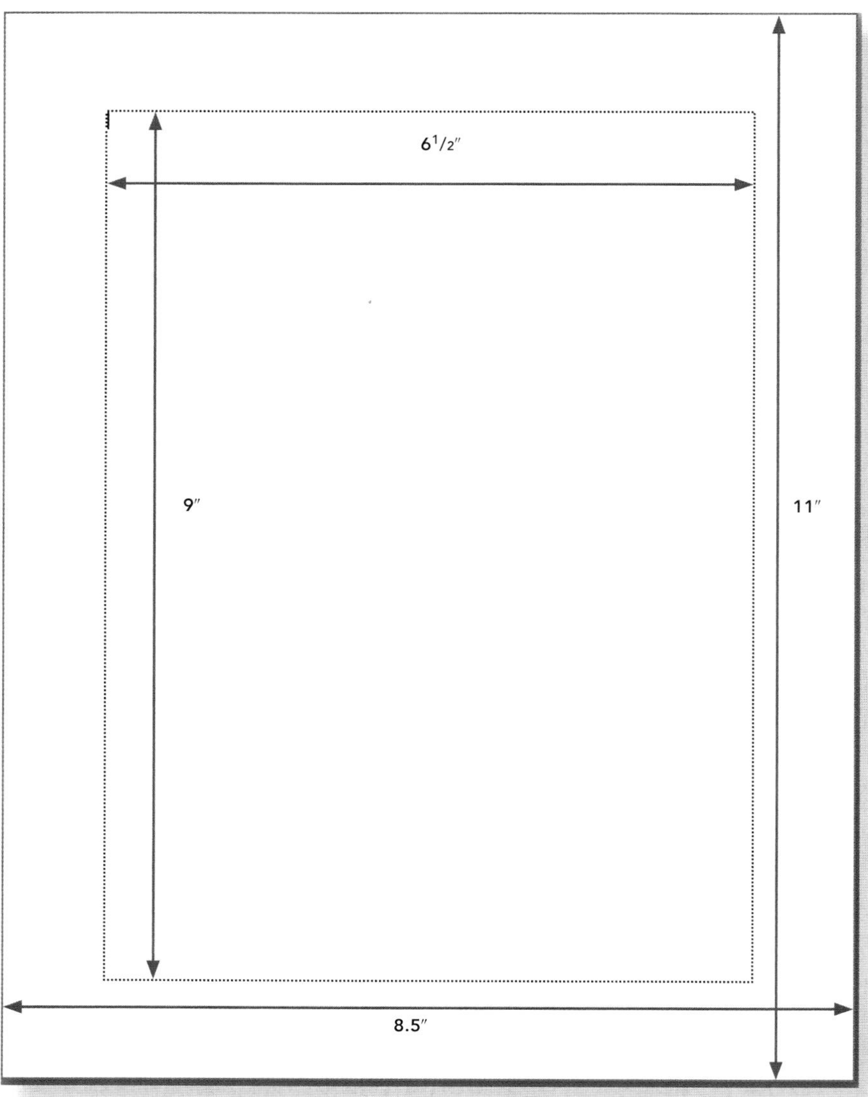

Exercise 9-1 CHANGE MARGINS FOR A DOCUMENT USING THE PAGE SETUP DIALOG BOX

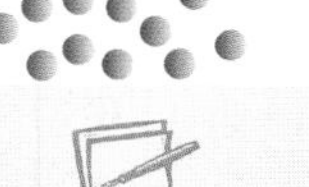

NOTE

The documents you create in this course relate to the case study about Campbell's Confections, a fictional candy store and chocolate factory (see the Case Study in the frontmatter of the book).

One way to change margins for a document is to use the Page Setup dialog box. You can change margins for an entire document or selected text. You can open the Page Setup dialog by clicking the Margins command or clicking the Page Setup Dialog Box Launcher.

1. Open the file **Corporate Gifts**. (Make sure no text is selected.)
2. Click the **Page Layout** tab and click the Margins button. Notice that the first option is **Normal**, which displays the default margin settings.
3. Click **Custom Margins** and click the **Margins** tab, if it is not active. The dialog box shows the default margin settings.

TIP

You can view page margins by opening the Word Options dialog box. Click **Advanced** and scroll to **Show document content**, and click **Show text boundaries**.

4. Edit the margin text box settings so they have the following values (or click the arrow boxes to change the settings). As you do so, notice the changes in the **Preview** box.

Top	1.5
Bottom	1.5
Left	2
Right	2

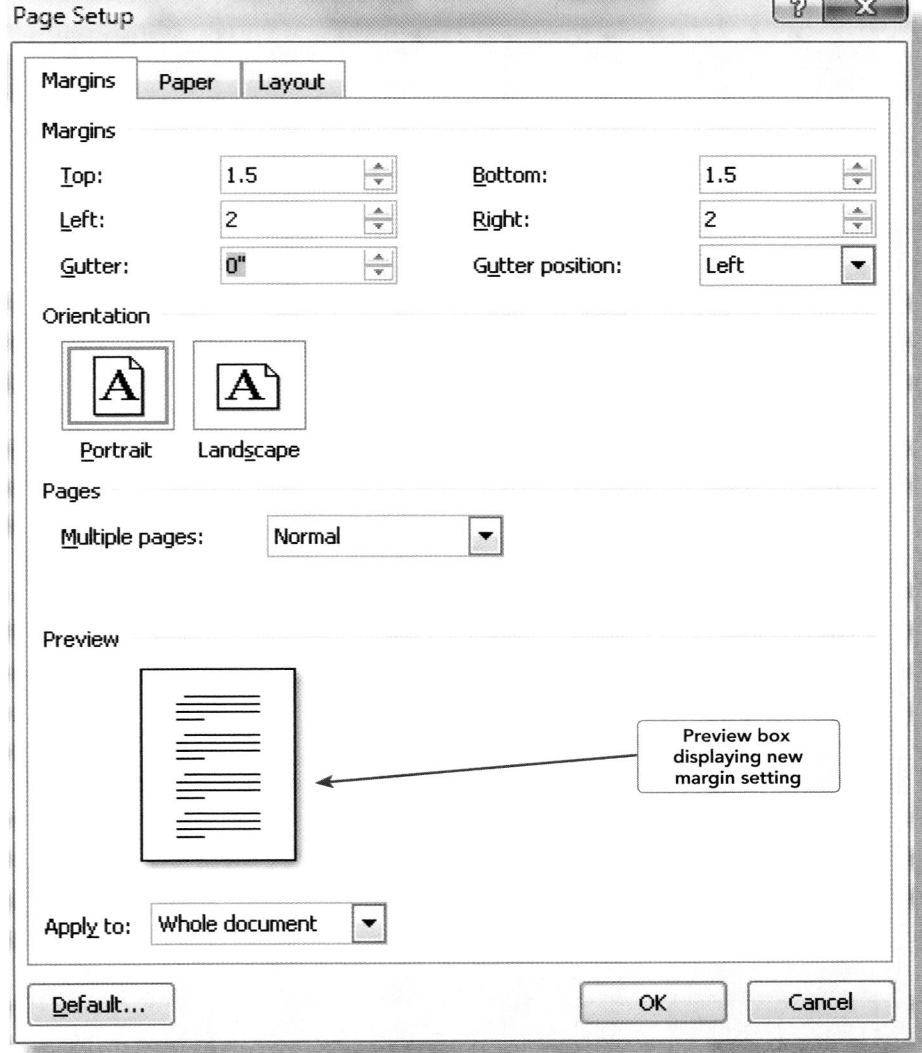

Figure 9-3
Changing margins in the Page Setup dialog box

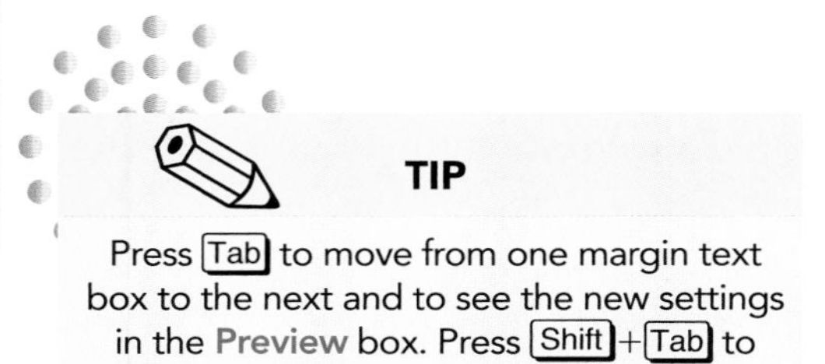

TIP

Press Tab to move from one margin text box to the next and to see the new settings in the **Preview** box. Press Shift+Tab to move to the previous margin text box.

5. Click the down arrow to open the **Apply to** drop-down list. Notice that you can choose either **Whole document** or **This point forward** (from the insertion point forward). Choose **Whole document** and click **OK** to change the margins of the entire document.

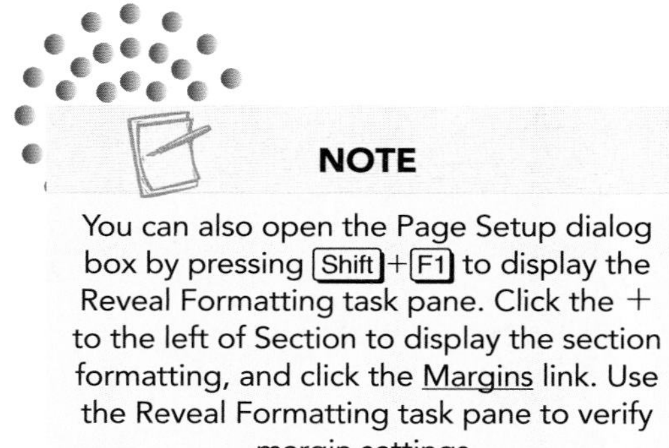

NOTE

You can also open the Page Setup dialog box by pressing Shift+F1 to display the Reveal Formatting task pane. Click the + to the left of Section to display the section formatting, and click the Margins link. Use the Reveal Formatting task pane to verify margin settings.

Exercise 9-2 CHANGE MARGINS FOR SELECTED TEXT BY USING THE PAGE SETUP DIALOG BOX

When you change margins for selected text, you create a new section. A *section* is a portion of a document that has its own formatting. When a document contains more than one section, *section breaks* indicate the beginning and end of a section. Section breaks in Draft view are represented by double-dotted lines.

1. Select the text from the second paragraph to the end of the document.
2. Click the **Page Layout** tab. Click the **Page Setup Dialog Box Launcher** to display the Page Setup dialog box.

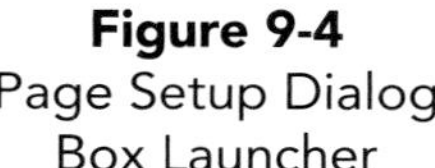

Figure 9-4
Page Setup Dialog Box Launcher

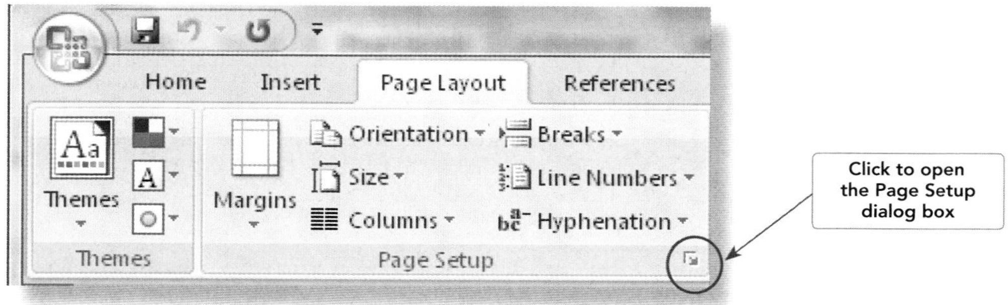

3. Change the margins to the following settings:

Top	2
Bottom	2
Left	1.5
Right	1.5

4. Choose **Selected text** from the **Apply to** box. Click **OK**.
5. Deselect the text, and scroll to the beginning of the selection. Word applied the margin changes to the selected text and created a new section. The section appears on a new page. The status bar displays section numbers and page numbers.

TIP

Display nonprinting characters if necessary, and switch to Draft view to see the section break double-dotted line in the document. Remember that Draft view does not show documents as they will appear when printed.

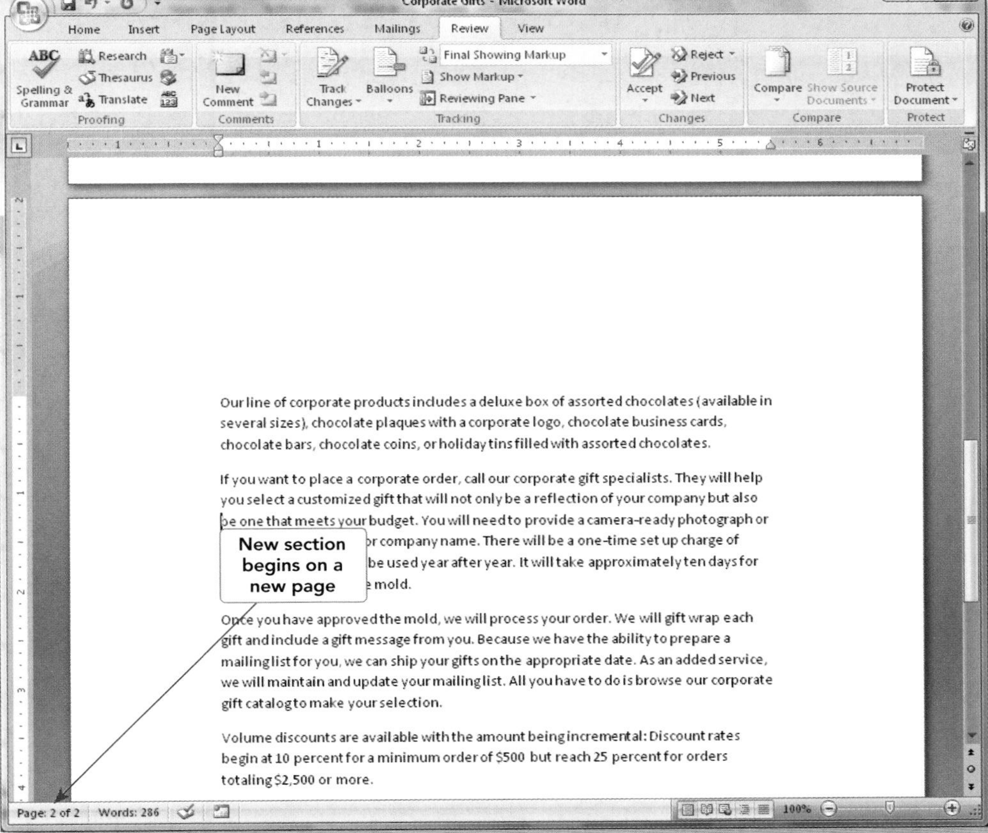

Figure 9-5
Changing margins for selected text creates a new section

Exercise 9-3 CHANGE MARGINS FOR A SECTION BY USING THE PAGE SETUP DIALOG BOX

After a section is created, you can change the margins for just the section (not the entire document) by using the Page Setup dialog box. To help you know which section you are formatting, customize the status bar to display sections.

1. Move the insertion point anywhere in the new section (section 2), and right-click the status bar. Click **Section** and click in the document to close the shortcut menu. Open the **Page Setup** dialog box.
2. Change the left and right margin settings to **1.25** inches.
3. Open the **Apply to** drop-down list to view the options. Notice that you can apply the new margin settings to the current section, to the whole document, or from the insertion point forward.
4. Choose **This section** and click **OK** to apply the settings to the new section.

Exercise 9-4 CHANGE MARGINS USING THE RULERS

To change margins using the rulers, use Print Layout view. The status bar includes five buttons for changing document views: The default view for Word documents is Print Layout, which displays text as it will appear on the printed page. Print Layout view displays headers, footers, and other page elements.

There are two ways to switch document views:

- Click a view button on the right side of the status bar.
- Click the View tab, and click a view button.

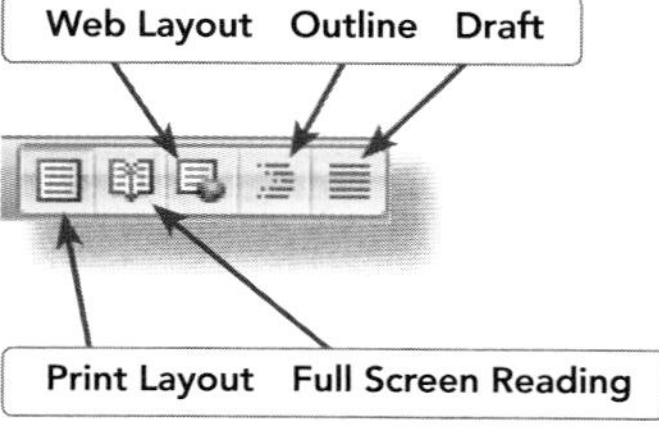

Figure 9-6
View buttons

1. Place the insertion point at the beginning of the document (Ctrl+Home). In bold uppercase letters, key **CORPORATE GIFTS** and then press Enter. Center the title.
2. Click the **View Ruler** button at the top of the vertical scroll bar if the rulers are not displayed.

3. Click in the new section (page 2). The status bar shows that the document contains two pages and two sections. Notice the extra space at the top of the page. The new section has a larger top margin (2 inches).
4. To see more of the page, including the margin areas, click the Zoom button 100% and then choose **Page width**. Click **OK**.
5. Move the insertion point to the top of the document (the first section). The blue area on the vertical ruler shows the 1.5-inch top margin. The blue areas on the horizontal ruler show the 2-inch left and right margins. The white area in the horizontal ruler shows the text area, which is a line length of 4.5 inches. (See Figure 9-7.)

Figure 9-7
Rulers in Print Layout view

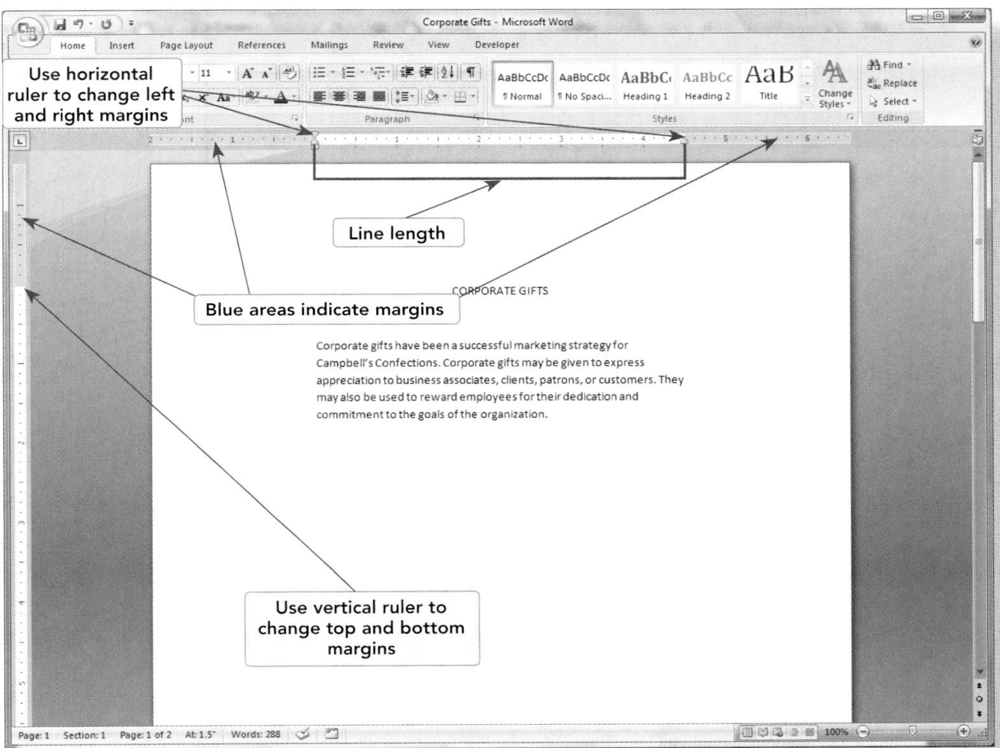

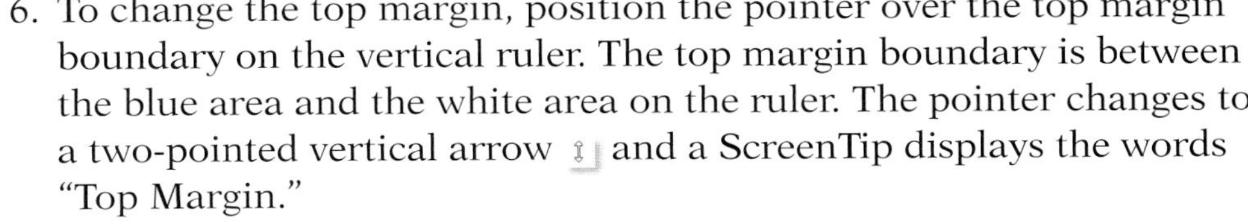

6. To change the top margin, position the pointer over the top margin boundary on the vertical ruler. The top margin boundary is between the blue area and the white area on the ruler. The pointer changes to a two-pointed vertical arrow and a ScreenTip displays the words "Top Margin."

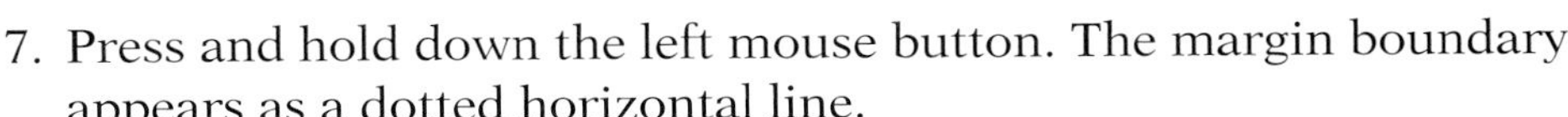

7. Press and hold down the left mouse button. The margin boundary appears as a dotted horizontal line.

8. Drag the margin boundary slightly up, and release the mouse button. The text at the top of the document moves up to align with the new top margin.

9. Click the Undo button to restore the 1.5-inch top margin.

10. Hold down the Alt key, and drag the top margin boundary down until it is at 2 inches on the ruler. Release Alt and the mouse button. Holding down the Alt key as you drag shows the exact margin and text area measurements.

11. To change the left margin, position the pointer over the left margin boundary on the horizontal ruler. The left margin boundary is between the blue area and the white area on the ruler. The pointer changes to a two-pointed horizontal arrow, and a ScreenTip displays the words "Left Margin."

Figure 9-8 Adjusting the left margin

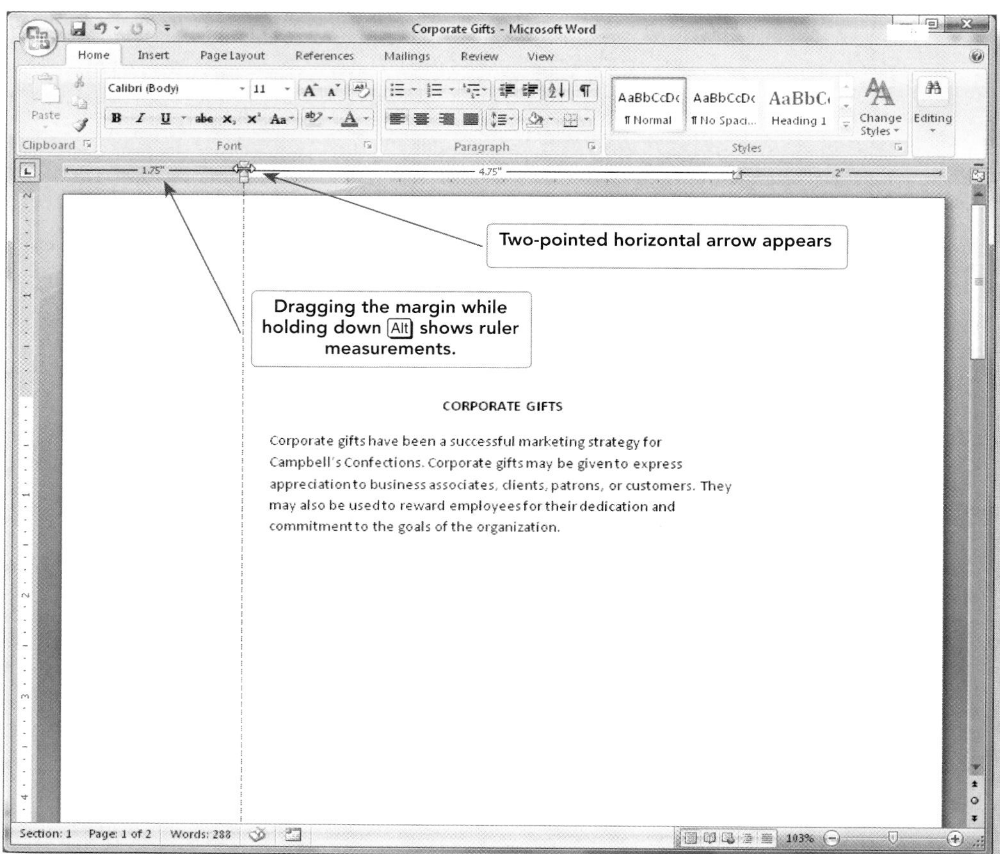

NOTE

You might have to fine-tune the pointer position to place it directly on the left margin boundary. Move the pointer slowly until you see the two-pointed arrow and the "Left Margin" ScreenTip.

12. Hold down the Alt key, and drag the margin boundary to the left to create a 1.75-inch left margin. (See Figure 9-8.)

13. Using the same procedure, drag the right margin boundary until it is located 1.75 inches from the right. Be sure to watch for the two-pointed arrow

before dragging. The first section now has 1.75-inch left and right margins and a 2-inch top margin.

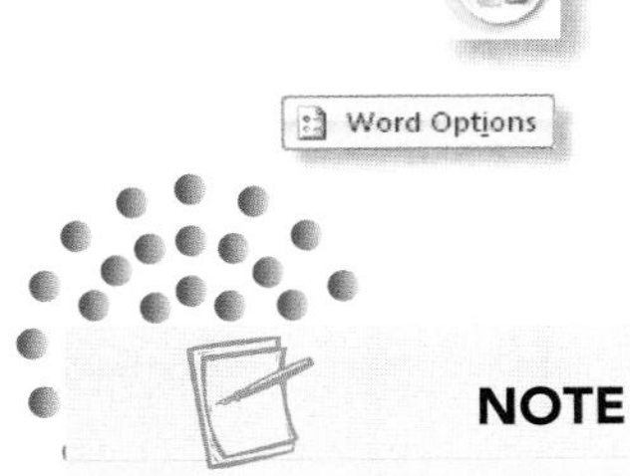

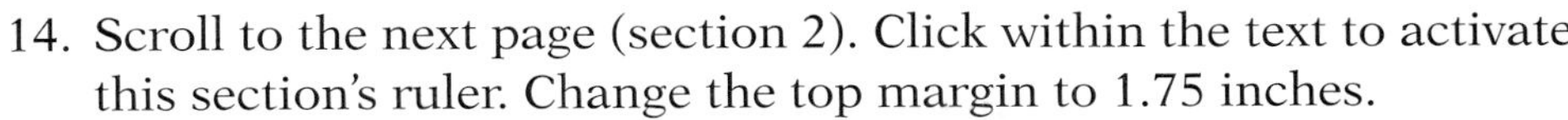

14. Scroll to the next page (section 2). Click within the text to activate this section's ruler. Change the top margin to 1.75 inches.

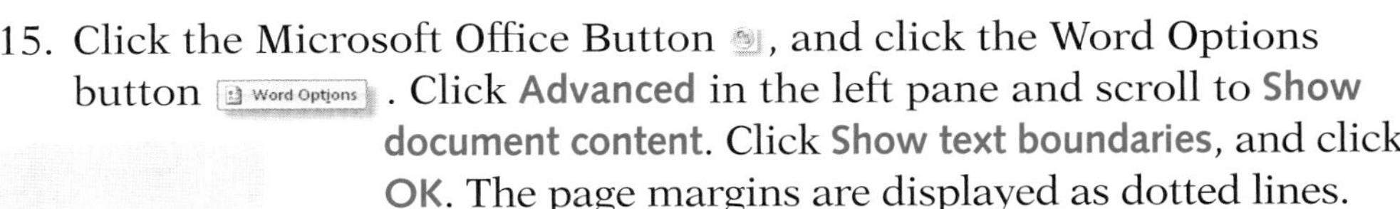

15. Click the Microsoft Office Button, and click the Word Options button Word Options. Click **Advanced** in the left pane and scroll to **Show document content**. Click **Show text boundaries**, and click **OK**. The page margins are displayed as dotted lines.

16. Remove the page margins from view by clicking the Microsoft Office Button, clicking the Word Options button Word Options, clicking **Advanced**, scrolling to **Show document content**, and deselecting **Show text boundaries**. Click **OK**.

17. Save the document as ***[your initials]*9-4** in a new Lesson 9 folder, and leave the document open for the next exercise.

NOTE

If you move the pointer to the top of the page in Print Layout view, you will see the Hide White Space button. Double click the button to hide the white space (the margin area) at the top and bottom of each page and the gray space between pages so you can see more document text. Point to the top of the page, and double-click the Show White Space button to restore the space.

Exercise 9-5 SET FACING PAGES WITH GUTTER MARGINS

If your document is going to be bound—put together like a book, with printing on both sides of the paper—you will want to use mirror margins and gutter margins. *Mirror margins* are inside and outside margins on facing pages that mirror one another. *Gutter margins* add extra space to the left or top margins to allow for binding.

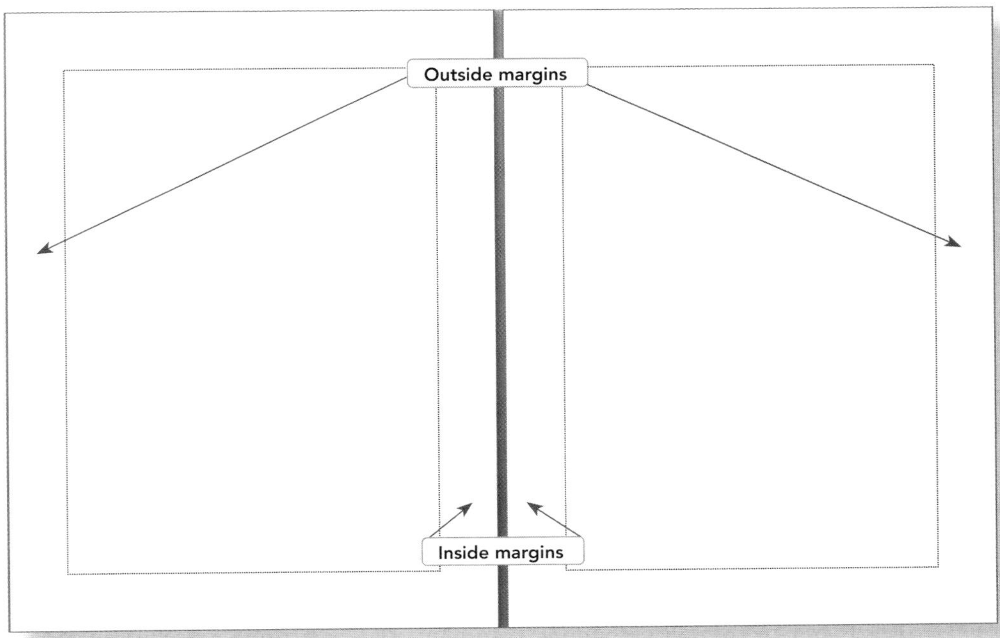

Figure 9-9
Mirror margins

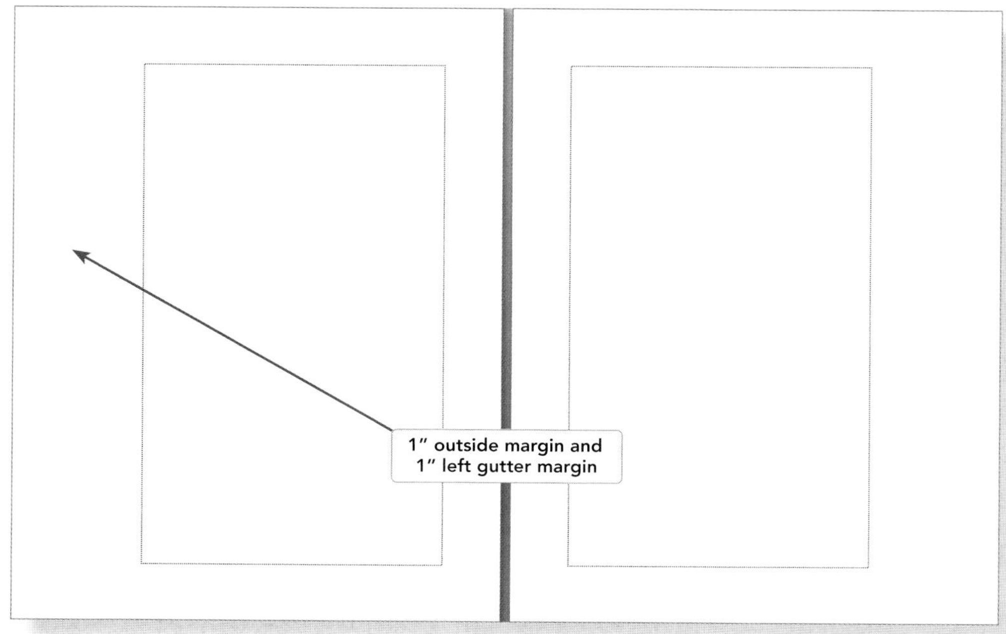

Figure 9-10
Gutter margins

1. Move the insertion point to the beginning of the document. Open the Page Setup dialog box, and open the **Multiple pages** drop-down list. Choose **Mirror margins**. Notice that the **Preview** box now displays two pages. The left and right margins are called the inside and outside margins.

2. Change the **Inside** margins to **1.25** inches and the **Outside** margins to **1** inch.

3. Set the **Gutter** margin to **1** inch, and press Tab to reflect the change in the Preview box. Click **OK**. A 1-inch gutter margin is added to the document. (Make sure you use at least 1-inch gutter margins to allow room for binding.)

TIP

Visualize the document as double-sided, facing pages in a book by placing the back of page 2 against the back of page 1 and placing page 3 beside page 2. The gutter margin of page 1 is on the left. The gutter margin on the right of page 2 and on the left of page 3 allows space for the binding and represents facing pages. *Facing pages* appear as a two-page spread with odd-numbered right pages and even-numbered left pages.

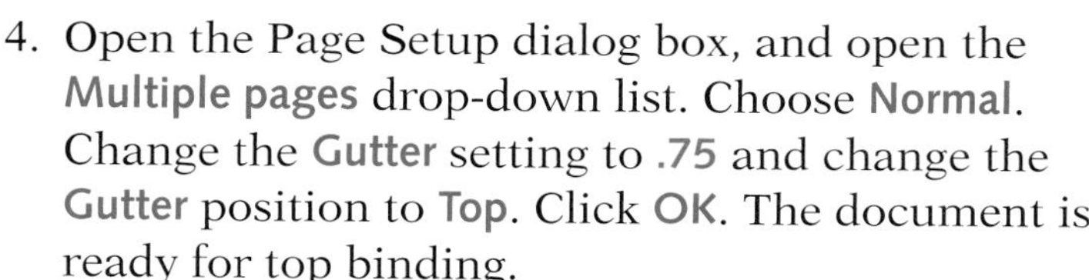

4. Open the Page Setup dialog box, and open the **Multiple pages** drop-down list. Choose **Normal**. Change the **Gutter** setting to **.75** and change the **Gutter** position to **Top**. Click **OK**. The document is ready for top binding.

5. Open the Page Setup dialog box. Change the **Left** and **Right** margins to **1.5** inches, change the **Gutter** setting to **0"**, and change the **Gutter position** to **Left**. Click **OK**.

6. Save the document as ***[your initials]*9-5** in your Lesson 9 folder.

7. Print the document, and keep it open for the next exercise.

Using Print Preview

Viewing a document in Print Preview is the best way to check how a document will look when you print it. You can view multiple pages at a time, adjust margins and tabs, and edit text.

To display a document in Print Preview, click the **Microsoft Office Button**, click the arrow beside **Print**, and click **Print Preview**. The keyboard shortcut for Print Preview is Alt+Ctrl+I.

Exercise 9-6 VIEW A MULTIPLE-PAGE DOCUMENT IN PRINT PREVIEW

Print Preview displays entire pages of a document in reduced size. You can view one page at a time or two pages at a time.

1. Move the insertion point to the beginning of the document.
2. Click the **Microsoft Office Button**, click the arrow beside **Print**, and click **Print Preview**. Click the One Page button on the Print Preview tab to display the first page of the document.

One Page

Two Pages

3. Click the Two Pages button to see both pages.

Figure 9-11 Viewing multiple pages in Print Preview

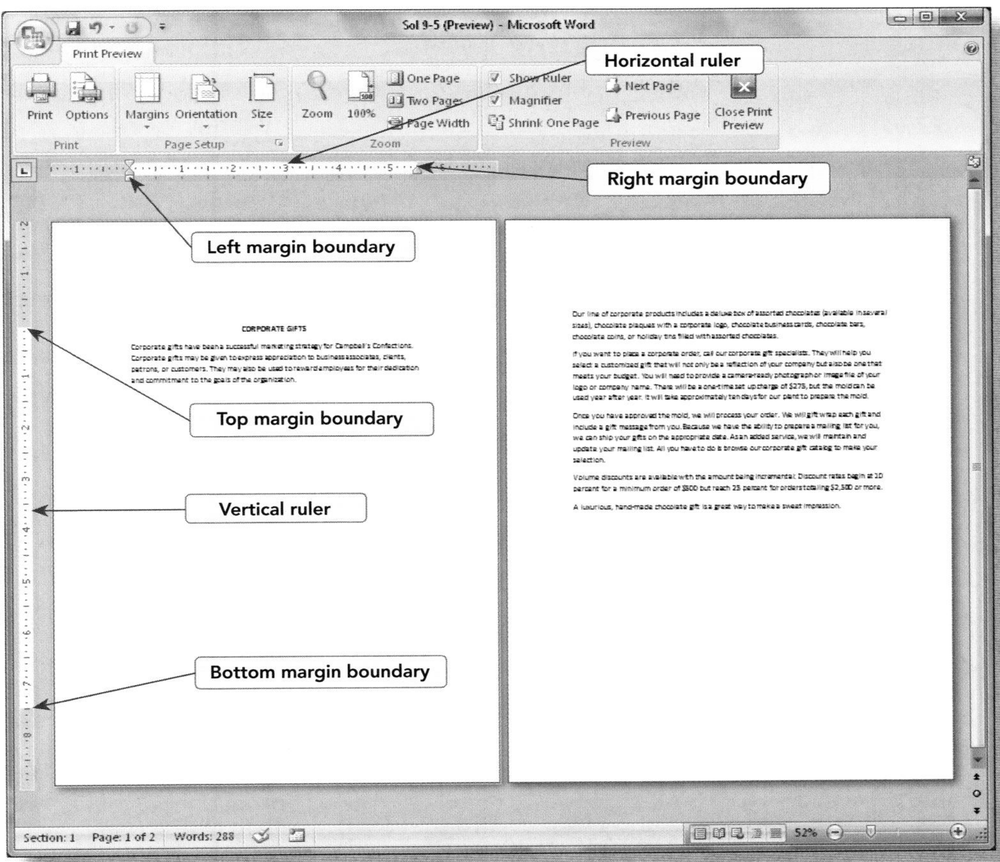

TIP

You use the Zoom box to view multiple pages of your document. Click the Zoom Level button on the status bar. Click Many Pages, and a grid appears to choose the number of pages you want to view and how they are configured in the window. If you drag the pointer as you move across the grid, you can expand the grid to display additional rows and pages, which is useful in a long document. Drag the Zoom Slider to 100% to return to a one-page view.

4. To zoom into page 2, click once on the page with the arrow pointer to make page 2 active and then click again with the magnifier pointer.
5. Click again to zoom out. Notice that the horizontal ruler shows the settings for page 2.
6. Click the Close Print Preview button to close the Print Preview window and to return to Print Layout view.

TABLE 9-1 Print Preview Toolbar

Button	Description	Function
	Print	Print the document in the Print Preview window.
	Options	List printing options.
	Margins	Change margin settings.
	Orientation	Switch between portrait and landscape orientation.
	Size	Select paper size.
	Zoom	Choose a magnification to reduce or enlarge the page or pages displayed.
	100%	Zoom document to 100 percent.
One Page	One Page	Display one page at a time.
Two Pages	Two Pages	Display two pages at a time.
Page Width	Page Width	Zoom the document to the width of the window.
Show Ruler	Show Ruler	Display or hide the Print Preview ruler, which you can use to change margins, tabs, and indents.
Magnifier	Magnifier	Change the I-beam pointer to a magnifying glass and vice versa. With the magnifying glass pointer, click in the document to zoom in and out. With the I-beam pointer, edit document text.
Shrink One Page	Shrink One Page	Shrink a document to fit on one less page when the last page contains only a few lines of text.
Next Page	Next Page	Move to the next page of the document.
Previous Page	Previous Page	Move to the previous page of the document.
	Close Print Preview	Close the Print Preview window and return to the previous view.

Exercise 9-7 CHANGE MARGINS IN PRINT PREVIEW

When you view a page in Print Preview, you can see all four margins and adjust margin settings using the horizontal and vertical rulers or by opening the Page Setup dialog box within the Print Preview window.

1. Move the insertion point to the beginning of the document (page 1, section 1).
2. Click the **Microsoft Office Button** and click the arrow beside **Print**. Click **Print Preview**.
3. Click the One Page button on the Print Preview tab to display only page 1. Click the Show Ruler button if it is not checked.
4. Move the pointer to the top margin boundary on the vertical ruler. The pointer changes to the two-pointed arrow, and the top margin is identified in a ScreenTip.

NOTE

Changing margins in Print Preview is similar to changing margins in Print Layout view. You use the vertical and horizontal rulers to drag the margins to the desired positions.

5. Hold down Alt as you drag the margin boundary to 1.5 inches on the blue area of the vertical ruler. Word adjusts the top margin to 1.5 inches.
6. Click the **Page Setup Dialog Box Launcher**.
7. Change the top margin to **2** inches and click **OK**.
8. Use the horizontal ruler to change the left and right margins to 1.25 inches.

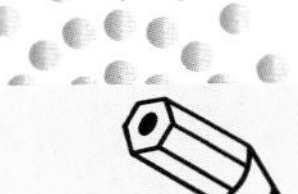

TIP

You can check the exact measurement of a margin in Print Preview or Print Layout view by moving the pointer over the margin boundary, holding down the left mouse button without dragging it, and holding down Alt.

Exercise 9-8 EDIT A DOCUMENT IN PRINT PREVIEW

To edit text in Print Preview, you magnify a page to the desired size and then switch to edit mode. You would not, however, want to make extensive changes in Print Preview.

1. Click on page 1 to zoom in. The view of the document is enlarged to 100 percent.

2. Click the Magnifier button to deselect the option and change the pointer to the I-beam.
3. Select "Campbell's Confections" in the first paragraph, and press Ctrl+I to apply italic formatting.

Magnifier

4. Click the Magnifier button to cancel edit mode.
5. Click **Close Print Preview** to close the Print Preview window.
6. Save the document as ***[your initials]*9-8**.
7. Submit the document, and leave it open for the next exercise.

Paper Size and Orientation

When you open a new document, the default paper size is 8.5 by 11 inches. Using the Page Setup dialog box, you can change the paper size to print a document on legal paper or define a custom-size paper.

The Page Setup dialog box also gives you a choice between two page orientation settings: portrait and landscape. A *portrait* page is taller than it is wide. This orientation is the default in new Word documents. A *landscape* page is wider than it is tall. You can apply page-orientation changes to sections of a document or to the entire document.

Exercise 9-9 CHANGE PAPER SIZE AND PAGE ORIENTATION

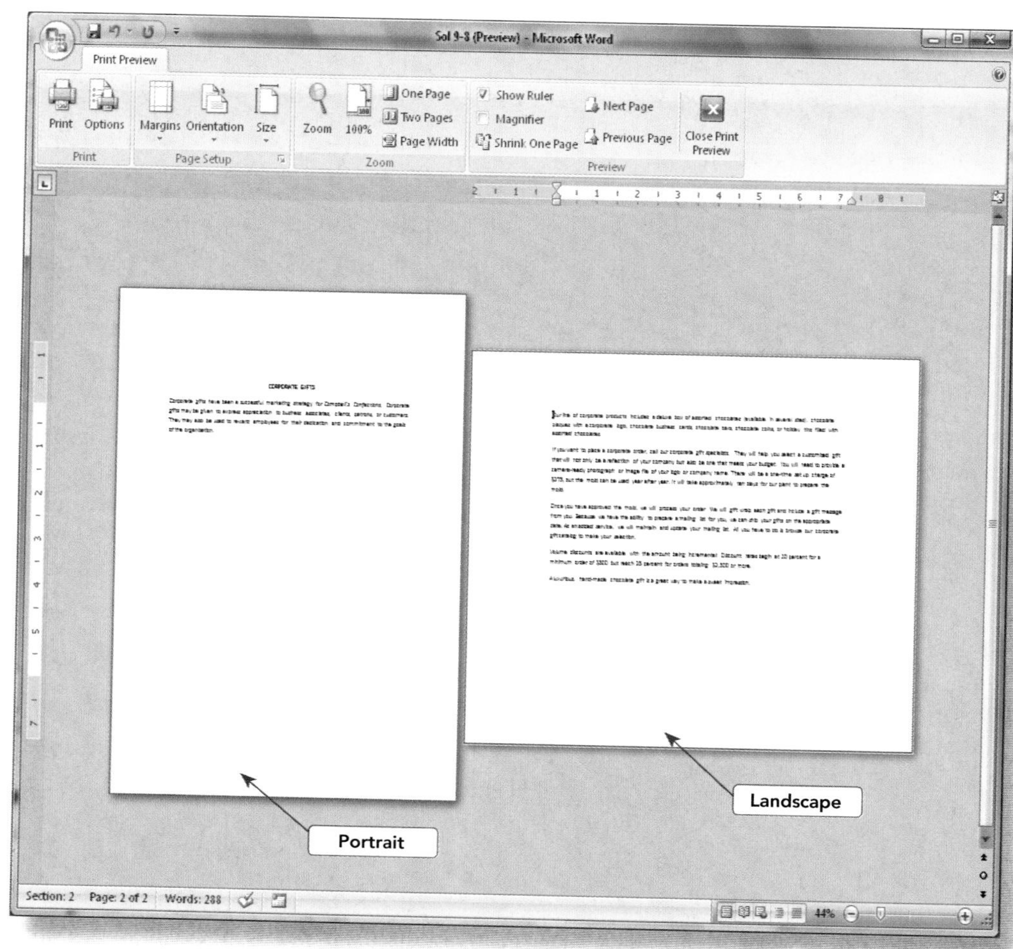

Figure 9-12
Changing page orientation

1. Open the **Page Setup** dialog box.
2. On the **Margins** tab, click **Landscape**.
3. Click the **Paper** tab. Notice the default paper size for letter paper.
4. Open the **Paper size** drop-down list and choose **Legal**. Click **OK**. Notice how the orientation and paper size changed.
5. Press Ctrl+Z to undo the changes to paper size and orientation.

6. Switch to Print Preview, and click the Two Pages button.

7. Click page 2, and click the Orientation button. Click **Landscape**. Section 2 on page 2 is formatted with landscape orientation and page 1 is formatted with portrait orientation. Click **Close Print Preview** to close the Print Preview window.
8. Save the document as ***[your initials]*9-9.**
9. Submit and close the document.

NOTE

You can change orientation for an entire document or from the insertion point forward by choosing an option from the **Apply to** drop-down list. When you choose **This point forward**, a new section is created with the orientation you choose. When selected text is formatted with a different orientation, a section break is automatically inserted before and after the selected text.

Printing Envelopes and Labels

Word provides a tool to print different-size envelopes and labels. Using the Envelopes and Labels command, you can:

- Print a single envelope without saving it or attach an envelope to a document for future printing. The attached envelope is added to the beginning of the document as a separate section.
- Print labels without saving them, or create a new document that contains the labels. You can print a single label or a full page of the same label.

Exercise 9-10 PRINT AN ENVELOPE

Printing envelopes often requires that you manually feed the envelope to your printer. If you print labels that are on other than 8 1/2 by 11 inch sheets, you might need to feed the labels manually. Your printer will display a code and not print until you feed an envelope or label sheet manually.

1. Open the file **Matthews**. This document is a one-page letter.
2. Click the **Mailings** tab, and locate the **Create** group. Click the Envelopes button.

3. Click the **Envelopes** tab if it is not active. Notice that Word detected the address in the document and placed this text in the **Delivery address** text box. You can edit this text as needed.

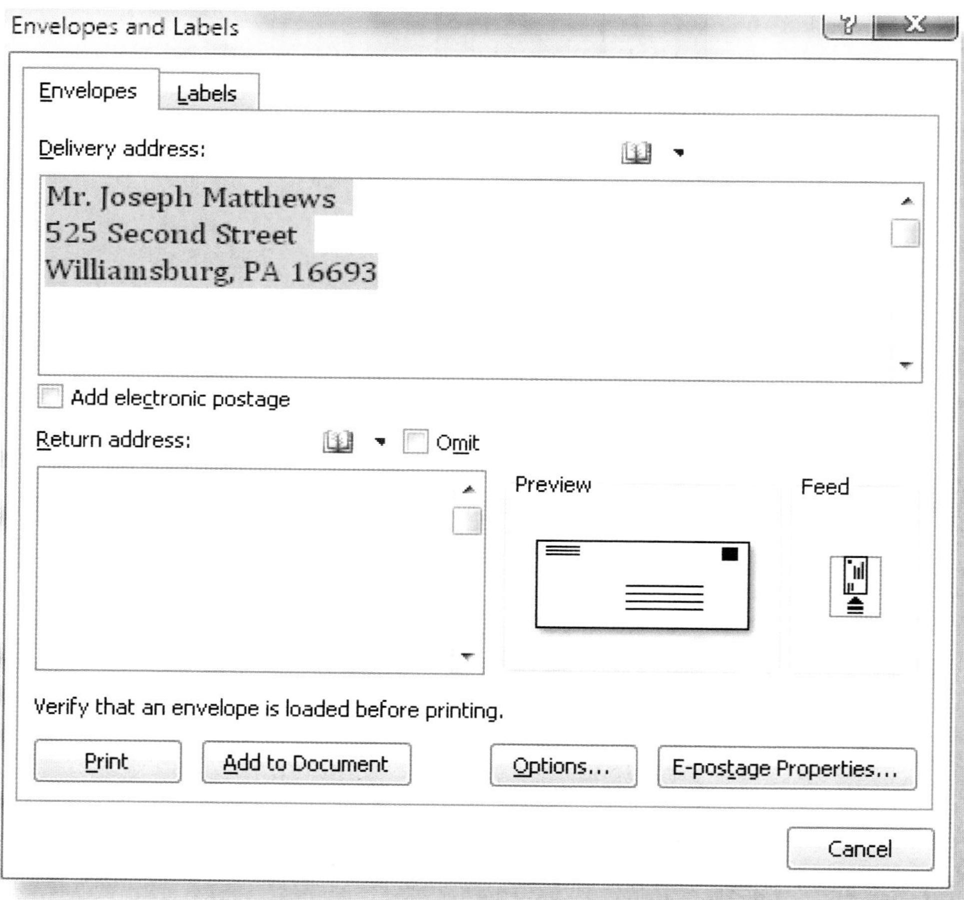

Figure 9-13 Envelopes and Labels dialog box

4. In the **Delivery address** text box, enter the full ZIP+4 Code by keying **-1129** after "16693."

5. Make sure the **Omit** box is not checked. Select and delete any text in the **Return address** text box, and then key the following return address, starting with your name:

   [your name]
   Campbell's Confections
   25 Main Street
   Grove City, PA 16127-0025

6. Place a standard business-size envelope in your printer. The **Feed** box illustrates the feeding method accepted by your printer.

7. Click **Print**. When Word asks if you want to save the return address as the default return address, click **No**. Word prints the envelope with the default font and text placement settings.

NOTE

If you don't have an envelope, you can use a blank sheet of paper to test the placement of the addresses. Ask your instructor how to proceed. You might have to feed the envelope or blank sheet manually.

NOTE

Check your printer to see what you need to do to complete a manual envelope feed. If the printer is flashing or displaying a message, you might have to press a button.

Exercise 9-11 CHOOSE ENVELOPE OPTIONS

Before printing an envelope, you can choose additional envelope options. For example, you can add the envelope content to the document for future use. You can also click the **Options** button in the Envelopes and Labels dialog box to:

- Change the envelope size. The default size is size 10, which is a standard business envelope.
- Change the font and other character formatting of the delivery address or return address.
- Verify printing options.

1. Open the **Envelopes and Labels** dialog box again.
2. Key your name and address in the **Return address** box.
3. Click the **Options** button in the Envelopes and Labels dialog box to open the Envelope Options dialog box. Click the **Envelope Options** tab if it is not active.

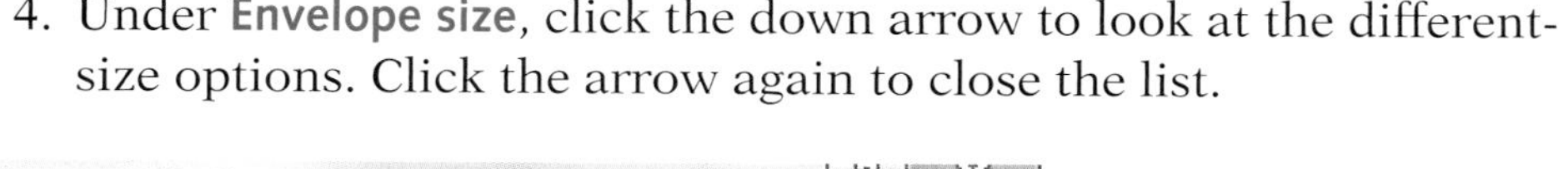

4. Under **Envelope size**, click the down arrow to look at the different-size options. Click the arrow again to close the list.

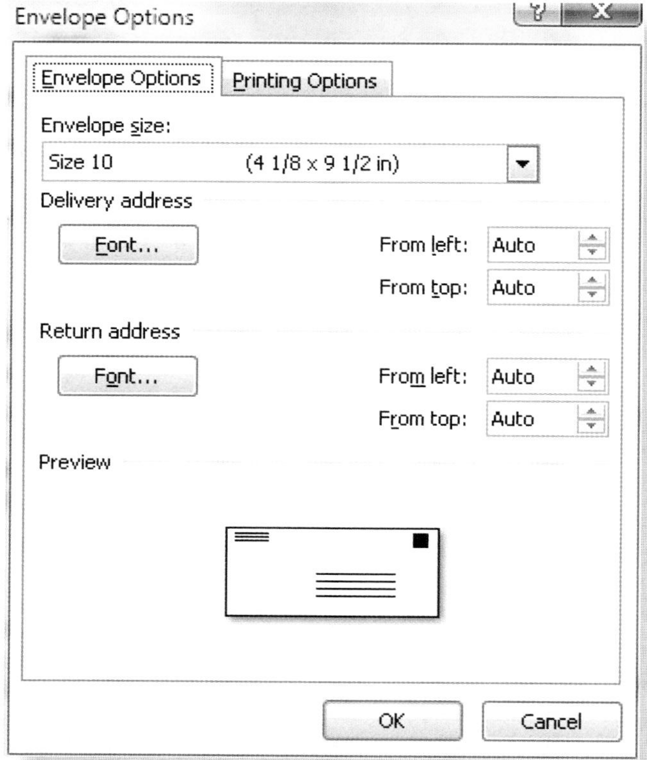

Figure 9-14 Envelope Options dialog box

5. Click the **Font** button for the **Delivery address**. The Envelope Address dialog box for the delivery address opens.

6. Format the text as bold and all caps and change the font size to **10**. Click **OK** to close the Envelope Address dialog box. Click **OK** to close the Envelope Options dialog box.

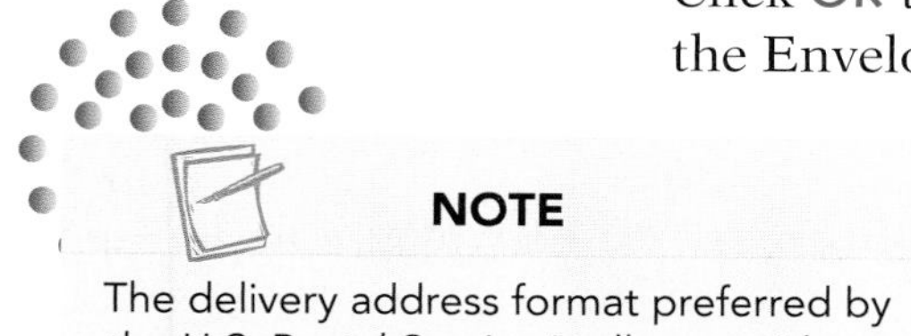

NOTE

The delivery address format preferred by the U.S. Postal Service is all caps with no punctuation.

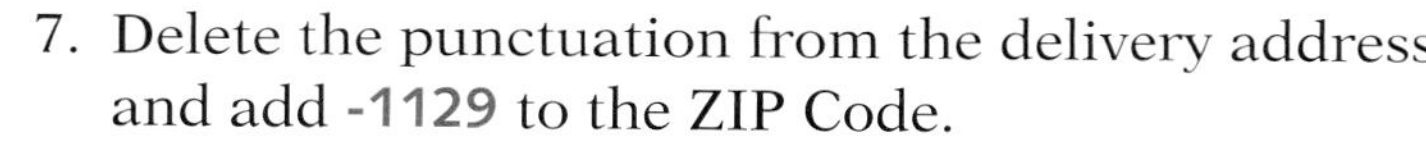

7. Delete the punctuation from the delivery address and add **-1129** to the ZIP Code.

8. Click **Add to Document** to add the envelope information to the top of the document as a separate section. Don't save the return address as the default address.

NOTE

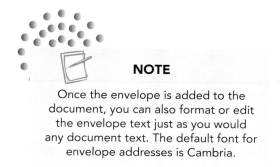

Once the envelope is added to the document, you can also format or edit the envelope text just as you would any document text. The default font for envelope addresses is Cambria.

9. Replace [Today's date] with the current date. Correct any spacing between the elements of the letter. Add your reference initials followed by **Enclosures (2)**. Review the letter to verify correct business letter format.
10. View the letter and envelope in Print Preview.
11. Close the Print Preview window, and save the document as ***[your initials]*9-11** in your Lesson 9 folder.
12. Print the document.
13. Leave the document open for use in the next exercise.

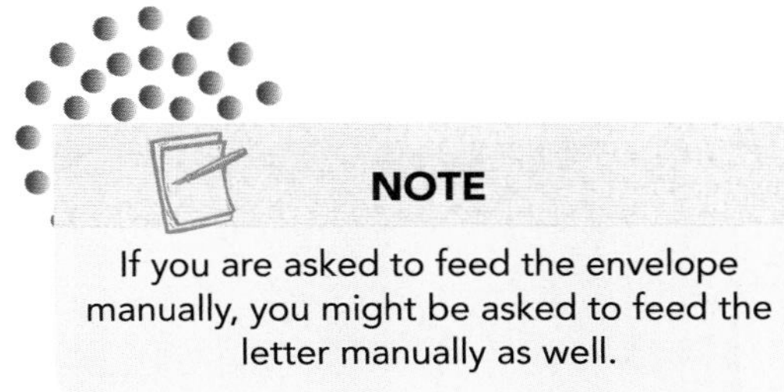

NOTE
If you are asked to feed the envelope manually, you might be asked to feed the letter manually as well.

Exercise 9-12 PRINT LABELS

The Labels tab in the Envelopes and Labels dialog box makes it easy to print different-size labels for either a return address or a delivery address.

1. Position the insertion point in the envelope section of the document. Click the **Mailings** tab. Click the Labels button.
2. Click the **Use return address** check box to create labels for the letter sender.
3. Select the address text, and press Ctrl+Shift+A to turn on all caps. Delete the comma after the city.
4. Click the option **Full page of the same label**, if it is not active, to create an entire page of return address labels.

5. Click the Options button to choose a label size.

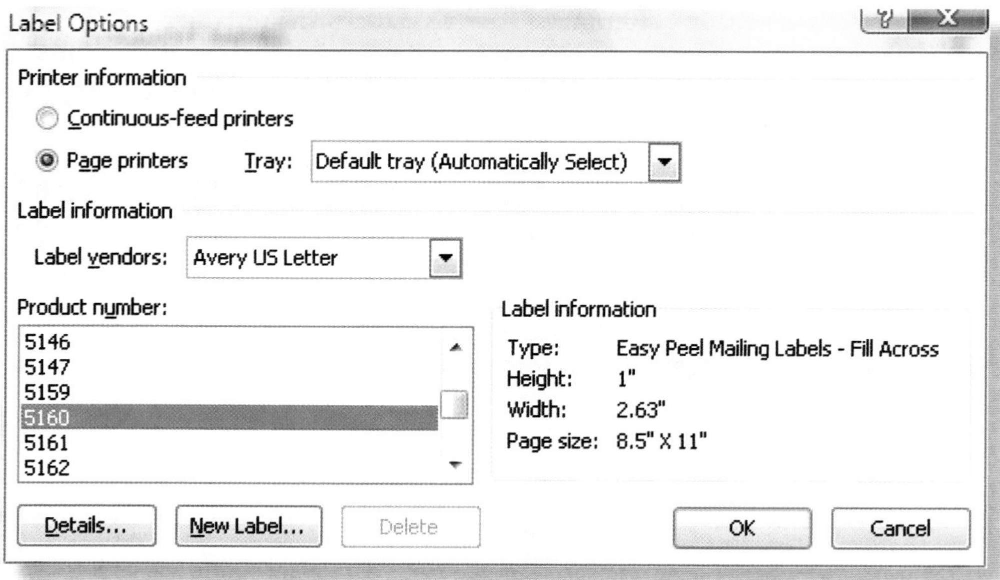

Figure 9-15
Label Options dialog box

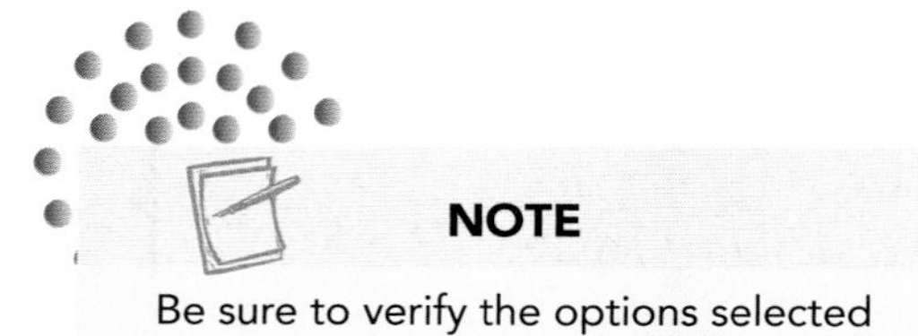

NOTE

Be sure to verify the options selected in the **Printer information** and **Label information** sections.

6. Verify that **Page printers** is selected under **Printer information** and that **Avery US Letter** is listed in the **Label vendors** box.
7. Scroll the **Product number** list to see the various label options, and choose **5160**, the product number for a standard Avery address label.
8. Click **OK**, and then click **New Document** to save the labels as a separate document. (If you click **Print**, you can print the labels without saving them.) Do not save the return address.
9. Select all text in the new document and reduce the font size to 11 points.
10. Save the document as ***[your initials]*9-12** in your Lesson 9 folder.
11. Switch to Print Preview to view the labels on the page.
12. Prepare the printer for a sheet of 5160-size labels or feed a blank sheet of paper into the printer, and then print the labels.
13. Close the document containing the full sheet of labels.

Setting Print Options

When you click the Quick Print option, Word prints the entire document. If you open the Print dialog box, however, you can choose to print only part of a document. You can also select other print options from the dialog box, including collating copies of a multipage document, printing selected text, or printing multiple document pages on one sheet of paper.

Exercise 9-13 CHOOSE PRINT OPTIONS FROM THE PRINT DIALOG BOX

1. Position the insertion point to the left of the date in the letter to Mr. Joseph Matthews (***[your initials]*****9-11**). Click the **Microsoft Office Button**, and click the arrow beside **Print** to view the print options. Click **Print** to open the Print dialog box. (You can also click **Print** to open the Print dialog box.)
2. Click **Current Page** and click **OK**. Word prints page 1 of the document.
3. Open the Print dialog box again. Key **1-2** in the **Pages** text box. You can also enter specific page numbers or page ranges.
4. In the **Number of copies** text box, use the up arrow to change the number of copies to **2**.
5. If the **Collate** check box is not active, click it to select it. Notice the change in the preview of the number of copies. Click the **Collate** check box to uncheck it (make sure it is unchecked). With this box not checked, Word will print two copies of page 1 and then two copies of page 2.
6. Change the number of copies back to 1.
7. Click the down arrow to open the **Print what** drop-down list. It shows the various elements you can print in addition to the entire document. Click again to close the list.
8. Click the down arrow to open the **Print** drop-down list, which gives you the option to print even or odd pages. Click again to close the list.
9. Click the down arrow to open the **Pages per sheet** drop-down list, which gives you the option to print your selection over a specified number of sheets. Choose the **2 pages** setting. This option prints two pages on one sheet of $8^1/_2$- by 11-inch paper, with each page reduced to fit on the sheet.

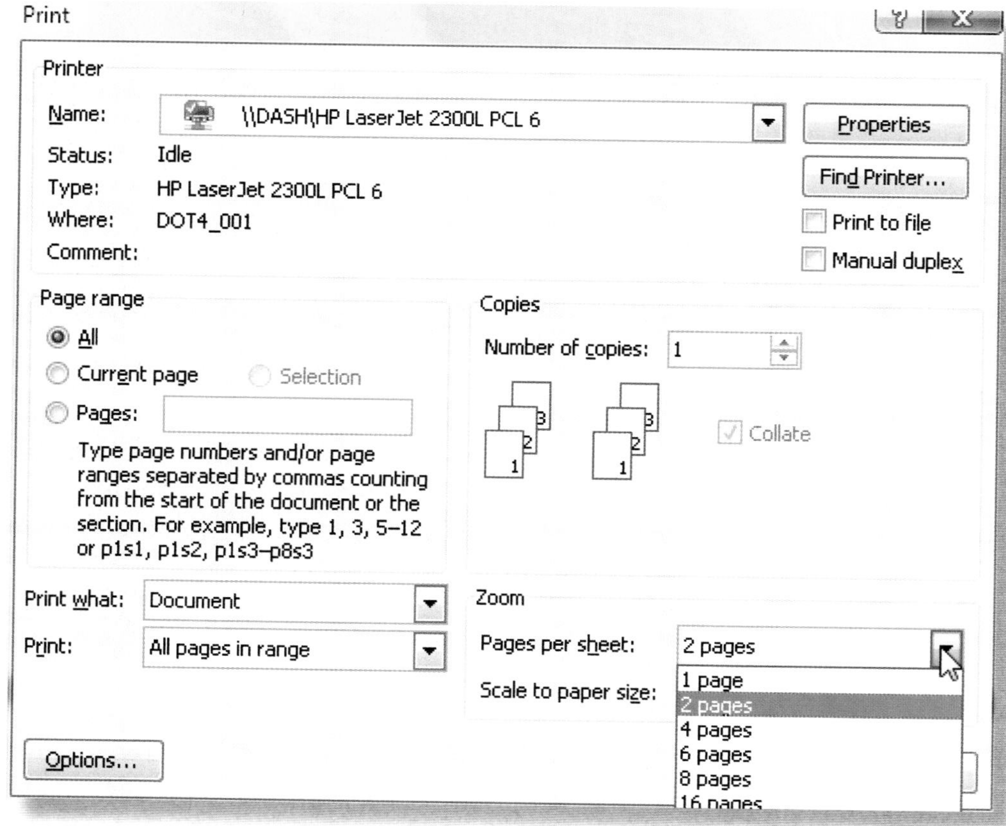

Figure 9-16
Print dialog box

10. Open the **Scale to paper size** drop-down list, which gives you the option to print on a different paper or envelope size (Word adjusts the scaling of the fonts, tables, and other elements to fit the new size). Close the drop-down list.
11. Click **OK**. Word prints reduced versions of pages 1 and 2 on one sheet of paper.
12. Close the document without saving.

Lesson 9 Summary

- In a Word document, text is keyed and printed within the boundaries of the document's margins. Margins are the spaces between the edges of the text and the edges of the paper.
- Change the actual space for text on a page by changing margins (left, right, top, and bottom). You can key new margin settings in the Page Setup dialog box.
- Changing margins for selected text results in a new section for the selected text. A section is a portion of a document that has its own formatting. When a document contains more than one section, you see

double-dotted lines, or section breaks, between sections to indicate the beginning and end of a section.

- Print Layout view shows how text is positioned on the printed page. Use the View buttons on the right of the status bar to switch between Print Layout view and Draft view.
- Print Preview shows how an entire document looks before printing. Use the One Page command, the Two Pages command, and the scroll bar to view all or part of the document. Change the Zoom as needed.
- Change margins in Print Layout view or in Print Preview by positioning the pointer over a margin boundary on a ruler and dragging. Press Alt to see the exact ruler measurement as you drag.
- Edit a document in Print Preview by clicking the Magnifier command to change the magnifier pointer to the I-beam pointer.
- For bound documents, use mirror margins and gutter margins. Mirror margins are inside and outside margins on facing pages that mirror one another. Gutter margins add extra space to margins to allow for binding.
- A document can print in either portrait ($8^1/_2$- by 11-inch) or landscape (11- by $8^1/_2$-inch) orientation. Choose an orientation in the Page Setup dialog box, Margins tab.
- A document can be scaled to fit a particular paper size. Choose paper size options in the Page Setup dialog box, Paper tab.
- Use Word to print different-size envelopes. You can change address formatting and make the envelope part of the document for future printing. Use Word to print different-size address labels—either a single label or a sheet of the same label.
- Choose print options such as printing only the current page, specified pages, selected text, collated copies of pages, and reduced pages by opening the Print dialog box.

LESSON 9 Command Summary

Feature	Button	Command	Keyboard
Print Preview		**Microsoft Office Button, Print, Print Preview**	Ctrl+F2 or Alt+Ctrl+I
Print Layout view		**View tab, Print Layout** command	Alt+Ctrl+P
Choose print options		**Microsoft Office Button, Print**	Ctrl+P
Print envelopes or labels		**Mailings tab, Envelopes** or **Mailings tab, Labels** command	

Lesson 10

Page and Section Breaks

OBJECTIVES

After completing this lesson, you will be able to:

1. Use soft and hard page breaks.
2. Control line and page breaks.
3. Control section breaks.
4. Format sections.
5. Use the Go To feature.

MCAS OBJECTIVES

In this lesson:

WW 07 1.1.6
WW 07 1.2.1
WW 07 2.3.1
WW 07 2.3.2
WW 07 5.1.1

Estimated Time: 1 hour

In Word, text flows automatically from the bottom of one page to the top of the next page. This is similar to how text wraps automatically from the end of one line to the beginning of the next line. You can control and customize how and when text flows from the bottom of one page to the top of the next. This process is called *pagination*.

Sections are a common feature of long documents and have a significant impact on pagination. This lesson describes how to use and manage sections.

Using Soft and Hard Page Breaks

As you work on a document, Word is constantly calculating the amount of space available on the page. Page length is determined by the size of the paper and the top and bottom margin settings. For example, using standard-size paper and default margins, page length is 9 inches. When a document exceeds this length, Word creates a *soft page break*. Word adjusts this automatic page break as you add or delete text. A soft page break appears as a horizontal dotted line on the screen in Draft view. In Print Layout view, you see the actual page break—the bottom of one page and the top of the next.

Draft view is frequently used to edit and format text. It does not show the page layout as it appears on a printed page, nor does it show special elements of a page such as columns, headers, or footers.

NOTE

When you format and edit a long document, check the status bar settings to make sure Section and Page Numbers display. To verify the settings, right-click the status bar and click to select the options.

NOTE

The page breaks described in this lesson might appear in slightly different locations on your screen.

Exercise 10-1 ADJUST A SOFT PAGE BREAK AUTOMATICALLY

1. Open the file **History**. Switch to Draft view by clicking the Draft button on the status bar. Change the zoom level to **100%** if necessary.
2. Scroll to the bottom of page 3. Notice the soft page break separating the heading "Gourmet Chocolate" from the paragraph below it.
3. Locate the paragraph just above the heading "Gourmet Chocolate" (it begins "In 2001"). Move the insertion point to the left of "The Web site has proven" in the middle of the paragraph, and press Enter to split the paragraph. Notice the adjustment of the soft page break. Undo the paragraph split.

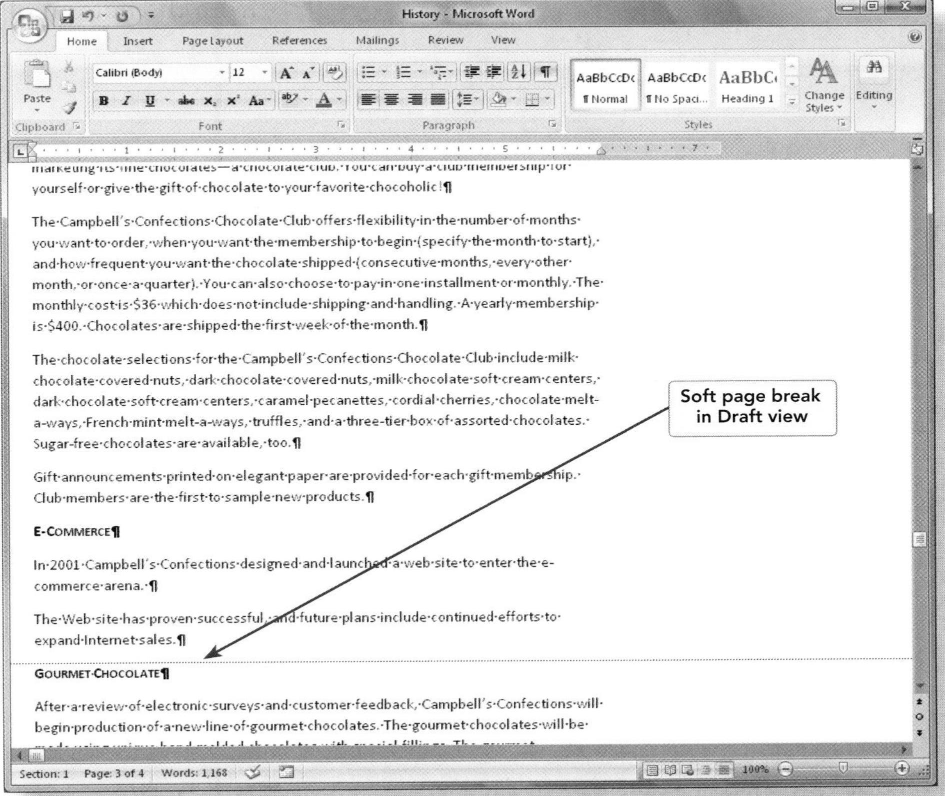

Figure 10-1 Adjusting the position of a soft page break

Exercise 10-2 INSERT A HARD PAGE BREAK

When you want a page break to occur at a specific point, you can insert a *hard page break*. In Draft view, a hard page break appears on the screen as a dotted line with the words "Page Break." In Print Layout view you see the actual page break.

There are two ways to insert a hard page break:

- Use the keyboard shortcut Ctrl+Enter.
- Click the **Insert** tab, and click the Page Break command.

1. Move the insertion point to the bottom of page 2, to the beginning of the paragraph that starts "The most popular."
2. Press Ctrl+Enter. Word inserts a hard page break so the paragraph and bulleted text are not divided between two pages.
3. Move to the middle of page 4, and place the insertion point to the left of the text that begins "Chronology."

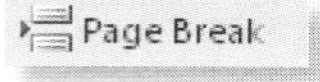

4. Click the **Insert** tab, and click the Page Break button to insert a page break. Word inserts a hard page break and adjusts pagination in the document from this point forward.

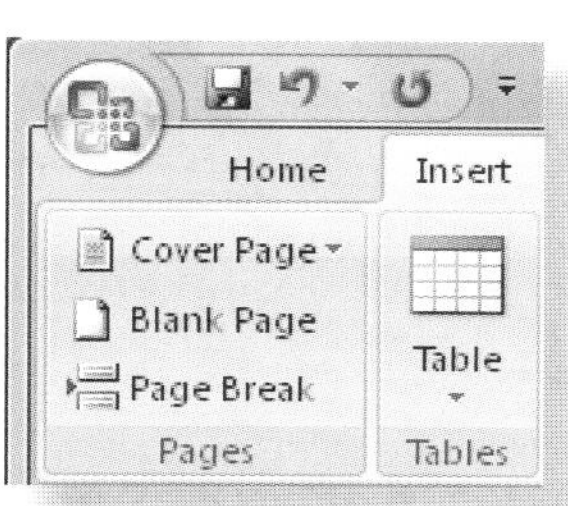

Figure 10-2
Insert tab, Pages group

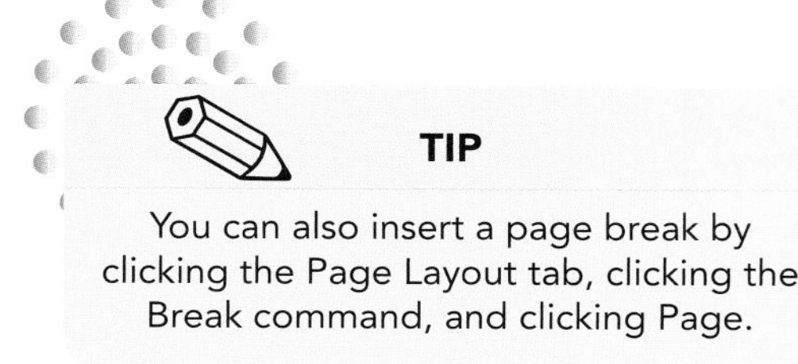

TIP

You can also insert a page break by clicking the Page Layout tab, clicking the Break command, and clicking Page.

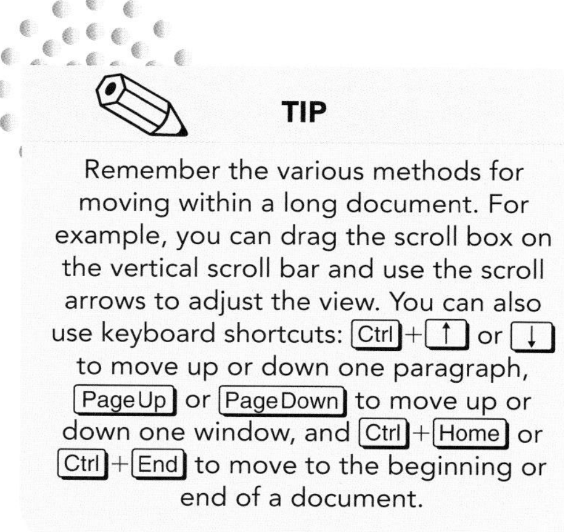

TIP

Remember the various methods for moving within a long document. For example, you can drag the scroll box on the vertical scroll bar and use the scroll arrows to adjust the view. You can also use keyboard shortcuts: Ctrl+↑ or ↓ to move up or down one paragraph, PageUp or PageDown to move up or down one window, and Ctrl+Home or Ctrl+End to move to the beginning or end of a document.

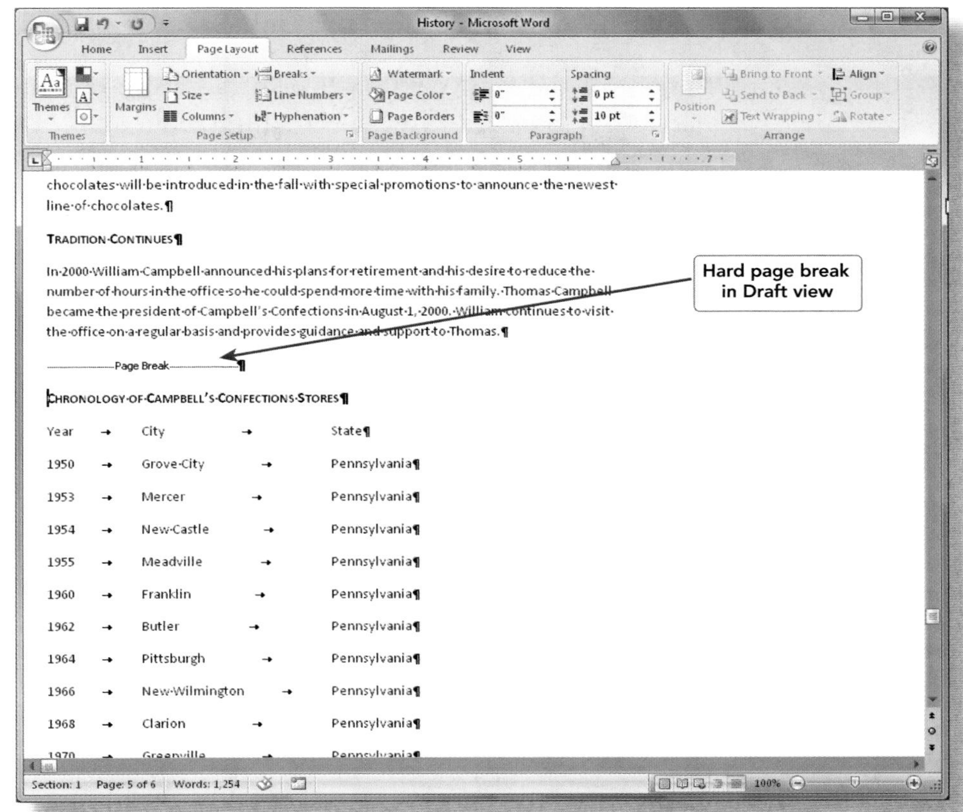

Figure 10-3
Inserting a hard page break

Exercise 10-3 DELETE A HARD PAGE BREAK

You cannot delete a soft page break, but you can delete a hard page break by clicking the page break and pressing Backspace or Delete.

1. Select the page break you just inserted by dragging the I-beam over the page break. Be sure to select the paragraph mark.
2. Press Delete to delete the page break.
3. Scroll back to the hard page break you inserted at the top of page 3. Position the insertion point to the left of "The most popular" and press Backspace two times (one time to delete the paragraph mark and one time to delete the page break). The page break is deleted, and Word adjusts the pagination.

Controlling Line and Page Breaks

To control the way Word breaks paragraphs, choose one of four line and page break options from the Paragraph dialog box:

- *Widow/Orphan control:* A *widow* is the last line of a paragraph and appears by itself at the top of a page. An *orphan* is the first line of a paragraph and appears at the bottom of a page. By default, this option is turned on to prevent widows and orphans. Word moves an orphan forward to the next page and moves a widow back to the previous page.
- *Keep lines together:* This option keeps all lines of a paragraph together on the same page rather than splitting the paragraphs between two pages.
- *Keep with next:* If two or more paragraphs need to appear on the same page no matter where page breaks occur, use this option. The option is most commonly applied to titles that should not be separated from the first paragraph following the title.
- *Page break before:* Use this option to place a paragraph at the top of a new page.

Exercise 10-4 APPLY LINE AND PAGE BREAK OPTIONS TO PARAGRAPHS

1. Close **History** without saving; then reopen the document. Switch to Draft view.
2. At the bottom of page 3, click within the heading "Gourmet Chocolate." You are going to format this heading so it will not be separated from its related paragraph.
3. Click the **Home** tab, and click the **Paragraph Dialog Box Launcher** to open the Paragraph dialog box. Click the **Line and Page Breaks** tab.

TIP

To reopen the file quickly, click the Microsoft Office Button and click the filename **History** under Recent Documents.

Figure 10-4
Line and Page Breaks options in the Paragraph dialog box

4. Click **Keep with next** to select it, and click **OK**. Word moves the soft page break, keeping the two paragraphs together.

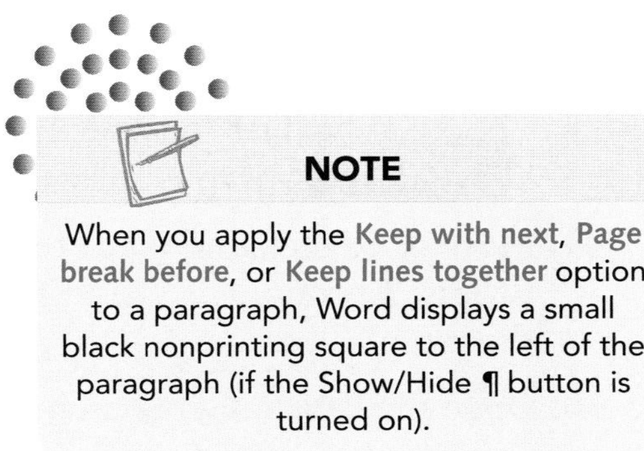

NOTE

When you apply the **Keep with next**, **Page break before**, or **Keep lines together** option to a paragraph, Word displays a small black nonprinting square to the left of the paragraph (if the Show/Hide ¶ button is turned on).

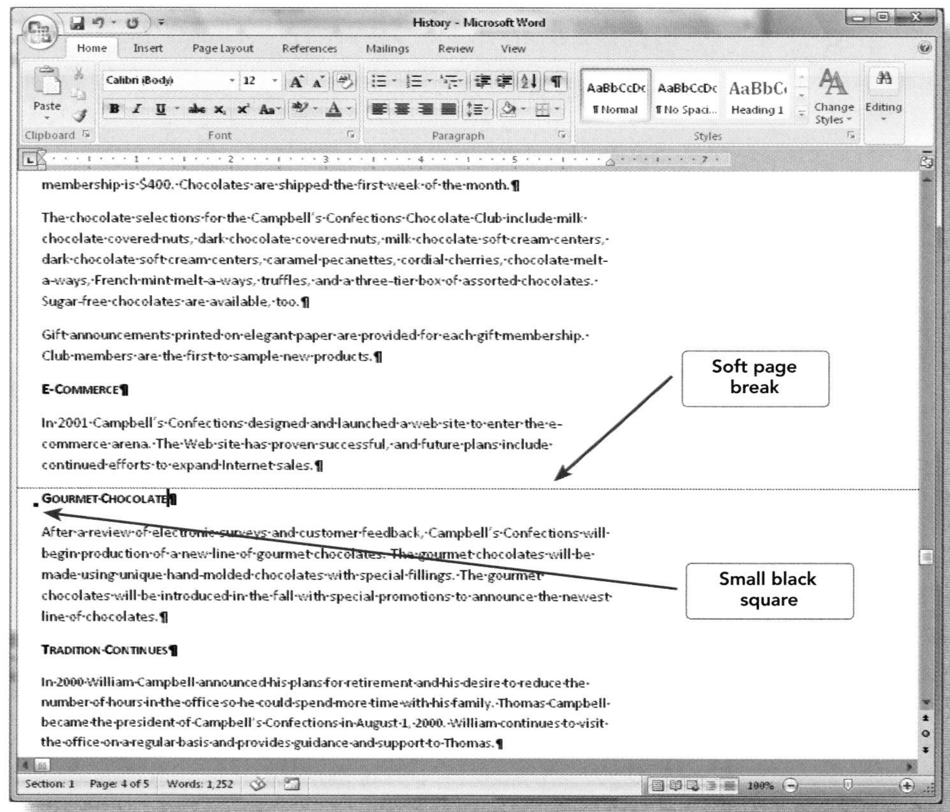

Figure 10-5
Applying the Keep with next option

5. Press Ctrl+Home to go to the top of the document. Select the title, and apply 72 points spacing before.

6. Locate the text at the bottom of page 1 that begins "By 1980." The paragraph is divided by a soft page break.

7. Right-click the paragraph to open the shortcut menu. Click **Paragraph**. Click the **Line and Page Breaks** tab if necessary.

8. Choose **Keep lines together** and click **OK**. The soft page break moves above the paragraphs to keep the lines of text together.

9. Move to page 4, and place the insertion point in the paragraph that begins "Chronology." You will format this paragraph so it begins at the top of the page.

10. Open the **Paragraph** dialog box, click **Page break before**, and click **OK**. Word starts the paragraph at the top of page 5 with a soft page break.

11. Press Shift+F1 to open the **Reveal Formatting** task pane. Click the + to the left of Paragraph to display the paragraph formatting. Notice the link for **Line and Page Breaks**. Close the task pane.

12. Save the document as ***[your initials]*10-4** in a new folder for Lesson 10. Leave it open for the next exercise.

Controlling Section Breaks

Section breaks separate parts of a document that have formatting different from the rest of the document. You may want to insert a section at the beginning of a document to include a title page with special formatting. A separate section is created when you change the left and right margins of selected text.

For better control in creating section breaks, you can insert a section break directly into a document at a specific location by using the Breaks command. You can also specify the type of section break you want to insert. Switch to Draft view to see the double-dotted section break lines.

TABLE 10-1 Types of Section Breaks

Type	Description
Next page	Section starts on a new page.
Continuous	Section follows the text before it without a page break.
Even page or Odd page	Section starts on the next even- or odd-numbered page. Useful for reports in which chapters must begin on either odd-numbered or even-numbered pages.

Exercise 10-5 INSERT SECTION BREAKS BY USING THE BREAKS COMMAND

1. Place the insertion point to the left of the paragraph at the top of page 5 that begins "Chronology."
2. Press Ctrl+Q. This clears the formatting for the paragraph, removing the soft page break you applied earlier.

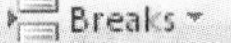

3. Click the **Page Layout** tab, and click the Breaks button. Under **Section Breaks**, click **Continuous**. Word begins a new section on the same page, from the position of the insertion point.
4. Click above and below the section mark. Notice that the section number changes on the status bar but the page number stays the same.

Figure 10-6
Inserting a continuous section break

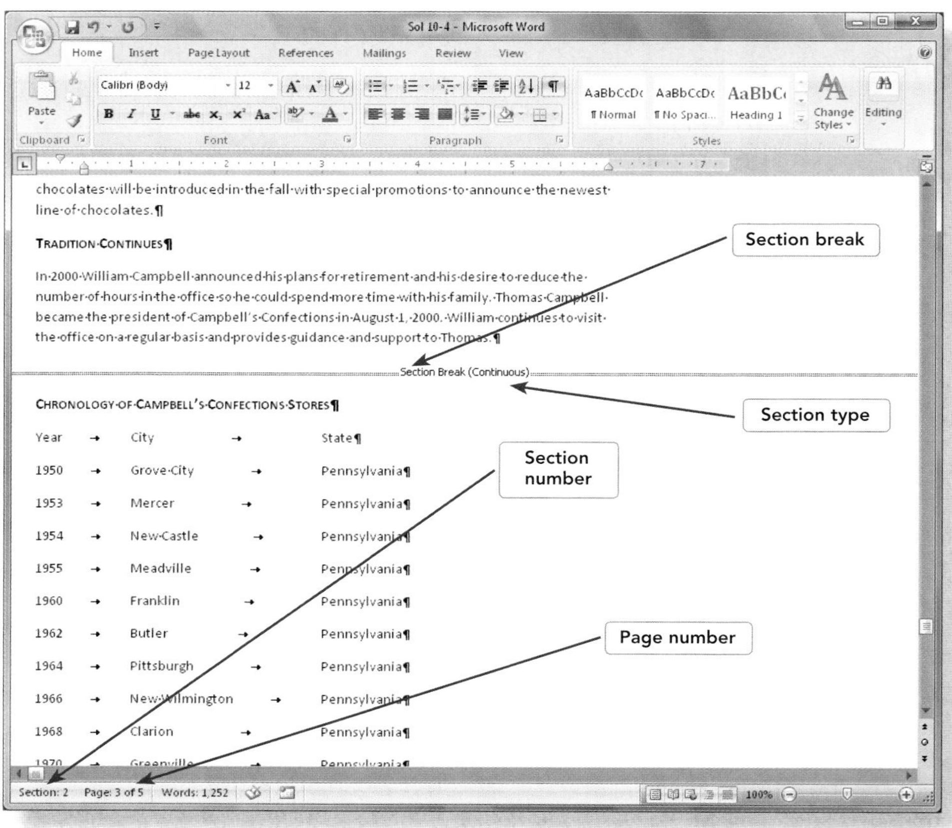

Formatting Sections

After you create a new section, you can change its formatting or specify a different type of section break. This is often useful for long documents, which sometimes contain many sections that require different page formatting, such as different margin settings or page orientation. For example, you can change a next page section break to a continuous section break, or you can change the page orientation of a section, without affecting the rest of the document.

NOTE

The formatting you apply to the section is stored in the section break. If you delete a section break, you also delete the formatting for the text above the section break. For example, if you have a two-section document and you delete the section break at the end of section 1, the document becomes one section with the formatting of section 2.

Exercise 10-6 APPLY FORMATTING TO SECTIONS

1. Position the insertion point before the text "Wholesale" on page 2. Use the **Page Layout** tab, Breaks button to insert a **Next page** section break.

2. With the insertion point in the new section (section 2), open the **Page Setup** dialog box by clicking the **Page Setup Dialog Box Launcher**.

3. Click the **Layout** tab, and click to open the **Section start** drop-down list. From this list you can change the section break from **Next page** to another type.
4. Choose **Continuous** so the section does not start on a new page.

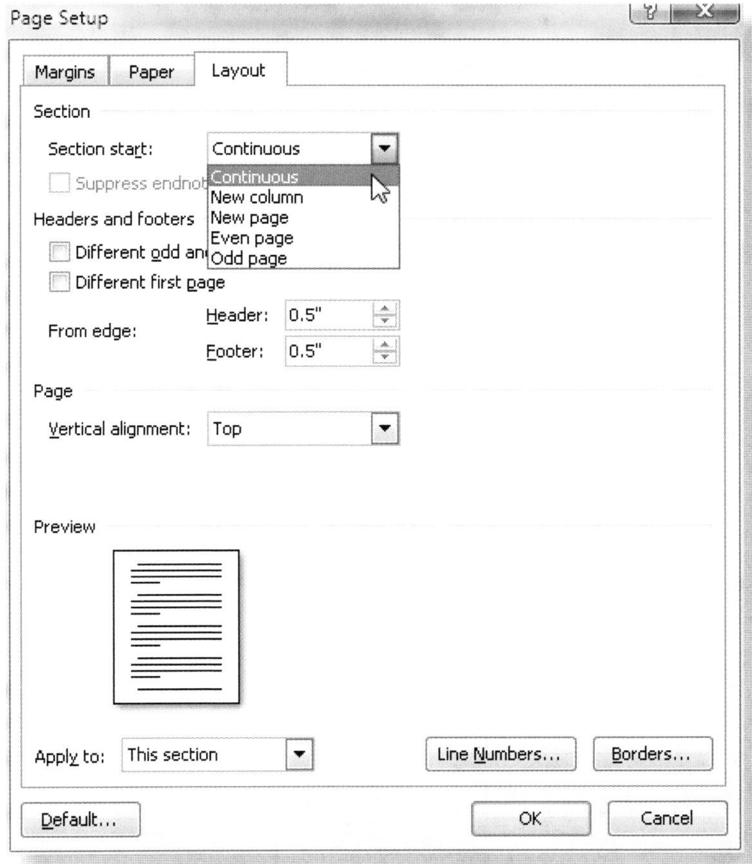

Figure 10-7
Using the Page Setup dialog box to modify the section

5. Click the **Margins** tab.
6. Set 1.5-inch left and right margins. Make sure **This section** appears in the **Apply to** box, and click **OK**. Section 2 of the document now has new margin settings.

Exercise 10-7 CHANGE THE VERTICAL ALIGNMENT OF A SECTION

Another way to format a section is to specify the vertical alignment of the section on the page. For example, you can align a title page so the text is centered between the top and bottom margins. Vertical alignment is a Layout option available in the Page Setup dialog box.

1. Move the insertion point to the last section of the document (which begins "Chronology"). Notice that, because this section does not start on a new page, a page break interrupts the list of stores.
2. Open the **Page Setup** dialog box and click the **Layout** tab.
3. Use the **Section start** drop-down list to change the section from **Continuous** to **New page**.
4. Open the **Vertical alignment** drop-down list and choose **Center**. Click **OK**.

TABLE 10-2 Vertical Alignment Options

Options	Description
Top	Aligns the top line of the page with the top margin (default setting).
Center	Centers the page between the top and bottom margins with equal space above and below the text.
Justified	Aligns the top line of the page with the top margin and the bottom line with the bottom margin, with equal spacing between the lines of text (similar in principle to the way Word justifies text between the left and right margins).
Bottom	Aligns the bottom line of a partial page along the bottom margin.

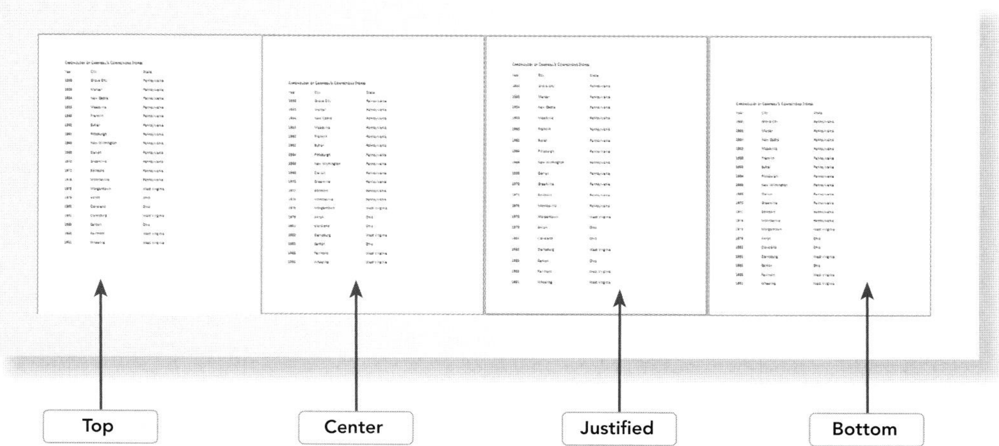

Figure 10-8 Vertical alignment options

Exercise 10-8 CHECK PAGINATION IN PRINT PREVIEW AND PAGE LAYOUT VIEW

After you apply page breaks, section breaks, or section formatting, use Print Preview or Print Layout view to check the document. Viewing the pages in relation to one another provides ideas for improvement before printing.

Remember, you can edit and change the formatting of a document in Print Layout view or Print Preview.

1. Click the **Microsoft Office Button** and click the arrow beside **Print**. Click **Print Preview** to preview the current section. Click the One Page button if necessary. Notice that the text is centered between the top and bottom margins. Notice also that Print Preview does not show the dotted lines of the section breaks, but it does show how the page will look when you print it.
2. While still in Print Preview, open the **Page Setup** dialog box, and change the vertical alignment to **Justified**. Click **OK**. Word justifies the last page of the document so the text extends from the top margin to the bottom margin.
3. Click the Previous Page button to scroll back, page by page, to page 2, section 1, of the document. (Check the status bar for location.)
4. Click the Zoom Level button, choose **Page width** and click **OK**. You cannot see the continuous section break before "Wholesale. . ." but you can check the formatting and see how the document will look when printed.
5. Click the Print Layout View button to close Print Preview and to switch to Print Layout view.
6. Scroll to page 2, section 1. Notice that in Print Layout view, page breaks are indicated by the actual layout of each page as it will look when printed.
7. Click the Zoom Level button on the status bar to open the Zoom dialog box. Click **Many Pages** and click on the grid to display **1 × 2** (one row, two pages). Click **OK**. This reduces the document display so you can see two pages at the same time.

8. Scroll to the end of the document. Click the Draft View button to switch to Draft view. Drag the **Zoom Slider** to **100%** if necessary.

Using the Go To Feature

You use Go To to move through a document quickly. For example, you can go to a specific section, page number, comment, or bookmark. Go To is a convenient feature for long documents—it is faster than scrolling, and it moves the insertion point to the specified location.

There are three ways to initiate the Go To command:

- Click the Home tab, and click the Find or Replace commands to open the Find and Replace dialog box. Click the Go To tab.
- Double-click on the status bar (anywhere to the left of "Words").
- Press Ctrl+G or F5.

Exercise 10-9 GO TO A SPECIFIC PAGE OR SECTION

1. With the document in Draft view, press F5. Word displays the **Go To** tab, located in the Find and Replace dialog box.

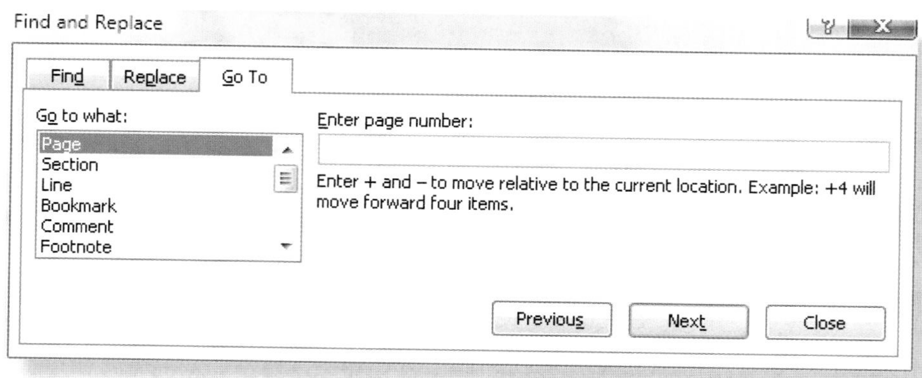

Figure 10-9 Using the Go To feature

2. Scroll through the **Go to what** list to review the options. Choose **Section** from the list, and click **Previous** until you reach the beginning of the document.
3. Click **Next** until the insertion point is located at the beginning of the last section, which is section 3.
4. Choose **Page** from the **Go to what** list and click **Previous**. The insertion point moves to the top of the previous page.
5. Key **2** in the **Enter page number** text box and click **Go To**. The insertion point moves to the top of page 2.
6. **Close** the dialog box.

Exercise 10-10 GO TO A RELATIVE DESTINATION

You can use the Go To command to move to a location relative to the insertion point. For example, with **Page** selected in the **Go to what** list, you can enter "+2" in the text box to move forward two pages from the insertion point. You can move in increments of pages, lines, sections, and so on.

Another option is to move by a certain percentage within the document, such as 50 percent—the document's midpoint.

1. Double-click the word "Page" on the status bar to reopen the Find and Replace dialog box.
2. Choose **Line** from the **Go to what** list, and key **4** in the text box. Click **Go To**. The insertion point moves to the fourth line in the document.

NOTE

You must select Page in the Go to what list to use a percentage.

TIP

You can use the Go To feature to delete a single page of content. Position the insertion point, and open the Find and Replace dialog box. Click the Go To tab, and key **\page** in the text box. Click Go To. Click Close (the text will be highlighted), and press Delete.

3. Key **+35** in the text box, and click **Go To**. The insertion point moves forward 35 lines from the previous location.
4. Key **-35** in the text box, and click **Go To**. The insertion point moves back to the previous location.
5. Click **Page** in the **Go to what** list, key **50%** in the text box, and click **Go To**. The insertion point moves to the midpoint of the document.
6. Close the dialog box.
7. Save the document as ***[your initials]*10-10** in a new Lesson 10 folder.
8. Open the Print dialog box, and choose **4 pages** in the **Pages per sheet** list box. Click **OK**.
9. Close the document.

Lesson 10 Summary

- Pagination is the Word process of flowing text from line to line and from page to page. Word creates a soft page break at the end of each page. When you edit text, you adjust line and page breaks. You can adjust the way a page breaks by manually inserting a hard page break (Ctrl+Enter).
- Delete a hard page break by clicking it and pressing Delete or Backspace.
- The Paragraph dialog box contains line and page break options to control pagination. To prevent lines of a paragraph from displaying on two pages, click in the paragraph and apply the **Keep lines together** option. To keep two paragraphs together on the same page, click in the first paragraph and apply the **Keep with next** option. To insert a page break before a paragraph, click in the paragraph and choose the **Page break before** option.

- Use section breaks to separate parts of a document that have different formatting. Apply a **Next page** section break to start a section on a new page or a **Continuous** section break to continue the new section on the same page. Apply an **Even page** or **Odd page** section break to start a section on the next even- or odd-numbered page.
- Change the vertical alignment of a section by clicking within the section and opening the Page Setup dialog box. On the **Layout** tab, under **Vertical alignment**, choose an alignment (Top, Center, Justified, or Bottom).
- Check pagination in Print Preview or Print Layout view. Scroll through the document or change the zoom level to display a different view.
- Use the Go To command to go to a specific page or section in a document. You can also go to a relative destination, such as the midpoint of the document or the 50th line.

LESSON 10		Command Summary	
Feature	**Button**	**Command**	**Keyboard**
Hard page break	Page Break	**Insert** tab, **Pages** group, **Page Break**	Ctrl+Enter
Line and page break options		**Home** tab, **Paragraph** group, **Paragraph** dialog box, **Line and Page Breaks** tab	
Section breaks	Breaks	**Page Layout** tab, **Page Setup** group, **Breaks** command	
Formatting sections		**Page Layout** tab, **Page Setup** group, **Page Setup** dialog box	
Go To	Find Replace	**Home** tab, **Editing** group, **Find** or **Replace** command, **Go To** tab	Ctrl+G or F5

Lesson 11

Page Numbers, Headers, and Footers

OBJECTIVES

After completing this lesson, you will be able to:

1. Add page numbers.
2. Change the starting page number.
3. Add headers and footers.
4. Work with headers and footers within sections.
5. Link section headers and footers.
6. Change starting page numbers.
7. Create continuation page headers.
8. Create alternate headers and footers.

MCAS OBJECTIVES

In this lesson:

WW 07 1.2.1
WW 07 1.2.2
WW 07 4.1.1
WW 07 4.1.3
WW 07 4.1.4

Estimated Time: 1 1/2 hours

Page numbers, headers, and footers are useful additions to multiple-page documents. Page numbers can appear in either the top or bottom margin of a page. The text in the top margin of a page is a *header;* text in the bottom margin of a page is a *footer*. Headers and footers can also contain descriptive information about a document, such as the date, title, and author's name.

Adding Page Numbers

Word automatically keeps track of page numbers and indicates on the left side of the status bar the current page and the total number of pages in a document. Each time you add, delete, or format text or sections, Word adjusts page breaks and page numbers. This process, called *background repagination,* occurs automatically when you pause while working on a document. Right-click the status bar to select **Formatted Page Numbers**, **Section**, and **Page Number** options when working with long documents.

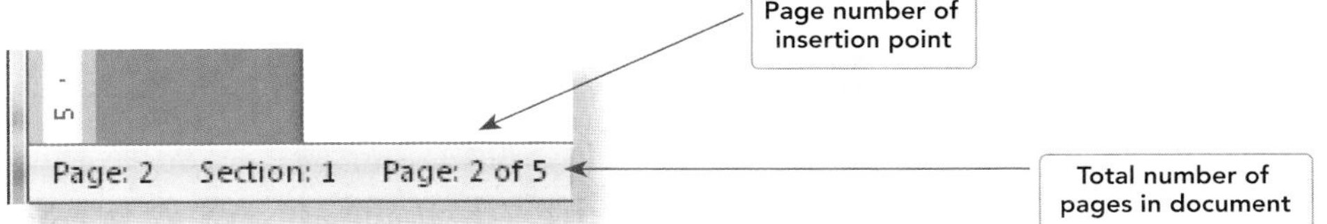

Figure 11-1
How Word paginates when you open a document

Exercise 11-1 ADD AND PREVIEW PAGE NUMBERS

Page numbers do not appear on a printed document unless you specify that they do. The simplest way to add page numbers is to click the Insert tab and click Page Number.

1. Open the file **History**.

2. With the insertion point at the top of the document, click the **Insert** tab and click the **Page Number** command. Word displays a list of options for placing your page number in the document. Notice that you can choose Top of Page, Bottom of Page, or Page Margins. Once you choose a position for the page number, you select a design from the gallery. A *gallery* is a list of design options for modifying elements of a page.

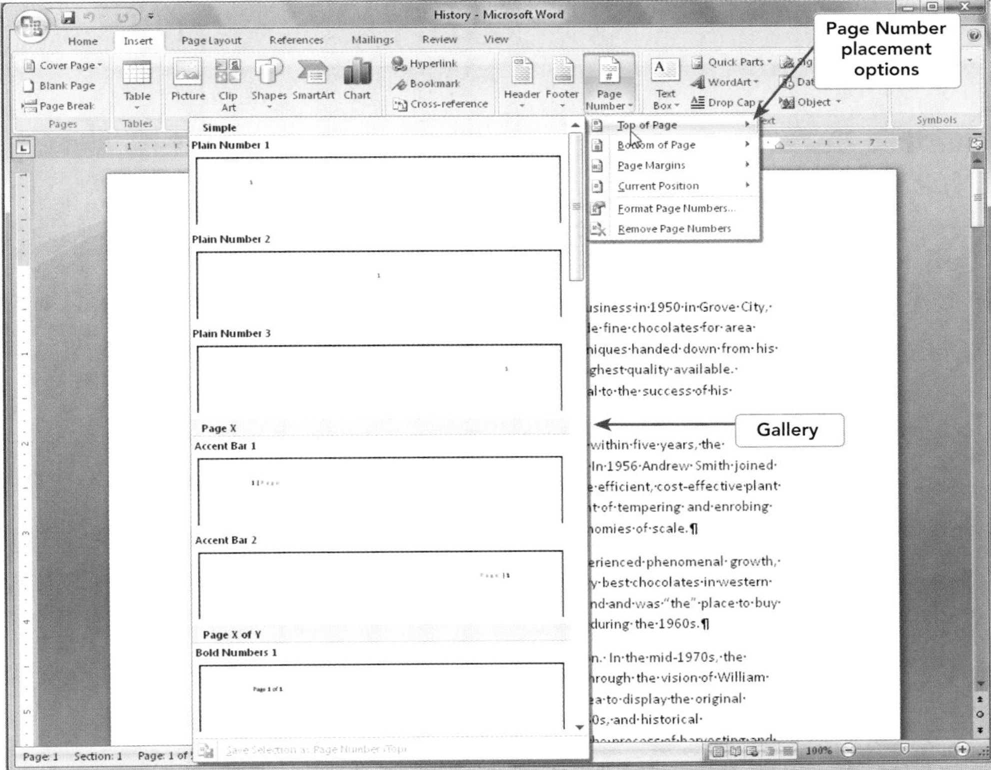

Figure 11-2
Page Number options

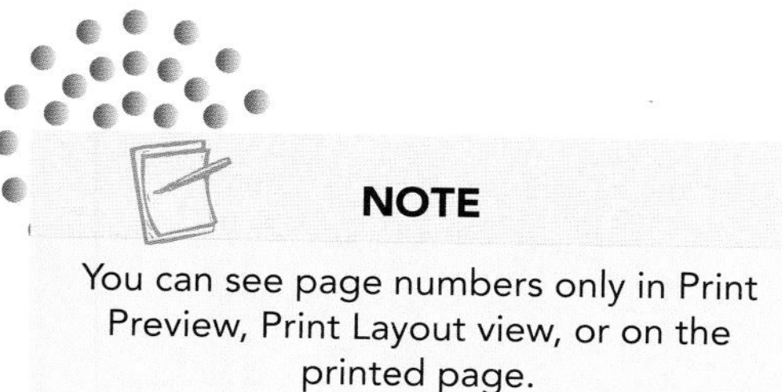

NOTE

You can see page numbers only in Print Preview, Print Layout view, or on the printed page.

3. Click **Top of Page** to display the gallery for placing numbers at the top of the page. Click **Plain Number 3** to place a page number in the upper right corner of the document.
4. Scroll through the document to view the page numbers. By default Word places page numbers on every page.
5. Notice that the **Ribbon** adds a new tab when page numbers have been added to a document. The **Header and Footer Tools Design** tab includes additional options for formatting the document.

6. Click the Close Header and Footer button.
7. Click the **Insert** tab and click the Page Number button. Click **Bottom of Page** and scroll to the bottom of the gallery. Click **Triangle 2**. A page number appears at the bottom right corner of each page.
8. Switch to Print Preview, and notice that page numbers appear in the header and footer of the page.
9. Use the magnifier pointer to click the upper right corner of the first page. The page number appears within the 1-inch top margin. Specifically, the page number is positioned 0.5 inch from the top edge of the page at the right margin.

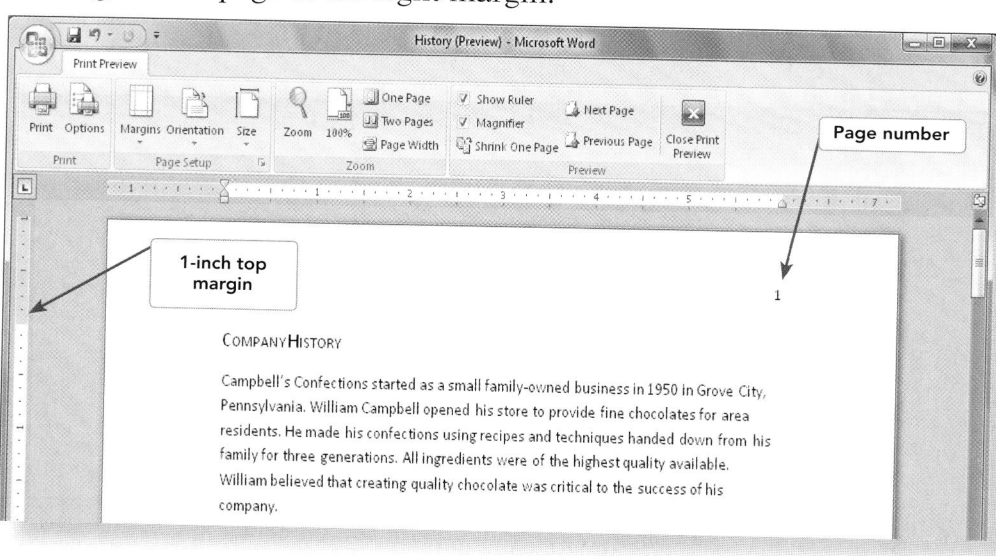

Figure 11-3 Viewing page numbers in Print Preview

NOTE

The available print area varies according to the type of printer. If your footer is not completely visible, ask your instructor about changing the footer position from 0.5 inch to 0.6 inch from the bottom edge of the page.

10. Close Print Preview. Click the Undo button to remove the page number in the footer.

Exercise 11-2 CHANGE THE POSITION AND FORMAT OF PAGE NUMBERS

Not only can you change the placement of page numbers and decide if you want to number the first page, but you can also change the format of page numbers. For example, instead of using traditional numerals such as 1, 2, and 3, you can use Roman numerals (i, ii, iii) or letters (a, b, c). You can also start page numbering of a section with a different value. For instance, you could number the first page ii, B, or 2.

1. Double click the header of page 1. This activates the header pane (the area at the top of the page that contains the page number), displays the Headers and Footer Tools Design tab, and dims the document text.
2. Select the page number, and change the format of the number to italic using the Mini toolbar. Press Ctrl+E to center the number. Click the Undo button to undo the center alignment.

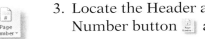

3. Locate the Header and Footer group on the Ribbon. Click the Page Number button and click **Format Page Numbers**.
4. Open the **Number format** drop-down list, and choose uppercase Roman numerals (I, II, III...). Click **OK**.

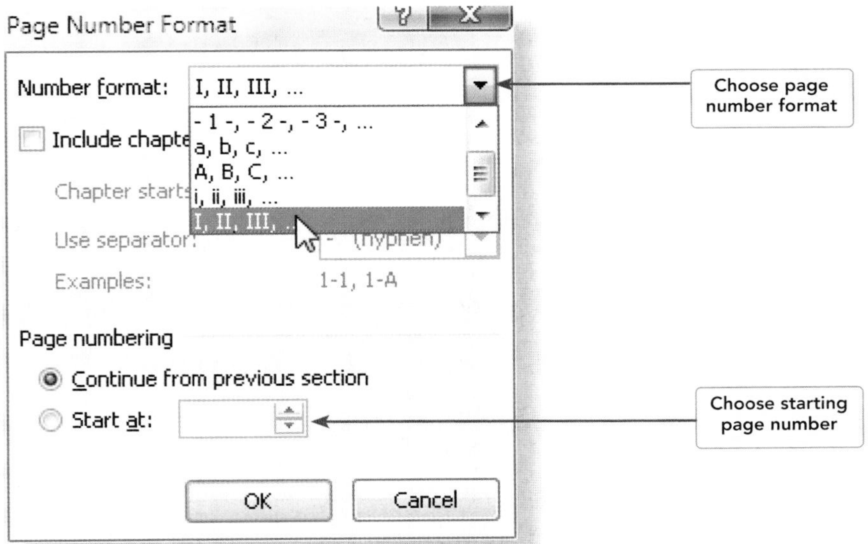

Figure 11-4 Page Number Format dialog box

5. Locate the **Options** group on the Ribbon, and click **Different First Page**. Selecting the Different First Page option removes the page number from page 1 of the document. Click the Close Header and Footer button .

6. View the document in Print Preview, and note that page 1 does not display a page number. The header page numbering is now italic, starting with Roman numeral II on page 2.
7. Close Print Preview.

Changing the Starting Page Number

In addition to formatting page numbers and changing the page number placement, you can change the starting page numbering. You can format a document with a cover page to display no page number on page 1 and define the actual page 2 of the document to display page number 1.

To add a cover page, click the Insert tab and click the Cover Page command. Select a design from the gallery, and the cover page automatically appears at the beginning of the document. You can also insert a blank page by clicking the Blank Page command on the Insert tab.

Exercise 11-3 ADD A COVER PAGE

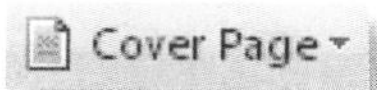

1. Position the insertion point at the beginning of the document. Click the **Insert** tab, and click the Cover Page button. Click the **Sideline** design from the gallery. Click the text "[Type the document title]" and key **History**.
2. Notice that the cover page is not numbered. The second page of the document is numbered page 2.

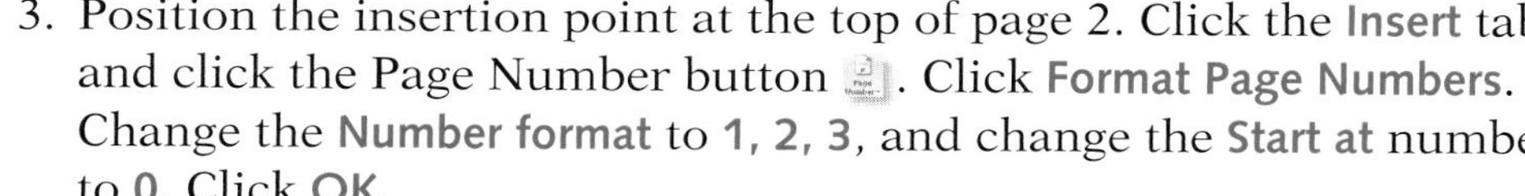

3. Position the insertion point at the top of page 2. Click the **Insert** tab, and click the Page Number button. Click **Format Page Numbers.** Change the **Number format** to **1, 2, 3**, and change the **Start at** number to **0**. Click **OK**.

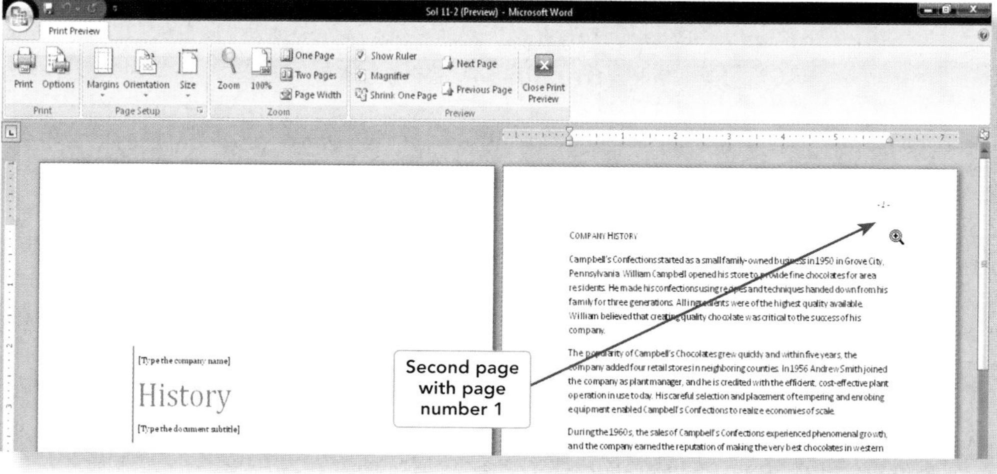

Figure 11-5
Preview page numbers

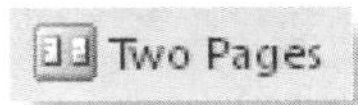

4. Switch to Print Preview, and click the Two Pages button. Notice that the cover page is not numbered and that page numbering starts with 1 on page 2. Close Print Preview.

NOTE

Changing one page number affects all page numbers.

5. Double-click the page number of page 2 of the document. Position the insertion point to the immediate left of the page number. Key **Page** and press Spacebar once.

6. Scroll to the header pane on page 3 to view the revised header text.

Figure 11-6
Formatted page number with "Page" added

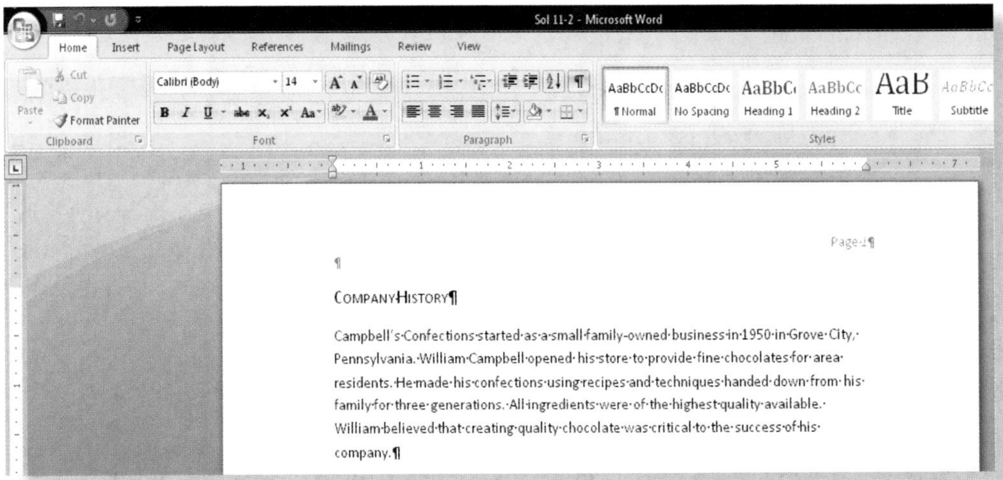

7. Save the document as ***[your initials]*11-3** in your Lesson 11 folder.

Exercise 11-4 REMOVE PAGE NUMBERS

To remove page numbers, delete the text in the header or footer area or click the Remove Page Numbers command.

1. Click the **Insert** tab, and click the Page Number button. Click **Remove Page Numbers**.

2. Scroll the document and notice that the page numbers in the header and footer are deleted.

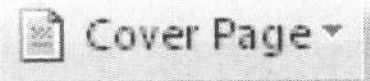

3. Click the Cover Page button, and click **Remove Current Cover Page**.

4. Close the document without saving it.

Adding Headers and Footers

Headers and footers are typically used in multiple-page documents to display descriptive information. In addition to page numbers, a header or footer can contain:

- The document name
- The date and/or the time you created or revised the document
- An author's name
- A graphic, such as a company logo
- A draft or revision number

This descriptive information can appear in many different combinations. For example, the second page of a business letter typically contains a header with the name of the addressee, the page number, and the date. A report can contain a footer with the report name and a header with the page number and chapter name. A newsletter might contain a header with a title and logo on the first page and a footer with the title and page number on the pages that follow.

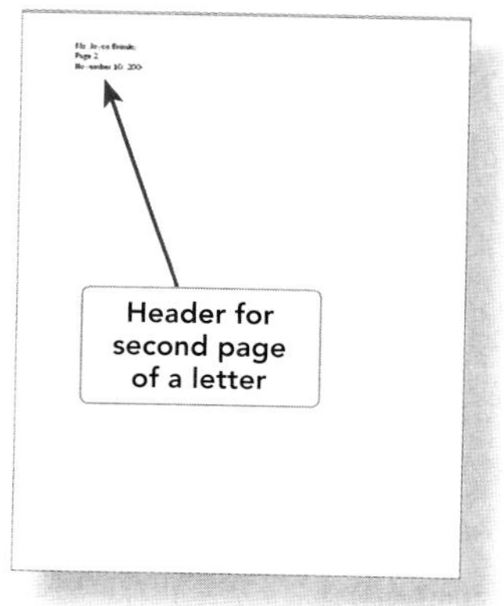

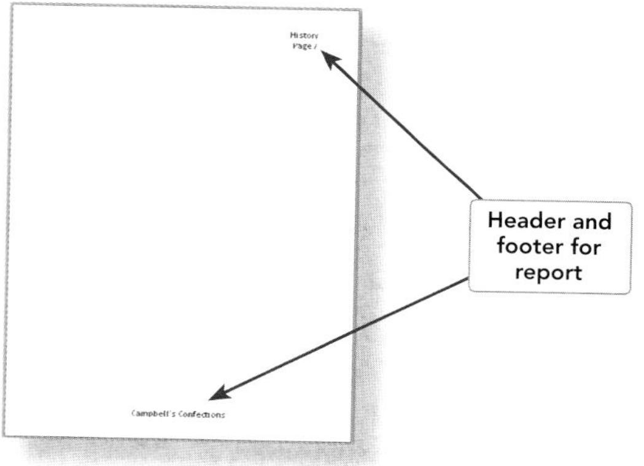

Figure 11-7
Examples of headers and footers

Exercise 11-5 ADD A HEADER TO A DOCUMENT

1. Open the file **History - 2**. This file is a six-page document with a title page. You will add a header and footer to pages 2 through 6.

2. Click the **Insert** tab, and click the Header button. Click the **Blank** design at the top of the Header gallery. Word displays the Header and Footer Tools Design tab, and the header pane is also visible.

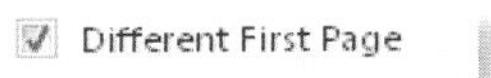

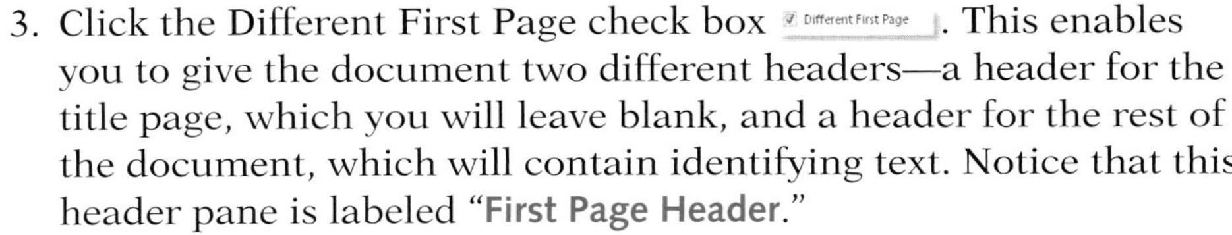

3. Click the Different First Page check box. This enables you to give the document two different headers—a header for the title page, which you will leave blank, and a header for the rest of the document, which will contain identifying text. Notice that this header pane is labeled "**First Page Header**."

Next Section

4. Click the Next Section button. Notice that this header pane is labeled "**Header**." The Previous Section button and the Next Section button are useful when you move between different headers and footers within sections of a document, as you will see later in the lesson.

> **NOTE**
>
> These preset tab settings are default settings for a document with the default 1-inch left and right margins. In such a document, the 3.25-inch tab centers text and the 6.5-inch tab right-aligns text. This document, however, has 1.25-inch left and right margins, so it is best to adjust the tabs.

5. Key **Campbell's Confections History** in the page 2 header pane. This text now appears on every page of the document except the first page.

6. Press Tab once. Notice that the ruler has two preset tab settings: 3.25-inch centered and 6.5-inch right-aligned. Drag the center tab marker to 3 inches on the ruler and the right-aligned tab marker to the right margin (6 inches). Press Tab again to move to the right-aligned tab setting.

Quick Parts

7. Click the Quick Parts button, and click **Building Blocks Organizer**. Click the **Gallery** heading to alphabetize the Building Blocks by Gallery.

8. Scroll through the Building blocks to locate the **Page Numbers** Gallery. Click to select **Bold Numbers 3** (Top of page) and to preview the page number Building Block.

9. Click **Insert**, and notice that the page number displays on the right margin, but the text on the left margin of the header disappeared. Click the Undo button.

10. Click the Quick Parts button, and click **Field**. Scroll the list of **Field names** to locate the **Page** field and click it one time. Click the **1, 2, 3 Format**, and click **OK**. Word inserts the page number. Click to the immediate left of the page number, and key **Page**, and press Spacebar.

Previous Section

11. Click the Previous Section button and notice that the first-page header pane is still blank. Click the Next Section button to return to the header you created.

TABLE 11-1 Header and Footer Tools Design Tab

Button	Name	Purpose
Header	Header	Edit the document header.
Footer	Footer	Edit the document footer.
Page Number	Insert Page Number	Insert the page number.
Date & Time	Date and Time	Insert the current date or time.
Quick Parts	Quick Parts	Insert common header or footer items, such as running total page numbers (for example, page 1 of 10).
Picture	Picture	Insert a picture from a file.
Clip Art	Clip Art	Insert clip art.
Go to Header	Go to Header	Activates header for editing.
Go to Footer	Go to Footer	Activates footer for editing.
Previous Section	Previous Section	Show the header or footer of the previous section.
Next Section	Next Section	Show the header or footer of the next section.
Link to Previous	Link to Previous	Link or unlink the header or footer in one section to or from the header or footer in the previous section.
Different First Page	Different First Page	Create a header and footer for the first page of the document.
Different Odd & Even Pages	Different Odd and Even Pages	Specify a header or footer for odd-numbered pages and a different header or footer for even-numbered pages.
Show Document Text	Show Document Text	Display or hide the document text.
Header from Top: 0.5"	Header from Top	Specify height of header area.
Footer from Bottom: 0.5"	Footer from Bottom	Specify height of footer area.
Insert Alignment Tab	Insert Alignment Tab	Insert a tab stop.

Exercise 11-6 ADD A FOOTER TO A DOCUMENT

1. With the header on page 2 displayed, click the Go to Footer button to display the footer pane.
2. Key your name and press Tab.
3. Save the document as ***[your initials]*11-6** in your Lesson 11 folder.
4. With the insertion point at the center of the footer, click the Quick Parts button on the Header and Footer Tools Design tab. Click **Field**. The Field dialog box displays.
5. Click **CreateDate** from the **Field names** list. Click the third item in the **Date formats** list. Click **OK**. A field is inserted that displays the date the document was created.
6. Press Tab and click Quick Parts. Click **Field** and scroll the list of **Field names** to locate **FileName**. Click **FileName** and notice that a list of **Field properties** appears. Click **First capital**. Click **OK**.

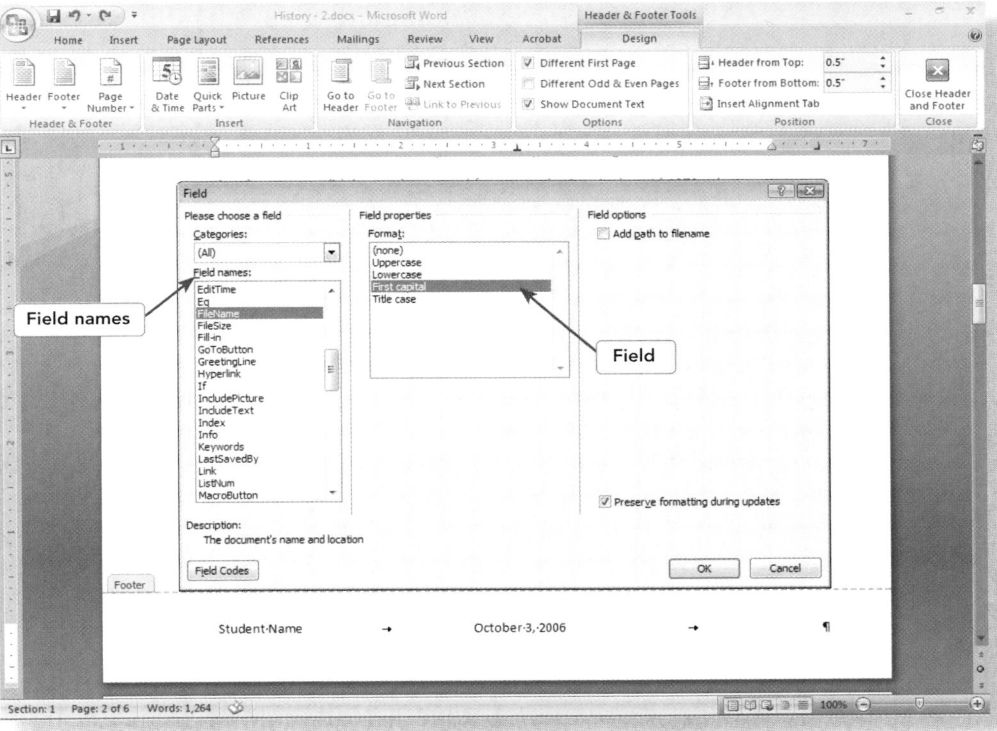

Figure 11-8
Field format

7. View the footer text. The document's filename is inserted. This footer information prints at the bottom of each page except the first.

8. Improve the tab positions by dragging the center tab marker to 3 inches and the right tab marker to 6 inches. (Remember, this document has 1.25-inch left and right margins, not the default 1-inch margins.)

9. Click the Close Header and Footer button to return to the document.

10. Switch to Print Preview. Check that no header or footer appears on the title page. Scroll through each page and view the header and footer.

11. Return to Page Layout view and save the document. Leave it open for the next exercise.

Adding Headers and Footers within Sections

Section breaks have an impact on page numbers, headers, and footers. For example, you can number each section differently or add different headers and footers.

When you add page numbers to a document, it is best to add the page numbers first and then add the section breaks.

Exercise 11-7 ADD SECTIONS TO A DOCUMENT WITH HEADERS AND FOOTERS

1. Delete the hard page break that follows the title page of the document, and insert a Next Page section break.

2. Insert a Next Page section break before the heading "Fundraising" on page 2 of section 2 (page 3 of the document) and a Next Page section break before the heading "Chronology" on page 2 of section 3 (page 5 of the document).

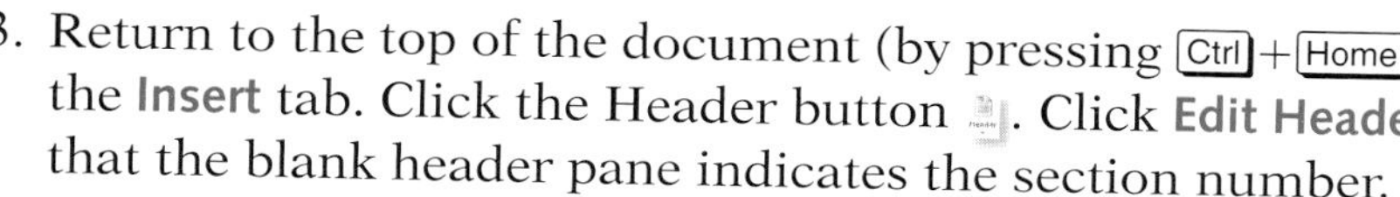

3. Return to the top of the document (by pressing Ctrl+Home), and click the **Insert** tab. Click the Header button. Click **Edit Header**. Notice that the blank header pane indicates the section number.

4. Click the Next Section button to move to the next header, in section 2, page 1. Notice that this header is also blank, because the Page Setup option **Different First Page** was selected for the entire document. This means the first page of each section can have a different header or footer than the rest of the pages in the section or it can have no header or footer.

5. Click the Next Section button [Next Section] again to move to section 2, page 2. The header and footer begin on page 3.

6. Click the Next Section button [Next Section] to move to section 3, page 1. Because the **Different First Page** option applies to the document, the first page of this section also has no header or footer.

7. Turn off the **Different First Page** option for section 3 by clicking the Different First Page button [Different First Page] on the Ribbon to clear the check box. Now page 1 of section 3 starts with the document header and footer. Turning off this option applies only to this section, as you will see in the next step.

[✓ Different First Page]

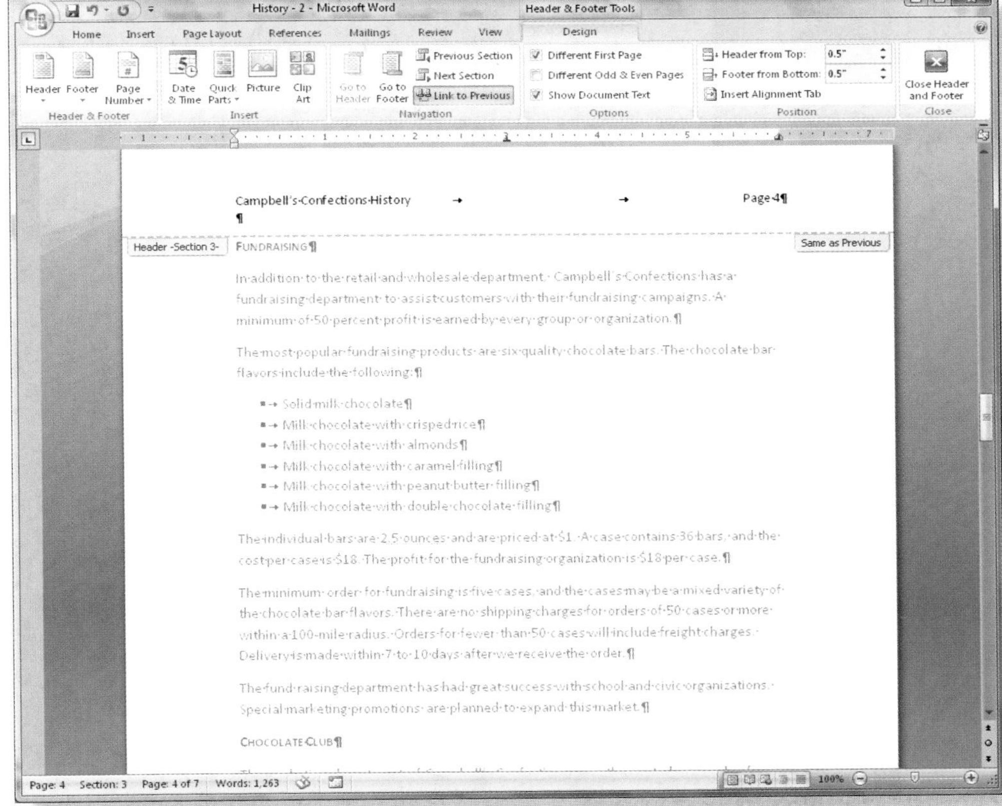

Figure 11-9
The header on page 1, section 3, of the document

[Previous Section]

8. Click the Previous Section button [Previous Section] twice to move to the header on page 1 of section 2. Notice that the header pane is still blank because the **Different First Page** option is still checked for this section.

9. Repeat step 7 to turn off the **Different First Page** option for this section. Now the header and footer start on page 1 of section 2. Repeat for section 4.

10. View each header in the document by dragging the scroll box (on the vertical scroll bar) down one page at a time. As you display each page's header, notice the page numbering. Also notice that the text "Same as Previous" appears on the header panes.

Linking Section Headers and Footers

By default, the Link to Previous command is "on" when you work in a header or footer pane. As a result, the text you originally enter in the header (and the footer) for the document is the same from section to section. Any change you make in one section header or footer is reflected in all other sections. You can use the Link to Previous command to break the link between header/footer text from one section to another section and enter different header or footer text for a section.

NOTE

Breaking the link for the header does not break the link for the footer. You must unlink them separately.

Exercise 11-8 LINK AND UNLINK SECTION HEADERS AND FOOTERS

1. Scroll to the header for section 3, page 1, select the text "Campbell's Confections History" and apply italic formatting.
2. Click the Previous Section button to move to the header in section 2. The header text is italic, demonstrating the link that exists between section headers and footers.
3. Click the Next Section button to return to section 3, page 1. Click the Link to Previous button to turn off this option. Now sections 2 and 3 are unlinked and you can create a different header or footer for section 3.

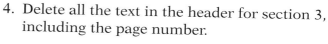

Link to Previous

TIP

To select text in a header or footer, you can point and click from the area to the immediate left of the header or footer pane.

4. Delete all the text in the header for section 3, including the page number.
5. Press Tab to move to the center tab setting and key **Supplement**. Press Tab again and click the **Quick Parts** button. Click **Field**, and select **Page** in the **Field names** list box. Select the first number format, and click **OK**. Drag the center tab marker to 3 inches and the right tab marker to 6 inches, as needed.

6. Click the Go to Footer button to switch to the footer. The footer text between sections 2 and 3 is still linked, so click the Link to Previous button to break the link.

Previous Section

Next Section

7. Delete all the footer text in section 3 except your name. Click the Previous Section button to see that the original footer text is still in section 2. Click the Next Section button to return to the section 3 footer.

NOTE

By default, page numbering continues from the previous section.

8. Click the Link to Previous button to restore the link between section footers. When Word asks if you want to delete the current text and connect to the text from the previous section, click **Yes**.

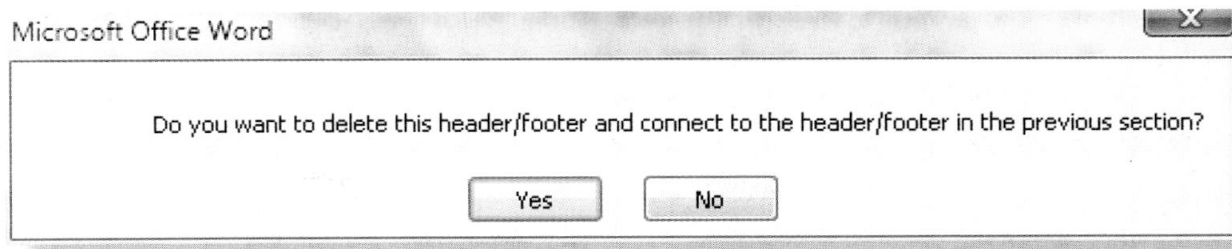

Figure 11-10 Restoring the link between section footers

9. With the link and the original footer text restored, click the Close Header and Footer button.
10. Format the title page attractively. Adjust page breaks throughout the document as needed.
11. Save the document as ***[your initials]*11-8**. Print the document six pages per sheet.

Changing the Starting Page Number

So far, you have seen page numbering start either with 1 on page 1 or 2 on page 2. When documents have multiple sections, you might need to change the starting page number. For example, in the current document, section 1 is the title page and the header on section 2 begins numbering with page 2. You can change this format so numbering starts in section 2, page 1, with page 1.

Exercise 11-9 CHANGE THE STARTING PAGE NUMBER

1. Double-click the page number on section 2, page 1 to display the header.

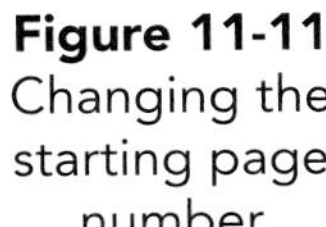

2. Click the Page Number button, and click **Format Page Numbers** to open the Page Number Format dialog box.
3. Change the **Start at** number to **1**.

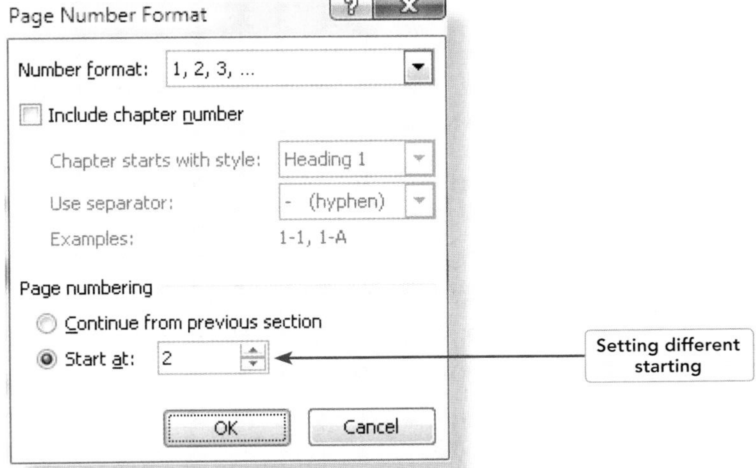

Figure 11-11 Changing the starting page number

4. Click **OK**. Section 2 now starts with page 1.

5. Click the Next Section button to move to section 3. Click the Link to Previous button and click **Yes** to restore the header from the previous section.

NOTE

You can change the starting page number for any document, with or without multiple sections. For example, you might want to number the first page of a multiple-page document "Page 2" if you plan to print a cover page as a separate file.

6. Open the **Page Number Format** dialog box. Choose the option **Continue from previous section** if necessary. Click **OK**. Notice that the section header begins with page 3.
7. Save the document as ***[your initials]*11-9** in your Lesson 11 folder.
8. Submit and close the document.

Creating Continuation Page Headers

It is customary to use a header on the second page of a business letter or memo. A continuation page header for a letter or memo is typically a three-line block of text that includes the addressee's name, the page number, and the date.

There are three rules for letters and memos with continuation page headers:

- Page 1 must have a 2-inch top margin.
- Continuation pages must have a 1-inch top margin.
- Two blank lines must appear between the header and the continuation page text.

Exercise 11-10 ADD A CONTINUATION PAGE HEADER TO A LETTER

The easiest way to create a continuation page header using the proper business format is to apply these settings to your document:

- Top margin: 2 inches.
- Header position: 1 inch from edge of page.
- Page Setup Layout for Headers and Footers: Different First Page.
- Additional spacing: Add two blank lines to the end of the header.

By default, headers and footers are positioned 0.5 inch from the top or bottom edge of the page. When you change the position of a continuation page header to 1 inch, the continuation page appears to have a 1-inch top margin, beginning with the header text. The document text begins at the page's 2-inch margin, and the two additional blank lines in the continuation header ensure correct spacing between the header text and the document text.

1. Open the file **Mendez**.
2. Add the date to the top of the letter, followed by three blank lines.
3. Open the **Page Setup** dialog box, and display the **Layout** tab. Check **Different first page** under **Headers and Footers**. Set the **Header** to 1 inch **From edge**.
4. Click the **Margins** tab, and set a 2-inch top margin and 1.25-inch left and right margins. Click **OK**.
5. Click the **Insert** tab, and click the Header button. Click **Edit Header** to display the header pane.
6. Click the Next Section button to move to the header pane on page 2.
7. Create the header in Figure 11-12, inserting the information as shown. Press Enter twice after the last line.

Figure 11-12

```
Ms. Isabel Mendez

Page [Click Quick Parts, Field, Page for the page number.]

[Click Date and Time for the current date.]
```

TIP

Letters and memos should use the spelled-out date format (for example, December 25, 2007), and the date should not be a field that updates each time you open the document. To insert the date as text, with the correct format, click the Date and Time command and clear the Update automatically check box.

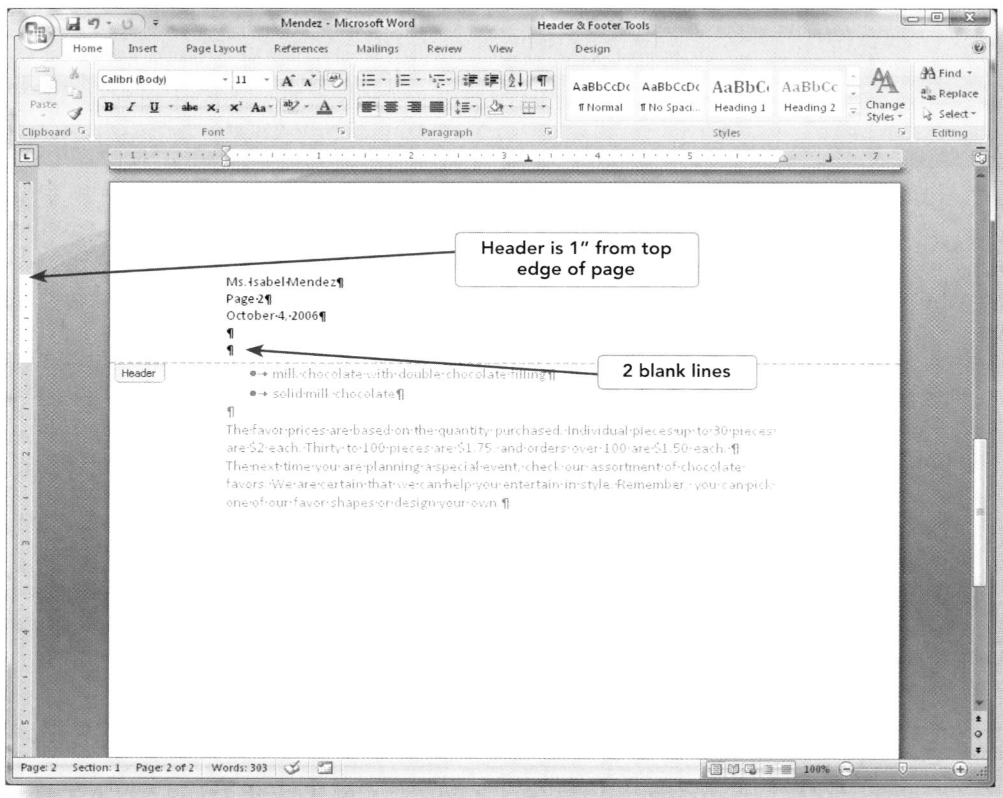

Figure 11-13 Continuation page header for a letter

8. Close the header pane, and view both pages in Print Preview. Close Print Preview.
9. Add a complimentary closing, and key **Lydia Hamrick** and the title **Customer Service** at the end of the letter, followed by your reference initials.
10. Save the document as ***[your initials]*11-10** in your Lesson 11 folder.
11. Submit, and close the document.

Creating Alternate Headers and Footers

In addition to customizing headers and footers for different sections of a document, you can also change them for odd and even pages throughout a section or document. For example, a textbook displays the unit name for even pages and displays the lesson name for odd pages.

Exercise 11-11 CREATE ALTERNATE FOOTERS IN A DOCUMENT

To create alternate headers or footers in a document, you use the **Different odd and even** check box and then create a header or footer for both even and odd pages.

1. Open the file **History - 2**. Delete the page break on page 1 and insert a next page section break.

2. Position the insertion point in section 1, click the **Insert** tab, and click the Footer button.
3. Click **Edit Footer**, and click the Different Odd and Even Pages button. Click the Different First Page button so the first page does not display a footer.
4. Click the Next Section button, and verify that the insertion point is in the Even Page Footer pane.
5. Click the Footer button, and scroll through the gallery. Select **Transcend (Even Page)**. The footer displays on page 2.

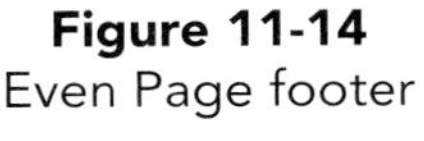

Figure 11-14
Even Page footer

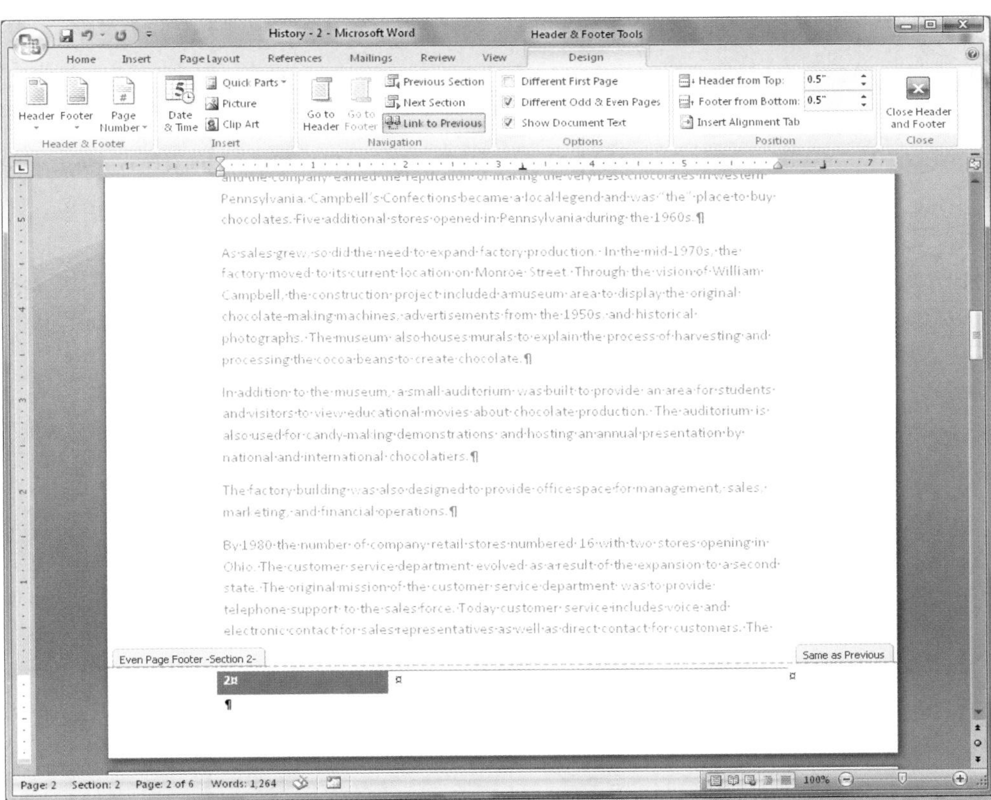

Word 2007

6. Click the Next Section button to move to the footer on page 3. The footer pane is labeled "**Odd Page Footer**" and is blank.

7. Click the Footer button, and scroll through the gallery. Select **Transcend (Odd Page)**. The footer displays on page 3.

8. Click the Close Header and Footer button, and switch to Print Preview.

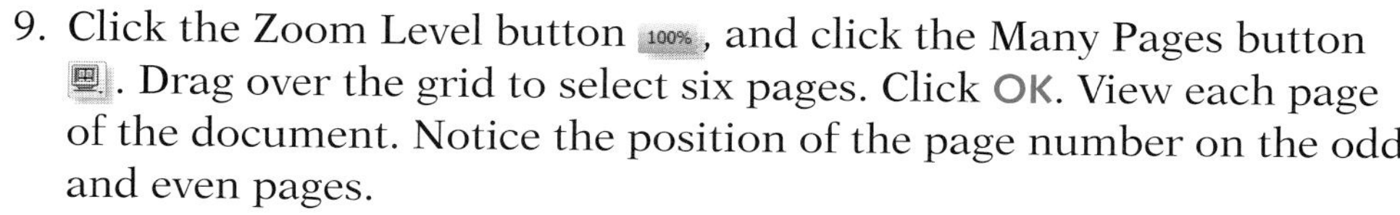

9. Click the Zoom Level button, and click the Many Pages button. Drag over the grid to select six pages. Click **OK**. View each page of the document. Notice the position of the page number on the odd and even pages.

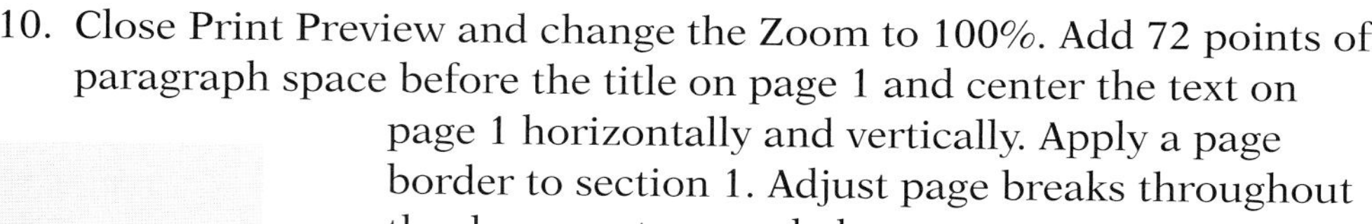

10. Close Print Preview and change the Zoom to 100%. Add 72 points of paragraph space before the title on page 1 and center the text on page 1 horizontally and vertically. Apply a page border to section 1. Adjust page breaks throughout the document as needed.

NOTE

To create different odd and even headers or footers within a section, you must first break the link between that section's header or footer and the previous section's header or footer.

11. Save the document as ***[your initials]*****11-11** in your Lesson 11 folder.

12. Print the document four pages per sheet, or submit the document, and then close it.

Lesson 11 Summary

- A header is text that appears in the top margin of the printed page; a footer is text that appears in the bottom margin. These text areas are used for page numbers, document titles, the date, and other information.
- Always add page numbers to long documents. You can choose the position of page numbers (examples: bottom centered or top right) and the format (examples: 1, 2, 3 or A, B, C). You can also choose to number the first page or begin numbering on the second page.
- Check page numbers in Print Preview or Print Layout view (they are not visible in Draft view). In Print Layout view, you can activate the header or footer pane that contains the page number by double-clicking the text and then modify the page number text (examples: apply bold format or add the word "Page" before the number).
- To remove page numbers, activate the header or footer pane that contains the numbering, select the text, and then delete it. You can also click the Page Number command and select Remove Page Numbers.

- To add header or footer text to a document, click the Insert tab, and click Header or Footer. Select a design from the gallery. Use the Header and Footer Tools Design tab buttons to insert the date and time or to insert Quick Parts for the filename, author, print date, or other information. See Table 11-1.
- Adjust the tab marker positions in the header or footer pane as needed to match the width of the text area.
- A document can have a header or footer on the first page different from the rest of the pages. Apply the Different first page option in the Page Setup dialog box (Layout tab), or use the Different First Page button on the Ribbon, Header & Footer Tools Design tab.
- Header and footer text is repeated from section to section because headers and footers are linked by default. To unlink section headers and footers, click the Link to Previous command. To relink the header or footer, click the button again.
- Sections can have different starting page numbers. Click the Page Number command to open the Page Number Format dialog box, and then set the starting page number.
- Memos or letters that are two pages or longer should have a continuation page header—a three-line block containing the addressee's name, page number, and date. Set the header to 1 inch from the edge, add two blank lines below the header, and use a 2-inch top margin. Apply the Different first page option, and leave the first-page header blank.
- Use the Ribbon, Header and Footer Tools Design Tab, or the Page Setup dialog box to change the position of the header or footer text from the edge of the page. The default position is 0.5 inch.
- A document can have different headers and footers on odd and even pages. Apply the Different odd and even option.

LESSON 11		Command Summary	
Feature	**Button**	**Command**	**Keyboard**
Add page numbers	Page Number	Insert tab, **Page Number**	
Change page number format		Insert tab, **Page Number, Format Page Numbers**	
Add or edit header	Header	Insert tab, **Header**	
Add or edit footer	Footer	Insert tab, **Footer**	
Change layout settings		**Page Layout** tab, **Page Setup** or **Header and Footer Tools Design** tab	

Lesson 12

Styles and Themes

OBJECTIVES

After completing this lesson, you will be able to:

1. Apply styles.
2. Create new styles.
3. Redefine, modify, and rename styles.
4. Use style options.
5. Apply and customize a theme.

MCAS OBJECTIVES

In this lesson:

WW 07 1.1.2
WW 07 1.1.3
WW 07 1.1.4
WW 07 2.1.1
WW 07 2.1.2

Estimated Time: 1 1/4 hours

A *style* is a set of formatting instructions you can apply to text. Styles make it easier to apply formatting and ensure consistency throughout a document.

In every document, Word maintains *style sets*—a list of style names and their formatting specifications. A style set, which is stored with a document, includes standard styles for body text and headings that appear in the Quick Style Gallery. You can apply styles, modify them, or create your own. A *theme* is a set of formatting instructions for the entire document. A theme includes style sets, theme colors, theme fonts, and theme effects. Themes can be customized and are shared across Office programs.

Applying Styles

The default style for text is called *Normal* style. Unless you change your system's default style, Normal is a paragraph style with the following formatting specifications: 11-point Calibri, English language, left-aligned, 1.15-line spacing, 10 points spacing after, and widow/orphan control.

To change the appearance of text in a document, you can apply five types of styles:

- A *character style* is formatting applied to selected text, such as font, font size, and font style.
- A *paragraph style* is formatting applied to an entire paragraph, such as alignment, line and paragraph spacing, indents, tab settings, borders and shading, and character formatting.
- A *linked style* formats a single paragraph with two styles. It is typically used to assign a heading style to the first few words of a paragraph.
- A *table style* is formatting applied to a table, such as borders, shading, alignment, and fonts.
- A *list style* is formatting applied to a list, such as numbers or bullet characters, alignment, and fonts.

Exercise 12-1 APPLY STYLES

There are two ways to apply styles:

NOTE

The keyboard shortcut to open the Styles task pane is Ctrl+Alt+Shift+S.

NOTE

Define a style set before you apply formatting to ensure you are using the appropriate styles.

NOTE

To apply a style to a paragraph, you can simply click anywhere in the paragraph without selecting the text. Remember, this is also true for applying a paragraph format (such as line spacing or alignment) to a paragraph.

- Open the Styles task pane and select a style to apply. To open the Styles task pane, click the Styles Dialog Box Launcher.
- Click the Home tab; click a Quick Style.

1. Open the file **Volume 1**.
2. Click the **Home** tab, and click the **Styles Dialog Box Launcher** to open the Styles task pane. The task pane lists formatting currently used in the document and includes some of Word's built-in heading styles.
3. Click the Change Styles button. Click **Style Set**, and click **Word 2007**.
4. Click in the line "Choc Talk," and place the mouse pointer (without clicking) over the Heading 1 style in the task pane. A ScreenTip displays the style's attributes.
5. Click the **Heading 1** style in the Styles task pane. The text is formatted with 14-point bold Cambria, blue, 24 points spacing before, and 1.15-line spacing.

Figure 12-1
Using the Styles task pane to apply a style

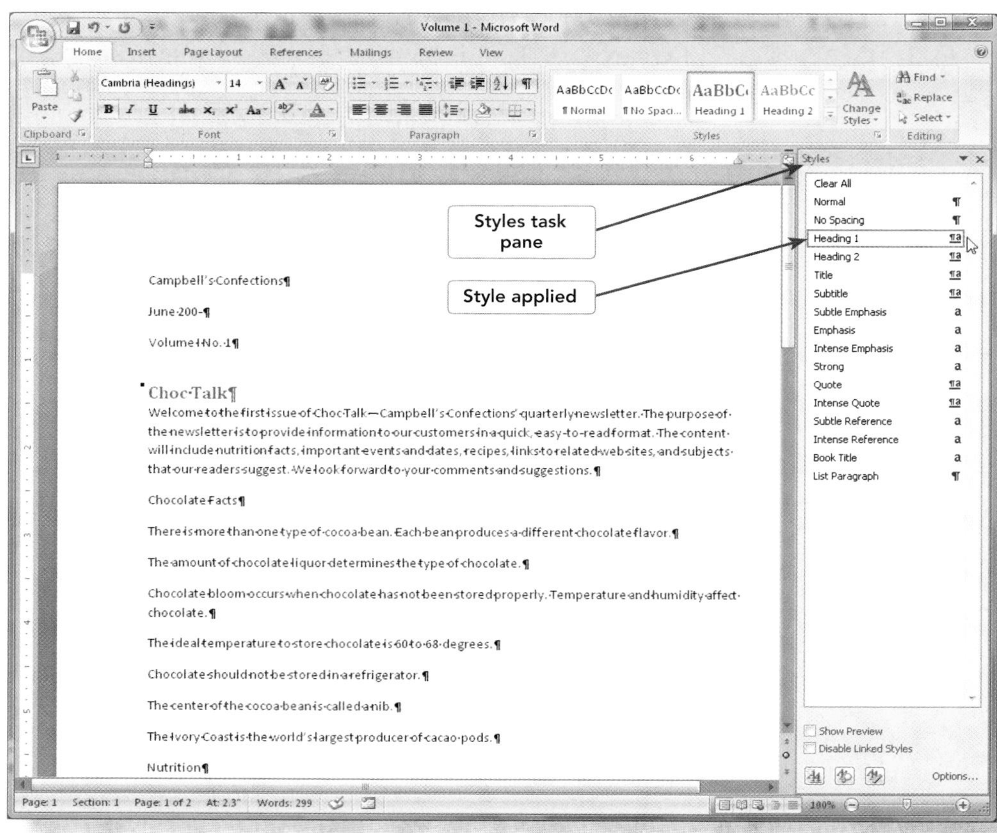

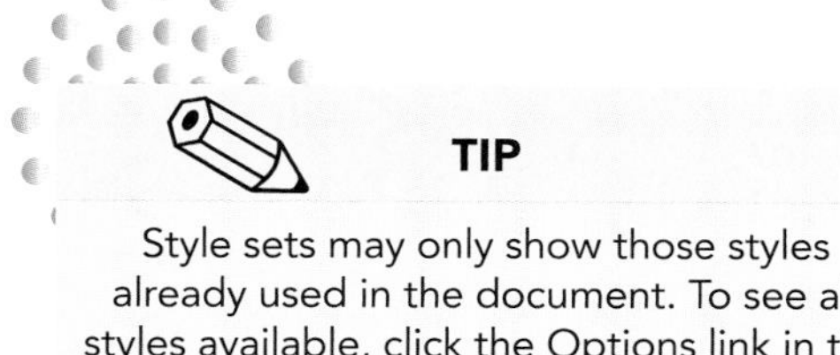

TIP

Style sets may only show those styles already used in the document. To see all styles available, click the Options link in the Style task pane, and click the arrow beside Select styles to Show. Select All styles.

6. Close the Styles task pane by clicking the Styles task pane Close button ×.

7. Position the insertion point in the text "Chocolate Facts."

8. Click the **Home** tab, and locate the **Styles** group. Click the More arrow to display all the styles in the Quick Style Gallery. Move the mouse pointer over each of the quick styles to preview the format.

9. Choose **Heading 2**. Notice the applied formatting.

Figure 12-2
Using the Quick Style Gallery

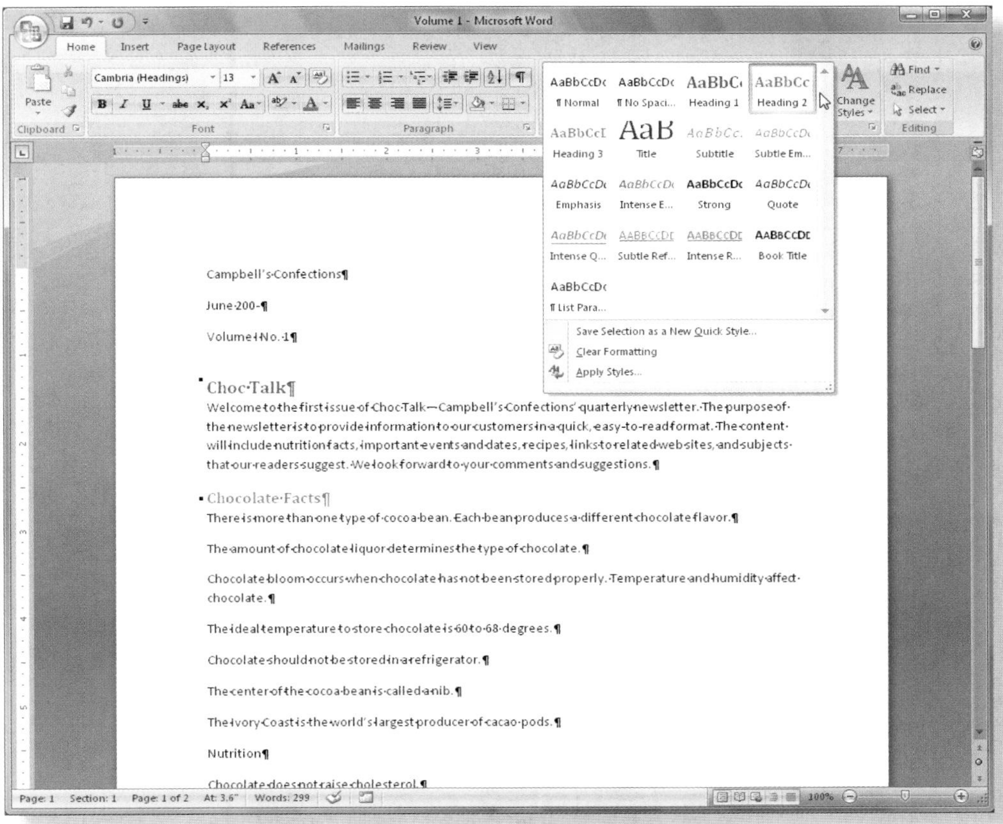

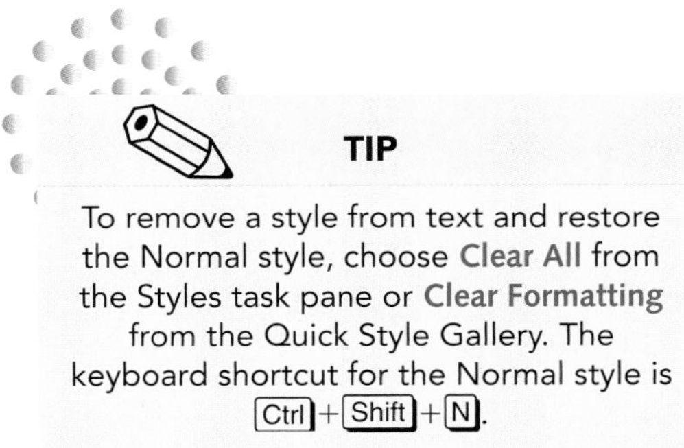

TIP

To remove a style from text and restore the Normal style, choose **Clear All** from the Styles task pane or **Clear Formatting** from the Quick Style Gallery. The keyboard shortcut for the Normal style is Ctrl+Shift+N.

10. Position the insertion point in the heading "Nutrition." Press F4 to repeat the Heading 2 style.

Creating New Styles

Creating styles is as easy as formatting text and then giving the set of formatting instructions a style name. Each new style name must be different from the other style names already in the document.

Word saves the styles you create for a document when you save the document.

Exercise 12-2 CREATE A PARAGRAPH STYLE

There are two ways to create a new paragraph style:

TIP

Click to the left of the text to select the entire paragraph. (Be sure your mouse is in the margin area and the mouse pointer changes into a white arrow.)

- Use the Quick Style Gallery.
- Click the **New Style** button in the Styles task pane.

1. Reopen the Styles task pane by clicking the **Styles Dialog Box Launcher**.
2. Select the heading "Chocolate Facts."
3. Increase the font size to 14 points, and press Ctrl+Shift+K to apply small caps.
4. Click the New Style button  at the bottom of the Styles task pane. The Create New Style from Formatting dialog box opens.
5. Key **Side Heading** in the **Name** box. Verify that **Paragraph** is the **Style type**.

NOTE

Click to select the **Show Preview** check box in the Style task pane to display style names with formatting.

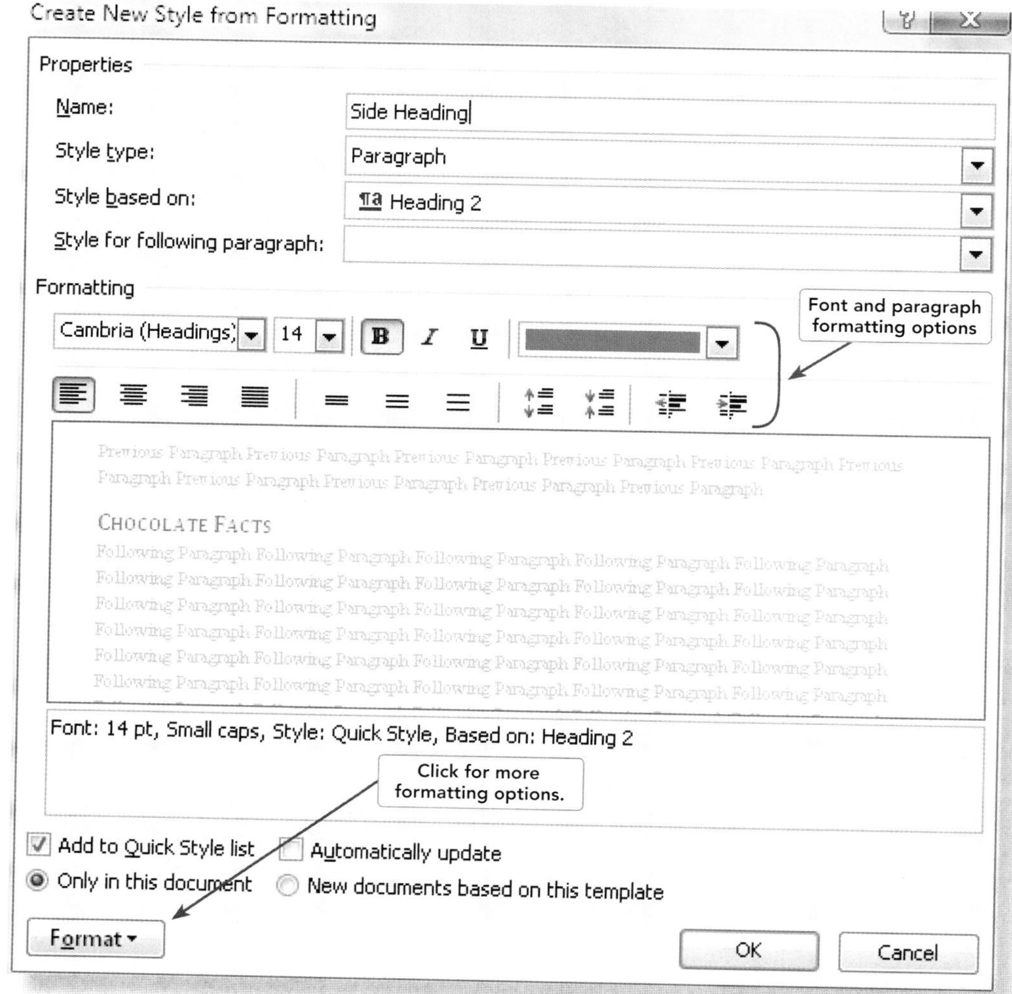

Figure 12-3
Create New Style from Formatting dialog box

NOTE

If you key a style name that already exists in the Style box, you apply the existing style; you do not create a new one.

TIP

Use the Formatting buttons in the New Style dialog box to apply basic font and paragraph formatting. For more formatting options, click the Format button, and choose Font, Paragraph, Tabs, Border, or Numbering to open the corresponding dialog boxes.

6. Notice the two rows of buttons under **Formatting**. The first row is for font formatting, and the second row is for paragraph formatting. Point to the buttons, and notice a ScreenTip appears to identify each button.
7. Click **OK**.
8. Locate the heading "Nutrition." Click in the paragraph, and click the **Side Heading** style in the task pane. The new style is applied.
9. Repeat the formatting to the side headings "Pets and Chocolate" and "Important Chocolate Dates."
10. Select the text "June 200-" and change the font size to 12.
11. Right-click the selected text, and click **Styles** in the shortcut menu. Click **Save Selection as a New Quick Style**.

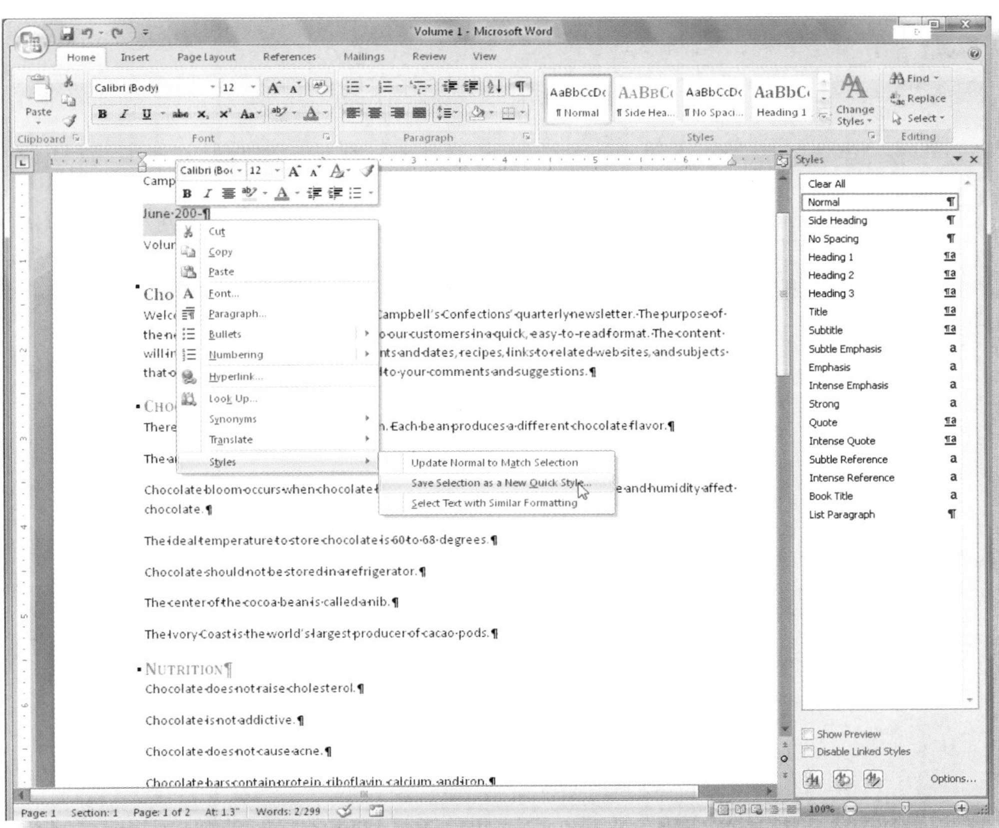

Figure 12-4
Creating a new style

12. Key **Issue Date** in the **Name** box, and click **OK**.
13. Notice that the Side Heading style and the Issue Date style appear in the Style task pane and the Quick Style Gallery.

NOTE

Press Shift+F1 to display the Reveal Formatting task pane. The Reveal Formatting task pane displays formatting of selected text. Expand or collapse the information in the task pane by clicking the plus or minus symbols. Click an underlined link to open a dialog box.

Exercise 12-3 CREATE A CHARACTER STYLE

A character style is applied to selected text and only contains character formatting.

1. Select the text "Choc Talk" in the first paragraph under the heading "Choc Talk." Open the Create New Style from Formatting dialog box and key **Accent** in the **Name** box.
2. Choose **Character** from the **Style type** drop-down list box.
3. Click the **Format** button, choose **Font**, and set the formatting to 11-point Calibri and italic.
4. Click **OK** to close the Font dialog box. Click **OK** to close the Create New Style from Formatting dialog box. The selected text is formatted, and the Accent style appears in the task pane.
5. Note that a character style is applied to selected text, not the entire paragraph.

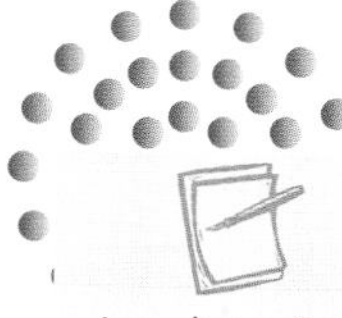

NOTE

In a list of styles, paragraph styles display a paragraph symbol (¶) and character styles display a text symbol (a) to the right of the style name. Linked styles display with a paragraph symbol (¶) and a text symbol (a).

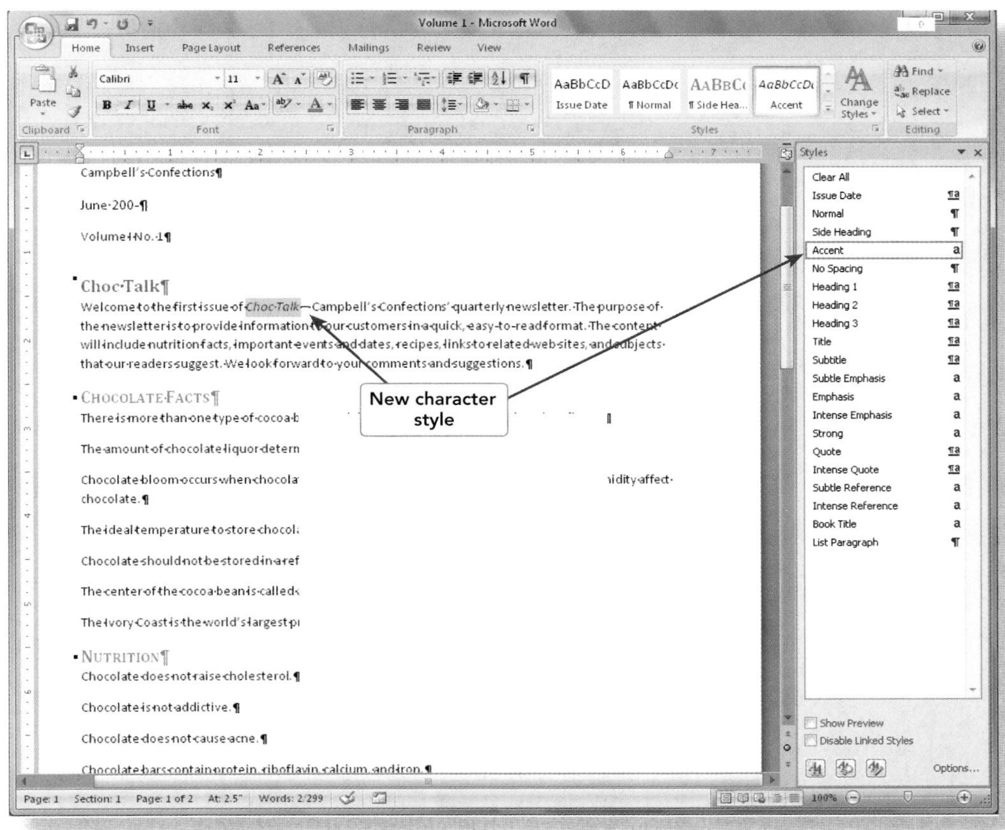

Figure 12-5
Applying the character style

6. Save the document as ***[your initials]*12-3** in a new folder for Lesson 12. Do not print the document; leave it open for the next exercise.

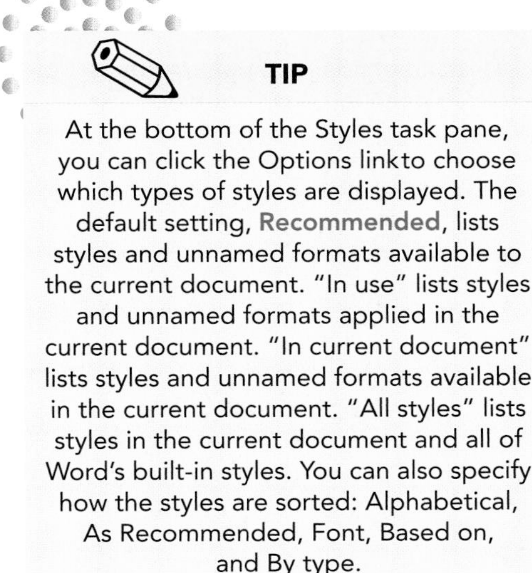

TIP

At the bottom of the Styles task pane, you can click the Options linkto choose which types of styles are displayed. The default setting, **Recommended**, lists styles and unnamed formats available to the current document. "In use" lists styles and unnamed formats applied in the current document. "In current document" lists styles and unnamed formats available in the current document. "All styles" lists styles in the current document and all of Word's built-in styles. You can also specify how the styles are sorted: Alphabetical, As Recommended, Font, Based on, and By type.

Modifying and Renaming Styles

After creating a style, you can modify it by changing the formatting specifications or renaming the style. When you modify a style, the changes you make affect each instance of that style. You can quickly replace one style with another by using the Replace dialog box.

NOTE

You can modify any of Word's built-in styles as well as your own styles. However, you cannot rename Word's standard heading styles.

Exercise 12-4 MODIFY AND RENAME STYLES

To modify a style, right-click the style in the Styles task pane and then choose Modify. Or select the styled text, modify the formatting, right-click the style name in the Styles task pane, and choose Update to Match Selection.

1. In the Styles task pane, right-click the style name **Heading 1**. Choose **Modify** from the drop-down list.
2. In the **Modify Style** dialog box, change the point size to 18, and click **OK** to update the style.
3. Select the text "June 200-" and open the **Paragraph** dialog box. Change the spacing after to 0 points and click **OK**. Right-click the style name **Issue Date** in the task pane. Choose **Update Issue Date to Match Selection**. The style is updated to match the selected text formatting.

TIP

Instead of using the right mouse button to open the drop-down list of style options, you can use the left mouse button to click the down arrow next to a style name. Remember, if you click a style name (not its down arrow) with the left mouse button, you will apply the style to the text containing the insertion point.

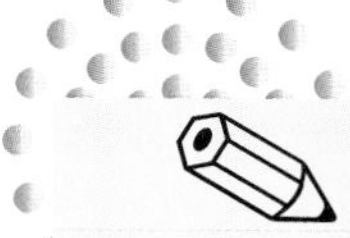

TIP

You can also click the Select All button in the Styles task pane to select all instances of a style.

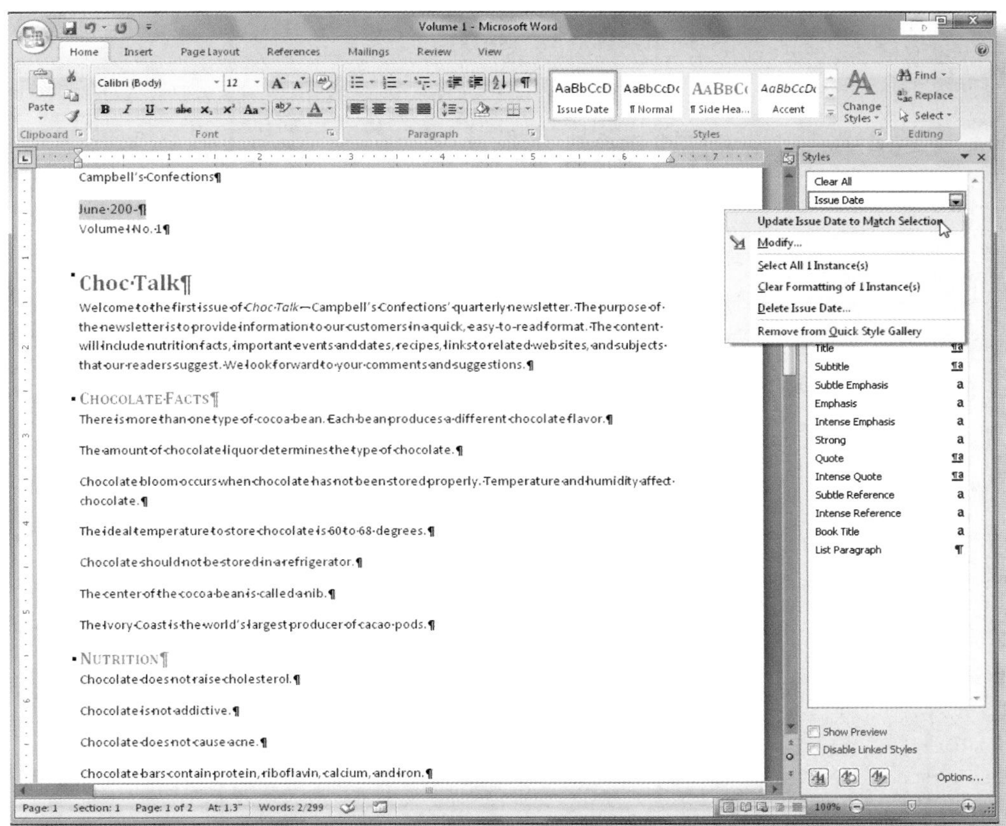

Figure 12-6
Modifying a style by updating it

NOTE

After modifying or renaming a style, you can undo your action (for example, click Undo from the Quick Access toolbar).

4. Position the insertion point in the text "June 200-." Right-click the **Issue Date** style in the task pane and choose **Modify**.
5. Rename the Issue Date style by keying **Pub Date** in the **Name** text box. Click **OK**. The style Pub Date appears in the task pane, replacing the style name Issue Date.

Exercise 12-5 REPLACE A STYLE

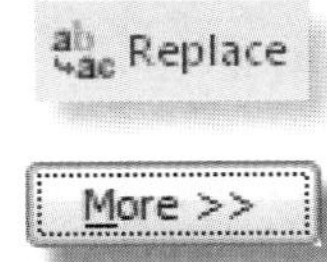

1. Click the Home tab, and locate the **Editing** group. Click the Replace button. Click the **More** button, if needed, to expand the dialog box. Clear any text or formatting from a previous search.
2. Click the **Format** button and choose **Style**. The Find Style dialog box displays.
3. Click **Side Heading** from the **Find what style** list, and click **OK**.

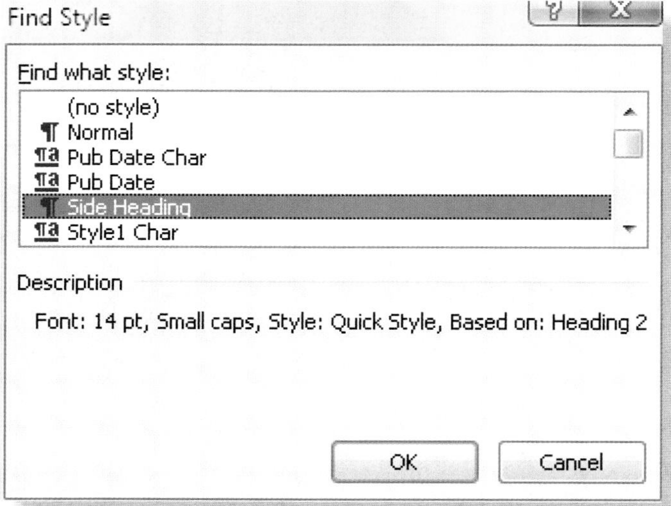

Figure 12-7
Find Style dialog box

TIP

You can also use the Styles task pane to replace one style with another style: Right-click a style name in the task pane, choose **Select All Instances**, and then click another style name in the task pane.

4. Click in the **Replace with** text box, click **Format**, and choose **Style**.
5. Choose **Heading 3** from the **Replace With Style** list, and click **OK**.
6. Click **Replace All**. Word replaces all occurrences of the Side Heading style with the Heading 3 style. Close the Find and Replace dialog box. Notice the change in the format. Click the Undo button.

Exercise 12-6 DELETE A STYLE

1. Click the Manage Styles button at the bottom of the Styles task pane. Click the **Edit** tab. Select the **Pub Date** style in the **Select a style to edit** list box. Click **Delete**.
2. Click **Yes** when prompted to verify the deletion. Click **OK**. The Pub Date style is deleted, and the paragraph returns to Normal, the default style.

NOTE

When you delete a style from the style sheet, any paragraph that contained the formatting for the style returns to the Normal style. You cannot delete the standard styles (Word's built-in styles) from the style sheet.

NOTE

A style deleted from the Quick Style Gallery is not deleted from the Style task pane.

Using Style Options

Word offers two options in the Style dialog box to make formatting with styles easier:

- *Style based on:* This option helps you format a document consistently by creating different styles in a document based on the same underlying style. For example, in a long document, you can create several different heading styles that are based on one heading style and several different body text styles that are based on one body text style. Then if you decide to change the formatting, you can do so quickly and easily by changing just the base styles.

NOTE

The standard styles available with each new Word document are all based on the Normal style.

- *Style for following paragraph:* This option helps you automate the formatting of your document by applying a style to a paragraph and specifying the style that should follow immediately after the paragraph. For example, you can create a style for a heading and specify a body text style for the next paragraph.

Exercise 12-7 USE THE STYLE FOR FOLLOWING PARAGRAPH OPTION

1. Go to the end of the document, and position the insertion point in the blank paragraph above "Copyright."

2. Click the **New Style** button in the Styles task pane.
3. Key **StaffName** in the **Name** text box.
4. Click **Format** and choose **Font**. Set the font to 11-point Cambria and click **OK** to close the Font dialog box. Click **OK** to close the Create New Style from Formatting dialog box.
5. Click the **New Style** button in the Styles task pane. Key **StaffTitle** in the name box. The **Style type** is **Paragraph**, and change the **Style based on** to **Normal**. Click **Format** and choose **Font**. Set the font to 12-point Calibri, with bold and small caps, and click **OK**.

6. Check that the Align Left button is selected. Change the spacing after to 0 points and the line spacing to single. Click the arrow for **Style for following paragraph**, and select **StaffName**. Click **OK**.

Figure 12-8
Choosing a style for the following paragraph

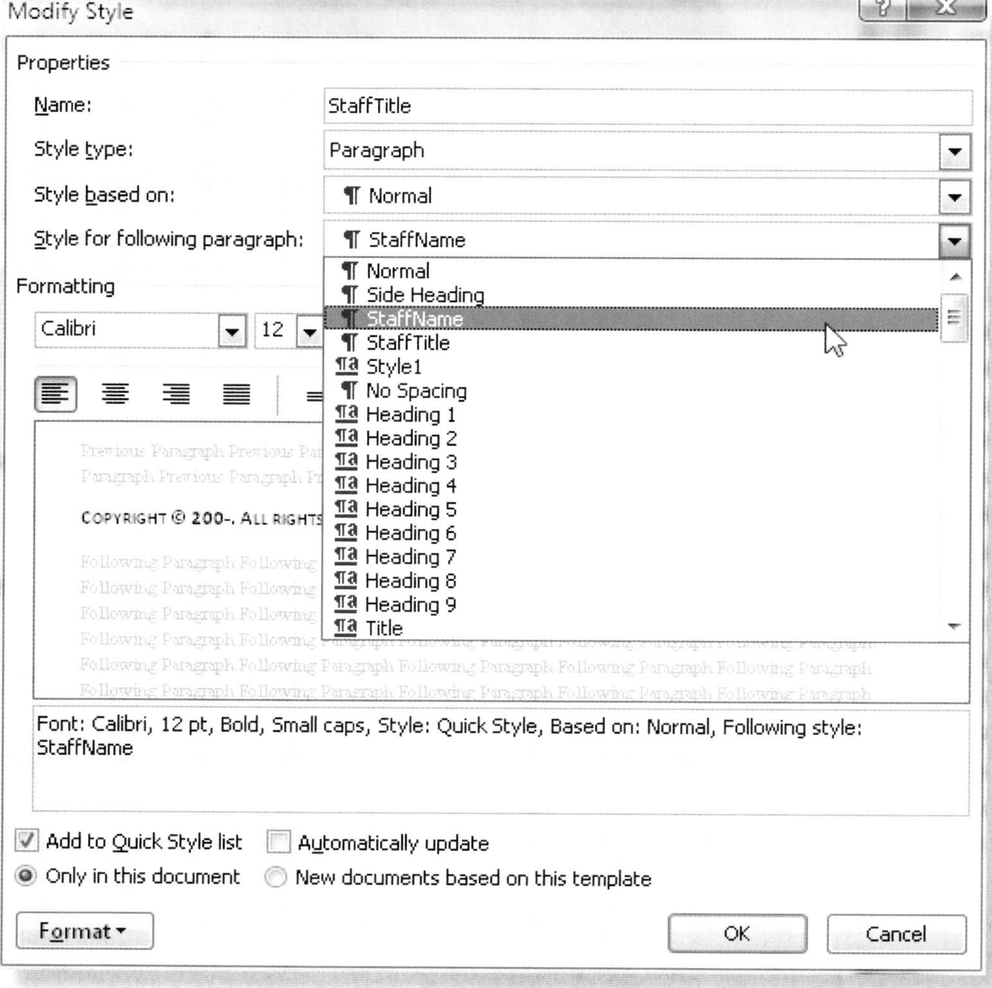

7. Key **President** and apply the **StaffTitle** style. Notice the format of the text. Press Enter. Key **Thomas Campbell**. Notice the change in the style name.
8. Press Enter. Note that the style automatically changes from StaffTitle to StaffName, which was the style indicated as the style for the following paragraph.
9. Key the text shown in Figure 12-9. Apply the appropriate styles.

Figure 12-9

```
Vice President        ← StaffTitle, Enter StaffName
Lynn Tanguay

Editor                ← StaffTitle, Enter StaffName
Margo Razzano
```

Exercise 12-8 USE THE BASED ON OPTION

1. Select the text near the bottom of page 2, from "Choc Talk" to "16127." Click the New Style button on the Style task pane. Key **BaseBody** in the **Name** box. Verify that **Paragraph** is selected for the **Style type**, and **Normal** is selected for **Style based on**.
2. Change the font to Times New Roman, 12 points. Change the paragraph formatting to 0 points spacing after and single spacing. Click **OK** to close the Create New Style from Formatting dialog box.
3. Click the **New Style** button in the task pane.
4. Key **Body2** as the name of the new style. Click the Italic button in the Create New Style from Formatting dialog box to change the font to italic. Check that Basebody appears in the **Style based on** box. Click **OK**.
5. Notice that the selected paragraph(s) are formatted with the Body2 style. Apply the BaseBody text to the text that was formatted by the new style. Deselect the text and press Enter after the ZIP Code.
6. Place the mouse pointer over (without clicking) the Body2 style in the task pane. The ScreenTip indicates that the Body2 style is based on the Basebody style.
7. Click the **New Style** button in the task pane to create another style.
8. Key **Body3** as the name of the new style. Choose **Basebody** from the **Style based on** list, if it is not already selected. Change the font size to 10 points. Click **OK**. Apply the BaseBody text to any text that was formatted by the new style.
9. Select the text from "June 200-" to "Volume 1 No. 1." Apply the Body2 style. Deselect the text.
10. Right-click the style **Basebody** in the task pane and choose **Modify**.
11. Change the font to Calibri. Click **OK**. All the text using or based on the Basebody style changes to Calibri.

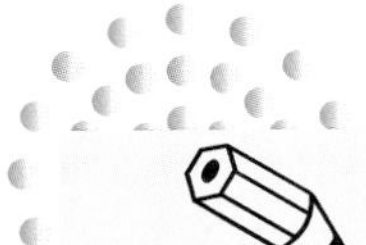

TIP

When you want to use an existing style as the based-on style, select the text with that style before opening the New Style dialog box. The style will automatically appear in the **Style based on** box.

Exercise 12-9 DISPLAY AND PRINT STYLES

To make working with styles easier, you can display a document's styles on the screen and print the style sheet. To see the styles, switch to Draft view.

1. Switch to Draft view. Open the **Word Options** dialog box, and click **Advanced** in the left pane. Scroll to the **Display** group of options.

NOTE

The style area is intended for on-screen purposes in Draft view only (it is not available in Print Layout view). If you switch to Print Preview, this area does not display or appear on the printed document. Additionally, when you display the style area, it will be displayed for any document you open unless you reduce the view to 0 inches. The default Style area width is 0 inches.

2. Set the **Style area width** box to **0.5"** and click **OK**. The style area appears in the left margin.
3. Right-click the Normal style in the Styles task pane. Click **Select All Instance(s)**. Click the Basebody style in the Styles task pane.
4. Select the text under "Chocolate Facts" beginning with "There is" through "cacao pods." Format the list as a bulleted list using a small square bullet.
5. Select the bulleted list you just formatted if necessary. Right-click the selected bulleted list, and select **Styles** from the shortcut menu. Select **Save Selection as a New Quick Style**. Name the style **Basebullet** that is based on Basebody.
6. Apply the Basebullet style to the text under the headings "Nutrition," "Pets and Chocolate," and "Important Chocolate Dates."
7. Change the Heading 2 style so it is based on Basebody. Apply the Heading 2 style to the first line of the document "Campbell's Confections." Move to the last page of the document, and repeat the Heading 2 format for the "Choc Talk" line.

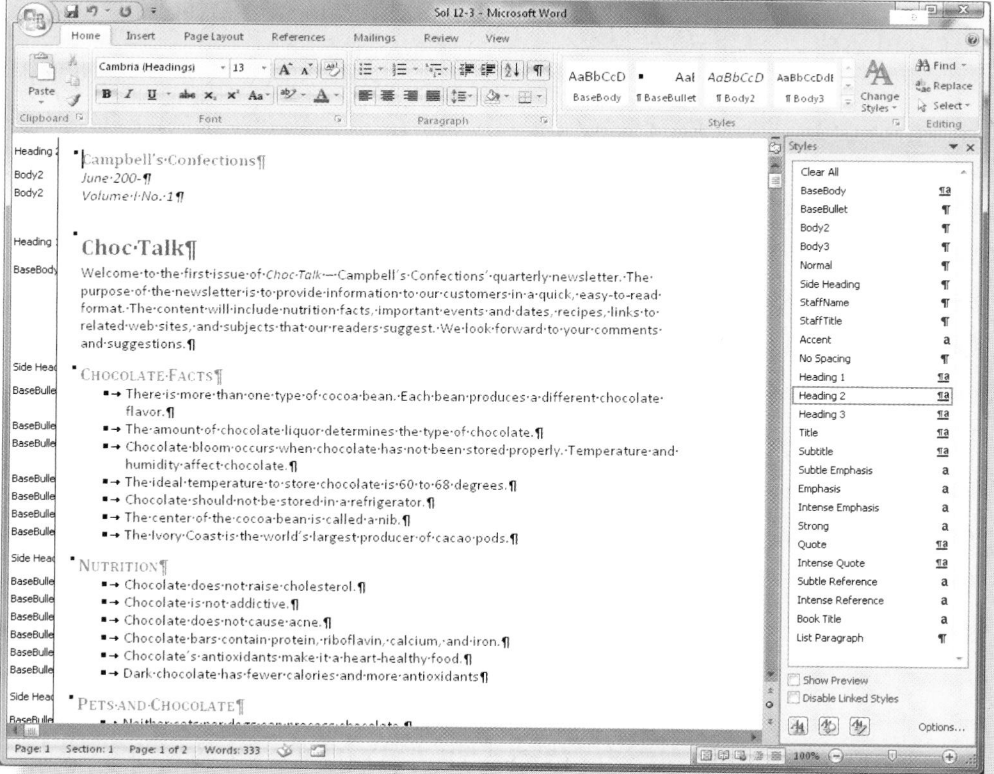

Figure 12-10
Styles shown in style area

NOTE

You can assign a shortcut key to a style you use frequently. In the Styles task pane, right-click the style to which you want to assign a shortcut key. Choose Modify. Click Format, and then click Shortcut key. In the Customize Keyboard dialog box, press an unassigned keyboard combination, such as Alt+B for a body text style. The shortcut key is saved with the document.

8. Open the **Word Options** dialog box, and click **Advanced**. Scroll to the **Display** section, and set the **Style area width** box to **0"** and click **OK**. Switch to Print Layout view.
9. Save the document as ***[your initials]*12-9** in your Lesson 12 folder.
10. Open the **Print** dialog box. Choose **Styles** from the **Print what** drop-down list and click **OK**. Word prints the styles for your active document.
11. Submit the document.

Exercise 12-10 CHANGE STYLE SET

Word provides several style sets to format your document. The number and types of styles available varies for each style set.

1. Position the insertion point at the top of the document. Click the Change Styles button and click **Style Set**. The default style set is currently selected. Click **Distinctive**, and scroll through the document to notice the changes in format.
2. Change the style set to the Word 2007 style.
3. Save and close the document.

Apply and Customize a Document Theme

You can use document themes to format an entire document quickly. A gallery of theme designs is available to format your document, or you can go to Microsoft Online for additional theme selections. Themes can also be customized and saved. Themes define the fonts used for body text and the fonts used for headings. For example, the default theme is Office, and Calibri is the default font for body text, and Cambri is the default font for headings. Themes affect the styles of a document.

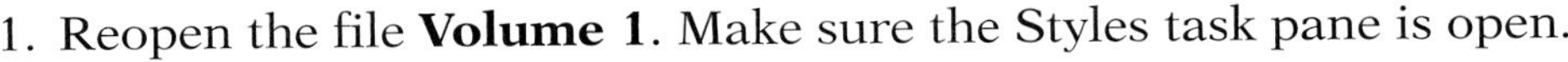

Exercise 12-11 APPLY A THEME

1. Reopen the file **Volume 1**. Make sure the Styles task pane is open.

2. Click the **Page Layout** tab, and click the Themes button. The design gallery for themes displays.

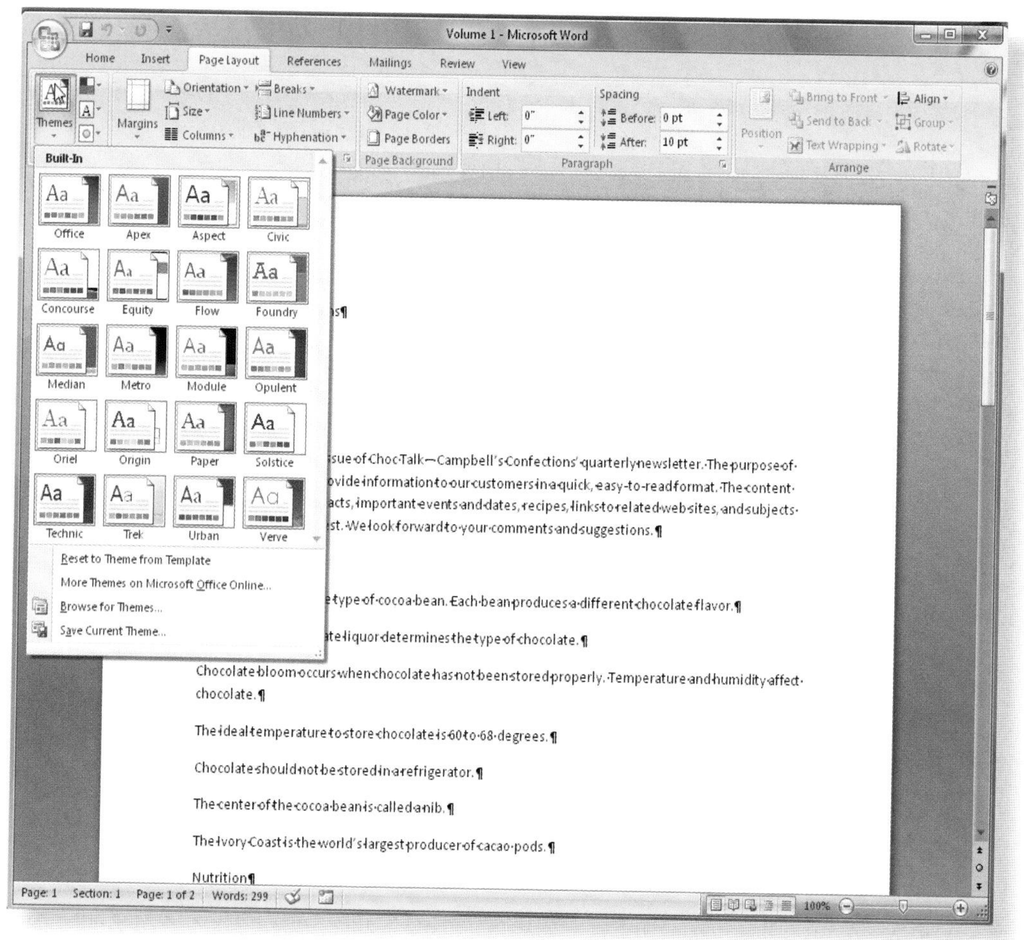

Figure 12-11
Theme gallery

NOTE

The design gallery includes a link for additional themes on Microsoft Office Online.

3. Move your mouse over each of the theme designs and preview the changes in your document. Click the **Technic** theme.
4. Scroll through the document, and notice the changes made. The default body text font is 11-point Arial, and the default heading font is Franklin Gothic Book.
5. View the style names in the Styles task pane. When you change a document theme, styles are updated to match the new theme.
6. Using the new styles, change the text "Campbell's Confections" at the beginning of the document to the Heading 2 style, and change "Choc Talk" to the Heading 1 style.

Exercise 12-12 CUSTOMIZE A THEME

Theme colors include text and background colors, accent colors, and hyperlink colors. The Theme Colors command displays the text and background colors for the selected theme.

1. Click the **Page Layout** tab, and locate the **Theme** group. Click the Theme Colors button. The design gallery for theme colors displays with the current theme colors selected.

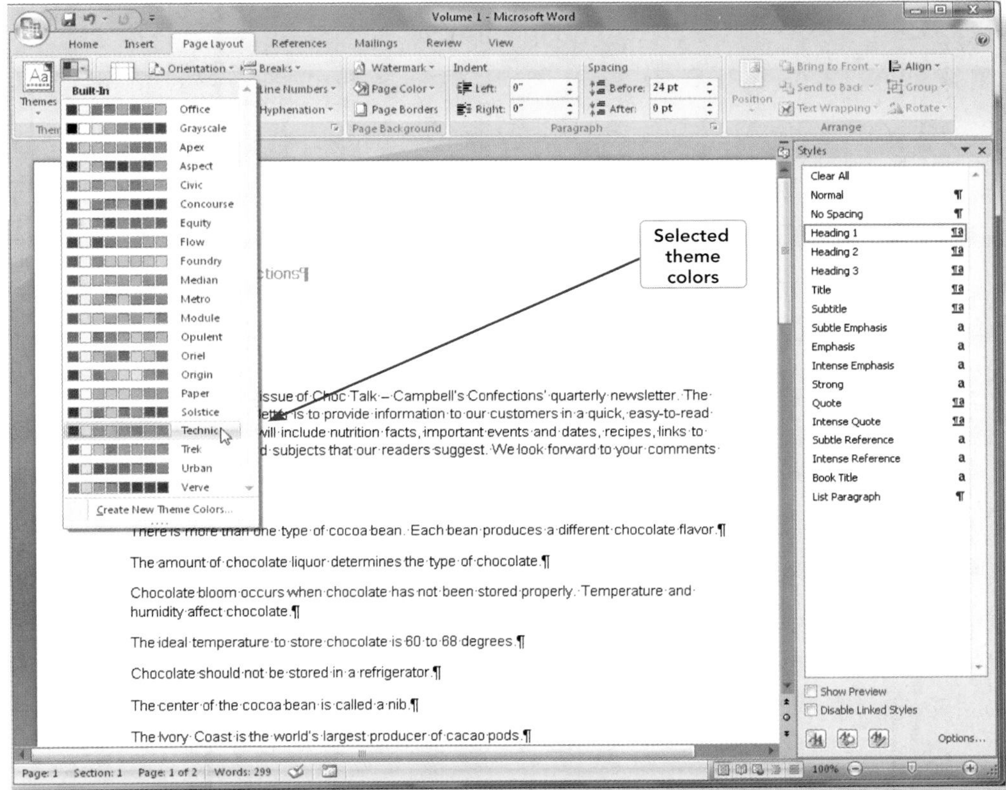

Figure 12-12
Theme colors

2. Click **Create New Theme Colors**. Notice that there is a button for each element of the theme. Click the down arrow beside the Accent 1 button, and notice that the first color in the fifth row of Theme Colors is selected. Click the last color in the fifth row, **Aqua, Accent 1, Darker 50%**. Key **Custom Accent 1** in the **Name** box. Click **Save**. The accent color for the heading text in the document changes.

Figure 12-13
Create New Theme Colors dialog box

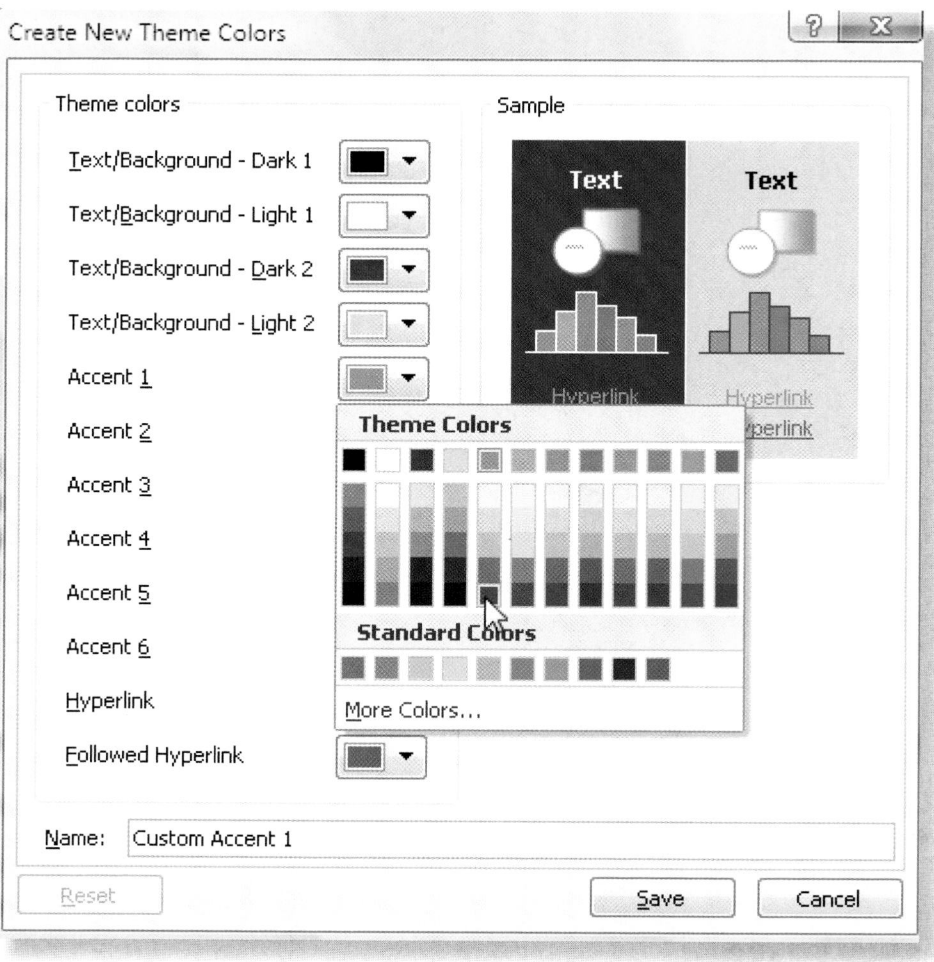

NOTE

The Sample area of the Create New Theme Colors dialog box displays the color changes for each element you change.

3. Click the Theme Colors button and notice that the Custom Accent 1 theme color appears at the top of the list. Right-click the Custom Accent 1 color, and click **Delete**. Click **No**.

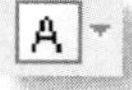

4. Click the **Page Layout** tab, and click the Theme Fonts button . The heading and body text font for each theme displays.

5. Click the option to **Create New Theme Fonts**. The current Heading font and Body font are selected in the Create New Theme Fonts dialog box.

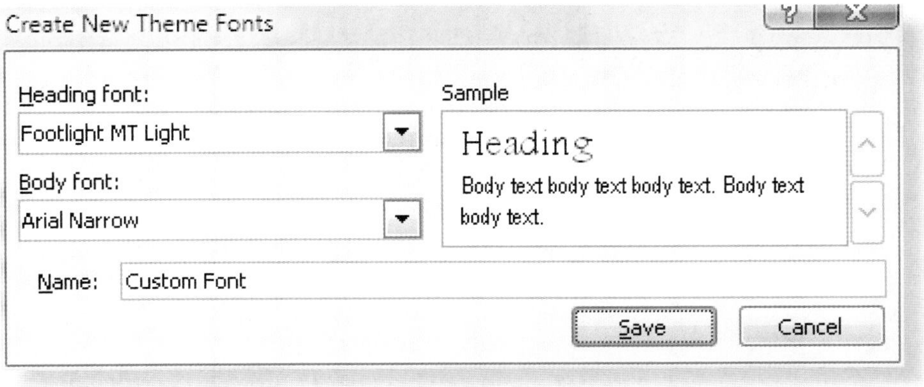

Figure 12-14
Create New Theme Fonts

6. Change the **Heading font** to **Footlight MT Light**, and change the **Body font** to **Arial Narrow**. Key **Custom Font** in the **Name** box. Click **Save**.
7. Click the Theme Fonts button, and notice that "Custom Font" appears at the top of the list. Right-click **Custom Font**, and click **Edit**. Change the **Heading font** to **Eras Medium ITC**, and change the **Body font** to **Footlight MT Light**. Click **Save**.
8. Apply the Heading 5 style to the second line "June 200-." Apply the Heading 4 style to the line that begins "Volume."
9. Select the headings "Chocolate Facts," "Nutrition," "Pets and Chocolate," and "Important Chocolate Dates," and apply the Heading 3 style.
10. Select the lines of text under each of the headings formatted with the Heading 3 style, and format the lines as a bulleted list.
11. At the end of the document, delete the text that begins "Choc Talk" through the end of the document.

12. Click the **Page Layout** tab, and click the Themes button. Click **Save Current Theme**. Key **Custom Theme** in the **File name** box. Click **Save**.

13. Click the Themes button, and notice that the design gallery displays Built In designs and Custom designs. Right-click the **Custom Theme** at the top of the gallery, and click **Delete**. Click **Yes** to delete the theme.
14. Save the document as ***[your initials]*12-12** in your Lesson 12 folder.
15. Submit and close the document.

Lesson 12 Summary

- A style is a set of formatting instructions you can apply to text to give your document a unified look. The five types of styles are character, paragraph, linked, table, and list.
- Word's default style for text is called the Normal style. The default settings for body text are 11-point Calibri, left-aligned, 1.15-line spacing, 10 points spacing after, with widow-orphan control. Word provides built-in heading styles (for example, Heading 1, Heading 2). The default font for heading text is Cambria.
- To apply a style, select the text you want to style (or click in a paragraph to apply a paragraph style). Then choose the style from the Styles task pane or the Quick Styles gallery.
- View the attributes of a style by placing the mouse pointer over the style name in the Styles task pane and reading the text in the ScreenTip.
- Select all instances of a style by clicking the arrow for the style name in the Styles task pane or by right-clicking a style name in the task pane and choosing Select All Instance(s).
- To create a new paragraph style: Select text, modify the text, right-click the text, select Styles, select Save Selection as a New Quick Style, key a new style name, and click OK. Or click the New Style button in the Styles task pane, and set the style's attributes in the Create New Style from Formatting dialog box. You must use the Create New Style from Formatting dialog box to create a character style and specify Character as the style type.
- To modify or rename a style, right-click the style name in the Styles task pane (or point to the style name and click the down arrow), choose Modify, and then change the attributes. Or select text that uses the style, change the format, right-click the style name in the task pane, and choose Update to Match Selection.
- After applying a style throughout a document, you can replace it with another style. Click Replace on the Home tab (in the dialog box, click Format, choose Style, and select the style name in both the Find what and Replace with boxes).
- You can also replace styles by using the Styles task pane (select all instances of a style and then choose another style).
- To delete a style, click the Manage Styles button in the Styles task pane, select the style, and click Delete. Click Yes to delete the style, and click OK.
- When creating new styles, you can specify that they be based on an existing style. You can also specify that one style follows another style automatically. Both these options are offered in the Create New Style from Formatting dialog box.
- Display styles along the left margin of a document in Draft view by opening the Word Options dialog box, clicking Advanced, and scrolling to the Display group. Change the Style area width box to 0.5 inch. Do the reverse to stop displaying styles.

- Print a style sheet by choosing Print from the File menu and choosing Styles from the Print what drop-down list.
- The Theme feature formats an entire document using design elements. Themes include theme colors, theme fonts, and theme effects.

LESSON 12		Command Summary	
Feature	**Button**	**Command**	**Keyboard**
Styles task pane		**Home** tab, **Styles** group, **Styles Dialog Box Launcher**	Shift+Ctrl+Alt+S
Apply styles		**Home** tab, **Styles** group	
View style area		**Word Options, Advanced, Display**	
Themes	Aa Themes	**Page Layout** tab, **Themes** group	

Lesson 13

templates

OBJECTIVES

After completing this lesson, you will be able to:

1. Use Word templates.
2. Create new templates.
3. Attach templates to documents.
4. Modify templates.
5. Use the Organizer.

MCAS OBJECTIVES

In this lesson:
WW 07 1.1.1
WW 07 1.1.5

Estimated Time: 1 1/2 hours

If you often create the same types of documents, such as memos or letters, you can save time by using templates. Word provides a variety of templates that contain built-in styles to help you produce professional-looking documents. You can also create your own templates and reuse them as often as you like.

Using Word's Templates

A *template* is a file that contains formatting information, styles, and sometimes text for a particular type of document. It provides a reusable model for all documents of the same type. Every Word document is based on a template. You can modify templates to include formatting and text that you use frequently.

The following features can be included in templates:

- Formatting features, such as margins, columns, and page orientation.
- Standard text that is repeated in all documents of the same type, such as a company name and address in a letter template.

- Character and paragraph formatting that is saved within styles.
- Macros (automated procedures).

Templates also include *placeholder text* that is formatted and replaced with your own information when you create a new document.

The default template file in Word is called **Normal**. New documents that you create in Word are based on the Normal template and contain all the formatting features assigned to this template, such as the default font, type size, paragraph alignment, margins, and page orientation. The Normal template differs from other templates because it stores settings that are available globally. In other words, you can use these settings in every new document even if they are based on a different template. The file extension for template files is .dotx or .dotm. (A .dotm file is used to enable macros in the file.)

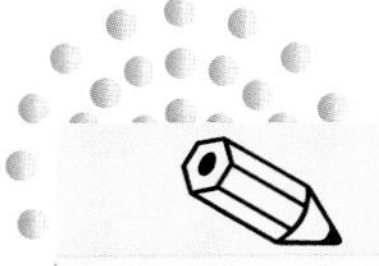

TIP

Pressing Ctrl+N or clicking the New button opens a new document but does not open the New Document dialog box. You can customize the Quick Access Toolbar to include a New button.

Exercise 13-1 USE A WORD TEMPLATE TO CREATE A NEW DOCUMENT

Starting Word opens a new blank document that is based on the Normal template.

1. Click the Microsoft Office Button, and click **New** to open the New Document dialog box.

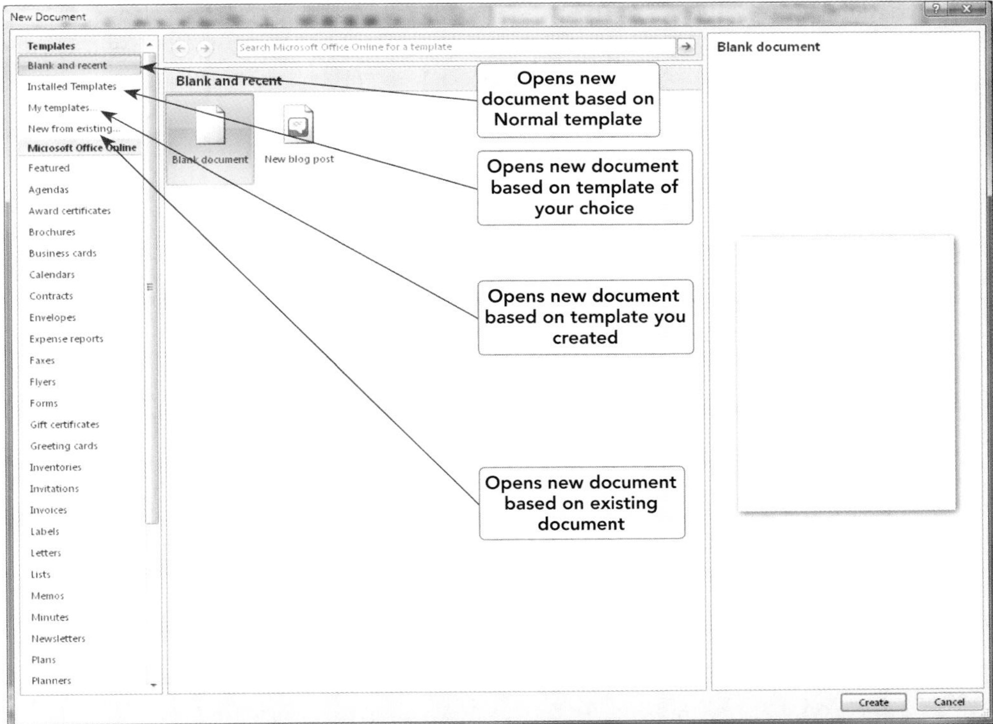

Figure 13-1
New Document dialog box

2. Under **Templates** in the New Document dialog box, click **Blank Document**, and click **Create**. Word opens a new document based on the default template Normal and closes the New Document dialog box. (You could also double-click **Blank Document**.)

NOTE

Some templates might not be installed on your computer. Check with your instructor for instructions on locating the template.

3. Close the document without saving it.
4. Reopen the New Document dialog box, and click **Installed Templates**.
5. Click the **Equity Fax** icon. Notice the design of the template in the **Preview** box.

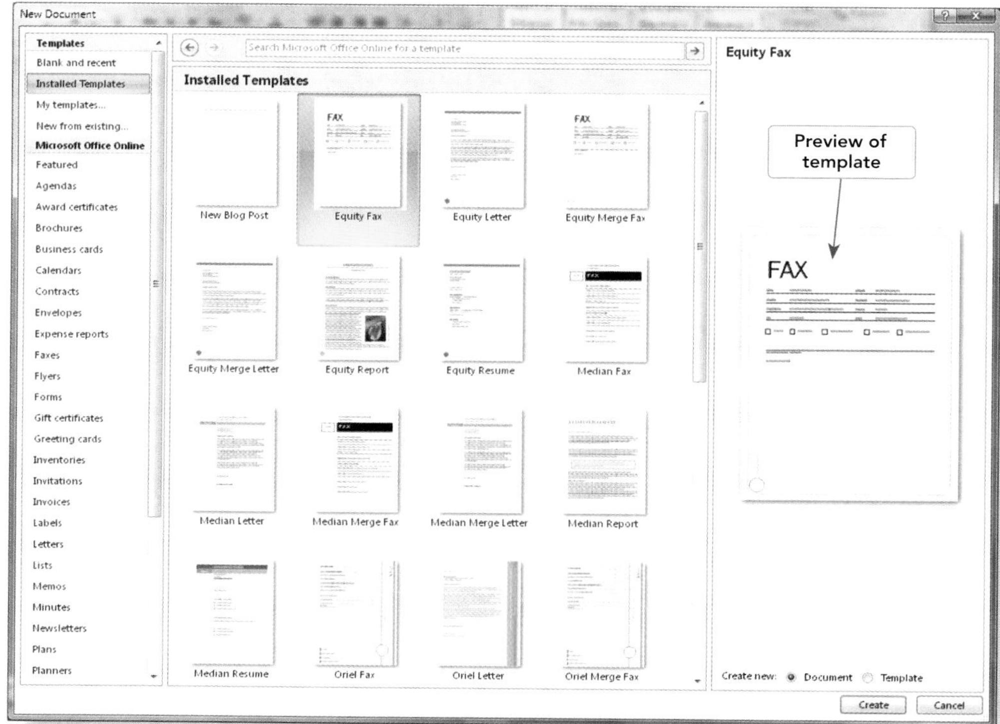

Figure 13-2
Installed Templates

6. Use the **Preview** box to view other Word templates in the dialog box.
7. Click **Letters** under **Microsoft Office Online**. Click **Business**, and click **To Suppliers and vendors**. Click **Acceptance of bid** to preview the letter. Click the Download button [Download]. Click **Continue**. The document displays in a new window.

Download

Figure 13-3
Creating a document from the downloaded template

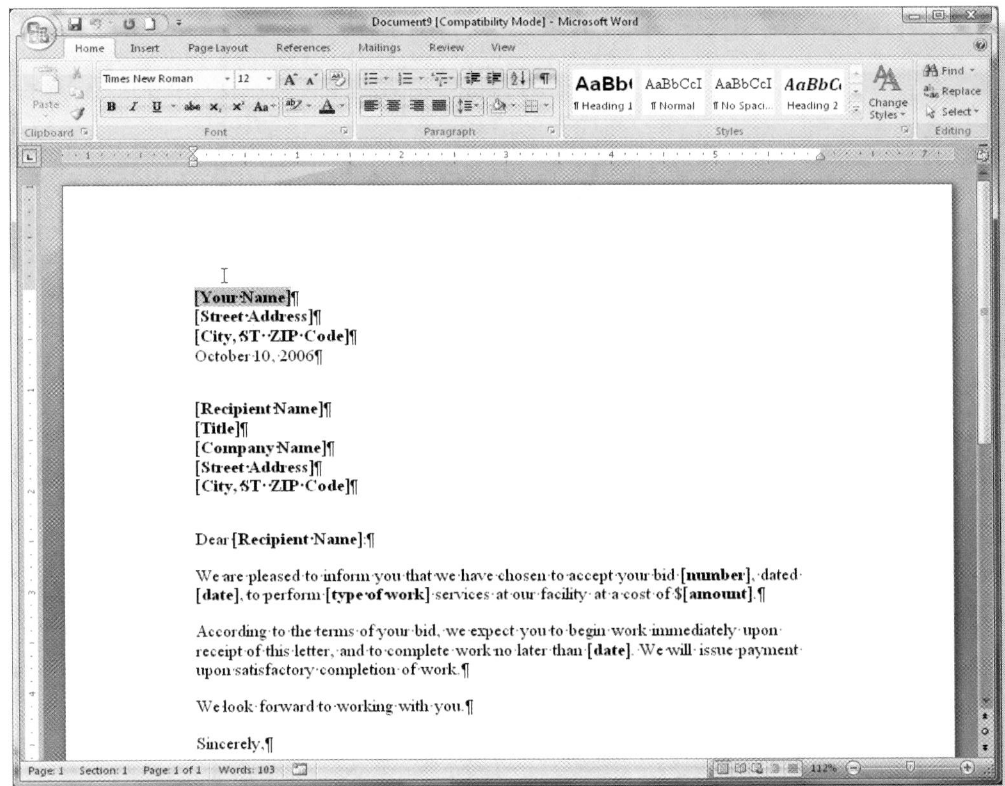

NOTE

The formatting stored in templates is often complex and highly stylized and does not necessarily conform to the traditional formatting for business documents as described in *The Gregg Reference Manual.*

NOTE

If you have difficulty locating or selecting the placeholder text, increase the zoom to 100%.

8. Select the first line of the return address, "[Your Name]," and key **Campbell's Confections**. Click to select the placeholder text that reads "[Street Address]." Key **25 Main Street**. Click to select the placeholder that reads "[City, ST ZIP Code]," and key **Grove City, PA 16127**.

9. Click each of the placeholders for the inside address, and key the following replacement text.

   Mr. Paul Sakkal
   President
   Liberty Storage
   1000 Millington Court
   Cincinnati, OH 45242

10. Click the placeholder in the salutation, and key **Mr. Sakkal**.

11. Edit the first paragraph that begins "We are pleased" as shown in Figure 13-4.

Figure 13-4

```
We are pleased to inform you that we have chosen to accept
your bid No. 876, dated February 1, to install chrome wire
shelving at our Grove City factory at a cost of $1,500.
```

12. Change the date placeholder in the second paragraph to **April 15**. Key **Robert Smith** in the [Your Name] placeholder and **Plant Manager** in the [Title] placeholder. Key your initials at the end of the document.

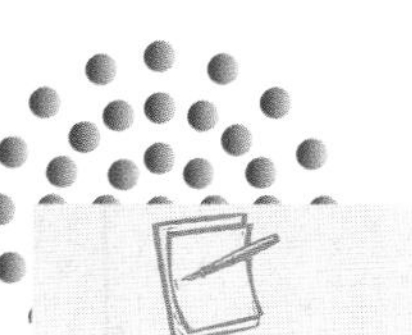

NOTE

If Word asks if you want to save the changes to the Acceptance of Bid template, click No.

13. Format the first line of the return address (Campbell's Confections) using 14-point bold and small caps.
14. Save the document as ***[your initials]*13-1** in a new Lesson 13 folder. Click **Yes**, if a message box appears.
15. Submit and close the document.

Creating New Templates

You can create your own templates for different types of documents by using one of three methods:

- Create a blank template file by using the default template, and define the formatting information, styles, and text according to your specifications.
- Open an existing template, modify it, and save it with a new name.
- Open an existing document, modify it, and save it as a new template.

Exercise 13-2 CREATE A NEW TEMPLATE

1. Open the **New Document** dialog box (by clicking the **Microsoft Office Button** and **then New**), and click **My templates** under Templates. Click the **Blank Document** icon.

Figure 13-5
New dialog box showing My Templates

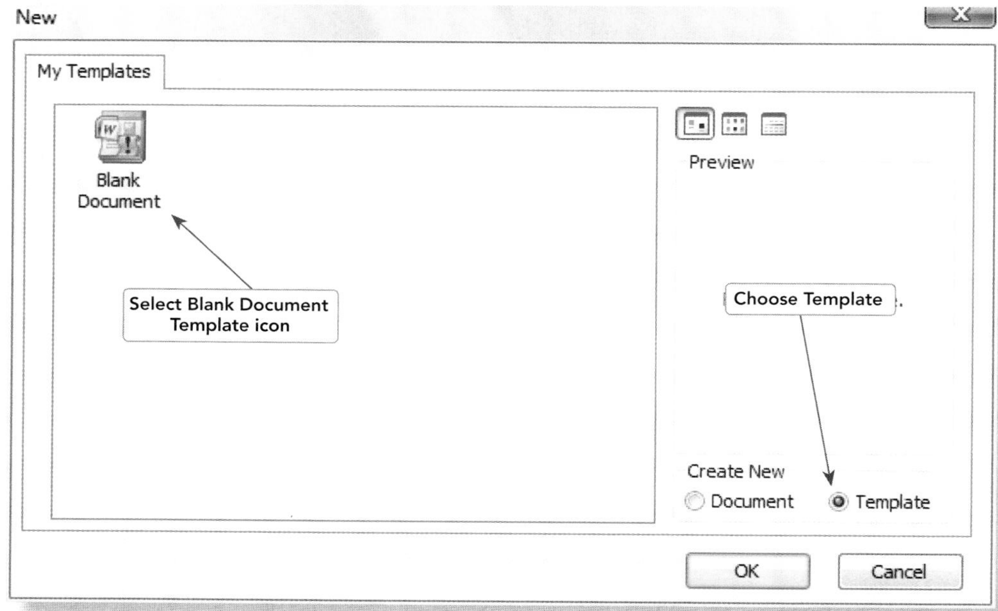

NOTE

If you select **Blank and recent** under **Templates**, you open a document window which can be saved as a template. If you select **My templates** under **Templates**, you can choose to open a document or template window.

2. In the lower right corner of the dialog box, under **Create New**, click **Template** and then click **OK**. A new template file opens with the default name Template1.
3. Change the top margin to 0.5 inch.
4. Key the text shown in Figure 13-6.

Figure 13-6

```
Campbell's Confections

25 Main Street

Grove City, PA 16127

Telephone: 724-555-2025

Fax: 724-555-2050

www.campbellsconfections.biz
```

5. Select the letterhead information, and center the text horizontally. Select the first line, and apply 14-point bold and small caps formatting.
6. Modify the Normal style to 0 points spacing after and single spacing. Press Enter three times to insert blank lines after the Web address, and change the paragraph alignment to left.
7. Insert the date as a field at the third blank paragraph mark after the letterhead by clicking the **Insert** tab, and clicking **Date and Time**. Use the third date format in the **Available formats** list in the Date and Time dialog box. Check **Update automatically** so the date field is updated each time the document is printed. Click **OK**.
8. Press Enter four times.
9. Click the last line of the letterhead text, and apply a bottom border.
10. Click the **Microsoft Office Button**, click the arrow beside **Save As** and click **Word Template**. A folder named "Templates" should appear in the **Save As** dialog box, and **"Word Template"** should appear in the **Save as type** box.

Figure 13-7
Save As dialog box

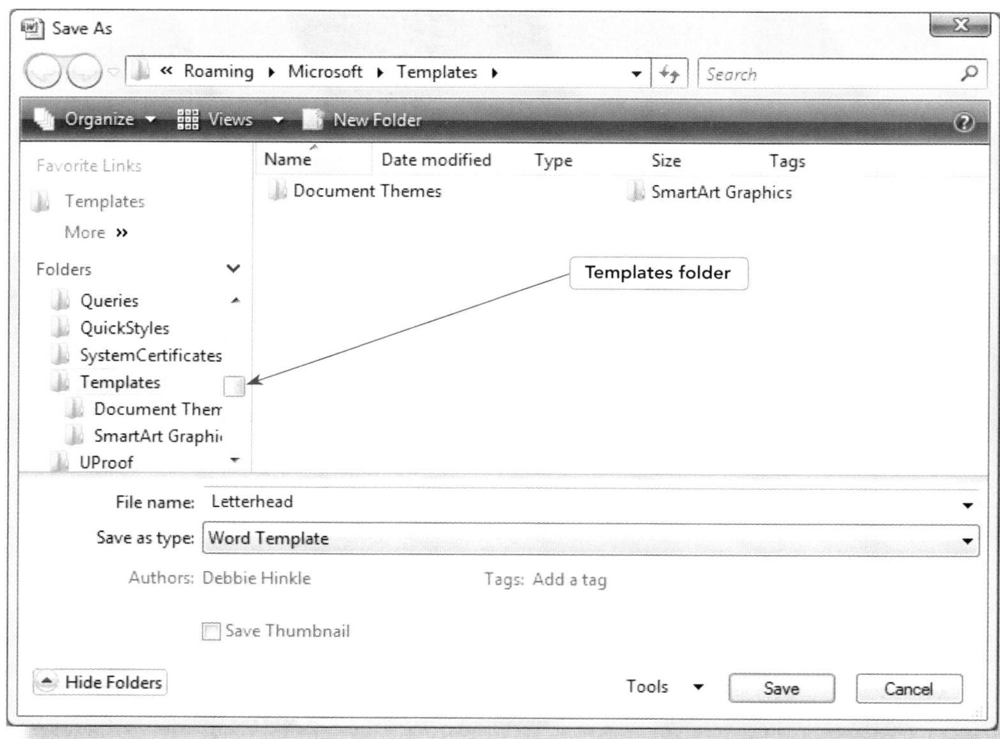

NOTE

By default, Word saves new templates in a User template folder on your hard disk. The specific location is C:\Users\ *Username*\Roaming\Microsoft\Templates (or a similar location in your computer). Before proceeding, ask your instructor where you should save your templates. If you use the default location, you can create new documents from your templates by using the New Document dialog box. If you use your Lesson 13 folder, you create new documents from your templates by using Windows Explorer or My Computer.

11. Save the template with the filename ***[your initials]*****Letterhead** in your Lesson 13 folder (unless your instructor advises you to save in the default Templates folder).

12. Close the template.

Exercise 13-3 CREATE A NEW TEMPLATE BY USING AN EXISTING DOCUMENT

Create New

1. Reopen the New Document dialog box by choosing New from the File menu. Under Templates, click New from existing.
2. Locate and click to select the student data file **Memo - 1**. Click the Create New button Create New. Word opens a copy of the document.
3. Change the top margin to 2 inches. Select the document, and change the font size to 12.
4. Delete all text to the right of each tab character in the memo heading.
5. Insert the date as a field; use the third date format. Check Update automatically so the date field is updated each time the document is printed.
6. Delete all the document paragraphs, but include the blank paragraph marks after the subject line.
7. Open the File menu, click the arrow beside Save As, and click Word Template. Verify that Word Template displays in the Save as type drop-down list box.
8. Save the file as ***[your initials]*****Memo** in your Lesson 13 folder (unless your instructor advises you to save in the default Templates folder).
9. Close the template.

Attaching Templates to Documents

All existing documents have an assigned template—either Normal or another template that you assigned when you created the document. You can change the template assigned to an existing document by *attaching* a different template to the document. When you attach a template, that template's formatting and elements are applied to the document, and all the template styles become available in the document.

Exercise 13-4 ATTACH A TEMPLATE TO A DOCUMENT

1. Open the New Document dialog box. Click the Memos link for the Microsoft Office Online templates.

Download

2. Click Memo (Professional design), and click the Download button Download. Click Continue.
3. Save the professional memo as a template file named ***[your initials]*****ProMemo** in your Lesson 13 folder (unless your instructor advises you to save in the default Templates folder). Click OK if necessary, and close the template.

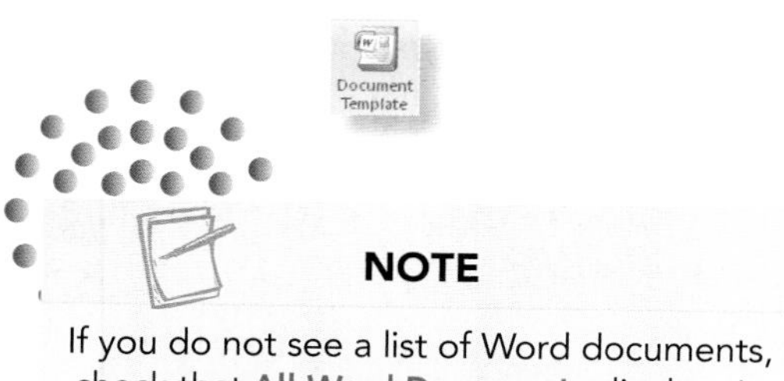

NOTE

If you do not see a list of Word documents, check that **All Word Documents** displays in the **Files of type** box.

4. Open the file **Memo - 4**.
5. Open the Word Options dialog box, and click **Popular** in the left pane. Click to select **Show Developer tab in the Ribbon**. Click **OK**.
6. Click the **Developer** tab in the Ribbon. Click the Document Template button. The Templates and Add-ins dialog box shows that the document is currently based on the Normal template.

Figure 13-8
Templates and Add-ins dialog box

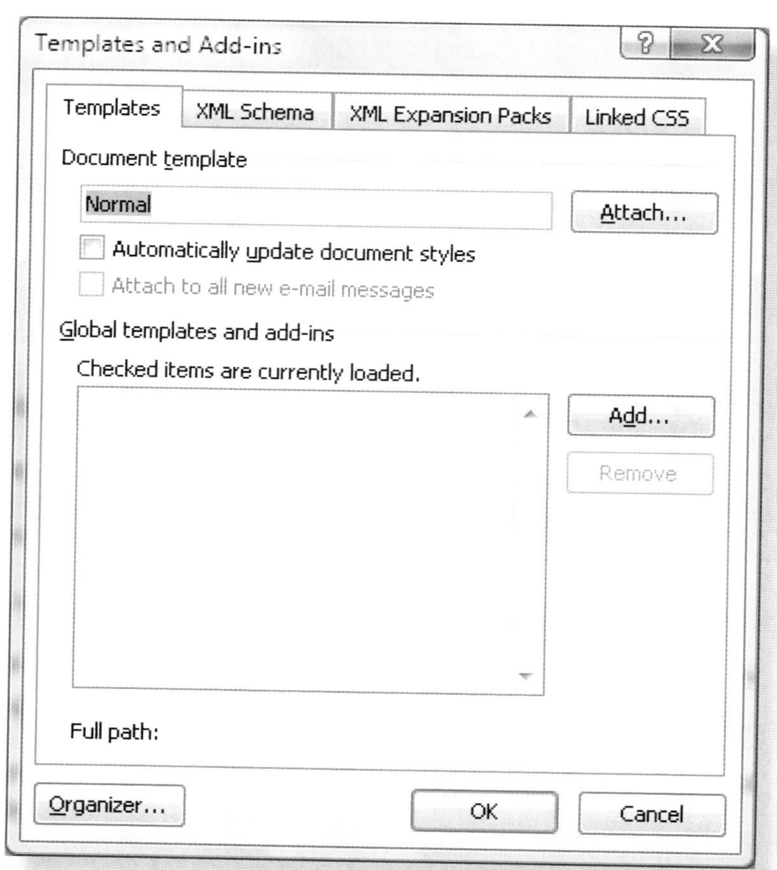

Attach...

7. Click **Attach**. The Attach Template dialog box opens, displaying available templates and folders in the current folder.
8. Change to the folder that contains Word templates. The full default path of this folder is C:\Program Files\Microsoft Office\Templates\1033. (The folder may not be on the C: drive of your computer. Check with your instructor.)
9. Locate your Lesson 13 folder, and display **All Word Templates** in the **Files of type** box.

Figure 13-9
Attach Template dialog box

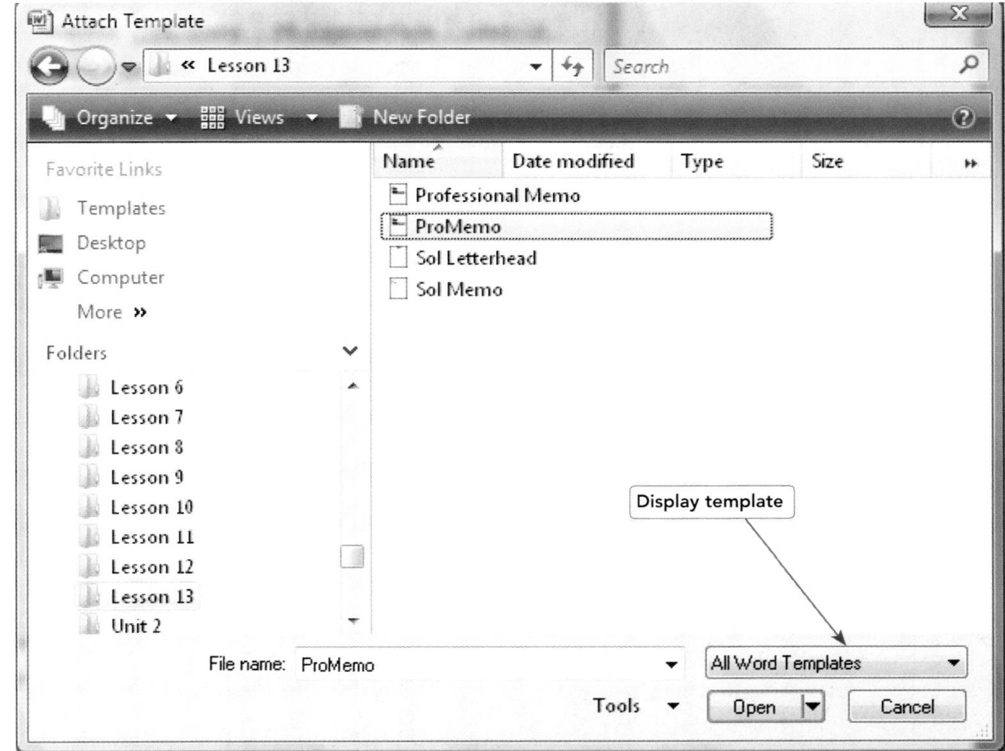

10. Double-click the template **ProMemo**.
11. Click the **Automatically update document styles** check box, and click **OK**. Formatting from the Professional Memo template is applied to this document, and you can now apply any of the Professional Memo styles.
12. Display the Styles task pane.
13. Position the insertion point in the subject line of the memo heading, and apply the style **Message Header Last**.
14. Position the insertion point immediately to the left of "TO:" in the memo heading, and press Enter. Place the insertion point in the first line of text ("MEMO"), and apply the style **Document Label**.
15. Apply the character style **Message Header Label** to the text "TO:," "FROM:," "DATE:," and "SUBJECT:" in the message header. (Remember, you must select text before applying a character style.) Select all four lines of the message header, and change the left tab setting to 1.5 inches to improve alignment.
16. Delete the text in the date line, and key today's date.
17. Set a 1-inch top margin and a 0.5 inch bottom margin.
18. Modify the Normal style to 12 points spacing after.

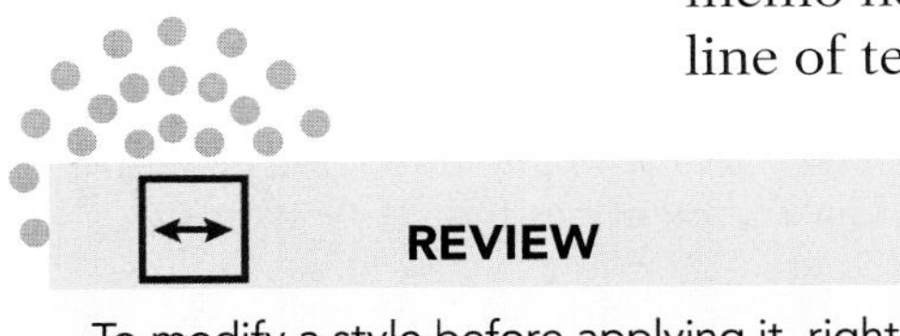

REVIEW

To modify a style before applying it, right-click the style name in the Styles task pane and choose **Modify**.

NOTE

Attaching a template replaces the template that is currently attached to the document.

19. Add your reference initials.
20. Save the document as ***[your initials]*****13-4** in your Lesson 13 folder.
21. Submit and close the document. If you are asked to save changes to the Professional Memo template, click **No**.

Modifying Templates

After you create a template, you can change its formatting and redefine its styles. You can also create new templates by modifying existing templates and saving them with a new name.

NOTE

Any changes you make to the formatting or text in a template affect future documents based on that template. The changes do not affect documents that were created from the template before you modified it.

Exercise 13-5 MODIFY TEMPLATE FORMATTING

1. Click the **Microsoft Office Button**, and click **Open**. From the **Files of type** drop-down list, choose **All Word Templates**.
2. Locate the folder you used to save your templates (for example, the Templates folder on your hard disk under either C:\Documents and Settings\<*your name*>\Application Data\Microsoft or your Lesson 13 folder).
3. Locate the file ***[your initials]*****Letterhead**.
4. Double-click the file ***[your initials]*****Letterhead** to open it. Display the Styles task pane.

5. Click the **Page Layout** tab, and click the Themes button. Change the document theme to **Flow**.

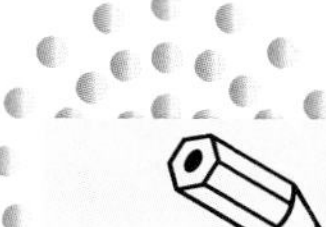

TIP

You can point to a file name to check its file type.

TIP

Opening a template through the Open dialog box opens the actual template. Double-clicking a template in Windows Explorer, My Computer, or the Templates dialog box opens a new document based on the template. Changes that you make to the new document do not affect the template.

NOTE

To create a new template based on an existing template, modify the existing template as desired, and then save the template with a new name.

6. Modify the Normal style font size to 12 points.
7. Click the Save button to save the changes. The earlier version of the template is overwritten by the new version.
8. Close the template.

Using the Organizer

Instead of modifying template styles, you can copy individual styles from another document or template into the current document or template by using the Organizer. The copied styles are added to the style sheet of the current document or template. When you copy styles, remember these rules:

- Copied styles replace styles with the same style names.
- Style names are case sensitive—if you copy a style named "HEAD" into a template or document that contains a style named "head," the copied style is added to the style sheet and does not replace the existing style.

Organizer...

You can also copy macros by using the Organizer. To open the Organizer, display and activate the Developer tab if necessary. Click the Document Template command. Click the Organizer button ; then select the Styles tab.

Exercise 13-6 COPY STYLES TO ANOTHER TEMPLATE

1. Open the **New Document** dialog box, and click **Installed Templates.** Click to select the **Equity Lettter** icon, and click **Create**.
2. Save the document as a template named ***[your initials]*****EquityLetter** in your Lesson 13 folder. Display the Styles task panel, and notice the list of styles. Close the document.
3. Open the template ***[your initials]*****Letterhead** revised in Exercise 13-5.

4. Click the **Developer** tab, and click the Document Template button . Click the **Organizer** button .
5. Click the **Styles** tab in the Organizer dialog box. On the left side of the dialog box, the Organizer lists the template and styles currently in use. You use the right side of the dialog box to copy styles to or from another template.

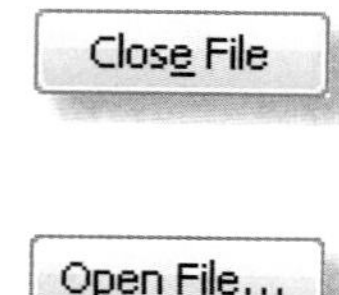

6. Click the **Close File** button on the right side of the dialog box. The Normal template closes, and the **Close File** button changes to **Open File**.

7. Click the **Open File** button. In the Open dialog box, make sure **All Word Templates** appears in the **Files of type** box.

8. Locate the folder that contains the ***[your initials]*****EquityLetter** template.

9. Double-click the ***[your initials]*****EquityLetter** template. You can now choose styles from this template to copy into your letterhead template.

Figure 13-10
Organizer dialog box

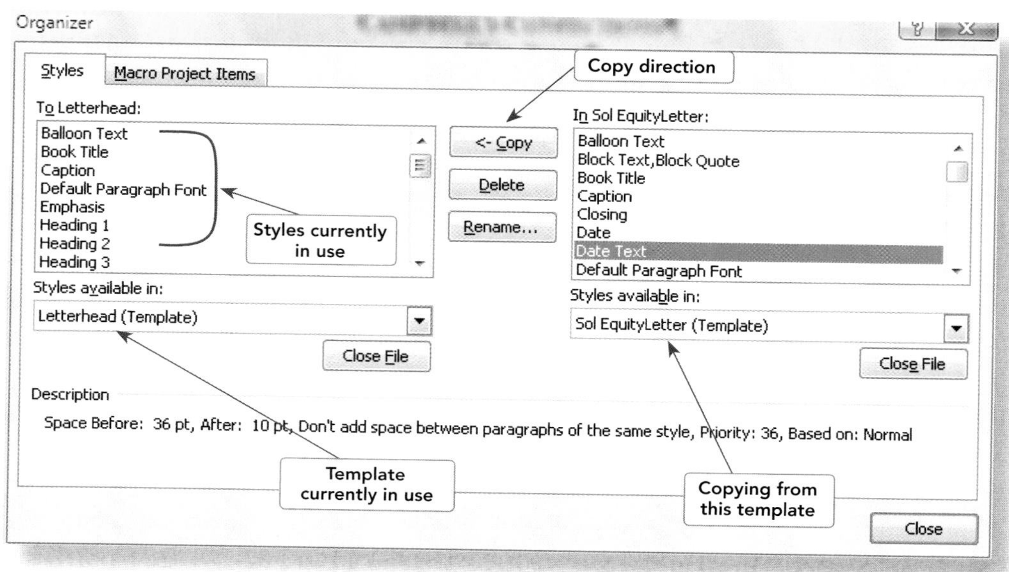

10. Scroll down the list of styles in the EquityLetter template. Click **Date Text**, and click **Copy**.

11. Choose the **Normal** style from the EquityLetter style list. Notice the style description.

12. Click **Copy**, and then click **Yes** to overwrite the existing style Normal.

13. Close the Organizer dialog box. The styles you chose from the EquityLetter template are copied to the current template. Notice that the Normal style from the EquityLetter template replaced the previous Normal style, so the text is formatted in Constantia 11 point with 8 points spacing after.

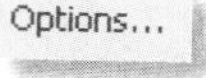

14. Click the Options link at the bottom of the Styles task pane. Click the arrow for **Select styles to show**, and select **All styles**. Click **OK**.

15. Apply the newly copied style Date Text to the date line.

16. Close the template without saving changes.

Lesson 13 Summary

- A template is a reusable model for a particular type of document. Templates can contain formatting, text, and other elements. By default, all new documents are based on the Normal template.
- Word provides a variety of templates upon which you can base a new document or a new template. You can modify any existing template and save it with a new name. You can also modify any existing document and save it as a new template.
- Every document is based on a template. You can change the template assigned to an existing document by attaching a different template to the document, thereby making the new template's styles available in the document.
- To modify a template you created, open it from the Open dialog box and choose All Word Templates from the Files of type drop-down list.
- Instead of modifying template styles, use the Organizer to copy individual styles from one document or template to another.

LESSON 13		Command Summary	
Feature	**Button**	**Command**	**Keyboard**
Use a template		**Microsoft Office Button, New**	
Attach template	Document Template	**Developer** tab, **Templates** group, **Document Template**	
Copy styles	Document Template	**Developer** tab, **Templates** group, **Document Template, Organizer**	

microsoft® office excel® brief

A Professional Approach

EXCEL 2007

Kathleen Stewart

There's more to learning a spreadsheet program like Microsoft Office Excel than simply keying data. You need to know how to use Excel in real-world situations. That's why all the lessons in this book relate to everyday business tasks.

As you work through the lessons, imagine yourself working as an intern for Klassy Kow Ice Cream, Inc., a fictional San Francisco business that manufactures and sells ice cream.

Klassy Kow Ice Cream, Inc.

Klassy Kow Ice Cream, Inc., was formed in 1985 by Conrad Steele, shortly after the death of his father. Since 1967, Conrad's father and mother had been dairy farmers in Klamath Falls, Oregon. As an addition to their farm, Archibald and Henrietta Steele opened a small ice cream shop. They made their own ice cream from fresh cream, eggs, and butter—starting simply with vanilla, chocolate, and strawberry flavors. They also sold cones, sundaes, shakes, and malts.

As word spread about their delicious ice cream, Archie and Henrietta's business blossomed from a seasonal shop to a year-round store. Eventually, the Steeles expanded the number of flavors and started to offer hand-packed ice cream pies and cakes. They also started to sell to small supermarkets in southern Oregon under the "Klassy Kow" name, allowing their many local customers to buy half-gallons at their favorite supermarkets.

The business continued to expand and soon reached into supermarkets in the Pacific Northwest. Archibald and Henrietta opened new ice cream shops in Medford, Oregon, and Eureka and Red Bluff, California.

After Archibald Steele died, Conrad and his mother sold the dairy farm but kept the ice cream shops. They continue to buy ice cream from the new owners (the Klamath Farm) and have expanded the ice cream business to include 33 franchised ice cream shops in the western United States.

In 1998, with Klassy Kow continuing to grow steadily, Conrad decided to move the corporate headquarters to San Francisco, California. His mother, Henrietta, is retired and still lives in Klamath Falls, where she continues to help create and test new flavors for the Klamath Farm.

The company now has more than 200 employees, but the number of employees in the San Francisco office is surprisingly small. Most employees work in the ice cream shops scattered across Washington, Idaho, Oregon, Nevada, and northern California.

Conrad Steele, who is now president and chief executive officer of Klassy Kow, is responsible for the general operations of the company. He says, "I love to see a big smile on a customer's face after the first lick. It makes it all worth it."

Conrad visits many of the ice cream shops and likes to keep in touch with customers. He visits Klamath Farms at least four times a year to keep in contact with his major supplier.

All the worksheets, data, and graphics you will use in this course relate to Klassy Kow Ice Cream, Inc. As you work with the worksheets in the text, take the time to notice the following:

- The types of worksheets needed in a small business to carry on day-to-day business.
- The formatting of worksheets. Real businesses don't always pay attention to formatting internal worksheets. However, they do focus on formatting worksheets that customers will see.
- The types of business activities required by a company such as Klassy Kow. For example, it must deal with employees, internal accounting, and suppliers.

As you use this text and become more experienced with Microsoft Office Excel, you will also gain expertise in creating, editing, and formatting the sort of worksheets generated in a real-life business environment.

Klassy Kow Klassics

Sugar Cones	Waffle Cones
Ice Cream	Frozen Yogurt
Shakes	Malteds
Ice Cream Sodas	Ice Cream Sundaes
Ice Cream Cakes	Ice Cream Pies
Ice Cream Sandwiches	Soda
Coffee	

Kowabunga
(An ice cream beverage available in several flavors)

KowOwow
(A cow-shaped ice cream bar)

unit 1

INTRODUCTION TO EXCEL

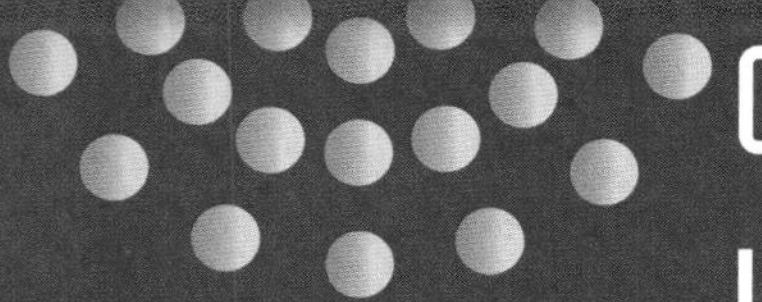

Lesson 1

Getting Started with Excel

OBJECTIVE

After completing this lesson, you will be able to:

1. Start Excel.
2. Navigate in a workbook.
3. Open an existing workbook.
4. Edit a worksheet.
5. Manage files.
6. Print Excel files.

MCAS OBJECTIVES

In this lesson:

XL07 1.3
XL07 1.4.1
XL07 1.4.3
XL07 5.4
XL07 5.4.2
XL07 5.5

Estimated Time: 1 hour

Microsoft Excel is *electronic spreadsheet software.* You can use Excel to create professional reports that perform business or personal calculations, display financial or scientific calculations, complete table management tasks, and show charts. Excel is powerful but easy to use. You'll become a productive Excel user as soon as you learn the basics.

Starting Excel

Excel opens showing a blank workbook, the Microsoft Office Button, the Quick Access toolbar, and the Ribbon (see Figure 1-1). New workbooks are named Book1, Book2, and so on during each work session.

NOTE

The command tabs in the Ribbon are similar to panes or tabs in a dialog box.

The *Ribbon* is a set of command tabs. Each command tab has buttons, galleries, or other controls related to a specific task group or object. Some command tabs

Figure 1-1
Excel screen

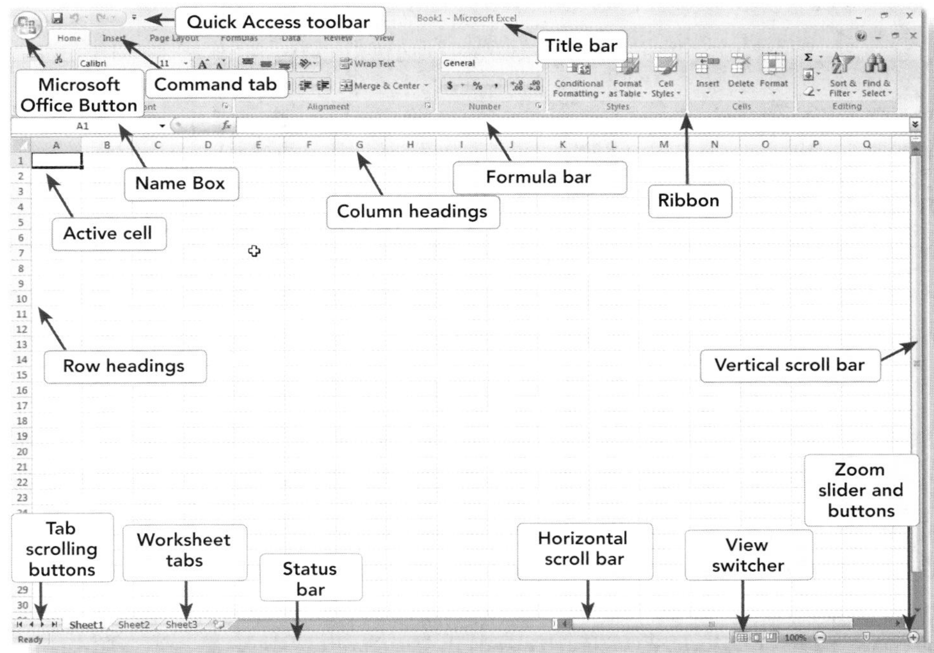

TABLE 1-1 Parts of the Excel Screen

Part of Screen	Purpose
Active cell	The cell outlined in a heavy black border. It is ready to accept new data, a formula, or your edits.
Column headings	Alphabetic characters across the top of the worksheet that identify columns.
Command tabs	A Ribbon tab control with command buttons, galleries, and other controls for creating, managing, editing, and formatting data.
Formula bar	Displays the contents of the active cell. You can also enter text, numbers, or formulas in the formula bar. It can be expanded and collapsed as needed.
Microsoft Office Button	Opens a menu with basic commands for working with the document.
Name Box	A drop-down combo box that shows the address of the active cell. You can also use it to move the pointer to a specific location.
Quick Access toolbar	Toolbar with shortcut command buttons for common tasks.
Ribbon	Organizes and displays command tabs.
Row headings	Numbers down the left side of the worksheet that identify rows.
Scroll bars	Used to move different parts of the screen into view.
Status bar	Displays information about the current task and mode of operation as well as View choices and the Zoom control.
Tab scrolling buttons	Navigation buttons to scroll through worksheet tabs.
Title bar	Contains the program name and the name of the workbook.
View switcher	Buttons to change the view of the current sheet among Normal, Page Layout, and Page Break Preview.
Worksheet tabs	Indicators at the bottom of the worksheet to identify sheets in the workbook.
Zoom controls	Buttons and slider to change the view magnification.

NOTE

Windows provides many ways to start applications. If you have problems, ask your instructor for help.

are context-sensitive and appear only when needed to accommodate what you are doing. The *Quick Access toolbar* provides one-click access to frequently used commands. You can add command buttons to this toolbar, and you can reposition it below the Ribbon. The *Microsoft Office Button* replaces the File menu in previous versions of Office, but it still lists commands such as Save and Print.

Exercise 1-1 WORK WITH THE EXCEL INTERFACE

There are several ways to start Excel, depending on how your software is installed. You can use the Start button on the Windows taskbar to choose Excel from the list of available programs. There may be an Excel icon on the desktop that you can double-click to start Excel.

Your screen size and resolution affects how the command buttons look and how much you see at once. Do not be concerned if your screen looks slightly different from illustrations in this text.

When the instructions tell you to "click" a tab, a command button, or a menu option, use the left mouse button. Use the left mouse button to carry out commands unless you are told explicitly to use the right mouse button.

1. Start Excel. A blank workbook opens.
2. Click the **Home** tab in the Ribbon. Commands on this tab are organized into seven groups: Clipboard, Font, Alignment, Number, Styles, Cells, and Editing.

NOTE

Super ScreenTips explain the purpose of the button, provide a keyboard shortcut, and when appropriate, describe when you might use the feature. They might also include a thumbnail image of a dialog box to be opened.

3. In the **Font** group, rest the mouse pointer on the Bold button **B**. A *Super ScreenTip* includes the button name, a brief description of the button's function, and its keyboard shortcut.
4. In the **Font** group, rest the mouse pointer on the Dialog Box Launcher. A Super ScreenTip describes and previews the dialog box that will be opened when you click this button. Many command groups have a Dialog Box Launcher.

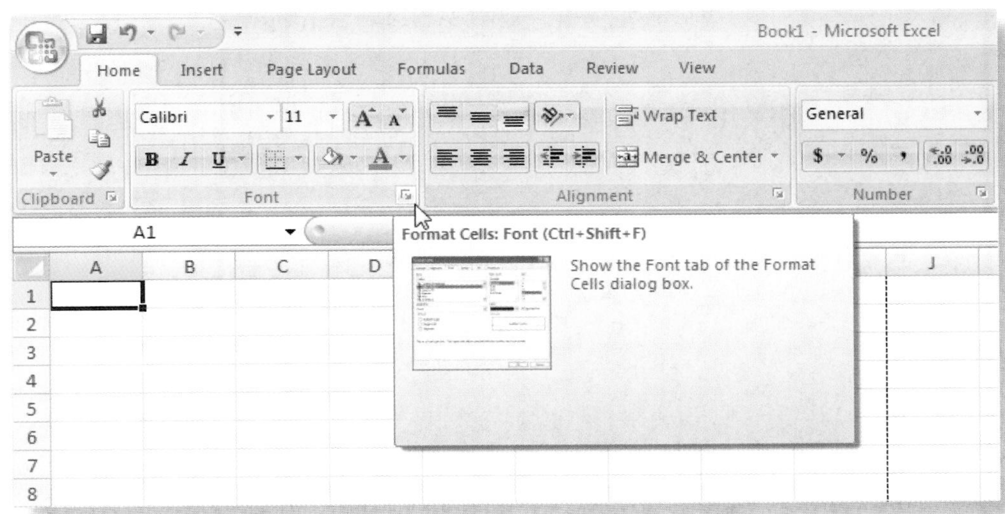

Figure 1-2
Dialog Box Launcher for the Font group

5. Click the Dialog Box Launcher for the **Font** group. The Format Cells dialog box opens with the **Font** tab visible.
6. Click **Cancel** to close the dialog box.

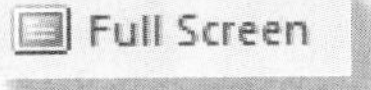

7. Click the **View** tab in the Ribbon. Commands on this tab are organized into five groups: Workbook Views, Show/Hide, Zoom, Window, and Macros.

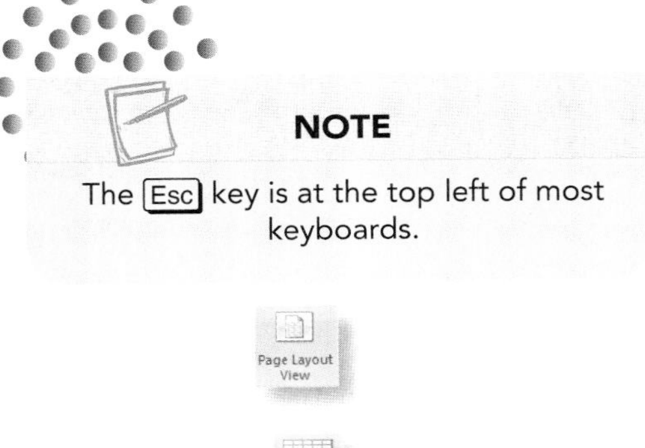

NOTE

The Esc key is at the top left of most keyboards.

8. In the **Workbook Views** group, move the mouse pointer to Full Screen and click. A Full Screen view shows only worksheet cells with row and column headings.
9. Press Esc on the keyboard to return to normal view.
10. Click the Page Layout View button. This view is an interactive preview of how the page will print and shows margins, the ruler, and header/footer areas. The grid does not print.
11. Click the Normal button.

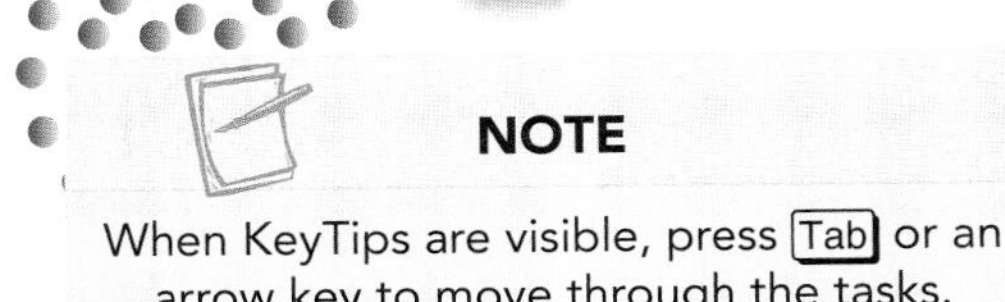

NOTE

When KeyTips are visible, press Tab or an arrow key to move through the tasks.

12. Press and release the Alt key. *KeyTips* appear over a command name when you press the Alt key. They show keyboard shortcuts.
13. Key **h** to activate the **Home** tab.
14. Press Tab four times. The active task cycles through the commands in the Clipboard group, and the KeyTips are no longer visible. The Clipboard group is now active.
15. Press Esc.
16. Press F10 and key **h**. This is another keyboard shortcut to display KeyTips. Each task now shows a key.

17. Key **1** to turn on bold. You can see that bold is applied by the button color.

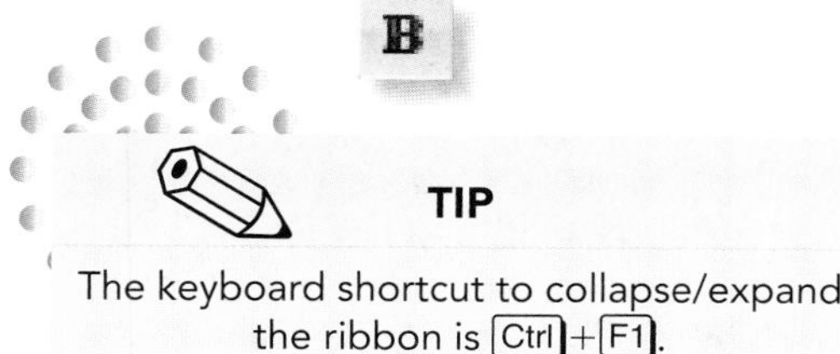

TIP

The keyboard shortcut to collapse/expand the ribbon is Ctrl+F1.

18. Click the Bold button **B**. Bold is toggled off.
19. Double-click the **Home** tab. The ribbon collapses and more working space is available.
20. Right-click the **Home** tab. Click to deselect **Minimize the Ribbon**. You can right-click any tab to expand or collapse the ribbon.

Navigating in a Workbook

A *workbook* is the file Excel creates to store your data. When you look at the screen, you are viewing a worksheet. A *worksheet* is an individual page or sheet tab. A new workbook opens with three blank worksheets. You can insert or delete worksheets in the workbook. A workbook must have at least 1 worksheet and can have as many as your computer's memory allows.

TABLE 1-2 Navigation Commands in a Workbook

Press	To Do This
Ctrl+Home	Move to the beginning of the worksheet.
Ctrl+End	Move to the last used cell on the worksheet.
Home	Move to the beginning of the current row.
PageUp	Move up one screen.
PageDown	Move down one screen.
Alt+PageUp	Move one screen to the left.
Alt+PageDown	Move one screen to the right.
↑, ↓, ←, →	Move one cell up, down, left, or right.
Ctrl+arrow key	Move to the edge of a group of cells with data.
Ctrl+G or F5	Open the Go To dialog box.
Click	Move to the cell that is clicked.
Tab	Move to the next cell in a left-to-right sequence.
Shift+Tab	Move to the previous cell in a right-to-left sequence.
Ctrl+Backspace	Move to the active cell when it has scrolled out of view.
Ctrl+PageUp	Move to the previous worksheet.
Ctrl+PageDown	Move to the next worksheet.

A worksheet is divided into *rows* and *columns*. The rows are numbered and reach row 1,048,576. There are 16,384 columns, lettered from A to Z, then AA to AZ, BA to BZ, AAA to AAZ, ABA to ABZ, and so on, up to column XFD.

NOTE

In a cell address, the column letter is first.

The intersection of a row and a column forms a rectangle known as a *cell*. You enter data (text, a number, or a formula) in a cell. Cells have *cell addresses* or *cell references*, which identify where the cell is located on the worksheet. Cell B2, for example, is the cell in column B, row 2.

The *active cell* is the cell that appears outlined with a thick border. It is ready to accept data or a formula, or if it already contains data or a formula, it is ready to be modified. It is the cell in which you are currently working. When you open a new workbook, the active cell is cell A1, the top-left cell in the worksheet. Cell A1 is referred to as "Home."

NOTE

Pointing and resting the mouse pointer on a button is known as "hovering."

The mouse pointer displays as a thick white cross when you move it across cells in the worksheet. When you point at a Ribbon or worksheet tab, a command button, or a menu item, the pointer turns into a white arrow.

Exercise 1-2 MOVE BETWEEN WORKSHEETS

A new workbook has three worksheets named **Sheet1**, **Sheet2**, and **Sheet3**. **Sheet1** is displayed when a new workbook is opened.

NOTE

Cell A1 is the active cell on all three worksheets in a new workbook.

NOTE

When keyboard combinations (such as Ctrl+PageUp) are shown in this text, hold down the first key without releasing it and press the second key. Release the second key and then release the first key.

1. Click the **Sheet2** worksheet tab. You can tell which sheet is active because its tab appears more white, and the tab name is bold.
2. Click the **Sheet3** worksheet tab. All three sheets are empty.
3. Press Ctrl+PageUp. This shortcut moves to the previous worksheet, **Sheet2**, in this case.
4. Press Ctrl+PageDown. This command moves to the next worksheet, **Sheet3**.
5. Click the **Sheet1** tab to return to **Sheet1**.

Exercise 1-3 GO TO A SPECIFIC CELL

When you move the mouse pointer to a cell and click, the cell you clicked becomes the active cell. It is outlined with a black border, and you can see the cell address in the *Name Box*. The Name Box is a drop-down combo box at the left edge of the formula bar. You can also determine the cell address by the orange-shaded column and row headings.

1. Move the mouse pointer to cell D4 and click. Cell D4 is the active cell, and its address appears in the Name Box. The column D and row 4 headings are shaded.

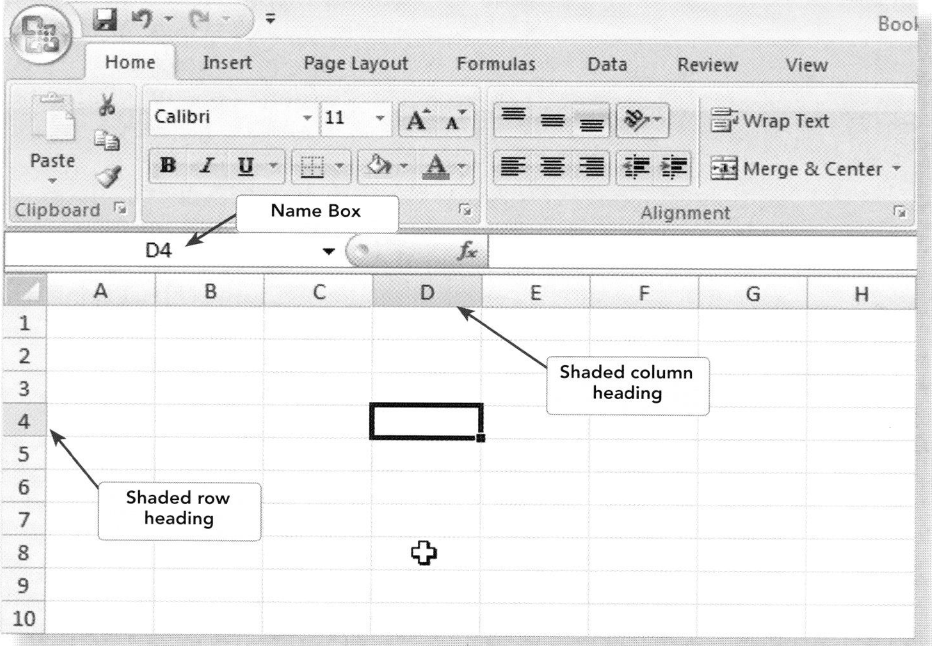

Figure 1-3
Active cell showing a thick border

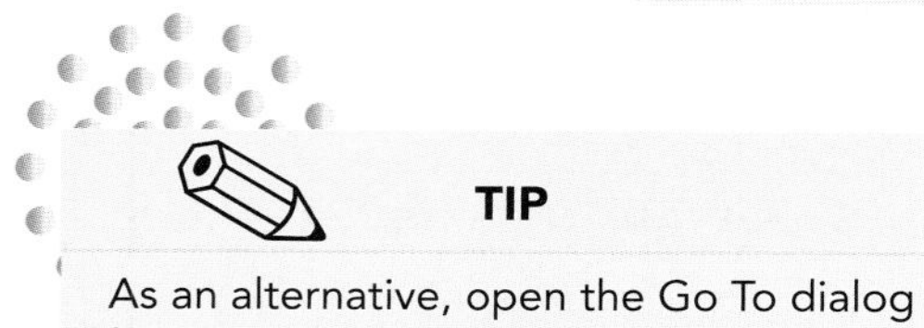

TIP

As an alternative, open the Go To dialog box by clicking the Find & Select button in the Editing group on the Home tab and choosing **Go To**.

2. Press Ctrl+Home. This shortcut makes cell A1 the active cell.
3. Press Ctrl+G to open the Go To dialog box.
4. Key **b19** in the **Reference** box and press Enter. Cell B19 becomes the active cell, and its address is shown in the Name Box.

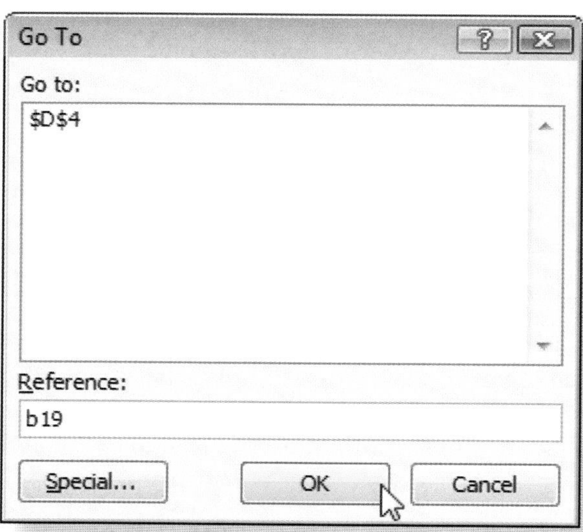

Figure 1-4
Go To dialog box

5. Press Ctrl+G. Recently used cell addresses are listed in the **Go to** list in the Go To dialog box.
6. Key **c2** and click **OK**.
7. Click in the **Name Box**. The current cell address is highlighted.
8. Key **a8** in the Name Box and press Enter.

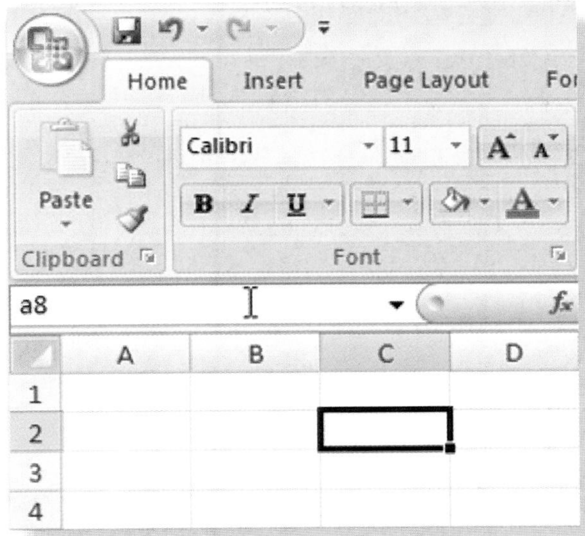

Figure 1-5
Using the Name Box

9. Press Ctrl+Home to return to cell A1.

Exercise 1-4 SCROLL THROUGH A WORKSHEET

When you scroll through a worksheet, the location of the active cell does not change. Instead, the worksheet moves on the screen so that you can see different columns or rows. The number of rows and columns you see at once depends on screen resolution and the Zoom size in Excel.

1. On the vertical scroll bar, click below the scroll box. The worksheet has been repositioned so that you see the next group of about 20 to 30 rows.
2. Click above the vertical scroll box. The worksheet has scrolled up to show the top rows.
3. Click the right scroll arrow on the horizontal scroll bar once. The worksheet scrolls one column to the right.
4. Click the left scroll arrow once to bring the column back into view.

NOTE

You cannot see the active cell (cell A1) during your scrolling.

5. Click the down scroll arrow on the vertical scroll bar twice.
6. Drag the vertical scroll box to the top of the vertical scroll bar. As you drag, a ScreenTip displays the row number at the top of the window. During all this scrolling, the active cell is still cell A1.

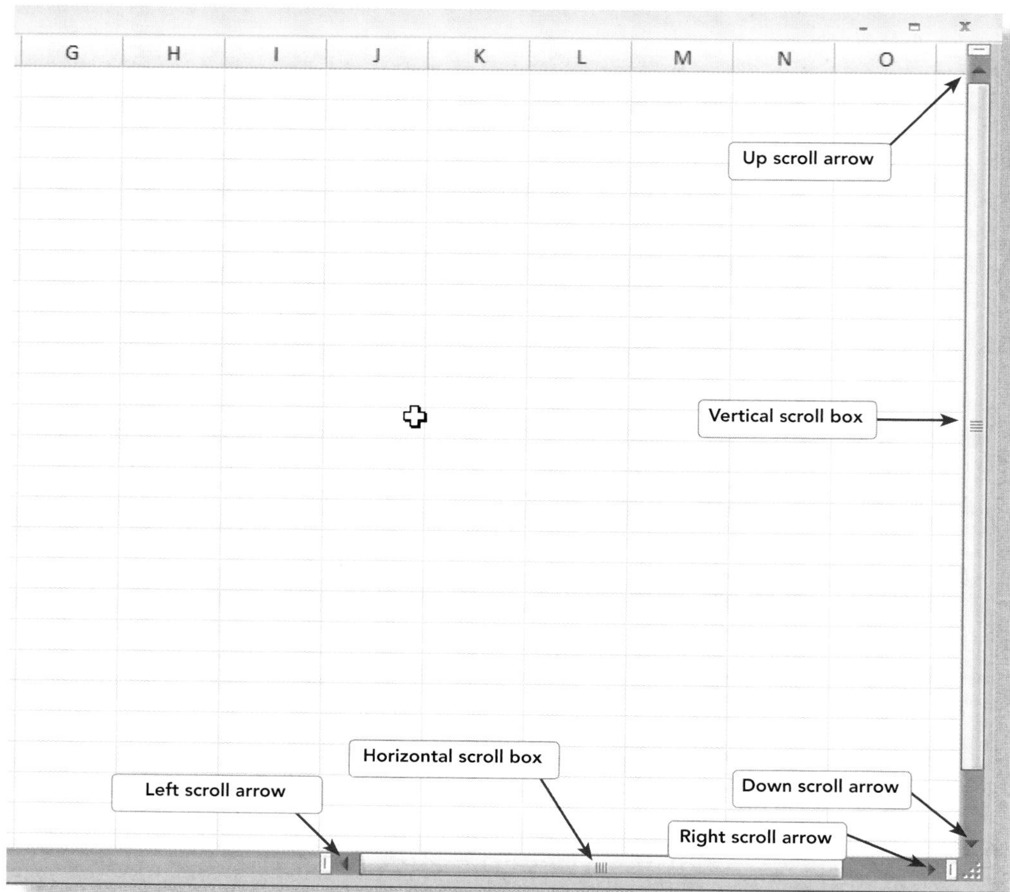

Figure 1-6
Using scroll bars

TABLE 1-3 Scrolling Through a Worksheet

To Move the View	Do This
One row up	Click the up scroll arrow.
One row down	Click the down scroll arrow.
Up one screen	Click the scroll bar above the scroll box.
Down one screen	Click the scroll bar below the scroll box.
To any relative position	Drag the scroll bar up or down.
One column to the right	Click the right scroll arrow.
One column to the left	Click the left scroll arrow.

Exercise 1-5 CHANGE THE ZOOM SIZE

The *Zoom size* controls how much of the worksheet you see on the screen. You can set the size to see more or less on screen and reduce the need to scroll. The **100%** size shows the data close to print size. A Zoom slider and two buttons are at the right edge of the status bar.

1. Click the Zoom In button on the status bar. The worksheet is resized to 110% and you see fewer columns and rows.

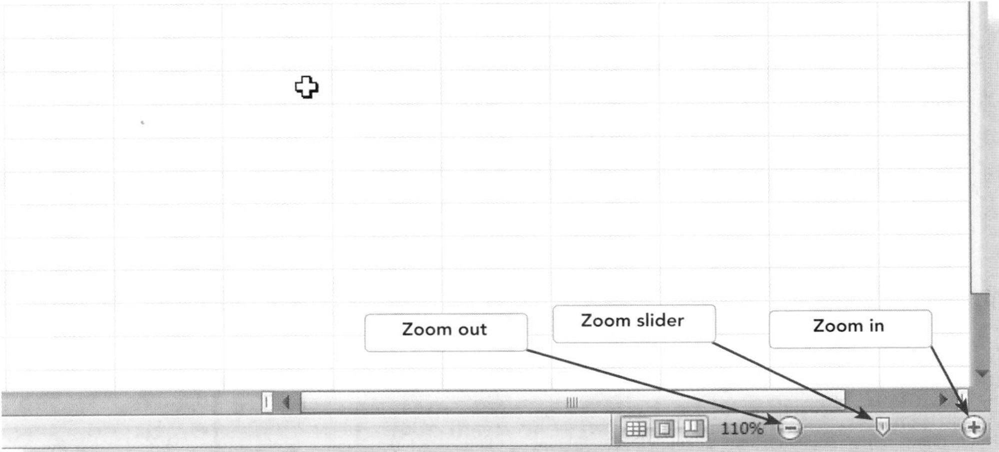

Figure 1-7
Changing the Zoom size

2. Click the Zoom Out button. The worksheet is reduced to 100% magnification.
3. Click the Zoom Out button again. Each click changes the magnification by 10%.

4. Point at the Zoom slider button, hold down the mouse button, and drag the slider slowly in either direction. You can set any magnification size.

5. Click the **View** tab in the Ribbon. There is a Zoom button on this tab.
6. Click the Zoom button. The Zoom dialog box opens.
7. Choose **200%**. Click **OK**.
8. Click **200%** in the status bar. The dialog box opens.
9. Choose **100%** and click **OK**.

TIP

It is usually quicker to change magnification by using the Zoom tools on the status bar.

Exercise 1-6 CLOSE A WORKBOOK

After you finish working with a workbook, you should save your work and close the workbook. You can close a workbook in several ways.

- Click the Microsoft Office Button and choose **Close**.
- Click the Close Window button at the right end of the Ribbon tabs.
- Use keyboard shortcuts, Ctrl+W or Ctrl+F4.

1. Click the Microsoft Office Button.
2. Choose **Close**. (If you have made a change to the workbook, a dialog box asks if you want to save the changes. Click **No** if this message box opens.) The workbook closes, and a blank blue screen appears.

Opening an Existing Workbook

There are several ways to open an existing workbook.

- Click the Microsoft Office Button and choose **Open**.
- Use the keyboard shortcut Ctrl+O or Ctrl+F12.
- Navigate through folders in Windows Explorer or Computer to find and double-click the filename.

Exercise 1-7 OPEN A WORKBOOK

1. Click the Microsoft Office Button and choose **Open**. The navigation line shows the most recently used folder.
2. Choose the drive/folder according to your instructor's directions.

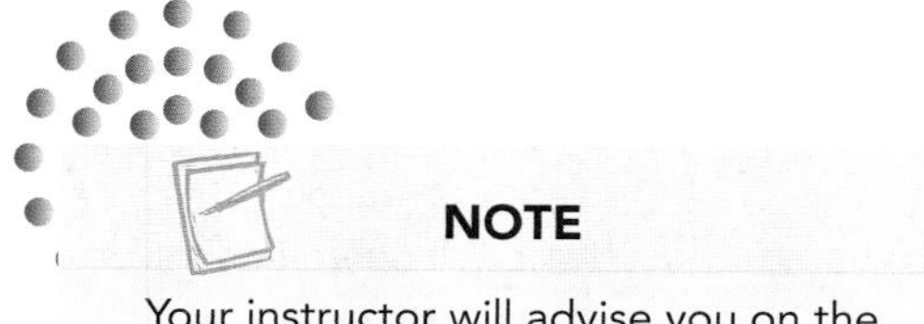

NOTE

Your instructor will advise you on the drive/folder to use for this course.

3. Click the arrow next to the Organize button and hover over **Layout**.
4. Click to select **Details Pane**. The Details pane is at the lower part of the dialog box. (Navigation Pane should also be selected. If it is not, repeat these steps to select it.)

5. Click the arrow next to the Views button and choose **Small Icons**.

Figure 1-8
Open dialog box

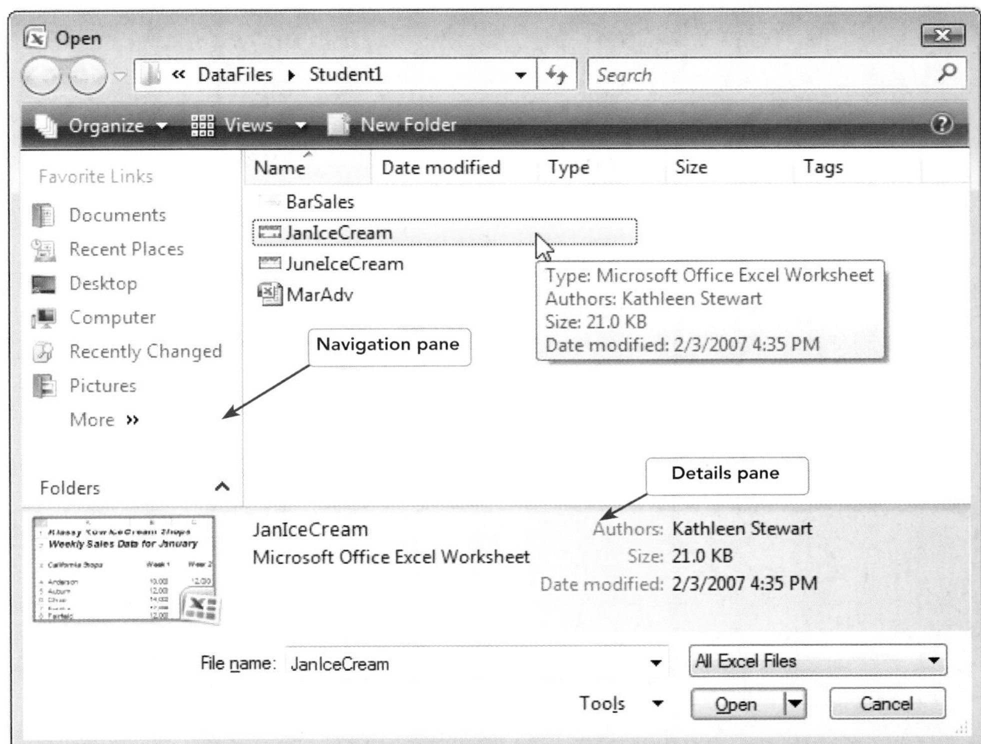

NOTE

The workbooks in this course relate to the Case Study about Klassy Kow Ice Cream, Inc., a fictional manufacturer of ice cream (see the Case Study in the frontmatter).

6. Find and click **JanIceCream**. The Details pane shows a thumbnail of the document.
7. Double-click **JanIceCream**. The workbook opens.

Editing a Worksheet

The **JanIceCream** workbook has three worksheets. The worksheets have been renamed **WeeklySales**, **Owners**, and **Chart** to better indicate what is on the sheet. For instance, the **WeeklySales** sheet shows sales for each city in each of the four weeks in January.

Worksheet cells contain text, numbers, or formulas. A formula calculates an arithmetic result. By simply viewing the worksheet, you might not know if the cell contains a number or a formula. However, you can determine a cell's contents by checking the formula bar. You can also use the formula bar to change the contents of cells.

Exercise 1-8 VIEW WORKSHEETS AND CELL CONTENTS

1. Click the **Owners** worksheet tab. The **Owners** worksheet shows the city and the name of the shop owner.
2. Click the **Chart** tab. This bar chart illustrates January sales for each city.
3. Press Ctrl+PageUp. This moves to the **Owners** worksheet.
4. Press Ctrl+PageDown. Now, the active tab is the **Chart** sheet.
5. Click the **WeeklySales** tab.
6. Press F5 to open the Go To dialog box.
7. Key **a5** and press Enter. The active cell is changed to cell A5. This cell contains the name of a city (Auburn), which you can see in the formula bar and on the worksheet.

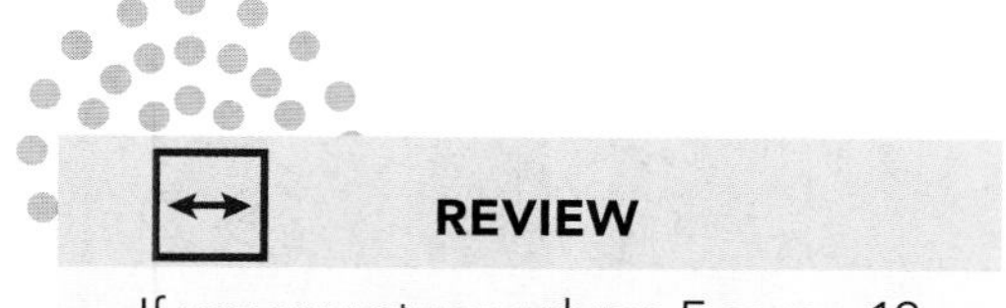

REVIEW

If you cannot see column F or row 19, adjust the Zoom size.

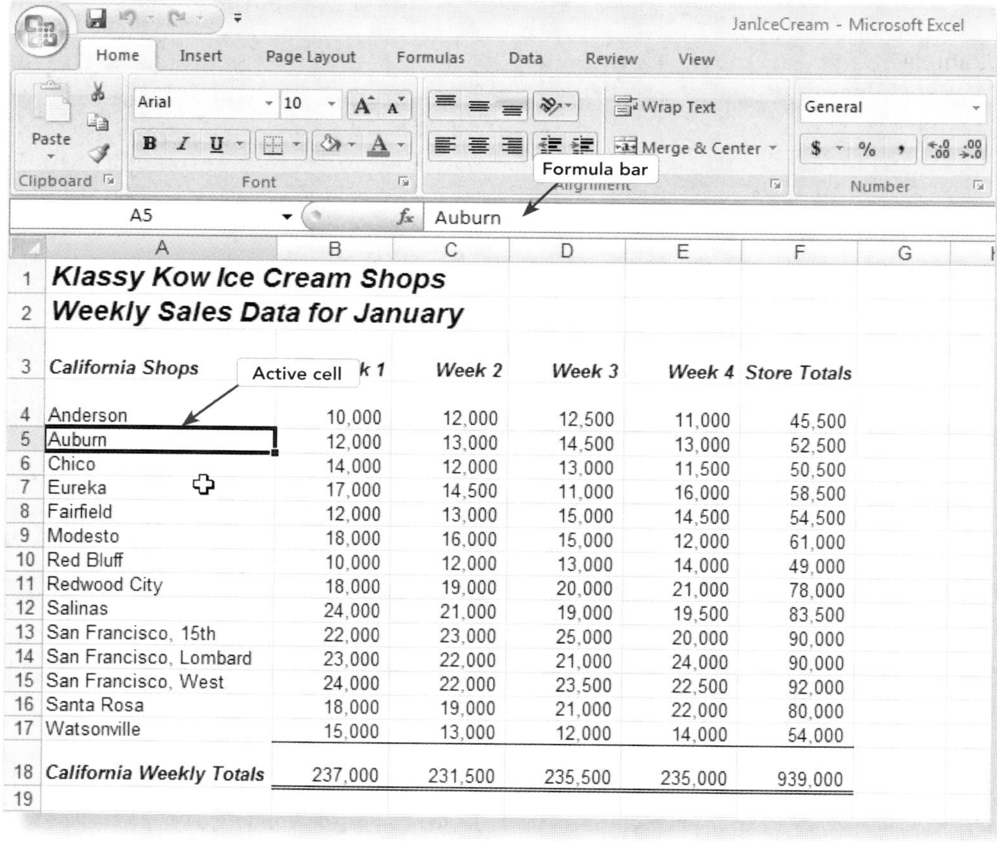

Figure 1-9
Cell contents and the formula bar
JanIceCream.xlsx
WeeklySales sheet

8. Press F5, key **c10**, and press Enter. Cell C10 contains a number. In the formula bar, the number does not show the comma.

9. Press F5, key **f17**, and press Enter. Cell F17 contains a formula, which you can see in the formula bar. Formulas calculate a result.

Exercise 1-9 REPLACE CELL CONTENTS

When the workbook is in Ready mode, you can key, edit, or replace the contents of a cell. To replace a cell's contents, make it the active cell, key the new data, and press Enter. You can also click the Enter button ✓ in the formula bar or press any arrow key on the keyboard to complete the replacement.

If you replace a number used in a formula, the result of the formula automatically recalculates when you complete your change.

1. Click cell B5 to make it the active cell.

2. Key **20000** without a comma. As you key the number, it appears in the cell and in the formula bar. The status bar shows **Enter** to indicate that you are in Enter mode.

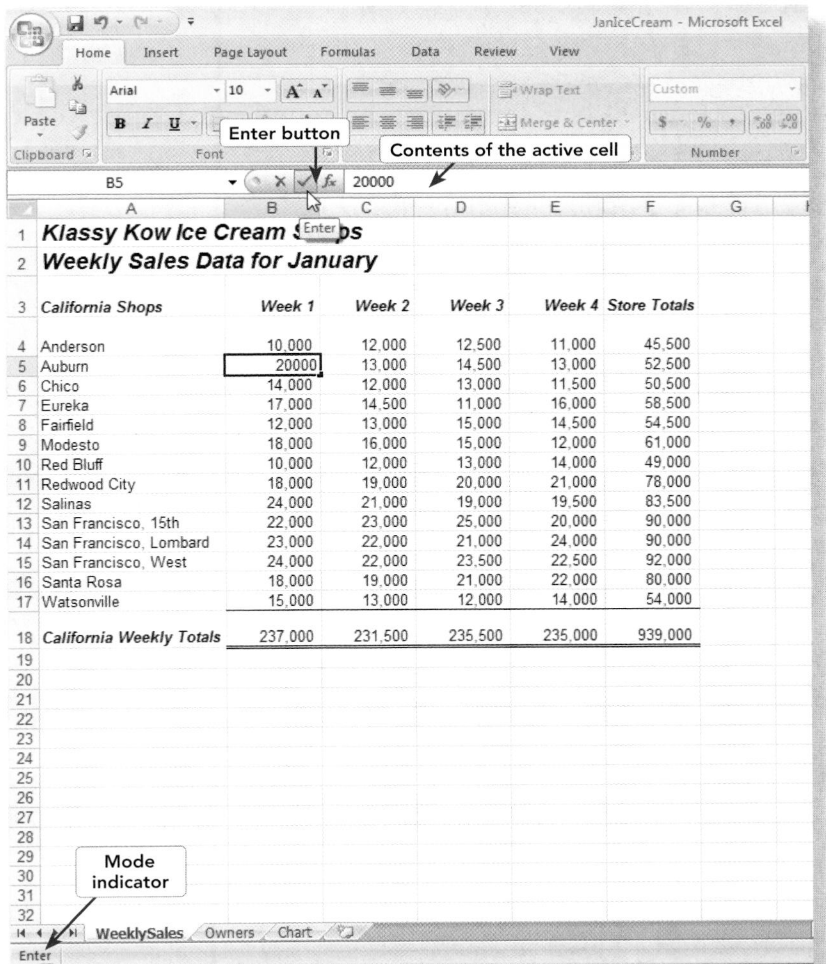

	A	B	C	D	E	F
1	*Klassy Kow Ice Cream Shops*					
2	*Weekly Sales Data for January*					
3	*California Shops*	*Week 1*	*Week 2*	*Week 3*	*Week 4*	*Store Totals*
4	Anderson	10,000	12,000	12,500	11,000	45,500
5	Auburn	20000	13,000	14,500	13,000	52,500
6	Chico	14,000	12,000	13,000	11,500	50,500
7	Eureka	17,000	14,500	11,000	16,000	58,500
8	Fairfield	12,000	13,000	15,000	14,500	54,500
9	Modesto	18,000	16,000	15,000	12,000	61,000
10	Red Bluff	10,000	12,000	13,000	14,000	49,000
11	Redwood City	18,000	19,000	20,000	21,000	78,000
12	Salinas	24,000	21,000	19,000	19,500	83,500
13	San Francisco, 15th	22,000	23,000	25,000	20,000	90,000
14	San Francisco, Lombard	23,000	22,000	21,000	24,000	90,000
15	San Francisco, West	24,000	22,000	23,500	22,500	92,000
16	Santa Rosa	18,000	19,000	21,000	22,000	80,000
17	Watsonville	15,000	13,000	12,000	14,000	54,000
18	*California Weekly Totals*	237,000	231,500	235,500	235,000	939,000

Figure 1-10
Replacing cell contents
JanIceCream.xlsx
WeeklySales sheet

3. Press Enter. Excel inserts a comma, and the next cell in column B is active. The "Store Total" (cell F5, 60,500) and the "California Weekly Totals" amounts (in cells B18 and F18, 245,000 and 947,000) are recalculated. The worksheet returns to Ready mode.

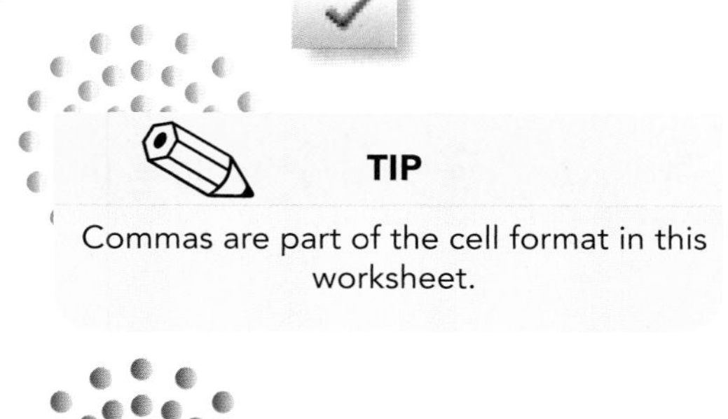

TIP

Commas are part of the cell format in this worksheet.

NOTE

Ctrl+Enter keeps the insertion point in the current cell.

4. Press ↑ to move to cell B5. Key **10000** without a comma. Click the Enter button ✓ in the formula bar. Notice that when you use the Enter button ✓, the pointer stays in cell B5.
5. Click the **Chart** tab. Notice the length of the Auburn bar, showing sales near $50,000.
6. Click the **WeeklySales** tab.
7. In cell B5, key **0**, and press Ctrl+Enter. A zero appears as a short dash in this worksheet.
8. Click the **Chart** tab. The chart on this worksheet is based on the data in the **WeeklySales** worksheet. Now that you have reduced sales, the Auburn bar is shorter.
9. Click the **WeeklySales** tab and key **10000** in cell B5. Press →.

Exercise 1-10 EDIT CELL CONTENTS

If a cell contains a long or complicated entry, you can edit it rather than rekeying the entire entry. Edit mode starts when you:

- Double-click the cell.
- Click the cell and press F2.
- Click the cell and then click anywhere in the formula bar.

TABLE 1-4 Keyboard Shortcuts in Edit Mode

Key	To Do This
Enter	Complete the edit, return to Ready mode, and move the insertion point to the next cell.
Alt+Enter	Move the insertion point to a new line within the cell, a line break.
Esc	Cancel the edit and restore the existing data.
Home	Move the insertion point to the beginning of the data.
End	Move the insertion point to the end of the data.
Delete	Delete one character to the right of the insertion point.
Ctrl+Delete	Delete everything from the insertion point to the end of the line.
Backspace	Delete one character to the left of the insertion point.
← or →	Move the insertion point one character left or right.
Ctrl+←	Move the insertion point one word left.
Ctrl+→	Move the insertion point one word right.

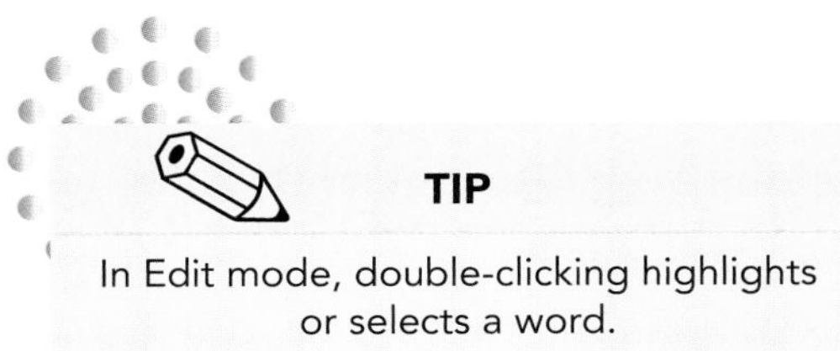

TIP

In Edit mode, double-clicking highlights or selects a word.

1. Click cell A2. The text in cell A2 is long, and its display overlaps into columns B and C.
2. Press F2. **Edit** mode is shown in the status bar. An insertion point appears in the cell at the end of the text.
3. Double-click "Data" in the cell. A Mini toolbar appears with buttons for font editing.
4. Point at the Mini toolbar. Its appearance brightens for easy viewing.

Figure 1-11
Using Edit mode
JanIceCream.xlsx
WeeklySales sheet

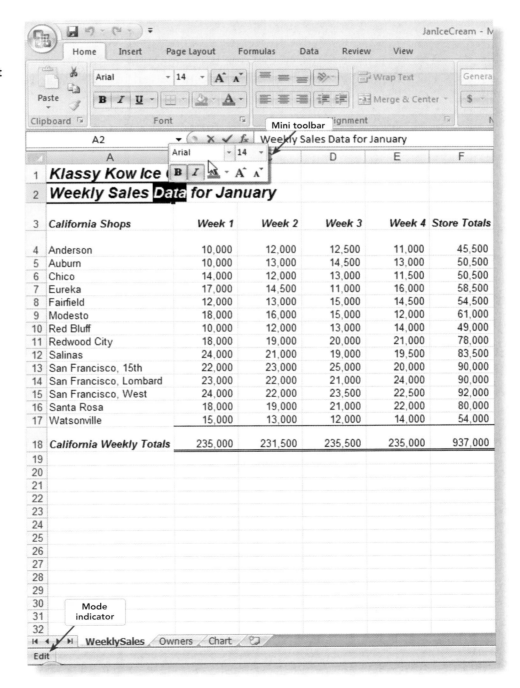

Mini toolbar

A2 | Weekly Sales Data for January

	A	B	C	D	E	F
1	*Klassy Kow Ice*					
2	*Weekly Sales Data for January*					
3	*California Shops*	*Week 1*	*Week 2*	*Week 3*	*Week 4*	*Store Totals*
4	Anderson	10,000	12,000	12,500	11,000	45,500
5	Auburn	10,000	13,000	14,500	13,000	50,500
6	Chico	14,000	12,000	13,000	11,500	50,500
7	Eureka	17,000	14,500	11,000	16,000	58,500
8	Fairfield	12,000	13,000	15,000	14,500	54,500
9	Modesto	18,000	16,000	15,000	12,000	61,000
10	Red Bluff	10,000	12,000	13,000	14,000	49,000
11	Redwood City	18,000	19,000	20,000	21,000	78,000
12	Salinas	24,000	21,000	19,000	19,500	83,500
13	San Francisco, 15th	22,000	23,000	25,000	20,000	90,000
14	San Francisco, Lombard	23,000	22,000	21,000	24,000	90,000
15	San Francisco, West	24,000	22,000	23,500	22,500	92,000
16	Santa Rosa	18,000	19,000	21,000	22,000	80,000
17	Watsonville	15,000	13,000	12,000	14,000	54,000
18	*California Weekly Totals*	235,000	231,500	235,500	235,000	937,000

WeeklySales | Owners | Chart

Mode indicator

Edit

5. Key **Information**. It replaces the word "Data." The Mini toolbar has disappeared.
6. Press Enter to complete the edit. Pressing Enter does not start a new line in the cell when the worksheet is in Edit mode.
7. Double-click cell A3. This starts Edit mode, and an insertion point appears in the cell.
8. In the cell, click to the left of the first "S" in "Shops."
9. Key **Retail** and press Spacebar. Press Enter.
10. Click cell F1. There is nothing in this cell.
11. Key your first name, a space, and your last name in the cell. Press Enter. If your name is longer than column F, part of its display might overlap into column G and even into column H.

Exercise 1-11 CLEAR CELL CONTENTS

When you clear the contents of a cell, you delete the text, number, or formula in that cell.

NOTE

A green triangle may appear in the corners of cells F5 and B18 to indicate that a formula error has occurred. Ignore the triangles for now.

1. Click cell B5. Press Delete on the keyboard. The number is deleted, and Excel recalculates the formula results in cells F5, B18, and F18.
2. Press → to move the pointer to cell C5.
3. On the **Home** tab in the **Editing** group, click the Clear button.
4. Choose **Clear Contents**. The number is deleted, and formulas are recalculated.

Exercise 1-12 USE UNDO AND REDO

The Undo command reverses the last action you performed in the worksheet. For example, if you delete the contents of a cell, the Undo command restores what you deleted. The Redo command reverses the action of the Undo command. It "undoes" your Undo.

To use the Undo command, you can:

- Click the Undo button on the Quick Access toolbar.
- Press Ctrl+Z or Alt+Backspace.

To use the Redo command, you can:

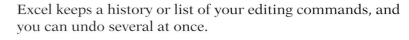

- Click the Redo button on the Quick Access toolbar.
- Press Ctrl+Y or F4.

Excel keeps a history or list of your editing commands, and you can undo several at once.

NOTE

The ScreenTip for the Undo button includes the most recent task, such as Undo Clear.

NOTE

Depending on the actions that have been undone and redone on your computer, your list might be different from the one shown in Figure 1-12.

1. Click the Undo button. The number in cell C5 is restored.
2. Click the Redo button. The number is cleared again.
3. Click cell A8 and key **Gotham**. Press Enter.
4. In cell A9 key **Los Angeles** and press Enter.
5. Click the arrow next to the Undo button to display the history list.
6. Move the mouse to highlight the top two actions and click. The last two changes are undone, and the original city names are restored.

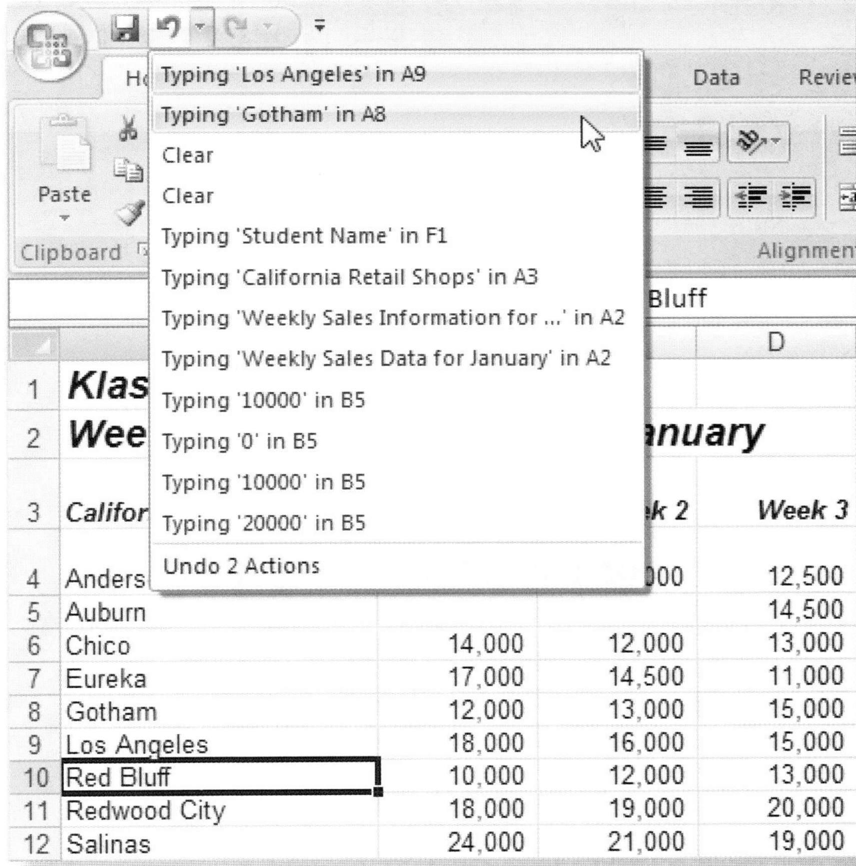

Figure 1-12
Undoing multiple edits
JanIceCream.xlsx WeeklySales sheet

TIP

If you place the pointer in cell A1 when you save a workbook, cell A1 is the active cell the next time you open the workbook.

7. Click the Redo button. The first action is restored.
8. Click the Redo button again.
9. Press Ctrl+Home to place the pointer in cell A1.

Managing Files

Workbook files are usually stored in folders. A *folder* is a location on a disk, network, or other drive. Folders are organized in a structure like a family tree. The top level of the tree is a letter such as C, F, or G to represent the disk or other storage device. Under each letter, you can create folders to help you organize and manage your work.

For your work in this text, you will save your files in a folder you create for each lesson.

Exercise 1-13 CREATE A NEW FOLDER AND USE SAVE AS

NOTE

Ask your instructor where to save lesson folders for this course.

1. Click the Microsoft Office Button and choose **Save As**. The Save As dialog box opens. You will save **JanIceCream** with a new filename in a lesson folder.
2. Choose the drive and folder location for your work.

3. Click the New Folder button. A New Folder icon opens.
4. Key *[your initials]*Lesson1. Press Enter. Your new folder's name now appears in the navigation line.

NOTE

JanIceCream may be a read-only file if you opened it from a protected or restricted location. You cannot resave such a file with its existing filename.

5. In the **File name** box, make sure the filename **JanIceCream** is highlighted or selected. If it is not highlighted, click to select it.

6. Key *[your initials]***1-13** and click **Save**. Your new filename now appears in the title bar.

Figure 1-13
Save As dialog box

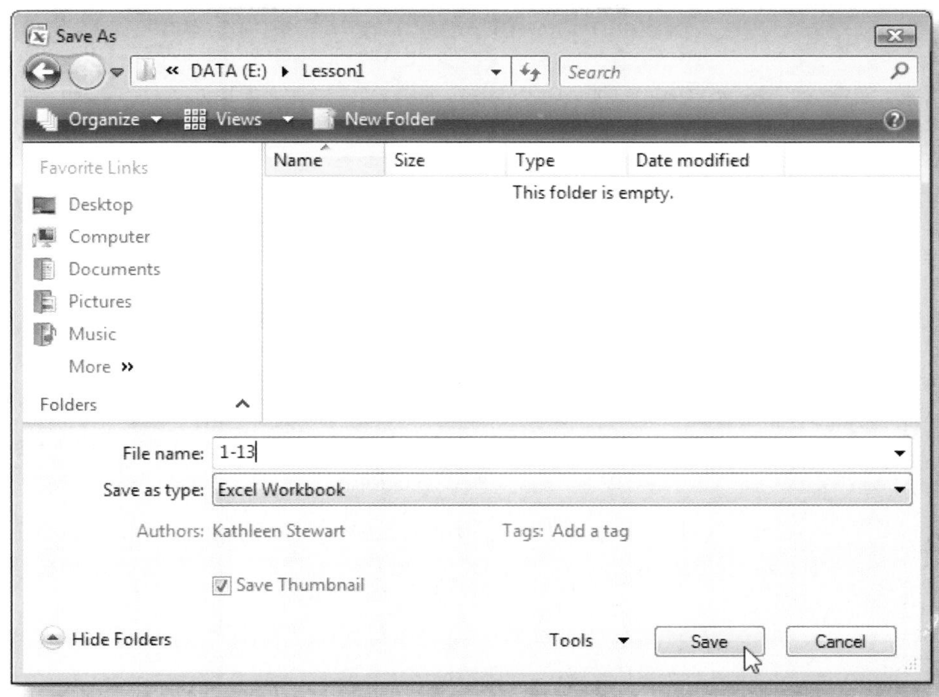

NOTE

Excel automatically assigns the **.xlsx** extension to files you save, but your computer may not be set to display filename extensions.

Printing Excel Files

You can use any of these methods to print a worksheet:

- Press Ctrl+P.
- Click the Microsoft Office Button and choose **Print** and then **Quick Print**.

- Click the Print button while in Print Preview.

- Click the Quick Print button on the Quick Access toolbar.

Some methods open the Print dialog box, in which you can change printing options. The Quick Print button, if it is on the Quick Access toolbar, and choosing Quick Print from the menu send the worksheet to the printer with default print settings.

Page Layout View displays your sheet with margin and header/footer areas. You can edit your work in Page Layout View. Print Preview also shows your worksheet as it will print in a normal or reduced view. You cannot make any changes in Print Preview.

Exercise 1-14 PREVIEW AND PRINT A WORKSHEET

1. In the status bar, click the Page Layout View button. The page shows margin areas and the rulers.
2. Click the Zoom Out button in the status bar. The worksheet is reduced to 90% magnification.
3. Click the Zoom Out button to reach 50% magnification. Unused pages appear grayed out.
4. Click **50%** in the status bar. Choose **100%** and click **OK**.

5. Click the Normal button in the status bar.
6. Click the Microsoft Office Button and hover over **Print**. A submenu opens.
7. Choose **Print Preview**. The worksheet is shown in a reduced size so that you can see the entire page.

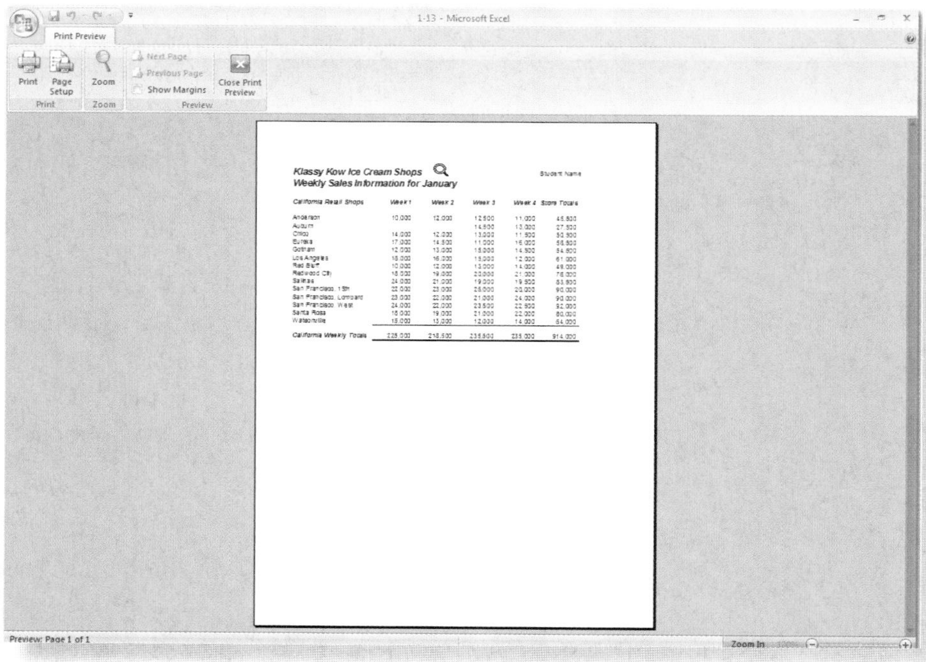

Figure 1-14
Worksheet in Print Preview
1-13.xlsx
WeeklySales sheet

8. Move the mouse pointer near the main headings. The pointer appears as a small magnifying glass icon.
9. Click while pointing at the headings. The worksheet changes to a larger size, close to the actual print size.

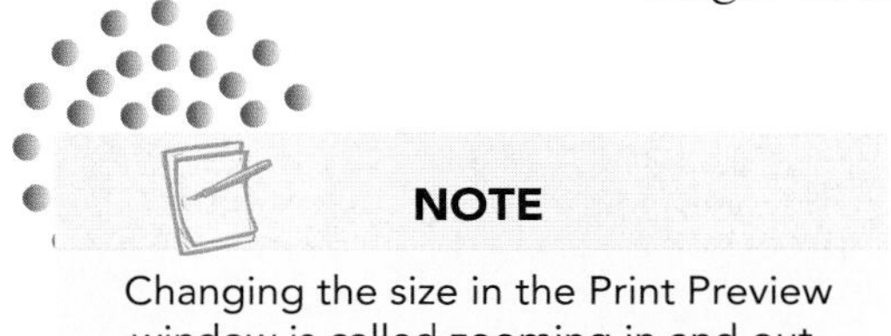

NOTE

Changing the size in the Print Preview window is called zooming in and out.

10. Click anywhere to return to a reduced size. The mouse pointer appears as a white solid arrow when it will zoom out.
11. Zoom in on the "California Weekly Totals" row. Click anywhere to zoom out.
12. Click the Print button. The Print dialog box opens.

13. Press Enter. A printer icon appears on the taskbar as the worksheet is sent to the printer. Only the **WeeklySales** worksheet is printed.

Exercise 1-15 PRINT A WORKBOOK

You can print all sheets in a workbook with one command from the Print dialog box.

1. Press Ctrl+P. The Print dialog box opens with your default settings.

Figure 1-15
Print dialog box

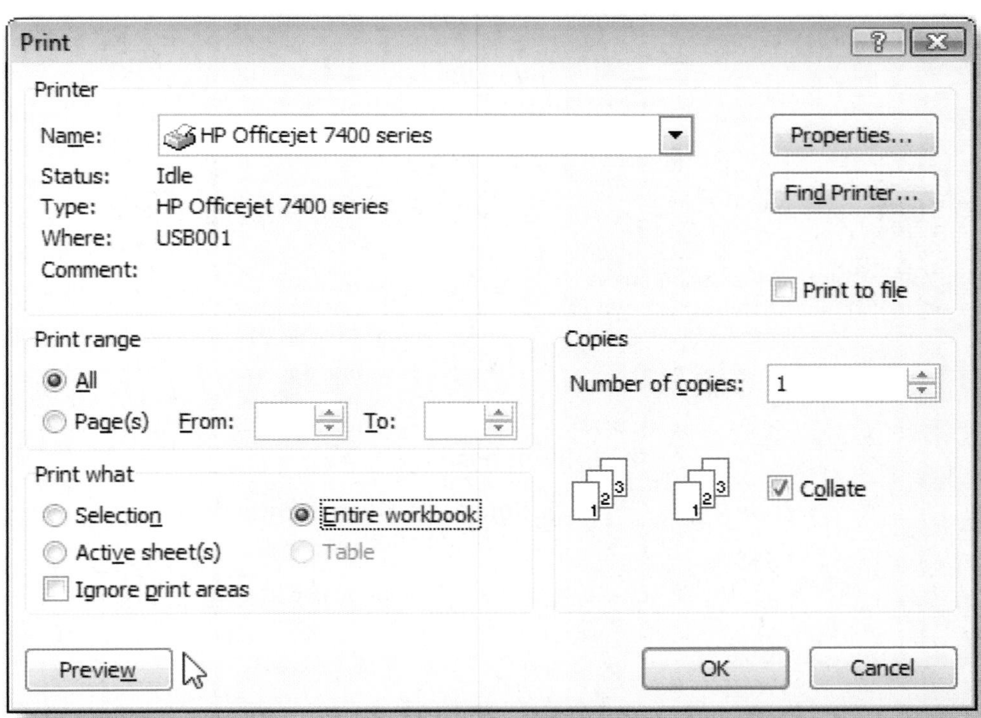

2. In the **Print what** section, choose **Entire workbook**.

3. Click **Preview**. The reduced size shows the first page, the **WeeklySales** sheet. The status bar shows that this is page 1 of 3.
4. Press PageDown. This is the second sheet, the **Owners** worksheet.
5. Press PageDown. This is the **Chart** sheet. It is set to print in landscape orientation.
6. Click **Previous Page** two times to return to the first sheet.
7. Click the Print button. All three sheets are sent to the printer and Print Preview closes.

Exercise 1-16 SAVE AN XPS FILE

XPS is *XML Paper Specification (XPS)*, a file type that maintains document formatting so that you or others can view or print the worksheet exactly as it was designed, with or without Excel. You need a viewer to open an XPS document, available in Windows Vista or free from Microsoft's Web site. To save a file as an XPS (or PDF) document, you must have installed this add-in at your computer.

1. Click the Microsoft Office Button and choose **Save As**. The Save As dialog box opens. If you have opened the Publish as PDF or XPS dialog box, close it and try again.
2. Choose ***[your initials]* Lesson1** as the location.
3. In the **File name** box, make sure the file name ***[your initials]*1-13** is highlighted or selected. If it is not highlighted, select it.
4. Key ***[your initials]*1-16**.

TIP

You can also save a document as an Adobe PDF file so that others can view it without Excel.

5. Click the **Save as type** arrow. A list of file types opens.
6. Find and choose **XPS Document**. The same document name is assumed, but it will have a different extension.
7. Choose **Standard** as the **Optimize for** option. Click to deselect **Open file after publishing**.
8. Click **Options** and choose **Entire workbook** in the **Publish what** group. Click **OK** (see Figure 1-16).
9. Click **Save**. Your workbook is still open, and the XPS file is saved separately.

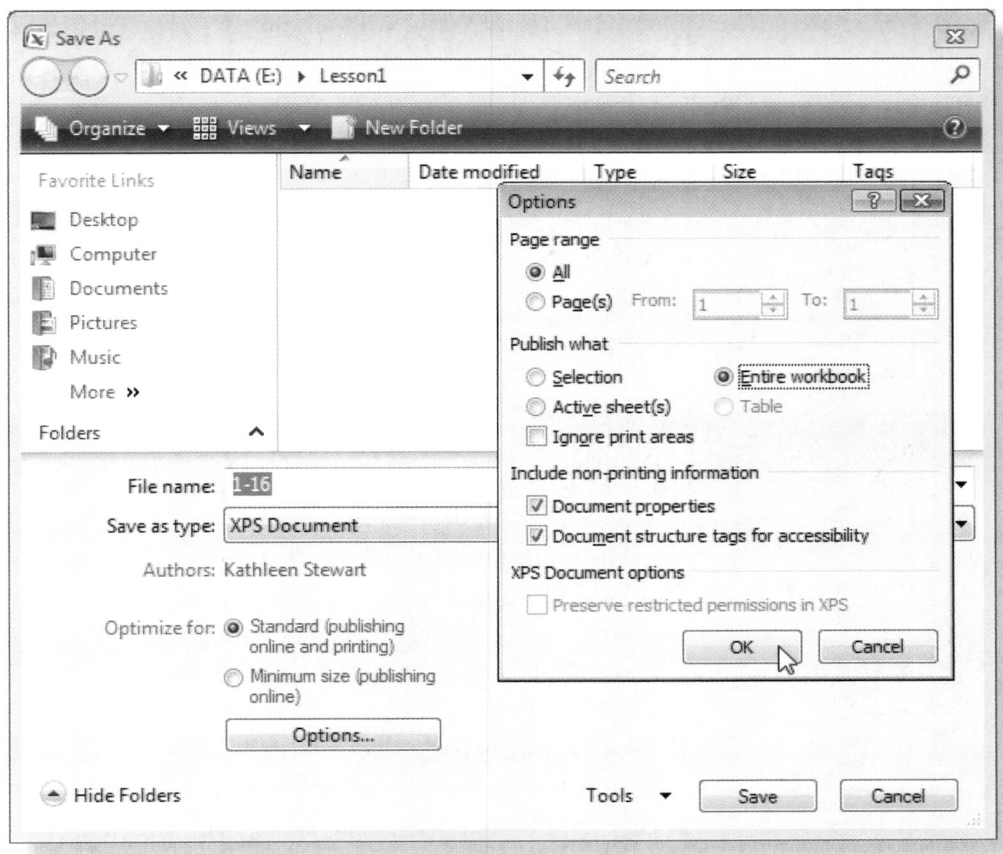

Figure 1-16
Saving an XPS document

Exercise 1-17 EXIT EXCEL

You can exit Excel and close the workbook at the same time. If you give the command to exit Excel, you will see a reminder to save the workbook if you have not yet done so.

There are several ways to close a workbook and exit Excel:

- Click the Microsoft Office Button and choose **Exit Excel**.
- Use the Close button to first close the workbook and then to close Excel.
- Use the keyboard shortcut Alt+F4 to exit Excel.

1. Click the Microsoft Office Button.
2. Choose **Exit Excel**. Do not save changes if asked.

Using Online Help

Online Help is available at your computer and on the Microsoft Office Web site. An easy way to use Help is to key a short request in the search text box at the top of the opening screen.

GET ACQUAINTED WITH USING HELP

1. Start Excel and click the Microsoft Office Excel Help button.
2. In the search box, key **get help** and press Enter.
3. From the list of topics, find a topic that will explain how to use help and click it. Click **Show All**.
4. Read the information and close the Help window.

Lesson 1 Summary

- Excel opens with a blank workbook and the Ribbon. The active command tab on the Ribbon changes depending on what you are doing.
- A new workbook opens with three worksheets. A worksheet is an individual page or tab in the workbook.
- Press Ctrl+PageUp and Ctrl+PageDown to move between worksheets in a workbook.
- Worksheets are divided into cells, which are the intersections of rows and columns. The location of the cell is its address (also called its cell reference).
- Move the pointer to a specific cell with the Go To command or by clicking the cell.
- The active cell is outlined with a black border. It is ready to accept new data or a formula or to be edited.
- The Name Box shows the address of the active cell. You can also use it to change the active cell.
- If you use the scroll box or arrows to reposition the worksheet on the screen, the active cell does not change.
- The Zoom size controls how much of the worksheet you can see at once.
- Replace any entry in a cell by clicking the cell and keying new data. Edit long or complicated cell data rather than rekeying it.
- The Undo button and the Redo button both have history arrows so that you can undo or redo multiple commands at once.
- Preview your worksheet or the entire workbook before printing it. To preview and print all the worksheets in a workbook, click the Microsoft Office Button and choose Print. Then choose **Entire workbook**.

LESSON 1		Command Summary	
Feature	**Button**	**Task Path**	**Keyboard**
Collapse ribbon			Ctrl+F1
Clear cell contents		Home, Editing, Clear, Clear Contents	Delete
Close workbook		Microsoft Office, Close	Ctrl+W or Ctrl+F4
Exit Excel		Microsoft Office, Exit Excel	Ctrl+F4
Full Screen	Full Screen	View, Workbook Views, Full Screen	
Go To	Find & Select	Home, Editing, Find & Select, Go To	Ctrl+G or F5
KeyTips			Alt or F10
Normal View	Normal	View, Workbook Views, Normal	
Open workbook		Microsoft Office, Open	Ctrl+O or Ctrl+F12
Page Layout View	Page Layout View	View, Workbook Views, Page Layout View	
Print		Microsoft Office, Print	Ctrl+P
Print Preview	Print	Microsoft Office, Print, Print Preview	Ctrl+F2
Redo			Ctrl+Y or F4
Save As		Microsoft Office, Save As	F12 or Alt+F2
Undo			Ctrl+Z or Alt+Backspace
Zoom In			
Zoom Out			
Zoom Size	Zoom	View, Zoom	

Lesson 2

Creating a Workbook

OBJECTIVES

After completing this lesson, you will be able to:

1. Enter labels.
2. Change the document theme.
3. Select cell ranges.
4. Modify column width and row height.
5. Enter values and dates.
6. Save a workbook.
7. Enter basic formulas.

Estimated Time: 1 1/2 hours

MCAS OBJECTIVES

In this lesson:

XL07 1.3
XL07 1.5.3
XL07 2.1.1
XL07 2.1.3
XL07 2.2.2
XL07 2.2.4
XL07 2.3.2
XL07 2.3.4
XL07 3.1.1
XL07 3.2.1
XL07 5.4

A new workbook opens with three blank worksheets. You can key text, numbers, or formulas in any cell in any of the worksheets. Excel uses a default document theme in a new workbook, but you can change the theme or any formatting elements used in the worksheet. You can also adjust the width and height of columns, edit colors, and more.

Entering Labels

When you key data that begins with a letter, Excel recognizes it as a *label*. Labels are aligned at the left edge of the cell and are not used in calculations.

As you key data, it appears in the active cell and in the formula bar. If you make an error, press Esc to start over. You can also press Backspace to edit the entry.

There are several ways you can complete an entry.

TABLE 2-1 Ways to Complete a Cell Entry

Key or Button	Result
Press Enter	Completes entry and moves the pointer to the cell below.
Press Ctrl+Enter	Completes entry and leaves the pointer in the current cell.
Press Tab	Completes entry and moves the pointer to the cell to the right.
Press Shift+Tab	Completes entry and moves the pointer to the cell to the left.
Press an arrow key	Completes entry and moves the pointer one cell in the direction of the arrow.
Click another cell	Completes entry and moves the pointer to the clicked cell.
Click the Enter button	Completes entry and leaves the pointer in the current cell.

Exercise 2-1 ENTER LABELS IN A WORKSHEET

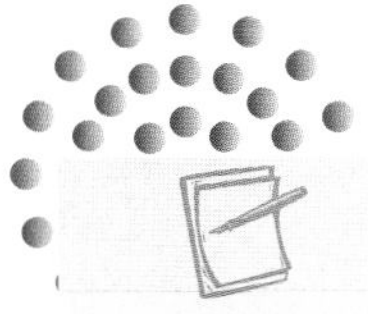

NOTE

The first new workbook in a work session is named **Book1** until you save it with another name. The next new workbook is **Book2**, and so on.

1. Start Excel with a blank workbook. Cell A1 on **Sheet1** is active.
2. In cell A1, key **Klassy Kow Sa** to start a label. The worksheet is in Enter mode, shown in the status bar. The label appears in the formula bar and in the cell.
3. Press Backspace to delete **Sa**.
4. Key **Promotions**. Notice that an Enter button  and a Cancel button  appear in the formula bar when you are in Enter mode.

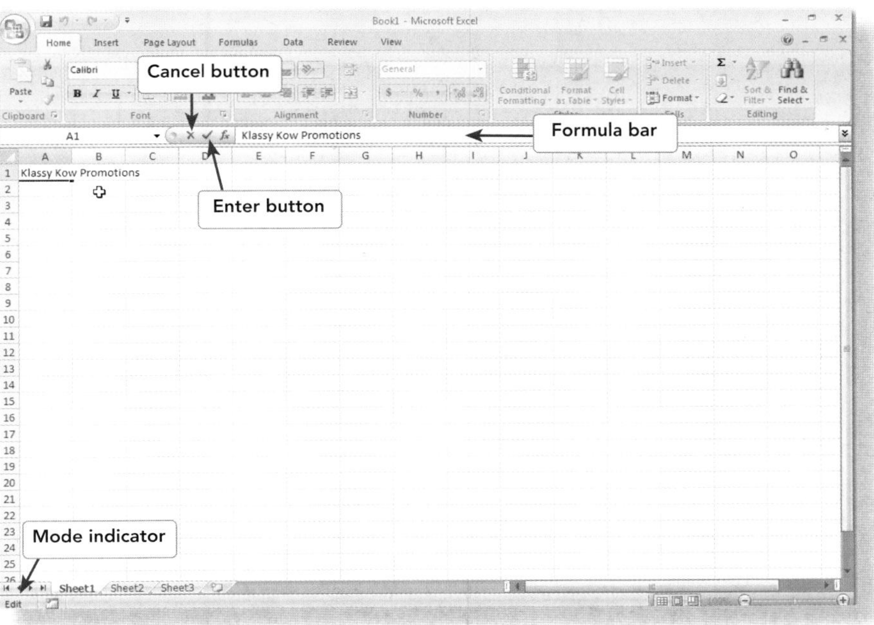

Figure 2-1
Label appearing in the formula bar and the cell

5. Press [Enter]. The label is completed in cell A1, and the pointer moves to cell A2. The label is longer than column A, so it appears to spill into columns B and C.

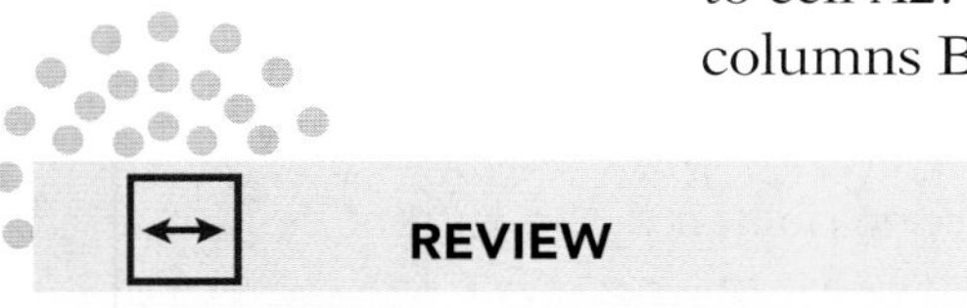

REVIEW

If you pressed [Enter] or moved away from the cell and need to edit it, click the cell. Key the new data and press [Enter].

6. In cell A2, key **Market** to start a label. Press [Esc] to delete your entry. You can use [Esc] to delete an entry if you haven't yet pressed [Enter] or moved away from the cell.
7. Key **Company Plan** and click the Enter button ✓ in the formula bar. The label appears to spill into cell B2.
8. Click cell A3 to make it active.
9. Key **Name** and press [→]. The pointer is now in cell B3.
10. Key **Starting Date** and press [Tab]. The label is too long for column B and spills into column C.

NOTE

Text display can spill into adjacent cells only if they are empty.

11. Key **Ending Date** in cell C3 and press [→]. This label cuts off the label from column B and spills into cell D3. You will fix these problems soon.
12. Key **Price** and press [Tab]. Key **Special Price** in cell E3 and press [Enter]. This label is not cut off, because there is nothing in the cell to the right.
13. Key the following labels in column A, starting in cell A4. Press [Enter] after each.

    Berry Kowabunga
    Easter Bunny Pie
    Triple-Scoop Cone
    24 oz. Shake

Changing the Document Theme

A *document theme* is a set of 2 fonts, 12 colors, and effects for shapes and charts. Each new workbook uses the Office document theme. The default body text font for this theme is 11-point Calibri. There is also a font for headings, Cambria.

NOTE

Although a theme includes 12 colors, 2 are for hyperlinks and do not appear in color palettes.

Document themes have been developed by designers to use fonts, colors, and effects that are coordinated and balanced. You can use any of the themes, or you can choose any available font, color, or effect.

Exercise 2-2 CHANGE THE THEME

If you have used theme fonts in your worksheet, you can change the document theme and immediately see font changes applied from the new theme. The *Live Preview* feature allows you to see the changes before they are applied.

NOTE

Your font list probably does not match the one in the text illustration.

1. Click cell A1. Click the **Home** tab. Hover over the **Font** box in the **Font** group to see the ScreenTip.
2. Click the arrow next to the **Font** box. The theme fonts are at the top of the list, Cambria for headings and Calibri for body data. Other fonts on your computer are listed below these two.

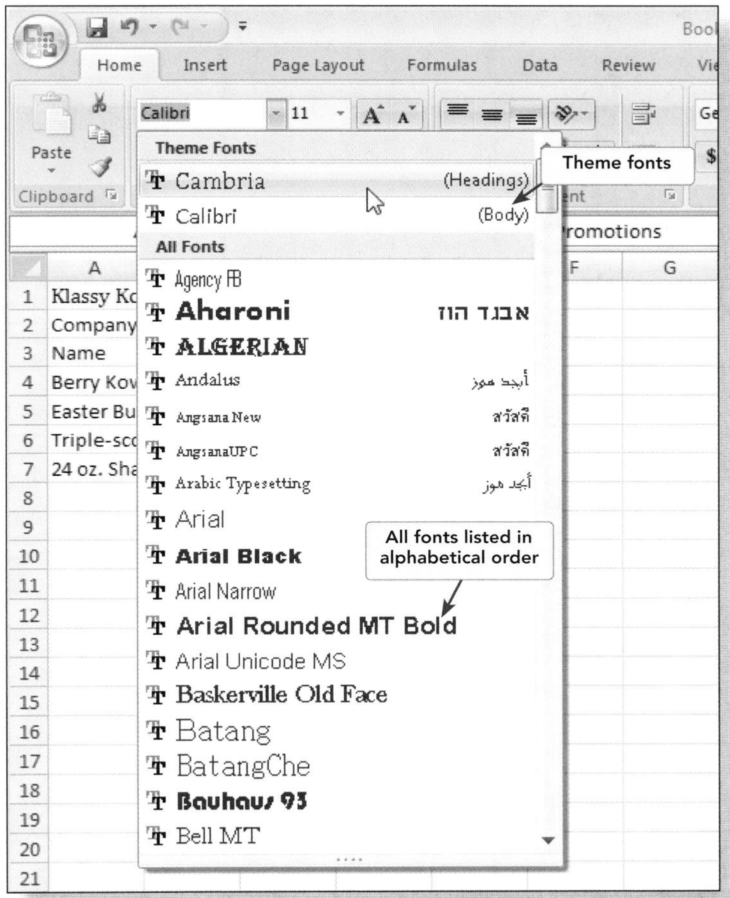

Figure 2-2
Choosing a theme font

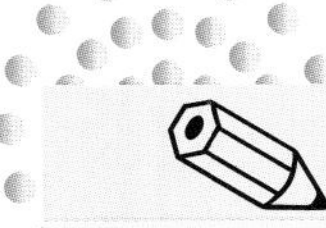

TIP

Calibri is a sans serif font; Cambria is a serif font. Serifs are tiny strokes at the end of a character.

3. Choose **Cambria**. The label in cell A1 is changed.
4. Choose the Cambria font for the label in cell A2. Your data now uses Cambria for these two labels and Calibri for the remaining data. These are both theme fonts.

5. Click the Zoom In button on the status bar four times. It will be easier to watch the changes in a larger view.
6. Click the **Page Layout** tab in the Ribbon. The first group is **Themes**.

7. Hover over the Themes button. The ScreenTip includes the current theme name.
8. Click the Themes button to open its gallery of built-in themes.

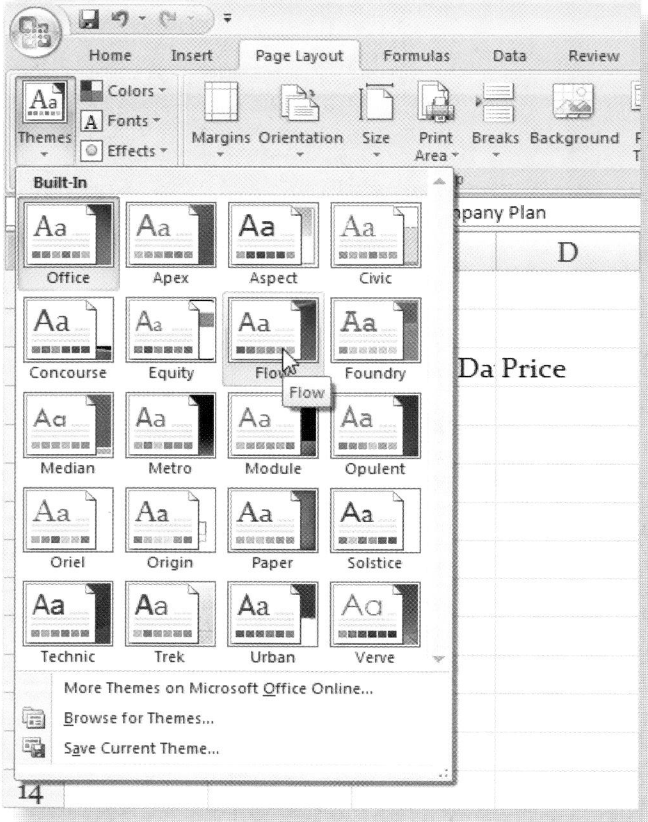

Figure 2-3 The Document Theme gallery

9. Hover over **Flow**. You can see a part of your data with the change.
10. Click **Flow**. The gallery closes, and the data uses new theme fonts.
11. Click the **Home** tab in the Ribbon.
12. Click the arrow next to the **Font** box. The theme fonts are Calibri for headings and Constantia for body text.

Exercise 2-3 CHANGE THE FONT, FONT SIZE, AND STYLE

You are not limited to the fonts in the document theme. You can use any font, font style, or size from the Font group on the Home tab or from the Format Cells dialog box. When you choose a larger font size, the height of the row is automatically made taller to fit the font. Font style includes bold, italic, and underline.

1. Click cell A1.
2. Click the arrow next to the **Font** box. A drop-down list box appears, showing font names for your computer.
3. Key **t** to move to the font names starting with "T." Live Preview shows the data in the new font as you scroll the list.
4. Find and choose **Times New Roman**.
5. Click the arrow next to the **Font Size** box. Choose **16**. Notice that row 1 is made taller to accommodate the larger font size.

NOTE

You can also scroll in the Font list to a new font.

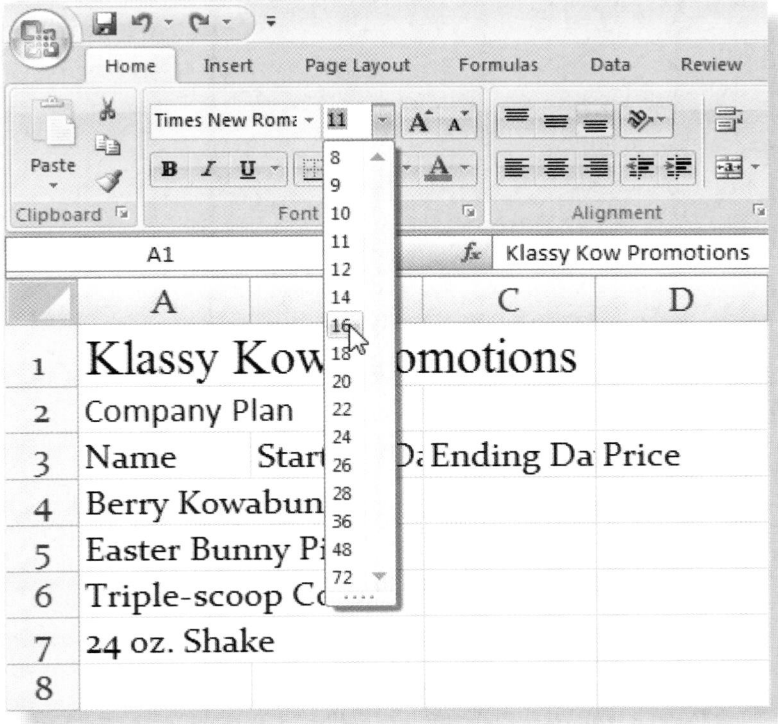

Figure 2-4
Choosing a font size

6. Click the Italic button *I*.

TIP

You can key a font size that is not in the list.

Exercise 2-4 USE THE FORMAT PAINTER

With the Format Painter, you can copy cell formats from one cell to another. This is often faster than applying formats individually.

To use the Format Painter, make the cell with formatting the active cell. Then click the Format Painter button in the Clipboard group on the Home tab. While the pointer is a white cross with a small paintbrush, click the cell to be formatted.

1. Make sure cell A1 is the active cell. Click the **Home** tab if necessary.
2. Hover over the Format Painter button and read the ScreenTip.
3. Click the Format Painter button. Cell A1 shows a moving marquee, and the pointer is a thick white cross with a paintbrush.

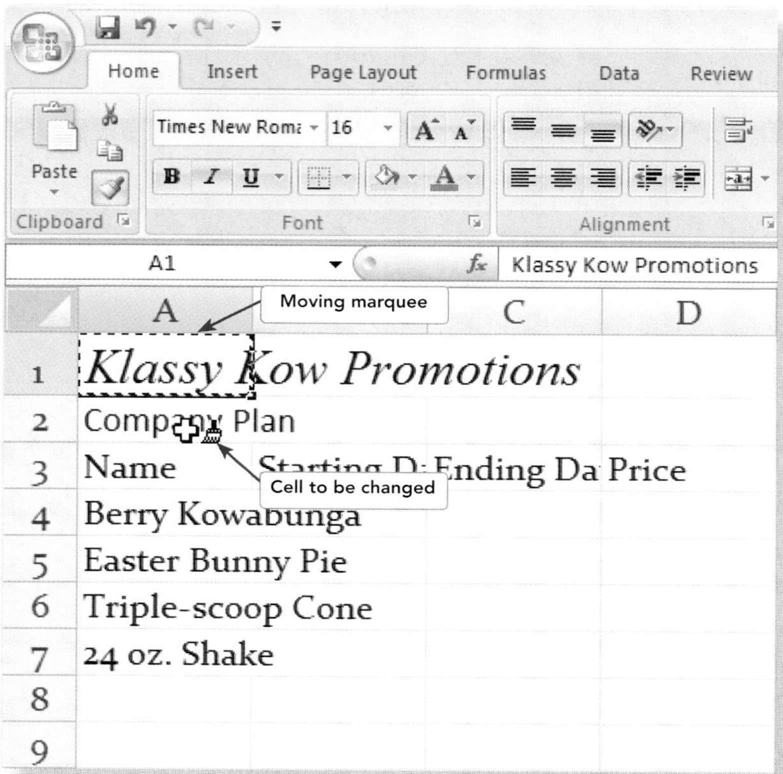

Figure 2-5
Using the Format Painter

4. Click cell A2. The font, size, and style are copied, and row 2 is made taller. The Format Painter command is canceled.
5. Make sure cell A2 is now the active cell.
6. Double-click the Format Painter button. This locks the painter on so that you can format more than one cell.

7. Click cell A3 to copy the format. Then click cell B3.
8. Click the Format Painter button to cancel the command.

9. Click the arrow next to the Undo button . Excel shows Format Painter as **Paste Special** in the Undo history list.
10. Undo two **Paste Special** commands. The labels in row 3 return to the theme font (11-point Constantia).
11. Press Esc to cancel the marquee.

12. Click the Zoom Out button to return to a 100% size.

Selecting Cell Ranges

A *range* is a group of cells that forms a rectangle on the screen. In many cases, you work with a range of cells. For example, you might need to format all the cells in rows 3 through 7 in the same style.

When a range is active, it is highlighted or shaded on the screen. Like an individual cell, a range has an address. A *range address* consists of the upper-left cell address and the lower-right cell address, separated by a colon.

TABLE 2-2 Examples of Range Addresses

Range Address	Cells in the Range
A1:B3	6 cells on 3 rows and in 2 columns
B1:B100	100 cells, all in column B
C3:C13	11 cells, starting at cell C3, all in column C
D4:F12	27 cells on 9 rows and in 3 columns
A1:XFD1	16,384 cells or the entire row 1

Exercise 2-5 SELECT RANGES WITH THE MOUSE

The *selection pointer* within the worksheet grid is a thick white cross shape. When you point at a row or column heading, the selection pointer appears as a solid black arrow. There are several ways to select a range of cells by using the mouse:

- Drag across adjacent cells to select the range.
- Click the first cell in the range. Hold down Shift and click the last cell in the range.
- Click a column heading letter to select a column or click a row heading number to select a row.

- Drag across adjacent column heading letters or row heading numbers to select multiple columns or rows.
- Click the Select All button (see Figure 2-6) to select every cell on the worksheet.

1. With the thick white cross-shaped pointer, click cell A3 and drag to the right to cell E3.

NOTE

If you do not select the correct cells, click cell A3 and try again.

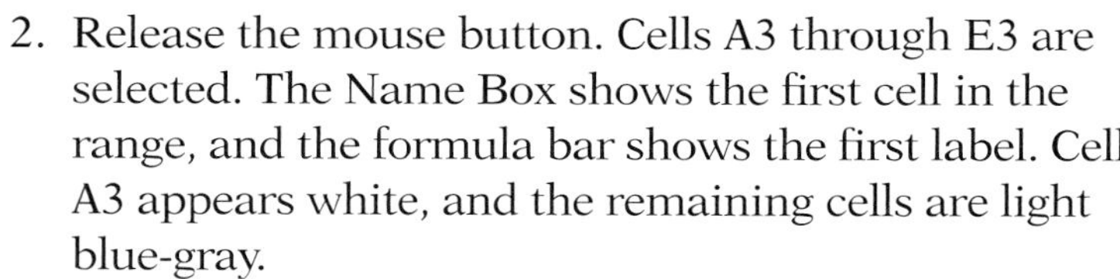

2. Release the mouse button. Cells A3 through E3 are selected. The Name Box shows the first cell in the range, and the formula bar shows the first label. Cell A3 appears white, and the remaining cells are light blue-gray.

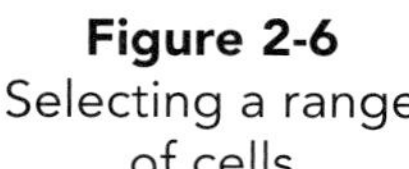

Figure 2-6
Selecting a range of cells

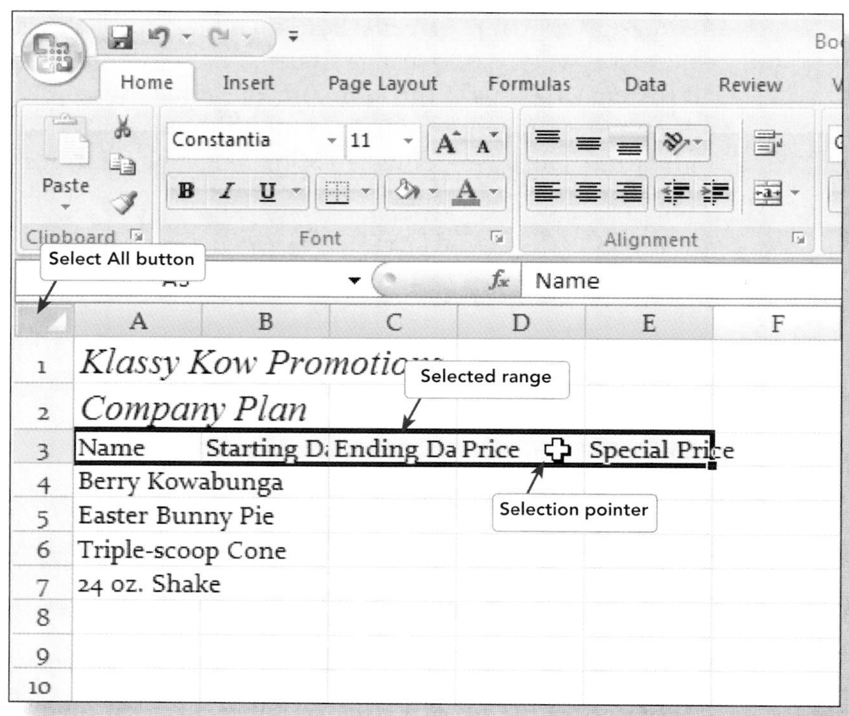

3. Click the Bold button **B**. The labels in the cells in the selected range are bold. Bold data is often slightly larger than data in the Regular style of the same font.

TIP

You can apply bold by using the keystroke combination Ctrl+B. You can apply italic by using Ctrl+I.

4. Click cell A1. This makes cell A1 active and deselects the range.
5. Click cell A1 and drag to cell F1. Do not release the mouse button.
6. Drag down to cell F3 and then release the mouse button. The selected range is A1:F3.
7. Click cell A1 to deselect the range and make cell A1 active again.

8. Point to the row 1 heading. The pointer changes shape and is a solid black arrow.
9. Click the row 1 heading to select the row.
10. Click cell B2. You can click any cell to deselect a range.
11. Point to the row 1 heading. Click and drag down through the row headings from row 1 to row 5.
12. Release the mouse button. Five rows are selected.
13. Click any cell to deselect the rows.
14. Click the column A heading. This selects the column.
15. Click any cell to deselect the column.
16. Click the column B heading and drag to the column G heading. This selects a range that includes all the cells in columns B through G.
17. Click cell B5. Hold down Shift and click cell E18. This is another way to select a range. This range is B5:E18.

Exercise 2-6 SELECT RANGES WITH KEYBOARD SHORTCUTS

You can select a range of cells by using keyboard shortcuts. These shortcuts work for selecting data in many Windows programs.

TABLE 2-3 Keyboard Shortcuts to Select Cell Ranges

Keystroke	To Do This
Shift+arrow key	Select from the active cell, moving in the direction of the arrow.
Shift+Spacebar	Select the current row.
Shift+PageDown	Extend selection from active cell down one screen in the same column.
Shift+PageUp	Extend selection from active cell up one screen in the same column.
Ctrl+A	Select the entire range with data or the entire worksheet.
Ctrl+Spacebar	Select the current column.
Ctrl+Shift+Home	Extend selection from active cell to beginning of data.
Ctrl+Shift+End	Extend selection from active cell to end of data.
F8	Start Extend Selection mode.
F8+arrow key	Extend selection from active cell in the direction of the arrow.
Esc	End Extend Selection mode.

1. Click cell A3. Hold down Shift and press → four times. The range is A3:E3.

NOTE

On a blank sheet, Ctrl+A selects every cell on the worksheet.

2. Click the arrow next to the Font box. Key **c** and choose **Calibri** (or scroll to the font).
3. Click the arrow next to the Font Size box. Choose **14**.
4. Click the Bold button **B** to remove bold.
5. Click cell A1. Hold down Shift and press ↓ once. Choose **Calibri** for the font.
6. Click cell A3 and press F8. This starts Extend Selection mode. Notice that **Extend Selection** appears in the status bar.
7. Press → four times. Press ↓ to reach row 15. The range A3:E15 is selected.

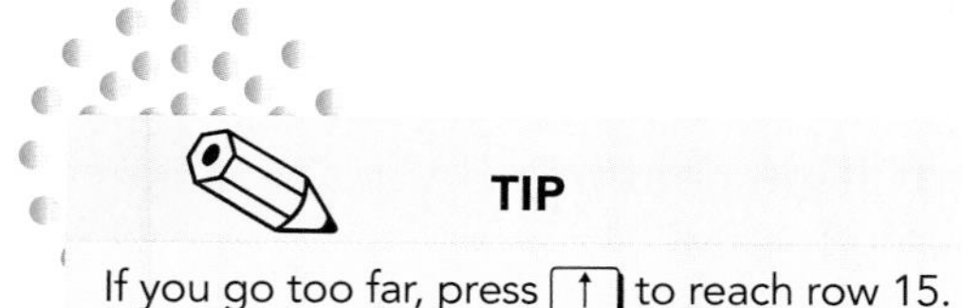

TIP

If you go too far, press ↑ to reach row 15.

8. Press Esc to cancel Extend Selection mode.
9. Click cell A3. Hold down Shift and click cell E15. This is another way to select the range.
10. Hold down Ctrl. Click cell A17 and drag across to cell E17.
11. Release the Ctrl key. Two different-sized ranges that are not next to each other are selected at the same time.

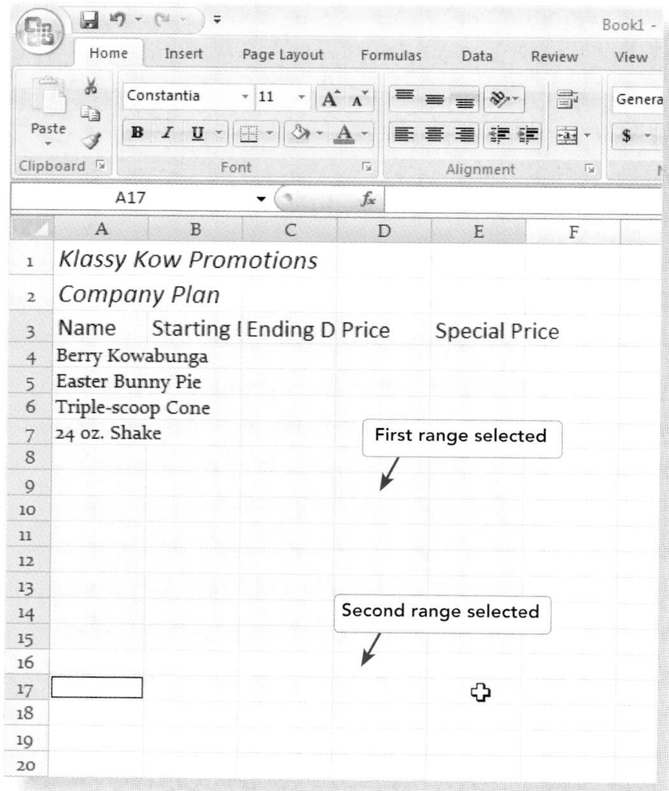

Figure 2-7
Selecting two ranges

12. Press Ctrl+Home.

Modifying Column Width and Row Height

In a new workbook with the Office document theme, columns are 8.43 spaces (64 pixels) wide. If the column on the right is empty, a label larger than 8.43 spaces spills into it so that you can see the entire label on screen. If the column on the right is not empty, you can widen the column so that the label is not cut off.

NOTE

If you change the document theme before keying any data, column width and row heights are set for the new theme.

Rows in a new workbook are 15.00 points (20 pixels) high to fit the default 11-point Calibri font. A *point* is 1/72 inch. Generally Excel resizes the row height as needed, but you can size it manually, too.

Here are the ways you can resize column widths and row heights:

- Drag a column or row border to a different size.
- Double-click a column's right border to AutoFit the column. *AutoFit* means the column is widened to fit the longest entry in the column.
- Double-click a row's bottom border to AutoFit the row height. A row is AutoFitted to fit the largest font size currently used in the row.
- On the Home tab in the Cells group, click the Format button Format and then choose Row Height or Column Width.

When you use the mouse to change the row height or column width, you will see the size in a ScreenTip. For rows, the height is shown in points (as it is for fonts) as well as in pixels. For columns, the width is shown in character spaces and in pixels. A *pixel* is a screen dot, a single point of color on the screen. A *character space* is the average width of a numeric character in the standard font used in the worksheet.

If you use Ribbon commands to change the column width or row height, you must key the entry by using points for row height or character spaces for column width.

Exercise 2-7 MODIFY COLUMN WIDTH

1. Place the pointer on the vertical border between the column headings for columns A and B. The pointer changes to a two-pointed arrow with a wide vertical bar.
2. Drag the sizing pointer to the right until the ScreenTip shows **15.63 (130 pixels)** and release the mouse button. At this width, the column should be wide enough for the longest promotion item.

Figure 2-8
Resizing columns

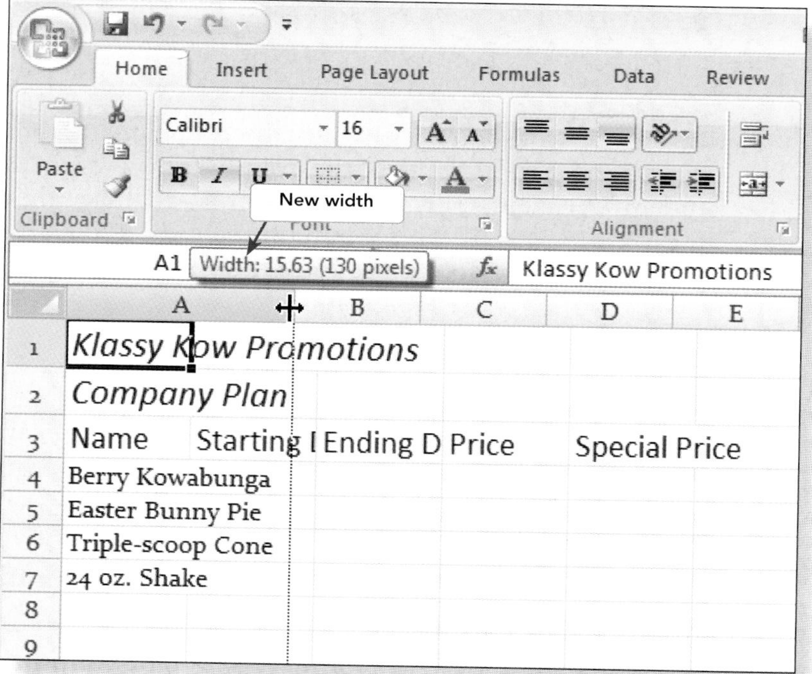

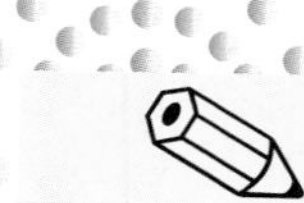

TIP

Be careful about AutoFitting columns that include titles in rows 1 or 2. Excel will AutoFit a column to accommodate long labels.

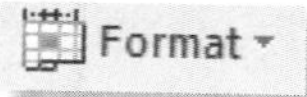

NOTE

If you change data in a column that you've AutoFitted, the column does not automatically AutoFit for the new entry.

3. Place the pointer between the column headings for columns B and C. Double-click. Excel AutoFits column B to fit the label.
4. Double-click the border between the column headings for columns C and D. Excel AutoFits column C.
5. Click anywhere in column D.
6. In the **Cells** group, click the Format button and then choose **Column Width**. The Column Width dialog box opens.
7. Key **10** and press Enter. The column width is changed to 10 spaces.
8. Double-click the border between the column headings for columns E and F to AutoFit column E.

Exercise 2-8 MODIFY ROW HEIGHT

1. Place the pointer on the horizontal border between the headings for rows 3 and 4. The pointer turns into a two-pointed arrow.
2. Drag down until the ScreenTip shows **22.50 (30 pixels)** and release the mouse button.

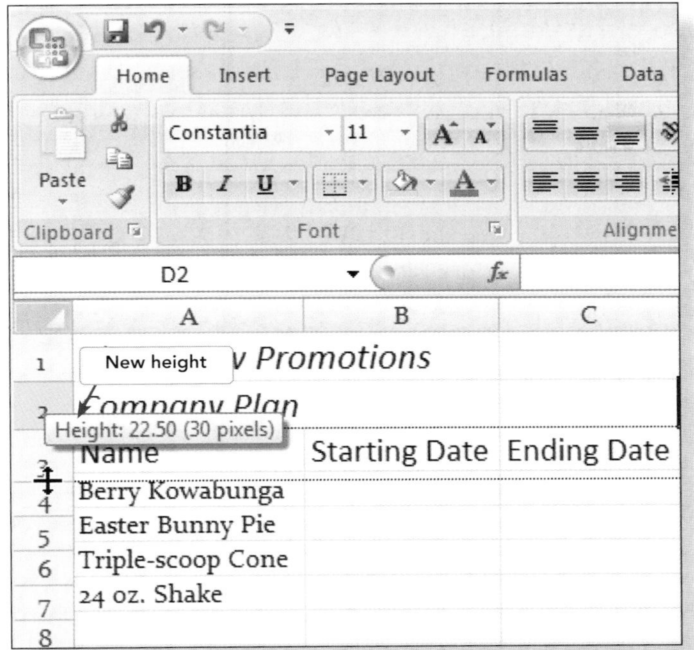

Figure 2-9
Resizing rows

3. Click anywhere in row 4.
4. In the **Cells** group, click the Format button and then **Row Height**. The Row Height dialog box opens.
5. Key **22.5** and press Enter. The row is 22.5 points (30 pixels) high.

Entering Values and Dates

When you key an entry that starts with a number or an arithmetic symbol, Excel assumes it is a *value*. A value is right-aligned in the cell and is included in calculations. Arithmetic symbols include =, −, and +.

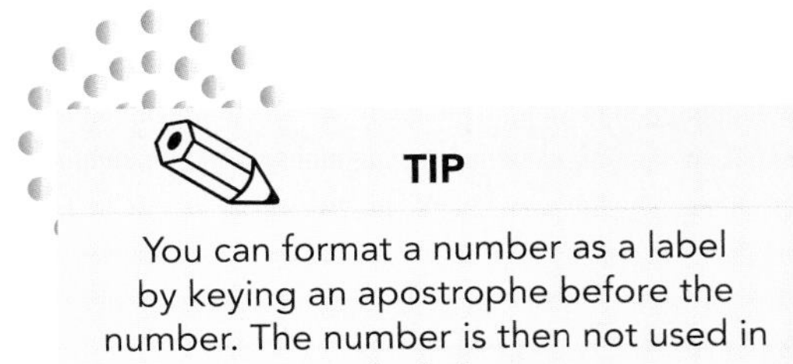

TIP

You can format a number as a label by keying an apostrophe before the number. The number is then not used in calculations.

Exercise 2-9 ENTER DATES AND VALUES

Excel recognizes dates if you key them in a typical date style. For example, if you key "1/1/08," Excel formats it as a date. Dates have special formats and can be used in date arithmetic.

1. Click cell B4.
2. Key **12/1/08** and press Enter. Excel recognizes the numbers as a date and shows four digits for the year. If SmartTags are enabled, you will see an indicator in the lower-right corner of the cell. Ignore the indicator for now.
3. Continue keying the following dates in column B. Press Enter after each one:
   3/15/08
   8/1/08
   10/15/08
4. Key these dates in cells C4:C7:
   12/31/08
   4/15/08
   8/31/08
   11/15/08
5. Click cell D4. Drag to select cells D4:E7. With the range selected, you can press Enter to move from cell to cell, going top to bottom and then left to right.
6. Key the prices shown in the "Price" and "Special Price" columns in Figure 2-10.

Figure 2-10
Worksheet data entry completed

	A	B	C	D	E	F
1	*Klassy Kow Promotions*					
2	*Company Plan*					
3	Name	Starting Date	Ending Date	Price	Special Price	
4	Berry Kowabunga	12/1/2008	12/31/2008	3.19	2.99	
5	Easter Bunny Pie	3/15/2008	4/15/2008	24.99	20.99	
6	Triple-scoop Cone	8/1/2008	8/31/2008	3.29	2.99	
7	24 oz. Shake	10/15/2008	11/15/2008	3.29	2.99	
8						

Exercise 2-10 APPLY NUMBER FORMATS FROM THE RIBBON

If you key only a value, it is formatted in a General style. This style shows only digits, no commas. If the value has a decimal point, it is shown with as many places after the decimal point as you key.

To increase the readability of your worksheet, you can apply common formats from the Ribbon. You first select the range of cells to be formatted and then click a task button in the Ribbon.

1. Click cell D4. Drag to select cells D4:E7.

2. In the **Number** group, click the Accounting Number Format button. The cells in the range are formatted to show a dollar sign and two decimal places. The dollar signs are aligned at the left edge of the cell.

Exercise 2-11 APPLY DATE FORMATS FROM THE DIALOG BOX

Excel includes many date formats in the Format Cells dialog box. You can open the Format Cells dialog box for the active cell or range by:

- Pressing Ctrl+1.
- Right-clicking the cell or range and choosing Format Cells from the shortcut menu.
- On the Home tab in the Cells group, clicking the Format button and then choosing Format Cells.

1. Click cell B4. Click and drag to select cells B4:C7.
2. Point at any of the selected cells and right-click. A shortcut menu opens with the Mini toolbar.
3. Choose **Format Cells**. The Format Cells dialog box opens; it should show the appropriate tab and category.
4. Click the **Number** tab if necessary.
5. Click **Date** in the **Category** list on the left if necessary. Many preset date formats are displayed in the **Type** box on the right.
6. Click a type in the list that shows the date first, a hyphen, an abbreviation for the month, another hyphen, and a two-digit year (example "14-Mar-01") and click **OK**. (See Figure 2-11 on the next page.) All of the dates are reformatted.

Figure 2-11
Choosing a date format

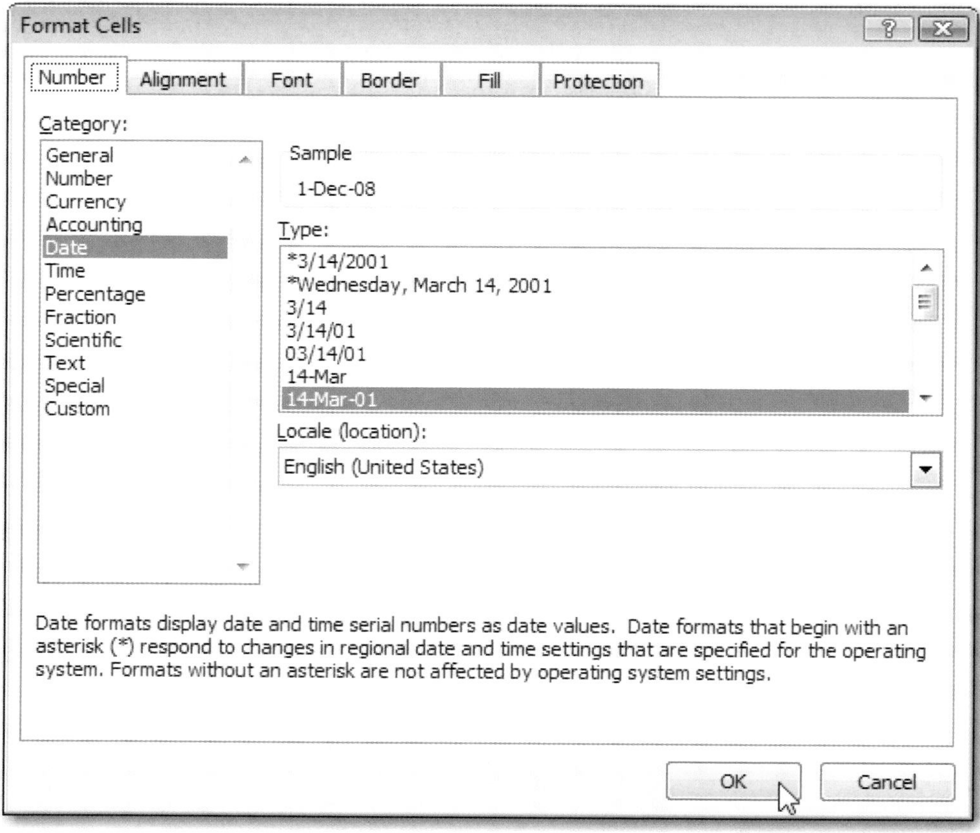

NOTE

Two-digit years between 00 and 29 are assumed to be the twenty-first century (2000, 2001, 2015). Two-digit years between 30 and 99 are assumed to be the twentieth century (1930, 1950, and 1999).

Exercise 2-12 CHANGE THE FONT COLOR

In addition to changing the font, size, and style, you can set a new font color. The document theme includes 12 colors and various intensities (or saturations) of that color. You can also choose from standard colors, too. You can change the font color for a selected cell or range by:

- On the Home tab in the Font group, clicking the Font Color button.
- Opening the Format Cells dialog box and choosing the Font tab.

NOTE

Two theme colors are for hyperlinks. These colors do not appear in the palettes. The color swatches in the palette have ScreenTips indicating the color's purpose, intensity, or name.

1. Select cells E4:E7 (the special prices).
2. Click the Font Color button. The color shown on the button is applied to the selected range, probably red.
3. Click the arrow next to the Font Color button. A color palette opens with 10 theme colors in the top row. The first 4 are text/background colors; the remaining 6 are accent colors. Standard colors are near the bottom of the palette.

4. Hover over several colors anywhere in the palette and watch the live preview in the worksheet.
5. Click **Dark Teal, Text 2** in the fourth column, first row. This is one of the theme colors. The palette closes, and the color is applied to the selected range.

TIP

Deselecting the range enables you to see the color more clearly.

6. Select cells A1:A2.
7. Press Ctrl+1 and click the **Font** tab.
8. Click the arrow for **Color**. The same theme colors are listed as well as the standard colors.
9. Choose **Dark Teal, Text 2** and click **OK**.

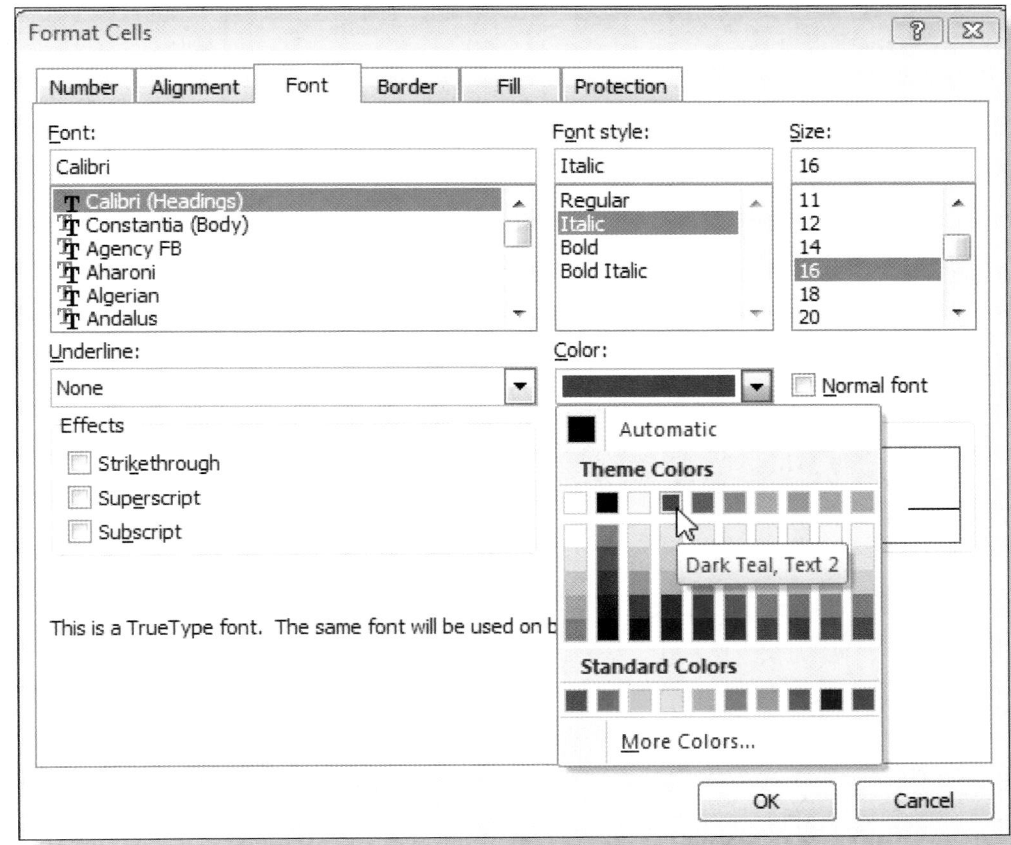

Figure 2-12
Changing the color from the Format Cells dialog box

Exercise 2-13 RENAME A WORKSHEET AND CHANGE THE TAB COLOR

You can rename a worksheet tab with a more descriptive name to help you and others remember the worksheet's purpose. Worksheet names can be up to 31 characters. You can use spaces in the name of a worksheet tab.

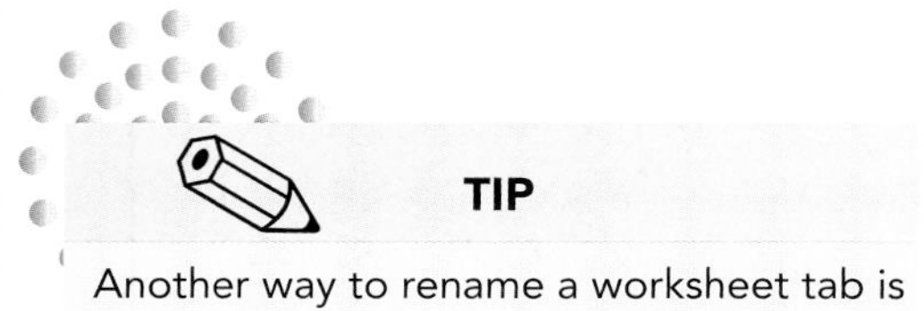

Another way to rename a worksheet tab is to right-click the tab and choose **Rename**.

1. Double-click the worksheet tab for **Sheet1**. The tab name is selected.
2. Key **Promos** and press Enter.
3. Double-click **Sheet2** and name it **Plans**. The **Plans** sheet is empty.
4. Right-click the **Promos** tab and choose **Tab Color**. The Theme Colors dialog box opens with the palette of colors.
5. Choose **Dark Teal, Text 2** as the tab color.

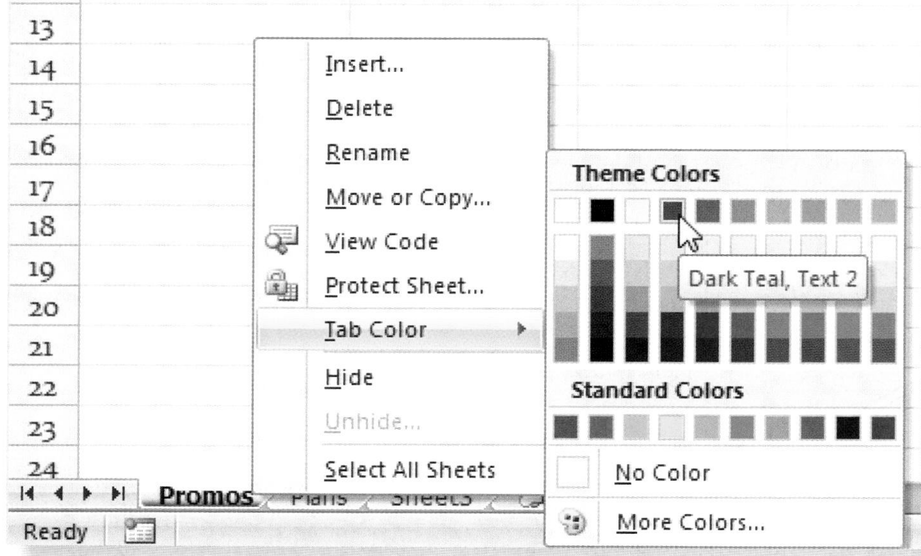

Figure 2-13
Changing the tab color

6. Click the **Plans** tab. Now you can see the color of the **Promos** tab better.
7. Click the **Promos** tab to make it the active sheet.

Saving a Workbook

When you create a new workbook or make changes to an existing one, you must save the workbook to keep your changes. Until you save your changes, your work can be lost if there is a power failure or computer problem.

To save a workbook, you must first give it a filename. A *filename* is the file identifier you see in the Open dialog box, Computer, or Windows Explorer. When you name a file in Windows, you can use up to 255 characters. Included in those 255 characters are the drive and folder names, so the actual filename is really limited to fewer than 255 characters. Generally, it is a good idea to keep filenames as short as possible.

You can use uppercase or lowercase letters, or a combination of both, for filenames. Windows is case-aware, which means it does recognize uppercase and lowercase that you key. However, it is not case-sensitive, so it does not distinguish between "BOOK1" and "book1." You can use spaces in a filename, but you cannot use the following characters: \ ?: * " <> |

Filenames are followed by a period and a three- or four-letter extension, supplied automatically by the software. Excel 2007 workbooks have the extension ".xlsx." Extensions identify the type of file.

For a new workbook, you can use either the Save or the Save As command to save and name the workbook. When you make changes to an existing workbook and want to save it with the same filename, use Save. If you want to save a workbook with a different filename, use Save As.

NOTE

You may not see filename extensions if your Folder Options (Organize button in the Explorer dialog box) are set to hide them.

Excel saves workbooks in the current drive or folder unless you specify a different location. You can easily navigate to the appropriate location in the Save dialog box.

Throughout the exercises in this book, filenames consist of two parts:

- *[your initials]*, which might be your initials or an identifier your instructor asks you to use, such as **kms**
- The number of the exercise, such as **2-14**

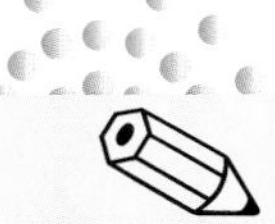

TIP

Wherever the pointer is when you save a workbook is where it appears the next time you open the workbook.

Exercise 2-14 SAVE A WORKBOOK

Depending on how difficult it would be to redo the work, you should save your file every 15 to 30 minutes.

1. Click cell A1.
2. Click the Save button on the Quick Access toolbar.
3. Choose the appropriate drive and folder location.
4. Click the New Folder button .
5. Key *[your initials]*Lesson2 and press Enter. The location is updated to your folder.
6. In the **File name** box, double-click **Book1** and key *[your initials]***2-14**.
7. Click **Save**. The title bar shows the new filename.

NOTE

Your instructor will tell you what drive/folder to use to save your workbooks.

Entering Basic Formulas

A *formula* is an equation that performs a calculation on values in your worksheet and displays an answer. You key a formula in a cell. After you press a completion key, the formula results appear in the cell. The formula itself is visible in the formula bar.

Formulas are one of the main reasons for using Excel, because a formula performs calculations for you. If you later change any of the numbers used for the calculations, Excel quickly recalculates the formula to show a revised answer.

Formulas begin with an = sign as an identifier. After the = sign, you enter the address of the cells you want to add, subtract, multiply, or divide. Then you use *arithmetic operators* in the 10-key pad or at the top of the keyboard to complete the calculation. You probably recognize all of the arithmetic operators shown in Table 2-4, with the possible exception of exponentiation. The *exponentiation* operator raises a number to a power. For example, 2^3 represents 2 to the third power, or 2^3, which means 2 × 2 × 2 or 8.

NOTE

Arithmetic operations are calculated in a specific order: first, exponentiation; second, multiplication and division; and finally, addition and subtraction.

TABLE 2-4 Arithmetic Operators

Key or Symbol	Operation
^	Exponentiation
*	Multiplication
/	Division
+	Addition
–	Subtraction

Exercise 2-15 KEY A BASIC FORMULA

In your workbook, you can calculate the difference between the regular price and the promotion price. This is a simple subtraction formula. You will be working in column F. If you cannot see column F, set your Zoom size to a smaller size so you can see it.

1. Click cell F3. Key **Difference** and press Enter. The label is formatted with the same style as other labels in the row.
2. Double-click the border between the column headings for columns F and G to AutoFit column F.
3. Key **=d** in cell F4 to start the formula. *Formula AutoComplete* shows a list of built-in formulas that begin with the letter "d." You can continue keying your own formula for now.

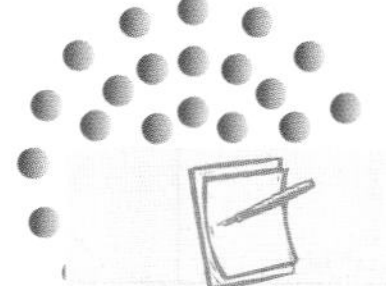

NOTE

Excel applies the same format to a cell in which you are entering data as the three or more cells to the immediate left or top of the cell.

Figure 2-14
Formula AutoComplete list
2-14.xlsx
Promos sheet

A	B	C	D		E		F	G
Klassy Kow Promotions								
Company Plan								
Name	Starting Date	Ending Date	Price		Special Price		Difference	
Berry Kowabunga	1-Dec-08	31-Dec-08	$	3.19	$	2.99	=d	
Easter Buni								
Triple-scoop Cone	1-Aug-08	31-Aug-08	$	3.29	$	2.99		
24 oz. Shake	15-Oct-08	15-Nov-08	$	3.29	$	2.99		

Returns the number that represents the date in Microsoft Office Excel date-time code

DATE
DATEVALUE
DAVERAGE
DAY
DAYS360
DB
DCOUNT
DCOUNTA
DDB
DEC2BIN
DEC2HEX
DEC2OCT

4. Key **4-e4** in cell F4. You'll see another Formula AutoComplete list when you key **e**. Your formula should be **=d4-e4**, and it appears in the cell and in the formula bar. The cells used in the formula are outlined in colors that match the colors of the formula in the cell.

Figure 2-15
Keying a formula
2-14.xlsx
Promos sheet

=d4-e4

B	C	D		E		F
motions						
Starting Date	Ending Date	Price		Special Price		Difference
1-Dec-08	31-Dec-08	$	3.19	$	2.99	=d4-e4
15-Mar-08	15-Apr-08	$	24.99	$	20.99	
1-Aug-08	31-Aug-08	$	3.29	$	2.99	
15-Oct-08	15-Nov-08	$	3.29	$	2.99	

NOTE

After you complete a formula, Excel capitalizes cell references.

5. Press Enter. The difference in price is 20 cents. It is shown in the same number format as the cells used in the formula.

6. Press ↑ to return to cell F4. Notice that the formula bar shows the formula, but the cell displays the result of the formula.

Exercise 2-16 ENTER A FORMULA BY POINTING

You can use the mouse to point to cells used in a formula. This increases accuracy, because you don't have to worry about keying the wrong cell address.

1. Click cell F5. Key = to start the formula.
2. Click cell D5. The address appears in cell F5 and in the formula bar. Cell D5 has a moving marquee.
3. Key – to subtract the next cell.
4. Click cell E5. It is placed in the formula after the minus sign and now has the moving marquee.

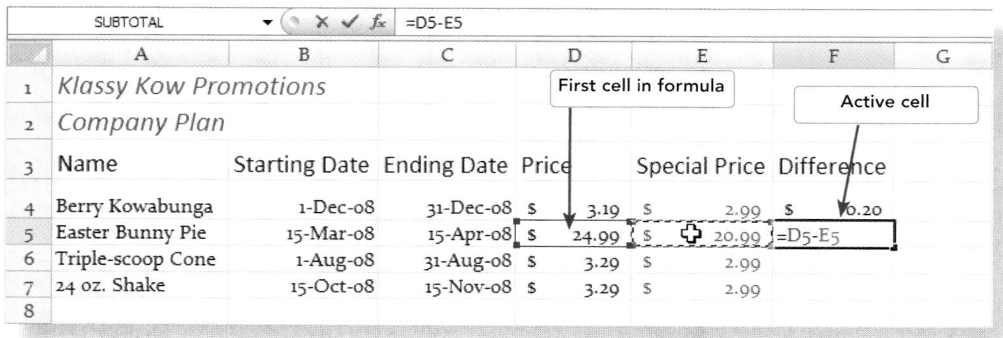

Figure 2-16
Entering a formula by pointing
2-14.xlsx
Promos sheet

5. Click the Enter button in the formula bar. The difference of $4 is calculated.

Exercise 2-17 COPY A FORMULA BY USING THE COPY AND PASTE BUTTONS

The formula in cell F5 is the same as the one in cell F4 except for the row references. The formula is relative to its location on the worksheet. When you copy a formula with row or cell references, Excel makes this adjustment automatically.

1. Click cell F5. Click the Copy button. The cell now has a moving marquee. The status bar tells you to select the destination for the copy.
2. Click cell F6 and drag to select the range F6:F7.

3. Click the Paste button. The formula is copied to both cells in the range. The Paste Options button appears just below the pasted data.

4. Hover over the Paste Options button. A down arrow appears next to the button. Click the down arrow; options for copying the data are listed. You need not change the option.

Figure 2-17
Copying a formula
2-14.xlsx
Promos sheet

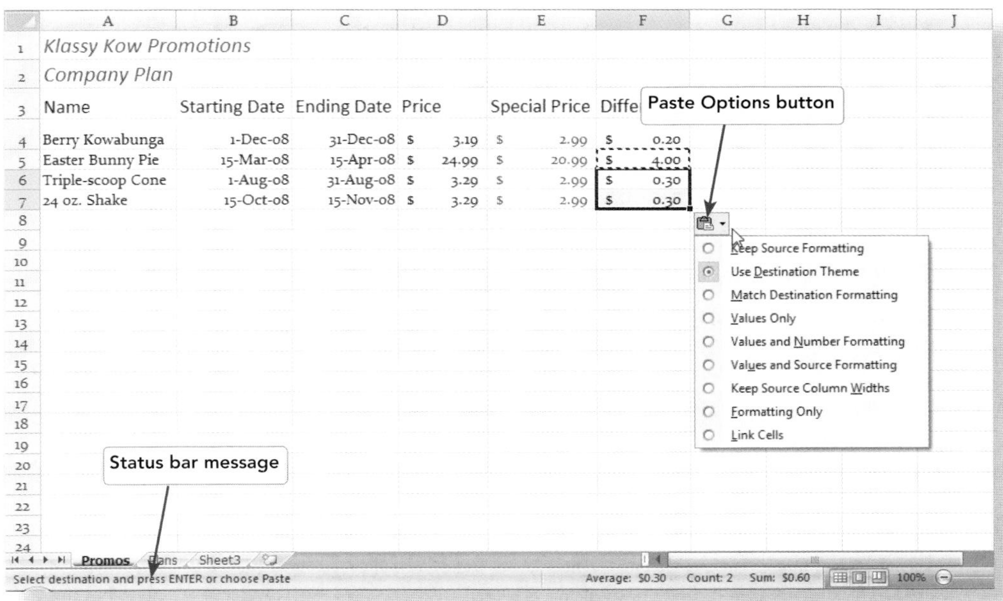

5. Press Esc twice to cancel the moving marquee and finish the Paste command.
6. Click cell F6 and review the formula. Notice that Excel has adjusted the formula to take into account the relative position of the cell.
7. Click cell F7. Review the formula. Excel has adjusted it as well.

NOTE

You can press Enter to complete a Copy or Paste command. This automatically cancels the moving marquee.

Exercise 2-18 USE AUTOSUM, AVERAGE, AND MAX

Some calculations are so common in business and personal use that Excel includes them as functions. A *function* is a built-in formula in Excel. An example of a function is "SUM," in which Excel automatically totals a column or row. A function starts with =, just like a formula. Excel has several "auto" functions available on the Formulas tab and the Home tab.

NOTE

The screen resolution at your computer affects how a button looks. It may include an icon and text, and the text may be below or next to the button. Check the ScreenTip when in doubt.

TABLE 2-5 Function Library Group

Button	Action
Insert Function	Opens the Insert Function dialog box
AutoSum	Displays the sum, average, count, maximum, or minimum of selected cells
Recently Used	Lists the most recently used functions
Financial	Displays a list of financial functions
Logical	Displays a list of logical functions
Text	Displays a list of text functions
Date & Time	Displays a list of date and time functions
Lookup & Reference	Displays a list of lookup and reference functions
Math & Trig	Displays a list of mathematical and trigonometry functions
More Functions	Displays a list of statistical, engineering, cube, and information functions

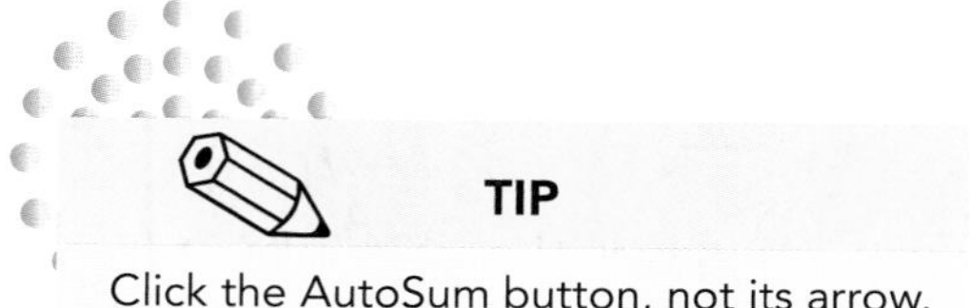

TIP

Click the AutoSum button, not its arrow.

1. Click the **Formulas** tab in the Ribbon. The Function Library group includes buttons for each major function category.

2. Click cell F8. Click the AutoSum button in the Function Library group. A formula is placed in the cell followed by the range that will be summed. A moving marquee surrounds cells that will be summed. A ScreenTip for the function appears.

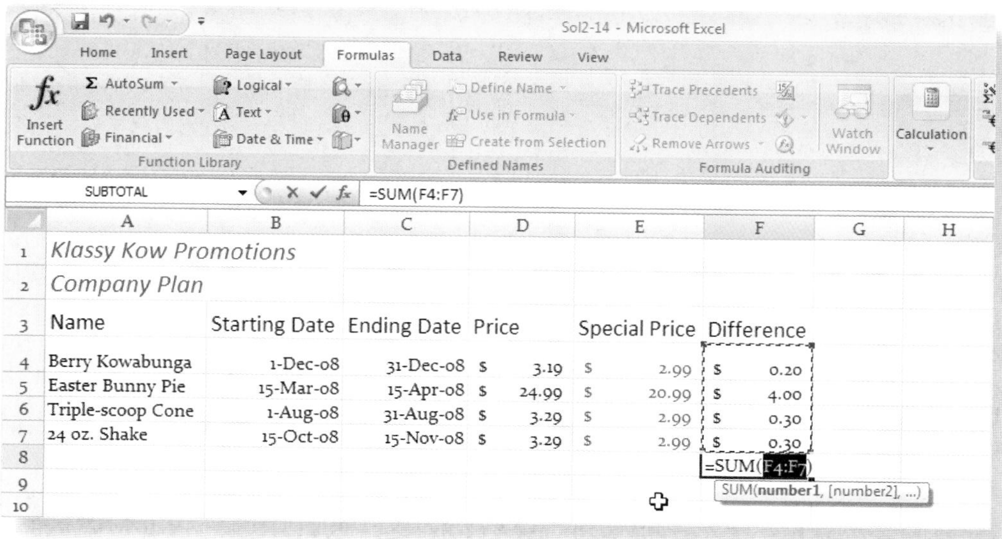

Figure 2-18
Using AutoSum
2-14.xlsx
Promos sheet

3. Press Enter. The formula is completed.
4. Click cell F8. Notice that the formula includes the function name SUM and an assumed range in parentheses.

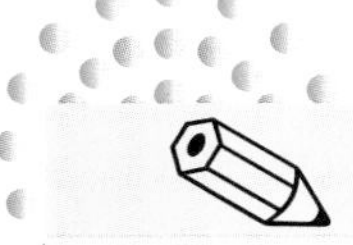

TIP

There is a Sum button in the Editing group on the Home tab. Both buttons are called AutoSum in this text.

NOTE

The SUM function adds the values in the cells. The AVERAGE function adds the values in the range and then divides by the number of cells in the range.

NOTE

Functions ignore titles in a column/row because they are not values; they are labels, which are not used in calculations.

5. Click cell D8.
6. Click the arrow with the AutoSum button Σ AutoSum.
7. Choose **Average**. The AVERAGE function appears in the formula bar and in the active cell. A moving marquee surrounds the cells in the assumed range.
8. Press Ctrl+Enter to complete the function. Notice that now the formula includes the function name AVERAGE and the range of cells that is averaged.
9. Click cell D9. Click the arrow with the AutoSum button Σ AutoSum.
10. Choose **Max**. A moving marquee surrounds the cells that will be used by the MAX function. The MAX function is used to determine the largest value in a range.
11. Click cell D4 and drag to select the range D4:D7. Don't include cell D8 in this function, because it is the average you just calculated.
12. Press Ctrl+Enter. The result of the formula shows the highest price in the column.

Exercise 2-19 CHECK RESULTS WITH AUTOCALCULATE

The *AutoCalculate* feature displays formula results for a selected range in the status bar. AutoCalculate can display sums, averages, counts, maximums, or minimums. You set AutoCalculate choices by right-clicking the status bar.

1. Right-click the status bar. Verify that there are check marks for **Average**, **Count**, and **Sum**. Press Esc.
2. Select the range F4:F7. AutoCalculate shows the average, a count, and the sum for the selected range in the status bar.

Figure 2-19
Using AutoCalculate
2-14.xlsx
Promos sheet

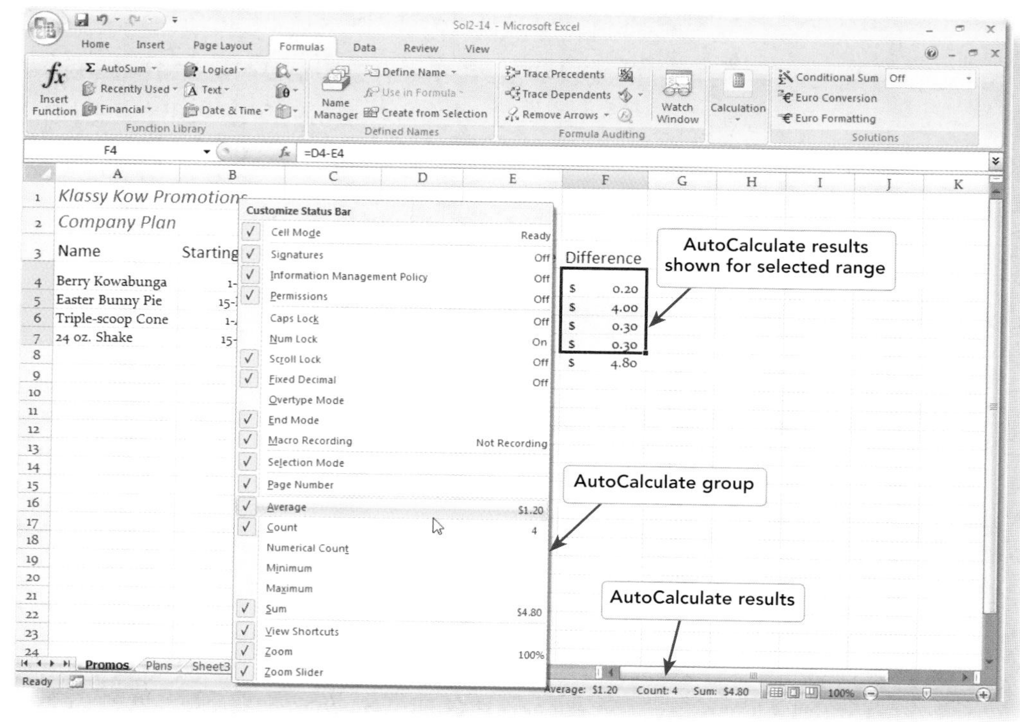

3. Right-click the status bar and click to select **Minimum** and **Maximum**. Press Esc.
4. Select the range D4:D7. AutoCalculate shows more information about these cells.
5. Select cells A4:A7. These are labels, so AutoCalculate only shows a count.
6. Right-click the status bar and click to deselect **Minimum** and **Maximum**. Press Esc.
7. Key your first and last name in cell A10.
8. Press F12 and save the workbook as ***[your initials]*2-19** in your Lesson 2 folder.
9. Prepare and submit your workbook.
10. Close the workbook.

NOTE

Your instructor will tell you how to submit your work for each lesson. Lesson 1 includes exercises with steps detailing how to print your work or save it as an XPS file.

Using Online Help

Building basic formulas is an important skill. You will use it as the basis for becoming a proficient Excel user.

LOOK UP FORMULAS

1. Start Excel and click the Microsoft Office Excel Help button .
2. Click in the Search box, key **create formula**, and press Enter.
3. In the list of topics, find and click a topic related to creating a formula.
4. Click **Show All** at the top of a Help window to expand all explanations.
5. When you finish investigating formulas, close the Help window.

Lesson 2 Summary

- In a blank workbook, you can key values, labels, dates, or formulas. Excel recognizes data by the first character you key in the cell.
- Labels are aligned at the left edge of a cell. If they are longer than the column width, they spill into the next column if it is empty. Otherwise, they appear cut off on the screen.
- To complete a cell entry, press Enter, Tab, or any arrow key or click another cell. You can also click the Enter button in the formula bar.
- New workbooks use the Office document theme. The default font for data is 11-point Calibri. You can change the font, the font size, the color, and the style.
- Use the Format Painter to copy formats from one cell to other cells.
- Many commands require that you first select a range of cells. You select a range of cells by using the mouse or keyboard shortcuts.
- The default row height matches the default font size in the document theme. The row height adjusts if you choose a larger font.
- Common formats, such as Accounting, can be applied to cells from the Number group on the Home tab. Many other formats are available in the Format Cells dialog box.
- It's usually a good idea to change the default worksheet tab name to a more descriptive name. You can also change the worksheet tab color for visual cues.
- You must save a new workbook to keep your work. For a new workbook, you can use the Save or the Save As command.
- To create a formula in a cell, you can key it or you can construct it by pointing to the cells used in the formula. All formulas begin with the = symbol.

- When you copy a formula, Excel adjusts it to match the row or column where the copy is located.
- Excel has functions for common calculations such as Sum, Average, Maximum, Minimum, and Count.
- You can see results for common functions without keying a formula if you use AutoCalculate.

LESSON 2		Command Summary	
Feature	**Button**	**Task Path**	**Keyboard**
Accounting Number	$	Home, Number	
AutoSum	Σ AutoSum	Formulas, Function Library	Alt+=
Column Width	Format	Home, Cells, Format, Column Width	
Copy		Home, Clipboard	Ctrl+C
Font		Home, Font	Ctrl+1
Font Color	A	Home, Font	Ctrl+1
Font Size		Home, Font	Ctrl+1
Format Painter		Home, Clipboard	
Paste	Paste	Home, Clipboard	Ctrl+V
Rename sheet	Format	Home, Cells, Format, Rename Sheet	
Row Height	Format	Home, Cells, Format, Row Height	
Save		Microsoft Office, Save	Ctrl+S
Tab color	Format	Home, Cells, Format, Tab Color	
Themes	Themes	Page Layout, Themes	

Lesson 3

Using Editing and Style Tools

OBJECTIVES

MCAS OBJECTIVES

In this lesson:

XL07 1.1.1
XL07 1.1.2
XL07 1.3
XL07 2.1.2
XL07 2.3
XL07 2.4.1
XL07 5.5.1
XL07 5.5.3
XL07 5.5.4

After completing this lesson, you will be able to:

1. Use AutoCorrect and Error Checking.
2. Check spelling.
3. Use Find and Replace.
4. Use series and AutoFill.
5. Apply table and cell styles.
6. Prepare headers and footers.

Estimated Time: 1 1/2 hours

Excel has many tools to increase your accuracy. Excel finds and flags common types of formula errors. It has electronic dictionaries that correct spelling errors as you type. Other tools enable you to quickly find and replace data or formats and to fill in data automatically.

Using AutoCorrect and Error Checking

AutoCorrect makes spelling corrections as you type. It recognizes common errors such as "teh," and changes it to "the." It capitalizes the days of the week and the months and corrects capitalization errors, such as THis. You can also set it to enter routine data automatically.

AutoCorrect makes its change when you press the spacebar, the Enter key, or a punctuation mark.

Exercise 3-1 USE AUTOCORRECT TO CORRECT ERRORS

The **KowaSales** workbook measures sales of the Kowabunga ice cream novelty over a three-year period. For the years 2008 and 2009, a percentage increase is estimated.

NOTE

As you key the labels for this exercise, be sure to key the errors that are shown.

1. Open **KowaSales**. The **Kowabunga** worksheet has a two-color scale applied to columns F and G.
2. Double-click the **Home** tab to collapse the ribbon. This provides more working space.

Figure 3-1
Keying a deliberate error
KowaSales.xlsx
Kowabunga sheet

3. In cell A1, key **KLassy KOw** and press [Spacebar]. The two incorrect uppercase letters are corrected. Notice that horizontal centering is preset for cell A1.
4. Key **Ice Cream Shops** to complete the label. Press [Enter].
5. Key **saturday and sunday Sales** and press [Enter]. As you can see, AutoCorrect capitalizes the days of the week.
6. Double-click the **Home** tab. Select cells A1:A2 and set them to Cambria 18 point.

NOTE

This workbook uses the Office document theme. Cambria is the headings font; Calibri is for body text.

7. In cell A3, change the font to 9-point Calibri.
8. Key **these aer sales fro all Kowagunga flavors**. Press [Enter]. Not all errors are found by AutoCorrect. "Aer" and "fro" have not been corrected, and neither has "Kowagunga." Leave these errors for now.

Exercise 3-2 SET AUTOCORRECT OPTIONS

If you key "acn," AutoCorrect changes your typing to "can." If "ACN" were the initials of an employee or a company, you would want to delete this correction from AutoCorrect. You can also add new corrections to AutoCorrect.

1. Click the Microsoft Office Button and choose **Excel Options**. There are nine panes with features that can be customized.

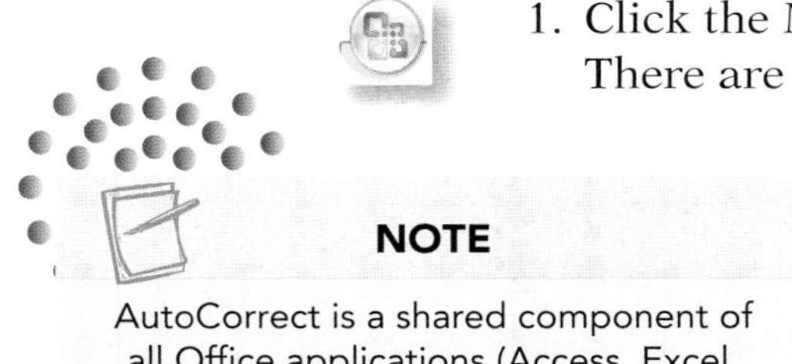

NOTE

AutoCorrect is a shared component of all Office applications (Access, Excel, PowerPoint, and Word). Each of these programs uses the same AutoCorrect.

2. Choose **Proofing**. Click **AutoCorrect Options**. The errors and corrections in AutoCorrect are listed in alphabetical order.
3. In the **Replace** box, key **kk**. Press Tab.
4. In the **With** box, key **Klassy Kow**. Click **Add** to add this entry to the AutoCorrect list. Click **OK**.

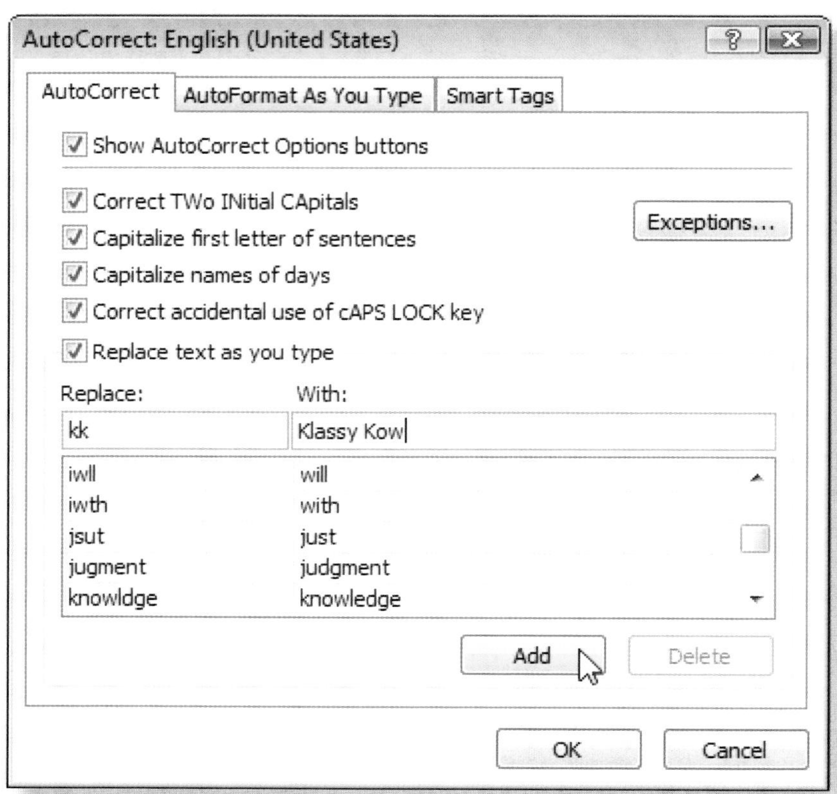

Figure 3-2
AutoCorrect dialog box

5. Click **OK** to close the Excel Options dialog box.
6. Click cell B25, key **kk**, and press Spacebar. The initials are changed to "Klassy Kow."
7. Key **Marketing Department** to finish the label. Press Enter.
8. Click the Microsoft Office Button and choose **Excel Options**. Choose **Proofing**. Click **AutoCorrect Options**.

9. In the **Replace** box, key **kk** to move to the "Klassy Kow" entry.
10. Click **Delete** to remove the entry. Click **OK**.

NOTE

You have been instructed to delete the "Klassy Kow" AutoCorrect entry so that students in other classes can use the computer without having this entry listed among the AutoCorrect entries.

11. Click **OK** to close the Excel Options dialog box.
12. Click cell G25, key **kk**, and press Enter. The initials are not changed, because the entry has been deleted from AutoCorrect.
13. Delete the contents of cells B25 and G25.
14. Press Ctrl+Home.

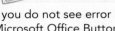

Exercise 3-3 REVIEW ERROR CHECKING

Excel automatically alerts you to problems with formulas by showing an error indicator and an Error Checking Options button. The error indicator is a small green triangle in the top-left corner of the cell. The Error Checking Options button is a small exclamation point within a diamond. It appears when you click the cell with the error indicator. When an error indicator warns of a potential error, you can review the type of error, fix it, or ignore the error.

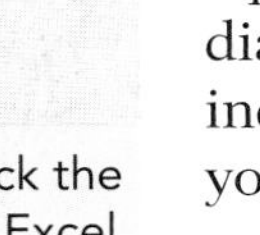

NOTE

If you do not see error indicators, click the Microsoft Office Button and choose Excel Options. In the Formulas pane, select Enable background error checking.

1. Click cell B11. The Error Checking Options button appears to the left of the cell.
2. Position the mouse pointer on the Error Checking Options button to see a ScreenTip.
3. Click the arrow next to the button. Its shortcut menu opens. The first menu item explains the error, that the formula omits adjacent cells. Excel assumes that a SUM formula in cell B11 would sum the cells directly above, cells B6:B10. However, the formula is correct because the year in cell B6 should not be included in the formula.

Figure 3-3
Error Checking options
KowaSales.xlsx
Kowabunga sheet

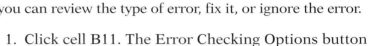

	A	B	C	D	E	F	G
1	Klassy Kow Ice Cream Shops						
2	Saturday and Sunday Sales						
3	these aer sales fro all Kowagunga flavors.						
4							
5		All Shop Sales				Increase	
6		2007	2008	2009		2008	2009
7	Qtr 1	$ 74,500	$ 77,300	$ 80,530		3.76%	4.18%
8	Qtr 2	70,130	80,100	87,000		14.22%	8.61%
9	Qtr 3	72,300	78,150	80,100		8.09%	2.50%
10	Qtr 4	77,500	82,350	84,560		6.26%	2.68%
11		$ 294,430	$ 317,900	$ 332,190			

Formula Omits Adjacent Cells
Update Formula to Include Cells
Help on this error
Ignore Error
Edit in Formula Bar
Error Checking Options...

actual and extimated
artr for 2007, 2008, and
ease is is computd by
s year from the current
the current year.

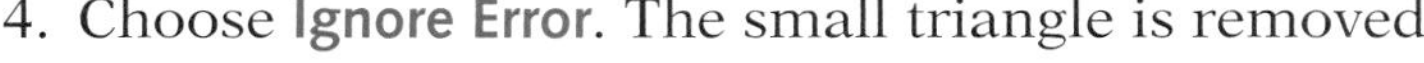

4. Choose **Ignore Error**. The small triangle is removed.
5. Click the **Formulas** command tab. There are four command groups on this tab.

6. In the Formula Auditing group, click the Error Checking button. The Error Checking dialog box opens with the next error noted, cell C11. This formula is correct.

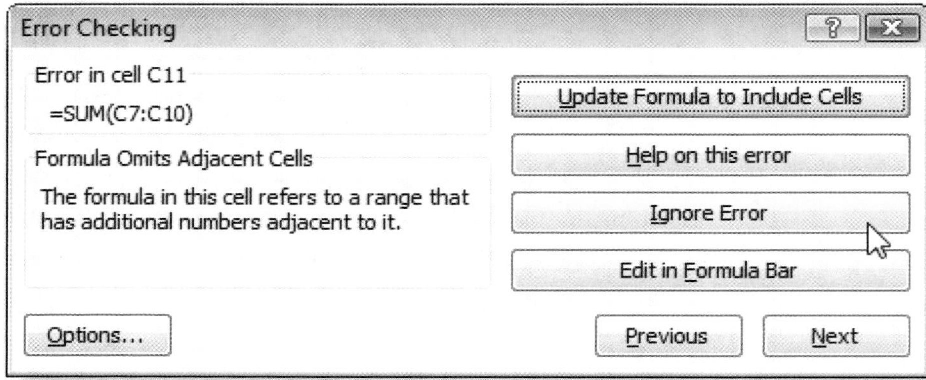

Figure 3-4
Error Checking dialog box
KowaSales.xlsx
Kowabunga sheet

7. Click **Ignore Error** in the dialog box. The error triangle in cell C11 is removed. Cell D11 is flagged.
8. Click **Ignore Error**. A message box notes that error checking is complete.
9. Click **OK**. Press Ctrl+Home.

Checking Spelling

Excel's Spelling feature scans the worksheet and finds words that do not match entries in its dictionaries. It also finds repeated words. The Spelling dialog box provides options for handling errors. These options are described in Table 3-1.

Exercise 3-4 SPELL-CHECK A WORKSHEET

Excel starts spell-checking at the active cell and checks to the end of the worksheet. When the spell-checker reaches the end of the worksheet, a dialog box opens, asking if you want to continue spell-checking from the beginning of the worksheet.

The **Kowabunga** worksheet has a text box below the data with several spelling errors. A text box is used for special text displays and notations. If you accidentally click the text box in this lesson, click any cell away from the box to continue working.

TABLE 3-1 Spelling Dialog Box Options

Command	Action
Ignore Once	Do not change the spelling of this occurrence of the word. If it is a repeated word, do not delete one of the words.
Ignore All	Do not change the spelling of any occurrences of the word. If it is a repeated word, do not delete the double word.
Add to Dictionary	Add this word to the dictionary so that Excel will not regard it as misspelled.
Change	Replace the current spelling with the highlighted alternative in the **Suggestions** box.
Delete	Appears only for repeated words. Click to delete one occurrence of the word.
Change All	Replace the current spelling with the highlighted alternative every time this misspelling occurs.
AutoCorrect	Add the misspelled word with its correction to the AutoCorrect list.
Undo Last	Reverse/undo the last spelling correction.
Options	Offers choices for changing the dictionary language, ignoring uppercase and words with numbers, and ignoring Internet addresses.

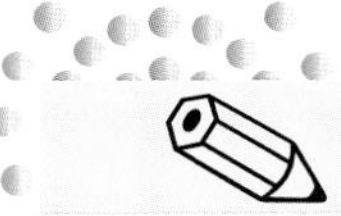

TIP

You can select a range of cells and then click the Spelling button to spell-check only that range.

1. Click the **Review** command tab. Three command groups on this tab are used to examine and annotate your worksheet.
2. Click the Spelling button. Excel finds "worksheet" in the text box. It offers a suggestion for the correct spelling.

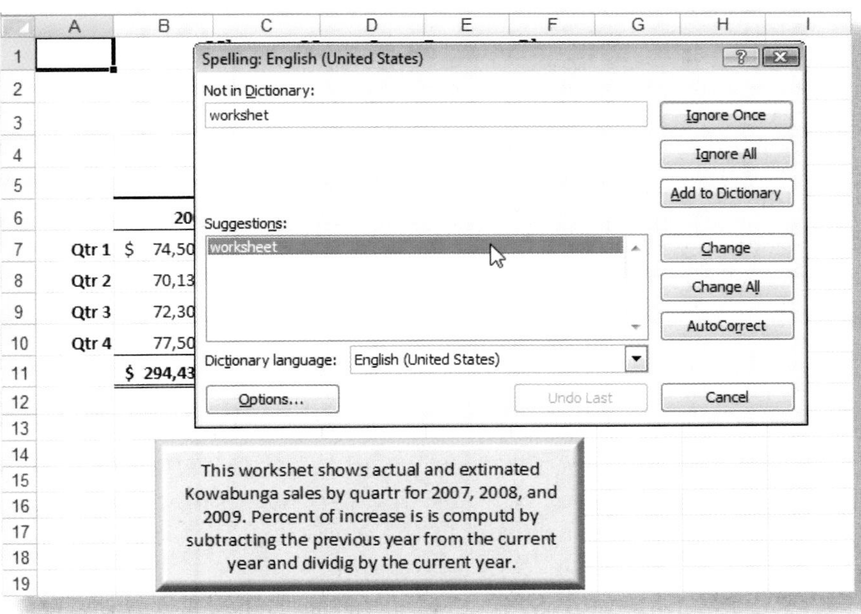

Figure 3-5
Spelling dialog box
KowaSales.xlsx
Kowabunga sheet

TIP

Move the dialog box so that you can see the text box. You can move a dialog box by dragging its title bar.

3. Double-click **worksheet** in the **Suggestions** list. A double-click is the same as clicking the word and then clicking **Change**. The correction is made, but you will not see it until you close the Spelling dialog box.
4. The next error is "extimated." Double-click **estimated** in the **Suggestions** list. "Kowabunga" in the text box is next. This word is correct.
5. Click **Ignore Once**. The word "quartr" appears next in the text box.
6. Double-click **quarter** in the **Suggestions** list. The next error is a **Repeated Word**, two occurrences of the word "is."
7. Click **Delete** to remove one occurrence of the word.
8. Correct "computd" and "dividng."
9. Excel shows "Klassy" in the **Not in Dictionary** box and offers one suggestion for the correct spelling. Since this is how the company spells its name, you can ignore all occurrences of this spelling.
10. Click **Ignore All**. Excel will ignore any more occurrences of "Klassy" in this worksheet. The word "Kow" is the next error. This is the same issue.
11. Click **Ignore All**. The word "aer" appears next with a list of possible corrections.
12. Click **are** in the **Suggestions** list and click **Change**. The next error is "Kowagunga."
13. Click in the **Not in Dictionary** box. There are no suggestions, but you can key the correction.
14. Edit the spelling to **Kowabunga** in the **Not in Dictionary** box.
15. Click **Change**. A message box notes that this word is not in the dictionary.

REVIEW

[F2] starts Edit mode. [Home] positions the insertion point at the beginning of the entry.

16. Click **Yes**. When Spelling is complete, a message box tells you that the spell check is complete. Click **OK**.
17. Click cell A3. Press [F2] and press [Home]. Spelling has not found all errors in this sheet.
18. Capitalize **These** and change "fro" to **for**. Press [Enter].

Using Find and Replace

You use the Find command to locate a *character string,* a sequence of letters, numbers, or symbols. You can also use the Find command to locate formats, such as everything in the worksheet that is bold.

You can use wildcards in a Find command when you are not sure about spelling or want to find a group of data. A *wildcard* is a character that represents one or more numbers or letters. Excel recognizes two common wildcard characters:

- * Represents any number of characters
- ? Represents any single character

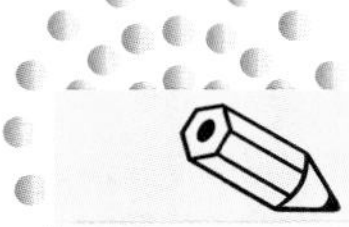

TIP

If you want to find a word or value that includes an asterisk or a question mark, precede the wildcard with a tilde (~). For example, "**25~***" would find **25***.

The character string "ce*" would find everything in the worksheet that includes the characters "ce" followed by any number of letters or values. This might include "central," "nice," and "ocean." The character string "s?t" would locate entries that have an "s" followed by any character and a "t." Examples are "sit," "reset," and "S4T."

There are two ways to start the Find command:

- Click the Find & Select button in the Editing group on the Home tab and choose **Find**.
- Press Ctrl+F or Shift+F5.

The Replace command locates occurrences of a character string and substitutes a replacement string. A *replacement string* is a sequence of characters that is exchanged for existing data. The Replace command can also search for a format, replacing it with another format.

There are two ways to start the Replace command:

- Click the Find & Select button in the Editing group on the Home tab and choose **Replace**.
- Press Ctrl+H or Shift+F5.

Find and Replace share a dialog box, so you can actually use any of these four methods to start either command.

Exercise 3-5 FIND DATA

In the Find and Replace dialog box, you can choose whether to search the worksheet or the workbook. You can search by column or row. If you know that the name you are looking for is in column A or B, it is faster to search by column. You can also choose to search formulas or the value results. Other options let you match capitalization or the entire cell contents. The Find command searches cells. It does not search *objects* in a worksheet such as the text box in **KowaSales**.

NOTE

An object is a separate, clickable element or part of a worksheet.

In Find and Replace character strings, do not key format symbols such as the dollar sign or a comma.

1. Press Ctrl+Home.
2. Press Ctrl+F. The Find and Replace dialog box opens. Notice that each command has a separate tab.
3. Key **2008** in the **Find what** box.

4. Click **Find All**. The dialog box expands to list information about two cells that include this string of numbers. The first occurrence is outlined in the worksheet and highlighted in the list.

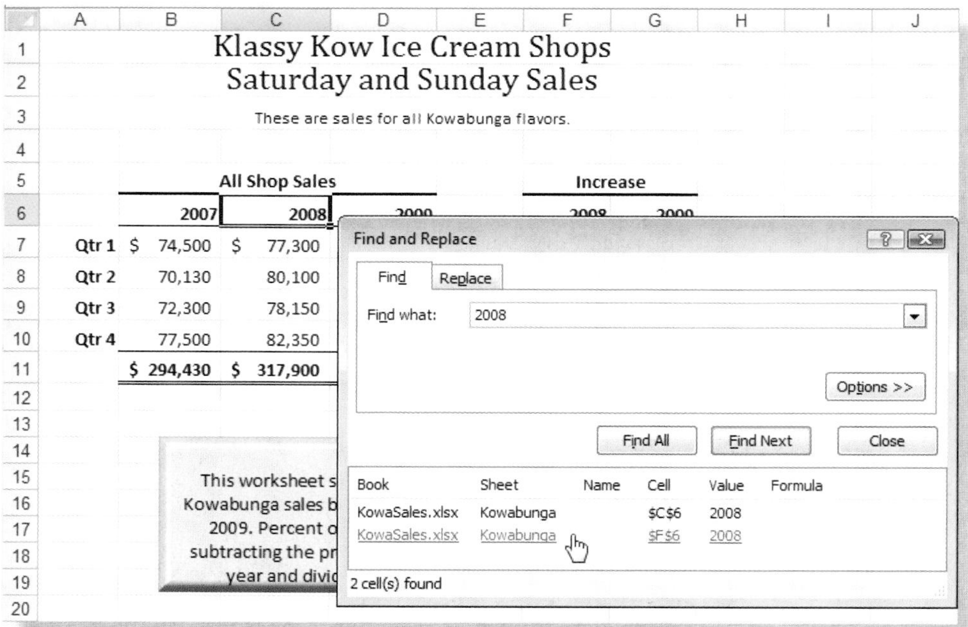

Figure 3-6
Find and Replace dialog box, Find tab

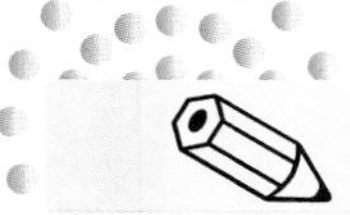

TIP

You can size the Find dialog box by dragging one of its corners.

5. Click the second cell identifier in the dialog box. The pointer moves to that cell in the worksheet.
6. Double-click **2008** in the **Find what** box and key **qtr**. Character strings you key in the **Find what** box are not case-sensitive unless you turn on the **Match case** option.
7. Click **Options >>**. The dialog box expands with additional settings.
8. Click the arrow next to the **Within** box. You can find data within the active sheet or the entire workbook.

NOTE

If the dialog box shows Options <<, it is expanded.

9. Choose **Sheet**.
10. Click the arrow next to the **Search** box. For many worksheets, you might not see much difference in speed if you search by columns or by rows.
11. Choose **By Rows**.
12. Click the arrow next to the **Look in** box. Excel searches the underlying formula or the values. A *comment* is a text message attached to a cell.
13. Choose **Formulas**.
14. Click **Find All**. Four cells include the "qtr" character string.
15. Drag the sizing handle at the lower-right corner of the dialog box to see the list.

Exercise 3-6 USE WILDCARDS

1. Double-click **qtr** in the **Find what** box and key ***500**. This character string is used to find all cells with an entry that ends in "500."
2. Click **Find All**. Two values in the worksheet match this character string.
3. Double-click ***500** in the **Find what** box and key **u*** (lowercase letter "U" and an asterisk). This character string is used to find all cells with an entry that includes the letter "u" followed by any number of other characters.
4. Click **Find All**. There are several cells with such entries. Some appear to be values.
5. Click the cell identifier for cell B11 in the dialog box. The value of **$294,430** is calculated from a SUM formula. That's the "u."
6. Click the arrow next to the **Look in** box. Choose **Values**.
7. Click **Find All**. The Values option checks the actual contents of the cells.
8. Double-click **u*** and key **t?e** in the **Find what** box.
9. Click **Find All**. There is one cell that includes this three-letter string.
10. Select **Match entire cell contents**. Click **Find All**. There are no cells that contain only this string. The message box says that Excel cannot find data to match.
11. Click **OK** to close the message box. Click **Close** to close the Find and Replace dialog box.

NOTE

Cell addresses in the Find and Replace dialog box are shown with dollar signs ($) to indicate an absolute reference. Absolute references are covered in another lesson.

Exercise 3-7 REPLACE DATA

You can replace a character string one occurrence at a time or all at once. Sometimes replacing them all at once can be a problem, because you might locate some character strings you didn't anticipate.

1. Press Ctrl+Home to make cell A1 active.
2. Press Ctrl+H. The same Find and Replace dialog box opens, this time with the **Replace** tab active. Excel remembers your most recent Find character string.
3. Double-click **t?e** in the **Find what** box and key **2009**.
4. Click in the **Replace with** box and key **2010**. This will change occurrences of "2009" to "2010."
5. Click to deselect **Match entire cell contents**.
6. Click **Find Next** to locate the first occurrence of "2009."

Figure 3-7
Find and Replace dialog box, Replace tab

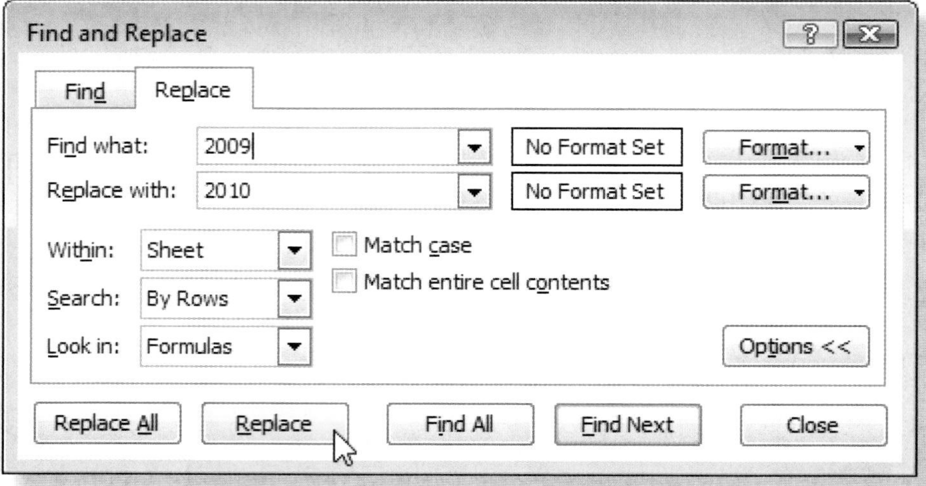

7. Click **Replace** to change "2009" to "2010." Excel locates the next occurrence.
8. Click **Replace**. The replacement is made.
9. Click **Replace**. There are no more occurrences of "2009."
10. Click **OK** in the message box.

Exercise 3-8 REPLACE A FUNCTION IN A FORMULA

1. Double-click **2009** in the **Find what** box and key **sum**.
2. Click **Find All**. Excel locates three cells with the SUM function.
3. Double-click **2010** in the **Replace with** box and key **avg**. This is not the correct spelling for the AVERAGE function.
4. Click **Replace**. The first occurrence is replaced. The cell shows **#NAME?**, a type of error.
5. Click **Replace All**. Two more replacements are made.
6. Click **OK**. You have replaced all instances of "sum" with a misspelled function name.
7. Click **Close** to close the Find and Replace dialog box. You will correct the errors in the next exercise.

Exercise 3-9 CORRECT ERRORS WITH REPLACE

1. Click cell B11. Position the pointer on the Error Checking Options button.
2. Click the arrow next to the button. This is an **Invalid Name Error**. The name of the function is "average," not "avg."

Figure 3-8
Error messages
KowaSales.xlsx
Kowabunga sheet

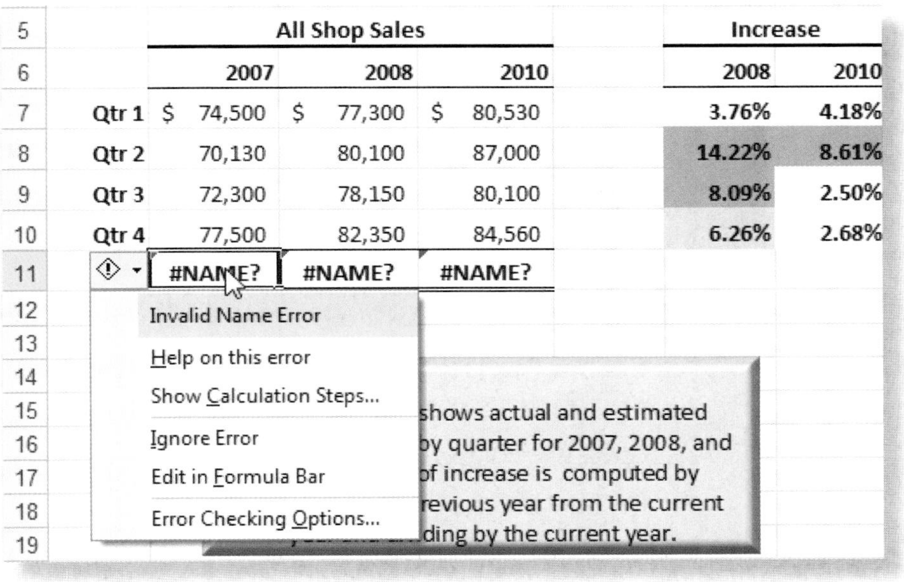

5		All Shop Sales				Increase	
6		2007	2008	2010		2008	2010
7	Qtr 1	$ 74,500	$ 77,300	$ 80,530		3.76%	4.18%
8	Qtr 2	70,130	80,100	87,000		14.22%	8.61%
9	Qtr 3	72,300	78,150	80,100		8.09%	2.50%
10	Qtr 4	77,500	82,350	84,560		6.26%	2.68%
11		#NAME?	#NAME?	#NAME?			

Invalid Name Error
Help on this error
Show Calculation Steps...
Ignore Error
Edit in Formula Bar
Error Checking Options...

shows actual and estimated
by quarter for 2007, 2008, and
of increase is computed by
revious year from the current
ding by the current year.

3. Click cell B11 to close the shortcut menu.
4. Press Ctrl+H. Double-click in the **Find what** box and key **avg**.
5. Press Tab. In the **Replace with** box, key **average**, the correct spelling.
6. Click **Find All**. All the cells with the misspelled function are listed.
7. Click **Replace All**. The replacements are made, and the function is now correct.
8. Click **OK** and then click **Close**. Another Error Checking Options button has appeared.
9. Click cell B11 and display the Error Checking Options menu. The AVERAGE function assumes that all cells immediately above the cell with the function should be included in the range, cells B6:B10. Cell B6 is the year and should not be included.
10. Drag to select the range B11:D11. Position the mouse pointer on the Error Checking Options button. Click the arrow and choose **Ignore Error**.

Exercise 3-10 FIND AND REPLACE FORMATS

In addition to finding or replacing characters, you can find and replace formats. For example, you can find labels and values that are 11-point bold Calibri and change them to bold italic. When you replace formats, you should not show any text or numbers in the Find what or Replace with boxes.

1. Press Ctrl+Home. Press Ctrl+H.
2. Double-click in the **Find what** box and press Delete. The box is empty.
3. Double-click in the **Replace with** box and press Delete.

4. Click the arrow next to **Format** to the right of the **Find what** box.
5. Click **Choose Format From Cell**. The dialog box closes, and the pointer shows the selection pointer with an eyedropper. This pointer will copy the format of the cell to the dialog box.
6. Click cell A7. The dialog box expands. The format from cell A7 (11-point bold Calibri) is shown in the **Preview** area for **Find what**. These cells are also right-aligned.
7. Click the arrow next to **Format** to the right of the **Replace with** box.
8. Choose **Format**. The Replace Format dialog box opens. You can set a new format here.
9. Click the **Font** tab. In the **Font** list, choose **Cambria (Headings)**.
10. In the **Font style** list, choose **Bold Italic**. In the **Size** list, choose **11**.
11. Click **OK**. The previews show what format will be found and how it will be replaced.
12. Click **Find All**. Four cells are listed.

Figure 3-9
Replacing formats

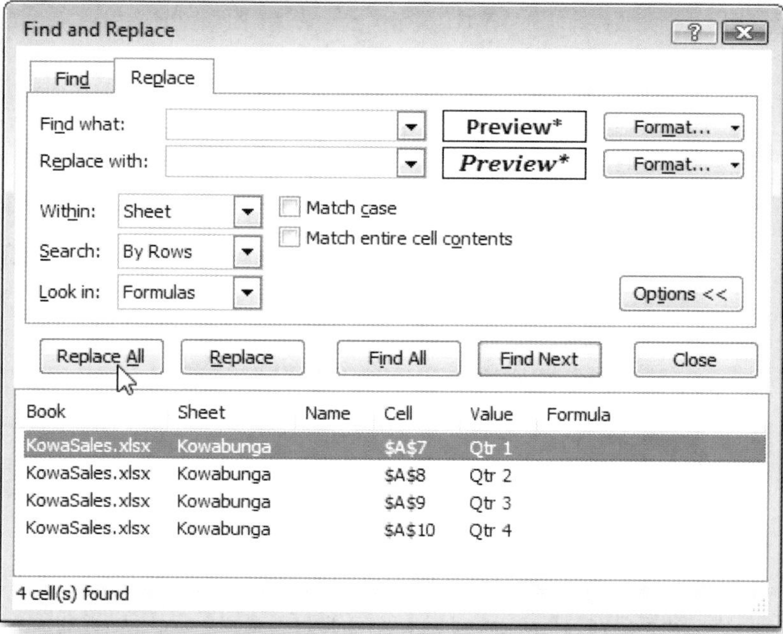

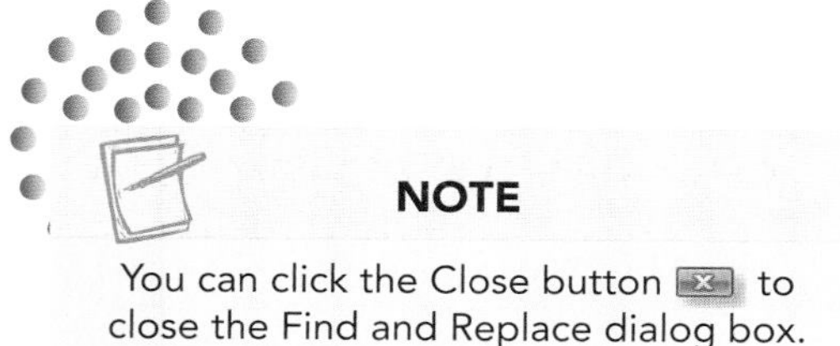

NOTE

You can click the Close button to close the Find and Replace dialog box.

13. Click **Replace All**. The replacements are made.
14. Click **OK** and then click **Close**. The labels in row 5 include a centering command, so they were not matched. Values in row 6 include top and bottom borders, and the other values include some type of number formatting.

Exercise 3-11 RESET FIND AND REPLACE FORMATS

After replacing formats, you should reset the dialog box. If you don't, the formats will be in effect the next time you use Find and Replace and could affect your results.

1. Press Ctrl+H.
2. Click the arrow next to **Format** for the **Find what** box.
3. Click **Clear Find Format**. The area shows **No Format Set**.
4. Click the arrow next to **Format** for the **Replace with** box.
5. Click **Clear Replace Format**. Click **Close**.

Using Series and AutoFill

A *series* is a list of labels, numbers, dates, or times that follows a pattern. The days of the week are a series that repeats every seven days. Months repeat their pattern every 12 months. These are common series that Excel recognizes if you key a label in the series.

You can create your own series by keying two values or labels to set an interval or pattern. The *interval* is the number of steps between numbers or labels. For example, the series "1, 3, 5, 7" uses an interval of two because each number is increased by 2 to determine the next number. The series "Qtr 1, Qtr 2, Qtr 3" uses an interval of one.

Exercise 3-12 CREATE MONTH AND WEEK SERIES

The easiest way to create a series is by using the *AutoFill command,* which copies and extends data from a cell or range of cells to adjacent cells. The AutoFill command uses the *Fill handle,* a small rectangle at the lower-right corner of a cell or range.

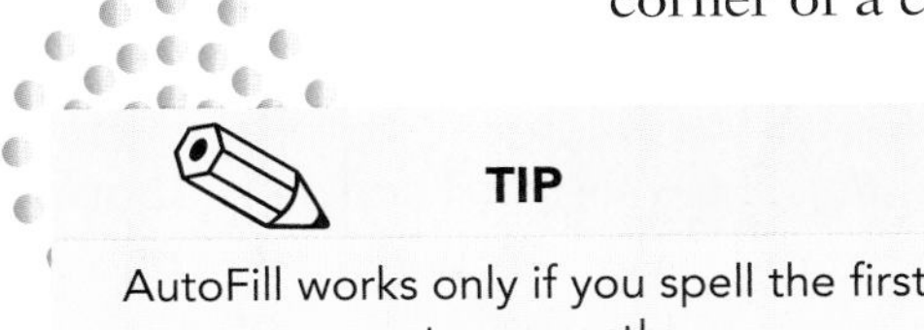

TIP

AutoFill works only if you spell the first entry correctly.

1. Press Ctrl+G. The Go To dialog box opens.
2. Key **a26** and press Enter. The insertion point is in cell A26.
3. Key **January** and press Enter.
4. Click cell A26. Scroll the worksheet until you can see rows 26 through 37.
5. Place the pointer on the Fill handle for cell A26. The pointer changes to a solid black cross.
6. Drag down to cell A37. As you drag, a ScreenTip shows each month as it is filled in.

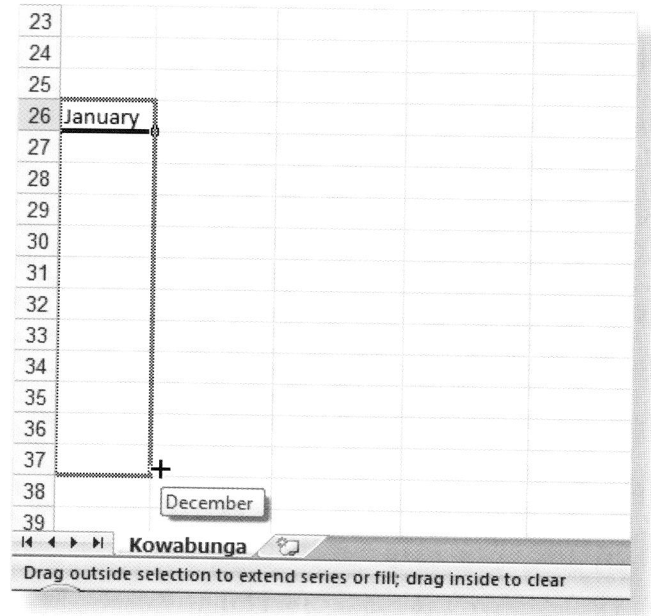

Figure 3-10
Creating a month series
KowaSales.xlsx
Kowabunga sheet

7. Release the mouse button. The series is filled. The AutoFill Options button appears below your filled selection. It includes options for filling data.
8. Hover over the AutoFill Options button and click its arrow.
9. Choose **Fill Series** for a regular AutoFill task.

Ctrl+Enter keeps the insertion point in the active cell.

10. In cell B25, key **Week 1** and press Ctrl+Enter.
11. Place the mouse pointer on the Fill handle for cell B25.
12. Drag right to cell E25. Release the mouse button. The series is filled.

Exercise 3-13 CREATE A NUMBER SERIES

To establish a value series, first key two values in the series. Then select both cells and drag the Fill handle. If you drag the Fill handle too far, just drag it back to where you wanted to finish.

1. Click cell B26. Key **5** and press Enter.
2. Key **10** in cell B27. This sets a pattern with an interval of 5, increasing each value by 5.
3. Click cell B26 and drag to select cell B27. There is one Fill handle for the range.
4. Place the pointer on the Fill handle for cell B27.
5. Drag down to cell B37 and release the mouse button. The series is filled in, and the range is selected.

6. Hover over the AutoFill Options button and click its arrow.
7. Choose **Copy Cells**. The series is adjusted to be a copy.
8. Click the arrow with the AutoFill Options button. Choose **Fill Series**.

Exercise 3-14 COPY DATA WITH THE FILL HANDLE

When there is no apparent pattern in the range, the Fill handle copies data rather than creating a series.

1. The series you just filled in should still be selected. The Fill handle for the range is located in cell B37. Place the mouse pointer on the Fill handle.
2. Drag right to column E and release the mouse button. The range is copied, because no pattern was set for going from one column to the next.

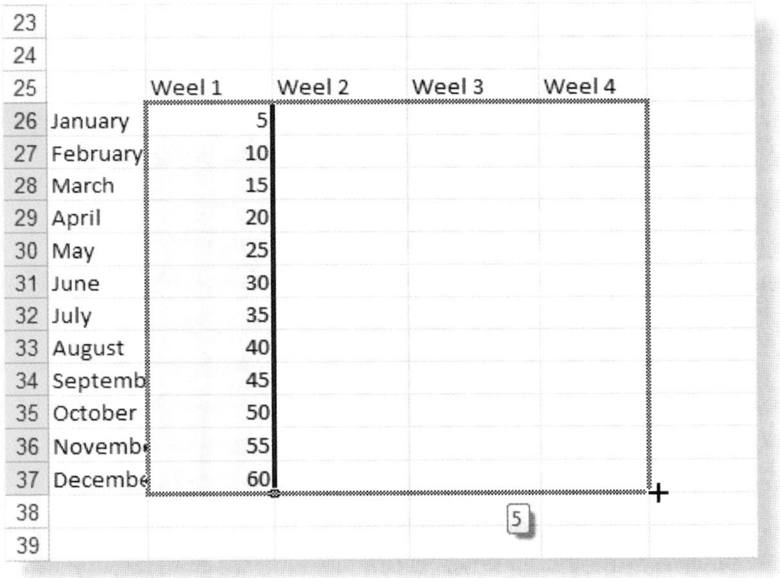

Figure 3-11
Using the Fill pointer to copy
KowaSales.xlsx
Kowabunga sheet

23					
24					
25		Weel 1	Weel 2	Weel 3	Weel 4
26	January	5			
27	February	10			
28	March	15			
29	April	20			
30	May	25			
31	June	30			
32	July	35			
33	August	40			
34	Septemb	45			
35	October	50			
36	Novemb	55			
37	Decembe	60			
38				5	
39					

3. Make column A **10.00 (75 pixels)** wide.

Exercise 3-15 COPY A FORMULA WITH THE FILL HANDLE

1. Click cell F26. Click the **Home** tab. 
2. In the **Editing** group, click the AutoSum button Σ. The SUM function shows the range to be summed as B26:E26.
3. Press Ctrl+Enter. The formula is completed.
4. Look at the formula bar. You can copy this formula to the rest of the rows by using the Fill handle.

5. Place the pointer on the Fill handle for cell F26.
6. Drag down to cell F37 and release the mouse. Excel copies the formula, and the AutoFill Options button appears.
7. Display the AutoFill Options menu. You do not need to make a change.
8. Click cell F27. The copied formula is relative to where it is on the worksheet, just as when you use Copy and Paste.

Applying Table and Cell Styles

A *table* is an arrangement of data in which each row represents one item or element. In your worksheet, each item is a month. Tables usually have a *header row* for each column to define the column's data. In this lesson, you will learn how to create a table from your data using built-in table styles.

Excel also has many cell styles for formatting labels and values based on the current document theme. These styles can include font and border settings, number formats, alignment settings, background colors, and more.

Exercise 3-16 CREATE A TABLE

1. In cell F25, key **Total** and press Enter. In cell A25, key **Month** and press Enter. Each column now has a header.
2. On the **Home** tab in the **Styles** group, click the Format as Table button. The Table Styles gallery opens with previews of many table styles. The styles are categorized as Light, Medium, or Dark based on the color scheme.

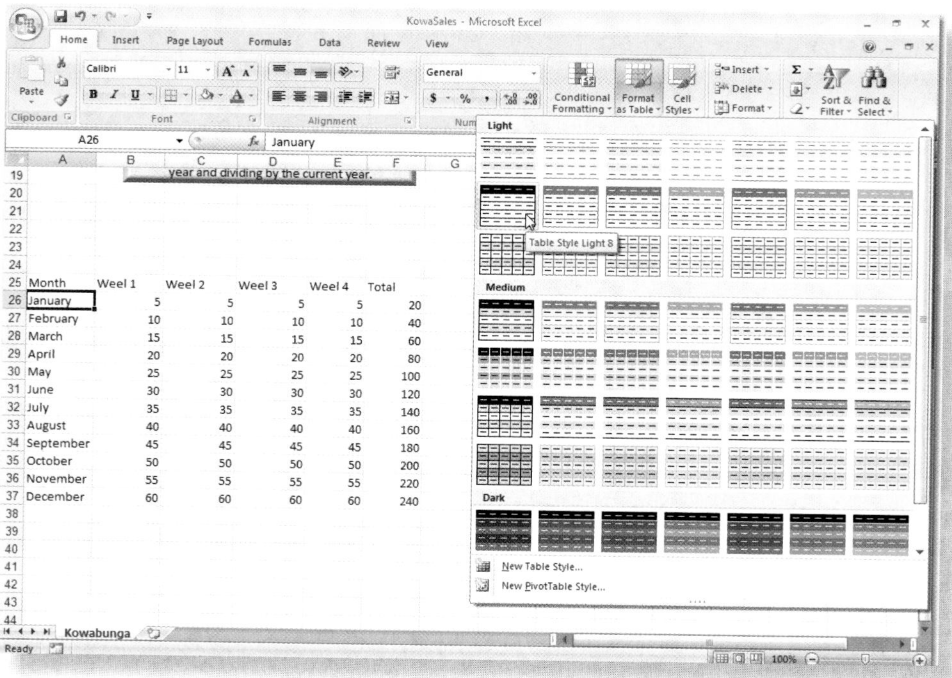

Figure 3-12
Table Styles gallery

3. Hover the mouse pointer over several thumbnails to find **Table Style Light 8** and click the icon. The gallery closes, your data is marqueed, and the Format As Table dialog box opens with a suggested range for your table.

Figure 3-13
Format As Table dialog box
KowaSales.xlsx
Kowabunga sheet

4. Make sure there is a check mark for **My table has headers**. Click **OK**. Excel applies the style, adds Filter buttons to the header labels, and displays the **Table Tools Design** command tab.

NOTE

Filter buttons are used to sort and filter the rows. The buttons do not print.

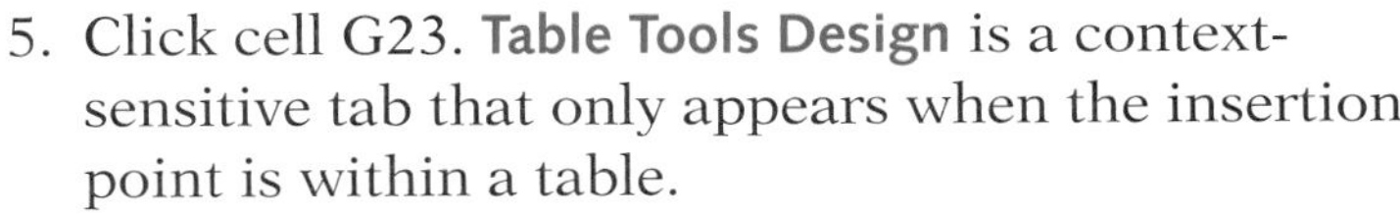

5. Click cell G23. **Table Tools Design** is a context-sensitive tab that only appears when the insertion point is within a table.
6. Click cell D27. The **Table Tools Design** tab appears.

Figure 3-14
New Table
KowaSales.xlsx
Kowabunga sheet

24						
25	Month	Weel 1	Weel 2	Weel 3	Weel 4	Total
26	January	5	5	5	5	20
27	February	10	10	10	10	40
28	March	15	15	15	15	60
29	April	20	20	20	20	80
30	May	25	25	25	25	100
31	June	30	30	30	30	120
32	July	35	35	35	35	140
33	August	40	40	40	40	160
34	September	45	45	45	45	180
35	October	50	50	50	50	200
36	November	55	55	55	55	220
37	December	60	60	60	60	240
38						

Exercise 3-17 CHANGE THE TABLE STYLE

You can easily change the style of a table and adjust several other design elements.

1. Click the **Table Tools Design** tab.

2. Click the More button in the **Table Styles** group to open the gallery.

3. Hover over several different styles. Live Preview shows the table as it would appear with each style as you hover.
4. Find **Table Style Medium 8** and click the icon. The gallery closes, and the table is restyled.
5. In the **Table Style Options** group, click to deselect **Header Row**. The header row is no longer visible.
6. In the **Table Style Options** group, click to select **Total Row**. A grand total is shown for the last column.
7. Click to deselect **Total Row**.
8. In the **Table Style Options** group, click to select **First Column**. The first column is styled differently for emphasis.
9. Click to deselect **First Column**.
10. Click to select **Header Row** to show the header row again.

Exercise 3-18 APPLY A CELL STYLE

1. In cell A23, key **Monthly Estimates** and press Enter.
2. Click cell A23. In the **Styles** group on the Home tab, click the Cell Styles button. The Cell Styles gallery opens. The styles are divided into five groups. You can use any style for any worksheet cell; the categories are just guidelines.

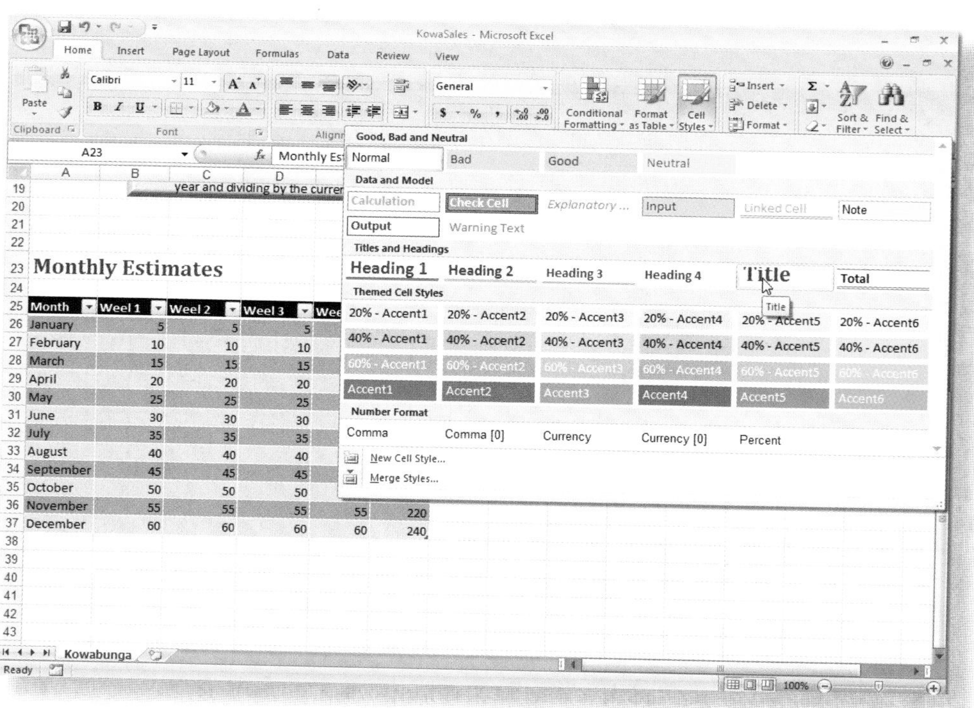

Figure 3-15
Cell Styles gallery
KowaSales.xlsx
Kowabunga sheet

3. Hover the mouse pointer over different thumbnails and watch cell A23. Live Preview shows how the label will appear with the style.
4. Find and click the **Title** style (under Titles and Headings). The label is reformatted as Cambria 18 point in a theme color.

5. In the **Font** group, click the Font Color button. The color on the button is applied (probably red). You can apply your own formatting after choosing a cell style.

Exercise 3-19 PRINT A SELECTION

In the current worksheet, you might want to print only the table. To print a portion of a worksheet, select the range of cells you want to print. Open the Print dialog box and choose **Selection**.

1. Go to cell A38 and key your first and last name. Excel assumes your name is another row in the table and formats it to match.
2. Rest the mouse pointer on the table-sizing handle in cell F38. The pointer changes to a two-pointed arrow.
3. Drag the handle up to row 37. Your name is no longer part of the table.
4. Click cell F38 and press Delete. The formula was copied, too.
5. Click cell A23 and press F8. Extend Selection mode starts.
6. Press → five times to reach column F.
7. Press Ctrl+↓ three times. Each press of this key combination highlights up to the current range of your data.
8. Press Ctrl+P. The Print dialog box opens.
9. Choose **Selection** in the **Print what** area.
10. Click **Preview**. The Print Preview shows the range that will be printed.
11. Click the Print button. Only the range that you specified is printed.
12. Save the workbook as ***[your initials]*3-19** in a folder for Lesson 3.

NOTE

A table has a sizing handle at the bottom right corner.

Preparing Headers and Footers

Headers and footers can be used to display a company name, a department, the date, or a company logo. A *header* prints at the top of each page in a worksheet. A *footer* prints at the bottom of each page. Excel has preset headers and footers, and you can create your own.

A header or footer can have up to three sections. The left section prints at the left margin. The center section prints at the horizontal center of the page. The right section aligns at the right margin.

You can create headers and footers by:

- Clicking the Header & Footer button in the Text group on the Insert tab.
- Clicking the Page Layout button on the status bar.
- Clicking the Page Layout button in the Workbook View group on the View tab.
- Clicking the Dialog Box Launcher in the Page Setup group on the Page Layout tab.
- Clicking the Page Setup button in Print Preview.

Exercise 3-20 SET HEADERS AND FOOTERS

1. With ***[your initials]*3-19** open, press Ctrl+Home.
2. Click the **Insert** tab in the Ribbon.
3. In the **Text** group, click the Header & Footer button. The Header/Footer Tools Design tab is a context-sensitive tab that opens when the insertion point is within a header or footer section. The worksheet is in Page Layout View.
4. Click the Header button to display a gallery of header arrangements. Header sections are separated by commas. If you choose a single item, it prints in the center section. Two items print in the center and at the right margin. Three items print at the left margin, in the center, and at the right margin.

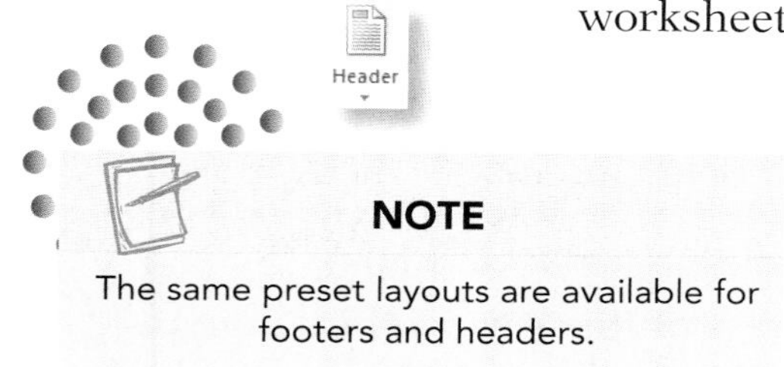

NOTE

The same preset layouts are available for footers and headers.

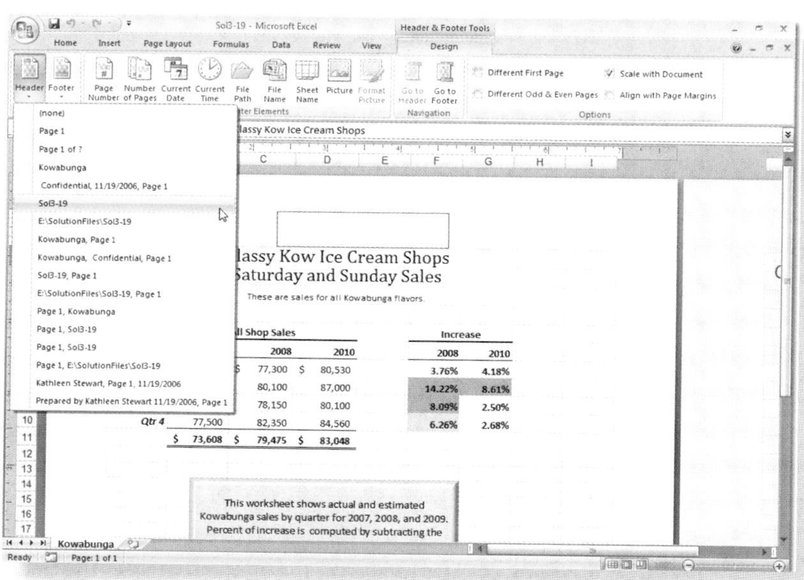

Figure 3-16
Choosing a preset header
3-19.xlsx
Kowabunga sheet

5. Find and click the first occurrence of your filename. You can see the header in the center section.

6. Point at the filename in the header and click. The code for displaying the filename is **&[File]**.

Go to Footer

7. In the **Navigation** group, click the Go to Footer button. The insertion point is in the center section.

8. Point at the left section and click. The insertion point moves there.

Page Number

9. Key your first and last name in the left section and press Tab. The insertion point moves to the center section.

Number of Pages

10. In the **Header and Footer Elements** group, click the Page Number button.

NOTE

You can use the buttons in the Ribbon or key the codes in the header/footer areas.

11. Press Spacebar, key **of**, and press Spacebar again.

12. In the **Header and Footer Elements** group, click the Number of Pages button.

13. Press Tab. The insertion point moves to the right section.

Current Date

14. Click the Current Date button. The code for displaying the current date is **&[Date]**.

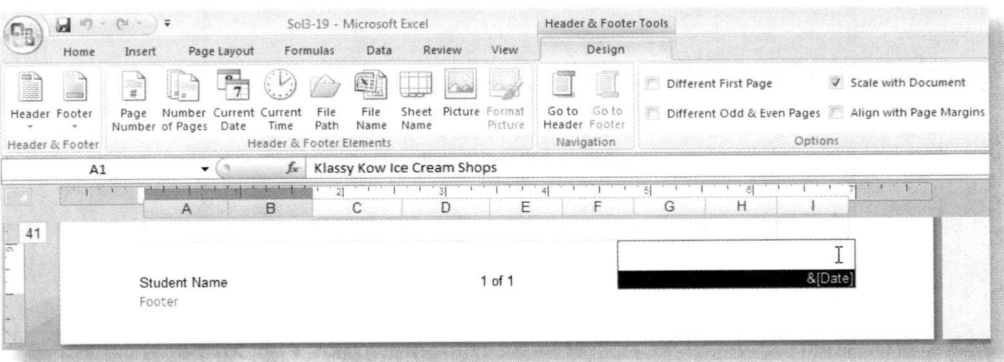

Figure 3-17
Creating a custom footer
3-19.xlsx
Kowabunga sheet

15. Click a cell above the footer area. This completes the footer and returns the focus to your worksheet.

16. Press Ctrl+Home. The worksheet is in Page Layout View while you work with headers and footers.

Exercise 3-21 PRINT GRIDLINES AND ROW AND COLUMN HEADINGS

Gridlines and row and column headings are visible while you work on a worksheet. They do not print as a default, but you can set them to print. Printing a worksheet with the gridlines and row and column headings makes it easy to locate data or to re-create a worksheet, if needed.

1. With ***[your initials]*3-19** in Page Layout view, click the **Page Layout** tab in the Ribbon.

2. In the **Sheet Options** group, click to select the **Print** box below **Gridlines**.

3. Click to select **Print** below **Headings**.

Exercise 3-22 CHANGE MARGINS AND COLUMN WIDTHS IN PAGE LAYOUT VIEW

Excel sets 0.75 inch for left and right margins in a new workbook. The top and bottom margins are both set at 0.7 inch. The header and footer are preset to print 0.3 inch from the top and bottom of the page, within the top and bottom margin areas.

You can change the margins and the column widths in Page Layout View by dragging a margin marker or a column heading border. As you drag, the margin setting or column width is shown in inches or character spaces.

1. Hover over the left margin marker. The pointer changes to a two-pointed arrow.

2. Click and drag right to set a left margin of about **1.00**. Watch the ScreenTip for the setting as you drag. Your margin setting does not need to be exact.

Figure 3-18
Changing page margins in Page Layout View
3-19.xlsx
Kowabunga sheet

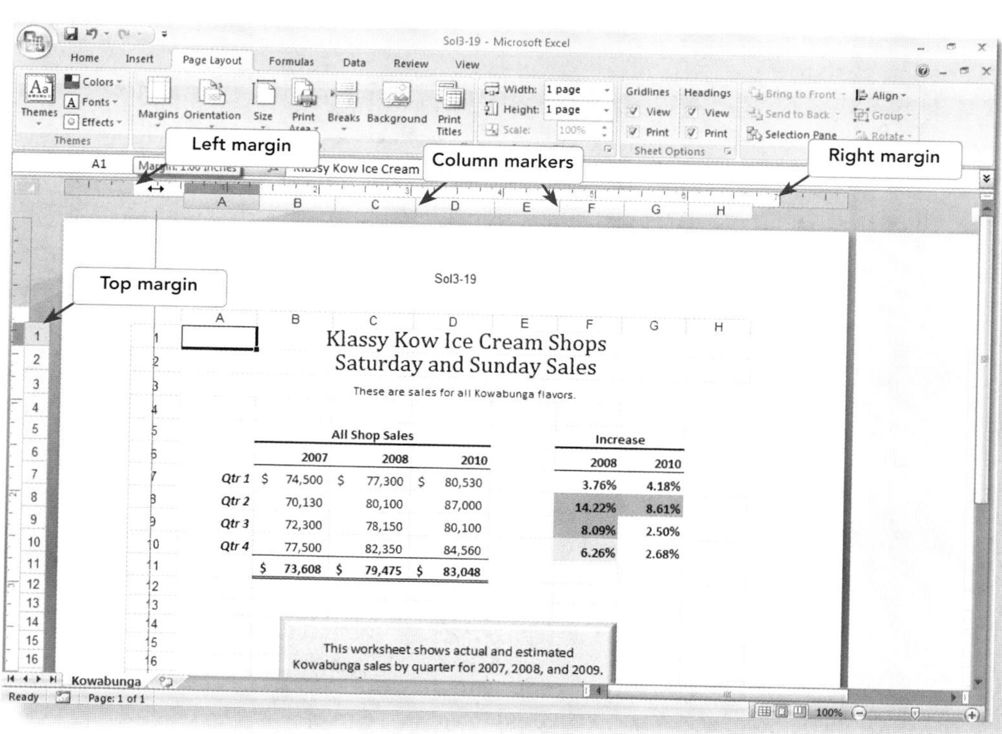

3. Hover the pointer over the right margin marker. Click and drag left to reach about **1.00**.

NOTE

The column headings for adjusting the width are just below the ruler.

4. Place the pointer on the column marker between columns A and B. The pointer changes to a two-pointed arrow. Drag right to make column A wider at **1.00 inches (101 pixels)**.
5. Make column E slightly less wide.
6. Press F12 and save the workbook as ***[your initials]*3-22** in your Lesson 3 folder.
7. Prepare and submit your work. Close the workbook.

Using Online Help

Series and AutoFill are time-saving features of Excel. They enable you to work more quickly and more accurately. Read more about series and the AutoFill command.

LOOK UP AUTOFILL AND SERIES

1. In a new workbook, press F1.
2. In the Search text box, key **autofill** and press Enter.
3. Find topics about filling in data in cells. Read the help information.
4. Close the Help window.

Lesson 3 Summary

- AutoCorrect corrects common typing errors as you work. You can add your own entries or delete existing ones.
- The Spelling command spell-checks a worksheet by comparing labels to dictionary entries. Options let you decide if and how to make the correction.
- The Find command locates and lists all occurrences of data that match your Find what character string. You can use wildcards in the character string.
- The Replace command locates and substitutes new data for existing data. You can complete the changes one at a time or all at once.
- Excel displays options buttons for some commands and formula errors. You can look at the message for the button, make a change, or ignore it.
- All cells have a Fill handle that can be used for filling in a series or for copying data.
- Excel recognizes common series for the days of the week, the months, and patterns such as "Week 1," "Week 2," and so on.

- You can create your own series with any interval by keying at least two cells that define the pattern.
- A table is a consistent pattern of data rows with a header row. Tables can be formatted with a style from the gallery.
- Cell styles apply colors, fonts, and other formatting options to a cell or range.
- Headers and footers print at the top or bottom of every page. There are preset headers and footers, or you can create your own.
- You can view and print a worksheet with or without the gridlines and row and column headings.
- You can change margins and column widths in Page Layout View and immediately see the results.

LESSON 3		Command Summary	
Feature	**Button**	**Task Path**	**Keyboard**
Error checking		Formulas, Formula Auditing	
Error checking options		Formulas, Formula Auditing	
Fill series		Home, Editing	
Find	Find & Select	Home, Editing, Find	Ctrl+F
Gridlines, print/view		Page Layout, Sheet Options	
Header/Footer	Header & Footer	Insert, Text	
Header, preset	Header	Header & Footer Tools Design, Header & Footer	
Headings, print/view		Page Layout, Sheet Options	
Print selection		Microsoft Office, Print	Ctrl+P
Replace	Find & Select	Home, Editing	Ctrl+H
Spelling	Spelling	Review, Proofing	F7
Style, cell	Cell Styles	Home, Styles	
Table, create	Format as Table	Home, Styles	Ctrl+T
Table, style		Table Tools Design, Table Styles	

Lesson 4

Exploring Home tab Commands

OBJECTIVES

MCAS OBJECTIVES

In this lesson:
XL07 1.2
XL07 1.3.1
XL07 1.4.2
XL07 1.5.1
XL07 1.5.5
XL07 2.2.1
XL07 2.2.3
XL07 2.3.2
XL07 2.3.3
XL07 2.3.4
XL07 2.3.6
XL07 2.3.7
XL07 4.3.1
XL07 4.3.3

After completing this lesson, you will be able to:

1. Insert and delete sheets and cells.
2. Use AutoComplete and Pick From Drop-Down List.
3. Copy, cut, and paste cell contents.
4. Work with columns and rows.
5. Work with alignment.
6. Apply borders and fill.
7. Use data bars.

Estimated Time: 1 1/4 hours

The Home tab includes commonly used tasks and commands. The groups on this tab are Clipboard, Font, Alignment, Number, Styles, Cells, and Editing. The Home tab is the active tab when you open a new workbook.

Inserting and Deleting Sheets and Cells

A new workbook opens with three blank sheets. You can insert and delete sheets as needed. You insert a new worksheet when you:

- Click the **Insert Worksheet** tab.
- Press Shift+F11.

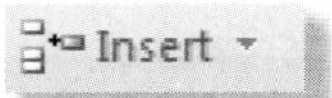

- In the Cells group, click the arrow with the Insert Cells button and choose **Insert Sheet**.
- Right-click a worksheet tab and choose **Insert**. Then choose **Worksheet** in the dialog box.

You delete a worksheet when you:

- Right-click the worksheet tab and choose **Delete**.

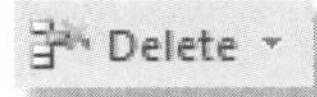

- In the Cells group, click the arrow next to the Delete Cells button and choose **Delete Sheet**.

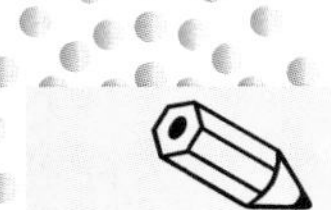

TIP

You can change the default number of sheets in a new workbook in the Popular pane in the Excel Options dialog box.

Exercise 4-1 INSERT WORKSHEETS

Excel names new sheets starting with the next number in sequence. For example, if the workbook already has **Sheet1**, **Sheet2**, and **Sheet3**, a new sheet would be named **Sheet4**.

1. Open **AcctRec**. This workbook has one worksheet named **AR2007** for Accounts Receivable in 2007. Notice that there is no **Sheet1**.
2. Click the **Insert Worksheet** tab.
3. Double-click the **Sheet1** worksheet tab.
4. Key **SalesReps** and press Enter. The worksheet tab is renamed.
5. Right-click the **SalesReps** tab. Choose a color different from the color of the **AR2007** sheet.
6. Press Shift+F11. A new worksheet named **Sheet2** is placed in front of the **SalesReps** sheet.

NOTE

Your sheet numbers might be different.

7. Right-click the **AR2007** tab and choose **Insert**. The Insert dialog box opens.
8. Click the **General** tab. This tab shows the types of objects you can insert in your workbook. You likely have objects different from the text figure.

Figure 4-1
Insert Worksheet dialog box

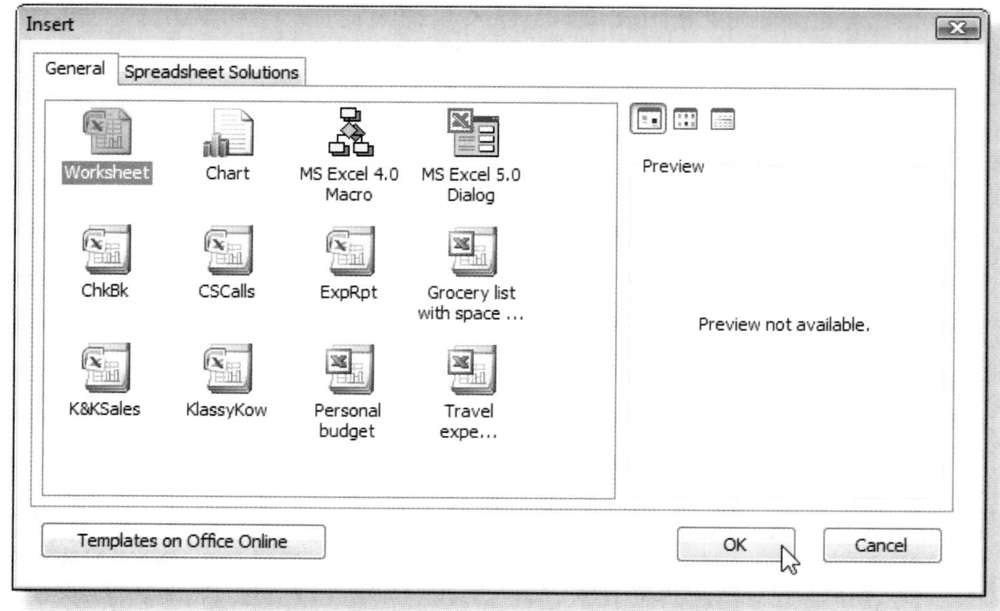

9. Click Worksheet and click OK. **Sheet3** is placed before the **AR2007** worksheet.

Exercise 4-2 MOVE AND DELETE WORKSHEETS

You can rearrange worksheet tabs in any order. Additionally, if you don't need all the sheets in a workbook, you can delete blank ones to conserve file space. You cannot delete the only sheet in a workbook.

1. Click the **AR2007** tab to make it active.
2. Point at the tab to display a white arrow pointer.
3. Click and drag the tab to the left of **Sheet3**. As you drag, you see a small sheet icon and a triangle that marks the new position of the sheet.
4. Release the mouse button. The **AR2007** sheet is now the leftmost tab.
5. Right-click the **Sheet3** tab. The sheet becomes the active sheet and a shortcut menu opens.
6. Choose Delete. The sheet is deleted, and **Sheet2** is active.
7. In the Cells group, click the arrow with the Delete Cells button [Delete]. Choose Delete Sheet. The sheet is deleted, and the **SalesReps** worksheet is active.

TIP

You can also move a sheet by right-clicking the tab and choosing Move or Copy from the shortcut menu.

Exercise 4-3 INSERT CELLS

When you insert or delete cells, you affect the entire worksheet, not just the column or row where you are working. You can accidentally rearrange data if you don't watch the entire sheet. When you insert or delete cells, you decide if existing cells should move up, down, left, or right.

NOTE

If you use a laptop computer that does not have a numeric keypad, press Ctrl+Shift++, using the + in the top row of keys.

1. Click the **AR2007** tab. Set the Zoom size so that you can see columns A through H.
2. Click cell B8.
3. Press Ctrl++ in the numeric keypad. (The *numeric keypad* is the set of number and symbol keys at the right side of the keyboard.) An Insert dialog box opens with choices about what happens after the cell is inserted.

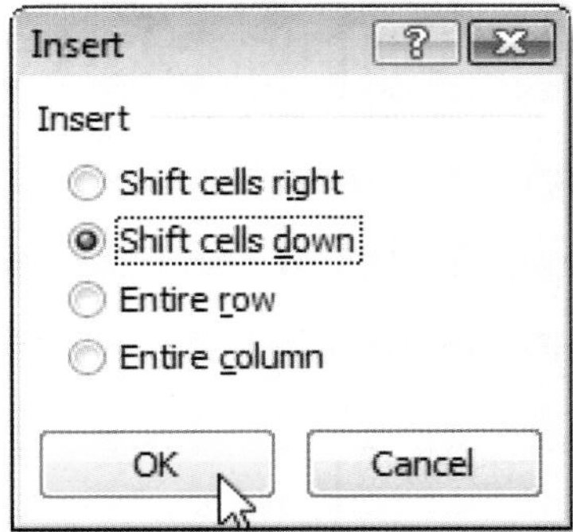

Figure 4-2
Insert dialog box
AcctRec.xlsx
AR2007 sheet

4. Choose **Shift cells down** if it's not already selected and click **OK**. A blank cell is inserted. The cells originally in cells B8:B15 have moved down to cells B9:B16. The data in the other columns did not shift.
5. Click cell C12. The reference number and related paid date are in the wrong columns.
6. Right-click cell C12 and choose **Insert**.
7. Choose **Shift cells right** and click **OK**. All the cells in the worksheet shift to the right, including those in column H and beyond.

NOTE

You will see the Mini toolbar when you right-click a cell; just ignore it for now.

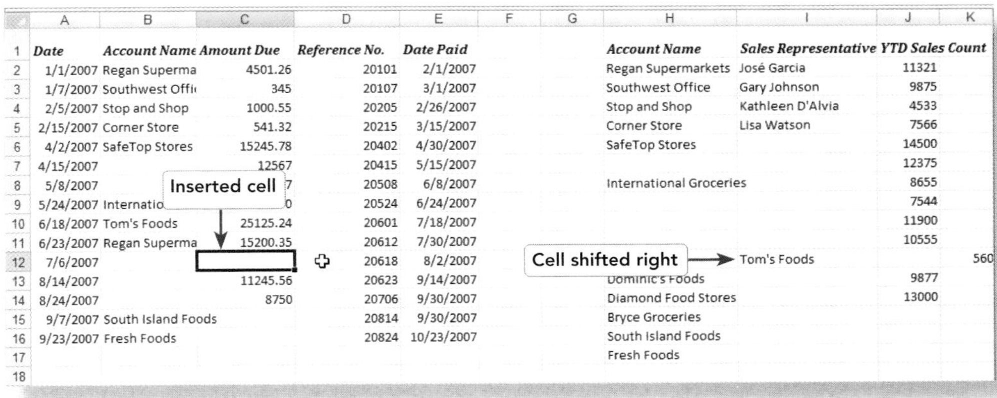

	A	B	C	D	E	F	G	H	I	J	K
1	*Date*	*Account Name*	*Amount Due*	*Reference No.*	*Date Paid*			*Account Name*	*Sales Representative*	*YTD Sales Count*	
2	1/1/2007	Regan Superma	4501.26	20101	2/1/2007			Regan Supermarkets	José Garcia	11321	
3	1/7/2007	Southwest Offi	345	20107	3/1/2007			Southwest Office	Gary Johnson	9875	
4	2/5/2007	Stop and Shop	1000.55	20205	2/26/2007			Stop and Shop	Kathleen D'Alvia	4533	
5	2/15/2007	Corner Store	541.32	20215	3/15/2007			Corner Store	Lisa Watson	7566	
6	4/2/2007	SafeTop Stores	15245.78	20402	4/30/2007			SafeTop Stores		14500	
7	4/15/2007		12567	20415	5/15/2007					12375	
8	5/8/2007		7	20508	6/8/2007			International Groceries		8655	
9	5/24/2007	Internatio	0	20524	6/24/2007					7544	
10	6/18/2007	Tom's Foods	25125.24	20601	7/18/2007					11900	
11	6/23/2007	Regan Superma	15200.35	20612	7/30/2007					10555	
12	7/6/2007			20618	8/2/2007				Tom's Foods		560
13	8/14/2007		11245.56	20623	9/14/2007			Dominic's Foods		9877	
14	8/24/2007		8750	20706	9/30/2007			Diamond Food Stores		13000	
15	9/7/2007	South Island Foods		20814	9/30/2007			Bryce Groceries			
16	9/23/2007	Fresh Foods		20824	10/23/2007			South Island Foods			
17								Fresh Foods			
18											

Figure 4-3
One cell inserted, with other cells shifted right
AcctRec.xlsx
AR2007 sheet

Exercise 4-4 DELETE CELLS

When you delete cells, watch the entire worksheet for changes.

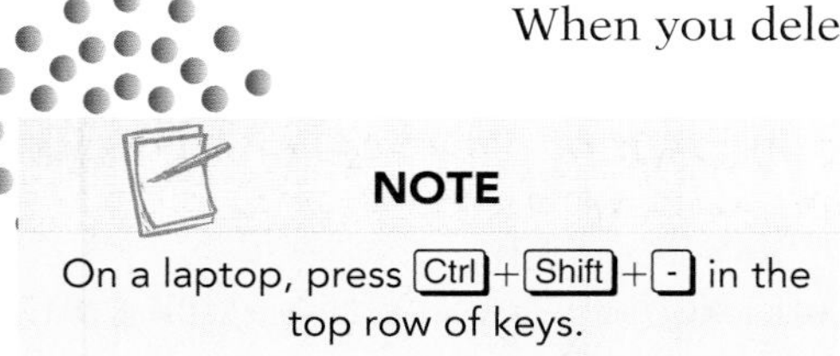

NOTE

On a laptop, press Ctrl+Shift+- in the top row of keys.

1. Scroll the worksheet so that you can see columns D through I.
2. Click cell H7.
3. Press Ctrl+- in the numeric keypad. The Delete dialog box opens.
4. Choose **Shift cells up** and click **OK**. Now there is no room to return "Tom's Foods" to column H.

5. Click the Undo button in the Quick Access toolbar.
6. Click cell H12. Press Ctrl+- on the numeric keypad.
7. Choose **Shift cells left** and click **OK**. Only the cells in columns H and beyond are shifted to the left.
8. Right-click cell H7 and choose **Delete**.
9. Choose **Shift cells up**, if it's not already selected, and click **OK**.
10. Select cells H8:H10. Right-click any cell in the range.
11. Choose **Delete** and **Shift cells up**. Click OK.
12. Press Ctrl+Home.

Using AutoComplete and Pick from Drop-Down List

Excel has two features that make it easy to enter labels in a column. Both features use text already in the column.

- *AutoComplete* displays a suggested label after you key the first character(s) in a cell. AutoComplete works for text and labels that are a combination of text and numbers.
- *Pick From Drop-Down List* displays a list of labels already in the column for your selection. This method is helpful when it is important that you use exactly the same data as already entered. It's a way to validate data as it is entered.

Exercise 4-5 USE AUTOCOMPLETE

When you key the first few characters of a label, Excel scans the column for the same characters. If it finds a match, it displays a proposed entry. If the suggestion is correct, press Enter. If the suggested label is not what you want, ignore it and continue to key the new label. You may need to key more than one character before Excel proposes a label.

TIP

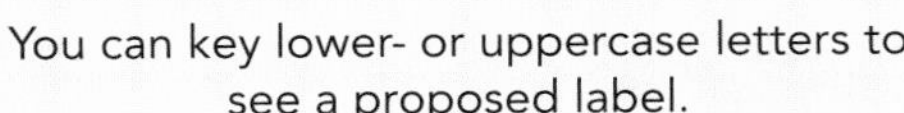

You can key lower- or uppercase letters to see a proposed label.

1. Click cell B7.
2. Key **r** to see an AutoComplete suggestion. In this case, Excel's suggestion is accurate.

Figure 4-4
An AutoComplete suggestion
AcctRec.xlsx AR2007 sheet

	A	B	C	D
1	*Date*	*Account Name*	*Amount Due*	*Reference No.*
2	1/1/2007	Regan Superma	4501.26	20101
3	1/7/2007	Southwest Offi	345	20107
4	2/5/2007	Stop and Shop	1000.55	20205
5	2/15/2007	Corner Store	541.32	20215
6	4/2/2007	SafeTop Stores	15245.78	20402
7	4/15/2007	regan Supermarkets		20415
8	5/8/2007		3677.87	20508
9	5/24/2007	International Gi	5590	20524
10	6/18/2007	Tom's Foods	25125.24	20601

3. Press Enter. The label is entered with the same capitalization as the existing label in the column.
4. Key **s** in cell B8. No suggestion is made, because several labels in the column start with "s." Excel needs more information.
5. Key **t** to see a suggestion for "Stop and Shop."
6. Press Enter.
7. Click cell B12 and key **south**. Excel has not found a match.
8. Press Spacebar. Excel suggests "South Island Foods," because the space distinguishes it from "Southwest."
9. Press Enter.

10. Key **PDQ Shop** in cell B13 and press Enter. No suggestion was made, because no existing label starts with "p."
11. Click cell C15 and key **87**. Excel does not make AutoComplete suggestions for values.
12. Press Esc.

Exercise 4-6 USE PICK FROM DROP-DOWN LIST

The Pick From Drop-Down List option appears on the shortcut menu when you right-click a cell.

1. Right-click cell I6.
2. Choose **Pick From Drop-Down List**. Excel displays a list of labels already in column I.
3. Click **José Garcia**.

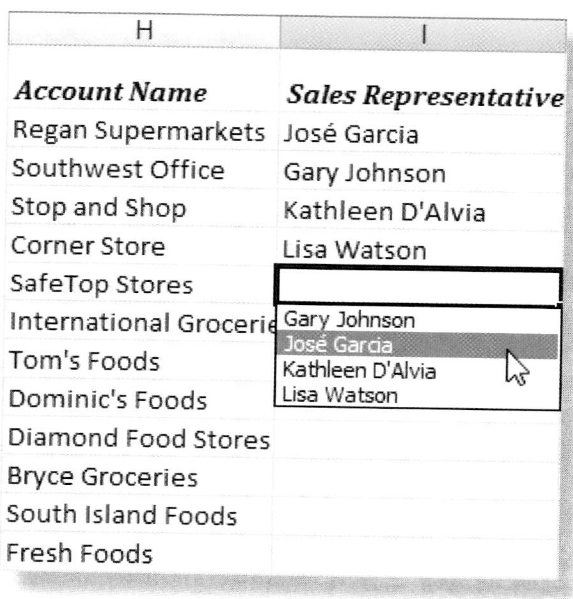

Figure 4-5
Using Pick From Drop-Down List
AcctRec.xlsx AR2007 sheet

4. Right-click cell I7. Choose **Pick From Drop-Down List**.
5. Click **Lisa Watson**.
6. Right-click cell B14. Choose **Pick From Drop-Down List**. The list is longer and includes a scroll bar.
7. Find and click **Tom's Foods**.
8. Right-click cell C12. Choose **Pick From Drop-Down List**. Excel does not display a list for values.
9. Press Esc.

Copying, Cutting, and Pasting Cell Contents

You can copy, cut (move), and paste cell contents in a worksheet. When you copy or cut a cell or range of cells, a duplicate of the data is placed on the *Windows Clipboard*. This is a temporary memory area used to keep data you have copied or cut.

Data that is cut can be pasted once. Data that is copied can be pasted many times and in many locations. Copied data stays on the Windows Clipboard until you copy or cut another cell or range. Then that data replaces the data on the Clipboard.

The Cut and Paste commands are used to move labels and values from one cell to another. To use Cut and Paste, first select the cells you want to cut, and then you can:

- Click the Cut button in the Clipboard group. Position the pointer at the new location and click the Paste button or press Enter.
- Press Ctrl+X. Position the pointer at the new location and press Ctrl+V or press Enter.
- Right-click the selected cells. Choose **Cut** from the shortcut menu. Right-click the new cell location and choose **Paste** from the shortcut menu.
- Select the cell or range. Drag it to a new location.

The Copy and Paste commands make a duplicate of the data in another location. To use copy and paste, select the cells you want to copy, and then you can:

- Click the Copy button in the Clipboard group. Position the pointer at the new location and click the Paste button or press Enter.
- Press Ctrl+C. Position the pointer at the new location and press Ctrl+V or press Enter.
- Right-click the selected cells. Choose **Copy** from the shortcut menu. Right-click the new cell location and choose **Paste**.
- Select the cell or range. While holding down the Ctrl key, drag it to a new location.

Exercise 4-7 CUT AND PASTE CELL CONTENTS

When you paste cells that have been cut, the cut data replaces existing data unless you tell Excel to insert the cut data.

1. Click cell C14. Click the Cut button . A moving marquee surrounds the cell.
2. Click cell C12 and then click the Paste button . The data is removed from cell C14 and pasted in C12. The marquee is canceled.
3. Select cells B15:B16. Press Ctrl+X. The range displays the moving marquee.

4. Click cell B17 and press [Enter]. The pasted range is selected.

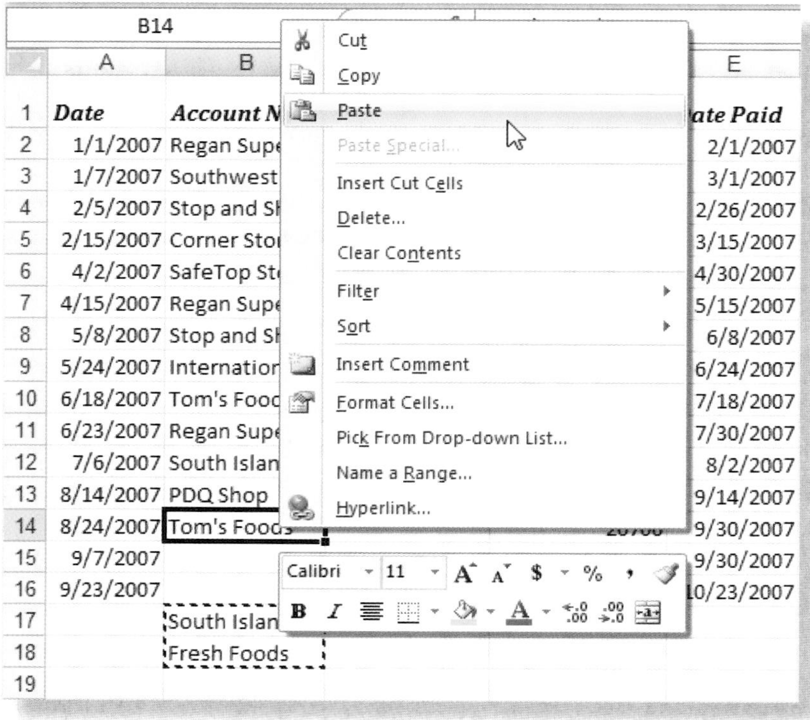

Figure 4-6
Cutting cell contents
AcctRec.xlsx
AR2007 sheet

5. Click the Cut button. The range displays the moving marquee.
6. Right-click cell B14. Choose **Paste**. A regular Paste command replaces existing data. "Tom's Foods" is gone from cell B14.
7. Select cells B5:B6. Press [Ctrl]+[X].
8. Right-click cell B4 and choose **Insert Cut Cells**. The data from cells B5:B6 is inserted before Stop and Shop, which has shifted down.

Exercise 4-8 COPY AND PASTE CELL CONTENTS

The Paste Options button appears below a pasted selection. When you click it, you see a list of options that establish how the selection can be pasted.

1. Click cell B1 and click the Copy button. The cell is surrounded by the moving marquee.
2. Click cell B13 and click the Paste button. The label is pasted, the original data is removed, and the Paste Options button appears.
3. Rest the mouse pointer on the Paste Options button. Click its arrow.

NOTE

Close the Clipboard pane if it opens.

4. Choose **Formatting Only**. This option copies only the formatting; it does not copy the actual label.

Figure 4-7
Using Paste Options
AcctRec.xlsx
AR2007 sheet

	A	B	C	D	E
1	*Date*	*Account Name*	*Amount Due*	*Reference No.*	*Date Paid*
2	1/1/2007	Regan Superma	4501.26	20101	2/1/2007
3	1/7/2007	Southwest Offi	345	20107	3/1/2007
4	2/5/2007	Corner Store	1000.55	20205	2/26/2007
5	2/15/2007	SafeTop Stores	541.32	20215	3/15/2007
6	4/2/2007	Stop and Shop	15245.78	20402	4/30/2007
7	4/15/2007	Regan Superma	12567	20415	5/15/2007
8	5/8/2007	Stop and Shop	3677.87	20508	6/8/2007
9	5/24/2007	International Gi	5590	20524	6/24/2007
10	6/18/2007	Tom's Foods	25125.24	20601	7/18/2007
11	6/23/2007	Regan Superma	15200.35	20612	7/30/2007
12	7/6/2007	South Island Fo	8750	20618	8/2/2007
13	8/14/2007	*Account Name*	11245.56	20623	9/14/2007
14	8/24/2007	South Island Foc		20706	9/30/2007
15	9/7/2007	Fresh Foods			/30/2007
16	9/23/2007				/23/2007
17					
18					
19					
20					
21					
22					
23					

- Keep Source Formatting
- Use Destination Theme
- Match Destination Formatting
- Values and Number Formatting
- Keep Source Column Widths
- Formatting Only
- Link Cells

TIP

The marquee is not automatically canceled after you click the Paste button. This enables you to paste the data again in a different location.

5. Click the Undo button. Press Esc.
6. Click cell I2 and drag to select the range I2:I7.
7. Press Ctrl+C. Excel displays a marquee around the range.
8. Click cell I8. You only need to click in the first cell for the copy as long as the destination range is empty.
9. Press Ctrl+V. The range of names is duplicated. The marquee is shown as well as the Paste Options button.
10. Click cell I14. Press Ctrl+V to paste the data again.
11. Press Esc to cancel the marquee.
12. Select the range C8:C10 and press Ctrl+C to copy the range.
13. Right-click cell C11.
14. Choose **Insert Copied Cells**. The Insert Paste dialog box opens.

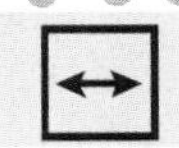

REVIEW

Copied cells replace existing data unless you choose the option to insert them.

15. Choose **Shift cells down**. Click **OK**. The copied cells are inserted, and the existing cells are shifted down in the column.
16. Press Esc to cancel the marquee.

Exercise 4-9 USE DRAG AND DROP

Use the drag-and-drop method to cut or copy data when you can see the original and the destination cell on screen. The *drag-and-drop pointer* is a four-pointed arrow.

1. Select cell C16. Place the pointer at the top or bottom edge/border of the cell. The drag-and-drop pointer appears.
2. Hold down the mouse button and drag to cell C17. A ScreenTip identifies the destination cell. You can also see a ghost highlight that shows where the data will be placed.

Figure 4-8
Using drag and drop to cut and paste
AcctRec.xlsx AR2007 sheet

10	6/18/2007	Tom's Foods	25125.24	20601
11	6/23/2007	Regan Superma	3677.87	20612
12	7/6/2007	South Island Fo	5590	20618
13	8/14/2007	PDQ Shop	25125.24	20623
14	8/24/2007	South Island Fo	15200.35	20706
15	9/7/2007	Fresh Foods	8750	20814
16	9/23/2007		11245.56	20824
17				
18			C17	
19				

3. Release the mouse button. You have used the drag-and-drop method to perform a cut and paste.
4. Place the pointer at the top or bottom edge/border of cell C17 to display the drag-and-drop pointer.
5. Hold down Ctrl. You will see a tiny plus sign (+) with a solid white arrow to signify this will be a copy and paste. Do not release Ctrl.
6. Click and drag to cell C16. Release the mouse button first and then release Ctrl. This is drag and drop to perform a copy and paste.
7. Select cells B6:B7. Place the pointer at the top or bottom edge of the range to display the drag-and-drop pointer.

NOTE

Drag and drop works in most Windows applications.

8. Hold down the Ctrl key to display the plus sign (+) and the white arrow pointer. Do not release the Ctrl key.
9. Click and drag down to cells B16:B17. Release the mouse button and then Ctrl. Both labels are copied.

Exercise 4-10 USE THE OFFICE CLIPBOARD

The *Office Clipboard* is a temporary memory area that can hold up to 24 copied items. It is separate from the Windows Clipboard. The Office Clipboard is available when any Office application (Excel, Access, Word, or PowerPoint) is running. It is shared among these programs, so something you copy in Excel can be pasted in Word. The options for the Office Clipboard allow you to set it to open automatically when you first copy an object and to show a screen message after copying.

1. Click the Dialog Box Launcher in the Clipboard group. The Clipboard task pane opens. You may see values and labels from your last copy task.

NOTE

If the Clear All button is grayed or dimmed, you have nothing on the Clipboard and can continue.

2. Click the Clear All button in the task pane.
3. Select the range A4:E4 and click the Copy button. An Excel icon and the data appear in the task pane. There is an icon in the lower-right corner of the Windows taskbar.
4. Select the range A6:A7 and click the Copy button. Another icon and data appear in the pane, above the first set.
5. Select the range A8:E8 and click the Copy button. Three items have been copied and are on the Office Clipboard.
6. Press Esc. The marquee is removed.
7. Click cell A17. Click the date object in the task pane to paste two dates (see Figure 4-9 on the next page).

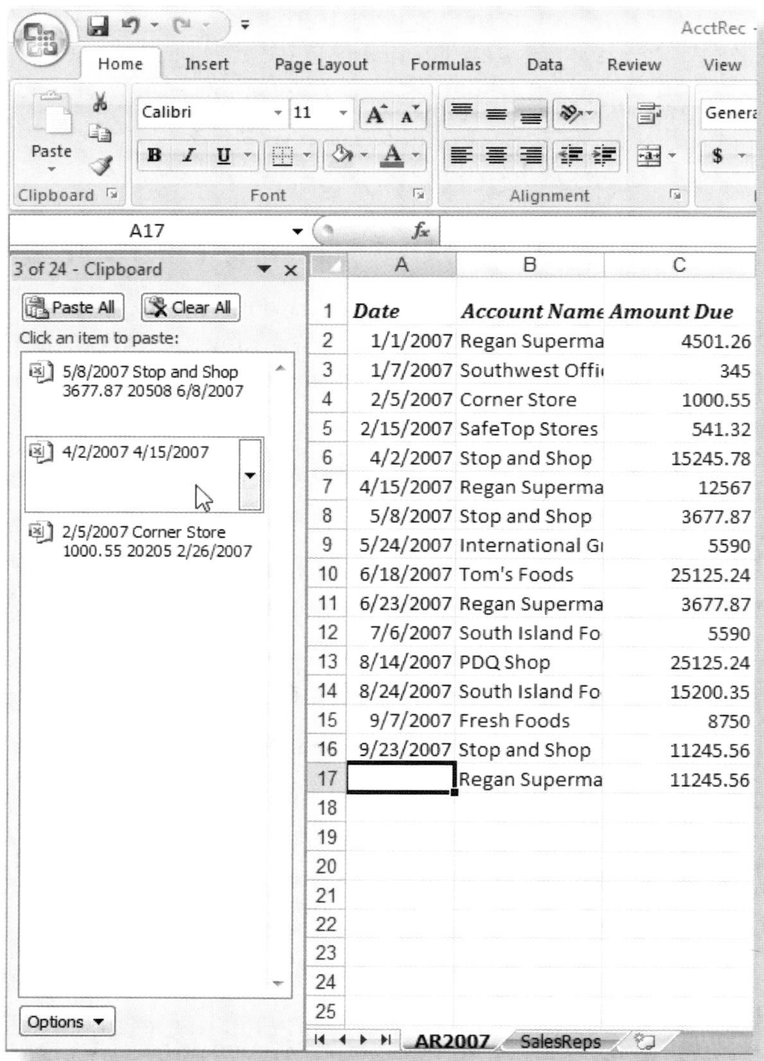

Figure 4-9
Using the Clipboard task pane
AcctRec.xlsx
AR2007 sheet

8. Click cell A19. Click the **Stop and Shop** object in the task pane to paste it.
9. Repeat these steps to paste the **Corner Store** object in cell A20.
10. Click the Clear All button in the task pane and then close the task pane.

Working with Columns and Rows

Inserted or deleted rows and columns extend across the entire worksheet. If you have used different parts of the worksheet, you could interrupt data elsewhere on the sheet after adding or deleting rows or columns.

When you insert a column or row, check formulas that might be affected. Excel updates formulas to include an inserted row or column if it falls within the original range used in the formula.

Exercise 4-11 INSERT ROWS

When you insert a row, it extends from column A to column XFD.

1. Click the Microsoft Office Button and choose **Excel Options**. Click **Formulas**.
2. Verify that all **Error checking rules** including **Formulas referring to empty cells** are active. Click **OK**.
3. In cell B18, key **p** and press Tab to insert **PDQ Shop**.
4. Key **345.7** in cell C18.
5. Click cell C21, click the AutoSum button Σ, and press Enter.
6. Click cell C21 and view the formula. The SUM function sums the range C2:C20.
7. Click cell J21 and click the AutoSum button Σ. Press Enter.
8. Click cell J21. Position the mouse pointer on the Error Checking Options button and click its arrow. The formula refers to empty cells.
9. Press Esc.
10. Click cell A12. Press Ctrl+\+ in the numeric keypad. The Insert dialog box opens.
11. Choose **Entire row** and click **OK**. A new row is inserted, and the existing rows shift down. Notice that the new row spans the worksheet.
12. Click cell C22. The formula has been updated to include rows 2 through 21 and now refers to empty cells (see Figure 4-10 on the next page).

Figure 4-10
Row inserted
AcctRec.xlsx
AR2007 sheet

	A	B	C	D	E	F
1	*Date*	*Account Name*	*Amount Due*	*Reference No.*	*Date Paid*	
2	1/1/2007	Regan Superma	4501.26	20101	2/1/2007	
3	1/7/2007	Southwest Offi	345	20107	3/1/2007	
4	2/5/2007	Corner Store	1000.55	20205	2/26/2007	
5	2/15/2007	SafeTop Stores	541.32	20215	3/15/2007	
6	4/2/2007	Stop and Shop	15245.78	20402	4/30/2007	
7	4/15/2007	Regan Superma	12567	20415	5/15/2007	
8	5/8/2007	Stop and Shop	3677.87	20508	6/8/2007	
9	5/24/2007	International Gi	5590	20524	6/24/2007	
10	6/18/2007	Tom's Foods	25125.24	20601	7/18/2007	
11	6/23/2007	Regan Superma	3677.87	20612	7/30/2007	
12						
13	7/6/2007	South Island Fo	5590	20618	8/2/2007	
14	8/14/2007	PDQ Shop		20623	9/14/2007	
15	8/24/2007	South Isla		706	9/30/2007	
16	9/7/2007	Fresh Foo		814	9/30/2007	
17	9/23/2007	Stop and S		824	10/23/2007	
18	4/2/2007	Regan Sup				
19	4/15/2007	PDQ Shop				
20	5/8/2007	Stop and S		508	6/8/2007	
21	2/5/2007	Corner Sto		205	2/26/2007	
22			154452.72			
23						

Formula Refers to Empty Cells
Trace Empty Cell
Help on this error
Ignore Error
Edit in Formula Bar
Error Checking Options...

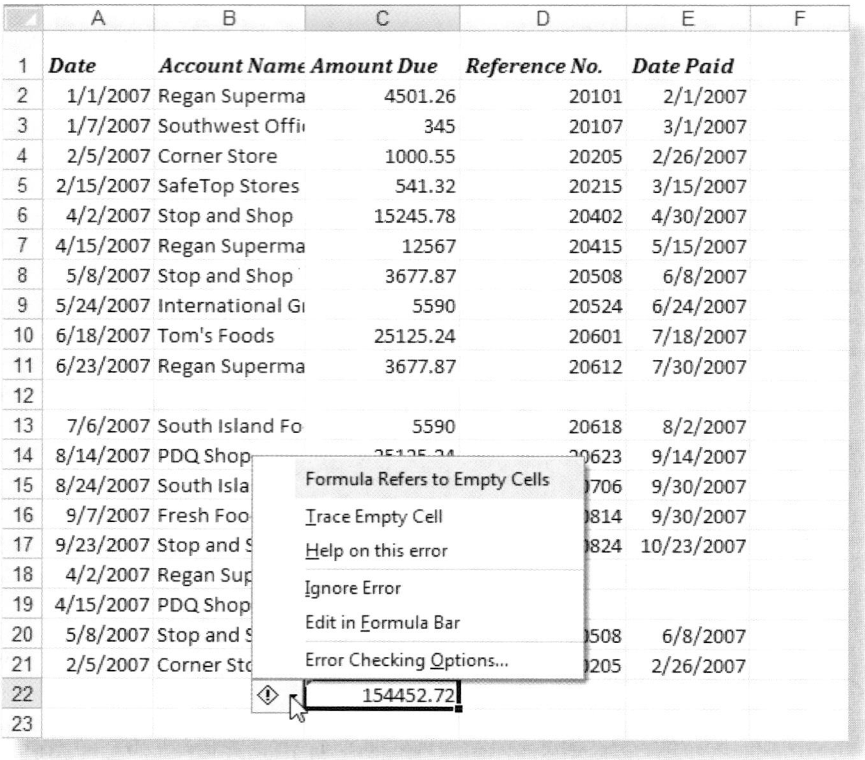

13. Click the row heading for row 15.
14. With the black right-arrow pointer, drag to select the row headings for rows 15 through 17. Three rows are selected or highlighted.
15. Right-click any of the selected row headings. The shortcut menu opens.
16. Choose **Insert**. Three rows are inserted, because you selected three rows before giving the Insert command.

Figure 4-11
Inserting three rows at once
AcctRec.xlsx
AR2007 sheet

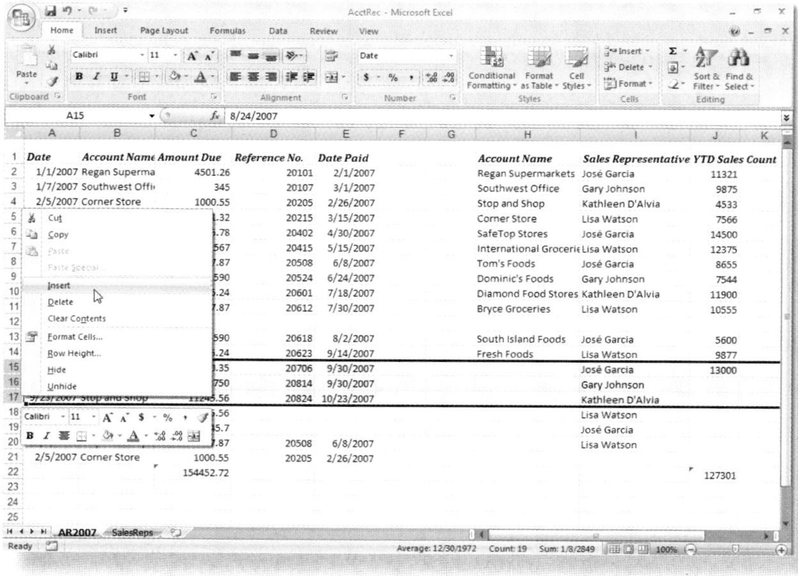

Exercise 4-12 DELETE ROWS

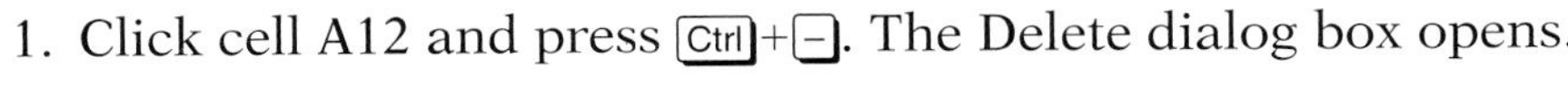

1. Click cell A12 and press Ctrl+-. The Delete dialog box opens.

NOTE

You can use the - in the numeric keypad or in the top row of keys to delete cells.

2. Choose **Entire row** and click **OK**. The row is deleted.
3. Select the range A6:E7.
4. Drag the range to the new range A14:E15 and drop it.
5. Click the row heading for row 6. Drag to select the row headings for rows 6 and 7.
6. Right-click one of the selected row headings. Choose **Delete**. Two rows are deleted. Data is now missing from columns H, I, and J.
7. Click anywhere in row 14. In the **Cells** group, click the arrow with the Delete Cells button Delete and choose **Delete Sheet Rows**. One row is deleted.
8. Click cell C21. The formula has been updated to sum the correct rows.

Exercise 4-13 INSERT AND DELETE COLUMNS

When you insert a column, it extends to row 1,048,576.

1. Right-click the column D heading. The column is selected and the shortcut menu opens.

NOTE

When you choose **Insert** or **Delete** from the shortcut menu, the dialog box does not open.

2. Choose **Insert**. One column is inserted, and existing columns move right.
3. Key **Discount** in cell D1 and press Enter. Excel copies the format from the three columns that precede the new column.
4. Click anywhere in column G. Press Ctrl+-.
5. Choose **Entire column** and click **OK**. Column G is deleted, and the other columns move left to fill the space.

Exercise 4-14 HIDE AND UNHIDE COLUMNS AND ROWS

Since you have not filled in discount amounts, you can temporarily hide the column. In that way, your worksheet does not print with an empty column taking up space. You can hide columns or rows with data that need not be viewed or printed. Even though a row or column is hidden, its values are used in calculations.

You can determine when columns or rows are hidden, because their column or row headings are hidden. There is also a slightly thicker border between the column/row headings.

1. Right-click the column heading for column D to select the column.
2. Choose **Hide** from the shortcut menu. Column D is hidden.
3. Drag across the row headings for rows 12 through 14.
4. In the **Cells** group, click the Format button. Hover over **Hide & Unhide**. Choose **Hide Rows**.
5. Click cell C21. Notice that the formula sums all the rows, even though three are hidden from view.
6. Drag across the column headings for columns C through E. Column D is hidden between these two columns.
7. Point at the column heading for either column and right-click. Choose **Unhide** from the shortcut menu.

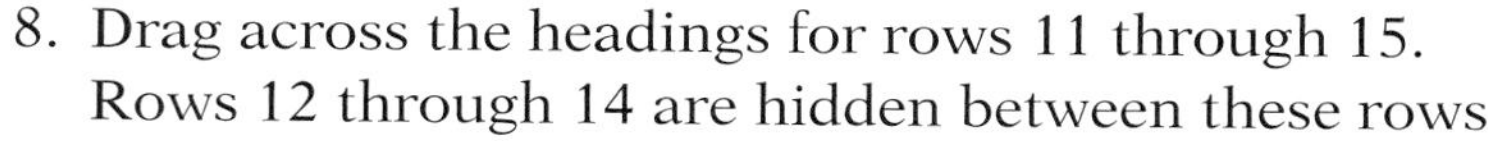

NOTE

To unhide a column or row, select the rows or columns on both sides of the hidden rows or columns.

8. Drag across the headings for rows 11 through 15. Rows 12 through 14 are hidden between these rows.
9. In the **Cells** group, click the Format button. Hover over **Hide & Unhide**. Choose **Unhide Rows**.
10. Press Ctrl+Home.

Exercise 4-15 FREEZE AND SPLIT THE WINDOW

In large worksheets, seeing related columns or rows on-screen at the same time can be difficult if they are not close to each other. You can keep data in view by freezing one of the columns or rows. You can also split the window and show different parts of the same sheet in separate panes.

REVIEW

KeyTips appear only when you press Alt or F10.

1. Click the Zoom In button in the status bar to reach **130%**. This enlarges the display so that you cannot see all the rows. (Use a higher Zoom setting if you still see all the rows.)
2. Click cell A2. Press Alt and key **w** to open the **View** tab.

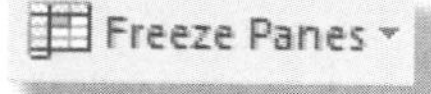

3. In the **Window** group, click the Freeze Panes button.
4. Choose **Freeze Top Row**. A solid horizontal line identifies where the row(s) are locked in position, between rows 1 and 2. This line does not print.
5. Press the ↓ arrow to reach row 30. The labels in row 1 do not scroll out of view.

6. Press Ctrl+Home. The pointer returns to the first unfrozen cell (cell A2).

7. In the **Window** group, click the Freeze Panes button. Choose **Unfreeze Panes**.

8. Click cell C1. In the **Window** group, click the Freeze Panes button. Choose **Freeze Panes**. The solid line is vertical to show that columns A and B are frozen.

9. Press → to reach column K. Columns A and B do not scroll.

TIP

To freeze a column, click the column letter or the cell in row 1 to the immediate right of the last column to be frozen. To freeze a row, click the row number or the cell in column A immediately below the last row to be frozen.

10. Press Ctrl+Home. The pointer returns to the first unfrozen cell.

11. In the **Window** group, click the Freeze Panes button. Choose **Unfreeze Panes**.

12. In the **Window** group, click the Split button. The window splits at column C.

13. Rest the mouse on the vertical split bar. The pointer displays a two-pointed arrow.

14. Drag the split bar to be between columns C and D.

15. Click in the pane on the right and press Tab or → to position the sales reps' names as the first visible column on the left.

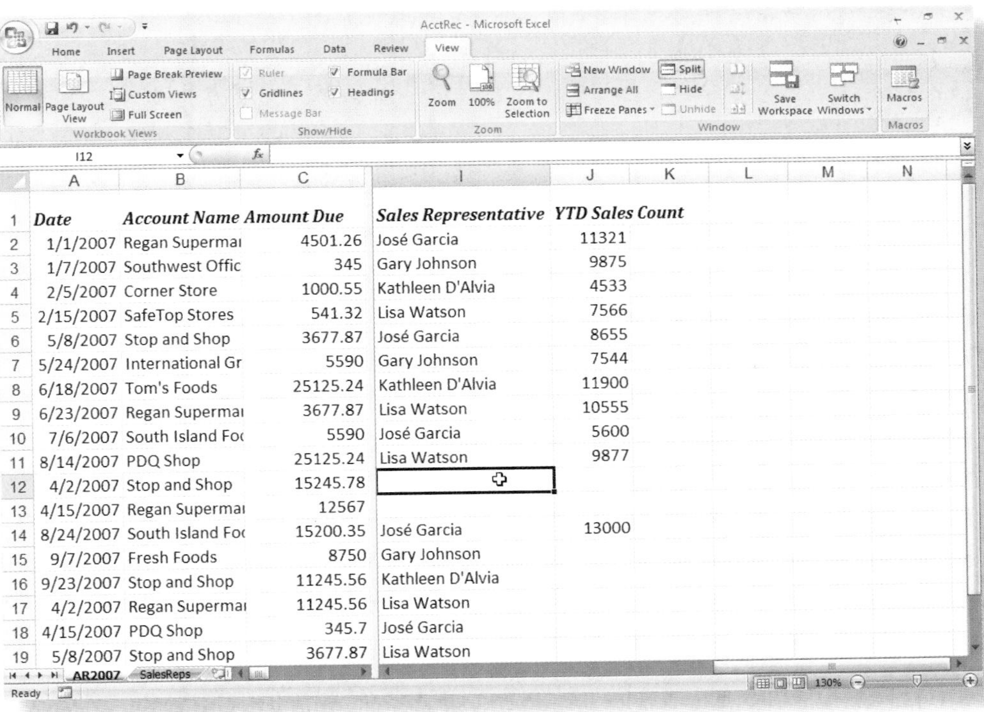

Figure 4-12
Splitting the window
AcctRec.xlsx
AR2007 sheet

16. Click the Split button [Split] to remove the split.
17. Set the Zoom size to **100%**.
18. Press Ctrl+Home. Save the workbook as ***[your initials]*4-15** in a new folder for Lesson 4.

Working with Cell Alignment

Cell alignment establishes how the contents of a cell are positioned in the cell. Cell contents can be aligned horizontally and vertically.

TABLE 4-1 Horizontal Alignment Options

Setting	Result
General	Aligns numbers and dates on the right, text on the left, and center-aligns error and logical values.
Left (Indent)	Aligns cell contents on the left of the cell indented by the number of spaces entered in the Indent box.
Center	Aligns contents in the middle of the cell.
Right (Indent)	Aligns cell contents on the right side of the cell indented by the number of spaces entered in the Indent box.
Fill	Repeats the cell contents until the cell's width is filled.
Justify	Spreads text to the left and right edges of the cell. This works only for wrapped text that is more than one line.
Center across selection	Places text in the middle of a selected range of columns.
Distributed (Indent)	Positions text an equal distance from the left and right edges including the number of spaces entered in the Indent box.

If a label is too wide for a cell, it generally spills into the cell to the right if that cell is empty and if the label is left-aligned. If the adjacent cell is not empty, the label is partially visible in the cell but completely visible in the formula bar.

TABLE 4-2 Vertical Alignment Options

Setting	Result
Top	Aligns cell contents at the top of the cell.
Center	Aligns cell contents in the vertical middle of the cell.
Bottom	Aligns cell contents at the bottom of the cell.
Justify	Spreads text to fill to the top and bottom edges of the cell. This works only for wrapped text that is more than one line.
Distributed	Positions text an equal distance from the top and bottom edges.

Exercise 4-16 CHANGE THE HORIZONTAL ALIGNMENT

The Alignment group on the Home tab contains three horizontal alignment buttons: the Align Text Left button, the Center button, and the Align Text Right button.

1. Press Alt and key **h** to open the **Home** tab.
2. Click cell A1. This label is left-aligned, but the dates in the column are right-aligned.

3. Click the Align Text Right button. The label is aligned at the right edge of the cell and balances the dates better.
4. Double-click the border between the column headings for columns B and C. The column title and the entries are left-aligned labels.

5. Click cell B1 and click the Center button. Column titles are often centered over labels.
6. Click cell C1. Click the Align Text Right button. Now the label better aligns with the values in the column.

Exercise 4-17 USE CENTER ACROSS SELECTION

The Center Across Selection command allows you to horizontally center multiple rows of labels across a part of the worksheet.

1. Point at the row 1 heading and drag to select rows 1 and 2.
2. Right-click either row heading and choose **Insert**. Two rows are inserted.
3. In cell A1, key **Klassy Kow Accounts Receivable** and press Enter.

NOTE

The Mini toolbar does not display ScreenTips. It fades from view as soon as you start another command.

4. In cell A2, key **Commercial Accounts.**
5. Select cells A1:A2 and right-click either cell. The Mini toolbar appears above the shortcut menu. Choose **Cambria** from the Font list (see Figure 4-13 on the next page).

6. Click the Increase Font Size button in the Mini toolbar three times to reach 16 point. Watch the Font size box in the Font group to check the size.

Figure 4-13
Using the Mini toolbar
4-15.xlsx
AR2007 sheet

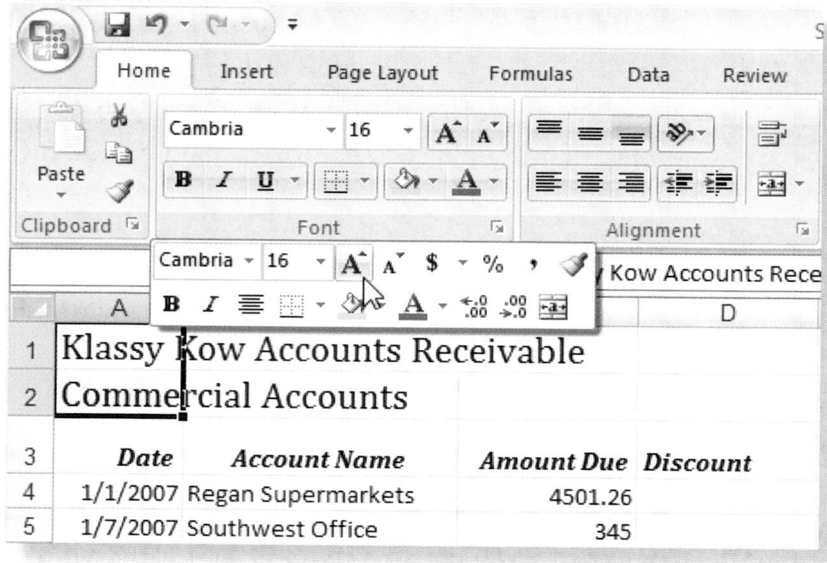

7. Click cell A2. In the **Font** group on the **Home** tab, click the Decrease Font Size button to reach 14 point.
8. Select cells A1:F2. This includes the labels and the range over which they will be centered.
9. Right-click any cell in the range and choose **Format Cells**.
10. Click the **Alignment** tab.
11. Click the arrow for the **Horizontal** box to display the options.

Figure 4-14
Alignment tab in the Format Cells dialog box

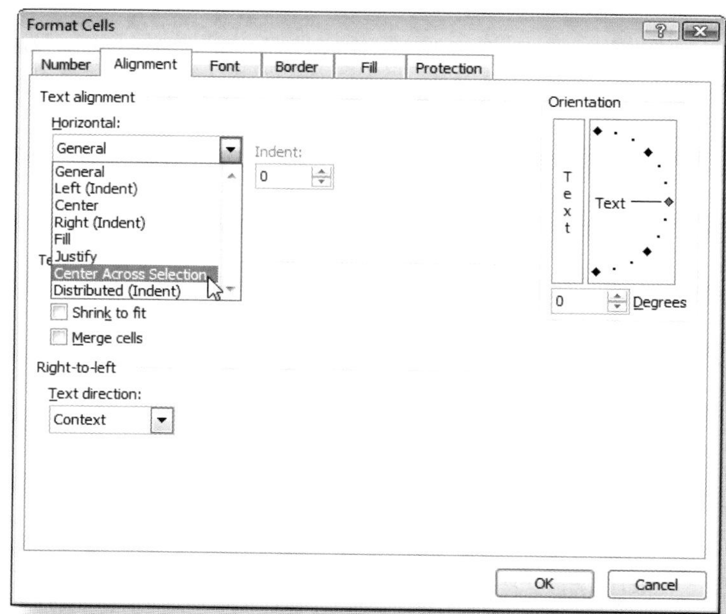

12. Choose **Center Across Selection**. Click **OK**. The labels are centered over the columns you selected.

Exercise 4-18 CHANGE THE VERTICAL ALIGNMENT

The Alignment group contains three vertical alignment buttons: Top Align, Middle Align, and Bottom Align. You can also set any alignment choice from the Format Cells dialog box.

1. Change row 1 to **37.50 (50 pixels)** high. You can see that the label is aligned at the bottom of the cell.
2. Click cell A1. Press Ctrl+1 to open the Format Cells dialog box.
3. On the **Alignment** tab, click the arrow for the **Vertical** box.
4. Choose **Center** and then click **OK**. The label is centered in the row.

Exercise 4-19 WRAP TEXT AND CHANGE INDENTS

Multiple-word labels can be split into multiple lines in a cell using the **Wrap Text** setting. With this choice, a narrow column can accommodate a wider label. The label will, of course, occupy more vertical space.

You can improve the readability of adjacent labels and values by adding an indent to one or the other. This moves the data away from the edge of the cell but maintains the alignment.

NOTE

Your screen size and resolution setting affect how buttons look in the Ribbon. They may or may not include both an icon and text. The arrow may be next to or below the icon, too.

TIP

While keying a label, press Alt+Enter to force a line break between words. Then adjust column width and row height as needed.

1. Change column E to **10.71 (80 pixels)** wide. Notice that this is wide enough for the data, but not wide enough for the label.
2. Click cell E3 and click the Wrap Text button in the **Alignment** group. The label splits into two lines, but now the row isn't high enough.
3. Change row 3 to **30.00 (40 pixels)** high.
4. Click cell E3 and click the Center button. The wrapped label looks better centered.
5. Click cell B3. Press F8 to start Extend Selection mode.
6. Press Ctrl+↓. This shortcut selects contiguous cells with data in the column.
7. Press Ctrl+1. On the **Alignment** tab, click the arrow for the **Horizontal** box.
8. Choose **Left (Indent)**. Click the up arrow for **Indent** to change it to **1**.
9. Click **OK**. The labels are indented one space from the left edge of the cell, leaving some space between them and the right-aligned dates in column A.
10. Double-click the border between the column headings for columns B and C.

Exercise 4-20 USE MERGE AND CENTER

The Merge and Center command combines a selected range of cells into one cell that occupies the same amount of space and centers the contents. You can merge any number of columns and rows to create special effects and alignment settings. The range of cells to merge should be empty except for the top-left cell.

1. Select the range H1:J23 and click the Cut button.
2. Click the **SalesReps** worksheet tab and press Enter. The data is moved.
3. AutoFit each column.
4. Select the range B16:C23 and press Delete.
5. In cell A1, key **Supermarket Sales Associates**. Press Ctrl+Enter.
6. Select the range A1:C1.
7. In the **Alignment** group, click the Merge and Center button. Cells A1:C1 are now one cell (A1), and the label is centered.

NOTE

You can unmerge cells by clicking the Merge and Center button to turn off the command.

8. Right-click the row 2 heading and choose **Delete**.
9. Click cell C2 and point at an edge to show the drag-and-drop pointer.
10. Click and drag the cell to cell D3.
11. Select cells D3:D12.
12. Click the Merge and Center button. Cells D3:D12 are now one cell (D3) that occupies the same amount of space, and the label is horizontally centered at the bottom.

Exercise 4-21 CHANGE CELL ORIENTATION

The label in the merged cell D3 is horizontal like the rest of your data. Because the cells were merged vertically, you should change the data's rotation to match.

1. Right-click cell D3 and choose **Format Cells**.
2. On the **Alignment** tab, click the red diamond in the **Orientation** box.
3. Drag the red diamond down to show −90 degrees (that's "minus 90 degrees"). Click **OK**. The text is rotated −90 degrees. Now you should change the vertical centering as well.

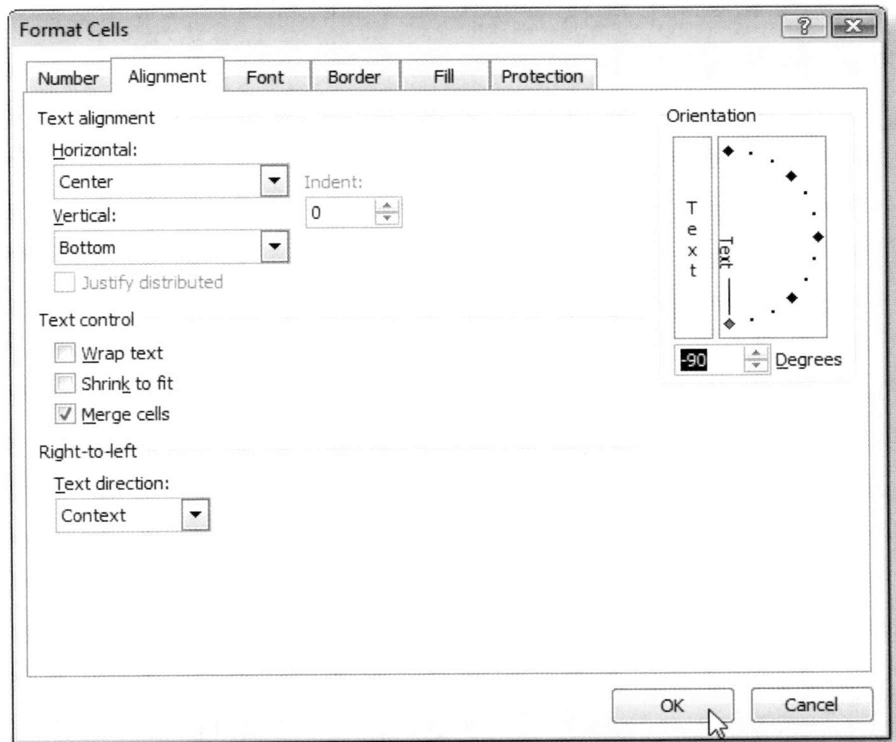

Figure 4-15
Rotating text −90 degrees

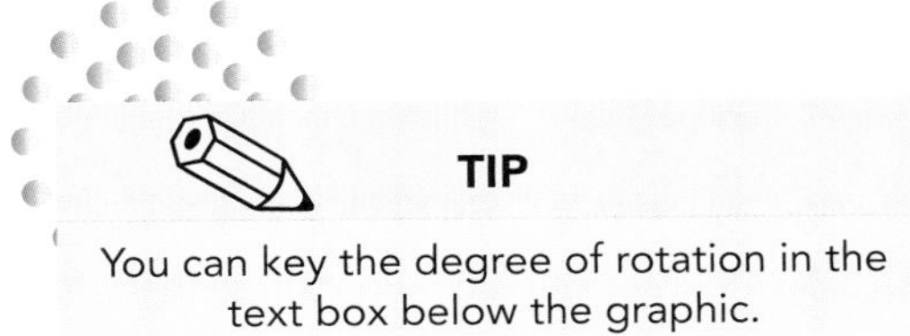

TIP

You can key the degree of rotation in the text box below the graphic.

4. Press Ctrl+1. On the **Alignment** tab, click the arrow next to the **Vertical** box. Choose **Center** and click **OK**.
5. Change column C to **11.43 (85 pixels)** wide.
6. Make cell A1 14-point Cambria.

Applying Borders and Fill

A *border* is a line around a cell or a range of cells. You can use borders to draw attention to a part of a worksheet, to show totals, or to group information in your worksheet.

Shading or *fill* is a background pattern or color for a cell or a range of cells. You can use fill in much the same way as a border—to group data or to add emphasis.

Exercise 4-22 APPLY BORDERS USING THE BORDERS BUTTON

Cells share borders, so adding a border to the bottom of cell A1 has the same effect as adding a border to the top of cell A2.

Excel provides two methods to apply a border to a cell or a range of cells:

- Use the Borders button in the Font group.
- Use the Format Cells dialog box.

1. Click cell C12.
2. Click the arrow with the Borders button . A gallery of border styles opens.

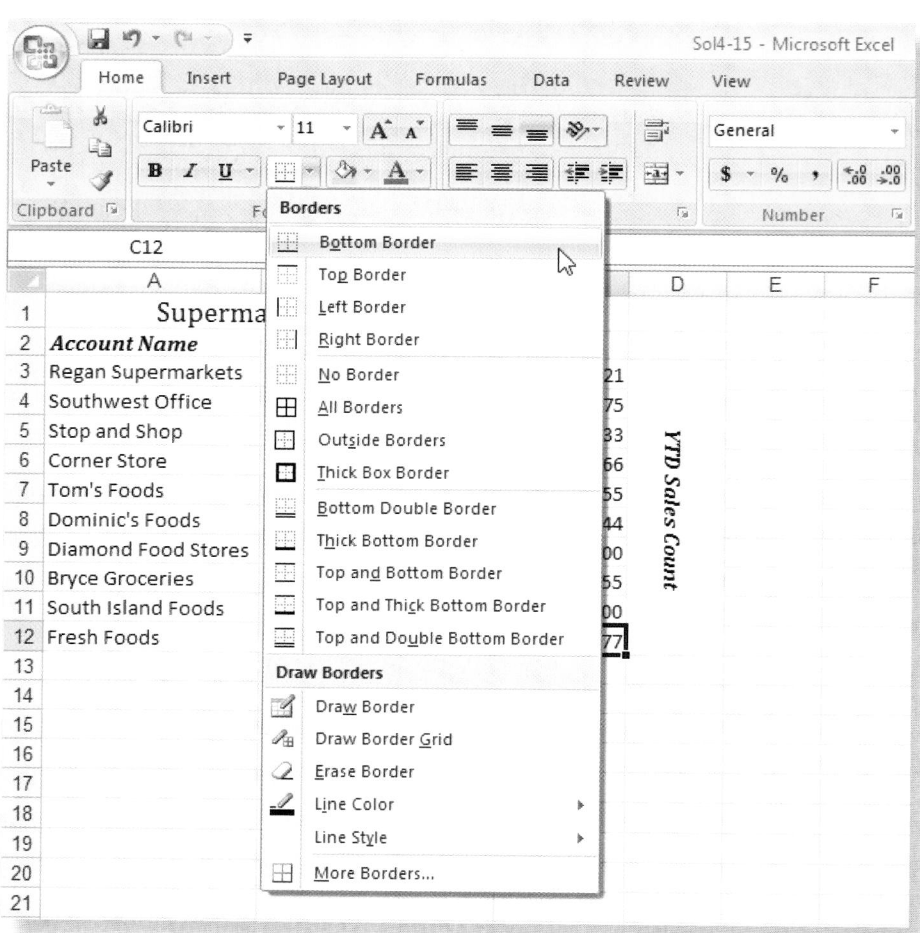

Figure 4-16
Borders gallery
4-15.xlsx
SalesReps sheet

3. Choose **Bottom Border**. A thin solid bottom border is applied to the cell.
4. Click cell C14 to better see the border. Notice that the border fills the width of the cell.

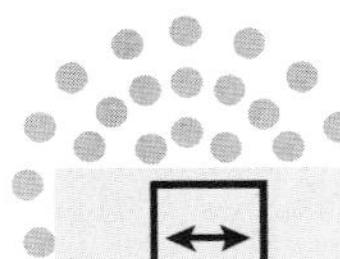

REVIEW

Press Ctrl+Enter to keep the insertion point in the current cell.

5. Select cell C13 and click the AutoSum button. Press Ctrl+Enter.
6. Click the arrow next to the Borders button. Click **Bottom Double Border**.
7. Click cell B13 to see the border. Notice that the Borders button shows the last-used style.

TIP

Totals in accounting and financial reports are often shown with a single border above and a double border below. There is a border style called Top and Double Bottom.

Exercise 4-23 APPLY BORDERS USING THE DIALOG BOX

The Format Cells dialog box provides more choices for designing borders.

1. Click the **AR2007** worksheet tab and press Ctrl+Home.
2. Press F5. Key **c23** and press Enter.
3. Press Ctrl+1. Click the **Border** tab. There are presets for **None**, **Outline**, or **Inside**.
4. Click **Outline**. The Border buttons around the preview show the top, bottom, and left and right side borders active in an outline border.
5. Click **None** to remove the border in the preview.
6. Click the arrow for the **Color** box. Choose **Red, Accent 2** in the first row, sixth column.
7. In the **Style** box, choose a single line (first column, last line).
8. In the **Text** preview area, click where the top border will be located. A preview of the red/brown single-line border is shown (see Figure 4-17 on the next page).

TIP

Inside borders are applied to multiple cells, not to a single cell.

NOTE

Choose the **Color** and **Style** of line before setting the location of borders in the Format Cells dialog box.

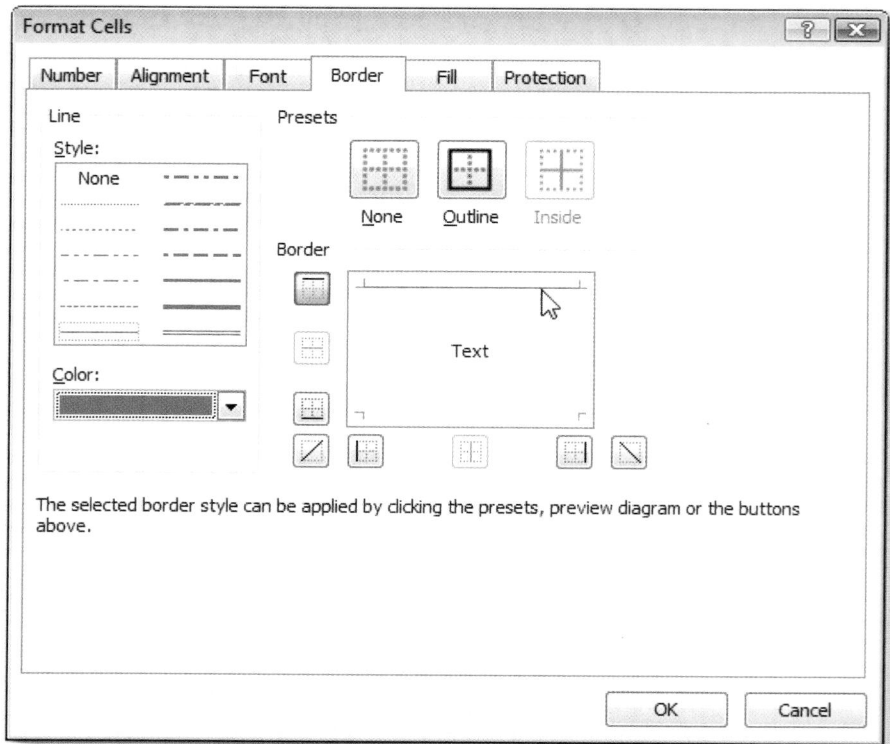

Figure 4-17
Border tab in the Format Cells dialog box
4-15.xlsx
AR2007 sheet

NOTE

Click in the **Text** preview to turn the borders on and off.

9. In the **Style** box, choose a double line (second column, last line). The color is still red/brown.
10. In the **Text** preview area, click where the bottom border will be located.
11. Click **OK**.
12. Deselect the cell to see the borders.
13. Click the Page Layout View button in the status bar.
14. Set the Zoom size to **70%**. It will be easier to preview your work in this size and view.

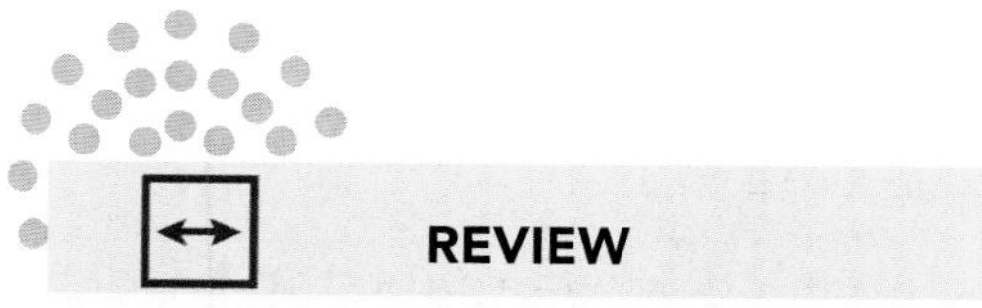

REVIEW

Borders appear in a shade of gray if your default printer is a non-color printer.

15. Select cells A1:F2 and press Ctrl+1. Click the **Border** tab.
16. Click the arrow for the **Color** box. Choose **Red, Accent 2**.
17. In the **Style** box, choose a single line (first column, last line).
18. Click **Outline**. Click **OK**.

Exercise 4-24 ADD SOLID FILL

The background of a cell or a range of cells can be shaded with a solid color or a pattern. Excel provides two methods for applying fill to a cell or a range of cells:

- Use the Fill Color button in the Font group.
- Use the Format Cells dialog box.

1. Click the **SalesReps** worksheet tab. This worksheet is in Normal view.
2. Select the range A3:C3. In the **Font** group, click the Fill Color button. Excel applies the color shown beneath the paint bucket icon.
3. Click in row 5 to see the shading.
4. Click the Undo button. The fill is removed, and the range is still selected.
5. Click the arrow next to the Fill Color button. The color palette opens.
6. Choose **White, Background 1, Darker 25%** in the first column.
7. Select the range A5:C5. Press Ctrl+1 and click the **Fill** tab.
8. For the **Background Color**, choose the first color in the third row below the theme colors. Click **OK**.

9. Double-click the Format Painter button. This locks the painter on, and a marquee appears around the selected range.
10. Select the range A7:C7 to paint the format. Then select cells A9:C9 and A11:C11.
11. Click the Format Painter button to turn it off.

Exercise 4-25 USE PATTERN FILL

A pattern might be dots or crisscrossed lines. Patterns are acceptable for cells that do not contain data or for cells with minimal data.

1. Click cell D3 and press Ctrl+1.
2. Click the **Fill** tab.
3. Click the arrow for the **Pattern Style** box. Patterns include dots, stripes, and crosshatches.
4. Choose **12.5% Gray** in the first row of patterns, second from the right. This is a dotted pattern (see Figure 4-18 on the next page).

TIP

Many patterns can make it difficult to read data in the cell.

Figure 4-18
Changing the pattern
4-15.xlsx
Sales Reps sheet

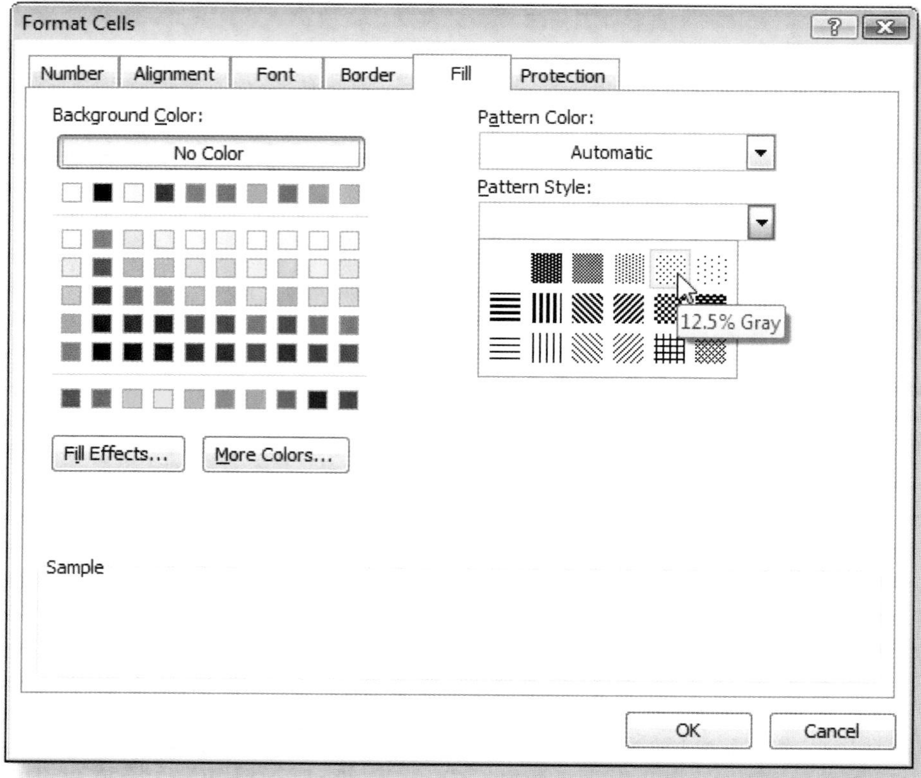

5. Click **OK**.
6. Right-click the column A heading and choose **Insert**. Right-click the row 1 heading and choose **Insert**.

TIP

Empty rows and columns around data can be used to create space between a border and the data. The empty rows/columns might be called separators.

7. Make both columns A and F **5.00 (40 pixels)** wide. Set the height of rows 1 and 15 at **15.00 (20 pixels)**.
8. Select cells A1:F15 and press Ctrl+1. Click the **Border** tab.
9. Choose a double-line style and an outline. Click **OK**.
10. Click the Page Layout View button in the status bar. Click cell A1.

Exercise 4-26 COMPLETE THE NUMBER FORMATTING

The Comma Style button inserts commas and two decimal places in a value. If you want fewer decimal places, you can use the Decrease Decimal button to remove positions one at a time.

You can build your own number formats from the Format Cells dialog box. For example, you can create a format that shows a *leading zero*, which is a zero (0) as the first digit in a number, typically a decimal number (example "0.59"). Normally, Excel does not show a leading zero because it has no value.

1. Select the range D4:D14. On the **Home** tab in the **Number** group, click the Comma Style button. Commas and two decimal places are added to the values.
2. In the **Number** group, click the Decrease Decimal button. One decimal position is removed.
3. Click the Decrease Decimal button again. The values still have the commas, but no decimals.
4. Click the **AR2007** worksheet tab.
5. Click cell C4. Hold down Ctrl and click cell C23.
6. Press Ctrl+1. Click the **Number** tab.
7. Choose **Accounting** in the **Category** list. A sample is displayed in the dialog box.
8. Click **OK**. This is the same format applied by the Accounting Number Format button.
9. Select the range C5:C22. Click the Comma Style button.
10. Select the range E4:E22. Press Ctrl+1 and click the **Number** tab.
11. Choose **Custom** in the **Category** list. Click **0** in the **Type** list. The zero appears in the entry box under **Type**.
12. Click after the **0** in the box and key **00000** to show six zeros. Zero (0) means that a digit is required. This format requires that the entry be six digits. If the value uses only five digits, Excel inserts a zero in the first position.

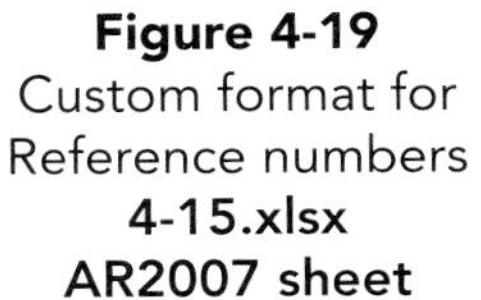

Figure 4-19
Custom format for Reference numbers
4-15.xlsx
AR2007 sheet

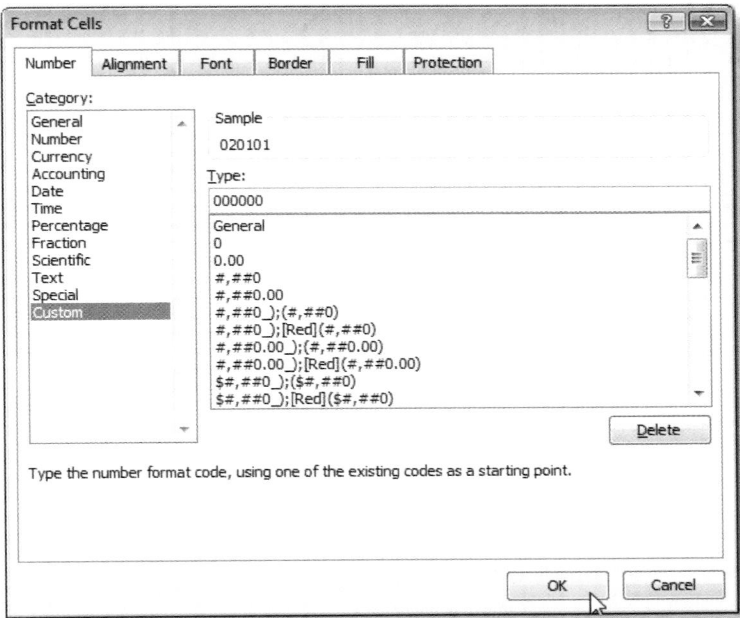

13. Click **OK**.

Using Data Bars

The Styles group on the Home tab includes Conditional Formatting tasks. These commands enable you to set formatting for a range of cells based on cell contents. For example, if a value is over 100, you can format it to appear in a particular color or with a fill. As part of the conditional formatting features, you can apply a data visualization. A *visualization* is a format element that displays bars, colors, or icons with the values. The formatting identifies trends and exceptions or compares values. It is a quick way to analyze data across many rows.

Excel has three types of visualizations.

- *Data bars* fill each cell with varying lengths of a color based on the highest and lowest values.
- A *color scale* shades each cell with varying colors based on the values. There are two- and three-color scales.
- An *icon set* displays an icon at the left of each cell based on the values. There are sets of three, four, and five icons.

Exercise 4-27 USE DATA BARS

With data bars, you can determine the value of a cell relative to the other cells in the range. The highest value displays the longest bar, and the lowest value displays the shortest bar.

1. Return to Normal view.
2. Select cells C4:C22.

3. In the **Styles** group, click the Conditional Formatting button. A subgroup of formatting rules and visualizations opens.
4. Hover over **Data Bars**. Choose the first icon for **Blue Data Bar**. You can see the visualization immediately on screen.

Figure 4-20
Choosing a Data Bar format
4-15.xlsx
AR2007 sheet

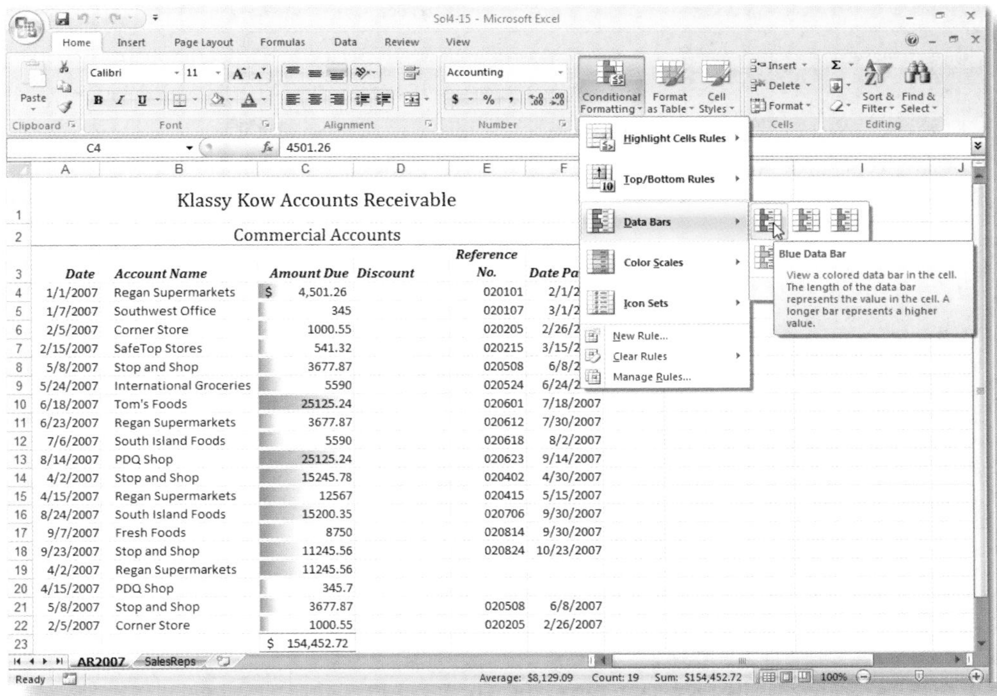

5. Click in column D. You can better see the bars.

Exercise 4-28 EDIT THE DATA BAR RULE

You can edit the rules used to build data bars by choosing colors, setting a value, a percent, a percentile, or by building a formula.

1. Select cells C4:C22.
2. In the **Styles** group, click the Conditional Formatting button.
3. Choose **Manage Rules**. The Conditional Formatting Rules Manager dialog box opens. Your current selection uses a data bar.

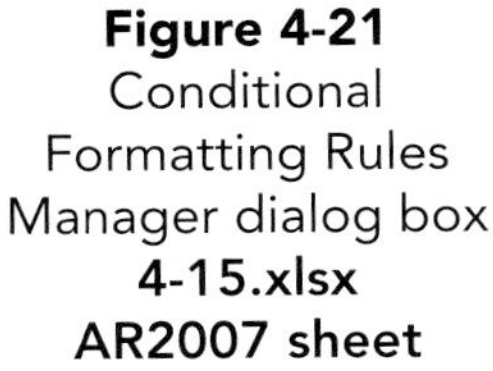

Figure 4-21
Conditional Formatting Rules Manager dialog box
4-15.xlsx
AR2007 sheet

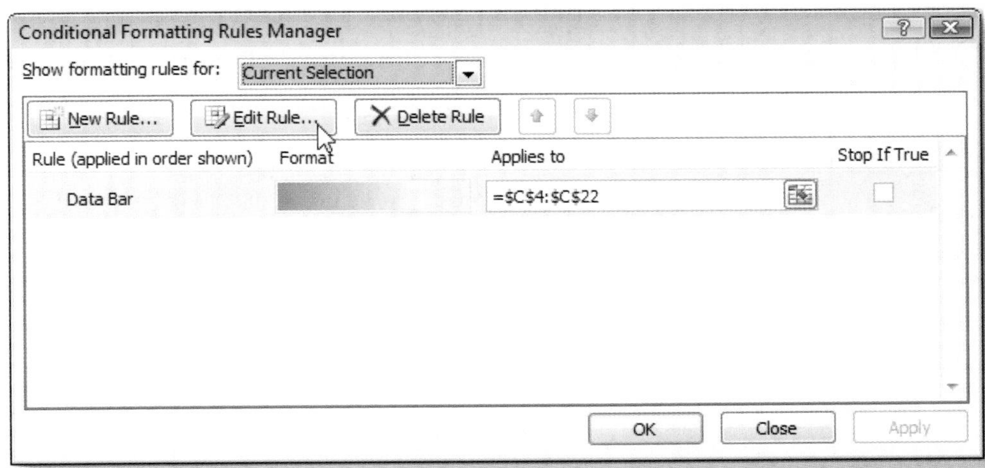

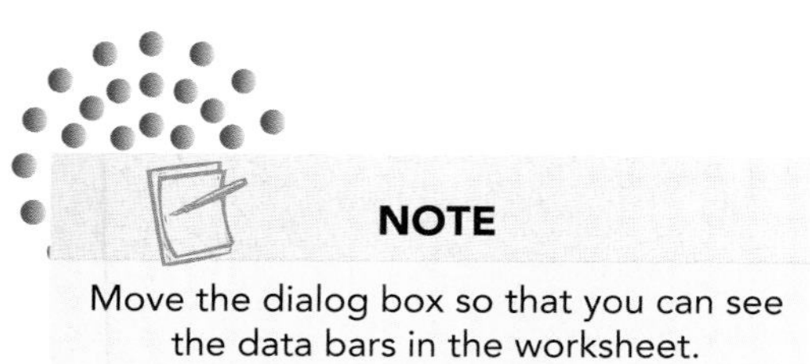

NOTE

Move the dialog box so that you can see the data bars in the worksheet.

4. Choose **Edit Rule**. The Edit Formatting Rule dialog box shows that the cells are formatted based on the lowest and highest value with a blue bar.
5. Click the arrow for **Bar Color**. Choose **Red, Accent 2, Lighter 40%** in the sixth column.
6. Click to select **Show Bar Only**. Click **OK**. Click **OK** again. This option hides the values.

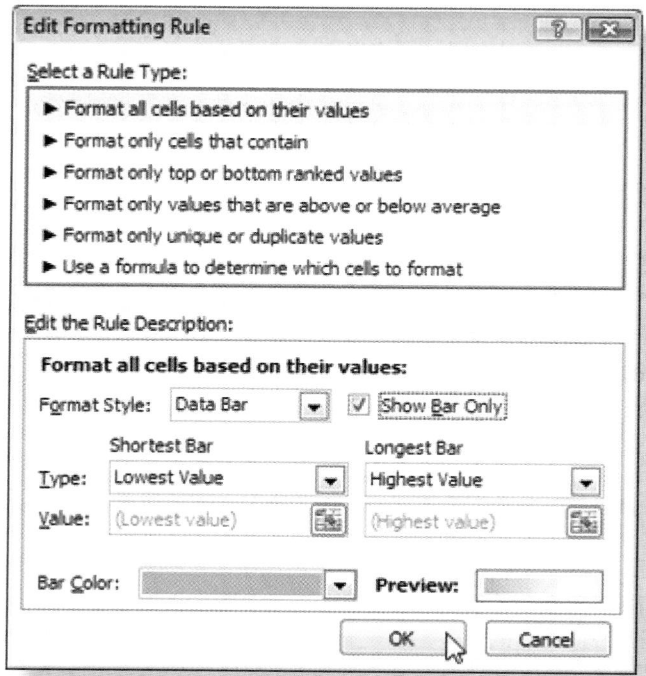

Figure 4-22
Edit Formatting Rule dialog box
4-15.xlsx
AR2007 sheet

7. Click the Conditional Formatting button. Choose **Manage Rules** and then **Edit Rule**.
8. Click to deselect **Show Bar Only**. Click **OK**. Click **OK** again.
9. Key your first and last name in cell A24. Key your first and last name in cell B17 on the **SalesReps** worksheet.
10. Press Ctrl+Home. Save the workbook as ***[your initials]*4-28** in your Lesson 4 folder.
11. Prepare and submit your work. Then close the workbook.

Using Online Help

In addition to data bars, color scales and icon sets are quick ways to add conditional formatting to your data.

EXPLORE CONDITIONAL FORMATTING

1. In a new workbook, press F1.
2. In the Search box, key **conditional formatting** and press Enter.
3. Find and review topics to learn more about data bars, color scales, icon sets, and other rules. Read the help information.
4. Close the Help window.

Lesson 4 Summary

- You can insert, delete, move, and rename worksheets in a workbook.
- Insert or delete cells when you need space for missing data or have blank rows or columns in a worksheet.
- The AutoComplete feature makes suggestions when you key a label that begins with the same characters as labels already in the column.
- The Pick From Drop-Down List displays a list of all labels already in the current column.
- When you cut or copy data, it is placed on the Windows Clipboard and the Office Clipboard. Copied data can be pasted more than once.
- The Office Clipboard stores up to 24 copied elements. It is shared among Word, Excel, Access, and PowerPoint.
- When you delete or insert a row or column, it is inserted across the entire worksheet. Be careful about data that is on the sheet but out of view.
- Change the cell alignment to make data easier to read and more professional-looking. There are several horizontal and vertical alignment choices.
- You can use the Mini toolbar to apply cell formats.
- Text can be wrapped, indented, or rotated.
- The Merge and Center command combines a range of cells into one cell.
- Borders outline a cell or range of cells with a variety of line styles and colors.
- Shading is the background pattern or color for a cell or range of cells.
- Data bars are data visualization that applies conditional formatting based on the cell's value.
- You can edit the color of a data bar and the way in which it is applied.

LESSON 4		Command Summary	
Feature	**Button**	**Task Path**	**Keyboard**
Bottom Align		Home, Cells, Format, Format Cells	Ctrl+1
Align Text Left		Home, Cells, Format, Format Cells	Ctrl+1
Middle Align		Home, Cells, Format, Format Cells	Ctrl+1
Align Text Right		Home, Cells, Format, Format Cells	Ctrl+1
Top Align		Home, Cells, Format, Format Cells	Ctrl+1
Borders		Home, Font	Ctrl+1
Center		Home, Alignment	Ctrl+1
Center across selection	Format	Home, Cells, Format, Format Cells	Ctrl+1
Comma Style	,	Home, Number	Ctrl+1
Copy		Home, Clipboard	Ctrl+C
Cut		Home, Clipboard	Ctrl+X
Data bars		Home, Styles, Conditional Formatting	
Data bars, edit	Conditional Formatting	Home, Styles, Conditional Formatting, Manage Rules	
Decrease Decimal		Home, Number	Ctrl+1
Decrease Font Size		Home, Font	Ctrl+1
Delete cell, row, column	Delete	Home, Cells, Delete	Ctrl+-
Fill color		Home, Font	Ctrl+1
Freeze rows/columns	Freeze Panes	View, Window	
Hide/unhide row/column	Format	Home, Cells, Format	
Increase Font Size		Home, Font	Ctrl+1
Indent text		Home, Cells, Format	Ctrl+1
Insert cell, row, column	Insert	Home, Cells, Insert	Ctrl++
Merge and Center		Home, Alignment	
Paste		Home, Clipboard	Ctrl+V
Split window	Split	View, Window	
Text orientation		Home, Cells, Format, Format Cells	Ctrl+1
Unfreeze rows/columns	Freeze Panes	View, Window	
Wrap text		Home, Alignment	Ctrl+1

unit 2

WORKING WITH FORMULAS AND FUNCTIONS

Lesson 5

Exploring Formula Basics

OBJECTIVES

MCAS OBJECTIVES

In this lesson:
XL07 1.2
XL07 1.5.1
XL07 2.1.4
XL07 2.3.1
XL07 2.3.4
XL07 2.3.7
XL07 3.1
XL07 3.1.1
XL07 3.8
XL07 4.3.3
XL07 5.4.2
XL07 5.5.5
XL07 5.5.6

After completing this lesson, you will be able to:

1. Use a template to create a workbook.
2. Build addition and subtraction formulas.
3. Build multiplication and division formulas.
4. Use order of precedence in a formula.
5. Use relative, absolute, and mixed references.
6. Work with the Page Layout tab.

Estimated Time: 1 1/2 hours

NOTE

The workbooks you create and use in this course relate to the Case Study (see the Case Study in the frontmatter of the book) about Klassy Kow Ice Cream, Inc., a fictional ice cream company.

Formulas use common arithmetic operations (addition, subtraction, multiplication, and division). When building formulas, you should keep in mind mathematical order of precedence, which determines how Excel completes a series of calculations.

Excel usually updates a reference in a formula relative to its position when the formula is copied. It also has other types of references for copying formulas.

Using a Template to Create a Workbook

A *template* is a model workbook that can include labels, values, formulas, themes, styles, alignment settings, borders, and more. A template is used as the starting point for routine workbooks.

NOTE

Copy the templates to the folder Users\UserName\AppData\Roaming\Microsoft\Templates. Check with your instructor if you need help locating the templates used in this lesson.

You can use a template as the model for a workbook by:

- Choosing My Templates in the Templates group of the New Workbook dialog box.
- Choosing Installed Templates in the Templates group of the New Workbook dialog box.
- Choosing the template name from the Blank and Recent pane in the New Workbook dialog box.

Templates are saved with an **.xltx** filename extension in a Templates folder for your computer. Templates must be in this Templates folder to be listed in the New Workbook dialog box.

Exercise 5-1 CREATE A WORKBOOK FROM A TEMPLATE

When you create a new workbook from a template, a copy of the template opens as the new workbook. It has the same name as the template, followed by a number.

1. Click the Microsoft Office Button and choose New. The New Workbook dialog box opens.

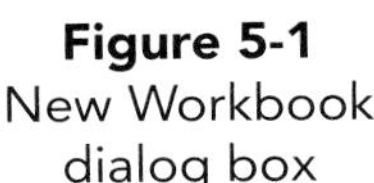

Figure 5-1 New Workbook dialog box

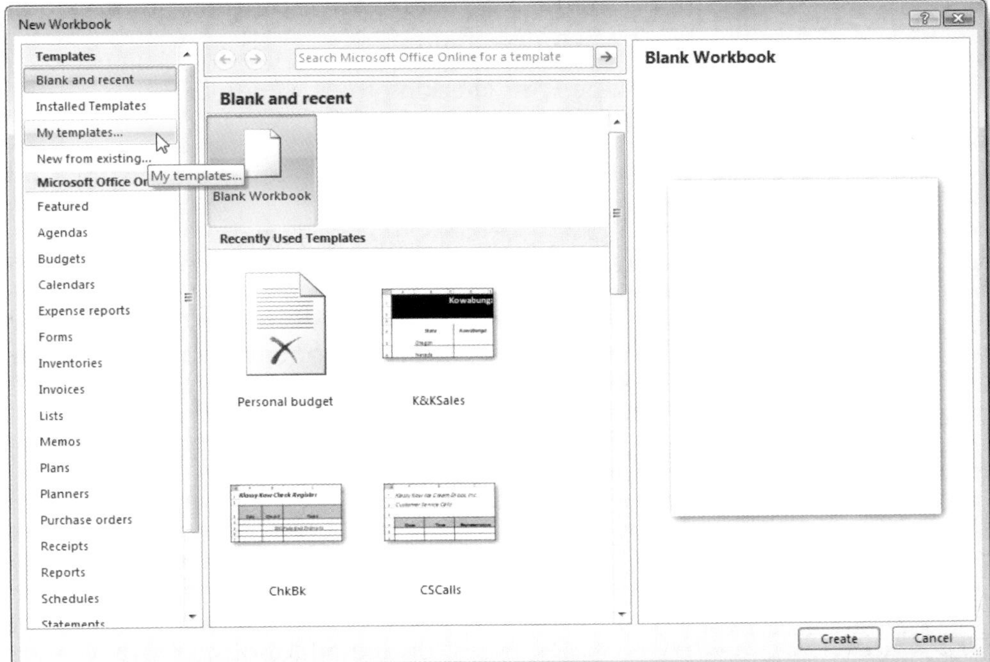

TIP

Excel includes several professionally designed templates, and you can download more from the Microsoft Office Web site.

2. Click **My templates**. The New dialog box opens.
3. Find the template **KlassyKow**.
4. Click **KlassyKow** and click **OK**. A new workbook opens with labels, values, and images. The title bar shows the template name with a number, probably 1.

Building Addition and Subtraction Formulas

Addition formulas total or sum cell values using the plus sign (+). Subtraction formulas compute the difference between cell values using the minus sign (−).

TIP

When cells are next to each other in a row or a column, it is usually faster to use AutoSum than to key a formula for addition.

Exercise 5-2 CREATE AND COPY ADDITION FORMULAS

This worksheet tracks monthly expenses of sales representatives. The budgeted amounts are part of the template, but expenses are keyed.

1. Click the Microsoft Office Button and choose **Excel Options**. Open the **Formulas** pane.
2. In the **Error checking rules**, verify that all rules show a check mark. Click **OK**.
3. Set the Zoom size so that you can see rows 1 through 30. Then click cell B27.
4. Press = to start a formula.
5. Click cell B8, the budget amount for the first week for Kim Tomasaki. A marquee appears around the cell, and it is outlined in a color.
6. Key + and click cell B13, the second week budget amount.
7. Key + and click cell B18, the third week.
8. Key + and click cell B23, the fourth week. This addition formula determines the monthly total budgeted amount for this salesperson.

TIP

You can use + on the numeric keypad or at the top of the keyboard to key the plus symbol in a formula.

Figure 5-2
Entering an addition formula
KlassyKow.xltx
Expenses sheet

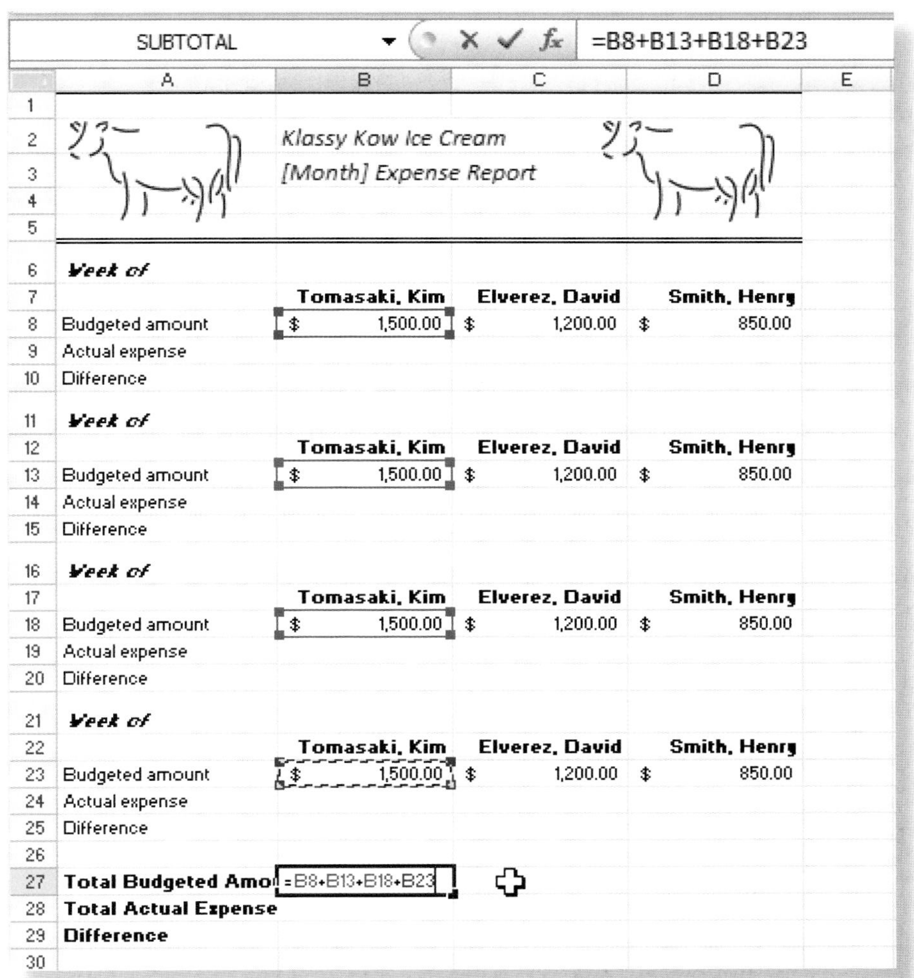

9. Press Enter. The result is $6,000.
10. In cell B28, key = to start the formula.

REVIEW

You can click the Enter button in the formula bar to complete a formula.

11. Click cell B9, the cell where the first week's actual amount will be keyed.
12. Key + and click cell B14, the second week.
13. Key + and click cell B19, and then key + and click cell B24.
14. Key + again to make a deliberate error.
15. Press Enter. A message box opens. The last plus sign is not necessary, and Excel proposes a correction, eliminating it.

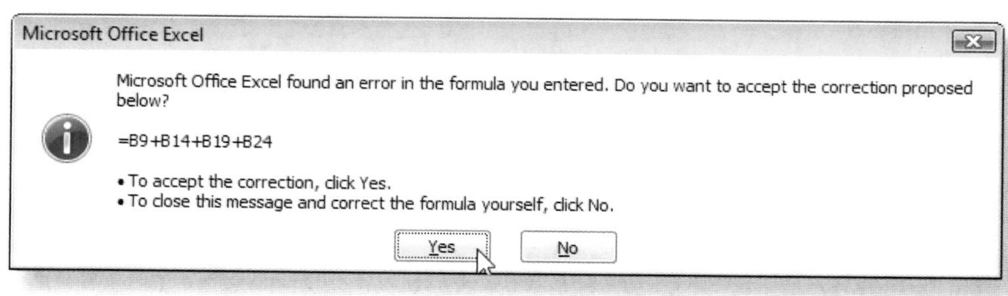

Figure 5-3
Error message box about incorrect formula

16. Choose **Yes**. This worksheet displays a single dash to indicate zero, and the cell shows a small green triangle indicating an error.

17. Click cell B28 and position the mouse pointer on the Error Checking Options button.
18. Click the arrow next to the button to see that the formula refers to empty cells.
19. Choose **Ignore Error**.
20. Select cells B27:B28. Position the mouse pointer on the Fill handle.

21. Drag the Fill handle to cell D28 to copy the formulas. The AutoFill Options button appears below the filled range. Results appear in row 27, and green triangles mark errors in cells C28:D28.
22. Select cells C28:D28 and ignore the errors.

Exercise 5-3 CREATE AND COPY SUBTRACTION FORMULAS

The difference between budgeted and actual expenditures is computed by subtracting the actual amount from the budgeted amount. You can use [-] on the numeric keypad or at the top of the keyboard.

NOTE

Because there are no actual values, the difference is the same as the budget total.

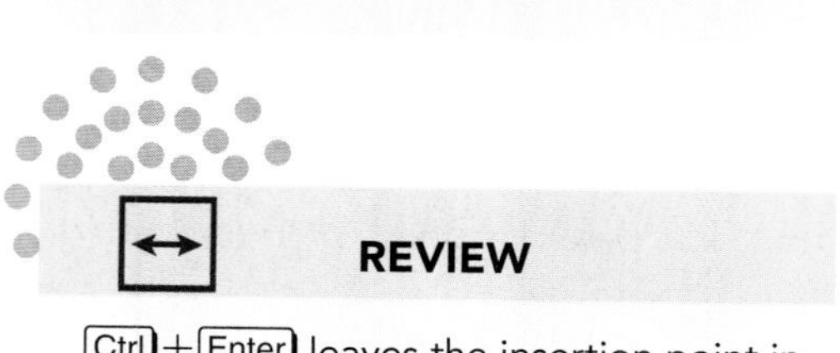

REVIEW

[Ctrl]+[Enter] leaves the insertion point in the cell.

1. Click cell B29 and key = to start a formula.
2. Click cell B27, the budget total.
3. Key – and click cell B28, the actual total. Press [Enter].
4. Copy the formula in cell B29 to cells C29:D29.
5. Click cell B10. Key = and click cell B8, the budgeted amount for the week.
6. Key – and click cell B9, the actual amount. Press [Ctrl]+[Enter].

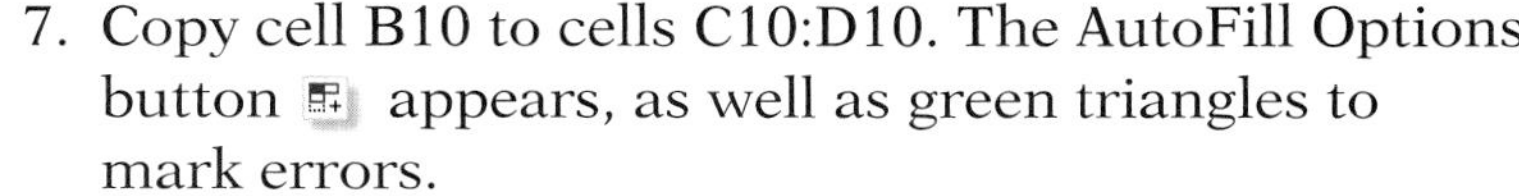

NOTE

Error triangles do not print and have no effect on your worksheet, so you can ignore them when you know that nothing is wrong.

7. Copy cell B10 to cells C10:D10. The AutoFill Options button appears, as well as green triangles to mark errors.
8. While cells B10:D10 are selected, click the Copy button.
9. Click cell B15 and click the Paste button.
10. Click cell B20 and click the Paste button. Paste again in cell B25.

11. Press Esc to cancel the marquee. The differences are the same as the budget amounts, because no actual expenses are shown yet.

Building Multiplication and Division Formulas

A multiplication formula can calculate an employee's weekly wages by multiplying hours worked by the rate of pay. Multiplication formulas use an asterisk (*).

TIP

You can use * and / on the numeric keypad or * at the top of the keyboard and / at the bottom.

Division formulas can be used to determine percentages, averages, individual prices, and more. A division formula uses a forward slash (/).

The result of a multiplication or division formula is formatted with decimals if the result is not a whole number. A *whole number* is a value without a fraction or decimal.

Exercise 5-4 CREATE MULTIPLICATION FORMULAS

You can multiply the current total amounts by 10 percent to determine next year's amounts, assuming a 10 percent increase. When you multiply by a percent, you can key the value with the percent sign (%) in the formula. If you do not key the percent sign, you must key the decimal equivalent of the value.

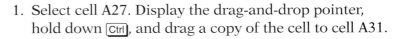

TIP

Convert a percent to its decimal equivalent by dividing the percent amount by 100. For example, 89% is 89/100 or 0.89.

1. Select cell A27. Display the drag-and-drop pointer, hold down Ctrl, and drag a copy of the cell to cell A31.
2. Click cell A31 and press F2. Press Home and key **Increased**.
3. Delete **Total** and press Enter.
4. Widen column A to fit the label.
5. Click cell B31 and key =.
6. Click cell B27, key *, and then key **10%**. Press Ctrl+Enter. This amount is the increase in dollars, but not the new total.

REVIEW

Display the drag-and-drop pointer by pointing at the top or bottom edge of a selection.

Exercise 5-5 EDIT A FORMULA IN THE FORMULA BAR

To determine the new total amount, multiply by 110%, because 110% is the current amount (100%) plus the increase (10%).

1. With cell B31 active, click in the formula bar. A text insertion point appears, and the cell in the worksheet is outlined in the same color as the cell address in the formula bar.
2. Click between the **1** and the **0** in the formula bar.
3. Key **1** to change the percent to **110%**.

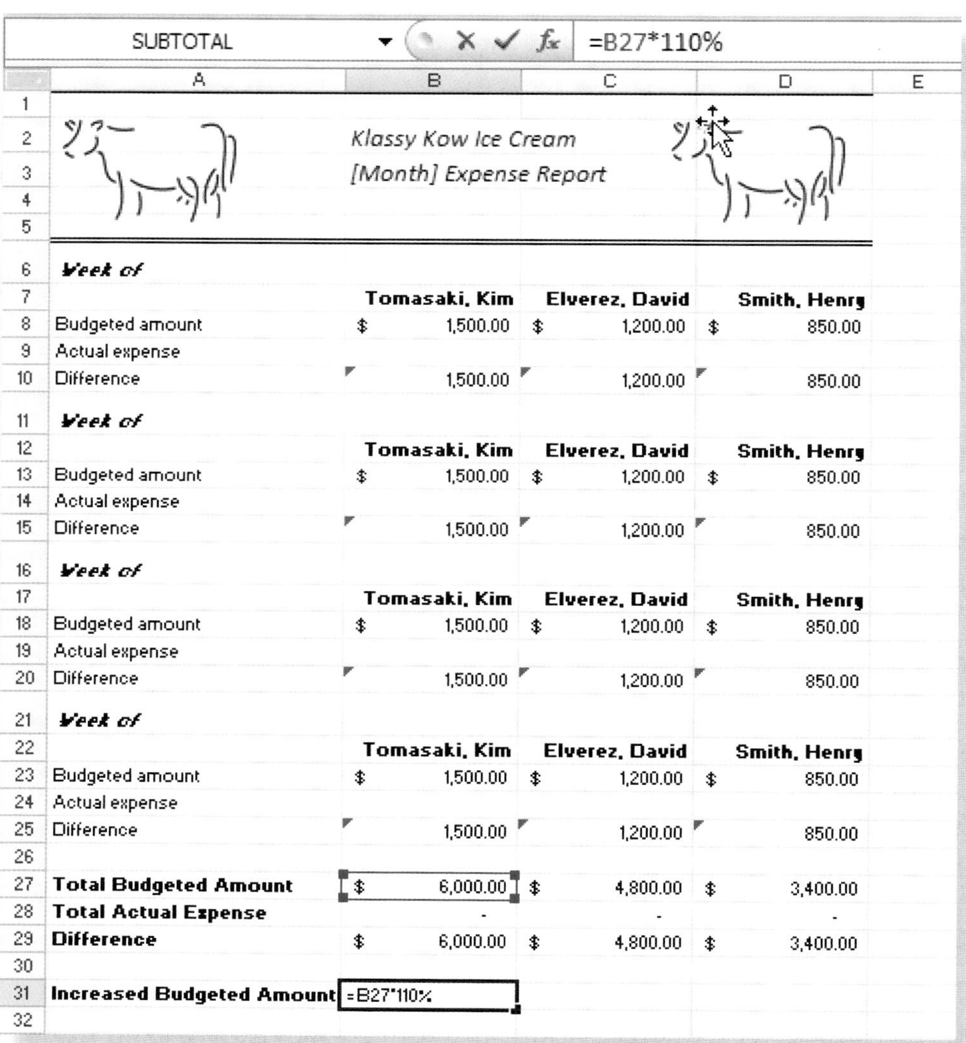

Figure 5-4
Editing a formula in the formula bar
KlassyKow.xltx
Expenses sheet

4. Press Ctrl+Enter. The new total ($6,600) is calculated.
5. Copy cell B31 to cells C31:D31.

Exercise 5-6 CREATE DIVISION FORMULAS

If you select a range before keying data, you can press Enter to move from one cell to the next in top-to-bottom, left-to-right order.

NOTE

The template includes formatting for cells B9:D9.

1. Select cells B9:D9.
2. Key **1000** and press Enter.
3. Key **950** and press Enter.
4. Key **725** and press Enter. As you fill in the amounts, the difference is calculated.
5. Select cells B14:D14 and key these values:

1300	1250	925

6. Key these values in cells B19:D19 and cells B24:C24. The totals are calculated in rows 28 and 29 as you key the values:

900	850	625
1000	750	575

7. Click cell B30 and key = to start a formula.
8. Click cell B28 and key / for division. Dividing the actual amount (cell B28) by the budget amount (cell B27) determines the percent actual expenses are of the budget amount.
9. Click cell B27 and press Enter. The result is formatted as a decimal.

Exercise 5-7 APPLY THE PERCENT STYLE AND INCREASE DECIMAL POSITIONS

Excel converts a decimal to a percent when you apply the Percent Style. It multiplies the decimal value by 100. For example, 0.7 is 0.7*100 or 70%.

1. Click cell B30. In the **Number** group on the **Home** tab, click the Percent Style button %. The percent symbol is added, and the value is converted.

2. Click the Increase Decimal button two times. A decimal position is added with each click.
3. Copy the formula in cell B30 to cells C30:D30.
4. In cell A30, key **Actual as % of Budget** and press Enter. Because three rows precede this row, the format of those rows is applied.
5. Press Ctrl+Home. Press F12 and save the workbook as ***[your initials]*5-7** in a new folder for Lesson 5.
6. Close the workbook.

Using Order of Precedence in a Formula

Excel follows mathematical rules as it calculates a formula. These rules include an *order of precedence,* sometimes called *order of operation* or *math hierarchy.* The order of precedence determines what part of a formula is calculated first. Generally, a formula is calculated from left to right, but some arithmetic operators take priority over others. For example, if you key a formula with both a multiplication symbol (*) and an addition symbol (+), Excel calculates the multiplication first even if it is the second symbol as you move from left to right. You can override the order of precedence by enclosing parts of the formula within parentheses.

When two operators have the same order of precedence—for example, multiplication and division—the operations are performed from left to right (see Table 5-1).

Figure 5-5 shows three formulas with the same values and the same operators. The results differ depending on the placement of the parentheses.

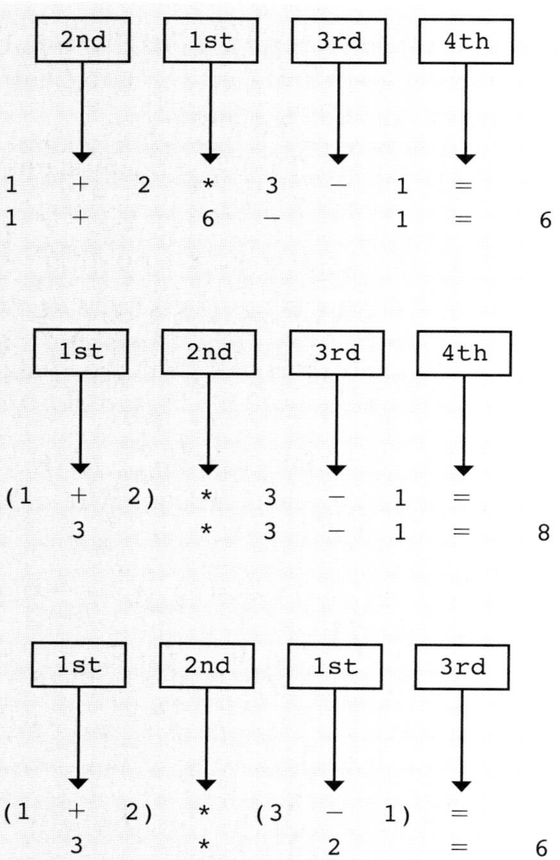

Figure 5-5
Parentheses change the order of operations

TABLE 5-1 Operator Precedence in Excel

Operator		Precedence Description
^	1st	Exponentiation
*	2nd	Multiplication
/	2nd	Division
+	3rd	Addition
–	3rd	Subtraction
&	4th	Concatenation (symbol used to join text strings)
=	5th	Equal to
<	5th	Less than
>	5th	Greater than

Exercise 5-8 USE MULTIPLICATION AND ADDITION IN A FORMULA

TIP

You can memorize the order of precedence for parentheses and the first five operators: "Please excuse my dear Aunt Sally" (parentheses, exponentiation, multiplication, division, addition, subtraction).

In this exercise, you use a formula that seems logical to determine a dollar amount of sales. You will see, however, that it results in an incorrect total.

1. Open **DrinkSize**. Click cell E15. You need to total the items for each state and multiply by the price.
2. Key = and click cell C6, the price for a 16-ounce soda.
3. Key * to multiply the price by the number sold.
4. Select cell D6 and key +.
5. Click cell E6, key +, click cell F6, key +, and click cell G6. This part of the formula adds state unit totals.
6. Press Enter. The result looks reasonable, but it is wrong.
7. Click cell E15. The formula includes a multiplication symbol, so cell C6 is first multiplied by cell D6. Then the other cells are added to the result of C6*D6.
8. Right-click the AutoCalculate area and verify that **Sum** is selected.
9. Select cells D6:G6. Check AutoCalculate for the sum of 30,000.
10. Click cell J6 and key = to start a formula. You are temporarily using this empty cell to calculate the correct amount.

REVIEW

AutoCalculate results are visible in the status bar.

11. Click cell C6, key *30000, and press Enter. This is the correct amount—the total number sold (30,000) multiplied by the price.
12. Delete the contents of cell J6.

Exercise 5-9 SET ORDER OF PRECEDENCE

1. Double-click cell E15 to start Edit mode. The formula is in the cell and in the formula bar. The referenced cells are outlined in color.
2. In the worksheet cell, click in front or to the left of D6.
3. Key a left parenthesis (in front of D6.
4. Press End. The insertion point moves to the end of the formula.
5. Key a right parenthesis).
6. Press Enter. These parentheses force the additions to be calculated first. That result is multiplied by the value in cell C6.

Figure 5-6
Changing the order of precedence
DrinkSize.xlsx
DrinkSales sheet

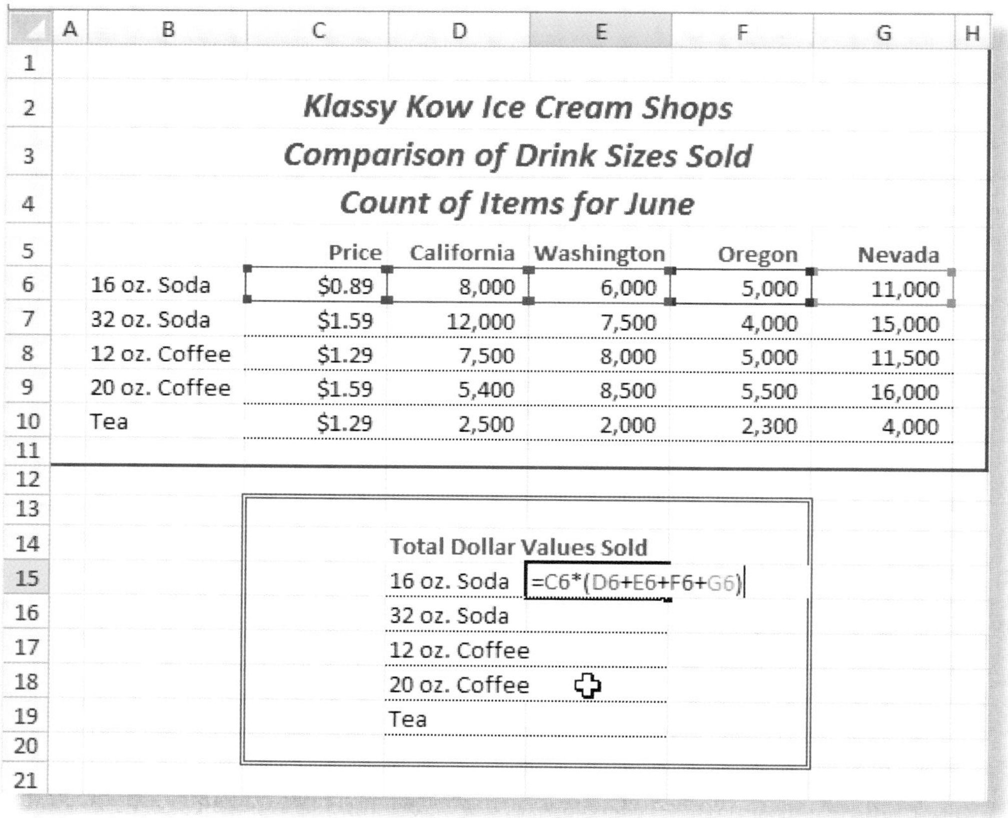

	A	B	C	D	E	F	G	H
1								
2				*Klassy Kow Ice Cream Shops*				
3				*Comparison of Drink Sizes Sold*				
4				*Count of Items for June*				
5			Price	California	Washington	Oregon	Nevada	
6		16 oz. Soda	$0.89	8,000	6,000	5,000	11,000	
7		32 oz. Soda	$1.59	12,000	7,500	4,000	15,000	
8		12 oz. Coffee	$1.29	7,500	8,000	5,000	11,500	
9		20 oz. Coffee	$1.59	5,400	8,500	5,500	16,000	
10		Tea	$1.29	2,500	2,000	2,300	4,000	
11								
12								
13								
14				Total Dollar Values Sold				
15				16 oz. Soda	=C6*(D6+E6+F6+G6)			
16				32 oz. Soda				
17				12 oz. Coffee				
18				20 oz. Coffee				
19				Tea				
20								
21								

7. Apply Accounting format to cell E15 but show no decimals.
8. Copy the formula in cell E15 to cells E16:E19.

9. Click cell E16. Notice that the formula multiplies the price in cell C7 by the values in row 7 for a 32-ounce soda. This is correct.
10. Widen columns as needed. Press Ctrl+Home.
11. Save the workbook as ***[your initials]*5-9** in your Lesson 5 folder.
12. Close the workbook.

Using Relative, Absolute, and Mixed References

When you copy a formula, Excel adjusts the formula relative to the row or column where the copy is located. This is known as a *relative reference*.

There are situations, however, when you want Excel to copy the formula exactly. A formula with an *absolute reference* does not change when it is copied into another cell. An absolute reference uses two dollar signs ($) in its address, one in front of the column reference and one in front of the row reference. B5 is an absolute reference to cell B5.

Excel can also use a *mixed reference,* in which a dollar sign is placed in front of the reference for either the row or the column. In a mixed reference, part of the cell reference is adjusted when a formula is copied; the other is not. $B5 is a mixed reference with an absolute reference to column B but a relative reference to row 5.

Dollar signs used in a cell address do not signify currency. They are a reserved symbol used to mark the type of cell reference.

TABLE 5-2 Cell References

Address	Type of Reference	
B1	Relative	
B1	Absolute	
$B1	Mixed	Column letter is absolute; row number is relative.
B$1	Mixed	Row number is absolute; column letter is relative.

Exercise 5-10 USE A LINE BREAK

You can place labels on two lines in a cell by pressing Alt+Enter at the point where you want the second line to start. This is known as a *line break* in a cell. You often need to adjust the row height or the column width if you use line breaks.

1. Open **ShopDownTime**.
2. In cell G5, key **Cost per** and press Alt+Enter.

3. Key **Down Hour** and press Enter.
4. Adjust the column width so that the label splits only between "per" and "Down."
5. Click cell G5 and look at the formula bar. It is not tall enough to show the complete label.
6. Rest the mouse pointer on the splitter bar above the column headings.

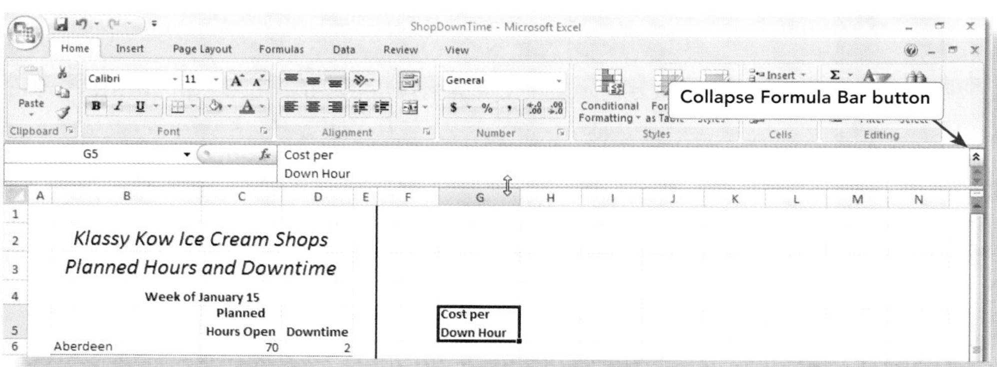

Figure 5-7
Sizing the formula bar
ShopDownTime.xlsx AllStates sheet

7. Drag down until you see the label in the formula bar. The formula bar occupies more space and your data rows occupy less.
8. In cell G6, key **25** and format it as Accounting with two decimals.

Exercise 5-11 COPY A FORMULA WITH A RELATIVE REFERENCE

1. Insert a column at column E. In cell E5, key **Cost**. Its formatting matches the preceding columns.
2. Click cell E6. Key = to start the formula.
3. Click cell D6, key *, and then click cell H6. This formula uses relative references.
4. Press Enter. The result is $50.
5. Drag the Fill handle for cell E6 to copy the formula to cell E25. The copied formulas show a dash for zero and an error triangle. The cells that should show a total cost do not.
6. Click each copied cell in column E and look in the formula bar. Each time the formula went down a row, the row reference adjusted. That works for column D, but not for column H.
7. Click the Undo button.

Exercise 5-12 CREATE A FORMULA WITH AN ABSOLUTE REFERENCE

REVIEW

F2 starts Edit mode, the same as double-clicking the cell.

Because absolute references are common to many calculations, Excel has a quick way of adding dollar signs to a cell reference. It's the F4 key.

1. Click cell E6 and press F2.
2. Click between **H** and **6** in the worksheet cell.
3. Press F4. Two dollar signs are inserted, one before **H** and one before **6**.

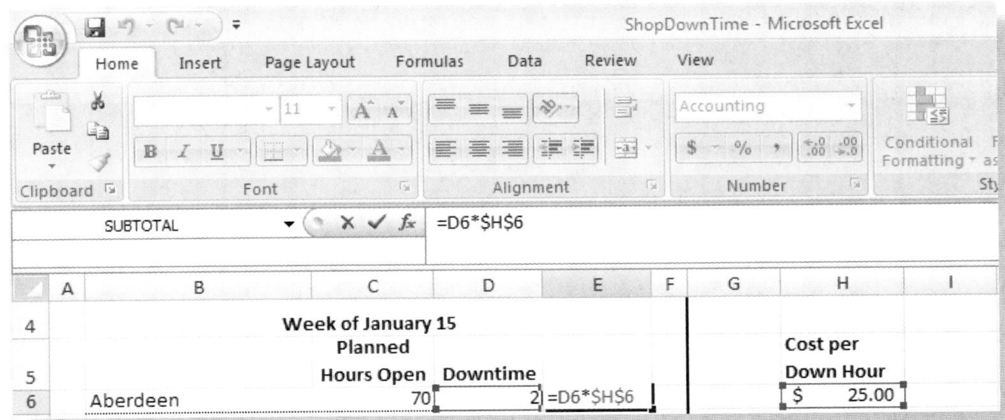

Figure 5-8
Making a cell reference absolute
ShopDownTime.xlsx
AllStates sheet

4. Press F. The dollar sign appears only with **6**.
5. Press F again. The dollar sign appears only with **H**.
6. Press F again. The dollar signs are removed.
7. Press F once more. The absolute reference appears again.
8. Press Ctrl+Enter. Look in the formula bar.
9. Use the Fill handle for cell E6 to copy the formula into cells E7:E37.
10. Click each copied cell and look in the formula bar. Cell H6 did not change in any of the copies.
11. Select cells E6:E37 and apply a dashed middle and bottom horizontal border.

Exercise 5-13 USE A COLOR SCALE

In addition to data bars, the Conditional Formatting command includes color scales. This command applies fill to the range based on the values. You can use two- or three-color arrangements.

NOTE

Color scales can show the largest or the smallest value with the darkest color.

1. Select cells E6:E37. In the **Styles** group on the **Home** tab, click the Conditional Formatting button.
2. Choose **Color Scales** and the **Red – Yellow Color Scale** in the second row, second icon. This scale shows the highest values in the darkest color.

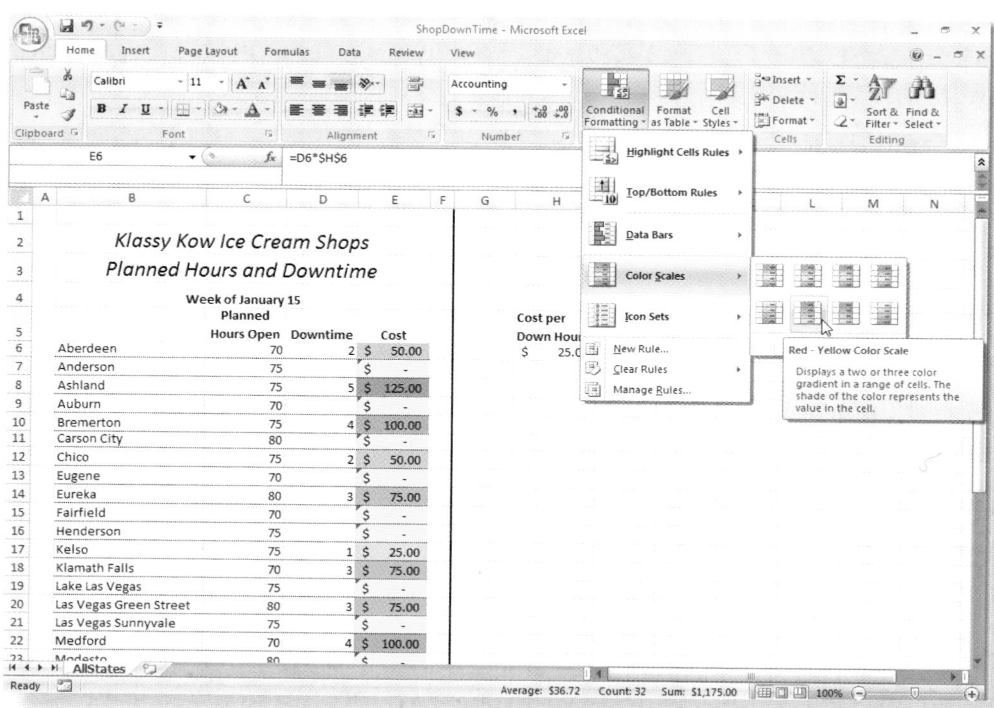

Figure 5-9
Choosing a color scale
ShopDownTime.xlsx AllStates sheet

3. Click in column H to better see the color scale.
4. Select cells E6:E37 and click the Conditional Formatting button.
5. Choose **Manage Rules**. The Conditional Formatting Rules Manager dialog box opens.
6. Click **Edit rule**. The Edit Formatting Rule dialog box is the same as the one for data bars.
7. Choose a different light and dark color from the same hue.
8. Click **OK** twice to see your changes.
9. Press Ctrl+Home. Save the workbook as ***[your initials]*5-13** in your folder.
10. Close the workbook.
11. At the right end of the formula bar, click the Collapse Formula Bar button. The formula bar collapses to its default height.

Exercise 5-14 USE MIXED REFERENCES

A multiplication table will be printed as a promotional item and posted on the company's Web site. This multiplication table uses mixed references.

1. Open **MultTable**.
2. Set the Zoom percent to a size that lets you see the entire worksheet.
3. Click cell B3. You want to show the result of multiplying 1 by 1 in cell B3.
4. Key = and click cell A3. This will be a mixed reference.
5. Press F4 three times to show **$A3**. This part of the formula will always use column A, but the row will change.
6. Press * and click cell B2.
7. Press F4 two times to show **B$2**. This part of the formula will always use row 2, but the column will change.

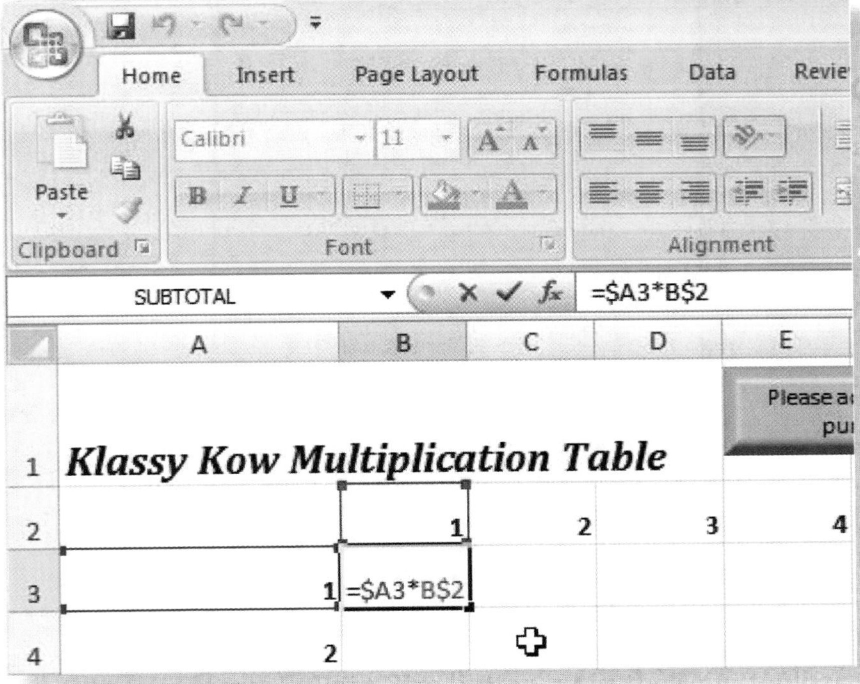

Figure 5-10
Mixed reference formula
MultTable.xlsx
Sheet1 sheet

8. Press Ctrl+Enter.
9. Use the Fill handle to copy cell B3 to cell K3.
10. Use the Fill handle to copy cells B3:K3 down to row 12.

Exercise 5-15 ADD BORDERS AND FILL FOR PRINTING

Borders and fill will make it easier to follow numbers across a wide layout.

1. Select cells A2:K12 and press Ctrl+1.
2. Click the **Border** tab.
3. In the **Border** preset group, click the Top Border button.
4. Click the Middle Horizontal Border and then the Bottom Border buttons. Click the Left Border and the Right Border buttons. Click **OK**.

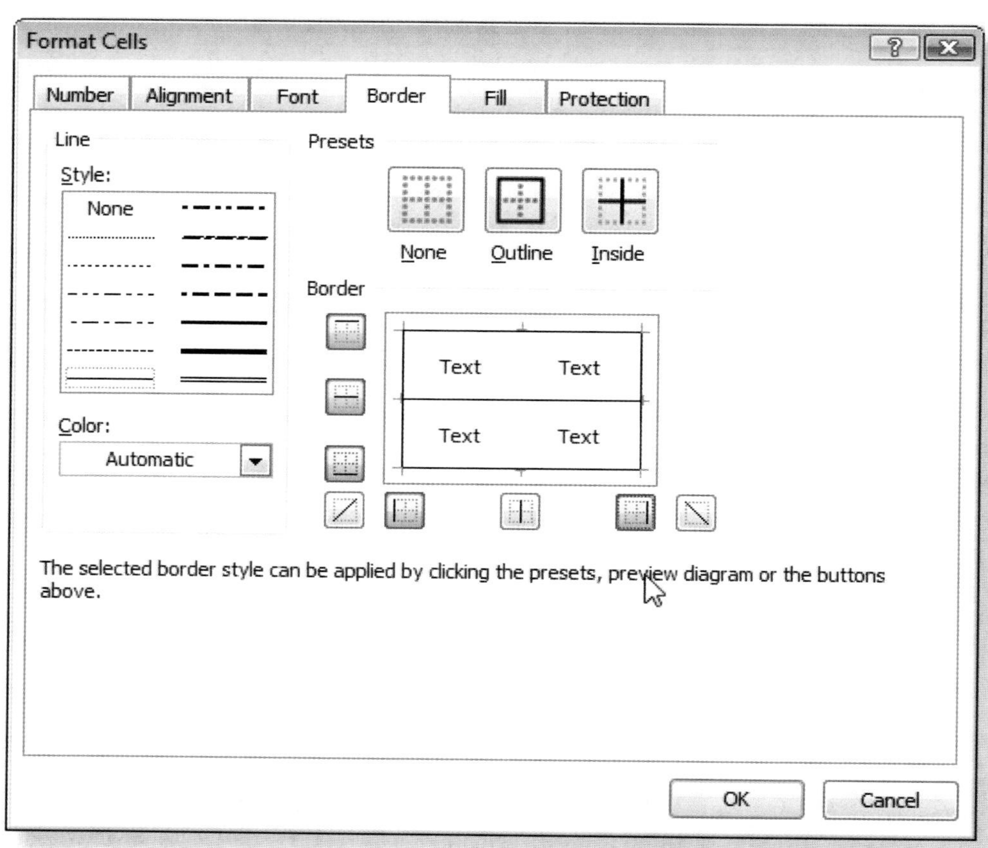

Figure 5-11
Setting top, middle, bottom, left, and right borders

Hold down the Ctrl key to select noncontiguous cell ranges.

5. Select cells A2:K2 and cells A3:A12.
6. Click the arrow next to the Fill Color button.
7. Choose **White, Background 1, Darker 25%** in the first column.
8. Press Ctrl+Home.

Working with the Page Layout Tab

There are many options for how to print a worksheet as well as several ways to change these options. From the Page Layout tab, you can:

- Change margins.
- Change the page orientation.
- Choose a paper size.
- Set a print area or print titles.
- Scale the worksheet to fit the page or print larger than the page.
- Change page breaks.
- Add a background image.

Page orientation determines if the worksheet prints landscape or portrait. The default is *portrait* orientation, one that is taller than it is wide.

Scaling commands enable you to set a size percentage for the printed page. This size can be smaller or larger.

Exercise 5-16 CHANGE PAGE ORIENTATION

Many worksheets are too wide to fit portrait orientation on 8½ by 11 inch paper. A *landscape* orientation is horizontal—the page is wider than it is tall.

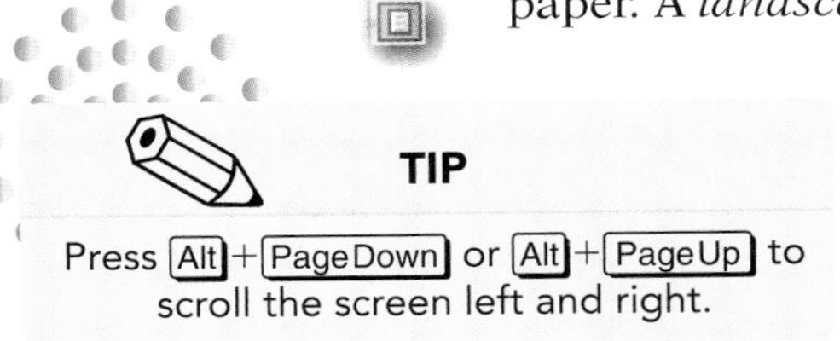

Press Alt+PageDown or Alt+PageUp to scroll the screen left and right.

1. Click the Page Layout View button in the status bar. The worksheet does not fit on a single page in portrait orientation. You can see in the status bar (at the left) that the worksheet requires more than one page.

2. Click the Zoom Out button to reach **80%**. Excel splits the worksheet between columns.
3. Click the **Page Layout** command tab.

4. In the **Page Setup** group, click the Page Orientation button. Choose **Landscape**. The worksheet fits on a single page in landscape orientation.

Exercise 5-17 CHANGE SCALING AND PAGE MARGINS

You can set a worksheet to print at 50 percent of its size or 150 percent of its size. You might need to do this if you want to print the worksheet on a 5- by 7-inch card or if you want to enlarge it for a special display. When you enlarge a worksheet, the output device will split the pages between columns so that you can tape the parts together.

You change margins by dragging the margin markers in Page Layout View. If you need to set a precise margin, you can use the Margins tab in the Page Setup dialog box to key a specific setting.

1. In the **Scale to Fit** group, double-click **100** and key **75**. Click any cell or press Enter. The worksheet is reduced to 75 percent of its normal size. This is only an output adjustment and does not change any format settings.

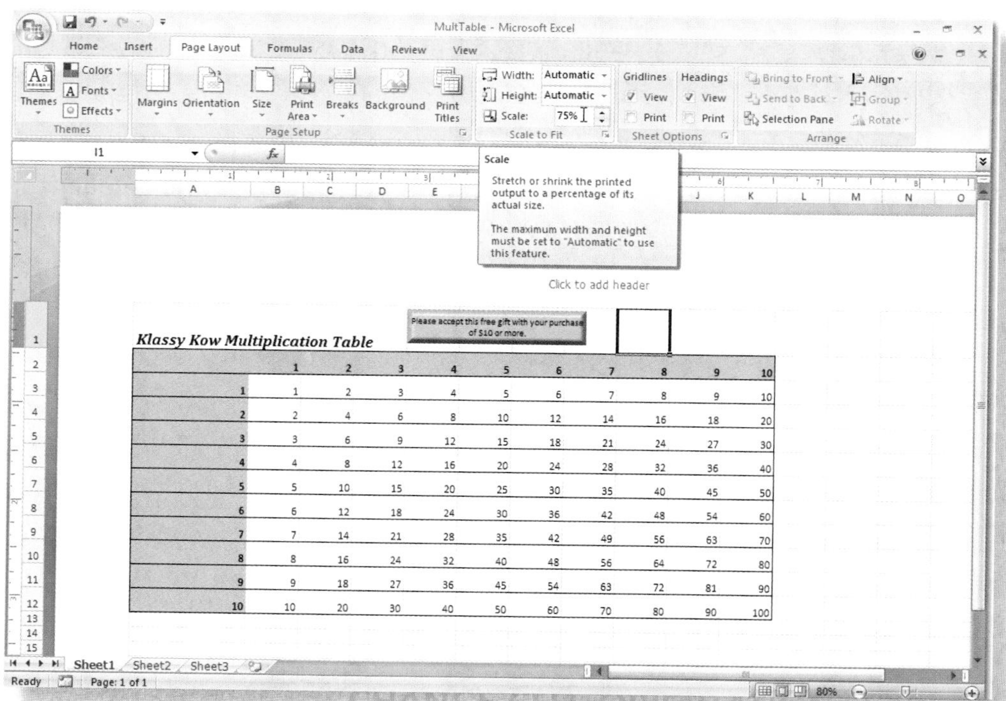

Figure 5-12
Scaling the worksheet
MultTable.xlsx Sheet1 sheet

2. In the **Page Setup** group, click the Margins button. Choose **Custom Margins**. The Page Setup dialog box opens with the **Margins** tab active.
3. Double-click in the **Left** box and key **2.25**.
4. Double-click in the **Right** box and key **1**. Click **OK**.
5. Zoom out to **70%**.
6. In the **Sheet Options** group, click to deselect **Gridlines: View** and **Headings: View**. This represents how the worksheet will print.
7. Save the workbook as ***[your initials]*5-17** in your folder.

Exercise 5-18 COPY A WORKSHEET AND DISPLAY FORMULAS

You can easily review and troubleshoot formulas by displaying them all at once on screen. A copy of the worksheet with formulas visible also provides clear documentation for your work.

In order to keep the original version of your worksheet, you'll make a copy and show formulas on the copy.

1. Rename **Sheet1** as **PrintTable**.
2. Right-click the **PrintTable** tab and choose **Move or Copy**.
3. In the Move or Copy dialog box, click to select **Create a copy**. Click **OK**. The copy is named **PrintTable (2)** and is inserted in front of the original.
4. Press Ctrl+~. The formulas in each cell are visible.
5. In the **Sheet Options** group on the **Page Layout** tab, click to select **Gridlines: View**, **Gridlines: Print**, **Headings: View**, and **Headings: Print**.
6. Click the column A heading. Scroll right and hold down Shift while clicking the column K heading. All the columns are selected.
7. Double-click the border between columns K and L. Excel AutoFits each column to its longest entry.
8. In the **Scale to Fit** group, double-click **75**, key **100**, and click any cell. The worksheet occupies two pages, because formulas require more space than values.
9. Click the Margins button. Choose **Custom Margins**. Double-click in the **Left** box and key **.5**. Press Tab and key **.5** in the **Right** box.
10. Click the **Page** tab. In the **Scaling** section, click to select **Fit to**.
11. Choose **1 page(s) wide** by **1 tall**.
12. Click **OK**. Excel fits the worksheet to a single landscape page with 0.5-inch left and right margins (see Figure 5-13 on the next page).

NOTE

The tilde (~) is located at the top left of the keyboard. You can display formulas by clicking the Microsoft Office Button and choosing **Excel Options**, **Advanced** pane (Display Options for this Worksheet).

NOTE

Column headings are above the header area.

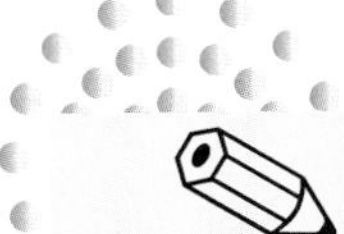

TIP

You can set your own scaling percentage or choose the **Fit to** option.

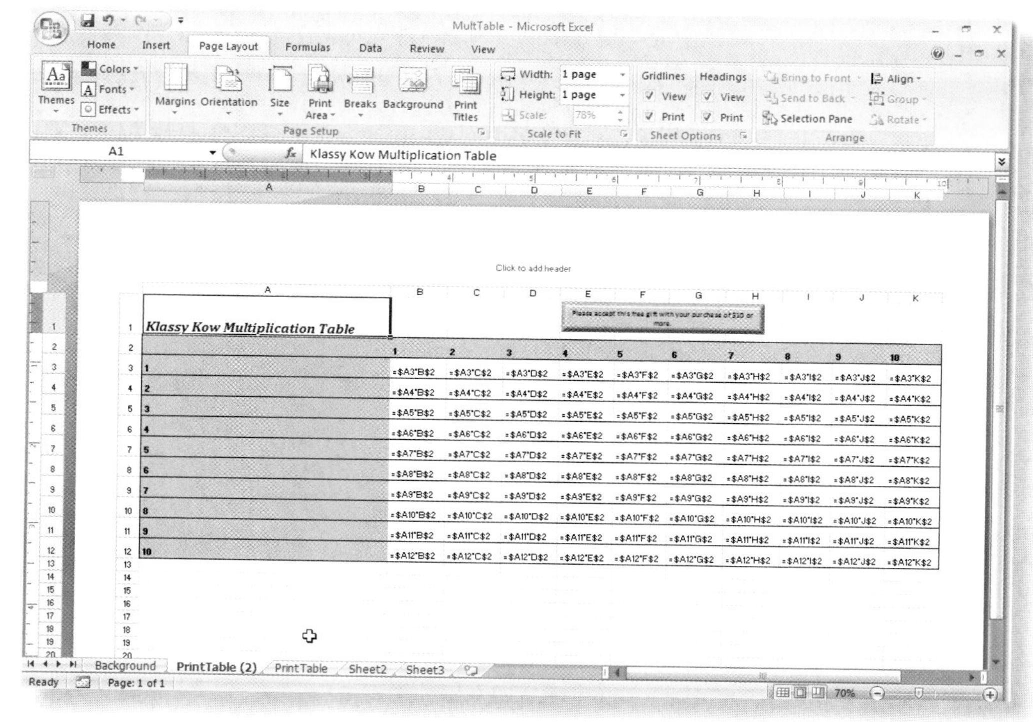

Figure 5-13
Formulas visible
5-17.xlsx
PrintTable (2) sheet

13. Press Ctrl+Home. Save the workbook as ***[your initials]*5-18** in your folder.

Exercise 5-19 ADD A BACKGROUND

A *background* is an image that appears on screen and on the Web. It fills or spans the entire worksheet. It does not print.

1. Right-click the **PrintTable** tab and choose Move or Copy.
2. In the Move or Copy dialog box, click to select Create a copy. Click OK. The copy is named **PrintTable (3)**.
3. Rename **PrintTable (3)** as **Background**.
4. Click the Normal button on the status bar.
5. On the Page Layout tab, click to select Gridlines: View and Headings: View.

6. Click the Background button in the Page Setup group. The Sheet Background dialog box opens.
7. Navigate to the folder with the **KKBack** file. Click to select the file.

Figure 5-14
Using a sheet background
5-18.xlsx
Background sheet

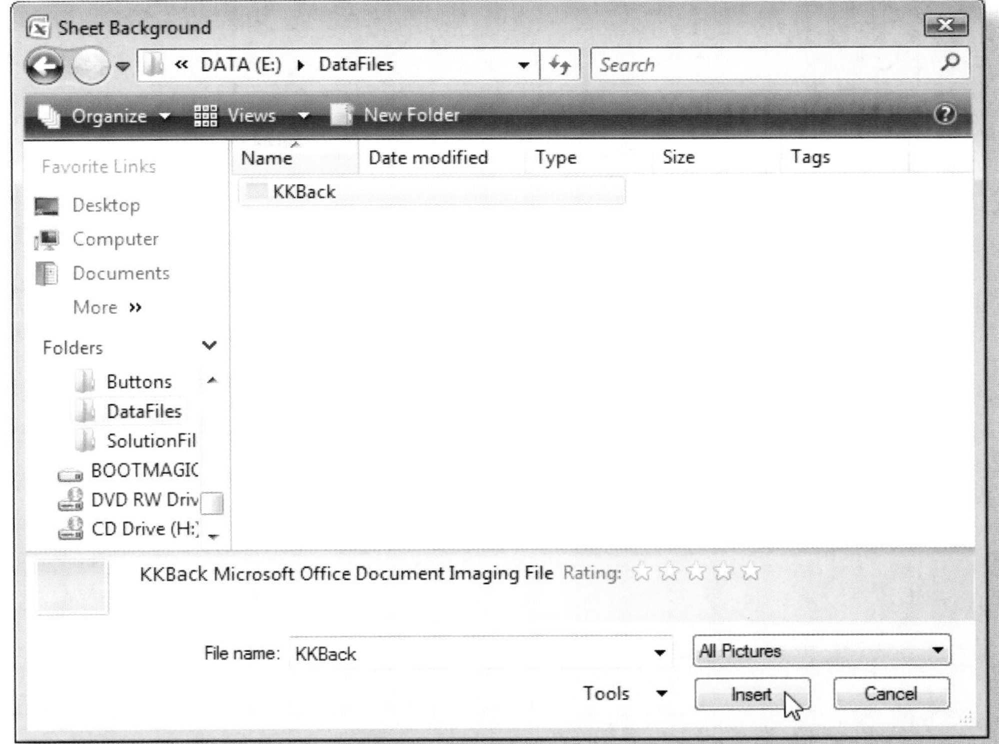

8. Click **Insert**. The background is a blend of colors and fills the worksheet.
9. Select cells A2:K2 and cells A3:A12.
10. Click the **Home** tab. Click the arrow with the Fill Color button and choose **No Fill**. You don't need a fill color with the background.
11. Press Ctrl+Home.
12. Press Ctrl+P. The Print dialog box opens.
13. Press Alt+W to open Print Preview. Backgrounds do not print; they are visible on screen and on a Web site.
14. Close Print Preview.

Exercise 5-20 SAVE A WORKBOOK AS A WEB PAGE

You can save an Excel workbook as an HTML file so that it can be viewed on the World Wide Web. An *HTML* file uses *Hypertext Markup Language*, a widely used and recognized format for Web pages. Web pages are saved with an **.htm** extension. You can save the entire workbook or an individual worksheet as a Web page. When you save the entire workbook, the Web page shows the worksheet tabs.

NOTE

Do not use Single File Web Page to save a Web page unless you are familiar with HTML and can edit it on your own.

1. Press F12. The Save As dialog box opens.
2. Click the arrow for **Save as type** and choose **Web Page**.
3. Set the **Save in** folder to your Lesson 5 folder.
4. In the **Save** area, choose **Entire Workbook**.
5. Click **Change Title**. The title appears in the title bar of the browser.
6. Key **Klassy Kow Multiplication Table** and click **OK**.

Figure 5-15
Saving a Web page

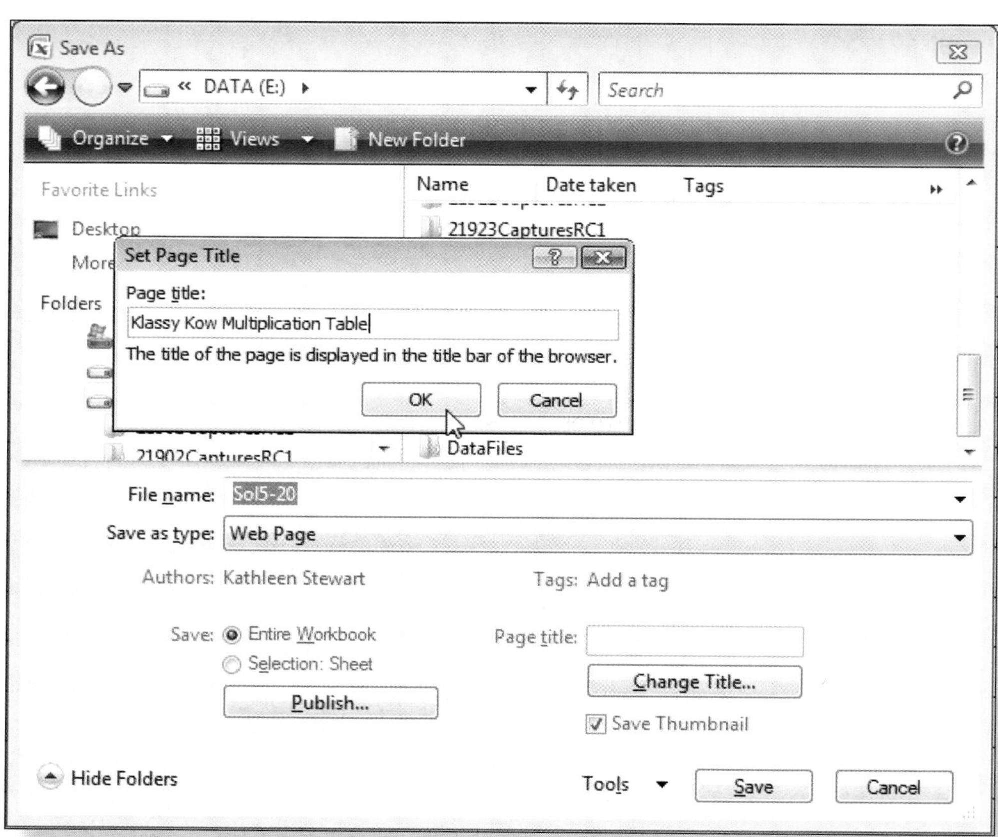

7. Name the file ***[your initials]*5-20**. Click **Save**. If a message box opens about incompatible features, choose **Yes**.
8. Close the workbook.
9. Start your Web browser and maximize the window.
10. Press Ctrl+O. Click **Browse** and navigate to your folder. Find and click ***[your initials]*5-20** and click **Open**. Click **OK**.

11. Look for the title and at each of the tabs in the browser.
12. Click the Close button to close the browser.

Using Online Help

USE HELP TO VIEW ADDITIONAL INFORMATION ABOUT FORMULAS

1. In a new workbook, press F1.
2. In the Search box, key **create formula** and press Enter.
3. Find and review topics to learn more about building formulas. Read the help information.
4. Close the Help window.

Lesson 5 Summary

- Use a template to create workbooks that use the same labels and other basic information on a routine basis.
- Templates can include labels, values, formatting, formulas, and pictures.
- You can edit a formula in the formula bar and within the cell in Edit mode.
- The Percent Style converts a decimal value to its percent equivalent.
- In calculating formulas, Excel follows mathematical order of precedence.
- You can establish a different order of precedence in a formula by keying parentheses around the calculations that you want performed first.
- Excel has relative, absolute, and mixed references. These references determine what happens when a formula is copied.
- A color scale is a conditional formatting rule that fills a range of cells with various intensities of a color based on the values.
- A portrait orientation prints a vertical page. A landscape page prints a horizontal page.
- The Scale to Fit group on the Page Layout tab enables you to print the worksheet in a reduced or enlarged size. You can also choose to have Excel fit the worksheet on a page.

- To set a precise margin, use the Margins tab in the Page Setup dialog box.
- You can print a worksheet with formulas displayed for documentation or help in locating problems.
- You can add an image as a sheet background for display on a Web page.
- You can save a workbook as a Web page for viewing in most browsers.

LESSON 5		Command Summary	
Feature	**Button**	**Task Path**	**Keyboard**
Absolute reference			F4
Background	Background	Page Layout, Page Setup	
Collapse formula bar			Ctrl+Shift+U
Color scale	Conditional Formatting	Home, Styles, Conditional Formatting	
Copy sheet		Home, Cells, Format, Move or Copy Sheet	
Show/hide formulas	Show Formulas	Formulas, Formula Auditing	Ctrl+~
Edit mode			F2
Fit to page	Height: Automatic Width: Automatic	Page Layout, Scale to Fit	
Increase Decimal		Home, Number	Ctrl+1
Margins	Margins	Page Layout, Page Setup	
New, from template		Microsoft Office, New	
Page Orientation	Orientation	Page Layout, Page Setup	
Percent Style	%	Home, Number	Ctrl+1 or Ctrl+Shift+%
Scaling		Page Layout, Scale to Fit	
Web page		Microsoft Office, Save As	F12

Lesson 6

Working with Functions

OBJECTIVES

After completing this lesson, you will be able to:

1. Use math and trig functions.
2. Use statistical functions.
3. Use icon sets.
4. Group worksheets.
5. Use date and time functions.

MCAS OBJECTIVES

In this lesson:

XL07 1.3.1
XL07 1.5.1
XL07 1.5.2
XL07 1.5.5
XL07 2.3.1
XL07 2.3.2
XL07 3.2
XL07 3.2.1
XL07 3.4.1
XL07 4.3.1
XL07 4.3.3
XL07 5.5

Estimated Time: 1 1/2 hours

Excel has several categories of functions that perform common mathematical, statistical, financial, and other calculations. A *function* is a built-in formula.

Many functions do things automatically that would be difficult or time-consuming for you to do manually. For example, in a list of accounts with each customer's amount due, Excel can quickly calculate a total, find the largest amount due, or calculate an average amount due.

Using Math and Trig Functions

All functions have a *syntax,* which defines the necessary parts of the formula and the order of those parts. The syntax consists of an equal sign and the name of the function, followed by parentheses. Inside the parentheses, you place arguments.

An *argument* is the information the function needs to complete its calculation, usually one or more values or cell ranges. A few functions do not have arguments, but most have at least one argument. If a function has more than one argument, the arguments are separated by commas. A function's arguments can consist of:

- Cell references (individual cells or ranges)
- Constants (a number keyed in the formula)
- Another function (known as a nested function)
- Range names

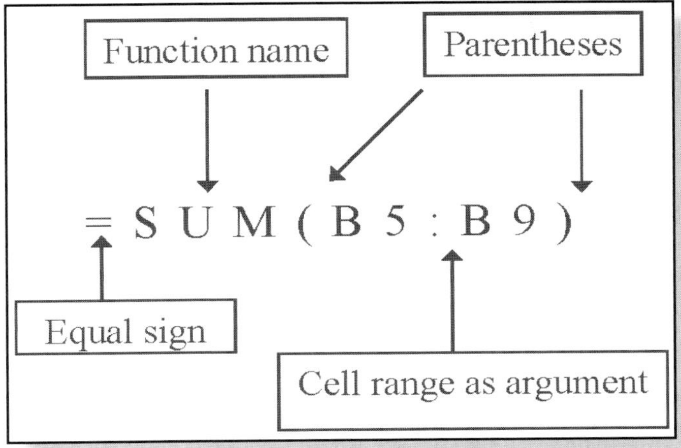

Figure 6-1
Syntax for the SUM function

Exercise 6-1 USE SUM AND THE FORMULA BAR

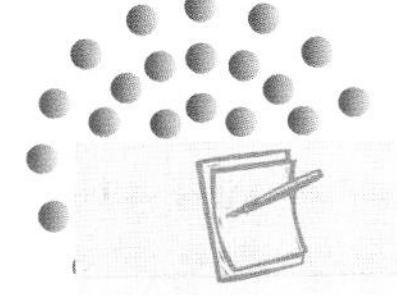

NOTE

Excel inserts the SUM function when you use the AutoSum button.

The SUM function in the Math & Trig category adds columns or rows of values. The SUM function ignores cells with:

- Text
- Error values such as #NAME?

TABLE 6-1 Examples of the SUM Function

Function(argument/s)	Cell Data	Result
=SUM(A1:A3)	A1=10, A2=20, A3=30	60
=SUM(50,60)	None	110
=SUM(A1,250)	A1=25	275
=SUM(A1,B2,C1:C2)	A1=10, B2=20, C1=10, C2=30	70
=SUM(A1,B2)	A1=25, B2="Ice Cream"	25
=SUM(A1,B2)	A1=25, B2=#NAME?	25

1. Open **DownTime**.
2. Click cell E17.
3. Key =su. *Formula AutoComplete* displays a list of functions that match what you have keyed so far. There is also a descriptive ScreenTip for the highlighted function.

Figure 6-2
Formula AutoComplete
DownTime.xlsx Jan15Plan sheet

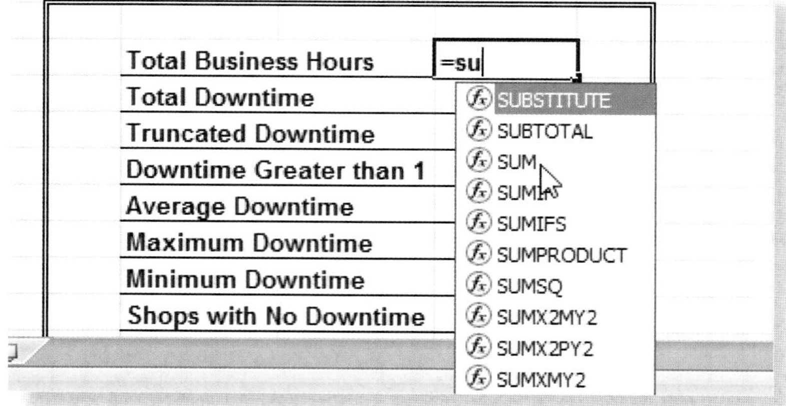

TIP

You can click the function name to highlight it in the Formula AutoComplete list and then press Tab to insert it.

4. Double-click **SUM** in the list. The opening parenthesis is inserted with the function name. An Argument ScreenTip illustrates the syntax for the function with the first argument shown in bold.
5. Click cell C7 and drag to select cells C7:C14. As you drag, the ScreenTip shows the number of rows and columns. The function will sum the range C7:C14.

Figure 6-3
SUM function with its Argument ScreenTip
DownTime.xlsx Jan15Plan sheet

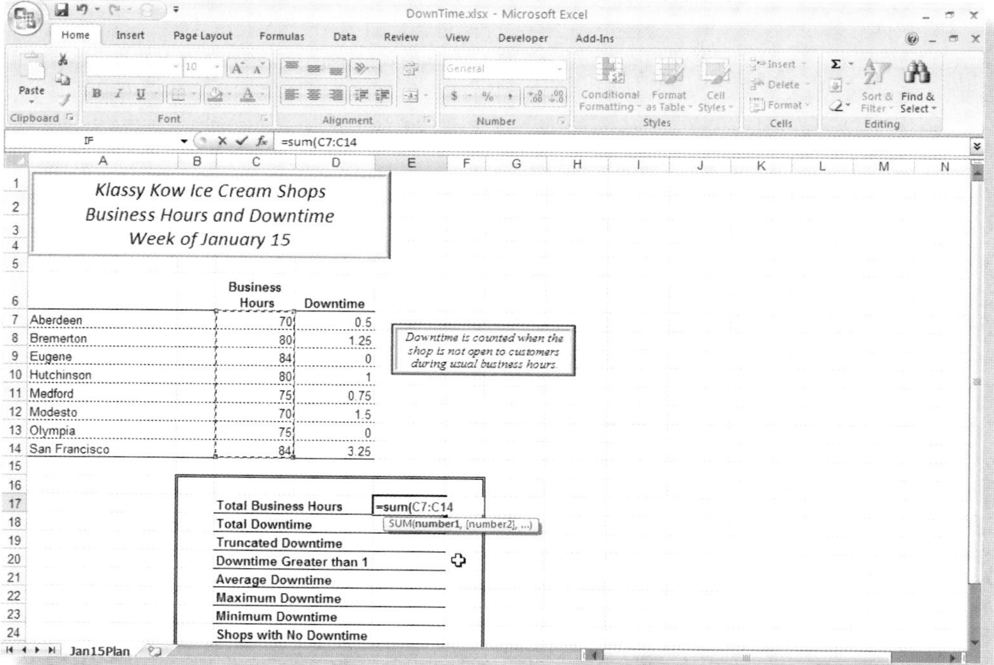

6. Press Ctrl+Enter. The result is 618.
7. Look in the formula bar. For the SUM function, Excel adds a closing parenthesis for you. This formula is the same as keying **=c7+c8+c9+c10+c11+c12+c13+c14**.

Exercise 6-2 USE INSERT FUNCTION

The Insert Function dialog box enables you to choose a function from all available. After you choose a function, the Function Arguments dialog box opens and guides you in building the formula. An Insert Function button appears at the left of the formula bar. There is also an Insert Function button on the Formulas tab.

1. Click cell E18. This will be a sum of the values from column D.
2. Click the Insert Function button in the formula bar. The Insert Function dialog box opens.

TIP

Categories and functions are listed in alphabetical order.

3. Click the arrow next to the **Or select a category** list. Choose **Math & Trig**.
4. In the **Select a function** list, scroll to find **SUM**.
5. Click **SUM** to see its syntax and a description in the dialog box.

Figure 6-4
Insert Function dialog box

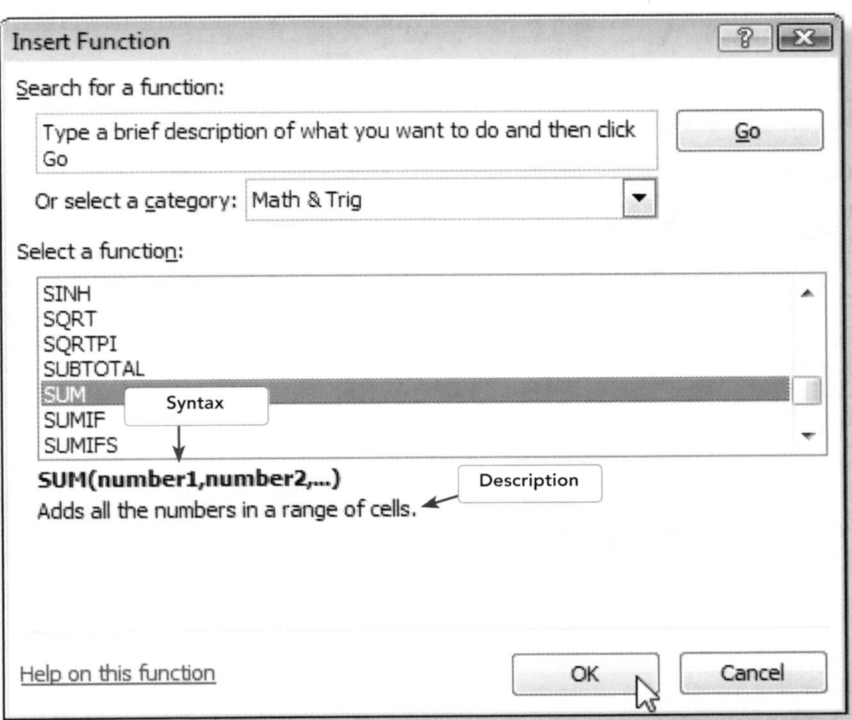

Drag a dialog box by pointing at its title bar.

6. Click **OK**. The Function Arguments dialog box opens. In the **Number1** box, Excel assumes that you want to sum the range above cell E18.
7. Move the dialog box so that you see columns C and D (see Figure 6-5).

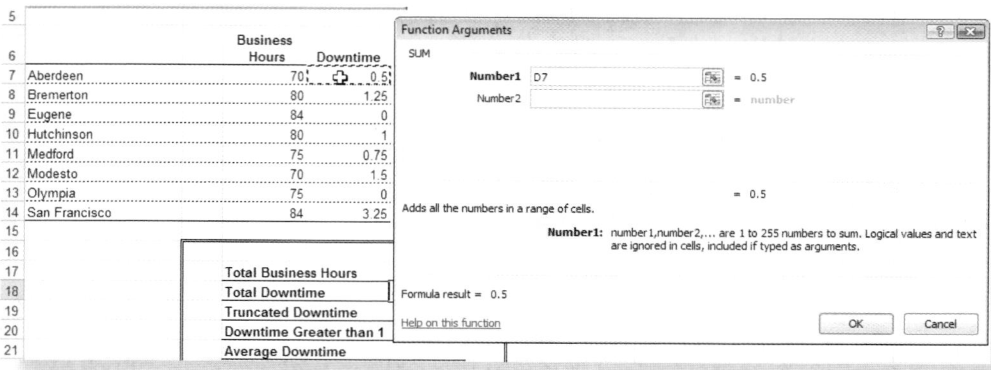

Figure 6-5
Function Arguments dialog box
DownTime.xlsx
Jan15Plan sheet

NOTE

If you click in the wrong cell or number box, reposition the pointer and click again in the correct location.

8. Click cell D7. A marquee appears around the cell, and its address is entered in the **Number1** box in the Function Arguments dialog box.
9. Click in the **Number2** box and click cell D8. Notice that the formula appears in both the formula bar and the cell. When cells are listed one by one, they are separated by commas in the function.
10. Click in the **Number3** box and click cell D9.
11. Click in the **Number4** box and click cell D10.
12. Click in the **Number5** box and click cell D11.
13. Scroll in the Function Arguments dialog box and complete the arguments up to **Number8** with cell D14.

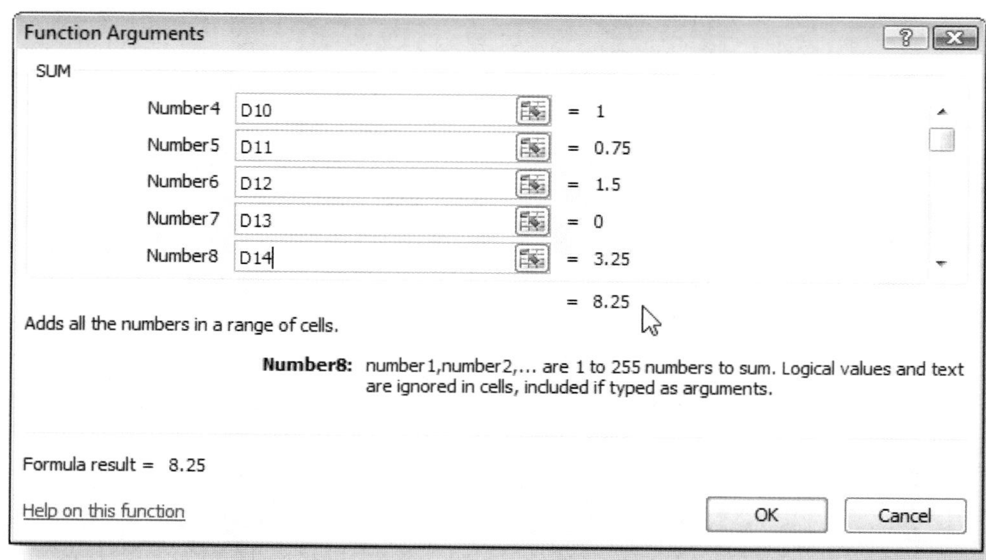

Figure 6-6
Function Arguments dialog box with cells entered separately

14. Press Enter. The dialog box closes; the result (8.25) is displayed in the cell.

Exercise 6-3 USE TRUNC

The TRUNC function removes the decimal part of a number or shows a certain number of decimal positions without adjusting the value.

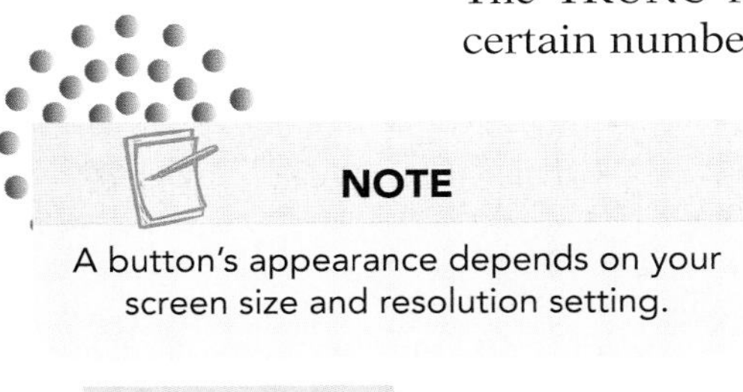

NOTE

A button's appearance depends on your screen size and resolution setting.

Math & Trig

1. Click cell E19. You are going to truncate the results in cell E18 to show no decimals.
2. Click the **Formulas** tab in the Ribbon.
3. In the **Function Library** group, click the Math & Trig button Math & Trig. The list of functions opens.

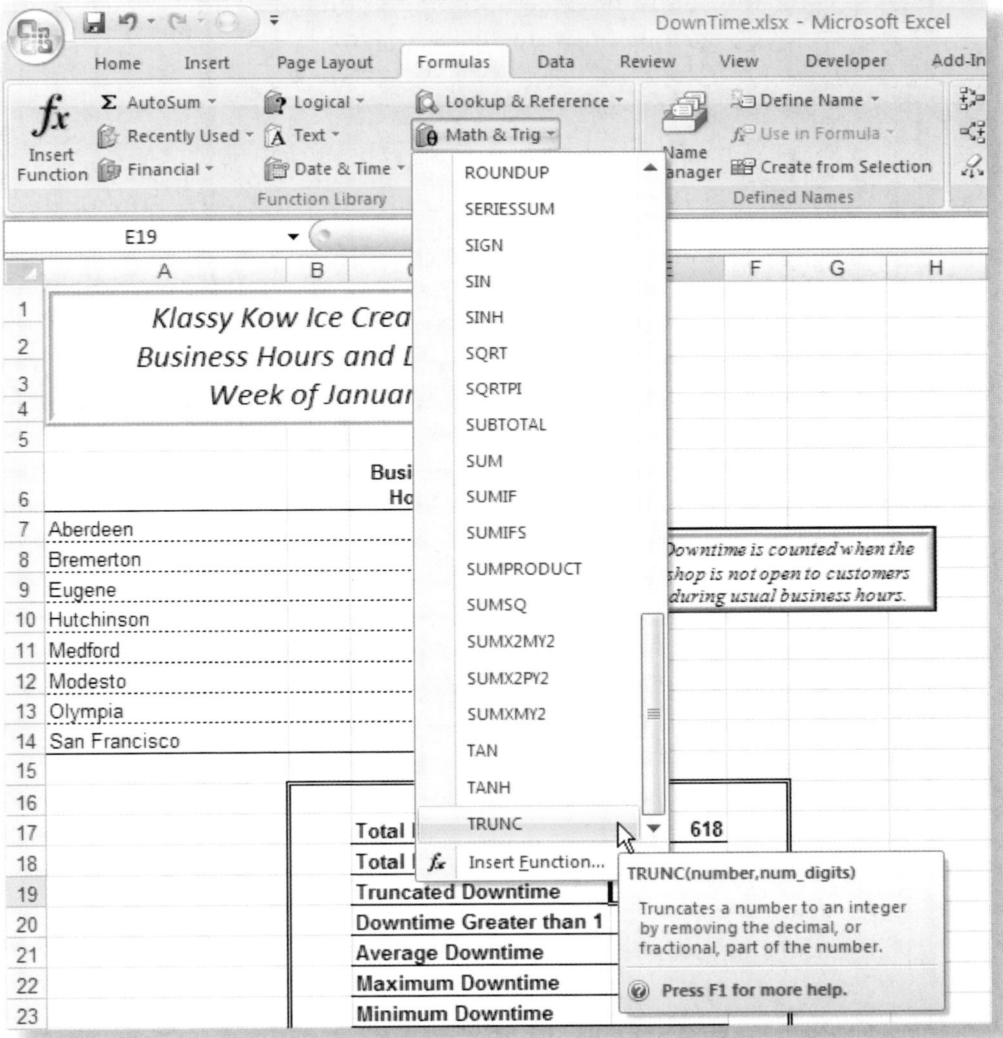

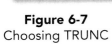

Figure 6-7
Choosing TRUNC

4. Scroll to find **TRUNC** and click. The TRUNC Function Arguments dialog box opens. The insertion point is in the **Number** box.
5. Click cell E18. Its address appears in the **Number** box.

6. Click in the **Num_digits** box. Key **0** to truncate the value to show no decimal positions.
7. Click **OK**. The truncated value of cell E18 is 8.

Exercise 6-4 USE SUMIF

The SUMIF function adds cell values only if they meet a condition. In this case, you will determine the total number of down hours for shops with downtime greater than one hour. The SUMIF function has two required arguments, Range and Criteria. The range is the group of cells to be added. The criteria is a condition that must be met for the cell to be included in the addition. The optional argument is Sum_range, which allows for additional limits on which cells to add.

1. Click cell E20. Click the **Formulas** tab.
2. Click the Math & Trig button Math & Trig .
3. Scroll to find **SUMIF** and click. The Function Arguments dialog box opens with the insertion point in the **Range** entry box.
4. Click cell D7 and drag to select the range D7:D14. As you drag, the dialog box collapses so that you can see your work better.
5. Release the mouse button. The dialog box expands, and the range you selected is entered in the **Range** box.
6. Click in the **Criteria** box. Key **>1** to set a rule that the value in the range D7:D14 be greater than 1 to be included in the sum.

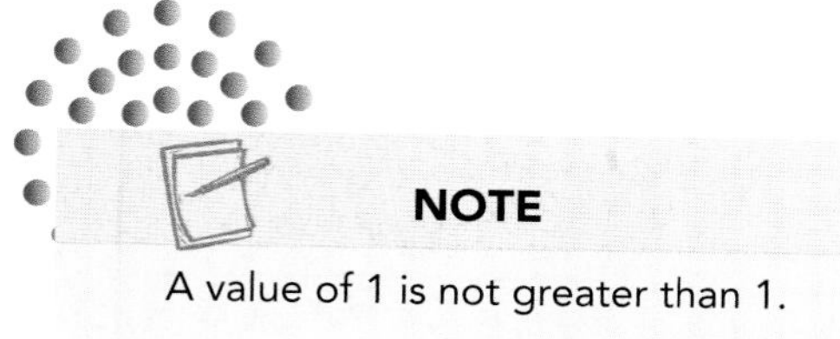

NOTE

A value of 1 is not greater than 1.

Function Arguments

SUMIF

Range D7:D14 = {0.5;1.25;0;1;0.75;1.5;0;3.25}

Criteria >1 =

Sum_range = reference

=

Adds the cells specified by a given condition or criteria.

Criteria is the condition or criteria in the form of a number, expression, or text that defines which cells will be added.

Formula result =

Help on this function OK Cancel

Figure 6-8
SUMIF function in the Function Arguments dialog box

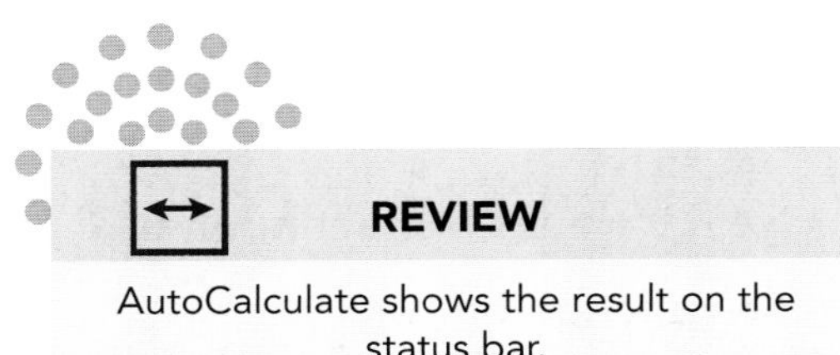

REVIEW

AutoCalculate shows the result on the status bar.

7. Click **OK**. The result is 6 because only the values in cells D8, D12, and D14 are totaled. You can verify this result with AutoCalculate.
8. Click cell D8. Hold down Ctrl and click cells D12 and then D14. These are values greater than 1. The sum appears in the status bar.
9. Click cell E20 and view the formula in the formula bar. The criteria has been inserted with quotation marks. Note that the values in cells E19 and E20 are not aligned.
10. Copy the format from cell E19 to cell E20 to adjust the alignment.

Using Statistical Functions

Another category of Excel functions is the Statistical group. Some of these functions are useful even if you are not a statistician.

Exercise 6-5 USE THE AVERAGE FUNCTION

The AVERAGE function calculates the arithmetic mean of a range of cells. The *arithmetic mean* adds the values in the cells and then divides by the number of values. The AVERAGE function ignores:

NOTE

A logical value is "True," "False," "Yes," or "No."

- Text
- Blank or empty cells (but not zeros)
- Error values such as #NAME?
- Logical values

TABLE 6-2 Examples of the AVERAGE Function

Function(argument/s)	Cell Data	Result
=AVERAGE(A1:A3)	A1=10, A2=20, A3=30	20
=AVERAGE(50,60)	None	55
=AVERAGE(A1,250)	A1=25	137.5
=AVERAGE(A1,B2,C1:C2)	A1=10, B2=20, C1=10, C2=30	17.5
=AVERAGE(A1, B2)	A1=25, B2="Ice Cream"	25
=AVERAGE(A1, B2)	A1=25, B2=#NAME?	25
=AVERAGE(A1:A3)	A1=20, A2=0, A3=TRUE	10
=AVERAGE(A1:A3)	A1=20, A2=Empty, A3=40	30

1. Right-click the row 21 row heading and choose **Insert**. A row is inserted.
2. Key **Average Business Hours** in cell C21.
3. Click cell E21. This cell should average the values from column C.

4. Click the **Formulas** tab. Click the Insert Function button.
5. Choose **Statistical** in the **Or select a category** list. In the **Select a function** list, locate **AVERAGE**.
6. Click **AVERAGE** to see its syntax and description. Click **OK**.
7. Move the dialog box until you can see column C. The **Number1** box shows the range directly above cell E21.
8. Click cell C7 and drag to select cells C7:C14 to reset the range.
9. Release the mouse button. The dialog box expands, and the range you selected is entered in the **Number1** box.
10. Click **OK**. The result is 77.25.

Exercise 6-6 USE AVERAGEIF

The AVERAGEIF function averages cell values only if they meet a condition. Like SUMIF, AVERAGEIF has two required arguments, Range and Criteria.

1. Click cell E22. Click the Insert Function button.
2. Choose **Statistical**. In the **Select a function** list, find **AVERAGEIF**.
3. Click **AVERAGEIF** and click **OK**. The Function Arguments dialog box opens with the insertion point in the **Range** entry box.
4. Click cell D7 and drag to select the range D7:D14.
5. Click in the **Criteria** box. Key **>0** to set a rule that the value in the range D7:D14 must be greater than 0 to be included in the average.
6. Click **OK**. The result is 1, formatted without any decimals.

7. Click the **Home** tab. Click the Increase Decimal button three times. The values are not properly aligned.
8. Press Ctrl+1 and click the **Number** tab. Click **General** and click **OK**.

Exercise 6-7 USE THE MIN AND MAX FUNCTIONS

MIN and MAX are statistical functions that show the minimum (smallest) value or the maximum (largest) value in a range. The MIN and MAX functions ignore:

- Text
- Blank or empty cells (but not zeros)
- Error values such as #NAME?
- Logical values

TABLE 6-3 Examples of the MIN and MAX Functions

Function(argument/s)	Cell Data	Result
=MAX(A1:A3)	A1=10, A2=20, A3=30	30
=MAX(50,60)	None	60
=MIN(A1,250)	A1=25	25
=MIN(A1,B2,C1:C2)	A1=10, B2=20, C1=10, C2=30	10
=MAX(A1, B2)	A1=25, B2="Ice Cream"	25
=MAX(A1, B2)	A1=25, B2=#NAME?	25
=MIN(A1:A3)	A1=20, A2=10, A3=FALSE	10
=MIN(A1:A3)	A1=20, A2=Empty, A3=40	20

1. Click cell E23.
2. Press Shift+F3. This shortcut opens the Insert Function dialog box.
3. Choose **Statistical** and **MAX**. In the Function Arguments dialog box, the **Number1** box shows the range directly above cell E23.
4. Select cells D7:D14 to determine the largest value from column D. The range is shown as **Number1**. Click **OK**. The maximum value is 3.25.
5. Click cell E24 and key **=min** to start the MIN function. Formula AutoComplete shows the function and its ScreenTip.

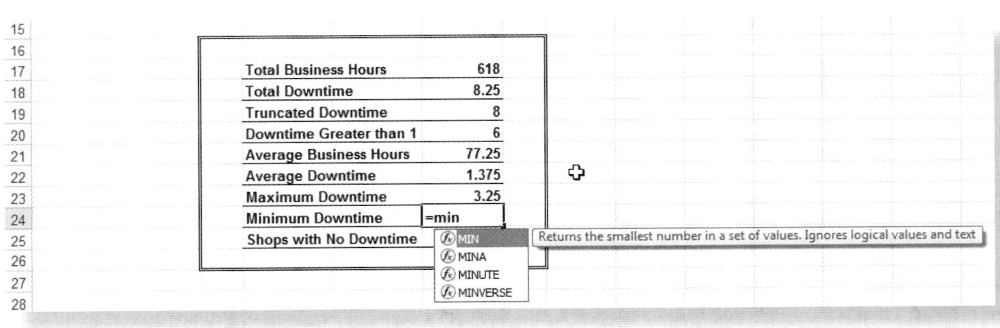

Figure 6-9
Formula AutoComplete and descriptive ScreenTip
DownTime.xlsx Jan15Plan sheet

6. Press Tab. The opening parenthesis is inserted.
7. Select cells D7:D14 and press Enter. The function does not ignore zeros, so the minimum value is zero.
8. Delete the contents of cells D9 and D13. The results in cell E24 are recalculated and some cells show error triangles because the formulas now refer to empty cells.

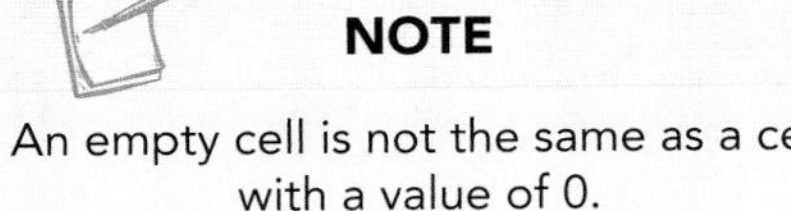

NOTE

An empty cell is not the same as a cell with a value of 0.

Exercise 6-8 USE COUNT AND COUNTBLANK

The COUNTBLANK function counts empty cells in a range. The COUNT function tallies the number of values in a range. The COUNT function ignores:

- Text
- Blank or empty cells (but not zeros)
- Error values such as #NAME?
- Logical values

TABLE 6-4 Examples of the COUNT Function

Function(argument/s)	Cell Data	Result
=COUNT(A1:A3)	A1=Empty, A2=20, A3=30	2
=COUNT(A1:A3)	A1=30, A2=Empty, A3=#NAME?	1
=COUNT(A1:A3)	A1=25, A2="Ice Cream," A3=3	2
=COUNT(13, 21, 111)	None	3
=COUNT(A1, B2, C1:C2)	A1=25, B2=0, C1="Hello," C2=4	3

1. Key **0** (zero) in cells D9 and D13. The results in cell E24 change.
2. Click cell E25 and click the **Home** tab. Click the Insert Function button [fx] in the formula bar.
3. Choose **Statistical** and **COUNT**. Click **OK**.
4. Select cells D7:D14. The range appears in the **Value1** box.
5. Click **OK**. The cells with zero (0) are included in the count.
6. Delete the contents of cells D9 and D13. The count tallies the cells with downtime. Blank cells are not included.
7. Edit the label in cell C25 to delete **No**.
8. Right-click the row heading for row 25 and insert a row.
9. Click cell E25 and click the Insert Function button [fx].
10. Choose **Statistical** and **COUNTBLANK**. Click **OK**. Select cells D7:D14. Click **OK**.
11. Key **Shops with No Downtime** in cell C25.
12. Insert a row at row 27. Key **Number of Shops** in cell C27.
13. Click cell E27, key **=count**, and press [Tab].
14. Drag to select cells A7:A14. The range is **value1** in the ScreenTip.

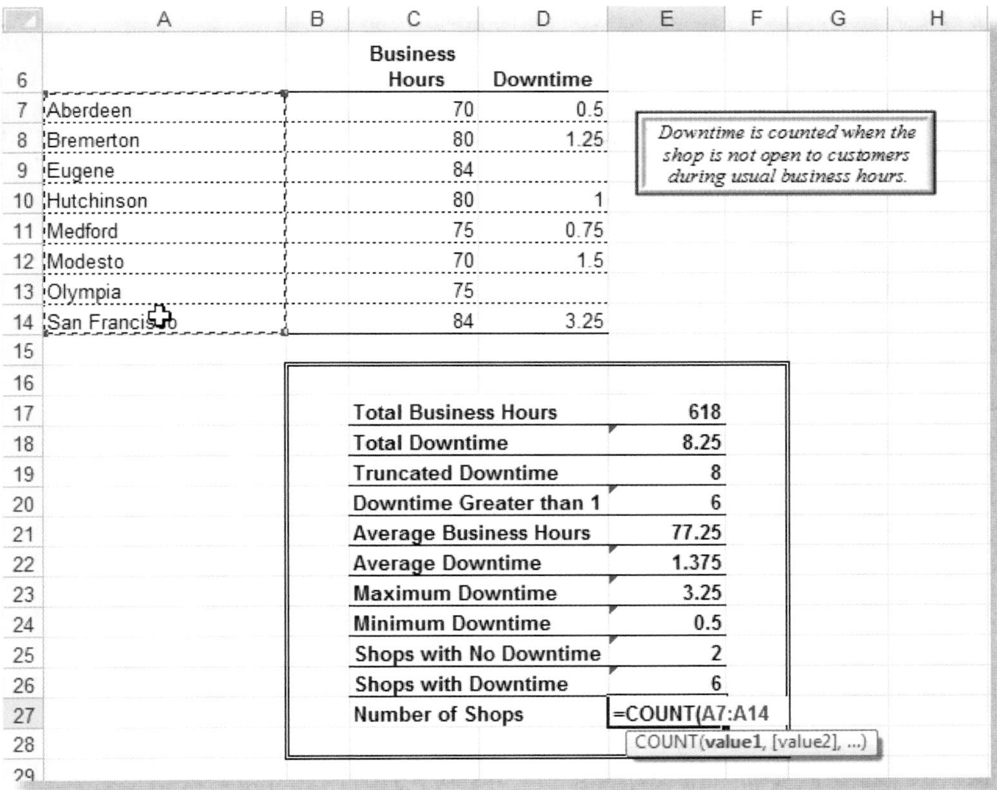

Figure 6-10
Keying the COUNT function
DownTime.xlsx
Jan15Plan sheet

15. Press Enter. The result is 0, because the COUNT function ignores text.

Exercise 6-9 USE THE COUNTA FUNCTION

The COUNTA function tallies values and labels. The COUNTA function ignores:

- Blank or empty cells (but not zeros)
- Error values such as #NAME?
- Logical values

TABLE 6-5 Examples of the COUNTA Function

Function(argument/s)	Cell Data	Result
=COUNTA(A1:A3)	A1=Empty, A2=20, A3=30	2
=COUNTA(A1:A3)	A1=30, A2=Empty, A3=#NAME?	1
=COUNTA(A1:A3)	A1=25, A2="Ice Cream," A3=3	3
=COUNTA(13, 21, 111)	None	3
=COUNTA(A1, B2, C1:C2)	A1=25, B2=0, C1="Hello," C2=TRUE	3

NOTE

The Count option in AutoCalculate shows the same results as the COUNTA function. AutoCalculate's Numerical Count option shows the same results as the COUNT function.

1. Double-click cell E27.
2. Position the insertion point and key **a** after **COUNT**.
3. Press Enter. The new function COUNTA includes labels; there are eight shops in the list.
4. Add a bottom border to the data in row 27.
5. Save the workbook as ***[your initials]*6-9** in a folder for Lesson 6.

Using Icon Sets

Data visualizations are simple conditional formatting rules. They use data bars, color scales, and icon sets. An icon set consists of three to five icons that appear in a range of cells based on the value in the cell.

Exercise 6-10 APPLY ICON SETS

1. With ***[your initials]*6-9** open, click the **Home** tab.
2. Select cells D7:D14. In the **Styles** group, click the Conditional Formatting button.

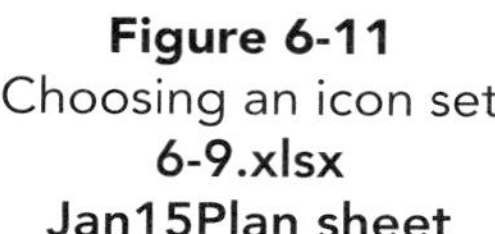

3. Hover at **Icon Sets**. A gallery opens with the available styles.
4. Hover at several sets to see the results. Live Preview displays the icon sets before you apply them.

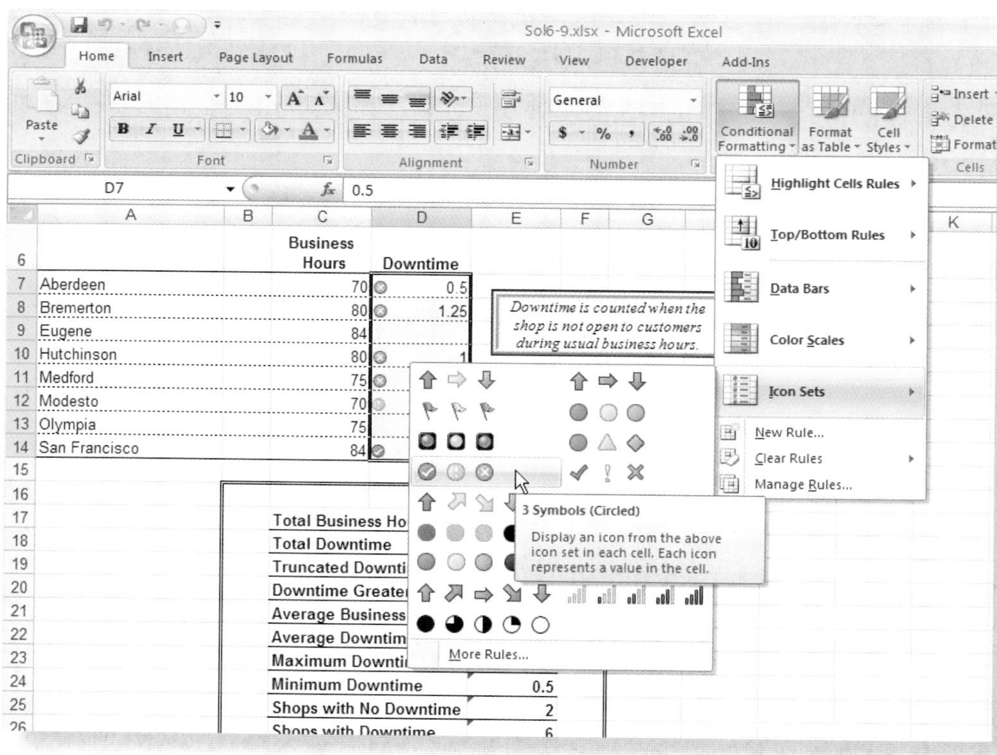

Figure 6-11
Choosing an icon set
6-9.xlsx
Jan15Plan sheet

5. Choose **3 Symbols (Circled)** in the first column. The icons appear at the left edge of the cell. The highest value has the green check mark.

Exercise 6-11 EDIT THE ICON FORMATTING RULE

1. Select cells D7:D14 and click the Conditional Formatting button.
2. Choose **Manage Rules**. The icon set is listed in the Conditional Formatting Rules Manager dialog box.
3. Click **Edit Rule**. The Edit Formatting Rule dialog box includes options that you can edit for this rule.
4. Click the arrow with **Percent** for the first icon. Choose **Number**. This will set the rule to use a specific value rather than a percent.
5. Change the **Type** for the second icon to **Number**.
6. Click to select **Reverse Icon Order**. This will set the rule to show the green check mark for the lowest value.
7. Key **10** in the **Value** box for the first icon (red X). There are no values greater than or equal to 10 in your list, so this icon won't be shown at all.
8. Key **1** in the **Value** box for the second icon (yellow exclamation point).

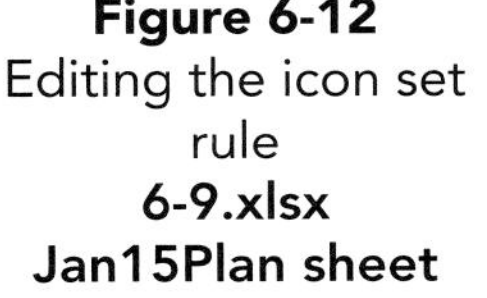

Figure 6-12
Editing the icon set rule
6-9.xlsx
Jan15Plan sheet

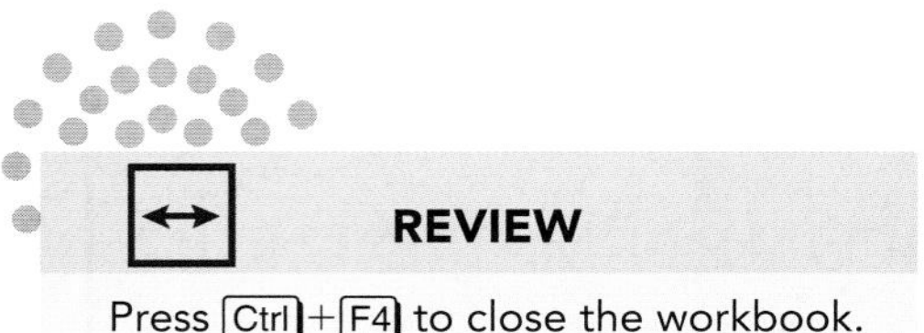

REVIEW

Press Ctrl+F4 to close the workbook.

9. Click **OK**. Click **OK** again. Empty cells are not formatted; they have no value.
10. Key **0** in cells D9 and D13. The icons are inserted.
11. Press Ctrl+Home. Save the workbook as ***[your initials]*6-11** in your folder. Close the workbook.

Grouping Worksheets

An Excel workbook can have as many worksheets as your machine's memory allows. Multiple sheets enable you to separate related data when necessary but have it available for managing information. When you work with multiple sheets, you can group the sheets to edit or format them as a group.

TIP

Some tasks do not work on grouped sheets. For example, you cannot add data visualizations (data bars, color scales, icon sets) to grouped sheets.

Exercise 6-12 GROUP AND DELETE WORKSHEETS

When worksheets are grouped, editing and formatting commands affect all sheets in the group. This is an efficient way to make changes to several worksheets at once, as long as the sheets are identical.

NOTE

The **CSCalls** template file should be copied to the appropriate Templates folder on your computer.

1. Choose the Microsoft Office Button and choose **New**. Choose **My templates** in the New Workbook dialog box.
2. Choose **CSCalls** and click **OK**.
3. Click the **Sheet2** tab, hold down Ctrl, and click the **Sheet3** tab. Both worksheets are selected or active. The word **[Group]** appears in the title bar. The tabs appear more white.

Figure 6-13
Grouped worksheets
CSCalls.xltx

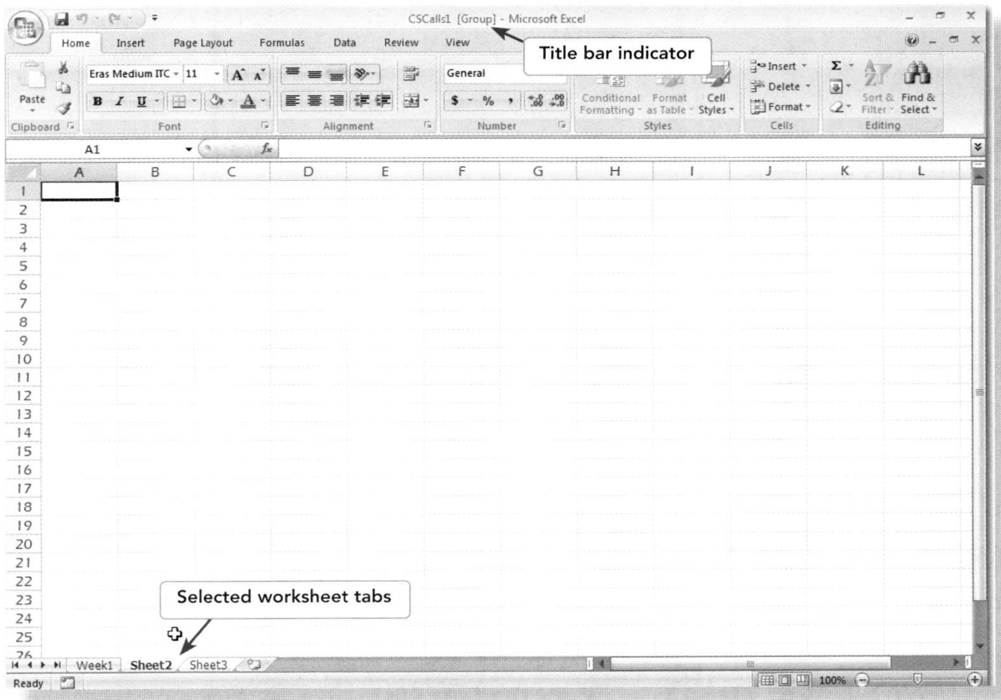

TIP

You can ungroup sheets by clicking a sheet that is not in the group or by right-clicking a sheet in the group and choosing Ungroup Sheets.

4. Click the **Week1** tab. Selecting a tab outside the group ungroups the sheets.
5. Click **Sheet2**, hold down Ctrl, and click **Sheet3** again.
6. Right-click either tab in the group and choose **Delete**. Both sheets are deleted.

Exercise 6-13 MANAGE WORKSHEETS

When you copy a worksheet with the Move or Copy dialog box, formatting and data are included.

1. Right-click the **Week1** tab. Choose **Move or Copy**. The **To book** list includes the names of open workbooks as well as a new book. The **Before sheet** list allows you to move or copy the sheet to a specific location in the tabs.
2. Select **(move to end)** in the **Before sheet** list.
3. Click to select **Create a copy**.
4. Click **OK**. The new worksheet named **Week1 (2)** is an exact duplicate of the **Week1** sheet.

NOTE

If you do not select **Create a copy**, the worksheet is moved.

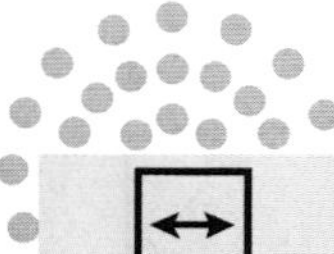

REVIEW

You can double-click or right-click a sheet tab to rename it.

5. Rename **Week1 (2)** tab as **Week2**.
6. Make two more copies of the **Week1** sheet and name them **Week3** and **Week4**.
7. Click the **Week1** tab and press Shift+F11. A blank worksheet is inserted in front of (to the left of) the **Week1** sheet. New sheet numbers start at the next available number in the workbook.
8. Rename the new sheet as **FirstQuarter**.
9. Right-click the **FirstQuarter** tab and choose **Move or Copy**. Choose **(move to end)** and click **OK**. This moves the sheet without making a copy.
10. Choose a different accent color for each tab.
11. Save the workbook as **[your initials]6-13** in your Lesson 6 folder.

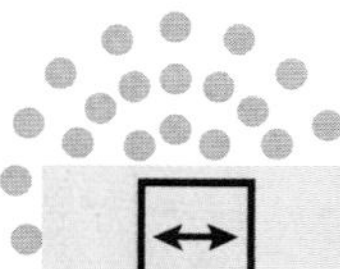

REVIEW

You can insert a sheet by right-clicking a worksheet tab and choosing Insert or by clicking the Insert Worksheet tab.

Using Date and Time Functions

Date and time functions can be used to display the current date and time, determine ages, and calculate hours worked, days passed, and future dates.

With dates and times, Excel uses a *serial number* system. A serial number is a date shown as a value. Excel's date system numbers January 1, 1900, as 1 and January 2, 1900, as 2; it assigns a number to every date up to December 31, 9999.

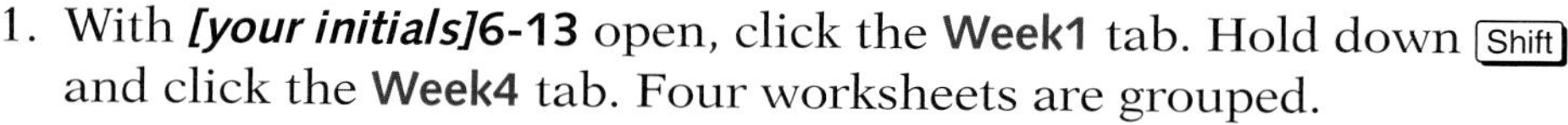

Exercise 6-14 USE THE TODAY() FUNCTION

The TODAY() function displays the current date, using the computer's clock. This function has no arguments, and Excel formats the results in a standard date style. The TODAY() function is *volatile,* which means that the formula results depend on the computer on which the workbook is opened.

1. With ***[your initials]*6-13** open, click the **Week1** tab. Hold down Shift and click the **Week4** tab. Four worksheets are grouped.
2. Click cell A3. Key **=today()** and press Enter. The current date is inserted. The ##### symbols indicate that the column is not wide enough to show the date in the current font size.
3. Click cell A3 and look in the formula bar. Excel capitalizes function names after you complete the cell.
4. Press Ctrl+1 and click the **Number** tab. In the **Category** list, choose **General**. The sample box shows the serial number for today.

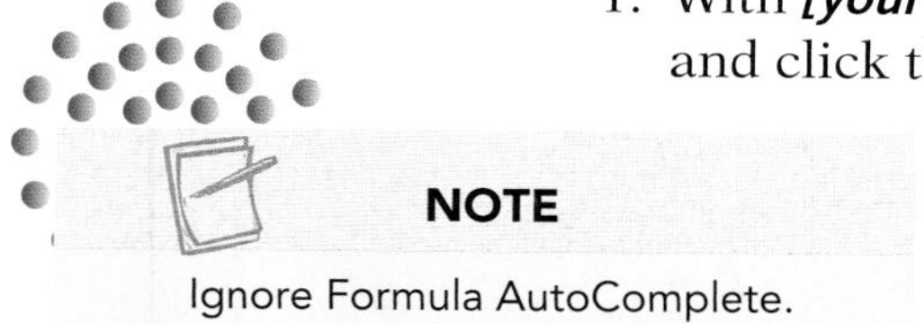

NOTE

Ignore Formula AutoComplete.

5. Click **OK**. The serial number that represents today's date is shown.
6. Click the Undo button. The format change is reversed.
7. Press Ctrl+1 and click the **Alignment** tab.
8. In the **Text control** group, click to select **Shrink to fit**.
9. Click **OK**. The display date is sized to fit the column width, but the font size still shows the original size.

Exercise 6-15 KEY AND FORMAT DATES

When you key a date, Excel assigns the closest matching date format to the date you key. The resulting format may not match what you key. You can, however, use one of many built-in date formats or create your own format.

TABLE 6-6 Sample Keyed Dates and Initial Screen Display

Keyed Characters	Screen Display
1-1-08	1/1/2008
1/1/08	1/1/2008
1-jan-08	1-Jan-08
january 1, 2008	1-Jan-08
jan 1, 2008	1-Jan-08

NOTE

Remember that four worksheets are grouped.

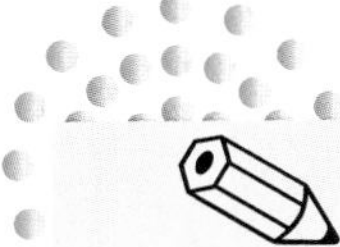

TIP

While keying a date, you generally do not need to capitalize months; Excel will do so automatically.

1. In cell A5, key **01/01/08** and press Enter. The date is formatted without leading zeros and shows the year with four digits.
2. In cell A6, key **1-jan-08** and press Enter. The format matches what you keyed.
3. In cell A7, key **january 1, 2008** and press Enter.
4. In cell A8, key **1-1-08** and press Enter.
5. Select cells A5:A8. Press Ctrl+1.
6. Click the **Number** tab and choose **Date** in the **Category** list.
7. Choose **March 14, 2001** in the **Type** list.
8. Click **OK**. Widen column A. All the dates are formatted in the same style.

9. Click cell A3.
10. Right-click the **Week4** tab. The **Week4** sheet becomes the active sheet.
11. Choose **Ungroup Sheets**. The **Week4** worksheet shows the dates.
12. Click the **Week1** tab, then the **Week2** tab, then the **Week3** tab. All sheets have the same formatting and data.

Exercise 6-16 USE FILL ACROSS WORKSHEETS

Another way to copy selected data from one worksheet to another is the Fill Across Worksheets command. To use this command, you first select the worksheet with the data and the one(s) where the data should be copied.

1. Click the **FirstQuarter** tab. This is the blank sheet you inserted.
2. Click the **Week4** tab.
3. Hold down the Ctrl key and click the **FirstQuarter** worksheet tab. The title bar shows **[Group]**.
4. On the **Week4** sheet, select cells A1:D8. These are the cells that will be copied to the **FirstQuarter** sheet.

5. On the **Home** tab, click the Fill button in the **Editing** group. Its submenu opens.
6. Choose **Across Worksheets**. The Fill Across Worksheets dialog box has options to copy everything, only the data, or only the formatting.

Figure 6-14
Using Fill Across Worksheets
6-13.xlsx
Week4 sheet

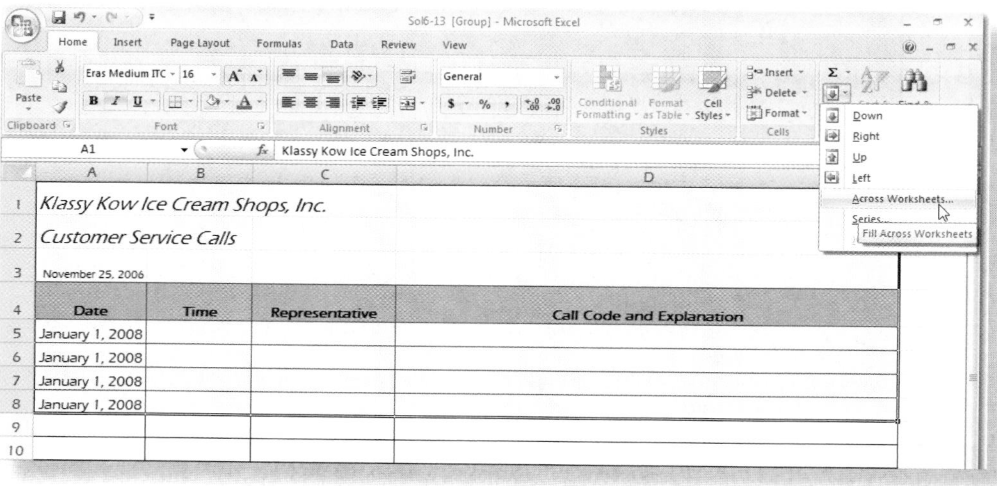

7. Choose All and click OK.
8. Right-click the **Week4** worksheet tab. Choose Ungroup Sheets.
9. Click the **FirstQuarter** worksheet tab. The data and some formatting have been copied. Column widths and row heights are not copied.
10. Make columns A:C 12.56 (120 pixels) wide. Make column D 57.56 (525 pixels) wide.
11. Make row 4 30.00 (30 pixels) tall. Make rows 5:8 18.75 (25 pixels) tall.

Exercise 6-17 CREATE A CUSTOM DATE FORMAT

To create your own date format, you key formatting codes in the Custom category. You can see formatting codes and samples in the Format Cells dialog box.

1. Select cells A5:A8 and press Ctrl+1.
2. Click the Number tab and choose Date in the Category list.
3. Scroll through the Type list. There is no preset format to show the date, the month spelled out, and a two-digit year (14 March 01).
4. Click Custom in the Category list. The Type list shows the codes for a variety of formats, not just dates. You can choose one as a starting point to build your own format.
5. Scroll the Type list to find d-mmm.
6. Click the code to select it. The Sample box shows the date with that format.
7. Click in the Type box above the Type list.
8. Delete the hyphen and press Spacebar.
9. Edit the code to show dd mmmm y. Two **dd**'s show the date with a leading zero. Four **mmmm**'s spell out the month. A single **y** shows a two-digit year.
10. Look at the Sample box.

Figure 6-15
Creating a custom date format

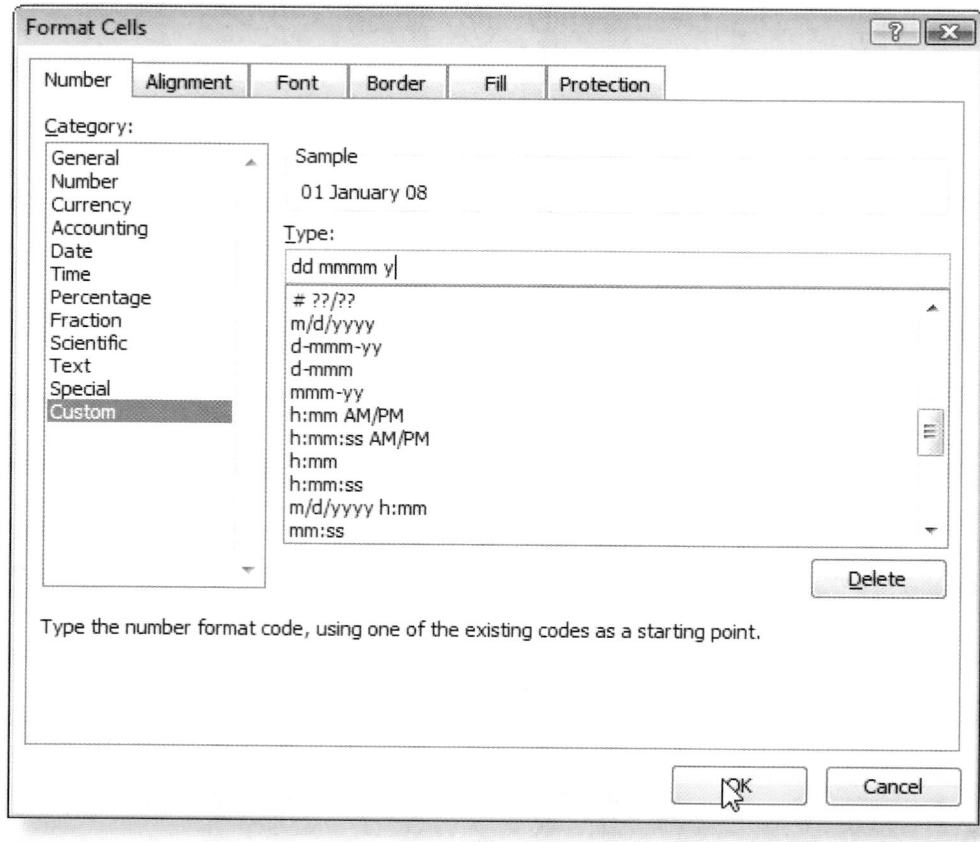

11. Click **OK**. The dates are reformatted. Widen the column if necessary.

Exercise 6-18 KEY AND FORMAT TIMES

TIP

It does not matter which worksheet is on top when you edit data in grouped worksheets.

1. Click the **Week1** tab. Hold down Shift and click the **Week4** tab. Four worksheets are grouped.
2. Click cell B5 and key **11 am**.
3. Press Ctrl+Enter. The time is shown and AM is capitalized.
4. Look in the formula bar to see minutes and seconds.
5. Click cell B6 and key **4:30** and press Ctrl+Enter.
6. Look at the time in the formula bar. If you do not key **am** or **pm**, Excel assumes morning.
7. In cell B7 key **4:30 pm** and press Enter.
8. In cell B8 key **13:30** and press Enter. Excel shows the time using the 24-hour clock.

9. In cell B9 key **2:45 pm**, and in cell B10 key **14:30**.
10. Select cells B5:B10.
11. Press Ctrl+1. Click the **Number** tab and choose **Time** in the **Category** list.
12. Scroll the **Type** list. Then choose **1:30 PM** and click **OK**.

Exercise 6-19 USE THE NOW() FUNCTION

The NOW() function is similar to the TODAY() function. It uses the computer's clock to show the current date and time.

1. Click cell A11. Key **=now(** and press Enter. Excel supplies the closing parenthesis.
2. Widen the column as needed. The default format may not include the time.
3. Click cell A11 and press Ctrl+1.
4. Click the **Number** tab and choose **Time** in the **Category** list.
5. Scroll through the **Type** list. Then choose **3/14/01 1:30 PM** and click **OK**. The function shows the current date and time.

Exercise 6-20 CREATE A CUSTOM TIME FORMAT

1. Click cell A11 and press Ctrl+1.
2. Click **Custom** in the **Category** list.
3. Scroll the **Type** list to find **m/d/yyyy h:mm**.
4. Click the code to select it. The **Sample** box shows the date and time with that format.
5. Click in the **Type** box before the first **m**.
6. Edit the code to show **mmm d, yyyy- -h:mm AM/PM**. Be sure to insert the spaces, the comma, and the hyphens. Check the **Sample** box to verify your format as you build it.

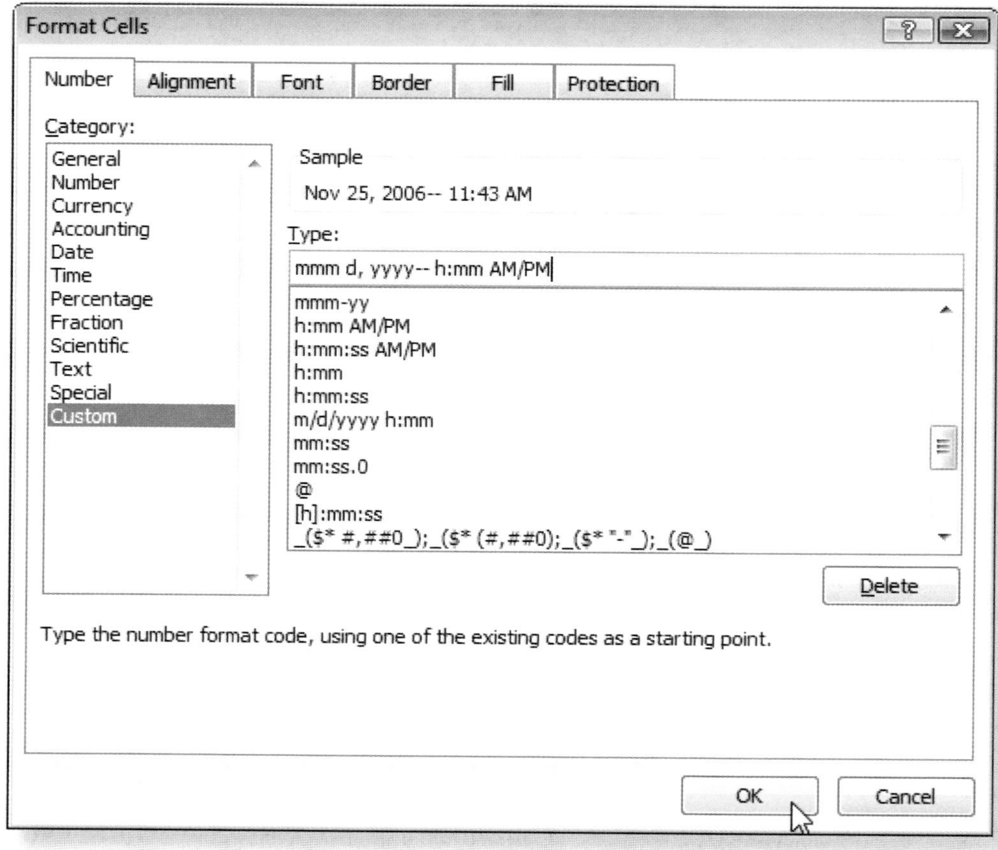

Figure 6-16
Creating a custom time format

7. Click the **Alignment** tab. In the **Text control** group, click to select **Shrink to fit**.
8. Click **OK**. The time is reformatted and shrunk.
9. Right-click any sheet and choose **Ungroup Sheets**.

Exercise 6-21 ADD A HEADER TO GROUPED SHEETS

You can add the same header or footer to all sheets in a group through the Page Setup dialog box. You can also center the sheets at the same time.

1. Click the **Week1** tab. Hold down Shift and click the **FirstQuarter** tab.
2. Click the **Page Layout** tab. Click the Dialog Box Launcher for the **Page Setup** group. The Page Setup dialog box opens.
3. Click the **Header/Footer** tab. Click **Custom Header**. The Header dialog box includes the usual three sections.
4. Key your name in the left section.
5. Click in the center and click the Insert Sheet Name button. Click in the right section and click the Insert Date button.

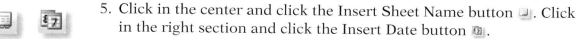

Figure 6-17
Adding a header in the Header dialog box

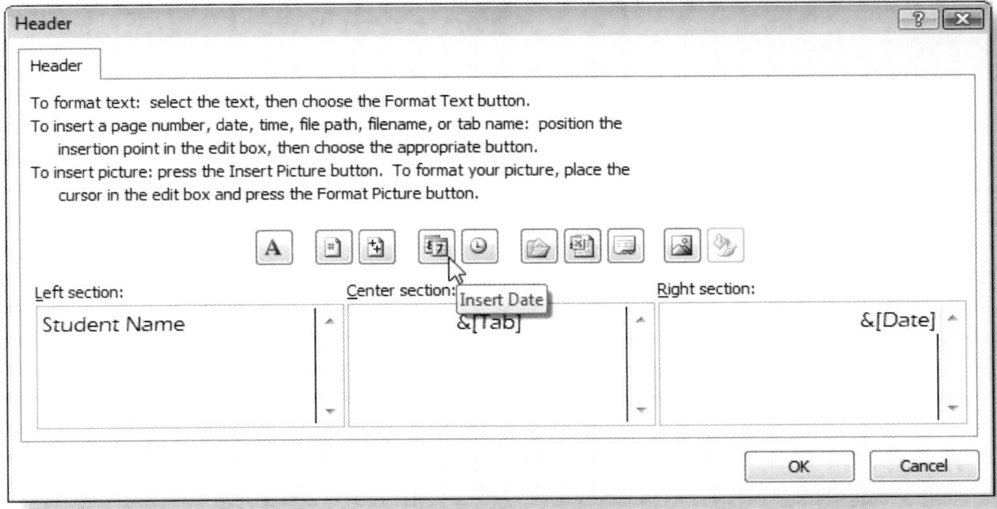

6. Click **OK**. The Page Setup dialog box includes a preview of your header.
7. Click the **Margins** tab. In the **Center on page** group, click to select **Horizontally**.
8. Click **Print Preview** in the **Page Setup** dialog box. This is the first page of five.
9. Press PageDown to see the next sheet. Press PageUp to return to previous pages.

TIP

A workbook is saved with the sheets grouped.

10. Click **Close Print Preview**.
11. Save the workbook as ***[your initials]*6-21** in your folder.
12. Click the Microsoft Office Button. Choose **Print** and then **Quick Print** while the worksheets are grouped. All five sheets print with the same header.
13. Close the workbook.

Using Online Help

USE HELP TO VIEW ADDITIONAL INFORMATION ABOUT FORMAT CODES

1. In a new workbook, press F1.
2. In the Search box, key **format codes** and press Enter.
3. Find and review topics to learn more about format codes. Read the help information.
4. Close the Help window.

Lesson 6 Summary

- Excel has several categories of date, time, mathematical, and statistical functions. You can key them or use the Insert Function dialog box.
- When you key a function name, Formula AutoComplete displays a list of functions that match your keystrokes.
- Functions have a syntax that must be followed. The syntax includes an equal sign, the name of the function, and arguments inside parentheses.
- The SUM function adds the values of the cells indicated in its argument.
- The TRUNC function removes the decimal part of a number.
- The AVERAGE function calculates the arithmetic mean.
- The SUMIF and the AVERAGEIF functions add and average values only if they meet the criteria specified in the argument.
- The MIN function displays the smallest value in a range. The MAX function displays the largest value in a range.
- The COUNT function counts the number of values in a range. The COUNTA function does the same and includes labels. COUNTBLANK counts empty cells in a range.
- The TODAY and NOW functions show the current date and time. Both functions can be formatted using preset or custom formats.
- An icon set is a data visualization that displays an icon at the left edge of the cell based on the value.
- Icon sets can use three, four, or five icons to represent the values.
- Copy selected data from one worksheet to another using the Fill Across Worksheets command.
- You can group multiple worksheets to edit, format, or print several sheets at once.
- Use the Page Setup dialog box to add a footer or header to grouped sheets.

LESSON 6		Command Summary	
Feature	**Button**	**Task Path**	**Keyboard**
Custom format	Format	Home, Cells, Format, Format Cells	Ctrl+1
Custom header/footer		Page Layout, Page Setup, Dialog Box Launcher	
Fill across worksheets		Home, Editing, Fill	
Icon set	Conditional Formatting	Home, Styles, Conditional Formatting	
Insert Function	fx		Shift+F3
Insert Function	fx Insert Function	Formulas, Function Library	Shift+F3

Lesson 7

Using Logical and Financial Functions

OBJECTIVES

After completing this lesson, you will be able to:

1. Use the IF function.
2. Use the AND, OR, and NOT functions.
3. Work with cell styles.
4. Work with page breaks.
5. Use the PMT and FV functions.
6. Use the Depreciation functions.

MCAS OBJECTIVES

In this lesson:
XL07 2.3.1
XL07 2.3.3
XL07 3.1
XL07 3.6.1
XL07 5.5
XL07 5.5.2
XL07 5.5.4

Estimated Time: $1^1/_2$ hours

A *logical function* is a formula that calculates if an expression is true. There are seven logical functions: AND, FALSE, IF, IFERROR, NOT, OR, and TRUE. Except for the IF and IFERROR functions, a logical function shows the word "TRUE" or "FALSE" as a result.

A *financial function* performs a business calculation that involves money. These include how to figure loan payments and how to determine depreciation.

Using the IF Function

The IF function is a simple analysis and decision-making tool. When working with accounts receivable, for example, you can determine if a late fee should be assessed.

The IF function has three arguments. It follows the form "If X, then Y; otherwise Z." X, Y, and Z represent the arguments.

The syntax for the IF function is:

=IF(logical_test, value_if_true, value_if_false)
Example: =IF(C5>50,C5*2, "None")

- Logical_test is the first argument, the condition. It's a statement or expression that is either true or false. In the example, the expression C5>50 is either true or false, depending on the value in cell C5.
- Value_if_true, the second argument, is what the formula shows if the logical_test is true. In the example, if C5 is greater than 50, the value in cell C5 is multiplied by 2. The value_if_true can be a formula, a value, text, or a cell reference.
- Value_if_false, the third argument, is what the formula shows if the logical_test is not true. The value_if_false can be a formula, a value, text, or a cell reference. In the example, if the value in cell C5 is 50 or less, the result is the word "None."

Exercise 7-1 USE IF TO SHOW TEXT

You can create an IF function to display text. When you use the Function Arguments dialog box, Excel inserts quotation marks around text in an IF function. When you key an IF function, you must key quotation marks.

IF functions can use relational or comparison operators as well as the arithmetic operators.

TABLE 7-1 Relational (Comparison) Operators

Operator	Description
=	Equal to
<>	Not equal to
>	Greater than
<	Less than
>=	Greater than or equal to
<=	Less than or equal to

1. Open **BonusPay** and click cell C4. If a salesperson sells more than $60,000 in goods, this cell should display "Yes."
2. Click the **Formulas** tab.
3. Click the Logical button 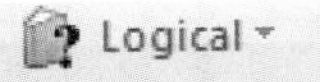.
4. Choose **IF** in the list. The insertion point is in the **Logical_test** box.
5. Click cell B4. The address appears in the **Logical_test** box.
6. Key **>60000** in the **Logical_test** box after **B4**. This logical test will determine if the value in cell B4 is greater than 60000.
7. Click in the **Value_if_true** box.

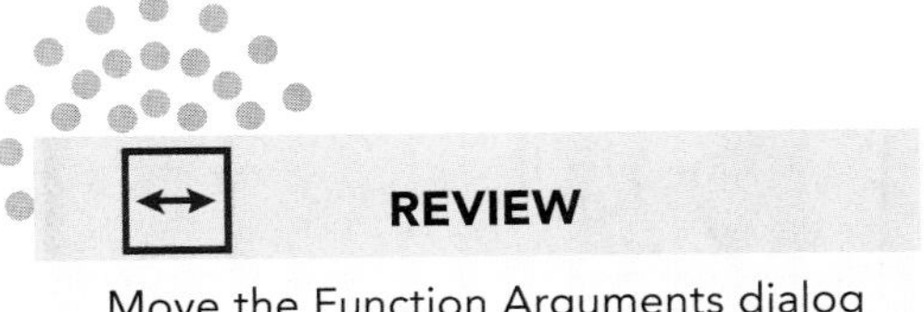

REVIEW

Move the Function Arguments dialog box so that you can see the cells you want to click.

8. Key **Yes**. If the value in cell B4 is greater than 60000, cell C4 will display the word "Yes."
9. Click in the **Value_if_false** box. Note the quotation marks for "Yes."
10. Key **No**. If the value in cell B4 is not greater than 60000, cell C4 will display the word "No."

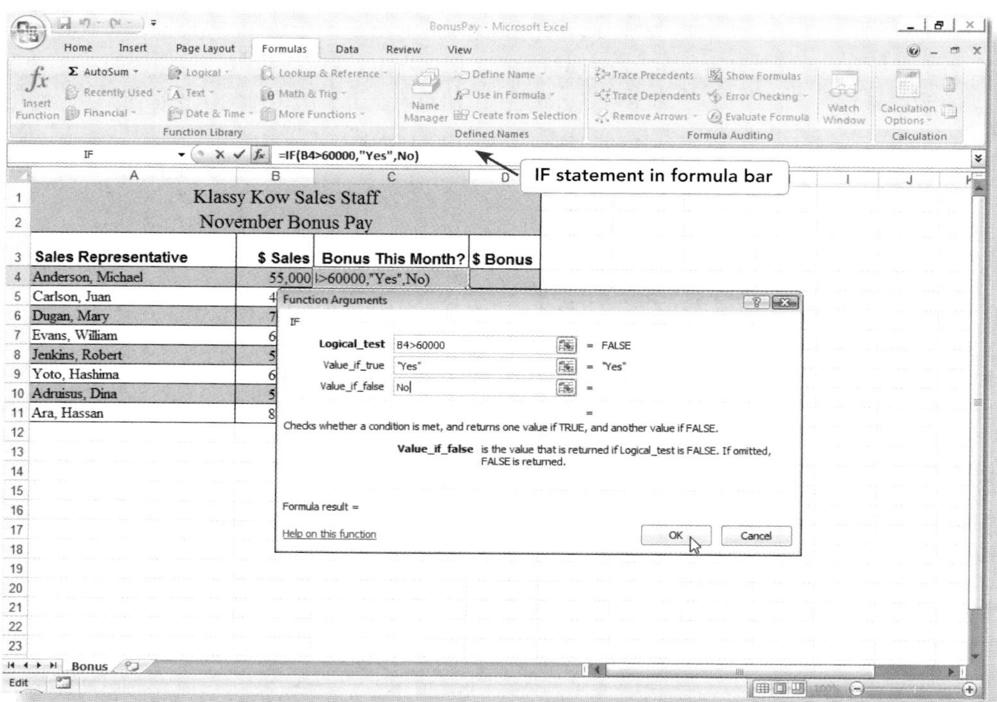

Figure 7-1
Function Arguments dialog box for IF
BonusPay.xlsx
Bonus sheet

11. Click **OK**. The result of this IF formula for cell C4 is **No**.
12. Look at the formula in the formula bar. You can see the quotation marks for **No** now.

13. Click the **Home** tab and then the Center button. Copy the formula to cells C5:C11. Formatting is copied with the formula.

14. Click the Undo button. Press Esc if you see a marquee.
15. Click cell C4 and press Ctrl+C.
16. Select cells C5:C11 and right-click one of the selected cells.
17. Choose **Paste Special**. Choose **Formulas** and click **OK**.
18. Click the Center button for the selected range.

Exercise 7-2 USE IF TO CALCULATE A VALUE

Excel can calculate the bonus if a salesperson is eligible. In this case, the bonus will be 2.5% of the sales value.

1. Click cell D4. Key **=if** to see the Formula AutoComplete list.
2. Press Tab. The ScreenTip displays the syntax for the function, and the argument to be keyed next is bold.
3. Click cell C4. A marquee appears around the cell, and the address appears after the left parenthesis. This starts the **Logical_test**.

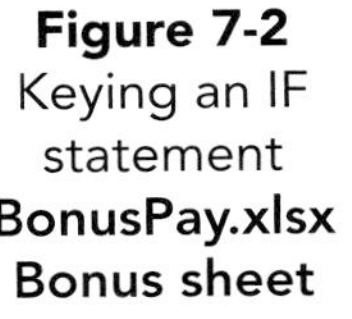

NOTE

When you key text as part of the Logical_test, you must include quotation marks.

4. Key **="yes"** after **C4**. This logical test will determine if cell C4 shows "Yes." Text in a logical test is not case-sensitive.
5. Key a comma after **"yes"** to separate the logical test from the value_if_true. **Value_if_true** in the ScreenTip is bold.
6. Click cell B4. A marquee appears around the cell, and the address appears after the comma.
7. Key ***2.5%** after **B4**. The formula multiplies the value in cell B4 by 2.5% if cell C4 shows "Yes." This is what the function will do if the test is true (C4 does show "yes").
8. Key a comma after **2.5%** to separate the value_if_true from the value_if_false. Value_if_false in the ScreenTip is bold.
9. Key **""** (two quotation marks with nothing between them). This represents no text, or nothing. If cell C4 does not show "Yes," cell D4 will show nothing. It will be blank.

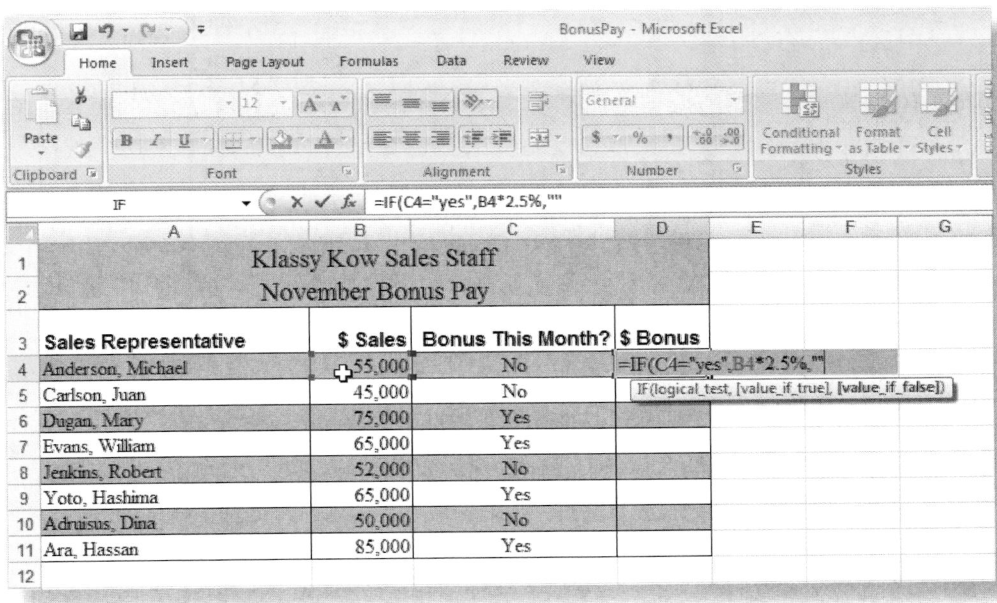

Figure 7-2
Keying an IF statement
BonusPay.xlsx
Bonus sheet

10. Press Enter. Excel added the closing right parenthesis for you. Cell D4 shows nothing, because this sales rep does not receive a bonus.
11. Click cell D4 and press Ctrl+C.
12. Select cells D5:D11 and right-click. Choose **Paste Special**. Choose **Formulas** and click **OK**. Press Esc to remove the marquee.
13. Select cells D4:D11 and click the Comma Style button.
14. Click the Decrease Decimal button two times.
15. Add a footer and save the workbook ***[your initials]*7-2** in a folder for Lesson 7. Close the workbook.

Using AND, OR, and NOT Functions

AND, OR, and NOT are logical functions that show either "TRUE" or "FALSE" as a result. These functions ignore labels and empty cells, so you use them only with values (numbers).

Exercise 7-3 USE THE AND FUNCTION

In an AND function, you can use multiple logical tests. All tests or expressions must be true for the result cell to show TRUE. Otherwise, it shows FALSE.

TABLE 7-2 Examples of the AND Function

Expression	Result
AND(C4>10, D4>10)	TRUE if both C4 and D4 are greater than 10; FALSE if either C4 or D4 is 10 or less.
AND(C4>10, C4<100)	TRUE if C4 is greater than 10 but less than 100; FALSE if C4 is 10 or less than 10 or 100 or greater than 100.
AND(C4>10, D4<10)	TRUE if C4 is greater than 10 and D4 is less than 10; FALSE if C4 is equal to or less than 10 or if D4 is equal to or greater than 10.
AND(C4=10, D4<100)	TRUE if C4 is equal to 10 and D4 is less than 100; FALSE if C4 is equal to any value except 10.

1. Open **CustCount**.
2. In cell J3, key **All Over 150 on** and hold down Alt and press Enter.
3. Key **on Weekend?** and press Enter.
4. Make the label bold. Make row 3 **30.00 (40 pixels)** tall. AutoFit the column.

5. Click cell J4. Click the **Formulas** tab.
6. Click the Logical button [Logical]. Choose **AND** in the list. The insertion point is in the **Logical1** box.
7. Click cell G4. The address appears in the **Logical1** box.
8. Key > in the **Logical1** box after **G4**.
9. Key **150** but don't press [Enter]. This test will determine if the value in cell G4 is greater than 150.
10. Click in the **Logical2** box. Click cell H4 and key **>150**. The second condition is that the value in cell H4 be greater than 150.
11. Click in the **Logical3** box. Click cell I4 and key **>150**. The third condition is that the value in cell I4 be greater than 150.

NOTE

If you click OK or press [Enter] before completing arguments in the Function Arguments dialog box, click either Insert Function button.

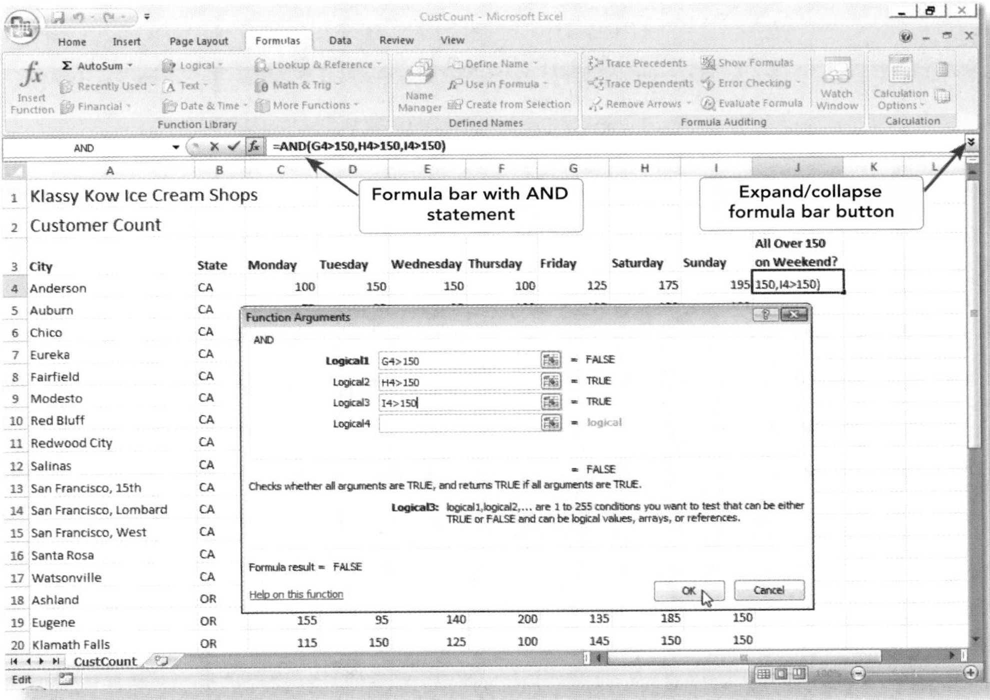

Figure 7-3
Function Arguments dialog box for AND
CustCount.xlsx
CustCount sheet

12. Click **OK**. The customer count must be greater than 150 each weekend day to show TRUE; it's not. Look at the formula in the formula bar.
13. Copy the formula to cells J5:J35. Only weekends in which all three days had greater than 150 customers show TRUE (Las Vegas Green Street, Reno, and Olympia). A day's count equal to 150 is not greater than 150.

TIP

Change the Zoom size to see more on screen at once.

Exercise 7-4 USE THE OR FUNCTION

In an OR function, any one of your logical tests can be true for the result cell to show TRUE. If they are all false, the result is FALSE.

TABLE 7-3 Examples of the OR Function

Expression	Result
OR(C4>10, D4>10)	TRUE if either C4 or D4 is greater than 10; FALSE only if both C4 and D4 are less than or equal to 10.
OR(C4>10, D4<100)	TRUE if C4 is greater than 10 or if D4 is less than 100; FALSE only if C4 is equal to or less than 10 and if D4 is equal to or greater than 100.
OR(C4>10, D4=10)	TRUE if C4 is greater than 10 or if D4 is equal to 10; FALSE if C4 is equal to or less than 10 and if D4 is any value other than 10.

1. Copy the label in cell J3 to cell K3.

2. Click the Expand Formula Bar button. Click in the formula bar and edit the label to **Any Over 150 on Weekend?**
3. Press Enter and AutoFit the column.
4. In cell K4, key **=or** and press Tab.
5. Click cell G4. A marquee appears around the cell, and the address appears in the formula.
6. Key **>150** after **G4**. This logical test will determine if the value in cell G4 is greater than 150.
7. Key a comma after **150**.
8. Click cell H4. Key **>150**. The second condition will test if the value in cell H4 is greater than 150.
9. Key a comma and click cell I4. Key **>150** as the third logical test.

Figure 7-4
Keying an OR function
CustCount.xlsx
CustCount sheet

F	G	H	I	J	K	L
Thursday	Friday	Saturday	Sunday	All Over 150 on Weekend?	Any Over 150 on Weekend?	
100	125	175	195	FALSE	=or(G4>150,H4>150,	
100	135	150	100	FALSE	I4>150	
225	135	175	1	OR(logical1, [logical2], **[logical3]**, [logical4], ...)		
100	125	135	150	FALSE		
100	135	150	100	FALSE		

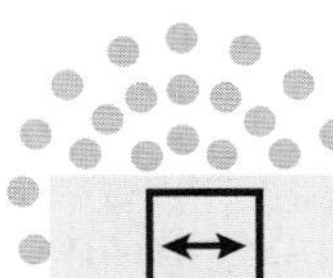

REVIEW

You can click the Enter button in the formula bar to complete a formula.

10. Press Enter. If the customer count is greater than 150 people on any one of the weekend days, the result is TRUE.
11. Copy the formula into cells K5:K35.
12. Click the Collapse Formula Bar button.

Exercise 7-5 USE THE NOT FUNCTION

In a NOT function, the reverse or opposite of your logical_test must be true for the result cell to show TRUE. The NOT function has one argument.

TABLE 7-4 Examples of the NOT Function

Expression	Result
NOT(C4>10)	TRUE if C4 is 10 or less than 10; FALSE if C4 is 11 or greater.
NOT(C4=10)	TRUE if C4 contains any value other than 10; FALSE if C4 is 10.

1. Click cell L3. Key **Sunday>150?**
2. Click cell L4. Key **=not(** and click cell I4.
3. Key **<150**. The formula tests if the value in cell I4 is less than 150. If the value is 150 or a value greater than 150, cell L4 will show TRUE.

Figure 7-5
Keying a NOT function
CustCount.xlsx
CustCount sheet

H	I	J	K	L	M
Saturday	Sunday	All Over 150 on Weekend?	Any Over 150 on Weekend?	Sunday>150?	
175	195	FALSE	TRUE	=NOT(I4<150	
150	100	FALSE	FALSE	NOT(logical)	
175	150	FALSE	TRUE		
135	150	FALSE	FALSE		
150	100	FALSE	FALSE		

4. Press Enter.
5. Copy the formula to cells L5:L35. Look at the results for counts of 150 or more on Sunday.

Working with Cell Styles

A *cell style* is a set of formatting specifications for labels or values. A cell style can contain number format, font, border, alignment, fill, and cell protection. You used cell styles when you clicked the Accounting Number Format button, the Comma Style button, or the Percent Style button. The default cell style for all new data keyed in a workbook is Normal.

Exercise 7-6 USE CELL STYLES

1. Click the **Home** tab.
2. Select cells C36:I36 and click the AutoSum button.

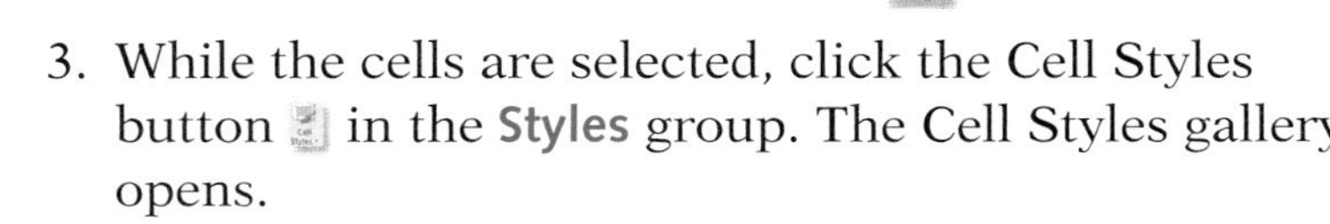

3. While the cells are selected, click the Cell Styles button in the **Styles** group. The Cell Styles gallery opens.
4. Hover over several cell styles to see the change in row 36.

NOTE

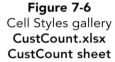

Live Preview shows the data with the style as you hover over the style button.

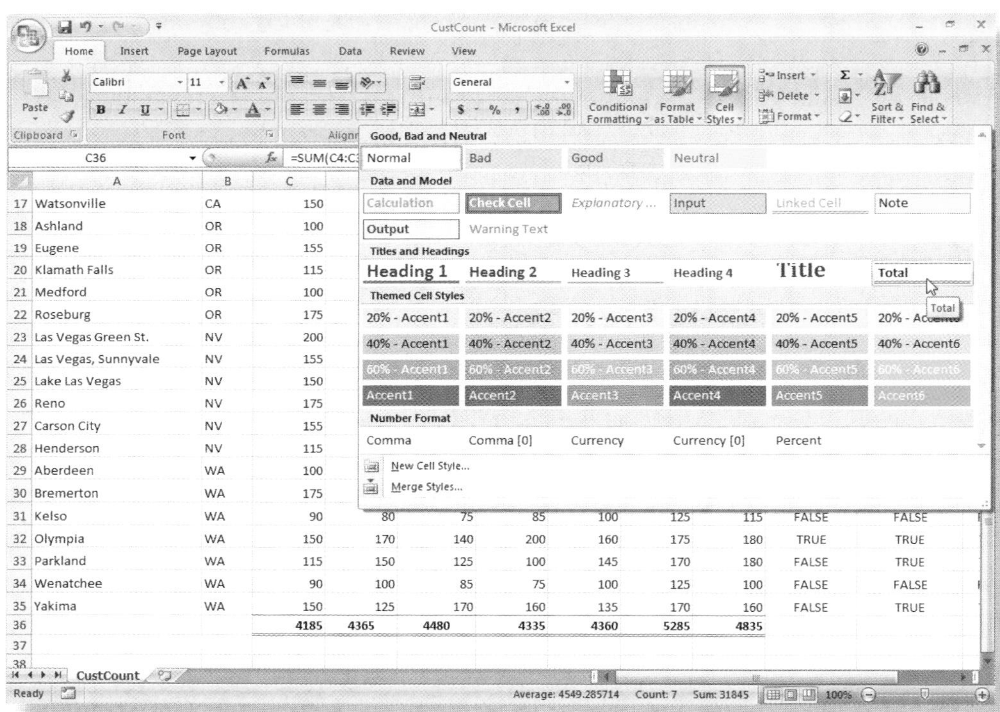

Figure 7-6
Cell Styles gallery
CustCount.xlsx
CustCount sheet

5. Find **Total** in the **Titles and Headings** category. Click to select it. The gallery closes and the style is applied.
6. Click a cell away from the range to see the style. The values are bold and have a top and double bottom blue border.

7. Select cells C36:I36 again. Click the Cell Styles button again. Number styles are near the bottom of the gallery.
8. Choose **Comma [0]**. This is the comma style with no decimal places. It overwrites the previous style. Notice that these cells are not right-aligned with other values in the columns. Other values use a different style.

Exercise 7-7 CLEAR AND REAPPLY CELL STYLES

You can remove a cell style or your own formatting from a cell or a range of cells. The cells then return to the default Normal style.

1. While cells C36:I36 are selected, click the Clear button in the **Editing** group. Choose **Clear Formats**. The cells are returned to the Normal style.
2. Click cell C4 and press F8 to start Extend Selection mode.
3. Press → six times to select up to column I.
4. Hold down Ctrl and press ↓. This shortcut selects to the last row of data.
5. Click the Cell Styles button.
6. Choose **Comma [0]**. The style is applied, and all values are aligned.
7. Select cells C36:I36 and apply the **Total** cell style.
8. Select cells A1:A2 and apply the **Title** cell style.
9. Press Ctrl+Home.

Exercise 7-8 CREATE A STYLE

You can create your own styles. Styles that you create are listed in the **Custom** category and saved with the workbook.

1. Click the Cell Styles button. Click **New Cell Style**.
2. In the **Style name** box, key **Mine** and click **Format**. The Format Cells dialog box opens.
3. Click the **Font** tab. Choose 11-point regular Calibri. Do not click **OK** yet.
4. Click the **Border** tab. Set a single bottom black border. Do not click **OK** yet.
5. Click the **Fill** tab. Choose a light shaded accent color to match the blue in cells A1:A2. Click **OK**. This style will apply fill and a bottom border.
6. Click **OK** again.
7. Select cells A4:L4. Hold down Ctrl and select cells A6:L6. Repeat these steps to cells A8:L8 to the selection.

NOTE

Cell styles use the document theme colors.

8. Click the Cell Styles button. Choose **Mine** at the top of the gallery. Notice that the alignment of values is not correct. The number format in your style does not match the **Comma [0]** style. You'll fix this in the next exercise.

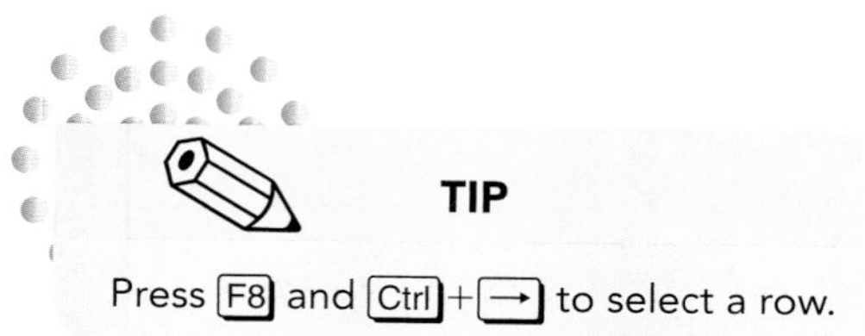

TIP

Press F8 and Ctrl+→ to select a row.

9. Select cells A10:L10. Press Ctrl+Y. This is the keyboard shortcut to repeat the most recent command.
10. Repeat these steps to apply the style to every other row in the sheet, up to and including row 34.
11. Make row 36 the same height as the other rows.

Exercise 7-9 EDIT A STYLE

If you edit a style, all cells with the style are reformatted.

1. Click cell C5 and press Ctrl+1. Click the **Number** tab. The **Number** format (from **Comma [0]**) uses the Accounting option with no decimals and no symbol. Close the dialog box.
2. Click cell C4. This is your style.
3. Click the Cell Styles button. Right-click **Mine** and choose **Modify**.
4. Click **Format**. The Format Cells dialog box opens.
5. Click the **Number** tab. Choose **Accounting**, **0** decimals. In the **Symbol** box, choose **None**. Do not click **OK**.
6. Click the **Fill** tab. Choose a different color if your first choice was too dark. Click **OK**.
7. Click **OK** again. All the cells with the Mine style are restyled. The values are properly aligned, but the number alignment is affecting the labels in columns A:B (cities and states).
8. Select cells A4:B35 and press Ctrl+1. On the **Number** tab, choose **General** and click **OK**. You can override an individual setting of any style.

9. Click the **Page Layout** tab. Click the Margins button. Choose **Custom Margins**.
10. Set the left and right margins at 1 inch; set the top and bottom margins at 1.25 inches. Click **OK**.

Working with Page Breaks

A *page break* is a code that tells the printer to start a new page. When a worksheet is too wide or too tall to fit on the paper, Excel inserts an automatic page break. This page break appears as a dashed line on the screen. You can accept Excel's location for page breaks, you can move the break to a new location, or you can insert your own.

Exercise 7-10 PREVIEW AND CHANGE PAGE BREAKS

1. Click the Microsoft Office Button. Hover over the **Print** arrow and choose **Print Preview**.

NOTE

In Print Preview, PageDown moves to the next page if your screen is showing a reduced view.

2. Point at the page and click anywhere to zoom in/out. The worksheet is too large to print on a single page in portrait orientation.
3. Click to set a reduced view and press PageDown. Rows(s) that do not fit on the first page are on page 2.
4. Press PageDown again. Columns that do not fit on the first two pages are on page 3. Look at page 4, too.
5. Close Print Preview.

NOTE

The background page number does not print.

6. Click the Page Break Preview button in the status bar. A message box explains how you can adjust page breaks.
7. Click **OK**. Pages are arranged in top-to-bottom, left-to-right order with a background page number. Page breaks are blue dashed lines.

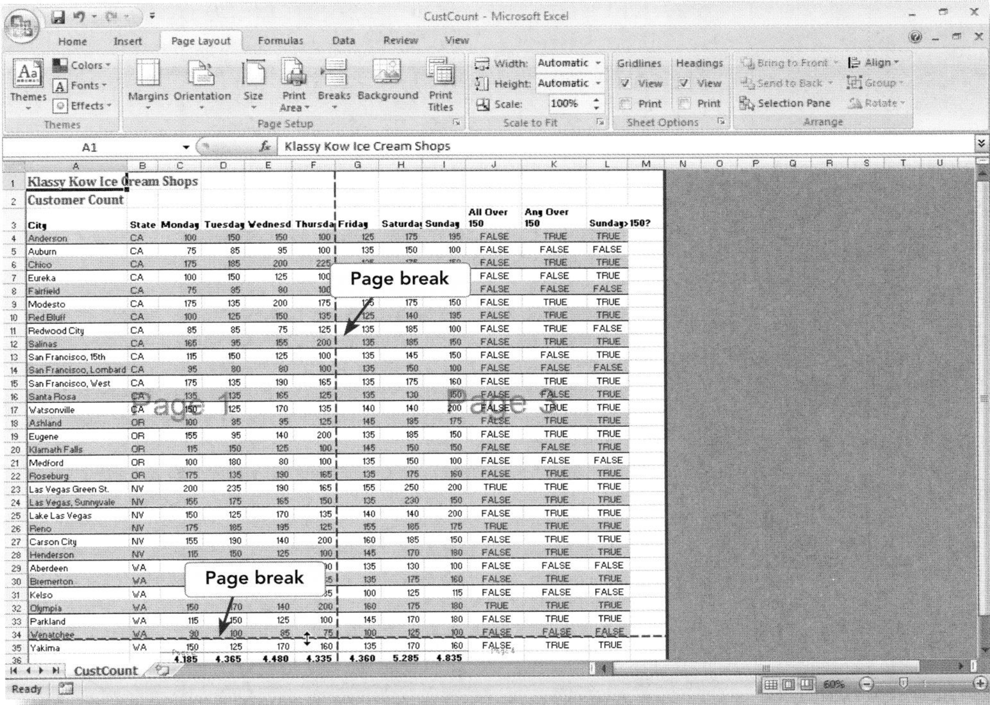

Figure 7-7
Page Break Preview
CustCount.xlsx
CustCount sheet

8. Place the pointer on the horizontal blue dashed line below row 35 to display a two-pointed arrow. Your dashed line might be anywhere between rows 33 and 36.

TIP
You can AutoFit columns and rows while in Page Break Preview.

9. Click and drag the dashed blue line up so that it is between rows 22 and 23. The line becomes solid blue if you manually set or adjust it.
10. Click and drag the vertical blue dashed line between columns F and G to the left so that it is between columns E and F.
11. Widen any column in which the label in row 3 is not visible.
12. Click the Normal button in the status bar. You can see dashed lines for page breaks in Normal view.

Exercise 7-11 REMOVE AND INSERT PAGE BREAKS

You can delete page breaks if necessary, or you can insert your own breaks where you want. When you insert a page break, it is placed to the left of the active cell or column. The placement of page breaks is affected by the currently installed printer, so your worksheet may have different breaks than those shown in this lesson.

1. Click the Page Break Preview button. Click **OK** in the message box.
2. Click and drag the page break below row 22 down and below row 36. You should now have only two pages.
3. Click cell J1. If you insert a page break here, it will be between columns I and J.

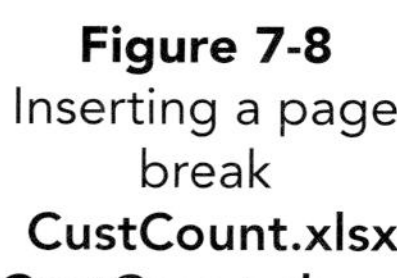

4. Click the **Page Layout** tab. In the **Page Setup** group, click the Breaks button.

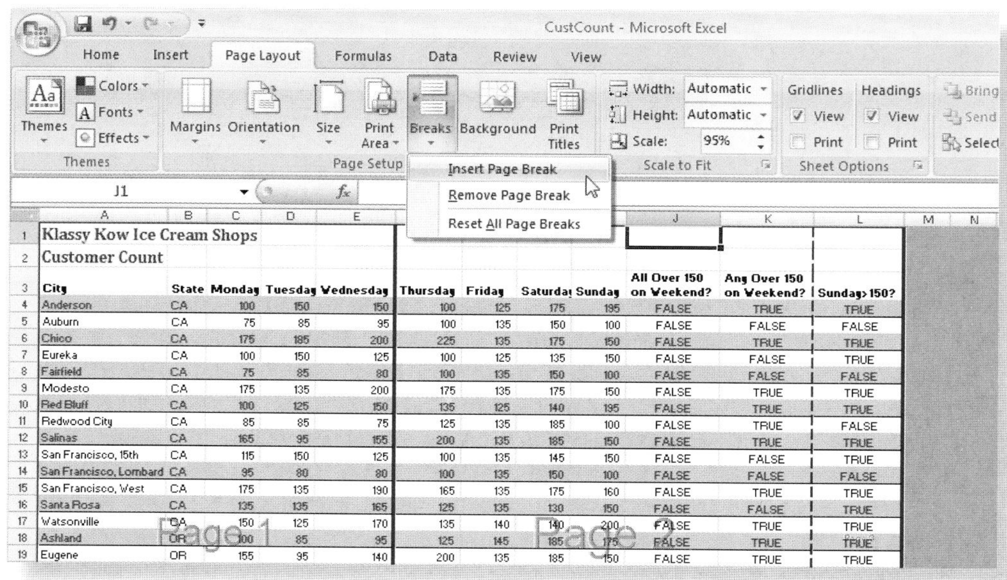

Figure 7-8
Inserting a page break
CustCount.xlsx
CustCount sheet

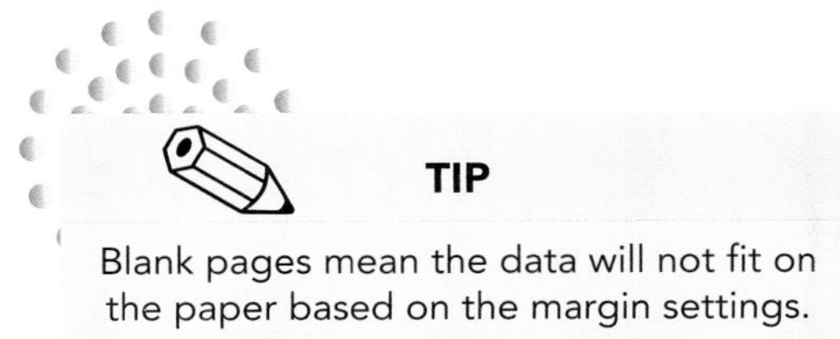

TIP

Blank pages mean the data will not fit on the paper based on the margin settings.

5. Choose **Insert Page Break**. The page break is solid blue because you inserted it manually. Your worksheet should now occupy three pages. If your worksheet is longer, you probably have some blank pages.
6. Click the Microsoft Office Button. Hover over the **Print** arrow and choose **Print Preview**. Press PageDown to view the pages.
7. In Print Preview, click to select **Show Margins**. The page shows markers for all margins, including the header and footer. The top margin is the lower of the two horizontal lines; the marker is the tiny rectangle at either edge.
8. Click the top margin marker and drag it up to reach about **.75**. The setting is shown in the status bar as you drag.

Figure 7-9
Changing margins in Print Preview
CustCount.xlsx
CustCount sheet

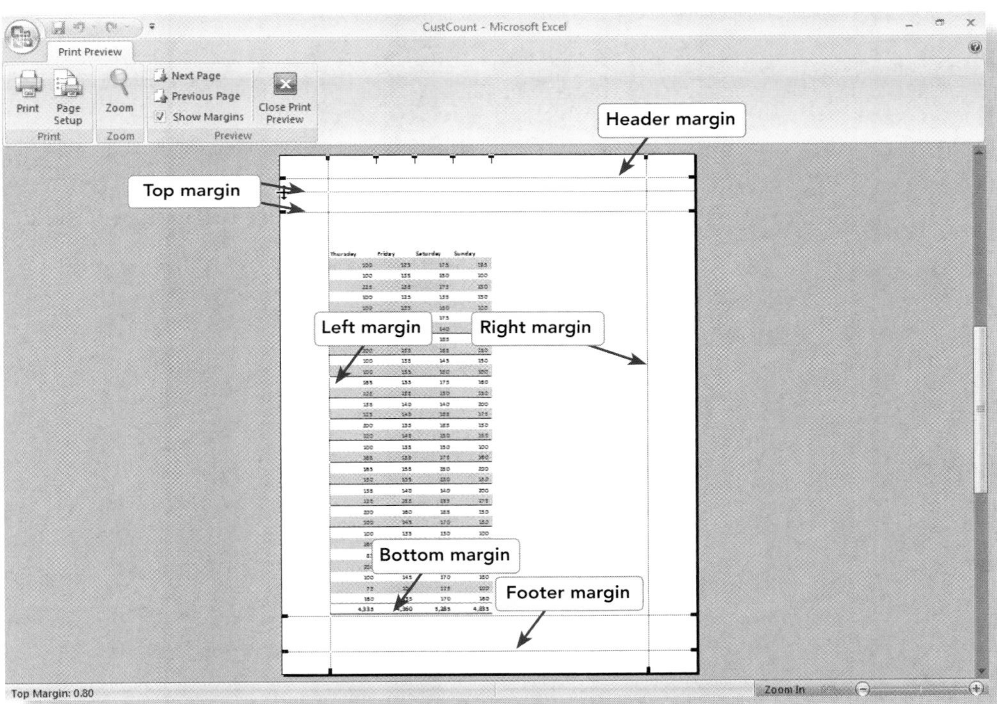

9. Do the same for the bottom margin. Less margin space eliminates any blank pages. Now the worksheet fits on three pages.
10. Close Print Preview.

Exercise 7-12 SET PRINT TITLES

You can repeat the labels in column A on each printed page to make this three-page worksheet easier to read. You will see the city name on each page so that it is easy to determine which values belong with each city.

1. Click the Print Titles button on the **Page Layout** tab. The Page Setup dialog box opens with the **Sheet** tab active.
2. Click in the **Columns to repeat at left** text box.
3. Click anywhere in column A. The dialog box shows **$A:$A** as the range for print titles.

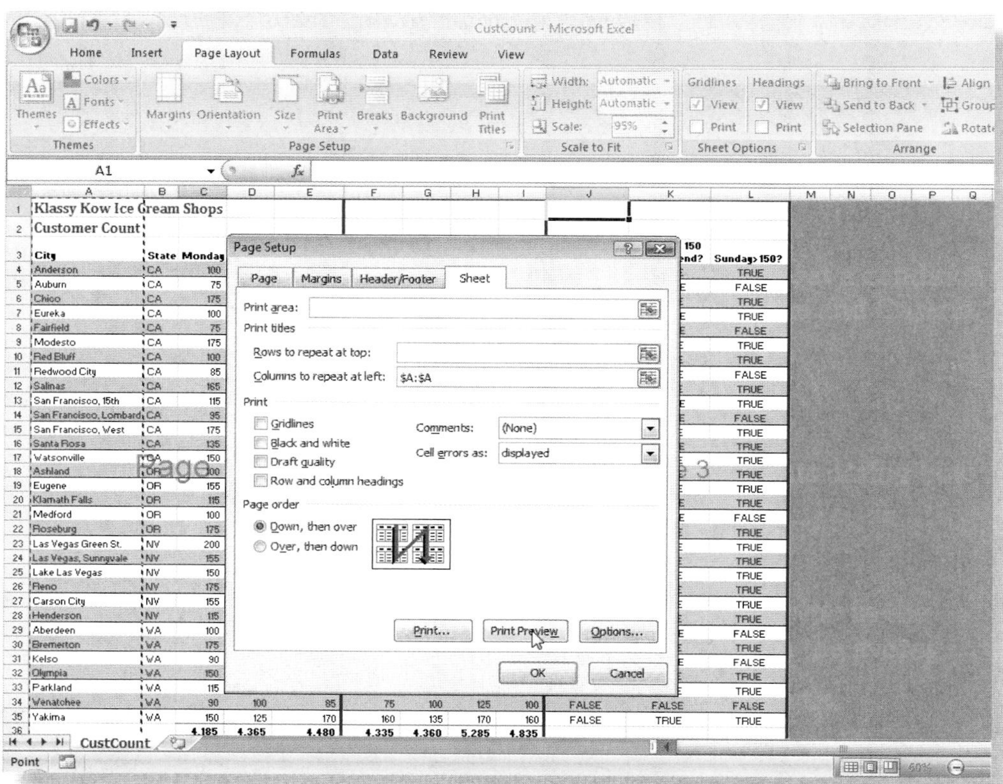

Figure 7-10
Setting print titles
CustCount.xlsx
CustCount sheet

4. Click **Print Preview** in the dialog box.
5. Press PageDown and PageUp to view the pages. Notice that the label in cell A1 is cut off on pages 2 and 3.
6. Close Print Preview. AutoFit column A. Hide column B. Excel probably inserted a new automatic page break, because column A is wider now.

Exercise 7-13 CENTER A PAGE

Although you can change the left and right margins to make a page appear centered, Excel can center a worksheet horizontally or vertically on the printed page. Centering occurs between the margins.

1. On the **Page Layout** tab, click the Margins button. Choose **Custom Margins**.
2. In the **Center on page** section, click to select **Horizontally**.
3. Click to select **Vertically**.
4. Change the left and right margins to **.50**. Change the top and bottom margins to **.75**.
5. Click **Print Preview** in the dialog box. All pages are horizontally centered, and the smaller margins better fit the first page.
6. Close Print Preview.
7. Click the Normal button in the status bar.

Exercise 7-14 CHANGE THE FOOTER FONT AND PRINT PAGE NUMBERS

The default font for data in headers and footers is 11-point Calibri for the default Office theme. You can change the formatting for any section in the footer to any font and size available on your computer.

1. Click the **Insert** tab, and then click the Header & Footer button.
2. Click the Go To Footer button in the **Navigation** group. Click in the left section.

3. Click the **Home** tab. Click the Font Size arrow and choose **8**.
4. Key ***[your first and last name]***. The font size is applied as you type.
5. Click in the center section. Click the **Header & Footer Tools Design** tab.

6. Click the Page Number button. The code is **&[Page]**, and it is 11-point Calibri.
7. Press Spacebar to insert a space after **&[Page]**.
8. Key **of** and press Spacebar.

9. Click the Number of Pages button. The code is **&[Pages]**. This footer will display **Page 1 of 3** on the first page.
10. Drag across **&[Page] of &[Pages]** to select all of it. The Mini toolbar appears.

11. Click the Decrease Font Size button three times. Each click reduces the size by 1 point.

Figure 7-11
Printing page numbers
CustCount.xlsx
CustCount sheet

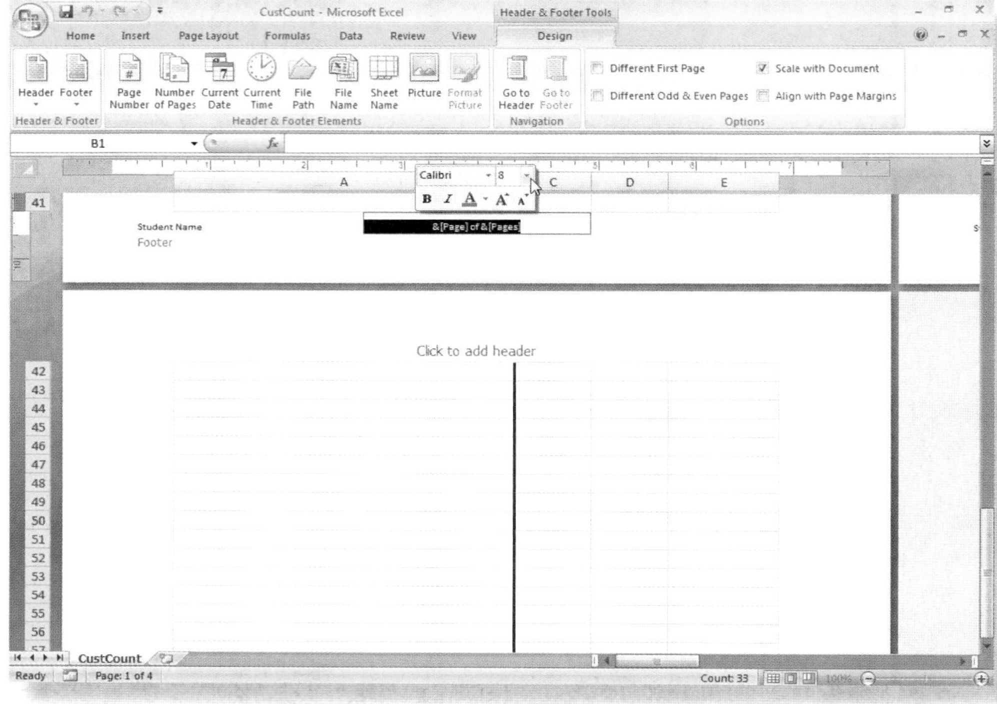

12. Insert the filename in the right section with the same font. Click a worksheet cell.
13. Click the Normal button in the status bar.
14. Save the workbook as ***[your initials]*****7-14** in your Lesson 7 folder.

Exercise 7-15 REMOVE A PAGE BREAK

You can remove a manual page break and let Excel resume automatic page breaks.

1. Click the Page Break Preview button. Click **OK** in the message box.
2. Click cell J1. The page break is to the left of this column.
3. Click the **Page Layout** tab. Click the Breaks button and choose **Remove Page Break**. An automatic page break is inserted, probably after column J.
4. Click the Normal button in the status bar.
5. Save and close the workbook.

Using the PMT and FV Functions

Financial functions analyze money transactions such as loans and savings or investment plans. Many financial functions, including PMT and FV, use the concept of an annuity. An *annuity* is a series of equal payments made at regular intervals for a specified period of time.

Many of Excel's financial functions use these arguments:

- *Rate* is the interest for the period. If you make monthly payments, you must divide the rate by 12 to find the monthly interest rate.
- *Nper* is the total number of periods during which a payment is made. It represents the total number of payments. A five-year loan with monthly payments would have an Nper of 60 (12 months a year * 5 years).
- *PV* is present value or the amount of the loan. It is the current cash value of the money transaction.
- *FV* is future value or the cash balance at the end of the time period. For an investment, FV is how much you will have at the end of your savings or investment time. For a loan, the FV is 0 because you must pay back every penny.
- *Type* specifies whether payments are made at the beginning or the end of the period.

Exercise 7-16 USE THE PMT FUNCTION

The PMT (Payment) function can be used to determine monthly payments if you borrow money to buy a computer, a car, or a house.

1. Open **CU**.
2. In cell C7, key **4** to plan a four-year loan.
3. In cell C8, key = to use a formula to compute the number of payments.

TIP

By using a formula in cell C8 to determine the number of payments, you only need to change the number of years to test different loan lengths.

4. Click cell C7 and key ***12**. Press Enter. You will make a total of 48 payments (4 years * 12 months in a year).
5. In cell C9, key **20000**, the amount of money borrowed.
6. In cell C10, key **4.9%** as the interest rate.
7. Click cell C12. Click the **Formulas** tab.

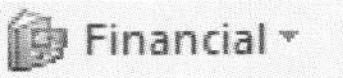

8. Click the Financial button. Scroll and click **PMT**. The PMT Function Arguments dialog box opens with the insertion point in the **Rate** box, the first argument.

9. Click cell C10, the interest rate. The cell address appears in the **Rate** box.
10. Key **/12** in the **Rate** box after **C10**. An annual interest rate must be divided by 12 to figure a monthly payment.
11. Click in the **Nper** box. This argument is the total number of payments.
12. Click cell C8 for the number of payments.
13. Click in the **Pv** box and click cell C9. The present value is cash you receive now.

TIP

Most loans use Type 1 because it costs less to pay at the beginning of the month than at the end.

14. Click in the **Fv** box. Future value for a loan is what you will owe at the end of the loan, 0. You do not need to enter anything in this box.
15. Click in the **Type** box and key **1** for a payment at the beginning of the month.

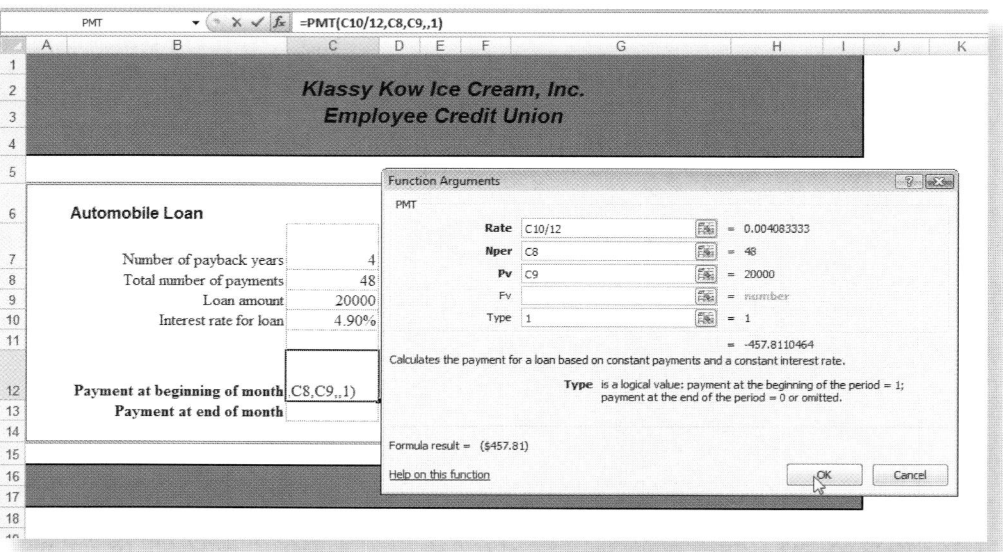

Figure 7-12
Function Arguments dialog box for PMT
CU.xlsx
CreditUnion sheet

16. Click **OK**. The result ($457.81) is a negative number, because it is money that you have to pay. It is money out of your pocket. Negative formula results are shown in red with parentheses in this worksheet.

Exercise 7-17 KEY A PMT FUNCTION

Key a PMT function from scratch in this exercise to determine the payment if made at the end of the month.

1. Click cell C13.
2. Key **=pm** to display the Formula AutoComplete list and press Tab. The ScreenTip reminds you that the first argument is the **Rate**.

3. Click cell C10 for the rate.
4. Key **/12** to divide the rate by 12.
5. Key a comma to separate the arguments. The second argument, **Nper**, is bold in the ScreenTip.
6. Click cell C8 for the number of payments.
7. Key a comma. The ScreenTip shows the next argument as bold, which is the present value or the amount of the loan.
8. Click cell C9. The square brackets with **[fv]** and **[type]** in the ScreenTip mean that these two arguments are optional. If you do not key a future value, Excel assumes the FV is 0. If you do not key a type, it is assumed to be a 0 type.
9. Press Enter. Notice that payment at the end of the month is slightly more than at the beginning of the month.

Figure 7-13
Keying a PMT function
CU.xlsx CreditUnion sheet

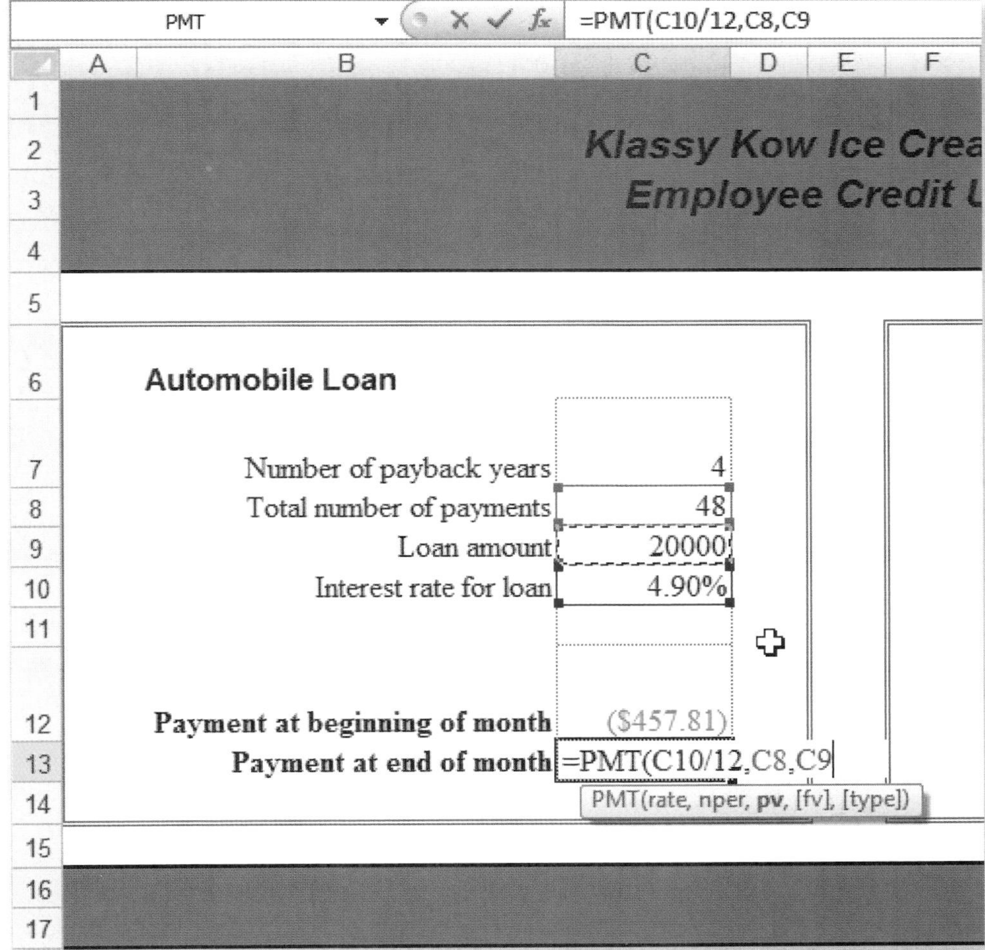

10. Click cell C7. Key **5** and press Enter for a five-year loan. Both functions are recalculated as well as the total number of payments.
11. In cell C10, key **3.9%** and press Enter. Payments with a lower interest rate are lower.
12. Click cell C9 and press F2 to edit the value.
13. Press Home to position the insertion point and key – to make this a negative number.
14. Press Enter. The payments now are positive numbers.

Exercise 7-18 USE THE FV FUNCTION

The FV (Future Value) function can be used to determine such things as how much you will have in your savings account at some point in the future if you make regular deposits. You can include money already in the account when you start your savings program.

1. Click cell H7 and key **5** to plan a five-year savings plan.
2. In cell H8, key = and click cell H7. Key ***12** and press Enter. You would make 60 total deposits if you save monthly for five years.
3. In cell H9, key **50** as the amount saved each month.
4. In cell H10, key **1000** as the amount of money already in the account.
5. In cell H11, key **5.25%** as the interest rate.
6. In cell H12, click the Financial button Financial. Scroll and click **FV**. The insertion point is in the **Rate** box for the first argument.
7. Click cell H11 for the **Rate**. Key **/12** in the **Rate** box after **H11** to divide the rate by 12.
8. Click in the **Nper** box and then click cell H8.
9. Click in the **Pmt** box and click cell H9. The payment is the amount you plan to deposit into your savings account each month.
10. Click in the **Pv** box and click cell H10. The present value is the amount in the account to start.
11. Click in the **Type** box and key **1** for a deposit at the beginning of the month.

REVIEW

If you do not key the % sign, you must key the decimal equivalent of the value.

NOTE

The Function Arguments dialog box shows the syntax and a description of each argument when you click its box.

TIP

In a savings plan, Type 1 pays more interest.

Figure 7-14
Function Arguments dialog box for FV
CU.xlsx
CreditUnion sheet

Function Arguments

FV

Rate	H11/12	= 0.004375
Nper	H8	= 60
Pmt	H9	= 50
Pv	H10	= 1000
Type	1	= 1

= -4736.486919

Returns the future value of an investment based on periodic, constant payments and a constant interest rate.

Type is a value representing the timing of payment: payment at the beginning of the period = 1; payment at the end of the period = 0 or omitted.

Formula result = -4736.486919

Help on this function

OK Cancel

12. Click **OK**. The result is shown as a negative number, because the FV function assumes the bank's or lender's point of view. This is money that they would have to pay to you.

Exercise 7-19 FORMAT NEGATIVE NUMBERS

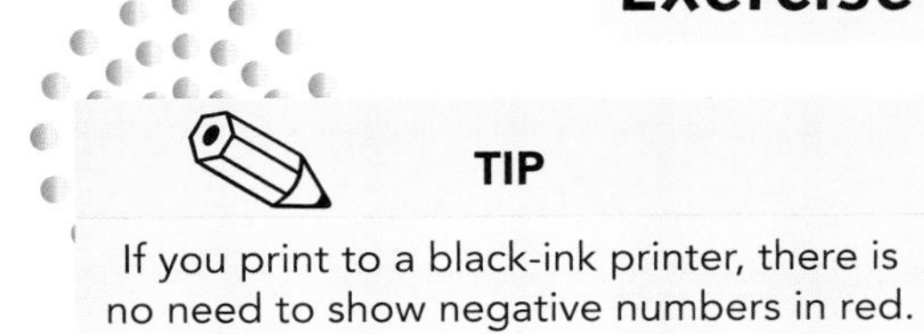

TIP

If you print to a black-ink printer, there is no need to show negative numbers in red.

Many business reports show negative numbers in red. Excel's number formats can show negative numbers in red or black, with or without parentheses, or with a leading minus sign.

1. Select cells C9, C12:C13, H9:H10, and H12.
2. Press Ctrl+1. Click the **Number** tab and choose **Currency**. Verify that there will be two decimals and a dollar sign.
3. In the **Negative numbers** list, choose the non-red **($1,234.10)**. Click **OK**.
4. Make cells C12 and H12 bold.
5. Press Ctrl+Home. Add a header.
6. Save the workbook as **[your initials]7-19** in your Lesson 7 folder. Close the workbook.

Using Depreciation Functions

Depreciation is the decline in value of an asset. Your car depreciates. You pay an amount for the car, but it is not worth that amount in three years because it has been used. In a business, depreciation is an expense that can reduce income taxes. There are widely accepted methods of determining depreciation, and Excel has several functions to calculate the amounts.

Excel's depreciation functions use these basic arguments:

- *Cost* is the original price of the item.
- *Salvage* is the value of the item after it has been depreciated. It is what the item is worth at the end of its life.
- *Life* is the number of periods over which the item will be depreciated. This is usually expressed in years for expensive assets.
- *Period* is the time for which depreciation is calculated. It uses the same units as Life. If an asset has a 10-year life, you would usually figure depreciation for a single year (the period).

Exercise 7-20 USE THE DB FUNCTION

The DB (Declining Balance) function calculates depreciation at a fixed rate and assumes that the value declines each year. You calculate depreciation for each year separately.

1. Open **Depreciation**.
2. Select cells B11:B12. Use the Fill handle to extend the labels down column A to "10th Year." Extend the values in column C to match.
3. Click the **Formulas** tab.
4. In cell D11, click the Financial button Financial.
5. Hover over **DB** and read the ScreenTip.
6. Click **DB**. The insertion point is in the **Cost** box for the first argument.
7. Click cell D7 for the **Cost**.
8. Click in the **Salvage** box and then click cell D8. This is the value of the tanks after 10 years.
9. Click in the **Life** box and click cell D9. The life is how long the tanks are expected to last.
10. Click in the **Period** box and click cell C11 to calculate depreciation for the first year.
11. Click in the **Month** box. This allows you to start depreciating an asset in the middle of a year. The label "Month" is not bold, which means this argument is optional. Leave it empty.

Figure 7-15
Function Arguments dialog box for DB
Depreciation.xlsx Sheet1 sheet

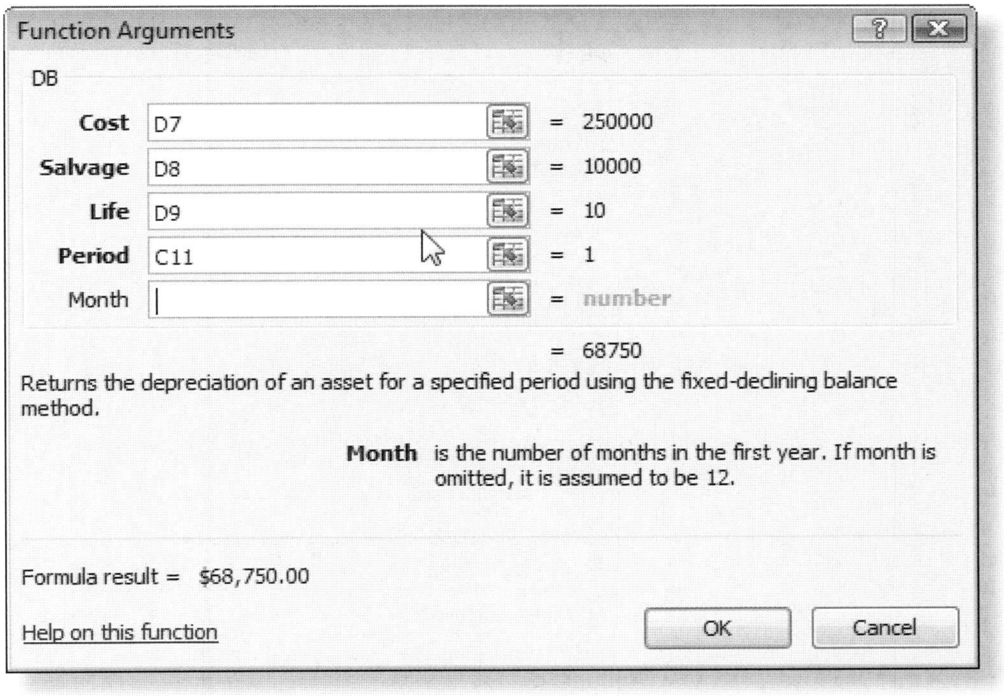

Function Arguments

DB

Cost	D7	= 250000
Salvage	D8	= 10000
Life	D9	= 10
Period	C11	= 1
Month		= number

= 68750

Returns the depreciation of an asset for a specified period using the fixed-declining balance method.

Month is the number of months in the first year. If month is omitted, it is assumed to be 12.

Formula result = $68,750.00

Help on this function — OK — Cancel

12. Click **OK**. The depreciation for the first year is $68,750.
13. Click cell D12 and key **=db(** to start the function. The ScreenTip shows that the first argument is the **cost**.
14. Click cell D7.
15. Key a comma to separate the arguments. The second argument, **salvage**, is bold in the ScreenTip.
16. Click cell D8 for the salvage value.
17. Key another comma. The ScreenTip reminds you that the next argument is the **life** of the asset.
18. Click cell D9 and key a comma. The **period** argument is next.
19. Click cell C12 for the second year. The next argument in square brackets is **[month]** in the ScreenTip. Do not enter anything here.

Figure 7-16
Keying a DB function
Depreciation.xlsx
Sheet1 sheet

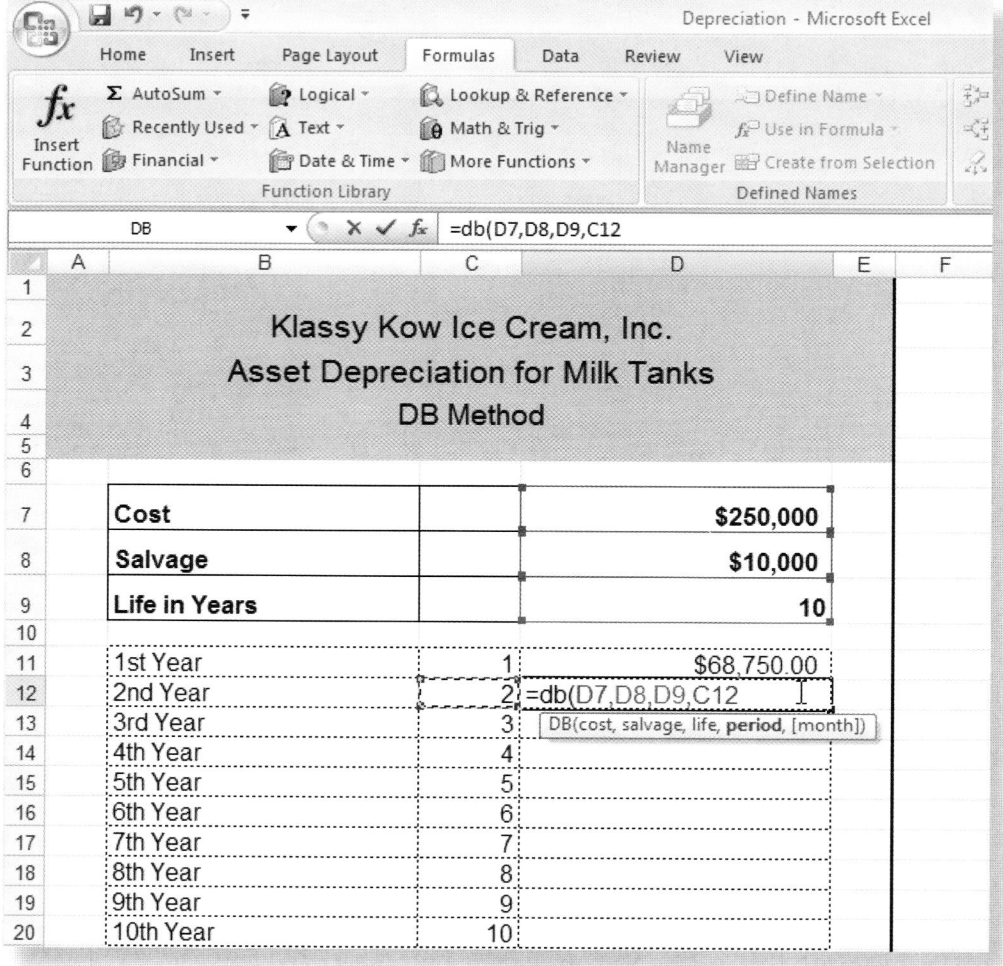

20. Press Enter. The depreciation for the second year is less because the asset was worth less at the beginning of the second year.

Exercise 7-21 EDIT AND COPY THE DB FUNCTION

With absolute references to the first three cells, you can copy the formula.

1. Click cell D12.
2. Press F2. The references to cells D7, D8, and D9 should be absolute.
3. Click between the **D** and the **7** and press F4. The reference is absolute.
4. Do the same for D8 and D9 in the formula and press Enter.
5. Copy the formula in column D and hide column C.
6. Press Ctrl+Home. Edit the footer to show your name and save the workbook as **[your initials]7-21** in your folder.
7. Close the workbook.

Using Online Help

Excel has many financial functions that calculate common business arithmetic, including several methods for determining depreciation.

USE HELP TO VIEW ADDITIONAL INFORMATION ABOUT DEPRECIATION

1. In a new workbook, click the Microsoft Office Excel Help button .
2. In the Search box, key **depreciation** and press Enter.
3. Find and review topics about the SLN, SYD, and VDB functions.
4. Close the Help window.

Lesson 7 Summary

- The IF function enables you to create formulas that test whether a condition is true. If it is true, you specify what should be shown or done. You also set what appears or is done if the condition is false.
- The IF function can show text in its result, it can calculate a value, or it can show a cell reference.
- AND, OR, and NOT are logical functions that show either TRUE or FALSE as a result.
- Logical functions use relational or comparison operators.
- A style is a set of formatting attributes for labels and values.
- Cell styles appear in a gallery with Live Preview. They are coordinated with the document theme.
- You can remove all formatting from a cell and return to the default Normal style.
- You can create your own style and save it with the worksheet.
- Page breaks determine where a new page starts. Excel inserts page breaks based on the paper size and the margins.
- You can insert and delete your own page breaks.
- Page Break Preview shows the page breaks as solid or dashed blue lines.
- If a worksheet requires more than one page, you can repeat column or row headings from page to page to make it easier to read the worksheet.
- The Margins tab in the Page Setup dialog box includes options to center a page horizontally or vertically.
- You can print each page number as well as the total number of pages in a worksheet as a header or a footer.
- Financial functions include PMT and FV and other common business calculations such as depreciation.

- The PMT function calculates a regular payment for a loan, using an interest rate.
- The FV function calculates how much an amount will be worth in the future at a given interest rate.
- The DB function calculates how much of its value an asset loses each year during its life.
- Negative numbers can be shown in red, within parentheses, or with a leading minus (−) sign.

LESSON 7		Command Summary	
Feature	**Button**	**Task Path**	**Keyboard**
Apply cell style	Cell Styles	Home, Styles, Cell Styles	
Center page	Margins	Page Layout, Page Setup, Margins, Custom Margins	Ctrl+1
Collapse formula bar			Ctrl+Shift+U
Create cell style	Cell Styles	Home, Styles, Cell Styles, New Cell Style	
Delete page break	Breaks	Page Layout, Page Setup, Breaks, Remove Page Break	
Edit cell style	Cell Styles	Home, Styles, Cell Styles	
Expand formula bar			Ctrl+Shift+U
Insert page break	Breaks	Page Layout, Page Setup, Breaks, Insert Page Break	
Page break preview		View, Workbook Views	
Print titles	Print Titles	Page Layout, Page Setup	
Repeat command			Ctrl+Y

Lesson 8

Rounding and Nesting Functions

OBJECTIVES

MCAS OBJECTIVES

In this lesson:
XL07 1.5.4
XL07 2.3.7
XL07 2.3.8
XL07 3.1.1
XL07 4.3.3
XL07 5.4.1
XL07 5.5.4

After completing this lesson, you will be able to:

1. Use the INT function.
2. Use the ROUND function.
3. Use date and time arithmetic.
4. Create nested functions.
5. Create a hyperlink.

Estimated Time: 1½ hours

The INT and ROUND functions can be used with formulas or functions to convert a value with decimals. You will learn about these two functions as well as how to nest one function inside another to solve complex problems.

Using the INT Function

Excel stores the full number of decimals that are keyed or calculated in a cell, even if the cell is formatted to show fewer decimal places. For example, if you key 1.2345 and format the cell for two decimal places, Excel displays 1.23 in the cell. In a calculation, however, Excel uses the full value, 1.2345, which you see in the formula bar.

If you want Excel to use the value shown in the cell (not the one in the formula bar), you can use the INT or ROUND functions.

INT stands for "Integer." An *integer* is a whole number, a number with no decimal or fractional parts. The INT function (in the Math & Trig category) shows only the nondecimal portion of a number. To do this, it truncates or cuts off all digits after the decimal point. The INT function has one argument, the value or cell to be adjusted.

TABLE 8-1 Examples of the INT Function

Expression	Cell Data	Result
INT(C4)	C4=9.7	9
INT(9.792)	None	9
INT(A1)	A1=−9.7	−9

Exercise 8-1 USE INT WITH A CELL REFERENCE

1. Open **Recipes.**
2. On the **Recipes** sheet in cell C7, key **=int** to see the Formula AutoComplete list and the ScreenTip.
3. Press Tab to select the INT function. The argument is the value.
4. Click cell B7.

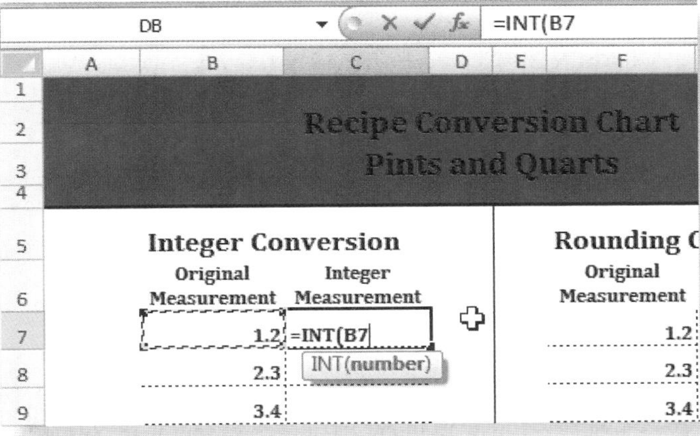

Figure 8-1
Keying an INT function
Recipes.xlsx
Recipes sheet

5. Press Enter. The integer value of 1.2 is 1.
6. Copy the formula in cell C7 to cells C8:C12.

Exercise 8-2 COMPARE VALUES WITH INT

1. Key = in cell B14 and click cell B7.
2. Key ***2** and press Enter. This is a multiplication formula, doubling the value in cell B7.
3. Use the Fill handle to copy the formula to cells B15:B19.
4. Key = in cell C14 and click cell C7.
5. Key ***2** and press Enter. This doubles the integer value in cell C7.

6. Copy the formula to cells C15:C19. Compare the values in columns B and C. There are some noticeable differences between doubling the original value and doubling the integer value.
7. Delete the contents of cells C14:C19.
8. In cell C14, key **=int(** and click cell B14. Press Enter. This is the integer value of 2.4.
9. Copy the formula to cells C15:C19.

Using the ROUND Function

The ROUND function "rounds" a value to a specified digit to the left or right of the decimal point. *Rounding* a number means that it is made larger or smaller, a greater or lesser value. The ROUND function uses two arguments: the value to be rounded and the number of digits used for rounding. If the second argument is zero or a negative number, the rounding occurs to the left of the decimal point.

TABLE 8-2 Examples of the ROUND Function

Expression	Cell Data	Result
ROUND(C4, 1)	C4=9.736	9.7
ROUND(C4, 2)	C4=9.736	9.74
ROUND(C4, 0)	C4=9.736	10
ROUND(C4, −1)	C4=9.736	10

TIP

Rounding can be used in financial calculations to round to the nearest dollar.

Exercise 8-3 USE ROUND

1. Click the **Formulas** tab and click cell G7.
2. Click the Math & Trig button Math & Trig. Hover over **ROUND** to read the ScreenTip.
3. Choose **ROUND**.
4. In the **Number** box, click cell F7.
5. In the **Num_digits** box, key **0**. The value in cell F7 will be rounded to show no decimal positions.

Math & Trig

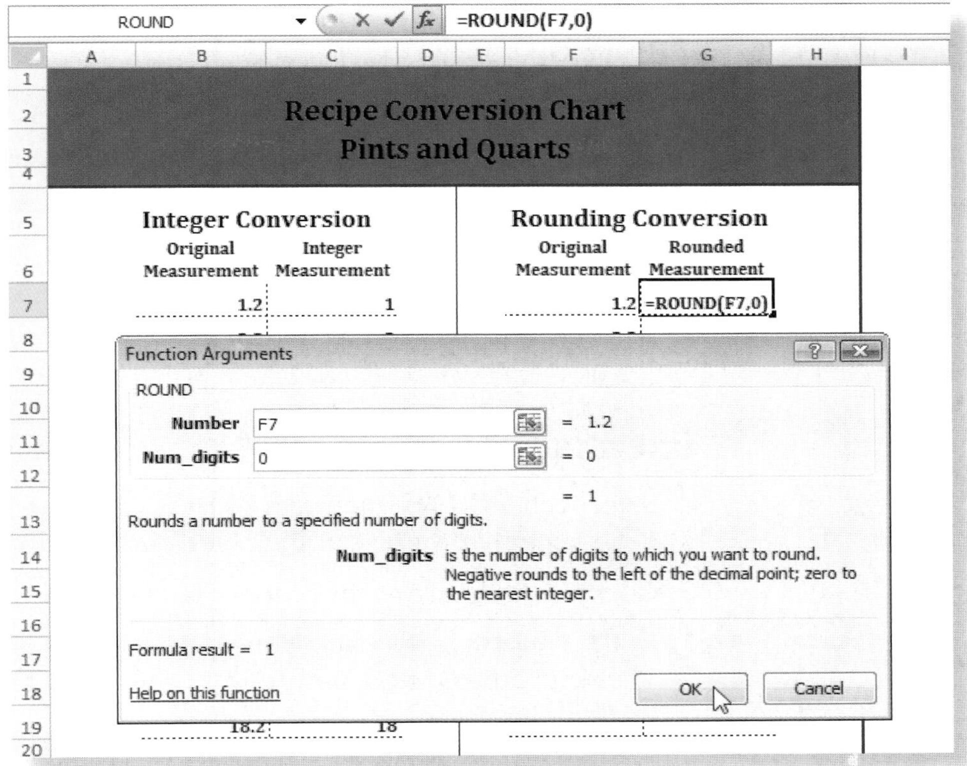

Figure 8-2
Using ROUND in the dialog box
Recipes.xlsx
Recipes sheet

6. Click **OK**. The value 1.2 is rounded to 1. It rounds down because the value after the decimal point is less than 5.
7. Copy the formula down to cell G12.
8. Edit cells F8:F11 to show the following values. As you do, notice how the values in column G are rounded up or down.
   1.6
   3.2
   5.5
   7.2
9. Click the arrow next to the Undo button and undo the last four edits.

Exercise 8-4 COMPARE ROUNDED VALUES

Note the difference between doubling the rounded values and rounding the doubled values in this exercise.

1. Key = in cell F14 and click cell F7. Key ***2** and press Enter.
2. Copy the formula to cells F15:F19.
3. Key = in cell G14 and click cell G7. Key ***2** and press Enter. This doubles the rounded value in cell G7.

4. Copy the formula to cells G15:G19. Compare the values in columns F and G.
5. Delete the contents of cells G14:G19.
6. Click the **Formulas** tab. In cell G14, click the Math & Trig button. Choose **ROUND**.

7. In the **Number** box, click cell F14.
8. In the **Num_digits** box, key **0**. Click **OK**. The value **2.4** is rounded to **2**.
9. Copy the formula to cells G15:G19.

Exercise 8-5 CHANGE COLORS AND BORDERS

1. Select cells A1:H21 and press Ctrl+1. Click the **Border** tab. You can determine that there is a thick blue outline border.
2. Click the **Color** arrow and choose **Blue, Accent 1** for a softer blue.
3. In the **Presets** group, click None button to remove all borders. Then click the Outline button. Click **OK**. The same border thickness is used.

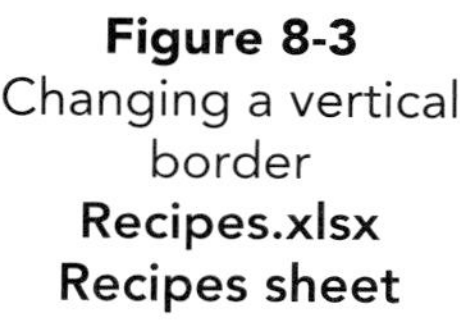

4. Click the **Home** tab. Select cells A1:H4 and click the arrow next to the Fill Color button.
5. Choose **Blue, Accent 1**.
6. Select cells D5:D21. There should be a vertical border for these cells. Since columns D and E share borders, you can edit this border from either column.

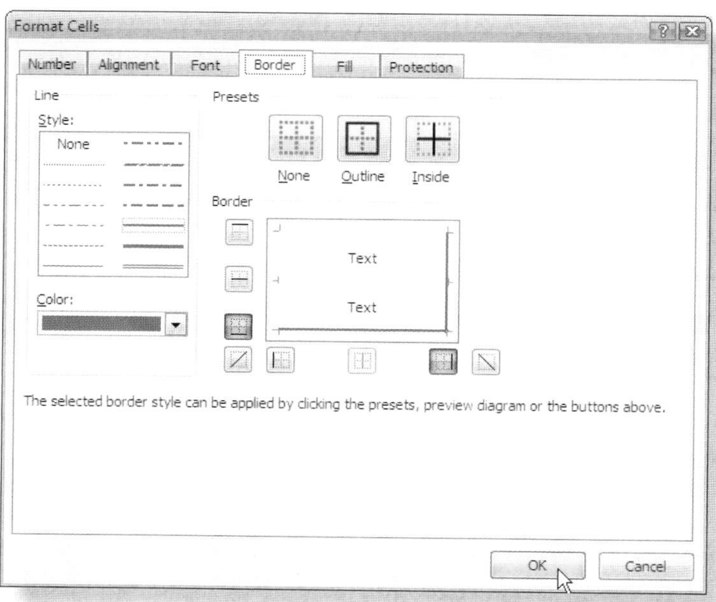

Figure 8-3
Changing a vertical border
Recipes.xlsx
Recipes sheet

7. Press Ctrl+1. Click the **Border** tab.

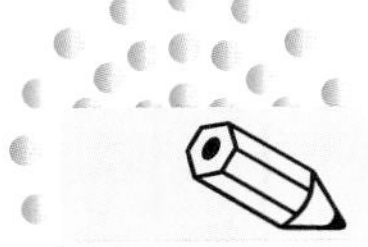

8. Click the **Color** arrow and choose **Blue, Accent 1**.
9. Click the right vertical border preview area or the Right Vertical button. Click **OK**.
10. Change the sheet tab color to **Blue, Accent 1**.
11. Save the workbook as ***[your initials]*8-5** in a new folder for Lesson 8.

Using Date and Time Arithmetic

TIP

Macintosh systems start counting at January 1, 1904.

Because of its serial number system, Excel's Date & Time functions can calculate ages, hours worked, or days passed. The serial number system treats dates as values. January 1, 1900, is 1; January 2, 1900, is 2; and so on.

Exercise 8-6 DETERMINE AGES AND DATES

To determine a product's age, subtract the manufacture date from today. The result is a serial number that can be converted to an age in years.

1. In ***[your initials]*8-5**, click the **ExpireDate** tab. Replace all occurrences of the year in column A with last year.
2. In cell C4, key **=today()-** to start the formula.
3. Click cell A4. The formula subtracts the manufacture date from today.

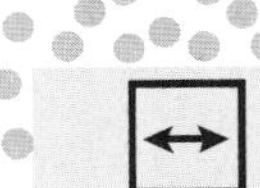

REVIEW

A series of #### symbols in a cell means that the value is too wide to be displayed in the currently selected font size.

4. Press Enter. The age is formatted as a date and is probably too wide to display.
5. Click cell C4 and press Ctrl+1. On the **Number** tab, choose **Number** with two decimal places and click **OK**. This is the age in days.
6. Press F2. Press Home and → to position the insertion point after the equal sign.
7. Key a left parenthesis **(** after the equal sign.
8. Press End and key a right parenthesis **)** after **A4** in the formula.

REVIEW

Excel calculates division before subtraction.

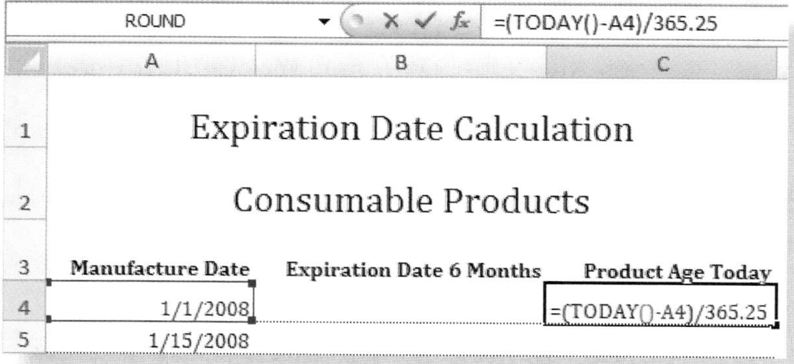

Figure 8-4
Converting the age formula to years
8-5.xlsx
ExpireDate sheet

NOTE

Dividing by 365.25 includes a leap year once every four years.

9. Key **/365.25** to divide by the number of days in a year. Press Enter.
10. Copy the formula in cell C4 to row 19.
11. Click cell B4 and key = to start a formula.
12. Click cell A4 and key + to add days to the manufacture date.
13. Key **6** and press Enter. This adds six days to the date.
14. Click cell B4, press F2, and edit the formula to add 180 days.
15. Copy the formula to row 19.

Exercise 8-7 DETERMINE TIME PASSED

Calculating time passed is similar to determining an age. You subtract the beginning time from the ending time. Excel usually shows time results as a fraction of a 24-hour day. To convert to hours, multiply the results by 24.

1. Click the **FreezerTime** tab.
2. In cell C6, key **8:30 am** and press →. Excel capitalizes the AM/PM reference.
3. In cell D6, key **4:30 pm**. Excel shows times as you key them, using a 12-hour AM/PM clock.
4. Key the following times in columns C and D.

	C	D
7	9 am	5 pm
8	10:30 am	6:15 pm
9	12 pm	8:30 pm
10	6 am	4 pm
11	1 pm	11 pm

5. In cell E6, key = and click cell D6, the ending time.

6. Key a minus sign (–) and click cell C6, the starting time. Press Enter.
7. Click cell E6 and press Ctrl+1. Click the **Number** tab.

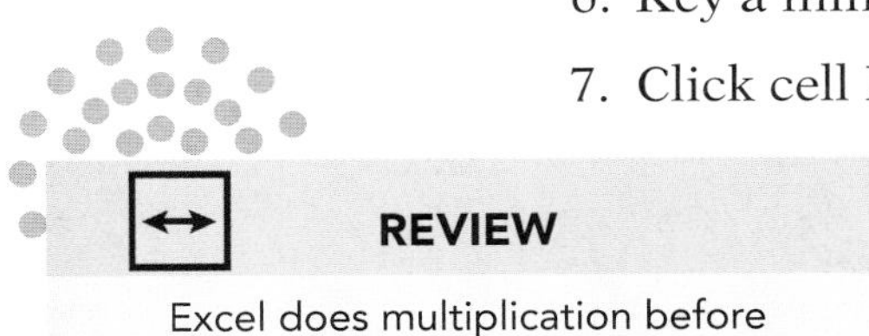

REVIEW

Excel does multiplication before subtraction unless you insert parentheses.

8. Choose **Number** with **3** decimal places. Click **OK**. The result is **.333**, representing one-third of a day.
9. Press F2 and press Home.
10. Press → and key a left parenthesis **(** after the equal sign.
11. Press End and key a right parenthesis **)**.

Figure 8-5
Converting time to hours
8-5.xlsx
FreezerTime sheet

ROUND =(D6-C6)*24

	A	B	C	D	E	F
1						
2		Freezer Time Calculation				
3		Special Flavors				
4						
5		Flavor	Time In	Time Out	Freezer Time	
6		Raspberry Roll	8:30 AM	4:30 PM	=(D6-C6)*24	
7		Macadamia Custard	9:00 AM	5:00 PM		

12. Key ***24** to multiply by the number of hours in a day. Press Enter.
13. Copy the formula to row 11, and fix the borders.

Exercise 8-8 GROUP SHEETS TO ADD FOOTERS

1. Save the workbook as ***[your initials]*8-8** in your Lesson 8 folder.
2. While the **FreezerTime** sheet is active, hold down Shift and click the **Recipes** tab.
3. Click the **Page Layout** tab. Click the Dialog Box Launcher for the **Page Setup** group.
4. Click the **Header/Footer** tab. Click **Custom Footer**.

5. Click the Format Text button A and choose 9-point regular Calibri. Key your name in the left section.

6. In the center section, click the Format Text button A and choose 9-point regular Calibri. Click the Insert Sheet Name button.
7. Insert the date using the same font in the right section. Click **OK**.
8. In the **Page Setup** dialog box, click the **Margins** tab. In the **Center on page** section, click to select **Horizontally**.

9. Click **Print Preview** in the **Page Setup** dialog box. This is the first page of three.
10. Press PageDown to see the other worksheets. Press PageUp to return to previous pages.
11. Click **Close Print Preview**.
12. Print while the worksheets are grouped. All three sheets print with the same footer.

Exercise 8-9 HIDE AND UNHIDE A WORKSHEET

You can hide a worksheet so that you do not see its tab while the workbook is open. This allows you to hide sheets that include sensitive information.

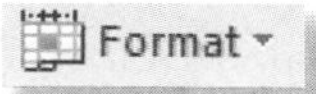

1. Right-click any worksheet tab and choose **Ungroup Sheets**.
2. Click the **ExpireDate** sheet. Click the **Home** tab.
3. In the **Cells** group, click the Format button Format. Choose **Hide & Unhide** and then choose **Hide Sheet**. The **ExpireDate** sheet no longer appears in the workbook.
4. Save and close the workbook. If you save and close a workbook with hidden sheets, the workbook will reopen just like that.
5. Open ***[your initials]*8-8**. There is no **ExpireDate** sheet visible.
6. In the **Cells** group, click the Format button Format. Choose **Hide & Unhide** and then choose **Unhide Sheet**. The Unhide dialog box lists the names of hidden sheets.
7. Choose **ExpireDate** in the list and click **OK**. The sheet is visible.
8. Save and close the workbook.

Creating Nested Functions

A *nested* function is a function inside another function. The argument for the main function is another function. The IF function is a function that is often used in nested functions as well as the ROUND function.

Exercise 8-10 NEST SUM AND ROUND

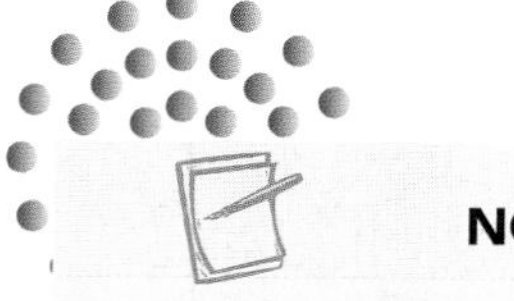

NOTE

A 5 percent increase multiplies the previous month's sales by 105 percent.

1. Open **CookieCrunch**.
2. Click cell C6 and notice the formula. Click cell D6 and check its formula. This worksheet uses a formula to compute a 5 percent sales increase from one month to the next and results in decimal values for most of the months.

3. Click cell H11. Click the Insert Function button in the formula bar.

TIP

You must choose the function category and immediately key the first letter of the function name to scroll the function list.

4. In the **Select a category** box, choose **Math & Trig**. Key **r** to move to the functions that begin with "r." Scroll and choose **Round**. Click **OK**.
5. Move the Function Arguments dialog box to see column headings and column H.
6. In the **Number** argument box, you will nest the SUM function. With the insertion point in the **Number** box, click the arrow for the **Name Box**.
7. Choose **SUM**. The Function Arguments dialog box now shows the SUM function, but it is nested in the ROUND function in the formula bar. The SUM function is bold in the formula bar, and the suggested range for the argument is highlighted and is correct (H6:H10).

NOTE

If SUM is not in the Name Box list, click **More Functions** and find it in the Math & Trig or Most Recently Used category.

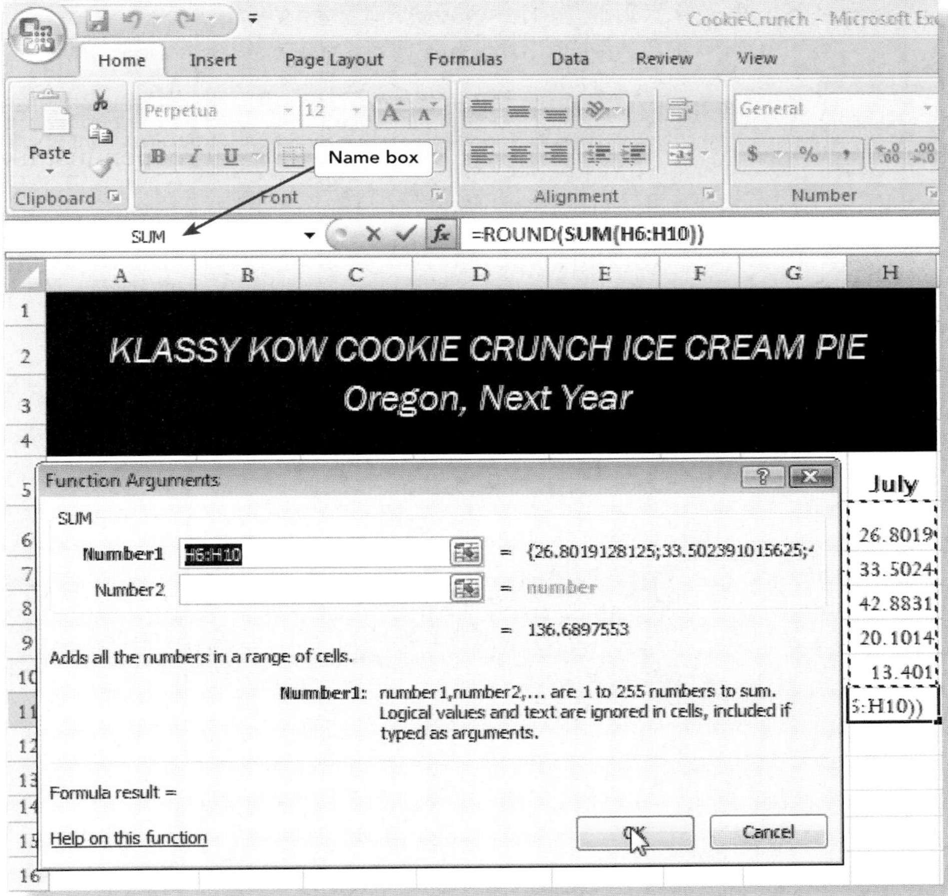

Figure 8-6
Nesting SUM in a ROUND function
CookieCrunch.xlsx PieSales sheet

8. Click anywhere in the word **ROUND** in the formula bar. The Function Arguments dialog box returns to the ROUND function and displays **SUM(H6:H10)** as the **Number** argument.

9. Click in the **Num_digits** argument box and key **0**. Click **OK**.
10. Display the Fill handle for cell H11 and drag left to copy the formula to cells G11:B11. All results are rounded to show no decimal places.

Exercise 8-11 CREATE A NESTED IF FUNCTION

A nested IF function tests for more than one logical test. In your worksheet, you will first check to see if the monthly total is greater than 110, and then you'll test if it is greater than 120.

1. Click cell B12 and click the **Formulas** tab. Click the Logical Logical . Choose **IF**.
2. In the **Logical_test** box, click cell B11. Key **>=120** after **B11** in the box. This tests if the value in cell B11 is equal to or greater than 120.
3. Click in the **Value_if_true** box. Key **120 or More**. If the value in cell B11 is greater than 120, the text "120 or More" will be shown.
4. Click in the **Value_if_false** box. If the value is not over 120, you will check if it is equal to or over 110. This is another IF function.
5. While the insertion point is in the **Value_if_false** box, click **IF** in the Name Box. The Function Arguments dialog box updates to show another IF statement. The second IF function is bold in the formula bar to show that it is the one you are now building.
6. In the **Logical_test** box, click cell B11. Key **>=110** after **B11**. Now you are determining if the value in cell B11 is equal to or greater than 110.
7. Click in the **Value_if_true** box. Key **110 or More** as the result text.
8. Click in the **Value_if_false** box. Key **Less than 110** and click **OK**.

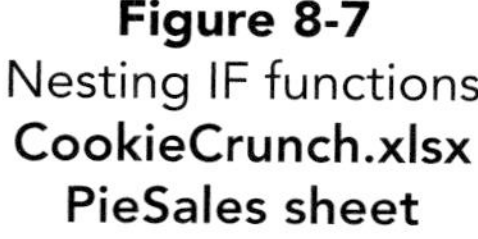

Figure 8-7
Nesting IF functions
CookieCrunch.xlsx
PieSales sheet

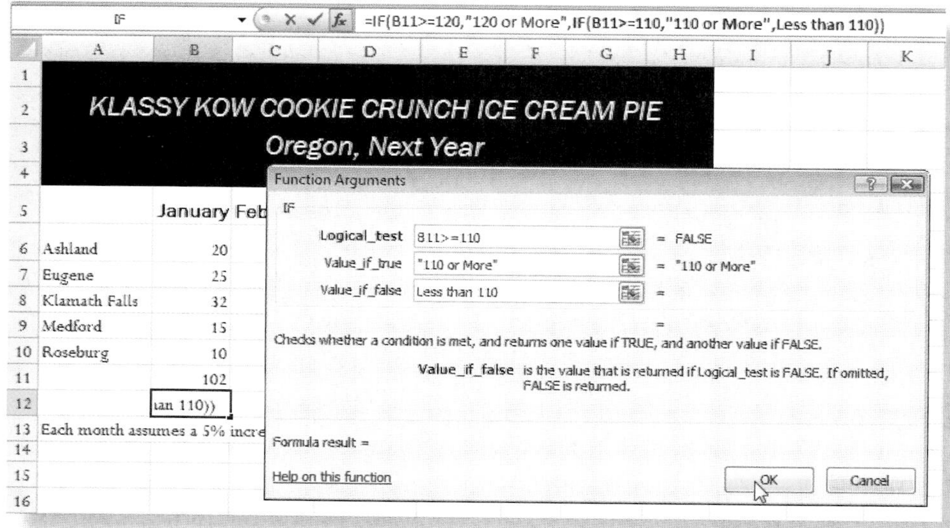

9. Copy the formula to cells C12:H12 and AutoFit columns B:H.
10. Set the height of row 13 to **67.50 (90 pixels)**.
11. Click the **Home** tab. Select cells A13:H13. In the **Alignment** group, click the Merge & Center button. Click the Middle Align button.
12. Right-align the data in row 12.
13. Set the page to landscape orientation and use horizontal centering.

Exercise 8-12 SET TOP/BOTTOM CONDITIONAL FORMATTING

In addition to data visualizations, you can use conditional formatting to display cells with a particular format based on common numerical rankings. The Top/Bottom Rules command has options to format the top or bottom number of items or a percentage. It can also distinguish values above or below average.

1. Select cells B6:H10. On the Home tab in the Styles group, click the Conditional Formatting button.
2. Choose **Top/Bottom Rules** and then **Top 10 Items**. The Top 10 Items dialog box allows you to set how many and which format.

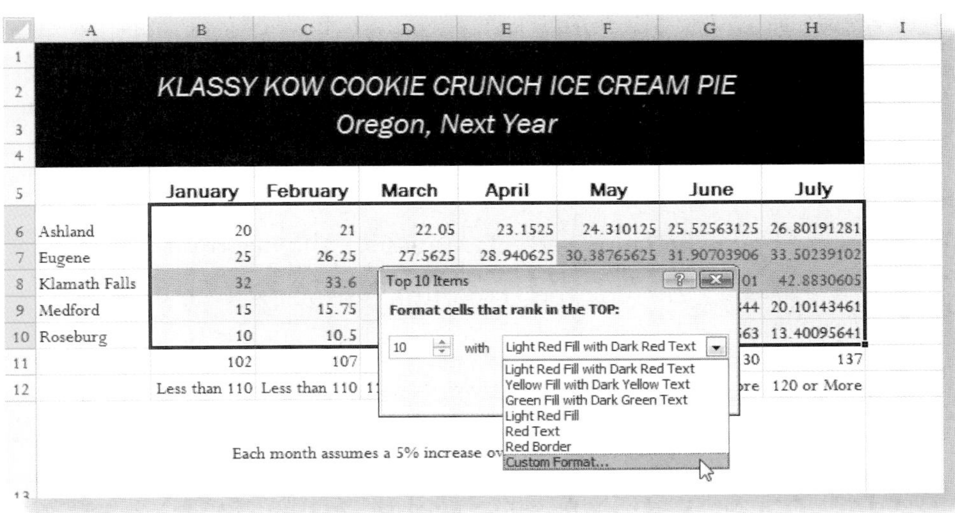

Figure 8-8
Setting top/bottom conditional formatting
CookieCrunch.xlsx PieSales sheet

3. Click the arrow next to the **With** box and choose **Custom Format**. The Format Cells dialog box opens. You cannot change the font, but you can change the style, color, fill, and borders.
4. Choose **Bold Italic** on the **Font** tab.

5. Click the **Fill** tab. Choose a medium gray color and click **OK**.
6. Click **OK**. Click a cell away from the values to better see the formatting.
7. Select cells B6:H10. Click the Conditional Formatting button and choose **Manage Rules**.
8. Click **Edit Rule**. The Edit Formatting Rule dialog box opens.
9. Click **Format**. Set the font to be bold, but not italic. Click **OK** to return to your worksheet.
10. Save the workbook as ***[your initials]*8-12** in your Lesson 8 folder.

Creating a Hyperlink

A *hyperlink* is a clickable object or text that, when clicked, displays another file, opens another program, shows a Web page, or displays an e-mail address. A hyperlink is a shortcut to files on your computer, your network, or the World Wide Web. As you insert hyperlinks in your work, Excel keeps a list of the addresses in the Insert Hyperlink dialog box. You can key a new entry or choose an existing link from the list.

A text hyperlink is shown in color and is underlined. There are several ways to add a hyperlink to your worksheet:

- Click the Hyperlink button on the **Insert** tab.
- Right-click the cell and choose **Hyperlink** from the shortcut menu.
- Press Ctrl+K.

Exercise 8-13 CREATE A HYPERLINK

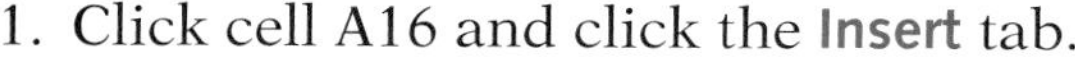

1. Click cell A16 and click the **Insert** tab.

2. Click the Hyperlink button. The Insert Hyperlink dialog box opens.
3. Click the **E-mail Address** button in the **Link to** bar. Key YourE-MailAddress in the **E-mail address** text box. Excel adds **mailto:** for e-mail addresses and shadows your address in the **Text to display** box.
4. Drag to select the address in the **Text to display** box.
5. Key **Click here to contact our office.**
6. Click the **ScreenTip** button. Key **Oregon Shops Only**. Click **OK**.

Figure 8-9
Insert Hyperlink dialog box
8-12.xlsx
PieSales sheet

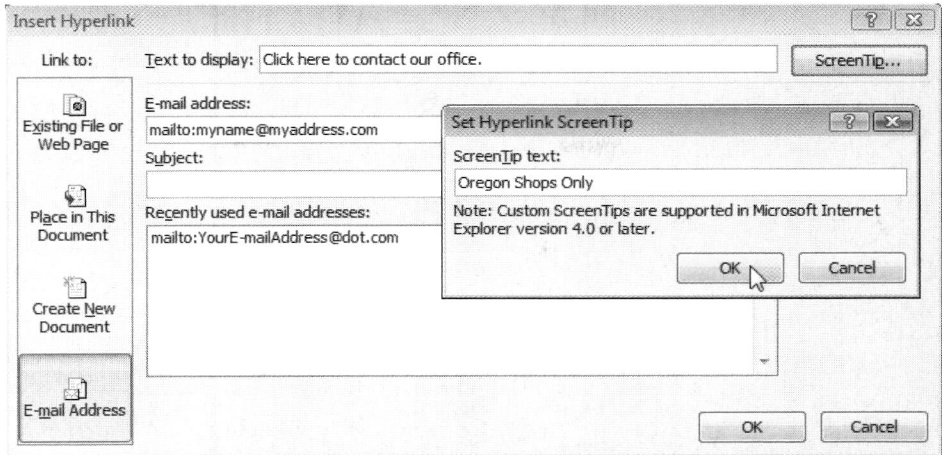

NOTE

If you click this hyperlink, Excel opens your e-mail program with your e-mail address inserted as the recipient.

7. Click **OK** again. Hyperlink text appears in color and is underlined. Hyperlink text is styled by the document theme, but its font and color are not shown in any galleries.
8. Position the mouse pointer on cell A16 to see the ScreenTip.

Figure 8-10
Hyperlink and ScreenTip
8-12.xlsx
PieSales sheet

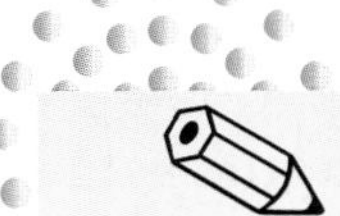

TIP

To edit or delete a hyperlink, right-click the cell and choose **Edit Hyperlink** or **Remove Hyperlink**. You can also right-click and choose **Format Cells** to change the appearance of the hyperlink text.

9. Press Ctrl+Home. Save the workbook as ***[your initials]*8-13** in your folder.

Exercise 8-14 RUN THE COMPATIBILITY CHECKER

If you work with people who use previous versions of Excel, you can save your work in an appropriate format for them. Two formats that are fairly common are *XLS* (earlier Excel version) and CSV (comma-separated values).

Before saving a workbook as an XLS file, you can determine if any of its elements won't be effective or visible in the previous version.

CSV files are simple text files with commas to separate the columns. CSV files generally do not include any type of formatting. Many software applications, including Word, can open a CSV file.

1. Click the Microsoft Office Button and hover over **Prepare**.
2. Choose **Run Compatibility Checker**. The dialog box opens and shows which features will not be functional in the earlier Excel file. Although earlier versions of Excel do have conditional formatting, they do not include all the subtleties of this version.

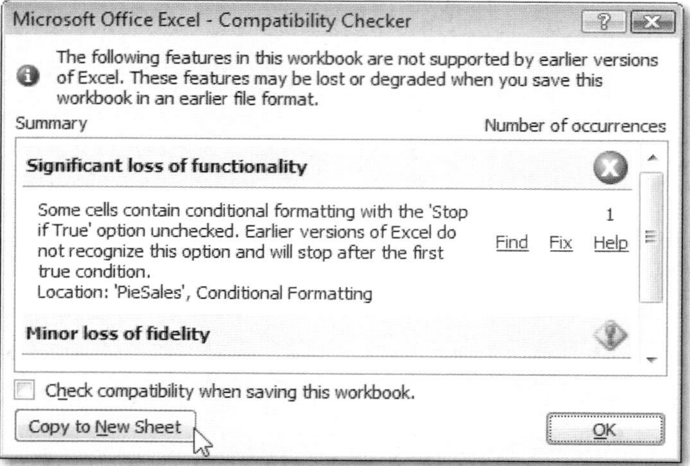

Figure 8-11
Compatibility Checker dialog box
8-13.xlsx
PieSales sheet

3. Click **Copy to New Sheet**. This creates a documentation sheet that explains the compatibility issues. These issues are more related to formatting than to the actual data.
4. Click the **PieSales** tab.
5. Press F12. Click the **Save as type** arrow.
6. Choose **Excel 97-2003 Workbook**. This workbook will have the **xls** extension, so you can use the same name.
7. Click **Save**. The Compatibility Checker runs automatically when you choose this file type.
8. Click **Continue**. The file has been saved. To really see the difference, you need to open the **.xls** file in an earlier version of Excel.

9. Press F12. Click the **Save as type** arrow.
10. Choose **CSV(Comma delimited)** for a different format. The filename is the same, but the workbook will have the **csv** filename extension.
11. Click **Save**. A message box alerts you that the second sheet will not be included.
12. Click **OK**. There are more problems in converting the file to this format.

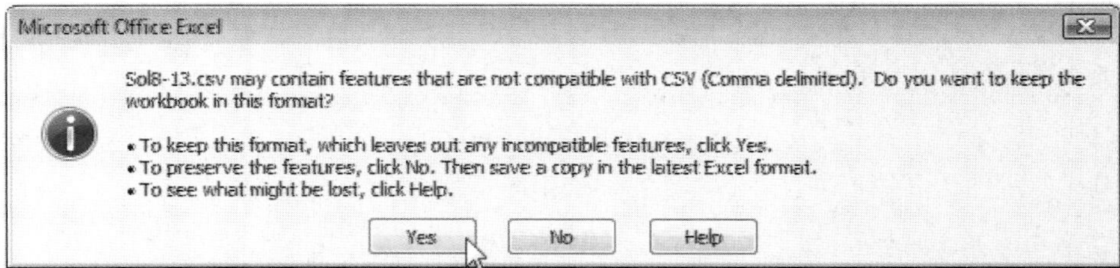

Figure 8-12
Message box about converting file **8-13.xlsx PieSales sheet**

13. Click **Yes**. The file is saved.
14. Close the workbook without saving.

Using Online Help

Excel is a *mail-enabled* program, which means you can e-mail a workbook to a coworker from within Excel.

USE HELP TO LEARN ABOUT EXCEL'S E-MAIL CAPABILITIES

1. In a new workbook, click the Microsoft Office Excel Help button.
2. In the Search box, key **e-mail** and press Enter. Find and review topics about sending a workbook in e-mail.
3. Close the Help window when you are finished reading about e-mail.

Lesson 8 Summary

- Use the INT function to display a value with no decimal positions.
- The ROUND function adjusts a value up or down, depending on how many digits you use for rounding. It can round to the left or right of the decimal point.
- Excel uses a serial number system for dates and times. This allows it to make date and time calculations.

- In most date and time calculations, you need to convert the results to the proper format. This may require additional arithmetic to change days to years or fractional days to hours.
- You can hide a worksheet so that its tab is not visible.
- A nested function is a function used as an argument for another function.
- The Conditional Formatting command includes a Top/Bottom Rules setting that formats the highest or lowest values or percentages in a range.
- Hyperlinks enable you to jump to other files, e-mail addresses, or Web sites.
- Workbooks can be saved in a variety of file formats for exchanging data with others. These include CSV text files and earlier versions of Excel.
- The Compatibility Checker scans a workbook before it is saved as an earlier Excel file. It notes features and commands that will not work in the earlier version.

LESSON 8		Command Summary	
Feature	**Button**	**Task Path**	**Keyboard**
Compatibility Checker		Microsoft Office, Prepare	
CSV file		Microsoft Office, Save As	F12
Hide sheet	Format	Home, Cells, Format, Hide & Unhide	
Insert hyperlink	Hyperlink	Insert, Links	Ctrl+K
Top/Bottom Rule	Conditional Formatting	Home, Cells, Conditional Formatting	
Unhide sheet	Format	Home, Cells, Format, Hide & Unhide	
XLS file		Microsoft Office, Save As	F12

unit 3

ENHANCING WORKSHEET APPEARANCE

Lesson 9

Building Charts

OBJECTIVES

After completing this lesson, you will be able to:

1. View and print charts.
2. Work with chart elements.
3. Create charts.
4. Edit chart data.
5. Use images, gradients, and textures for a data series.
6. Create a combination chart.

MCAS OBJECTIVES

In this lesson:

XL07 4.1
XL07 4.1.1
XL07 4.1.2
XL07 4.1.3
XL07 4.2
XL07 4.2.1
XL07 4.2.2
XL07 4.2.3

Estimated Time: 2 hours

A *chart* is a visual representation of information in a worksheet. Charts can help you make comparisons, identify patterns, and recognize trends.

You can create a chart on the same sheet as its data or on its own sheet in the workbook. In either case, a chart is linked to the data used to create it and is updated when you edit the data.

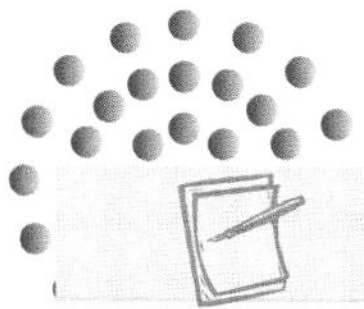

NOTE

The workbooks you create and use in this course relate to the Case Study (see the frontmatter of the book) about Klassy Kow Ice Cream, Inc., a fictional ice cream company.

Viewing and Printing a Chart

A chart that appears on the same sheet as the data is a graphic object and can be selected, sized, moved, and edited. An object is a separate, clickable element or part of a worksheet or chart. When a workbook has objects, you can use the Selection pane to select, view, and rearrange them.

Exercise 9-1 VIEW A CHART OBJECT

When you select a chart, the Chart Tools are activated. These tools include three command tabs: the Design tab, the Layout tab, and the Format tab.

1. Open **SeptChart**. The Zoom size is set to 75% so that you can see more of the worksheet and the chart without scrolling.
2. Click in the white chart background area to select the chart. The Chart Tools command tabs are now visible. The chart is surrounded by a light frame.
3. Press Alt to see the KeyTips. Key **jo** to select the Chart Tools Format tab. The Current Selection group shows that the chart area is the active chart element.

4. In the **Arrange** group, click the Selection Pane button. This worksheet has a chart and a text box. The Eye button toggles the object's visibility on/off.

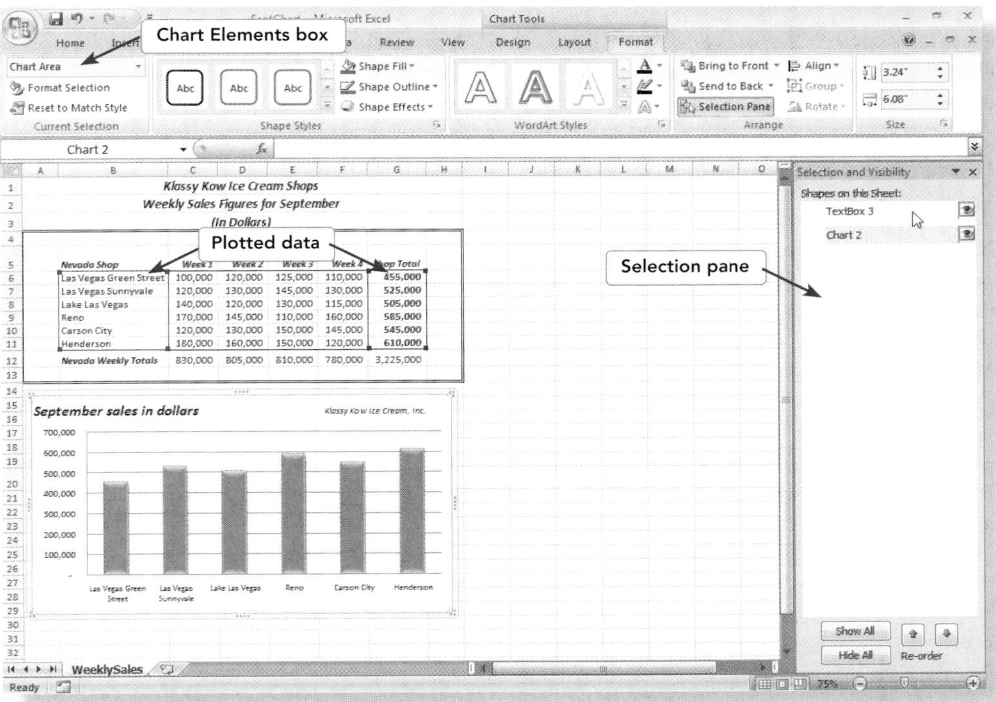

Figure 9-1
Chart selected in the worksheet
SeptChart.xlsx
WeeklySales sheet

NOTE

In this worksheet, the text box is on top of the chart; otherwise it would be hidden by the chart's white background.

5. Click the Eye button for **TextBox 3**. The text box is the company name in the top-right corner of the chart. It's hidden now.
6. Click the Eye button for **TextBox 3** again to display it.
7. Toggle the visibility of **Chart 2** on/off.

Exercise 9-2 PRINT A CHART OBJECT

1. Click cell A1 to deselect the chart. The background frame is removed from the chart.
2. Press Alt and key **n**. The Insert tab is active.
3. Key **h** to choose **Header & Footer**.
4. Click the Header button. A list of header arrangements opens.
5. Choose the second option from the bottom of the list—the user name, the page number, and the date.
6. Click the user name and change it to your name.
7. Click cell A1 and print the sheet. The worksheet and the chart print on a single page.
8. Click in the white background chart area to select the chart.
9. Press Ctrl+P. In the **Print what** group, **Selected Chart** is chosen. Click **OK**. The chart prints by itself in landscape orientation. When you print a selected element, the header is not included, because a header is a page setting.
10. Click cell A1. Click the Normal button in the status bar.
11. Click the Close button in the **Selection & Visibility** pane.

NOTE

The user name in a classroom setting is set by the class or network administrator.

Working with Chart Elements

A chart is composed of many clickable elements or objects. These elements are formatted by the current layout and style, but you can change each object on its own, too. Here is a brief description of Excel chart elements:

- The *chart area* is the background for the chart. It can be filled with a color or pattern.
- An *axis* is the horizontal or vertical line that encloses the data.

- The *horizontal (category) axis* is created from row or column headings in the data. A category describes what is shown in the chart.
- The *vertical (value) axis* shows the numbers on the chart. Excel creates a range of values (the *scale*) based on the data.
- An *axis title* is an optional title for the categories or values.
- The *plot area* is the rectangular area bounded by the horizontal and vertical axes.
- The *chart title* is an optional title or name for the chart.
- A *data series* is a collection of related values from the worksheet. These values are in the same column or row and translate into the columns, lines, pie slices, and so on.
- A *data point* is a single value or piece of data from the data series.
- A *data marker* is the object that represents individual values. The marker can be a bar, a column, a point on a line, or an image.
- A *legend* is an element that explains the symbols, textures, or colors used to differentiate series in the chart.
- A *gridline* is a horizontal or vertical line that extends across the plot area to make it easier to read and follow the values.
- A *tick mark* is a small line or marker on the horizontal (category) and vertical (value) axes to help in reading the values.

Figure 9-2
Excel chart elements

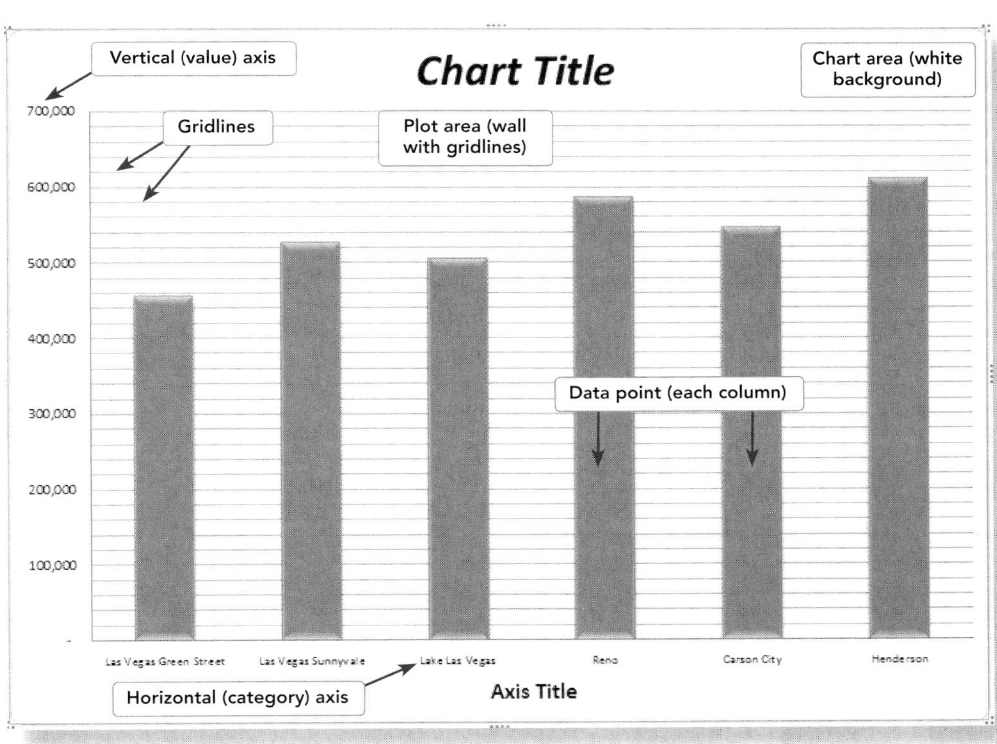

Exercise 9-3 CHANGE THE CHART LAYOUT

The Chart Tools command tabs include layout and style choices to help you build a professional-looking chart. The Chart Layouts gallery offers various arrangements of chart elements for each chart type.

1. Click the chart background. Click the **Chart Tools Design** tab.
2. In the **Chart Layouts** group, click the More button. The Chart Layout gallery opens.
3. Click **Layout 2**. The chart is redesigned to show values above the columns with no values along the vertical axis.

Figure 9-3
The Chart Layouts gallery
SeptChart.xlsx
WeeklySales sheet

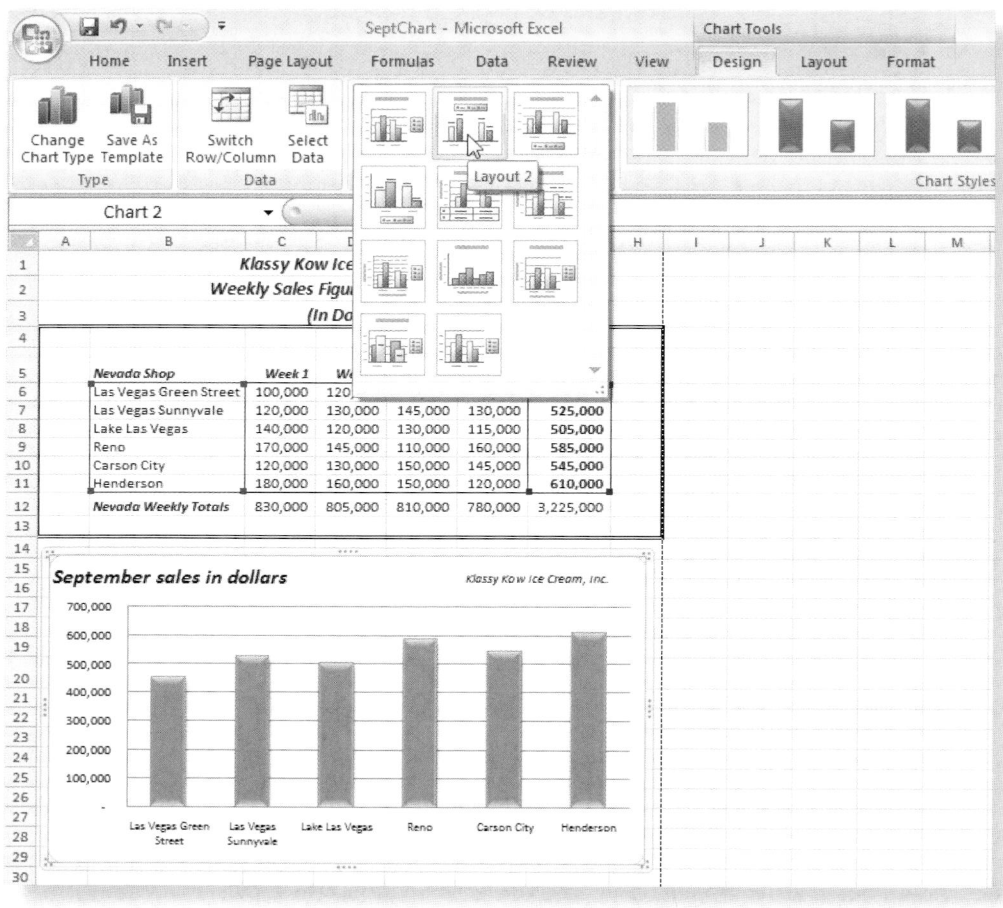

TIP

In a column chart with one series, you do not need a legend.

4. In the **Chart Layouts** gallery, click **Layout 3**. This is similar to Layout 1 but with a legend at the bottom (**Series 1**).
5. In the **Chart Layouts** group, click the More button. Click **Layout 4**. This layout does not include a chart title.
6. Choose **Layout 3**. The chart title object is a placeholder and will need to be rekeyed (later in the lesson). There is a legend at the bottom.

Exercise 9-4 CHANGE THE CHART STYLE

The Chart Styles gallery provides variations in colors and effects for chart elements using the document theme. There are many predefined styles that combine theme colors and effects.

1. In the **Chart Styles** group, click the More button. The Chart Styles gallery opens. Your chart uses Style 19, but the column colors were modified.
2. Click **Style 34**. The columns show a flat effect in a new color.

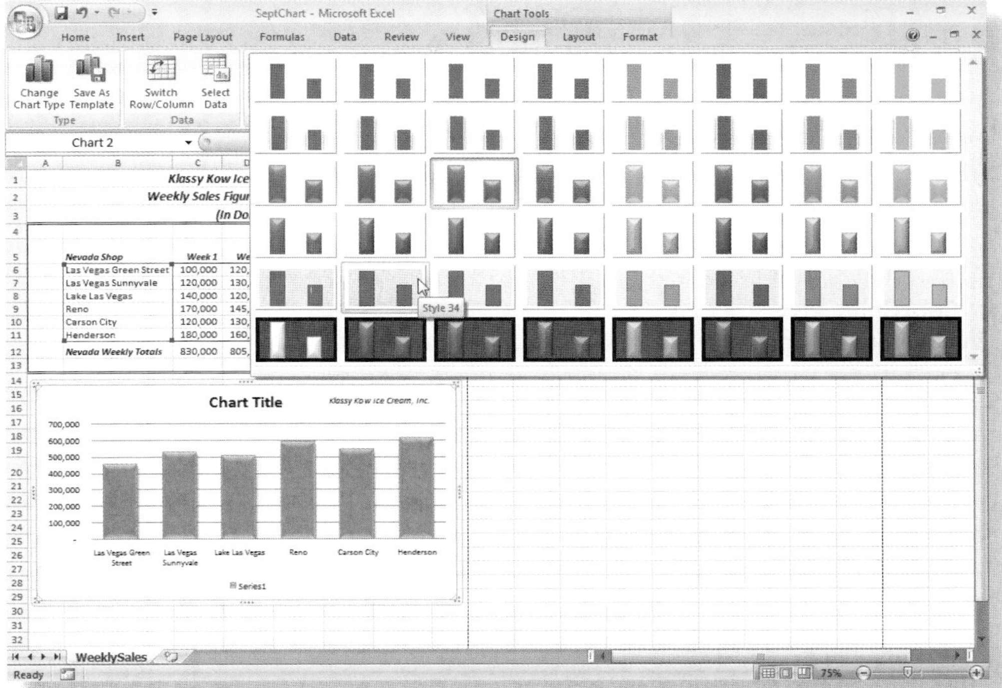

Figure 9-4
The Chart Styles gallery
SeptChart.xlsx
WeeklySales sheet

3. In the **Chart Styles** group, click the More button. Click **Style 44**. This style changes the background color, too.
4. Choose **Style 20**. The columns again have a beveled effect.

Exercise 9-5 EDIT AND FORMAT THE CHART TITLE

Chart elements show a ScreenTip when you hover over them. To edit an element, select it by pointing and clicking. When an element is selected, it shows a bounding frame and selection handles, and its name appears in the Chart Elements box on the Chart Tools Format tab. *Selection handles* are small circles, rectangles, or dots at the corners and along each border of the bounding frame. They can be used to size the element.

NOTE

The bounding box and selection handles do not print.

1. Click the **Chart Tools Format** tab.
2. Point at the placeholder text **Chart Title** on the chart and click. The object is selected and shows a bounding border with four selection handles. Its name appears in the Chart Elements box in the Current Selection group.
3. Point at an edge of the object to display a four-pointed arrow. This is the move pointer.
4. Drag the object left to align with the values on the vertical axis.
5. Triple-click **Chart Title**. This is placeholder text.
6. Key **Nevada sales for September**. The placeholder text is replaced.
7. Triple-click **Nevada sales for September** to select it. Point at the Mini toolbar.
8. Click the Italic button *I*. Change the font size to 16.

Figure 9-5
Editing the chart title
SeptChart.xlsx
WeeklySales sheet

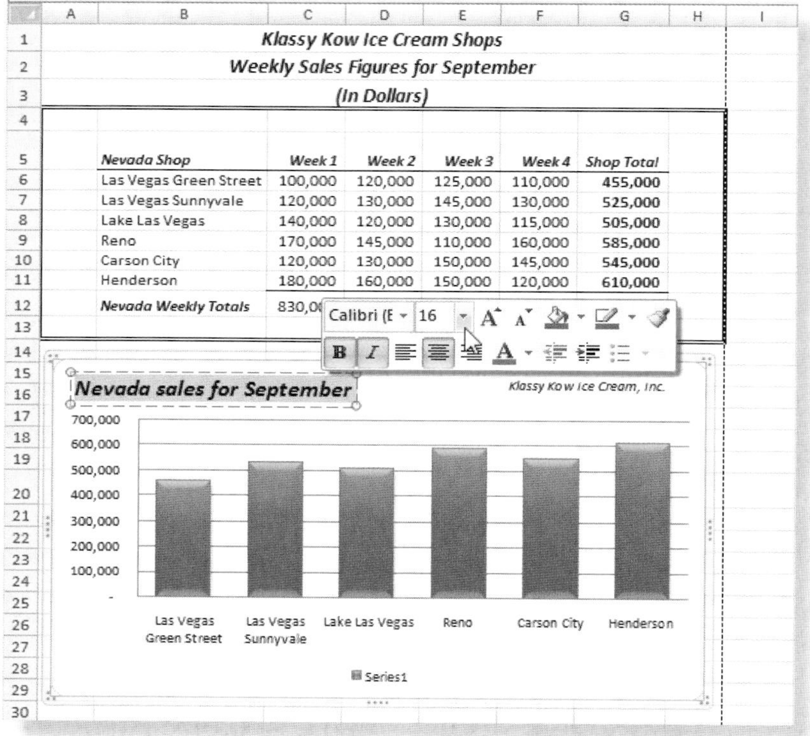

Klassy Kow Ice Cream Shops
Weekly Sales Figures for September
(In Dollars)

Nevada Shop	Week 1	Week 2	Week 3	Week 4	Shop Total
Las Vegas Green Street	100,000	120,000	125,000	110,000	**455,000**
Las Vegas Sunnyvale	120,000	130,000	145,000	130,000	**525,000**
Lake Las Vegas	140,000	120,000	130,000	115,000	**505,000**
Reno	170,000	145,000	110,000	160,000	**585,000**
Carson City	120,000	130,000	150,000	145,000	**545,000**
Henderson	180,000	160,000	150,000	120,000	**610,000**
Nevada Weekly Totals	830,0				

NOTE

If you accidentally select the text box with "Klassy Kow Ice Cream, Inc.," the Drawing Tools Format command tab is activated. Click away from that area in the chart background.

9. Click the white background area of the chart to deselect the title.

Exercise 9-6 SET SHAPE FILL AND EFFECTS

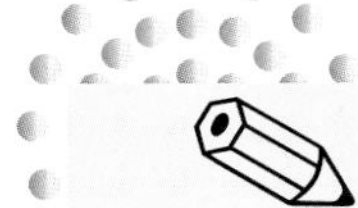

TIP

Many chart experts refer to the value axis as the y-axis and the category (horizontal) axis as the x-axis.

The data series in this chart are the values from column G. Each value is represented by the height of its column. The values are plotted against the value (vertical) axis, the column of numbers at the left. The category for this chart is the city name, shown along the horizontal axis.

1. Make sure the chart is selected.
2. Rest the mouse pointer on the Reno column to see its ScreenTip. It is one data point from the series.
3. Click the Reno column. The entire data series is selected, and the Chart Elements box shows **Series 1**. This is the first (and only) series in this chart.
4. In the **Shape Styles** group on the **Chart Tools Format** tab, click the More button for the **Shape Styles**. The styles include some with an outline and no fill, some with both outline and fill, and beveled and shadow styles.

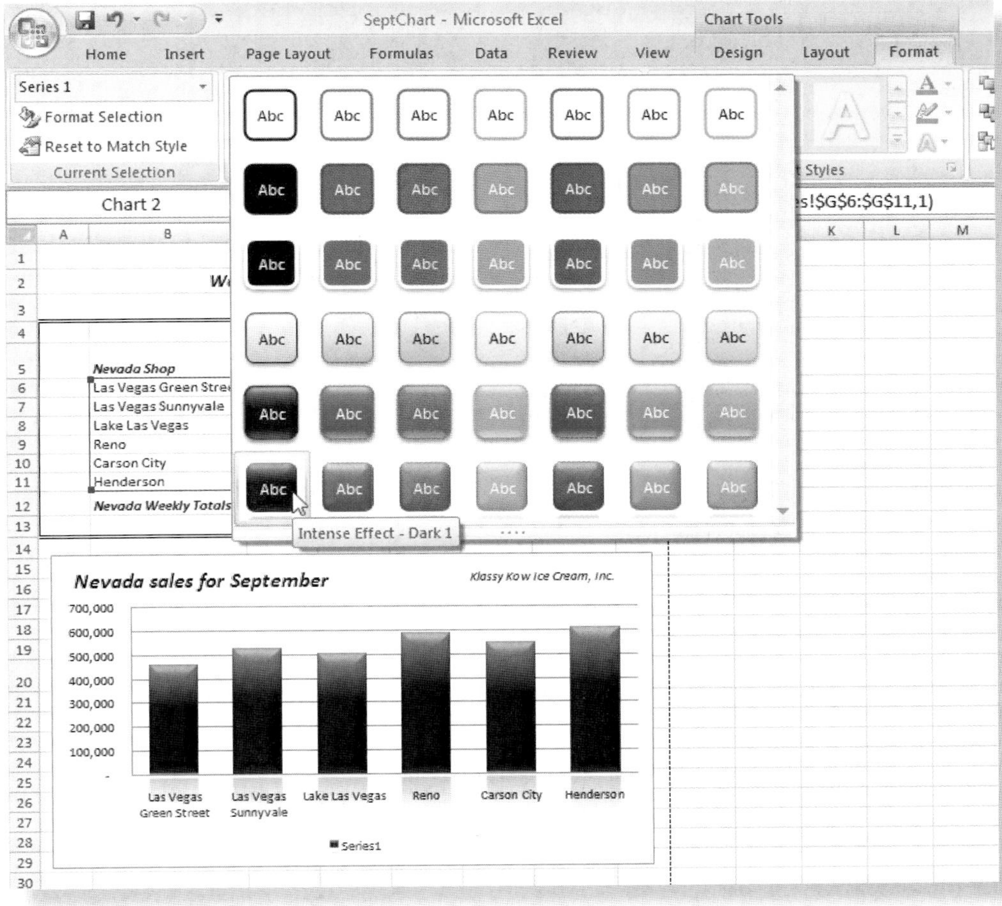

Figure 9-6
Changing the shape's style
SeptChart.xlsx
WeeklySales sheet

5. Choose **Intense Effect, Dark 1**. Each column now has a reflection, too.
6. In the **Shape Styles** group, click the Shape Fill button.
7. Choose **White, Background 1, Darker 35%** in the first column.
8. In the **Shape Styles** group, click the Shape Effects button. Most effects are available for this shape.

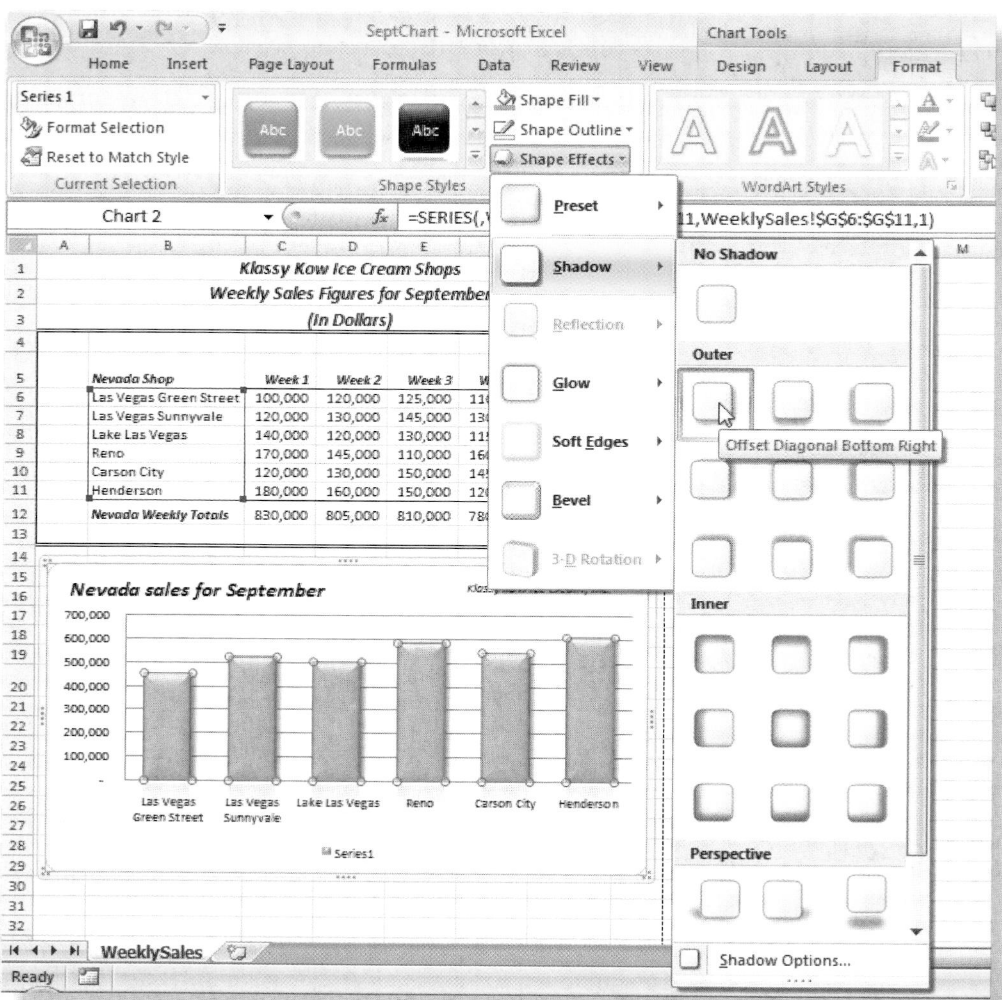

Figure 9-7
Changing the shape's effect
SeptChart.xlsx WeeklySales sheet

9. Hover over **Shadow** to display its gallery. Then choose **Offset Diagonal Bottom Right** (first effect in the Outer group).
10. Click the white chart background.

Exercise 9-7 SET AND FORMAT DATA LABELS

A *data label* is an optional title shown for each value. It is the value from column G in this case. The Chart Tools Layout tab provides options for setting and positioning individual chart elements.

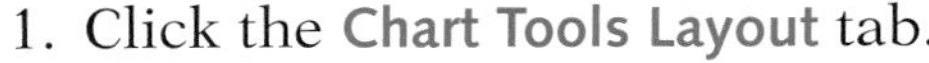

1. Click the **Chart Tools Layout** tab.

2. Hover over the Data Labels button and read its ScreenTip. Click one of the labels.
3. Click the Data Labels button and choose **Outside End**. The value of each data point appears above its column.
4. Rest the mouse pointer on one of the data labels to see the ScreenTip.
5. Click the **Chart Tools Format** tab. Click the arrow next to the **Chart Elements** box and choose **Series 1 Data Labels**. The data labels are selected and show bounding boxes and selection handles.
6. Click the **Home** tab and change the font size to 9 points.

NOTE

The Chart Elements box is in the Current Selection group on both the Layout and Format command tabs.

Exercise 9-8 FORMAT THE AXES

The Horizontal (Category) Axis is the x-axis in this chart, the city names.

1. Position the mouse pointer on a city name to see its ScreenTip.
2. Click the **Chart Tools Format** tab. Click the **Chart Elements** arrow and choose **Horizontal (Category) Axis**. The city names are selected and show a bounding box and selection handles.
3. On the **Home** tab, change the font size to 8 points.
4. Click one of the values along the Vertical (Value) Axis, the y-axis, the sales in dollars.

5. Click the **Chart Tools Layout** tab. Click the Axes button. Choose **Primary Vertical Axis** and **None**. With the data labels displayed, you don't need the axis values.
6. Right-click one of the data labels (above the columns). Choose **Format Data Labels**.
7. Click **Number**. Choose **Currency** with **0** decimals and **$** as the **Symbol**. Click **Close**.

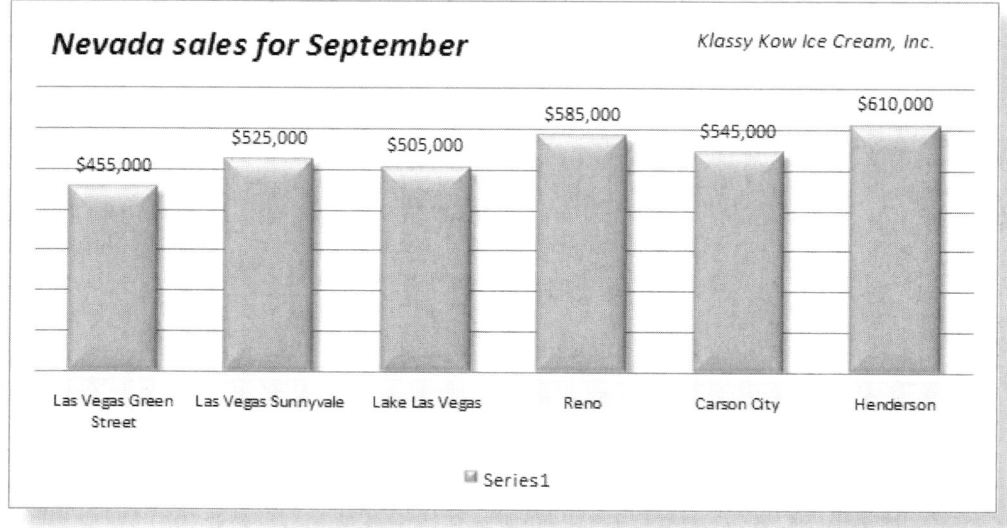

Figure 9-8
Formatted data labels
SeptChart.xlsx
WeklySales sheet

8. Click a cell in column I to better see the chart.

Exercise 9-9 FORMAT THE PLOT AND CHART AREAS

1. Click **Series 1** at the bottom of the chart. This is the legend. There is one series in this chart, the amount shown by each column.
2. Press Delete.
3. Click the **Chart Tools Format** tab. Click the **Chart Elements** arrow and choose **Plot Area**. The plot area is the background grid for the columns, currently white. It is selected.

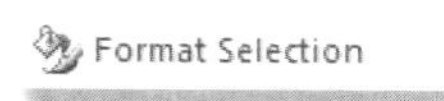

TIP

Choosing no background color means your chart will print faster than with a white background color and look the same on white paper.

4. In the **Current Selection** group, click the Format Selection button.
5. On the **Fill** pane, choose **No fill**. Click **Close**. The color (white) is removed but is not noticeable yet.
6. Click the **Chart Elements** arrow and choose **Chart Area**. The chart's background is selected; it is white, too.
7. Click the Format Selection button.
8. On the **Fill** pane, choose **No fill**. Click **Close**. You can now see that there is no fill color.
9. Click cell A1.
10. Save the workbook as ***[your initials]*****9-9** in a folder for Lesson 9.
11. Close the workbook.

Creating Charts

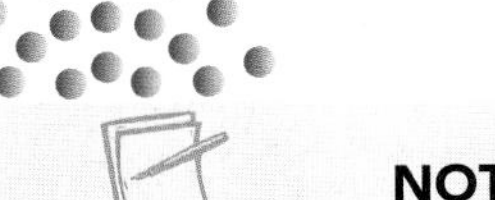

Before you build your own chart, you must consider two questions. First, what data should you use for the chart? And, second, what type of chart is best for that data? With practice and experience, you can develop a good sense of how to identify data and choose chart types.

You can create basic chart types such as column charts, bar charts, pie charts, and line charts. You can also create specialized charts such as doughnut and radar charts. Table 9-1 describes the chart types available.

NOTE

The appearance of a button in the Ribbon is affected by the screen size and resolution setting. All buttons have ScreenTips for clarification.

TABLE 9-1 Chart Types in Excel

Type	Definition
Column	A column chart is the most popular chart type. Column charts show how values change over a period of time or make comparisons among items. They can be prepared with 3-D effects or stacked columns. Categories are on the horizontal axis (x), and values are on the vertical axis (y). The shape can also be a cone, a cylinder, or a pyramid.
Line	Line charts show trends in data over a period of time. They emphasize the rate of change. 3-D effects are available. Lines can be stacked and can show markers, a symbol that indicates a single value.
Pie	Pie charts show one data series and compare the sizes of each part of a whole. Pie charts should have fewer than six data points to be easy to interpret. A pie chart can use 3-D effects and can show exploded slices.
Bar	Bar charts illustrate comparisons among items or show individual figures at a specific time. Bar charts can use 3-D effects and stacked bars. Categories are on the vertical axis (y). Values are on the horizontal axis (x). The shape can also be a cone, a cylinder, or a pyramid.
Area	Area charts look like colored-in line charts. They show the rate of change and emphasize the magnitude of the change. 3-D effects are available.
Scatter	Scatter charts are used to show relationships between two values, such as comparing additional advertising to increased sales. Scatter charts do not have a category; both axes show numbers/values.
Stock	Stock charts are often called "high-low-close charts." They use three series of data in high, low, close order. They can also use volume as a fourth series.
Surface	Surface charts illustrate optimum combinations of two sets of data. They show two or more series on a surface. Surface charts can use 3-D effects.
Doughnut	Doughnut charts compare the sizes of parts. A doughnut chart has a hole in the middle. A doughnut chart shows the relative proportion of the whole. A doughnut chart can show more than one data series, with each concentric ring representing a series.
Bubble	Bubble charts compare sets of three values. They are like scatter charts with the third value displayed as the size of the bubble. Bubble charts can be 3-D.
Radar	Radar charts show the frequency of data relative to a center point and to other data points. There is a separate axis for each category, and each axis extends from the center. Lines connect the values in a series.

Exercise 9-10 CREATE AND EDIT A CHART SHEET

After you select values and labels, press F11 to create a chart sheet with the default chart type. It is inserted on a new sheet, and you can edit it like any chart.

1. Open **MayChart**. There is no chart yet.
2. Select cells B6:C11. This range includes the province/country category and the values.
3. Press F11. A column chart is inserted on its own sheet.
4. On the **Chart Tools Design** tab in the **Chart Layouts** group, click the More button.
5. Choose **Layout 3**. This layout includes a chart title and a legend (at the bottom).
6. Click the chart title object. Its bounding box and selection handles are visible.
7. Triple-click the placeholder text. Key **Number of Kowabungas Sold**.
8. Click any column and notice that the entire series is selected.
9. While all columns are selected, click the "British Columbia" column. It is selected alone.
10. Click the **Chart Tools Format** tab. In the **Shape Styles** group, click the Shape Fill button.

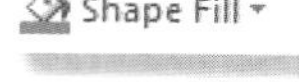

11. Choose **Red, Accent 2** in the sixth column. Only the selected column is changed.

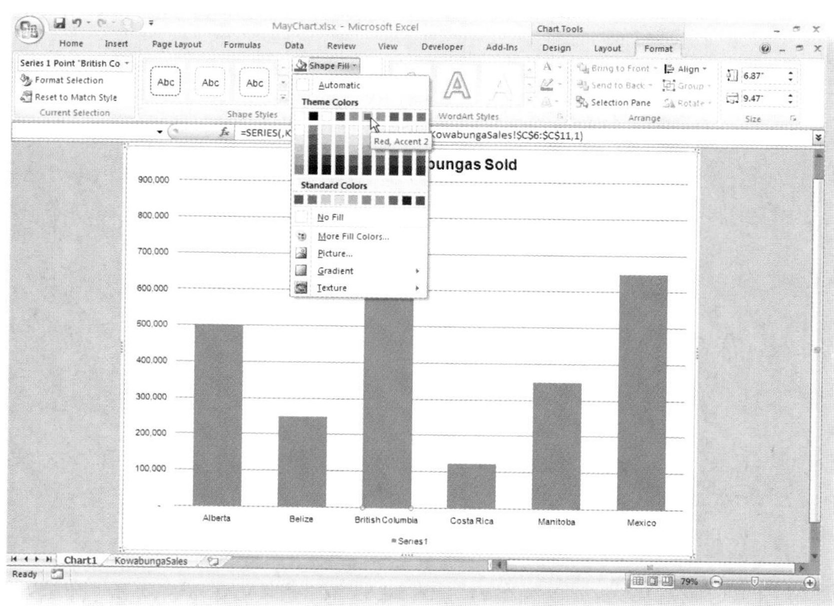

Figure 9-9
Changing an individual column
MayChart.xlsx
Chart1 sheet

12. Click the legend at the bottom of the sheet and press Delete.

Exercise 9-11 CREATE A CHART OBJECT

A *chart object* appears on the same sheet as the data; it may also be called an *embedded chart*. You create it by choosing the chart type from the Insert command tab.

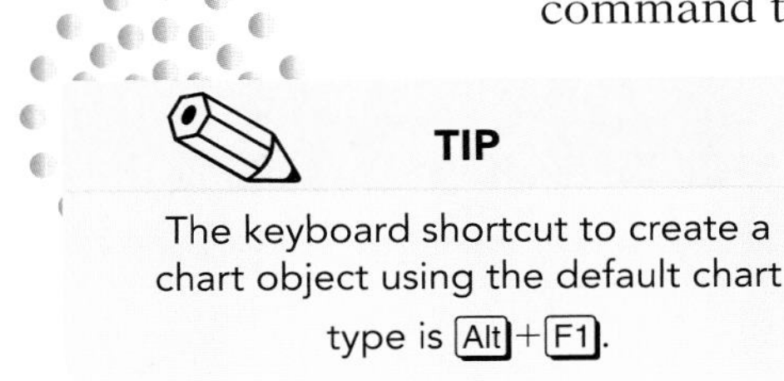

TIP
The keyboard shortcut to create a chart object using the default chart type is Alt+F1.

1. Click the **KowabungaSales** tab. Cells B6:C11 are still selected.

2. Click the **Insert** tab. The Charts group includes buttons for the most commonly used chart types.

3. Click the Pie button. You can create two- or three-dimensional charts. A ScreenTip describes each type when you hover over the icon.

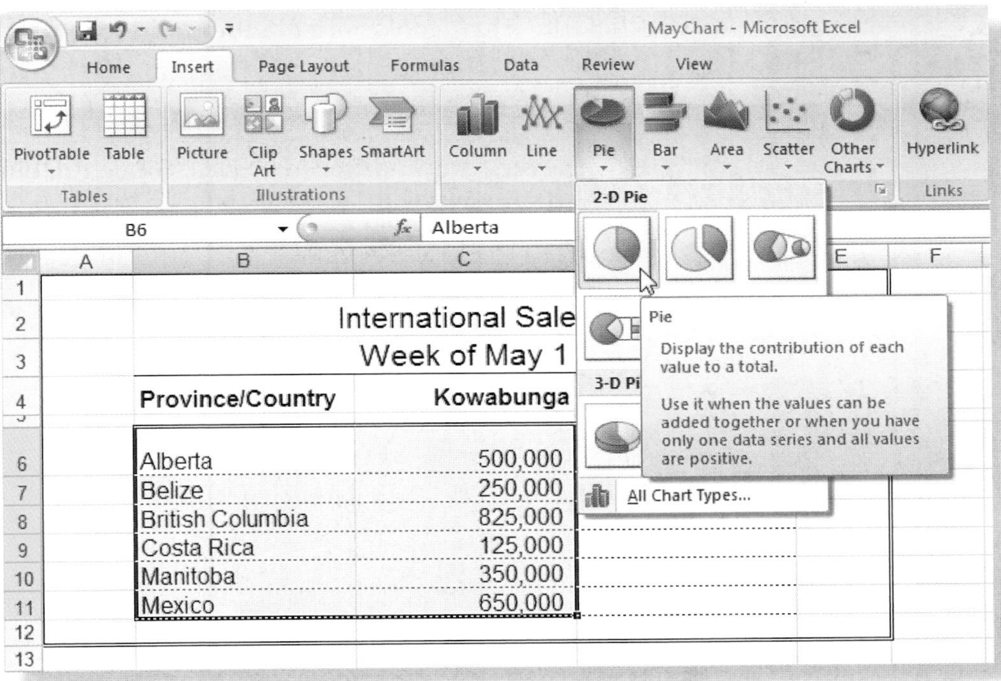

Figure 9-10
Creating a pie chart
MayChart.xlsx
KowabungaSales sheet

4. In the **2-D** list, choose **Pie**. The chart is on the worksheet with its data.

Exercise 9-12 MOVE AND SIZE A CHART OBJECT

The selection handles for the chart object are three dots arranged in a triangle shape on the corners. The handles are four dots arranged in a row in the middle of each edge. The move pointer is a four-pointed arrow; the sizing pointer is two-pointed.

1. Point at the top edge of the chart object to display a four-pointed arrow. Drag the chart so that its top-left corner aligns at cell A14.

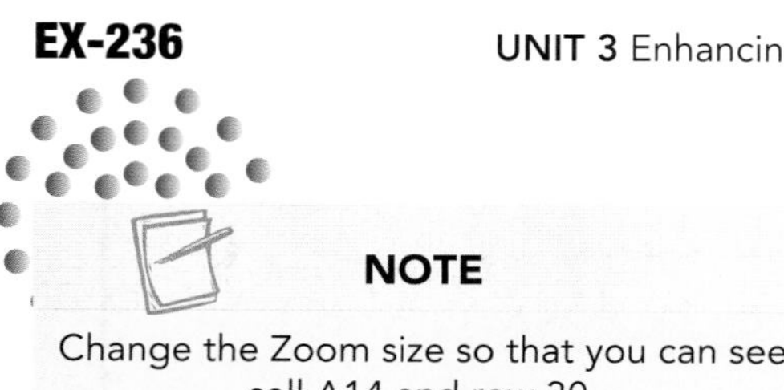

NOTE

Change the Zoom size so that you can see cell A14 and row 30.

2. Point at the bottom-right selection handle. A two-pointed sizing pointer appears.
3. Click and drag the bottom-right selection handle to cover cell E32. As you drag, the chart is made larger.

Exercise 9-13 CHANGE THE LAYOUT AND STYLES

1. Click the **Chart Tools Design** tab. In the **Chart Layouts** group, click the More button.
2. Choose **Layout 5**. This layout includes a chart title, no legend, and data labels inside the pie slices.
3. In the **Chart Styles** group, click the More button.
4. Choose **Style 17**. The slices are shown in shades of gray.
5. Click the **Chart Tools Format** tab. Make sure that the chart area is the current selection.
6. For **Shape Styles**, click the More button.
7. Hover over several different styles. Since the chart area is selected, the entire object is affected.
8. Press Esc to close the gallery without making a change.
9. Point at any pie slice, but away from the label and click.
10. For **Shape Styles**, click the More button.
11. Hover over several styles. Now the slices would be affected, not the background.
12. Press Esc to close the gallery without making a change.
13. While the slices are selected, click only the Alberta slice. You should see selection handles for just this slice.

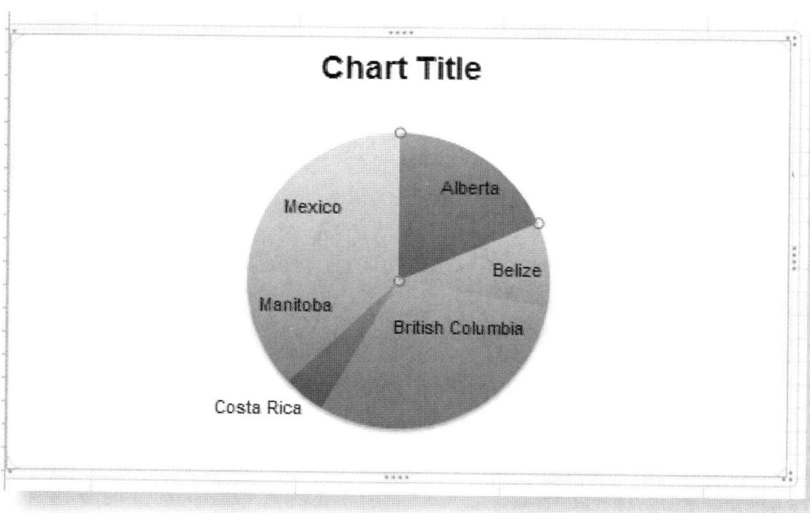

Figure 9-11
Pie chart with a single slice selected
MayChart.xlsx KowabungaSales sheet

14. Click the More button for **Shape Styles**.
15. Hover over several styles. Now just one slice would be affected.
16. Press Esc.
17. Click the chart title object.
18. Triple-click the placeholder text and key **Kowabunga Sales**.
19. Right-click the pie and choose **Format Data Labels**.
20. On the **Label Options** pane, click to select **Percentage**.
21. Click **Close**. The slices now show the name and the percentage.

Exercise 9-14 CREATE A BAR CHART SHEET

You can create a chart object and later move it to its own sheet. It is still linked to the data in the worksheet.

1. Select cells B6:C11 and click the **Insert** tab.
2. In the **Charts** group, click the Bar button .
3. In the **3-D** group, choose **Clustered Bar in 3-D**, the first icon. The chart object appears on your worksheet.

4. In the **Location** group, click the Move Chart button . The Move Chart dialog box allows you to move the chart to its own sheet or to another worksheet in the workbook.

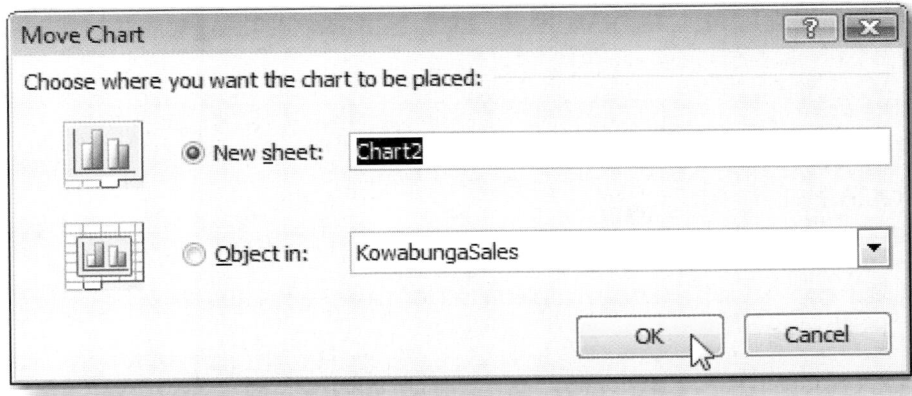

Figure 9-12
Move Chart dialog box
MayChart.xlsx KowabungaSales sheet

5. Choose **New sheet** and click **OK**. The chart is placed on a new sheet.
6. Click **Series 1** and press Delete. That was the legend.

7. Click the **Chart Tools Layout** tab. In the **Labels** group, click the Chart Title button .
8. Choose **Above Chart**. A placeholder object is inserted.

9. Triple-click **Chart Title** and key **Comparison of Weekly Sales**.
10. Click anywhere in the side panel to deselect the chart.

Exercise 9-15 ADD GRIDLINES AND A DATA TABLE

A data table lists the values and names displayed in the chart. It is separate from the chart and appears below the horizontal axis. Gridlines appear on the plot area to make it easy to relate values to the bars or columns. Only major vertical gridlines are shown in this chart.

Gridlines

Data Labels

1. Click the white chart background to select the chart.
2. On the **Chart Tools Layout** tab, click the Gridlines button.
3. Choose **Primary Vertical Gridlines** and then choose **Major and Minor Gridlines**.
4. Click the Data Table button.
5. Choose **Show Data Table**. It appears below the chart and shows "Series 1" as the name.
6. Right-click anywhere in the data table and choose **Select Data**. The source worksheet data is active and the Select Data Source dialog box opens.
7. Click **Series 1** in the Legend Entries list and then click **Edit**. There is no series name at this point.
8. Key **$ Sales** and click **OK**. Click **OK** again. The data table shows the new series name.

Figure 9-13
Editing the series name
MayChart.xlsx
KowabungaSales sheet

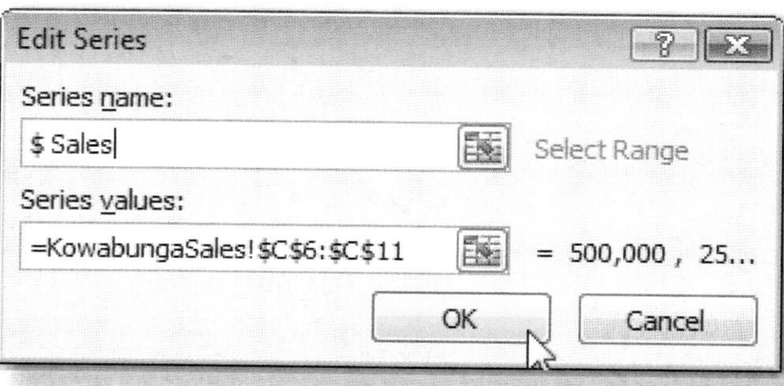

REVIEW

You can right-click a tab to rename it.

9. Name the sheet **BarChart**.
10. Save the workbook as ***[your initials]*9-15** in your folder.

Editing Chart Data

Because a chart is linked to its data, changes that you make in the worksheet are reflected in the chart. You can add categories or value series to your data and then to its chart.

Exercise 9-16 EDIT CHART DATA

1. Click the **KowabungaSales** tab in ***[your initials]*****9-15**. Notice the pie-slice size for Manitoba and its corresponding value in the worksheet.
2. Click the **BarChart** tab. Note the length of the bar for Manitoba.
3. Click the **Chart1** tab. Note the height of the Manitoba column.
4. Click the **KowabungaSales** tab.
5. Click cell C10, key **900000**, and press Enter. Notice the larger pie slice for Manitoba.
6. Click the **Chart1** tab. The height of the Manitoba column is increased.
7. Click the **BarChart** tab. Note the length of the Manitoba bar.

Exercise 9-17 ADD A DATA POINT

If you add another country and its total to the worksheet, you add a data point to the data series. If you insert the new data within the chart's current data range, it appears automatically in all charts linked to the data. If you add data below or above the chart's original source data range, you need to reset the data range for each chart.

1. On the **KowabungaSales** sheet, insert a row at row 12.
2. Key **Ontario** in cell B12. Key **1000000** in cell C12. This data is not within the existing data range for the charts.
3. Right-click the white background area for the pie chart. Choose **Select Data**. The Select Data Source dialog box opens, and a moving marquee encloses the current data range.
4. Click **Cancel**. The data range shows sizing handles at each corner.
5. Position the pointer on the bottom-right handle for cell C11. A two-pointed sizing arrow appears.
6. Drag the sizing arrow to include the Ontario information. The chart is updated when you release the mouse button.

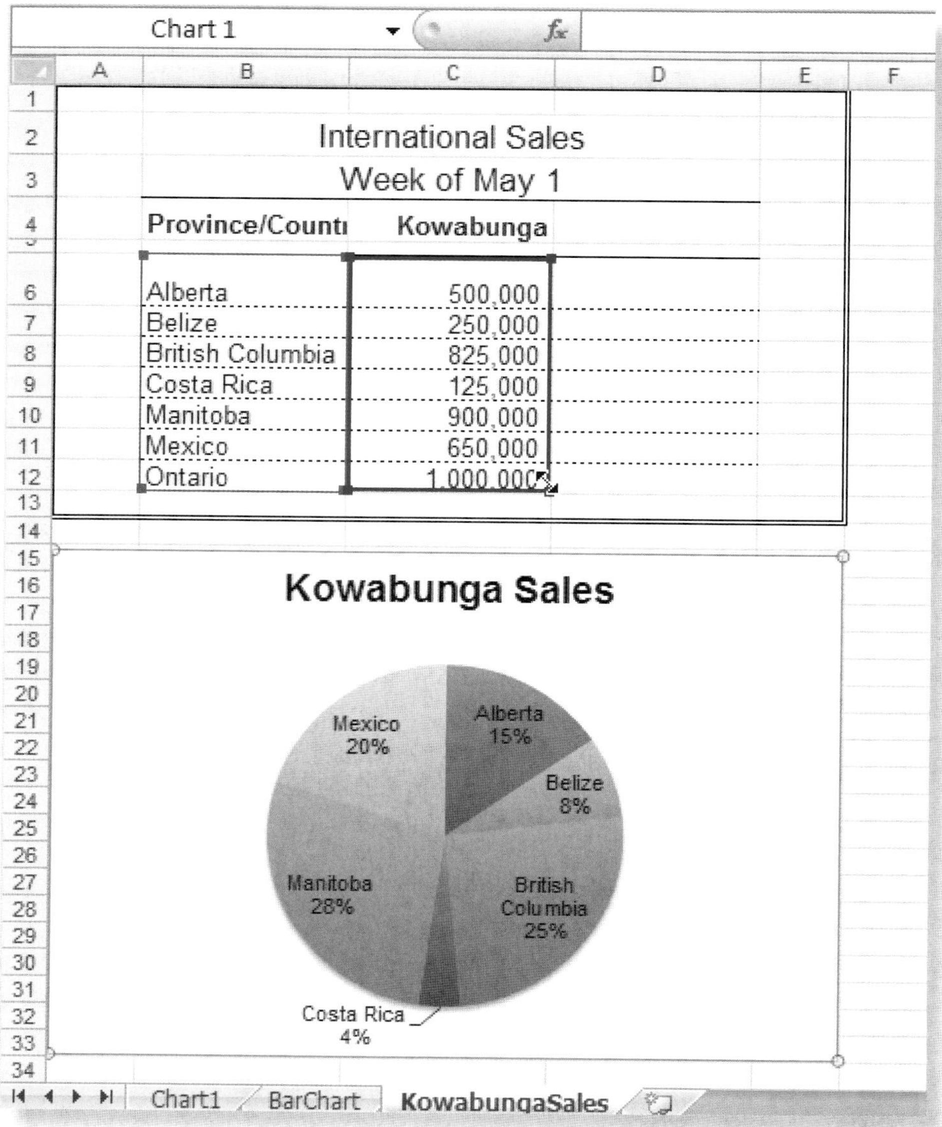

Figure 9-14
Adding a data point
9-15.xlsx
KowabungaSales
sheet

7. Click the **Chart1** tab.
8. Right-click the white chart background. Choose **Select Data**. The Select Data Source dialog box opens on top of the **KowabungaSales** tab with the current data range selected.
9. In the **Chart data range** entry box, edit the address to show **C12** instead of C11. Click **OK**. The column chart is updated to include Ontario.

Figure 9-15
Edit Data Source dialog box
9-15.xlsx
KowabungaSales sheet

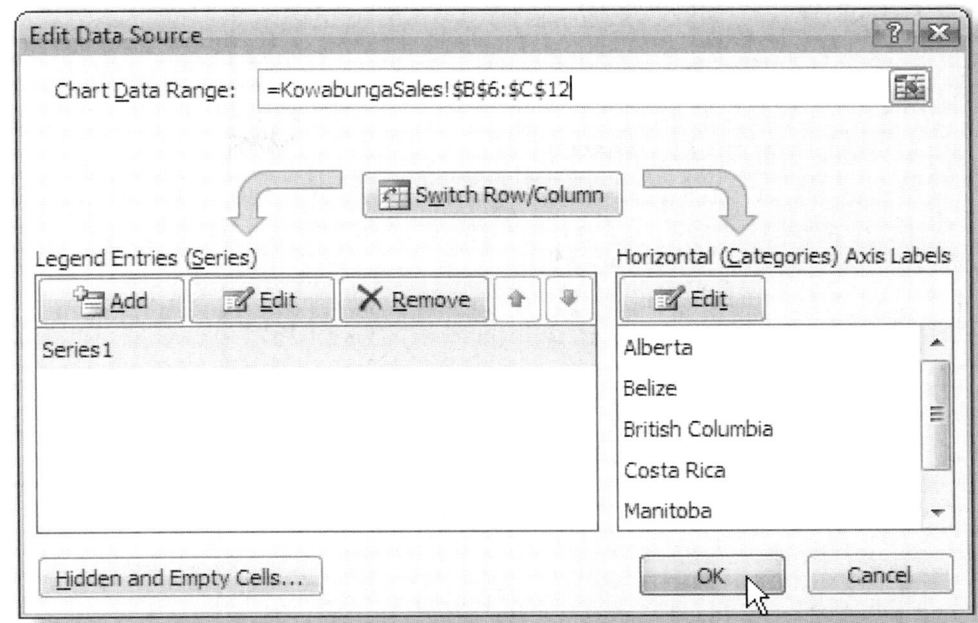

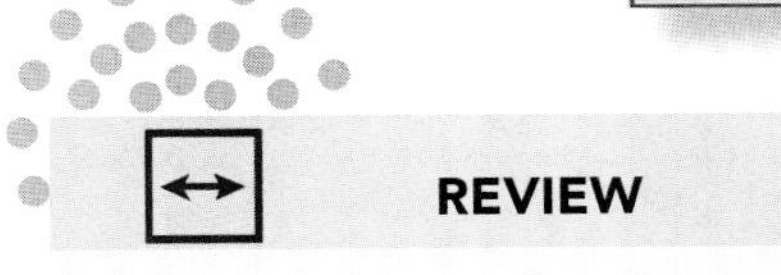

REVIEW

The dialog box collapses as you drag. It expands when you release the mouse button.

10. Click the **BarChart** tab. Right-click the white chart background.
11. Choose **Select Data**. Move the dialog box so that you can see the range.
12. Click cell B6 and drag to select cells B6:C12. Click **OK**. There is now an Ontario bar.
13. Insert a row at row 10 on the **KowabungaSales** sheet.
14. Key **Great Britain** in cell B10 and **250000** in cell C10. This data point is within the existing data range for the charts.
15. Click each sheet tab to see the Great Britain data.

Exercise 9-18 ADD AND RENAME DATA SERIES

NOTE

A pie chart has only one series.

If you add a second product to the data, you can then create a second series for the column and bar charts.

1. On the **KowabungaSales** sheet, key **KowOwow** in cell D4.
2. Key the following values in cells D6:D13:

D6	60000
D7	120000
D8	45000
D9	150000
D10	300000
D11	250000
D12	100000
D13	750000

3. Format the label and values to match the rest of the worksheet.
4. Click the **Chart1** tab. Right-click the white chart background and choose **Select Data**.
5. In the **Chart data range** entry box, edit the address to show **B6:d13**. Click **OK**. The column chart now shows two columns for each province/country, one for each product. The British Columbia data has a different color scheme due to your earlier change. Your colors may be different from the text figures.

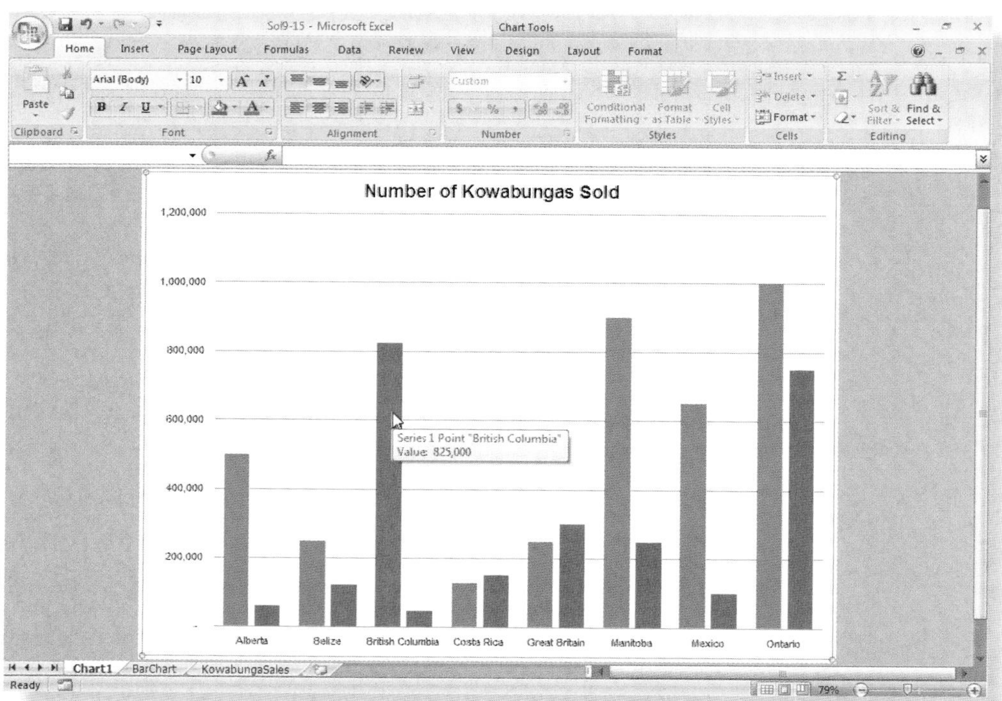

Figure 9-16
Adding a data series
9-15.xlsx
KowabungaSales sheet

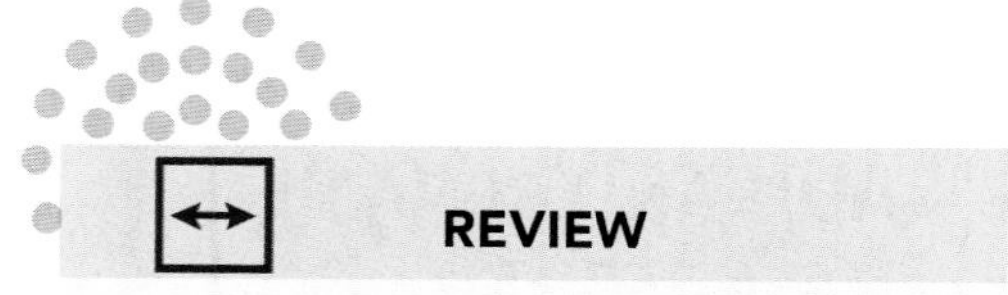

REVIEW

Hover over a column to determine which one represents "Series 1."

6. Right-click any column for **Series 1** (Kowabunga). Choose **Select Data**.
7. Click **Series 1** in the Legend Entries list and click **Edit**.
8. Key **Kowabunga** and click **OK**.
9. Click **Series 2** in the list and click **Edit**. Key **KowOwow** and click **OK**.
10. Click **OK** again. Hover over several columns to view the series' names.
11. Right-click the **Kowabunga** column for British Columbia. Choose **Reset to Match Style**.
12. Click the white background.
13. On the **Chart Tools Design** tab, choose **Style 6**.

Exercise 9-19 DELETE DATA POINTS AND A DATA SERIES

1. Click the **KowabungaSales** tab.
2. Delete rows 8 and 9. The pie chart is updated.
3. Click the **BarChart** tab. Click the **Chart1** tab. The British Columbia and Costa Rica data is removed from all charts.

NOTE

You can delete any chart object or the entire chart by selecting it and pressing Delete.

4. Click the **KowabungaSales** tab.
5. Delete cells D6:D11. This is an entire data series.
6. Click the **Chart1** tab. The second column (KowOwows) is gone, but the category labels appear out of alignment with the columns.
7. Right-click any column and choose **Select Data**. KowOwow is still listed as a series.
8. Click **KowOwow** in the Legend Entries list and click **Remove**.
9. Click **OK**.

Using Images, Gradients, and Textures for a Data Series

You can change from a solid color to a gradient or an image for columns, bars, pie slices, and other chart objects. Gradients and textures can be used to better distinguish bars, columns, or slices on a black-and-white printer. Images allow you to show a picture to represent the data.

You can insert an image, a gradient, or a texture by selecting the chart object and:

- Clicking the Shape Fill button on the Chart Tools Format tab.
- Clicking the Format Selection button on the Chart Tools Format tab or the Chart Tools Layout tab.
- Right-clicking the object and choosing Format Data Series or Format Data Point.

Exercise 9-20 USE AN IMAGE FOR A DATA SERIES

If you want to use an image in a bar or column chart, it looks best if you use a two-dimensional chart rather than 3-D.

1. Click the **BarChart** tab. Select the chart and then click the **Chart Tools Design** tab.

2. Click the Change Chart Type button. The Change Chart Type dialog box lists all the available types.
3. In the **Bar** group, choose **Clustered Bar** (first icon, first row) to change the chart to a two-dimensional chart. Click **OK**.
4. Click any bar in the chart. All the bars show selection handles.
5. Click the **Chart Tools Format** tab. Click the Format Selection button Format Selection. The Format Data Series dialog box opens.
6. On the **Fill** pane, choose **Picture or texture fill**.
7. In the **Insert from** group, click **File**.
8. Navigate to the folder with **Kowabunga** to find the image.
9. Choose **Kowabunga** and click **Insert**. The picture is inserted in the bars and stretched to fit the length of the bar. Move the dialog box to see.
10. In the dialog box, click to select **Stack**. The image is scaled to fit and repeat across the bars.

Figure 9-17
Inserting a picture
9-15.xlsx
BarChart sheet

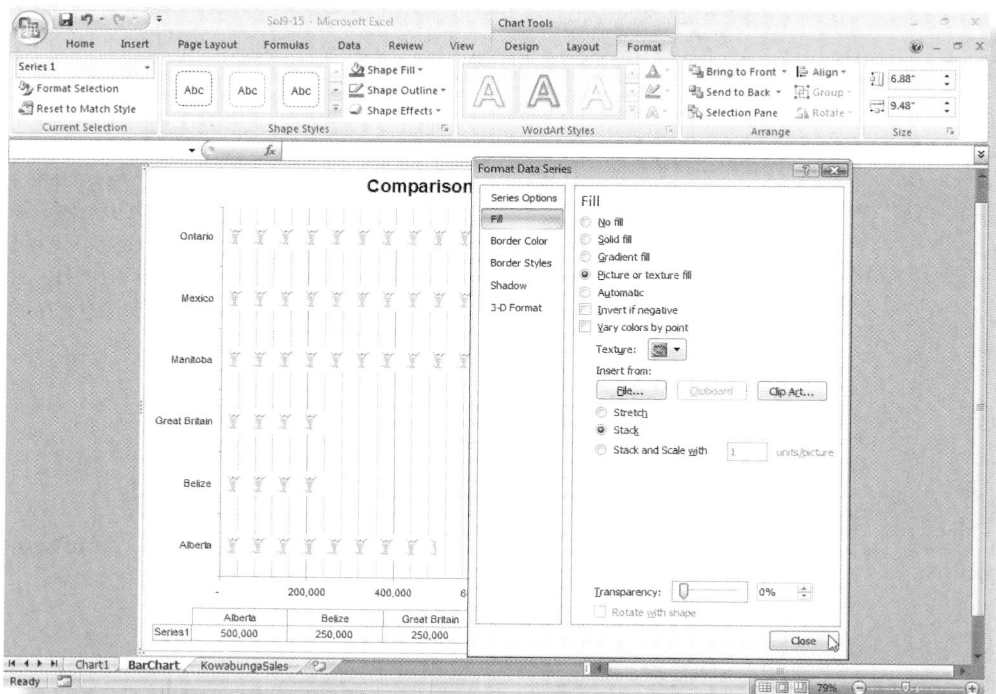

11. Click **Close**.

Exercise 9-21 USE A GRADIENT FOR A DATA SERIES

A *gradient* is a blend of colors. A gradient can give a special effect to bars, columns, or pie slices in a chart. In Excel, you can build blends that use one, two, or more colors, or you can choose from preset gradients.

1. Click the **Chart1** tab.
2. Right-click any column and choose **Format Data Series**.
3. On the **Fill** pane, choose **Gradient fill**. The dialog box updates to show the related options.
4. Click the arrow for **Preset colors**. A gallery of preset color blends opens.
5. Find and click **Moss** (first tile, third row). Click **Close**.
6. Right-click any column again and choose **Format Data Series**. Click **Fill**.
7. In the **Gradient stops** group, verify that **Stop 1** is current. A *stop* is a color in a gradient and refers to a position on a color scale.
8. Click the arrow for **Color** and choose **White, Background 1**.
9. Click the arrow next to **Stop 1** and choose **Stop 2**. This will be your second color.
10. Click the arrow for **Color** and choose **Black, Text 1**.
11. Click the arrow next to **Stop 2** and choose **Stop 3**. This is a third color from the **Moss** gradient.

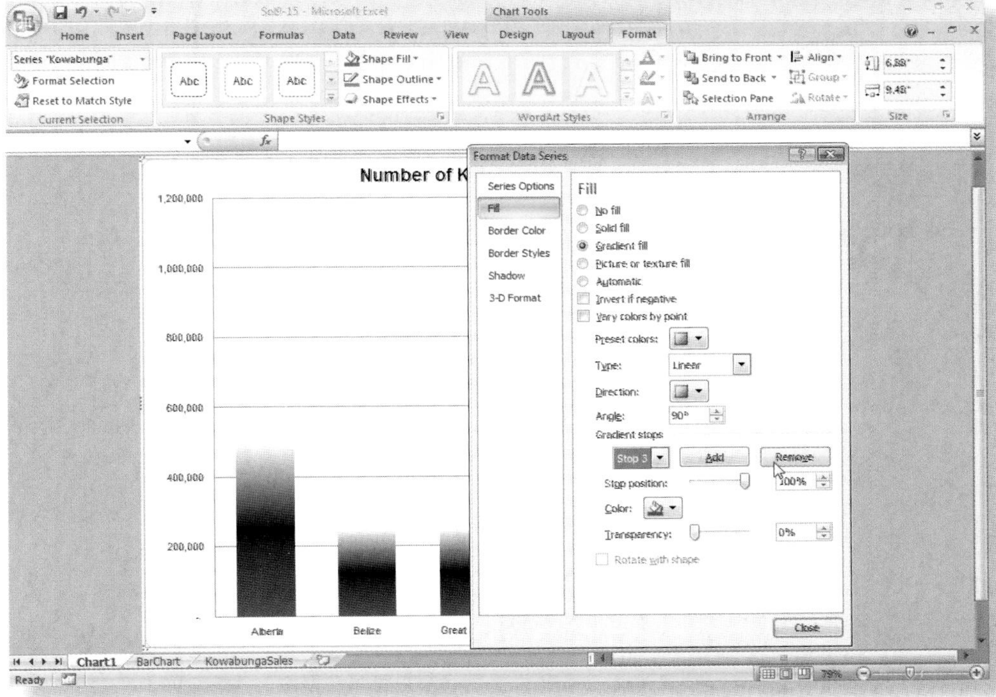

Figure 9-18
Building a gradient fill
9-15.xlsx
BarChart sheet

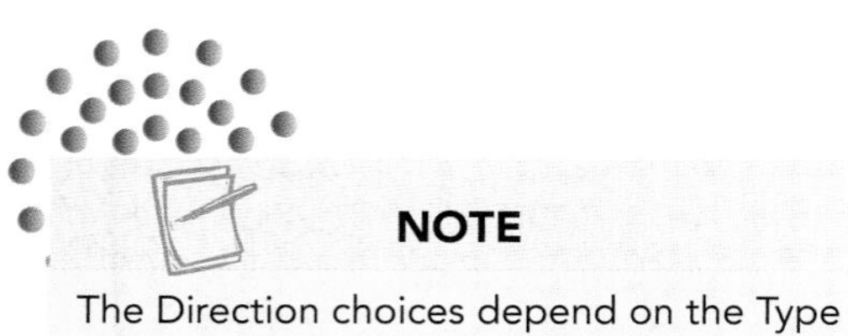

NOTE

The Direction choices depend on the Type of gradient.

12. Click **Remove** to use only two colors (two stops).
13. Click the arrow for **Direction**. Several variations of the way in which the colors blend are shown in a gallery.
14. Find and choose **Linear Up**.
15. Click **Close**.

NOTE

If you're using a black-and-white printer, colorful gradients print as shades of gray.

Exercise 9-22 USE A TEXTURE FOR A DATA POINT

A *texture* is a background that appears as a grainy, nonsmooth surface.

TIP

Point at the slice, not the data label within the slice.

1. Click the **KowabungaSales** tab.
2. Click the pie to select it. Click the Manitoba slice to select that slice only.
3. Right-click the slice and choose **Format Data Point**.
4. On the **Fill** pane, choose **Picture or texture fill**.
5. Click the arrow with **Texture**. A gallery of available textures opens. Notice that textures look similar to marble, wood, or canvas.

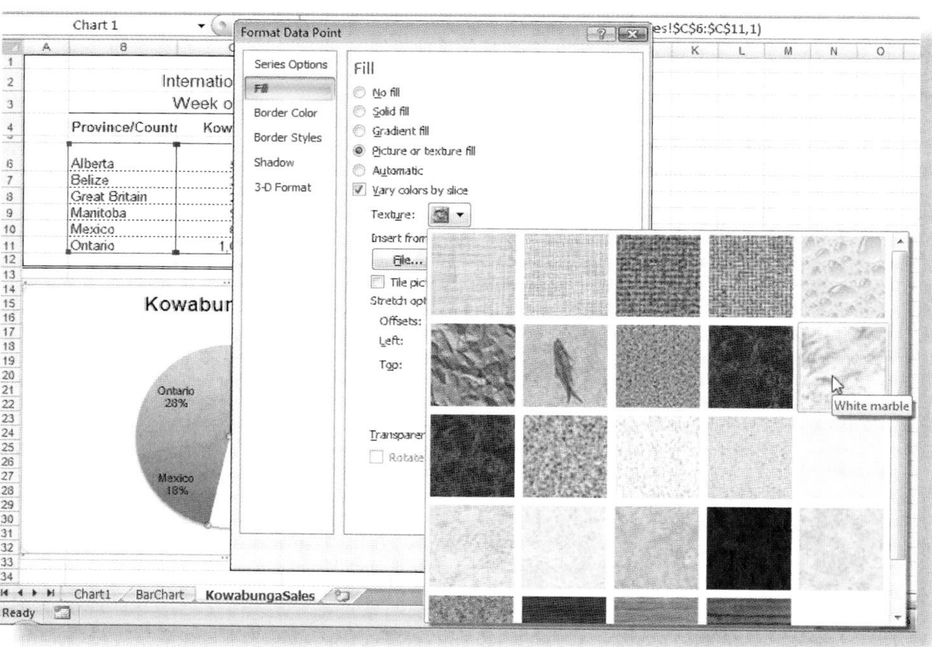

Figure 9-19
Using a texture as fill
9-15.xlsx
KowabungaSales sheet

6. Hover over several texture tiles. A description appears with the name.
7. Choose **White marble**. Click **Close**.
8. Select only the Ontario slice. Click the **Chart Tools Format** tab and then click the Format Selection button.

Format Selection

9. On the **Fill** pane, choose **Picture or texture fill**.
10. Click the arrow with **Texture** and choose a different texture. Click **Close**.
11. Click a cell in the worksheet. Save your workbook as ***[your initials]*9-22** in your folder.
12. Close the workbook.

Creating a Combination Chart

A *combination chart* is a single chart that uses more than one chart type or different number scales. A combination chart has at least two series or sets of values. Some combination charts use the same chart type for each series, but a secondary number scale. A *secondary axis* is a set of axis values that is different from the first (primary) set.

Exercise 9-23 CREATE A CHART WITH TWO CHART TYPES

NOTE

The formulas in columns D and E multiply the price by the number sold.

1. Open **ComboChart**.
2. Select cells A4:C9 and press F11. A new chart sheet is inserted and plots two products.
3. On the **Chart Tools Design** tab, click the Select Data button.

4. Choose **Series 1** in the Legend Entries list and click **Edit**.
5. Key **Kowabunga** and click **OK**.
6. Edit **Series 2** to display **KowOwow** and click **OK**.
7. Click **OK** again. The legend is updated.
8. Right-click any Kowabunga bar and choose **Change Series Chart Type**.
9. In the **Line** category, choose **Line with Markers**. Click **OK**. The Kowabunga series is now a line chart.

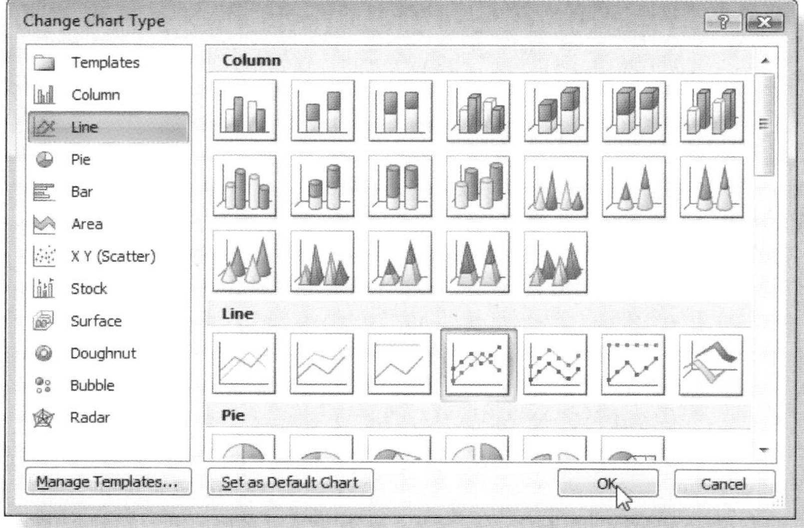

Figure 9-20
Changing the chart type for a data series
ComboChart.xlsx
Chart1 sheet

10. Right-click the line and choose **Format Data Series**.
11. On the **Line Style** pane, set the **Width** to **2 pt**.
12. On the **Line Color** pane, choose **Black Text 1** as the **Color**.
13. On the **Marker Options** pane, choose **Built-in**. Set the **Size** to **10**. Click **Close**.
14. Click the white chart background. The markers should be the same color as the line.
15. Right-click the line and choose **Format Data Series**. On the **Marker Fill** pane, choose **Solid fill**. Then set the color to match the line color.
16. On the **Marker Line Color** pane, choose **Solid fill** and the same color. Click **Close**.
17. Save the workbook as ***[your initials]*9-23**.

Exercise 9-24 BUILD A CHART WITH TWO SERIES

You can show the dollar sales and the number of items sold on the same chart. These values will be two different series on the chart.

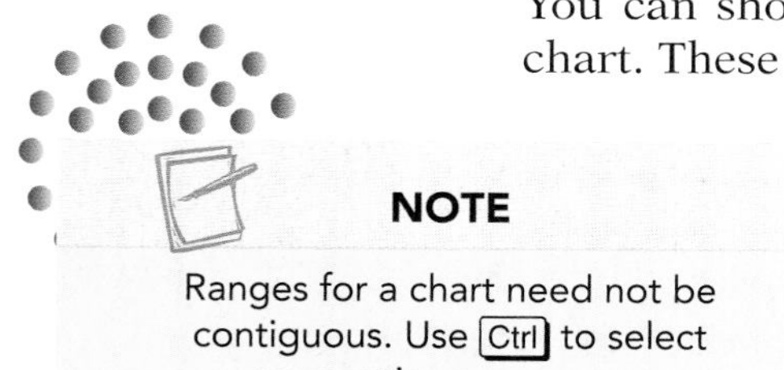

NOTE

Ranges for a chart need not be contiguous. Use Ctrl to select noncontiguous ranges.

1. Click the **KowabungaSales** tab.
2. Select cells A4:A9, C4:C9, and E4:E9. This represents the number of KowOwows sold and the sales dollars.
3. Click the **Insert** tab. Choose a **Clustered Column** 2-D chart.

4. Click the Move Chart button and place the chart on its own sheet. There are two series, one for the product and one for the dollars. Both series use the same value axis, so the dollar column is disproportionately taller.

5. Right-click the legend and choose **Select Data**.
6. Change **Series 1** to display **Number Sold**.
7. Change **Series 2** to **Dollar Sales** and click **OK**. Click **OK** again.

8. On the **Chart Tools Layout** tab, click the Chart Title button. Choose **Above Chart**.
9. Edit the placeholder to show **Units and Dollars**.

Exercise 9-25 ADD A SECONDARY AXIS

Because the values are very different, you should use two axes on the chart, one for the number of items and one for the dollar amounts. To use a secondary axis, use different chart types for each data series.

1. Right-click any Dollar Sales column and choose **Change Series Chart Type**.

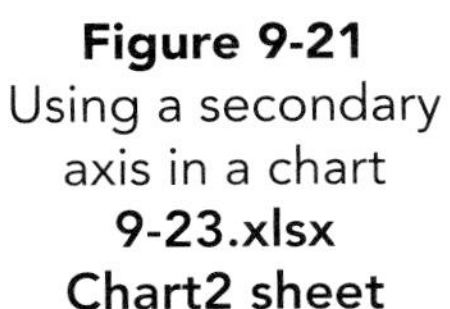

NOTE

Some chart types cannot be combined. Excel displays a message if you choose charts that cannot be combined.

2. In the **Area** category, choose **Area**. Click **OK**.
3. Right-click somewhere in the area and choose **Format Data Series**.
4. On the **Fill** pane, choose **Gradient fill**. Click the arrow with **Preset colors** and choose **Moss**. Click **Close**.
5. Right-click a Number Sold column and choose **Format Data Series**.
6. On the **Series Options** pane, choose **Secondary axis**. The selected series will be plotted on a separate value axis. Click **Close**.

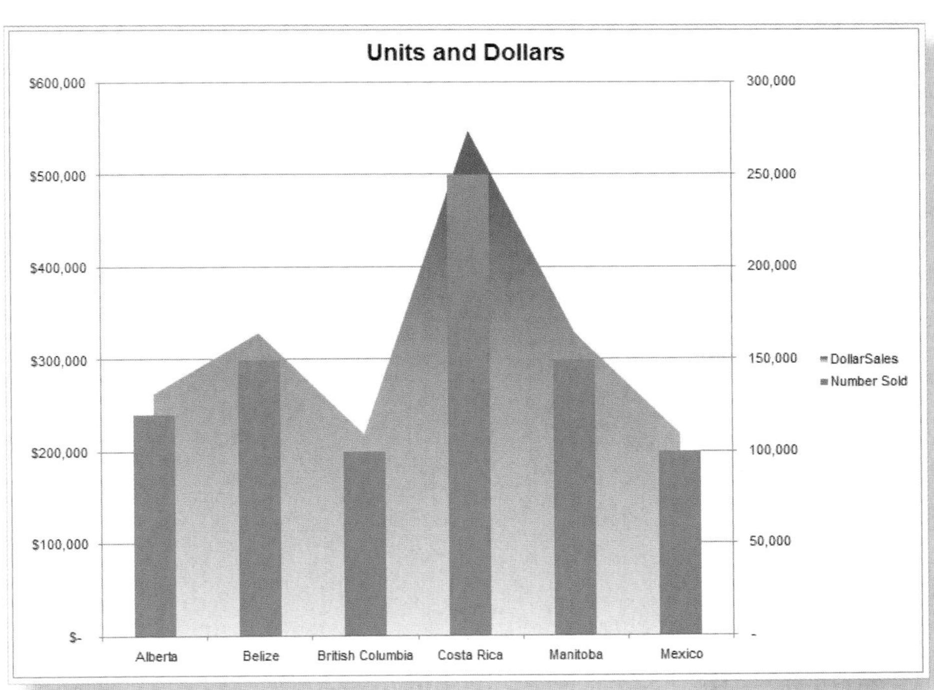

Figure 9-21
Using a secondary axis in a chart
9-23.xlsx
Chart2 sheet

7. Right-click the legend and choose **Format Legend**.
8. On the **Legend Options** pane, choose **Bottom** and click **Close**.
9. Save the workbook as ***[your initials]*9-25**. Close the workbook.

Using Online Help

In addition to charts, you can use many types of images and graphics in a worksheet. Unlike charts, SmartArt graphics and shapes are usually not based on worksheet data.

USE HELP TO LEARN ABOUT GRAPHICS

1. In a new workbook, press F1.
2. Find and review topics about using SmartArt Graphics in a worksheet. Then find topics about shapes.
3. Close the Help window when you are finished reading about graphics and shapes.

Lesson 9 Summary

- Charts can be objects in a worksheet, or they can be separate chart sheets.
- A chart is linked to the data that it is plotting. If the data is edited, the chart reflects the changes.
- A chart includes many individual elements that can be formatted and edited.
- Right-click a chart element to see its shortcut menu.
- Charts show data series, which are the chart's values. A pie chart can have only one series, but other types of charts can show multiple data series.
- You can make many chart changes directly on the chart.
- If you select data and press F11, Excel creates an automatic column chart sheet.
- Excel's standard types of business charts include bar, column, line, and pie charts.
- Move a chart by selecting it and dragging it. Size a chart by dragging one of its selection handles.
- After a chart is created, you can add a data point or an entire series to it.
- Although charts typically use solid color for columns, slices, and bars, you can use images, textures, or gradients to add visual appeal to your charts.

- You can apply effects to the shapes used in a chart to include shadows, glows, bevels, and more.
- A combination chart has at least two series and uses different chart types for each series.
- Some combination charts use a single chart type with a secondary axis because the series values are disproportionate.

LESSON 9		Command Summary	
Feature	**Button**	**Task Path**	**Keyboard**
Axis, add	Axes	Chart Tools Layout, Axes	
Axis, format	Format Selection	Chart Tools Format, Current Selection	Ctrl+1
Axis titles, add	Axis Titles	Chart Tools Format, Labels	
Chart object, create		Insert, Charts	Alt+F1
Chart sheet, create		Insert, Charts	F11
Chart title, add	Chart Title	Chart Tools Layout, Labels	
Chart type	Change Chart Type	Chart Tools Design, Type	
Data labels, add	Data Labels	Chart Tools Layout, Labels	
Data labels, format	Format Selection	Chart Tools Format, Current Selection	Ctrl+1
Data series, edit	Select Data	Chart Tools Design, Data	
Data series, format	Format Selection	Chart Tools Format, Current Selection	Ctrl+1
Data table, add	Data Table	Chart Tools Layout, Labels	
Legend, add	Legend	Chart Tools Layout, Labels	
Legend, format	Format Selection	Chart Tools Format, Current Selection	Ctrl+1
Move chart	Move Chart	Chart Tools Design, Location	
Selection pane	Selection Pane	Chart Tools Format, Arrange	

microsoft® office powerpoint® brief

A Professional Approach

POWERPOINT 2007

Pat R. Graves

Amie Mayhall

There is more to learning a presentation graphics program like Microsoft Office PowerPoint 2007 than simply keying text on colored backgrounds and calling the result a presentation. You need to know how to use PowerPoint in a real-world situation. That's why all the lessons in this text relate to everyday business tasks. The text will show you how to create well-organized presentations that are designed effectively, too.

As you work through the lessons, imagine yourself working as an intern for Good 4 *U*, a fictional New York restaurant.

Good 4 *U* Restaurant

The Good 4 *U* restaurant has been in business for only a little more than three years, but it's been a success from the time it served its first veggie burger. The restaurant, which features healthy food and has as its theme the "everyday active life," seems to have found an award-winning recipe for success. (Figure CS-1 shows the interior of the largest dining room in the restaurant. It features plants and a wide expanse of windows looking out over Central Park South, a tree-lined avenue on the south side of New York's Central Park.)

Figure CS-1 Interior of Good 4 *U* restaurant and a sampling of the fresh food prepared daily

The food at Good 4 *U* is all low-fat. The menu features lots of vegetables (all organic, of course) as well as fish and chicken. The restaurant doesn't serve alcohol, instead offering fruit juices and sparkling water. Good 4 *U*'s theme of the "everyday active life" is reflected on the restaurant's walls with running, tennis, and bicycling memorabilia. This theme reflects the interests of the two co-owners: Julie Wolfe, who led the New York Flash to two Women's Professional Basketball Association championships in her 10 years with the team, and Gus Irvinelli, who is an avid tennis player and was selected for the U.S. amateur team. Even the chef, Michele Jenkins, leads an everyday active life—she rides her bicycle 10 miles a day in and around Central Park.

Two years ago, Roy Olafsen was a marketing manager for a large hotel chain. He was overweight and out of shape. In the same week that his doctor told him to eat better and exercise regularly, Roy received a job offer from Good 4 *U*. "It was too good to pass up," he said. "It was my chance to combine work and a healthy lifestyle." As you work through the text, you'll discover that Good 4 *U* is often involved in health-oriented as well as athletic events.

In your work as an intern at Good 4 *U* restaurant, you will meet many of the people who work at Good 4 *U* and will interact with the four key people shown in Figure CS-2. You will be doing most of your work for Roy Olafsen, the marketing manager.

All the presentations you will use and create in this course relate to the Good 4 *U* restaurant. As you work with the presentations in the text, note the following things:

- The types of presentations needed in a small business to carry on day-to-day business.
- The design of presentations. Real businesses must often focus on designing eye-catching, informative presentations for customers. The business's success often depends on developing attractive and compelling presentations that sell its services to customers.

Figure CS-2 Key employees

Julie Wolfe
Co-Owner

Gus Irvinelli
Co-Owner

Michele Jenkins
Head Chef

Roy Olafsen
Marketing Manager

As you use this text and become more experienced with Microsoft Office PowerPoint 2007, you will also gain experience in creating, editing, and designing the sort of presentations generated in a real-life business environment.

In your first meeting with Roy Olafsen, he gave you the following tips for designing presentations. These guidelines can be applied to any presentation.

Tips for Designing Presentations

- Prepare a distinctive title slide. Make sure the title identifies the presentation content.
- Maintain a consistent color scheme throughout the presentation for a sense of unity.
- Keep the background simple, and modify it to help create a unique theme for your presentation.
- Choose colors carefully so all text can be seen clearly. You must have a high contrast between background colors and text colors for easy reading.
- Write lists with parallel wording and be concise. Limit bulleted text to no more than seven words on a line and no more than seven lines on a slide.
- Avoid small text. Body text on slides, such as for bulleted lists, should be no smaller than 24 points. Text for annotations may be slightly smaller, but not less than 20 points. Establish a hierarchy for text sizes based on text importance and then use those sizes consistently.
- Think and design visually to express your message. Use graphics such as boxes, lines, circles, and other shapes to highlight text or to create SmartArt graphics that show process diagrams and relationships. Illustrate with pictures and clip art images.
- Select all images carefully to make your presentation content more understandable. They should not detract from the message. Avoid the temptation to "jazz up" a slide show with too much clip art.
- Keep charts simple. The most effective charts are pie charts with three or four slices and column charts with three or four columns. Label charts carefully for easy interpretation.
- Provide some form of handout so your audience can keep track of the presentation or make notes while you are talking.
- Include multimedia elements of animation, transitions, sound, and movies if these elements strengthen your message, engage your audience, aid understanding, or make your presentation more compelling.
- Your final slide should provide a recommendation or summary to help you conclude your presentation effectively.

unit 1

BASIC SKILLS

Lesson 1

Getting Started in PowerPoint

OBJECTIVES

After completing this lesson, you will be able to:

1. Explore PowerPoint.
2. View a presentation.
3. Add text using placeholders.
4. Name and save a presentation.
5. Prepare presentation supplements.
6. End your work session.

MCAS OBJECTIVES

In this lesson:

PP07 4.3.6

PP07 4.4.2

See Appendix

Estimated Time: 2 hours

PowerPoint is an easy-to-use presentation graphics program you can use to create professional-quality presentations. PowerPoint can be used in a variety of settings by people in many different career fields. For example, a day care worker may develop a presentation showing parents pictures of their children in all of the year's activities, or a minister may utilize PowerPoint to display notes on the sermon or song lyrics for the congregation. An instructor may use it for notes for a lecture to help students keep focused and their notes organized, or a hotelier may develop a presentation to help market the hotel at conferences and meetings. PowerPoint is also an effective tool for creating flyers and other printed products because of its versatile drawing and layout tools.

This lesson begins with an overview of many PowerPoint features and will help you become accustomed to the application window.

Exploring PowerPoint

If you are already familiar with other Microsoft Office 2007 programs, you'll feel right at home with PowerPoint. Although a number of new features appear in the PowerPoint window shown in Figure 1-1, it's easy to recognize similarities to Microsoft Word and Microsoft Excel.

TABLE 1-1 Main Parts of the PowerPoint Window

Part of Window	Purpose
Title bar	Contains the name of the presentation.
Quick Access toolbar	Located by default at the top of the PowerPoint window and provides quick access to commands that you use frequently.
Microsoft Office Button	Located in the upper left-hand corner and contains commands to open, save, print, and share your PowerPoint file with others.
Ribbon	Consists of task-oriented tabs with commands organized in groups.
Tabs	Task-oriented collections of commands. In addition to the standard tabs, there are other tabs which appear only when they are useful for the type of task you are currently performing.
Groups	Logical sets of related commands and options.
Command buttons	Buttons designed to perform a function or display a gallery of options.
Slide pane	The area where you create, edit, and display presentation slides.
Notes pane	The area where you can add presentation notes for the presenter.
Slides and Outline pane	The area that can display either an outline of the presentation's text or *thumbnails*—miniature pictures—of the presentation's slides. You choose either Outline or Slides by clicking the appropriate tab. (If this pane is not displayed, click the Normal view button.)
Scroll bars	Used with the pointer to move a slide or outline text right or left and up or down. You can also use the vertical scroll bar to move from slide to slide.
Status bar	Displays information about the presentation you are working on.
View buttons	Buttons used to switch between Normal view, Slide Sorter view, and Slide Show view.

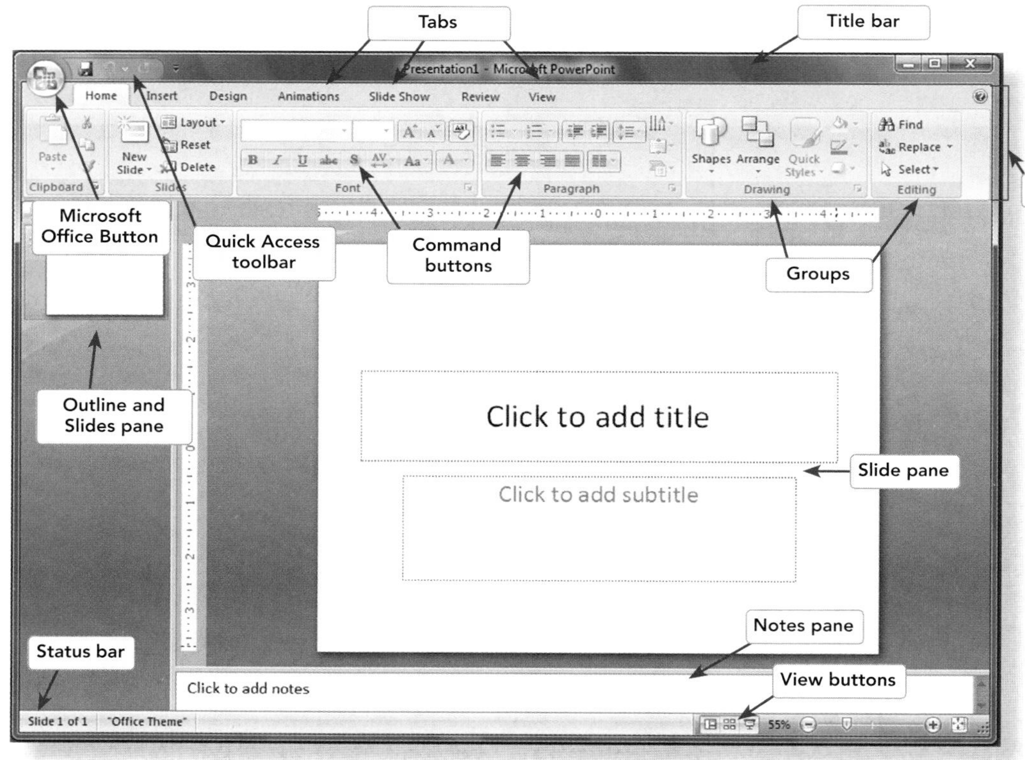

Figure 1-1 Main features in PowerPoint's Normal view

Exercise 1-1 IDENTIFY PARTS OF THE POWERPOINT WINDOW

The first step to becoming familiar with PowerPoint is to identify the parts of the window. The *Ribbon* contains seven task-oriented tabs: Home, Insert, Design, Animations, Slide Show, Review, and View. Commands are organized in logical groups with command buttons and other controls. ScreenTips will help you identify command buttons and other objects. A *ScreenTip* is the box displaying an object's name and sometimes a brief description that appears under a command button or other object when you point to it. Within the Ribbon groups are drop-down galleries that easily present formatting options, graphics choices, layouts, and more.

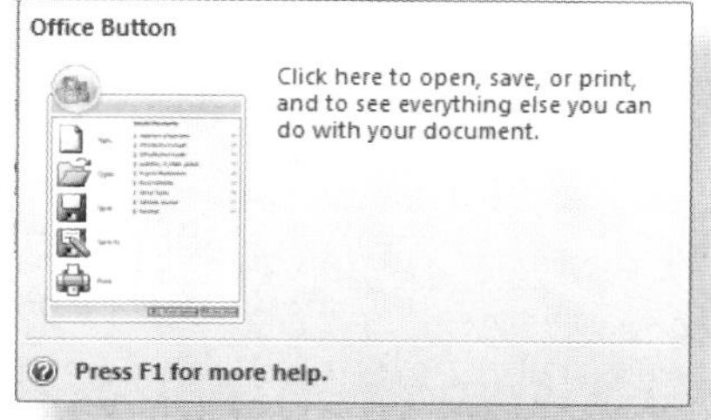

Figure 1-2 ScreenTip over the Microsoft Office Button

1. Using Figure 1-1 as a guide, move your pointer over items in the PowerPoint window to identify them by name using ScreenTips similar to Figure 1-2.

Exercise 1-2 USE THE QUICK ACCESS TOOLBAR

The *Quick Access toolbar* is a customizable toolbar containing a set of common commands that function independently of the tab that is currently displayed. This toolbar's default location is above the Ribbon. It can be moved under the Ribbon, but this location requires more space.

1. Click the drop-down arrow at the end of the Quick Access toolbar.
2. Choose **Show Below the Ribbon**.
3. Click the drop-down arrow again and choose **Show Above the Ribbon** to return to the default position.

Exercise 1-3 OPEN AN EXISTING PRESENTATION

When you first open PowerPoint, a new blank presentation automatically appears, ready for you to add text and graphics. However, in this exercise you open an existing PowerPoint presentation. The presentation was created for this lesson to give you an overview of many PowerPoint features.

NOTE

When downloading student data files online, data files are zipped. You must right-click this folder and extract all files before moving on with Exercise 1-3.

1. Point to the Microsoft Office Button and click the left mouse button to open a menu.
2. Choose **Open**.
3. In the Open dialog box, navigate to the appropriate drive and folder for your student files according to your instructor's directions.
4. When you locate the student files, click the arrow next to the Views button (see Figure 1-3) in the Open dialog box to display a menu of view options.

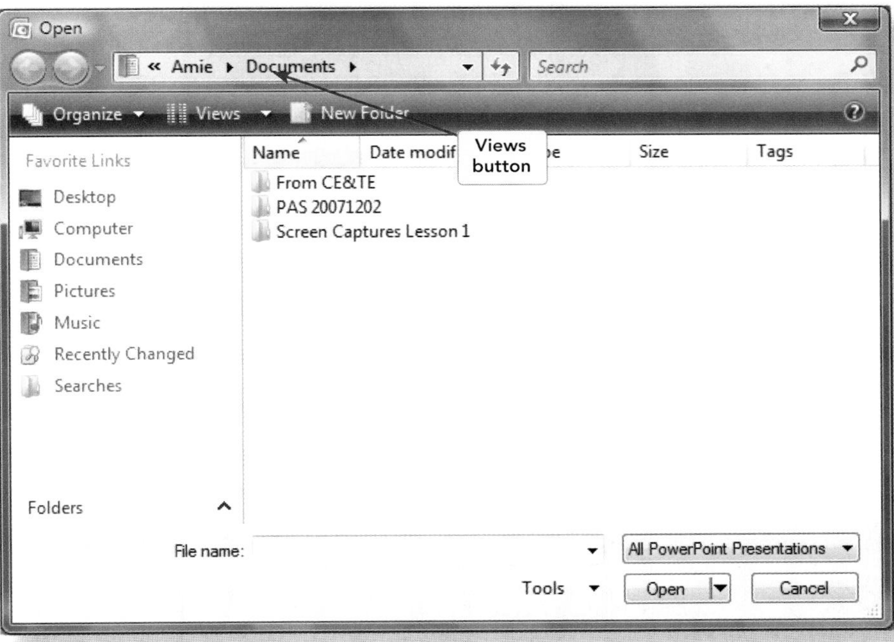

Figure 1-3
Folders listed in the Open dialog box

NOTE

Your instructor will advise you where to locate the files for this course. For more information about working with files, folders, and directories in Windows, refer to "File Management" at the Professional Approach Online Learning Center at **www.mhhe.com/pas07brief**.

5. Choose **Small Icons** to list all files by name.
6. Click the Views button again and choose **Details** to see the type of file and the date when it was last modified.
7. Locate the file **ThreeYr1** (use the scroll bar if you need to) and click once to select the file.
8. Click **Open**. (You can also double-click the file's name to open it.) PowerPoint opens the file in Normal view.

NOTE

The presentations you create in this course relate to the case study at the front of this text about Good 4 U, a fictional restaurant.

Exercise 1-4 WORK WITH RIBBONS, TABS, GROUPS, AND COMMAND BUTTONS

PowerPoint organizes command buttons in a logical way. On the Ribbon, the tabs reflect tasks or activities you commonly perform and provide easy access to the commands. Within each tab, the commands are divided into related groups of buttons and other controls.

Live Preview is a feature that allows you to see exactly what your changes will look like before clicking or selecting an effect. Sometimes the available effects are presented in a *gallery* that displays thumbnails of different options you can choose.

1. Click the Insert tab on the Ribbon.
2. Identify each of the groups located on the Insert tab: Tables, Illustrations, Links, Text, and Media Clips.
3. These groups each contain command buttons that either provide options through dialog boxes or through galleries of options.

Exercise 1-5 USE MICROSOFT OFFICE POWERPOINT HELP

Microsoft Office provides a *Help* feature that is an excellent reference tool for reinforcing skills presented in a lesson and for finding more information on any PowerPoint feature. Each program in Microsoft Office has a separate Help window.

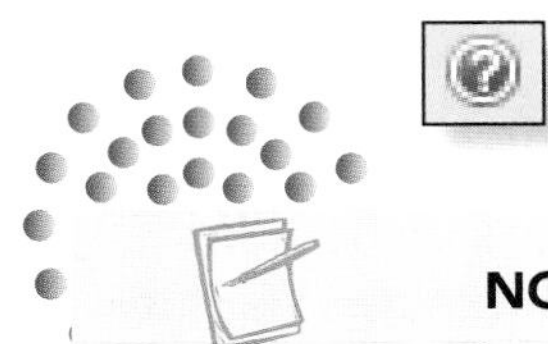

NOTE

If you are connected to the Internet, Help will automatically open a browser and search your topic. If this happens, you will have to close the browser and the Help window.

1. Click Microsoft Office PowerPoint Help button located on the upper-right of the Ribbon or you can press F1. The Help window will appear on top of your open PowerPoint presentation.
2. Key **Ribbon** in the search box located on the Help window, and then press Enter.
3. Scroll through the list of options that display and select **Use the Ribbon**.
4. Read and scroll through the entire Help window.

5. When you have finished, click the Close button in the upper-right corner of the Help window to close it and return to PowerPoint.

Viewing a Presentation

PowerPoint provides multiple views for working with your presentations. Using these various views, you can work in outline format, rearrange slides in *Slide Sorter view*, or work on an individual slide in the Slide pane of Normal view.

Exercise 1-6 USE NORMAL AND SLIDE SORTER VIEWS

The Normal view is the best for entering text directly on a slide and planning the design of your presentation. *Normal view* is the default view when you open PowerPoint. The *Slide Sorter view* presents a window of *slide thumbnails*, which are miniature versions of the slides. To rearrange slides, you can click on a thumbnail and then hold down the left mouse button while you *drag* it to a new position. Slide Sorter view makes it easy to apply special slide-show effects.

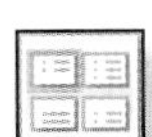

1. From the View tab, in the Presentation Views group, choose the Slide Sorter button .
2. Click and drag slide 7 to place it before slide 6. You will be able to tell where your slide is when dragging by the vertical line that appears.

3. From the View tab, in the Presentation Views group, choose the Normal button to return to Normal view.

Exercise 1-7 USE THE SLIDES AND OUTLINE PANE

In Normal view, the *Slides and Outline pane* is at the left of the Slide pane. It provides some alternative ways to work with your presentation. The Outline tab shows only slide titles and listed text with *bullets*, small circular shapes, in front of each listing. The Outline tab allows you to enter just your text content as an outline without modifying the design or adding graphics to

Figure 1-4
Working with the Slides and Outline pane

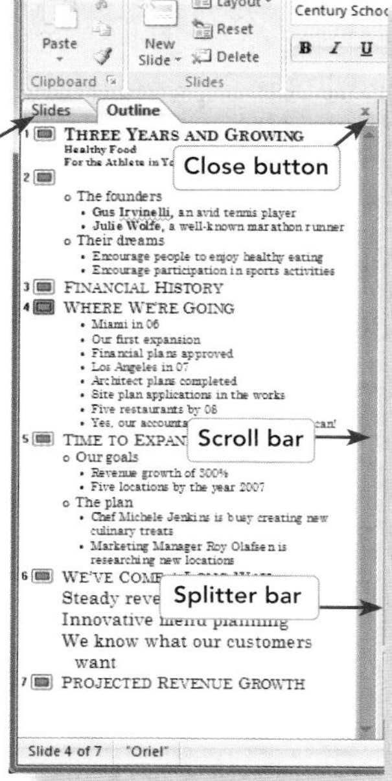

your slide. The Slides tab provides thumbnails similar to the Slide Sorter view.

1. Click the **Outline** tab at the top of the Slides and Outline pane. The Outline pane displays the presentation's text in an outline format.
2. Point to the right border of the Slides and Outline pane. When the splitter appears, drag the border about an inch to the right. This increases the size of the Slides and Outline pane.
3. Scroll in the outline text until you see the text for slide 4.
4. Working in the Outline tab, change each of the years (06, 07, and 08) to **2007**, **2008**, and **2009**. The first line, for example, should read **Miami in 2007**. Notice that as you work, your changes are reflected in the Slide pane.

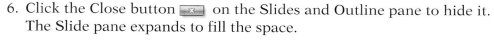

NOTE

When you have several bulleted lists, you can key them all in outline format if that's the way you like to work.

5. Click in front of Miami, then from the Home tab, in the Paragraph group, choose the Decrease List Level button to promote the item by moving it to the left. Apply this same treatment to Los Angeles in 2008 and Five Restaurants by 2009. This distinguishes the main items in the list from the more detailed items under them.
6. Click the Close button on the Slides and Outline pane to hide it. The Slide pane expands to fill the space.

7. From the View tab, in the Presentation Views group, choose the Normal view button. The Slides and Outline pane is displayed again.
8. Click the **Slides** tab at the top of the Slides and Outline pane. The Slides and Outline pane becomes smaller and the size of the Slide pane increases.

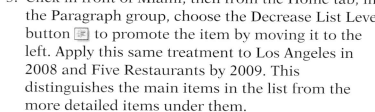

Exercise 1-8 MOVE FROM SLIDE TO SLIDE

PowerPoint provides several ways to move from slide to slide in a presentation:

- Use the pointer to drag the scroll box.
- Use the pointer to click the Previous slide or Next slide buttons.
- Use the PageUp and PageDown keys on the keyboard.

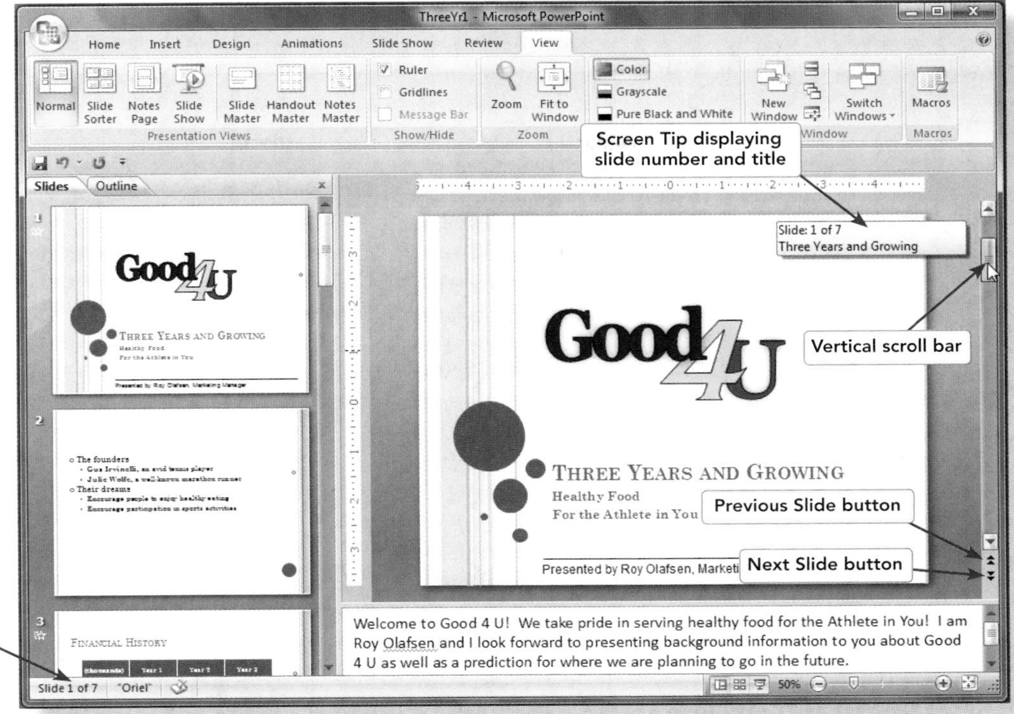

Figure 1-5
Moving from slide to slide

1. Drag the vertical scroll box on the Slide pane to the bottom of the scroll bar. Notice the box that displays slide numbers and slide titles as you drag. When you release the mouse button at the bottom of the scroll bar, slide 7 appears in your window. Notice slide 7 has a highlighted border around it in the Slide pane. This identifies it as the current slide.

2. Drag the scroll box up to display slide 6. Notice that Slide 6 of 7 is indicated on the left side of the status bar.

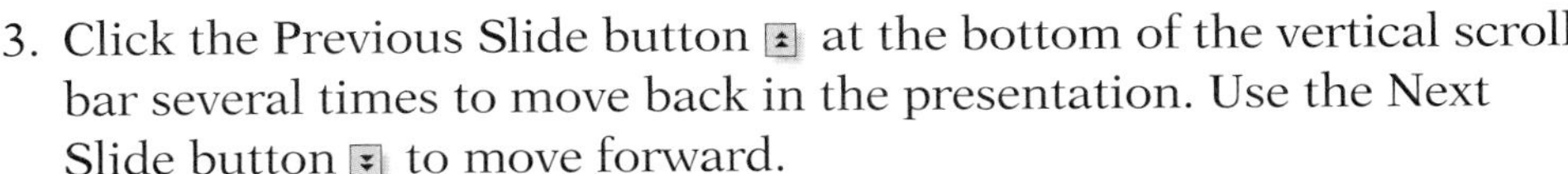

3. Click the Previous Slide button at the bottom of the vertical scroll bar several times to move back in the presentation. Use the Next Slide button to move forward.

4. As an alternative to clicking the Next Slide button and the Previous Slide button, press PageDown and PageUp on your keyboard several times. Use this method to move to slide 2. Check the status bar for the slide number.

Exercise 1-9 USE THE ZOOM AND FIT TO WINDOW

PowerPoint provides two different ways to *zoom* and *Fit to Window*. Zoom is a great tool for magnifying your slide so you can see small details for precise alignment and corrections. The Fit to Window command will change from the current zoom settings to fit in the window that is open.

- From the View tab, in the Zoom group, choose the Zoom or Fit to Window command buttons.
- Use the Zoom slider and Fit to Window buttons on the right end of the status bar.

1. From the View tab, in the Zoom group, click the Zoom button .
2. On the Zoom dialog box, click the Radial button beside **200%** and click OK. You can use the zoom feature in Normal or Slide Sorter view to change the percentage of what you are viewing.

TIP

You can also click and drag the Zoom slider toward the minus to zoom out and toward the plus to zoom in.

3. On the right end of the status bar is a Zoom slider. Click the Zoom out button (a minus) until you reach **170%**.
4. From the View tab, in the Zoom group, choose the Fit to Window button . This reduces the size of your slide to be viewable in the window.

Exercise 1-10 RUN A SLIDE SHOW

A *slide show* displays slides sequentially in full-screen size. One way to start a slide show is to click the Slide Show command button. After you begin running a slide show, PowerPoint provides navigation tools to move from slide to slide. You may start a slide show from any slide by moving to the slide you wish to start on and clicking the Slide Show command button.

TIP

As an alternative to clicking the left mouse button, you can press the Spacebar to move forward. Also, you can press N, which means "next" to move forward and P, which means "previous" to move backward. You can also use the right and left arrow keys or PageDown and PageUp to move forward and backward.

1. Move to slide 1 if it is not currently displayed. Click the Slide Show button located on the status bar to the left of the Zoom slider. The first slide in the presentation fills the screen.
2. Click the left mouse button to move to slide 2. The left mouse button is one of many ways to move forward in a slide presentation.
3. Press N on the keyboard to move to the next slide, slide 3.

Exercise 1-11 OBSERVE ANIMATION EFFECTS

Animation effects are the special visual or sound effects used as objects are displayed on the screen or removed from view. *Transition effects* are the effects seen in the process of changing between slides.

1. Press N again to move to slide 4, which is titled "Where We're Going."
2. Using the left mouse button, click anywhere to see a sample of a PowerPoint text animation. Click twice more to see the remaining text on this slide.
3. Press N again to move to slide 5. Notice the Box Out transition effect between slides 4 and 5.
4. Click the left mouse button two times to bring in the text from slide 5.
5. Press N to move to slide 6. Press N three more times to bring in the text for slide 6. Notice the Entrance and Emphasis effects placed on this text. If your sound is on, you should also hear sound effects with each text item.
6. Press N to move to slide 7 and N again to finish the presentation.
7. Press Esc or - (minus) to end the slide show.

Adding Text Using Placeholders

Adding and editing text in PowerPoint is very similar to editing text in a word processing program. You click an *I-beam* to position the *insertion point* where you want to key new text. An I-beam is a pointer in the shape of an uppercase "I." An insertion point is a vertical blinking bar indicating where the text you key will be placed. You can also drag the I-beam to select existing text. The keys Enter, Delete, and Backspace work the same way as in a word processing program.

It is important to understand that you *activate* a placeholder when you click the I-beam in it, making it ready to accept text.

Exercise 1-12 KEY PLACEHOLDER TEXT

Text on the slide is contained in text *placeholders*. Placeholders are used for *title text* (the text that usually appears at the top of a slide), *body text* (text in the body of a slide), and other objects, such as pictures. Placeholders help keep design layout and formatting consistent within a presentation.

Body text often contains *bullets* (small dots, squares, or other symbols) to indicate the beginning of each item in a list; therefore, this text is sometimes called bulleted text. Bullets can be decorative, also, for an attention-getting effect.

1. Move to slide 2, click in the Title text placeholder to activate the placeholder. Notice the box that surrounds the text. The border is made up of tiny dashed lines, and sizing handles indicates that the text box is activated and in edit mode, meaning you can edit and insert text.

NOTE

Notice that the pointer changes from an I-beam inside the border to an arrow pointer outside the border. When the pointer rests on top of the border, it becomes a four-pointed arrow, which can be used to move the text placeholder. When the pointer rests on top of a sizing handle, a two-pointed arrow appears.

2. Key the text **Where We Came From**.
3. Click anywhere on the line of text that begins "Gus Irvinelli."
4. Without clicking, move the pointer outside the border to the right and then back inside.
5. Drag the I-beam across the text "an avid" to select it as shown in Figure 1-6. (Click to the left of "an avid," hold down the left mouse button, drag the I-beam across the two words, and then release the mouse button.)

Figure 1-6
Selecting text to edit it

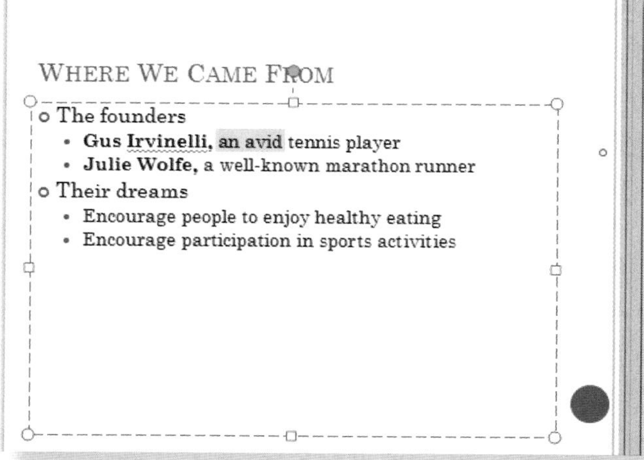

NOTE

Bulleted text lists the points being made in a slide presentation. This presentation uses open circle and solid dot bullets. Bullets can be changed to fit your presentation needs.

6. Key **a professional** to replace the selected text. (You don't need to delete selected text before keying new text.)
7. Click the I-beam to place the insertion point to the right of the words "healthy eating," near the bottom of the slide.
8. To insert a new line, press Enter. Notice that a new dimmed bullet appears at the beginning of the new line.
9. Key **Make their financial investment grow** on the new blank bullet line.
10. Click a blank part of the slide area to deactivate the text box. To make sure you are clicking a blank area, click when the pointer is a simple arrow, not an I-beam or a four-pointed arrow.

Exercise 1-13 CHANGE AND RESET PLACEHOLDER LAYOUT

Placeholders can be moved, resized, and rearranged on your slide. The layout feature of PowerPoint can be used to choose different layouts or reset the placeholder back to the original.

1. Still working on slide 2, click in the Title placeholder to activate it.
2. Move your pointer to the outer border of the Title placeholder.
3. When your pointer turns to a four-pointed arrow (see Figure 1-7), click and drag the Title placeholder to the bottom of the slide.

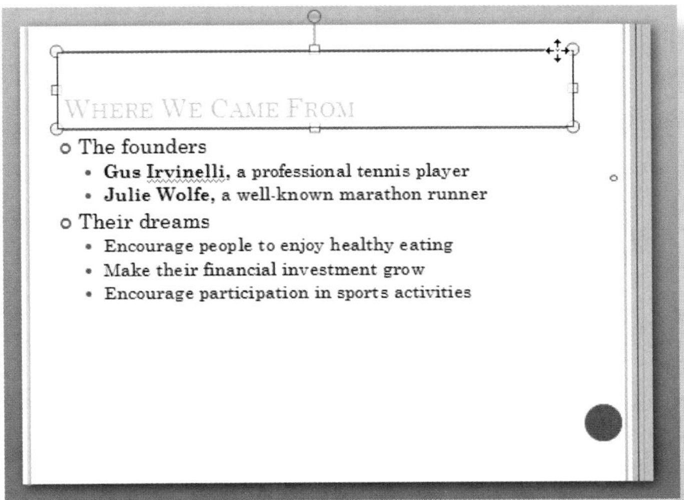

Figure 1-7 Selecting a placeholder

4. From the Home tab, in the Slides group, click the Layout command button, and choose the **Title and Content Layout** to reposition the placeholders to their original position.

Naming and Saving a Presentation

In PowerPoint, presentations are saved as files. When you create a new presentation or make changes to an existing one, you must save the presentation to make your changes permanent. Until your changes are saved, they can be lost if there's a power failure or a computer problem.

The first step in saving a document is to give it a *filename*. Filenames can be up to 255 characters long.

Throughout the exercises in this book, your document filenames will consist of two parts:

- The number of the exercise, such as **1-15**.
- **Your initials**, which might be your initials or an identifier your instructor asks you to use, such as **rst**.

When you're working with an existing file, choosing the **Save** command (or clicking the Save button on the Quick Access toolbar) replaces the file with the file on which you're working. After saving, the old version of the file no longer exists and the new version contains all your changes.

You can give an existing presentation a new name by using the **Save As** command. The original presentation remains unchanged and a second presentation with a new name is saved as well.

Exercise 1-14 CREATE A FOLDER FOR SAVING YOUR FILES

NOTE

Your instructor will advise you of the proper drive or folder to use when creating your lesson folders.

Before saving a file, you need to decide where you want to save it: in a folder on your fixed disk drive, on a jump drive, floppy disk or other removable medium, or on a network drive.

When you save a file, it's a good idea to create separate folders for specific categories to help keep your work organized. For example, you might want to create folders for different projects or different customers. In this course, you will follow these steps to create a new folder for each lesson's work before you begin the lesson.

NOTE

Even though you clicked Cancel to close the Save As dialog box, your new folder has been created. You could have saved your presentation before closing the Save As dialog box, but you will do that in the next exercise instead.

1. Click the Microsoft Office Button, choose **Save As** then **PowerPoint Presentation**. The Save As dialog box appears.
2. Using the list box at the top or links on the left, follow your instructor's directions to navigate to the location where you should create your folder. If you will be using a jump drive or other media, put it in your computer's drive now.

3. Click the Create New Folder button on the Save As dialog box toolbar as shown in Figure 1-8.

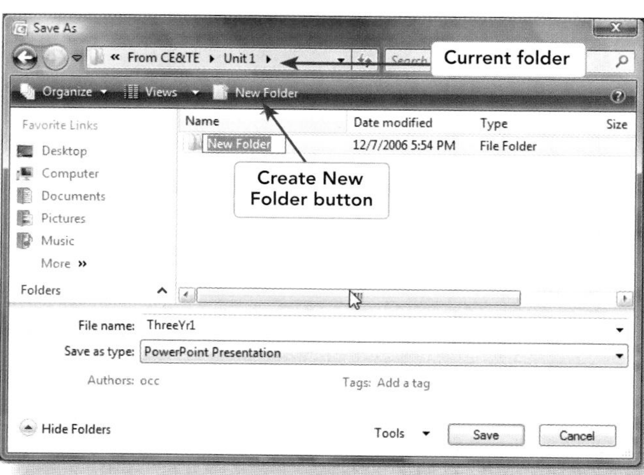

Figure 1-8
Creating a new folder in the Save As dialog box

4. With the words New Folder selected, key **Lesson 1** and click off of the folder. A yellow folder icon with the name "Lesson 1" appears.
5. Click **Cancel** to close the Save As dialog box.

Exercise 1-15 NAME AND SAVE A PRESENTATION

To name files, you can use uppercase letters, lowercase letters, or a combination of both. Filenames can also include spaces. For example, you can use "Good 4 U Sales Report" as a filename.

1. Click the Microsoft Office Button, choose **Save As** to reopen the Save As dialog box.
2. Navigate to the drive and folder where you created your new Lesson 1 folder.
3. Double-click the **Lesson 1** folder to open it.
4. In the **File name** text box, key **[1-15your initials]**.
5. Click **Save**. Your document is saved and named for future use. Notice that the title bar displays the new filename.

Preparing Presentation Supplements

Although the primary way of viewing a presentation is usually as a slide show, you can also print PowerPoint slides, just as you print Word documents or Excel worksheets. PowerPoint provides a variety of print options, including printing each slide on a separate page or printing several slides on the same page. You should utilize the PowerPoint Print Preview option when preparing to print.

Throughout this course, to conserve paper and speed up printing, you usually print a *handout* instead of full-size slides. A handout contains several scaled-down slide images on each page (one, two, three, four, six, or nine to a page) and is often given to an audience during a presentation.

Exercise 1-16 PREVIEW A PRESENTATION

The PowerPoint *Print Preview* feature lets you see what your printed pages will look like before you actually print them. You can view preview pages in black and white, grayscale, or color.

1. Click the Microsoft Office Button.
2. Point to the arrow next to **Print**.
3. Click **Print Preview**. The Preview window opens, showing you how the printed slide will appear on paper. The Print Preview Ribbon (see Figure 1-9) is displayed at the top of the window.

Figure 1-9
Print Preview Ribbon

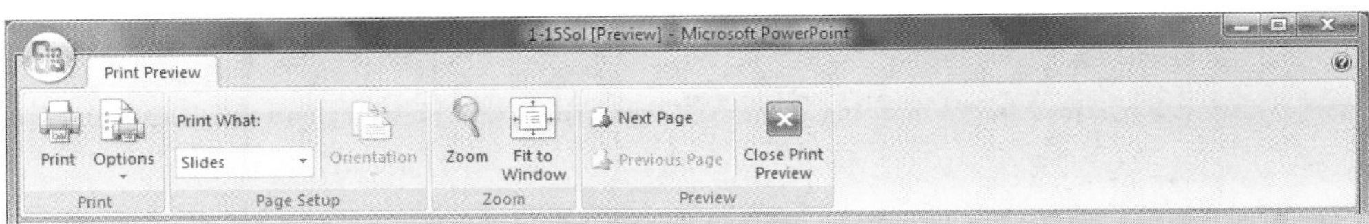

TABLE 1-2 Print Preview Ribbon Buttons

Toolbar Button	Name	Purpose
	Print	Open the Print dialog box.
	Options	Choose from a variety of options and preview them before printing.
	Print what	Choose between printing slides, handouts, notes pages, or an outline.
	Orientation	Switch the pages between portrait (vertical) and landscape (horizontal) layouts.
	Zoom	Change the magnification in the Preview window.
	Fit to window	Zoom the presentation so that the slide fills the window.
	Next page	Display the next page to be printed.
	Previous page	Display the previous page to be printed.
	Close Print Preview	Close the Print Preview window and return to Normal view.

4. From the Print Preview tab, in the Preview group, click the Next Page button. Page 2 of the printout is displayed.

5. Move your pointer to the middle of the slide. Notice that the pointer is in the shape of a magnifying glass.
6. Click the magnifying glass pointer in the center of the slide. The display is magnified.
7. Click again. The display returns to its regular size.

8. Click the Close the Print Preview window button.

Exercise 1-17 PRINT A SLIDE, NOTES PAGE, OUTLINE, AND HANDOUT

You can start the printing process in one of the following ways:

- Click the Microsoft Office Button, point to the arrow next to **Print**, and choose **Print Preview**. From the Print Preview Ribbon, in the Print group, click the Print button.
- Click the Microsoft Office Button, and choose **Print**.

- Press Ctrl+P.
- From the Quick Access toolbar, click the Quick Print button.

The first method opens the Print Preview window, which you learned in Exercise 1-16. The next two methods open the Print dialog box, where you can choose printing options. The last method, Quick Print, should be used with caution. You must first customize the Quick Access toolbar to make the button available. This feature prints a presentation with the most recently used print options and does not open the Print Options dialog box. Usually this will result in printing your entire presentation with one slide on a page.

Printing an outline view is a nice feature if you want to print text only and avoid the slide thumbnails. Printing notes pages allows the speaker to record notes and print them along with an image of the slide. Printing several slides on a single page is a handy way to review your work and to create audience handouts. It's also a convenient way to print class assignments. You can create handouts in the Print Preview window or in the Print dialog box.

1. To print the first slide in your presentation, display slide 1, click the Microsoft Office Button, and then choose **Print**. The Print dialog box displays PowerPoint's default settings and indicates the designated printer as shown in Figure 1-10.

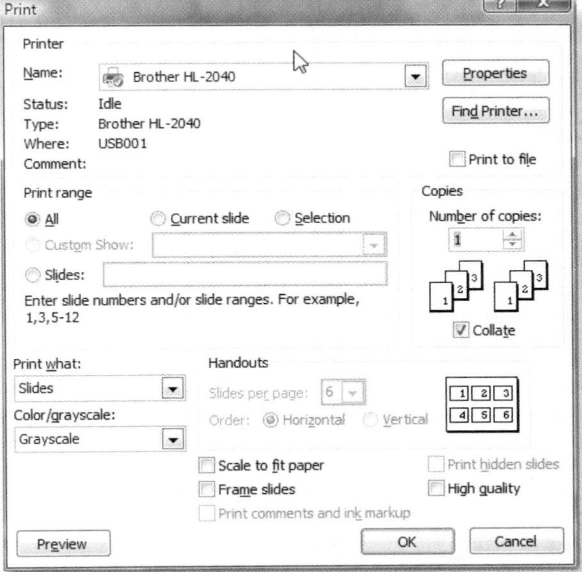

Figure 1-10
Print dialog box

NOTE

The information below the Name box applies to the selected printer. For example, "Status" indicates if the printer is idle or currently printing other documents.

2. At the top of the Print dialog box, click the down arrow in the **Name** box. This is where you choose another printer, if one is available. Follow your instructor's directions to choose an appropriate printer from the list.
3. In the **Print range** option box, choose **Current Slide**.
4. From the **Print what** drop-down list box, choose **Slides**.

5. Click **OK** to start printing.
6. Click the Microsoft Office Button, point to the arrow next to **Print**, and choose **Print Preview**. From the Print Preview tab, in the Page Setup group, click the arrow next to the **Print what** list box and then choose **Handouts (2 Slides per page)**. Only one slide is shown in Print Preview due to previous exercise choice of current slide only. To see both slides, return to the Print dialog box and choose All under Print Range. This screen displays how your handouts would look if printed with the selected options.
7. Still working in the Page Setup group, click the Orientation button and choose **Landscape**.
8. Open the **Print what** list box and then choose **Outline View** (this provides text only).
9. Open the **Print what** list box and then choose **Notes Pages** (this provides a snapshot of the slide as well as speaker notes).
10. Open the **Print what** list box again and choose **Handouts (9 Slides per page)**. Now the entire presentation is displayed on one page.
11. From the Print Preview tab, in the Preview group, click the Close Print Preview button.

TIP

You can create a presentation that uses overhead transparencies by printing your slides on transparency film. Before printing, insert transparency sheets directly into your printer (choosing the correct type of transparency for a laser or ink-jet printer).

TIP

If two slides are not displayed in the Print Preview screen, click the **Print** button, and under **Print range**, choose **All**. In the **Print what** drop-down list, choose **Handouts**. Then, under the **Handouts** heading, choose **2** from the drop-down list. Last of all, click **Preview** to return to **Print Preview**. This reverses the action where you chose Current Slide.

Exercise 1-18 CHOOSE PRINT OPTIONS

In addition to the options covered previously, there are two options for printing in black and white. The *Grayscale* option converts the presentation colors to shades of gray. The *Pure Black and White* option converts all colors to either black or white, eliminating shades of gray. Multiple copies can be printed, too, and the *Collate* option will print the slides in sequence.

The Print dialog box is divided into several areas: Printer, Print range, Copies, Print what, and Handouts. Each area presents choices that let you print exactly what you want in a variety of layouts.

NOTE

Because the Pure Black and White option simplifies your presentation graphics, it can sometimes speed up printing time.

1. Still working in **1-15your initials**, click the Microsoft Office Button and choose **Print** to open the Print dialog box.
2. Under **Print range**, click **Slides** and key **1,2** in the text box to print only slides 1 and 2.
3. Under **Copies**, in the **Number of copies** box, key **2**. The **Collate** check box is selected by default to print the slide show from beginning to end two times.

TIP

To print consecutive slides, you can use a hyphen. For example, key **2-4** to print slides 2 through 4. To print a combination of slides, you can key the range **1,3, 5-9, 12** to print slides 1, 3, 5 through 9, and 12.

4. From the **Print what** drop-down list box, choose **Notes Pages**.
5. If you have a black-and-white printer, choose **Grayscale** from the **Color/grayscale** list box. If you have a color printer, you can choose Color from the list box but the grayscale will conserve your colored ink/toner.
6. Click the **Scale to fit paper** check box to expand items to the full width of the page.
7. Click **OK**.
8. Open the Print dialog box again and set the following options:
   - For **Print range**, choose **All** to print all slides.
   - For **Number of copies**, key **1**.
   - In the **Print what** list box, choose **Handouts**.
   - Under **Handouts**, choose **3 Slides per page**.
   - From the **Color/grayscale** list box, choose **Pure Black and White**.
   - Click the **Frame slides** check box if it is not already checked.
9. Click **OK** to print the presentation handout and close the Print dialog box.
10. Click the Microsoft Office Button, and choose **Save As**.
11. In the **File name** text box, key **[1-18your initials]**.
12. Click **Save**. Your document is saved and named for future use. Notice that the title bar displays the new filename.

NOTE

You are still on landscape orientation since you set that in a previous exercise.

Ending Your Work Session

After you finish working on a presentation and save it, you can close it and open another file or you can exit the program.

To close a presentation and exit PowerPoint, you can:

- Click the Microsoft Office Button and choose **Close** or **Exit PowerPoint**.
- Use keyboard shortcuts. Ctrl+W closes a presentation and Alt+F4 exits PowerPoint.
- Use the Close button in the upper-right corner of the window.

Exercise 1-19 CLOSE A PRESENTATION AND EXIT POWERPOINT

1. Click the Microsoft Office Button.
2. Choose **Close** to exit the presentation.
3. Click the Close button in the upper-right corner of the window to exit PowerPoint.

Lesson 1 Summary

- Microsoft PowerPoint is a powerful graphics program used to create professional-quality presentations for a variety of settings.
- Identify items in the PowerPoint window by pointing to them and waiting for their ScreenTips to appear.
- PowerPoint command buttons are arranged in groups that can be accessed by clicking tabs on the Ribbon.
- The Quick Access toolbar contains a set of commands independent of the tab that is currently displayed. The toolbar includes commonly used commands such as save, undo, redo, and print.
- PowerPoint Help window is a great place to look for additional information on a topic or steps to completing a task.
- Key and edit text on a slide in the same way as you would in a word processing program.
- Use the Slide Show button to run a slide show. A slide show always starts with the slide that is currently selected.
- To print handouts that contain more than one slide on a page, use the Print dialog box or Print Preview window to select from the **Print what** options.
- Printing options provide a variety of ways to print your presentation: as slides, handouts, notes pages, and outline view.

LESSON 1 Command Summary

Feature	Button	Ribbon	Keyboard
Open a presentation		Microsoft Office Button, Open	Ctrl+O
Display Slides and Outline pane		View tab, Presentation Views group, Normal	
Zoom		View tab, Zoom group, Zoom	
Help		Help button	F1
Normal view		View tab, Presentation Views group, Normal	
Slide Sorter view		View tab, Presentation Views group, Slide Sorter	
Next Slide			PageDown
Previous Slide			PageUp
Slide Show		View tab, Presentation Views group, Slide Show	F5
Save		Microsoft Office Button, Save; Quick Access toolbar, Save button	Ctrl+S
Save with a different name		Microsoft Office Button, Save As	
Next Slide (Slide Show view)		Right-click, Next	N, PageDown
Previous Slide (Slide Show view)		Right-click, Previous	P, PageUp, Backspace
End a slide show		Right-click, End Show	Esc or -
Layout		Home tab, Slides group, Layout	
Print Preview		Microsoft Office Button, Print arrow, Print Preview	
Print		Microsoft Office Button, Print; Quick Access toolbar, Quick Print button	Ctrl+P
Close a presentation		Microsoft Office Button, Close	Ctrl+W or Ctrl+F4
Exit PowerPoint	Exit PowerPoint	Microsoft Office Button, Exit PowerPoint	Alt+F4

Lesson 2

Developing Presentation Text

OBJECTIVES

After completing this lesson, you will be able to:

1. Create a new blank presentation.
2. Use the font group commands.
3. Adjust text placeholders.
4. Work with bullets and numbering.
5. Work with text boxes.

MCAS OBJECTIVES

In this lesson:
PP07 1.1.1
PP07 1.5
PP07 2.1.1
PP07 2.1.2
PP07 2.1.3
PP07 2.1.4
PP07 2.2.3
PP07 2.2.5
PP07 2.2.6
See Appendix

Estimated Time: 1$^{3}/_{4}$ hours

You can add interest to a PowerPoint presentation by varying the appearance of text—that includes changing the font, text style, bullet shape, or position of text. You can change text appearance before or after you key it. Always strive for readability and continuity within your presentation.

In this lesson you will learn how to change text attributes such as color, font, font style, and font size. You will also work with bullets and numbering for easy-to-read lists and use different ways of indenting your text. You will change the indent settings, set tab stops, adjust line spacing, and manipulate text in other ways. Several keystrokes you will use to quickly move around on slides or within your presentation are shown in Table 2-1.

Creating a New Blank Presentation

To create a new blank presentation, you can begin with either:

- A *design theme,* which adds uniform colors and design background to each slide in the presentation.
- A blank presentation (simple text on a plain background), to which you can later apply a design template.

You build each slide by choosing a slide layout and keying slide text.

Exercise 2-1 START A NEW BLANK PRESENTATION

NOTE

If PowerPoint is already open and a blank title slide is not displayed, click the Microsoft Office Button and choose **New**. Choose Blank Presentation and click **Create**.

One way to create a presentation is to start with a blank slide, focusing first on content, and then adding color and other design elements later.

1. Start PowerPoint. A blank title slide appears, ready for your text input, as shown in Figure 2-1.

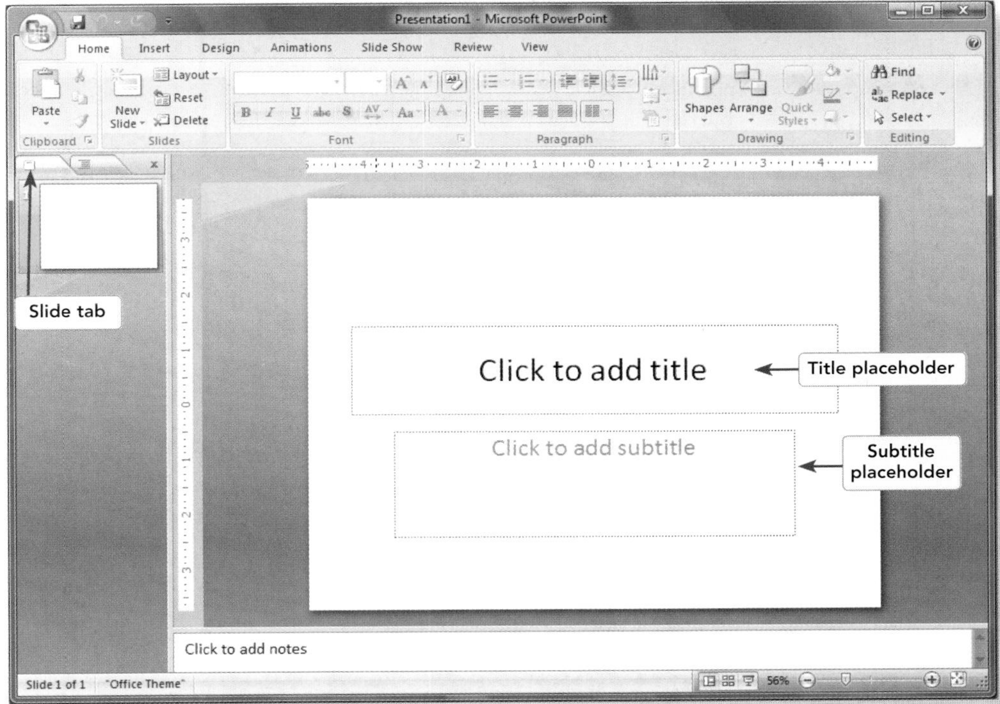

Figure 2-1
Title slide

2. Click the title placeholder to activate it and key **For the Pleasure of Your Company**.

3. Click the subtitle placeholder and key **Plan Your Next Event with Good 4 U**.

NOTE

The documents you create in this course relate to the case study in the front of this text about Good 4 U, a fictional restaurant business.

4. Position the insertion point after the word "Event" in the subtitle; then press Shift+Enter. The subtitle is now split into two lines. Delete the space before "with" on the second line of the subtitle.

5. Split the title text into two lines so that "Your Company" appears on the second line.

TABLE 2-1 Using the Keyboard to Navigate on a Slide and in a Presentation

Keystrokes	Result
Ctrl+Enter	Selects and activates the next text placeholder on a slide. If the last placeholder (subtitle or body text) is selected or activated, pressing Ctrl+Enter inserts a new slide after the current slide. Pressing Ctrl+Enter never selects other objects on a slide (including text boxes) that are not placeholders.
Esc	Deactivates the currently activated text placeholder or text box and selects the entire text box instead. If a text box is selected but not activated, pressing Esc deselects the text box.
Tab	If a text placeholder or text box is activated, inserts a tab character at the insertion point; if not activated, selects the next object on the slide. If the insertion point is between a bullet and the first text character on a line, pressing Tab demotes the bulleted text. Pressing Tab repeatedly when no objects are activated cycles through all the objects on a slide but never moves to another slide.
Shift+Tab	If a text box or text placeholder is not activated, selects the previous object on a slide. If the insertion point is between a bullet and the first text character on the line, promotes the bulleted text.
Esc, Tab	Moves to the next object on a slide, regardless of whether a text box is activated. It never inserts a new slide.
Shift+Enter	If a text box or text placeholder is activated, inserts a new line (but not a new paragraph) at the insertion point.
Enter	If a text box or text placeholder is activated, inserts a new paragraph, including a bullet if in a body text placeholder. If a text box or text placeholder is selected but not activated, selects all the text in the object.
Ctrl+M	Inserts a new slide after the current slide.

Exercise 2-2 ADD NEW SLIDES AND USE SLIDE LAYOUTS

To add a new slide after the current slide in a presentation, you can do one of the following:

- From the Home tab, in the Slides group, click the New Slide button.
- Press Ctrl+M.
- When a placeholder is selected, press Ctrl+Enter one or more times until a new slide appears.

When a new slide first appears on your PowerPoint window, you don't need to activate a placeholder to start keying text. When no placeholder is selected, as long as your Slide pane is active, the text you key automatically goes into the title text placeholder. Knowing this can speed up the process of developing a presentation.

1. From the Home tab, in the Slides group, click the top of the New Slide button. A new slide appears, containing a title text placeholder and a body text placeholder.

2. Key **Excellent Service**. The text appears automatically in the title placeholder.

Figure 2-2
Keying text on a slide

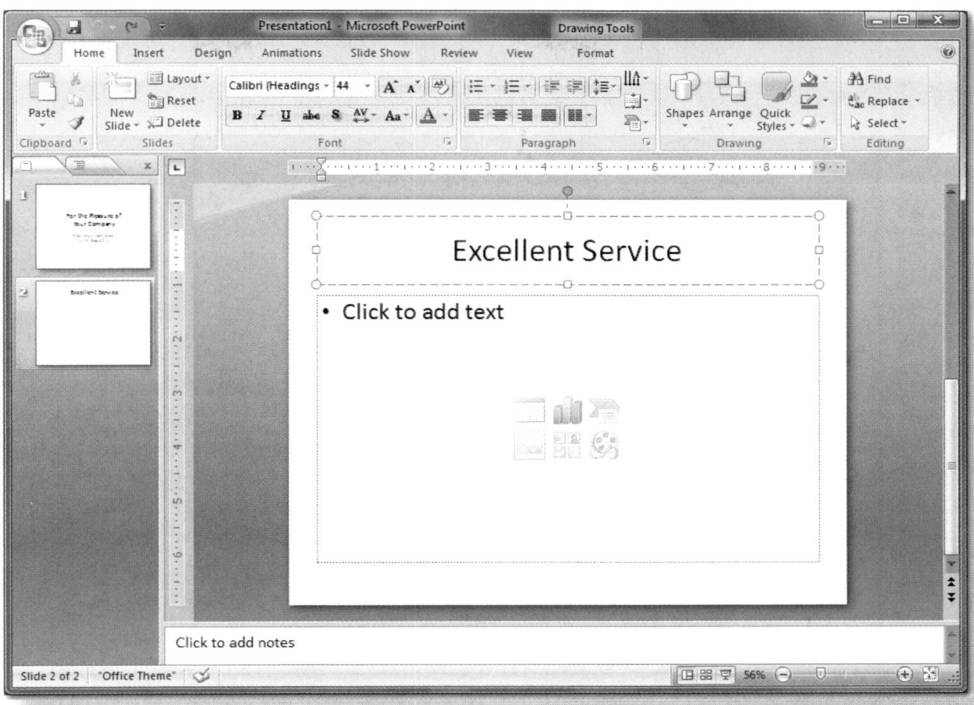

3. Press Ctrl+Enter or click the body text placeholder to activate it and key the following text, pressing Enter at the end of each bulleted line:
   - **We put your employees and guests at ease**
   - **We make your company look good**
   - **We adhere to promised schedules**
   - **We provide a professional and courteous staff**
   - **We guarantee customer satisfaction**

TIP

When you insert a new slide in a presentation, it uses the same layout as the previous slide (unless the previous slide was the title slide). You learn how to change slide layouts later in this lesson.

4. Press Ctrl+M to create a new text slide.
5. Key **A Delightful Menu** as the title and then key the following body text:
   - **High-quality, healthy food**
   - **Variety to appeal to a broad range of tastes**
6. From the Home tab, in the Slides group, click the down arrow on the New Slide button to see thumbnail *slide layouts* with their names, as shown in Figure 2-3. Layouts contain placeholders for slide content such as titles, bulleted lists, charts, and shapes that you will learn about in other lessons.

Figure 2-3
Inserting a new slide by using the slide layouts

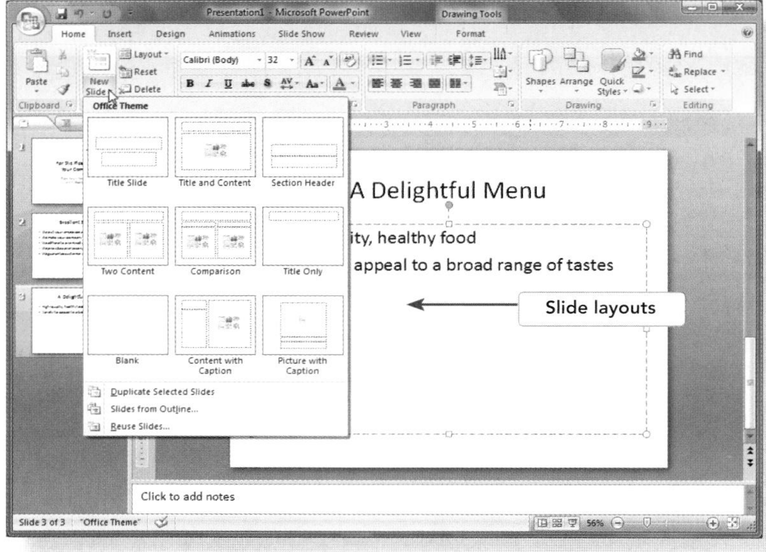

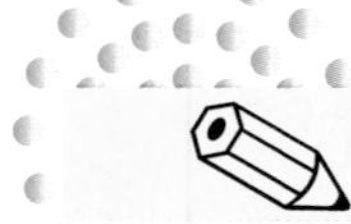

TIP

PowerPoint's *AutoCorrect* feature automatically corrects common spelling and other errors as you key text. It can be turned on or off, and you can customize it so it will find errors that you frequently make.

7. Click the **Title and Content** slide layout.
8. Key **High-Energy Fun** as the title and then key the following body text:
   - **Athletic decor**
   - **Sports promotions**
9. Notice that PowerPoint's AutoCorrect feature automatically adds the accent mark to the word "décor."
10. Press Ctrl+M to insert another slide; then key **A Healthy Atmosphere** as the title and key the following body text:
    - **Smoke-free**
    - **Alcohol optional**
    - **We sell none**
    - **We'll gladly serve your own**
11. Move to slide 4 ("High-Energy Fun") and from the Home tab, in the Slides group, click the down arrow on the New Slide button. Click the **Two Content** slide layout.
12. Key **Events That Are Good 4 U** as the title and then key the following bulleted text in the left body text placeholder:
    - **High-energy meetings**
    - **Productive lunches**
    - **Company celebrations**
    - **Celebrity promotions**

13. Key the following bulleted text in the right body text placeholder:
    - **Entertaining customers**
    - **Demonstrating products**
14. Notice how each slide is numbered in the Slides and Outline pane.
15. Create a new folder for Lesson 2 and save the presentation **[2-2your initials]** in your new Lesson 2 folder.
16. Close the presentation.

Using the Font Group Commands

One way to change the appearance of text in your presentation is by changing the font. A font is a set of characters with a specific design. You can change the *font face* (such as Times New Roman or Arial) and the *font size*. Fonts are measured in *points* (there are 72 points to an inch) indicating how tall a font is.

It is useful to understand that different fonts can take up different amounts of horizontal space, even though they are the same size. For example, a word formatted as 20-point Arial will be wider than a word formatted as 20-point Garamond, as shown in Figure 2-4.

Figure 2-4
Comparing fonts

20 point Arial: Formatting

20 point Garamond: Formatting

Another way to change the appearance of text is by applying text attributes. For example, you can apply a text style (such as bold or italic) and effect (such as underline or shadow). You use the Font group commands, shown in Figure 2-5 and described in Table 2-2, to change selected text.

Figure 2-5
The Font group on the Home tab

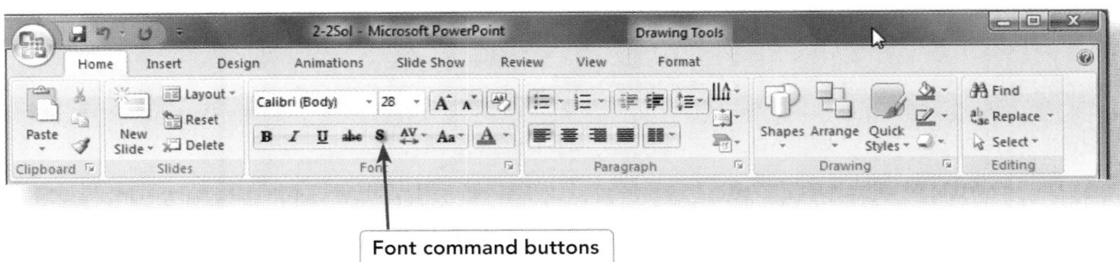

TABLE 2-2 The Font Group Formatting Command Buttons

Button	Purpose
Font	Enables you to choose a font face for selected text or for text to be keyed at the insertion point.
Font Size	Enables you to choose a font size for selected text or for text to be keyed at the insertion point.
Increase Font Size	Increases the size of selected text by one font size.
Decrease Font Size	Decreases the size of selected text by one font size.
Clear All Formatting	Removes all formatting from the selected text.
Bold	Applies the bold attribute to text.
Italic	Applies the italic attribute to text.
Underline	Applies the underline attribute to text.
Shadow	Applies a text shadow.
Strikethrough	Draws a line through selected text.
Character Spacing	Increases or decreases the space between characters.
Change Case	Applies different capitalizations such as uppercase, lowercase, or sentence case.
Font Color	Changes text color.

Exercise 2-3 CHANGE THE FONT FACE AND FONT SIZE

One convenient way to apply text formatting is to first key the text, focusing on content, and then select the text and apply formatting, such as by changing the size or font. Keep in mind that no more than two or three fonts should be used in a presentation. Also remember that the font size should be large enough for easy reading when the presentation is displayed on a large projection screen.

Another thing to be aware of is the type of font you choose. The font drop-down list displays all the fonts available for your computer. On the left side of each font is a symbol indicating the font type. *Truetype* fonts have the following symbol: . If you plan to show your presentation on a different computer or print it with a different printer, it is best to choose a Truetype font.

The Increase Font Size and Decrease Font Size buttons change the size of all the text in a selected placeholder by one font size increment as shown in the font size box on the formatting toolbar. If several sizes of text are used in the placeholder, each size is changed proportionately. For example, if a text placeholder contains both 24-point text and 20-point text, clicking the Increase Font Size button will change to the point sizes 28 and 24 at the same time.

Many of the buttons used to format text are toggle buttons. A *toggle button* switches between on and off when you click it. The Shadow button is an example of a toggle button: click it once to apply a shadow, once again to remove it. Other examples of toggle buttons are Bold, Italic, and Underline.

Figure 2-6
Font drop-down list

1. Open the file **Health1**.
2. Examine the Font group and locate the command buttons listed in Table 2-2.
3. On slide 1, click the title placeholder to activate it and key **Heart**.
4. Select the word you just keyed.
5. In the Font group, click the down arrow next to the Font box. A drop-down list of available fonts appears, as shown in Figure 2-6.
6. From the drop-down list, choose **Arial Black**. As you can see, text formatting in PowerPoint is similar to text formatting in a word processing program.

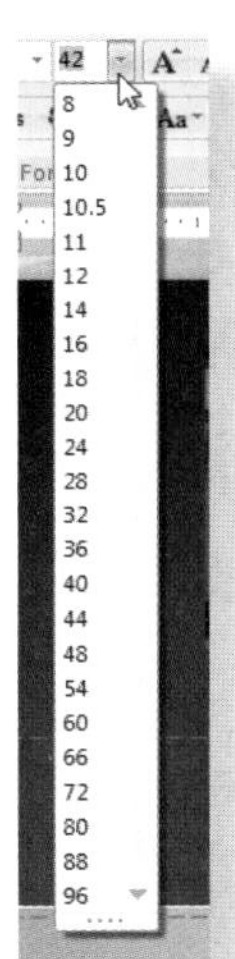

Figure 2-7
Font size drop-down list

7. With "Heart" still selected, click the down arrow next to the Font Size box, as shown in Figure 2-7. Choose **66**. The text size increases to 66 points.
8. Click the Decrease Font Size button. The font size decreases by one size increment. Notice the number "60" displayed in the Font Size box.
9. Click the Increase Font Size button twice. The font size increases by two size increments, to 72 points (the equivalent of 1 inch tall).

NOTE

Theme colors are preselected groups of colors that provide variations suitable for many presentation needs. However, font colors or other graphic colors may need more emphasis than using the Theme colors will provide.

Exercise 2-4 APPLY BOLD, ITALIC, COLOR, AND SHADOW

Sometimes it's convenient to apply text formatting as you key. This is particularly true with bold, italic, and underline if you use the following keyboard shortcuts:

- Ctrl+B for bold
- Ctrl+I for italic

- Ctrl+U for underline
- Ctrl+S for shadow

TIP

A shadow can help to make the shapes of characters more distinctive. Be sure you always have a high contrast in color between your text colors and your background colors (light on dark or dark on light) for easy reading. Apply a shadow when it helps to make your text stand out from the background color and apply the same type of shadow in a similar way for unity of design in your presentation.

1. Position the insertion point to the right of "Heart" and press Spacebar. Click the Bold button (or press Ctrl+B) and then the Italic button (or press Ctrl+I) to turn on these attributes.
2. Key **Smart!** The word is formatted as bold italic as you key. Notice that this word is also 72-point Arial, like the previous word.
3. Double-click the word "Heart"to select it then press Ctrl+B to make it bold.
4. Select the word "Heart."

5. From the Home tab, in the Font group, locate the Font Color button. Click its down arrow to open the Font Color menu showing Theme colors and Standard colors, as shown in Figure 2-8.
6. Drag your pointer over the row of standard colors and you will see the live preview of that color before it is applied. Click the red box and the color is applied.

Figure 2-8
Font color menu

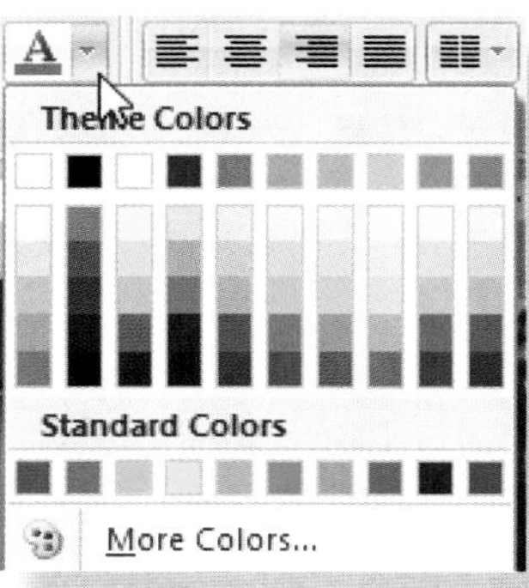

7. Click in the word "Smart" to deselect "Heart." "Heart" is now red.
8. Select both of the two words in your title placeholder. From the Home tab, in the Font group, click the Shadow button. Now the text appears to "float" above the slide background with a soft shadow behind it.

Exercise 2-5 CHANGE THE CASE OF SELECTED TEXT

If you find that you keyed text in uppercase and want to change it, you don't have to re-key it. By using the Change Case button, as shown in Figure 2-9, you can change any text to **Sentence case, lowercase, UPPERCASE, Capitalize Each Word**, or **tOGGLE cASE**. You can also cycle through uppercase, lowercase, and either title case or sentence case (depending on what is selected) by selecting text and pressing Shift+F3 one or more times.

Figure 2-9
Change Case dialog box

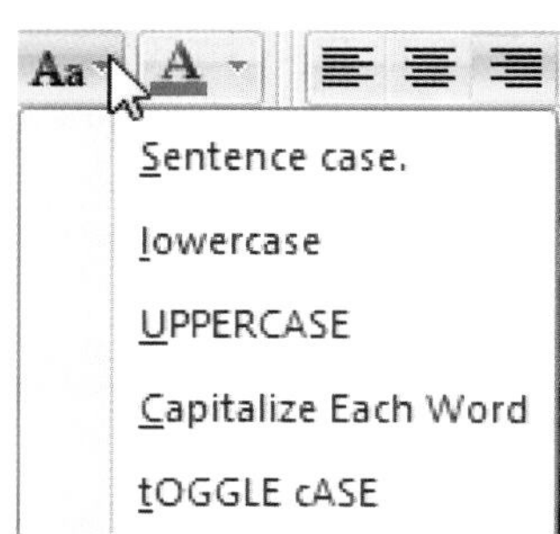

1. Move to slide 3.
2. Use the I-beam pointer to select the title "walk to good health," which has no letters capitalized.

3. From the Home tab, in the Font group, click the down arrow on the Change Case button. Choose **Capitalize Each Word**. This option causes each word to begin with a capital letter.
4. Select the word "To" in the title. Press Shift+F3 two times to change it to lowercase.
5. Select the first item in the body text placeholder by clicking its bullet. This text was keyed with Caps Lock accidentally turned on.
6. From the Home tab, in the Font group, click the Change Case button and choose **tOGGLE cASE**. This option reverses the current case, changing uppercase letters to lowercase, and lowercase letters to uppercase.
7. Select the two bulleted items under "Walking" (beginning with "reduces" and "lowers") by dragging your I-beam across all the words.
8. From Home tab, in the Font group, click the Change Case button and choose **Sentence case**. Now only the first word in each item is capitalized.

Exercise 2-6 CHANGE LINE SPACING WITHIN PARAGRAPHS

You can control *line spacing* by adding more space between the lines in a paragraph or by adding more space between paragraphs. Increased line spacing can make your text layout easier to read and enhance the overall design of a slide.

To change spacing between lines within a paragraph, you can use the Line Spacing button to change the space between lines within a paragraph by increments of 0.5 lines.

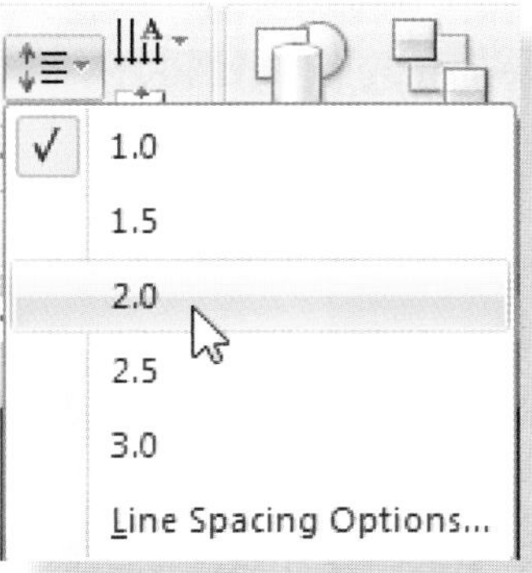

Figure 2-10
Line spacing sizes

1. Move to slide 2. Click within the first bulleted item, which is considered a paragraph in the placeholder.
2. From the Home tab, in the Paragraph group, click the Line Spacing button and a drop-down list of sizes appear, as shown in Figure 2-10.
3. Click 2.0 and the line spacing of the first paragraph increases.
4. Usually you will want to change the line spacing for an entire text placeholder. Select the placeholder.
5. From the Home tab, in the Paragraph group, click the Line Spacing button , and change the line spacing to 1.5 lines.

Exercise 2-7 CHANGE LINE SPACING BETWEEN PARAGRAPHS

The default paragraph line spacing measurement is single. Using the Paragraph dialog box, you can add space by inserting points for before or after paragraphs to expand the space between them. In PowerPoint, each bulleted item in a list is treated as a paragraph.

1. Still working on slide 2, click within the second bulleted item. In the Paragraph group, click the Dialog Box Launcher to open the Paragraph dialog box, as shown in Figure 2-11.

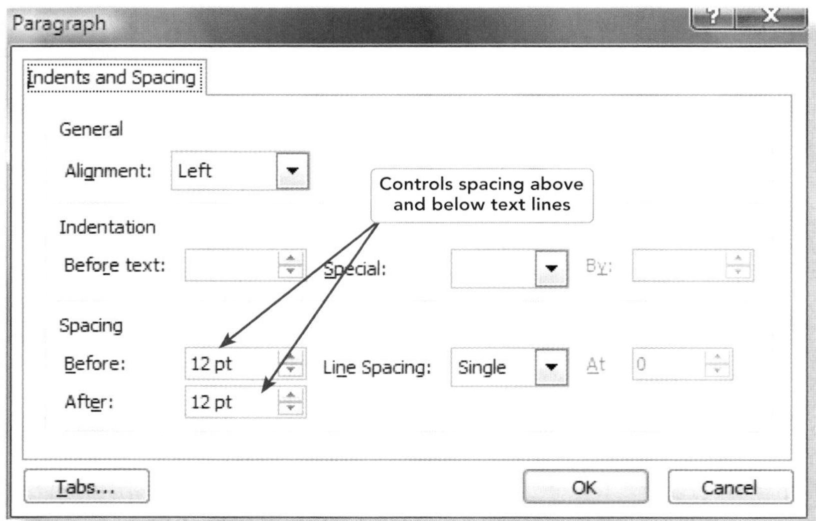

Figure 2-11 Paragraph dialog box

2. In the Spacing section, change the **Before** setting by clicking the spin-box up arrow twice to 18 points. Click **OK**.
3. To make all paragraph spacing uniform, select the entire text placeholder and open the Paragraph dialog box. Change the **Before** spacing to 12 points and the **After** spacing to 12 points. Change the Line spacing setting to **Single**. Click **OK**. The text is now evenly spaced in the placeholder.
4. Save the presentation as [**2-7your initials**] in your Lesson 2 folder but do not print it. Leave the presentation open for the next exercise.

Exercise 2-8 USE THE FONT DIALOG BOX TO MAKE MULTIPLE CHANGES

The Font dialog box is a convenient place to apply several font attributes all at one time. In addition to choosing a font, font style, and font size, this dialog box enables you to choose various effects, such as underline or shadow, and a font color.

1. Go to slide 1 and select the words "Diet and Exercise" in the subtitle. Notice that handles appear around the entire subtitle placeholder, but the colored area showing selection appears only around the text. This has happened because the placeholder is much bigger than the three words that are keyed in it.

2. Right-click the selected text to display the shortcut menu. Choose **Font** to open the Font dialog box, as shown in Figure 2-12.

TIP

Underlining is not the best way to emphasize text. Underlining can cut through the bottom of letters (the descenders) causing the text to be more difficult to read. And because underlining is used so much for hyperlinks on the Internet, underlining seems to have the connotation of a hyperlink. So emphasize your text in different ways, such as by using a larger font size, more dramatic color, or bold.

3. Choose the following options in the Font dialog box:
   - From the **Latin text font** list box, choose **Arial**.
   - From the **Font style** list box, choose **Bold Italic**.
   - From the **Size** list box, key **48**.
   - For **Underline style**, choose **Wavy heavy line**.
   - For **Underline color**, choose **Dark red**.
   - Notice the additional options available in this dialog box.

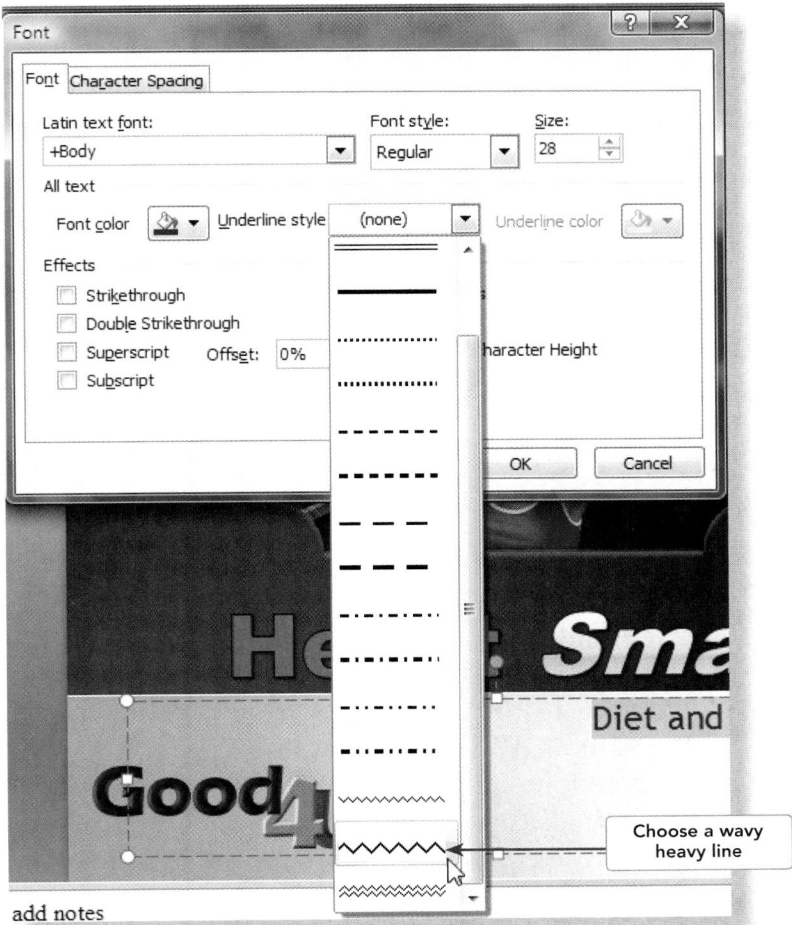

Figure 2-12
Font dialog box

4. Click **OK** to close this dialog box.
5. Select the word "Heart" and then from the Home tab, in the Font group, click the Underline button to turn on underlining. Click the Underline button again to turn off this attribute.
6. With the word "Heart" still selected, change the size to 80 points.
7. Save the presentation as **[2-8your initials]** in your Lesson 2 folder.
8. Preview and then print the title slide only, grayscale, framed.

NOTE

You can change text attributes in the Outline tab in the same way as in the Slide tab.

Adjusting Text Placeholders

You can change formatting features for an entire placeholder by first selecting the placeholder and then choosing the formatting. For example, you can change the text size, color, or font.

You can select placeholders several ways:

- Click the border of an active placeholder with the four-pointed arrow.
- Press Esc while a placeholder is active (when the insertion point is in the text).
- Press Tab to select the next placeholder on a slide (only when a text box or text placeholder is not active).

You can deselect placeholders several ways:

- Press Esc to deselect a placeholder or other object. (Press Esc twice if a text placeholder or text box is active.)
- Click an area of the slide where there is no object.

Exercise 2-9 SELECT A TEXT PLACEHOLDER

Selecting and applying formatting to an entire placeholder can save time in editing.

1. On slide 3, click anywhere in the title text to make the placeholder active. Notice that the placeholder is outlined with small dashes to create a border showing the size of the rectangle. Circles are positioned on the corners and squares are positioned at the midpoint of all four sides, as shown in Figure 2-13. When the placeholder looks like this, the insertion point is active (an I-beam) and you are ready to edit the text within the placeholder.

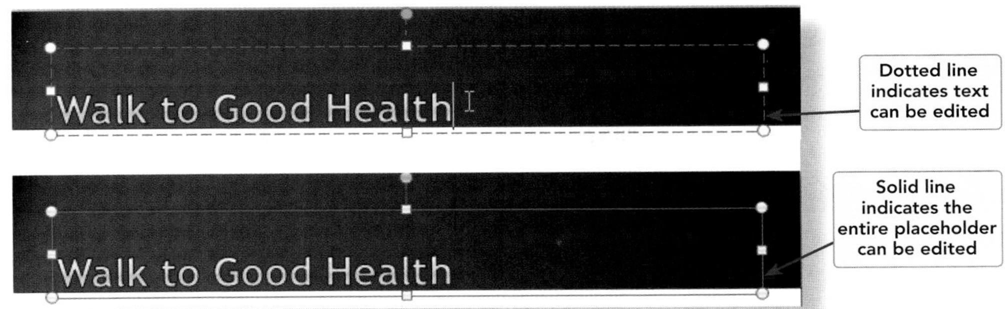
Walk to Good Health
Dotted line indicates text can be edited
Walk to Good Health
Solid line indicates the entire placeholder can be edited

Figure 2-13 Selecting a text placeholder

2. Point to any place on the dotted line border but not on a circle or square. When you see the four-pointed arrow, click the border. Notice that the insertion point is no longer active and the border's appearance has changed slightly—it is now made up of a solid line instead of a dashed line. This indicates that the placeholder is selected. You can make changes to all of the text within it, the fill color of the placeholder, the size of the placeholder, or the position of the placeholder.

NOTE

Pressing Tab cycles through all objects on a slide, not just text placeholders. If a slide contains a graphic object, Tab selects that as well.

3. Press Tab. Now the body text placeholder is selected.
4. Press Esc to deselect the body text placeholder. Now nothing on the slide is selected.
5. Still working on slide 3, click inside the title placeholder text and then press Esc. This is another way to select an active placeholder.
6. Click the Increase Font Size button five times. The font size increases to 60 points.
7. Click the Decrease Font Size button two times until the font size is 48 points.
8. Press Tab to select the body text placeholder. Notice the 23+ in the Font Size box. This indicates that there is more than one font size in the placeholder, and the smallest size is 23 points.
9. Click any text in the first bullet. Notice that its font size is 26 points. Notice also that when you click text inside a placeholder, its border is no longer selected. (The dashed line returns to the border showing that you are editing the text.)
10. Click the first sub-bullet text, which is 23 points.
11. Press Esc to reselect the entire placeholder.
12. Click the Increase Font Size button twice so that 28+ appears in the Font Size box.

TIP

Another way to increase or decrease font size is to press Ctrl+Shift+> or Ctrl+Shift+<.

13. From the Home tab, in the Font group, click the down arrow on the Font Color button and choose Standard color dark blue (the color sample second from the right), making all the body text on this slide dark blue.

14. Still working in the Font group, click the Shadow button to test that effect. Now all the text has a shadow, but with the colors being used, the text looks blurred. Remove the shadow by clicking the Shadow button again.
15. Leave the presentation open for the next exercise.

Exercise 2-10 CHANGE TEXT HORIZONTAL ALIGNMENT

Bulleted items, titles, and subtitles are all considered paragraphs in PowerPoint. Just as in a word processing program, when you press Enter, a new paragraph begins. You can align paragraphs with either the left or right placeholder borders, center them within the placeholder, or justify long paragraphs so that both margins are even. However, the last alignment option should be reserved for longer documents such as reports when you want a formal appearance. Fully justified text is not appropriate for presentation slides.

You can change text alignment for all the text in a placeholder or for just one line, depending on what is selected.

1. Move to slide 5 and select the body text placeholder.
2. Position the insertion point in the first line, "Earn Good 4 U discounts."

3. From the Home tab, in the **Paragraph** group, click the Align Right button. The text in the first line aligns on the right.

4. Click the Align Left button and the paragraph aligns on the left.

5. Select the placeholder border and click the Center button. Both lines are centered horizontally within the placeholder. Because the lines are centered, remove the bullets by clicking on the Bullet list button.
6. Make the text bold.
7. Leave the presentation open for the next exercise.

Exercise 2-11 RESIZE A PLACEHOLDER

At times you will want to change the way text is positioned on a slide. For example, you might want to make a text placeholder narrower or wider to control how text wraps to a new line, or you might want to move all the text up or down on a slide. You can change the size and position of text placeholders in several ways:

- Drag a *sizing handle* to change the size and shape of a text placeholder. Sizing handles are the four small circles on the corners and the squares on the border of a selected text placeholder or other object.
- Drag the placeholder border to move the text to a new position.
- Change placeholder size and position settings by using the Format Shape dialog box.

To change the size or shape of a placeholder, you must first select it, displaying the border as a solid line with sizing handles. It is important to make sure that you're dragging a sizing handle when you want to change a placeholder's size.

By dragging a corner sizing handle, you can change both the height and width of a placeholder at the same time.

1. Display slide 5 and select the body text placeholder. Notice the small white circles and squares on the border. These are the sizing handles, as shown in Figure 2-14.
2. Position the pointer over the bottom center sizing handle.

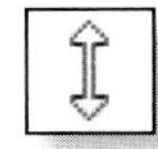

3. When the pointer changes to a two-pointed vertical arrow, hold down your left mouse button and drag the bottom border up until it is just below the second line of text.

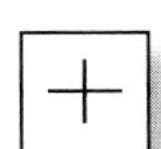

4. As you drag, the border moves and the pointer turns into a crosshair. When you release the mouse, the border adjusts to the new position.

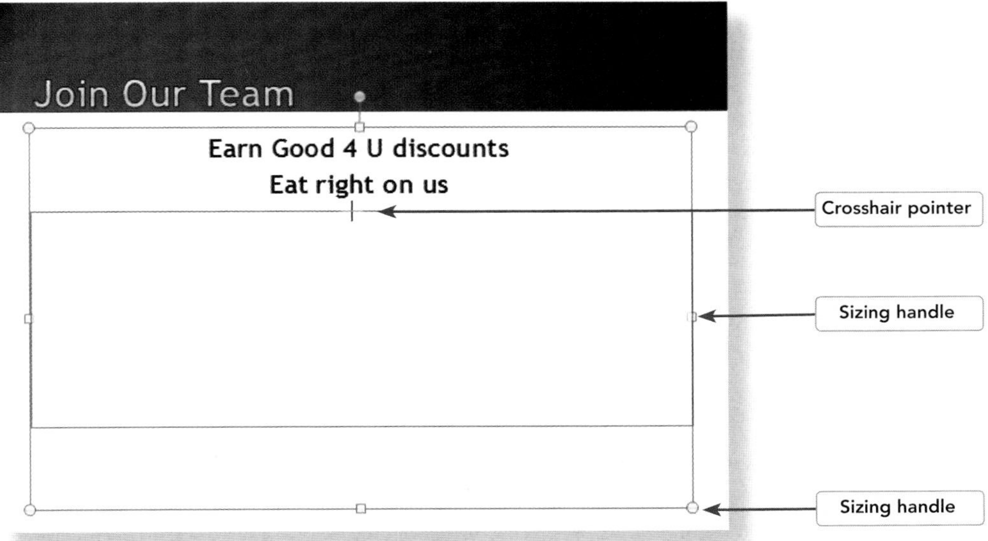

Figure 2-14 Resizing a placeholder

5. Position your pointer over the lower-left-corner sizing handle; then drag it toward the center of the text. Both the height and width of the placeholder change.

6. Click the Undo button once to restore the placeholder to its previous size.
7. Leave the presentation open for the next exercise.

Exercise 2-12 MOVE A PLACEHOLDER

As with changing the size of a placeholder, to change a placeholder's position you must first select it. Drag any part of the placeholder border except the sizing handles when you want to change its position.

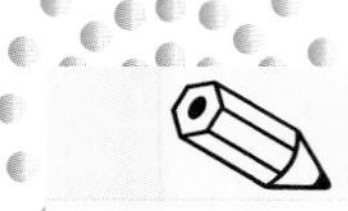

TIP

To fine-tune the position of an object, hold down Alt while dragging or press the arrow keys to "nudge" an object. Press Ctrl+ arrow keys to nudge an object in very small increments.

1. Select the body text placeholder on slide 5.
2. Position the pointer over the placeholder border anywhere except on a sizing handle. The pointer changes to the four-pointed arrow.
3. Drag the four-pointed arrow down until the placeholder appears vertically centered on the white area of the slide, as shown in Figure 2-15.

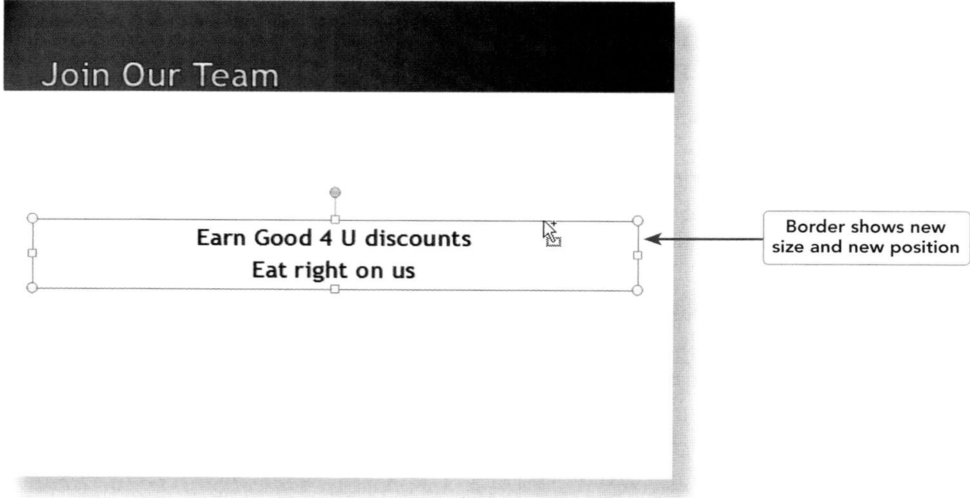

Figure 2-15 Moving a placeholder

4. Deselect the placeholder. The text is now attractively placed on the slide.
5. Move to slide 1 and save the presentation as **[2-12your initials]** but do not print it.
6. Leave the presentation open for the next exercise.

Working with Bullets and Numbering

When you work with body text placeholders, each line automatically starts with a bullet. However, you can turn bullets off when the slide would look better without them. You can remove bullets, add new ones, change the shape and color of bullets, and create your own bullets from pictures. The Bullets and Numbering buttons are both found in the Paragraph group.

Exercise 2-13 REMOVE BULLETS

As you have learned in previous exercises, the Bullets button can turn bullets off and on. Depending on how your text is selected, you can affect a single bullet or all the bulleted lines in a body placeholder when you use the Bullets button. The Bullets button is another example of a toggle button.

1. Display slide 2. Click within the body text to activate the placeholder. Press Esc to select the entire placeholder.
2. From the Home tab, in the Paragraph group, click the Bullets button. This turns bullets off for the entire placeholder and moves the text to the left.
3. Click the Bullets button again to reapply the bullets.
4. Click within the first bulleted item, "Exercise regularly," and click the Bullets button to turn off the bullet.
5. Click the Bullets button again to reapply the bullet.

Exercise 2-14 PROMOTE AND DEMOTE BULLETED TEXT

As you create bulleted items, a new bullet is inserted when you press Enter to start a new line. When you want to expand on a slide's main points, you can insert indented bulleted text below a main point. This supplemental text is sometimes referred to as a sub-bullet or a level 2 bullet. PowerPoint body text placeholders can have up to five levels of indented text, but you will usually want to limit your slides to two levels.

To *demote* body text, you increase its indent level by moving it to the right. To *promote* body text, you decrease its indent level by moving it to the left. These changes can be made by moving the insertion point before the text and pressing Tab to demote (increase indent) or Shift+Tab to promote (decrease indent) or by using the Increase List Level or Decrease List Level buttons found on the Home tab, in the Paragraph group.

1. With slide 2 displayed, move your insertion point after "regularly" then press Enter to create a new bulleted line.
2. Press Tab to indent to the second-level bullet and key **Walk 30 minutes daily**, then press Enter.
3. Notice that the text is now indented automatically to the second-level bullet.
4. Key **Alternate aerobic and weight training**, then press Enter.
5. To return to the first-level bullet, press Shift+Tab.
6. Key **Get sufficient rest**.
7. Leave the presentation open for the next exercise.

NOTE

If you press Tab when the insertion point is within the text placeholder, you insert a tab character instead of demoting text.

Exercise 2-15 CHANGE THE COLOR AND SHAPE OF A BULLET

The Bullets gallery provides just a few choices to change the shape of a bullet. The Bullets dialog box provides many more choices to change the bullet shape by choosing a character from another font. Fonts that contain potential bullet characters include Symbol, Wingdings, and Webdings. Another source of bullet characters is the Geometric Shapes subset available for most other fonts.

1. Working on slide 2, select the body text placeholder.
2. From the Home tab, in the Paragraph group, click the down arrow on the Bullets button to see the gallery options, as shown in Figure 2-16.
3. Click the checkmark bullet option.

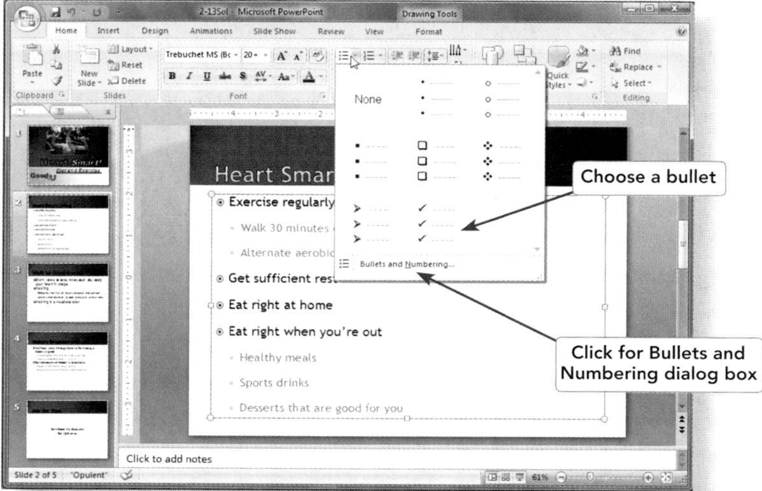

Figure 2-16
Bullets and Numbering gallery

4. With the body text placeholder still selected, click the Bullets button again, and then choose **Bullets and Numbering** at the bottom.
5. In the Bullets and Numbering dialog box, as shown in Figure 2-17, click the **Bulleted** tab.

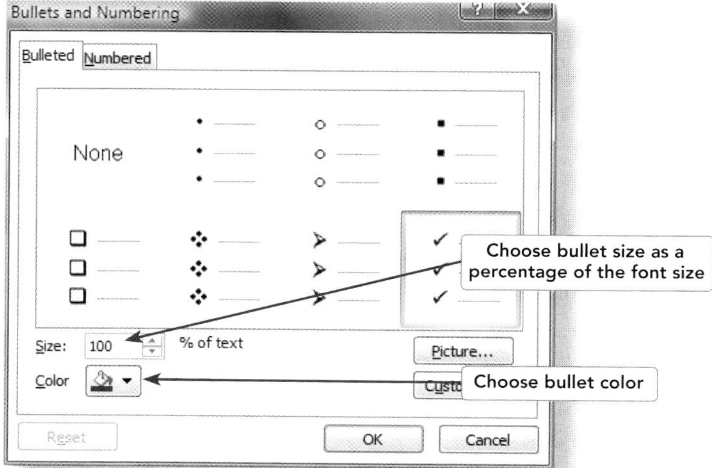

Figure 2-17
Bullets and Numbering dialog box

6. In the **Color** box, choose a Standard red.
7. In the **Size** box, click the down arrow several times until **80** is displayed. Click **OK**. All bullets on slide 2 are now red checks, sized at 80 percent of the font size.
8. Select the first line of bulleted text then press Ctrl while you use your I-beam pointer to select the text of the remaining three level-one bulleted text lines.
9. From the Home tab, in the Paragraph group, click the Bullets button down arrow then choose **Bullets and Numbering**.
10. Click **Customize** to open the Symbol dialog box, shown in Figure 2-18.
11. In the **Font** drop-down list (upper-left corner of the dialog box), scroll to the top and choose **Monotype Corsiva** if it is not displayed.
12. In the **Subset** drop-down list (upper-right corner), choose **Geometric Shapes** (near the bottom of the list). Several characters suitable for bullets appear in the dialog box grid.

Figure 2-18
Symbol dialog box

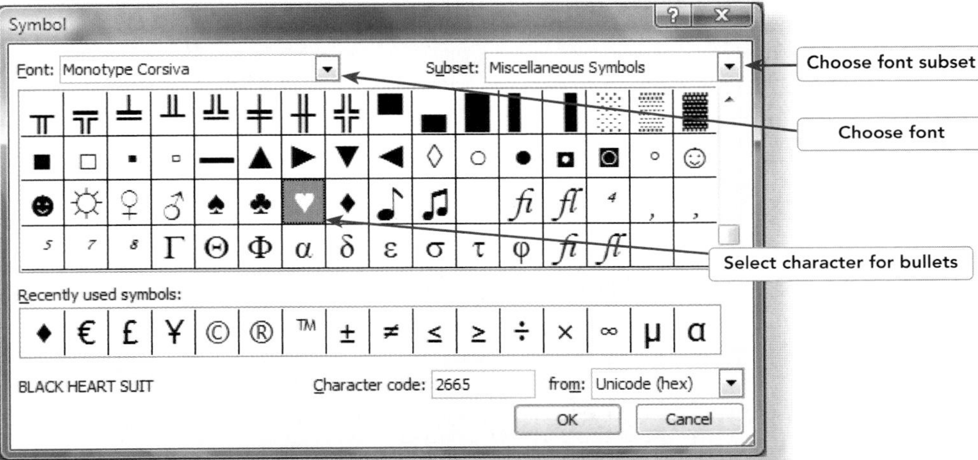

13. Click the heart bullet to select it; then click **OK**. The Symbol dialog box closes, and the Bullets and Numbering dialog box reappears.
14. Change the **Size** to **110%** and leave the **Color** on a Standard **red**. Click **OK**. The selected three bullets on the slide change to red hearts. While the percentage you use is related to the size of the font for that bulleted item, symbols vary in size. So you may need to try more than one adjustment before you accept a size that is pleasing to you.
15. Leave your presentation open for the next exercise.

Exercise 2-16 CREATE A BULLET FROM A PICTURE

A picture bullet can add a unique or creative accent to your presentation. A picture bullet is made from a graphic file and can be a company logo, a special picture, or any image you create with a graphics program or capture with a scanner or digital camera.

1. Display slide 3 and select the text of the first two bullets (but not the sub-bullets).
2. From the Home tab, in the Paragraph group, click the Bullets button down arrow then choose **Bullets and Numbering**.
3. Click the **Picture** to open the Picture Bullet dialog box. The Picture Bullet dialog box displays a variety of colorful bullets. You can choose from one of these bullets, or you can import a picture file of your own.
4. Key the search text **walking**. Click the check box to include content from Office Online, then click **Go**.
5. Look through the images to find a simple one that would represent a person walking for exercise, as shown in Figure 2-19.
6. Click the picture of a person walking to select it and then click **OK**. The bullets are replaced with picture bullets, but they are too small.

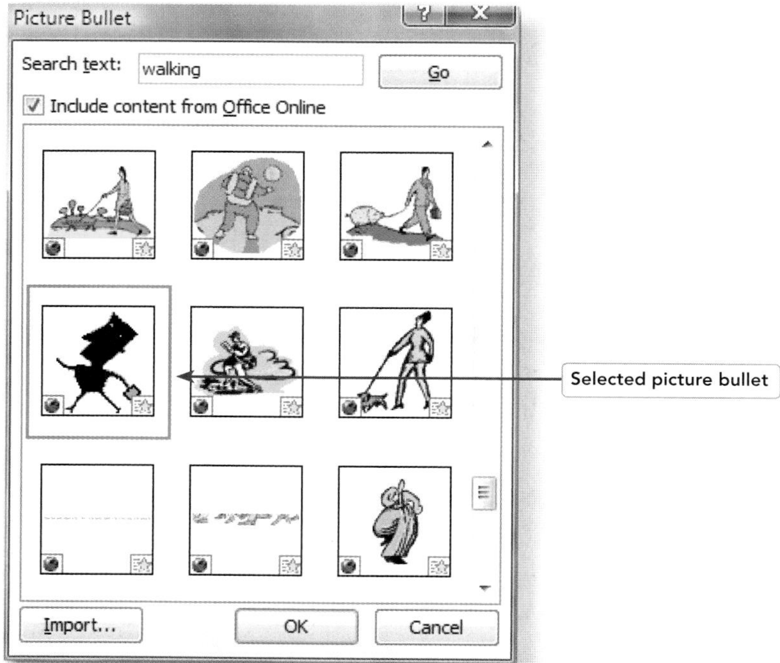

Figure 2-19 Inserting a picture bullet

7. With the two bullet items still selected, reopen the Bullets and Numbering dialog box. In the **Size** box, change the size to **200%**. Click **OK**.

NOTE

If the AutoFit Options button appears near the placeholder, click it and choose **AutoFit Text to Placeholder.**

8. Using the steps outlined previously, change the bullet for the last bulleted item ("Walking is a mood elevator") to the picture of the walker and size it to match the other bullets.
9. Leave your presentation open for the next exercise.

Exercise 2-17 CREATE NUMBERED PARAGRAPHS

Instead of using bullet characters, you can number listed items. A numbered list is useful to indicate the order in which steps should be taken or to indicate the importance of the items in a list.

Using the **Numbered** tab in the Bullets and Numbering dialog box, you can apply a variety of numbering styles, including numbers, letters, and Roman numerals. You can also create a numbered list automatically while you key body text.

1. Display slide 5 and select the body text placeholder.
2. From the Home tab, in the Paragraph group, click the Align Text Left button.
3. Select all the text in the placeholder and delete it.
4. With the placeholder activated, key **1** and press Tab. Key **Walk with us**.
5. Press Enter. The second line is automatically numbered "2."
6. Key **Eat with us** and press Enter.
7. Key **Do what's Good 4 U**. The slide now has three items, automatically numbered 1 through 3.
8. Your text may have resized to be smaller because earlier you made this placeholder just tall enough for two text lines. Press Esc to select the placeholder, then use the bottom sizing handle to drag down and increase the placeholder size to see all three items.
9. From the Home tab, in the Paragraph group, click the down arrow on the Numbers button to see several different numbering styles. Then click **Bullets and Numbering** to open the Bullets and Numbering dialog box and click the **Numbered** tab.

10. Click the first numbered option. In the **Color** box, choose **Red** and change the size to **100%** of text. Click **OK**.

TIP

You can control the numbering style that is applied automatically by keying your first item with the style you want, such as 1. or A.

11. Move to slide 1 and save the presentation as **[2-17your initials]** in your Lesson 2 folder.
12. Preview and then print the presentation as handouts, six slides per page, grayscale, framed. Leave the presentation open for the next exercise.

Exercise 2-18 USE THE RULER TO ADJUST PARAGRAPH INDENTS

A text placeholder will have one of three types of paragraph indents that affect all text in a placeholder. These paragraph indents are:

- *Normal indent*—where all the lines of the paragraph are indented the same amount from the left margin.
- *Hanging indent*—where the first line of the paragraph extends farther to the left than the rest of the paragraph.
- *First-line indent*—where only the first line of the paragraph is indented.

These paragraph indents are controlled by the Paragraph dialog box shown in Figure 2-20 that is accessed through the Paragraph Dialog Box Launcher.

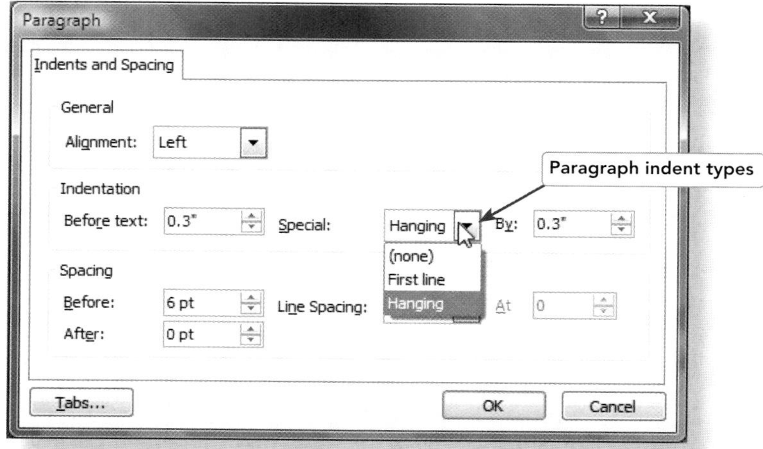

Figure 2-20 Paragraph Indent dialog box

You can also set indents by using the ruler. If the ruler is displayed, you can see and manipulate *indent markers* when you activate a text object for editing. Indent markers are the two small triangles and the small rectangle that appear on the left side of the ruler.

At times you might want to change the distance between the bullets and text in a text placeholder. For example, when you use a large bullet (as you did in Exercise 2-16), the space that it requires may cause the text that follows it to word-wrap unevenly. You can easily adjust this spacing by dragging the indent markers. The following steps will guide you through this process.

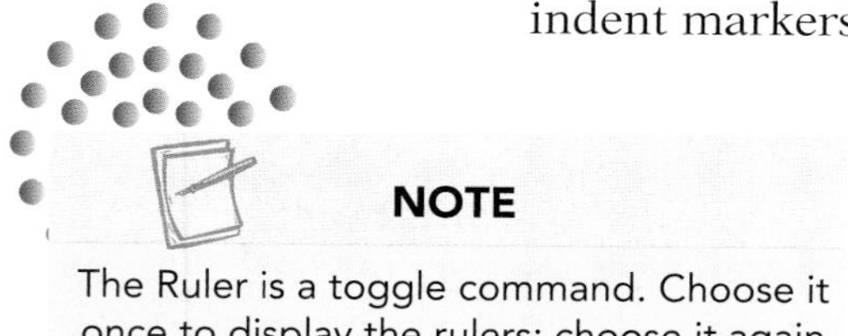

NOTE

The Ruler is a toggle command. Choose it once to display the rulers; choose it again to hide them.

1. Display slide 3. Notice how the text does not align correctly and the square second-level bullets are not indented enough.
2. From the View tab, in the Show/Hide group, click to select the **Ruler**. The vertical and horizontal rulers appear, as shown in Figure 2-21.

Figure 2-21
Horizontal and vertical rulers

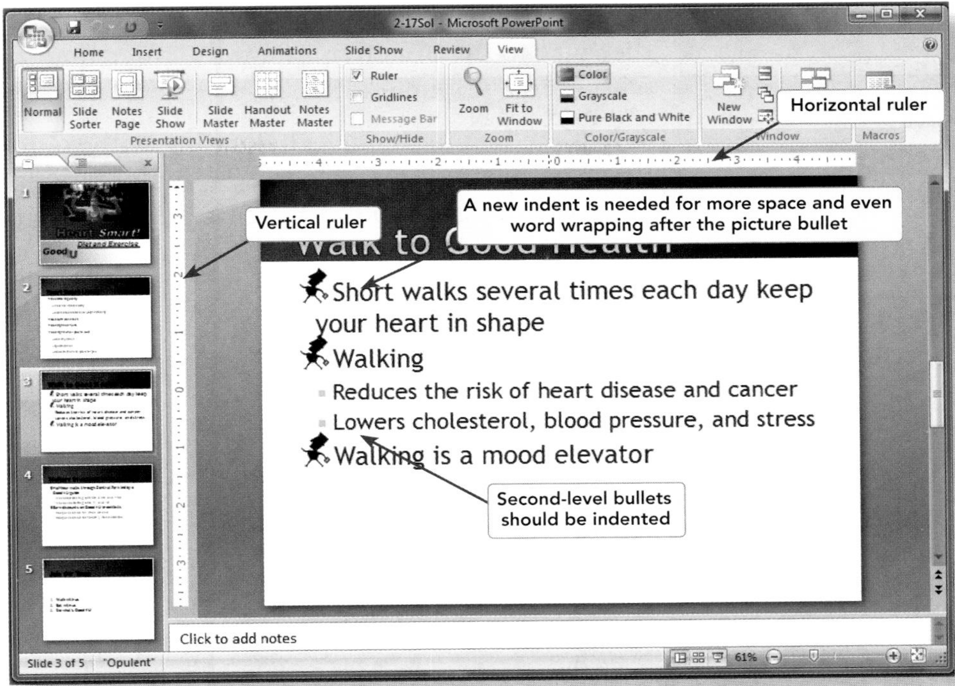

NOTE

You must have an insertion point somewhere inside a text box to change settings on the ruler. The appearance of the ruler reflects whether the entire placeholder is selected or the insertion point is active within the placeholder. If text is already in the placeholder, it must be selected for any ruler changes to apply to the text.

3. Click anywhere within the placeholder as if you were planning to edit some text. Notice the indent markers that appear on the horizontal ruler. Also notice that the white portion of the ruler indicates the width of the text placeholder.
4. Select all of the text in the placeholder.
5. Point to the first-line indent marker on the ruler (triangle at the top of the horizontal ruler, shown in Figure 2-22) and drag it to the right, to the 1-inch mark. The first line of each bulleted item beginning with the picture bullet is now indented the same way.

Figure 2-22
Indent markers

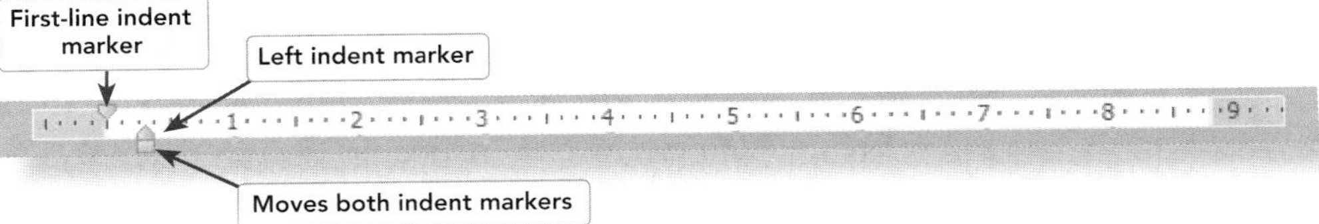

6. Drag the small rectangle (below the triangle on the bottom of the ruler) to the 1-inch mark on the ruler. Notice that both triangles move when you drag the rectangle.

7. Drag the left indent marker (triangle at the bottom of the ruler) to the right to the 2-inch mark on the ruler, and the text will word-wrap with even alignment after the picture bullet.

8. Select the text in the lines beginning with square bullets. Drag the first-line indent marker to the 2.5-inch mark on the ruler. Drag the left indent marker to the 3-inch mark on the ruler. Now the text has much better alignment.

9. Save the presentation as **[2-18your initials]** in your Lesson 2 folder but do not print it. Leave the presentation open for the next exercise.

Working with Text Boxes

Until now, you have worked with text placeholders that automatically appear when you insert a new slide. Sometimes you'll want to use *text boxes* so you can put text outside the text placeholders or create free-form text boxes on a blank slide.

You create text boxes by clicking the Text Box button found on the Insert tab, in the Text group, and then dragging the pointer to define the width of the text box. You can also just click the pointer, and the text box adjusts its width to the size of your text. You can change the size and position of text boxes the same way you change text placeholders.

NOTE

You can also click and drag the text tool pointer to create a text box in a specific width. The text you key will wrap within the box if it does not fit on one text line. You can use the resizing handles to increase or decrease the text box width. You can practice making other text boxes on this slide, and then click Undo as needed to return to just the first text box.

Exercise 2-19 CREATE A TEXT BOX

When you use the Text Box button to create a single line of text, you are free to place that text anywhere on a slide, change its color and font, and rotate it. This type of text is sometimes called floating text.

1. Display slide 5.

2. From the Insert tab, shown in Figure 2-23, in the Text group, click the Text Box button.

Figure 2-23
Insert tab

3. Place the pointer below the "G" in "Good 4 U" and click. A small text box containing an insertion point appears, as shown in Figure 2-24.

1. Walk with us
2. Eat with us
3. Do what's Good 4 U

Figure 2-24
Creating floating text

4. Key **Join Our Team Today!** Notice how the text box widens as you key text.

5. Leave the presentation open for the next exercise.

Exercise 2-20 CHANGE THE FONT AND FONT COLOR

You can select the text box and change the font and font color using the same methods as you did with text placeholders.

1. Click the text box border to select it. Change the text to 44-point, bold, shadowed.

Figure 2-25
Placement for floating text

2. With the text box selected, choose an attractive script font such as Monotype Corsiva or Script MT Bold.
3. Using the Font color button, change the text color to red.
4. Using the four-pointed arrow, move the floating text box to the bottom-right corner of the slide. See Figure 2-25 for placement.

Exercise 2-21 ROTATE AND CHANGE TEXT DIRECTION

You can *rotate* almost any PowerPoint object—including text boxes, placeholders, and clip art—by dragging the green rotation handle that appears at the top of a selected object. You can also control rotation of text boxes and placeholders by using the Format Shape dialog box.

To *constrain* the rotation of an object to 15-degree increments, hold down Shift while rotating.

When text is in a rotated position, it can be awkward to edit. Fortunately, when you select a rotated text box for editing, it conveniently returns to a horizontal position while you revise the text.

TIP

You can key a precise angle of rotation measurement on the 3-D Rotation tab of the Format Shape dialog box in the Z area.

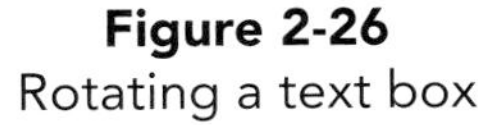

1. On slide 5, click "Join Our Team Today!" and drag the text box up slightly so that you will have enough space to angle it on the slide.

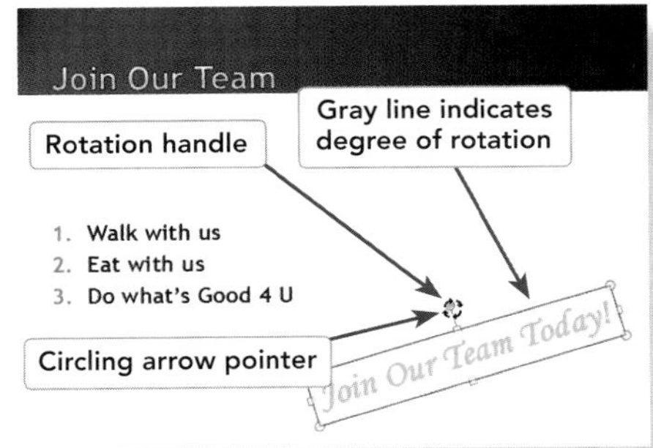

Figure 2-26
Rotating a text box

2. Point to the green rotation handle at the top of the text box and drag it to the left. Notice the circling arrow pointer that appears while you drag.
3. Position the text box as shown in Figure 2-26.

4. With the "Join Our Team Today!" text box selected, press Ctrl+C to copy.
5. Move to slide 4 and press Ctrl+V to paste.
6. Rotate the copied text box to make it straight again, then change the text to read **Offered Daily!** The text box should resize itself to fit this text.
7. With the text box selected, from the Home tab, in the Paragraph group, click Text Direction then choose **Rotate All Text 270°** to make the text read from the bottom up.
8. Reposition this rotated text on the right of the slide.
9. Save the presentation as **[2-21your initials]** in your Lesson 2 folder but do not print it. Leave the presentation open for the next exercise.

Exercise 2-22 WRAP TEXT AND CHANGE ALIGNMENT

When you drag the pointer to define the width of a text box, *word wrapping* is automatically turned on. As you key, your insertion point automatically jumps to a new line when it gets to the right side of the box. The height of the box automatically adjusts to accommodate additional text lines.

1. Move to slide 2, "Heart Smart Living."
2. From the Insert tab, in the Text group, click the Text Box button .
3. Position your pointer to the right of "Exercise regularly"; then drag to the right to create a rectangle that is about 2 inches wide (use the ruler as a guide).
4. In the text box, key **Be consistent wherever you are!**
5. Click the text box border to select it; then increase the font size to 28 points, bold, and red; and then right-align the text. Resize the text box if necessary to match Figure 2-27 and position the text box as shown.

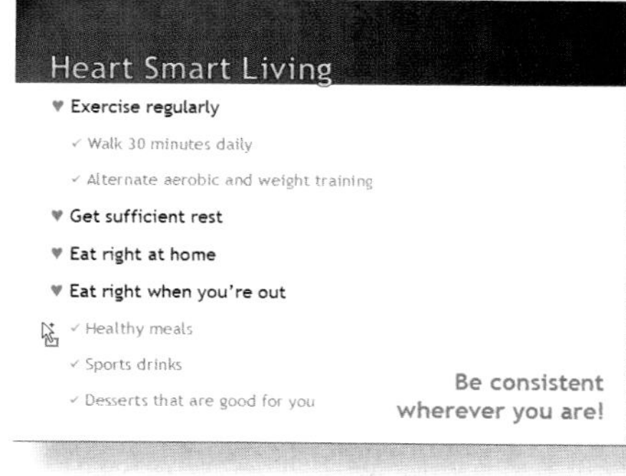

Figure 2-27
Text wrapped in a text box

6. Save the presentation as **[2-22your initials]** in your Lesson 2 folder and print a handout page with six slides per page, grayscale, and framed.

Lesson 2 Summary

- Creating a presentation by starting with a blank presentation lets you concentrate on textual content. Anytime during the process, you can choose a design and color theme.
- Keyboard shortcuts are a big time-saver when creating a presentation. For example, Ctrl+Enter moves to the next text placeholder and Ctrl+M inserts a new slide.
- When you add a new slide, you can choose a slide layout. Slide layouts can be either text layouts or content layouts containing different arrangements of placeholders.
- After a slide is added, you can change the layout of the current slide or of a group of selected slide thumbnails.
- Before keying text in a placeholder, activate it by clicking inside it.
- Using the Outline pane is a quick way to enter slide titles and bulleted text.
- A font is a set of characters with a specific design, for example, Arial or Times New Roman.
- Font size (the height of a font) is measured in points, with 72 points to an inch. Fonts of the same size can vary in width, some taking up more horizontal space than others.
- Many formatting buttons are toggle buttons, meaning that the same button is clicked to turn an effect on and clicked again to turn it off.
- Change text attributes and effects such as bold, italic, and text color by first selecting the text and then clicking the appropriate buttons on the Home tab in the Font group. Or, apply formatting before you key text.
- The Font dialog box, accessible through the Font Dialog Box Launcher, enables you to apply multiple formatting styles and effects all at one time.
- When a text placeholder is selected, formatting that you apply affects all the text in the placeholder.
- Text in placeholders can be aligned with the left or right side of the placeholder, centered, or justified.
- Body text placeholders are preformatted to have bulleted paragraphs. Bullets for selected paragraphs or placeholders are turned on or off by clicking the Bullets button.
- Use the Bullets and Numbering dialog box to change the shape, size, and color of bullets or numbers.
- Graphic files can be used as picture bullets.
- Paragraph indents can be adjusted in text placeholders and text boxes by dragging indent markers on the ruler when a text object is selected.
- To display the ruler for a text object, from the View tab, in the Show/Hide group, choose **Ruler**, and then activate the text object as if to edit the text.
- Bulleted text always uses a hanging indent. Changing the distance between the first-line indent marker (top triangle) and the left indent marker (bottom triangle) on the ruler controls the amount of space between a bullet and its text.

- Indent and tab settings apply only to the selected text object and all the text in the text box. To create more than one type of indent or tab setting, you must create a new text object.
- Line spacing and the amount of space between paragraphs are controlled using the Line Spacing button and dialog box. Line and paragraph spacing can be applied to one or more paragraphs in a text object, or to the entire object.
- Text boxes enable you to place text anywhere on a slide. From the Insert tab, in the Text group, click the Text Box button, then click anywhere on a slide or draw a box and then start keying text.
- Text in a text box can be formatted by using standard text-formatting tools. Change the width of a text box to control how the text will word-wrap.
- When you select a text box on a slide, a green rotation handle appears slightly above the top-center sizing handle. Drag the rotation handle left or right to rotate the object.

LESSON 2 — Command Summary

Feature	Button	Menu	Keyboard
Create new presentation		Microsoft Office Button, New	Ctrl+N
Insert new slide		Home tab, Slides group, New Slide	Ctrl+M
Activate placeholder			Ctrl+Enter
Deactivate placeholder			Esc
Insert line break			Shift+Enter
Move to next placeholder			Ctrl+Enter
Decrease List Level			Shift+Tab or Alt+Shift+←
Increase List Level			Tab
Decrease Font Size		Home tab, Font group, Decrease Font Size	Ctrl+Shift+<
Increase Font Size		Home tab, Font group, Increase Font Size	Ctrl+Shift+>
Bold		Home tab, Font group, Bold	Ctrl+B
Italic		Home tab, Font group, Italic	Ctrl+I
Underline		Home tab, Font group, Underline	Ctrl+U

continues

LESSON 2	Command Summary *continued*		
Feature	**Button**	**Menu**	**Keyboard**
Shadow	S	Home tab, Font group, Shadow	
Font Color	A	Home tab, Font group, Font Color	
Apply a font	Century Gothic	Home tab, Font group, Font	Ctrl+Shift+F
Change font size	36	Home tab, Font group, Font Size	Ctrl+Shift+P
Change case	Aa	Home tab, Font group, Change Case	Shift+F3
Align Text Left		Home tab, Paragraph group, Align Text Left	Ctrl+L
Center		Home tab, Paragraph group, Center	Ctrl+E
Align Text Right		Home tab, Paragraph group, Align Text Right	Ctrl+R
Justify		Home tab, Paragraph group, Justify	Ctrl+J
Turn bullets on or off		Home tab, Paragraph group, Bullets	
Turn numbering on or off		Home tab, Paragraph group, Numbering	
Change paragraph spacing		Home tab, Paragraph group, Line Spacing	
Text Box	A	Insert Tab, Text group, Text Box	
Change text box options		Drawing Tools Format tab	

Lesson 3

Revising Presentation Text

OBJECTIVES

After completing this lesson, you will be able to:

1. Select, rearrange, and delete slides.
2. Use the clipboard.
3. Check spelling and word usage.
4. Insert headers and footers.
5. Apply a consistent background and color theme.
6. Add movement effects.

Estimated Time: 1 1/2 hours

MCAS OBJECTIVES

In this lesson:

PP07 1.2.1
PP07 1.3
PP07 1.4.2
PP07 1.5
PP07 2.2.1
PP07 2.2.4
PP07 2.3.2
See Appendix

When using PowerPoint, it is important to review your presentation to ensure that it flows logically, is free of errors in spelling and grammar, and is consistent in its visual representation. Many PowerPoint tools will help with this important task.

Selecting, Rearranging, and Deleting Slides

Just as you frequently rearrange paragraphs or sentences in a word processing document, you will often need to rearrange or delete slides in a PowerPoint presentation. You can change the arrangement of slides by dragging them to a new position in the Slides tab, in the Outline tab, or in Slide Sorter view.

You can delete selected slide thumbnails by pressing Delete on your keyboard.

Exercise 3-1 SELECT MULTIPLE SLIDES

If you select multiple slides, you can move them to a new position all at one time. You can also delete several selected slides at one time. In addition, you can apply transitions, animations, and other effects to a group of selected slides.

There are two ways to select multiple slides:

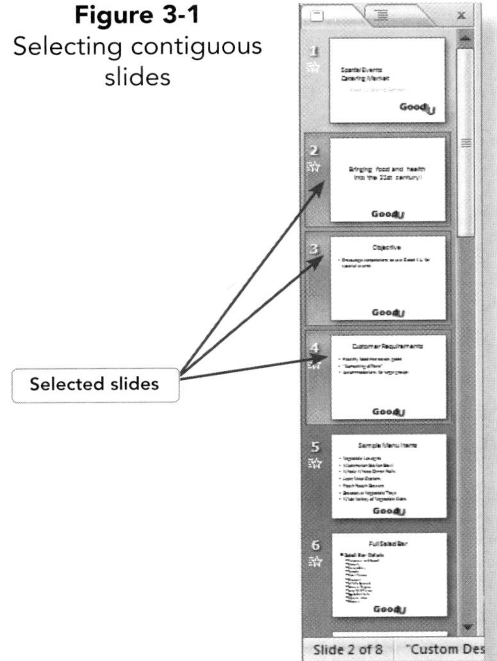

Figure 3-1 Selecting contiguous slides

- To select *contiguous slides* (slides that follow one after another), click the first slide in the selection and then hold down Shift while you click the last slide in the selection.
- To select *noncontiguous slides* (slides that do not follow one after another), click the first slide and then hold down Ctrl while you click each slide you want to add to the selection, one at a time.

1. Open the file **SpEventCatering**.
2. In the Slides and Outline pane, click the Slides tab to display slide thumbnails if they are not already displayed.
3. Without clicking, point to each thumbnail one at a time and notice that a ScreenTip appears displaying the title of the slide.
4. Click the thumbnail for slide 2 ("Bringing Food and Health . . .") to select it.
5. Hold down Shift and click the slide 4 thumbnail ("Customer Requirements"). Release Shift.

   Slides 2, 3, and 4 are all selected, as indicated by the heavy borders around their thumbnails, as shown in Figure 3-1. This is a contiguous selection.
6. With Shift released, click slide 3. Now it is the only slide selected.
7. Hold down Ctrl and click slide 1. Slide 1 and slide 3 are both selected. This is a noncontiguous selection.
8. While holding down Ctrl, click slide 5. Now three noncontiguous slides are selected, as shown in Figure 3-2. You can add as many slides as you want to the selection if you hold down Ctrl while clicking a slide thumbnail.

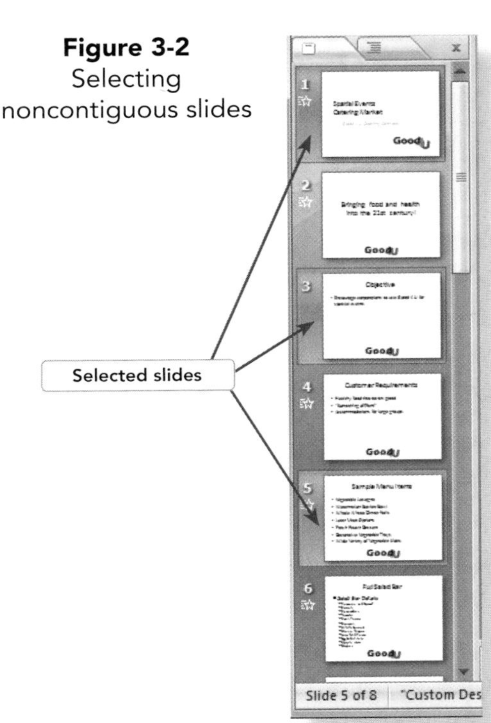

Figure 3-2 Selecting noncontiguous slides

Exercise 3-2 REARRANGE SLIDE ORDER

The Slides tab is a convenient place to rearrange slides. You simply drag selected slide thumbnails to a new position. *Slide Sorter View* enables you to see more thumbnails at one time and is convenient if your presentation contains a large number of slides. You select slides in Slide Sorter view in the same way as in the Slides tab.

1. Click the Slide Sorter View button.
2. Click the slide 2 thumbnail to select it.

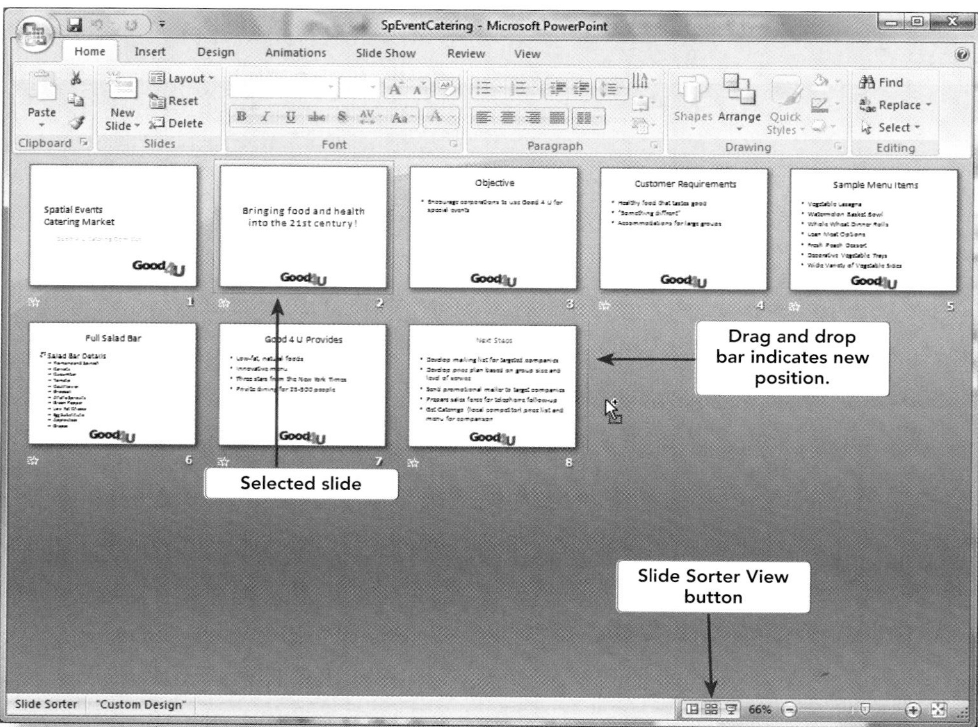

Figure 3-3
Moving a slide in the Slide Sorter view

NOTE

While you are dragging, be sure not to release the left mouse button until it is pointing where you want the selection to go. Otherwise, you might either cancel the selection or drop the slides in the wrong place.

3. Position the pointer within the selected slide's border, press the left mouse button, and drag the pointer after the eighth slide, as shown in Figure 3-3. Notice the drag-and-drop bar (the vertical line) as you drag. The vertical line indicates where the slide will go.
4. Release the mouse button. Slide 2, titled "Bringing Food and Health . . . ," becomes slide 8.
5. Using Ctrl, make a noncontiguous selection of slides 3 ("Customer Requirements") and 6 ("Good 4 U Provides").

6. Point to either slide in the selection and drag the selection after the first slide. Both slides move to the new position.
7. Check to make sure your slides are in the following order. If not, rearrange your slides to agree.

   Slide 1: Special Events Catering Market (This slide has a spelling error that you will correct later.)

   Slide 2: Customer Requirements

   Slide 3: Good 4 U Provides

   Slide 4: Objective

   Slide 5: Sample Menu Items

   Slide 6: Full Salad Bar

   Slide 7: Next Steps

   Slide 8: Bringing Food and Health into the 21st Century!
8. Double-click slide 1 to display it in Normal view.

Exercise 3-3 DELETE SLIDES

When you want to delete slides, you first select them (in the Slides tab or in Slide Sorter view) the same way you select slides you want to move. You delete them by pressing Delete on your keyboard or clicking the Delete button on the Home tab, in the Slides group.

REVIEW

To advance through a slide show, click the left mouse button, press the Spacebar, press PageDown, or press N.

1. Working in Normal view, display the Slides tab if it is not already showing.
2. Click the slide 4 thumbnail to select it. The slide 4 title should be "Objective."
3. Press Delete on your keyboard. Slide 4 is deleted and the new slide 4 becomes selected.

4. Move to slide 1 and click the Slide Show button to start a slide show.
5. Advance through the slides (using any method), reading the text and observing the built-in animation effects.
6. Create a new folder for Lesson 3. Save the presentation as **[3-3your initials]** in the Lesson 3 folder. Do not print the presentation at this point, and do not close it.

Using the Clipboard

The *Cut*, *Copy*, and *Paste* commands are almost universally available in computer programs. When you cut selected text or a selected object, it is removed from the presentation and placed on the *Clipboard*, a temporary storage space. When you copy text or an object, it remains in its original place and a copy is placed on the Clipboard. When you paste a Clipboard item, a copy of the item is placed at the location of the insertion point and the item remains on the Clipboard to use again if needed.

Each item you cut or copy is stored on the Clipboard, which can hold up to 24 items at a time. Clipboard items can be viewed and managed by using the Clipboard task pane. When working with the Office Clipboard, it is important to understand that unlike the Cut command, Delete does not save items to the clipboard.

The following cut, copy, and paste keyboard shortcuts are big time-savers when you do extensive editing:

- Ctrl+C Copy
- Ctrl+X Cut
- Ctrl+V Paste the most recent item stored on the clipboard.

Exercise 3-4 USE CUT, COPY, AND PASTE TO REARRANGE SLIDES

In the previous objective, you learned how to rearrange slides by dragging their thumbnails. This exercise presents another way to arrange slides by using the Clipboard. From the Home tab, in the Clipboard group, you can open the Clipboard task pane by clicking the Dialog Box Launcher.

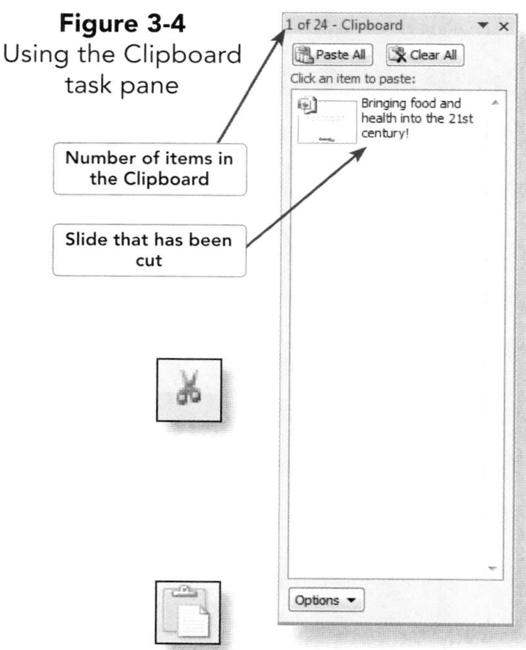

Figure 3-4 Using the Clipboard task pane

1. With the **[3-3your initials]** presentation open, from the Home tab, in the Clipboard group, click the Dialog Box Launcher to display the Clipboard task pane, as shown in Figure 3-4.
2. On the Slides tab, click the thumbnail of slide 7 ("Bringing Food and Health into the 21st Century!").
3. From the Home tab, in the Clipboard group, click the Cut button. This removes the slide and stores it on the Clipboard.
4. Select the thumbnail for slide 1 ("Spatial Events Catering Market"). Later you will change the spelling of the first word.
5. From the Home tab, in the Clipboard group, click the Paste button. The cut slide (on the Clipboard) is inserted (or pasted) after slide 1. This accomplishes the same thing as if you moved the slide by dragging its thumbnail.

6. Select the slide 1 thumbnail ("Spatial Events Catering Market"). From the Home tab, in the Clipboard group, click the Copy button. Notice that two slides are stored on the Clipboard task pane.

If the Outline tab and Slides tab are not visible, click the Normal view button.

7. Move to slide 7 ("Next Steps"). From the Home tab, in the Clipboard group, click the Paste button to paste ("Spatial Events Catering Market"). A copy of the slide is inserted at the end of the presentation to use for making a concluding comment.
8. Move to slide 8, the pasted slide.
9. Delete the subtitle text, and key the following text in its place on four lines:

   Catering Market Slogan:
   Make Your Event Special
   Call Good 4 U at
   800-555-1234

10. Move to slide 1 and save the presentation as **[3-4your initials]**. Keep the presentation open for the next exercise.

Exercise 3-5 USE CUT, COPY, AND PASTE TO REARRANGE TEXT

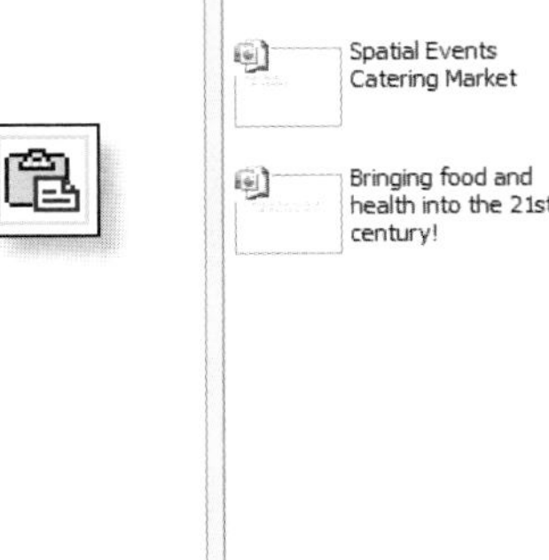

Figure 3-5 Text and slides stored on the Office Clipboard

Just as you cut, copy, and paste slides, you can cut, copy, and paste text, and store it on the Office Clipboard. The Paste Options button appears near a pasted item if the item's *source* formatting is different from the formatting of similar elements in its *destination* presentation. A Clipboard item's source is the presentation or other document from which it was cut or copied. Its destination is the presentation or other document in which it is pasted.

1. Display slide 7 ("Next Steps").
2. Activate the body text placeholder; then click the second bullet to select all its text.
3. Press Ctrl+X to cut the text from the slide. It appears on the Clipboard task pane. Notice the difference between text and slides on the Clipboard, as shown in Figure 3-5.

4. Click in front of the text in the first bulleted item.
5. Click the first item on the Clipboard task pane ("Develop price plan . . .") to insert that text as the first bulleted item.
6. Move to slide 6 ("Full Salad Bar").
7. Select the title text "Full Salad Bar," and press Ctrl+C to copy the text from the slide.
8. Move to slide 5, and click after the text "Wide Variety of Vegetable Sides," press Enter to create a new bullet, and press Ctrl+V. Notice that a Paste Options button appears each time you paste.
9. Click the Paste Options button that appears underneath the new bulleted item, and choose **Keep Source Formatting** from the drop-down list. Notice that the new bulleted item font size does not match that of the other bullets.
10. Click the Paste Options button again. This time choose **Use Destination Theme**, as shown in Figure 3-6. The bullet design changes to match the size of the other bulleted items.

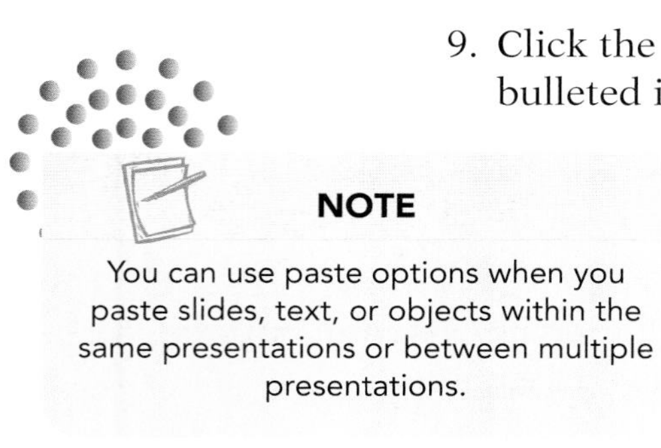

NOTE

You can use paste options when you paste slides, text, or objects within the same presentations or between multiple presentations.

Figure 3-6
Viewing the Paste Options button

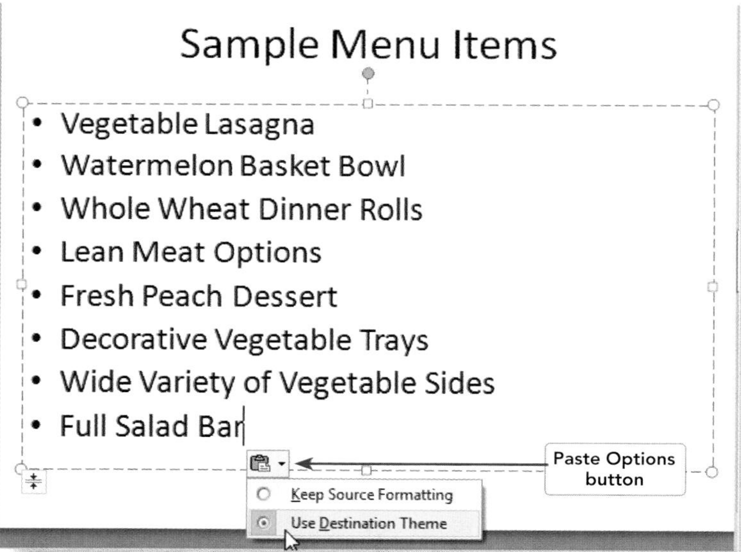

Exercise 3-6 CLEAR THE CLIPBOARD TASK PANE

The Clipboard task pane is a quick way to see a series of items that have been cut or copied to the Clipboard. The advantage of using the Clipboard to paste items is that you can have several items on the Clipboard and then choose which ones you want to paste instead of having to paste immediately after copying or cutting. If you have copied a lot of items, however, you may want to clear the Clipboard task pane.

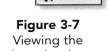

The Clipboard Options button allows you to control the settings of the Clipboard task pane.

1. If the Clipboard task pane is not open, from the Home tab, in the Clipboard group, click the Clipboard Dialog Box Launcher.
2. Click the Clipboard Options button at the bottom of the task pane, as shown in Figure 3-7.
3. Choose **Show Office Clipboard Automatically** to enable the Clipboard to automatically pop up when you use the cut, copy, or paste commands.

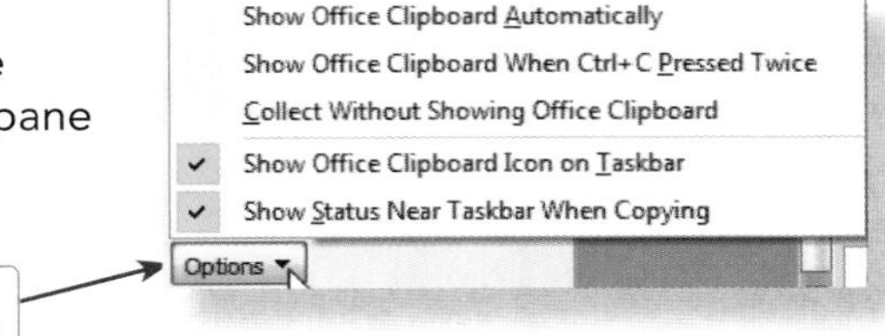

Figure 3-7 Viewing the Clipboard task pane options

Clipboard Options button

4. At the top of the Clipboard task pane, click the Clear All button on to clear all of the contents held in the Clipboard.
5. Click Close on the Clipboard task pane.

Exercise 3-7 USE UNDO AND REDO

The *Undo* button on the Quick Access toolbar reverses the last action you took. You can undo a series of editing actions, including keying or deleting text, promoting or demoting items, or deleting slides. By using Undo more than once, you can undo multiple actions. The *Redo* button found beside the Undo button reapplies editing commands in the order you undid them.

TIP

By default, PowerPoint can undo the last 20 actions. You can increase or decrease this number by choosing the Microsoft Office Button, PowerPoint Options, Advanced tab, and changing the Maximum number of undos. Increasing the number uses up more RAM on your computer.

In PowerPoint, unlike Word, Undo and Redo are cleared when you save a presentation. In other words, you cannot undo or redo actions performed before saving a presentation. Therefore, in PowerPoint, don't save unless you are sure you won't want to undo an action.

1. Move to slide 7 ("Next Steps"). Click at the end of the second bulleted line and press Enter.
2. Click the Undo button. Notice the new bullet is removed and your insertion point is back at the end of the first line.
3. Click the Redo button. The bullet is back and ready to accept text beside it.
4. On the new bulleted line, type the text below:

   Fully develop a menu choices plan

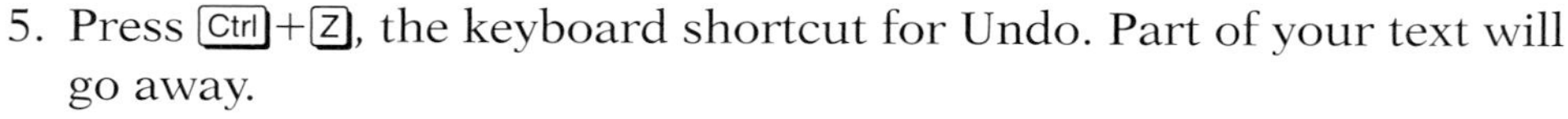

5. Press Ctrl+Z, the keyboard shortcut for Undo. Part of your text will go away.

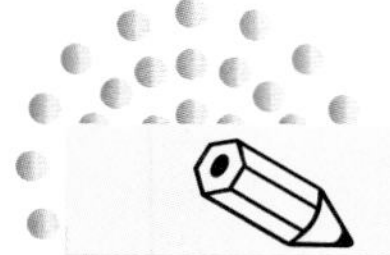

TIP

It's fairly common to make unintentional deletions and unintentional text moves. The Ctrl+Z key combination is very handy to use when the unexpected happens.

6. Press Ctrl+Y, the keyboard shortcut for Redo. The text that was taken away in step 5 is now back on your screen.
7. In the Slides and Outline pane, click on slide 6, and press Delete on your keyboard. Notice the slide is deleted.
8. Press Ctrl+Z to undo this deletion and put the slide back into place.

Exercise 3-8 USE FORMAT PAINTER

If you use Word or Excel, you may be familiar with the *Format Painter* tool. This tool makes it easy to copy the formatting, for example, the font size, color, and font face, from one object to another object on the same slide or within a presentation.

When you copy the format of an object, many default settings associated with that object are copied as well.

1. On slide 6, select the title "Full Salad Bar."

2. From the Home tab, in the Clipboard group, click the Format Painter button. The Format Painter picks up the font formatting of this title.
3. Click within the word "cucumber" on the same slide. The text appears with the same formatting as the title. Click the Undo button.
4. Select the title "Full Salad Bar" once again and double-click the Format Painter button. Double-clicking keeps the Format Painter active, so you can copy the formatting to more than one object.
5. Move to slide 7, and click on "Next" in the title. Notice when you just click a word, it changes only that single word.
6. Click "Steps" to format it the same way.
7. Click the Format Painter button again, or press Esc to restore the standard pointer.

Checking Spelling and Word Usage

PowerPoint provides many tools to edit and revise text, and improve the overall appearance of a presentation:

- *Spelling Checker*, which corrects spelling by comparing words to an internal dictionary file.

- *Research*, which allows you to search through reference materials such as dictionaries, encyclopedias, and translation services to find the information you need.
- *Thesaurus*, which offers new words with similar meanings to the word you are looking up.
- *Find* and *Replace*, which allows you to find a certain word or phrase and replace it with a different word or phrase.

Exercise 3-9 CHECK SPELLING

The *Spelling Checker* in PowerPoint works much the same as it does in other Microsoft Office applications. It flags misspelled words with a red wavy underline as you key text. It can also check an entire presentation at once. The Spelling Checker is an excellent proofreading tool, but it should be used in combination with your own careful proofreading and editing.

1. In slide 1, a word in the subtitle has a red wavy underline indicating a spelling error. Right-click the word. Choose the correct spelling ("Committee") from the short-cut menu and click to accept it.
2. Notice the spelling of "Spatial" in the title. This is an example of a word that is correctly spelled but incorrectly used. The Spelling Checker can't help you with this kind of mistake. Change the spelling to **Special**. Do this on slide 8 also.
3. Move to slide 1 and run the Spelling Checker for the entire presentation. From the Review tab, in the Proofing Group, click the Spelling button or press F7.

4. PowerPoint highlights "diffrent," the first word it doesn't find in its dictionary. It displays the word in the Spelling dialog box and suggests a corrected spelling, as shown in Figure 3-8.

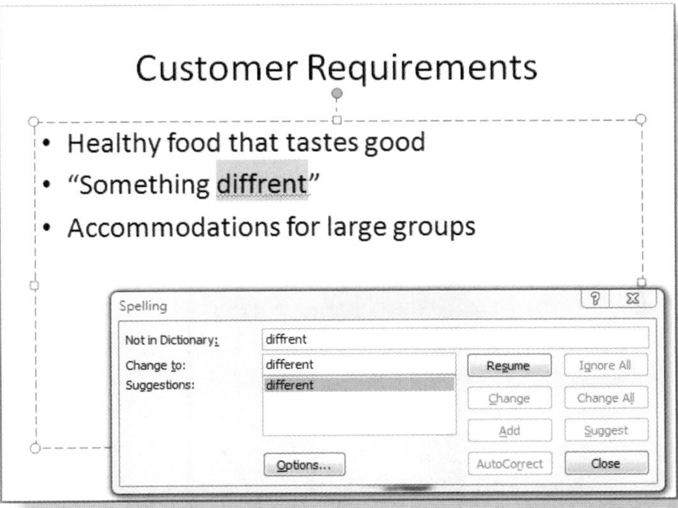

Figure 3-8
Using the spelling checker

NOTE

If the Spelling dialog box is hiding a misspelled word, move the dialog box to a different position by dragging its title bar.

5. Click **Change** to apply the correct spelling of "different."
6. When the spelling checker locates "Privite," click **Change** on the correct spelling of "Private."
7. At the next spelling error "Caterngo," click **Ignore** because this is the correct spelling of the company name.
8. Click **OK** when the spelling check is complete.

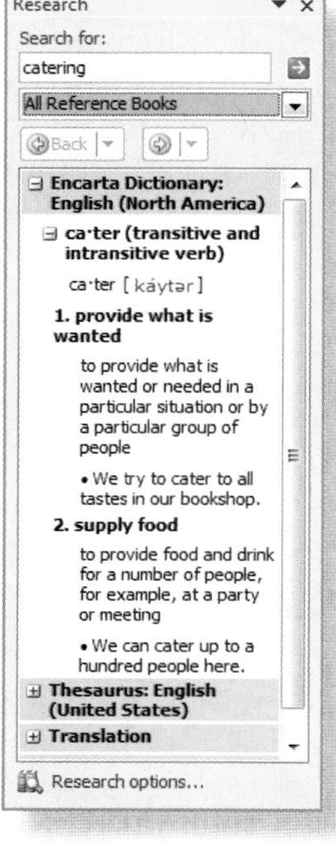

Figure 3-9
Research task pane with definitions

Exercise 3-10 USE RESEARCH

Research is a handy reference tool to look up many facets of a word. For example, when you research the word "catering," you find information about the definition of the word from the dictionary, synonyms in the thesaurus, and an area where you can translate this word into another language.

1. From the Review tab, in the Proofing group, click the Research button.
2. On the Research task pane in the **Search for** box, type **catering** and press Enter.
3. Look in the definition area and notice that the context for the word "catering" is definition number 2, as shown in Figure 3-9.
4. On the Thesaurus task pane, click the Close button.

Exercise 3-11 USE THE THESAURUS

The *Thesaurus* is used to find words with similar meanings. This tool is extremely helpful when the same word becomes repetitious and you would like to use a similar word, or if you are looking for a more appropriate word with a similar meaning.

1. On slide 6, put your insertion point on the word "Full." From the Review tab, in the Proofing group, click the Thesaurus button. On the Research task pane, the word "full" is automatically placed in the **Search for** box, a search has already been performed, and the results displayed, as shown in Figure 3-10.

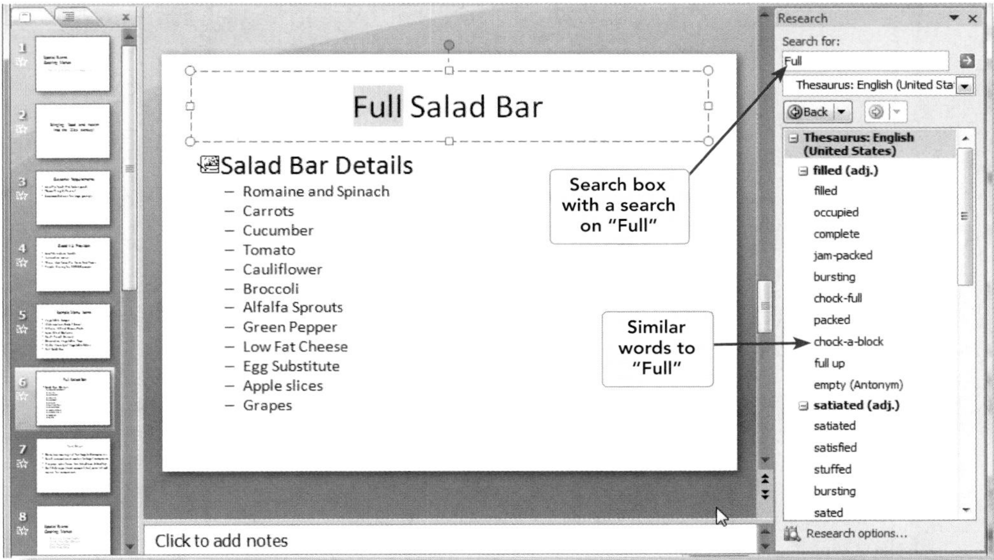

Figure 3-10
Search word highlighted and Thesaurus task pane

TIP

If you click on any word in the Thesaurus list, you will see another list of words that are related to that word.

2. Scroll down until you find the word "extensive." Click the down arrow beside extensive, and choose **Insert**. Notice that the word "Full" is replaced by the word "Extensive," and the slide now reads "Extensive Salad Bar."
3. Click the Thesaurus task pane Close button.

Exercise 3-12 USE FIND AND REPLACE

When you create presentations—especially long presentations—you often need to review or change text. In PowerPoint, you can do this quickly by using the Find and Replace commands.

The *Find* command locates specified text in a presentation. The *Replace* command finds the text and replaces it with a specified alternative.

1. Move to slide 1. From the Home tab, in the Editing group, click the Find button (or press Ctrl+F) to open the Find dialog box.
2. In the **Find what** text box, key **full**, as shown in Figure 3-11.

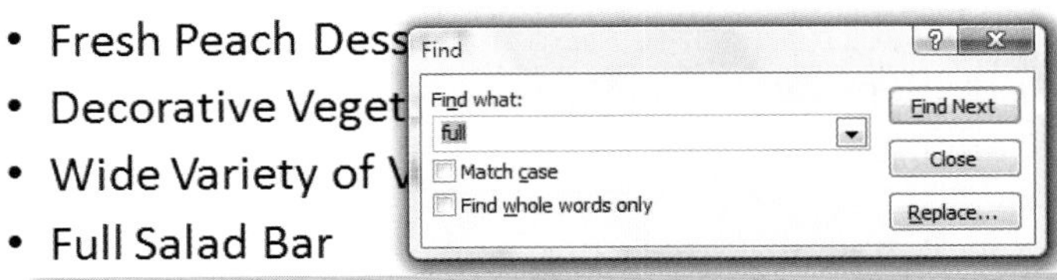

Figure 3-11
Find dialog box with text selected

3. Click the Find Next button and PowerPoint locates and selects the text. This could be used if you were looking for a particular word in the presentation.
4. Click the Close button to close the Find dialog box.
5. Move back to slide 1. From the Home tab, in the Editing group, click the Replace button (or press Ctrl+H) to open the Replace dialog box.
6. In the **Find what** text box, key **Full** if it is not displayed already. In the **Replace with** text box, key **Extensive** as shown in Figure 3-12.
7. Check **Match case** and **Find whole words only**, to ensure that you find only the text "Full" and not words that contain these letters (such as "fuller" or "fullest").

Figure 3-12
Replace dialog box

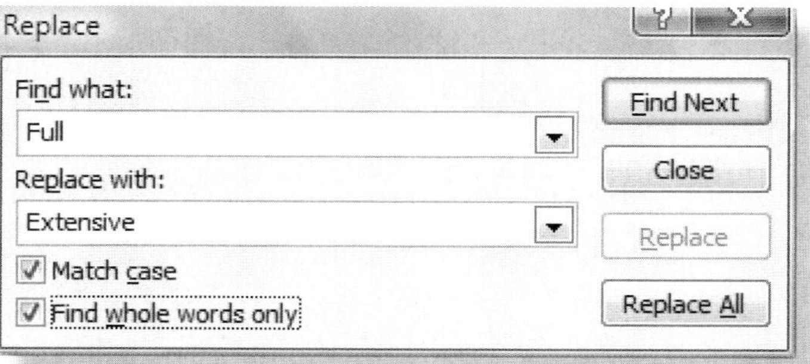

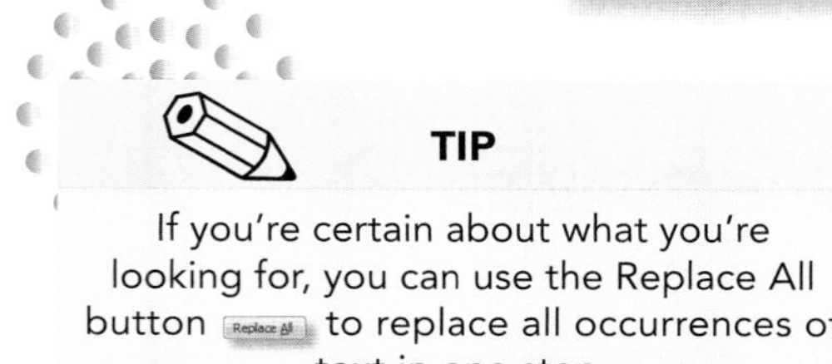

If you're certain about what you're looking for, you can use the Replace All button to replace all occurrences of text in one step.

8. Click the Find Next button and PowerPoint finds the first occurrence of "Full." Click the Replace button. Click the Find Next button once again. A dialog box appears to tell you the search is completed. Click **OK**.
9. Click the Close button to close the Replace dialog box.
10. Return to slide 1 and save the presentation as **[3-12your initials]** in your Lesson 3 folder. Leave the presentation open for the next exercise.

Inserting Headers and Footers

You can add identifying information to your presentation, such as header or footer text, the date, or a slide or page number. See Table 3-1. A *header* is text that appears at the top of each notes page or handouts page. A *footer* is text that appears at the bottom of each slide, notes page, or handouts page. Header and footer text appears in special header and footer placeholders.

As is true in Word and Excel, the Header and Footer button is on the Insert tab in the Text group. In PowerPoint, this command opens the Header and Footer dialog box, which has two tabs: the Slide tab and the Notes and Handouts tab.

TABLE 3-1 Adding Identifying Information to Presentations

Information	Description
Date and Time	Current date and time—can be updated automatically or keyed
Header	Descriptive text printed at the top of the page on notes and handouts pages only
Page Number	Number placed in the lower-right corner of notes and handouts pages by default
Slide Number	Number placed on slides, usually in the lower-right corner
Footer	Descriptive text printed at the bottom of slides, notes pages, and handouts pages

Exercise 3-13 ADD SLIDE DATE, PAGE NUMBER, AND FOOTER

Using the Slide tab in the Header and Footer dialog box, you can add information to the footer of all slides in a presentation by clicking **Apply to All**, or you can add footer information to only the current slide by clicking **Apply**.

1. Working on the presentation **[3-12your initials]**, from the Insert tab, in the Text group, click the Header and Footer button. Notice the two tabs in the Header and Footer dialog box, one for adding information to slides and one for adding information to notes and handouts, as shown in Figure 3-13. Click the Slide tab.

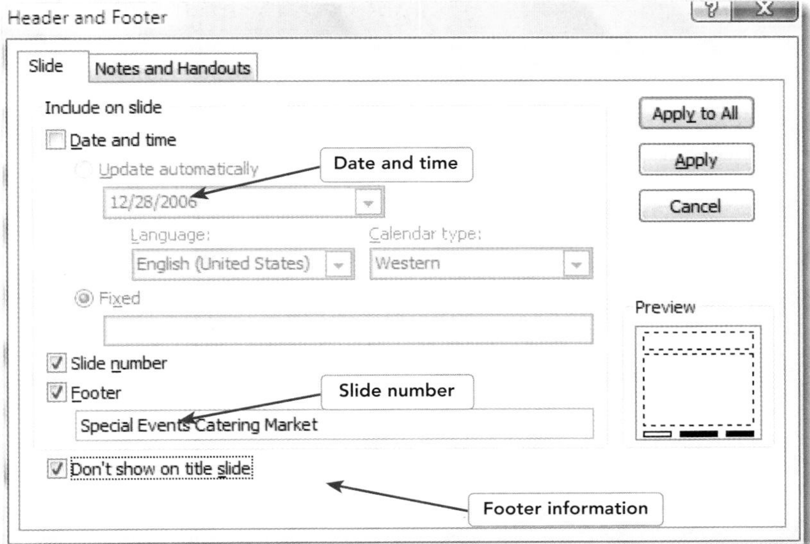

Figure 3-13
Header and Footer dialog box, Slide tab

2. In the **Preview** box, notice the positions for the elements you can place on a slide. As you enable each element by selecting its check box, PowerPoint indicates where the element will print with a bold outline.
3. Click the **Slide number** check box to select it.
4. Click the check box labeled **Don't show on title slide**. When this box is checked, footer and page number information does not appear on the slides using the title slide layout.
5. Clear the **Date and Time** check box so there is no check.
6. Click the **Footer** check box and key **Special Events Catering Market**.
7. Click **Apply to All**. The presentation now has footer information including slide numbers at the bottom of each slide except the title slide.
8. Move to slide 1 and click the Slide Show button on the Status bar to view the presentation. Notice the footer information and slide number at the bottom of the slide when you reach slide 3.

Exercise 3-14 ADD HANDOUT DATE, PAGE NUMBER, AND HEADER

Using the Notes and Handouts tab, you can insert both header and footer information on notes pages and handouts that are usually printed.

1. From the Insert tab, in the Text group, click the Header and Footer button . On the Header and Footer dialog box, click the Notes and Handouts tab as shown in Figure 3-14.
2. Under the **Date and time** option, click **Update automatically** to add today's date. Each time you print the presentation handout, it will include the current date. You can choose different date and time formats from the drop-down list.

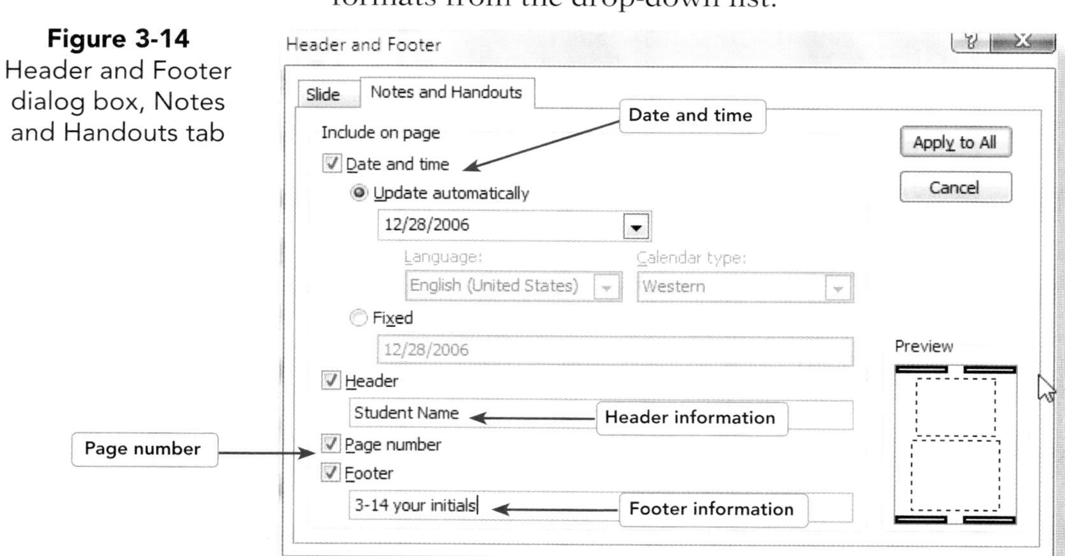

Figure 3-14
Header and Footer dialog box, Notes and Handouts tab

3. Make sure **Header** is checked and key **Your Name** in the header text box. The header is printed in the upper-left corner of a notes or handouts page.
4. Make sure the **Page number** option is checked. Page numbers are printed at the bottom right of the page.
5. Make sure the **Footer** check box is selected. Then key the filename **[3-14your initials]** in its text box.
6. Click **Apply to All** to add this information to all handouts pages you print (but not to individual slides).
7. Save the presentation as **[3-14your initials]** in your Lesson 3 folder.

Applying a Consistent Background and Color Theme

When you create a new blank presentation, the presentation contains no special formatting, colors, or graphics. Sometimes it's convenient to work without design elements so that you can focus all your attention on the presentation's text. Before the presentation is completed, however, you will usually want to apply a *design theme* to add visual interest. You can apply a design theme or change to a different one at any time while you are developing your presentation.

Exercise 3-15 SELECT A DESIGN THEME

The presentation that you have been working on in this lesson contains no theme. To select a design theme, from the Design tab, in the Themes group, click a design theme. The process to change a design theme is the same as to apply it for the first time.

1. From the Design tab, in the Themes group, click the More button to display the theme choices shown as thumbnails.

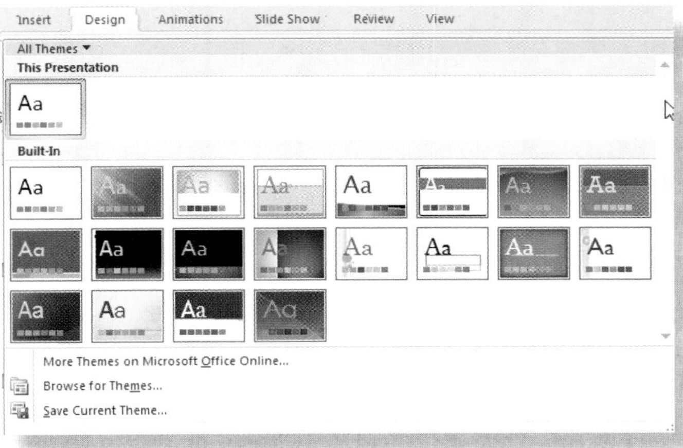

Figure 3-15
Applying a design theme

2. Use the vertical scroll bar in the All Themes window to view the many design thumbnails. The window is divided by "This Presentation" and "Built-In." Links are available for "More Themes on Microsoft Office Online," "Browse for Themes," and "Save Current Theme," as shown in Figure 3-15.
3. Point to one of the design theme thumbnails. Notice the live preview working as you point to one of the design themes; PowerPoint automatically previews what that design theme will look like applied to your presentation. A ScreenTip also appears to indicate the name of the theme you are previewing or choosing.
4. Point to several design themes to sample what your presentation will look like with them applied.
5. Right-click any design theme thumbnail. Notice that you can apply the slide design to matching slides, all slides, or selected slides.
6. Click **Apply to All Slides**. The design theme that you selected is applied to all the slides in your presentation.
7. Locate the **Flow** design theme in the list of design theme thumbnails and click it. By clicking on the design theme, it automatically changes all slides in the presentation. (If **Flow** is not available on your computer, use a different theme.)
8. Notice that each thumbnail on the Slides tab shows the new theme design. Note also that the name of the template appears at the left on the status bar below the slide.
9. Move to slide 1 and view the presentation as a slide show; then return to slide 1 in Normal view.

Exercise 3-16 CHANGE THEME COLORS

You can apply different built-in colors to the current design theme by changing the *theme colors*. To display the built-in theme colors, from the Design tab, in the Themes group, click the Colors button.

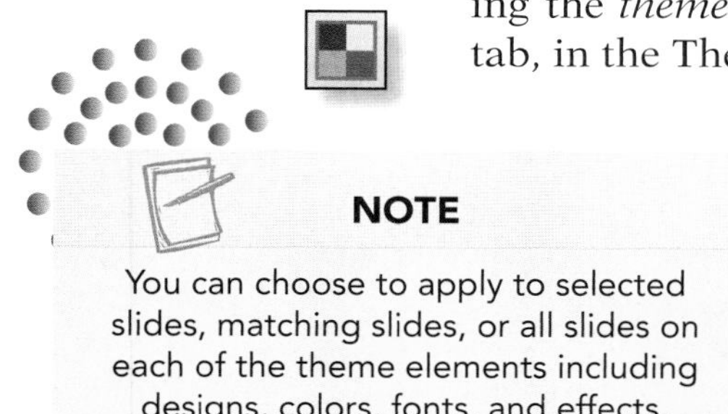

NOTE

You can choose to apply to selected slides, matching slides, or all slides on each of the theme elements including designs, colors, fonts, and effects.

1. From the Design tab, in the Themes group, click the Colors button. Several choices for theme colors are available, as shown in Figure 3-16.
2. Point to any theme color set to see a live preview of what it will look like applied to your presentation.

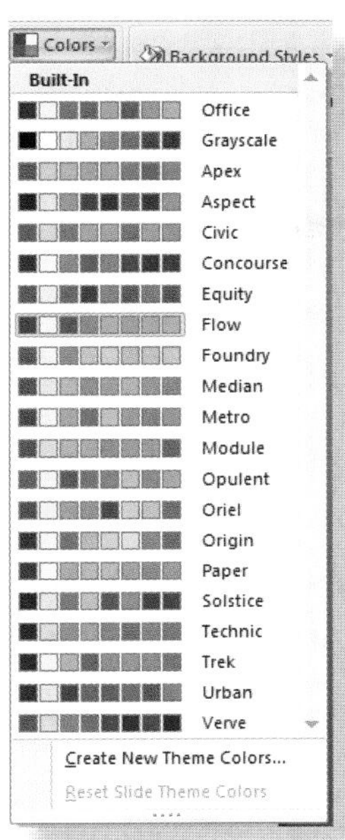

Figure 3-16
Theme Colors drop-down list

3. Click any theme color to apply it to your presentation.
4. Click the **Aspect** theme color to apply it to your presentation.
5. View the presentation as a slide show; then return to Normal view.
6. Move to slide 8.
7. From the **Design** tab, in the Themes group, click the Colors button.
8. Right-click on the **Office** theme color and choose **Apply to Selected Slides**. Notice that the color of only slide 8 changes to make this closing slide look a little different from the other slides.

Exercise 3-17 CHANGE THEME FONTS

You can apply different built-in fonts to the current design theme by changing the *theme font*. To display the built-in theme fonts, from the Design tab, in the Themes group, click the Fonts button.

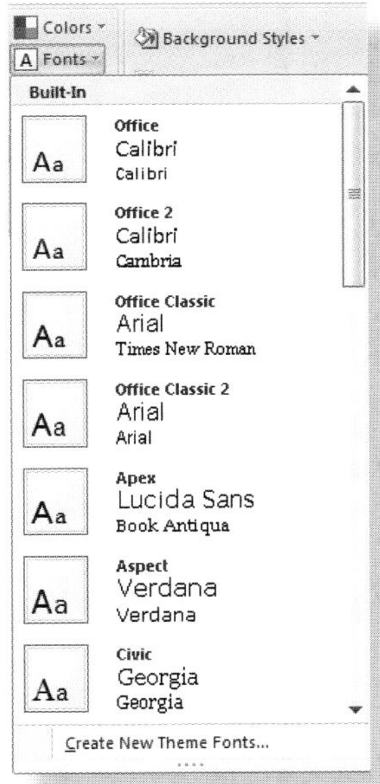

Figure 3-17
Theme Font drop-down list

1. From the Design tab, in the Themes group, click the Fonts button. Several choices for theme fonts are available, as shown in Figure 3-17.
2. Point to any theme font to see a live preview of what it will look like applied to your presentation. A ScreenTip will pop up showing the name of the theme font.
3. Click any theme font to apply it to your presentation.
4. Click the **Oriel** Theme Font (Century Schoolbook) to apply it to your presentation.
5. View the presentation as a slide show; then return to Normal view.

Exercise 3-18 CHANGE THEME EFFECTS

You can apply different built-in effects to the current design theme by changing the *theme effects*. To display the built-in theme effects, from the Design tab, in the Themes group, click the Effects button.

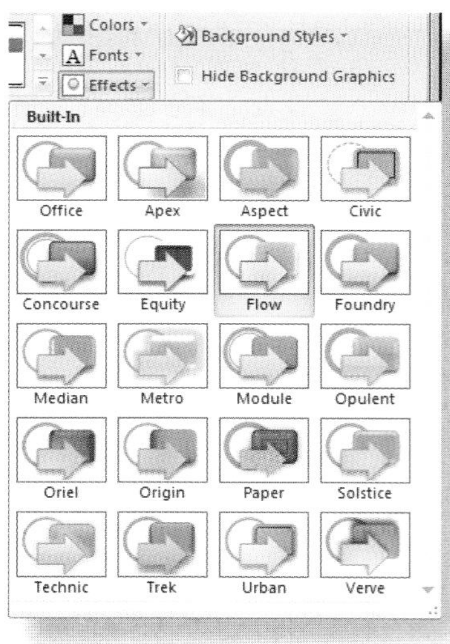

Figure 3-18
Theme Effect drop-down list

1. From the Design tab, in the Themes group, click the Effects button. Several choices for theme effects are available, as shown in Figure 3-18.
2. Click any set of theme effects to apply them to your presentation. Right now you may not see any changes because these effects are most noticeable when applied to graphics you will use in later lessons.
3. Click the **Metro** theme effects to apply it to your presentation.
4. View the presentation as a slide show; then return to Normal view.

Exercise 3-19 CREATE NEW THEME FONTS

Although many built-in theme fonts are available, it is sometimes better to choose your own. You can accomplish this by creating new theme fonts.

1. From the Design tab, in the Themes group, click the Fonts button.
2. Click **Create New Theme Fonts** at the bottom of the Font Theme drop-down list.
3. Click the drop-down arrow under **Heading font**, and choose **Gloucester MT Extra Condensed**, as shown in Figure 3-19.
4. Click the drop-down arrow under **Body font**, and choose **Goudy Old Style**.
5. In the Name box, key **Special Event Presentation Font Theme**.

Figure 3-19
Create New Theme Fonts dialog box

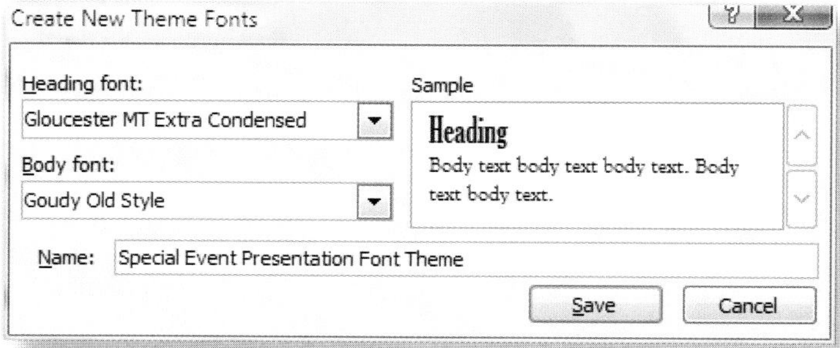

Create New Theme Fonts
Heading font: Gloucester MT Extra Condensed
Body font: Goudy Old Style
Sample
Heading
Body text body text body text. Body text body text.
Name: Special Event Presentation Font Theme
Save Cancel

6. Click **Save**. Notice the change in the fonts of your presentation.
7. Save the presentation as **[3-19your initials]** in your Lesson 3 folder.

Adding Movement Effects

A *slide transition* is an effect that appears between two slides as they change during a slide show. You can choose to make one slide blend into the next in a checkerboard pattern, a fade pattern, or choose from many other effects. Transitions can have an effect like turning pages of a book. Movement can be applied to all slides in a presentation to control how they enter and exit the screen.

Exercise 3-20 APPLY SLIDE TRANSITIONS

Transitions can be applied to individual slides, to a group of slides, or to an entire slide show. To apply transitions, from the Animations tab, in Transition to This Slide group, click the More button to display transition options. Click on the transition that you would like to apply.

1. Move to slide 1 and from the Animations tab, in the Transition to This Slide group, click the More button to view all of the transition options shown as thumbnails.

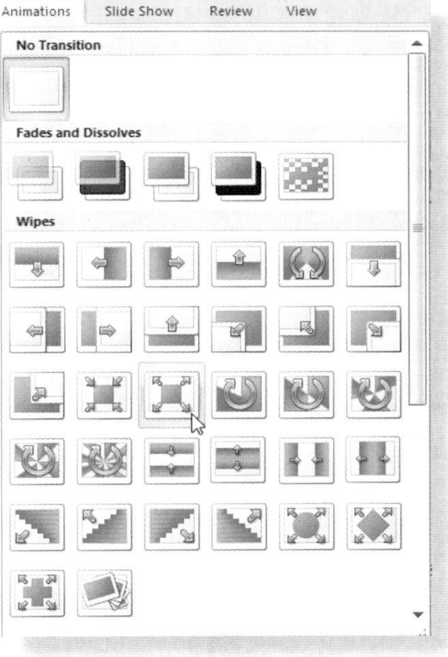

Figure 3-20
Choosing the Box Out transition

2. Point to several transitions and notice that the live preview shows you how this transition effect will look applied to your slide.
3. Choose **Box Out** from the list of transitions, as shown in Figure 3-20. This applies the transition to slide 1 only.
4. From the Animations tab, in the Transitions to This Slide group, click the Apply to All button . This applies the transition to all slides in the presentation.
5. View the presentation as a slide show, and notice the Box Out transition between slides.

Exercise 3-21 ADJUST SOUNDS AND SPEEDS

Transitions also have the option to include sounds during the transition, and you can adjust the speed at which the transition occurs.

1. Move to slide 1. From the Animations tab, in the Transitions to This Slide group, click the drop-down arrow in the Transition Speed list box.

2. Choose **Medium** to slow the speed of the transition a little. This applies only to slide 1.

3. From the Animations tab, in the Transitions to This Slide group, click the Apply to All button. This applies the transition speed to all slides in the presentation.

4. Click the drop-down arrow in the Transition Sounds list box, and point to several sounds to listen to the possibilities for transition sounds.

5. Move to slide 1 and choose **Applause** from the Transition Sounds list box to apply the applause sound.

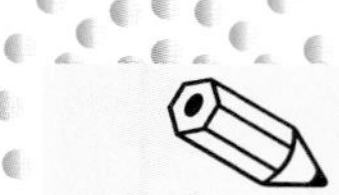

TIP

Try not to apply transition effects randomly. You might choose one transition for most of your presentation and then select one or two other effects to better emphasize the slide content as it appears. Be careful about using sounds, too, because they may detract from your presentation unless specifically suited to your content.

6. Still working in the Transitions to this Slide group, for **Advance slide** select **On mouse click** if it is not already checked.

7. View the presentation as a slide show to hear this sound as slide 1 appears.

8. Save the presentation as **[3-21your initials]** in your Lesson 3 folder.

9. Print the presentation as handouts, grayscale, framed, three slides per page.

Lesson 3 Summary

- To change the order of slides in a presentation, use either the Slides and Outline pane or the Slide Sorter view. Select the slides you want to move; then drag them to a new location. You can also delete selected slides.
- The Clipboard can store up to 24 items that you cut or copy from a presentation. The items can be text, entire slides, or other objects. Insert a Clipboard item at the current location in your presentation by clicking the item.
- Text can be moved or copied by using the Cut, Copy, and Paste commands. Slides can also be rearranged by using these commands.
- The Paste Options button enables you to choose between a pasted item's source formatting and its destination formatting. The source is the slide or placeholder from which the item was cut or copied, and the destination is the location where it will be pasted.
- PowerPoint enables you to undo—and if you change your mind—redo multiple editing actions. The default number of available undos is 20. When you save a presentation, the list of undos is cleared.
- The Format Painter button enables you to copy formatting from one object to another. This is a great time-saver if you applied several effects to an object and want to duplicate the effects.

- Double-clicking the Format Painter button keeps it active, so that multiple objects can receive the copied format. Click the Format Painter button again to turn it off.
- Right-clicking a word flagged with a red wavy line provides a shortcut list of suggested spelling corrections. You can spell check an entire presentation at one time by using the Spelling dialog box.
- Use the Research task pane to research items in the dictionary, thesaurus, and translator all at once.
- Use the Thesaurus task pane to find words with similar meanings.
- The Find command and the Replace command search your entire presentation for specified text. The Replace feature enables you to automatically make changes to matching text it finds.
- Headers and Footers can appear at the top and bottom of notes and handouts pages. Footers can also appear at the bottom of slides. They are commonly used to provide page numbers, dates, and other identifying information common to an entire presentation.
- Design themes are a great way to add color, design, fonts, and effects all at once.
- There are several built-in Theme Colors, Theme Fonts, and Theme Effects. You can access these from the Design tab, in the Theme group.
- Design themes, Theme Colors, Theme Fonts, and Theme Effects can be applied to individual slides, to a group of selected slides, or to an entire presentation.
- Slide transitions add visual interest to slide shows. They can be applied to individual slides, a group of slides, or an entire slide presentation.
- Transition sounds and speed can be adjusted to add interest in a presentation.

LESSON 3 — Command Summary

Feature	Button	Ribbon	Keyboard
Select contiguous slides			Shift+click left mouse button
Select noncontiguous slides			Ctrl+click left mouse button
Delete selected slides		Home, Slides group, Delete	Delete
Cut selected object or text		Home, Clipboard group, Cut	Ctrl+X
Copy selected object or text		Home, Clipboard group, Copy	Ctrl+C
Paste (insert) cut or copied object or text		Home, Clipboard group, Paste	Ctrl+V

continues

LESSON 3	Command Summary *continued*		
Feature	**Button**	**Ribbon**	**Keyboard**
Paste options			
Display Clipboard task pane		Home, Clipboard group, Dialog Box Launcher	
Clear the Clipboard task pane	Clear All	Clipboard task pane, Clear All	
Copy formatting of an object		Home, Clipboard group, Format Painter	
Undo		Quick Access toolbar, Undo	Ctrl+Z
Redo		Quick Access toolbar, Redo	Ctrl+Y
Spelling checker	ABC	Review, Proofing group, Spelling	F7
Research definitions		Review, Proofing group, Research	
Thesaurus		Review, Proofing group, Thesaurus	
Find		Home, Editing group, Find	Ctrl+F
Replace	Replace	Home, Editing group, Replace	Ctrl+H
Header and footer		Insert, Text group, Header and Footer	
Apply Design Theme		Design, Themes group, Design Theme	
Choose Theme Colors		Design, Themes group, Colors	
Choose Theme Fonts	A	Design, Themes group, Fonts	
Choose Theme Effects		Design, Themes group, Effects	
Slide transition		Animation, Transition to This Slide group	

unit 2

PRESENTATION ILLUSTRATION

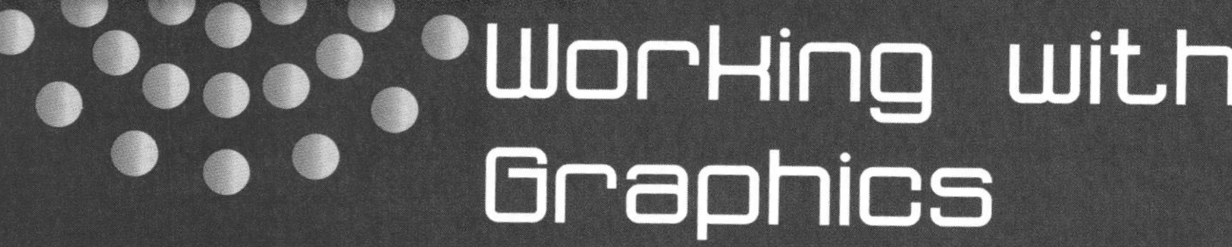

Lesson 4

Working with Graphics

OBJECTIVES

After completing this lesson, you will be able to:

1. Work with shapes.
2. Insert clip art images.
3. Insert and enhance pictures.
4. Create WordArt.
5. Create a photo album.

MCAS OBJECTIVES

In this lesson:
PP07 2.2.2
PP07 2.2.7
PP07 3.3.1
PP07 3.3.2
PP07 3.3.3
PP07 3.3.4
PP07 3.4.1
PP07 3.4.2
PP07 3.5.1
PP07 3.5.2
PP07 3.5.3
See Appendix

Estimated Time: 2 hours

An effective presentation slide show consists of more than text alone. Although text may carry most of the information, you can use several types of objects to help communicate your message or draw attention to key points. For example, you can add shapes, free-floating text objects, clip art images, and photographs to help illustrate your presentation.

After you add an object to a slide, you can change its size, position, and appearance. In this lesson, you will concentrate on some basic drawing skills and begin to explore some of the many special effects made possible in PowerPoint 2007.

Working with Shapes

PowerPoint provides a variety of tools you can use to create original drawings. These tools are available in three tabs: Home, Insert, and Drawing Tools Format. In this lesson, you learn basic drawing skills. In later lessons, you learn how to enhance simple shapes and create more complex drawings.

When drawing shapes, the ruler can help you to judge size and positioning. When the ruler is displayed, it appears in two parts: the horizontal measurement is across the top of the slide and the vertical measurement is on the left. By default, the ruler measures in inches; the center of the slide (vertically and horizontally) appears as zero. A dotted line on each ruler indicates the horizontal and vertical position of your pointer.

TABLE 4-1 Tools for Basic Drawing

Button	Name	Purpose
	Select	Selects an object. This tool is automatically in effect when no other tool is in use.
	Picture	Inserts a bitmap or photo image from a file.
	Clip Art	Inserts a clip art object, which could be drawings, sounds, movies, or stock photography.
	Photo Album	Creates a presentation made of pictures with each one on a separate slide.
	Shapes	Opens the Shapes gallery, which contains predefined shapes you can draw.
	Line	Draws a straight line.
	Arrow	Draws an arrow.
	Rectangle	Draws a rectangle or square.
	Oval	Draws an oval or circle.
	Text Box	Inserts text anywhere on a slide.
	WordArt	Creates a Microsoft WordArt object on a slide.
	Shape Fill	Fills a shape with colors, patterns, or textures.
	Shape Outline	Changes the color of a shape's outline or the color of a line.
	Shape Effects	Adds a visual effect such as shadow, glow, or bevel.

Exercise 4-1 DRAW SHAPES—RECTANGLES, OVALS, AND LINES

In this exercise, you practice drawing several *shapes* on a blank slide. To draw a shape, click the appropriate drawing tool button (such as the Line, Rectangle, or Oval); then drag the *Crosshair pointer* on your slide until the shape is the size you want.

You can draw multiple shapes with the same drawing tool by using the *Lock Drawing Mode* option. This keeps the button activated, so you can draw as many of the same shapes as you want without the need to reclick the button. This feature is deactivated when you click another button.

If you don't like an object that you created, you can easily remove it from your slide. Simply select the object by clicking it, and then press Delete on your keyboard.

As you draw with different tools, the ones you have used appear at the top of the list in a **Recently Used Shapes** category of the Shapes gallery; however, each tool is also shown in a related group when you access the entire Shapes gallery.

NOTE

Three of the slides in this presentation were created by using the Blank slide layout. The Blank slide layout contains no text placeholders. The text that appears on the slides is placed in text boxes as shown in Lesson 2.

1. Open the presentation file **Opening1**.
2. Insert a new slide after slide 2 and use the **Blank** layout. You will use this slide to practice drawing.
3. If the rulers are not showing, right-click on the blank slide and choose **Ruler** from the shortcut menu.
4. While watching the horizontal ruler at the top of the slide, move your pointer back and forth, observing the dotted line on the ruler indicating the pointer's position. While moving your pointer up and down, observe the dotted line on the vertical ruler. From the Home tab, in the Drawing group, click the Shapes button then click the Rectangle button. The pointer changes to a crosshair pointer.

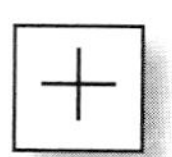

5. Notice that zero is placed at the midpoint of the slide on both the vertical ruler and the horizontal ruler. Move the crosshair pointer to the 3-inch mark on the horizontal ruler to the left of the zero and to the 2-inch mark on the vertical ruler above the zero.

NOTE

The green handle just above the rectangle is a *rotation handle*. It can be used to rotate a shape in the same way it was used to rotate a text box in the previous lesson.

6. Click and hold the left mouse button. Drag diagonally down and to the right until you reach the 2-inch mark below the zero on the vertical ruler and the 3-inch mark to the right of the zero on the horizontal ruler. Release your mouse button. A blue rectangle with a white outline appears. See Figure 4-1 to compare the size and placement of the completed rectangle.

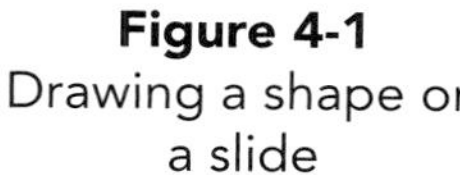

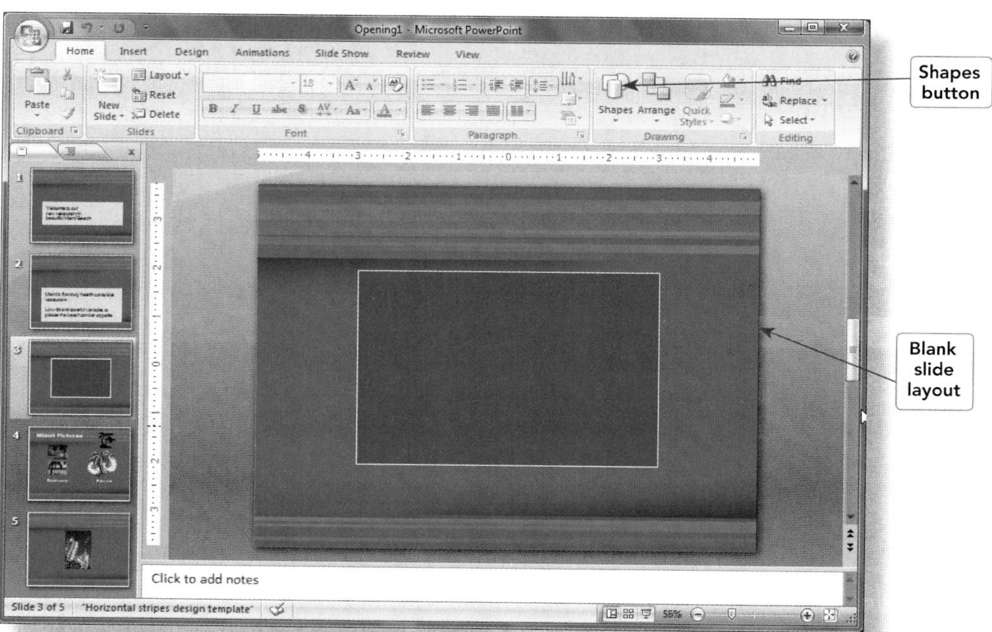

Figure 4-1
Drawing a shape on a slide

7. From the Home tab, in the Drawing group, click the Shapes button, and then choose the Oval button.
8. Draw a small oval (approximately one-inch wide) on the inside of the rectangle that you previously drew, using the same method that you used to draw the rectangle.
9. From the Home tab, in the Drawing group, click the Shapes button, and then right-click the Line button and choose **Lock Drawing Mode**. Drag your pointer diagonally to draw a line from the left corner of the rectangle to the outline of the oval.
10. Because the drawing mode is locked, notice that the pointer is still the crosshair pointer showing that the Line button is still selected. Draw three more lines from each corner of the rectangle to the outline of the oval.
11. Your screen should look similar to the back of an envelope with a seal, as shown in Figure 4-2.

Figure 4-2
Drawing an oval and lines

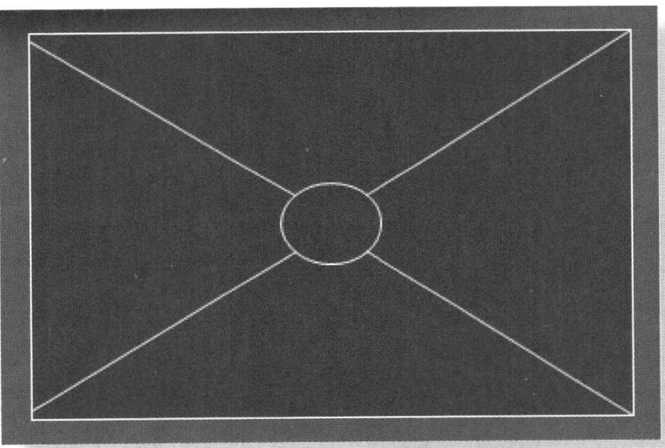

12. Click the Line button again to deactivate it.
13. Hold Shift down while you click to select all four lines and the oval then press Delete to remove them all at once. The slide should now contain one rectangle only.

Exercise 4-2 DRAW HORIZONTAL CONSTRAINED LINES

You use Shift to *constrain* a shape as you draw it on a slide. For lines, constraining enables you to make perfectly straight horizontal or vertical lines. If you try to angle a constrained line, lines are limited to angles in increments of 45 degrees.

When using Shift to constrain a shape, it's important to release your mouse button before releasing Shift. Otherwise, you might accidentally move the pointer when Shift is no longer in effect, resulting in a shape that is no longer constrained.

NOTE

Depending on the settings of your computer and the size of your screen, you may need to use a different percent so you can focus on the rectangle and not the entire slide.

REVIEW

To insert a footer on one slide only, move to the slide before opening the Header and Footer dialog box; then click **Apply** instead of **Apply to All**.

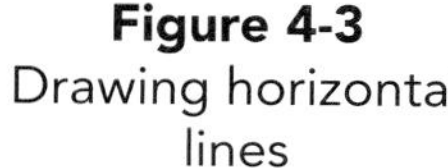

NOTE

The documents you create in this course relate to the case study about Good 4 U, a fictional restaurant business described at the beginning of this text.

1. Still working on slide 3, from the View tab, in the Zoom group, click the Zoom button. On the Zoom dialog box, key **150** percent and click **OK**. Scroll as needed to display the rectangle. Zooming in on the area will make it easier to see what you're doing when you work on detailed objects.
2. From the Home tab, in the Drawing group, right-click the Line button then choose **Lock Drawing Mode**. You're going to draw several constrained lines without needing to reclick the Line button each time you draw.
3. Position the crosshair pointer on the left side of the rectangle on the vertical ruler's zero marker, hold down Shift, and drag straight across to the right side of the rectangle. (As you drag, notice that the line remains straight, even if you move the pointer up or down a little.)
4. Release the mouse button first, and then release Shift.
5. With the Line button still activated, position the crosshair pointer at the left end of the rectangle again about a half inch above where you drew the last line. Hold down Shift and drag to the right edge of the rectangle. Release the mouse button, and then release Shift. Continue this process until the rectangle is full of horizontal lines a half inch apart, as shown in Figure 4-3.
6. Press Esc to release the locked drawing mode.
7. From the View tab, in the Zoom group, click **Fit to Window** to display the entire slide.

Figure 4-3
Drawing horizontal lines

8. Insert a footer only on slide 3 that contains Your Name, a comma, and the text **[4-2your initials]**. (Do not include the date.)
9. Create a new folder for Lesson 4. Save the presentation as **[4-2your initials]** in the new Lesson 4 folder. Print only slide 3, full size, grayscale, and framed. Keep the presentation open for the next exercise.

Exercise 4-3 ADD CONNECTOR LINES

Sometimes two or more shapes need to be connected with a line; therefore, PowerPoint provides a variety of *connector lines* for this purpose. These lines are either straight connectors, elbow connectors (with 90-degree angles between connected shapes), or curved connector lines. Some lines have arrowheads on one or both ends to show a relationship or movement between the shapes when creating a diagram.

1. Insert a new slide after slide 3 using the **Blank** layout.
2. On the new slide 4, from the Home tab, in the Drawing group, click the Shapes button and then choose the Rounded Rectangle button. Notice that a ScreenTip will appear that labels each drawing tool button.
3. Position the crosshair pointer on the left of your slide then click and drag to create a rectangle as shown in Figure 4-4.
4. Repeat this process to create a similar rectangle on the right of the slide.
5. Now select the Elbow Connector button. Point to the left rectangle and you will see a red square appear on all four sides of this rectangle. These are *connection sites* where the line and rectangle can be joined.
6. Click the red square at the bottom. This step connects the beginning portion of your line.
7. Now drag the line to the right until you connect to the red square on the left side of the second rectangle.
8. Notice that the connector line has two yellow diamond shapes. These are *adjustment handles* that enable you to change the horizontal or the vertical portions of the line. Adjust the line as shown in Figure 4-4.

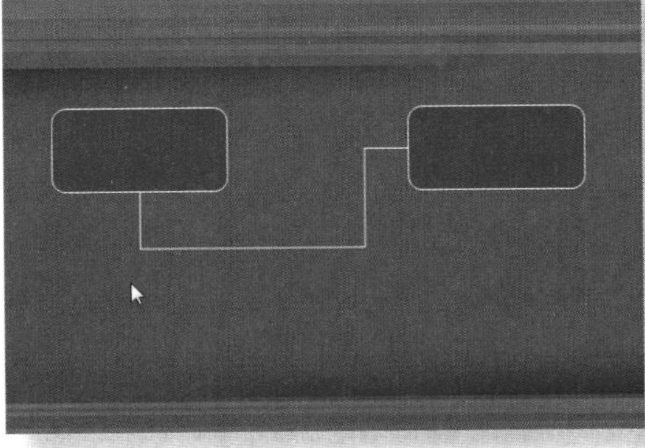

Figure 4-4
Elbow connector lines

9. With the connector line still selected, press Delete to remove the connector line.
10. Now add a different connector line. Click the Curved Double-Arrow Connector button and repeat the process of connecting the bottom of the left rectangle with the left side of the rectangle on the right.

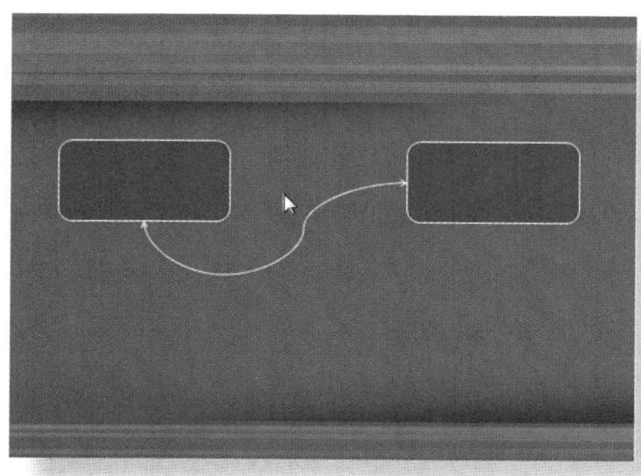

Figure 4-5 Double-arrow connector line

11. Notice how the adjustment handles affect the curve of the line as you move them horizontally or vertically. Adjust the line as shown in Figure 4-5.

Exercise 4-4 CREATE SQUARES AND CIRCLES

When you constrain other shapes, such as rectangles or ovals, they grow at an equal rate horizontally and vertically as you draw, creating symmetrical objects such as squares and circles.

NOTE

Your square might look more like a rectangle if your monitor's horizontal size and vertical size are not perfectly synchronized. Your square will print correctly, even if it is distorted on your screen.

1. Insert a new slide after slide 4 using the **Blank** layout.
2. On the new slide 5, from the Home tab, in the Drawing group, click the Shapes button and then choose the Rectangle button.
3. Position the crosshair pointer. on the left of your slide.
4. Press and hold Shift then drag diagonally down and to the right, ending near the center of the slide. Release the mouse button first, and then release Shift. See Figure 4-6 for the approximate size and placement of the completed square.

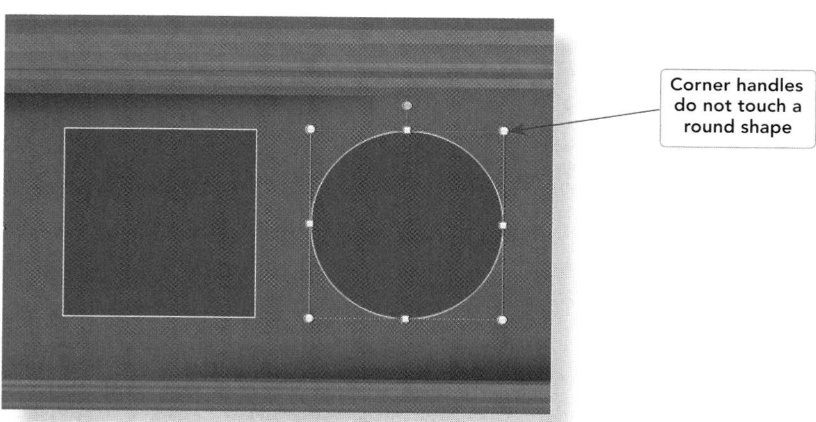
Corner handles do not touch a round shape

Figure 4-6 Drawing a circle and a square

5. From the Home tab, in the Drawing group, click the Shapes button and choose the Oval button.
6. Position your pointer to the right of the square.

7. While pressing Shift, drag diagonally down and to the right to create a circle the same size as the square. Your screen should resemble Figure 4-6. Both the square and the circle in this example have a **Height** and **Width** measurement of 3.5 inches.
8. Notice that with a circular shape, the corner handles do not touch the shape.
9. Save the presentation as **[4-4your initials]** in your Lesson 4 folder, but do not print it. Leave it open for the next exercise.

Exercise 4-5 RESIZE AND MOVE SHAPES

A shape that you draw is resized in the same way that you resize a text placeholder: Select it, and then drag one of its sizing handles. Holding down Shift and/or Ctrl while dragging a sizing handle has the following effects on an object:

- Shift preserves a shape's *proportions,* meaning that its height grows or shrinks at the same rate as its width, preventing shapes from becoming too tall and skinny or too short and wide.
- Ctrl causes a shape to grow or shrink from the center of the shape, rather than from the edge that's being dragged.
- Ctrl+Shift together cause a shape to grow or shrink proportionately from its center.

You reposition a shape by dragging it with the four-pointed arrow. Point anywhere in the shape and when you see the four-pointed arrow, drag the shape to another place on your slide.

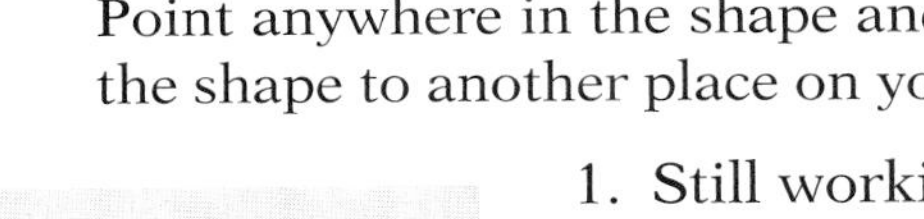

NOTE

These techniques also apply to resizing and moving clip art and photo images, too.

1. Still working on slide 5, select the circle by clicking anywhere inside it, and then point to its bottom center sizing handle. Your pointer changes to a two-pointed vertical arrow.
2. Drag the handle down. As you drag, the pointer changes to a crosshair. The circle has changed into an oval and is now larger.
3. Drag the bottom-left corner handle diagonally up and to the left. The oval is now wider and flattened, taking on an entirely new shape.
4. Click the Undo button twice to restore the circle to its original size and shape.
5. Point to the circle's lower-left corner sizing handle. While holding down Shift, drag diagonally out from the circle's center, making it larger. (Don't worry if the circle overlaps the rectangle.) The circle retains its original shape. Press Ctrl+Z to Undo this action and revert the circle to the original size.

6. While holding down both Ctrl and Shift, drag the lower-left corner sizing handle toward the center of the circle. The circle becomes smaller, shrinking evenly from all edges. With this technique, all expanding and contracting of the size occurs from the shape's center, as shown in Figure 4-7.

Figure 4-7
Resizing a shape from its center

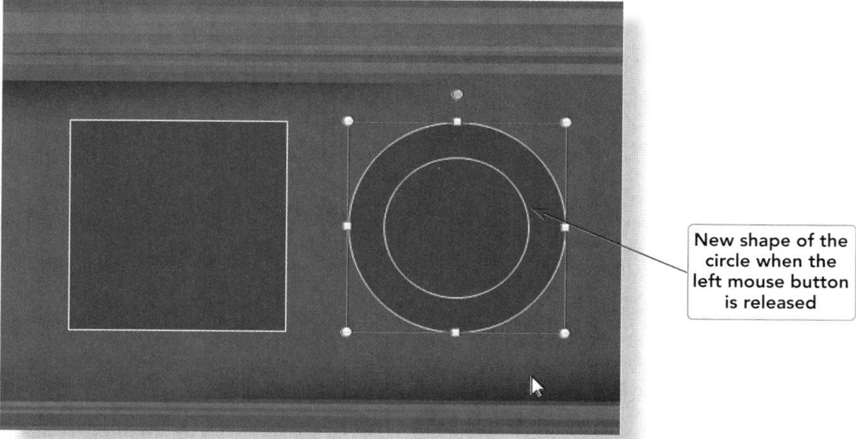

7. Select the circle and press Delete to remove it.
8. Select the square shape and then from the the Drawing Tools Format tab, in the Size group, key **4.5** in both the **Height** and **Width** boxes.
9. Point in the square so you see the four-pointed arrow then drag the square to the middle of the slide
10. To control precise sizing and positioning, click the **Dialog Box Launcher** in the Size group.
11. On the Size tab in the **Size and Position** dialog box, click the **Lock aspect ratio** option to keep the vertical and horizontal sizing in the same ratio as a shape (or other object) is resized. This can be very important when working with photographs.
12. Click the Position tab, then change the **Horizontal** position of the square to be 2.75 inches from the top left corner and the **Vertical** position to be 1.75 inches down from the top left corner.
13. Click the Close button .
14. Save the presentation as **[4-5your initials]** in your Lesson 4 folder, but do not print it. Leave it open for the next exercise.

TIP

If you like working with the ruler measurements, you can precisely size and position objects without the need to open the Size and Position dialog box, but keep in mind that the rulers measure distances from the center of the slide. So, if you point to the two-inch mark at the right of the zero mark on the horizontal ruler, you need to do some math to figure out how far you are from either edge of the slide. The Position tab on the Size and Position dialog box lets you choose to measure either from the center of the slide or from its top left corner.

Exercise 4-6 USE ADJUSTMENT HANDLES TO MODIFY SHAPES

The rectangles, ovals, and lines that you have created are very simple shapes. Many additional shapes are available, as shown in Figure 4-8.

Shape tools are arranged in nine different categories, as shown in Figure 4-8. You resize all of these shapes in the same way, and many shapes include one or more adjustment handles which enable you to change the shape dimensions after it is drawn.

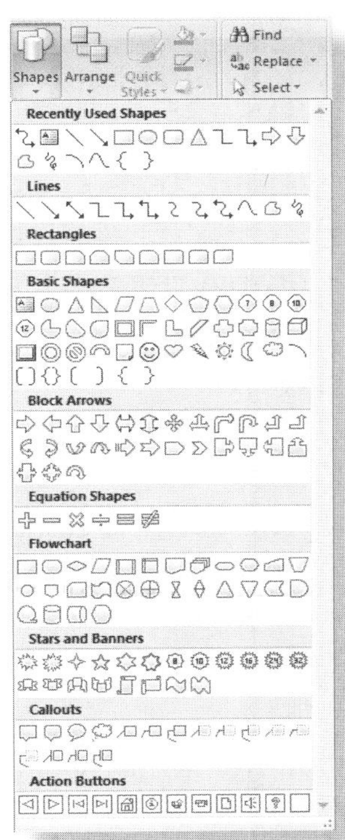

Figure 4-8
Additional shapes in the Shapes gallery

1. You no longer need slides 3 and 4 where you practiced making shapes. From the Slides and Outline pane, select each of these slide thumbnails and press Delete to remove them.
2. Now working on slide 3, from the Home tab, in the Drawing group, click the Shapes button to display the Shapes gallery.
3. In the **Stars and Banners** category, point to the various shape buttons and read their ScreenTips to see what each one is called.
4. Right-click the 5-Point Star button and choose **Lock Drawing Mode**. Draw several stars in different sizes positioned randomly on the slide with some stars overlapping. Place stars on the rectangle and on the blank area of the slide.
5. Press Esc to exit the locked drawing mode.
6. Select one of the stars and drag its yellow diamond-shaped adjustment handle toward the center to make the points more narrow, as shown in Figure 4-9.
7. Press Ctrl+Z several times until there is only a square left on the slide.

TIP

Use Shift to create a symmetrical shape in the same way that you use Shift when you draw a circle or square.

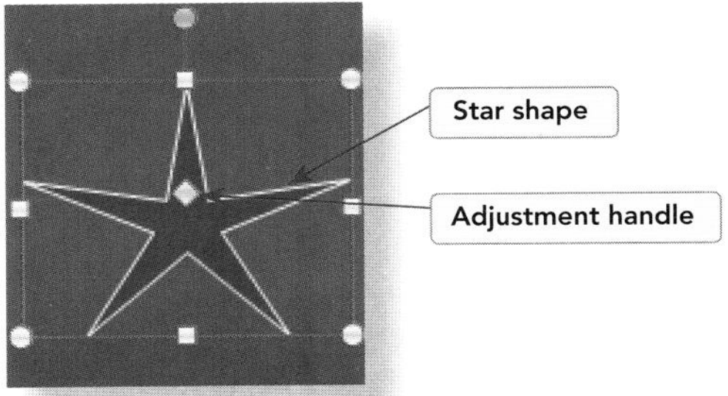

Figure 4-9
Dragging an adjustment handle

8. From the Home tab, in the Drawing group, click the Shapes button and in the **Basic Shapes** category, click the Sun button. Draw a sun, about two inches in diameter, in the upper right corner of the slide.
9. Drag the adjustment handle toward the center of the sun shape to make the center circle smaller and the points longer.

Exercise 4-7 PLACE TEXT IN A SHAPE AND ROTATE

You can easily transform a shape into an attention-getting background for text. Simply select the shape and key the text (or paste it from the clipboard). You can format and edit the text in the same way as in a text placeholder. The text in a shape is centered by default.

1. Select the sun shape on slide 3 and press Delete.
2. From the Home tab, in the Drawing group, click the Shapes button to display the Shapes gallery.

3. In the **Stars and Banners** category, choose the 16-Point Star button then click and drag to draw this shape in the upper right of the slide. It should slightly overlap the large square.
4. Key **Grand Opening**. The text automatically appears in the center of the star in the same color as the star's outline. Notice the dashed-line border similar to a text placeholder border.
5. Click the star's outline anywhere between two sizing handles to select it.
6. From the Home tab, in the Font group, change the size from 18 points to 28 points and apply bold. The text becomes too large for the star.
7. Drag the center sizing handle on the left side to make the star wide enough to contain the text without word wrapping. Part of the star shape will be over the square shape.

Figure 4-10
Inserting text in a shape

8. Drag the top-center sizing handle down to flatten the star, as shown in Figure 4-10.
9. Click on the green rotation handle and drag it slightly to the left to rotate the star.
10. Drag the star down until it overlaps the lower-right corner of the square, as shown in Figure 4-11.

Figure 4-11
Rotating a shape with text

11. Compare slide 3 with Figure 4-11 and make any necessary adjustments.
12. Create a handout header and footer: Include the date and your name as the header, and the page number and text **[4-7your initials]** as the footer.
13. Move to slide 1 and save the presentation as **[4-7your initials]** in your Lesson 4 folder.

Inserting Clip Art Images

Included with Microsoft Office is a collection of ready-to-use images known as clip art, also called *clips*, that you can insert on PowerPoint slides. The *clip art* collection includes *vector drawings*—images made up of lines, curves, and shapes that are usually filled with solid colors. It also includes *bitmap pictures*—photographs made up of tiny colored dots that are made from scanned photographs or a digital camera. These photographs can be accessed from the Insert Clip Art task pane.

You can insert clip art and picture images into a PowerPoint presentation in two ways:

- Search for Clip Art. On the Insert tab, in the Illustrations group, click the Clip Art button to display the Clip Art task pane where you can search for appropriate images from Microsoft's Clip Organizer collection. Also, if your slide uses a layout that includes a content placeholder, double-click the Clip Art button to display the Clip Art task pane.
- Insert Picture from File. On the Insert tab, in the Illustrations group, click the Picture button to insert picture files stored on a hard drive, removable drive, or network drive. This method is useful for inserting your own images that you have stored on your computer and that are not part of the Microsoft Clip Organizer collection.

Exercise 4-8 FIND CLIP ART, THEN MODIFY A SEARCH

Each clip art image that Microsoft provides has *keywords* associated with it that describe the subject matter of the picture. You use keywords to find the art you need for your presentation.

Clip art images (and other media such as photographs, sound, and movie files) are organized into collections and media types. You can choose to search all collections and types or to select a particular type. If you know that you want a photograph only, be sure to select that type of media only to make the search more efficient.

If you search for a keyword and don't find any images, or you don't find one you like, you can modify your search and try again.

1. If you have Internet access, but are not connected, make a connection now (unless your instructor tells you otherwise).

2. Move to slide 2, and then from the Insert tab, in the Illustrations group, click the Clip Art button. The Clip Art task pane, as shown in Figure 4-12, is displayed on the right.

Figure 4-12
Clip Art task pane

3. In the Clip Art task pane, click the **Search in** list box arrow. Be sure that **Everywhere** is checked. All categories in the Microsoft Clip Organizer will be searched and, if you are connected to the Internet, Microsoft Office Online will be searched, too.
4. Close the list box by clicking anywhere on your screen.
5. Click the **Results should be** list box arrow. In this list box, you can choose to search all media types or limit your search to specific types. These options are helpful if you have a large number of media files stored on your computer, or you are searching on the Internet. Check only the Clip Art category and remove all other checks.
6. In the **Search for** text box at the top of the Clip Art task pane, key **food** and then click **Go**. The **Results** box shows thumbnails (miniature images) of clips that match the search word, as shown in Figure 4-13.

Figure 4-13
Search results

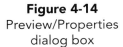

7. Use the scroll bar to review some of the thumbnails.
8. In the **Search for** box, key **bananas** and then click **Go**. Thumbnails of pictures with bananas should appear in your **Results** box. If you do not find a picture you like, modify the search using a different keyword.

Exercise 4-9 PREVIEW AND INSERT CLIP ART IMAGES

You can preview images in a larger format, so you can see more detail before choosing one of them.

1. Without clicking, point to a clip art thumbnail in the task pane. As your pointer is over an image, a ScreenTip showing keywords, image dimensions, size, and file format appears. A gray bar with a downward pointing triangle appears on the right side of the thumbnail that changes to blue when you point to it.
2. Choose a picture you would like to insert.
3. Click the gray bar beside the picture you have chosen to display a menu of options. You can also display this menu by right-clicking a thumbnail.
4. Choose **Preview/Properties**. In addition to displaying an enlarged picture, this dialog box also shows you the filename and more detailed information about the image, as shown in Figure 4-14.

NOTE

Clips from the Microsoft Office Online collection have an online icon in the lower left corner of the image thumbnail. When you do a search from all categories, some clips will have a musical note, indicating that they are sound files. Some clips will have an animation icon displayed in the lower right corner, indicating that they are movies.

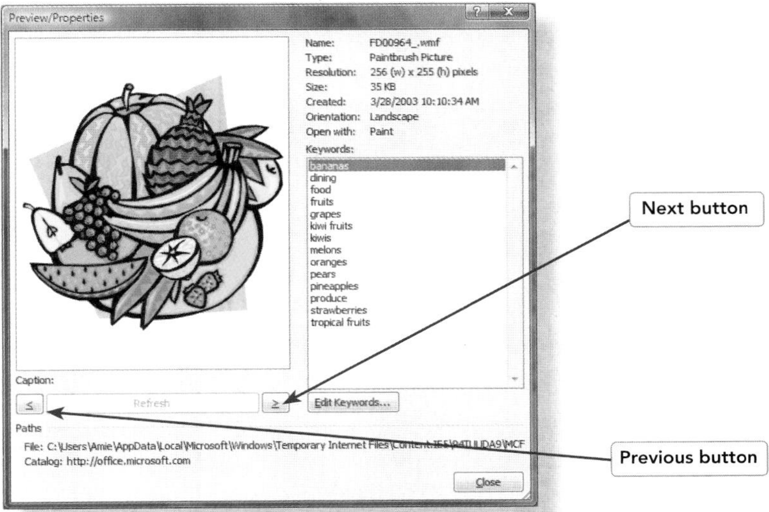

Figure 4-14
Preview/Properties dialog box

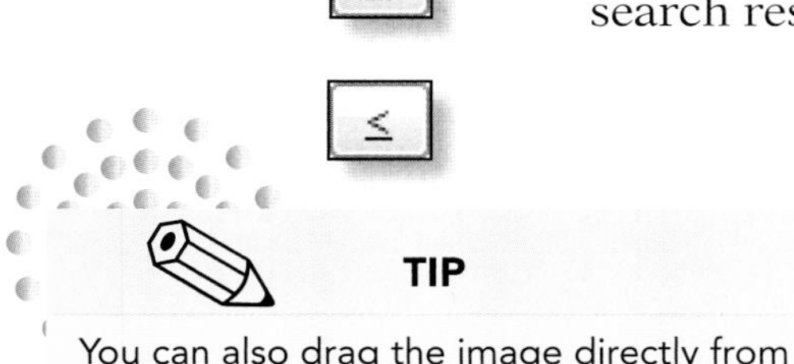

5. Click the Next button below the picture. The next picture in the search results pane is displayed.

6. Click the Next button several times more; then click the Previous button. When you find a picture of health-conscious food that you like, such as the one in Figure 4-14 or Figure 4-15, click **Close**. Notice that the last picture you previewed has a blue selection box around it.

7. With your left mouse button, click the thumbnail for the image you chose. The clip art image is inserted on the current slide.

TIP

You can also drag the image directly from the task pane onto your slide or select **Insert** from the bar that appears next to the thumbnail.

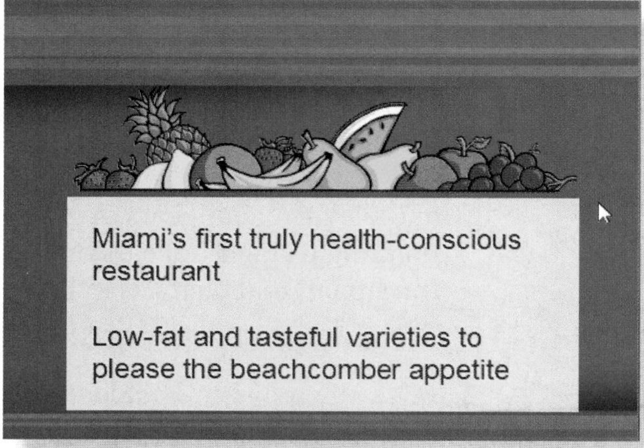

Figure 4-15 Positioning of clip art

8. Drag the image above the text box and resize it as necessary for a pleasing appearance. The image in Figure 4-15 was increased in size and centered on the top edge of the text box. If you used a different image, then decide how to position it attractively on the slide.

9. Move to slide 1, and search for another image that would be appropriate for Miami Beach. Search for a palm tree and choose the Photograph media option in the **Results should be** box.

10. When you find a photograph of a palm tree that you like, insert it on slide 1. Close the Clip Art task pane.

Exercise 4-10 REARRANGE, DELETE, COPY, PASTE, AND DUPLICATE CLIP ART IMAGES

When developing a presentation you might insert an image on one slide and later decide to move it to a different slide. You can rearrange, delete, copy, paste, and duplicate clip art images.

1. Still working on slide 1, click on the photograph to select it. When you see the four-pointed arrow, drag the photograph down to center it vertically on the right edge of the text box.

2. Move to slide 4. This slide has four clip art images that have been previously inserted. On the left, select the sunset beach scene on the top and notice that it has a green rotation handle at the top. Practice dragging this handle to rotate the image.
3. Press Delete to remove the sunset beach scene from this slide.
4. On the right, select the palm tree image on the top and press Ctrl+C to copy it, then Delete to remove it from this slide. The image is still in your clipboard, however.
5. Move to side 1 press Ctrl+V to insert the palm tree on the first slide.

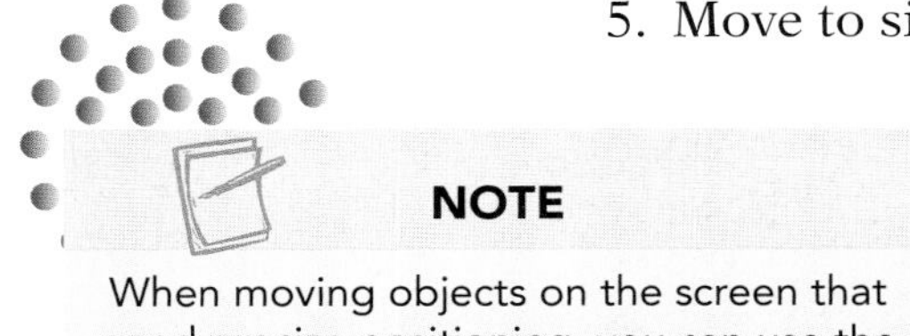

NOTE

When moving objects on the screen that need precise positioning, you can use the directional arrow keys on the keyboard to *nudge* the image gradually.

6. When this image first appears, the size is 1.84 inches for both the height and width. From the Picture Tools Format tab, in the Size group, change both height and width to 1.5 inches.
7. Drag the palm tree to the upper left of the slide, aligning the bottom of the image with the darkest blue color on the background and the left edge of the image even with the left of the slide as shown in Figure 4-16.

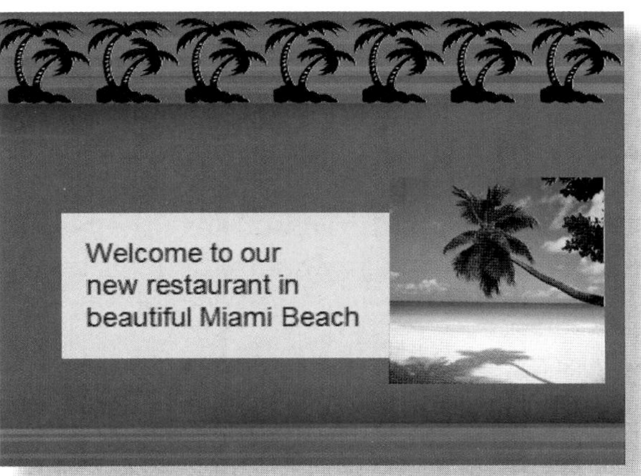

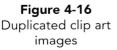

Figure 4-16 Duplicated clip art images

8. Press Ctrl+D to *duplicate* this image. Move the second image over so it aligns with the bottom of the first image and the branches almost touch.
9. With the second image selected, press Ctrl+D. Because the positioning information from your first duplication is remembered by PowerPoint, this image should go into the same alignment.

NOTE

Using the duplicate command is faster than using copy/paste when you want a second image on the same slide. Copy/paste works best when you want to copy an image from one slide and paste it on another slide.

10. Repeat this process of pressing Ctrl+D five more times to create a row of palm trees across the top of the slide as shown in Figure 4-16.
11. Update your footer text to **[4-10your initials]**. Save the presentation as **[4-10your initials]**, but do not print it. Keep the file open for the next exercise.

Exercise 4-11 GROUP AND UNGROUP IMAGES AND TEXT

When you *group* objects, you combine two or more shapes or images so they behave as one. If you then move one object of the group, all the other objects move with it. Grouping assures that objects meant to stay together don't accidentally get moved individually or deleted. When you apply formatting to a group, all the objects in the group receive the same formatting. If you need to work on the objects separately, then you can *ungroup* them. *Regrouping* can combine the objects again.

1. Move to slide 4. Press Shift while you click on both the beach scene image and the text below it. Now selection handles appear on both images.

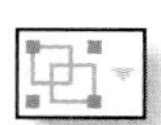

2. From the Picture Tools Format tab, in the Arrange group, click Group then select **Group**. Now the clip art image and the text are combined as one object.
3. Resize the group by stretching the corner sizing handle on the top right to make the image about as large as the palm tree on the right.
4. By resizing the group, the text has moved and is not in the best position. From the Picture Tools Format tab, in the Arrange group, click the Group button, then choose **Ungroup**. Now you can move the image and text separately.
5. Arrange the beach scene image on the left so the bottom aligns evenly with the palm tree on the right. Move the beach scene text to be centered under the image and aligned with the palm tree text. You may need to resize the beach scene text box.
6. Now select the beach scene text and the image. From the Picture Tools Format tab, in the Arrange group, click the Group button and choose **Regroup**.
7. Select the palm tree image and the palm tree text and group them.
8. Move to slide 5. Select the picture of Miami buildings and press Ctrl+C.
9. Move to slide 3 and press Ctrl+V. Position the picture to be in the center of the square shape.

Figure 4-17
Grouped shapes and picture

10. Resize the left and right sides of the square shape to change it to a rectangle that evenly frames the picture.

11. Select the **16-Point Star** shape. From the Drawing Tools Format tab, in the Arrange group, click Bring to Front button so the star is on top of the picture and rectangle as shown in Figure 4-17.

12. With the star selected, press Shift while you click on the picture and the rectangle to select all three objects.
13. From the Drawing Tools Format tab, in the Arrange group, click the Group button, and choose **Group**.

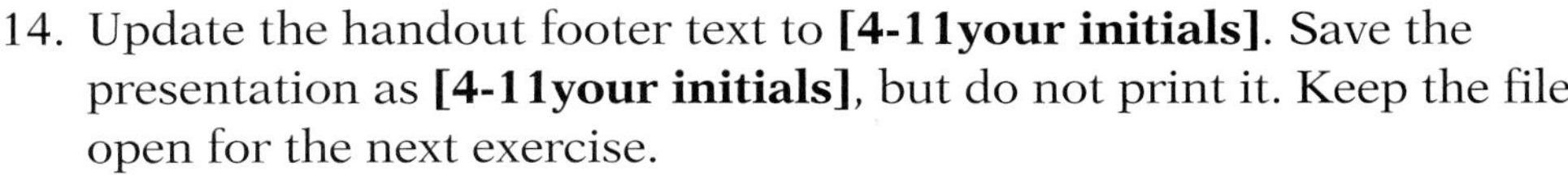

14. Update the handout footer text to **[4-11your initials]**. Save the presentation as **[4-11your initials]**, but do not print it. Keep the file open for the next exercise.

Inserting and Enhancing a Picture

More than any other graphic element, pictures can add a sense of realism to a presentation. Microsoft's online collection offers an abundance of photo images, which are referred to as *stock photography,* that you can search for just as you search for clip art images. Pictures that you take with a digital camera also can be inserted. Or pictures that are already printed can be turned into an appropriate digital format by scanning.

Once the picture is inserted into PowerPoint, you have many options for improving its appearance, as shown by the picture tools in Figure 4-18 and Table 4-2. In the next exercises you will learn to crop to remove unwanted details, adjust brightness and contrast, and apply many different styles and special effects.

Figure 4-18
Picture tools format Ribbon

TABLE 4-2 Format—Picture Tools

Button	Name	Purpose
	Brightness	Increases or decreases a picture's overall lightness.
	Contrast	Increases or decreases the difference between the lightest and darkest areas of a picture.
	Recolor	Enables you to change the color mode (grayscale, sepia, washout, or black-and-white) and color variations of a picture.
	Compress Pictures	Strips unnecessary information from a picture file to make a presentation file size smaller.
	Change Pictures	Changes to a different picture in the same size and format as a selected picture.
	Reset Picture	Restores a picture's original attributes if changes were made by using the Picture Adjustment tools.
	Picture Styles	Provides a gallery of preset effects to quickly add interest.

continues

TABLE 4-2 Format—Picture Tools *continued*

Button	Name	Purpose
	Picture Shape	Enables you to change the rectangular appearance of a picture into a shape.
	Picture Border	Places an outline around a picture in different colors, weight, or line styles.
	Picture Effects	Provides the effects of shadow, reflection, glow, soft edges, bevel, or 3-D rotation.
	Bring to Front	Adjusts stacking order of pictures and other objects.
	Send to Back	Adjusts stacking order of pictures and other objects.
	Selection Pane	Used to select individual pictures and other objects and to change the visibility or order.
	Align	Used to make multiple objects evenly spaced.
	Group	Fastens multiple objects together to act as one object.
	Rotate	Used to angle pictures and other objects.
	Crop	Enables you to cut away the edges of a picture.
	Height	The vertical size dimension.
	Width	The horizontal size dimension.

Exercise 4-12 INSERT STOCK PHOTOGRAPHY

To search for a photograph image, use the same steps as you did for searching for clip art images except choose Photographs instead of Clip Art under the **Results should be** heading.

1. Move to slide 5 and delete the photo displayed on the slide.
2. From the Insert tab, in the Illustrations group, click the Clip Art button so the Clip Art task pane is displayed on the right.
3. In the Clip Art task pane, the **Search in** list box should say **All collections**.
4. In the Clip Art task pane, in the **Results should be** list box check only the Photograph category and remove other checks.
5. In the **Search for** text box at the top of the Clip Art task pane, key **Miami** and then click **Go**. The **Results** box shows thumbnails (miniature images) of clips that match the search word.
6. Double-click the Miami night image. Drag the corner sizing handle to increase the picture height to about 4 inches. Notice that the width automatically adjusts to keep the image in proportion.

Figure 4-19
Picture inserted from search

7. Position the image as shown in Figure 4-19.
8. Close the Clip Art task pane. Keep the presentation open for the next exercise.

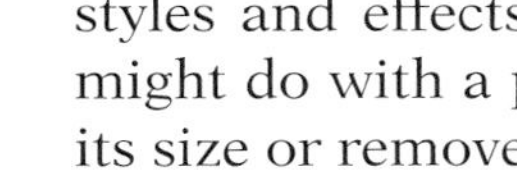

Exercise 4-13 CROP A PICTURE

When a picture is selected and you click the Picture Tools Format tab, many options become available to you for adjusting the picture or applying picture styles and effects. You can also *crop* (trim) parts of a picture, just as you might do with a page from a magazine by using a pair of scissors to reduce its size or remove unwanted details around the edge.

When you click the cropping tool, a picture's sizing handles change to *cropping handles*—short black markers that you drag to trim a picture.

TIP

Try holding down Alt as you crop. This enables you to make very fine adjustments.

TIP

If you crop too far, use the cropping tool to drag the handle in the opposite direction to restore that part of the picture, or click the Undo button.

1. On slide 5, select the night scene picture. The colors of the lighted buildings and water reflections can be featured more if the picture is trimmed across the top and bottom.
2. From the Picture Tools Format tab, in the Size group, click the Crop button. The cropping handles appear around the edges of the picture and your pointer changes to a cropping tool.
3. Position the cropping tool on the top center handle and drag the handle down until the cropping line is positioned a little closer to the top of the tallest building, as shown in Figure 4-20.

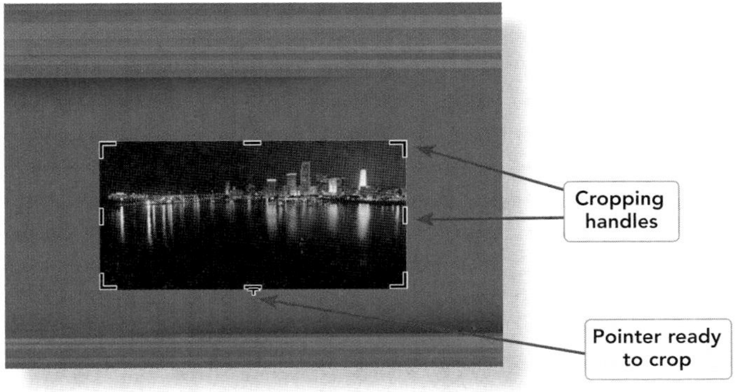

Figure 4-20
Cropping a picture

4. Repeat this process to crop from the bottom to make the bottom edge of the picture just below where the reflections end.
5. Click on a blank area of the slide to turn off the crop function.
6. Update the handout footer text to **[4-13your initials]**. Save your presentation as **[4-13your initials]**, but do not print it. Keep the file open for the next exercise.

Exercise 4-14 RECOLOR A PICTURE, THEN RESET COLORS

Color settings can be applied to *recolor* pictures using different color modes and light or dark variations of the presentation's theme colors. These effects might be used to create a subtle image that is placed behind other slide objects.

1. On slide 5, select the picture. From the Picture Tools Format tab, in the Adjust group, click the Recolor button. A gallery of color options will appear, as shown in Figure 4-21.

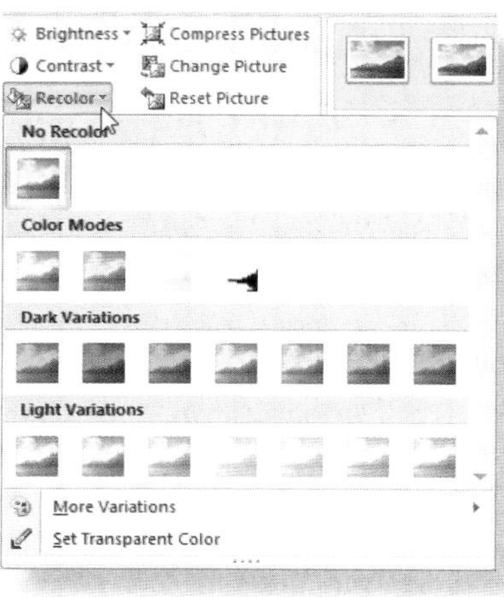

Figure 4-21 Recolor gallery

2. On the gallery, slowly drag your pointer over each of the options. A live preview showing the result of that option will be displayed on the picture before it is actually accepted.
   - In **Color Mode** you have options for **Grayscale, Sepia, Washout,** or **Black and White.**
   - Variations have options for **Light** and **Dark** settings.
3. Click **Accent color 2 Dark** to select this color change.
4. Now restore the colors to their original colors. With the picture selected, click the Recolor button and choose **No Recolor.**
5. Keep the presentation open for the next exercise.

Exercise 4-15 APPLY A PICTURE STYLE

Many different *picture styles* are available to display your pictures in beautiful and interesting ways. As with any of the creative techniques you are using, be careful that the styles and other treatments you apply to your pictures add to the appearance of the picture and do not distort it or diminish its effectiveness.

1. On slide 5, select the picture. From the Picture Tools Format tab, in the Picture Styles group, slowly drag your pointer over each of the Picture Styles options and the results of that option will be displayed on the picture.

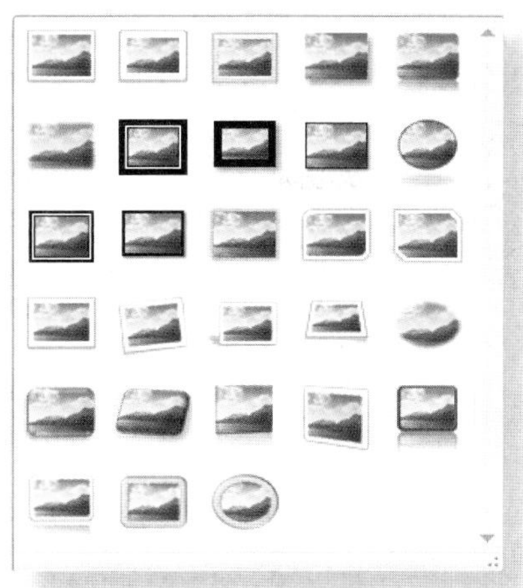

Figure 4-22
Picture Styles

2. Click the More button to see additional styles that are available, as shown in Figure 4-22.
3. Now click the Picture Style **Double Frame, Black**, as shown in Figure 4-23.

Figure 4-23
Cropped picture with Double Frame effect

4. Update the handout footer text to **[4-15your initials]**. Save the presentation as **[4-15your initials]** in your Lesson 4 folder, but do not print it. Leave the presentation open for the next exercise.

Exercise 4-16 INSERT A PICTURE FROM FILE

When you begin to acquire a collection of digital images, you need to keep them organized in some logical way in folders on your computer that are appropriately named to identify the folders' contents. These folders might be saved in the Pictures folder that is automatically created on your computer when Microsoft Office is installed.

However, for this exercise you have a picture file stored in the same folder as all the other files for this lesson.

1. Display slide 5, then from the Home tab, in the Slides group, click the New Slide button to add a new slide with a **Blank** layout.

2. On slide 6, from the Insert tab, in the Illustrations group, click the Picture button.
3. In the Insert Picture dialog box, locate where your student data files for this lesson are stored and select the file **Restaurant1.jpg**. Click **Insert**.

4. With the Picture selected, click the Picture Tools Format tab. Change the Height to **5 inches** and the Width will automatically change to **3.7 inches**.
5. Move the picture to the left of the slide.
6. Keep your presentation open for the next exercise.

Exercise 4-17 ADJUST CONTRAST AND BRIGHTNESS

Sometimes a picture may be too dark to show needed details, or colors are washed out from too much sunshine when the picture was taken. PowerPoint's *Brightness* and *Contrast* adjustments can fix these problems. Adjusting the brightness changes the picture's overall lightness while adjusting contrast affects the difference between its lightest and darkest areas.

Figure 4-24
Brightness drop-down list

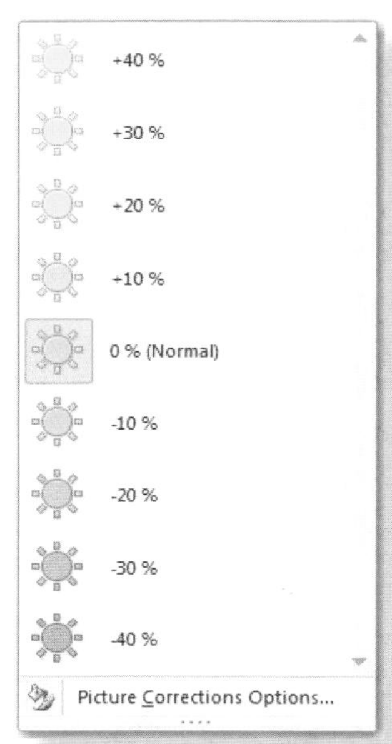

1. On slide 6, select the picture and press Ctrl+D to duplicate it. Position the second image on the right of the slide. Use it to make the color adjustments in this exercise so you can compare your changes to the original.
2. With the second picture selected, from the Picture Tools Format tab, in the Adjust group, click the Brightness button. A drop-down list appears showing adjustments in 10 percent increments, as shown in Figure 4-24, to increase or decrease the brightness of the picture.
3. Drag your pointer over the various amounts and study the effect on the picture. Click on **+10%** to increase the brightness.

Figure 4-25
Contrast drop-down list

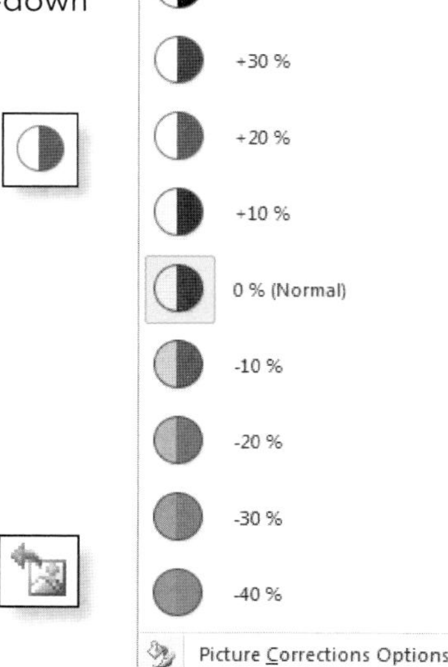

4. Click the Contrast button. Again, a drop-down list appears showing adjustments in 10 percent increments, as shown in Figure 4-25, to increase or decrease the lightness of the picture.
5. Drag your pointer over the various amounts and study the effect on the picture. Click on **+20%** to increase the contrast.
6. Now click the Reset Picture button to restore the picture's original colors and size. Change the height to 5 inches again.

7. Sometimes these 10 percent increments change a picture's colors too much, so you might need to adjust them more gradually to get good results. Click the Brightness button then choose **Picture Correction Options** to open the Format Picture dialog box. Move this dialog box away from the picture so you can see the results of your changes as you make them.
8. Both the Brightness and Contrast can be adjusted by dragging the sliders to the left or right. You can also enter numbers in the spin boxes or click up or down to change in 1 percent increments.
9. This time change the Brightness to **14%** and the Contrast to **24%**. Click **Close**.
10. The picture appears a little clearer now when you compare the one changed on the right with the original version on the left, as shown in Figure 4-26.

Figure 4-26
Image-adjusted picture

11. Update the handout footer text to **[4-17your initials]**. Save the presentation as **[4-17your initials]** in your Lesson 4 folder, but do not print it. Leave the presentation open for the next exercise.

Exercise 4-18 CHANGE A PICTURE SHAPE

Any picture that is inserted on a slide can be made to fill a shape for an unusual and creative treatment.

1. On slide 6, from the Home tab, in the Slides group, click the New Slide button to add a new slide with a **Blank** layout.
2. On slide 7, insert another picture from your Clip Art task pane. If the search from earlier in the lesson is not displayed, then search again for Miami photograph images.
3. Click the image that shows a beach and buildings. It has an unusual appearance because the image is angled.

4. With this image selected, from the Picture Tools Format tab, in the Picture Styles group, click the Picture Shape button. Try several of these shapes by clicking on the buttons in any of the categories. The image becomes the fill for that particular shape.
5. In the **Basic Shapes** category, select the **Heart** shape.
6. Continue to the next exercise.

Exercise 4-19 ADD A BORDER TO A PICTURE

The line that surrounds pictures is referred to as a Picture Border. This line can be shown in different colors and *line weights* (thicknesses) or in different styles (solid lines or dashes) to create a border around a picture just as you have used an outline on other shapes.

1. With the heart-shaped picture selected, from the Picture Tools Format tab, in the Picture Styles group, click the Picture Border button. As you drag your pointer over these colors, you can see how the color will look if selected.

Figure 4-27
Picture in a shape with a border

2. From the colors that appear, in the **Standard Colors** group, click the **Red** color.
3. Click the Picture Border again and click **Weight**. Choose **3 pt** for a thicker red line, as shown in Figure 4-27.
4. Continue to the next exercise.

Exercise 4-20 APPLY PICTURE EFFECTS

Special effects can be applied to pictures as well as other shapes you create. To apply these effects to pictures, you will use the Picture Effects button on the Picture Tools Format tab. Many different customized settings are possible. Picture effects are available in seven categories:

- *Preset*—a collection of images with several different settings already applied.
- *Shadow*—displays a shadow behind the picture that can be adjusted in different ways to change direction, thickness, and blurring effect.
- *Reflection*—causes a portion of the image to be displayed below the image as though reflecting in a mirror or on water.
- *Glow*—adds a soft color around the picture edges that makes the picture stand out from the background.
- *Soft Edges*—changes a picture's normal hard edges to a soft, feathered appearance that gradually fades into the background color.

- *Bevel*—makes the picture look dimensional with several different options available such as a raised button.
- *3-D Rotation*—enables the picture to be angled in different ways with perspective settings that change the illusion of depth.

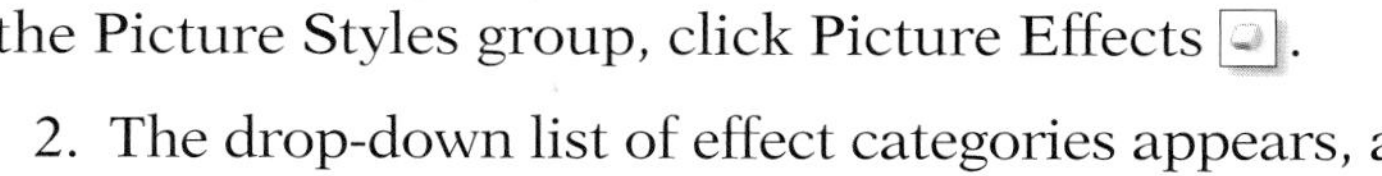

1. On slide 7, select the heart-shaped picture. From the Picture Tools Format tab, in the Picture Styles group, click Picture Effects.

Figure 4-28 Picture Effects categories

2. The drop-down list of effect categories appears, as shown in Figure 4-28. Each of these categories has several variations that you can see on your image as you drag your pointer over the effect thumbnail.
3. From the **Shadow** category, in the **Outer** subcategory, click the shadow named **Offset Diagonal Bottom Right** to apply a soft shadow.
4. Adjustments can be made to how the shadow appears. Click the Picture Effects button, click **Shadow** and then choose the **Shadow Options** at the bottom of this gallery.
5. From the dialog box that appears, key these numbers for each of the following settings:
   - Transparency **20%**
   - Size **100%**
   - Blur **10 pt**
   - Angle **40°**
   - Distance **15 pt**

TIP

You may also use the Dialog Box Launcher for Picture Styles to access the Format Picture dialog box.

6. Click **Close** to accept these settings. Your heart shape should now look like Figure 4-29.

Figure 4-29 Format Picture shadow settings and shadow effects

7. Update the handout footer text to **[4-20your initials]**. Save the presentation as **[4-20your initials]** in your Lesson 4 folder, but do not print it. Leave the presentation open for the next exercise.

Creating WordArt

WordArt can create special effects for decorative text that are not possible with standard text-formatting tools. You can stretch or curve text and add special shading, 3-D effects, and much more.

Exercise 4-21 CREATE AND MODIFY WORDART TEXT

In this exercise, you create a WordArt object, and then modify it by changing its shape and size. Make sure you key and proofread WordArt objects carefully.

1. Display slide 3 with the building photograph.

Figure 4-30 WordArt Styles gallery

2. From the Insert tab, in the Text group, click the WordArt button. The WordArt Styles gallery appears, as shown in Figure 4-30.
3. Point to the blue WordArt style that is called **Fill – Accent 2, Warm Matte Bevel** and click to select it. WordArt appears in the middle of your slide with sample text. At this point, you edit the text to replace the sample text, as shown in Figure 4-31, with the words you wish to display.

Figure 4-31 WordArt as it first appears

4. With the WordArt object selected, key **Good For You** and delete any extra letters.

TIP

Many different styles are displayed in the WordArt gallery using the colors of your current theme. When applied, some of the styles may need color adjustments so the text is easily readable on the background color.

5. Click anywhere on the blank part of the slide to accept these changes, and the bevel effect of this style becomes more evident.
6. To edit WordArt text, simply select the text and change it. In this case change the wording to **Good 4 U**.
7. Move the WordArt object to the upper left of the slide above the picture as shown in Figure 4-32.

Figure 4-32
WordArt showing positioning

8. Update the handout footer text to **[4-21your initials]**. Save the presentation as **[4-21your initials]** in your Lesson 4 folder, but do not print it. Leave the presentation open for the next exercise.

Exercise 4-22 APPLY WORDART EFFECTS

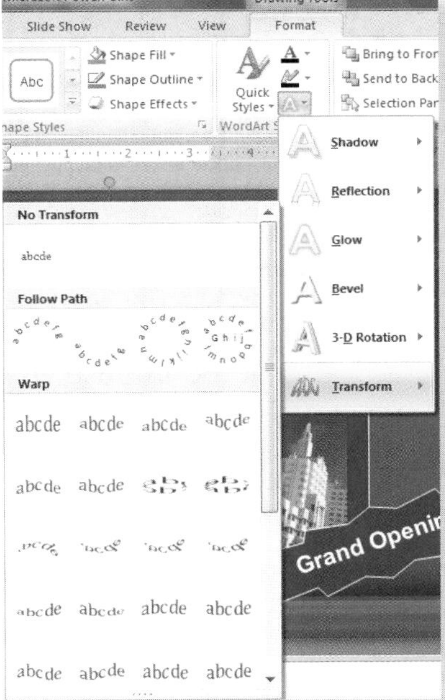

Figure 4-33
Text Effects

The same types of effects you have applied to pictures can be applied to WordArt. From the Drawing Tools Format tab, in the WordArt Styles group, the Text Effects [button] are shown in Figure 4-33. In Exercise 4-20 you were introduced to these effects when applying them to a picture: Shadow, Reflection, Glow, Bevel, and 3-D Rotation. But the last category, *Transform*, is unique to WordArt because it enables you to change your text into different shapes.

1. Still working on slide 3, with the Good 4 U WordArt selected, click the Drawing Tools Format tab, in the WordArt Styles group, click the Text Effects button [button] and choose **Transform**.

2. The default for WordArt text is No Transform because text will appear straight. When you drag your pointer over the various effects shown in this gallery, you will see that effect being applied to your text. The text sample on each of the buttons gives you an indication of the particular effect.

Figure 4-34 Using Transform to apply the Deflate Bottom Warp effect

3. From the Warp category, choose the effect **Deflate Bottom** that causes the text in the middle of the WordArt to become smaller.
4. Move the WordArt to the top of the picture so the letters G and U just slightly overlap with the blue rectangle as shown in Figure 4-34.
5. Keep your presentation open and continue to the next exercise.

Exercise 4-23 EDIT WORDART TEXT FILL AND TEXT OUTLINE COLORS

The *Text Fill* color of WordArt text can be changed as well as the *Text Outline* color and the weight of the outline. The outline goes around the edge of each letter. Making it thick emphasizes the outline; making it thin provides less emphasis but still makes the text look quite different than if no outline is applied.

1. Move to slide 7.
2. From the Insert tab, in the Text group, click the WordArt button. For the style, click the white WordArt style that is called **Fill – White, Warm Matte Bevel** and click to select it.
3. Key **We Love Miami Beach!** then select the text. From the Home tab, in the Font group, change the font size to 44 points.
4. Move the WordArt object above the heart, centered horizontally on the slide.

5. With the WordArt selected, from the Drawing Tools Format tab, in the WordArt Styles group, click the Text Fill button. From the Standard Colors, choose **Red**.
6. Now the WordArt color is almost too intense with such a bright red on the blue background. So apply a line color to tone down this effect.

7. With the WordArt selected, from the Drawing Tools Format tab, in the WordArt Styles group, click the Text Outline button.
8. Choose **More Outline Colors**, and then from the Colors dialog box, choose **Black**. Click **OK**.

9. Click the Text Outline button, click **Weight**, and choose **1 pt**.
10. Now change the shadow effect so it better matches the heart shape. From the Drawing Tools Format tab, in the WordArt Styles group, click the Dialog Box Launcher button.
11. From the Format Text Effects dialog box, choose **Shadow**. Change to these settings: Transparency **20%**, Size **100%**, Blur **4 pt**, Angle **45°**, distance, **2 pt**. Click **Close**.
12. From the Drawing Tools Format tab, in the WordArt Styles group, click the Text Effects button, click **Transform**, and from the Warp category, choose **Wave 2**.
13. Resize and adjust any necessary spacing so your slide resembles Figure 4-35.

Figure 4-35
Completed WordArt object

14. Update the handout footer to show **[4-23your initials]**.
15. Save the presentation as **[4-23your initials]** in your Lesson 4 folder and print it as handouts with nine slides per page. Close the presentation.

Creating a Photo Album

A presentation consisting of mostly pictures can be created quickly using PowerPoint's *Photo Album* feature. Picture files can be inserted from different locations on your computer and will be displayed with one picture on a slide. The pictures can be displayed at full screen size or framed in different shapes. Also, text can accompany each picture at the time you create the photo album, or text can be added to the individual slides. When complete, your saved photo album can be displayed just as any other presentation.

While this feature can be important for business situations, it could also be very helpful for creating a display for open house functions, or even wedding or birthday celebrations.

Exercise 4-24 CREATE ALBUM CONTENT BY INSERTING NEW PICTURES

In your Lesson 4 student data files you have a folder named **Salads** containing five pictures for this exercise. Copy the **Salads** folder to your storage location.

1. Open PowerPoint if necessary. Start a new blank presentation.

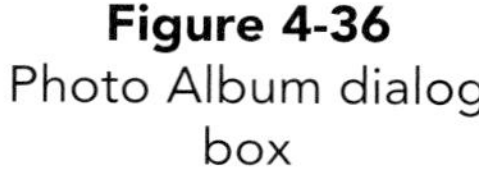

2. From the Insert tab, in the Illustrations group, click the top of the Photo Album button. The Photo Album dialog box appears, as shown in Figure 4-36.

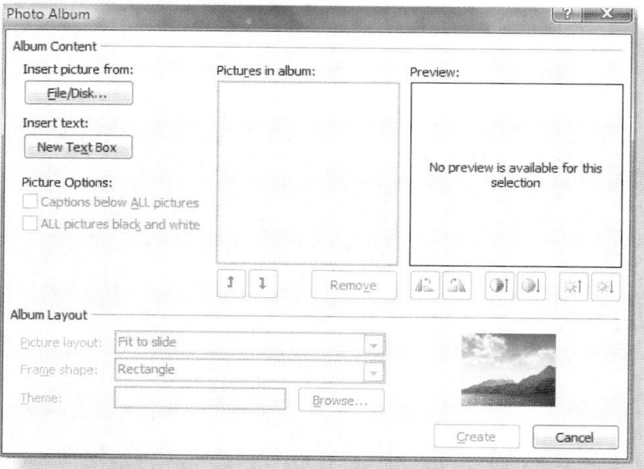

Figure 4-36
Photo Album dialog box

3. Click the File/Disk button, then choose the storage location where you have the **Salads** folder. Select the folder name, then click **Open**.
4. Select all of the picture files and click **Insert**.
5. At the bottom of the dialog box, notice the **Album Layout** options. By default, the **Picture layout** is **Fit to slide**. This option will expand each picture to fill your computer's screen. Click **Create**.
6. Each picture appears on a separate slide and a title slide has been created.
7. Continue to the next exercise to edit the Photo Album settings.

Exercise 4-25 ADJUST PICTURE ORDER, BRIGHTNESS, AND CONTRAST

Using the Format Photo Album dialog box, pictures can easily be reordered by selecting the picture name and clicking the up or down arrows. Pictures can be rotated if their orientation needs to change, and even the brightness and contrast can be adjusted. These changes can be made at the time you create the Photo Album or later by editing it.

1. From the Insert tab, in the Illustrations group, click the lower half of the Photo Album button, then click **Edit Photo Album**.
2. In the Pictures in album list, highlight the picture named **tuna**. Click the reorder arrows as needed to move tuna to picture 3.
3. Highlight the picture named **avocado,** then click twice on the Increase Contrast button.
4. Highlight the picture named **apples,** then click once on the Increase Brightness button and click twice on the Increase Contrast button.
5. Click **Update** to accept these changes.
6. Continue to the next exercise.

Exercise 4-26 CONTROL ALBUM LAYOUT

Album Layout allows you to change the Picture layout from **Fit to slide** to different options with one to four pictures on a slide. You can choose to display titles for each slide or change to one of seven different Frame shapes for the pictures. Using Picture Options, you can choose to place captions below all pictures.

1. From the Insert tab, in the Illustrations group, click the lower half of the Photo Album button, then click **Edit Photo Album.**
2. For **Picture Layout**, change to **1 picture**.
3. Now **Picture Options** are available. Click **Captions below ALL pictures**.
4. For **Frame shape**, select several of the available options and notice how the effect is displayed in the thumbnail area on the right. Select **Simple Frame, White**.

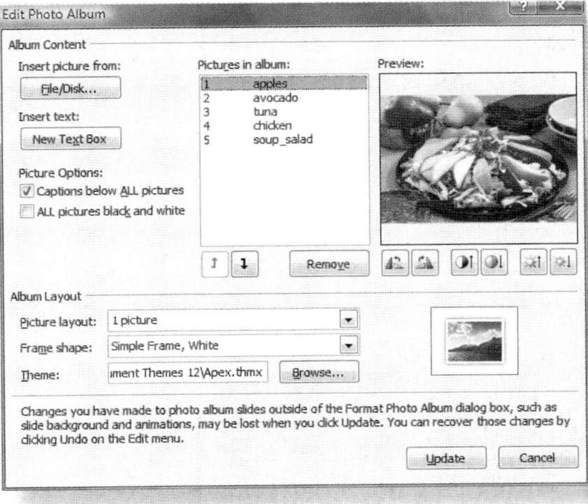

Figure 4-37
Photo Album edited options

5. Now apply a background theme that will provide soft coloring on the background behind the pictures. For the Theme, click Browse and choose **Apex**, then click **Select**. (You may have to navigate to your themes for Office 2007.)
6. Be sure the options on your Edit Photo Album dialog box match Figure 4-37. Click **Update**.

7. Now the pictures appear a little smaller on the slide and have a white frame with a subtle shadow effect, as shown in Figure 4-38. The **Apex** theme provides a soft background that is subtle and does not detract from the pictures.

Figure 4-38 Slide with framed picture

8. Notice that the file names for each picture now appear in text boxes below each picture. This text could now be changed to a more descriptive title for each salad.
9. On slide 1, key **New Salads** for the presentation title and key **Good 4 U** for the subtitle. Change the subtitle text size to 36 points and apply bold.
10. Add a header on the handout page with **[4-26your initials]** and nothing in the footer.
11. Save the presentation as **[4-26your initials]** in your Lesson 4 folder.
12. Highlight the picture named **apples,** then click once on the Increase Brightness button and click twice on the Increase Contrast button.
13. Close your presentation.

Lesson 4 Summary

- In addition to text placeholders, PowerPoint provides a variety of objects that you can use to enhance the visual appearance of your slides. These include shapes, text boxes, clip art, and pictures.
- PowerPoint's drawing tools enable you to create a variety of shapes including squares, circles, rectangles, ovals, and straight lines drawn at any angle.
- To draw a shape, from the Insert tab, in the Illustrations group, click the Shapes button, choose a shape, and then drag diagonally on your slide to create the shape in the size you need.
- If you don't like a shape you drew, select it and press Delete to remove it from your slide, or press Ctrl+Z to undo the action.

- Press Shift while drawing a line or other shape to constrain it. Constraining a shape makes it perfectly symmetrical, for example, a circle or a square, or it can make a line perfectly straight.
- Press Ctrl while drawing a shape to make it grow in size from the center instead of from one edge.
- Change the size of a drawn object by dragging one of its sizing handles (small white circles on its border) with a two-pointed arrow.
- To preserve an object's proportions when resizing it, hold down Shift while dragging a corner sizing handle.
- Move a drawn object by pointing to it and when the four-pointed arrow appears, drag the object to a new position.
- The Shapes gallery has many predefined shapes that are organized into several categories.
- When a shape is selected, text that you key appears inside the shape.
- Use the Clip Art task pane to search for clip art and photograph images. If you are connected to the Internet, the task pane's **Search** command will automatically search the Microsoft Office Online collection.
- To see the file properties of a clip art image or photograph, point to a clip art thumbnail in the Clip Art task pane, and then click the vertical bar that appears on the right side of the thumbnail (or right-click the thumbnail).
- Using the **Cut, Copy,** and **Paste** commands, you can easily move or copy clip art or other images from one slide to another or from one presentation to another.
- Using the **Duplicate** command is the quickest way to create a copy of an object on the same slide.
- Resize a clip art image by dragging one of its sizing handles. If you want to preserve proportions, drag a corner handle. If you want to distort the proportions, drag one of the side handles.
- From the Picture Tools Format tab, in the Adjust group, use tools to change a picture's brightness, contrast, and colors.
- Clip art images (vectors, bitmaps, or scanned images) can be cropped. Cropping is trimming away edges of a picture, much like using scissors to cut out a picture from a newspaper or magazine.
- WordArt enables you to create special effects with text that are not possible with standard text-formatting tools.
- WordArt is modified by using the WordArt Styles and Text Effects to change its appearance in many different ways. These options are available on the Drawing Tools Format tab when a WordArt object is selected.
- PowerPoint's Photo Album feature can be used to quickly create a presentation consisting mostly of pictures. One or more pictures can be placed on each slide with a choice of different framing techniques.
- Once a photo album is created, it can be modified by choosing the Edit Photo Album option to rearrange pictures, request captions, and add a theme. A photo album is saved as any other presentation.

LESSON 4 Command Summary

Feature	Button	Ribbon
Rectangle		
Oval		
Line		
Constrained line	Shift +	
Square	Shift +	
Circle	Shift +	
Shapes		Home tab, Drawing group, Shapes or Insert tab, Illustrations group, Shapes
Search for Clip Art and Photographs		Clip Art task pane, Search
Insert Pictures		Insert tab, Illustrations group, Picture
Adjust Picture Brightness		Picture Tools Format tab, Adjust group, Contrast
Adjust Picture Contrast		Picture Tools Format tab, Adjust group, Brightness
Adjust Picture Color		Picture Tools Format tab, Adjust group, Recolor
Change Picture Shape		Picture Tools Format tab, Picture Styles group, Picture Shape
Apply Picture Border		Picture Tools Format tab, Picture Styles group, Picture Border
Picture Effects		Picture Tools Format tab, Picture Styles group, Picture Effects
Crop a Picture		Picture Tools Format tab, Size group, Crop
Insert WordArt		Insert tab, Text group, WordArt
Apply WordArt Styles		Drawing Tools Format tab, WordArt Styles group, Quick Styles
Change WordArt Color		Drawing Tools Format tab, WordArt Styles group, Text Fill
Change WordArt Outline		Drawing Tools Format tab, WordArt Styles group, Text Outline
Apply WordArt Text Effects		Drawing Tools Format tab, WordArt Styles group, Text Effects

Lesson 5

Creating Tables

OBJECTIVES

After completing this lesson, you will be able to:

1. Create a table.
2. Draw a table.
3. Modify a table structure.
4. Align text and numbers.
5. Enhance the table.
6. Create a tabbed table.

MCAS OBJECTIVES

In this lesson:
PP07 2.1.6
PP07 3.7
PP07 3.7.1
PP07 3.7.2
PP07 3.7.3
PP07 3.7.4
See Appendix

Estimated Time: 2 hours

Tables display information organized in rows and columns. Once a table is created, you can modify its structure by adding columns or rows, plus you can merge and split cells to modify your table's design. Table content can be aligned in different ways for easy-to-read layouts. Color can be applied to highlight selected table cells or to add table borders. Working with tables in PowerPoint is similar to working with them in Word.

Creating a Table

A *table* consists of rows, columns, and cells. *Rows* consist of individual cells across the table horizontally. *Columns* consist of individual cells aligned vertically down the table. The *cell* is the intersection between the column and a row.

PowerPoint provides several convenient ways to create a table. With each method, you specify the number of columns and rows that you need.

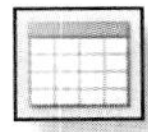

- Insert a new slide, choose the **Title and Content** layout, and click the Insert Table button.
- From the Insert tab, in the Tables group, click the Table button and choose **Insert Table**.
- From the Insert tab, in the Tables group, click the Table button, and drag the mouse to select the correct number of rows and columns.
- Draw a table using the Draw Table pen tool. To access this tool, click the Insert tab then in the Tables group, choose the Table button and then click **Draw Table**. Using the Pencil pointer, click and drag to create the size of the table and then divide it into columns and rows.
- Create a tabbed table using tab settings.

When you insert a table into your presentation, your Ribbon will change to show the Table Tools Design and Layout tabs. These tabs contain many options for formatting and modifying the table you have created.

Exercise 5-1 INSERT A TABLE

When you use the Insert Table button, you may define a table's dimensions by dragging down and across a grid to determine the number of rows and columns.

1. Open the file **Briefing1**. Insert a new slide after slide 1 that uses the **Title Only** slide layout. Key the title **Employment Levels 2006**. Resize the placeholder so the title fits on one row.
2. From the Insert tab, in the Tables group, choose the Insert Table button. A grid appears for defining the size of the table by selecting squares that represent table cells.
3. Drag your pointer down three squares and across four squares to define a 4 by 3 Table (four columns by three rows), as shown in Figure 5-1, then click your left mouse button to accept the table size.

Figure 5-1
Defining a table

4. Point to the table's border and use the four-pointed arrow to move the table down and to the right about one-half inch.
5. Key the text shown in Figure 5-2. Use your pointer to click into the first cell of the table, and then press Tab to move from cell to cell. Entering text in a PowerPoint table is similar to entering text in a Word table.
6. Leave the presentation open for the next exercise.

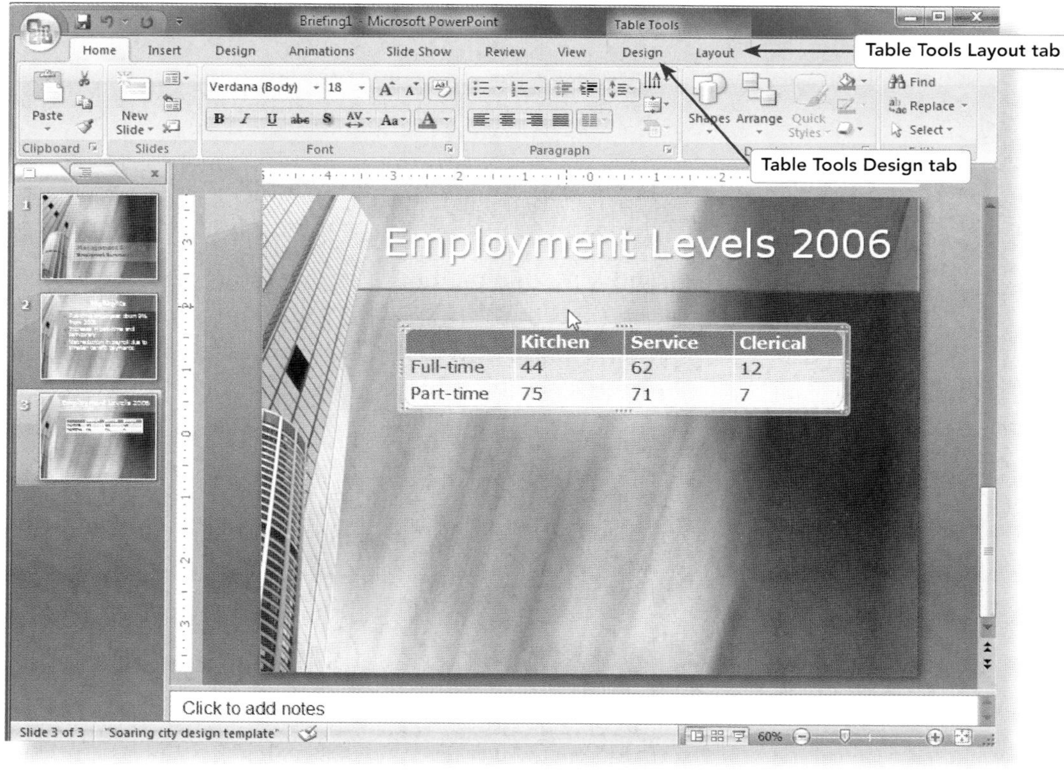

Figure 5-2
Table with text

Exercise 5-2 NAVIGATE IN A TABLE

NOTE

When a cell is blank, pressing the left arrow key ← or the right arrow key → moves the insertion point left or right one cell. If text is in a cell, the left and right arrow keys move the insertion point one character to the left or right.

NOTE

If you reach the end of the table move to step three. If you accidentally press Tab at the end of the table, it will add a new row to the table. Use the Undo Button to reverse this action.

There are several ways to navigate in a table:

- Click the cell with the I-beam.
- Use the arrow keys ←, →, ↑, or ↓.
- Press Tab to move forward or Shift+Tab to move backward.

1. Click in the first table cell. Notice the insertion point in the cell you clicked.
2. Press Tab several times. The insertion point moves through cells from left to right. When you reach the end of a row, pressing Tab moves the insertion point to the beginning of the next row.
3. Press Shift+Tab several times. The insertion point moves through cells from right to left.
4. Press each arrow key several times and observe the movement of the insertion point.
5. Leave the presentation open for the next exercise.

Exercise 5-3 SELECT TABLE STYLES

A *Table Style* is a combination of formatting options, including color combinations, based on your theme colors. A table style is applied automatically to any table that you add through the Insert Table feature. Thumbnails of table styles are shown in the Table Styles gallery found on the Table Tools Design tab in the Table Styles group, as shown in Figure 5-3. When your pointer is over any thumbnail in the gallery, you will see a live preview of what your table will look like if you apply this style.

1. Right-click in any of the table cells and choose **Select Table** from the shortcut menu.

2. From the Table Tools Design tab, in the Table Styles group, choose the More button to open the Table Styles Gallery.

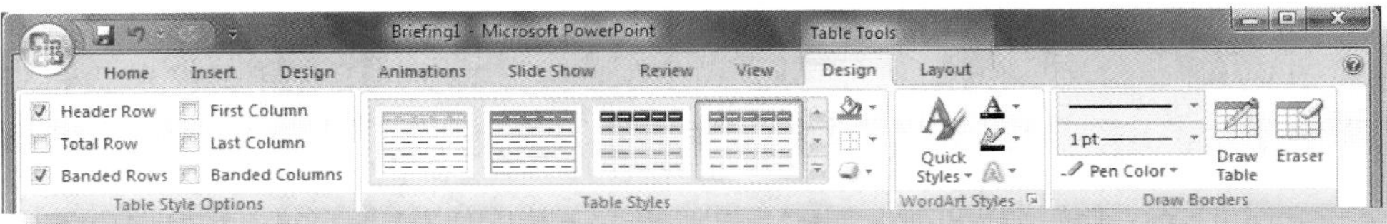

Figure 5-3
Table Tools Design tab

3. Place your pointer over several of the styles to see the ScreenTip with the name of the style, and preview the effect on your table.
4. From the **Best Match for Document** category, choose **Themed Style 1, Accent 6** by clicking on the thumbnail. Notice how this table style blends well with the background.
5. Leave the presentation open for the next exercise.

Exercise 5-4 APPLY TABLE STYLE OPTIONS

Table Style Options can be used to apply a table style to specific parts of your table.

- To emphasize the first row of the table, select the **Header Row** check box.
- To emphasize the last row of the table, select the **Total Row** check box.
- To have alternating striped rows, select the **Banded Rows** check box.
- To emphasize the first column of the table, select the **First Column** check box.
- To emphasize the last column of the table, select the **Last Column** check box.
- To have alternating striped columns, select the **Banded Column** check box.

1. With the table selected, from the Table Tools Design tab, in the Table Style Options group, click the **First Column** check box. Notice that the text in the first column now appears bold.

TIP

If you were comparing the number of kitchen staff versus the number of clerical staff, this formatting style would make the document easier to read. However, if you were comparing the number of full-time versus the number of part-time employees, the Banded Rows would be a better choice.

2. Click the **Header Row** check box to uncheck the box. Notice that the deep brown disappears and the banded rows alternate starting with the first row.
3. Click the Undo button to reapply the Header Row formatting.
4. Click the **Banded Rows** check box to uncheck the box.
5. Click the **Banded Columns** check box to apply a check in the box.
6. Leave the presentation open for the next exercise.

Drawing a Table

The Draw Table feature in PowerPoint provides a different method of creating a table. From the Insert tab, in the Tables group, click the Table button, and choose **Draw Table**. Using this method allows you to control the exact size of the table using the Pencil pointer to draw.

Exercise 5-5 USE PENCIL POINTER TO DRAW A TABLE

To draw a table, you first drag the *Pencil pointer* diagonally down and across to create a rectangle the approximate size of the table's outside border. Then you draw horizontal and vertical lines within the table to divide it into columns and rows.

1. Insert a new slide after slide 3 that uses the **Title Only** slide layout. Key the title **Employment Levels 2007**. Resize the placeholder to fit the text on one row.
2. From the Insert tab, in the Tables group, click the Table button, and then choose **Draw Table**.
3. Using the Pencil pointer, drag from under the left edge of the title (down and to the right) to create a rectangle that fills the available space. See Figure 5-4 for size and placement. At this point, you have a one-cell table.

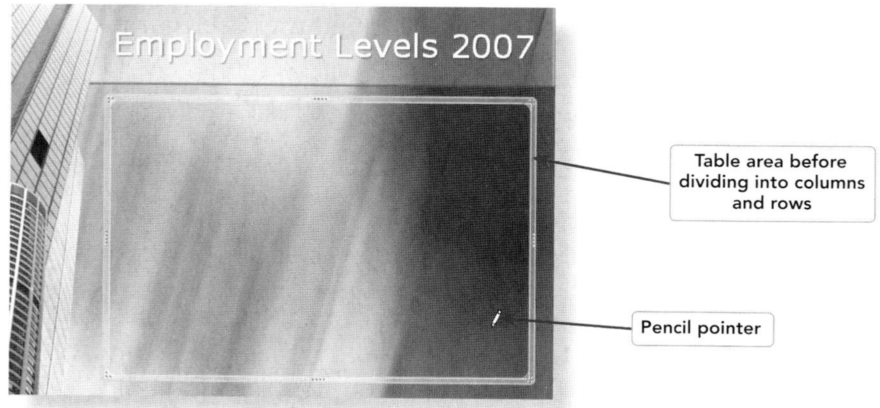

Figure 5-4
Using the Pencil pointer

4. The Pencil pointer creates rows and columns when you draw borders within the table area. Be sure the pointer is inside the table before you start drawing so the lines you draw divide the table space. If the pointer touches the table border, a new table will be created. (If this happens, press Ctrl+Z to undo the action and try again.)

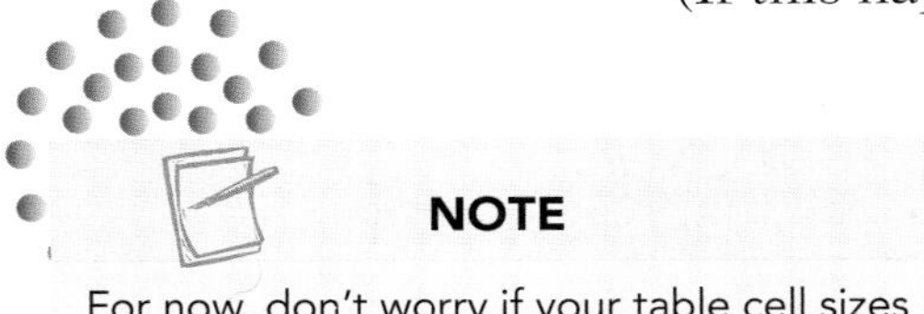

NOTE

For now, don't worry if your table cell sizes do not perfectly match Figure 5-5 or if your text wraps within the cell. You will learn how to adjust cell sizes later in the lesson.

5. With the table selected, from the Table Tools Design tab, click the Draw Table button and draw a line through the middle of the table area. Each time you draw a line, one cell is split into two cells. Because you are drawing horizontal lines now, the cells you are splitting create the table rows. Draw two more horizontal lines to create four rows in the table as shown in Figure 5-5.
6. Now, split the table with four vertical lines extending from the top of the table to create 5 columns.
7. From the Table Tools Design tab, in the Draw Borders group, click **Draw Table** to turn off the Pencil pointer.
8. Key the table text shown in Figure 5-5. Leave the presentation open for the next exercise.

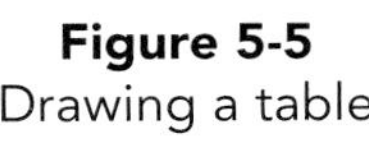

Figure 5-5
Drawing a table

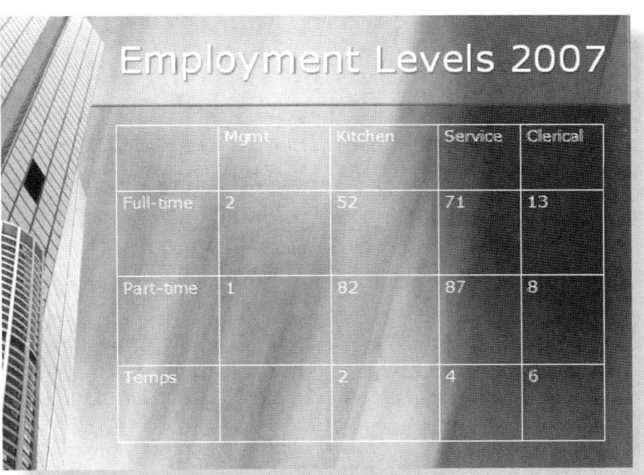

Exercise 5-6 CHANGE TABLE TEXT DIRECTION

Text direction changes can affect the appearance of a table and how it fits within a given space. If the title is the only long part about the column, changing the column title text direction allows you to fit more columns in a given area. Text direction in a table can be changed in two ways:

NOTE

Some of your titles may wrap onto the next line even in the middle of words. You will fix this in a later exercise.

- From the Table Tools Layout tab (see Figure 5-6), in the Alignment group, select the Text Direction button.
- From the Home tab, in the Paragraph group, select the Text Direction button.

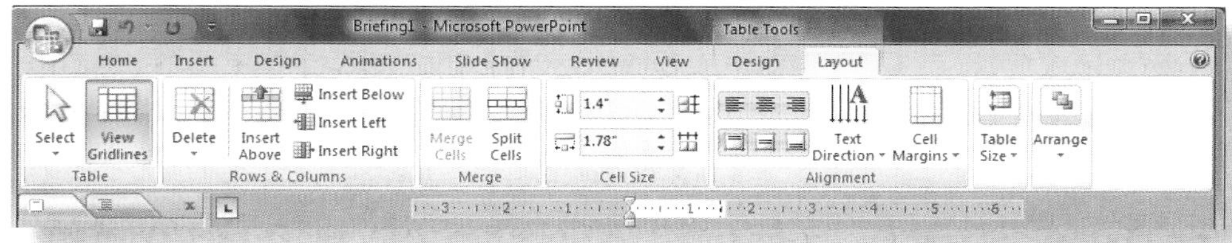

Figure 5-6 Table Tools Layout tab

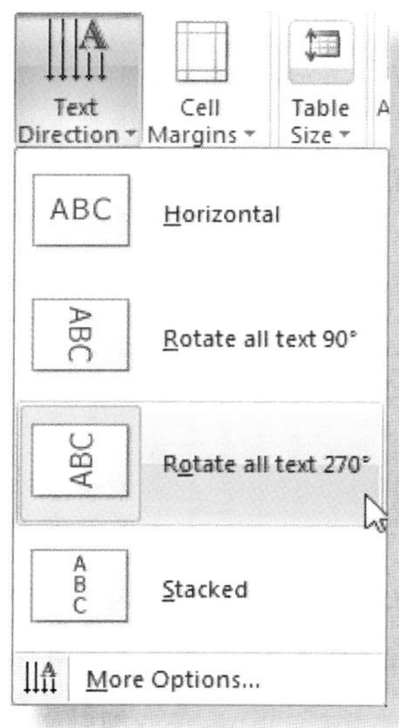

Figure 5-7 Text Direction drop-down list

1. Click in the cell that reads **Mgmt**.
2. From the Table Tools Layout tab, in the Alignment group, click Text Direction button.
3. From the drop-down list, choose **Rotate all text 270°** as shown in Figure 5-7.
4. Notice how the text reads going up in the cell. Change the text direction in the same manner for **Kitchen**, **Service**, and **Clerical**.

Exercise 5-7 APPLY SHADING AND BORDERS

When you first draw a table, the table cells contain no shading, allowing the slide's background to show. You can apply a shading color or other shading alternatives, such as a gradient, or picture effect to one or more cells in your table. Applying shading to a table is similar to applying shading to other PowerPoint objects. All of the shading options are available from Table Tools Design tab, in the Table Styles group, from the Shading button drop-down list. Applying shading involves two-steps:

- First, select the cells to which you want to apply the shading effect.
- Second, click the Shading button and choose the shading you wish to apply.

Table borders are the lines forming the edges of cells, columns, rows, and the outline of the table. From the Table Tools Design tab, in the Table Styles group, the Borders button drop-down list enables you to apply borders to all the cells in a selection, to just an outside border, or to just the inside borders separating one cell from another. Applying table borders is a three-step process:

- First, select the cells to which you want to apply the border effect.
- Second, select the border style, border width, and border color you want.
- Third, click the Borders button and choose an option from the drop-down list.

1. On slide 4, with the table active, select all the cells in the top row by moving your pointer to the left of row 1 until you get a solid black arrow pointing at the row. Click to select the whole row.
2. From the Table Tools Design tab, in the Table Styles group, click the Shading button and choose **Gray-25%, Accent 4, Darker 25%** from the Theme Colors area.
3. Change the font color for the selected row to **Gray-25%, Accent 4, Darker 90%**.

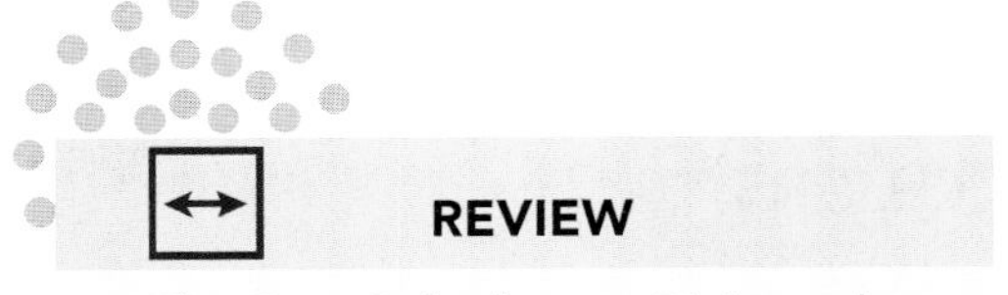

REVIEW

The Font Color button is on the Home tab, in the Font group. You can also right-click to access the floating font group to make font changes.

4. Select the first column in the table by pointing to the top of the first column until you get a solid black arrow pointing down at the column. Apply the same **Gray-25%, Accent 4, Darker 25%**, and change the font color to **Red, Accent 1, Darker 50%**.
5. Select all the cells that contain numbers by clicking in the first number cell and dragging your pointer down and to the right to the last number cell.
6. From the Table Tools Design tab, in the Table Styles group, click the Shading button and apply a white color. With these cells still selected, change the font color to the **Red, Accent 1, Darker 50%** matching the first column.
7. Click outside the table to observe the effect. Now the table has an appearance that distinguishes it from the slide background. Compare your table to Figure 5-8.

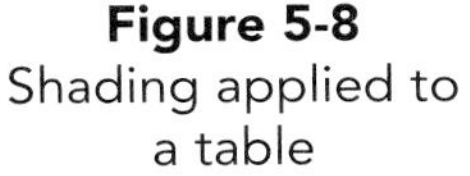

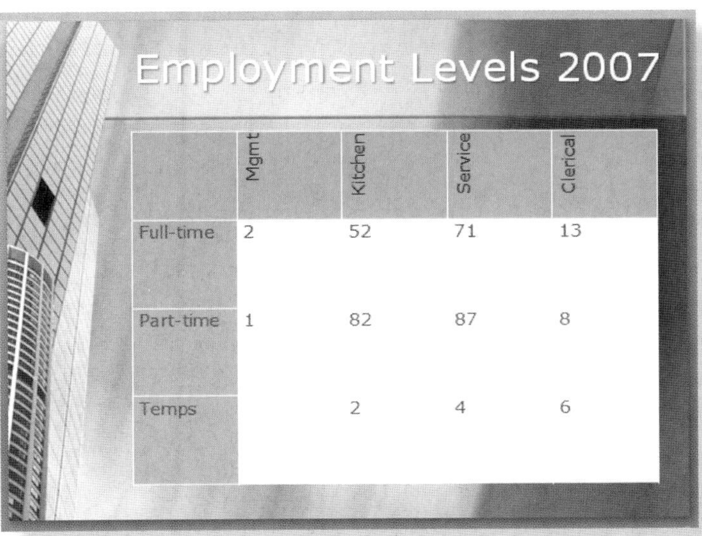

Figure 5-8
Shading applied to a table

8. Select the whole table by right-clicking any cell within the table and choosing **Select Table** from the shortcut menu.

9. From the Table Tools Design tab, in the Draw Borders group, click the Pen Weight button and change to **2¼ pt**.

10. Still working in the Draw Borders group, click the Pen Color button, and choose **Red, Accent 1**.
11. Click the Borders button in the Table Styles group, and choose **Top Border**. Repeat this step for the **Bottom Border** and the **Inside Horizontal Border**. Click outside the table to deselect the table and notice the difference in the table with some added borders.

Exercise 5-8 CHANGE BORDER AND SHADING COLORS

Table Border and Shading styles can be changed at any point while creating your presentations.

1. Select any cell in your table. From the Table Tools Design tab, in the Draw Borders group, click Pen Style and choose the second style down (a dashed line).

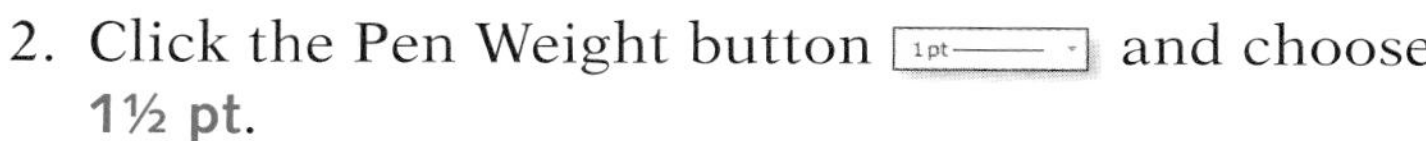

2. Click the Pen Weight button and choose **1½ pt**.
3. Click the Pen Color button and choose **Gray-25%, Accent 4**.
4. Right-click in the table and choose **Select Table**.
5. Click the drop-down list arrow for the Borders button, and choose **Inside Borders**, as shown in Figure 5-9. The inside borders of the table are now dashed lines.

TIP

You can use the pencil tool to change the color and style of a border. Set the border options in the Draw Borders group. Then, instead of clicking the Borders button, use the pencil to click the borders you want to change.

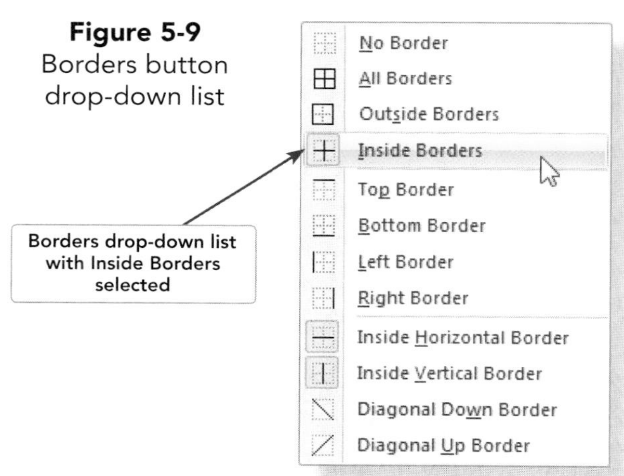

Figure 5-9 Borders button drop-down list

6. Still working on slide 4, select row 2 of the table. From the Table Tools Design tab, in the Table Styles group, click the Shading button and choose **White, Text 1** to change the Shading to white for row 2.
7. Select row 3 of the table. Still working in the Table Styles group, click the Shading button and choose **Gray-25%, Accent 4, Darker 25%** to change the shading to gray for row 3.
8. Select row 4 of the table. Click the Shading button and choose **White, Text 1** to change the Shading to white for row 4, as shown in Figure 5-10.

Figure 5-10
Completed table

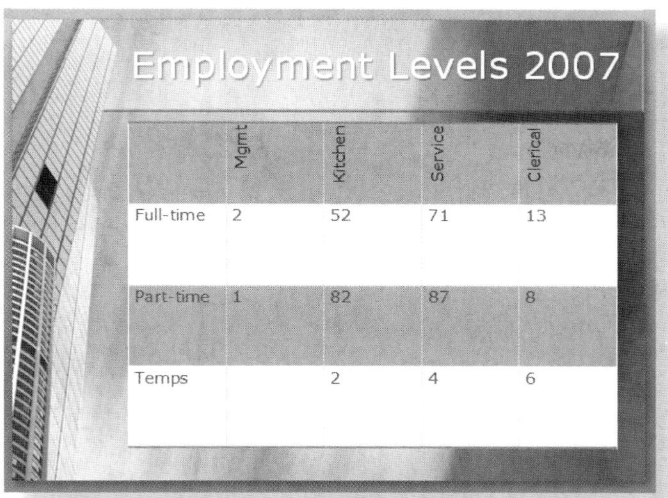

Exercise 5-9 ERASE CELL BORDERS

The *Eraser* can be used to delete borders between cells.

1. Click in the last cell of the table on slide 4. Click Tab one time. Notice that PowerPoint automatically inserts another row below the last row in the table.
2. From the Table Tools Design tab, in the Draw Borders group, choose the Eraser .
3. Click each of the four borders that divide the last row of the table into five cells. Notice that as you click each border, it disappears. When all four are removed, the last row is turned into one cell.
4. Press Esc to turn off the Eraser. Click in the last row and key **Estimated Projection**. Your table may now extend past the bottom of the slide. This will be corrected later.
5. Create a new folder for Lesson 5 and save the presentation as **[5-9your initials]** in your new Lesson 5 folder.
6. Leave the presentation open for the next exercise.

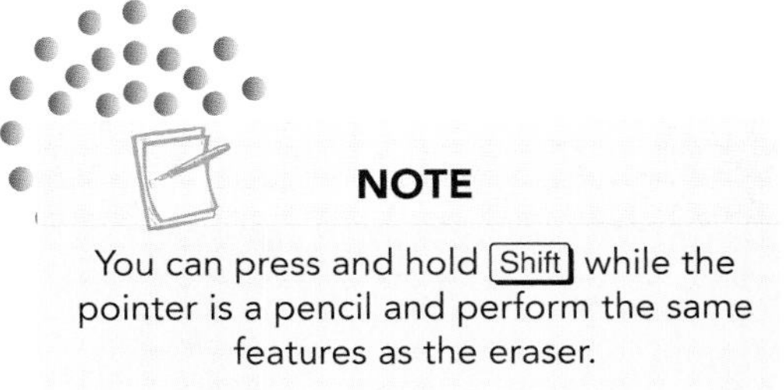

NOTE

You can press and hold Shift while the pointer is a pencil and perform the same features as the eraser.

Modifying Table Structure

When you create a table, you decide how many rows and columns the table should have. After entering some data, you might discover that you have too many columns or perhaps too few rows. Or, you might want one row or column to have more or fewer cells than the others. You can modify your table structure by inserting or deleting columns, merging a group of cells, or splitting an individual cell into two or more cells.

Exercise 5-10 INSERT AND DELETE ROWS AND COLUMNS

Columns and rows can be inserted using three methods:

- From the Table Tools Layout tab, in the Rows & Columns group, choose which option you would like to insert.
- Right-click a cell in the table and use commands on the shortcut menu.
- Insert a row at the bottom of the table by pressing Tab if you're in the last cell of the last table row. This is convenient if you run out of rows while you're entering data.

Columns can be inserted either to the right or the left of the column that contains the active cell. The column formatting of the active column is copied to the new column or the table style is applied. Rows can be inserted above or below the row that contains the active cell. The row formatting of the active row is copied or the table style is applied to the new row.

1. Move to slide 2, select the "Kitchen" column.
2. Right-click the selected column and click **Insert** and choose **Insert Columns to the Left** from the shortcut menu, as shown in Figure 5-11. A new column appears to the left of "Kitchen." It is the same size as the "Kitchen" column and has the formatting of the table style applied. The table is wider to accommodate the extra column.

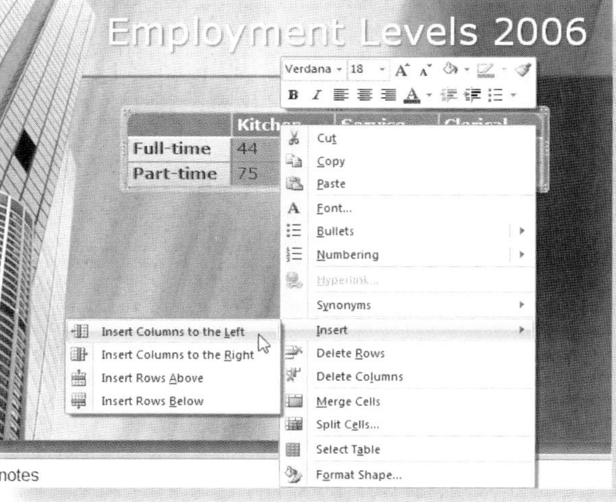

Figure 5-11
Inserting a column through the shortcut menu

3. Click the blank cell in the upper-left corner of the table.
4. From the Table Tools Layout tab, in the Rows & Columns group, click the Insert Right button. A new column appears to the right of the selected cell, and it is the same size and formatted with the selected table style.

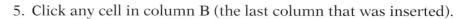

5. Click any cell in column B (the last column that was inserted).

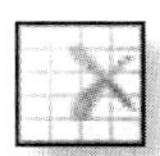

6. From the Table Tools Layout tab, in the Rows & Columns group, click the Delete button then choose **Delete Columns**. The new column is deleted, and the table is resized. Your table should now have one blank column located to the left of the "Kitchen" column and some of your titles may be wrapped to two lines. This will be fixed later.

NOTE

If more than one column is selected when you use the **Delete Columns** command, all the selected columns will be deleted.

7. Still working on the Table Tools Layout tab, in the Rows & Columns group, select one cell in the second table row and click the Insert Below button.

8. Click the last cell in the last row, containing the number "7." Press Tab. A new row is inserted at the bottom of the table.

9. Select cells in the blank row below the text "Full-time," right-click the selected cells, and choose **Delete Rows** from the shortcut menu.

10. Complete the table by keying the information shown in Figure 5-12 into the blank row and blank column.

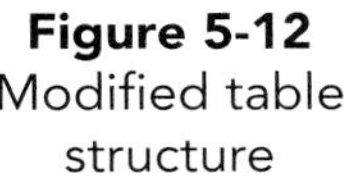

Figure 5-12
Modified table structure

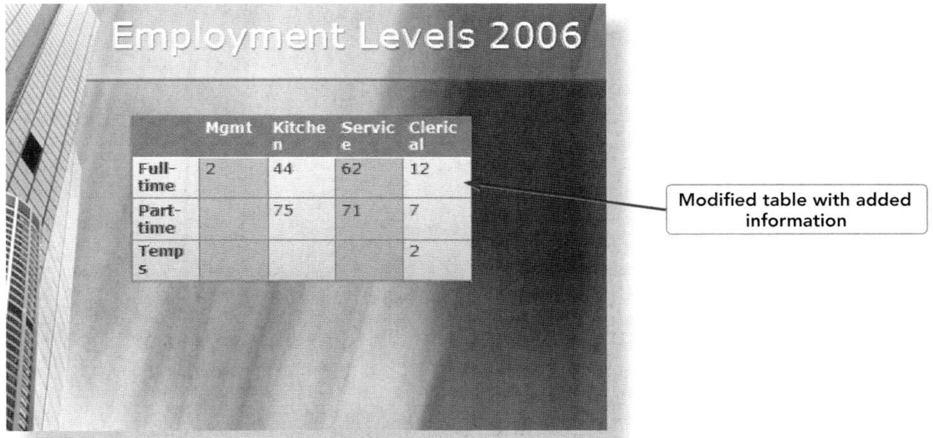

Exercise 5-11 MERGE AND SPLIT CELLS

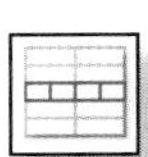

As you discovered when drawing the table, you can split cells by drawing a line through them with the Pencil pointer. You can also split a cell by using the *Split Cells* button on the Table Tools Layout tab in the Merge group, or by right-clicking the cell and choosing **Split Cells** from the shortcut menu.

Cells can be merged together in several ways. As you learned in a previous exercise, the Eraser button removes borders between two adjacent cells to create one cell. You can merge cells by selecting two or more cells, and then from the Table Tools Layout tab, in the Merge group, click the *Merge Cells*

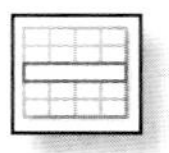

button or by right-clicking the selected cells and choosing **Merge Cells** from the shortcut menu.

1. Move to slide 4. At the bottom of the table, click the cell containing the text "Estimated Projection."
2. From the Table Tools Layout tab, in the Merge group, click the Split Cells button. Change the number of columns to **1** and the number of rows to **2**. The selected cell becomes two cells.
3. Click **OK**.
4. In the new cell, key **Revised Figures**.
5. Select the first three cells in the second row that begins "Full-time."
6. Still working on the Table Tools Layout tab, in the Merge group, click the Merge Cells button. The three cells transform into one wide cell. The text and numbers from the merged cells all appear in one cell.
7. Click the Undo button to return the merged cells to their previous state.
8. Leave the presentation open for the next exercise.

Exercise 5-12 APPLY A DIAGONAL BORDER

Borders can be placed diagonally within a cell. For example, if you are using a PowerPoint table to create a calendar, you might want to put two dates in the same square, separated by a diagonal line. Applying a diagonal border in this way does not create two separate cells, but is merely a line drawn within one cell. You can make it look like two cells by carefully placing text inside the cell.

1. Still working on slide 4, select the two rows at the bottom of the table, and then right-click and choose **Merge Cells** from the shortcut menu to combine the two cells into one. The text "Revised Figures" now appears on a separate line below "Estimated Projection" in one cell.
2. With the table active, move to the bottom of the table in the center at the sizing handle, and click and drag up to fit within the slide.
3. From the Table Tools Design tab, in the Draw Borders group, change the pen style to a **dashed line**, **1½-point**, **Gray-25%**, **Accent 4**, **Darker 50%** gray line. Your pointer has been changed to a pencil.
4. Position the pencil tool near, but not touching, the lower-left corner of the cell in the last row. Draw a diagonal line across the cell to the upper-right corner, as shown in Figure 5-13.

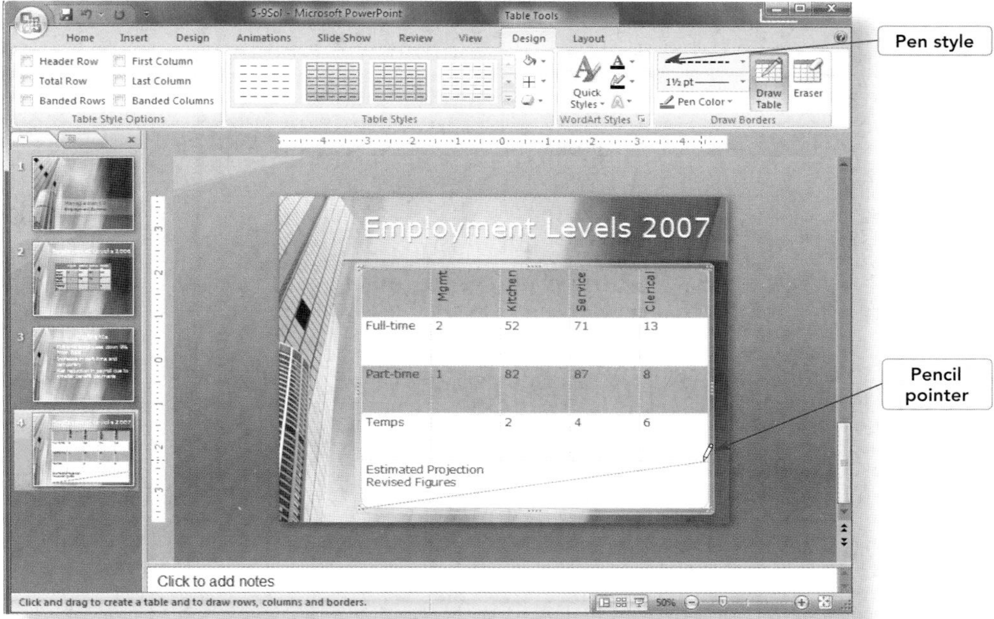

Figure 5-13
Using the Pencil pointer to add a diagonal border

NOTE

Be careful where you start drawing. If you touch one of the cell borders with the pencil, the formatting of that border might change. If that happens, use Undo to restore it.

5. Press Esc to turn off the Pencil pointer. Deselect the table to see the result. In a later exercise, you will apply text alignment to give this the appearance of a split cell.

Exercise 5-13 DISTRIBUTE COLUMN WIDTH AND ROW HEIGHT

If you decide to add rows or columns, or if you decide to make a column wider, the table may no longer fit on a slide. You can make a table smaller or larger by dragging its sizing handles, and you can change the height of rows and the width of columns individually by dragging cell borders. You can also choose the exact height and width of the cells by using the Cell Size group on the Table Tools Layout tab.

From the Table Tools Layout tab, in the Cell size group, use the *Distribute Columns* button to easily adjust several columns to be the same width. The *Distribute Rows* button works in a similar way.

1. Move to slide 2, move your pointer over the right border of the first column until the pointer changes to a two-pointed arrow.

2. Using this pointer, click and drag the column border to the right making the column wide enough so that the text "Part-time" appears on one line, as shown in Figure 5-14. The column width increases, and the adjacent column becomes smaller. Now the second column might be too narrow for the word "Kitchen."
3. Use the arrow pointer to double-click the right border of the "Kitchen" column. Double-clicking a right border makes the column wide enough to accommodate the widest text line in the column.
4. Double-click the right border of each of the remaining columns to allow the widest text to be all on one line.
5. Position your pointer on the bottom border of the first row. When the pointer changes to, click and drag the bottom border down, so that the row is approximately half again its original height.

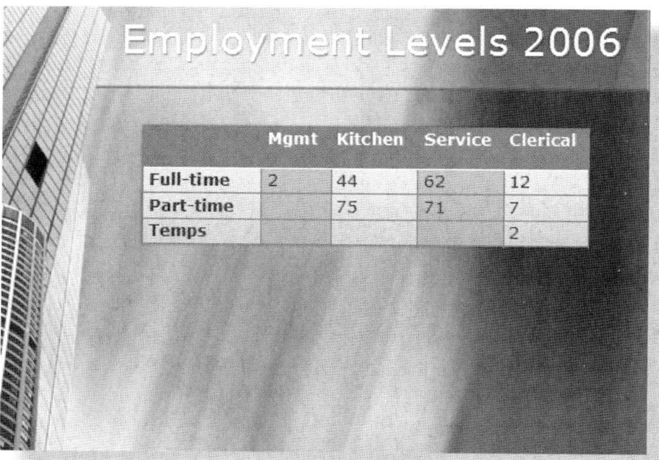

Figure 5-14
Resizing column width and row height

6. Move to slide 4. Select the "Mgmt," "Kitchen," "Service," and "Clerical" columns by dragging across the second, third, fourth, and fifth cells in any row (or drag the small, black, down-facing arrow just above the top border of the four columns).
7. From the Table Tools Layout tab, in the Cell Size group, click the Distribute Columns button. The four selected columns are now all the same width.
8. Select the second through fourth cells in the first column.
9. Click the Distribute Rows button. Now the second through fourth rows are exactly the same height.
10. Select the last row of the table. From the Table Tools Layout tab, in the Cell Size group, change the height to **.7"** so the table fits better on the slide.

11. Create a handout header and footer: Include the date and your name as the header, and the page number and text **[5-13your initials]** as the footer.
12. Save the presentation as **[5-13your initials]** in your Lesson 5 folder.

Aligning Text and Numbers

Text and numbers in a table cell can be aligned vertically or horizontally. You can specify that text or numbers appear at the top, middle, or bottom of a cell, and be horizontally left-, center-, or right-aligned.

In addition, you can use *Cell Margin* settings to refine even further the position of text and numbers in a cell. A cell margin is the space between the text in a cell and its borders.

Exercise 5-14 ALIGN TEXT AND NUMBERS HORIZONTALLY

Text is aligned horizontally within cells in the same manner that you align text in other PowerPoint objects by using the alignment buttons on the Home tab, in the Paragraph group, or by right-clicking to access the floating font group.

1. On slide 2, select the cells in the first row that contain the text "Mgmt," "Kitchen," "Service," and "Clerical."
2. From the Home tab, in the Paragraph group, click the Center button. The text is horizontally centered in each cell.
3. Select all the cells that contain numbers and right-click. From the floating font group that appears, click the right-align button.
4. Move to slide 4. In the last row of the table, select the text "Revised Figures." From the Home tab, in the Paragraph group, click the right-align button. This gives the appearance that the cell is actually split instead of just having a border in it.

Exercise 5-15 CHANGE THE VERTICAL POSITION OF TEXT IN A CELL

The appearance of a table is often improved by changing the vertical alignment of text or objects within cells.

1. On slide 4, select the cells in the first row that contain the text "Mgmt," "Kitchen," "Service," and "Clerical."

2. From the Table Tools Layout tab, in the alignment group, choose the Center Vertically button. The text in the selected cells is now in the center of the cells.
3. Select all the cells in the second, third, and fourth rows.

4. Click the Align Bottom button. The text moves to the bottom edge of the cells.

Exercise 5-16 USE MARGIN SETTINGS TO ADJUST THE POSITION OF TEXT IN A CELL

Sometimes, the horizontal and vertical alignment settings do not place text precisely where you want it to be in a cell. You might be tempted to use Spacebar to indent the text, but that usually doesn't work well.

You can precisely control where text is placed in a cell by using the cell's margin settings, combined with horizontal and vertical alignment, as shown in Figure 5-15. For example, you can right-align a column of numbers and also have them appear centered in the column.

1. Move to slide 2. Select all the cells that contain numbers (blank cells in the third and fourth rows, too).

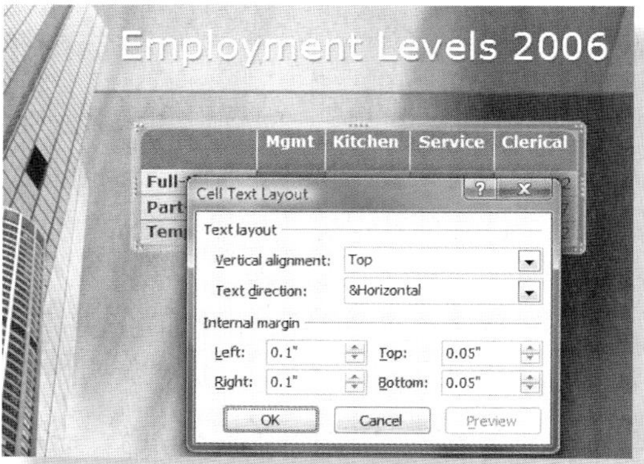

Figure 5-15
Using the Cell Text Layout dialog box to control cell margins

2. From the Table Tools Layout tab, in the Alignment group, click Cell Margins. From the drop-down list, click **Custom Margins**.
3. Click the **Vertical alignment** list box arrow to see the other settings. Choose **Middle**.
4. Under Internal margin, change the **Right** setting to **0.5"** and then click **OK**. The numbers are still right-aligned, but some space is between the cell border and the numbers, as shown in Figure 5-16.
5. Select all the cells in the first column containing text, and change the left margin to **0.2"**.

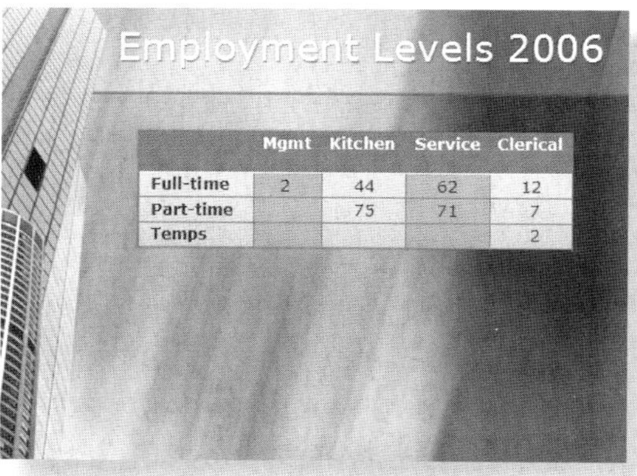

Figure 5-16
Table with improved alignment

Exercise 5-17 RESIZE A TABLE

To resize the entire table, drag one of the sizing handles. When you drag, make sure the pointer is one of these shapes , , , and not the pointer used for changing column width or row height .

If you hold down Shift while dragging a corner sizing handle, the table will resize proportionately. Whenever possible, depending on how large or small you make the table, the relative proportions of row heights and column widths are preserved.

1. Move to slide 4, and click anywhere inside the table. Notice the eight sizing handles around the border (one in each corner, and one in the middle of each side). They work just like sizing handles on other PowerPoint objects.
2. Using the diagonal two-pointed arrow , drag the lower-right corner up and to the left about ½ inch. The table becomes smaller, and the relative size of the rows and columns is preserved. Notice that your titles are wrapping onto two lines again.
3. Select the entire table and change the font size to 24 points. Resize the first row and first column as necessary to get the titles all on one row, as shown in Figure 5-17.
4. Position the table attractively on the slide by using the same method that you use to move text boxes or other objects.

TIP

Click in the table and then move your pointer to an outside border. When you get a four-pointed arrow, you may click and drag the table to position it.

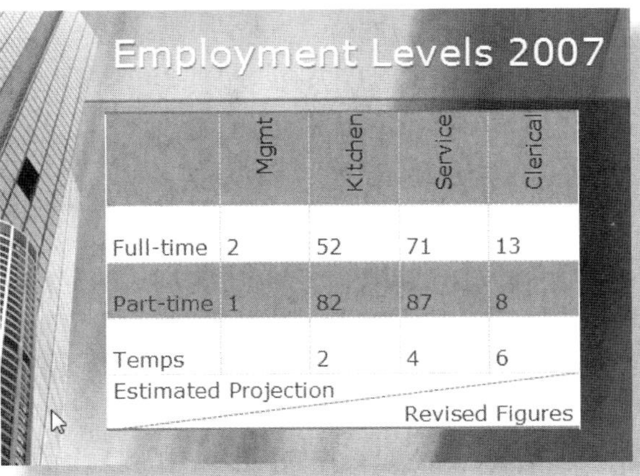

Figure 5-17
Resized table

Enhancing the Table

You can enhance a table by adding one of the many three-dimensional effects available in PowerPoint 2007. Graphic images and shading effects also improve the appearance of tables.

Images can be added in open cells or across the full table; shading effects can be applied in the same manner.

Exercise 5-18 APPLY AND MODIFY A CELL BEVEL EFFECT

The *Cell Bevel* effect is a dimensional effect that can be applied to make cells look raised and rounded or pressed in, as shown in Figure 5-18. The Cell Bevel effect is found on the Table Tools Design tab, in the Table Styles group, under the Effects button.

1. On Slide 4, select the whole table. From the Table Tools Design tab, in the Table Styles group, click the Effects button. A drop-down list displays effects that can be applied to a table.
2. Choose **Cell Bevel** then choose **Riblet**. Notice the effect that is applied to the table.
3. With the table still selected, click the Effects button and choose **Cell Bevel** and **No Bevel**. This removes the bevel effect.
4. Click the Effects button again, choose **Cell Bevel**, then choose **Relaxed Inset**.

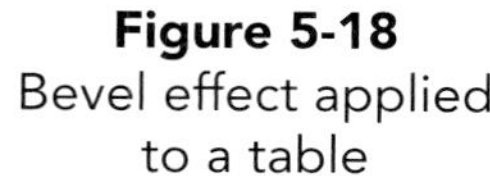

Figure 5-18
Bevel effect applied to a table

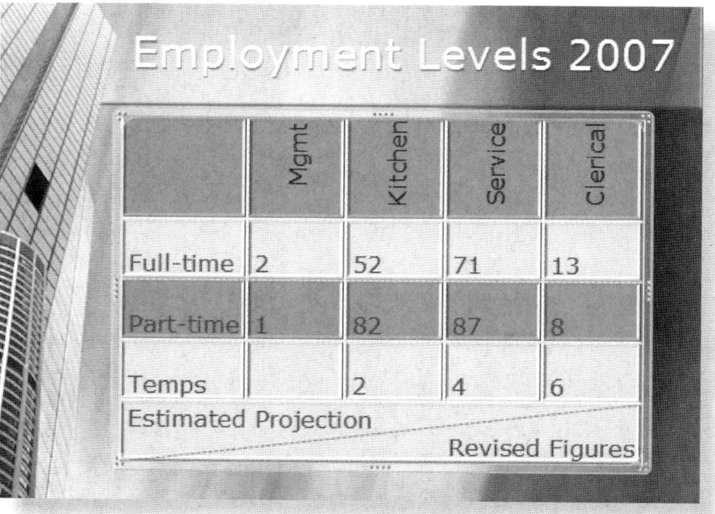

Exercise 5-19 APPLY AND MODIFY A SHADOW EFFECT

Another dimensional effect is the *Shadow* effect. You may modify where the shadow is cast, what color the shadow is, and many other aspects of the shadow. The shadow effect can be applied from the Table Tools Design tab in the Table Styles group, under the Effects button.

1. Still working on slide 4, select the table. From the Table Tools Design tab, in the Table Styles group, click the Effects button. A drop-down list displays effects that can be applied to a table.
2. Choose **Shadow** and move your pointer over several of the options. Notice the effect that the shadow has on the table.

3. Without selecting a shadow, choose **Shadow Options** at the bottom of the drop-down list. The Format Shape dialog box appears and allows you to control every aspect of the shadow.
4. Under **Presets**, in the **Outer** group, choose **Offset Diagonal Bottom Right**.
5. Under **Color**, choose **Red, Accent 1, Darker 25%**.
6. Change the other settings as follows:
   - Transparency, **34%**
   - Size, **100%**
   - Blur, **4 pt.**
   - Angle, **180°**
   - Distance, **13 pt.**
7. Click **Close** on the dialog box to return to your presentation. Notice the effect that the shadow applies to your table, as shown in Figure 5-19.

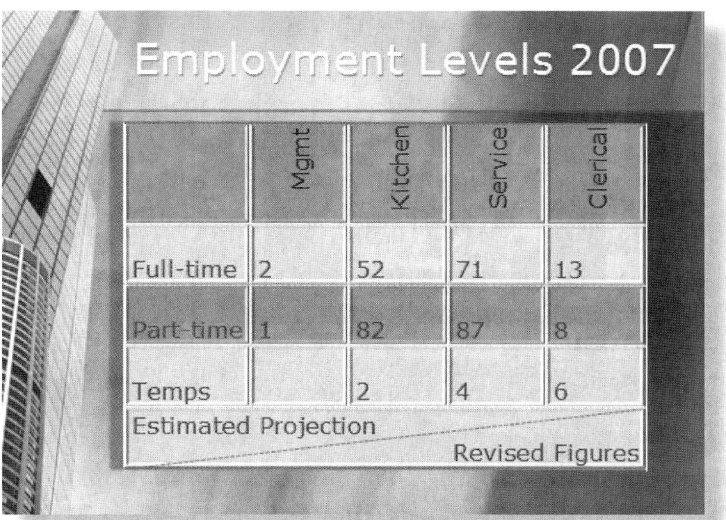

Figure 5-19
Shadow effect applied to table

Exercise 5-20 APPLY AND MODIFY A REFLECTION EFFECT

The *Reflection* effect makes the table appear to be reflecting on a body of water or a mirror. Several preset reflection effects are available to be applied to a table. The Reflection effect is found on the Table Tools Design tab, in the Table Styles group, under the Effects button.

1. Move to slide 2, and select the table.
2. From the Table Tools Design tab, in the Table Styles group, click the Effects button. A drop-down list displays effects that can be applied to a table.

3. Choose **Reflection** and move your pointer over several of the options. Notice the effect that each reflection has on the table.
4. Choose the **Half Reflection, 8 pt Offset** option. The lower half of the table is reflected and the reflection is offset from the bottom of the table, as shown in Figure 5-20.
5. Leave the presentation open for the next exercise.

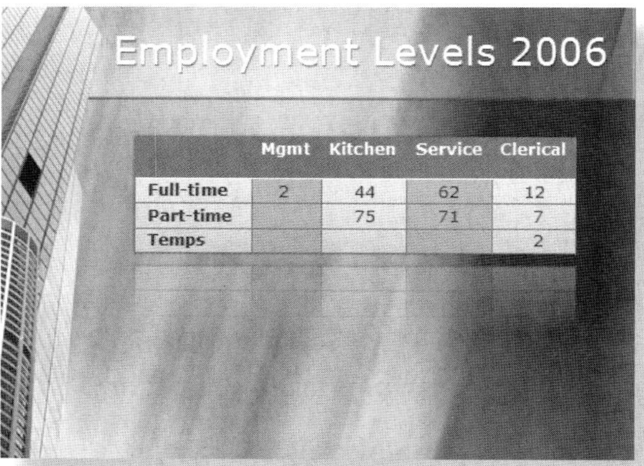

	Mgmt	Kitchen	Service	Clerical
Full-time	2	44	62	12
Part-time		75	71	7
Temps				2

Figure 5-20
Reflection effect applied to a table

Exercise 5-21 INSERT A PICTURE AND APPLY GRADIENT SHADING

Pictures within a table can help viewers understand the context of the data in the table. Gradient shading on rows or columns can add interest or perhaps make text easier to read.

1. On slide 4, with the table active, click in the first cell of the table.
2. From the Table Tools Design tab, in the Table Styles group, click the Shading button and choose **Picture**. A picture can be inserted in one cell, a selection of cells, or an entire table.
3. Locate your student files for Lesson 5, and double-click on **Employees** to insert the picture into the table.
4. Select the last four cells in the first row in the table. Still working on the Table Tools Design tab, in the Table Styles group, click the Shading button and choose **Gradient**.
5. In the **Light Variation** category, choose the **Linear Down** pattern of gradient fill.
6. Select row three and apply the **Linear Down** pattern of gradient fill.
7. Select row five and apply the color **Gray-25%, Accent 4, Darker 25%** first, then repeat the process of applying a **Linear Down** pattern of gradient fill for row five.
8. Click outside the table to observe the effects. Compare your table to Figure 5-21.

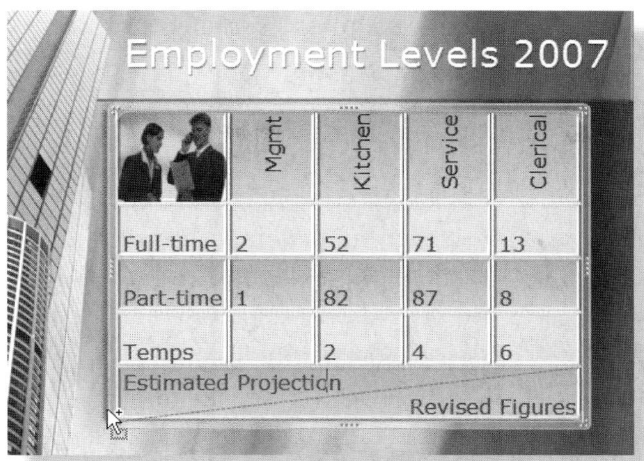

Figure 5-21
Gradient shading effects applied to a table

9. Update the handout footer to include the text **[5-21your initials]**.
10. Save the presentation as **[5-21your initials]** in your Lesson 5 folder. Leave it open for the next exercise.

Creating a Tabbed Table

In this lesson, you have learned several ways to create tables using PowerPoint's table tools. You can also create tables through tab settings using the *Ruler*. Sometimes information can be effectively displayed with just a very simple table.

Exercise 5-22 SET AND EDIT TABS

In PowerPoint you set tabs on the Ruler the same way you set tabs in Word, and they are left-aligned by default. However, PowerPoint's default tabs are set at one-inch intervals. To set your own tabs, click the Tab Type button (in the upper-left corner of the Slide pane, where the two rulers meet) to choose the alignment style. Then click the ruler at the location where you want to set a tab.

1. Insert a new slide after slide 4 that uses the **Title Only** slide layout.
2. From the View tab, in the Show/Hide group, check the box beside the **Ruler** if the Ruler is not displayed already.
3. Key the title **Employment Change Summary**. The title will appear on two lines.
4. Draw a text box starting an inch to the left and below the word "Employment" and extending it to the right to a similar position (approximately seven inches wide).

5. Key the following, pressing Tab where indicated: **Department** Tab **Status** Tab **2006** Tab **2007** Tab **% Change**.
6. Select the text box, apply bold, and change the font color to **Brown, Accent 6**.

NOTE

Tabs are set when the Tab Type symbol appears on the ruler. The tabs you set override the default tabs, and the default tabs are removed. It might take some practice before you are comfortable with tab type selection and tab placement.

7. Click anywhere within the text box to activate the text box ruler. If the ruler is still not showing, click the View tab and choose **ruler** in the show/hide group.
8. Click the Tab Type button at the left end of the horizontal ruler. Each time you click the button, a different tab type icon appears, enabling you to cycle through the four tab type choices, as shown in Table 5-1 and Figure 5-22.

TABLE 5-1 Types of Tabs

Tab	Purpose
	Left-aligns text at the tab setting
	Centers text at the tab setting
	Right-aligns text at the tab setting
	Aligns decimal points at the tab setting

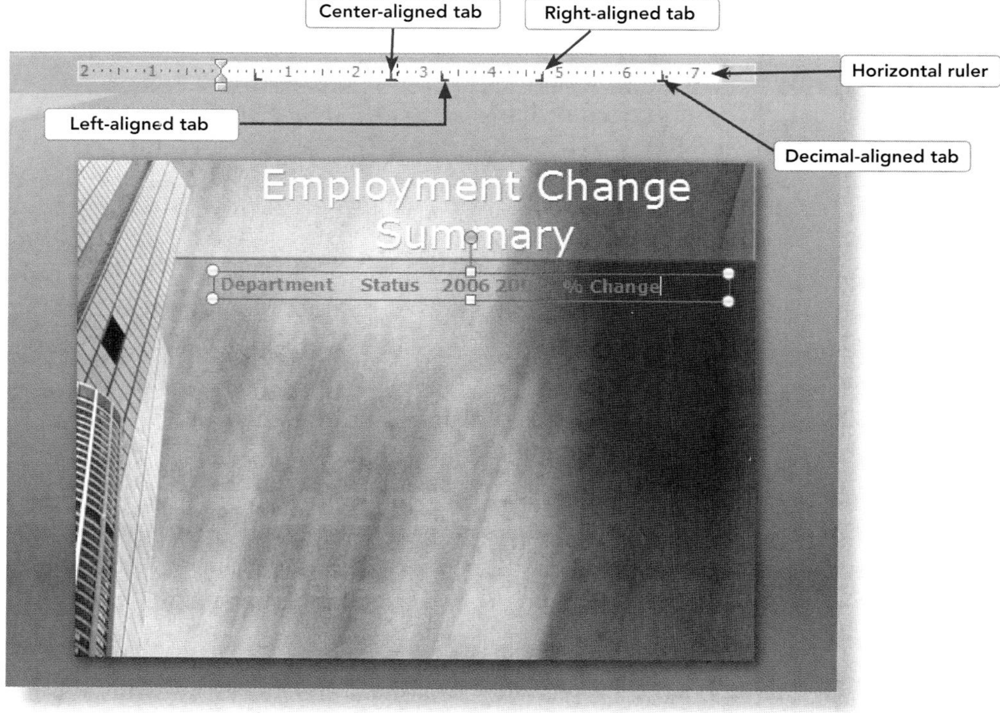

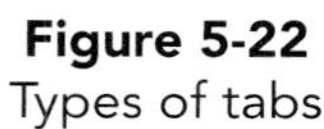

Figure 5-22
Types of tabs

9. Click the Tab Type button one or more times until the left-aligned tab button appears. Click the ruler at the .5-inch position to set a left tab.

10. Click the Tab Type button once until the center-aligned tab button appears. Click the ruler at the 2.5-inch position. The text "Status" moves so that it is centered under the tab marker.

TIP

When setting tabs, you might want to increase the zoom setting for an enlarged view of the ruler. After tabs are set, tabbed text that you key will automatically align under the tab markers you placed on the ruler.

11. Click the Tab Type button once or more until the left-aligned tab marker appears. Click the ruler at the 3.25-inch mark to set a left tab.

12. Click the Tab Type button once or more until the right-aligned tab marker appears. Click the ruler at the 4.75-inch mark to set a right-aligned tab.

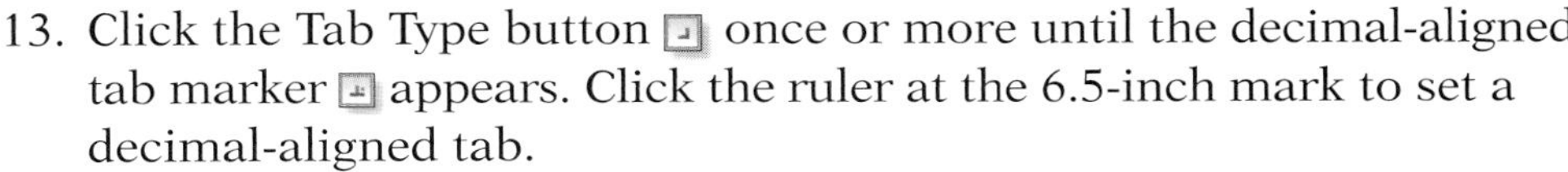

13. Click the Tab Type button once or more until the decimal-aligned tab marker appears. Click the ruler at the 6.5-inch mark to set a decimal-aligned tab.

14. Click on the first tab setting, a left-aligned tab marker, and click and drag it down and off the ruler. This removes the tab.

15. Leave the presentation open for the next exercise.

Exercise 5-23 CREATE A TABBED TABLE

A tabbed table is created by making a series of tabs within a text box. Since you have set the tabs, now you just need to enter text using the set tabs.

1. Working in the text box you created on slide 5, position the insertion point at the end of the text line and press Enter to start a new line of text.

2. Key the table text shown in Figure 5-23, pressing Tab between columns and pressing Enter at the end of each line. The text box will increase in size as the text is keyed.

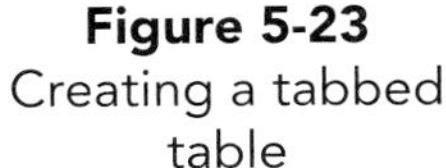

Figure 5-23 Creating a tabbed table

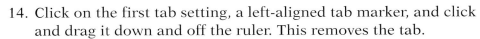

Employment Change Summary

Department	Status	2006	2007	% Change
Mgmt	Full-time	2	2	0.00%
Mgmt	Part-time	0	1	100.00%
Kitchen	Full-time	44	52	18.18%
Kitchen	Part-time	75	82	9.33%
Kitchen	Temps	0	2	200.00%
Service	Full-time	62	71	14.52%
Service	Part-time	71	87	22.54%
Service	Temps	0	4	400.00%
Clerical	Full-time	12	13	8.33%
Clerical	Part-time	7	8	14.29%
Clerical	Temps	2	6	300.00%

3. Select the entire text box by clicking its border. From the Drawing Tools Format tab, in the Shape Styles group, click the Shape Fill button and add shape fill of **Brown, Accent 6, Lighter 60%**.
4. From the Drawing Tools Format tab, in the Shape Styles group, click the Shape Outline button and add a shape outline of **Brown, Accent 2**.
5. Select the text in the table, and from the Home tab, in the Paragraph group, change the line spacing to **1.5**.
6. Highlight the text in the text box. Drag the center-aligned tab marker from the 2.5-inch position on the ruler to 2.25 inches. The entire column moves to the left.
7. Drag the center-aligned marker down and off the ruler to remove it. The table realigns in an unattractive way that does not make sense.
8. Click the Undo button once to restore the table's appearance.
9. Update the handout footer text to **[5-23your initials]** as the footer.
10. Save the presentation as **[5-23your initials]** in your Lesson 5 folder.
11. View the presentation as a slide show; then preview and print the presentation as handouts, six slides per page, grayscale, landscape, scale to fit paper, framed.

Lesson 5 Summary

- Tables offer a convenient way to quickly organize material on a slide. From the Insert tab, in the Table group, you can use the Insert table button to insert a table. You can insert a table by choosing a content slide layout. You can "draw" a table directly on a slide by using the Draw Table button. Lastly, you can create a tabbed table through setting tabs.
- Before you can apply special formatting to table cells, you must first select those cells. You can select individual cells, groups of cells, or the entire table.
- Use the buttons on the Table Tools Design tab, in the Table Styles group, to apply fill effects and border effects to individual cells, a group of cells, or the entire table.
- Change the overall size of a table by dragging one of its sizing handles with a two-pointed arrow.
- Change the width of a column by dragging or double-clicking its border. Change the height of a row by dragging its border.

- Rows and columns can be easily inserted or deleted as you develop a table. Select at least one cell in the row or column where you want to insert or delete; then use buttons on the Table Tools Layout tab.
- While keying text in a table, a quick way to insert a new row at the bottom is to press Tab when you reach the last table cell.
- Occasionally, you might want one row or column to have more or fewer cells than the others. You can make this happen by merging a group of cells or splitting an individual cell into two cells.
- A diagonal line can be added to a cell to make it appear to be split into two cells. Careful placement of text within the cell completes this illusion.
- Applying and removing shading effects is similar to applying shading effects to other PowerPoint objects. Table and cell fills can be gradients, textures, or pictures.
- Before applying a border to cells or the entire table, choose the border style, border width, and border color from the Table Tools Design tab in the Draw Borders group. Then select cells and choose an option from the Borders button drop-down list or use the Pencil pointer to apply it to the borders you want to change.
- Use the text alignment buttons on the Home tab in the Paragraph group to control the horizontal position of text in a cell.
- Use the Align Top, Center Vertically, and Align Bottom buttons on the Table Tools Layout tab in the Alignment group to control the vertical position of text within a cell.
- To fine-tune the horizontal or vertical position of text, change a cell's margin settings by using the Cell Margins button on the Table Tools Layout tab in the Alignment group.
- Add and modify 3-D effects by selecting the table and clicking the Effects button on the Table Tools Design tab.
- Click the Tab Type button on the left edge of the ruler to change the type of tab. The button cycles through four tab types: left-aligned, centered, right-aligned, and decimal.
- Create a tabbed table by using a text box and setting tabs to control how the information is indented. Remove tabs or move tabs as needed by clicking and dragging.

LESSON 5		Command Summary	
Feature	**Button**	**Ribbon**	**Keyboard**
Insert table		Insert, Tables group, Table	
Navigate in a table			Tab; Shift+Tab; ↓; ↑; ←; →
Column, select		Table Tools Layout, Table group, Select, Select Column	

continues

LESSON 5 Command Summary *continued*

Feature	Button	Ribbon	Keyboard
Row, select		Table Tools Layout, Table group, Select, Select Row	
Table, select		Table Tools Layout, Table group, Select, Select Table	
Apply Shading Effect to cells		Table Tools Design, Table Styles group, Shading	
Select Table Styles		Table Tools Design, Table Styles group, More	
Change Table Style		Table Tools Design, Table Style group, More	
Add Header Row		Table Tools Design, Table Style Options group	
Change Text Direction		Table Tools Layout, Alignment group, Text Direction	
Apply Border Effects		Table Tools Design, Draw Borders group	
Erase Cell Borders		Table Tools Design, Draw Table group, Eraser	
Align Table Text Vertically	or	Table Tools Layout, Alignment group	
Set Table Cell Margins		Table Tools Layout, Alignment group, Margins	
Distribute Columns Evenly		Table Tools Layout, Cell Size group, Distribute Columns	
Distribute Rows Evenly		Table Tools Layout, Cell Size group, Distribute Rows	
Insert Table Columns		Table Tools Layout, Rows & Columns group	
Insert Table Rows		Table Tools Layout, Rows & Columns group	
Delete Table Columns		Table Tools Layout, Rows & Columns group, Delete	
Draw a Table		Insert, Tables group, Table, Draw Table	
Merge Table Cells		Table Tools Layout, Merge group, Merge Cells	
Split a Table Cell		Table Tools Layout, Merge group, Split Cells	
Apply 3-D Effects		Table Tools Design, Table Styles group, Effects	

Lesson 6

Creating Charts

OBJECTIVES

After completing this lesson, you will be able to:

1. Create a chart.
2. Format a column chart.
3. Use different chart types.
4. Work with pie charts.
5. Enhance chart elements.

MCAS OBJECTIVES

In this lesson:
PP07 3.6
PP07 3.6.1
PP07 3.6.2
PP07 3.6.3
PP07 3.6.4
See Appendix

Estimated Time: 1½ hours

Charts, sometimes called graphs, are diagrams that display numbers in pictorial format. Charts illustrate quantitative relationships and can help people understand the significance of numeric information more easily than when they view the same information in a table or in a list. Charts are well suited for making comparisons or examining the changes in data over time.

Creating a Chart

PowerPoint provides several ways to start a new chart. You can add a chart to an existing slide, or you can select a slide layout with a chart placeholder at the time you create a new slide. Here are two methods of inserting a chart:

- From the Insert tab, in the Illustrations group, click the Chart button.
- On a new slide with the Title and Content layout, click the Insert Chart icon in the center of the placeholder.

Microsoft Excel is opened using either method of creating charts. Microsoft Excel holds the chart data in a *worksheet* and this data is linked to Microsoft PowerPoint where the chart is displayed. If changes are made to the data in Microsoft Excel, the chart is automatically updated in Microsoft PowerPoint.

If Microsoft Excel is not installed on your computer when you start a new chart, Microsoft Graph will open with a sample *datasheet*. A datasheet provides rows and columns in which you key the numbers and labels used to create a chart. Advanced features of charting with Excel are not available with Microsoft Graph.

Exercise 6-1 CHOOSE A SLIDE LAYOUT FOR A CHART

Several slide layout choices are suitable for charts. For example, the **Title and Content** layout works well for one chart on a slide; the **Two Content** layout works well for a chart combined with text or an image.

1. Open the file **Finance1**.
2. Insert a new slide after slide 1 that uses the **Title and Content** slide layout, as shown in Figure 6-1. Key the slide title **Sales Forecast**. This layout contains a placeholder suitable for one chart. When you want to place more than one chart or other element on a slide, use one of the other Content layouts.

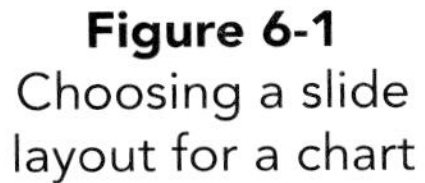

Figure 6-1
Choosing a slide layout for a chart

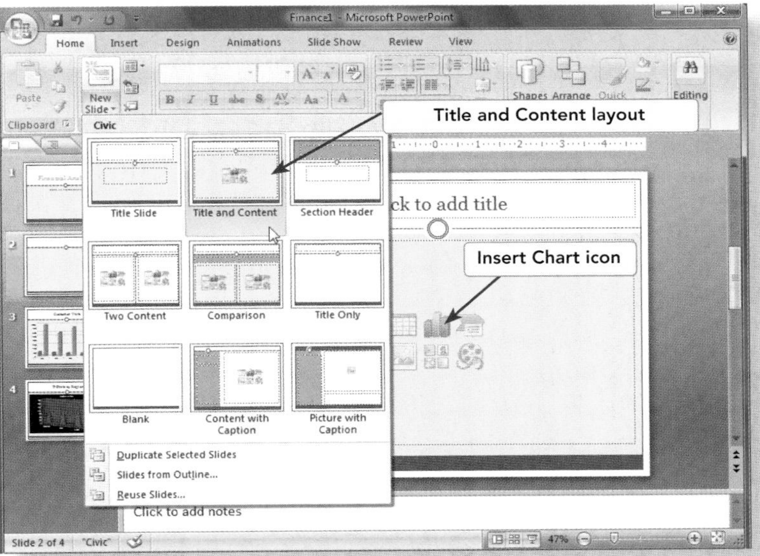

3. Click the Insert Chart icon in the center of the content placeholder.
4. Point to the options in the Insert Chart dialog box, and notice the different chart types displayed. Choose the **3-D Clustered Column Chart**, and click **OK**. Microsoft Excel opens displaying a worksheet with sample data, and a chart is inserted into PowerPoint. Chart-related tabs appear on the Ribbon.

Exercise 6-2 EDIT THE DATA SOURCE

Each worksheet contains rows and columns. Each number or label is in a separate *cell*—the rectangle formed by the intersection of a row and a column.

As you enter data, you can monitor the results on the sample chart. You key new information by overwriting the sample data or by deleting the sample data and keying your own data.

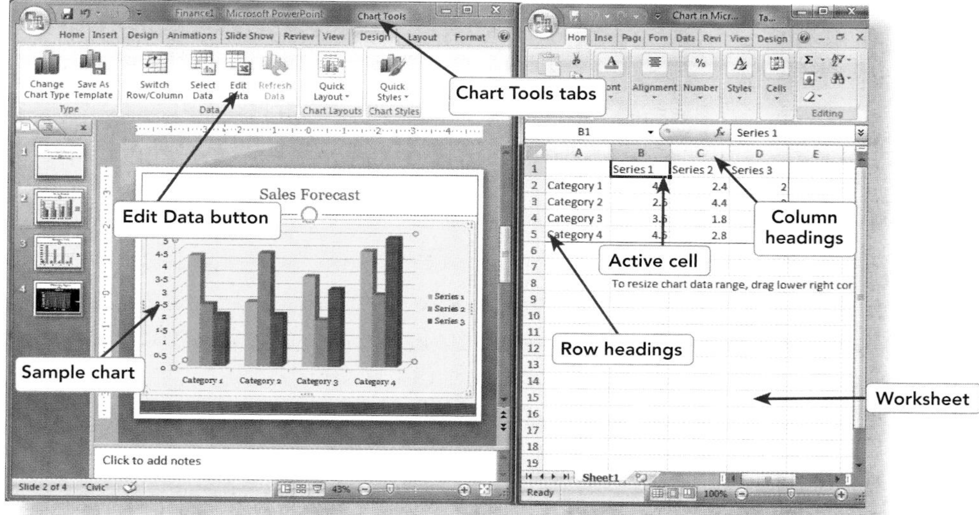

Figure 6-2
Creating a chart

NOTE

If Microsoft Excel is not installed on your computer, Microsoft Graph will open a datasheet that contains gray column headings and row headings with a button-like appearance that indicate column letters and row numbers. If you like, you can move the datasheet by dragging its title bar, and you can resize it by dragging its borders.

1. On the worksheet, click the words "Series 1." A heavy black border, which indicates that this is the active cell, surrounds the cell that contains "Series 1," as shown in Figure 6-2. Notice that when working on the worksheet, your pointer is a white cross ✚, called a *cell pointer*.
2. Move around the worksheet by clicking on individual cells. Then try pressing Enter, Tab, Shift+Enter, Shift+Tab, and the arrow keys to explore other ways to navigate in a worksheet.
3. Click cell B2 (the cell in column B, row 2 that contains the value 4.3) then key **10** and press Enter. The chart data will automatically update in PowerPoint.
4. Click cell B2 with the value "10," which represents Category 1 of Series 1.
5. Press Delete to delete the contents of cell B2 and press Enter. Notice that the first column in the chart is no longer displayed.

6. Click and drag the pointer from cell B3 to cell B5 to select the rest of the numbers in the Series 1 column.

7. Press Delete and then for Series 1 no columns are displayed in the chart. Because the Series 1 column is still included on the worksheet, however, space still remains on the chart where the columns were removed and Series 1 shows in the legend.

NOTE

If you leave gaps between columns or rows as you enter data, your chart will not display correctly.

8. Click the box in the upper-left corner of the worksheet where the row headings meet the column headings, as shown in Figure 6-3. The entire worksheet is selected.

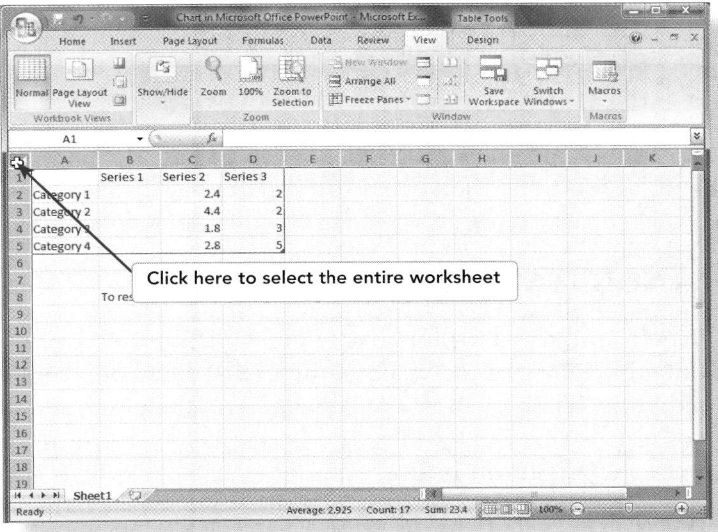
Click here to select the entire worksheet

Figure 6-3 Editing the worksheet

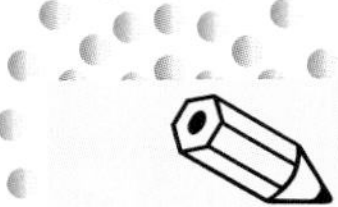

TIP

You do not need to be concerned about number formatting in the worksheet. If any of the labels or numbers do not fit in a cell, move to the right of the column heading for the cell until you get the two-pointed arrow and double-click. This will adjust the column to fit the longest line of text.

9. Press Delete. The worksheet is now blank and ready for you to key new data. Notice that the columns in the chart are removed.

10. Click the first cell in the upper-left corner. All the cells in the worksheet are deselected. Your computer may have made these changes automatically. If so, you may omit this step.

11. Close Microsoft Excel. The worksheet is not visible. The worksheet can be closed at any point and accessed when you wish.

12. From the Chart Tools Design tab, in the Data group, choose the Edit Data button. This reopens the worksheet and you can now enter new data.

13. Key the numbers and labels shown in Figure 6-4. Be sure to put the labels in the top row and left-most column. Notice how the chart grows as you key data.

Figure 6-4
Worksheet with new data

	A	B	C	D	E
1		2008	2009	2010	
2	New York	920	1130	1450	
3	Miami	500	850	1210	
4	Los Angeles	350	760	990	
5 ← Row heading					

14. Notice on the chart in Microsoft PowerPoint, there is a blank area on the chart. In the sample chart, there were four categories. To fix this, row 5 must be deleted. Click on the row heading number for row 5. Right-click, and choose **Delete**. This will update the chart to remove the blank space where the fourth category columns were displayed before, and the remaining columns will expand to fill the chart area.

15. Leave both files open for the next exercise.

Exercise 6-3 SWITCH ROWS/COLUMN DATA

When you key data for a new chart, Microsoft Excel interprets each row of data as a *data series*. On a column chart, each data series is usually displayed in a distinct Theme color. For example, on the current chart, the 2008 worksheet column is one data series and is displayed in orange on the chart. The 2009 worksheet column is a second data series, displayed in blue on the chart, and the 2010 worksheet column is a third data series, displayed in dark red.

When creating your worksheet, you might not know whether it is best to arrange your data in rows or columns. Fortunately, you can enter the data and easily change the way it is displayed on the chart.

1. In PowerPoint, click on the slide 2 chart area to continue modifying this chart.

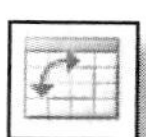

2. From the Chart Tools Design tab, choose the Switch Row/Column button. The chart columns are now grouped by year instead of by city. The years are displayed below each group of columns.

3. Click the Switch Row/Column button again to group the chart columns by city. Your chart should look like the one shown in Figure 6-5.

4. Create a slide footer for the current slide (slide 2 only) containing today's date and the text your name, **[6-3your initials]**.

5. Create a new folder for lesson 6. Save the presentation as **[6-3your initials]** in your folder for Lesson 6.

6. Print the current slide (slide 2) in full size. If you have a color printer, print it in color.

Figure 6-5
Chart with new data

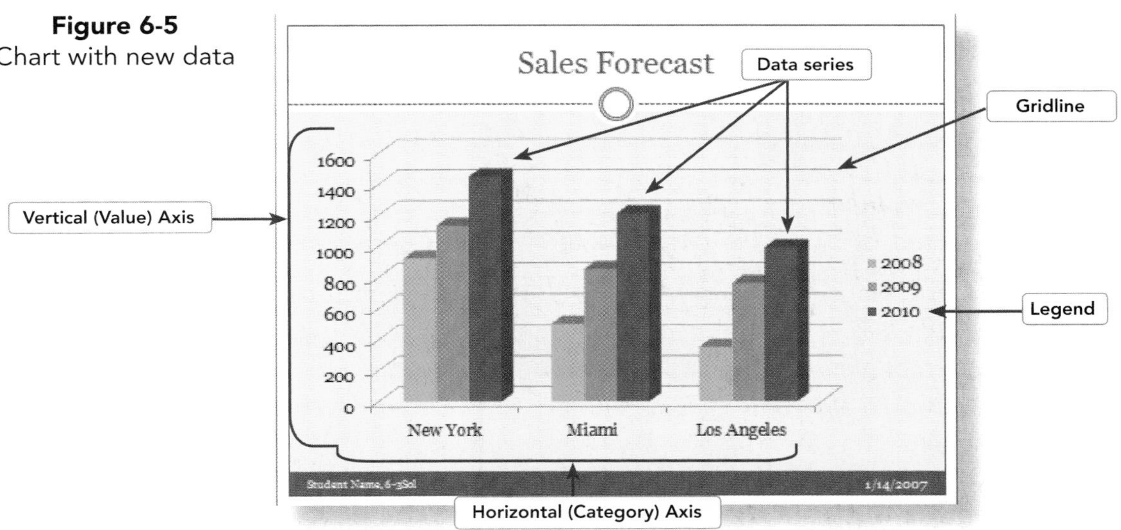

Formatting a Column Chart

You can apply a wide variety of format options to charts by changing the colors, gradients, fonts, and number formats of a chart. Some of these options are appropriate based on the particular chart type being used. In this lesson, you have been working with a **3-D Clustered Column** chart.

You can alter the appearance of your chart's axes by changing text color, size, font, and number formatting. You can also change scale and tick mark settings. The *scale* indicates the values that are displayed on the value axis and the intervals between those values. *Tick marks* are small measurement marks, similar to those found on a ruler, that can show increments on the *Vertical (Value) Axis* (on the left for column charts) and the *Horizontal (Category) Axis* (on the bottom for column charts).

To make these changes, use the Format Axis dialog box, which you display in one of the following ways:

TIP

Ctrl+1 opens the Format dialog box that is appropriate for whatever chart element is currently selected.

- Click on the Chart Tools Format tab, in the Current Selection group, choose the area you want to format and click the Format Selection button.
- Right-click an axis and choose Format Axis from the shortcut menu.

Exercise 6-4 EXPLORE PARTS OF A CHART

PowerPoint provides several tools to help you navigate around the chart and ScreenTips to help you select the part of the chart on which you want to work.

1. Click on the chart to select it.

Figure 6-6
Chart elements list

2. Move the pointer over the words "New York." The ScreenTip identifies this part of the chart as the Horizontal (Category) Axis.
3. Point to one of the horizontal gray lines (gridlines) within the chart. The ScreenTip identifies these lines as Vertical (Value) Axis Major Gridlines.
4. Move the pointer around other parts of the chart to find the Plot Area, Chart Area, and Legend Entries. Each of these areas can be formatted with fill colors, border colors, and font attributes.
5. From the Chart Tools Format tab, in the Current Selection group, the chart element that is currently selected is displayed. Click the **Chart Elements** list box arrow to see a list of the various chart elements as shown in Figure 6-6.
6. Choose **Floor** from the list to select the chart floor. Sometimes it's easier to select the chart's smaller elements this way.
7. Close the Excel worksheet, but keep the chart open for the next exercise.

Exercise 6-5 CHANGE CHART STYLES

Microsoft PowerPoint provides preset *Chart Styles* that can be applied to a chart to enhance its appearance.

1. On slide 2, click anywhere inside the chart to select it.

2. From the Chart Tools Design tab, in the Chart Styles group, click the More button.
3. Move your pointer over several of the style samples. Click the **Style 4** chart style, as shown in Figure 6-7.

Figure 6-7
Chart styles drop-down gallery

4. Notice the effect that applying a style has on the selected chart. The chart still coordinates with theme colors, but has three blue colors applied.
5. Leave the presentation open for the next exercise.

Exercise 6-6 FORMAT THE VERTICAL (VALUE) AND HORIZONTAL (CATEGORY) AXES

The Vertical (Value) Axis and the Horizontal (Category) Axis can be formatted through the Format Axis dialog box to change fonts, scales, units, and more options.

1. On slide 2, point to one of the numbers on the left side of the chart. When you see the Vertical (Value) Axis ScreenTip, right-click to open the shortcut menu.
2. Using the floating font group, change the font to **Arial, Bold, 18 points.**
3. Right-click on the value axis again to reopen the shortcut menu and choose **Format Axis**. Click the **Number** option at the left of the dialog box, then in the **Category** box, choose **Currency**. Change the decimal places to **0** because all numbers in the worksheet are even numbers. Change the Symbol to **$ English (U.S.).**
4. Click **Axis Options** at the left of the dialog box. In the **Maximum** box, choose **Fixed** and key **1500** to set the largest number on the value axis.
5. In the **Major unit** box, choose **Fixed** and key **500** to set wider intervals between the numbers on the value axis.
6. Click **Close**. The chart now shows fewer horizontal gridlines, and each value is formatted as currency with a dollar sign, as shown in Figure 6-8.

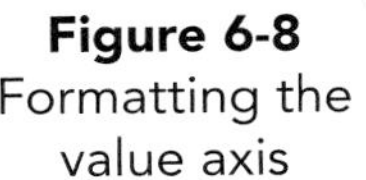

Figure 6-8
Formatting the value axis

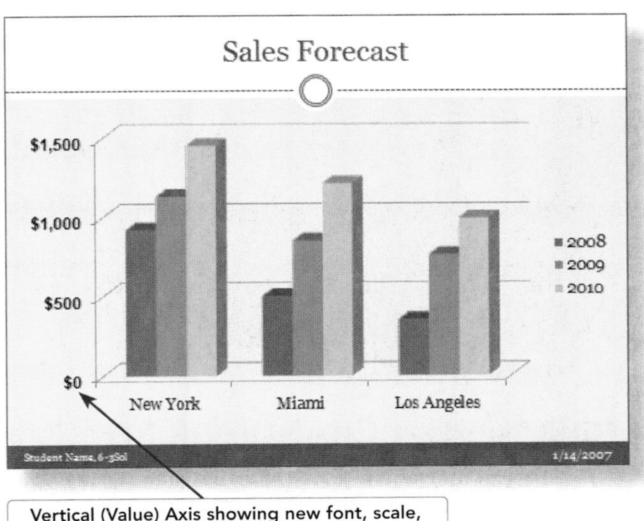

7. Right-click the text “New York” on the horizontal (category) axis.
8. Using the floating font group, change the font to **Arial, Bold, 18 points**.
9. Leave the presentation open for the next exercise.

Exercise 6-7 APPLY DIFFERENT CHART LAYOUTS

Chart Layouts control the position where different chart elements appear on the chart. PowerPoint provides many different preset layouts.

1. Move to slide 3 and click anywhere within the chart area.
2. From the Chart Tools Design tab, in the Chart Styles group, click **Style 2**.
3. From the Chart Tools Design tab, in the Chart Layouts group, click the Quick Layout button.
4. Select **Chart Layout 2**. Notice the new position of several chart elements. Also, the vertical (value) axis is gone and it has been replaced with data labels showing the values on the columns, as shown in Figure 6-9.

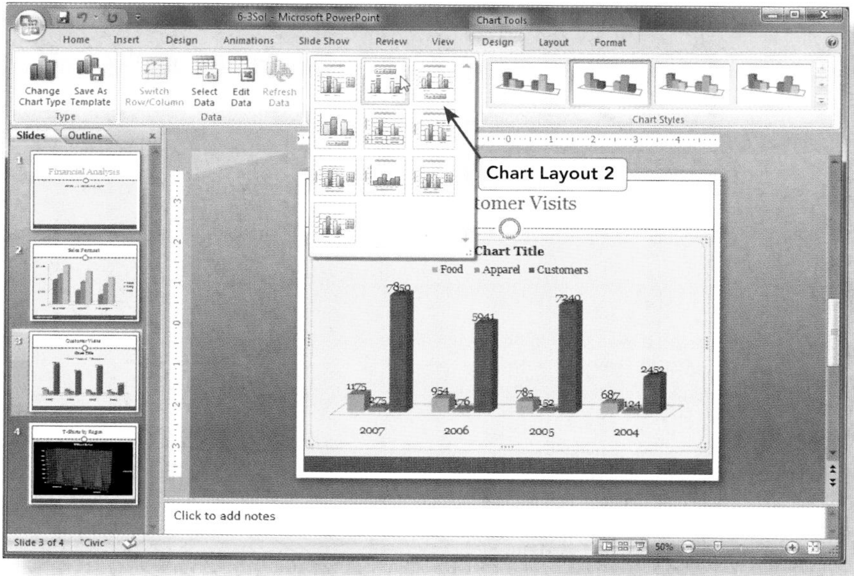

Figure 6-9
Choosing a chart layout

5. Select the “Chart Title” text box, and press Delete to remove it.
6. Leave the presentation open for the next exercise.

Exercise 6-8 CHANGE OR REMOVE THE LEGEND

A *Legend* is a box showing the colors assigned to the data series. You can customize a chart's legend by changing the border, background colors, and font attributes.

1. Move to slide 2, and right-click the legend box.
2. Using the Floating Font group, change the font to **Arial, Bold, 18 points**.
3. Right-click the legend box again and choose **Format Legend** so you can make several changes at once. Click the **Fill** option at the left of the dialog box, choose **Solid Fill**, and select the gold accent color to change the legend background.

TIP

Choosing a fill color, even if it is the same as the background, can make it difficult to choose good grayscale settings for printing.

4. Click **Legend Options** at the left of the dialog box and under legend position, choose **Top**. Click **Close**. The legend appears above the chart with gold background color. Note that sizing handles surround the legend.
5. Using a right or left sizing handle, resize the legend box to make it wider so there is more space between the legend items and all three items are still visible.
6. Point to the center of the legend and click to select it once the four-headed arrow appears. Drag the legend down so it fits below the top gridline and above the columns, as shown in Figure 6-10. Adjust the width of the legend if it overlaps any columns.

Figure 6-10
Legend repositioned

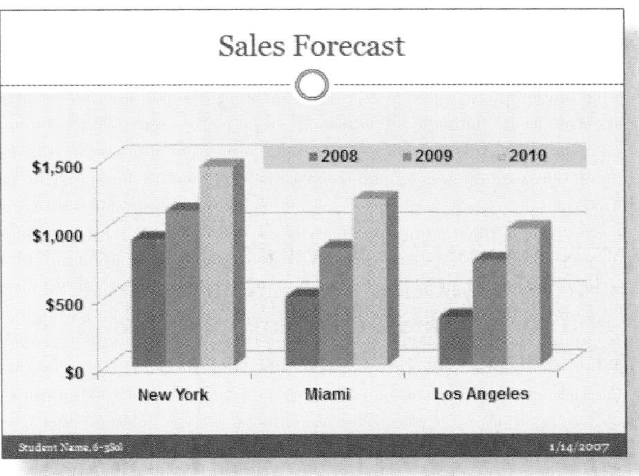

Exercise 6-9 APPLY OR REMOVE GRIDLINES

The chart style you used on slide 3 removed the chart gridlines. In situations where numbers are displayed within the chart, gridlines may not be needed. *Gridlines* are the thin lines that can be displayed for major and minor units on vertical or horizontal axes. They align with major and minor tick marks on the axes when those are displayed. Gridlines make quantities easier to understand.

1. Still working on slide 2, click anywhere within the chart area.

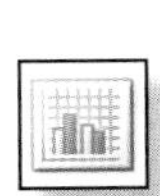

2. From the Chart Tools Layout tab, in the Axes group, choose the Gridlines button.

3. Choose **Primary Horizontal Gridlines** and **Minor Gridlines**. Notice that there are many horizontal gridlines now instead of only gridlines on the major units, as shown in Figure 6-11.

Figure 6-11
Gridlines options

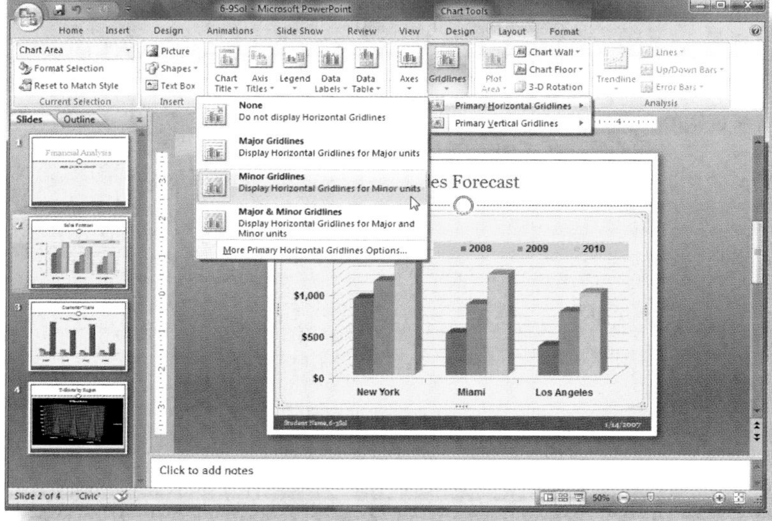

4. Update your slide footer for the current slide (slide 2 only) containing today's date and the text your name, **[6-9your initials]**.

5. Save the presentation as **[6-9your initials]** in your Lesson 6 folder.

Using Different Chart Types

In addition to the 3-D Clustered Column chart, PowerPoint offers a wide variety of chart types. Other types include bar, area, line, pie, and surface, in both two- and three-dimensional layouts. In addition, you can include more than one chart type on a single chart, such as a combination of lines and columns.

If you are working on a two-dimensional (2-D) chart, you can add a secondary axis, so that you can plot data against two different scales. For example, air temperature could be compared to wind speed, or number of customers could be compared to dollar sales. A secondary axis is also a good choice if you need to display numbers that vary greatly in magnitude. For example, sales generated by a small local brand could be compared with national sales trends.

Exercise 6-10 SWITCH TO OTHER CHART TYPES

Sometimes a different chart type can make data easier to understand. You can change chart types in the following ways:

- From the Chart Tools Design tab, in the Type group, click the Change Chart Type button to open the Change Chart Type dialog box.
- Right-click the chart area; then choose **Change Chart Type** from the shortcut menu.

1. Move to slide 3 and click the chart area to activate the chart. This chart compares dollar sales to number of customer visits. Because of the different types of data, the sales figures are not easy to understand.
2. Right-click the chart and choose **Change Chart Type** from the shortcut menu. On the Change Chart Type dialog box, chart types are organized by category, as shown in Figure 6-12.

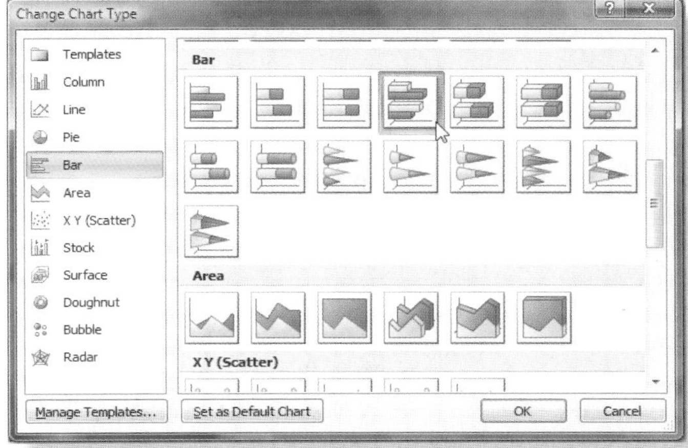

Figure 6-12
Changing to a different chart type

3. Click **Bar** at the left of the dialog box and choose the **Clustered Bar in 3-D** thumbnail and click **OK**. The chart's vertical columns change to horizontal bars.
4. Here is another way to change to a different chart type. From the Chart Tools Design tab, in the Type group, choose the Change Chart Type button. The Change Chart Type dialog box opens again.
5. Click **Column** at the left of the dialog box and several column chart thumbnails appear. Point to different thumbnails and notice the description that appears in the ScreenTip.
6. Select the **Clustered Column** type in the upper left of this category. Click **OK**. The chart changes to a two-dimensional column chart.
7. Leave the presentation open for the next exercise.

Exercise 6-11 ADD A SECONDARY CHART AXIS

The chart on slide 3 ("Customer Visits") contains dollar values for apparel and food sales, and also unit values for number of customer visits. Plotting customer visits on a secondary axis will improve the chart by making it easier to interpret.

If you are working with a 3-D chart, you must change it to a 2-D chart (as you did in the previous exercise), before you can add a secondary axis.

1. Select the chart on slide 3.
2. From the Chart Tools Design tab, in the Chart Layouts group, change the chart layout to **Layout 1** and delete the Chart Title text box.
3. Right-click one of the "Customers" columns, and choose **Format Data Series** from the shortcut menu. Click **Series Options** at the left of the dialog box.
4. In the **Plot Series On** area of the dialog box, select **Secondary axis**. Click **Close**. Now the orange and blue columns have become taller, and a new scale has been added on the right, as shown in Figure 6-13. In the following exercises you will improve the appearance of this chart.
5. Leave the presentation open for the next exercise.

NOTE

If the Format Data Series dialog box does not contain a **Plot Series On** area, your current chart type does not support a secondary axis. Make sure you are working with a 2-D chart.

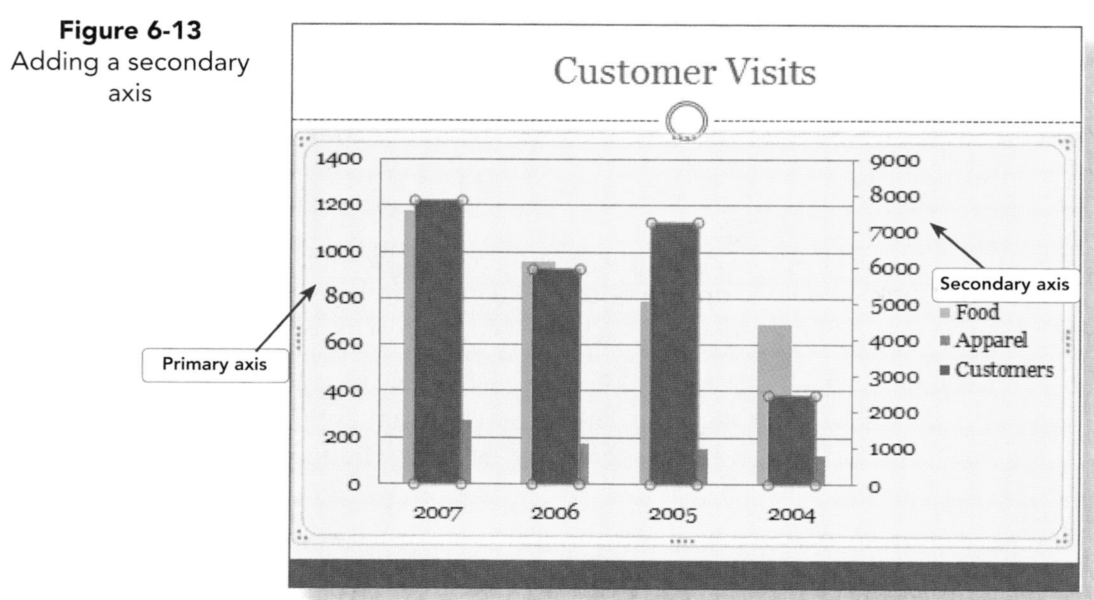

Figure 6-13
Adding a secondary axis

Exercise 6-12 COMBINE CHART TYPES

A good way to distinguish between different data types on a single chart is to assign different chart types. For example, with the current chart, the "Customers" data series can be shown as a line or an area, while the sales data can remain as columns, as shown in Figure 6-14.

1. Still working on slide 3, select the "Customers" data series if not already selected.
2. Right-click the data series, and choose **Change Series Chart Type** from the shortcut menu. Click the **Area** category at the left of the dialog box, and choose the **Area** chart type. Click **OK**.

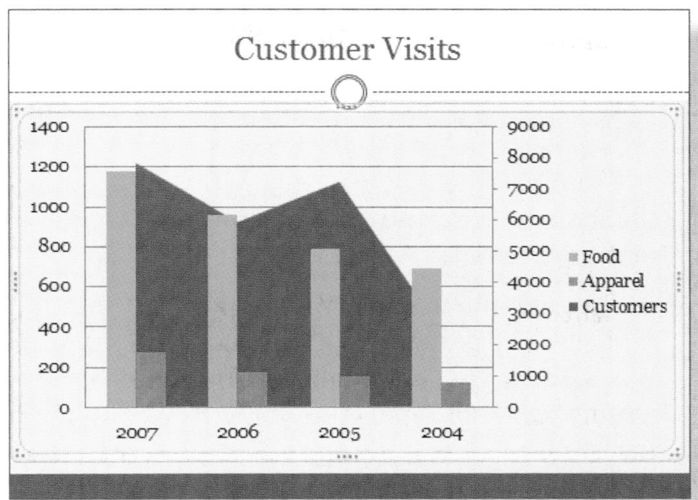

Figure 6-14 Area and column combination chart

3. Click the "Customers" area to select it, then right-click and choose **Change Series Chart Type** from the shortcut menu. Choose the **Line** category at the left of the dialog box, and click the **Line** chart type. Click **OK**.
4. Right-click the red line representing "Customers," and choose **Format Data Series** from the shortcut menu.
5. Click **Line Style** option at the left of the dialog box, and change the **Width** to **3 points**.
6. Choose the **Line Color** option at the left of the dialog box, and change the **Color** to **Red Accent 3, Darker 50%**. Click **Close**.
7. Leave the presentation open for the next exercise.

Exercise 6-13 FORMAT A PRIMARY AND SECONDARY AXIS

Proper formatting and labeling on a chart is always important to ensure that viewers understand the information you want to convey. This is even more important when you have both a primary and secondary axis scale on the chart.

1. On slide 3, click the chart area to select it.

2. From the Chart Tools Layout tab, in the Labels group, click the Axis Titles button and choose the **Primary Vertical Axis Title** and **Rotated Title**.
3. In the Axis Title text box located on the primary vertical axis, delete the text and key **Sales (thousands)**. The size of the text box will adjust automatically. Figure 6-15 indicates the position of the text on the chart.

4. From the **Chart Tools Layout** tab, in the Labels group, click the Axis Titles button and choose the **Secondary Vertical Axis Title** and **Rotated Title**. An Axis Title text box appears beside the secondary axis scale on the left.
5. In the Axis Title text box, delete the text and key **Customer Visits (hundreds)**. Descriptive titles now appear next to both the primary and the secondary axes.
6. Right-click the **Vertical (Value) Axis** (the Sales numbers on the left) and choose **Format Axis**. Click **Axis Options** at the left of the dialog box; then in the **Major unit** text box, choose **Fixed** and key **500**. Under **Major Tick Mark Type**, choose **Outside** from the list box. This will insert tick marks and numbers on the axis.
7. Click **Number** at the left of the dialog box. In the **Category** list box, choose **Currency**. Change the **Decimal places** to **0**. Under symbol, choose **$ English (U.S.)**. Click **Close**.
8. Right-click the **Secondary Vertical (Value) Axis** (the Customers numbers on the right), and choose **Format Axis**. Click **Axis Options** at the left of the dialog box, and change the value in the **Major unit** text box to **Fixed** and **1500** to reduce some of the number labels. Click **Close**.
9. Click outside the chart area to return to view your changes.
10. Click the Legend, then right-click and choose **Format Legend**. For the Legend Position choose **Top**. Click **Close**. Now the chart appears more balanced with the scales evenly spaced on each side.

TIP

It is best to avoid using red and green in the same chart to distinguish between data on column and bar charts. Some individuals have difficulty distinguishing between those two colors.

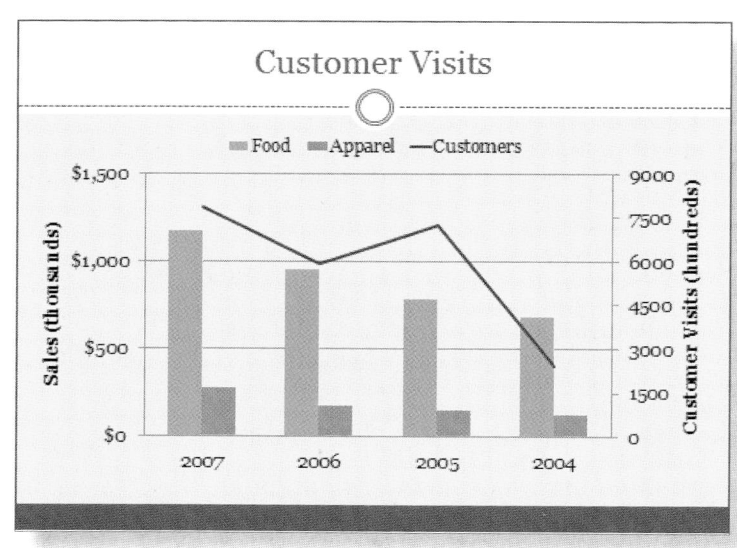

Figure 6-15 Completed combination chart

11. Create a slide footer for only slide 3 that includes the date and the text your name, **[6-13your initials]**. Save the presentation as **[6-13your initials]** in your Lesson 6 folder.

12. Print slide 3 only in full size. Leave the presentation open for the next exercise.

Working with Pie Charts

A *pie chart* is a simple, yet highly effective, presentation tool that shows individual values in relation to the sum of all the values—a pie chart makes it easy to judge "parts of a whole." Each value is displayed as a slice of the pie.

A pie chart can show only one data series. To show more than one data series, use more than one pie chart.

Exercise 6-14 CREATE A PIE CHART

In this exercise, you create a pie chart to display the breakdown of the restaurant's sales by category.

If your worksheet contains more than one series, a pie chart uses the first column of numbers. You can change to a different row or column by selecting the series you wish to use.

1. Insert a new slide after slide 3 that uses the **Title Only** layout. This layout provides a white background.

2. Key the title **2007 Sales Categories**.

3. From the Insert tab, in the Illustrations group, click the Chart button.

4. Click the **Pie** category at the left of the dialog box, and choose the first chart type that appears in the pie chart category called **Pie**. Click **OK**. Microsoft Excel opens and displays a sample worksheet, and in PowerPoint you will see a sample pie chart reflecting that data.

5. On the worksheet, click the box in the upper-left corner to select all the sample data, and then delete it.

6. Key the data shown in Figure 6-16.

7. Close the Excel worksheet to view the chart and leave the presentation open for the next exercise.

Figure 6-16
Worksheet for pie chart

	A	B	C
1		2007 Sales	
2	Food	3339	
3	Beverage	2933	
4	Apparel	1529	
5	Other	906	

Exercise 6-15 ADD PIE SLICE LABELS

You can add labels to the chart's data series and edit those labels individually.

1. Click one of the pie slices to select the Chart Series data.
2. From the Chart Tools Layout tab, in the Labels group, click the Data Labels button and click **More Data Label Options**.

3. Click **Label Options** at the left of the dialog box, and make several changes under the **Label Contains** heading:
   a. Select both **Category name** and **Percentage**.
   b. Deselect **Value** and **Show Leader Lines**.
   c. Click **Close**.
4. Data labels now appear on the pie slices. With the addition of the data labels, the pie is now smaller; however, the legend is no longer needed since the slices are each labeled, as shown in Figure 6-17.

NOTE

Depending on the pie chart, sometimes parts of the data labels might be hidden by the edges of the chart placeholder. In this case, you need to resize the pie by using the plot area sizing handles.

5. Right-click the legend box and choose **Delete** from the shortcut menu. The pie chart becomes a little larger.
6. Click any data label. All the data labels are selected. Right-click on one of the labels, and use the floating font group to change the font to Arial, 16 points, bold, and italic. Click outside the pie to turn off this selection.
7. Click the data label "Other 10%" twice to select just that label. As with columns, click once to select all labels, and click again to select just one. You can now edit the selected label's text.
8. Click within the text to display an insertion point. Delete the word "Other" (but not "10%"), and key in its place **Take-out**.
9. Click anywhere within the chart to deselect the label that now appears separated from the pie.
10. Click on the "Take-Out 10%" label two times to select just that label. Right-click and choose **Format Data Label**. Under the Label Position heading, choose **Inside End**. Click **Close**. Now the label is positioned on the slice.
11. Because the slide title identifies what the pie contains, the pie chart title for 2007 sales can be removed. Select this text box and press Delete. The pie will expand to fill the available space.

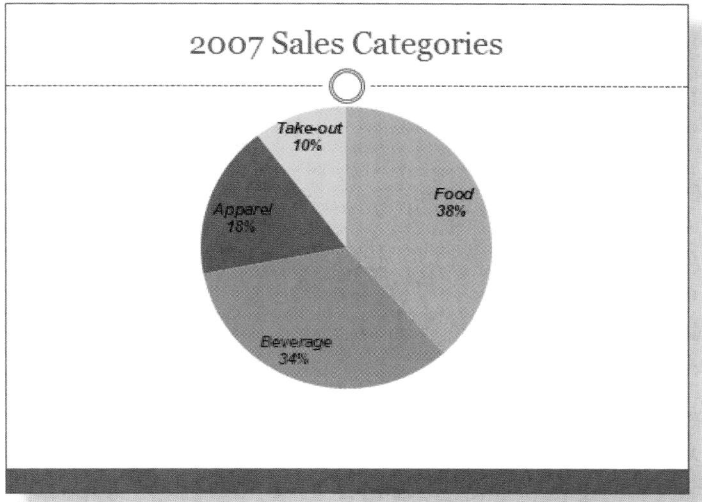

Figure 6-17
Pie chart with data labels

Exercise 6-16 APPLY 3-D ROTATION

You can enhance the appearance of your pie chart with additional effects, such as changing to a 3-D appearance and rotating the angle of the pie or *exploding* a slice (dragging it out from the center of the pie) for emphasis.

1. Click to select the chart. From the Chart Tools Design tab, in the Type group, click the Change Chart Type button and select **Pie in 3-D**. The pie now has a perspective treatment. Click **OK**.
2. From the Chart Tools Layout tab, in the Background group, click the 3-D Rotation button. At the bottom of the Format Chart Area dialog box, click **Default Rotation** and the pie becomes more dimensional but almost flat.
3. In the **Perspective** box, key **0.1°**.
4. Under the Rotation heading, change the **X degree** to **35°** to move the "Take-out" slice to the right. Click **Close**.
5. Click the center of the pie once to select all the slices. Notice that each slice has selection handles where the slices join.
6. Click the "Take-out" slice so you have handles on that slice only (be careful not to select the label), and drag it slightly away from the center of the pie. This is called *exploding a slice*.
7. The labels for two slices move away from their respective slices. Select just the "Apparel 18%" label, right-click, choose **Format Data Label**, and select the Label Position of **Inside End**. Click **Close**.
8. Select just the "Take-out 10%" label and drag it over to fit on top of the exploded slice, as shown in Figure 6-18.

Figure 6-18
Pie chart with 3-D rotation and exploded slice

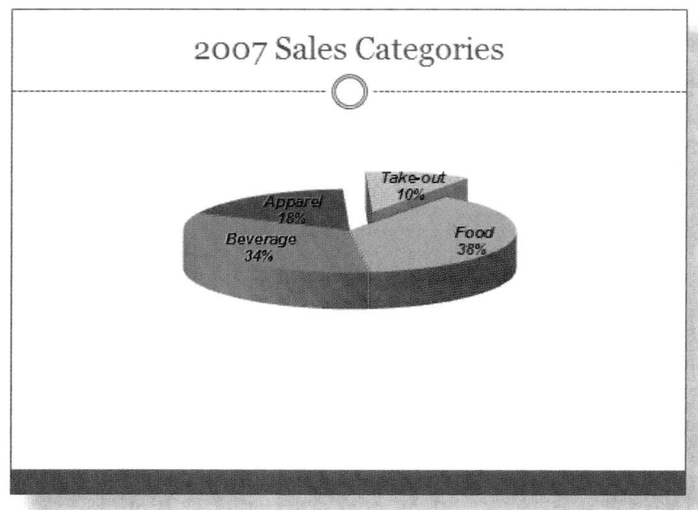

9. In Normal view, select the chart area and use the corner sizing handles to increase its size to make the pie chart larger to fill the slide.
10. Create a slide footer for slide 4 only that includes the date and the text your name, **[6-16your initials]**.
11. Save the presentation as **[6-16your initials]** in your Lesson 6 folder.
12. Print slide 4 only in full slide size. Leave the presentation open for the next exercise.

Enhancing Chart Elements

You can add many interesting effects to charts. In addition to changing colors, you can add shapes or pictures that help you make a particular point or highlight one aspect of the data. You can also annotate your charts with text to clarify or call attention to important concepts.

Exercise 6-17 ADDING SHAPES FOR EMPHASIS

Shapes can be combined with text or layered in some way to emphasize the point you need to make. For this exercise, you will combine an arrow and text.

1. Move to slide 5 ("T-Shirts by Region").
2. Because this chart reflects only one data series, the legend at the side is not needed. Select the legend and press Delete.
3. Because the slide title identifies the content of this chart, the chart title is redundant; therefore, select the chart title and press Delete.

4. From the Insert tab, in the Text group, click the Text Box button; click and drag above the Miami column to create a space to enter the text, change the font color to white, and key **L.A. may top Miami in 2008**.

5. Select the text inside the text box, right-click, and use the floating font group to change the text to 18-point Arial, bold, italic.

6. From the Insert tab, in the Illustrations group, click the Shapes button; then from the Block Arrow category, click the **Left Arrow** shape. Draw an arrow above the Los Angeles chart shape. Change the shape fill color to a gold that coordinates with the theme, and remove the shape outline. Reposition and resize the arrow and text box as needed to appear as shown in Figure 6-19.

TIP

You may want to use Zoom to enlarge the slide so you can more easily use the arrow's rotation handle.

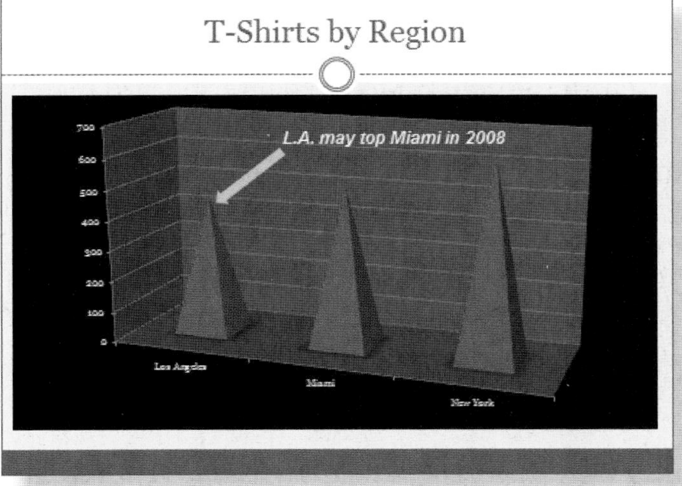

Figure 6-19
Chart with arrow and text box

7. Create a slide footer for slide 5 that includes the date and the text your name, **[6-17your initials]**.

8. Save the presentation as **[6-17your initials]** in your Lesson 6 folder.

9. Print slide 5 in full size. If you have a color printer, print it in color. Leave the presentation open for the next exercise.

Exercise 6-18 CHANGE COLORS IN CHART AREAS

You can change the colors of individual chart areas, columns, or an entire data series. Shape fill effects, including textures and gradient fills, can be used the same way you use them for other PowerPoint shapes. You can also change the outline style of columns, bars, and other chart elements.

1. Move to slide 2 and click to select the chart. Point to one of the darkest blue columns, the 2008 series. Notice the ScreenTip that appears, identifying the data series.
2. Click any light blue column, the 2010 series. All the light blue columns are selected, as indicated by the box that is displayed around each selected column.
3. Click the light blue column for Los Angeles. Now the Los Angeles column is the only one selected. Clicking once selects all the columns in a series; clicking a second time (not double-clicking) changes the selection to just one column.
4. Click one of the darkest blue columns to select all of the 2008 series.
5. From the Chart Tools Format tab, in the Shape Styles group, click the Shape Fill button. Click a darker blue.

6. Click the darker blue column for Los Angeles, and then change to **Orange, Accent 1**. The Los Angeles column is now a different color from the other columns in its series. Click the Undo button to return the column to the darker blue to match the other columns in the series.

TIP

You can change colors and fills on each part of the chart. Be sure to select the element that you would like to change before beginning to change colors or gradients, or add a picture.

7. Select the columns that contain the light blue fill color, the 2010 series. Click the Shape Fill button and choose **Ice Blue, Accent 5**. Click the Shape Fill button again and choose **Gradient**. Under the Light Variations category, select **Linear Up** so the lightest color is at the top of the column.

Exercise 6-19 ADD A PICTURE FILL BEHIND CHART

A picture can help communicate the meaning of the chart by illustrating the data in some way. For instance, if you are discussing T-shirts as in this exercise, it is appropriate to have a shirt picture in the chart background.

1. Move to slide 5.
2. Change the font color of the text on both axes and in the text box to black to make it easier to read once a picture has been added.
3. With the chart active, from the Chart Tools Layout tab, in the Current Selection group, choose **Chart Area** from the Chart Elements drop-down list. Click the Format Selection button.
4. Choose **Fill** at the left of the dialog box; then choose **Picture or texture fill** and click **File** under the Insert from heading.

5. Navigate to your student files and click the file **t-shirt**. Click Insert. Click Close. The picture fills the background of your chart. You need to recolor other parts of the chart so the T-shirt is visible in the background, as shown in Figure 6-20.
6. Click the gray area behind the chart shapes, the Back and Side Walls. Right-click and choose Format Walls. Choose No Fill and click Close.
7. Right-click the Vertical (Value) Axis numbers and change the font to Arial, 18 points, and bold.
8. Right-click the Horizontal (Category) Axis labels and change the font to Arial, 18 points, and bold.
9. Adjust the position of the text box or arrow if necessary.
10. Update the slide footer for slide 5 to include the text **[6-19your initials]**.

Figure 6-20
Chart with picture background

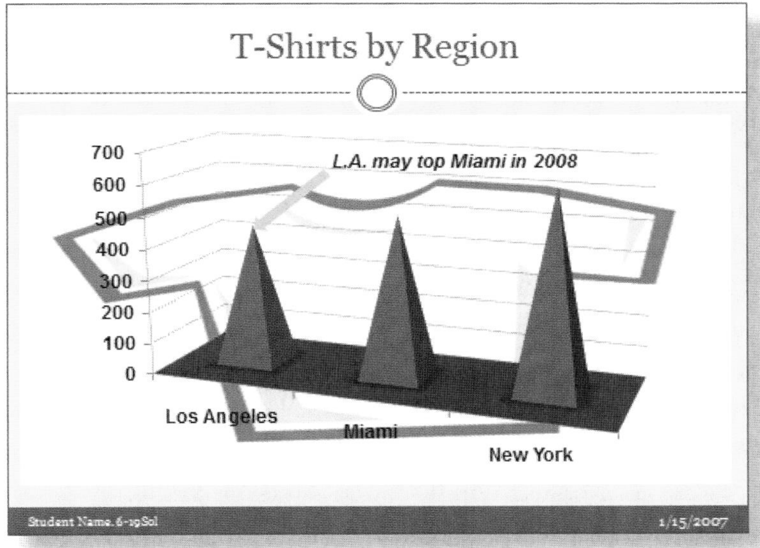

11. View the presentation as a slide show, starting with slide 1.
12. Create a handout header and footer: Include the date and your name as the header, and the page number and text **[6-19your initials]** as the footer.
13. Move to slide 1 and save the presentation as **[6-19your initials]** in your Lesson 6 folder.
14. Preview, and then print the presentation as handouts, six slides per page, grayscale, landscape, scale to fit paper, and framed. Close the presentation.

Lesson 6 Summary

- Charts are diagrams that display numbers in pictorial format. Charts illustrate quantitative relationships and can help people understand the significance of numeric information more easily than viewing the same information as a list of numbers.
- When you start a new chart, a sample worksheet appears in Microsoft Excel. A worksheet is where you key the numbers and labels used to create a chart.
- The worksheet contains rows and columns. You key each number or label in a separate *cell*—the rectangle formed by the intersection of a row and a column.
- On the worksheet, key labels are in the first row and column.
- A data series is a group of data that relates to a common object or category. Often, more than one data series is displayed on a single chart.
- Use the Switch Row/Column button to change how a data series is displayed on a chart.
- A wide variety of chart types are available including column, bar, area, line, pie, and surface with many different chart format options.
- Several Content Layouts are suitable for charts. Two Content Layouts also make it easy to combine a chart and body text on the same slide.
- Use the Chart Elements drop-down list to select specific parts of a chart or you can use ScreenTips to identify parts as you point to them.
- Special fill and border effects, including textures and gradient fills, can be used in charts the same way you use them for other PowerPoint objects.
- Use the Format Axis dialog box to modify the units, font, and number format of the value axis or secondary value axis. Modify the unit settings to specify the range of numbers displayed and increments between numbers.
- Axis titles are an important part of charts. Careful labeling ensures that your charts will be interpreted correctly.
- A legend is a box showing the colors assigned to each data series. Customize a chart's legend by changing the border, background colors, and font attributes.
- Use a secondary axis when you need to plot two dissimilar types of data on the same chart. A secondary axis is available only for a 2-D chart type.
- Proper formatting and labeling on a chart is important when your chart has both a primary and secondary axis.
- A good way to distinguish between different data types on a single chart is to assign different chart types. For example, use columns for one type of data and lines for the other type.
- A pie chart shows individual values in relation to the sum of all the values. Each value is displayed as a slice of the pie.
- A pie chart can show only one data series. To show more than one data series, use more than one pie chart.

- The plot area of a chart is the area containing the actual columns, bars, or pie slices. It can be formatted with or without a border and a fill effect.
- Exploding a pie slice (dragging it out from the center of the pie) emphasizes the slice.
- Use the Insert tab to add shapes and text boxes. Use text boxes wherever annotation is needed to clarify the chart's meaning.
- Charts can be enhanced by adding pictures, colors, and 3-D effects.

LESSON 6 — Command Summary

Feature	Button	Task Path	Keyboard
Insert a chart		Insert, Illustrations group, Chart	
Display worksheet		Chart Tools Design, Data group, Edit Data	
Insert axis titles		Chart Tools Layout, Labels group, Axis Titles	
Insert or remove a legend		Chart Tools Layout, Labels group, Legend	
Switch data series between columns and rows		Chart Tools Design, Data group, Switch Row/Column	
Format a chart object		Chart Tools Format, Current Selection group, Format Selection	Ctrl+1
Change the chart type		Chart Tools Design, Type group, Change Chart Type	
Add a secondary axis		Chart Tools Format, Current Selection group, Format Selection (with Data series selected)	
Add data labels		Chart Tools Layout, Labels group, Data Labels	
Change chart style		Chart Tools Design, Chart Styles group, Chart Layout	
Apply different chart layouts		Chart Tools Design, Chart Layouts group, More	
Add/Remove gridlines		Chart Tools Layout, Axes group, Gridlines	

Lesson 7

Creating Diagrams with SmartArt Graphics

OBJECTIVES

After completing this lesson, you will be able to:

1. Choose SmartArt graphics.
2. Enhance diagrams.
3. Prepare an organization chart.
4. Create other diagrams with SmartArt.
5. Change diagram types and orientation.

MCAS OBJECTIVES

In this lesson:

PP07 3.1.1
PP07 3.1.2
PP07 3.2.1
PP07 3.2.2
PP07 3.2.3
PP07 3.2.4
PP07 3.2.5
PP07 3.2.6
PP07 3.2.7
PP07 3.3.1
PP07 3.5.1
See Appendix

Estimated Time: 1½ hours

Using diagrams is a very important way to illustrate presentation content. *Diagrams* provide a visual representation of information that can help an audience understand a presenter's message. For example, diagrams can be used to show the steps of a process or the relationship between managers and subordinates. An audience can see the process or relationship because it is portrayed with graphic shapes and connecting lines or layered in some way to show these sequences and relationships. In this lesson you will create diagrams using SmartArt, a new feature of PowerPoint that contains a wide range of predesigned diagrams that can be customized in many different ways.

Choosing SmartArt Graphics

A *SmartArt graphic* is a diagram that can be inserted on your slide and then the parts of the diagram can be filled in with identifying text. Or if you have text in a bulleted list or in text shapes, the text items can be converted to a SmartArt diagram. You will use both of these techniques in this lesson.

From the Insert tab, in the Illustration group, click the SmartArt button to see the Choose a SmartArt Graphic dialog box shown in Figure 7-1. You can display thumbnails of all possible diagrams, or you can click one of the seven categories to look at them by diagram type. On the right side of this dialog box, the diagram is displayed in a larger size with a definition below to help you decide if this is the right type of illustration for your communication needs. The white lines that you see on the sample diagram represent where your text will appear when you label each part of the diagram.

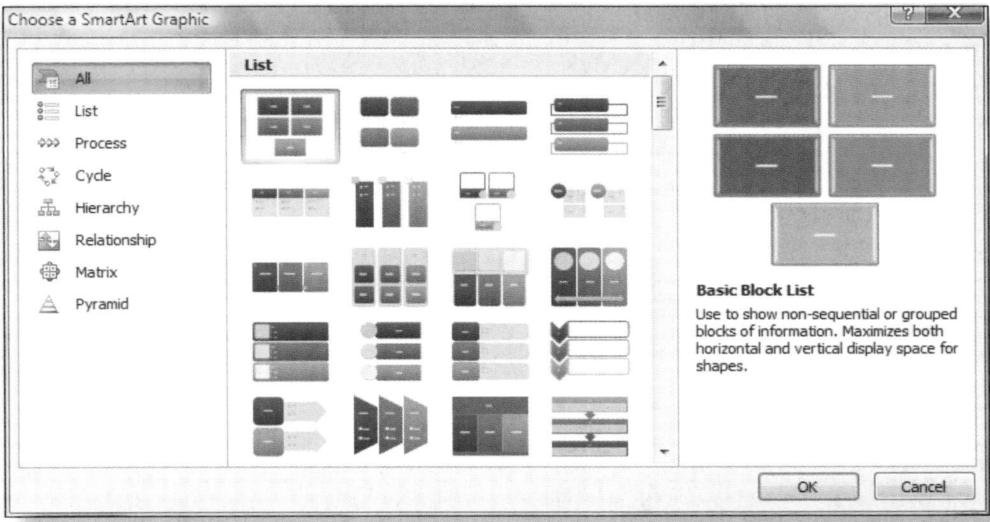

Figure 7-1
Choose a SmartArt Graphic dialog box

Exercise 7-1 USE DIAGRAMS FOR COMMUNICATION PURPOSES

Preparing a few bulleted lists is a simple way to create a series of slides for a presentation. However, a presentation including only bulleted lists is not very appealing to an audience from a visual standpoint and may not be the best way to communicate the meaning of your message an audience needs to understand.

As you develop your presentation content, you should be considering your message from the viewpoint of the audience and not just thinking about what you need to say. To help your audience visualize these concepts and remember them, plan alternative ways to illustrate concepts, such as including pictures, charts, and shapes, to draw attention to key points. Also, you can choose from an extensive array of SmartArt graphics. These graphics are diagrams that are arranged in seven categories, as listed in Table 7-1.

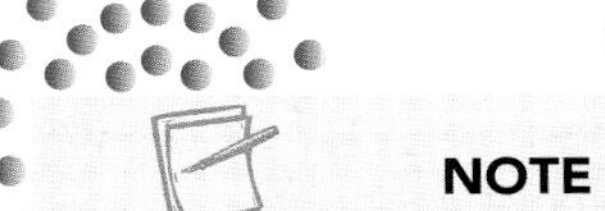

NOTE

Search for SmartArt descriptions in PowerPoint's Help to find a comprehensive list of all SmartArt graphics organized by category. Each graphic is displayed with descriptions of the layout and tips for situations where each would be appropriate.

TABLE 7-1 SmartArt Graphics Diagram Types

Diagram Type	Purpose
List	Provides an alternative to listing text in bulleted lists. List diagrams can show groupings, labeled parts, and even directional concepts through how the shapes are stacked. Several diagrams show main categories and then subtopics within those categories.

continues

TABLE 7-1 SmartArt Graphics Diagram Types *continued*

Diagram Type	Purpose
Process	Shows a sequence of events or the progression of workflow such as in a flowchart. These diagrams show connected parts of a process or even converging processes using a funnel technique. Several diagrams with arrows can portray conflict or opposing viewpoints.
Cycle	Represents a continuous series of events such as an ongoing manufacturing or employee review process. A cycle can be arranged in a circular pattern or with slices or gears to reflect interconnected parts. A radial cycle begins with a central part and then other parts extend from the center.
Hierarchy	Illustrates reporting relationships or lines of authority between employees in a company such as in an organization chart. These connections are sometimes called parent-child relationships. Hierarchy diagrams can be arranged vertically or horizontally such as in a decision tree used to show the outgrowth of options after particular choices are made.
Relationship	Shows interconnected, hierarchical, proportional, or overlapping relationships. Some of these diagrams also appear in different categories.
Matrix	Allows placement of concepts along two axes or in related quadrants. Emphasis can be on the whole or on individual parts.
Pyramid	Shows interconnected or proportional relationships building from one direction such as a foundational concept on which other concepts are built.

Exercise 7-2 USE LISTS TO SHOW GROUPS OF INFORMATION

In this exercise you will create a List diagram in two different ways:

NOTE

If you added a fourth bulleted item, the shapes on the slide would become a little smaller so all shapes could be displayed.

- Start with a blank slide and key SmartArt content using a Text pane.
- Start with existing bulleted text and convert to SmartArt.

1. Open the file **Organize**.
2. Move to slide 1. From the Home tab, in the Slides group, click the New Slide button to insert a new slide using the **Title and Content layout**. On the content placeholder, click the SmartArt button.
3. Click the **List** category. Click the **Vertical Box List** thumbnail then click **OK**.
4. From the SmartArt Tools Design tab, in the Create Graphic group, click the Text pane button. A text box will appear on the left, as shown in Figure 7-2, where you can key the text after each bullet for each of the shapes in this diagram.

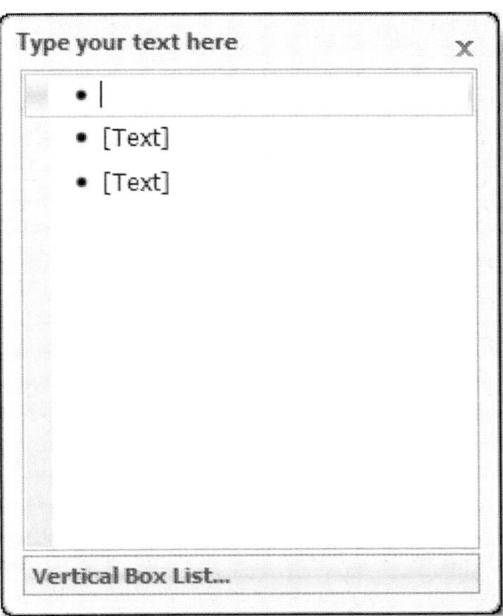

Figure 7-2
Entering SmartArt text

5. For the first item, key **New Procedure**.
6. Click after the second bullet and key **New Philosophy**; click after the third bullet and key **New Department**. Notice that the text you keyed as bulleted items now appears on the shapes.
7. Close the Text pane.
8. For the slide title, key **Organizational Changes** as shown in Figure 7-3. This type of list diagram will work best when you have limited information for first-level bulleted points and no subpoints in a list.

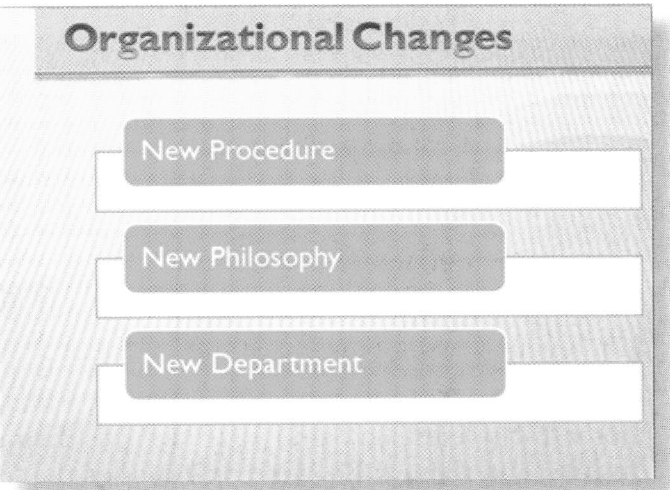

Figure 7-3
Vertical Box List diagram

NOTE

If you already have bulleted text on a slide, then that text can be converted to a SmartArt diagram. In the following steps, you will show both the first-level and second-level text shown on slide 3.

9. In the Slides and Outline pane, click slide 3 and press Ctrl+D to duplicate the slide. Once your diagram is prepared on slide 3 and you have confirmed that all the text is appropriately displayed, you can delete slide 4 with the bulleted list. But for now, it is a good idea to leave one slide as originally prepared so it is available for comparison.
10. Now highlight all of the bulleted text on slide 3.

11. From the Home tab, in the Paragraph group, click the Convert to SmartArt Graphic button.

12. Click **More SmartArt Graphics** to access all categories, and click the **List** category.
13. Click the **Horizontal Bullet List** thumbnail, then click **OK**.
14. The first-level bulleted items appear in the top rectangles and the second-level bulleted items appear in the bottom rectangles with bullets. The color treatment of the first-level words is more dominant than what appears for the subpoints, as shown in Figure 7-4.

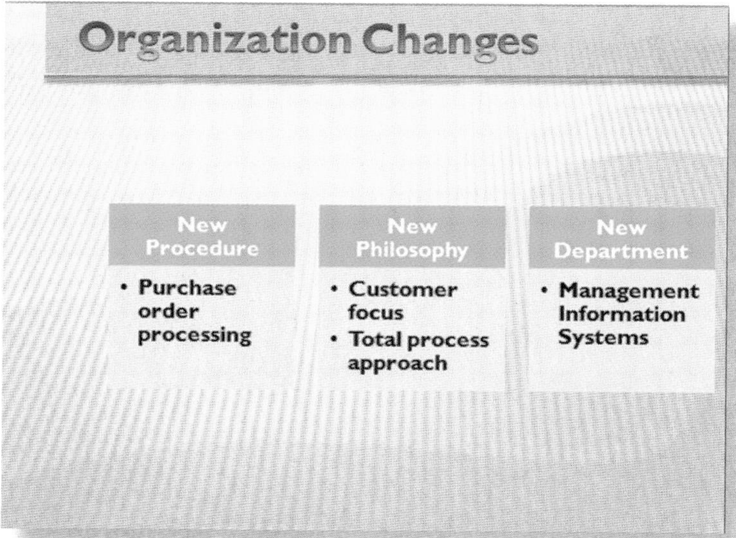

Figure 7-4
Horizontal Bullet List diagram

15. Now confirm that all the same text is included in the diagram on slide 3 that is in the duplicated slide 4 bulleted list.
16. When you are sure that everything matches, delete slide 4.
17. Create a new folder for Lesson 7. Create a handout header and footer. Include the date and your name as the header, and the page number and the text **[7-2your initials]** as the footer. Save the presentation as **[7-2your initials]** in your new Lesson 7 folder. Leave the presentation open for the next exercise.

Exercise 7-3 USE PROCESS DIAGRAMS TO SHOW SEQUENTIAL WORKFLOW STEPS

A *process diagram* reflects concepts or events that occur sequentially. Generally speaking, one part must be finished before the next part begins. Many variations for how these processes can be portrayed are available through SmartArt.

1. Move to slide 3. From the Home tab, in the Slides group, click the New Slide button.
2. On the slide 4 content area, click the SmartArt button, then choose the **Process** category.

3. Examine the different options in this category and then click the **Basic Process** thumbnail and click **OK**. A three-part diagram appears as shown in Figure 7-5. You can enter text directly in the placeholders on each diagram shape, or you can click the Text pane button on the left to open enter text.
4. For this exercise, key directly in each of the shapes. As you key, the text will automatically word-wrap in the shape and become smaller to fit within that shape. Therefore, you need to be careful when using this method to keep the words you enter very concise.
5. Click in the first rectangle shape and key **Survey customer needs**.
6. Click in the second rectangle shape and key **Analyze survey results**.
7. Click in the third rectangle shape and key **Develop product plan**.

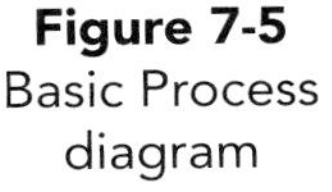

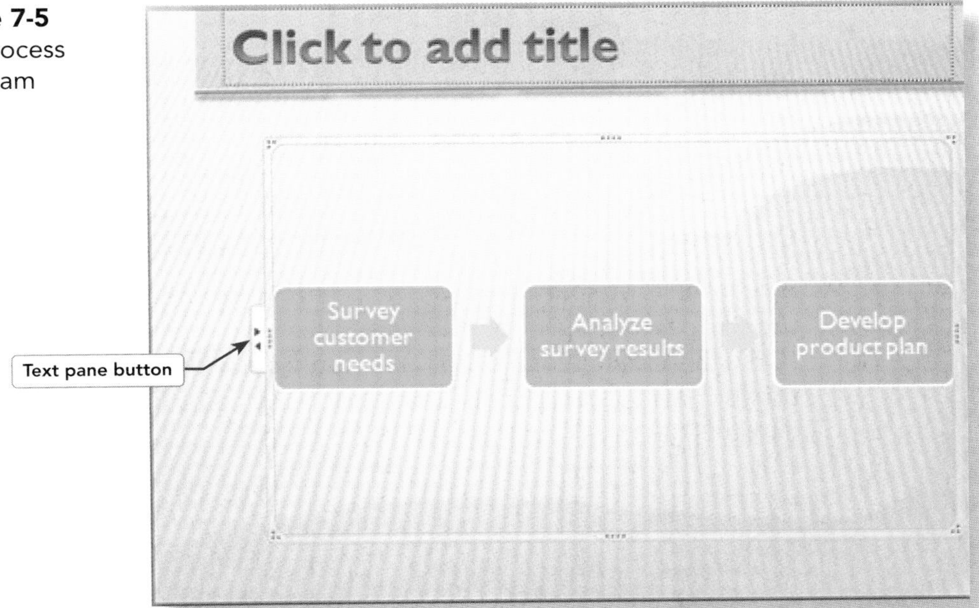

Figure 7-5
Basic Process diagram

8. Because you need to include a fourth step in this process, you need to increase the size of the SmartArt area. Point to the top left corner of the SmartArt border and drag it close to the left edge of the slide.
9. Select the third shape in the diagram, then click the Text pane button to open the bulleted text dialog shape. Notice that this text is highlighted in the bulleted text dialog shape.
10. Click at the end of the word "plan" and press Enter, then key **Introduce new products**. A fourth shape is added and text size automatically adjusted again.
11. Close the Text pane.

NOTE

When creating diagrams like this, be careful that your text does not become too small for easy reading. Later in this lesson you will make the text larger on this slide.

12. For the slide title, key the text New Development Process.
13. Update the handout footer text to **[7-3your initials]**. Save the presentation as **[7-3your initials]** in your Lesson 7 folder. Leave the presentation open for the next exercise.

Exercise 7-4 USE CYCLE DIAGRAMS TO SHOW A CONTINUING SEQUENCE

The *cycle diagram* is used to communicate a continuing sequence. In this exercise you will use the same information as you did in slide 4, but display it in a cycle. Instead of creating the diagram first, however, you will enter text using a bulleted list and then convert the list into a SmartArt graphic.

1. Insert a new slide after slide 4, and key the title New Development Cycle.
2. In the content placeholder, key four bulleted items:

   Survey customer needs
   Analyze survey results
   Develop product plan
   Introduce new products

3. Select the listed text and right-click. From the pop-up menu choose Convert to SmartArt, then click the Basic Cycle thumbnail.
4. Select the four shapes. From the SmartArt Tools Format tab, in the Shape Styles group, click the Shape Fill button and choose (Orange, Accent 1, darker 25%) to apply a darker theme fill color. Select the four arrows and apply a darker theme color (Orange, Accent 1, darker 50%), as shown in Figure 7-6.

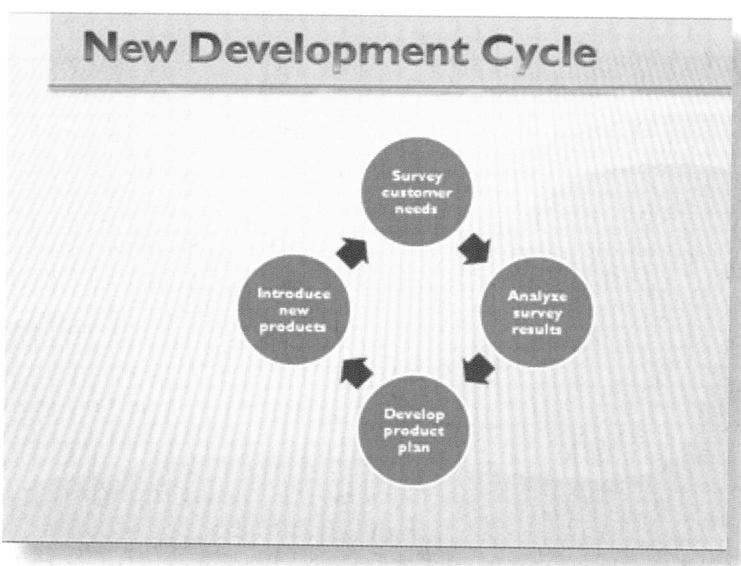

Figure 7-6
Completed Basic Cycle diagram

5. Update the handout footer text to **[7-4your initials]**.

6. Move to slide 1 and save the presentation as **[7-4your initials]** in your Lesson 7 folder.
7. Preview, and then print the entire presentation as handouts, six slides per page, grayscale, framed. Leave the presentation open for the next exercise.

Enhancing Diagrams

Once a SmartArt graphic is inserted on your slide, its appearance can be altered using the effects you have learned to apply to shapes. However, additional options exist for customizing these diagrams, and you will work with these design options in the next exercises.

Exercise 7-5 APPLY SHAPE QUICK STYLES

One of the quickest ways to change the appearance of shapes within a diagram is to apply *Quick Styles*. These styles include more than one preset adjustment.

1. On slide 2, select the three rectangle shapes that contain text content.

2. From the Home tab, in the Drawing group, click the Quick Styles button. A gallery of preset styles appears in an array of theme colors, as shown in Figure 7-7.

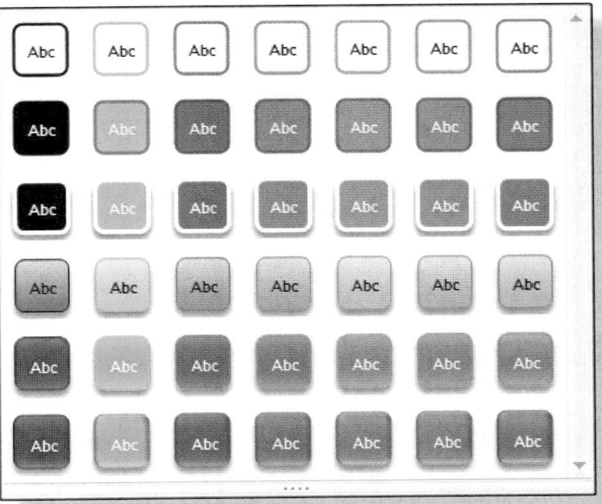

Figure 7-7
Shape Quick Styles

3. As you move your pointer horizontally, you will see different colors applied to the selected shapes. As you move your pointer vertically, you will see different effects such as outlines, beveling, and shadows.
4. To use a darker color and apply a shadow effect to the shapes, click on **Light 1 Outline, Color Fill - Accent 2**.

Exercise 7-6 ADJUST 3-D FORMAT AND ROTATION

In the previous exercises, the shapes have a *2-D* orientation—you see the shapes in dimensions of height (up/down measurement) and width (left/right measurement). Three-dimensional (*3-D*) settings add a perspective dimension to create the illusion of depth. For example, a square can look like a cube. Rotation settings enable you to tilt shapes on the screen.

1. Move to slide 4 and select the four rectangles.

2. From the Home tab, in the Drawing group, click the Shape Effects button, then choose **3-D Rotation**.
3. From the gallery of options, choose **Perspective Heroic Extreme Left**, as shown in Figure 7-8.

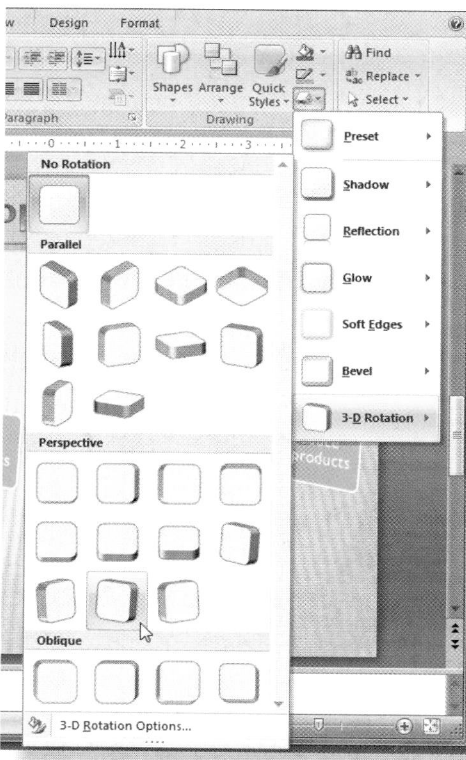

Figure 7-8
3-D Rotation effects

4. Now add two more shape effects to customize this diagram. With the rectangle shapes selected,
   a. click the Shape Effects button, choose **Bevel**, and then choose the **Circle** bevel.
   b. click the Shape Effects button, choose **Shadow**, and then from the Outer category choose **Offset Diagonal Top Right**.
   c. click anywhere on the slide to turn off the selection.
5. Select the three arrows and apply the same **Bevel** and **Shadow** effects that were applied to the shapes in step 4.

Exercise 7-7 ADJUST THE OVERALL SIZE AND LAYOUT OF THE DIAGRAM

Diagrams can be resized like any other PowerPoint object. However, you must always be sure the text is still readable if the size of shapes is reduced. You may need to use only a single word on small shapes if their size becomes small. In this exercise, you will experiment with a couple of sizing techniques.

1. Duplicate slide 4, then make the following changes on the slide 5 diagrams.
2. Notice that the four rectangles and connecting arrows extend across the complete slide so you don't have any extra horizontal room

unless the shapes become smaller. Resize the SmartArt area by dragging the right side about a half inch to the left. The text on the shapes becomes slightly smaller.

3. Resize the top and bottom of the SmartArt area so it is just large enough to contain the shapes.
4. Drag this diagram up to fit directly under the slide title.
5. With the diagram selected, press Ctrl+D to duplicate the diagram. Position the second diagram evenly below the first one. Duplicating is a quick way to make a second diagram because you can simply edit the text on each shape for new wording without having to reset the Shape Effects.
6. On the second diagram, expand its space, then change the position of the shapes, as shown in Figure 7-9. Follow these steps:
   a. Resize the bottom border of the duplicated SmartArt area to increase the size of available space for positioning shapes.
   b. Select the first rectangle and drag it to the upper left. Notice that the arrow between this rectangle and the second one automatically repositions itself.
   c. Select the second rectangle and move it to the left.
   d. Select the third rectangle and move it to the left and down slightly. Be careful that you allow enough space for the arrow.
   e. Select the fourth rectangle and move it to the left and down slightly.
   f. Adjust rectangle positioning by nudging (using the arrow keys) so the arrows remain approximately the same size.
7. Now you are still portraying the four-step process because of the connecting arrows that show the direction. But with only one diagram in this arrangement, you would have enough room on the slide for a picture or some other graphic element to accompany the diagram.

Figure 7-9
A Process diagram arranged two ways

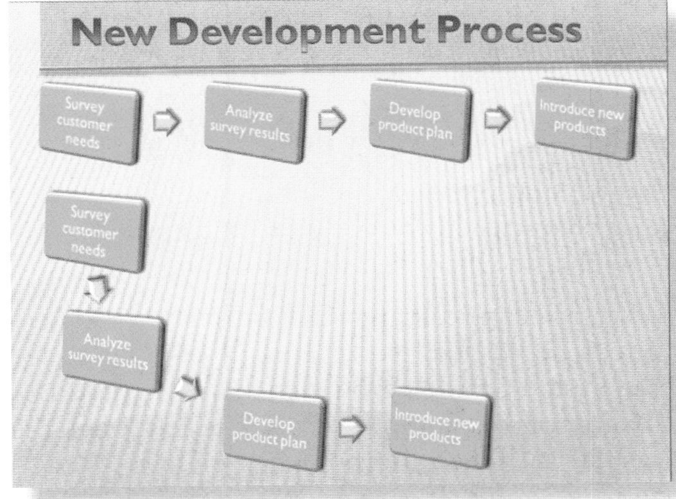

8. Update the handout footer text to **[7-7your initials]**.
9. Move to slide 1 and save the presentation as **[7-7your initials]** in your Lesson 7 folder. Leave the presentation open for the next exercise.

Exercise 7-8 ADD SHAPES

In Exercise 7-3, you added a shape so you already have some experience in modifying SmartArt. The different diagrams add shapes in different places, so the shape you have selected when you add another shape is important because the new shape is normally connected to the selected one in some way.

1. Move to slide 6 and create a new slide with the **Title and Content** layout. Key **Adding SmartArt Shapes** as the slide title. Click the SmartArt button in the content placeholder.
2. From the List category, choose the **Stacked List** then click **OK**.
3. Now edit the text on each shape as follows:
   a. In the circle on the left, key **One**, then for the related text key **First item** and **Second item**.
   b. In the circle on the right, key **Two**, then for the related text key **First item** and **Second item**.
   c. Notice that the text will automatically resize and word-wrap for each shape.

4. Now under the left circle labeled "One," click the "First item" text to select that shape. From the SmartArt Tools Design tab, in the Create Graphic group, click the bottom part of the Add Shape button then choose **Add Shape After**. A new shape appears below the first item, and the diagram has been resized. Key **New item** in this shape.
5. Now select the left circle labeled "One." Click the bottom part of the Add Shape , then choose **Add Shape After**. This time a second circle with a related rectangle shape is added, as shown in Figure 7-10.
6. In the added circle, key **New**; in the related shape, key **New item**.
7. Notice that you have the options of before and after as well as above and below when you are adding shapes, so it is very important that you choose where you want the shape to go.

8. Also, you can rearrange the order of the shapes in a diagram. Select the circle labeled "New." From the SmartArt Tools Design tab, in the Create Graphic group, click the Right to Left button and the diagram is displayed from right to left. Click the button again to display the diagram from left to right.

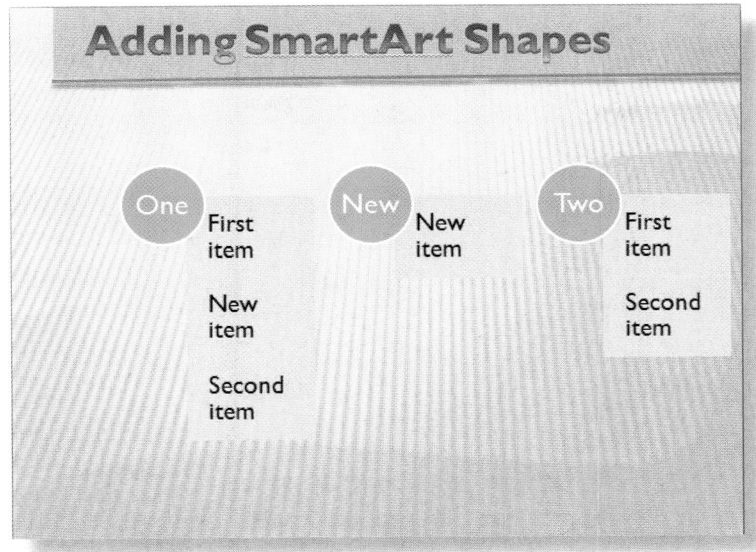

Figure 7-10 Adding SmartArt shapes

Exercise 7-9 CHANGE COLORS AND RESET THE GRAPHIC

You have already used Quick Styles to change a diagram's appearance. Many more options are available from the SmartArt Tools Design tab, in the SmartArt Styles group, as shown in Figure 7-11.

1. On slide 7, select the SmartArt diagram. From the SmartArt Tools Design tab, in the SmartArt Styles group, click the More button to see the complete gallery of SmartArt Styles arranged in two categories, Best Match for Document and 3-D. As you point to these thumbnails you will see that effect applied to your diagram.

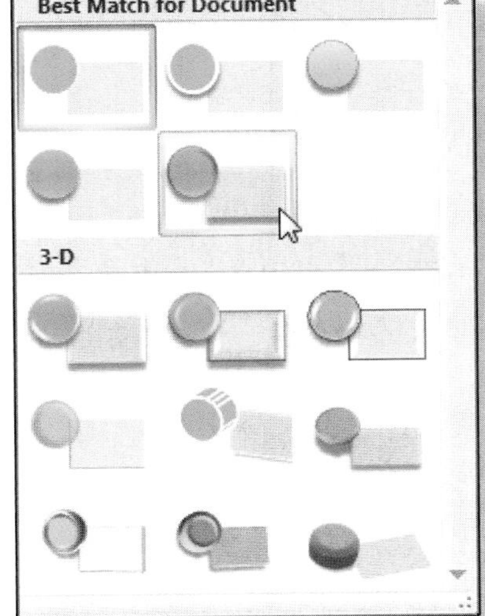

Figure 7-11 SmartArt Styles

2. Click the **Intense Effect** thumbnail and this effect is automatically applied.
3. With your SmartArt diagram selected, from the SmartArt Tools Design tab, in the SmartArt Styles group, click the Change Colors button. Colors are arranged in eight categories: Primary Theme Colors, Colorful, and six Accent colors. The current color is selected, as shown in Figure 7-12.

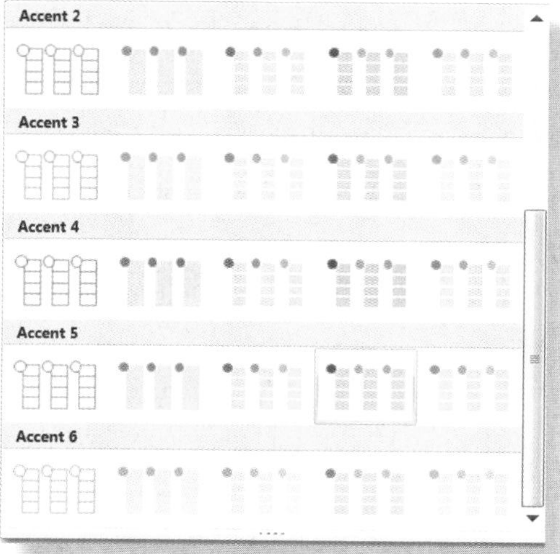

Figure 7-12
Change colors for a SmartArt diagram

4. Point to different thumbnails in this gallery of colors, and consider the changes on your slide. Notice that colors change as you go down the list between the various accent colors in the presentation's design theme. Then as you go across, different line and shading treatments are used.
5. Select the **Gradient Loop – Accent 5** color.
6. If you are not pleased with your change, it is always easy to remove it. From the SmartArt Tools Design tab, in the Reset group, click the Reset Graphic button and the original style of your diagram is restored.

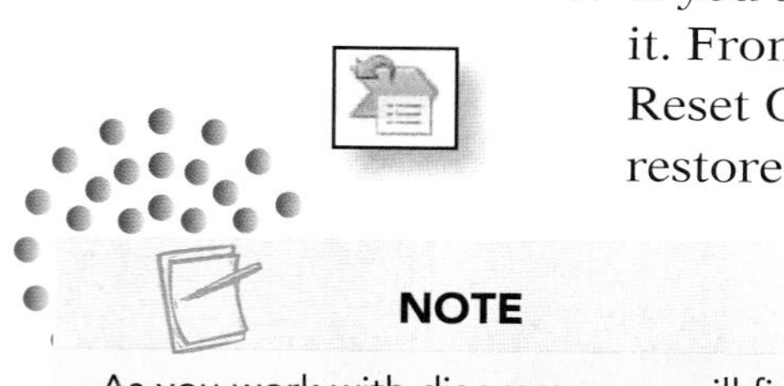

NOTE

As you work with diagrams, you will find the keyboard shortcuts listed in Table 7-2 helpful because they provide a quick way to move between shapes, select shapes, or select the text within the shapes.

7. Update the handout footer text to **[7-9your initials]**.
8. Move to slide 1 and save the presentation as **[7-9your initials]** in your Lesson 7 folder. Leave the presentation open for the next exercise.

TABLE 7-2 Using the Keyboard to Navigate in SmartArt Graphics

Key	Result
F2	Toggles the current shape between being selected and activated.
Esc	Deactivates a selected shape.
Enter	Activated shape: Inserts a new text line.
← or →	Selected shape: Nudges the position of the shape left or right.
↑ or ↓	Selected shape: Nudges the position of the shape up or down.
Tab	Selected shape: Moves to the next shape. Activated shape: Inserts a tab character at the insertion point.
Shift+Tab	Selected shape: Moves to the previous shape. Activated shape: Inserts a tab character at the insertion point.

Preparing an Organization Chart

Organization charts are most commonly used to show a hierarchy such as the lines of authority or reporting relationships in a business. You start an organization chart in the same way as other SmartArt graphics, but it is important to consider superior and subordinate relationships.

Exercise 7-10 CREATE AN ORGANIZATION CHART

When you start a new organization chart, you begin with a default arrangement of five rectangular shapes. Each shape is positioned on a *level* in the chart, which indicates its position in the hierarchy. The top shape indicates the highest level with a direct line down to the second level (such as the president of a company and the managers who report to the president). The shape that branches from the central line reflects a supporting position (such as an assistant to the president).

1. Insert a new slide after slide 7 that uses the **Title and Content** layout. Key the title **New Management Structure**.
2. In the content placeholder, click the SmartArt button .
3. Choose the **Hierarchy** category then click the **Organization Chart** thumbnail and click **OK**. A chart with five shapes appears with text placeholders that show text in a large size. The text size will become smaller as you key text.
4. Move your pointer to the top shape in the chart and click inside the text placeholder. Notice the dashed outline that indicates the shape is activated.
5. Key **Julie Wolfe &**, then press Enter and key **Gus Irvinelli** to position the names on two lines. You will later format this text to fit on one line.
6. Press Enter to start a new line and key **Co-owners**.
7. Press Esc to deactivate text editing. The shape now has a solid outline.
8. Press Tab to move to the first lower-level shape.
9. Key the following three items on three lines:

   Administration
   Michael Peters
   Administration Mgr

10. The text becomes smaller to fit in the shape. Press F2 to deactivate text editing.

11. Press Tab to move to the second shape on the lower level. Key the following items on three lines:

    Sales & Marketing
    Roy Olafsen
    Marketing Mgr

12. Press F2, then press Tab to move to the third shape and key the following items on three lines:

    Operations
    Michele Jenkins
    Head Chef

13. Press F2, then press Tab to move to the shape that branches from the central line and press Delete.
14. Click outside the SmartArt area to deactivate the organization chart, as shown in Figure 7-13.

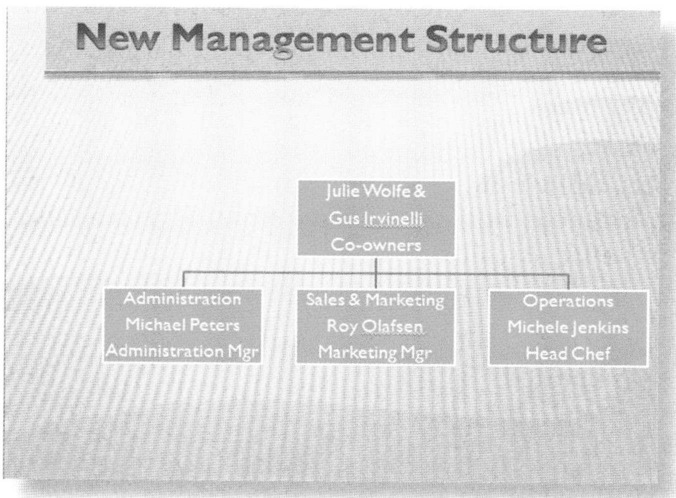

Figure 7-13
Organization chart

15. Update the handout footer text to **[7-10your initials]**.
16. Save the presentation as **[7-10your initials]** in your Lesson 7 folder. Leave the presentation open for the next exercise.

Exercise 7-11 INSERT SUBORDINATE SHAPES

The organization of many companies changes frequently. You might need to promote, demote, or move organization chart shapes as the reporting structure changes or becomes more complex.

To expand your organization chart as shown in Figure 7-14, you can insert additional shapes of the following types:

- *Subordinate shapes*—shapes that are connected to a superior shape (a shape on a higher level).

- *Coworker shapes*—shapes that are connected to the same superior shape as another shape.
- *Assistant shapes*—shapes that are usually placed below a superior shape and above subordinate shapes.

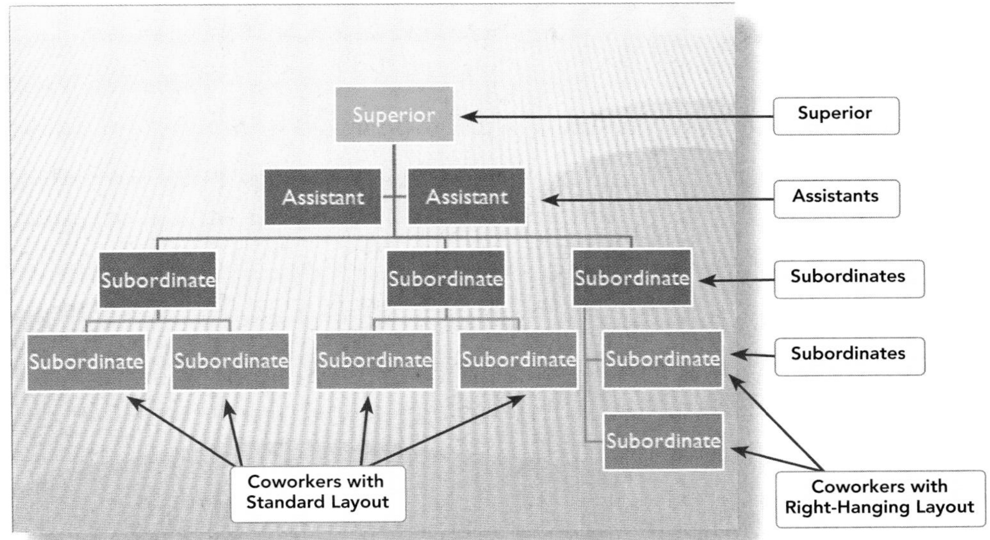

Figure 7-14 Structure of an organization chart

To add *subordinate shapes*, first select the shape that will be their superior; then from the SmartArtTools Design tab, in the Create Graphic group, click the Add Shape button.

1. Still working on slide 8, select the first shape on the second level, with the name "Michael Peters."

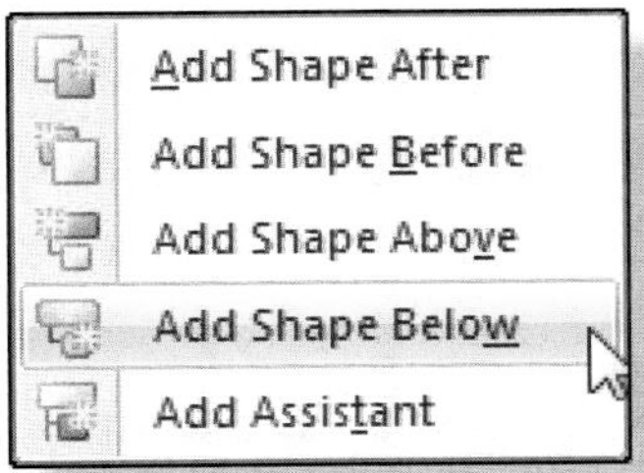

Figure 7-15 Adding organization chart shapes

2. From the SmartArt Tools Design tab, in the Create Graphic group, click the lower half of the Add Shape button, then from the pop-up list select **Add Shape Below**. A shape appears below the selected shape with a connecting line and now the new shape is selected.

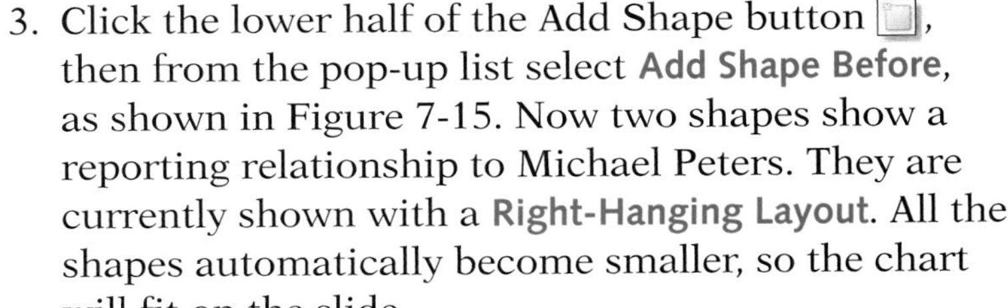

3. Click the lower half of the Add Shape button, then from the pop-up list select **Add Shape Before**, as shown in Figure 7-15. Now two shapes show a reporting relationship to Michael Peters. They are currently shown with a **Right-Hanging Layout**. All the shapes automatically become smaller, so the chart will fit on the slide.
4. Repeat this process to add one shape under Roy Olafsen and three shapes under Michele Jenkins. Once again the shapes are resized to fit, but the text is now too small to read. This will be corrected later.

NOTE

Both Add Shape After and Add Shape Before insert new shapes at different levels. Add Shape Above inserts a new shape in the level above, which would be a superior position. Add Shape Below inserts a new shape in the level below, which would be a subordinate position. Add Assistant inserts a new shape between levels.

Exercise 7-12 ADD ASSISTANT AND COWORKER SHAPES

Assistant shapes are used for positions that provide administrative assistance or other support. They are inserted below a selected shape, but above the next-lower level.

Coworker shapes are inserted at the same level as the selected shape and report to the same superior as the selected shape.

1. On slide 8, select the level 1 shape.
2. From the SmartArt Tools Design tab, in the Create Graphic group, click the Add Shape button and choose **Add Assistant**. A new shape is inserted between levels 1 and 2.
3. Select the shape below Michael Peters to add another shape at the same level. From the SmartArt Tools Design tab, in the Create Graphic group, click the Add Shape button and choose **Add Shape Before**. A new shape is inserted at the same level—this represents a coworker.
4. Repeat step 3 to add one shape under Roy Olafsen.
5. Now increase the slide size so you can more easily see the text. From the View tab, in the Zoom group, click the Zoom button and choose **200%**, then click **OK**.
6. On the enlarged slide, scroll to locate the assistant shape below the level 1 shape. Key **Troy Scott**, press Enter, then key **Assistant** so this text fits on two text lines.
7. In the three shapes under Michael Peters, key the following employee information on two text lines in each shape. After the text is entered, press F2 or Esc to deactivate the shape and then press Tab to move to the next shape.

MIS	**Billing**	**HR**
Chuck Warden	**Sarah Conners**	**Chris Davis**

8. After keying the text in Chris Davis's shape, press Esc to deactivate the text shape. Press Tab one time to move to Roy Olafsen's shape, and press Tab to move to the first shape under Roy Olafsen.
9. In the two shapes under Roy Olafsen, key the following employee information:

Events	**Marketing**
Ian Mahoney	**Evan Johnson**

10. In the first two shapes under Michele Jenkins, key the following and leave the last shape blank:

Kitchen	**Purchasing**
Eric Dennis	**Jessie Smith**

11. Notice that the organization chart again adjusted the text to a smaller size, as shown in Figure 7-16. From the View tab, in the Zoom group, click the Fit to Window button .

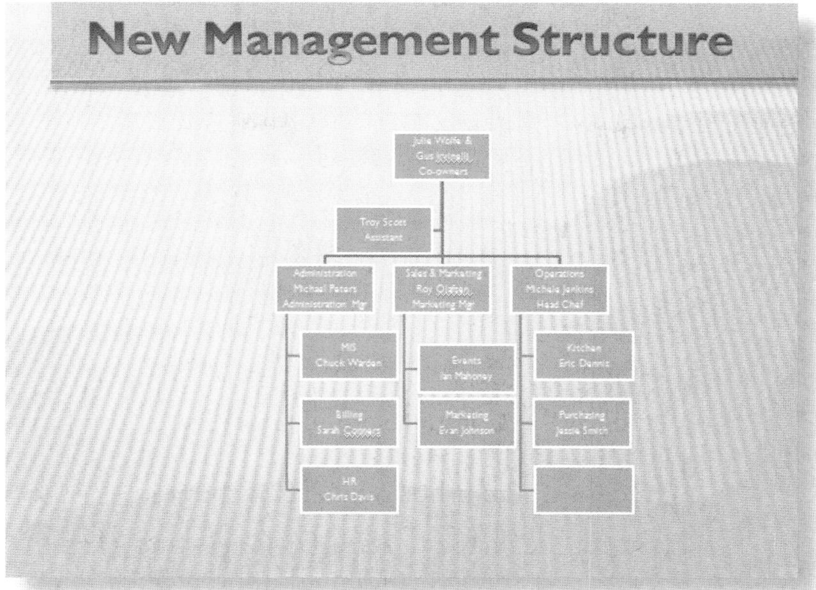

Figure 7-16
Organization chart with text

Exercise 7-13 CHANGE LAYOUT, DELETE, AND REARRANGE SHAPES

The layout of the organization chart can be changed to show subordinates in a *standard* format or a *hanging indent* format. A shape can be repositioned to a higher level by promoting (moving up) or repositioned to a lower level by demoting (moving down). An entire group of connected shapes can be moved right or left. If you have more shapes than necessary, you can delete them at any time.

1. On slide 8, select the shape for Michael Peters. From the SmartArt Tools Design tab, in the Create Graphic group, click the Layout button and choose **Standard**. The subordinate shapes below Michael Peters (coworkers) are now arranged side by side instead of in a vertical, hanging arrangement.
2. Select the blank subordinate shape below Michele Jenkins and press Delete.
3. Select the shape for Eric Dennis and click the Promote button. It moves up a level and the connected shape moves with it. Click the Undo button.
4. Click Roy Olafsen's shape and change the Layout to **Standard**. Repeat this process to change the Layout for Michele Jenkins's shape to **Standard**.
5. This arrangement communicates nicely the three levels of the organization as shown in Figure 7-17; however, the text is very small. The next steps will rearrange the layout so each shape can be a little larger.

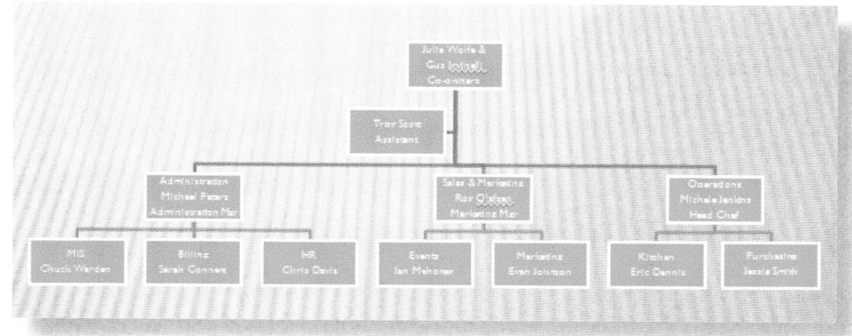

Figure 7-17
Organization chart with standard layout

6. Select the shape for Michael Peters. From the SmartArt Tools Design tab, in the Create Graphic group, click the Layout button and choose **Right Hanging**. Repeat this process to apply the **Right Hanging** indent to the other two level 2 shapes.
7. Select the shape of Sarah Conners and click the Demote button. Now this shape is indented under Chuck Warden.
8. Select the shape for Michael Peters and click the Right to Left button, and this entire branch of the chart is reordered to appear on the right, as shown in Figure 7-18.

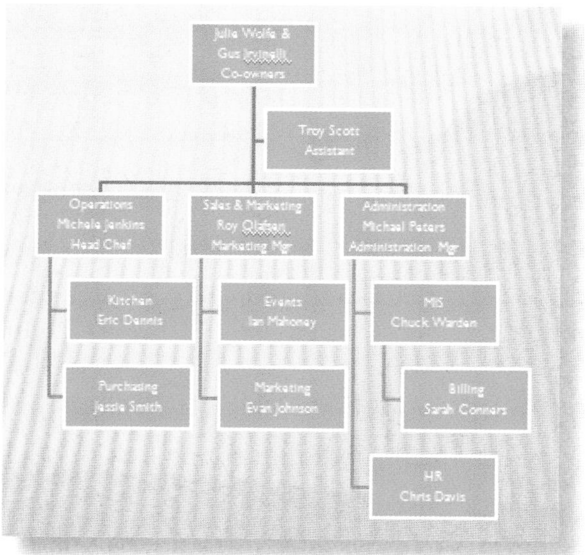

Figure 7-18
Organization chart with hanging indent layout

9. Update the handout footer text to **[7-13your initials]**.
10. Save the presentation as **[7-13your initials]** in your Lesson 7 folder. Leave the presentation open for the next exercise.

Exercise 7-14 CHANGE SHAPE SIZING AND STYLES

The entire SmartArt area can be made larger to accommodate charts with several levels. Selected shapes can be resized, and connected shapes repositioned so the text fits better. Text can be made larger, too.

1. On slide 8, resize the SmartArt area by dragging its border to expand it horizontally on both sides as well as vertically.
2. Select the level 1 shape and resize it horizontally to make it wider so both names fit on one line.
3. Select all three level 2 shapes and resize horizontally and vertically to allow a little more room in each shape.
4. Select all of the chart's shapes and increase the font size to 16 points in bold. Adjust the horizontal size of shapes if the text word-wraps.
5. Now spread apart the related shapes in the chart for easier reading. Select the Michael Peters shape and the related shapes below him. Press Ctrl and the right arrow about five times to move this branch to the right. The connecting lines automatically adjust.
6. Select the Michele Jenkins shape and the related shapes below her. Press Ctrl and the left arrow about five times to move this branch to the right.
7. With the SmartArt area selected, from the SmartArt Tools Design tab, in the SmartArt Styles group, click the Change Colors button and select the **Colorful – Accent Colors** thumbnail.
8. You can also change the color of individual shapes. Select the Assistant shape and then from the SmartArt Tools Format tab, in the Shape Styles group, choose a Shape Fill that will make the fill color a little lighter.
9. From the SmartArt Tools Design tab, in the SmartArt Styles group, examine the effect of different SmartArt Styles on the chart. Click the SmartArt Styles More button then choose the **Intense Effect**, as shown in Figure 7-19.
10. Update the handout footer text to **[7-14your initials]**. Save the presentation as **[7-14your initials]** in your Lesson 7 folder. Leave the presentation open for the next exercise.

Figure 7-19 Completed organization chart

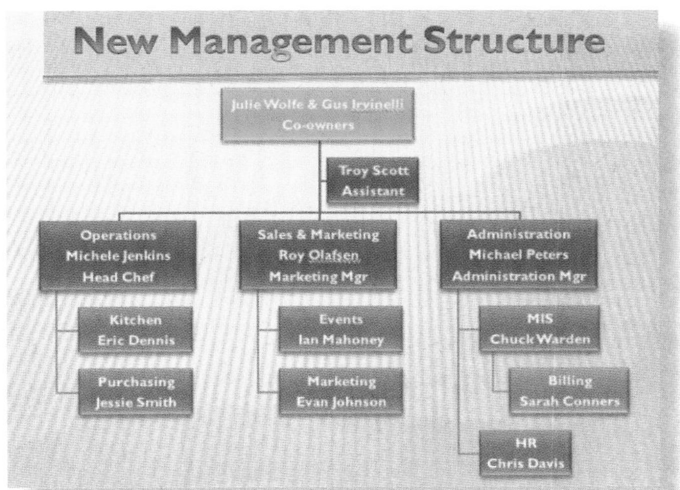

Creating Other Diagrams with SmartArt

The seven categories of PowerPoint SmartArt graphics offer many options to illustrate your thoughts in a visual way. This exercise will focus on three diagrams in the Relationship category.

Exercise 7-15 CREATE A RADIAL DIAGRAM

A *radial diagram* starts with a central circle (level 1) with four circles (level 2) connected to and surrounding the center circle. You can insert as many additional circles as you need to illustrate your message.

1. Insert a new slide after slide 8 that uses the **Title and Content** layout. Key the title **New Customer Philosophy**.
2. From the content placeholder click the SmartArt button.
3. Choose the **Relationship** category, then click the **Basic Radial** thumbnail and click **OK**. A chart appears with four circle shapes that radiate from the center circle with text placeholders.
4. Click the center circle, then from the SmartArt Tools Design tab, in the Create Graphic group, click the Add Shape button and a new circle is added to the diagram. It becomes the selected circle.
5. Press Delete to remove this new shape.
6. With the center circle selected, key **Customer**.
7. Think about your positioning as though referring to the face of a round clock. Click the top outer circle (12 o'clock position) and key the information shown under "12 o'clock" in Figure 7-20. Press Enter after the individual words, so the information appears on three text lines.
8. Click the circle at the 3 o'clock position and key the corresponding text.
9. Working in a clockwise direction, key the remaining text shown in Figure 7-20 in the remaining outer circles.

NOTE

If PowerPoint automatically capitalizes the second and third word in each circle, change the letters to lowercase. Automatic capitalization is caused by the AutoCorrect in PowerPoint. You can turn off this feature, if you wish, by clicking the Microsoft Office Button, click the PowerPoint Options button, choose **Proofing**, click **AutoCorrection Options**, deselect **Capitalize first letter of sentences**, then click **OK**.

Figure 7-20
Radial diagram text

12 o'clock	3 o'clock	6 o'clock	9 o'clock
Satisfy	Provide	Provide	Resolve
customer	courteous	excellent	problems
needs	service	quality	promptly

10. From the SmartArt Tools Design tab, in the SmartArt Styles group, click the Change Colors button and choose **Colored Fill – Accent 6**. Then click the SmartArt Styles More button and look at the effect of different options as you point to them. Choose the **Cartoon** style.
11. Drag the borders of the SmartArt area to increase the size of the diagram.
12. Choose the center shape, then from the SmartArt Tools Format tab, in the Shape Styles group, choose a darker shade of the shape fill color to emphasize the center, as shown in Figure 7-21.
13. Update the handout footer text to **[7-15your initials]**. Save the presentation as **[7-15your initials]** in your Lesson 7 folder. Leave the presentation open for the next exercise.

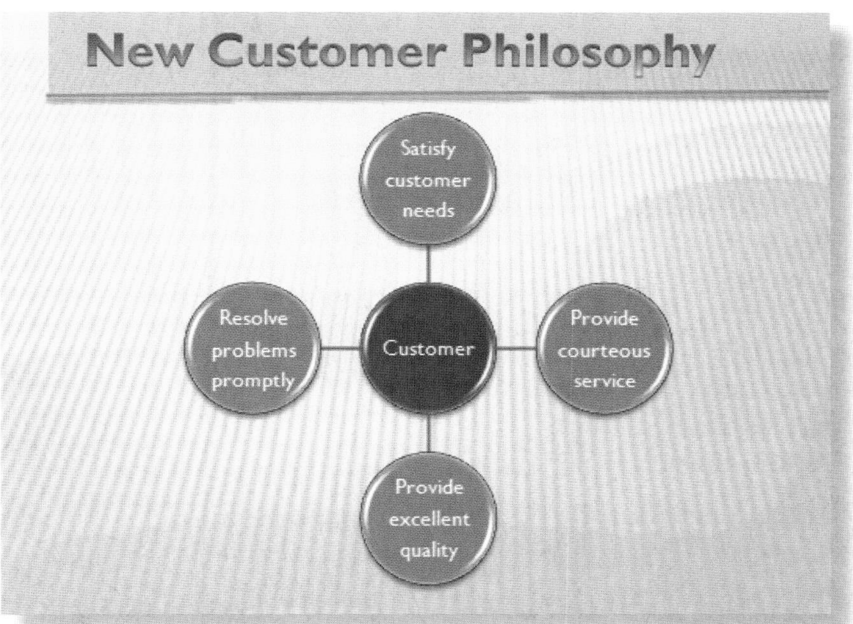

Figure 7-21
Radial diagram

Exercise 7-16 CREATE A GEAR DIAGRAM

Gears have spokes that stick out and lock with other gears to make them turn. The turning of each gear is dependent on the other gears. Therefore, the *gear diagram* communicates interlocking ideas that are shown as shapes.

1. Insert a new slide after slide 9 that uses the **Title and Content** layout. Key the title **Interlocking Ideas**.
2. From the content placeholder, click the SmartArt button .
3. Choose the **Relationship** category, then click the **Gear** thumbnail and click **OK**. A chart with three shapes and directional arrows appears. Key the text as shown in Figure 7-22.

4. From the SmartArt Tools Design Tab, in the SmartArt Styles group, choose the SmartArt Styles More button and choose the **3-D Inset style**.
5. Resize and reposition the SmartArt graphic attractively.

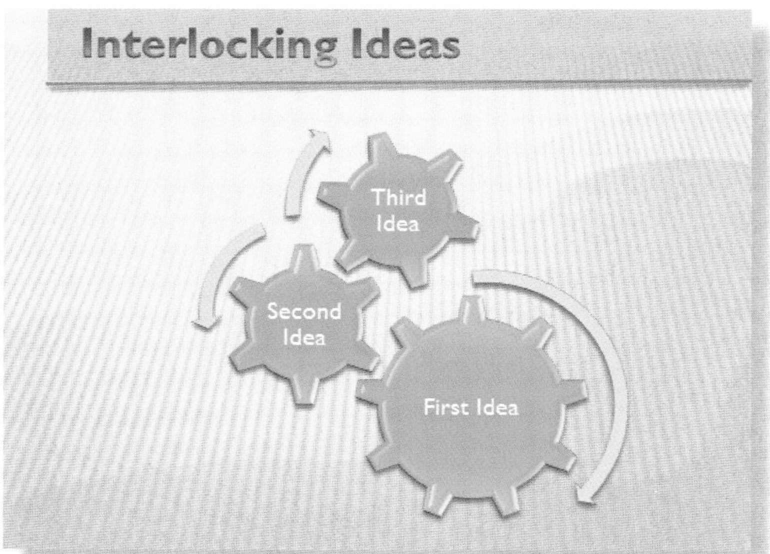

Figure 7-22 Completed Gear diagram

6. Update the handout footer text to **[7-16your initials]**. Save the presentation as **[7-16your initials]** in your Lesson 7 folder. Leave the presentation open for the next exercise.

Exercise 7-17 INSERT A CONTINUOUS PICTURE LIST

The *Continuous Picture List* contains round placeholders for pictures and a horizontal arrow to communicate that the items shown represent interconnected information.

1. Insert a new slide after slide 10 that uses the **Title and Content** layout. Key the title **New Desserts**.
2. From the content placeholder, click the SmartArt button.
3. Choose the **Relationship** category, then click the **Continuous Picture List** thumbnail and click **OK**. A chart appears with three shapes that each contain a small circle with a picture placeholder.
4. Click the first picture placeholder to access the Insert Picture dialog shape. Navigate to where your student files are located, select the **cake** picture, and click **Insert**.
5. Repeat this process on the next two placeholders, inserting the **cookies** picture in the middle shape and the **strawberry** picture in the right shape.

6. Now key text below each of the pictures as shown in Figure 7-23 and the text will automatically resize:

   Fruit Cake Holiday Delight
   Oatmeal and Raisin Cookies
   Cream Cake and Strawberries

7. From the SmartArt Tools Design tab, in the SmartArt Styles group, click the More button and select the **3-D, Polished** style.
8. Resize and reposition the SmartArt graphic attractively on the slide.
9. Update the handout footer text to **[7-17your initials]**. Save the presentation as **[7-17your initials]** in your Lesson 7 folder. Leave the presentation open for the next exercise.

Figure 7-23
Continuous Picture List

Changing Diagram Types and Orientation

Once a SmartArt diagram is created, the type of diagram can easily be changed by selecting a thumbnail from a different category. However, the levels of your information may not translate well into some layouts. The orientation of a diagram can be changed if an appropriate layout can be used. Shapes within the SmartArt area can also be repositioned by dragging them.

Exercise 7-18 CHANGE DIAGRAM TYPES

At any time during the development of your SmartArt diagram, you can apply a different SmartArt graphic to create a different diagram. Level 1 information and level 2 information will be reformatted to fit the new layout, so the layout you choose must have matching levels.

NOTE

Because this is a List diagram, you see those choices first. You could access all diagrams by clicking the More button.

1. Move to slide 3, and select it in the Slides and Outline pane. Press Ctrl+C to copy the slide, move to the end of your slide series, and press Ctrl+V to paste the slide after slide 11.
2. Now working on slide 12, select the SmartArt graphic, then from the SmartArt Tools Design tab,

in the Layouts group, click on several different Layout thumbnails to consider the different diagrams that are available. Notice how the level 1 and level 2 information is arranged, and consider the emphasis that each level receives. The next three steps will point out specific diagrams to try and what you should notice in each one.

3. Click the **Table Hierarchy** thumbnail. This layout does not distinguish between the levels; level 1 information is placed above level 2, but no color or lines are used to show any connecting effect or relationship between the levels.

4. Click the **Grouped List** thumbnail. Now it is easy to see that certain items relate to other items because the shapes used for level 1 create a sort of container for the shapes used for level 2 information. It tends to emphasize level 2 text.

5. Click the **Vertical Arrow List**. This layout clearly distinguishes between the two levels and it works well for bulleted lists of information. The arrows on which level 2 information is displayed communicate that the level 2 information is an outgrowth of level 1.

6. The fill color on the arrows blends too much with the slide background to be easily visible, so change the colors and the style to make the arrows stand out more. From the SmartArt Tools Design tab, in the SmartArt Styles group, click Change Colors then choose **Colorful Range – Accent Colors 5 to 6**. Then click the SmartArt Style More button and choose the **3-D, Polished** style.

NOTE

Although the current text fits nicely on the slide, if you need more space for level 2 bulleted text, the size of level 2 shapes could be increased and the size of the text on the level 2 shapes could be reduced.

7. Select the three arrows, then from the SmartArt Tools Format tab, in the Shape Styles group, click the Shape Fill button and choose the **Orange, Accent 6, Lighter 40%** color. Now the arrows still blend with the theme design, but they are easier to see, as shown in Figure 7-24.

8. Leave your presentation open for the next exercise.

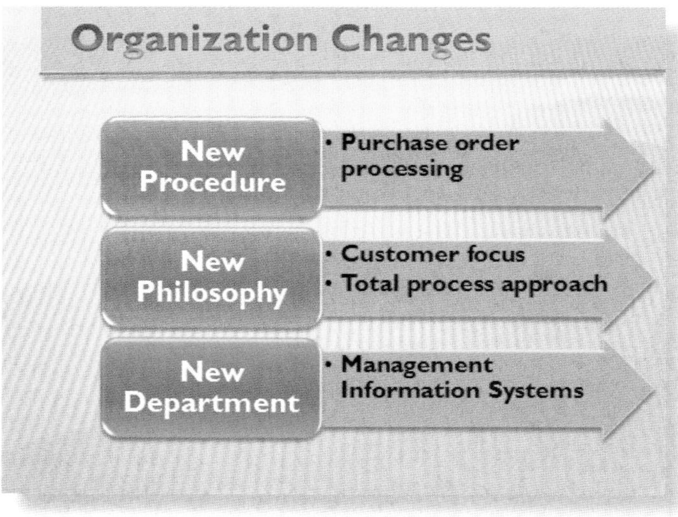

Figure 7-24 Diagram with changed layout

Exercise 7-19 CHANGE THE ORIENTATION OF DIAGRAMS

Because of the particular information a diagram must contain, the information may need to be displayed in a different orientation than the original SmartArt shape provides. For example, instead of a top to bottom orientation, it might need to be left to right.

1. From the Slides and Outline pane, select slide 8 and copy it. Move to the last slide in your presentation and paste the slide.
2. Now on slide 13, select the SmartArt diagram. From the SmartArt Tools Design tab, in the Layouts group, click the More button and choose the **Horizontal Hierarchy** layout. The shapes are now positioned horizontally as in a decision-tree diagram.
3. While the shapes are still connected, the sizes should be adjusted on some of them.

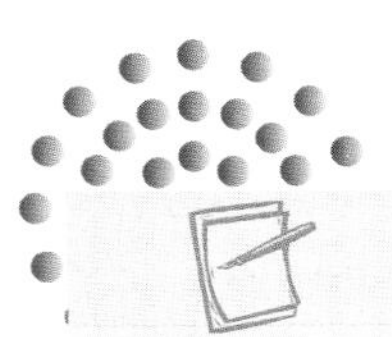

NOTE

Within the SmartArt area, shapes can be repositioned; therefore, a diagram such as the one on slide 7 could be redesigned manually to show the circles in a vertical arrangement and the shapes extending horizontally to the right.

4. Select the three shapes for Michael Peters, Roy Olafsen, and Michele Jenkins. Resize them horizontally and vertically to increase the shape size so all text prints on three lines and there is sufficient space above and below the text in each shape.
5. Select the MIS shape and all the ones below it and the Billing shape. Resize these shapes horizontally so each name fits on one text line, as shown in Figure 7-25.
6. Increase the vertical size of the Julie Wolfe & Gus Irvinelli shape.

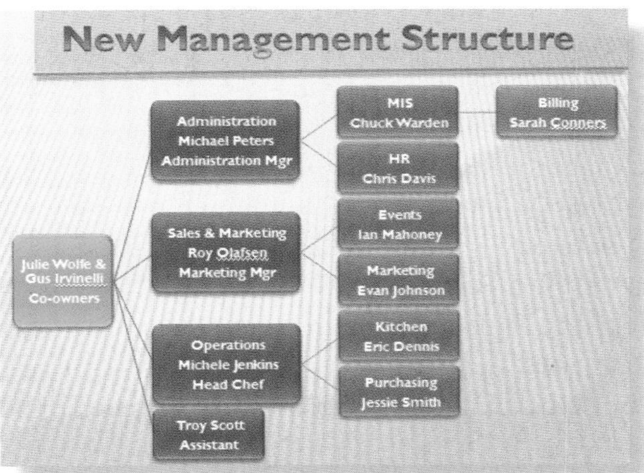

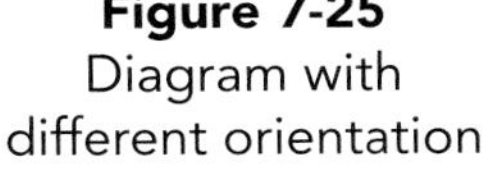

Figure 7-25
Diagram with different orientation

7. Update the handout footer text to **[7-19your initials]**.
8. Save the presentation as **[7-19your initials]** in your Lesson 7 folder. Print the presentation as handouts in landscape orientation with nine slides on a page.
9. Close the presentation.

Lesson 7 Summary

- SmartArt graphics are used to represent information in a visual manner.
- SmartArt graphics are arranged into seven different categories that include a wide variety of diagrams such as organization charts, radial diagrams, list diagrams, and relationship diagrams.
- The SmartArt Tools Design tab has command buttons to insert shapes and modify the predefined diagram layouts. Shapes can be added and removed.
- List diagrams provide an alternative to listing information in a bulleted list because concise text can be placed on shapes that help to communicate categories and subtopics.
- Process diagrams show a sequence of events or the progression of workflow.
- Cycle diagrams communicate a continuous or ongoing process.
- Hierarchy diagrams are used to describe a hierarchical structure, showing who reports to whom, and who is responsible for what function or task.
- Pyramid diagrams show interconnected or proportional relationships.
- Relationship diagrams contain interconnected shapes that reflect relationships in some way.
- Matrix diagrams display two axes in related quadrants that emphasize the whole or the individual parts.
- An organization chart is a type of hierarchy chart in a tree structure, branching out to multiple divisions in each lower level.
- When a chart shape is promoted, it moves up a level. When a chart shape is demoted, it moves down a level.
- A SmartArt Text pane provides a quick way to enter the text that labels diagram shapes.
- List diagrams can show both level 1 and level 2 information, but text must be concise for easy reading.
- Text entered in SmartArt shapes automatically resizes to fit the shape; if shapes increase in size, the text they contain increases in size.
- An existing bulleted list can be converted to a SmartArt graphic.
- Quick Styles provide choices for color and effect changes such as outlines, beveling, and shadows that can be applied to any selected shape.
- SmartArt Styles consist of predefined effects that work well together for diagrams.
- An illusion of depth is created with 3-D style options.
- Shapes can be repositioned within the SmartArt area.
- The Change Colors option provides many possible variations of theme colors.

- If color changes made to a SmartArt graphic are unacceptable, the colors can be reset to their original colors.
- Several layouts in the List category have placeholders for pictures.

LESSON 7		Command Summary
Feature	**Button**	**Ribbon**
Create a graphical list or diagram on a slide.		Insert, Illustrations group, Insert SmartArt Graphic
Change text from a bulleted list to a diagram		Home, Paragraph group, Convert to SmartArt Graphics
Pick from choices for shape color and effects		Home, Drawing group, Quick Styles
Rearrange diagram direction or sequencing of shapes		SmartArt Tools Design, Create Graphic group, Right to Left
Open a gallery of thumbnails showing available options		Available on many Ribbons, More
Select from variations of theme colors		SmartArt Tools Design, SmartArt Styles group, Change Colors
Change back to original formatting		SmartArt Tools Design, Reset group, Reset Graphic
Create additional shapes within a diagram		SmartArt Tools Design, Create Graphic group, Add Shape
Change organization chart layout		SmartArt Tools Design, Create Graphic group, Layout
Increase the level of a selected bulleted item or shape		SmartArt Tools Design, Create Graphic group, Promote
Decrease the level of a selected bulleted item or shape		SmartArt Tools Design, Create Graphic group, Demote
Change the color of a selected shape		SmartArt Tools Format, Shape Styles group, Shape Fill

microsoft® office access® brief
A Professional Approach

ACCESS 2007

Jon Juarez

John Carter

Database programs such as Microsoft Access are very powerful. There's more to learn about databases than just how to enter data or execute simple queries. You also need to know how to use Access in a real-world situation. Therefore, this book focuses on everyday business tasks. As you work through the lessons, imagine yourself working as an intern for Carolina Critters, Inc., a fictional company that manufactures stuffed animals, located in Charlotte, North Carolina.

Carolina Critters, Inc.

Carolina Critters, Inc., was formed in 1946 by Hector Fuentes upon his return from serving in the U.S. Navy in World War II. Hector's son Carlos took over the company in 1962 and ran it until 1997, when Carlos's daughter Lisa assumed the presidency.

Originally, Carolina Critters produced stuffed teddy bears, rabbits, squirrels, and other cuddly animals. The company has branched out over the years and now offers five product lines and 25 products, producing more than $25 million in annual sales. Today, the stuffed animals from Carolina Critters—ranging from traditional teddy bears and cats and dogs to dinosaurs and endangered species—sell in department stores and toy stores across the nation. The company also sells products via the Internet.

In your work as an intern at Carolina Critters, you interact primarily with the four key people shown in Figure CS-1. The databases you use relate to Carolina Critters. As you work, take the time to notice the following:

- The unusual method Carolina Critters has for manufacturing its stuffed animals.
- The types of database activities required in a small business to carry on its day-to-day activities.

Figure CS-1

Lisa Fuentes
President

James McCluskie
Vice President, Chief Financial Officer

Frances Falcigno
Sales and Marketing Manager

Jin Yan
Manufacturing Manager

Method of Manufacturing

Carolina Critters, Inc., uses an unusual method of manufacturing. It does not buy each individual component for a stuffed animal (e.g., material for the outer shell, plastic joints for arms and legs, felt pads for paws, specially made eyes, extruded plastic components for the nose or claws, clothes, stuffing). Instead, it has approached a small number of suppliers and contracted with them for kits that contain all the precut, preweighed, preformed materials required to manufacture a specific stuffed animal. For example, Robinson Mills, Inc., a supplier in Passaic, New Jersey, provides the kit for "Granny Bear."

unit 1

UNDERSTANDING ACCESS DATABASES

Lesson 1

Getting Started with a Database

OBJECTIVES

After completing this lesson, you will be able to:

1. Identify basic database structure.
2. Work with a Microsoft Access database.
3. Identify components of Access.
4. Navigate Access recordsets.
5. Modify datasheet appearance.
6. Print and save a recordset.
7. Manage Access files.

MCAS OBJECTIVES

In this lesson:

AC07_3.2
AC07_5.6
AC07_5.5
AC07_6.1.2
AC07_6.1.3
AC07_6.2.2

Estimated Time: 1 1/2 hours

Databases are part of your daily life. Telephone directories are databases that you can use to find phone numbers for people or companies. Banks use databases to track account balances. Information about you is stored in many databases. Your school keeps track of where you live, when you enrolled, what courses you've taken, what grades you've received, and when you will graduate, as well as other important academic information.

A *database* is a logically organized collection of data. The most common type of database in use today follows the relational model. Other types of models include flat, hierarchical, network, and dimensional.

Identifying Basic Database Structure

Microsoft Access follows the relational model for its design. In a relational model database like Access, all data are stored in tables. A *table* is the major database object that stores all data in a subject-based list of rows and columns. A database table looks similar to a table displayed in a spreadsheet program or a word processor.

Tables are made up of records and fields. A *record* is a complete set of related data about one entity or activity. A record is displayed as a row in a table. Examples of records include a phone directory listing, a sales transaction, or a bank deposit. Records are composed of related fields. A *field* is the smallest storage element that contains an individual data element within a record. A field is displayed as a column in a table.

Figure 1-1
Data organization

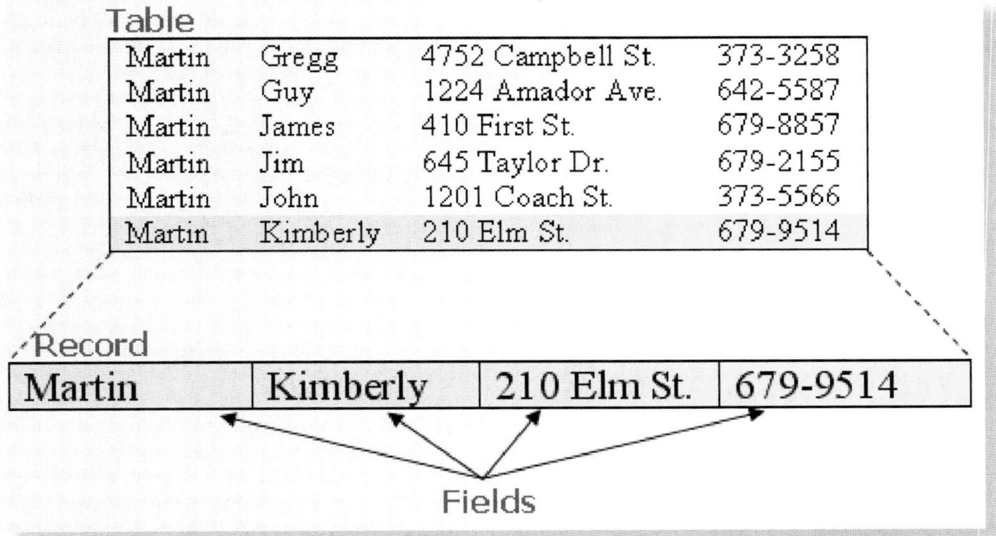

A group of related fields make up a record. A group of related records make up a table, and a group of related tables make up a relational model database.

Figure 1-2
Data hierarchy

Although all data are stored in tables, most often you use other objects to locate, organize, and modify recordsets. A *recordset* is a Microsoft object-oriented data structure consisting of grouped records. A recordset can be as small as a single field or as large as two or more combined tables.

Major objects in an Access database include the following:

- Tables store data about people, activities, items, and events. A table consists of records made up of fields. The information in a table appears in rows (records) and columns (fields), similar to an Excel worksheet.
- Queries organize data in the database. You can specify criteria or conditions to show records and fields from one or more tables. You can also create queries to perform actions.
- Forms display data. With a form you can view, add, and edit fields and records in a table.

- Reports are used to print data. When designing a report, you can sort records, calculate totals, and add graphics to make the report attractive and easy to read.

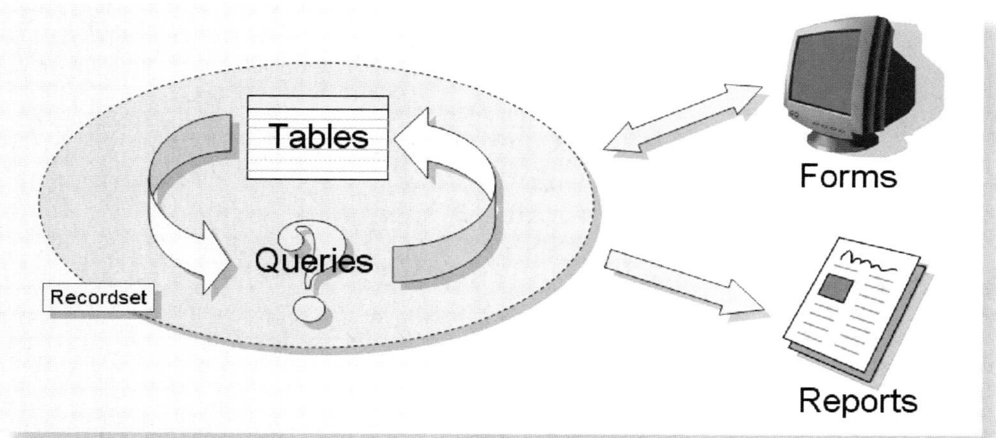

Figure 1-3
Major object orientation

NOTE

In this course, the database with which you work involves a Case Study about Carolina Critters, a fictional company that manufactures stuffed animal kits (see the front matter of the book).

A recordset is most often displayed as either a form or a report. A form is a major database object used to display information in an attractive, easy-to-read screen format. Forms can be used to display, add, edit, or delete recordsets. A report is a major database object used to display information in a printable page format. Reports can only display recordsets.

Working with a Microsoft Access Database

Because of the complexity of a database, Access limits certain file operations. When a database is open, you cannot move or rename the file. Therefore, before you begin working with a database, you must place the file in a suitable location. The storage medium in which the file is located must provide enough space to allow the database to grow, and you must have rights to modify the file.

Exercise 1-1 MANAGE A DATABASE

At the beginning of each lesson, you will be required to copy the lesson files into a folder on your hard drive or another storage device such as a USB drive. Student files are located online or are available from your instructor. The files you need for a lesson can be found in its corresponding folder. For example, in the first lesson, you will need the folder **Lesson 01**, which contains the database

NOTE

Check with your instructor for the specific location of files used in this lesson.

CC01. If you need help copying files to your computer, ask your instructor or lab manager for assistance.

1. Locate the **Lesson 01** folder.
2. Double-click the folder **Lesson 01** to see its content.
3. Right-click the file **CC01** and from the shortcut menu, choose **Copy**.
4. Right-click an unused part of the folder and from the shortcut menu, choose **Paste**.
5. Right-click the new file and from the shortcut menu, choose **Rename**. Rename the file to *[your initials]*-CC01.
6. Right-click ***[your initials]*-CC01** and from the shortcut menu, choose **Properties**. Make certain that the Read-only attribute check box is not checked.

Figure 1-4 Properties dialog box

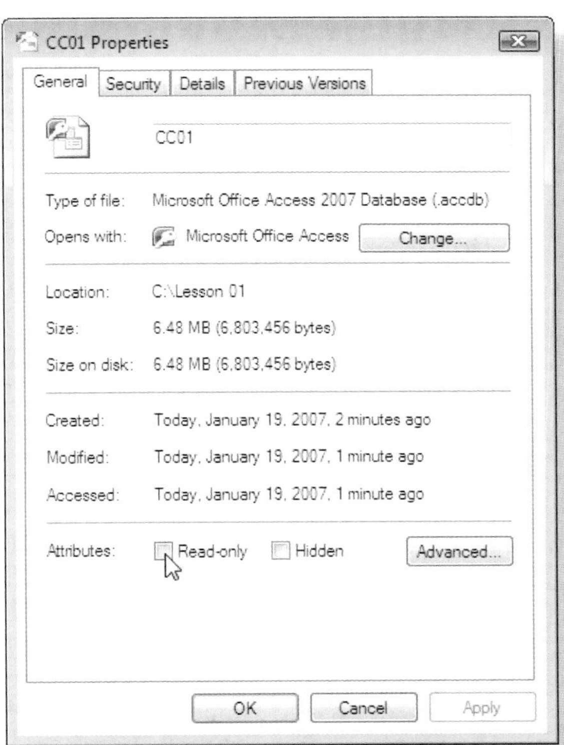

7. Click **OK** to close the dialog box. Close Windows Explorer.

NOTE

Windows provides many ways to start applications. If you have problems, ask your instructor for help.

Exercise 1-2 START A DATABASE

The first screen that appears after starting Access is Getting Started with Microsoft Office Access. From this screen, you can create a new database, open an existing database, or view featured content from Microsoft Office Online.

1. Click the Start button and choose **All Programs**.
2. Click on the Microsoft Office folder and choose Microsoft Office Access 2007. This will start Access.

Figure 1-5
Getting Started window

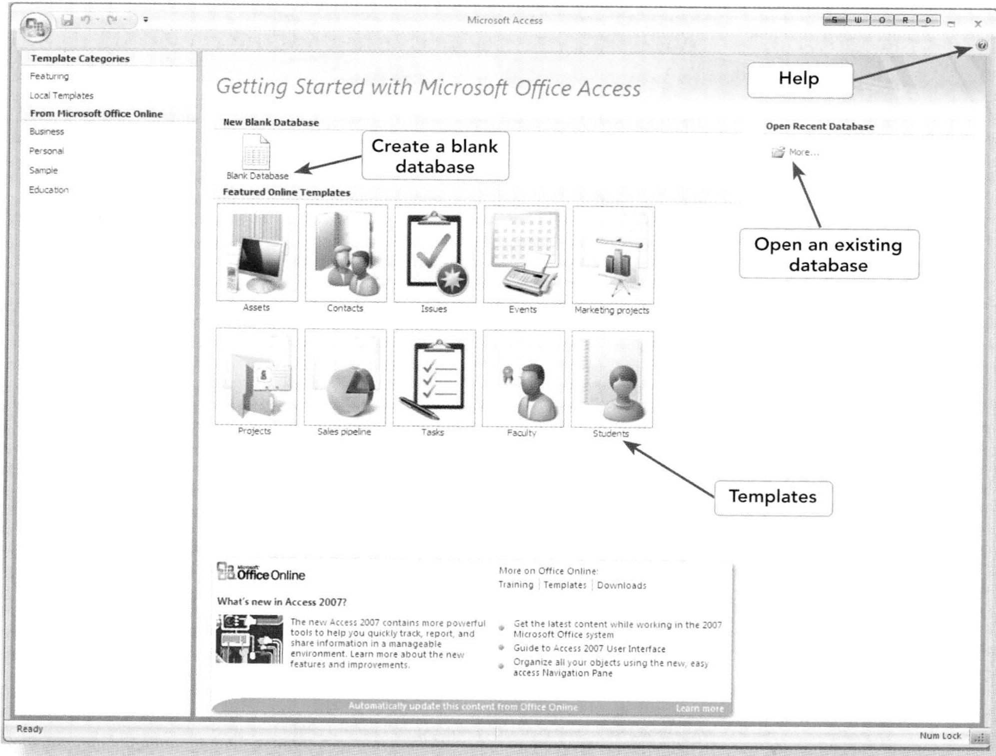

Exercise 1-3 OPEN A DATABASE

By double-clicking on the file icon of a database, you open it in the default mode. The default mode is set to Shared for most databases. Shared mode is a method of opening a database in which multiple users can read and write to the database at the same time. Access databases can be opened in several different modes, including Shared, Read-only, Exclusive use, and Exclusive Read-only.

Each time you open a database, a security alert displays on the Message Bar. The Message Bar alerts you that the database may contain malicious code. Because all Access databases contain program code, this message normally displays.

1. In the **Open Recent Database** section, click **More**.
2. Locate the folder **Lesson 01**. Select the file ***[your initials]*-CC01** and click **Open**.
3. In the Message Bar a **Security Warning** message states that certain content is disabled. Click **Options**. The **Microsoft Office Security Options** dialog box appears.
4. Click **Enable this content** and click **OK**.

Identifying Components of Access

You will use the Office Button to print and manage file operations. You will use command tabs and ribbons to complete specific tasks. The commands in each Ribbon are organized by command groups.

You will use the Navigation Pane to control major database objects. The Navigation Pane is the rectangular area on the left side of the database window that organizes major database objects. All major objects are accessed through the Navigation Pane.

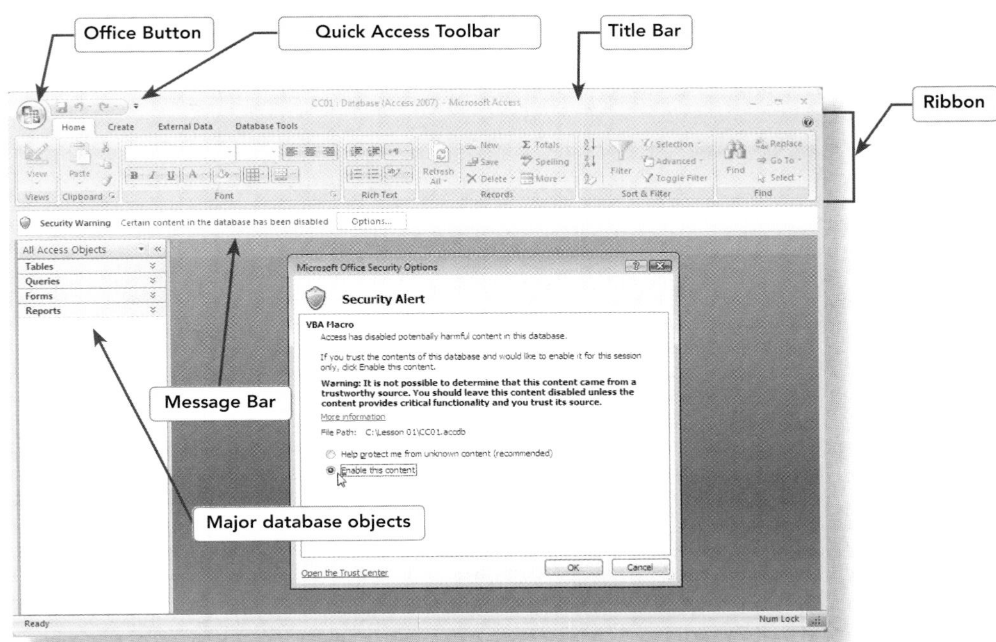

Figure 1-6 Getting Started window CC01.accdb

Exercise 1-4 MANIPULATE THE NAVIGATION PANE

The Navigation Pane displays the major database objects. Access allows you to organize these objects by categories and groups. You can open an object by double-clicking it or by right-clicking and selecting **Open** from the shortcut menu.

The Carolina Critters database organizes objects by the category **Object Type** and grouped by **All Access Objects**. Access allows you to change the layout of the Navigation Pane.

1. In the Navigation Pane, click the **Tables** group. This will expand the group and show all the tables in this database.

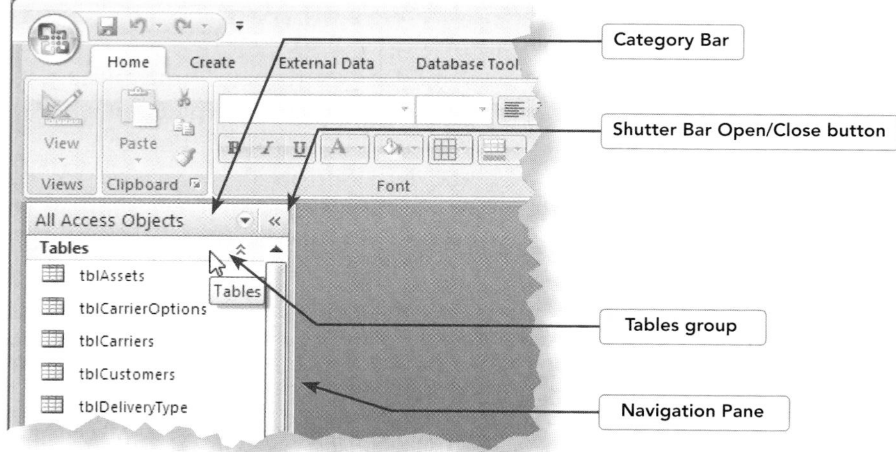

Figure 1-7
Navigation Pane
CC01.accdb

2. Click the **Tables** group again. This collapses the group.
3. Click the **Reports** group to expand the group.
4. Click the **Forms** group. You can have multiple groups expanded at any time.

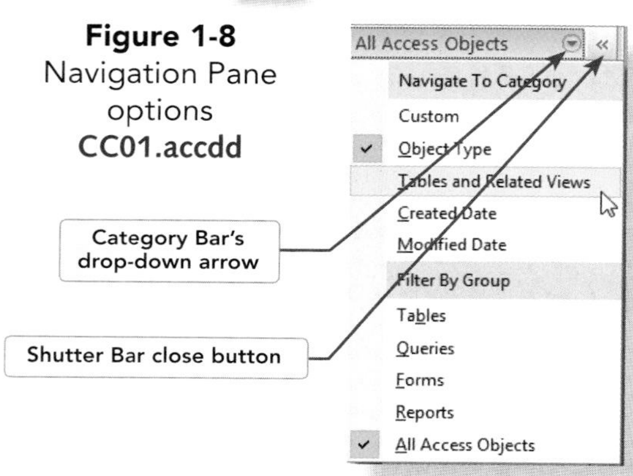

Figure 1-8
Navigation Pane options
CC01.accdd

5. Click on the Category Bar's drop-down arrow and select **Tables and Related Views**. Objects are now grouped by related major objects.
6. Click on the Category Bar's drop-down arrow and select **Object Type** to return the Navigation Pane to its original layout.
7. Click the Shutter Bar button « to collapse the Navigation Pane. This allows you to see more data on the screen.
8. Click the Shutter Bar button » to expand the Navigation Pane.

Exercise 1-5 EXPLORE TABS, RIBBONS, AND GROUPS

Access uses tabs, ribbons, and groups, similar to other Microsoft Office applications. Some Access commands are the same as in Word and Excel. Other commands are unique to Access. Hovering over a command displays its ScreenTip. A *ScreenTip* is the name of or information regarding a specific object. This information can include images, shortcut keys, and descriptions.

When you click on a command tab, a unique set of command groups will appear in the Ribbon. A *command group* is a collection of logically organized commands.

1. In the command tab **Home**, in the **Clipboard** group, you will find the Cut command. Hover your mouse pointer over this command to display its ScreenTip.

Figure 1-9
Viewing ScreenTips
CC01.accdb

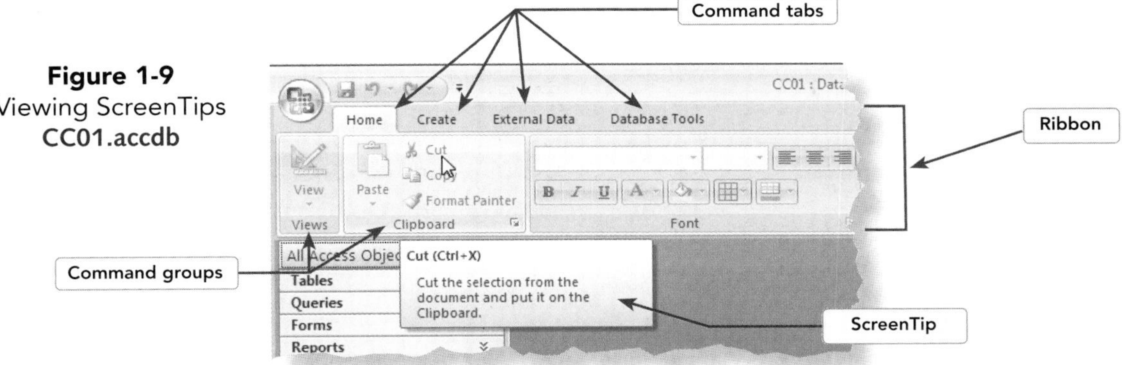

2. In the command tab **Create**, in the **Forms** group, hover your mouse pointer over the Form command. Read the ScreenTip.
3. Click the **Home** command tab.

Exercise 1-6 OPEN AND CLOSE MAJOR OBJECTS

In this textbook, the names of the database objects use the Leszynski Naming Convention. The Leszynski Naming Convention is a method of naming objects that emphasizes the use of three-letter prefixes to identify the type of object. This convention does not use spaces or underscores and is widely used by software developers and programmers worldwide.

Table 1-1 Leszynski Naming Convention for Major Objects

Prefix	Object Type	Example
tbl	Table	**tblEmployees**
qry	Query	**qryKitSuppliers**
frm	Form	**frmStuffedAnimals**
rpt	Report	**rptQuarterlySales**

1. In the Navigation Pane, expand the **Tables** group.
2. Double-click the table **tblEmployees** to open it. The table that contains the employee's information is now open.

Figure 1-10
Open a table
CC01.accdb
tblEmployees

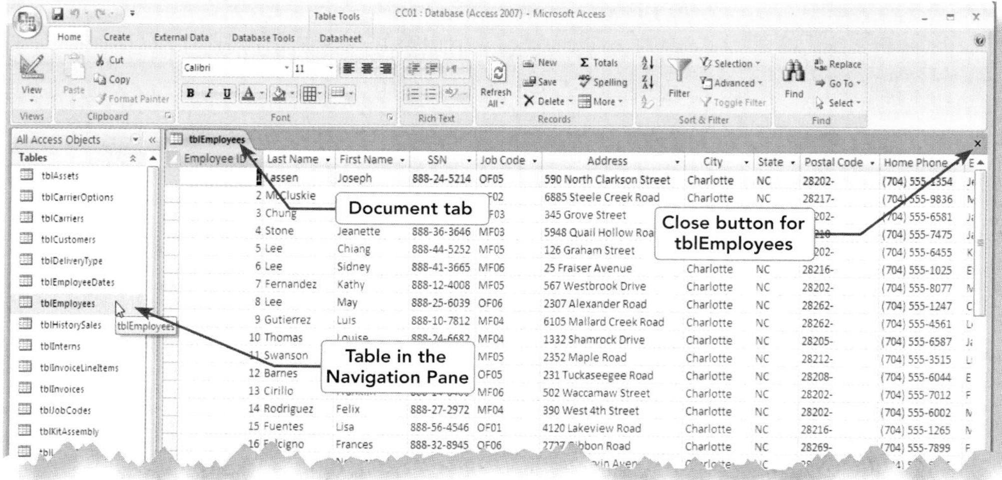

3. Click the Close button × to close the table **tblEmployees**.
4. In the Navigation Pane, collapse the **Tables** group.
5. Expand the **Queries** group, right-click the query **qryCustomerContact**, and select **Open** from the shortcut menu.
6. Right-click the document tab for **qryCustomerContact**, then select **Close** from the shortcut menu.

Exercise 1-7 EXPLORE DATASHEET AND DESIGN VIEWS

Each major database object has multiple views. The view that allows you to see a recordset is called the Datasheet View. A *Datasheet View* is a screen view used to display data in rows and columns, similar to a spreadsheet. Records are displayed as rows and fields are displayed as columns.

In addition to the Datasheet View, objects can be displayed in Design View. A *Design View* is a screen view used to modify the structure of a major object.

Switching between different views can be completed by

- Selecting, from the **Home** command tab in the **View** command group, the option arrow for the View command.
- Using the View Shortcut buttons (lower right corner of the screen.)
- Right-clicking the object and selecting the view.

1. In the **Queries** group of the Navigation Pane, double-click **qryProductPrice**. This will open the query in Datasheet View.

2. In the command group **Views**, click the option arrow for the View command and select Design View. In this view, you can see the tables that are used to create this query.

Figure 1-11
Switching views
CC01.accdb
qryProductPrice

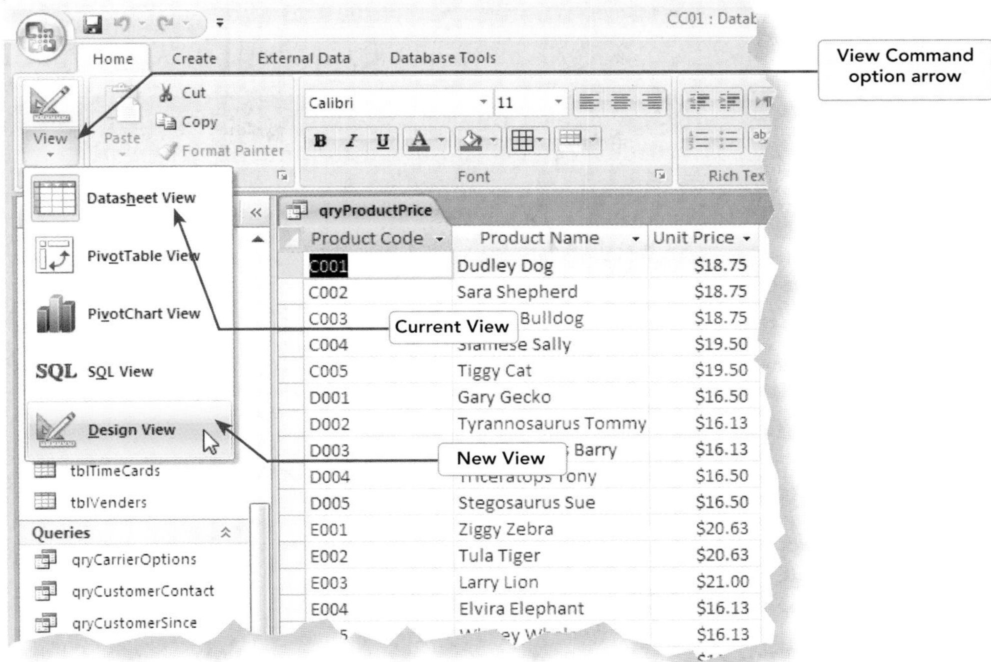

3. Right-click the document tab for the query, then select Datasheet View.
4. In the Navigation Pane, expand the **Tables** group.
5. Double-click **tblAssets**. This opens the table in Datasheet View. In the message dialog box, click **Yes**.
6. Right-click the document tab for the table, then select Design View. This is where you define the structure of the table.
7. Right-click the document tab for the table, then select **Close All**. This will close all open documents.
8. Collapse both the **Tables** and **Queries** groups.

Navigating Access Recordsets

Datasheet View has two modes: Edit mode and Navigation mode. *Edit Mode* is the mode in which changes to the content of a field can be made and the insertion point is visible. The insertion point looks like an I-beam. *Navigation Mode* is the mode in which an entire field is selected and the insertion point is not visible.

By using the scroll bars, navigation buttons, and keyboard shortcuts, you can navigate around large datasheets.

Access 2007

Exercise 1-8 USE NAVIGATION BUTTONS IN A TABLE

In Navigation mode, you can move between fields by using the keyboard shortcuts or record navigation buttons. A *record navigation button* is an icon that moves the pointer within a recordset to the next, previous, first, or last record. The record navigation buttons are located on the Navigation Bar near the bottom of the window.

1. Expand the **Tables** group. Double-click the table **tblKitAssembly** to open it. By default, the first record, first field, is selected.

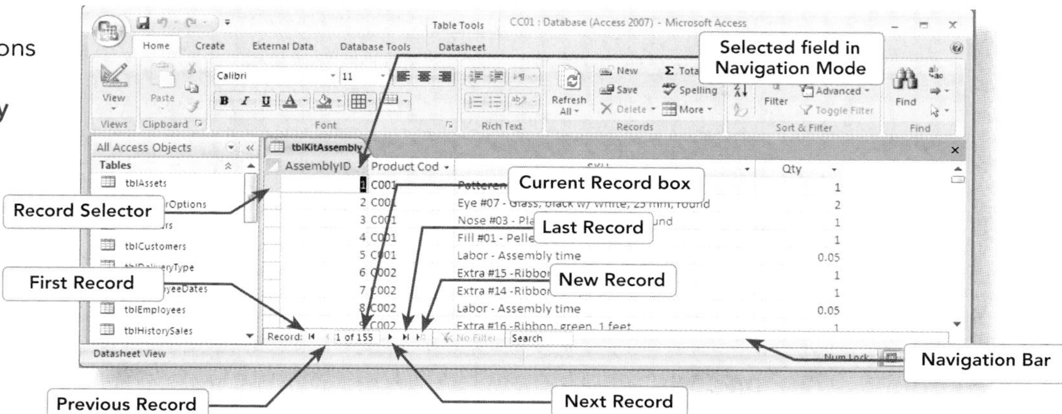

Figure 1-12 Navigation buttons CC01.accdb tblKitAssembly

2. In the Navigation Bar, click the Next Record button once. The **AssemblyID** for the second record is highlighted.
3. Click the Previous Record button to return to the previous record.
4. Click the Last Record button to move to the last record in the table.
5. Click in the **Current Record** box. Delete the number in the box and key **75** and press Enter. The pointer moves to the seventy-fifth record.
6. Right-click the document tab for the table, then select **Close**. Collapse the **Tables** group.

Exercise 1-9 USE NAVIGATION SHORTCUT KEYS IN A QUERY

Just as in a table's Datasheet View, you can use both the navigation buttons and keyboard shortcuts to navigate through a recordset.

1. Expand the **Queries** group. Double-click the query **qrySales** to open it.
2. Press Ctrl+End to move to the last field in the last record.
3. Press Home to move to the first field in the current record.

4. Press Ctrl+Home to move to the first field in the first record.
5. Press End to move to the last field in the current record.
6. Press ↓ to move to the last field of the second record.
7. Right-click the document tab for the table, then select **Close**, and collapse the **Queries** group.

Table 1-2 Keyboard Shortcuts

Action	Shortcut
Move down one screen	PageDown
Move to the current field in the first record	Ctrl+↑
Move to the current field in the last record	Ctrl+↓
Move to the current field in the next record	↓
Move to the current field in the previous record	↑
Move to the first field in the current record	Home
Move to the first field in the first record	Ctrl+Home
Move to the last field in the current record	End
Move to the next field	Tab or →
Move to the previous field	Shift+Tab or ←
Move up one screen	PageUp
Place the pointer in the Current Record Box	F5

Modifying Datasheet Appearance

In Access, a datasheet appears similar to a table displayed in Excel or Word. Just as in the other applications, in Access, you can hide, display, and resize columns and rows. You can also use formatting tools to change the appearance of text. Each format setting globally affects all text in every column and row.

Exercise 1-10 HIDE AND UNHIDE COLUMNS

When a table contains more fields than can be viewed on a single screen, you must scroll horizontally through the window. To reduce the number of fields shown at one time, you can hide columns within the datasheet.

1. Expand the **Tables** group. Double-click the table **tblHistorySales** to open it. There are nine fields in this table.
2. Click on the column header for the field **Employee** and drag through **ShipDate**. The four selected columns are highlighted.

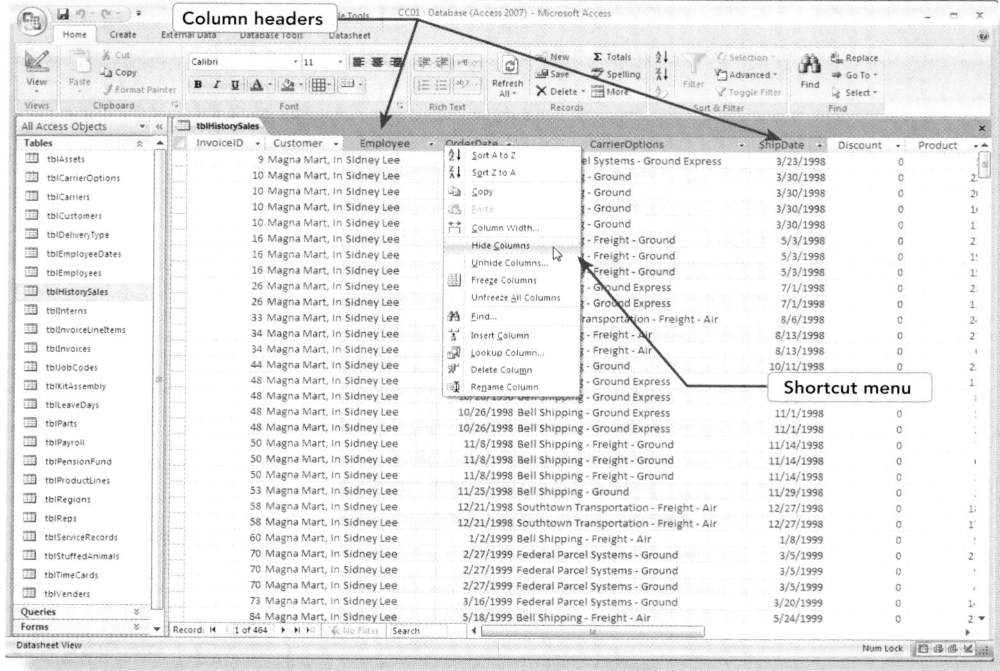

Figure 1-13
Selecting multiple columns
CC01.accdb
tblHistorySales

3. Right-click on the column header for the field **Employee** and select **Hide Columns**.
4. Right-click on the column header for the field **Customer** and select **Unhide Columns**.

5. Select the check box for **OrderDate** and **ShipDate**.
6. Click **Close**.
7. Right-click the document tab for the table, then select **Close**. A dialog box appears, prompting you to save the changes to the table. Click **Yes** to accept the changes.

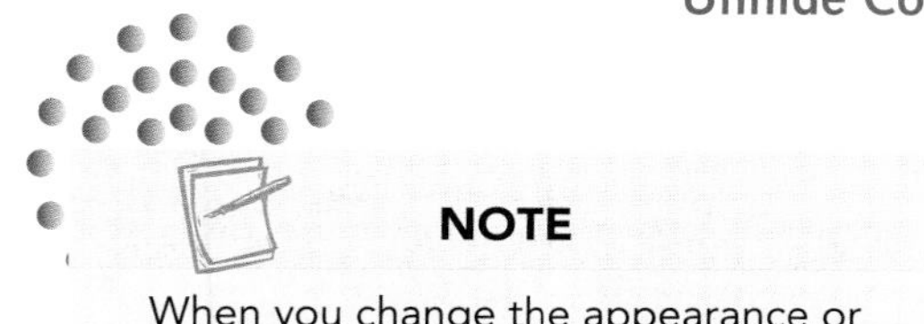

NOTE

When you change the appearance or design of a major database object, Access prompts you to save the changes.

Exercise 1-11 CHANGE COLUMN WIDTHS AND ROW HEIGHTS

By default, all columns in a datasheet are the same width. You can change the width of each column to optimize your view of the data or the title for each field. You also can make columns narrower if too much blank space is included in a field.

You adjust row heights similarly to adjusting column widths. Although column widths can be set individually, row heights cannot. The row height is a global setting that applies to all rows in the entire datasheet.

1. Double-click the table **tblHistorySales** to open it.
2. Place the pointer on the vertical border between the column headers for **Customer** and **OrderDate**. Notice that the pointer changes to a vertical bar between a two-headed arrow. This is the resize pointer.
3. Drag the pointer to the right approximately one inch to allow enough space so the complete customer name is displayed for each record.

Figure 1-14
Resize a column
CC01.accdb
tblHistorySales

4. Right-click on the Record Selector for the first row.
5. From the shortcut menu, select **Row Height**.
6. In the **Row Height** dialog box, key **25** and click **OK**. Notice that all rows are now taller.
7. Right-click on the Record Selector for any record and select **Row Height**.
8. Click the **Standard Height** check box and click **OK**.

Exercise 1-12 USE THE FONT COMMAND GROUP

You can increase the readability of data by applying specific format commands from the Font command group. Some commands, such as bold, underline, and italics, apply to the entire datasheet. Other commands, such as **Align Text Left**, **Center**, and **Align Text Right**, can be applied to selected fields in the datasheet.

1. In the command group **Font**, hover your mouse pointer over the word **Calibri**. The ScreenTip states that this is the **Font** command.
2. Click the **Font**'s drop-down arrow and select **Microsoft Sans Serif**. The font has been applied to the entire datasheet.
3. The command to the right of **Font** is **Font Size**. Change the **Font Size** to **16**.
4. Place the resize pointer on the vertical border between the column headers for **OrderDate** and **ShipDate**.
5. Double-click to automatically adjust the column width of **OrderDate**.
6. Double-click the right side of the column header for **ShipDate** to automatically adjust its width.

7. Select the field **InvoiceID** by clicking its column header. Click the Center command. Only one field has been affected.
8. Press Home to deselect the column.

9. In the lower right corner of the command group **Font**, is a command called Alternate Fill/Back Color. Click its drop-down arrow to show the available colors.
10. In the **Standard Colors**, select **Brown 2** (row 3, last column) as the alternate color.

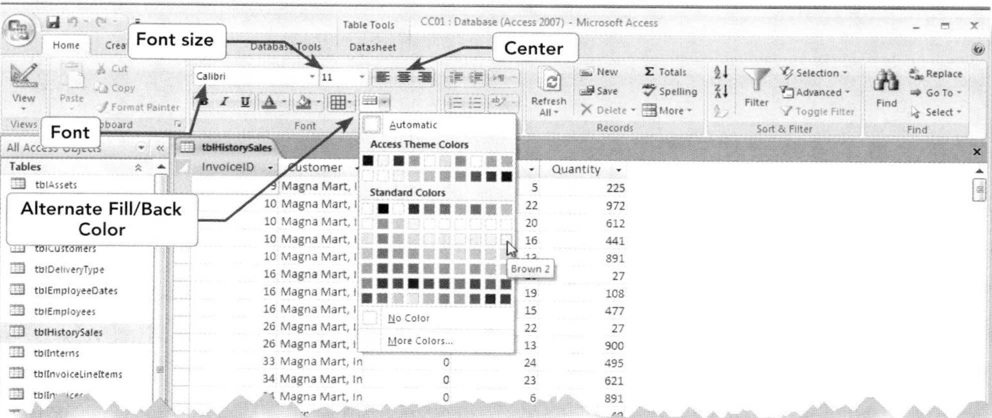

Figure 1-15
Changing datasheet appearance
CC01.accdb
tblHistorySales

11. To the far right of the document tab for the table **tblHistorySales**, click the Close button. Click **Yes** to save the changes.
12. Collapse the **Tables** group.

Printing and Saving a Recordset

You can print or save the Datasheet View of a table or query. The steps you take to print a datasheet are similar to the steps for printing in other Microsoft Office applications such as Word or Excel. You can also create an electronic XPS file of your printout. *XPS* is an XML Paper Specification (XPS) file format that preserves document formatting and enables file sharing of printable documents. The XPS format ensures that when the file is viewed online or is printed, it retains the original format.

Exercise 1-13 PRINT A QUERY

You can print a table or a query as it appears in Datasheet View. You can use any of these methods:

- Click the Office Button and then choose **Print**.
- Press Ctrl+P.

When you use the Office Button or the keyboard method, the Print dialog box displays to allow you to change print options.

1. Expand the **Queries** group. Double-click the table **qryProductPrice** to open it.
2. Press Ctrl+P to open the **Print** dialog box.

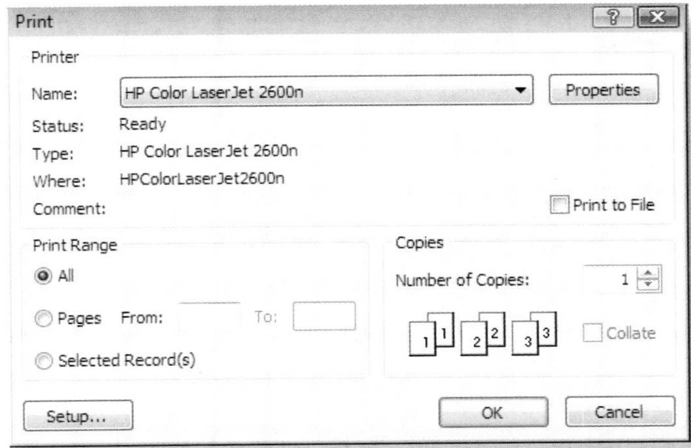

Figure 1-16
Print dialog box
CC01.accdb
qryProductPrice

3. Based on your classroom procedure, you can either print the table or cancel the print process. To cancel, click **Cancel**. To print the datasheet, click **OK**. If you are uncertain, ask your instructor.
4. To the far right of the document tab for the query **qryProductPrice**, click the Close button.
5. Close the query and collapse the **Queries** group.

Exercise 1-14 PRINT A TABLE

Before printing a datasheet, you can use Print Preview to determine whether to change the page orientation from portrait (vertical layout) to landscape (horizontal layout). Landscape is often the better option when a datasheet contains numerous fields or wide columns.

1. Expand the **Tables** group. Double-click the table **tblInterns** to open it.
2. Click the Office Button. From the **Print** option, choose **Print Preview**.
3. Click the Last Page navigation button to display the last page.
4. From the **Print Preview** command tab, in the command group **Zoom**, click the Two Pages command to view both pages.

Figure 1-17
Print Preview
CC01.accdb
tblInterns

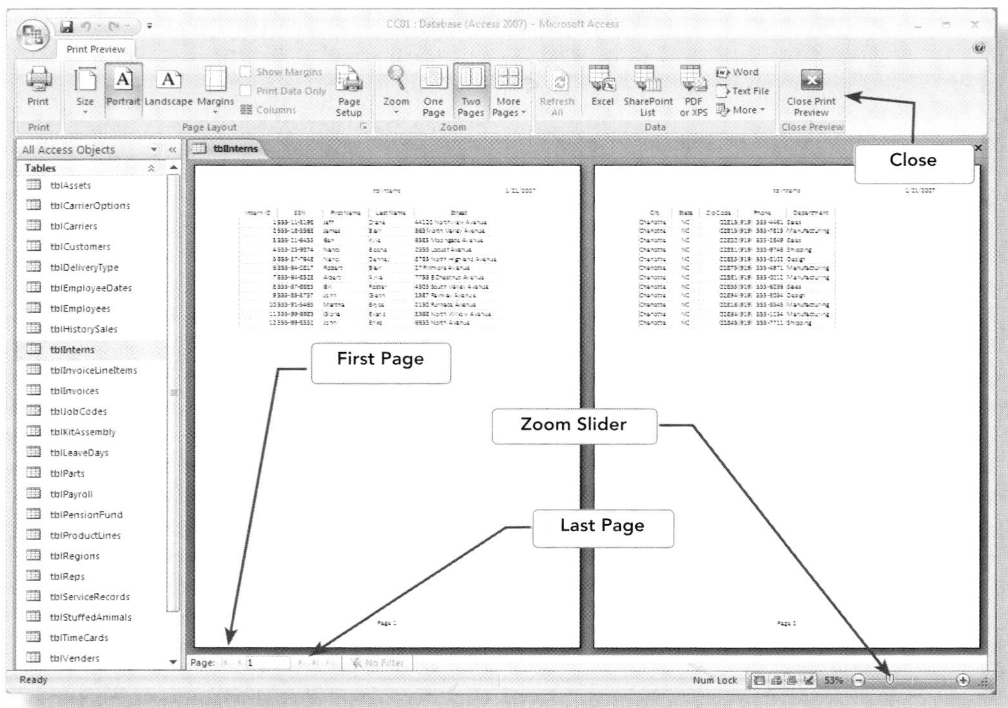

5. From the **Print Preview** command tab, in the command group **Page Layout**, click the Landscape command to reduce the total number of pages to print.

6. Based on your classroom procedure, you can either print the table or cancel the print process. To cancel, click **Cancel**. To print the datasheet, click **OK**. If you are uncertain, ask your instructor.

7. From the **Print Preview** command tab, in the **Command** group **Close Preview**, click the Close Print Preview command. This will return you to the table Datasheet View.

Exercise 1-15 PUBLISH A TABLE

In addition to printing a paper copy, you can create an electronic XPS file. The XPS format preserves document formatting and enables file sharing of printable documents. You can publish a document in high quality or reduced quality. Reduced quality is similar to draft quality printing. High quality produces a better printout but also increases the size of the file saved.

1. Double-click the table **tblKitAssembly** to open it.

2. Click the Office Button. Hover your mouse pointer over the More Options arrow of the **Save As** option and choose **PDF or XPS**.

Figure 1-18
Office Button options
CC01.accdb
tblKitAssembly

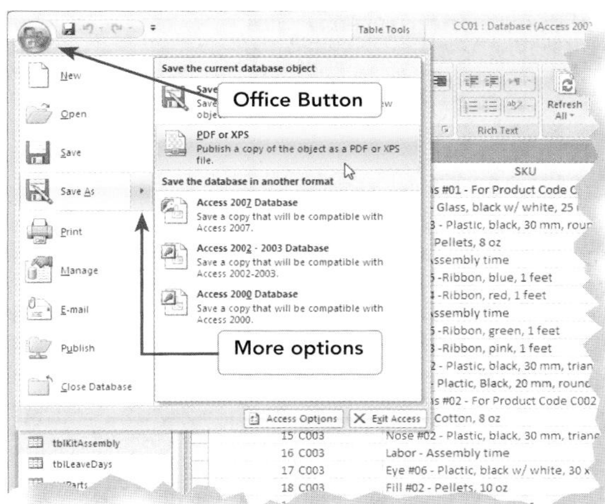

3. Change the location to the location where you will be storing your homework.
4. Click to the right of the file name and key in a hyphen and your initials.
5. Click the **Open file after publishing** check box.
6. Click **Publish** to create the XPS file. Your file has been opened in Internet Explorer.
7. Close Internet Explorer.
8. Right-click the **tblKitAssembly** tab and select **Close All**.
9. Collapse the **Tables** group.

NOTE

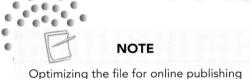

Optimizing the file for online publishing and printing increases the size of the file.

Managing Access Files

Access, similar to many database applications, is designed to utilize space quickly, but not necessarily effectively. Normal database activities, such as adding, deleting, and moving data, can make the file unnecessarily large. After performing extensive work on a database, you should compact the data to save disk space.

The database expands and is usually not as efficiently organized on the disk as it could be. After compacting, you can back up the database to a new location, back it up with a new name, close it, or exit the program.

Exercise 1-16 USE COMPACT AND REPAIR

The Compact and Repair Database command reclaims unused space and improves database efficiency. After compacting an inefficient database, many activities will perform quicker.

1. Click the Office Button .
2. From the **Manage** option, choose **Compact and Repair Database**.

Exercise 1-17 BACK UP A DATABASE

By default, the backup file is saved to the same location as the original file. The default name is the original database name with the current date appended to the end. You can change both default values.

1. Click the Office Button .
2. From the **Manage** option, choose **Back Up Database**.
3. Click **Save**.

Exercise 1-18 CLOSE A DATABASE AND EXIT ACCESS

Now that you have compacted and backed up your database, you can close your database and Access.

1. Click the Office Button .
2. Click **Close Database**. This closes your database but not Access.
3. Click the Office Button .
4. Click **Exit Access**.

Lesson 1 Summary

- An Access database is relational, the most common type of database in use today.
- Major Access database objects include tables, queries, forms, and reports.
- A record is composed of related fields, a table is composed of related records, and a database is composed of related tables.
- A recordset is a Microsoft object-oriented data structure consisting of grouped records.
- A recordset is most often displayed as either a form or a report.
- An opened database cannot be moved or renamed.
- Shared mode is the default mode for most databases. This mode allows multiple users to use the database simultaneously.
- When opening a database, a security alert displays on the Message Bar alerting you that the database may contain malicious code.
- In the Navigation Pane, major objects are organized by categories and groups.
- The Leszynski Naming Convention is a method of naming objects that emphasizes the use of three-letter prefixes to identify the type of object.
- Datasheet View and Design View are two methods of displaying each major object.
- Edit mode allows contents of fields to be changed.
- Navigation mode allows movement between fields.
- The columns and rows of a datasheet can be hidden, displayed, or resized.

- Format changes to a datasheet affect all text in every column and row.
- In a datasheet, column widths can be changed individually; row heights must all be the same.
- In a datasheet, some format commands can be applied to individual fields; other commands apply to the entire datasheet.
- The Quick Print command sends a document directly to the default printer without allowing changes to the print options.
- Documents can be printed or published in portrait or landscape orientation.
- Publishing a document as an XPS file in either reduced quality or high quality preserves document formatting.
- Normal database activities such as adding, deleting, and moving data can unnecessarily increase the size of a database file.
- The Compact and Repair Database command reclaims unused space and improves database efficiency.

LESSON 1 — Command Summary

Feature	Button	Task Path	Keyboard
Close active object	×		Ctrl+W or Ctrl+F4
Close database		Office Button, Close Database	
Column width		Shortcut menu, Column width	
Collapse Navigation Pane	«		
Compact database		Office Button, Manage, Compact, and Repair Database	
Database Properties		Shortcut menu, Properties	
Datasheet View		Views, View, Datasheet View	
Design View		Views, View, Design View	
Exit Access	X	Office Button, Exit Access	Alt+F4
Expand Navigation Pane	«		
Font Face		Font, Font	
Font Size		Font, Font Size	
Go to record			F5
Hide Columns		Shortcut menu, Hide Columns	

continues

LESSON 1		Command Summary *continued*	
Feature	**Button**	**Task Path**	**Keyboard**
Jump to next screen or record			PageDown
Jump to pervious screen or record			PageUp
Move to beginning of field text			Home
Move to end of field text			End
Move to first record			Ctrl+Home
Move to last record			Ctrl+End
Move to next field			Tab
Move to next record			
Move to previous field			Shift+Tab
Move to previous record			
Open database			Ctrl+O
Page Layout		Office Button, Print, Print Preview, Page Layout	
Print Preview		Office Button, Print, Print Preview	
Print		Office Button, Print	Ctrl+P
Row Height		Shortcut menu, Row Height	
Save		Office Button, Save	Ctrl+S
Unhide Columns		Shortcut menu, Unhide Columns	

Lesson 2

Viewing and Modifying Records

OBJECTIVES

After completing this lesson, you will be able to:

1. Modify recordsets in a table.
2. Modify recordsets through a query.
3. Use Office editing tools.
4. View and modify recordsets through a form.
5. Manage attachments.
6. Preview, print, and save data using a report.

MCAS OBJECTIVES

In this lesson:
AC07_3.1
AC07_3.2
AC07_3.4
AC07_5.5
AC07_5.6

Estimated Time: 1 1/2 hours

In Lesson 1, you learned about the database environment including major objects such as tables, queries, forms, and reports. In this lesson, you learn to add, edit, delete, and print data. You learn how to use time-saving edit commands like duplicate, copy, and paste. You also learn how to store images in tables.

You will work directly with data in a table or as a recordset through a query, form, or report. A query creates a recordset based upon an entire table, a portion of a table, or a combination of one or more tables. Although you can look at an entire table in Datasheet View, more often it is easier to use a query and form.

Modifying Recordsets in a Table

Records are routinely added to a database. For example, when a new student enrolls in your school, a record is added to your school's database. If a new employee begins working at Carolina Critters, the company must add the person's information to the database. On other occasions, a record might be deleted if the information will no longer be used.

Exercise 2-1 OPEN A DATABASE

In addition to the database file, in this lesson you will use several text and image files. These files are located in the **Lesson 02** folder. Before opening the Access database, you must move and rename the file.

1. Locate the folder **Lesson 02**. Double-click the folder **Lesson 02** to see its contents.
2. Right-click the file **CC02** and, from the shortcut menu, choose **Rename**. On the keyboard, press Home to move to the beginning of the file name. Key your initials and then a hyphen. Press Enter to accept the new name.
3. Double-click ***[your initials]*-CC02** to open the database.
4. In the **Security Warning** message bar, click the **Option** button. The **Microsoft Office Security Options** dialog box appears.
5. Click **Enable this content** and click **OK**.

TIP

If a Read only message appears in the Message Bar, you will need to close the database, deselect the Read-only property, and reopen the file.

Exercise 2-2 EDIT FIELDS IN A TABLE

You do not need to "save" when you make changes to a record. Access automatically saves your changes as soon as you move the insertion point to another record.

You can determine if a record has been saved by the shape of the Pointer in the Record Selector. Two shapes can appear in the Record Selector:

- A pencil icon appears while you are adding or editing text. This indicates the record changes have not been saved.
- An asterisk marks a new record.

1. In the Navigation Pane, expand the **Tables** group and double-click **tblCustomers** to open it in Datasheet View.

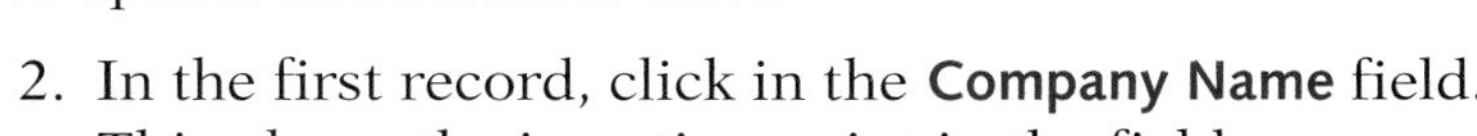

2. In the first record, click in the **Company Name** field. This places the insertion point in the field.
3. Press End to move the insertion point to end of the data in the field.
4. Press Ctrl+Backspace to delete "Inc."

NOTE

Notice the pencil icon in the Record Selector indicates that the record has been modified.

Figure 2-1
Modifying a record
CC02.accdb
tblCustomers

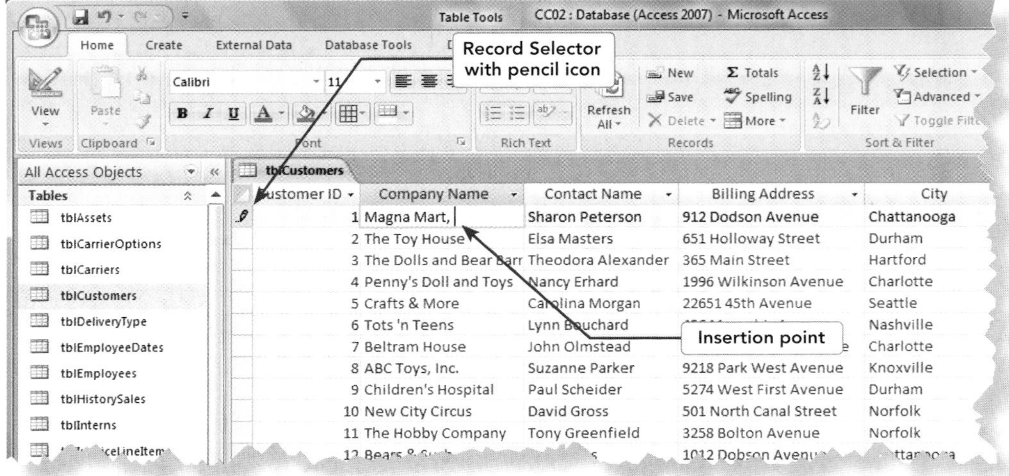

5. Key **LLC**.

6. In the **Contact Name** field of the first record, double-click on "Peterson" to select the word.

7. Key **Butler** to change the last name.

8. In the **Billing Address** field for **Customer ID** #7's record, click between the "7" and the "6."

9. Press [Delete] once and key **1**. You have changed "2876" to "2871."

10. Press [Tab] to move to the field **City**. Press the space bar to delete the data.

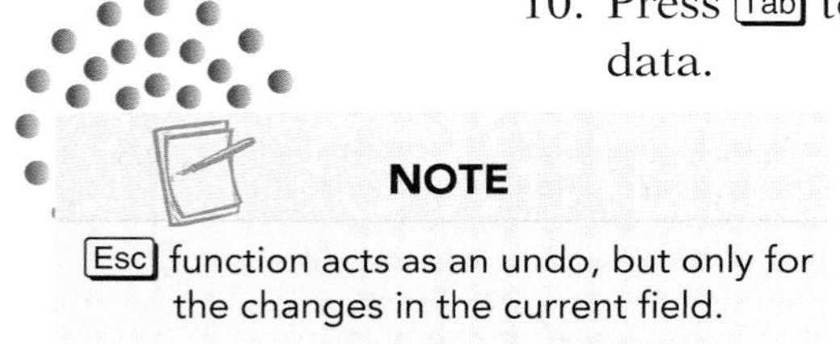

NOTE

[Esc] function acts as an undo, but only for the changes in the current field.

11. Press [Esc] to undo the deletion of the data.

12. Press [↓] to save the changes to the record. Notice that the pencil icon has disappeared from the Record Selector.

Exercise 2-3 ADD A RECORD IN A TABLE

When adding records in Datasheet View, you add the records to the end of the table. The last row of the table in which the new record will be added is marked by an asterisk in the Record Selector. You move to the new record row by any of the following steps:

- Right-click the selected record and, on the shortcut menu, select **New Record**.
- Click the New Record command.
- From the **Home** command tab, in the command group **Records**, select the New command.
- [Ctrl]+[+].

1. From the command tab **Home**, in the command group **Records**, click the New command. This moves the insertion point to the empty record at the bottom of the table.

2. Key the customer information below to create a new record. Press Tab to move from one field to the next.

NOTE

The first column lists field names. The second column contains data to be entered along with special characters and instructions. **Red** text is entered exactly as shown. **Black** symbols automatically appear and do not need to be keyed. *Orange italic* indicates specific instructions for the field.

Customer ID:	21
Company Name:	Checker Toys
Contact Name:	Kathy Prince
Billing Address:	8854 Elm Street
City:	Knoxville
State:	TN
ZIP Code:	39725-6458
Region Name:	1
Phone Number:	(423)555-3456
Fax Number:	(423)555-3457
After Hours:	*Press* Tab
Tax Exempt:	*Press* Spacebar *to add a checkmark*
Initial Order:	8/5/07

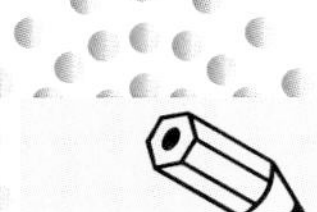

TIP

In a check box field, you can toggle back and forth from "checked" to "not checked" by pressing the space bar.

3. Press ↑ to leave the new record, which will save the changes.

4. Press Ctrl+PageUp to return to the first field in the record.

Exercise 2-4 DELETE A RECORD IN A TABLE

There are times when you find that records are no longer needed and should be removed from a table. An example might be that you find a record that was entered into the wrong table.

To delete one or more records, you must first select the record(s) that you intend to delete. After selecting the record(s), you can use one of four methods:

- Select a record and press Delete.
- Right-click a selected record and, on the shortcut menu, select **Delete Record**.
- From the command tab **Home**, in the command group **Records**, select the Delete command .
- Ctrl+-.

REVIEW

The Record Selector is the narrow gray column to the left of the first field in the **Datasheet View** of a table or query.

1. In the **Datasheet View** of the table **tblCustomers**, click on the Record Selector to select the record for "Crafts & More."

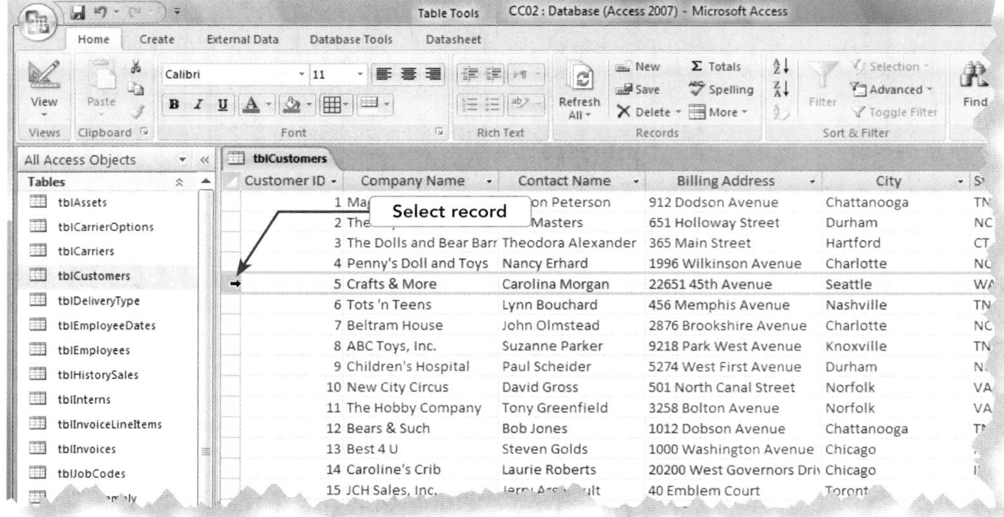

Figure 2-2
Selecting a record for deletion
CC02.accdb
tblCustomers

2. Press Delete. The record disappears, and a dialog box opens asking you to confirm the deletion.

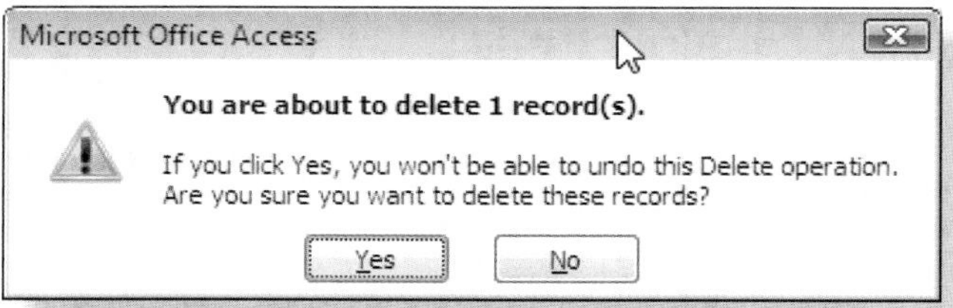

Figure 2-3
Dialog box confirming deletion
CC02.accdb
tblCustomers

3. Click **Yes**. Access deletes the record.
4. Click anywhere in the **Company Name** field for "New City Circus" to make it the current record.
5. Press Ctrl+- and then click **Yes** to confirm the deletion.
6. In the Navigation Pane, collapse the **Tables** group.

Modifying Recordsets through a Query

When you use a query to make changes to data, you are making changes to the recordset. Although the records display in a query, the data are actually stored in a table. When you edit a record in a query, the data in the underlying table are changed automatically.

Although records can be added directly into a table, more often queries are used to enter data. An advantage to editing through a query over a table is that the recordset of a query does not have to display all the records or fields in the table. Using a query allows you to view only the relevant fields and records.

Exercise 2-5 EDIT FIELDS THROUGH A QUERY

When editing a record, you can insert text or use the Overtype mode to key over existing text. Use Insert to switch between Insert and Overtype mode.

1. In the Queries group of the Navigation Pane, double-click the **qryCustomerContact**. Notice that there are only 19 records.
2. In the record for **Customer ID** #11, in the field **Contact Name**, click to the right of the "n" in Greenfield.
3. Press Insert to switch to Overtype mode.

Figure 2-4
Overtype mode
CC02.accdb
qryCustomerContact

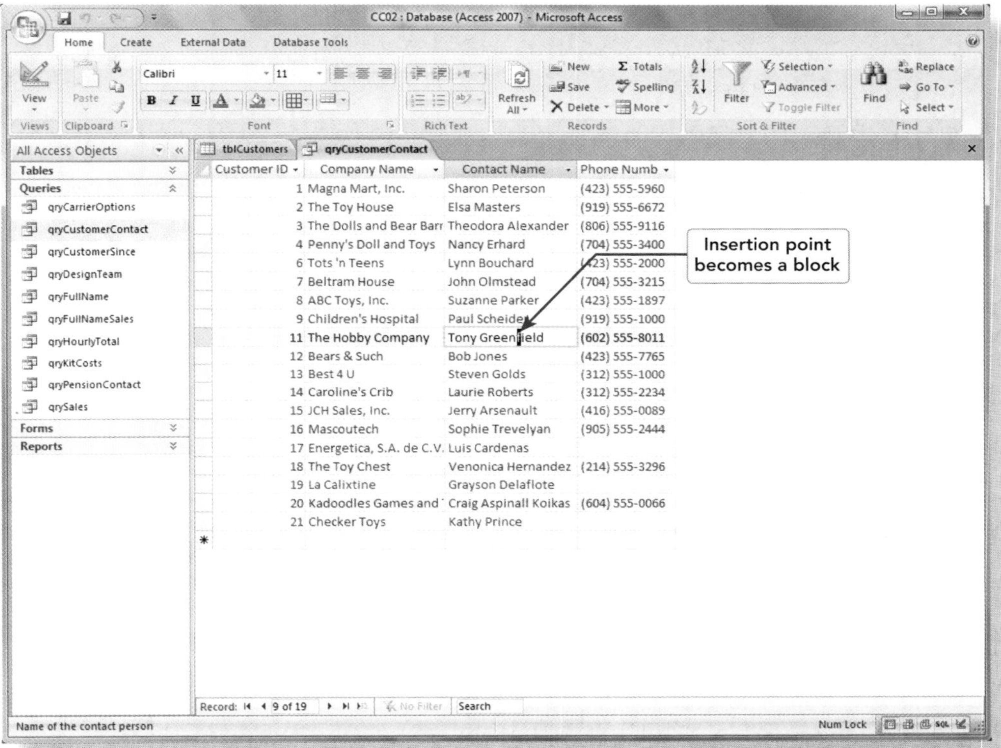

4. Key stein.
5. In the "Tots 'n Teens" record, in the Contact Name field, select "B" of "Bouchard."
6. Key Leachman over the old name.
7. Press Insert to return to Insert mode.
8. Press Ctrl+S to save the record.
9. Click the **tblCustomers** tab to see the changes made through the query.

NOTE

Overtype mode stays on until Insert is pressed, even when the query is closed.

Exercise 2-6 ADD A RECORD THROUGH A QUERY

The additions made in the query's recordset are simultaneously made to the underlying table. The corresponding fields in a table are updated through a query even when the query recordset does not include all the fields in the source table.

1. Click on the **qryCustomerContact** tab and press Ctrl+[+] to move to a new record.
2. Key the customer information below to create a new record. Press Tab to move from one field to the next.

Customer ID:	22
Company Name:	New City Circus
Contact Name:	*Key [your full name]*
Phone Number:	(602) 555-1800

NOTE

In this text, to help identify your work, you often are asked to key an identifier such as your name or initials.

3. Press Shift+Enter to save the record.
4. Click the **tblCustomers** tab and look for the New City Circus record.

5. From the command tab **Home**, in the command group **Records**, click the Refresh All command.
6. You should now see **Customer ID** "22." Because the query did not use all the fields in the table, the record is incomplete.

Exercise 2-7 DELETE A RECORD THROUGH A QUERY

Similarly to adding a record through a query, you can delete a record through a query.

1. Click the **qryCustomersContact** tab and click the record selector for New City Circus.
2. Right-click the selected record. From the shortcut menu, select **Delete Record.** Click **Yes** to confirm the deletion.

NOTE

When you deleted the record while in the query **qryCustomersContact**, Access automatically refreshed the query. By selecting **Refresh All**, you tell Access to refresh the data being displayed in all open objects.

3. Click the **tblCustomer** tab. Notice that the record for New City Circus has "#Deleted" in each cell.
4. From the command tab **Home**, in the command group **Records**, click the Refresh All command.
5. Right-click the **tblCustomer** tab. From the shortcut menu, select **Close All**.
6. In the Navigation Pane, collapse the **Queries** group.

Using Office Editing Tools

Similar to Word and Excel, Access uses AutoCorrect. *AutoCorrect* is an application feature that automatically corrects commonly misspelled words. The AutoCorrect Options button appears next to text being automatically corrected. Choices within the button allow you to customize the correction process. You can undo the correction, cancel future automatic corrections for this error, or turn off the AutoCorrect option completely.

The Office Clipboard is a feature available in Microsoft Word, Excel, PowerPoint, Access, and Outlook. You can use this clipboard to collect and paste multiple items. The contents of the Office Clipboard are deleted when you close Access. If you have multiple Office programs running, the contents of the Office Clipboard are deleted after you close the last Office program. You can copy items while using any program that provides copy and cut functionality, but you can only paste items into a Microsoft Office application.

Exercise 2-8 USE AUTOCORRECT

Text edit commands are used to make changes to the data within a record. AutoCorrect corrects commonly misspelled words as you key text. For example, if you type "teh," AutoCorrect will change it to "the." AutoCorrect also can fix many capitalization errors.

NOTE

Microsoft Office products share **AutoCorrect**. Changes you make in Access affect Word, Excel, and PowerPoint.

1. Click the Office Button and choose Access Options button.
2. In the left pane, click **Proofing**.
3. In the right pane, click the **AutoCorrect Options** button. This opens the AutoCorrect dialog box.

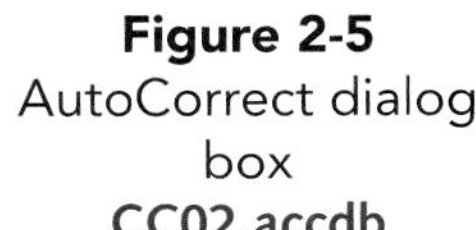

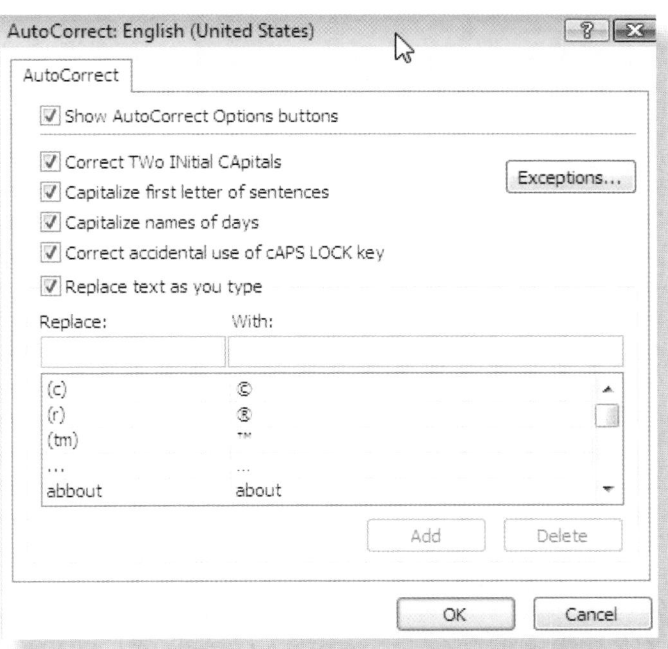

Figure 2-5
AutoCorrect dialog box
CC02.accdb

4. Make sure all check boxes are checked.
5. Scroll down the list of entries to see which words are in the **AutoCorrect** dictionary.

TABLE 2-1 AutoCorrect Options

Options	Description
Show AutoCorrect Option buttons	Option button appears after a word was automatically corrected.
Correct TWo INitial CApitals	Corrects words keyed with two initial capital letters, such as "THis."
Capitalize first letter of sentences	Capitalizes the first letter in a sentence.
Capitalize names of days	Capitalizes days of the week and months.
Correct accidental use of cAPS LOCK key	Corrects words keyed with Caps Lock on but Shift key pressed, such as cAPS.
Replace text as you type	Makes corrections as you work.

NOTE

The field **VenderID** has been set to assign a unique sequential number automatically. This unique number helps identify individual records.

6. Click **OK** to close the **AutoCorrect Options** dialog box.
7. Click **OK** to close the **Access Options** dialog box.
8. In the **Tables** group of the Navigation Pane, double-click the table **tblVenders**.
9. Press Ctrl+ + to add a new record.
10. Press Tab to move to the **Vender Name** field.
11. Key **ACN**.
12. Press the space bar. Notice that "ACN" changed to "CAN."
13. Place your pointer over the corrected word. Click the **AutoCorrect Options** icon when it appears and select **Change back to ACN**.
14. Key **Inc.** to complete the field.
15. Press Tab to move to the **Contact Name** field.
16. Key **TIm Herat**. Press Tab. Notice that AutoCorrect corrected the name to "Tim Heart."
17. Press ↑ to save changes to the record.

18. Click the Close command for the table.

Exercise 2-9 USE COPY, PASTE, AND THE OFFICE CLIPBOARD

You can copy a block of text from one part of a table to another. There are three ways to copy and paste text:

- From the Ribbon, click the Copy command and Paste command buttons.
- Press Ctrl+C (copy) and Ctrl+V (paste).
- Right-click and, from the shortcut menu, choose **Copy** and **Paste**.

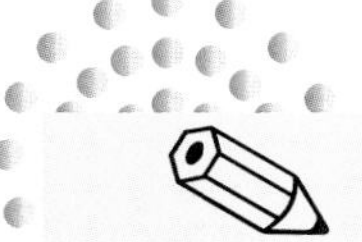

TIP

Unlike the Office Clipboard, the Windows Clipboard only stores the last item copied. On both Clipboards, text can be pasted repeatedly. However, when you copy new information using the Windows Clipboard, the old information on the Windows Clipboard is replaced by the new information.

When you copy the second text block, the Office Clipboard pane opens. You can use the Office Clipboard to paste multiple blocks of text. From that pane, you can select the item you want to paste.

You can duplicate the data from a field in the previous record to the same field in the current record by pressing Ctrl+' (apostrophe). The Duplicate command copies one field at a time.

You can also paste an entire record from one location to another by using the Paste Append command.

NOTE

F2 selects an entire content of a field.

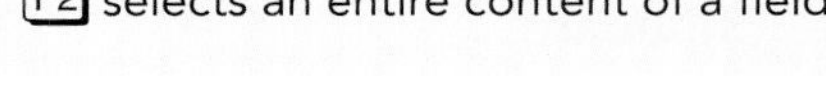

NOTE

When you press Ctrl+;, Access will enter the current system date, according to your computer.

1. In the Navigation Pane, double-click the query **qryCustomerSince**.
2. Find the record for "Energetica" and click in the field **Company Name**.
3. Press F2 to select the whole field.
4. Press Ctrl+' to copy the content field from the previous record.
5. Double-click the word "Hospital" and key **Corner**.
6. Press Tab to move to the next field.
7. Press Ctrl+; to replace the old date with today's date. Press Tab to save the changes.
8. From the command tab **Home**, in the lower-right corner of the command group **Clipboard**, click the Dialog Box Launcher to open the **Clipboard** pane.

Figure 2-6
Clipboard group
CC02.accdb
qryCustomerSince

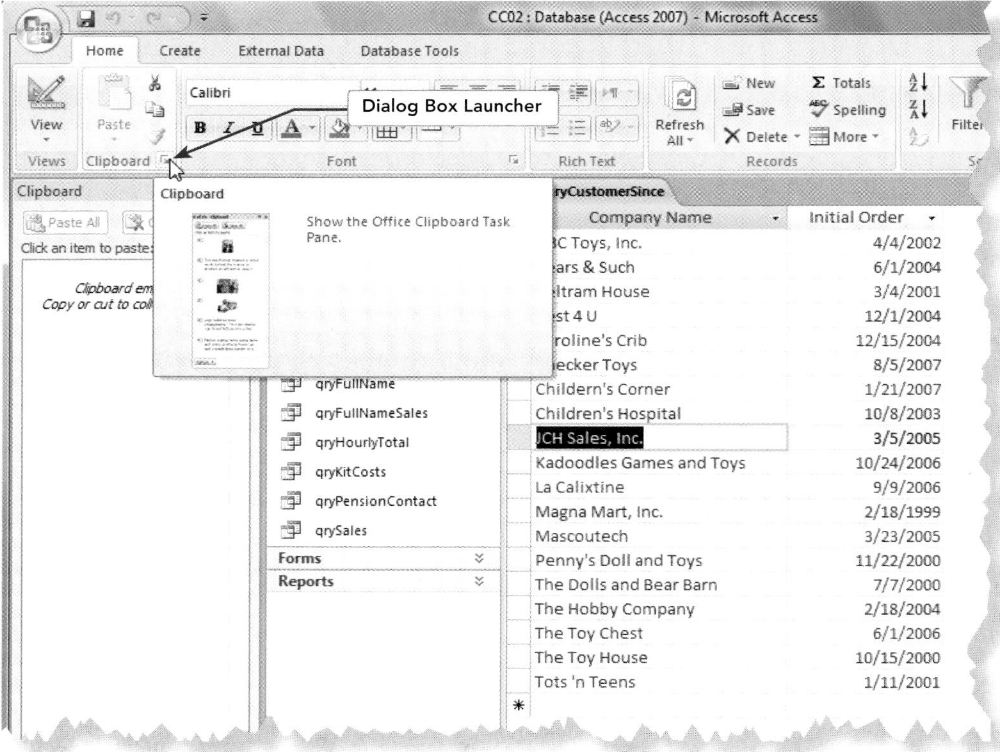

NOTE

The Office Clipboard holds up to 24 copied items.

TIP

In the Clipboard, the icon next to each copied item indicates the application from which the item was copied.

9. In the first record's **Company Name** field, click between the "s" and ",". Press Shift+End to select ", Inc."
10. Click Ctrl+C to copy. Notice that the selected text has been added to the **Clipboard**.
11. In the 16th record's (The Hobby Company) **Company Name** field, double-click the word "Company" to select it.
12. From the command tab **Home**, in the command group **Clipboard**, click the Copy command. There are now two items in the **Clipboard**.

13. In the 13th record's (Mascoutech) **Company Name** field, click to the right of the data and press the spacebar to add a space.
14. Press Ctrl+V to paste the last text copied.
15. In the 17th record's (The Toy Chest) **Company Name** field, click to the right of the data.
16. From the Clipboard pane, click ", Inc." to paste the text.
17. In the 18th record's (The Toy House) **Company Name** field, click to the right of the data.

18. From the Clipboard pane, click ", Inc." to paste the text.
19. Click the **Clipboard** Close command.
20. Right-click the **qryCustomerSince** tab. From the short-cut menu, select **Close**.
21. In the Navigation Pane, collapse the **Queries** group.

Exercise 2-10 USE UNDO

In a previous exercise you used Esc to cancel changes in a field. You will now use the Undo command, which can affect fields, records, or even major objects.

Access remembers changes to the record and lets you undo most edits. If you accidentally delete text in a field, you can use the Undo command to reverse the action. One exception to this is if you delete a record, it can't be undone. There are two ways to undo an action:

- From the **Quick Access Toolbar**, click the Undo command.
- Press Ctrl+Z.

1. In the Navigation Pane, double-click the table **tblRegions**.
2. In the field **Region Name**, double-click "Southeast."
3. Press Delete to delete the data.
4. From the **Quick Access Toolbar**, click the Undo command.

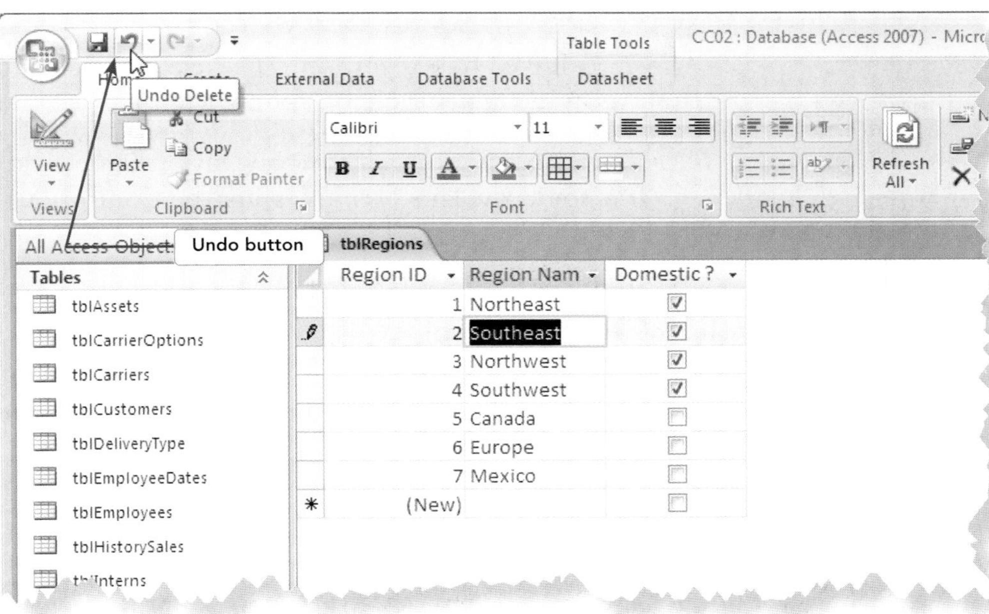

Figure 2-7
Undo a deletion
CC02.accdb
tblRegions

5. Click the Record Selector for Region ID "2" and press Delete.
6. Read the dialog box, and then click **Yes** to confirm the deletion.
7. Press Ctrl+Z to attempt to undo the deletion. Nothing happens because once a record is deleted, it can't be undone.
8. Right-click the **tblRegions** tab. From the shortcut menu, select **Close**.
9. In the Navigation Pane, click the table **tblRegions** to select it. Do not open the table.
10. From the command tab **Home**, in the command group **Records**, click the Delete command ×.
11. In the dialog box, click **Yes**. The table is deleted.
12. Press Ctrl+Z to undo the deletion.
13. In the Navigation Pane, collapse the **Tables** group.

Viewing and Modifying Recordsets through a Form

A form is a major Access object. A form is designed to be used on a computer screen. Through a form, you can enter, view, sort, edit, and print data. Most often when making changes to records, it is easier to use a form rather than a table. A form uses the same navigation buttons, scroll bars, and text editing features as a table.

Exercise 2-11 NAVIGATE THROUGH FORMS

A form is linked to a recordset. The fields displayed through a form are the same as in the table or query from which they originate.

1. In the **Forms** group of the Navigation Pane, double-click the form **frmInternList**. This form is using the Continuous Form view to display data.
2. In the **Forms** group of the Navigation Pane, double-click the form **frmInterns**. This form is using the Single Form view.
3. In the **Forms** group of the Navigation Pane, double-click the form **frmInternSplit**. This form is using the Split Form view.

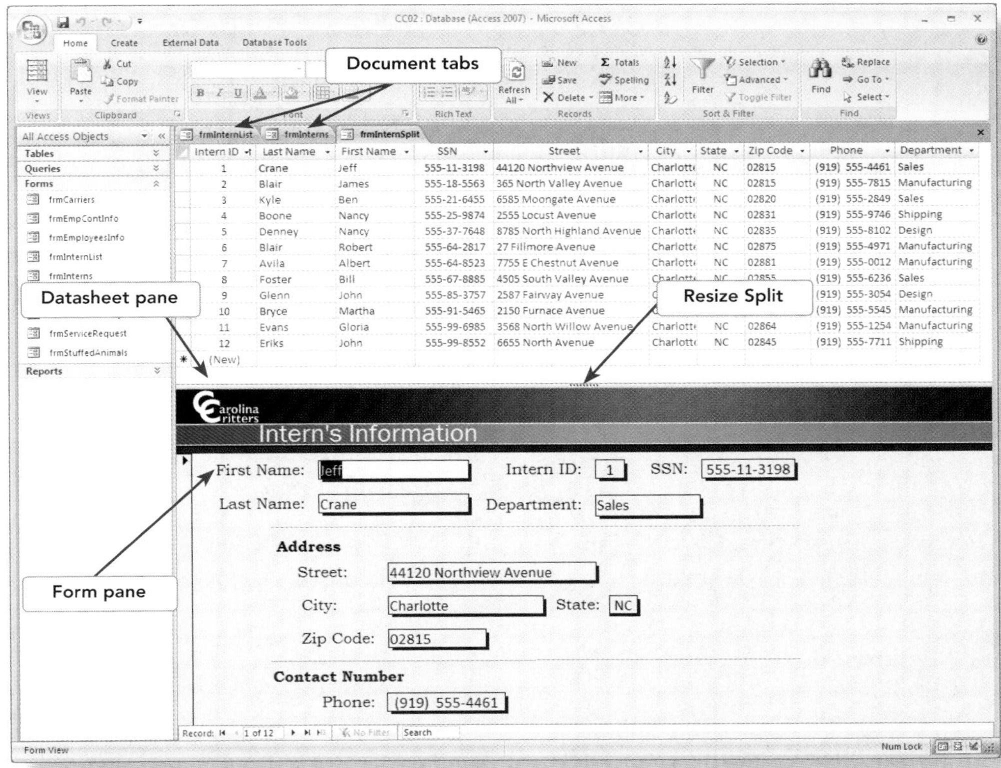

Figure 2-8
Multiple open documents
CC02.accdb
frmInternSplit

4. Click the document tab for the form **frmInternList**.
5. Press [Tab] to move the cursor to the second field (**SSN**) in the first record.
6. Press [Ctrl]+[PageDown] to move to the second record.
7. Press [Ctrl]+[End] to move to the last field in the last record.
8. Click the document tab for the form **frmInterns**.
9. Press [Tab] 5 times. Notice the selected field order is not always left to right or top down.
10. Press [PageDown] to move to the next record. Notice that the field Street is still selected.

11. In the Record Navigation tool, click the Last Record button. The record for John Eriks is now visible.
12. Click the document tab for the form **frmInternSplit**.
13. Press [Tab] to move through the first record. Notice that the fields in the form are not in the same order as in the datasheet.
14. Press [PageDown] to move to the next record. Notice that the information in the selected record and the form are the same.

Exercise 2-12 EDIT FIELDS THROUGH A FORM

You can edit data in a form with the same shortcuts you use in a table or a query. For example, Backspace deletes a single character and the keyboard combination Ctrl+Delete deletes everything to the right of the insertion point.

The data displayed in each field of a form are stored in a table. Just as you can change the data stored in a table through the table's Datasheet View, you can change the data through a form.

1. Click the document tab for the form **frmInternList**.
2. Click the Previous Record button until you get to the "Gloria Evens" (**Intern ID** 11) record.

NOTE

Record Selectors in forms are the same as in tables and queries.

3. In the **Street** field, click to the left of "Avenue" and press Ctrl+Delete.
4. Key **Boulevard**. Notice the pencil icon in the Record Selector.

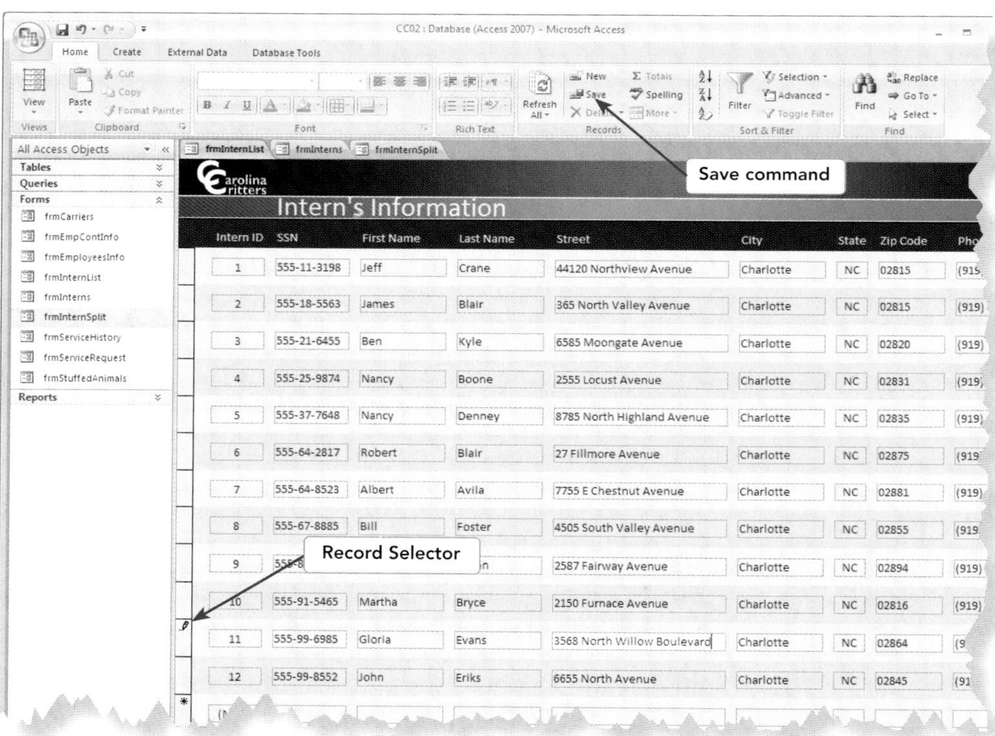

Figure 2-9
Edit data in a form
CC02.accdb
frmInternList

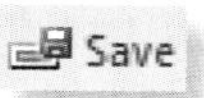

5. From the command tab **Home**, in the command group **Records**, click the Save command. Notice the pencil icon is no longer in the Record Selector.
6. Click the document tab for the form **frmInternSplit**.
7. In the datasheet at the top of the form, click anywhere in the record for "Nancy Boone" (**Intern ID** 4.)

8. Double-click the **City** field for the selected record to select all content.
9. Key **Garner** and press [Enter]. Notice that the data in the **City** field have changed in the lower part of the form.
10. Press [↓] to save the changes to the record.
11. Click in any field in the form (lower half).

Exercise 2-13 ADD RECORDS THROUGH A FORM

A form can make it easier for you to add records. A well-designed form utilizes field placement to improve the efficiency of data entry.

1. From the command tab **Home**, in the command group **Records**, click the New command [New]. The Record Selector will display an asterisk until you key new data.
2. Key the following new record, pressing [Tab] between entries:

First Name:	*Key [your first name]*
Last Name:	*Key [your last name]*
SSN:	555-99-7845
Department:	Administration
Street:	825 Canal Street
City:	Cary
State:	NC
Zip Code:	27513
Phone:	(919) 555-1601

Figure 2-10
Adding a new record
CC02.accdb
frmInternSplit

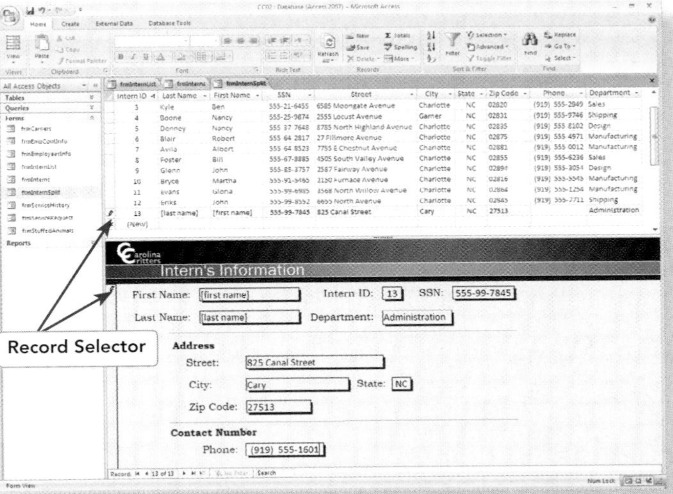

3. Press [Ctrl]+[S].

NOTE

In the split view of a form, data can be edited or added in either section.

Exercise 2-14 DELETE RECORDS THROUGH A FORM

You can delete the current record by using the same methods you used when deleting a record in a table.

1. Click the document tab for the form **frmInternList**.
2. Click in any field for the intern "James Blair" (**Intern ID** 2.)
3. From the command tab **Home**, in the command group **Records**, click the Delete command option arrow and choose the Delete Record command.

Figure 2-11
Delete options
CC02.accdb
frmInternList

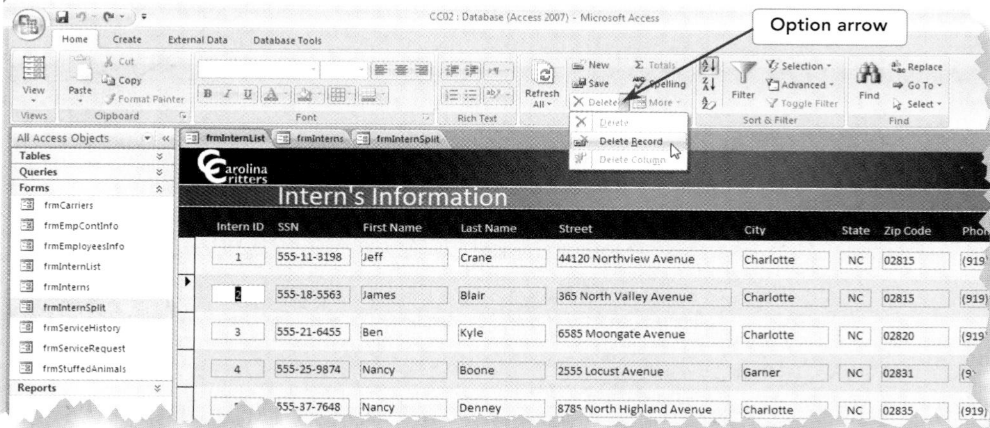

4. Click **Yes** to confirm the deletion.
5. Click the document tab for the form **frmInternSplit**. Notice that there is a row with "#Deleted" in each field.
6. From the command tab **Home**, in the command group **Records**, click the command Refresh All.
7. Right-click the **frmInternSplit** tab. From the shortcut menu, select **Close All**.
8. In the Navigation Pane, collapse the **Forms** group.

Managing Attachments

Some tables include an image with each record. The Stuffed Animals table includes a field with an illustration of the product. The Employees table includes a field with a photograph of the employee. Both the illustration and the photograph are images attached to a field. All attachment fields display as a paperclip in Datasheet View.

In addition to images, you can attach certain types of data files such as documents, worksheets, or text files. The **Attachments** window allows you to add, remove, open, or save an attachment. Attached files cannot be larger than 256 megabytes or be nondata files such as programs, system files, or batch files.

Exercise 2-15 ATTACH AN IMAGE

When attaching an image, you must know the location of the file and in which record the file will be stored.

1. In the **Tables** group of the Navigation Pane, double-click the table **tblStuffedAnimals**.
2. Locate the record for "Larry Lion" (**Product ID** 13.)
3. Double-click the attachment field. The **Attachments** dialog box appears.

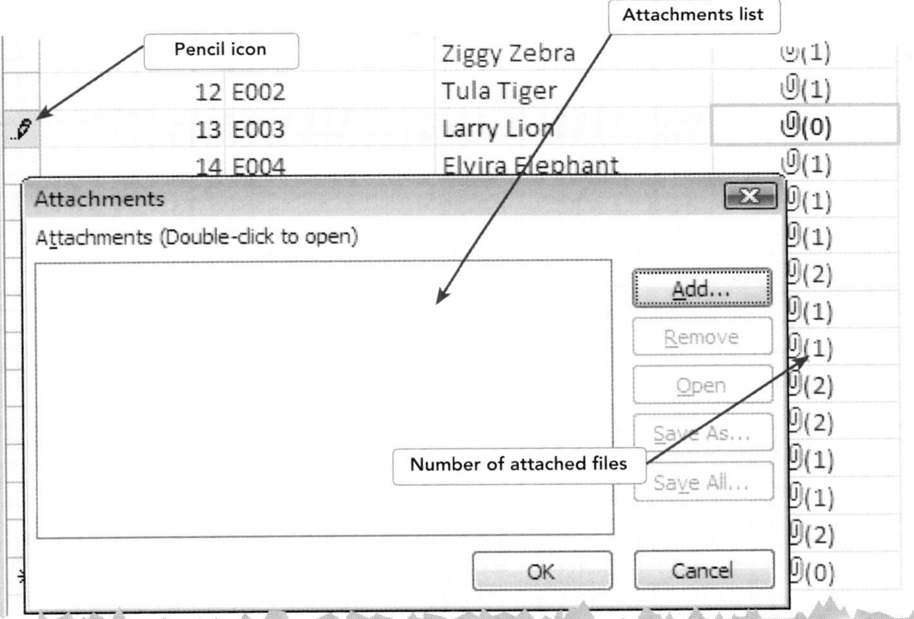

Figure 2-12 Adding an attachment **CC02.accdb tblStuffedAnimals**

4. The names of attached files appear in the Attachments list. Click **Add**.
5. Locate the **Lesson 02** folder. Double-click the file **Lin003**.
6. Click **OK**.
7. Press Ctrl+S to save the changes in the record.
8. Close the table by right-clicking the table's document tab and choosing **Close**.

9. In the Navigation Pane, collapse the **Tables** group.
10. In the **Forms** group of the Navigation Pane, double-click the form **frmStuffedAnimals**.
11. Press PageDown until you get to the "Larry Lion" record.
12. Click the picture. A Mini toolbar appears above the image.

Figure 2-13
Attachments in a form
CC02.accdb
frmStuffedAnimals

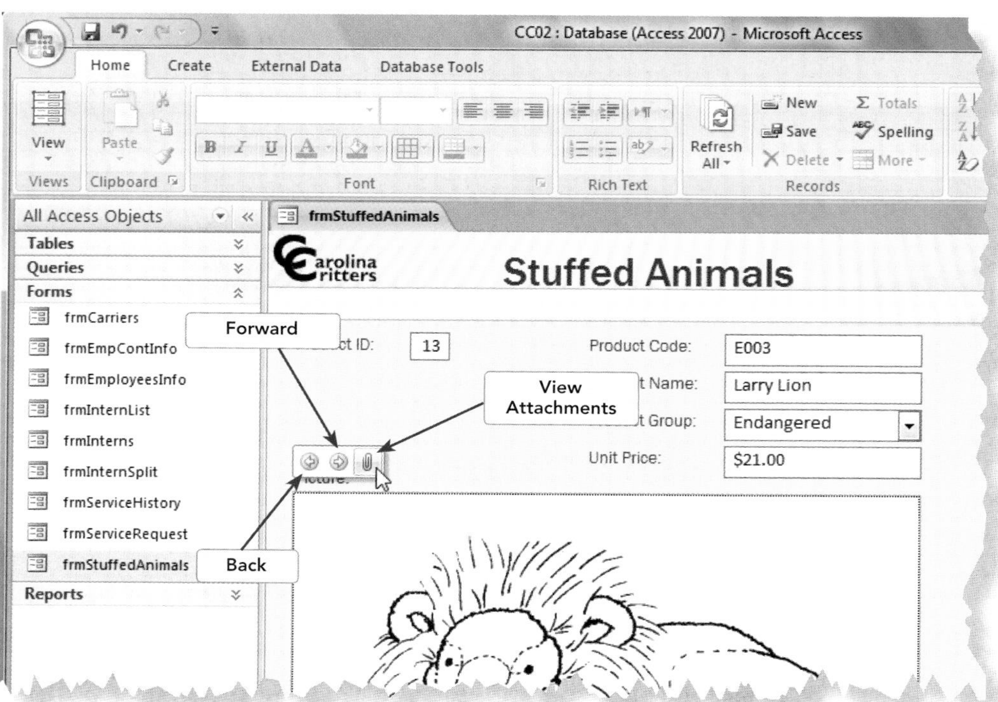

13. On the Mini toolbar, click the **View Attachments** button.
14. In the **Attachments** dialog box, click **Add**.
15. In the **Lesson 02** folder, double-click the file **Lin003c**. You now have two files attached to this record.
16. Click **OK**.
17. Click the picture to open the Mini toolbar.

18. On the Mini toolbar, click the Forward button to see the second file.

Exercise 2-16 EXTRACT AN IMAGE FROM THE DATABASE

Extracting is different than removing an image. When you remove an image, you delete that image from the record. When you extract an image, you save a copy of the image as an external file without affecting the original image.

1. Press PageDown until the data for "Theodore Bear" (**Product ID** 22) is displayed in the form.
2. Double-click the image of the product. This opens the **Attachment** dialog box.
3. Click **Save As**.
4. In the **Save Attachment** dialog box, change the **File name** to **Theodore Bear.bmp**.
5. Check the file path in the location bar. Change if needed.
6. Click **Save** to save a copy of the image outside of the database.

REVIEW

Closing a major object after modifying or adding a record will save the changes.

7. Click **OK** to close the **Attachment** dialog box.
8. Close the form by right-clicking the form's document tab and choosing **Close**.
9. In the Navigation Pane, collapse the **Forms** group.

Previewing, Printing, and Saving Data Using a Report

Just as forms are designed to view data on a screen, reports are designed to view data on paper. A form is designed to fit on a standard computer screen, while a report is designed to fit on a sheet of paper.

Use the Microsoft Office Button or keyboard methods to open the Print dialog box. From the Print dialog box, you can set a print range or change the page orientation.

Exercise 2-17 PREVIEW A REPORT

Print Preview shows you how the selected report prints on paper. *Print Preview* is a method for displaying on the screen how an object will appear if printed on paper.

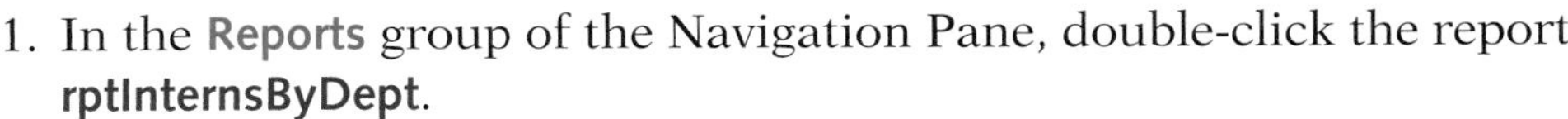

1. In the **Reports** group of the Navigation Pane, double-click the report **rptInternsByDept**.

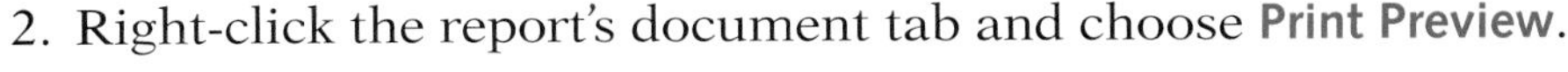

2. Right-click the report's document tab and choose **Print Preview**.

TIP

To use the Print Preview Ribbon for tables, queries, and forms, you must click the Office Button and click the **Print** option arrow.

3. From the command tab **Print Preview**, in the command group **Page Layout**, click the command **Portrait**.
4. In the lower-right corner is the zoom control. Click the Plus button twice to zoom to 120%.

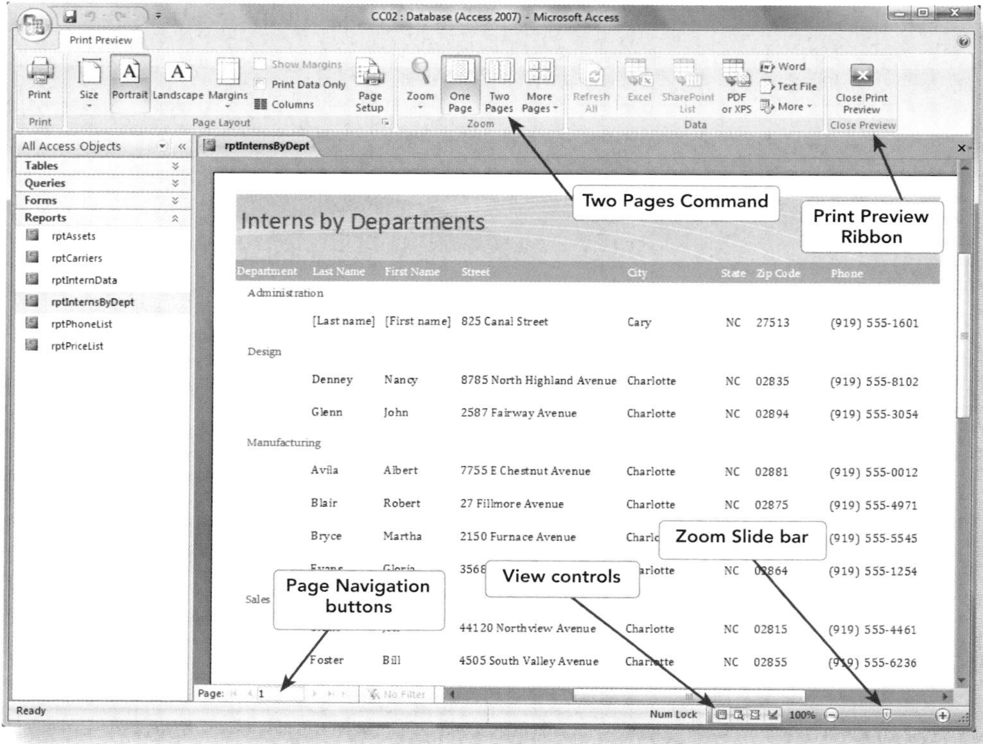

Figure 2-14
Print Preview
CC02.accdb
rptInternsByDept

5. Click the Two Pages command. Notice that this report fits onto one page.

Exercise 2-18 PRINT A REPORT

Depending on the size of the report, you may need to change the page orientation or the margins. You can set the print orientation to landscape for a report similar to when printing a datasheet. You most often change the page orientation when records contain more fields than can print in portrait orientation.

1. In the **Reports** group of the Navigation Pane, double-click the report **rptInternData**.

2. At the right end of the status bar are the Change View buttons. Click the **Print Preview** button.
3. Click the Two Pages button. Notice that this report has information on a second page.

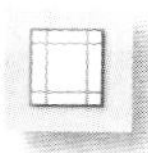

4. From the command tab **Print Preview**, in the command group **Page Layout**, click the Margins command option arrow and choose **Narrow**.

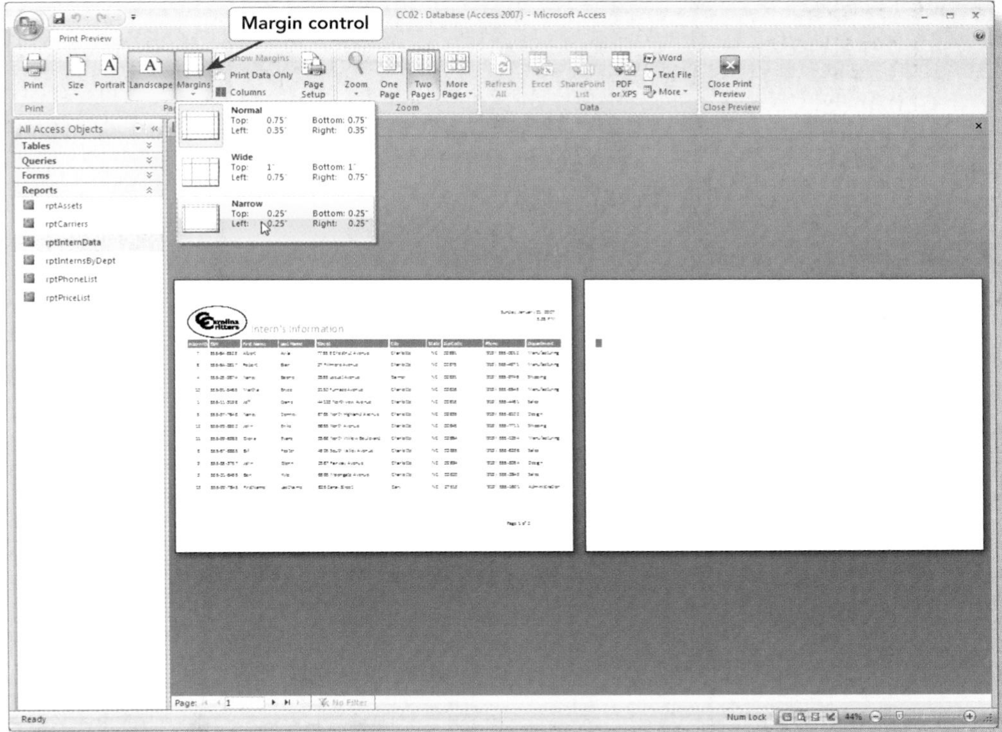

Figure 2-15
Changing margin settings
CC02.accdb
rptInternData

5. From the command tab **Print Preview**, in the command group **Print**, click the Print command. The **Print** dialog box opens.

6. Based upon your classroom procedure, you can either print the report or cancel the print process. To cancel, click **Cancel**. To print the report, click **OK**. If you are uncertain, ask your instructor.

Exercise 2-19 SAVE A REPORT TO A FILE

You can publish a report as an electronic XPS file just like when you publish a datasheet. A published report can be viewed or printed through Microsoft Internet Explorer.

1. From the command tab **Print Preview**, in the command group **Data**, click the PDF or XPS command.

2. Change the location to the location where you will be storing your homework.

TIP

Use the Browse Folder button to help you store files in nondefault locations.

3. Click to the right of the filename and key a hyphen and your initials.

4. Click the **Open file after publishing** check box.

Figure 2-16
Save a report to a file
CC02.accdb
rptInternDat

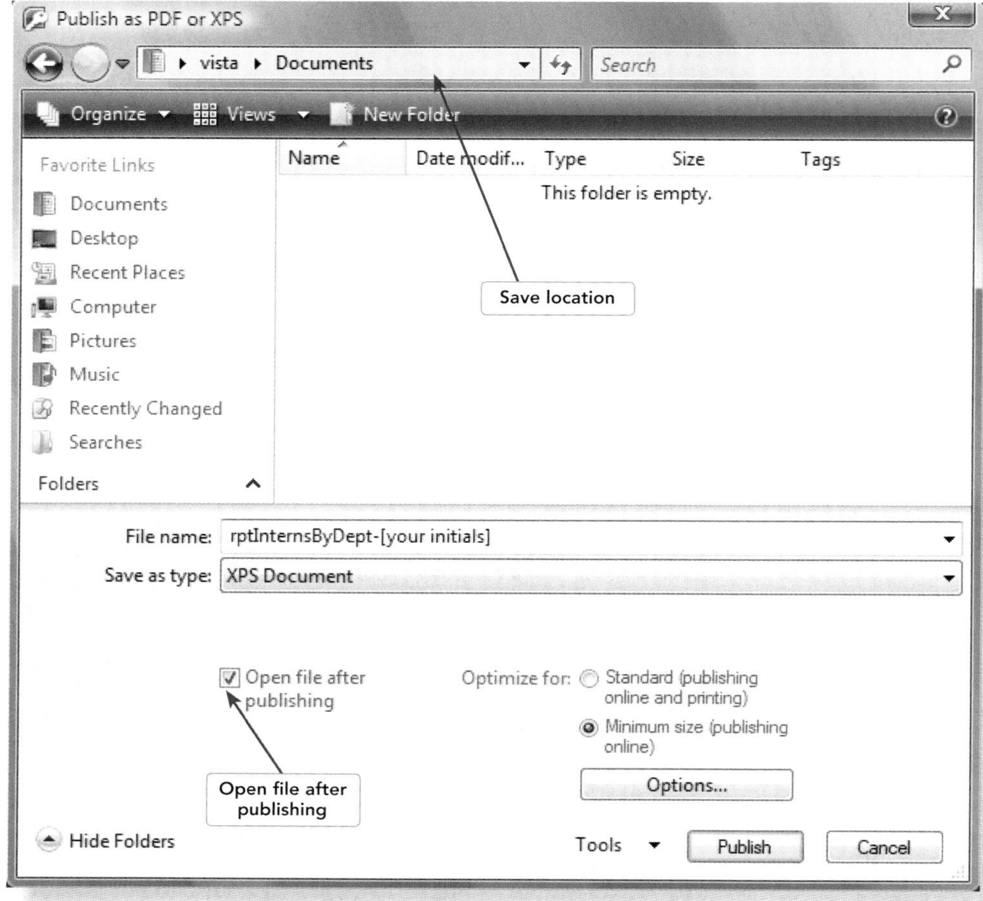

5. Click **Publish** to create the XPS file. Your file has been opened in Internet Explorer.
6. Close the Internet Explorer.
7. Right-click the **rptInternData** tab. From the shortcut menu, select **Close All**.

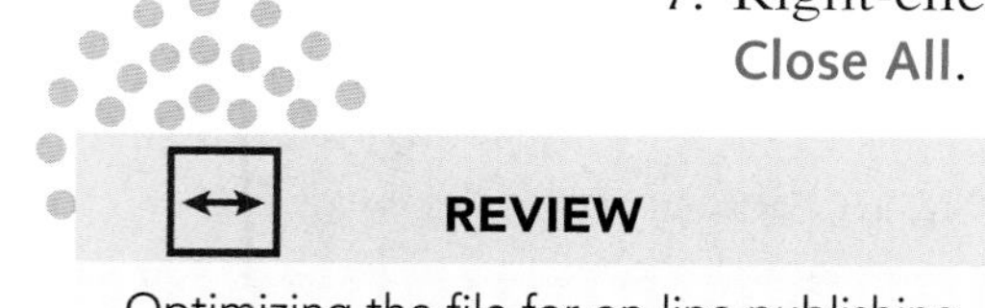

Optimizing the file for on-line publishing and printing increases the size of the file.

8. In the Navigation Pane, collapse the **Reports** group.
9. Click the **Office Button**.
10. Click **Exit Access**.

Lesson 2 Summary

- Access automatically saves changes to a record when you move the insertion point to another record.
- Records are stored in tables.
- Records can be added, edited, and deleted in a table, through a query, or through a form.
- You can delete records from a table by clicking on the Record Selector and pressing Delete.
- When editing a record, you can insert text or use the Overtype mode to key over existing text.
- AutoCorrect corrects commonly misspelled words.
- Press Ctrl+' to duplicate the contents in the field from the previous record.
- Press Ctrl+; to enter the current system date into a field.
- Press Ctrl+C to copy and Ctrl+V to paste text.
- Click the Undo button to restore the previously deleted text.
- You can attach an image or document file to a record.
- Print Preview displays on the screen how an object will be printed.
- A published object can be viewed or printed at a later time.

LESSON 2	Command Summary		
Feature	**Button**	**Task Path**	**Keyboard**
Add record	New	Home, Records, New	Ctrl+ +
Copy		Home, Clipboard, Copy	Ctrl+C
Delete record		Home, Records, Delete	Ctrl+ -
Duplicate field			Ctrl+'
Insert current date			Ctrl+;
Paste		Home, Clipboard, Paste	Ctrl+V
Print			Ctrl+P
Save		Office Button, Print Preview, Data, XPS	
Refresh All		Home, Records, Refresh All	
Save record	Save	Home, Records, Save	Ctrl+Enter
Undo		Edit, Undo	Ctrl+Z

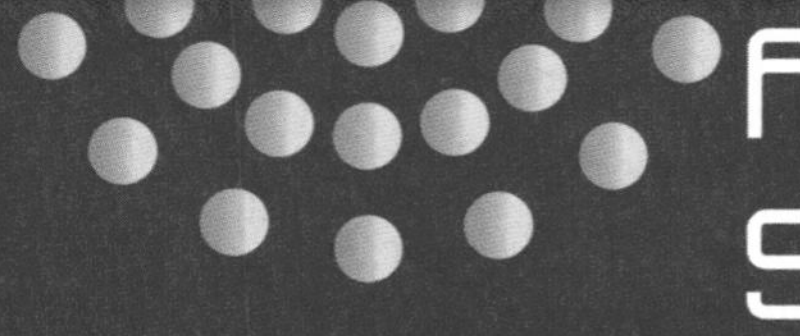

Lesson 3

Finding, Filtering, Sorting, and Summarizing Data

OBJECTIVES

After completing this lesson, you will be able to:

1. Find and replace data.
2. Use wildcards
3. Sort records.
4. Add and modify the Totals row in datasheets.
5. Use filters.
6. Use the Database Documenter.

MCAS OBJECTIVES

In this lesson:
AC07 70-605 2.3.5
AC07 70-605 3.3
AC07 70-605 5.1.1
AC07 70-605 5.1.2
AC07 70-605 5.1.3
AC07 70-605 5.1.4
AC07 70-605 5.2.1
AC07 70-605 5.2.2
AC07 70-605 5.2.3
AC07 70-605 5.2.4
AC07 70-605 5.5
AC07 70-605 6.2.5

Estimated Time: 1 1/2 hours

The main purpose of a database is to turn raw data into useful information. Often, databases are too complex to find specific information easily. To locate specific information, you can use Access tools to search, find, sort, and filter. By applying the proper combinations of tools, the cumbersome data becomes useful information.

Carolina Critters sells 24 different stuffed animal kits categorized into five different product lines. If you want to know which stuffed animal kits were most popular in Canada, you would total the quantities sold, sort the sales totals in descending order, and filter for only Canadian customers. You might often use a combination of tools to change data to information.

Finding and Replacing Data

Finding information can be time consuming if you have to scroll through several thousand records. Searches can be quicker when fields contain unique data. For example, if you know the social security number of a particular employee, you can find that person quickly because no two people share the same social security number. However, if you only know the person's last name, then the search can take quite a bit longer because your database may contain numerous employees who share the same last name.

Although most often, you will change single records, on occasion, you will find it necessary to update the same data listed in many records. Employees at Carolina Critters are classified by job titles. If the job title for a group of employees changes, then these changes need to be reflected throughout the entire table. To make the changes, you will need to find the original job titles and replace them with the updated job titles.

Exercise 3-1 USE THE SEARCH TOOL

Using the Search tool is a quick way to find data in a recordset. The Search tool begins its search at the first field of the first record and stops at the first match. If the recordset contains more than one match, only the first match is found. Because of this limitation, the Search tool is best used when searching for unique data, such as a social security number. The Search tool can be used on tables, queries, and forms.

1. Locate and open the **Lesson 03** folder.
2. Make a copy of **CC03** and rename it to *[your initials]*-**CC03**.
3. Open and enable content for ***[your initials]*-CC03**.
4. From the Navigation Pane, open the table **tblEmployees** in Datasheet View.
5. In the Navigation Bar, click in the **Search** tool.

NOTE

The Search tool is not case sensitive. Access treats uppercase and lowercase text the same.

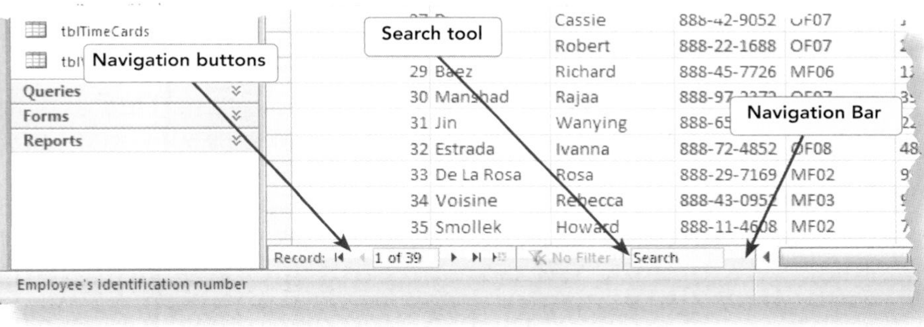

Figure 3-1 Search tool **CC03.accdb tblEmployees**

6. Key r. Starting from the upper left, the first "r" is selected.
7. Key o. Starting from the upper left, the first "ro" is selected.
8. Key c. The selection has moved to the 10th record.
9. Press Backspace three times to remove the content of the **Search** tool.
10. Key raj. The selection has moved to the **First Name** field of the 30th record.
11. Clear the content of the **Search** tool.
12. Key 888-5. The selection has moved to the **SSN** field of the 15th record.
13. Close **tblEmployees**.

NOTE

The content and application of the Search tool cannot be retained when you close an object.

Exercise 3-2 USE THE FIND COMMAND

Similar to the **Search** tool, the **Find and Replace** dialog box finds matches in a recordset. However, there are two major differences. The **Find and Replace** command begins a search at the insertion point and includes options for fine-tuning how text is matched.

TABLE 3-1 Find and Replace Dialog Box Options

Option	Description
Look In	Sets the search for the current field or the entire table.
Match: Any Part of Field	Finds records with matching characters anywhere in the field.
Match: Whole Field	Finds records in which an entire field matches the value in the Find What text box.
Match: Start of Field	Finds records in which the beginning of a field matches the Find What entry.
Search: All	Searches forward to the end of the table and wraps back to the beginning.
Search: Up	Searches in the Up (backward) direction only.
Search: Down	Searches in the Down (forward) direction only.
Match Case	Finds exact uppercase and lowercase matches.
Search Fields As Formatted	Enables you to key data in its display format. To find a date that is stored as 1/25/01, you can key 25-Jan-01. This is the slowest search.

There are two ways of opening the **Find and Replace** dialog box with focus on the **Find** tab:

- From the **Home** tab, in the **Find** group, choose the Find command.
- Press Ctrl+F.

1. In the Navigation Pane, open the table **tblEmployees** in Datasheet View.
2. From the **Home** tab, in the **Find** group, choose the Find command.
3. In the **Find What** control, key **robert**.

Figure 3-2
Find option of the Find and Replace dialog box
CC03.accdb
tblEmployees

Find and Replace
Find | Replace
Find What: robert
Find Next
Cancel
Look In: Employee ID
Match: Whole Field
Search: All
Match Case | Search Fields As Formatted

NOTE

To see the results of a search, you can drag the **Find and Replace** dialog box by its title bar to a location on the screen that doesn't conceal the results of the search.

4. Click **Find Next**. There is no "robert" found in the field **Employee ID**. Click the drop-down arrow for the control **Look In** and choose **tblEmployees**.
5. Click **Find Next.** The first occurrence of "robert" is located in the field **First Name**. To search in only one field, you must click in that field before starting the search.
6. Click anywhere in the datasheet and press PageUp. In the **Find and Replace** dialog box, click the drop-down arrow for the control **Match** and choose **Any Part of Field**.
7. Now the first occurrence of "robert" is located in the field **Emergency Contact.**
8. Click **Find Next** to find the next occurrence, until you reach the end of the table.
9. Read the message box and click **OK**.
10. Click **Cancel** to close the **Find and Replace** dialog box.

Exercise 3-3 USE THE REPLACE COMMAND

The **Replace** tab finds matches in the same way as the **Find** tab does. With Replace, you not only find the match, but you can also replace each matched value with a new value. You can replace either a single occurrence or every occurrence of the value.

When using the **Replace All** option, you must be careful that all occurrences in the recordset are values that you planned to replace. Sometimes, unanticipated errors can occur. For example, if you replace the word "form" with "report," then a field containing the word "information" will become "inreportation." You will not be able to use undo to correct these changes.

There are two ways of opening the **Find and Replace** dialog box with focus on the **Replace** tab:

- From the **Home** tab, in the **Find** group, choose the Replace command.
- Press Ctrl+H.

1. In the table **tblEmployees**, for the first record, click in the **Address** field.
2. Press Ctrl+H to open the **Find and Replace** dialog box.
3. In the **Find What** control, key **road**.
4. In the **Replace With** control, key **Street**.
5. Verify that the **Look In** control is set to **Address**.
6. Verify that the **Match** control is set to **Any Part of Field**.

7. Click **Find Next**. The first occurrence after the insertion point is selected.
8. Click **Replace** to replace the first occurrence of "road" with "Street" and to find the next occurrence of "road."
9. Click **Find Next** to skip this occurrence of "road" and move to the next.
10. Click **Replace**.
11. Change the content of the **Find What** control to **st.** Make sure that the **Look in** control is set to **Address** and the **Match** control is set to **Any Part of Field**.
12. Click **Find Next**. The abbreviation of "street" is selected.
13. Click **Replace All**.
14. Read the message box and click **Yes**.
15. Click **Cancel** to close the dialog box.

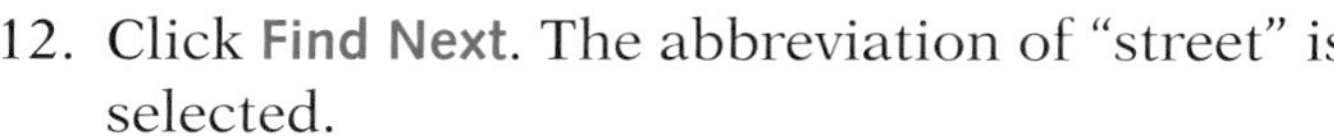

TIP

Make sure that you have keyed the period after "st."

Using Wildcards

Up to this point, you have used exact text when finding and replacing text. On occasion, you may not know the exact value you want to match. For example, you might need to find a particular stuffed animal. You may not know its exact name, but you know that the product name uses the word "dog." Not knowing the exact names, you would need to search using a wildcard. A *wildcard* is a character or group of characters used to represent one or more alphabetical or numerical characters.

Exercise 3-4 FIND DATA USING AN ASTERISK "*"

The asterisk (*) is a wild card that represents one or more characters. If you search for "Mar*" as a last name, you will match names such as "Mar," "Mart," "Martin," "Marigold," or "Marblestone." All fields matched will begin with "Mar," regardless of remaining characters in the field.

1. In the table **tblEmployees**, for the first record, click in the **Job Code** field.
2. Press Ctrl+F to open the **Find and Replace** dialog box.
3. In the **Find What** control, key **m***.
4. Click **Find Next.** "MF03" is selected.
5. Click **Find Next** twice. "MF05" is selected.
6. Click the drop-down arrow for the **Look In** control and choose **tblEmployees**.
7. Click **Find Next**. Notice that part of an address is now selected.
8. Click **Cancel** to close the dialog box.

Exercise 3-5 FIND DATA USING A QUESTION MARK "?"

The question mark (?) is a wildcard that represents a single character. If you search for "Mar?" as a first name, you will find names such as "Mari," "Mark," "Marv," or "Mary." All fields containing only four characters and starting with "Mar" will be matched. Fields containing more than four characters or not beginning with "Mar" will not be matched.

1. In the table **tblEmployees**, for the first record, click in the **Job Code** field.
2. From the **Home** tab, in the **Find** group, choose the Find command .
3. In the **Find What** control, key **OF??**.
4. In the **Look In** control, select **tblEmployees**.
5. In the **Match** control, select **Whole Field**.
6. Click **Find Next** to find the first occurrence of any field's content that is only four characters long that starts with "OF."
7. Click **Find Next** a few more times to see which different codes are found.
8. Click **Cancel**.

Sorting Records

In a table, records are displayed in the order in which they were entered. For example, whenever a new employee is hired, his or her name is added to the end of a table. Most often this order is not useful for all your needs.

You can change the sort order of the recordset depending on the information you need. When creating an employee phone list, you would sort the recordset by last and first name. When creating an organizational chart, you would sort by job title rather than by name.

Exercise 3-6 SORT RECORDS IN DATASHEET VIEW

You can sort data in three ways:

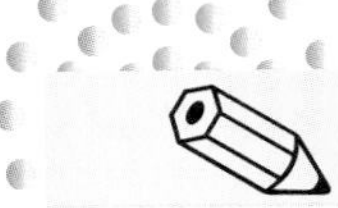

TIP

A small up or down arrow appears on the column header of a sorted column. This sort-order arrow appears to the right of the column header's drop-down arrow.

- From the **Home** tab, in the **Sort & Filter** group, choose Ascending or Descending .
- On a column selector, click the option arrow and select the **Sort A to Z** or Sort **Z to A**.
- In a field, right-click and select the **Sort A to Z** or **Sort Z to A**.

1. In the table **tblEmployees**, in the **Job Code** field, click the option arrow on the column header, and choose **Sort A to Z**.

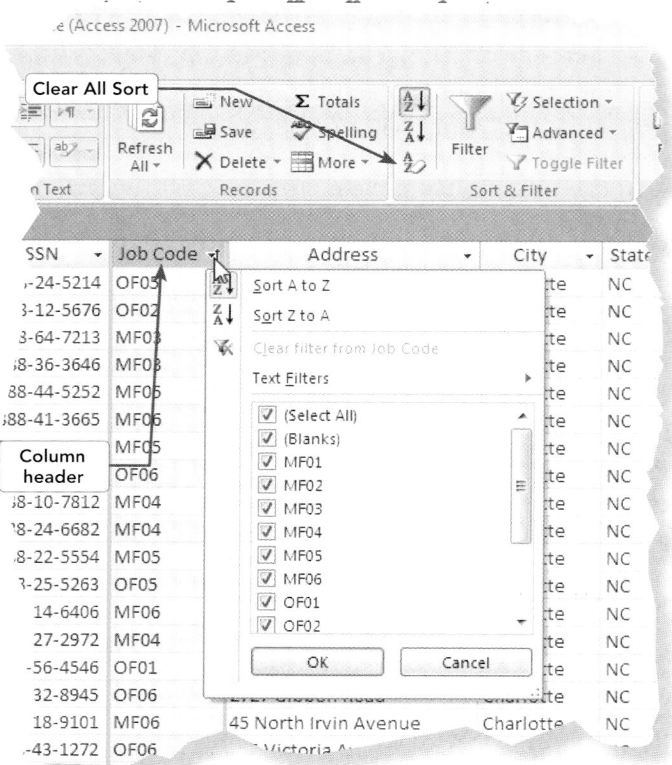

Figure 3-3
Apply Sort to a column
CC03.accdb
tblEmployees

2. From the **Home** tab, in the **Sort & Filter** group, choose the Clear All Sorts command. Notice that the sort-order arrow no longer displays in the column header.
3. Select both the **Last Name** and the **First Name** fields.
4. Right-click the selected column headers and choose **Sort Z to A**. The table is now sorted by last name and then by first name.
5. In the Navigation Pane, open the query **qryEmployeePhone** in Datasheet View. This query gets its data from **tblEmployees**.
6. Click in the **Employee ID** field, click the option arrow on the column header, and choose **Sort Largest to Smallest**.
7. Click the document tab for **tblEmployees**. Notice that the sort order on the table is not affected when a sort order is applied to the query.
8. Right-click any document tab and choose **Close All**. Do not save any changes.

Exercise 3-7 SORT RECORDS IN A FORM

A form can be set to view a single record at one time or multiple records all at once. All forms can be sorted. When multiple records are displayed in a form, the sort order is observable. To see the results of a sort to a single record form, you will need to navigate through the recordset one screen at a time.

1. From the Navigation Pane, open the form **frmStuffedAnimals** in Form View.
2. Click in the **Product Code** field.
3. From the **Home** tab, in the **Sort & Filter** group, choose **Ascending**. A different record now displays.
4. Press [PageDown] to move through all the records to see that the form is indeed sorted by **Product Code**.
5. Click in the **Product Name** field.
6. From the **Home** tab, in the **Sort & Filter** group, choose the Ascending command.
7. Use the Record Navigation buttons to move through the records to see the change.
8. From the **Home** tab, in the **Sort & Filter** group, choose the Clear All Sorts command.
9. Right-click the form's tab and select **Close All**. Do not save any changes.

Exercise 3-8 SORT RECORDS IN A REPORT

The recordset displayed in Layout View of a report can be sorted similarly to a recordset in Form View of a form. The Layout View of a report allows you to fine-tune the display of data, including sorting the fields and adjusting column widths.

1. From the Navigation Pane, open the report **rptEmployeePhone** in Report View. This report is sorted by Employee ID.
2. From the **Home** tab, in the **Views** group, click **View** and choose the **Layout View command**.

NOTE

When in Layout or Design Views, contextual tabs are added to the Ribbon.

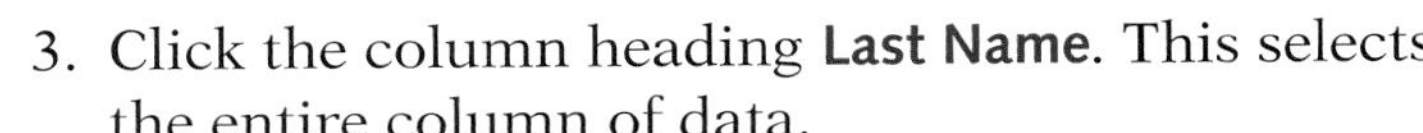

3. Click the column heading **Last Name**. This selects the entire column of data.
4. Click the **Home** tab.
5. In the **Sort & Filter** group, choose the Ascending command. (See Figure 3-4 on the next page.)
6. From the **Home** tab, in the **Views** group, click View, and choose the Report View command.

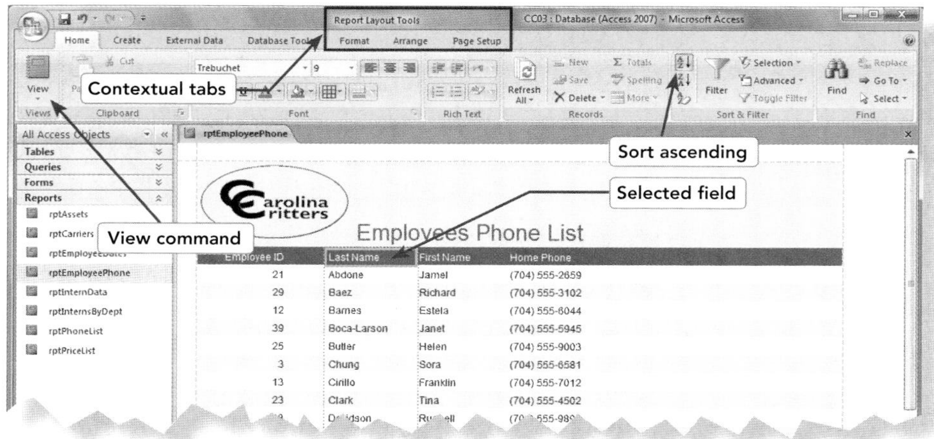

Figure 3-4 Sort in a report CC03.accdb rptEmployeePhone

7. Right-click the report's tab and select **Close**.
8. Click **Yes** to save the changes.

Adding and Modifying the Totals Row in Datasheets

The **Totals** row is a feature that you can use to summarize data quickly. For example, if you need to know the amount of federal income tax paid by your employees this year, you would need to create a sum total for the federal income tax field in the payroll table.

Exercise 3-9 ADD A TOTALS ROW TO A QUERY

The Totals row uses an aggregate function to summarize a field. An *aggregate function* is a dynamic mathematical calculation that displays a single value for a specific field. Any change to a recordset automatically triggers recalculations of the aggregate functions located in the **Totals** row.

TABLE 3-2 Totals Row Aggregate Functions

Function	Description
Average	Calculates the average value for a column containing numeric, currency, or date/time data.
Count	Counts the number of items in a column.
Maximum	Returns the item with the highest value. For text data, the highest value is the last alphabetic value.
Minimum	Returns the item with the lowest value. For text data, the lowest value is the first alphabetic value.
Standard Deviation	Measures how widely values are dispersed from an average value.
Sum	Adds the items in a column containing numeric or currency data.
Variance	Measures the statistical variance of all values in the column containing numeric or currency data.

1. From the Navigation Pane, open the query **qryYrPay** in Datasheet View.
2. From the **Home** tab, in the **Records** group, choose the Totals command Σ. This adds a **Totals** row below the new record row.
3. In the **Totals** row, click in the **Salary Total** field. A drop-down arrow appears to the left of the field.
4. Click the drop-down arrow to display the list of available functions.
5. Choose **Count** from the list. There are 16 records that have **Salary Total** data.

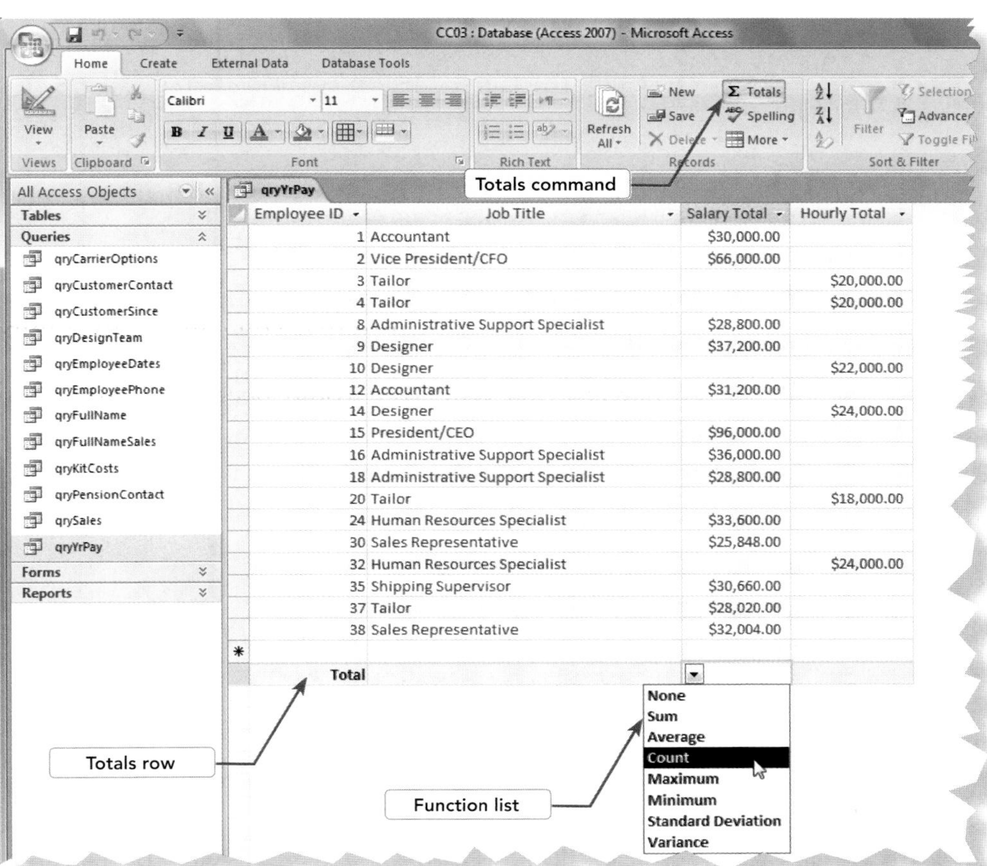

Figure 3-5
Adding a Totals row to a Datasheet
CC03.accdb
qryYrPay

Exercise 3-10 MODIFY A TOTALS ROW IN A QUERY

A Totals row is always present. Once you've created a Totals row in a datasheet, you can never truly delete it. You either modify it with a new function or hide it. Each time you display the Totals row, the functions that you last saved will appear.

1. In the query **qryYrPay**, click in the **Salary Total** field.
2. Click the drop-down arrow, and choose the function **Average**. The average of all data in the column displays.

3. In the **Totals** row, click in the **Hourly Total**.
4. Click the drop-down arrow and choose **Average**.
5. From the **Home** tab, in the **Records** group, choose the Totals command Σ to remove the **Totals** row.
6. Click the Close button × to close the query.
7. Click **Yes** to save the changes.
8. Reopen the query **qryYrPay**.
9. From the **Home** tab, in the **Records** group, choose the Totals command Σ to add the **Totals** row. Notice that the functions you added have been saved.
10. Click the Close button × and then click **Yes** to save the changes.

Using Filters

A *filter* is a database feature that limits the number of records displayed. A filter uses a criterion to determine which records will be displayed. A *criterion* is a rule or test placed upon a field. When the tested field in a record matches the filter criterion, the record is displayed.

Once you define a filter, you can toggle between Apply or Remove. When applied, a filter displays only matching records. When removed, the entire recordset displays. Whether applied or removed, the actual number of records in the underlying recordset remains constant.

Exercise 3-11 CREATE AND APPLY A FILTER BY SELECTION

Filter By Selection is a filter applied to a single field. The filter can be created to match the entire field or a portion of a field. The selection will be compared with field values in the recordset based upon a comparison option selected from a contextual menu. A *contextual menu* is a varying list of options based upon the item selected.

The filter options displayed depend upon the type of field and data selected. Options displayed for a date field differ from options displayed for a text field. Some options, such as "Begins With" or "Ends With," display only when the beginning portion or the ending portion of a text field is selected.

When filtering with more than one field, only records that match all filters will display. For example, if you need to list all employees who work as inspectors in the manufacturing department, you would create criteria for the department field and the job title field. Only records that match "Inspector" and "Manufacturing" will appear.

TABLE 3-3 Common Contextual Filter Options

Field Type	Filter Option
Date	Equals Does Not Equal On or Before On or After
Numeric	Equals Does Not Equal Less Than or Equal To Greater Than or Equal To Between
Text	Equals Does Not Equal Contains Does Not Contain Begins With Does Not Begin With Ends With Does Not End With

1. From the Navigation Pane, open the table **tblInvoices** in Datasheet View.
2. Click the Search tool and key **the t**. The Toy House customer is the first found.
3. Click in the highlighted field.
4. Press F2 to select the whole field.
5. From the **Home** tab, in the **Sort & Filter** group, click the Selection command.

6. From the menu, choose **Equals "The Toy House"**. There are 12 records for this customer.

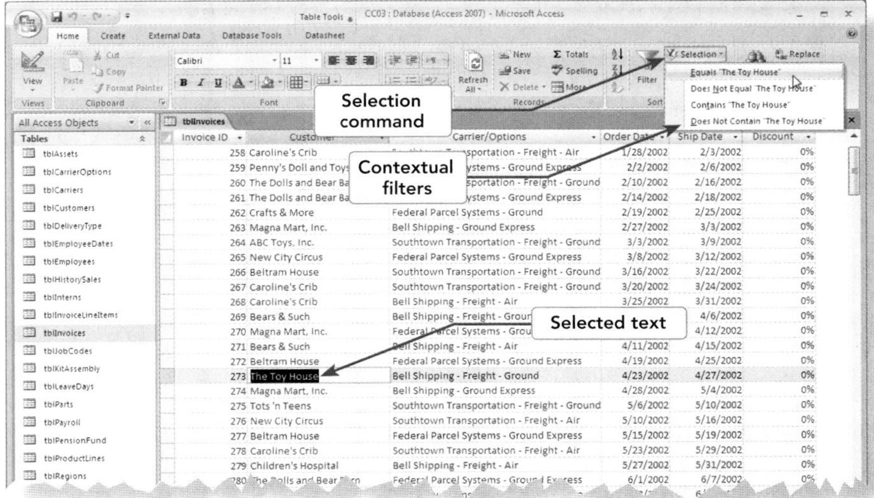

Figure 3-6
Creating a filter by selection
CC03.accdb
tblInvoice

NOTE

The field Customer ID now has a small icon of a funnel in the column header to indicate the table has a filter enabled for this field.

7. From the **Home** tab, in the **Sort & Filter** group, choose the Toggle Filter command. This disables the filter.
8. Press Ctrl+End to move to the last record in the table.
9. In the last record, select only the year (2007) in the **Order Date** field.
10. From the **Home** tab, in the **Sort & Filter** group, click the Selection command and choose **Ends With 2007**. There are 12 records for the year 2007.
11. From the **Home** tab, in the **Sort & Filter** group, click the Toggle Filter command to disable the filter.
12. Click in the **Carrier/Options** field of the first record. Make sure that no text is selected.

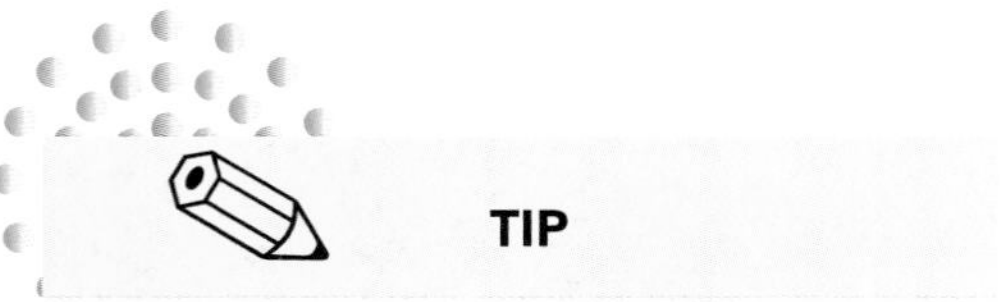

TIP

When the insertion bar is in a field with no characters selected, Filter By Selection assumes the whole field is selected.

13. From the **Home** tab, in the **Sort & Filter** group, click the Selection command and choose **Equals "Federal Parcel Systems – Groun..."**. Carolina Critter used this carrier 32 times.
14. Click the drop-down arrow next to the funnel icon in the column heading for the **Carrier/Options** field and choose **Clear filter from Carrier/Options**.

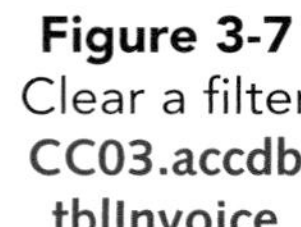

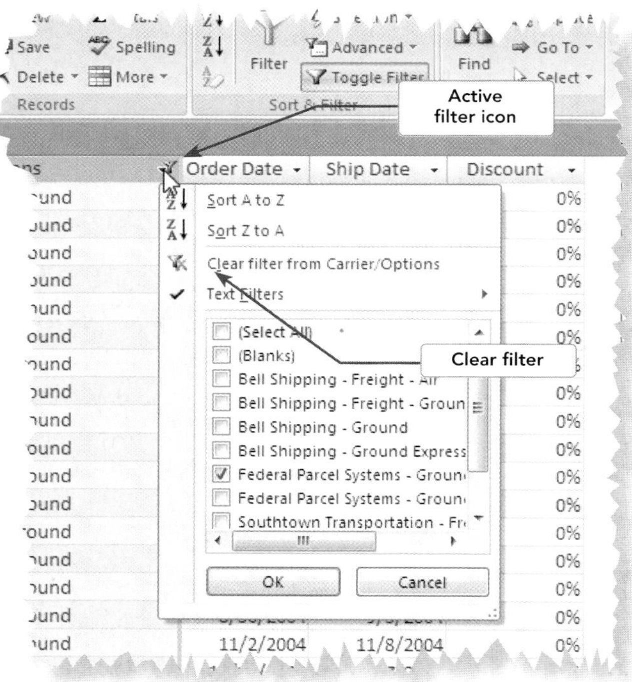

Figure 3-7
Clear a filter
CC03.accdb
tblInvoice

Exercise 3-12 FILTER FOR A SPECIFIC VALUE

When filtering for a specific value, you select one or more values from a predefined criteria list. Each item on a list can be "selected for" or "omitted from" the filter condition. When two or more criteria are selected, either criterion must match for the record to display. For example, if you select "NY" and "CA" for the state, then all records from New York and all records from California will display.

NOTE

When changing a filter for a field, the new filter replaces the old filter.

The criteria list is dynamically created on the basis of the unique values found in the field. The first two items in every criteria list will be "Select All" and "Blanks." "Select All" toggles between selecting and omitting all values. Selecting "Blanks" includes records where the criterion field is left empty.

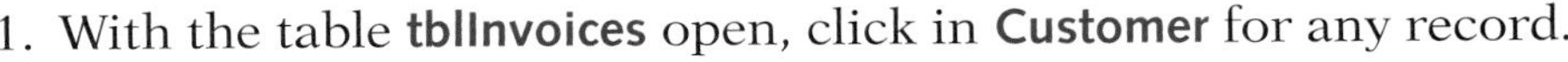

1. With the table **tblInvoices** open, click in **Customer** for any record.

2. From the **Home** tab, in the **Sort & Filter** group, click the Filter command.
3. In the menu, click the check box **(Select All)**. This removes all checkmarks.
4. Click the check boxes for **Crafts & More** and **Caroline's Crib**.
5. Click **OK**. All records for both customers display.

Figure 3-8
Filter Logic: Specific value
CC03.accdb

```
(Company Name="Crafts & More") or (Company Name="Carolina's Crib")
                            Condition
```

6. From the Navigation Pane, open the query **qryEmployeeDates** in Datasheet View.
7. Click in the **End Date** field for any record.
8. Click the drop-down arrow in the field's column header.
9. In the menu, uncheck the check box **(Select All)** and then check the check box for **(Blanks)**.
10. Click **OK** to apply the filter. Only records that do not have data in this field are shown.
11. Click the drop-down arrow in the **End Date** column header. From the menu, choose **Clear filter from End Date**.

Exercise 3-13 FILTER FOR A RANGE OF VALUES

Other contextual filter options, such as calendar filters, have even more options. If you filter on a date field, you can select to filter dates by days, weeks, months, quarters, or years. The options available will vary depending on the date selected and the current date. For example, if the date selected is within the current year, then "This Year" becomes an available filter option.

1. From the Navigation Pane, open the report **rptEmployeeDates**.
2. From the **Home** tab, in the **Views** group, click **View** and choose Layout View command.
3. Right-click the **Hire Date** column header, and from the menu, click **Data Filters**. From the menu, choose **Between...**

4. In the **Between Dates** dialog box, click in the **Oldest** control.
5. Key **1/1/2000** and press Tab.

Figure 3-9
Date Picker control
CC03.accdb
tblEmployeeDates

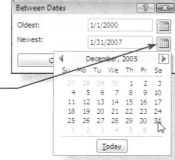

Date Picker button

6. Press the Date Picker button for the **Newest** control.
7. Use the left arrow to move through the calendar until you get to December, 2005. For the **Newest** control, click the 31st. This adds the date to the **Newest** control.
8. Click **OK**. Carolina Critters employees hired between 1/1/2000 and 12/31/2005 are shown.

Figure 3-10
Filter Logic: Range of values
CC03.accdb

```
(Hire Date >= 1/1/2000) and (Hire Date <= 12/31/2005)
                     Condition
```

9. From the **Home** tab, in the **Sort & Filter** group, choose the Toggle Filter command.
10. Right-click the table's tab and choose **Close All**.

Exercise 3-14 CREATE AND APPLY A FILTER BY FORM

Filter By Form allows you to define a collection of criteria for one or more fields using a template. When using Filter By Form in a form, the template appears as a blank form. Alternatively, when using Filter By Form in a datasheet, the template appears as a blank datasheet.

Collections in Filter By Form are organized by tabs. The first tab is called "Look for" and is located in the lower-left hand corner of the template. In a tab, all conditions must be met for a record to be displayed. For example, in the "Look for" tab, if you defined the criterion "NY" for the state and the criterion "Albany" for the city, then only records from "Albany, NY" will be included in the active recordset.

1. From the Navigation Pane, open the form **frmStuffedAnimals** in Form View.
2. From the **Home** tab, in the **Sort & Filter** group, click the Advanced command and choose **Filter By Form**.
3. Click the drop-down arrow for the **Product Group** and choose **Endangered**.

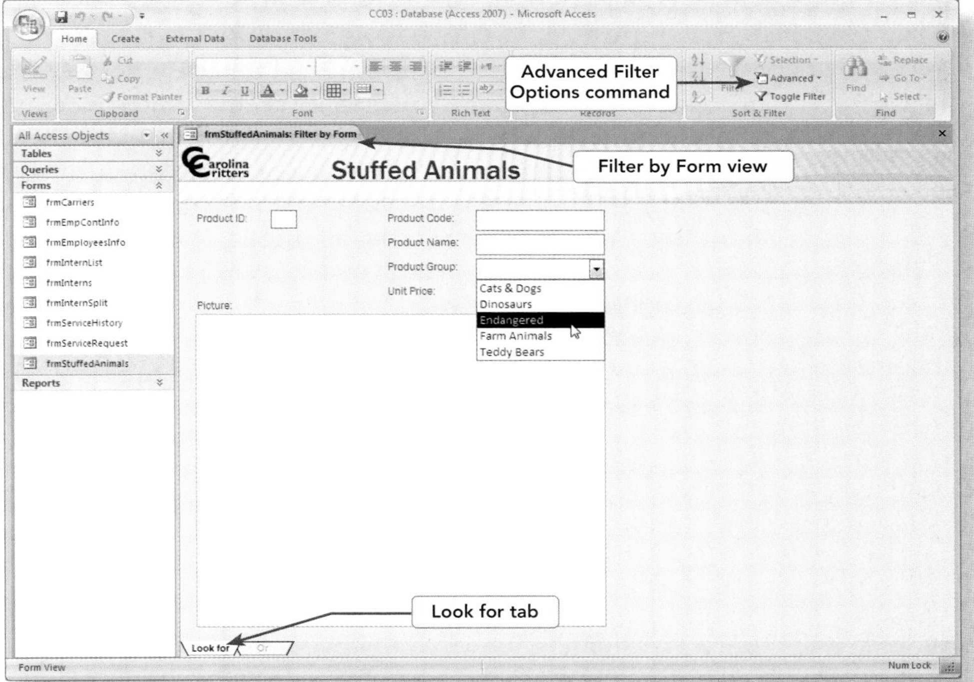

Figure 3-11
Filter By Form
CC03.accdb
frmStuffedAnimals

4. From the **Home** tab, in the **Sort & Filter** group, choose the Toggle Filter command. This returns you to the form and enables the filter. Five records match this filter.
5. Press Tab to move through the records.
6. From the **Home** tab, in the **Sort & Filter** group, click the Advanced command and choose **Filter By Form**. The last setting for Product Group is still present.
7. Click in the **Unit Price** field, and key **>20** and press Enter.
8. From the **Home** tab, in the **Sort & Filter** group, choose the Toggle Filter command. Only three records display.

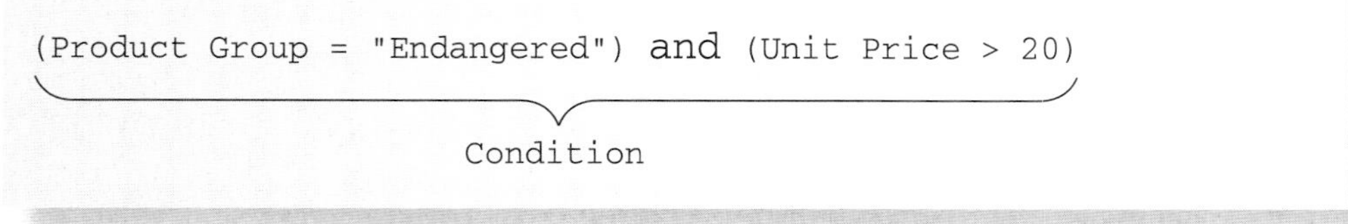

Figure 3-12
Filter Logic: Filter By Form
CC03.accdb

9. Press Tab to move through the records.

Exercise 3-15 USE FILTER BY FORM "OR" OPTION

In the previous exercise, you used Filter By Form to create a set of filters in a single tab. There are times that you may need to create a more complex filter using multiple tabs. The Filter By Form has the ability to add alternate sets of filters. Alternative collections of filters are located on the "Or" tab. When using multiple tabs, displayed records must match all conditions on the first tab or all conditions on the additional "Or" tabs.

Suppose that you need to display a list of stuffed animals in Product Groups D and E. Although you might say "D and E," this is actually an OR condition. You really want to display all the records that have "D" or "E" for a value in the Product Group field. Because both values are applied to the same field, you must place the first filter on the "Look for" tab and the second on the "Or" tab.

1. From the **Home** tab, in the **Sort & Filter** group, click the Advanced command and choose **Filter By Form**. The filter is set to find "Endangered" animal kits that cost greater than $20.
2. Click the **Or** tab next to the **Look for** tab. This opens an alternative collection of fields.
3. Click the drop-down arrow for the **Product Group** and choose **Teddy Bears**.
4. Click in the **Unit Price** field, and key **>20**.

Figure 3-13
Filter Logic: Filter By Form with Or
CC03.accdb

((Product Group = "Endangered") and (Unit Price > 20)) or ((Product Group = "Teddy Bear") and (Unit Price > 20))

Condition 1 Condition 2

5. From the **Home** tab, in the **Sort & Filter** group, choose the Toggle Filter command.
6. Press Tab to move through the records. There are seven records.
7. From the **Home** tab, in the **Sort & Filter** group, choose the Toggle Filter command to disable the filter.
8. Click the Close button and then **Yes** to save the changes.

Using the Database Documenter

External documentation helps a database administrator manage changes to a database. An easy way to document a database is to create a report using the Database Documenter. The *Database Documenter* is an Access tool that lists the indexes, properties, relationships, parameters, and permissions of major database objects.

Assume you are the database manager for Carolina Critters and are asked to track healthcare expenses for the dependents of all employees. Before beginning the task, you would find it beneficial to see a list of all fields used in every table.

Exercise 3-16 GENERATE A REPORT FOR A TABLE

When documenting a single object, you most often include details for fields and indexes. By default, the Database Documenter does not include fields or indexes in its report. It is always a good idea to check which options are selected before printing a report.

1. From the **Database Tools** tab, in the **Analyze** group, choose the Database Documenter command.
2. In the **Documenter** dialog box, on the **Tables** tab, click the checkbox for **tblEmployees**.

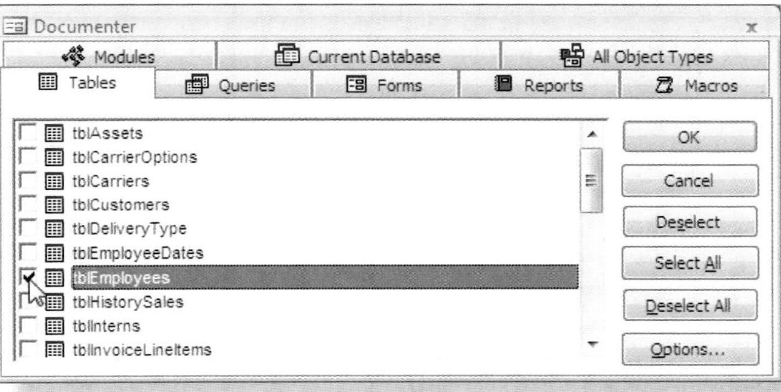

Figure 3-14
Database Documenter
CC03.accdb

3. Click **Options** to open the **Print Table Definition** dialog box.
4. For the **Include for Table** section, check the **Properties**, **Relationships**, and **Permissions by User and Group**.
5. For the **Include for Fields** section, select **Names, Data Types, Sizes, and Properties**.
6. For the **Include for Indexes** section, select **Names, Fields, and Properties**.
7. Click **OK** to accept the changes and close the dialog box.
8. Click **OK** to view the report. This report contains more information than is needed.

9. Click the Close Print Preview command.

Exercise 3-17 PRINT/SAVE REPORTS FOR MULTIPLE OBJECTS

When documenting multiple objects, you may not wish to include the same level of detail that you might for a single object report. For example, you may only need to see field names, data types, and sizes for all tables in your database.

1. From the **Database Tools** tab, in the **Analyze** group, choose the Database Documenter command.
2. In the **Documenter** dialog box, on the **Tables** tab, click **Select All**.
3. Click **Options** to open the **Print Table Definition** dialog box.
4. For the **Include for Table** section, only check **Properties**.
5. For the **Include for Fields** section, select **Names, Data Types, and Sizes**.
6. For the **Include for Indexes** section, select **Nothing**.

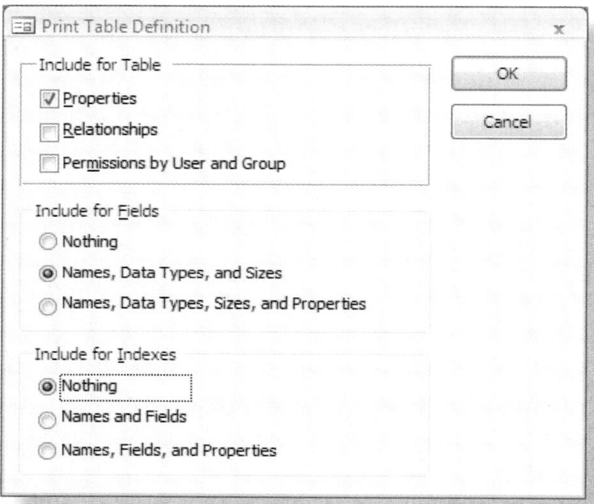

Figure 3-15
Print Table Definition
CC03.accdb

7. Click **OK** to accept the changes and close the dialog box.
8. Click **OK** to view the report. Notice that the information for each table now fits on one page.

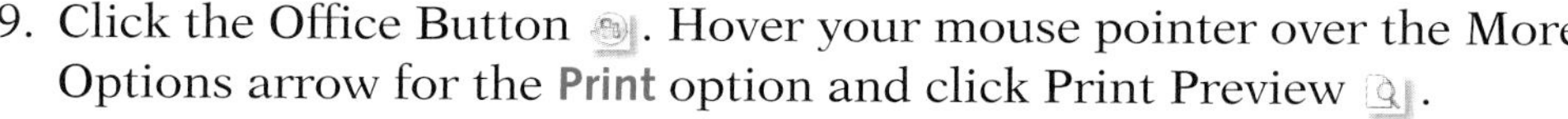

9. Click the Office Button. Hover your mouse pointer over the More Options arrow for the **Print** option and click Print Preview.

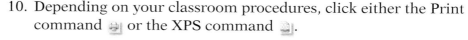

10. Depending on your classroom procedures, click either the Print command or the XPS command.

11. Click the Close button to close the database.

Lesson 3 Summary

- To locate specific information, you can use Access tools to search, find, sort, and filter.
- You can improve the search speeds by specifying unique data.
- The Search tool begins its search at the first field of the first record and stops at the first match.
- The **Find and Replace** command begins a search at the insertion point and includes options for fine-tuning how text is matched.
- A wildcard is a character or group of characters used to represent one or more alphabetical or numerical characters.
- The **Totals** row is a feature that you can use to calculate aggregate functions quickly.
- Each time you display the **Totals** row, the functions that you last saved will appear.
- A filter is a database feature that limits the number of records displayed.
- When applying a filter to a recordset, only records matching the criterion will display.
- The Filter By Selection options displayed depend upon the type of field and data selected.
- When filtering for a specific value, you select one or more values from a dynamically created list.
- The date filter options available vary depending on the date selected and the current date.
- Filter By Form allows you to define a collection of criteria for one or more fields using a template.
- The Filter By Form has the ability to add alternate sets of filters located on the "Or" tab.
- The Database Documenter is an Access tool that lists the indexes, properties, relationships, parameters, and permissions of major database objects.

LESSON 3		Command Summary	
Feature	**Button**	**Task Path**	**Keyboard**
Database Documenter		Database Tools, Analyze, Database Documenter	
Filter By Form		Home tab, Sort & Filter, Advanced, Filter By Form	
Filter Range of Values		Home, Sort & Filter, (data type) Filters	
Filter Selection		Home, Sort & Filter, Selection	

continues

LESSON 3		Command Summary *continued*	
Feature	**Button**	**Task Path**	**Keyboard**
Filter Specific Value		Home, Sort & Filter, Filter	
Find		Home tab, Find	Ctrl+F
Replace		Home tab, Find, Replace	Ctrl+H
Sort Ascending		Home, Sort & Filter, Ascending	
Sort Descending		Home, Sort & Filter, Descending	
Sort Remove		Home, Sort & Filter, Clear All Sorts	
Totals Rows	Σ	Home, Records, Totals	

Lesson 4

Creating New Databases and Tables

OBJECTIVES

After completing this lesson, you will be able to:

1. Create databases.
2. Create tables.
3. Add and delete fields in a table.
4. Control field appearance.
5. Control data integrity.
6. Manage external data.

MCAS OBJECTIVES

AC07 70-605 1.1.1
AC07 70-605 1.1.2
AC07 70-605 1.1.3
AC07 70-605 2.1.1
AC07 70-605 2.1.2
AC07 70-605 2.2.1
AC07 70-605 2.2.2
AC07 70-605 2.2.3
AC07 70-605 2.3.1
AC07 70-605 2.3.3
AC07 70-605 2.3.4
AC07 70-605 2.4.1
AC07 70-605 2.4.1
AC07 70-605 2.4.2
AC07 70-605 2.4.4
AC07 70-605 3.4.3
AC07 70-605 3.5.1
AC07 70-605 5.4.1
AC07 70-605 5.4.2
AC07 70-605 6.2.3

Estimated Time: 2 hours

Company databases maintain customer names, transaction histories, inventory levels, product pricing, and employee data. All of these data are vital pieces of information necessary to operate a company on a day-to-day basis.

The structure of a database is critical for a company's ability to convert data into useful information. A database must be both efficient and effective. It must be designed to improve data entry and protect the integrity of the data.

Creating Databases

Prior to creating a new database, you should analyze the needs of the people who will use it. You should plan for the type of data that will be stored, including how they will be entered and displayed.

There are two methods for creating a new database. One method uses templates to create a structured database containing major objects (e.g., tables, queries, forms, or reports). The second method creates a blank database without objects.

Exercise 4-1 CREATE A DATABASE USING A TEMPLATE

When creating a new database, you sometimes can find a database template on which to base your preliminary design. A *database template* is a ready-to-use database containing all the tables, queries, forms, and reports needed to perform a specific task.

For example, Access includes templates for tracking potential sales, organizing contact lists, and even maintaining grade sheets. Database templates can be useful even when you modify the pre-defined objects to better fit your needs.

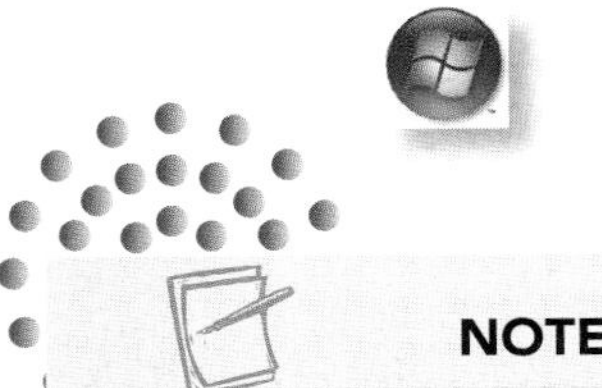

NOTE

You will not need to keep a copy of this database. At the end of this exercise, you will delete the file. It is used only to demonstrate database templates.

1. Click the Start button on the Windows task bar and point to **All Programs**.
2. Click **Office Access 2007** to start Access. (You might have to first point to a program group, such as Microsoft Office.)
3. Access opens into the **Getting Started with Microsoft Office Access** page.
4. Click in the **From Microsoft Office Online** section. Click **Business**.

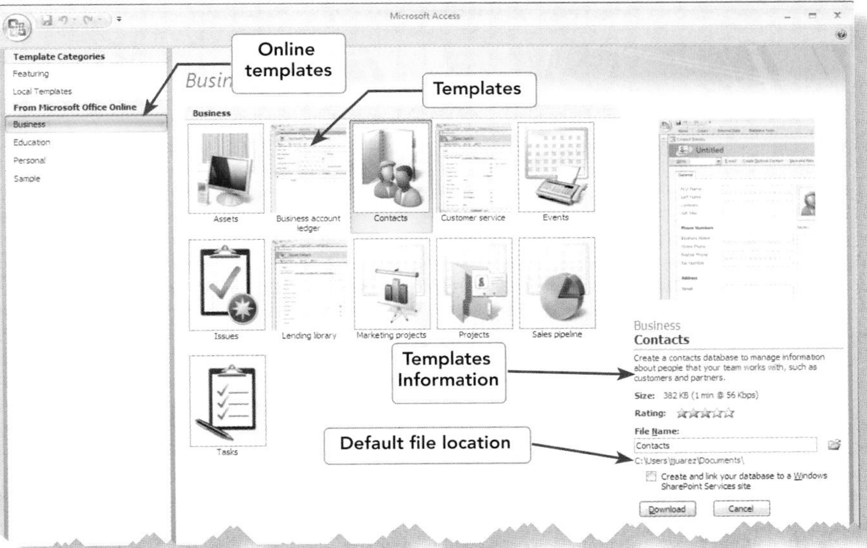

Figure 4-1
Business Templates

NOTE

Microsoft Templates do not follow the Leszynski Naming Convention when naming a major object.

5. Click the **Contacts** template. The template's information appears on the right.
6. Click the **File Name** text box and change the file name to *[your initials]*-**Contact**.
7. Click **Download** to download and launch the template.
8. Click the Shutter Bar Open/Close button to expand the Navigation Pane. The Navigation Bar is organized by **Contacts Navigation**.

NOTE

Microsoft Templates do not follow the Leszynski Naming Convention when naming a field.

9. Click the **Contacts Navigation** drop-down arrow and choose **Object Type**. This database has one table, one query, two forms, and two reports.
10. Right-click the document tab for the form **Contact List** and choose **Close**.
11. In the Navigation Pane, double-click the table **Contacts**.

12. From the **Home** tab, in the **Views** group, choose the View command. This is the Design View of the table.
13. Right-click the document tab for the table **Contacts** and choose **Close**.

Exercise 4-2 SET DATABASE PROPERTIES

Database properties do not change the functionality of the database. They only provide useful information to help identify the file. Some database properties, such as the title, author, and company, are defined when creating a new database. The information supplied comes from the operating system of the workstation on which the database is created.

1. Click the Office Button. Hover your mouse pointer over the **Manage** option and click Database Properties.
2. Click in the textbox for the **Title** property and key the name of your class.
3. Change the value for **Author** to *[your name]*.
4. In the property **Comments**, key **This database was created using the Microsoft Contacts template on** *[today's date]*.
5. Click **OK** to close the dialog box.

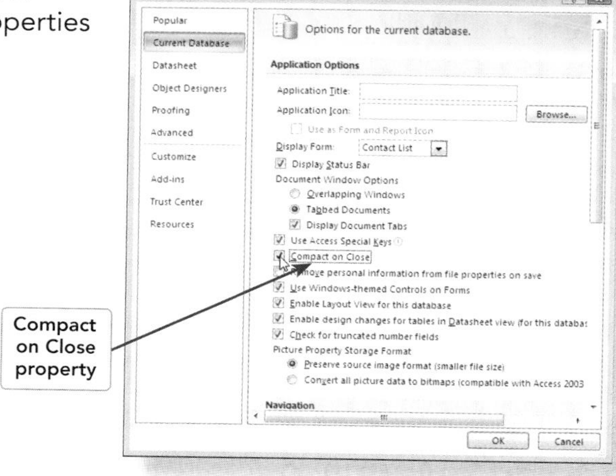

Figure 4-2
Changing properties

6. Click the Office Button and click the **Access Options** button.
7. On the left, click the **Current Database** category. Locate the **Compact on Close** property, and click the check box to add a checkmark.
8. Click **OK** to close the **Access Options** dialog box.
9. Click **OK** to close and reopen the database.

10. Click the Office Button and click the Close Database button to close the database but not Access.

Exercise 4-3 CREATE A BLANK DATABASE

If you cannot find a database template to meet your needs, you must create a blank database from scratch. The process requires you to name the database and specify a location in which to save it. Once the database is created, you will be able to add other major objects, such as tables, queries, reports, and forms.

1. In the Getting Started with Microsoft Office Access page, click the Blank Database button.

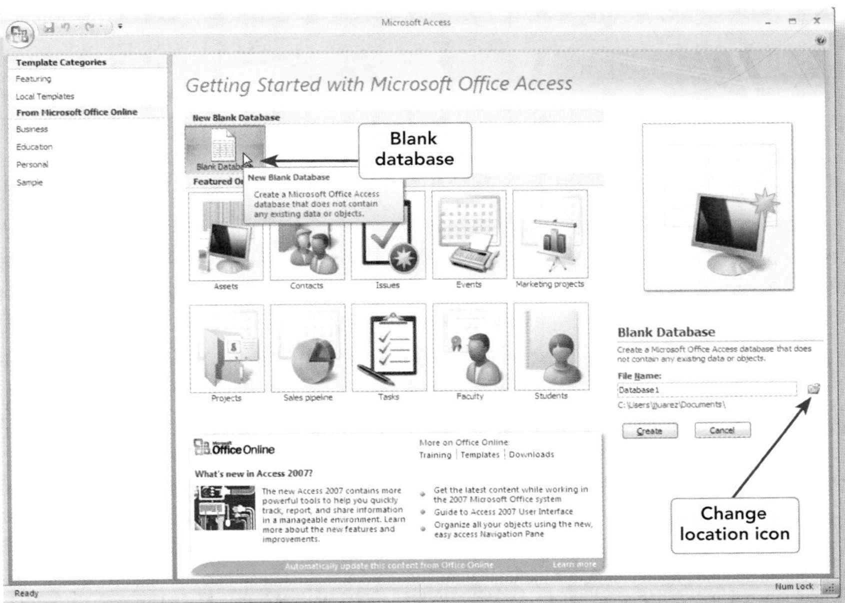

Figure 4-3 Create a blank database

REVIEW

Your instructor will tell you where to save the database. Because database files can be quite large, do not create a database on a diskette.

2. In the **File Name** textbox, key *[your initials]*-**Contacts2**.
3. Click **Create**. A new table opens in Datasheet View.
4. Click the Close button for the table. Notice that because the table does not contain fields, it is not listed in the Navigation Pane.

Creating Tables

In a well-designed database, each table should store data for a unique purpose. For example, Carolina Critters has a table for employees. The data for employees are similar to the data for interns; however, each table has a unique purpose. When creating a new table, you should test your design by adding a few sample records. You may find that you will need to modify the design.

There are two methods for creating a new table. One method uses templates to populate a table with fields. The second method creates a blank table without fields.

Exercise 4-4 CREATE A TABLE USING A TEMPLATE

Table Templates are similar to database templates. Table Templates provide a quick and easy method to produce a table containing commonly used fields based upon a specific need. Tables created with a template provide the structure that you can modify later.

1. From the **Create** tab, in the **Tables** group, click the Table Templates command and choose **Contacts** from the list.

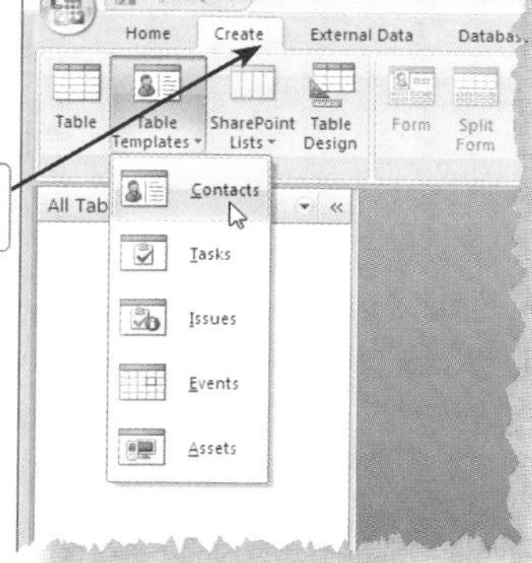

Figure 4-4
Table Wizard dialog box
Contacts2.accdb

2. In the Quick Access toolbar, click the Save button.
3. In the **Save As** dialog box, key **Contacts** and click **OK**.
4. In the Navigation Pane, click the **All Tables** drop-down arrow and choose **Object Type**.
5. Click the Close button for the table.
6. In the Navigation Pane, right-click the table **Contacts** and choose **Rename**.
7. Press Home and key **tbl**. Press Enter to accept that name change.

Exercise 4-5 CREATE A TABLE IN DESIGN VIEW

Design View offers you the greatest flexibility when defining field names, types, and properties. The type of field defined depends upon the data that will be stored. For example, prices will be stored as currency, names as text, and images as attachments. When data contains a mixed type of values, such as a street address that contains both numbers and text, you should use the Text data type.

TABLE 4-1 Access Data Types

Setting	Type of Data
Text	Alphanumeric characters. A text field can be a maximum of 255 characters long. Use Text as the data type for numbers that are not used in calculations, such as addresses or phone numbers.
Memo	Descriptive text such as sentences and paragraphs used for text greater than 255 characters in length or for text that uses rich text formatting.

continues

TABLE 4-1 Access Data Types *continued*

Setting	Type of Data
Number	Numbers (integer or real). Data in a number field can be used in arithmetic calculations. Use Number as the data type when values will be used in calculations.
Date/Time	Formatted dates or times used in date and time calculations. Each value stored includes both a date component and a time component.
Currency	Money values used for storing monetary values (currency). Values can be used in arithmetic calculations and can display a currency symbol.
AutoNumber	A unique numeric value automatically created by Access when a record is added. Use AutoNumber as the data type for generating unique values that can be used as a primary key.
Yes/No	Boolean value displayed as check boxes. Use Yes/No as the data type for True/False fields that can hold one of two possible values.
Attachment	Pictures, images, binary files, or Office files. Preferred data type for storing digital images and any type of binary file.
Hyperlink	Navigation element for Internet sites, e-mail addresses, or file path names. Use Hyperlink Data as the data type for storing hyperlinks to provide single-click access to Web pages through a URL (Uniform Resource Locator) or files through a name in UNC (universal naming convention) format.

NOTE

When a single field contains both alphabetic and numeric data characters, you must define the field as a text data type.

1. From the **Create** tab, in the **Tables** group, choose Table. A new table is created and the Ribbon now shows the contextual tab **Datasheet**.
2. In the **Views** group, choose Views to switch to Design View.
3. In the **Save As** dialog box, key **tblOrganization** and click **OK**. The table is now in Design View.

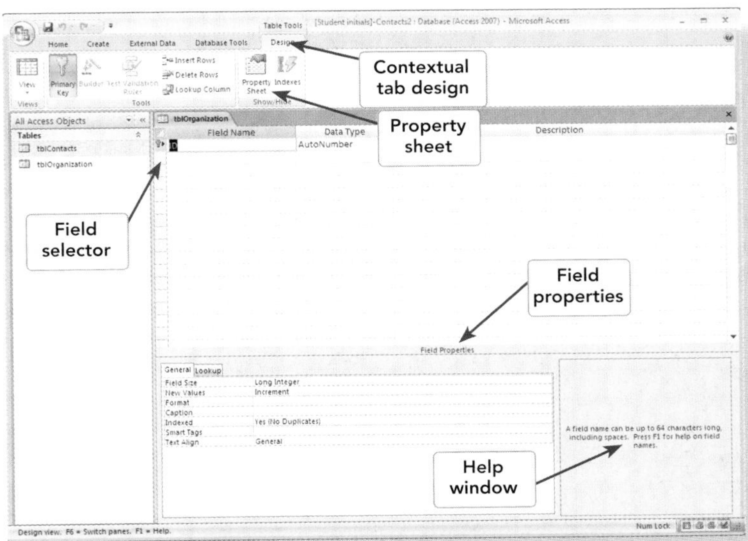

Figure 4-5
Design View of a table
Contacts2.accdb tblOrganization

4. In the second row, click the **Field Name** column, and key **OrgNum**.
5. Press [Tab] to move to the **Data Type** column.
6. Click the drop-down arrow and choose **Number**.
7. Press [Tab] to move to the **Description** column. Key **Member identification number**.
8. Press [Tab] to move to the third row in the **Field Name** column. Key **OrgName**.
9. Press [Tab] to move to the **Data Type** column. The default data type is **Text**.
10. Press [Tab] and key **Organization name**.
11. Enter the following fields:

Field Name	Data Type	Description
Dues	Currency	Organization dues
Phone	Text	Office phone number
StartDate	Date/Time	Member since
Email address	Hyperlink	Organization e-mail
MemPhone	Attachment	Member's phone lists

12. Click the Close button × for the table.

Figure 4-6
Structural changes to a table
Contacts2.accdb
tblOrganization

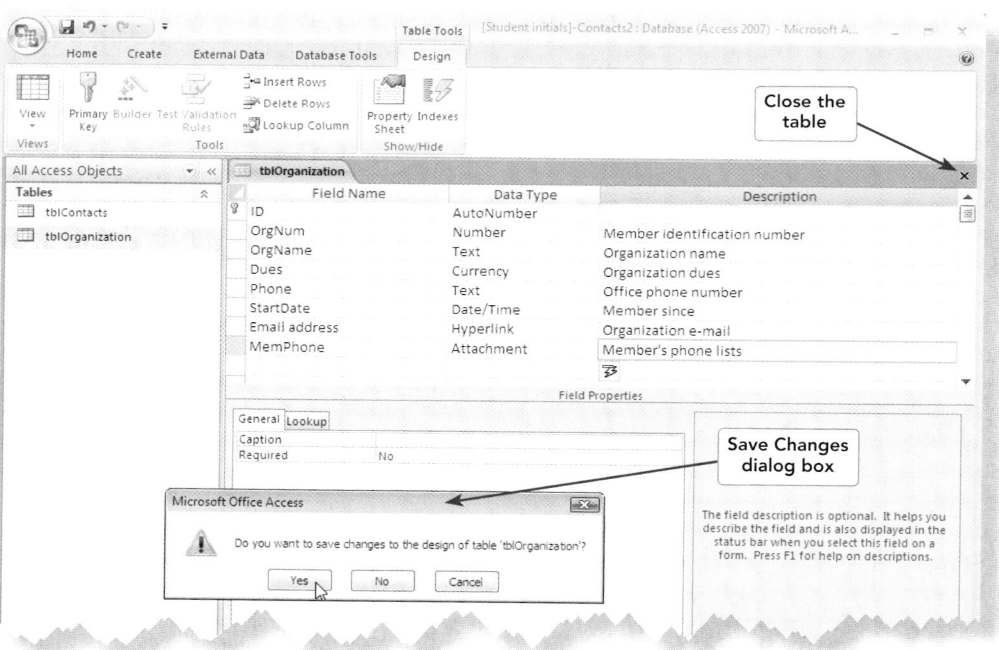

13. Click **Yes** to save the changes to the design of the table.

14. Click the Office Button and click the Exit Access button to close the database and exit Access.

Exercise 4-6 COPY A TABLE STRUCTURE

When copying a table, you have three options. You can select to include only the structure, the structure and the data, or only the data. When copying only the structure, you create a table with only fields but no records. When copying only the data, you will add the records to a similarly structured table.

1. Locate and open the **Lesson 04** folder.
2. Make a copy of **CC04** and rename it to *[your initials]*-CC04.
3. Open and enable content for ***[your initials]*-CC04**.
4. In the Navigation Pane, double-click the table **tblEmployees**. This table has 39 records.
5. Click the Close button for the table.
6. In the Navigation Pane, right-click the table **tblEmployees** and choose Copy from the menu.

7. From the Home tab, in the Clipboard group, click the Paste command.
8. In the Paste Table As dialog box, change the Table Name to tblRetirees.
9. In the Paste Options section, select Structure Only.
10. Click OK.
11. In the Navigation Pane, double-click the table **tblRetirees**. This table has no records. Only the structure of the employees table was copied.

Exercise 4-7 MODIFY TABLE PROPERTIES

Table properties do not change the functionality of the table. They only provide useful information to help identify the object. Most properties, such as owner or date/time modified, are automatically updated based upon the workstation settings.

1. In the Navigation Pane, right-click the table **tblRetirees**, and choose Table Properties.

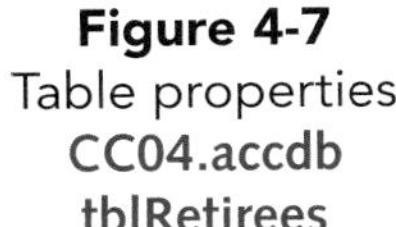

Figure 4-7
Table properties
CC04.accdb
tblRetirees

2. In the Description textbox, key This table stores the information of all Carolina Critters retirees.
3. Click OK.
4. In the Navigation Pane, double-click the table **tblRetirees**.
5. From the Home tab, in the Views group, choose the View command.

6. From the **Design** tab, in the **Show/Hide** group, click the Property Sheet command . The Property Sheet appears. Notice that the **Description** property contains the text from step 2.
7. From the **Design** tab, in the **Show/Hide** group, click the Property Sheet command to close the Property Sheet.
8. Right-click the document tab for **tblRetirees** and choose **Close**.

Adding and Deleting Fields in a Table

When your company's needs for information change, so should your database. Making periodic adjustments to the table structures, such as adding or deleting fields, occasionally may be necessary.

Before adding any field to a table, you first should make certain that it does not duplicate an existing field's data. Adding a new field in one table to store data already in another table creates inefficient data design and can lead to data entry errors.

Deleting a field can be much more dangerous than adding one. Before deleting a field from a table, make certain that the data in the field will never be needed in the future. Many database administrators would rather move data to an archive table than delete historical information.

Exercise 4-8 ADD AND DELETE FIELDS IN DATASHEET VIEW

You also can insert and delete fields in Datasheet View. When inserting a text field in a datasheet, the default width of the field is 255 spaces. Each field will be named Field*n*, where *n* is a sequential number starting with one (1). Although the task of deleting a field from a datasheet may appear similar to hiding the field, deleting a field is a permanent action that cannot be undone.

1. In the Navigation Pane, double-click the table **tblCustomers**.

2. From the **Home** tab, in the **Records** group, click the More command and choose **Unhide Columns** from the menu.
3. In the **Unhide Columns** dialog box, click the check box for **Add New Field**. Click **Close**.
4. Scroll horizontally to see the last field in the table.
5. In the **Add New Field**, for the first record, key **3.2%** and press Tab. The field is now called **Field1**, and a new **Add New Field** column was added.
6. Click on the column header for **Field1**.
7. From the **Datasheet** tab, in the **Fields and Columns** group, choose Rename .
8. Key **Discount** as the new field name.
9. Scroll horizontally to see the first field in the table.

10. Click on the column header for **After Hours**.

11. From the **Datasheet** tab, in the **Fields and Columns** group, choose Delete. Click **Yes** to confirm the deletion.

Exercise 4-9 ADD AND DELETE FIELDS IN DESIGN VIEW

NOTE

When you insert a field, the new row is placed in the row selected, and all fields below are moved down.

Adding fields through Design View is more flexible than through Datasheet View. In addition to text, numeric, and date fields, you can define and size all field types.

1. From the **Datasheet** tab, in the **Views** group, choose View to switch to Design View.
2. Click on the field selector for **CompanyName**.

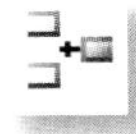

3. From the **Design** tab, in the **Tools** group, choose the Insert Row command.

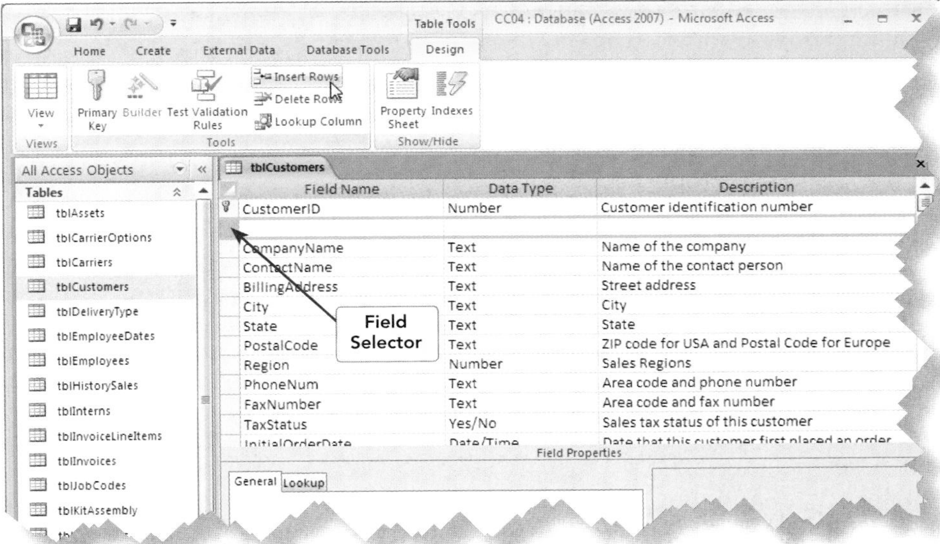

Figure 4-8
Inserting a row
CC04.accdb
tblCustomers

4. Click in the Field Name for the blank row and key **ID**.
5. Press Tab, click the drop-down arrow, and choose AutoNumber.
6. Click in the **Description** area for **CustomerID** and press F2 to select the whole description. Press Ctrl+C to copy.
7. Click in the **Description** area for **ID** and press Ctrl+V to paste.

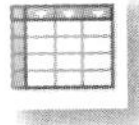

8. From the **Design** tab, in the **Views** group, choose View to switch to Datasheet View.
9. Click **Yes** to save the changes to the table's structure. The **ID** field has generated an incremental number starting at 1.

REVIEW

Changes to field data are saved automatically; however, you must save design changes to the table.

10. From the **Home** tab, in the **Views** group, choose View to switch to Design View.
11. Make certain the first field is selected.
12. From the **Design** tab, in the **Tools** group, choose Delete Rows. Click **Yes** to confirm the deletion.
13. Click in the **Field Name ID** and key **CustomerID**.

14. From the Quick Access Toolbar, click Save.

Controlling Field Appearance

NOTE

Spaces should not be used in field names. Spaces create additional requirements when using fields in advanced objects such as Macros and Modules.

Certain field properties control how a field appears to database users. A change to one of these properties only affects the field's appearance without changing the underlying structure or size of the field.

Changing a field's appearance may be for functional reasons, not merely cosmetic. For example, when most records use the same area code, you may change the default value for the phone number. This simple change may improve the speed, accuracy, and consistency of data entry.

TABLE 4-2 Text Field Properties

Property	Purpose
Field Size	Controls the size of a text field and can be up to 255 characters.
Format	Defines the appearance of data. Custom formatting changes the appearance of the data without changing the underlying record.
Input Mask	Displays a pattern for entering the data. Examples are the use of parentheses around an area code or hyphens in a social security number.
Caption	Sets a label or title for the caption. The caption replaces the field name as the column title in a datasheet and as the control label in forms and reports.
Default Value	Specifies the value that automatically appears in a field when creating a new record. The value can be accepted or changed.
Validation Rule	Condition specifying criteria for entering data into an individual field. A Validation Rule of ">100" requires values to be larger than 100.
Validation Text	Error message that appears when a value prohibited by the validation rule is entered. For the Validation Rule ">100," the Validation Text might be "You must enter a value greater than 100."
Required	Requires entry of a value in the field when set to "Yes."

Exercise 4-10 CHANGE FIELD PROPERTY CAPTION

When no caption is defined, the name of the field displays as its column heading on a datasheet or as its control label in a form or report. When a field caption is defined, the caption will be used instead.

1. In the Design View of **tblCustomers**, double-click the field **CustomerID** to select the **Field Name.** Press Ctrl+C.
2. In the **Field Properties** section, click in the **Caption** property.
3. Press Ctrl+V. Add a space between "Customer" and "ID."

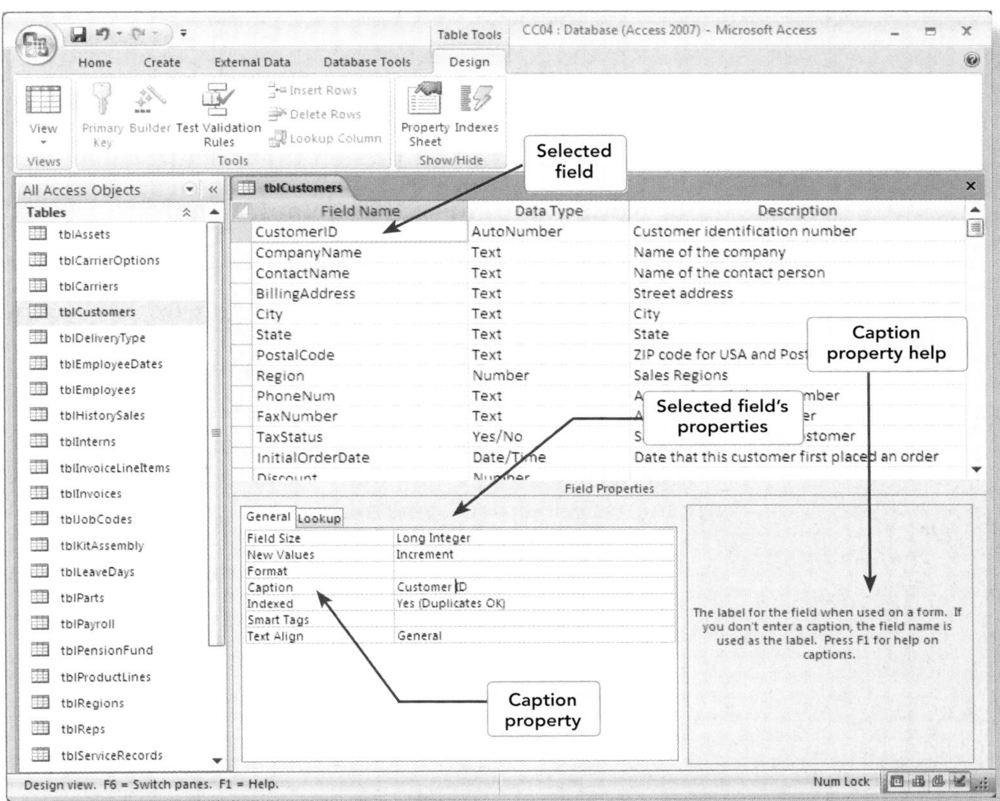

Figure 4-9
Change the Caption property
CC04.accdb
tblCustomers

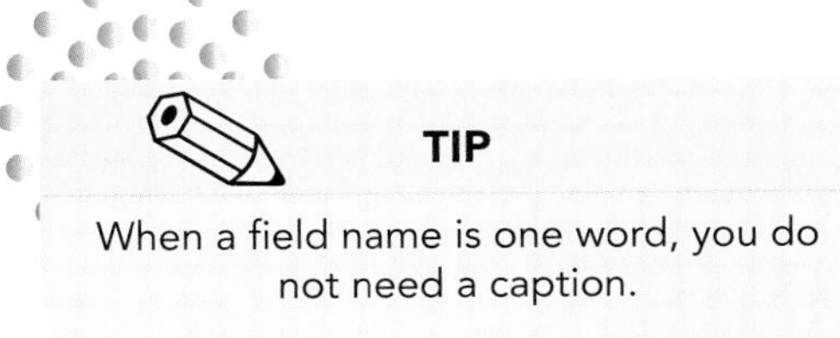

TIP

When a field name is one word, you do not need a caption.

4. Double-click the **Field Name PhoneNum** and press Ctrl+C.
5. Press F6 to move to the **Field Properties** section.
6. Press Tab three times to move to the **Caption** property.
7. Press Ctrl+V. Add a space between "Phone" and "Num."
8. Press End and key **ber**.

9. In the Quick Access Toolbar, click the Save button. Each column now has a more readable heading.

Exercise 4-11 CHANGE FIELD PROPERTY DEFAULT VALUE

Setting a default value is useful when a significant number of records contain the same field value. For example, if the majority of your employees live in the same state, you might choose to set a default value for the state field. All new records will display the default value, and previously entered records will not be changed. Whenever a record contains a different value for the field, the user can key a new value to replace the default value.

1. Click the field selector for **TaxStatus** and press F6.
2. Press Tab until you reach the **Default Value** property.
3. Key **no** to set the default to no tax exemption.
4. Click the field selector for **Discount** and press F6.
5. Press Tab until you reach the **Default Value** property.
6. Key **0** (zero) to set the default to a 0% discount.

Exercise 4-12 CHANGE FIELD PROPERTY FORMAT

You can improve data entry by specifying formats. For example, you can set the format for a date to display the name of the month, set the format for currency to show dollar signs, or set the format for text to display as uppercase letters. For some data types, you can select from predefined formats. For others, you must enter a custom format.

1. In the Design View of **tblCustomers**, click the field selector for **InitialOrderDate** and press F6.
2. In the **Format** property, click the drop-down arrow, and choose **Medium Date**.

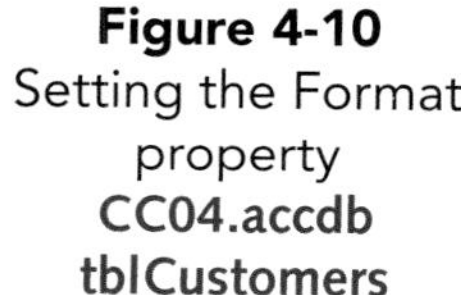

Figure 4-10
Setting the Format property
CC04.accdb
tblCustomers

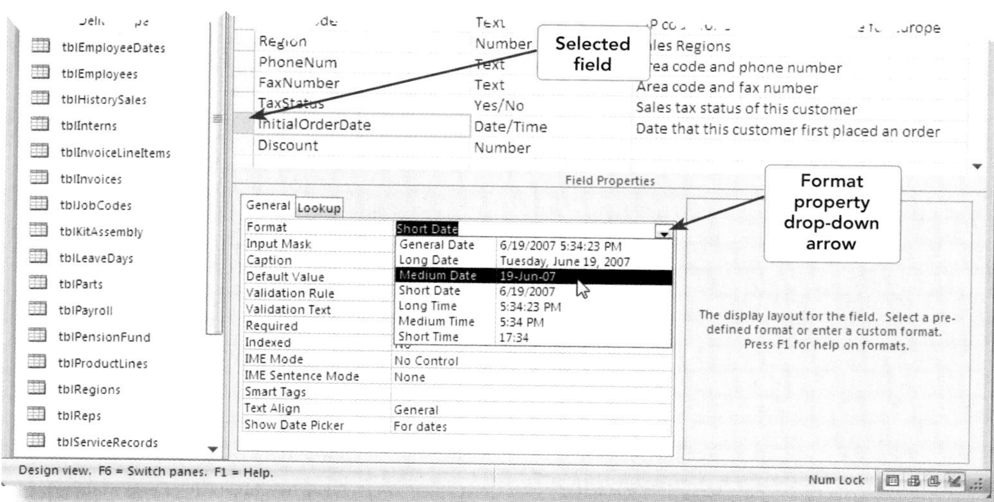

3. Press Ctrl+S to save the changes to the table.
4. From the **Design** tab, in the **Views** group, choose View to switch to Datasheet View. Scroll to see the **Initial Order** field. The appearance of the dates has changed.
5. From the **Home** tab, in the **Views** group, choose View to switch to Design View.
6. Click the field selector for **State** and press F6.
7. In the **Format** property, key >.
8. Press Ctrl+S to save the changes to the table.
9. From the **Design** tab, in the **Views** group, choose View to switch to Datasheet View.
10. In the **State** field for **Customer ID** "20", key **bc**. Press Tab. The data displays as upper case characters.
11. From the **Home** tab, in the **Views** group, choose View to switch to Design View.

TIP

A complete list of Text format symbols is located in the Appendix.

Exercise 4-13 CHANGE FIELD PROPERTY INPUT MASK

An input mask is used to format the display of data and control the format in which values can be entered. Input masks can be used for text or numeric data types. You can use the Input Mask Wizard for common formats such as telephone numbers and social security numbers.

TABLE 4-3 Input Masks

Character	Description
0	Digit (0 through 9, entry required; plus [+] and minus [−] signs not allowed).
9	Digit or space (entry not required; plus and minus signs not allowed).
#	Digit or space (entry not required; blank positions converted to spaces, plus and minus signs allowed).
L	Letter (A through Z, entry required).
?	Letter (A through Z, entry optional).

NOTE

A complete list of Input Mask symbols is located in the Appendix.

1. In the Design View of **tblCustomers**, click the field selector for **PhoneNum**, and press F6.
2. Click the **Input Mask** property row.
3. From the **Design** tab, in the **Tools** group, choose Builder.

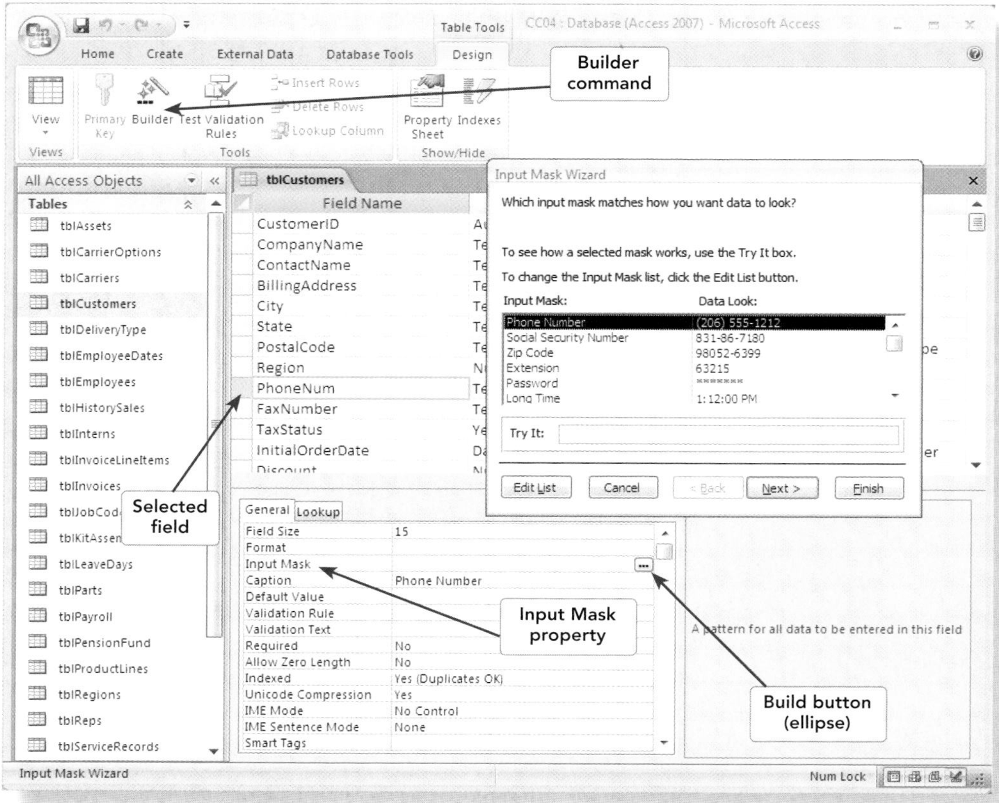

Figure 4-11
Input Mask Wizard dialog box
CC04.accdb
tblCustomers

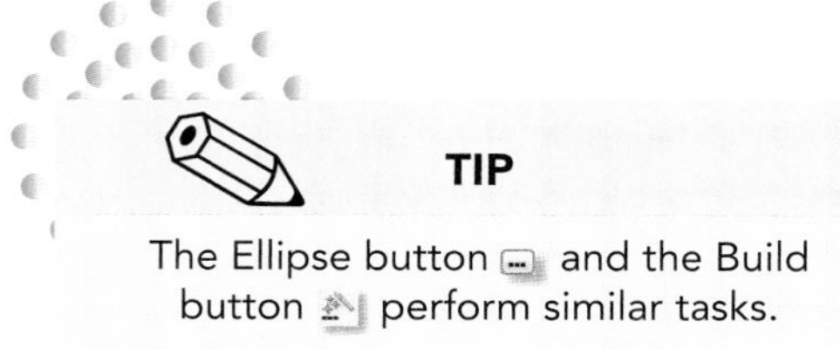

TIP

The Ellipse button and the Build button perform similar tasks.

4. The Input Mask Wizard lists several common masks and shows how the data are displayed. Select the **Phone Number** mask.
5. Click **Next**. The wizard asks if you want to change the **Input Mask**. Click in the **Try It** entry box.
6. Press Home. Key your phone number.
7. Click **Next**. The wizard asks how you want to store the data. Select **With the symbols in the mask, like this:**
8. Click **Next**. Read the final message and click **Finish**.
9. From the **Design** tab, in the **Views** group, choose View to switch to Datasheet View. Click **Yes**.

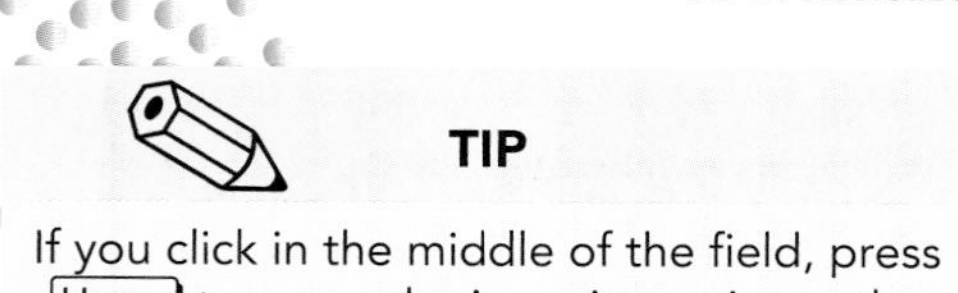

TIP

If you click in the middle of the field, press Home to move the insertion point to the beginning of the field.

10. Locate the **Customer ID** 17. Scroll to the **Phone Number** field and enter your phone number.
11. From the **Home** tab, in the **Views** group, choose View to switch to Design View.

Exercise 4-14 CHANGE FIELD PROPERTY DATE PICKER

Depending on the workstation's language settings, the date picker displays either to the right or left side of a Date/Time field. Clicking the date picker launches a calendar control from which you can select a date. If the field is empty, the Date Picker will default to the current date.

1. In the Design View of **tblCustomers**, click the field selector for **InitialOrder** and press F6.
2. Move to the **Show Date Picker** property, and click the drop-down arrow, and choose **For dates**.
3. From the **Design** tab, in the **Views** group, choose View to switch to Datasheet View. Click **Yes** to save the changes.

4. Click in the first record's **InitialOrder** and click the Date Picker button.

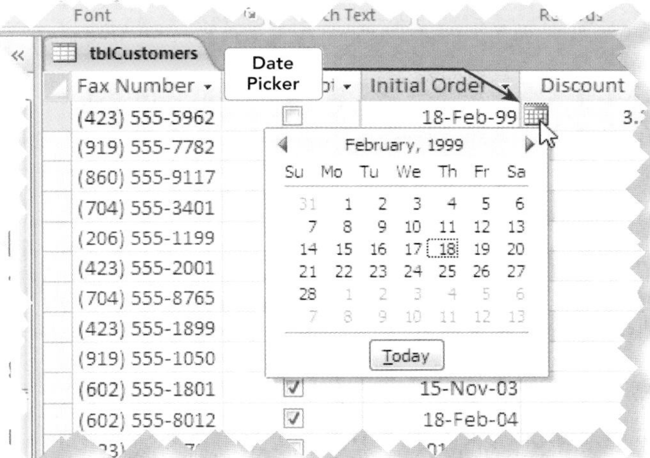

Figure 4-12
Date Picker
CC04.accdb
tblCustomers

5. Press Esc to exit the field without saving any changes.
6. From the **Home** tab, in the **Views** group, choose View to switch to Design View.

Controlling Data Integrity

Certain field properties restrict values stored in a field. A change to one of these properties can affect both the structure and the size of the field. Because these changes might alter your data, it's best to make them before adding data to a table. If a table already contains data and you are uncertain if your data will be affected, back up your database before making changes to the field properties.

Exercise 4-15 SET THE PRIMARY KEY

Most tables contain a primary key. A *primary key* is a field or set of fields in a table that provides a unique identifier for every record. Each record must store a unique value in a primary key field. Most often primary keys are numeric data types; however, other data types can be used.

1. In the Design View of **tblCustomers**, click the field selector for **CustomerID**.

2. From the **Design** tab, in the **Tools** group, choose the Primary Key command.

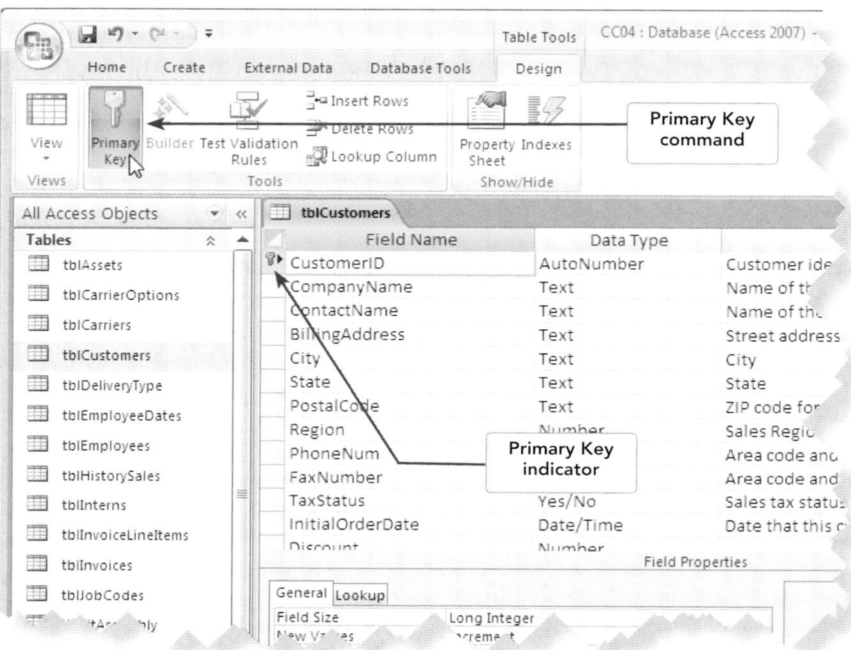

Figure 4-13
Set a Primary Key
CC04.accdb
tblCustomers

Exercise 4-16 SET THE FIELD PROPERTY FIELD SIZE

Changing the field size alters the space available to store data. The numeric value defined in the **Field Size** property is the maximum number of characters allowed for the storage of data. Changing the field size in Design View is different than changing the column width in Datasheet View.

1. In the Design View of **tblCustomers**, click the field selector for **CompanyName** and press F6.

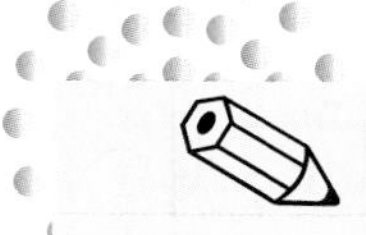

TIP

Text fields should be wide enough to hold most data, but not so unnecessarily wide that they waste space.

2. In the **Field Size** property, change 255 to **30**.
3. Read the message dialog box. Click **Yes**. If any record has stored more than 30 characters in the **CompanyName** field, characters beyond the first 30 characters would be deleted.

4. Select the **Discount** field selector and press F6.
5. For the **Field Size** property, click the drop-down arrow and choose **Single**. Changing from **Double** to **Single** reduces the field size from 8 bytes to 4 bytes.
6. Press Ctrl+S to save the changes to the table.
7. Click **Yes** to the message dialog box.

Exercise 4-17 SET THE FIELD PROPERTY VALIDATION TEXT AND RULES

A *Validation Rule* is a condition specifying criteria for entering data into an individual field. You define a validation rule to control what values can be entered into a field. You also can enter an optional validation text to match your rule. *Validation text* is an error message that appears when a value prohibited by the validation rule is entered.

For example, you could define the validation expression ">=100" for a quantity field to prevent a user from entering values less than 100. For the corresponding validation expression, you could enter "You must enter a number equal to or greater than 100."

When you set a validation rule for a field that contains data, Access will ask if you want to apply the new rule to the existing data. If you answer yes, Access evaluates the rule against the existing data in the table. If any record violates the validation rule, you will be notified that the data must be corrected before the rule can be applied.

The Test Validation Rule button checks the current data in the field to see if it matches the rule. If not, Access prompts you to resolve the conflict.

1. In the Design View of **tblCustomers**, click the field selector for **Discount** and press F6.
2. Tab to the **Validation Rule** property and key **<=.05**. This rule will restrict users to enter a discount equal to or less than 5%.
3. Press Enter to move to the **Validation Text** property.
4. Key **The maximum discount is 5%. Please try again.**
5. Save the changes to the table. A data integrity dialog box appears, asking if you want to test the existing data with the new rules. Click **Yes**.
6. Switch to Datasheet View. Scroll horizontally to see the **Discount** field.
7. In the second record's **Discount** field, key **6** and press Enter.

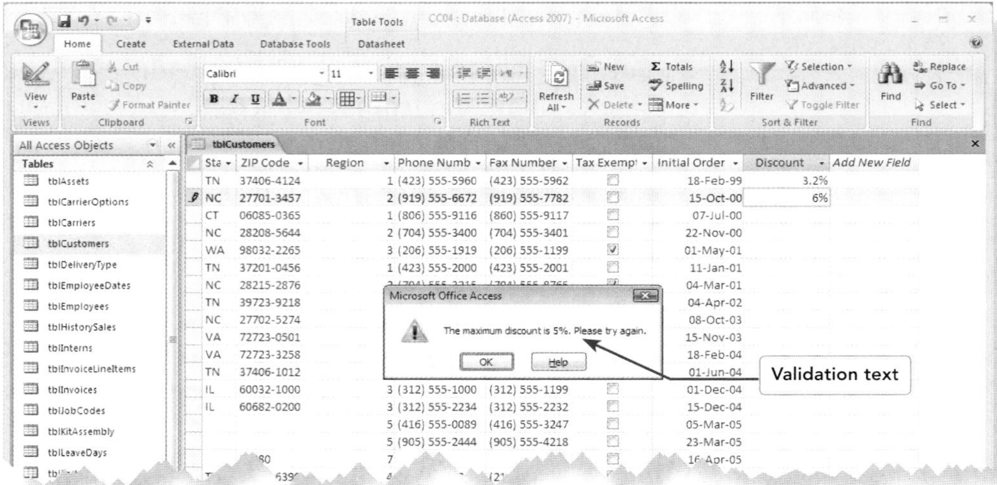

Figure 4-14
Validation Text dialog box
CC04.accdb
tblCustomers

8. Click **OK** to close the dialog box. Delete the 6 and key **5**.
9. Press [↓]. The new data meets the **Validation Rule**.
10. Close the table.

Managing External Data

Whenever possible, a goal of yours should be to avoid requiring users to re-enter data already stored in an electronic format. Rather than re-keying the data, users should transfer the electronic data by importing it into the database. Importing data prevents errors that may occur when re-keying data.

Each time you import data, you create a copy of the original data. The original data remains in the source application while you work with a copy of the data in your database.

Exercise 4-18 EXPORT A TABLE TO ACCESS

You can export an Access table directly to another Microsoft application such as Word or Excel. Access tables can also be exported directly to non-Microsoft applications such as dBASE and Paradox. For applications not supported by Access, you can export a table using a file format such as text, XML, or HTML. When exporting a table, you can save the steps used in the export operation. Saving the steps can greatly decrease the time it takes to export the same table next time.

NOTE

Check with your instructor to verify the location of your student data files and the location in which you will be working. The folder "Documents" is often the default folder when you're creating or storing files.

1. Select the table **tblInterns** in the Navigation Pane.
2. From the **External Data** tab, in the **Export** group, click the More command [More] and choose **Access Database** from the menu.

Figure 4-15
Export a table
CC04.accdb

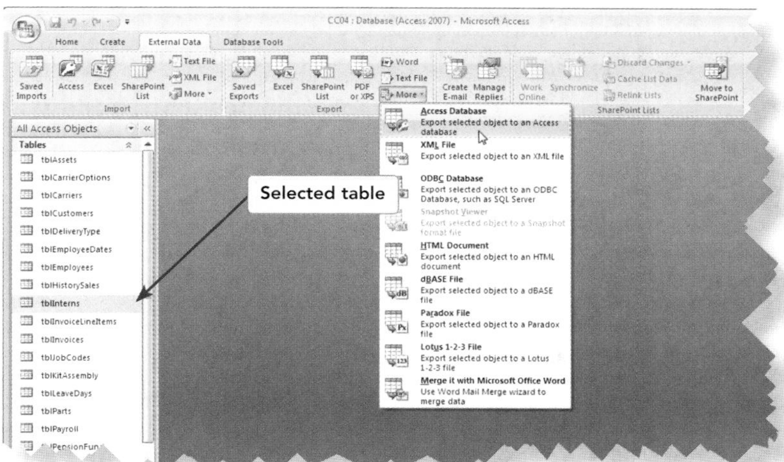

3. In the **Export – Access Database** dialog box, click **Browse**.

NOTE

You may want to open the database ***[your initials]*-Contacts2** to verify that the table has been exported.

4. In the **File Save** dialog box, locate ***[your initials]*-Contacts2,** that you created earlier in this lesson. Click **Save**.
5. Click **OK** to close the **Export – Access Database** dialog box.

Figure 4-16
Export dialog box
CC04.accdb

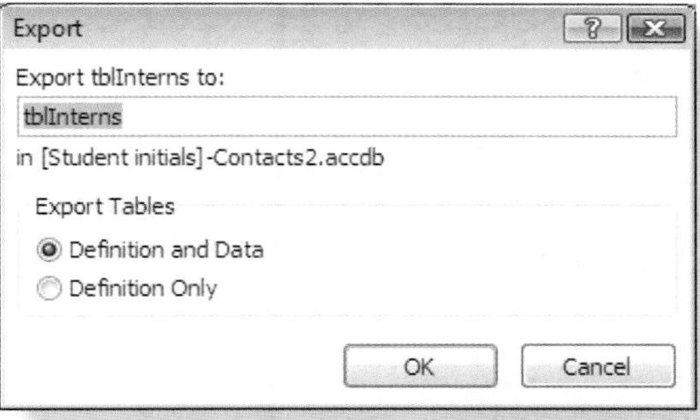

6. Click **OK** to export the table **tblInterns**.
7. Click **Close**.

Exercise 4-19 EXPORT DATA TO WORD

You can export a table, query, form, or report to Microsoft Word using the Access Export Wizard. A copy of the object's data will be stored as a Rich Text Format (RTF) file. For tables, queries, and forms, the visible fields and records appear as a table in the Word document. Hidden or filtered columns and records are not exported.

1. In the Navigation Pane, select the query **qryEmployeeDates**.

2. From the **External Data** tab, in the **Export** group, click the Word command.

3. In the **Export – RTF File** dialog box, delete the "qry" from the file name.
4. Click the check box **Open the destination file after the export operation is complete.** Click **OK**.
5. View the table in Word, then exit Word.
6. Click **Close** without saving the export steps.
7. Close the query.

Exercise 4-20 IMPORT DATA FROM EXCEL

For most non-Access applications, a wizard steps you through the import process. When importing from an Excel workbook, you may select all columns and rows from a worksheet or just a range of cells. The ease of importing data greatly depends upon how the information is stored in the source workbook. Blank columns and rows in the worksheet add unnecessary fields and records to the imported data.

1. In the Navigation Pane, double-click the table **tblEmployees**. Notice that there are 39 employees in this table.
2. Close the table.
3. From the **External Data** tab, in the **Import** group, click the Excel command.
4. In the **Get External Data – Excel Spreadsheet** dialog box, click **Browse**.
5. In the **File Open** dialog box, locate the folder **Lesson 04** and select the Excel file **Employees**.
6. Click **Open**.
7. Select the option **Append a copy of the records to the table:**, click the drop-down arrow, and choose **tblEmployees**.

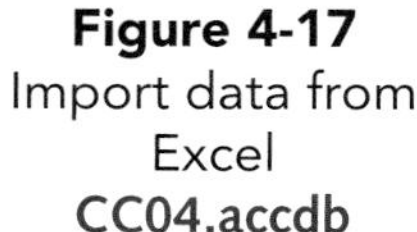

Figure 4-17
Import data from Excel
CC04.accdb

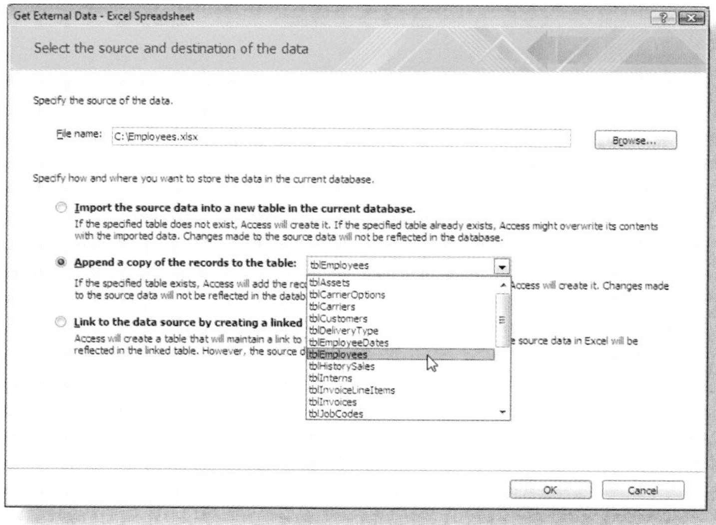
Get External Data - Excel Spreadsheet
Select the source and destination of the data
Specify the source of the data.
File name: C:\Employees.xlsx
Browse...
Specify how and where you want to store the data in the current database.
Import the source data into a new table in the current database.
If the specified table does not exist, Access will create it. If the specified table already exists, Access might overwrite its contents with the imported data. Changes made to the source data will not be reflected in the database.
Append a copy of the records to the table:
tblEmployees
Link to the data source by creating a linked
tblAssets
tblCarrierOptions
tblCarriers
tblCustomers
tblDeliveryType
tblEmployeeDates
tblEmployees
tblHistorySales
tblInterns
tblInvoiceLineItems
tblInvoices
tblJobCodes
OK
Cancel

8. Click **OK**. This action starts the **Import Spreadsheet Wizard**.
9. In the first step in the **Import Spreadsheet Wizard**, you see the data from the Excel file. Click **Next**.

TIP

If you have any problems with any of the steps in a Wizard, just click **Cancel** and start over.

10. Click **Next**.
11. Click **Finish** and click **Close**.
12. Open **tblEmployees** in Datasheet View. There are now 42 records. Close the table.

13. Click the Office Button. Click the **Manage** and choose the Compact and Repair Database command.
14. Click the Office Button and click **Exit Access** to close the database.

Lesson 4 Summary

- The two methods for creating a new database are using a template and creating a blank database.
- A database template is a ready-to-use database containing all the tables, queries, forms, and reports needed to perform a specific task.
- A new database created as a blank database does not contain objects or data.
- Some database properties come from the operating system of the workstation on which the database is created.
- Because database files can be quite large, you should not create a database on a diskette.
- The two methods for creating a new table are using a template and creating a blank table.
- Table Templates provide a quick and easy method to produce a table containing commonly used fields, based upon a specific need.
- When a single field contains both alphabetic and numeric data characters, you must define the field as text data type.
- When copying a table, you can select to include only the structure, the structure and data, or only the data.
- Before adding any field to a table, you first should make certain that it does not duplicate an existing field's data.
- When tables are created using Datasheet View, Access evaluates the data entered and determines the data type for each field.
- A caption is a field property that displays as a column heading in Datasheet View or as a control label in a form or report.
- Spaces should not be used in field names. Spaces create additional requirements when using fields in advanced objects such as macros and modules.

- An input mask is used to format the display of data and control the format in which values can be entered.
- Depending on the workstation's language settings, the Date Picker displays either to the right or left side of a Date/Time field.
- A primary key is a field or set of fields in a table that provides a unique identifier for every record.
- Changing the field size in Design View is different than changing the column width in Datasheet View.
- The data contained in a primary key field must be unique.
- A Validation Rule is a condition specifying criteria for entering data into an individual field.
- Validation text is an error message that appears when a value prohibited by the validation rule is entered.
- Importing data prevents errors that may occur when re-keying data.
- Data can be exported to another Microsoft application such as Word or Excel or non-Microsoft applications such as dBASE or Paradox.
- Data imported from another Access database, a non-Access database, or a nondatabase application can be added to an existing table or used to create a new table.
- The Manage Data Tasks dialog box displays and manages import and export operations previously saved.

LESSON 4 Command Summary

Feature	Button	Task Path	Keyboard
Data, Export		External Data, Export	
Data, Import		External Data, Import	
Database, Create		Microsoft Office Button, New	
Database, Create, Blank		New Blank Database	
Database, Properties		Microsoft Office Button, Manage	
Field, Properties		Home, Views, Design View	
Field, Properties, Toggle			F6
Primary Key		Design, Tools, Primary Key	
Table, Create		Create, Tables	
Table, Properties		Right-click Object, Properties	
Table, Template		Create, Tables, Table Templates	

unit 2

DESIGNING AND MANAGING DATABASE OBJECTS

Lesson 5

Managing Data Integrity

OBJECTIVES

MCAS OBJECTIVES

In this lesson:
AC07 70-605 1.2.1
AC07 70-605 1.2.3
AC07 70-605 1.2.2
AC07 70-605 2.4.3
AC07 70-605 2.3.2
AC07 70-605 6.2.4

After completing this lesson, you will be able to:

1. Create relationships between tables.
2. Work with referential integrity.
3. Work with subdatasheets.
4. Use the Lookup Wizard.
5. Use Analyzing tools.
6. Track object dependency.

Estimated Time: 1 1/2 hours

Relationships are critical for properly designed databases. A *relationship* is a link or connection between two tables sharing a common field. Relationships change a flat database, containing isolated data, into a relational database, containing linked data. For tables to relate to each other, they must share common data.

Relationships must be planned; they do not just happen. Understanding them—and how to set them—takes time and practice. As you work more extensively with databases, you will learn more about creating and maintaining relationships.

Creating Relationships Between Tables

Relationships between tables can be graphically viewed in the Relationships window. Tables display as field lists. Related fields from each table are connected by a join line. Each end of the join line connects to the related fields in linked tables.

The related field between the two tables must be of the same data type and the same size. The related fields do not need to use the same name.

However, you will find it much easier to create and recognize relationships when the common fields use the same field name in both tables.

When you select a primary key in both related tables, you create a One-To-One relationship. A One-To-One relationship occurs when the common field is a primary key in the first table and a primary key field in the second. This means one record in the first table can relate to only one record in the second table.

When you select a primary key in only one table, you create a One-To-Many relationship. A One-To-Many relationship occurs when the common field is a primary key in the first table and not a primary key field in the second. This means one record in the first table can relate to one or more records in the second table.

When you do not select a primary key in either table, you create an Indeterminate relationship. An Indeterminate relationship occurs when Access does not have enough information to determine the relationship between the two tables. The common fields in the first and the second table are not primary key fields.

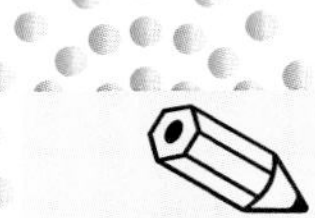

TIP

To resize a list box, you can use the left, right, and bottom borders. Clicking and dragging the top area (title bar) will move the list box

TIP

Make certain that you open the shortcut menu for the join line. The menu enables you to edit the relationship or delete the join line. If you accidentally open the shortcut menu for the Relationships window or for a field list, the menu displayed will not offer the option to edit relationships or to delete the join line.

NOTE

You will learn more about the types of relationships later in this lesson.

Exercise 5-1 LOOK AT AN EXISTING RELATIONSHIP

The Relationships window shows existing relationships in the current database. One or more relationships can be displayed at a time. When more than two tables are displayed, it is advantageous to arrange the tables to allow optimum viewing of all join lines.

1. Locate and open the **Lesson 05** folder.
2. Make a copy of **CC05** and rename it to *[your initials]*-CC05.
3. Open and enable content for ***[your initials]*-CC05**.
4. From the **Database Tools** tab, in the **Show/Hide** group, click the Relationships command. This opens the Relationship window.
5. From the **Design** tab, in the **Relationship** command group, click the **All Relationships** command. Any table that has a relationship with another table will open. The line connecting two tables represents the relationship between the tables.
6. Click and drag the bottom and right edges of the **tblEmployees** field list until all field names are visible.
7. Resize and move each field list to appear as shown in Figure 5-1.

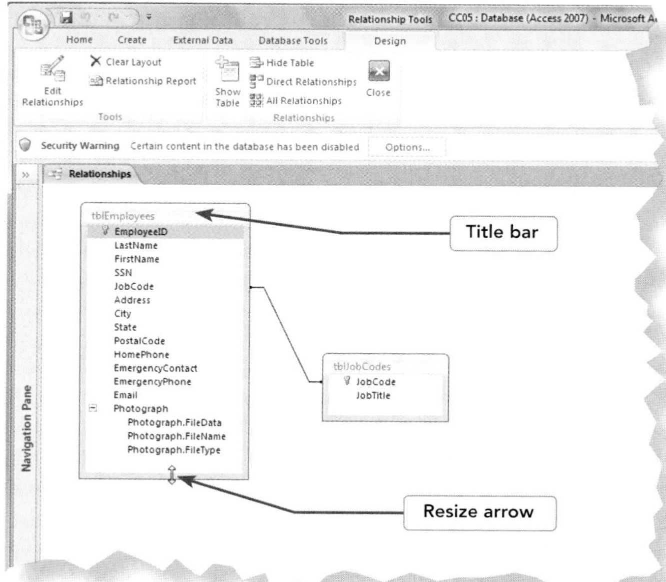

Figure 5-1
Relationships window with field lists rearranged
CC05.accdb
Relationships window

8. Right-click the sloping part of the join line between **tblEmployees** and **tblJobCodes** to open the shortcut menu for the join line.

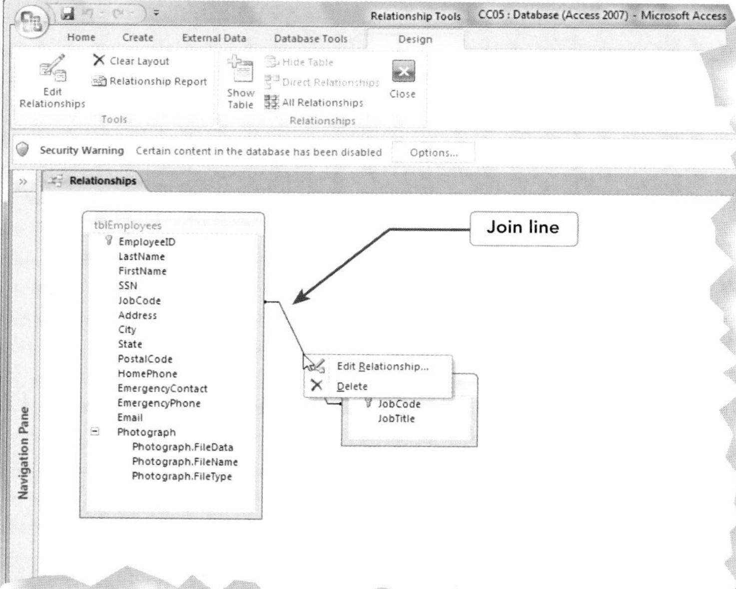

Figure 5-2
Shortcut menu
CC05.accdb
Relationships window

Edit Relationships
Table/Query: tblJobCodes
Related Table/Query: tblEmployees
JobCode JobCode
OK
Cancel
Join Type..
Create New..
Enforce Referential Integrity
Cascade Update Related Fields
Cascade Delete Related Records
Relationship Type: One-To-Many

Figure 5-3
Edit Relationships dialog box
CC05.accdb
Relationships window

9. Choose **Edit Relationship**.
10. Click **Cancel** to close the dialog box.

NOTE

The **Show Table** dialog box sometimes opens automatically when no relationships are present in the database.

TIP

If you cannot see the field lists, move the Show Table dialog box by its title bar.

Exercise 5-2 CREATE A RELATIONSHIP IN THE RELATIONSHIPS WINDOW

You can create different types of relationships depending on whether you choose a primary key as a common field. When a common field is a primary key in one table, it becomes a foreign key in the other table. A *foreign key* is a field that links to a primary key field in the related table.

1. From the **Design** tab, in the **Relationships** group, click the Show Table command. The **Show Table** dialog box lists the tables and queries that are in the database.
2. In the **Tables** tab, click **tblJobCodes**. Click **Add** to add its field list to the window.
3. Double-click **tblPayroll** and **tblTimeCards**.

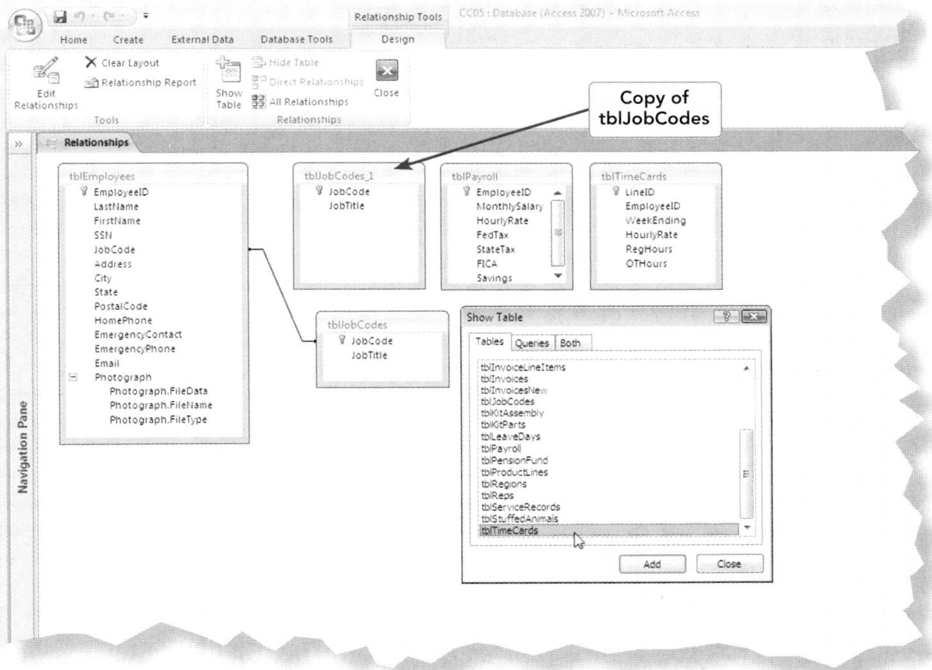

Figure 5-4 Show Table dialog box **CC05.accdb Relationships window**

NOTE

Copies of field lists have "_#" added to the end of the table or query. "#" stands for the number of copies.

4. In the **Show Table** dialog box, click **Close**.
5. The table **tblJobCodes** has been entered twice. Click on the field list **tblEmployees_1** and press Delete to remove the copy.
6. In the **tblEmployees** field list, click the **EmployeeID** field. The field name has a key symbol because it is the primary key in this table.
7. Click and drag the **EmployeeID** field from the **tblEmployees** field list to the **EmployeeID** field in the **tblTimeCards** field list.

8. The **Edit Relationships** dialog box opens. The Relationship Type is One-To-Many because the EmployeeID (the primary key) appears only once in the table **tblEmployees** but can appear many times in the table **tblTimeCards**.
9. Click **Create**. A join line links the common field names.
10. Click and drag the **EmployeeID** field from the **tblEmployees** field list to the **EmployeeID** field in the **tblPayroll** field list.
11. The **Edit Relationships** dialog box opens. The Relationship Type is One-To-One because the EmployeeID (the primary key) appears only once in the table **tblEmployees** and only once in the table **tblPayroll**.
12. Click **Create**. A join line links the common field names.
13. Resize and move each field list to appear as shown in Figure 5-5.

Figure 5-5
Show Table dialog box
CC05.accdb Relationships window

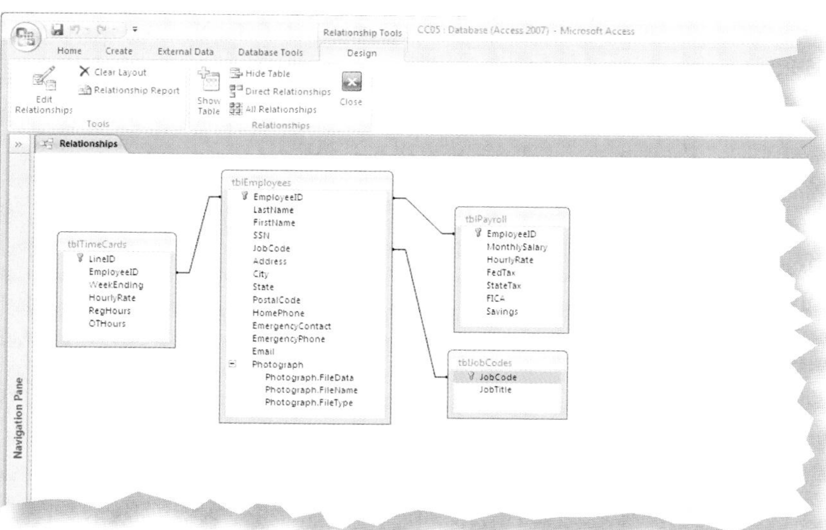

14. From the **Design** tab, in the **Tools** group, click the Clear Layout command.
15. Click **Yes** to clear the layout.
16. From the **Design** tab, in the **Relationships** group, click the All Relationships command.
17. From the **Design** tab, in the **Tools** group, click the Clear Layout command. Click **Yes** to clear the layout.

NOTE

The Clear Layout button clears the way tables are arranged but does not delete the relationships between them.

18. From the Navigation Pane, click and drag the tables **tblAssets** and **tblServiceRecords** into the Relationships window. Collapse the Navigation Pane.
19. Resize and move each field list so all fields are visible.
20. Click and drag the **AssetID** field from the **tblAssets** field list to the **AssetID** field in the **tblServiceRecords** field list. The Relationship Type is One-To-Many.

21. Click **Create**. From the Quick Access toolbar, click the Save button.

22. From the **Design** tab, in the **Relationships** group, click the Close command.

Exercise 5-3 PRINT/SAVE RELATIONSHIPS

Printing a Relationship Report helps a database administrator document and manage database integrity. A *Relationship Report* is a graphical report showing related tables. Each Relationship Report you create can be saved.

1. From the **Database Tools** tab, in the **Show/Hide** group, click the Relationships command.
2. From the **Design** tab, in the **Tools** group, click the Relationship Report command.
3. From the **Print Preview** tab, in the **Page Layout** group, click **Margins** and choose the Wide command from the menu.
4. From the Quick Access toolbar, click the Save button.
5. In the **Save As** dialog box, key **rptRelAssetsService** and press **OK**. This saved report can be opened or printed at any time.

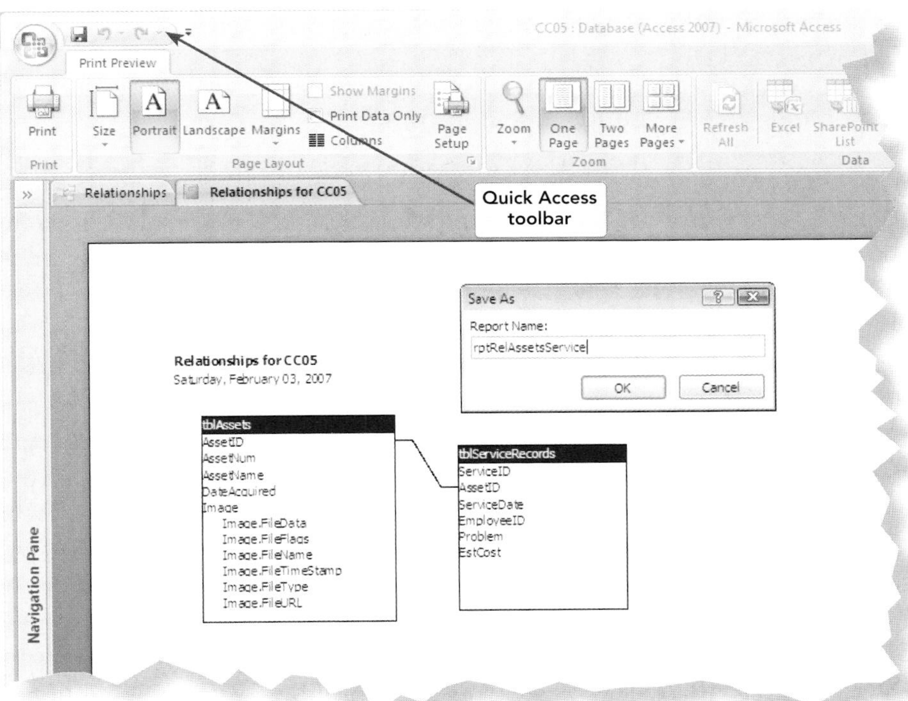

Figure 5-6
Save a Relationship report
CC05.accdb
rptRelAsstesService

6. Click the Relationships tab to return to the Relationships window.
7. From the **Design** tab, in the **Relationships** group, click the All Relationships command.
8. Resize and move each field list to appear as shown in Figure 5-7.

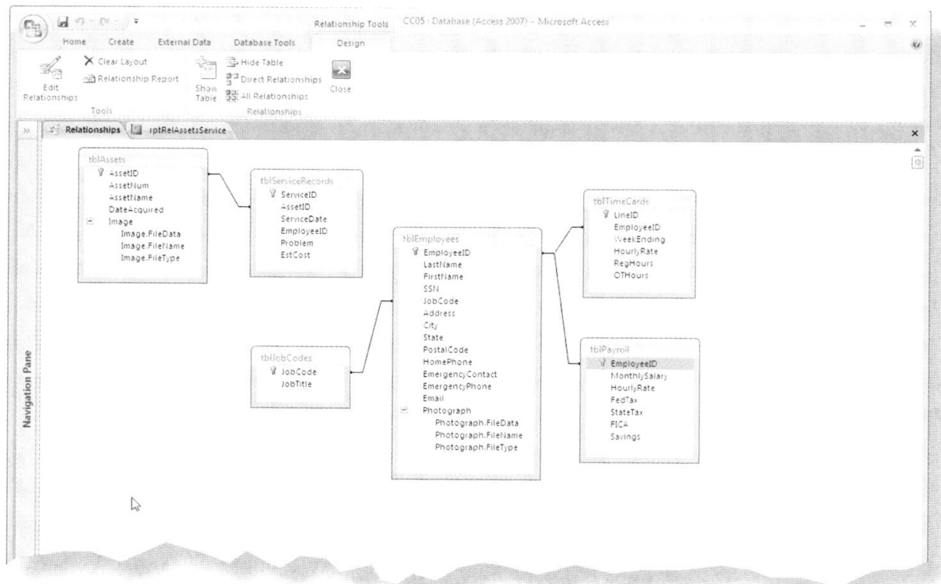

Figure 5-7 Organize the Relationships window
CC05.accdb Relationships window

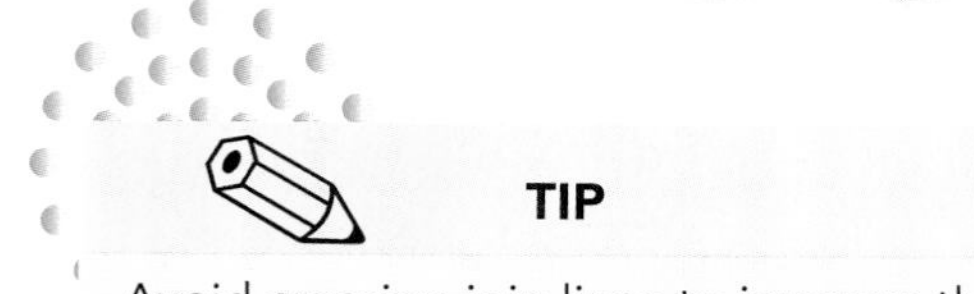

TIP

Avoid crossing join lines to improve the readability of the relationships.

9. From the **Design** tab, in the **Tools** group, click the Relationship Report command.
10. From the **Print Preview** tab, in the **Page Layout** group, click **Margins** and choose the Wide command from the menu.

11. From the **Print Preview** tab, in the **Page Layout** group, click the Landscape command.
12. From the Quick Access toolbar, click the Save button.
13. In the **Save As** dialog box, key **rptRelAll** and press **OK**.
14. Right-click the **rptRelAll** document tab, and select **Close All**.

Working with Referential Integrity

The use of referential integrity helps reduce human error through accidental deletions or other common errors. *Referential integrity* is a set of database rules for checking, validating, and keeping track of data entry changes in related tables. Enforcing referential integrity in two or more tables ensures that field values are consistent throughout the entire database.

For example, if you enforce referential integrity between the invoices table and the customers table, then you can prevent someone from creating an invoice without a corresponding customer. The enforced integrity also prevents someone from deleting a customer that has active invoices.

Exercise 5-4 ENFORCE REFERENTIAL INTEGRITY

You can enforce referential integrity between tables in a One-To-Many relationship. When referential integrity is enforced, the join line between the tables displays a 1 for the "one" side of the relationship and an infinity symbol (∞) for the "many" side. Referential integrity cannot be set for indeterminate relationships.

You can set referential integrity when the following conditions are met:

- The linking field from the main table is a primary key.
- The linked fields have the same data type.
- Both tables belong to the same Microsoft Access database.

1. Open **tblEmployees**. In the first record (EmployeeID # 1), change the **Job Code** to OF55.
2. Open **tblJobCodes**. Notice that there is no **Job Code** "OF55." Referential integrity would prevent this type of error from being made. Close both tables.
3. From the **Database Tools** tab, in the **Show/Hide** group, click the Relationships command.
4. Right-click the sloping part of the join line between **tblJobCodes** and **tblEmployees**. Select **Edit Relationship**. The Relationship Type is **One-To-Many**.
5. Click the check box to select **Enforce Referential Integrity** and click **OK**.

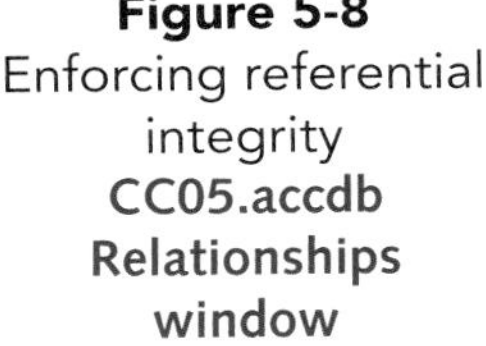

Figure 5-8
Enforcing referential integrity
CC05.accdb
Relationships window

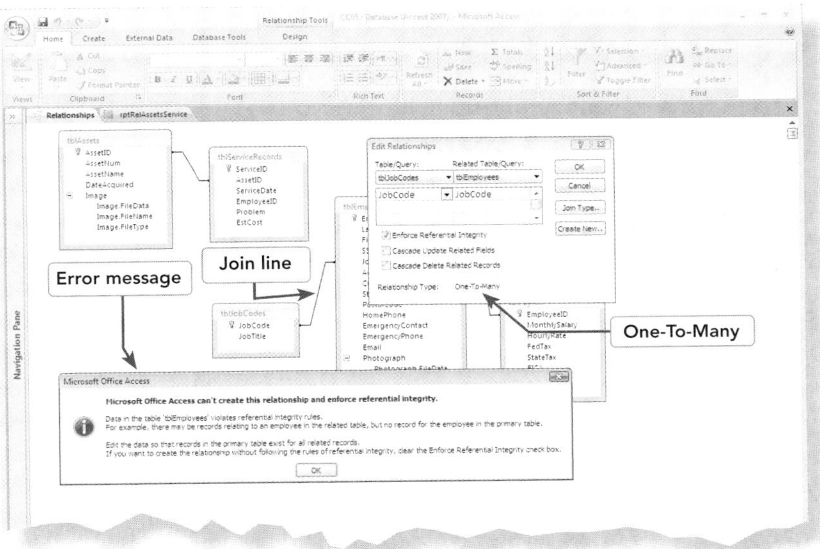

6. Read the error message and click **OK**.
7. Click **Cancel** to close the **Edit Relationships** dialog box without saving the changes.
8. Open **tblEmployees**. In the first record (EmployeeID # 1), change the **Job Code** back to OF05.
9. Close **tblEmployees**.

10. Click the **Relationships** tab to return to the Relationships window.
11. Right-click the sloping part of the join line between **tblJobCodes** and **tblEmployees**. Select **Edit Relationship**.
12. Click the check box to select **Enforce Referential Integrity**, and click **OK**. This time, the changes were accepted, and the symbols "1" and "∞" have been added to the join line.

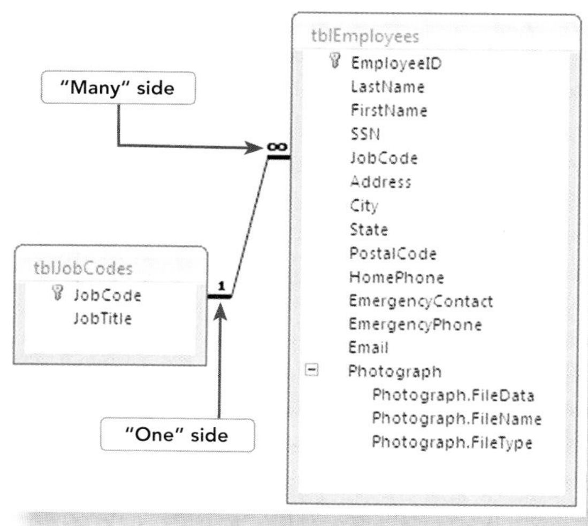

Figure 5-9
One-To-Many relationship
CC05.accdb Relationships window

13. From the **Design** tab, in the **Relationships** group, click the Close command.
14. Open **tblEmployees**. In the first record (EmployeeID # 1), change the **Job Code** to **OF55** and press ↓.
15. A message box alerts you to a problem.

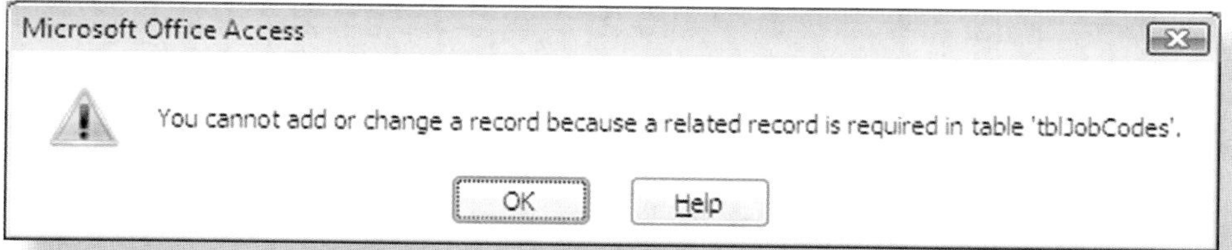

Figure 5-10
Referential Integrity finds an error
CC05.accdb Relationships window

16. Click **OK**. Key **OF06** and press ↓. This change was allowed because the job code "OF06" is found in **tblJobCodes**.
17. Close the table.

Exercise 5-5 REMOVE REFERENTIAL INTEGRITY

Referential integrity is a property of a relationship. When you remove referential integrity from a relationship, you merely remove the validation rules while preserving the original relationship between the tables.

1. From the **Database Tools** tab, in the **Show/Hide** group, click the Relationships command.

2. Right-click the sloping part of the join line between **tblEmployees** and **tblJobCodes**.
3. Choose **Edit Relationship** from the shortcut menu.
4. In the **Edit Relationships** dialog box, remove the checkmark from **Enforce Referential Integrity**. Click **OK**.
5. From the **Design** tab, in the **Relationships** group, click the Close command. Save changes to the layout.

Working with Subdatasheets

A table on the "one" side of a One-To-Many relationship, by default, has a subdatasheet. A *subdatasheet* is a datasheet linked within another datasheet. A subdatasheet contains data related to the first datasheet. The common field linking the two datasheets is the primary key field in the main datasheet and the foreign key field in the linked datasheet.

Exercise 5-6 INSERT A SUBDATASHEET

You can insert a subdatasheet into a main datasheet even when a relationship does not exist between the two objects. When a relationship does not exist, Access automatically creates one. You can insert a subdatasheet into the Datasheet Views of tables and queries.

1. Open **tblJobCodes** in Design View.

2. From the **Design** tab, in the **Show/Hide** group, click the Property Sheet command.
3. In the Property Sheet, the **Subdatasheet Name** property is set to **[None]**. Click on this property. Click the drop-down arrow and choose **Table.tblEmployees**.
4. Switch to Datasheet View, and save the changes to the table.
5. Notice that the record selector now has an Expand icon symbol. Click the Expand icon for the Job Code "MF04."

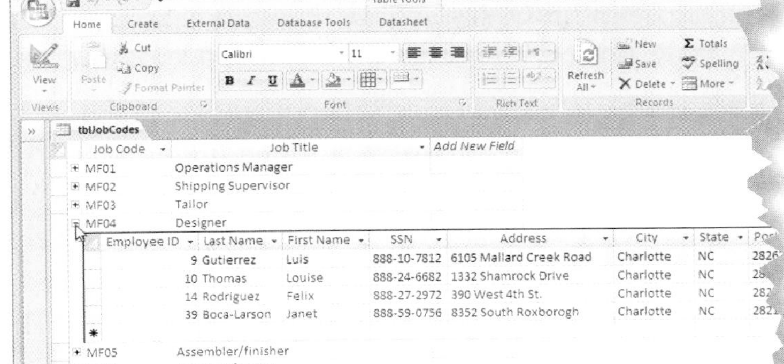

Figure 5-11
Expanding a subdatasheet
CC05.accdb
tblJobCodes

TIP

When the common fields in both tables have the same name, often Access automatically identifies the Master and Child fields.

6. Click in the subdatasheet's first record.
7. From the **Home** tab, in the **Records** group, click **More**, and choose **Subdatasheet**, then the Subdatasheet command from the menu.
8. In the **Insert Subdatasheet** dialog box, choose **tblPayroll**.

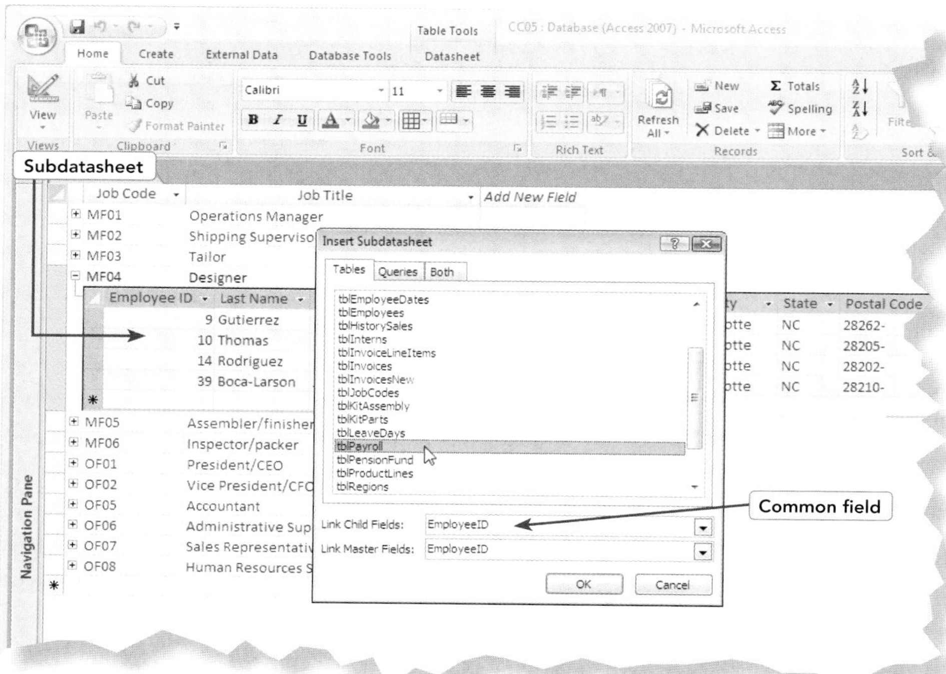

Figure 5-12
Inserting a subdatasheet
CC05.accdb
tblJobCodes

9. Click **OK**. Now the subdatasheet has its own subdatasheet.
10. Expand Employee #10 to see payroll information for that employee.
11. Click the Collapse icon button to collapse the subdatasheet.
12. Close **tblJobCodes**. A **Save** dialog box appears, asking if you want to save both **tblJobCodes** and **tblEmployees**. Click **Yes**.

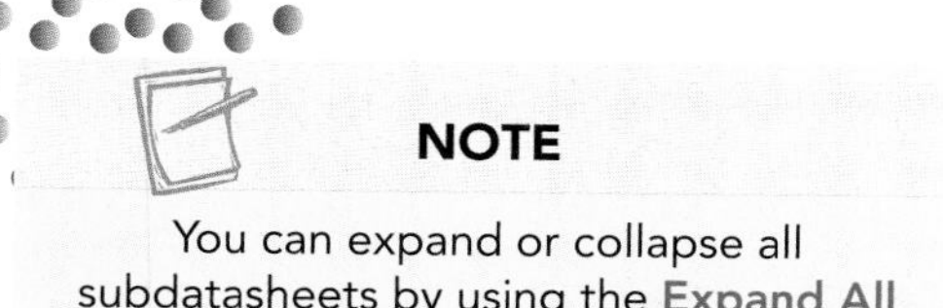

NOTE

You can expand or collapse all subdatasheets by using the **Expand All** or **Collapse All** commands found on the **Home** tab, in the **Records** group. Click **More** and choose **Subdatasheet**.

13. Open **tblEmployees**. This table now has the Expand icon ⊞. In the **tblJobCodes**, you added **tblEmployees** as the subdatasheet. Then you added **tblPayroll** as a subdatasheet for **tblEmployees**.
14. Click the Expand icon ⊞ for the first record. The payroll information for that employee is displayed.

Exercise 5-7 REMOVE A SUBDATASHEET

Not all subdatasheets need to be displayed in the main datasheet. If most database users do not need to use the subdatasheet, you should remove it from the main datasheet. Although a subdatasheet does not display in a main datasheet, the relationship between the two tables remains. You can remove a subdatasheet in Datasheet View.

1. While in the Datasheet View of **tblEmployees**, collapse the subdatasheet.
2. From the **Home** tab, in the **Records** group, click **More**, and choose **Subdatasheet**, then **Remove** from the menu.
3. Close **tblEmployees** and save the changes.
4. Open **tblJobCodes** and expand the subdatasheet for the first record. Notice that there is no longer a subdatasheet for the employee.
5. Close **tblJobcodes**. You were not asked to save because there were no changes to the table **tblJobCodes**.

Using the Lookup Wizard

Using lookup fields often improves data entry. A *lookup field* is a field property that displays input choices from another table and allows these choices to be selected from a list. Lookup fields are used often when specialized codes appear within databases.

Codes use less space than lengthy text describing the record. Some codes are readily understandable, such as two-letter abbreviations for state names. Other codes are less obvious and need a lookup field to become useful.

Exercise 5-8 CREATE A LOOKUP FIELD

In addition to reducing the amount of data stored in a table, a lookup field can improve the efficiency and consistency of data entry. The best fields to convert to a lookup value are those that contain a finite number of values. Lookup fields use list boxes to display a list of possible values. The Lookup Wizard guides you through a step-by-step process for creating the lookup field.

1. Open **tblInterns** in Datasheet View.
2. Click the column header for the field **Department**.

3. From the **Datasheet** tab, in the **Fields & Columns** group, click the Lookup Column command.
4. The Lookup Wizard dialog box appears. Verify that **I want the lookup column to look up the values in a table or query** is selected. Click **Next**.
5. From the list of tables, choose **Table: tblDepartments** and click **Next**.

6. Click the Add All button >> to move both fields from the Available Fields to the Selected Fields area.
7. Click **Next**. Click the first drop-down arrow and choose Department.
8. Click **Next**. Double-click the right edge of the column header to resize the column to fit the widest data.
9. Remove the checkmark from the **Hide key column** control. The **Department ID** field is also displayed.

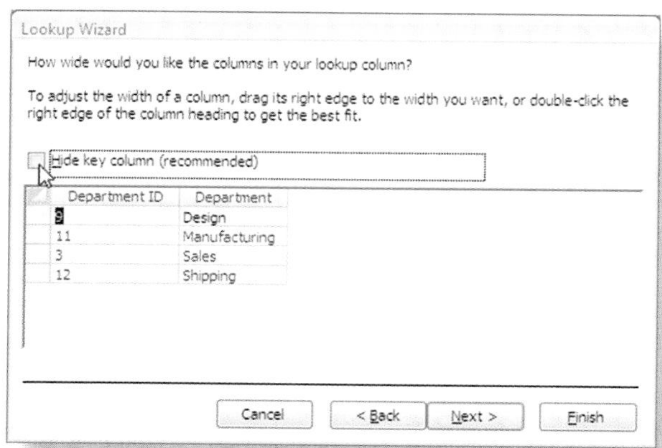

Figure 5-13
Showing the key column
CC05.accdb
tblInterns

10. Click to add the checkmark to the **Hide key column** control.
11. Click **Next**. Key **Dept** as the label for the column. Click **Finish**.

Exercise 5-9 ADD DATA WITH A LOOKUP FIELD

Adding data to a field through a lookup field reduces the number of keystrokes necessary to enter a value. In this example, values in the lookup fields are listed alphabetically in ascending order.

1. Click in the first record's **Dept** field and key **s**. The combo box will display Sales. Press Enter to select Sales.
2. Click in the second record's **Dept** field. Click the drop-down arrow of the combo box to display the list of departments and choose **Manufacturing**.

Figure 5-14
Choose the value from the lookup column.
CC05.accdb
tblInterns

3. Press ↓ and key **s**. Press ↓ to move to the next record.
4. Key **sh**. Because there are two departments that start with the letter "S," you must key a second letter.
5. Finish adding the departments to the **Dept** field.

6. Now that the data in the **Dept** field matches the **Department** field, we can delete the old data. Click the column header for the **Department** field to select the column.

7. From the **Datasheet** tab, in the **Fields & Columns** group, click the Delete command. Click **Yes** in response to the warning message.

Exercise 5-10 MODIFY A LOOKUP FIELD

The list of values displayed in a lookup field can be limited or editable. A limited list does not allow the user to enter new values. An editable list does allow for new values to be entered.

1. Click in the first record's **Education** field and key **AA**.
2. Press [Tab]. An error message states that "AA" is not on the list.
3. Click **OK**. The lookup list expands to show the valid options. Press [Esc] twice.
4. Switch to Design View.

NOTE

In order to prevent data entry errors, most database administrators set the Limit to List option to yes.

5. Click the field **Edu**.
6. Press [F6] to move to the field properties. Click the **Lookup** tab.
7. Notice that the **Limit To List** property is set to **Yes**. Read the description in the Help window.

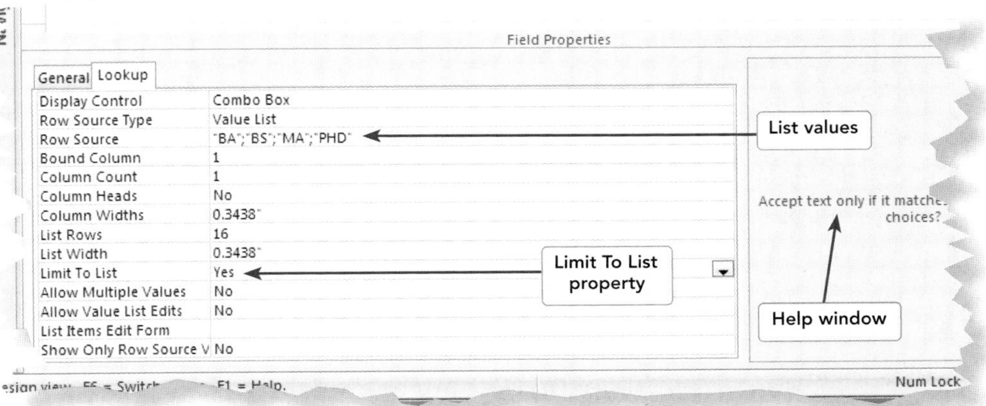

Figure 5-15
Limit To List property
CC05.accdb
tblInterns

NOTE

If a lookup field has more than one column, the **Allow Value List Edits** property is ignored.

8. Click in the **Allow Value List Edits** property. Read the description in the Help window.
9. Change the **Allow Value List Edits** property value from "No" to **Yes**.
10. Save the table and switch to Datasheet View.

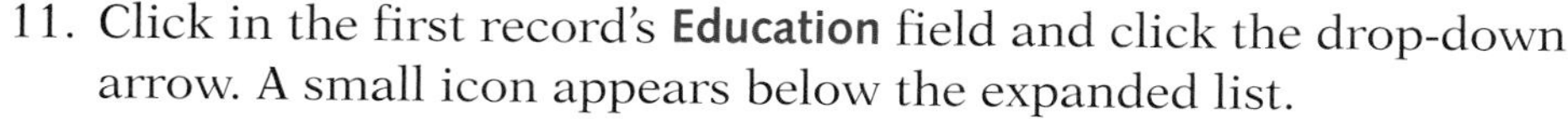

11. Click in the first record's **Education** field and click the drop-down arrow. A small icon appears below the expanded list.

12. Click the Edit List icon . The **Edit List Items** dialog box opens.

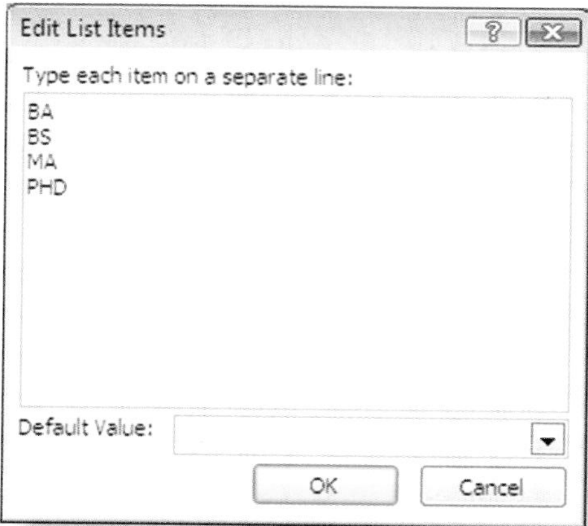

Figure 5-16
Edit a lookup field list
CC05.accdb
tblInterns

13. Press PageUp and key **AA**. Press Enter.
14. Click **OK**.
15. Click in the first record's **Education** field, and click the drop-down arrow. The list now has an Associates of Arts degree.
16. Key **A** and press Tab.
17. Close **tblInterns,** and save the changes.

Exercise 5-11 CREATE A MULTI-VALUED LOOKUP FIELD

A lookup field can be set to be a multi-valued lookup field. The idea behind multi-valued fields is to make it easy to support those instances in which you want to select and store more than one choice, without having to create a more advanced database design. Access 2007 doesn't actually store the values in a single field. Even though what you see is a single field, the values are actually stored independently and managed in hidden, system tables. The same wizard used to create lookup fields is used to create multi-valued lookup fields.

1. Open **tblRegions**. This table contains seven different sales regions.
2. Open **tblReps**. One sales representative can be assigned to many regions.
3. Switch to Design View.
4. Notice the field **Regions** has a **Data Type** of **Text**. Switch back to Datasheet View.
5. Select the **Regions** column.
6. From the **Datasheet** tab, in the **Fields & Columns** group, click the Lookup Column command .
7. In the **Lookup Wizard** dialog box, click **Next**.
8. From the list of tables, select **Table: tblRegions** and click **Next**.
9. In the **Available Fields** area, double-click **RegionID** and **RegionName** to move them to the **Selected Fields** area.
10. Click **Next**. Click the drop-down arrow and choose **RegionName**. Click **Next**.

11. Resize the **Region Name** column so all data can be seen. Click **Next**.
12. Name the field **Reg**.
13. Click to add the checkmark to the **Allow Multiple Values** control.
14. Click **Finish**.

Exercise 5-12 ADD DATA WITH A MULTI-VALUED LOOKUP FIELD

Each value stored in a multi-valued lookup field is linked to the source table or list. Values can be added or deleted from the field by using the check boxes next to each choice.

1. For the first record, click the drop-down arrow for the field **Reg**. Notice that this combo box has checkboxes next to each value.
2. Click the checkboxes for **Northeast** and **Northwest**.

Figure 5-17
Multi-Valued lookup field
CC05.accdb
tblReps

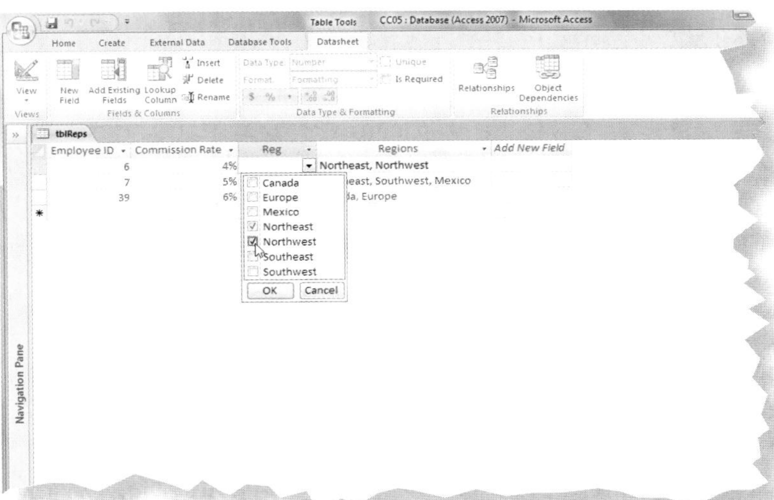

3. Close **OK**. Resize the column so you can see all the data.
4. Press [↓] to move to the next record.
5. Click the drop-down arrow, and add checkmarks to **Southeast**, **Southwest**, and **Mexico**. Click **OK**.
6. Press [↓]. Click the drop-down arrow, and add checkmarks to **Canada** and **Europe**. Click **OK**.
7. Select the **Regions** column.
8. From the **Datasheet** tab, in the **Fields & Columns** group, click the Delete command.
9. Click in the **Reg** field, on any record.

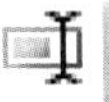

10. From the **Datasheet** tab, in the **Fields & Columns** group, click the Rename command and key **Regions**.

11. Switch to Design View.
12. Click in the **Regions** field. Notice the **Data Type** is **Number**. Only **RegionID** is being stored in this field.
13. Press F6. Click the **Lookup** tab. The **Allow Multiple Values** property is set to **Yes**.
14. Close both tables and save changes.

Exercise 5-13 VIEW RELATIONSHIPS CREATED BY LOOKUP FIELDS

When you create a lookup field, Access creates a relationship between the main table and the linked table. The relationship uses the lookup field as the common field. This relationship can be displayed in the Relationships window.

1. From the **Database Tools** tab, in the **Show/Hide** group, click the Relationships command.
2. From the **Design** tab, in the **Tools** group, click the Clear Layout command. Click **Yes** to clear the layout.
3. From the Navigation Pane, drag **tblInterns**, **tblDepartments**, **tblReps**, and **tblRegions** to the Relationships window. A join line appears between **tblReps** and **tblRegions**. Creating the lookup field produced this relationship.
4. Arrange the field lists so you can clearly see all fields and relationships.

NOTE

A multi-valued lookup field uses a One-To-Many control structure that is not compatible with older versions of Access.

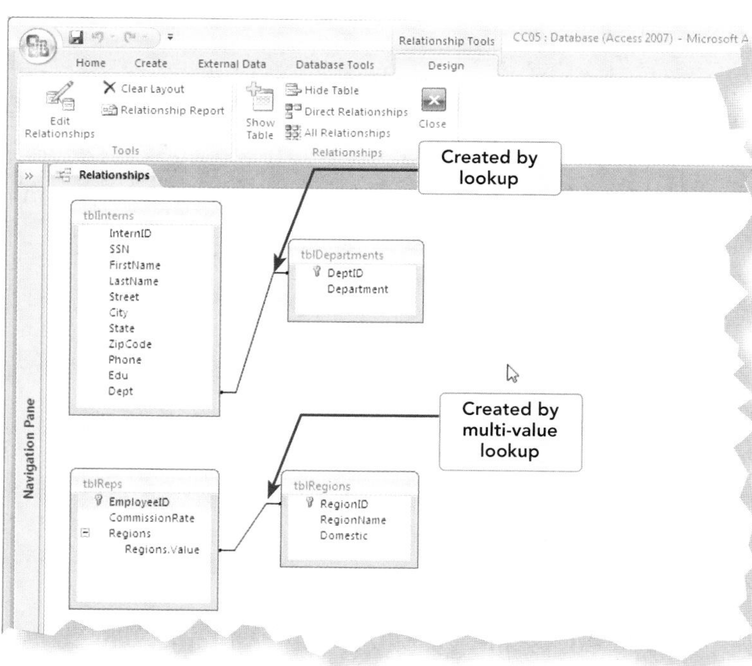

Figure 5-18
Relationships created by lookup fields
CC05.accdb Relationships window

5. Double-click the join line between **tblInterns** and **tblDepartments** to open the Edit Relationships dialog box. This is a One-To-Many relationship. The main table is **tblDepartments**; it has the primary key. Click **OK**.

6. Double-click the join line between **tblReps** and **tblRegions** to open the Edit Relationships dialog box. This is a One-To-Many relationship. The main table is **tblRegions**; it has the primary key. Click **OK**.

7. Close the Relationships window. A message box asks if you want to save the changes to the layout. Click **Yes**.

Using Analyzing Tools

The Table Analyzer Wizard analyzes a database and recommends changes for normalization. *Normalization* is the process of restructuring a relational database for the purposes of organizing data efficiently, eliminating field redundancy, and improving data consistency.

The wizard analyzes table structures and field values. When the wizard identifies duplicated data or improper table structures, you are given the option to allow the wizard to automatically make changes to your database or for you to manually make changes.

Exercise 5-14 ANALYZE A TABLE

The Table Analyzer Wizard evaluates the contents of tables in your database. When a significant number of records contain repeating field values, the Analyzer will recommend that you split the table into two new tables. The structure and contents of the original table will be preserved.

1. Open **tblKitParts** in Datasheet View. You can see that there is redundancy in the Vender information.

2. Close the table.

3. From the **Database Tools** tab, in the **Analyze** group, click the Analyze Table command .

4. In the **Table Analyzer Wizard** dialog box, read the description of the problems that this wizard will try to analyze.

5. Click **Next**. Read the description of how the wizard will try to solve them.

6. Click **Next**. From the list of tables, select **tblKitParts**.

7. Click **Next**. The default is to let the wizard decide what fields go in what tables.

8. Click **Next**.

9. Double-click the "Table1" field list header. Rename this table **tblParts**. This table will contain the part number (SKU), description of the part, and its cost.

10. Double-click the "Table2" field list header. Rename this table **tblVender**. This table will contain the unique data for the vender.

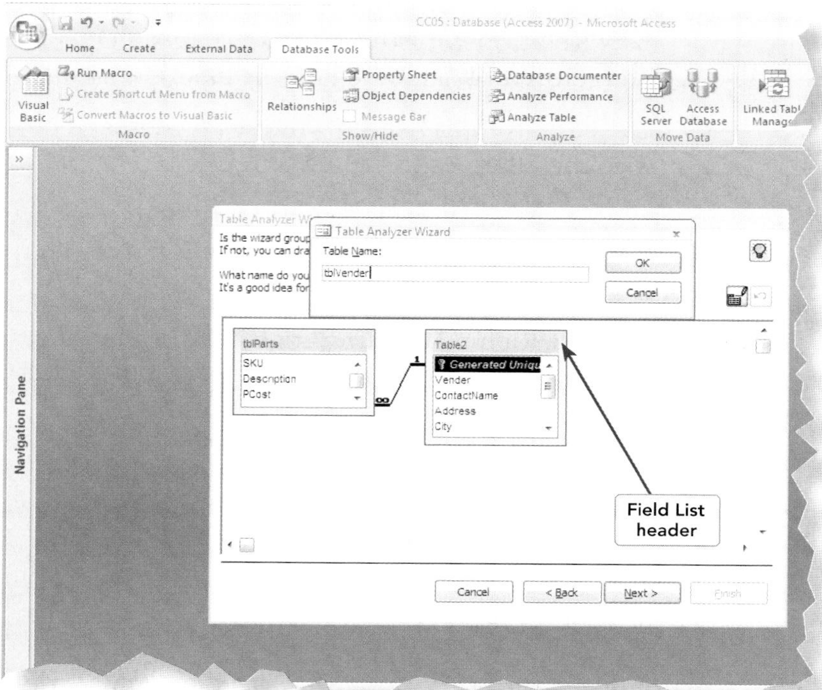

Figure 5-19 Table Analyzer Wizard **CC05.accdb Table Analyzer Wizard**

11. Click **Next**. In the field list **tblParts**, click **SKU** and click the Set Unique Identifier button. This action makes this field the Primary Key for the table.

12. Click **Next**.

13. If a dialog box appears identifying possible typographical errors, you will need to choose a value from the **Correction** list. For each record listed, in the **Correction** field, select **(Leave as is)**. Click **Next**.

14. In the last step, select **Yes, create the query option**.

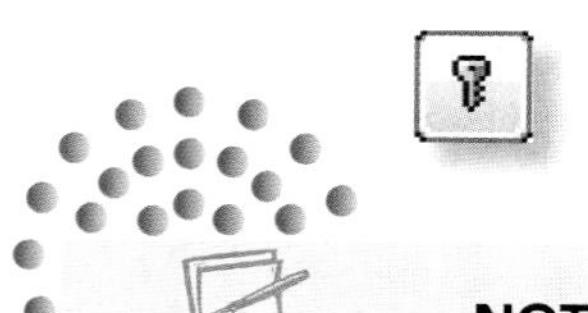

NOTE

The **Analyze Table Wizard** has renamed table **tblKitParts** to **tblKitParts_Old**. The newly created query has been named **tblKitParts**. The wizard does not follow the Leszynski naming convention.

15. Click **Finish**. If the Access Help appears, close the window.

16. The query opens in Datasheet View. Switch to Design View.

17. Notice that this query uses the two newly created tables. Resize the field lists so that all field names are visible.

18. Save and close the query.

19. In the Navigation Pane, right-click the query **tblKitParts** and choose **Rename**. Key **qryKitParts** and press Enter.

Exercise 5-15 ANALYZE PERFORMANCE

In addition to identifying redundant data, the Analyzer can identify data that can be converted to more efficient data types. Often the recommendations involve converting text data types to numeric values.

1. From the **Database Tools** tab, in the **Analyze** group, click the Analyze Performance command.
2. In the **Performance Analyzer** dialog box, on the **Tables** tab, click the check boxes for **tblEmployees** and **tblHistorySales.** Click **OK**.
3. In the **Analysis Results** section, you will see that the two tables that you selected have four **Ideas** and one **Recommendation**.
4. The table **tblHistorySales** is not indexed because the table does not contain a Primary Key field. Click the **Recommendation** for **tblHistorySales**.
5. Click **Optimize**. The red exclamation point has turned into a yellow checkmark.
6. The ideas that are listed refer to the fact that information stored as a number takes up less space than **Text** fields. Click on the first **Idea** in the section. Read the **Analysis Notes**.
7. This database needs these fields to stay **Text**. Click **Close**.

Tracking Object Dependency

Access provides a database tool to display information regarding dependencies among major objects. *Object dependency* is a condition of an object requiring the existence of another object. For example, the customers form depends upon the customers table.

Understanding dependencies helps you maintain database integrity. Before deleting an object, you first should track the dependencies for that object. For example, you might find a form is based upon a query rather than a table. Before deleting the query, you will need to decide if the form is necessary to the functionality of the database.

Exercise 5-16 VIEW OBJECT DEPENDENCY

An Object Dependency list can be generated for tables, queries, forms, and reports. The Object Dependency list displays:

- Objects that depend on the selected object.
- The object on which the selected object depends.

1. In the Navigation Pane, select **qryEmployeeDates**.

2. From the **Database Tools** tab, in the **Show/Hide** group, click the Object Dependencies command.

3. If a message dialog box appears, you will need to allow the wizard to analyze the database. The Object Dependencies Pane appears on the right side of the window.

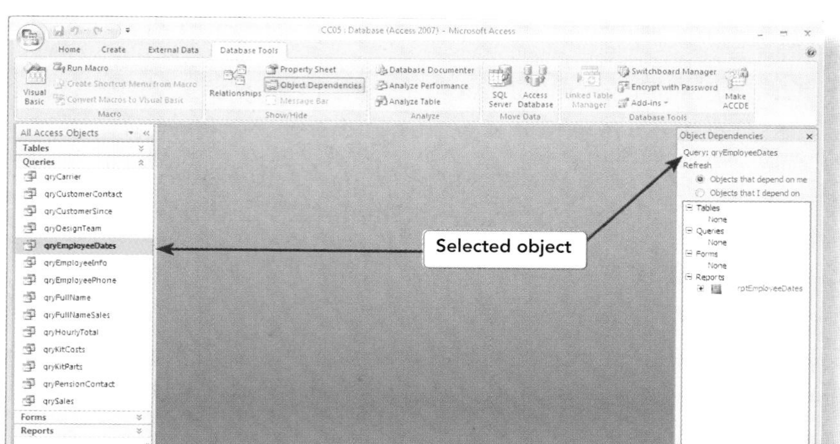

Figure 5-20 Object Dependencies Task Pane CC05.accdb Object Dependencies Task Pane

4. The first view is **Objects that depend on me**, and it shows that the form **rptEmployeeDates** depends on the query **qryEmployeeDates**.
5. Click **rptEmployeeDates** in the pane. The report opens in Design View.
6. From the **Design** tab, in the **Tools** group, click the Property Sheet command. Click the **Data** tab. Notice that the **Record Source** property is set to **qryEmployeeDates**.
7. Close the Property Sheet and the report.
8. In the Object Dependencies Pane, click **Objects that I depend on**. This shows that the query **qryEmployeeDates** depends on the tables **tblEmployeeDates** and **tblEmployees**.
9. Click **tblEmployeeDates** to open the table in Design View.
10. Close the table.

Exercise 5-17 VIEW A MISSING DEPENDENCY

If a database object is not functioning properly, you should look at its dependency list. For example, if a form does not display data, the record source upon which it depends might be missing. Viewing "Objects that I depend on" identifies the source recordset for an object.

1. In the Navigation Pane, select **qryEmployeeInfo**.
2. In the Object Dependencies Pane, click **Refresh**. Notice that this object needs the table **tblEmployees**.
3. Click **Objects that depend on me**. Notice that this query is needed by the report **rptEmployeeInfo**.

4. In the Navigation Pane, right-click **qryEmployeeInfo** and choose **Delete** from the menu. Click **Yes** to confirm the deletion.
5. In the Navigation Pane, select, but do not open, **rptEmployeeInfo**.

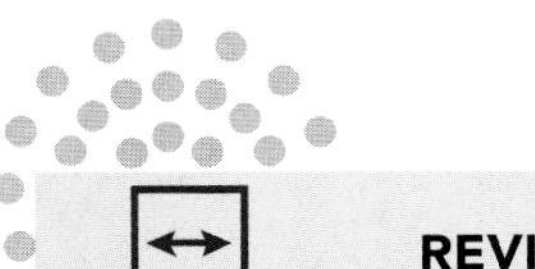

REVIEW

Remember to back up your database!

6. In the Object Dependencies Pane, click **Objects that I depend on**. Click **Refresh**. You can see that **qryEmployeeInfo** is now missing. For the report to work, a new query would need to be created.
7. Close the Object Dependencies Pane.
8. Compact and repair the database, and then close it.

Lesson 5 Summary

- Relationships between tables change a flat database containing isolated data, into a relational database containing linked data.
- Graphical relationships between tables can be viewed in the Relationships window.
- Related fields must be of the same data type and size, but not have the same name.
- A One-To-One relationship occurs when the common field is a primary key in the first table and a primary key field in the second.
- A One-To-Many relationship occurs when the common field is a primary key in the first table and not a primary key field in the second.
- An Indeterminate relationship occurs when Access does not have enough information to determine the relationship between the two tables.
- One or more relationships can be displayed in the Relationships window.
- When a common field is a primary key in the first table, it becomes a foreign key in the second table.
- A Relationship report is a graphical report showing related tables.
- Referential integrity is a set of database rules for checking, validating, and keeping track of data entry changes in related tables.
- A subdatasheet is a datasheet linked within another datasheet containing related data.
- A lookup field is a field property that displays input choices from another table and allows these choices to be selected from a list.
- A multi-valued lookup field is a lookup field that can store more than one value per record.
- The Table Analyzer Wizard displays options for improving the table structures of your database based upon the field types and the values stored.
- Object dependency is a condition of an object requiring the existence of another object.

LESSON 5		Command Summary	
Feature	**Button**	**Task Path**	**Keyboard**
Collapse Subdatasheet			
Expand Subdatasheet			
Layout, Clear		Design, Tools, Clear Layout	
Lookup field, Create		Datasheet, Fields & Columns, Lookup Column	
Lookup field, Limit To List		Design View, Lookup, Limit To List	
Lookup field, Multi-valued, Create		Design View, Lookup, Allow Multiple Values	
Object Dependency		Database Tools, Show/Hide, Dependencies	
Primary Key, Set			
Referential Integrity, Enforce		Database Tools, Show/Hide, Relationships, Edit Relationships, Enforce Referential Integrity	
Relationship Report, Create		Design, Tools, Relationship Report	
Relationships, Report		Database Tools, Show/Hide, Relationships	
Relationships, Show All		Database Tools, Relationships, All Relationships	
Relationships, Table, Hide		Database Tool, Show/Hide, Relationships, Hide Table	
Relationships, Table, Show		Database Tool, Show/Hide, Relationships, Show Table	
Relationships, View		Database Tool, Show/Hide, Relationships	
Subdatasheet, Insert		Design, Show/Hide, Property Sheet	
Subdatasheet, Remove		Home, Records, More, Subdatasheet, Remove	
Table, Analyze Table		Database Tools, Analyze, Analyze Table	
Table, Analyze Performance		Database Tools, Analyze, Analyze Performance	

Lesson 6

Designing Queries

OBJECTIVES

After completing this lesson, you will be able to:

1. Create and modify select queries.
2. Add criteria and operators to a query.
3. Apply logical operators.
4. Modify query properties.
5. Add calculations to a query.
6. Create queries with wizards.
7. Apply PivotChart / PivotTable Views.

MCAS OBJECTIVES

In this lesson:

AC07 70-605 2.5.6
AC07 70-605 4.1.1
AC07 70-605 4.1.2
AC07 70-605 4.1.4
AC07 70-605 4.2.1
AC07 70-605 4.2.2
AC07 70-605 4.2.4
AC07 70-605 4.2.5
AC07 70-605 4.2.6

Estimated Time: 1 1/2 hours

In most relational databases, queries locate, add, modify, and delete records. The effectiveness and efficiency of a query depends upon its ability to access information quickly. When you design a query, you must select necessary fields, specify appropriate criteria, and sort recordsets.

Because queries make data more manageable, they often become the record source for reports and forms. For example, a report based on an employee table with 10,000 employees would show all 10,000 records. A report based on a query would show a subset of the table's records. This subset could specify information such as who is eligible for retirement, who is scheduled for evaluation, or who is on vacation this week.

REVIEW

A query is similar to a filter in some respects. However, only a single filter can be saved per table, but multiple queries can be associated to a single table.

As with any computer application, executing a query demands processing resources. Large databases and complicated queries take more processing time than small databases and simple queries. A skilled database administrator will be knowledgeable with the numerous types of queries available in a Microsoft Access database.

Creating and Modifying Select Queries

The most common type of query is a select query. A select query locates data from one or more tables and displays the results as a datasheet. In addition to grouping records, a select query can calculate sums, averages, and other types of totals.

You can use a wizard to design queries, but usually you can build a query quickly in Design View. The Query Design window has an upper and lower pane. The upper pane is the Field List pane in which you choose the data source from one or more field lists. The lower pane is the design grid in which you specify criteria. The lower pane is also known as the QBE (Query by Example) grid.

Exercise 6-1 VIEW A SELECT QUERY AND ITS REPORT

Many reports and forms use a select query to limit the number of records and fields displayed. For example, rather than display all employees listed in the employee table, you can use a select query to display only names and phone numbers. When you view the results, the dynaset shows only the specified fields you specify in the design grid. A *dynaset* is a dynamic recordset that automatically reflects changes to its underlying data source.

1. Locate and open the **Lesson 06** folder.
2. Make a copy of **CC06** and rename it to *[your initials]*-CC06.
3. Open and enable content for ***[your initials]*-CC06**.
4. Open **qryEmployeePhone** in Design View. This query uses four fields from the table **tblEmployees**.

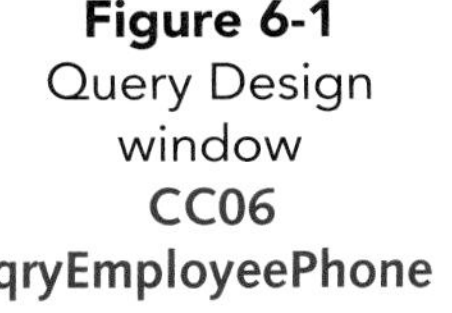

Figure 6-1 Query Design window CC06 qryEmployeePhone

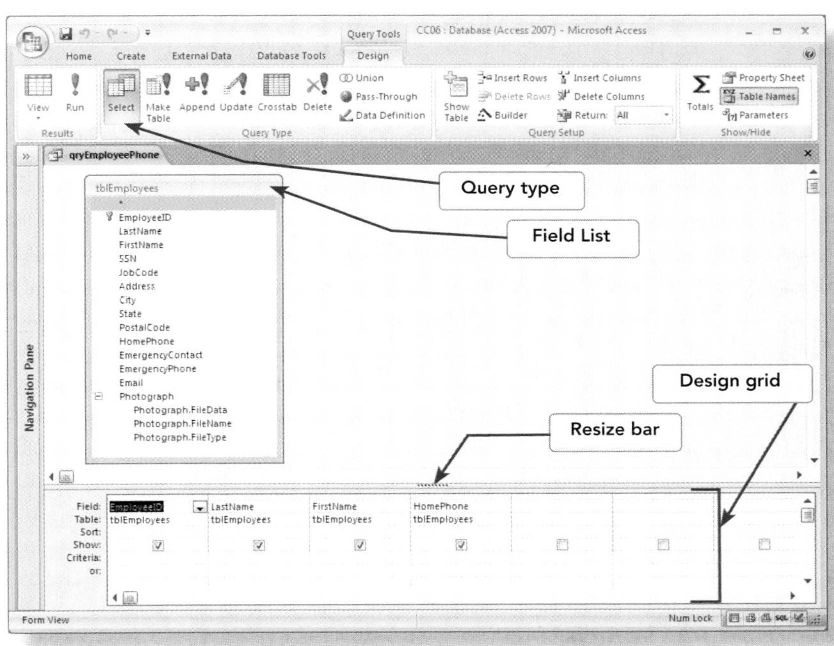

5. Open **rptEmployeePhone** in Design View.

6. From the **Design** tab, in the **Tools** group, click the Property Sheet command.

7. In the Property Sheet, click the **Data** tab. The **Record Source** property shows that this report is based on **qryEmployeePhone**.

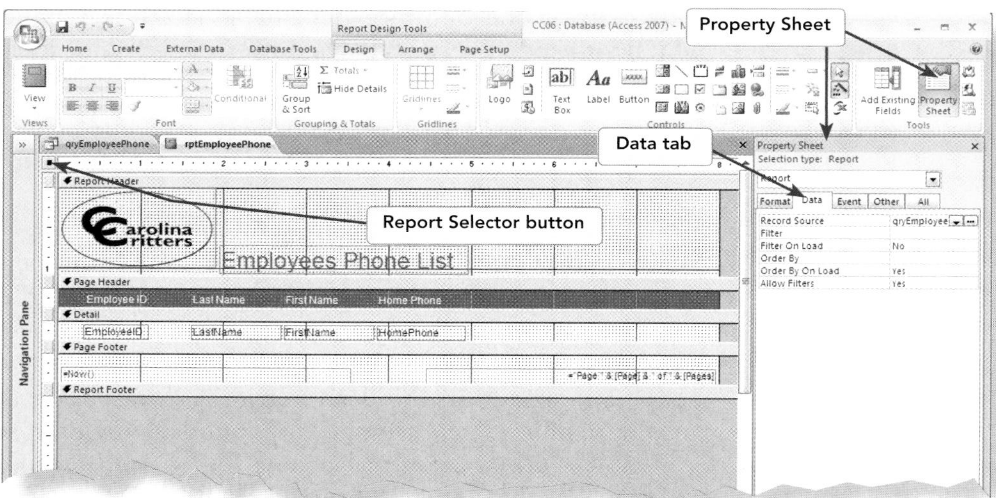

Figure 6-2
Report's Property Sheet
CC06
rptEmployeePhone

8. Right-click the document tab for **rptEmployeePhone**, and choose **Close All**.

Exercise 6-2 CREATE A SELECT QUERY BASED ON A SINGLE TABLE

You define criteria and field lists in the Design View of a query. You display the resulting recordset through the datasheet of the query. When you view the results, only the fields and records that you specified will display.

1. From the **Create** tab, in the **Other** group, click the Query Design command.

2. In the **Show Table** dialog box, double-click **tblStuffedAnimals**. The **tblStuffedAnimals** Field List appears in the upper pane of the Query Design window.

Figure 6-3
Show Table dialog box
CC06
qryAnimalPrices

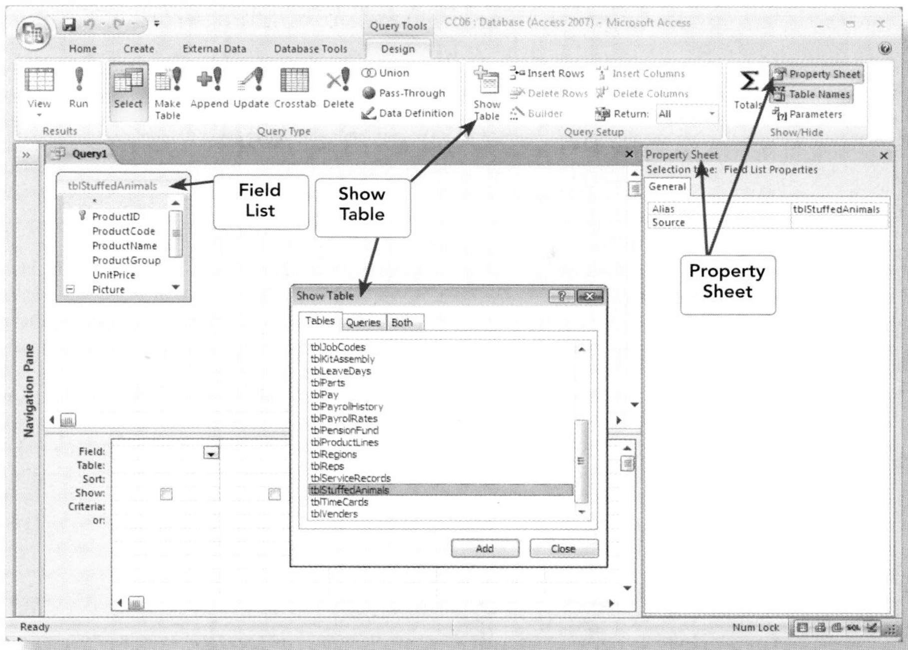

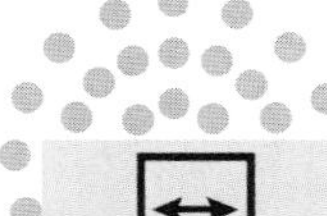

REVIEW

If you accidentally open two copies of the same Field List, right-click the second list and select **Remove Table**. You can also click the title bar of the Field List window and press Delete to remove the second copy.

3. Click **Close** in the **Show Table** dialog box.
4. Resize the Field List so all fields can be seen.
5. If the Property Sheet is not open, click the Property Sheet command.
6. Click the **tblStuffedAnimals** Field List. The Property Sheet is now showing the properties of the table.
7. Click the blank area to the right of the Field List. The Property Sheet now shows the properties of the query.

8. From the Quick Access toolbar, click the Save button.
9. In the **Save As** dialog box, key **qryAnimalPrices** and click **OK**.

Exercise 6-3 ADD FIELDS TO A QUERY

You can add fields to the design grid of a query by any of the three following ways:

- Double-click the field name in the Field List.
- Drag the field from the Field List to a **Field** row in the design grid.
- Click the **Field** row in the design grid and select a field name from the drop-down list.

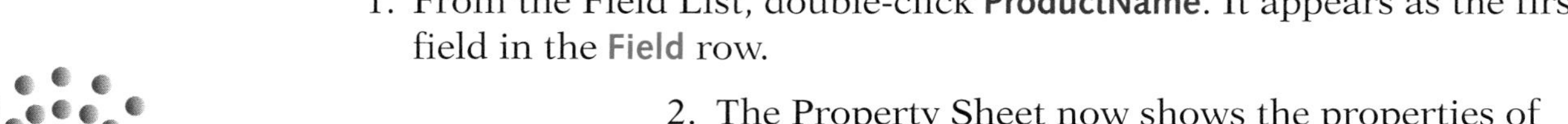

1. From the Field List, double-click **ProductName**. It appears as the first field in the **Field** row.

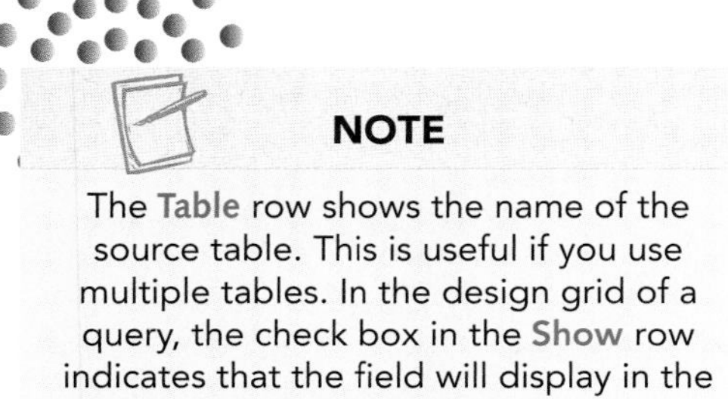

NOTE

The **Table** row shows the name of the source table. This is useful if you use multiple tables. In the design grid of a query, the check box in the **Show** row indicates that the field will display in the Datasheet View.

2. The Property Sheet now shows the properties of the field. Click the Property Sheet button to hide the Property Sheet.
3. Drag the **ProductGroup** field from the Field List to the **Field** row, second column.
4. In the third column, click the **Field** row, and then click its drop-down arrow. Choose **UnitPrice** from the list of field names.

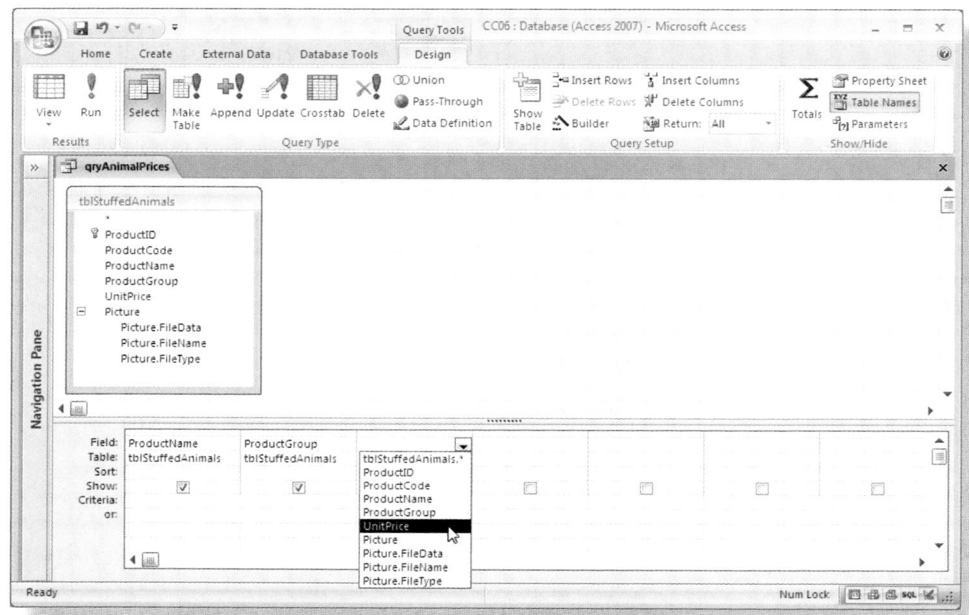

Figure 6-4
Adding fields to the design grid
CC06
qryAnimalPrices

5. Save and close the query.

Exercise 6-4 CREATE A SELECT QUERY BASED ON TWO TABLES

A query is based upon one or more field lists. Each field list is a recordset created by a table or query. When you use two or more field lists, you must link the field lists through a common field.

1. From the **Create** tab, in the **Other** group, click the Query Design command.
2. In the **Show Table** dialog box, double-click **tblStuffedAnimals** and **tblProductLines**.
3. Double-click **tblProductLines** again to add a second copy. Click **Close**.

NOTE

When using more than one table in a query, they must always show a join line.

NOTE

In a select query, the Run command ! and Datasheet View command produce the same results.

4. The second copy of **tblProductLines** ends with "_1."
5. Resize and move the Field Lists so all fields can be seen.
6. From the **tblStuffedAnimals** Field List, double-click **ProductID** and **ProductName**.
7. From the **tblProductLines** Field List, double-click **ProductLine**.
8. From the **Design** tab, in the **Results** group, click the Run command !.
9. This query results in a dynaset of 120 records. Notice the many copies of the **Product Name**. Switch to Design View.
10. Right-click the **tblProductLines_1** Field List, and choose **Remove Table**.
11. From the **Design** tab, in the **Results** group, click the Run command !.
12. The dynaset now contains only 24 records. The extra records come from having two unrelated tables in the query. Switch to Design View.
13. Save the query as **qryAnimalList**.
14. Close the query.

Adding Criteria and Operators to a Query

Adding criteria to a query is similar to adding criteria to a filter. One major difference is that more than one condition can be placed on multiple fields. When the query is executed, each condition placed as a criterion must be evaluated against field values for each record in the dynaset. The combination of conditions and operators is evaluated as a single criterion statement.

An *operator* is a word or symbol that indicates a specific arithmetic or logical relationship between the elements of an expression. Operators are used to create conditions. Operators can include arithmetic operators, such as the plus sign (+); comparison operators, such as the equals sign (=); or, logical operators, such as the word "And"; concatenation operators, such as "&" and "+"; and special operators such as "Like," "Between," or "In."

In addition to operators, a condition can also include one or more functions. A *function* is a procedure used in an expression. Most functions include multiple arguments. An *argument* is a reference in a function assigned as a single variable. Some functions such as "Date" do not require arguments. Other functions, such as "DateDiff," contain both required arguments and optional arguments.

TABLE 6-1 Types of Operators

Type	Definition	Examples
Arithmetic operator	A word or symbol that calculates a value from two or more numbers.	+, −, *, /, \, ^
Comparison operator	A symbol or combination of symbols that specifies a comparison between two values. A comparison operator is also referred to as a relational operator.	=, <>, <, <=, >, >=
Logical operator	A symbol, word, group of symbols, or group of words used to construct an expression with multiple conditions.	And, Or, Eqv, Not, Xor
Concatenation operator	A symbol, word, group of symbols, or group of words used to combine two text values into a single text value.	&, +
Special operators		Like, Between, In

Exercise 6-5 USE A SINGLE CRITERION

Text, numbers, or expressions can be used for criterion placed on a single field. Criterion using text values include leading and closing quotation marks. Criterion using date values include leading and closing pound signs (#). Numbers and expressions do not require leading or closing symbols.

1. Open **qryAnimalPrices** in Design View.
2. Click in the **Criteria** row for **ProductGroup**. Key **c**.

Figure 6-5
Entering criteria
CC06
qryAnimalPrices

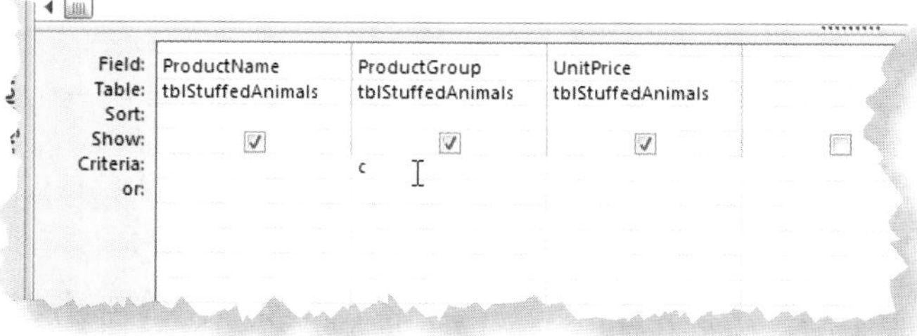

TIP

Text criterion is not case-sensitive.

3. From the **Design** tab, in the **Results** group, click the View command. Only those products in **Product Group** "C" (Cats & Dogs) are shown.

4. Switch to Design View.
5. Click in the **Criteria** row for **ProductGroup**, and press [F2] to select the criterion. Then press [Delete].
6. In the **Criteria** row for **ProductGroup**, key **t**.
7. From the **Design** tab, in the **Results** group, click the View command. Only those products in **Product Group** "T" (Teddy Bears) are shown.
8. Switch to Design View.
9. Click in the **Criteria** row for **ProductGroup** and press [F2]. Press [Delete] to remove the criteria.
10. Save and close the query.

TIP

After you run a query, Access places leading and closing quotation marks around the text used as the criterion.

NOTE

This query has reduced the dynaset from 24 records to 5 records.

Exercise 6-6 USE COMPARISON OPERATORS

Queries often use comparison operators to evaluate data. Comparison operators allow you to evaluate numbers, text, and dates. For example, the expression >10/17/07 would display all records with a date after October 17, 2007. The expression >=10/17/07 would display all records with a date on or after October 17, 2007.

When comparing text, fields are evaluated alphabetically. The expression <Smith would display all records that appear in a dictionary before the word "smith."

TABLE 6-2 Comparison Operators

Operator	Meaning
=	Equal
<>	Not equal
<	Less than
<=	Less than or equal to
>	Greater than
>=	Greater than or equal to

1. Open **qrySalesByOrderDate** in Datasheet View, and notice that the dynaset is sorted by **OrderDate**.
2. Switch to Design View. Click in the **Criteria** row for **OrderDate**.
3. Key **>=8/23/05** and press [↓]. Access adds "#" around the date criteria.
4. Switch to Datasheet View. Records for which the **OrderDate** is on or after August 23, 2005, are displayed.

5. Switch to Design View. Click in the **Criteria** row for **OrderDate**. From the **Design** tab, in the **Query Setup** group, click the Delete Rows command.
6. Click in the **Criteria** row for **ShipDate**. Key **<=10/15/03**, and display the dynaset. Records for which the **ShipDate** is on or before September 15, 2003, are displayed.
7. Delete the criteria.

Exercise 6-7 USE WILDCARDS IN CRITERIA

In much the same way you might use wildcards in the Find command, you can use wildcards in a query. When using a wildcard in the Criteria row of a query, the Like operator compares the criterion condition to each record. When the keyword "Like" is not included in the criterion, Access automatically adds it.

1. For the **qrySalesByOrderDate**, in the **Criteria** row for **CompanyName**, key **the***.

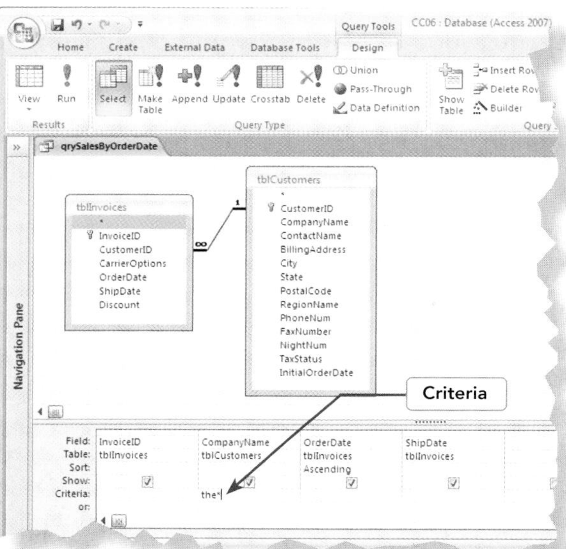

Figure 6-6
Using the * wildcard
CC06
qrySalesByOrderDate

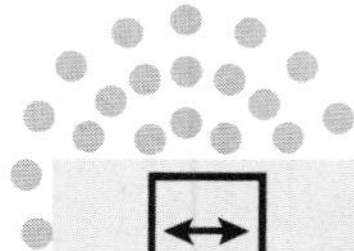

REVIEW

The wildcard * represents any amount of characters. Thus, the criterion "the*" specifies the word "the" followed by any number of characters.

2. From the **Design** tab, in the **Results** group, click the Run command **!**. Records for which the companies name starts with "the" are displayed.
3. Switch to Design View. Access inserts the keyword "Like" and formats the text with quotes.
4. Press F2 and Delete.
5. In the **Criteria** row for **CompanyName**, key ***inc***.

6. Switch to view the dynaset. Records for which the companies name contains "inc" are displayed.

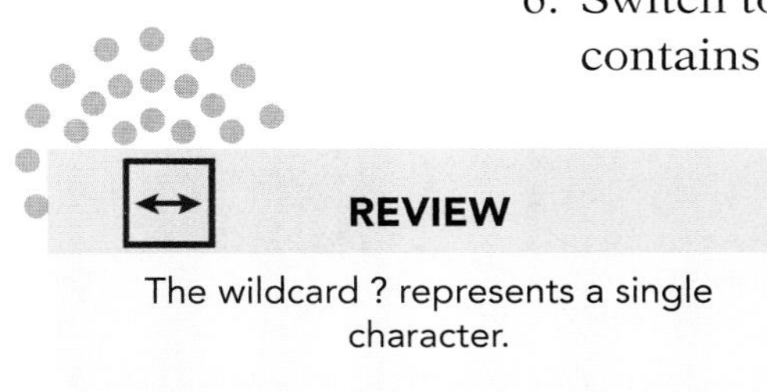

REVIEW

The wildcard ? represents a single character.

7. Switch to Design View. Delete the criteria.
8. In the **CompanyName Criteria** row, key *b??r*. This means that only companies that was a b followed by any two letters and then the letter "r" will display.

Figure 6-7
Using the * and ? wildcards
CC06
qrySalesByOrderDate

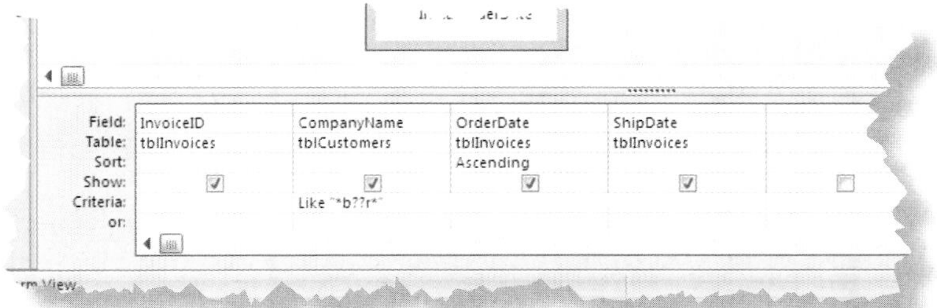

9. View the dynaset. Thirty-eight records are displayed.
10. Return to Design View and delete the criteria.

Exercise 6-8 USE KEYWORDS IN CRITERIA

Only the keywords "Like" and "Is" are automatically added to a criterion. All other keywords must be specified. Criterion expressions can be viewed in the Zoom box. You can open the Zoom box by pressing Shift+F2.

TABLE 6-3 Criteria Keywords

Keyword	Returns records in which the field . . .
Is Null	has no data, is "blank," or is "empty."
Between	value is between two numbers.
Like	value equals a defined text.
Not	value does not match the defined value.

1. With **qrySalesByOrderDate** in Design View, in the **tblInvoices** Field List, double-click the field **Discount** to add it to the Design Grid.
2. In the **Criteria** row for **Discount**, key **null** and press ↓. Access has added the keyword "Is" to the criteria.
3. View the dynaset. There are 310 sales that were not given a discount.

4. Return to Design View.
5. Edit the **Discount** criteria to show **Is Not Null**.
6. View the dynaset. There are 24 sales that were given discounts.
7. Return to Design View and delete the criteria.
8. Right-click in the **Criteria** row for **OrderDate** and choose **Zoom**.
9. In the **Zoom** dialog box, key **between 1/1/05 and 12/31/05** and click **OK**.
10. View the dynaset. There were 65 sales in 2005.
11. Switch to Design View.
12. In the **Show** row, click to remove the checkmark for **OrderDate** and **ShipDate**.
13. View the dynaset. The two dates are not showing.
14. Return to Design View and delete the criteria.
15. Close the query and do not save the changes.

Applying Logical Operators

An AND criterion or an OR criterion compares two conditions in a single criterion statement. You use an AND criterion when two conditions must occur simultaneously for the statement to be true. You use an OR criterion when either condition must occur for the statement to be true.

The design grid of a query allows for AND and OR statements without using AND or OR as keywords. When you create an AND criterion, you enter all conditions on the same Criteria row of the design grid. When you create an OR criteria, you enter the conditions on different Criteria rows of the design grid.

Exercise 6-9 USE THE "AND" CRITERION

An AND condition can be created for a single field or multiple fields. When an AND condition is placed on a single field, the keyword AND must be placed between the two conditions. When an AND condition is placed on multiple fields, the keyword is not entered. When more than one field contains a condition on the same Criteria row, then an AND condition is automatically created by Access.

1. From the **Create** tab, in the **Other** group, click the Query Design command.
2. From the **Show Table** dialog box, double-click **tblCustomers** and click **Close**.

3. Resize the Field List so all field names can be seen.
4. Add the following fields to the query design grid; **CompanyName**, **BillingAddress**, **City**, **State**, **PostalCode**.
5. In the **CompanyName** column, click the drop-down arrow in the **Sort** row and choose **Ascending**.
6. Switch to Datasheet View to see the results. Resize the columns so all data are visible.
7. Right-click the document tab for the query and choose **Save**. Key **qryCustomerAddress** and click **OK**.
8. Switch to Design View.
9. In the **City** column, key **charlotte** in the **Criteria** row.
10. Switch to Datasheet View to see how many customers are in Charlotte. Return to Design View.
11. In the **BillingAddress** column, key ***brook*** in the same **Criteria** row.

Figure 6-8
AND criteria on the same row in the design grid
CC06
qryCustomerAddress

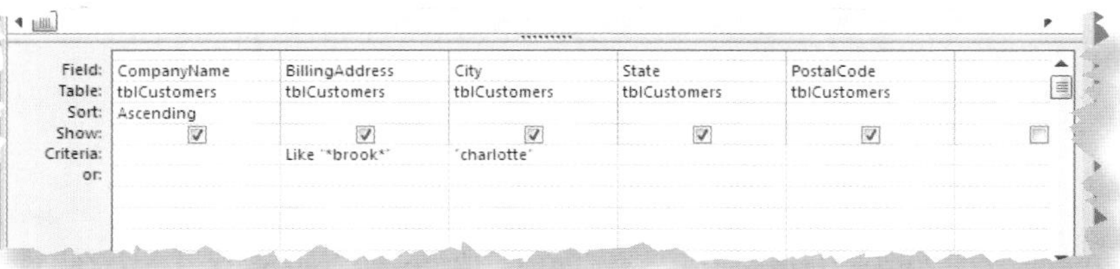

12. Switch to Datasheet View. Only records that matched both criteria are shown.
13. Switch to Design View. Click in the **Criteria** row for the **City** field. From the **Design** tab, in the **Query Setup** group, click the Delete Rows command.
14. Click in the **Criteria** row for the **State** field. Key **tn and nc**.
15. Switch to Datasheet View. No records match the criteria because no customer's state can be both TN and NC.

Exercise 6-10 USE THE "OR" CRITERION

An OR condition also can be created for a single field or multiple fields. When an OR condition is placed on a single field, the keyword OR must be placed between the two conditions. When an OR condition is placed on multiple fields, the keyword is not entered. When multiple conditions are placed on multiple **Criteria** rows, then an OR condition is automatically created by Access.

1. Switch to Design View. Point to the right of the word "Criteria" in the **Criteria** row to display a black, right-pointing arrow. Click to select the **Criteria** row and press Delete.

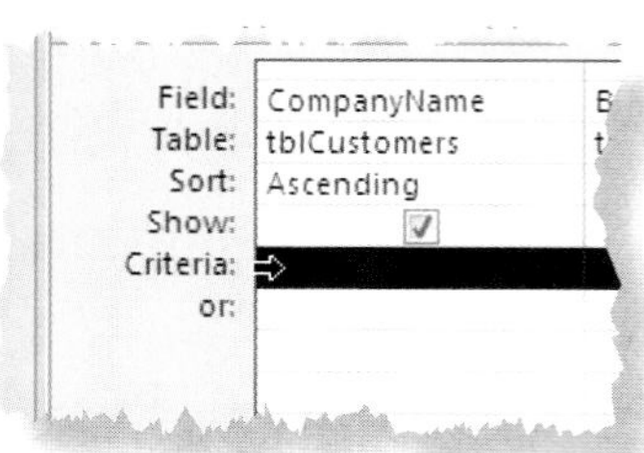

Figure 6-9 Selecting a Criteria row **CC06 qryCustomerAddress**

2. Click in the **Criteria** row for the **State** field and key **tn**. View the dynaset to see the four matching records. Return to Design View.

3. Key **nc** in the row below "tn" to enter a second condition. The first **or** row is directly below the **Criteria** row.

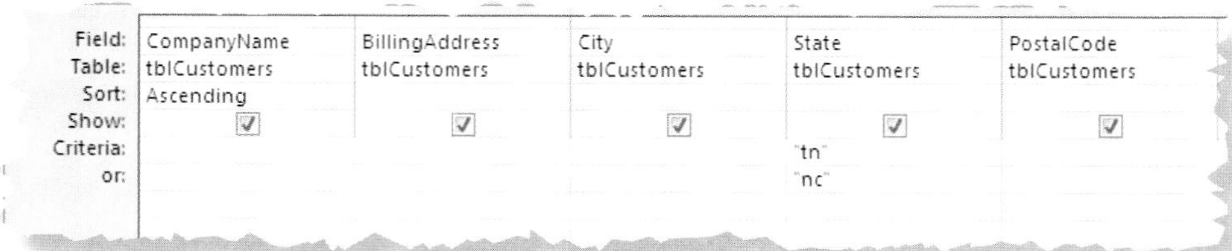

Figure 6-10 OR criteria on separate rows in the design grid **CC06 qryCustomerAddress**

4. View the dynaset. Each record meets one of the OR conditions. Return to Design View.

5. Save and close the query.

6. Open **qryCustomerAddress** in Design View. Notice that Access has combined the two criteria to one row using the OR keyword.

7. Delete the criteria. Save and close the query.

Modifying Query Properties

Queries display specific data and sorted data. By setting specific properties for a query, you can display top values and subdatasheets. For example, if you need to list the five least expensive stuffed animals, you would sort the stuffed animals table by price in ascending order and apply the Top Value property. If you want to find the customers who generate the most revenue for your company, you would also use the Top Value property in a query.

Exercise 6-11 FIND THE TOP AND BOTTOM VALUES

When using the Top Values property, Access displays records based upon the defined sort order. If a query is sorted by a numeric value, then the top values will be based upon the sorted numeric field. If a query is sorted by a text field, then the top values will be based upon the sorted text field.

The Top Values property displays either a static number of records (such as the top five) or a percentage of all records in the dynaset (such as the top 5%). Depending on the sort order, Top Values can display either the highest (top) or lowest (bottom) values. For example, when you sort a numeric field in ascending order, the "top" of the list will be the lowest numbers. When you sort a numeric field in descending order, the "top" values are the largest numbers.

1. Open **qrySalesByAnimal** in Datasheet View. The dynaset shows sales by customer and product sold.
2. Switch to Design View. Click in the **Sort** row for the **InvoiceID** field. Click the drop-down arrow and choose **(not sorted)**.
3. Click in the **Sort** row for the **Qty** field. Click the drop-down arrow and choose **Descending**.
4. Switch to Datasheet View. The largest quantities of items sold per invoice are located at the top of the list.
5. Switch to Design View.

TIP

The **Top Values** property also can be changed through the **Return** list box found on the **Design** tab in the **Query Setup** group.

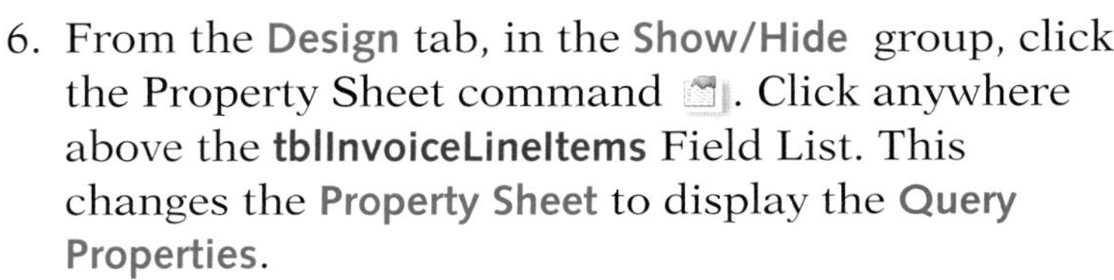

6. From the **Design** tab, in the **Show/Hide** group, click the Property Sheet command. Click anywhere above the **tblInvoiceLineItems** Field List. This changes the **Property Sheet** to display the **Query Properties**.
7. Click the **Top Values** property and the drop-down arrow. Choose **5**.

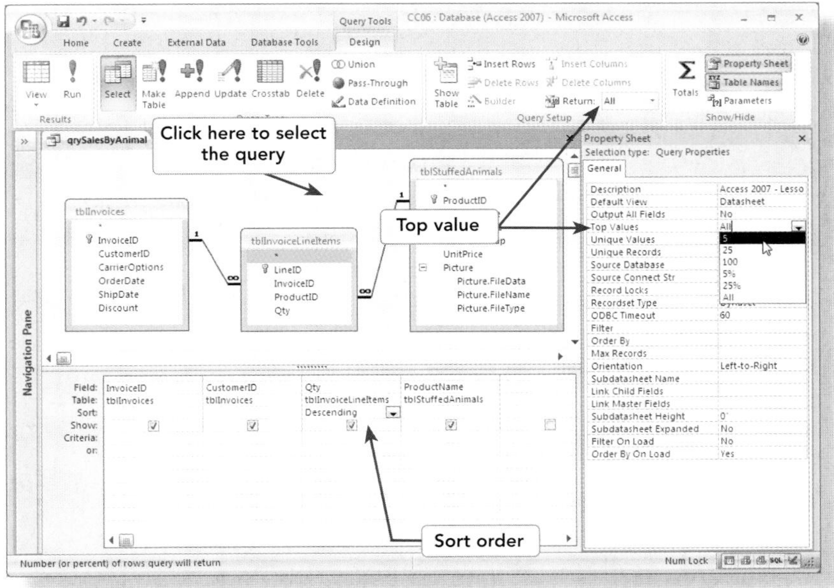

Figure 6-11
Top Values property
CC06
qrySalesByAnimal

NOTE

Remember to reset the **Top Values** property to "All." If you forget to reset the property and later prepare a report based on the query, you will print an incomplete dynaset.

8. Switch to Datasheet View. Since the field **Qty** field is sorted in descending order, the five largest quantities are shown.
9. Switch to Design View. From the **Design** tab, in the **Query Setup** group, click the Return list box (Top Value) and choose **5%**.
10. Switch to Datasheet View. The top 5% quantities of sales results in 33 records being displayed.

11. Switch to Design View, and reset the **Return** list box to **All**.
12. Close and save the query.

Exercise 6-12 CREATE A QUERY WITH A SUBDATASHEET

Just as a table can display a related table as a subdatasheet, a query can also contain a subdatasheet. A subdatasheet is created by defining a Subdatasheet Name as a query property.

1. From the **Create** tab, in the **Other** group, click the Query Design command.
2. From the **Show Table** dialog box, double-click **tblInvoices**. Click **Close**.
3. In the **tblInvoices** Field List, double-click the asterisk (*). This tells Access to use all the fields.
4. Switch to Datasheet View. All six fields have been included.

NOTE

If the Property Sheet shows "Field Properties," click again in the top pane. You may also need to resize the Property Sheet to see all values.

5. Save the query as **qryInvoices**.
6. Switch to Design View. Open the Property Sheet if it is not already visible.
7. In the Property Sheet for the query, click the property **Subdatasheet Name** and click the drop-down arrow. Choose **Table.tblInvoiceLineItems** from the list.
8. Click the **Link Child Fields** property, and key **InvoiceID**.
9. Click the **Link Master Fields** property, and key **InvoiceID**.
10. Close the Property Sheet, and switch to Datasheet View.

11. Click the Expand button for any record to see which products were ordered.
12. Collapse the subdatasheet.
13. Close the query and save the changes.

Adding Calculations to a Query

The queries you have created so far have been select queries. Select queries display the dynaset as individual records similar to the datasheet of a table. A query can also display calculations. To display a calculation in a query, you must use an aggregate function. An aggregate function is a sum, average, maximum, minimum, or count for a group of records.

A query can also have a calculated field. A *calculated field* is a field that uses an expression or formula as its data source. You can add calculated fields to queries, forms, and reports.

Exercise 6-13 USE A FORMULA IN A CALCULATED FIELD

A calculated field does not store data in a dynaset. The value of a calculated field is generated each time you run a query. Only the definition and properties of the calculated field are stored in the query object.

Since a calculated field is not part of the source dynaset, each calculated field must have a unique name. When a field does not have a name, Access assigns an alias name. The alias name for a calculated field displays as text followed by a colon. The alias displays in front of the calculation.

Calculated fields can be entered directly into the design grid or can be entered using the Expression Builder. The *Expression Builder* is an interface used to create a function, calculation, or expression.

TABLE 6-4 Parts of the Expression Builder

Part	Purpose
Expression box	White area at the top of the window that shows the formula as you build it. (Also called the preview area.)
Operator buttons	Set of buttons with common arithmetic and logical symbols below the Expression box.
Left panel	List of folders with objects available for use.
Middle panel	Contents of the folder selected in the left panel.
Right panel	Details or properties of the object selected in the middle panel.
Paste button	Command to paste a selected object, function, or expression into the expression box.

NOTE

If the Field List does not appear in the middle pane, close the Expression Builder, save the query, and re-open the Expression Builder.

1. Open **qryInvoiceLineItemCost** in Design View.
2. Click the empty **Field** row in the sixth column.
3. From the **Design** tab, in the **Query Setup** group, click the Builder command.

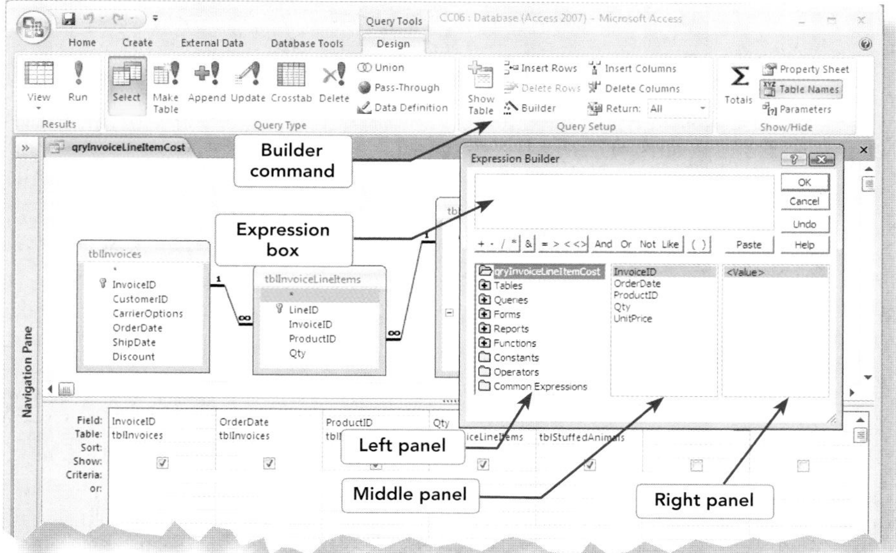

Figure 6-12
Building an expression for the query
CC06
qryInvoiceLineItemCost

4. The current query is at the top of the left panel. In the middle panel, click the field **Qty**.
5. In the right panel, double-click **[Value]**. This action pastes the value of the **Qty** field into the expression box.
6. Press [*] to add the multiply symbol to the expression box.
7. In the middle panel, double-click the field **UnitPrice**.

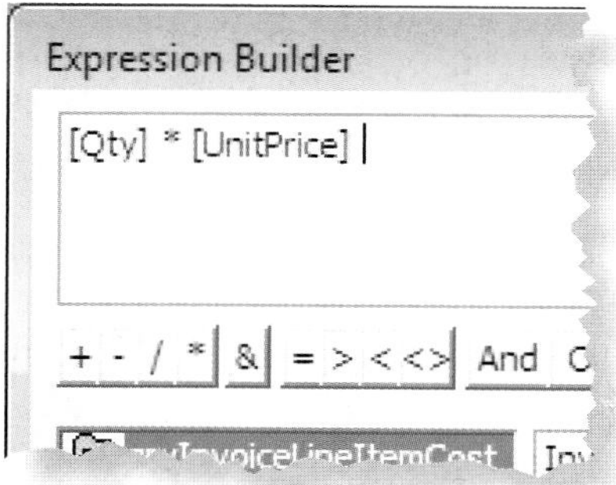

Figure 6-13
Building a formula
CC06
qryInvoiceLineItemCost

8. Click **OK** to close the **Expression Builder**.
9. Switch to Datasheet View. Notice that the last column shows the cost of each line item, or the unit price multiplied by the quantity.
10. Access has given the calculated field the alias of "Expr1." Switch to Design View.
11. Replace "Expr1" with **ItemCost**. Be certain to leave the colon after the field name.
12. From the **Design** tab, in the **Show/Hide** group, click the Property Sheet command. In the **Caption** property, key **Item Cost**.
13. In the **Format** property, click the drop-down arrow and choose **Currency**. In the **Decimal Places** property, key **2**.

REVIEW

To see the calculation more easily, you can open the Zoom window by using [Shift]+[F2].

14. Close the Property Sheet.
15. Switch to Datasheet View.
16. Save and close the query.

Exercise 6-14 USE A FUNCTION IN A CALCULATED FIELD

Calculated fields can be entered directly into the design grid or can be entered using the Expression Builder.

TIP

You can key expressions directly in the **Field** row without using the Expression Builder.

NOTE

Functions use leading and ending placeholders, << and >>. These placeholders identify the argument(s) used in the function.

1. Open **qrySalesByOrderDate** in Design View.
2. Click the empty **Field** row in the fifth column.
3. From the **Design** tab, in the **Query Setup** group, click the Builder command.
4. In the left panel, double-click **Functions** and click **Built-In Functions**.
5. In the middle panel, click **Date/Time**.
6. In the right panel, double-click **DateDiff**. This function has five parameters or values. We need to fill three of them.
7. In the expression box, click on **<<interval>>** and key **"d"**.
8. In the expression box, click on **<<date1>>**. In the left panel, click **qrySalesByOrderDate**. In the middle panel, double-click **OrderDate**.
9. In the expression box, click on **<<date2>>**. In the middle panel, double-click **ShipDate**.
10. Press Delete until you have deleted the remaining commas and placeholders. Do not delete the right parenthesis.

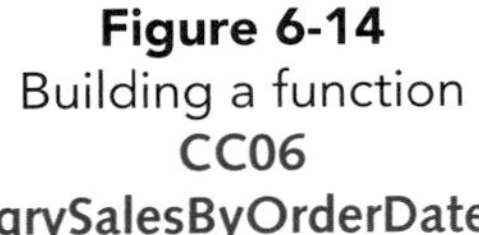

Figure 6-14
Building a function
CC06
qrySalesByOrderDate

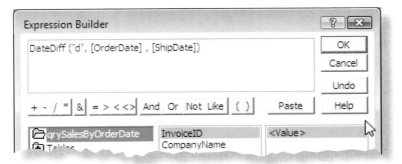

11. Click **OK**. Press [↓]. Access has added the alias "Expr1."
12. Replace the alias with **Turnover**.
13. From the **Design** tab, in the **Show/Hide** group, click the Property Sheet command. In the field **Turnover** Property Sheet, click in the **Format** property and key **#" Days"**.
14. Switch to Datasheet View. The difference between the order and shipping date is now listed in days.
15. Close and save the query.

Creating Queries with Wizards

Relationships and referential integrity prevent data duplication or unmatched relationships. However, when using data from other sources, such as an online Web site, the table you create might not follow your relationship rules. Access provides two query wizards to assist verifying the accuracy of your data. The Find Unmatched Records Query Wizard and the Find Duplicate Records Query Wizard create these special queries. Wizards can also be used to create a Crosstab query.

Exercise 6-15 USE THE SIMPLE QUERY WIZARD

When creating a query using a wizard, you must select the record source and the associated fields. The record source can be one or more related tables or queries.

1. From the **Create** tab, in the **Other** group, click the Query Wizard command.

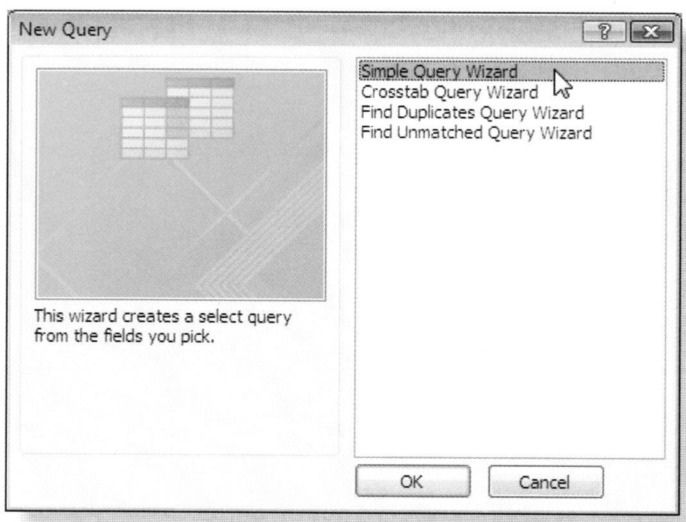

Figure 6-15
New Query Wizard collection
CC06

2. In the New Query dialog box, double-click Simple Query Wizard.
3. From the Tables/Queries list box, choose **Table: tblStuffedAnimals**.
4. In the Available Fields list, double-click **ProductName**.
5. From the Tables/Queries list box, choose **Table: tblKitAssembly**.
6. In the Available Fields list, double-click **Qty**.
7. From the Tables/Queries list box, choose **Table: tblParts**.
8. In the Available Fields list, double-click **Description** and **PCost**.
9. Click Next. The default type of select query is Detail. Click Next.
10. Delete the suggested title and key qryProductParts.
11. Click Finish. This dynaset lists the parts, quantity, and cost to make each kit.
12. Switch to Design View. Resize and move each Field List.

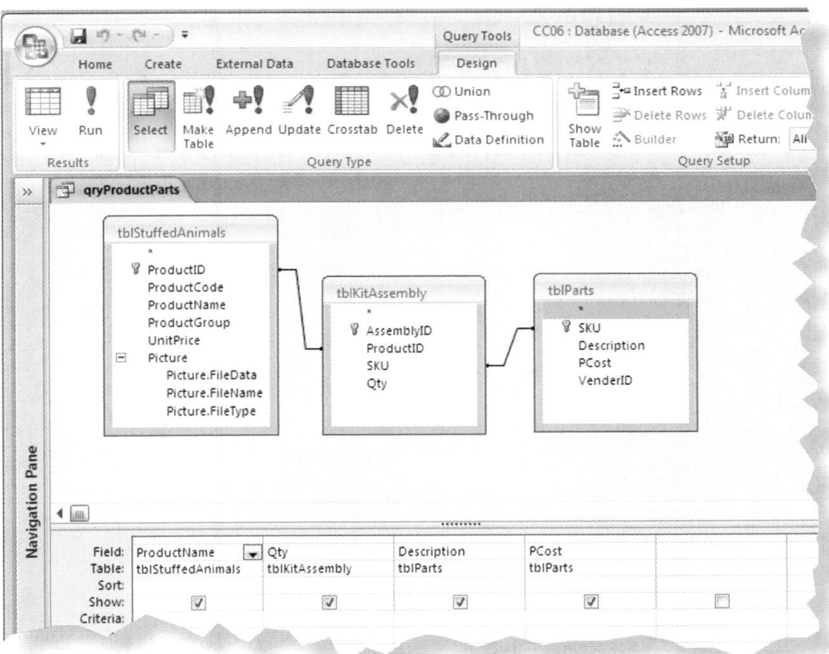

Figure 6-16
Query created by the Simple Query Wizard
CC06
qryProductParts

13. Close and save the query.

Exercise 6-16 USE THE CROSSTAB QUERY WIZARD

A Crosstab query displays information similar to a spreadsheet. The Total row calculates the sum, average, count, or other totals. The Crosstab row defines the fields used for the data, column headings, and row headings. Data are grouped by two fields, one listed on the left and the other listed across the top.

1. From the **Create** tab, in the **Other** group, click the Query Wizard command.

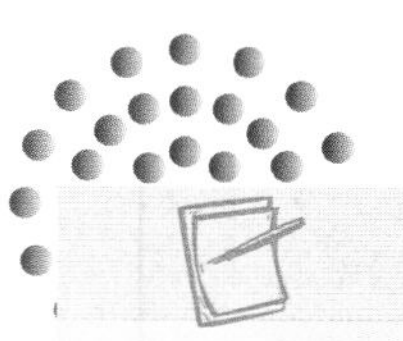

NOTE

Crosstab queries require that you have data suitable for summarizing. Many tables do not have fields appropriate to display as crosstabs.

2. In the **New Query** dialog box, double-click **Crosstab Query Wizard**.
3. In the **View** control, click **Queries**. From the list, select **Query: qryEmployeeLeave**. Click **Next**.
4. From the **Available Fields**, double-click **LastName** and **FirstName**. Click **Next**.
5. With **LeaveCategory** selected as the column heading, click **Next**.
6. With **LeaveDate** selected as the data to be shown, and **Count** as the **Function**, deselect the checkbox **Yes, include row sums**. Click **Next**.
7. Accept the suggested title, and click **Finish**.

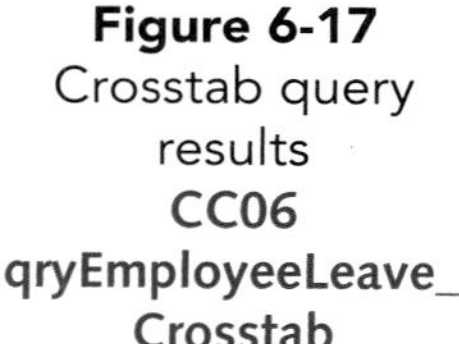

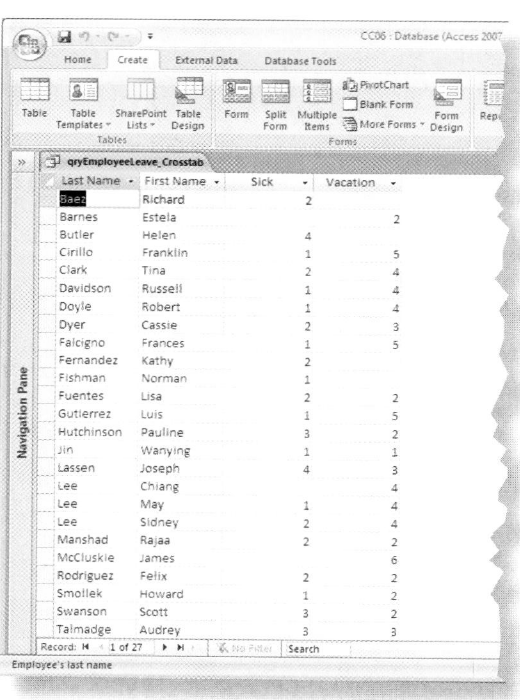

Last Name	First Name	Sick	Vacation
Baez	Richard	2	
Barnes	Estela		2
Butler	Helen	4	
Cirillo	Franklin	1	5
Clark	Tina	2	4
Davidson	Russell	1	4
Doyle	Robert	1	4
Dyer	Cassie	2	3
Falcigno	Frances	1	5
Fernandez	Kathy	2	
Fishman	Norman	1	
Fuentes	Lisa	2	2
Gutierrez	Luis	1	5
Hutchinson	Pauline	3	2
Jin	Wanying	1	1
Lassen	Joseph	4	3
Lee	Chiang		4
Lee	May	1	4
Lee	Sidney	2	4
Manshad	Rajaa	2	2
McCluskie	James		6
Rodriguez	Felix	2	2
Smollek	Howard	1	2
Swanson	Scott	3	2
Talmadge	Audrey	3	3

Figure 6-17
Crosstab query results
CC06
qryEmployeeLeave_ Crosstab

8. Switch to Design View. Two new rows were added to the design grid by the wizard: **Total** and **Crosstab**.
9. Close and save the query.

Exercise 6-17 USE THE FIND DUPLICATES QUERY WIZARD

The Find Duplicates Query Wizard analyzes a table for duplicate data. If duplicates are identified, you then decide what action to take, including deleting or editing the records. Because the Carolina Critters database has been normalized, you must first add a duplicate entry error to test the Find Duplicates Query that you will create.

1. Open **tblCustomers**. Copy the contents of the **Company Name** field for Customer "9."
2. Locate the record for the customer named "Magna Mart, Inc." Paste over "Magna Mart, Inc." Both records now have the same company name (a deliberate error). Close the table.
3. From the **Create** tab, in the **Other** group, click the Query Wizard command.
4. In the **New Query** dialog box, double-click **Find Duplicates Query Wizard**.
5. From the list of table, select **Tables: tblCustomers**. Click **Next**.
6. From the **Available fields** list, double-click **CompanyName**. Click **Next**.

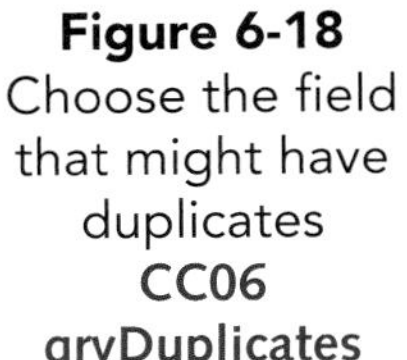

Figure 6-18
Choose the field that might have duplicates
CC06
qryDuplicates

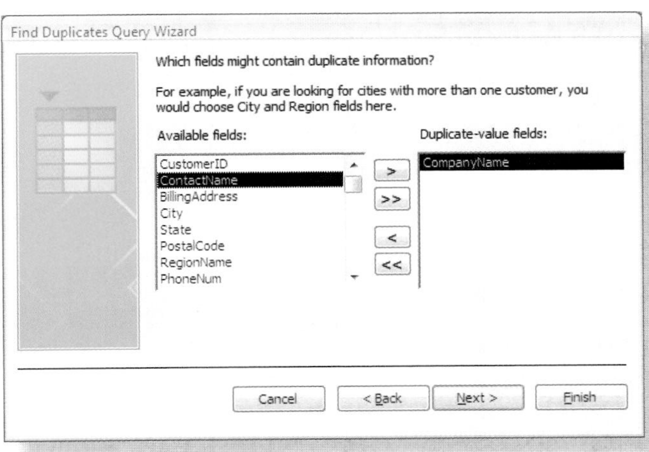

7. Click the Add All button to show all fields in the resulting dynaset. Click **Next**.
8. Delete the suggested title, key **qryDuplicates**, and click **Finish**. The query shows the duplicate records. You could delete one now if that were the appropriate thing to do; however, do not delete anything.
9. For the **Customer ID** # 9, in the **Company Name** field, key **Magna Mart, Inc.**

10. From the **Home** tab, in the **Records** group, click the Refresh All command. The query runs again, but this time, there are no duplicates.
11. Close the query.

Exercise 6-18 USE THE FIND UNMATCHED QUERY WIZARD

The Find Unmatched Query Wizard finds unmatched, or orphaned, records. Since your database does not have any unrelated data, you must first add a deliberate error (an unmatched record) to test the Find Unmatched Records Query that you will create.

1. Open **tblReps**, and add a new record for **Employee ID** **999**. There is, of course, no employee with that ID. It is a deliberate error. Close the table.
2. From the **Create** tab, in the **Other** group, click the Query Wizard command.
3. In the **New Query** dialog box, double-click **Find Unmatched Query Wizard**.
4. The first dialog box asks you to choose a table that might have unmatched records. You created the error in **tblReps**, so choose it. Click **Next**.
5. The next dialog box asks you to choose the table that should have the matching records. Choose **tblEmployees**, and click **Next**.

6. In both Field Lists, choose the common field **EmployeeID**. Click the Match button.

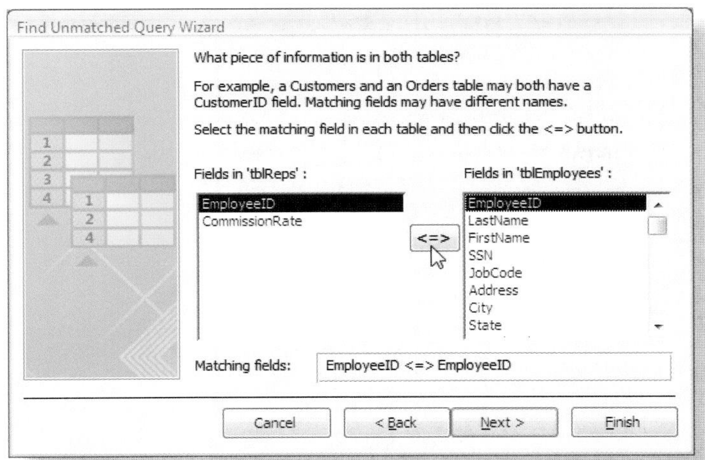

Figure 6-19
Match the common field
CC06
qryNoEmp

7. Click **Next**. Click the Add All button to show all three fields in the query results. Click **Next**.
8. Delete the suggested title, key **qryNoEmp**, and click **Finish**. The unmatched record you created is listed. The query shows you the problem record. Delete the record for **Employee ID** "999".
9. Close the query.

Applying PivotChart / PivotTable Views

PivotTables and PivotCharts are methods of viewing complex information in summarized formats. PivotTables and PivotCharts can automatically sort, count, and total data in a summarized format. You can change the summary's structure by dragging and dropping fields using a graphical interface.

You use PivotTables and PivotCharts to analyze related totals or to compare related information from a large data set. In a PivotTable or PivotChart, each column or field in your source data becomes a PivotTable field that summarizes multiple rows of information. When you rearrange the fields in a PivotTable, the changes reflect as changes to columns in the related PivotChart. You can print PivotTables and PivotCharts similar to other objects.

Exercise 6-19 USE PIVOTTABLE VIEW

A *PivotTable* is an interactive table that combines and compares data in a summarized view. You create a PivotTable by using a graphical interface to drag and drop fields into the appropriate column, row, and data locations.

1. Open **qryProductParts** in Design View.
2. From the **Design** tab, in the **Results** group, click the down arrow and choose PivotTable View .

3. From the PivotTable Field List, select **ProductName**. Click the drop-down arrow in the lower right corner. It contains a list of all drop zones in the chart. Choose **Row Area**. Click **Add to**.

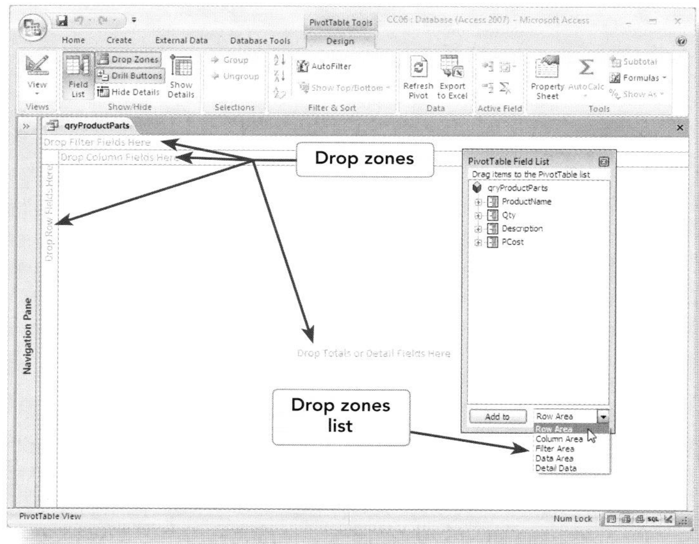

Figure 6-20 Adding a field to a PivotTable CC06 qryProductParts

4. Drag the **Description** field from the **PivotTable** Field List into the **Drop Totals or Detail Fields Here** zone of the PivotTable.

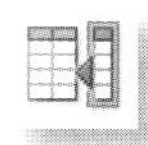

5. From the **Design** tab, in the **Show/Hide** group, click the Field List command.

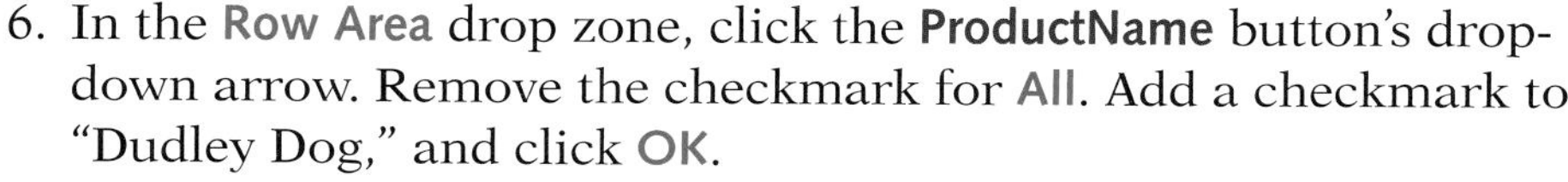

6. In the **Row Area** drop zone, click the **ProductName** button's drop-down arrow. Remove the checkmark for **All**. Add a checkmark to "Dudley Dog," and click **OK**.

7. Click the **ProductName** button's drop-down arrow. Add the checkmark for **All**, and click **OK**.

8. Close and save the query.

Exercise 6-20 USE PIVOTCHART VIEW

A PivotChart View displays the same information as a Crosstab query, including counts and sums of numeric fields. A *PivotChart View* is an interactive graphical representation of data displayed in a PivotTable.

A PivotChart displays field values which can be switched or pivoted to display different views of the same data. You set different levels of detail by dragging fields and items or by showing and hiding items in the field drop-down lists.

1. From the **Create** tab, in the **Other** group, click the Query Design command.
2. Double-click **tblStuffedAnimals** to add it to the grid, and then close the **Show Table** dialog box.
3. Size the Field List.
4. Double-click **UnitPrice**, **ProductGroup**, and **ProductID** to add them to the design grid.
5. Save the query as **qryProductGroupsD&F**.

6. From the **Design** tab, in the **Results** group, click the down arrow and choose PivotChart View.
7. Select **UnitPrice** from the Chart Field List. Click the drop-down arrow in the lower right corner. It contains a list of all drop zones in the chart. Choose **Data Area**.
8. Click **Add to**. An aggregate Sum function is automatically created.

NOTE

The Chart Field List displays a field name in a bold font whenever the field is used in the chart.

TIP

When dragging a field to a drop zone, make sure that the drop zone "lights up" before you release the field.

9. Drag the **ProductID** from the Chart Field List into the **Drop Category Fields Here** zone of the PivotChart. The Product IDs are listed at the bottom of the chart.
10. Drag the **ProductGroup** from the **Chart Field List** into the **Drop Series Fields Here** section of the PivotChart. Each product group has a different color.
11. From the **Design** tab, in the **Show/Hide** group, click the Field List command to remove the Field List.
12. Drag the **ProductGroup** field button on top of the **ProductID** field button and slightly to the left. Both fields are now being used for the X-axis of the chart.

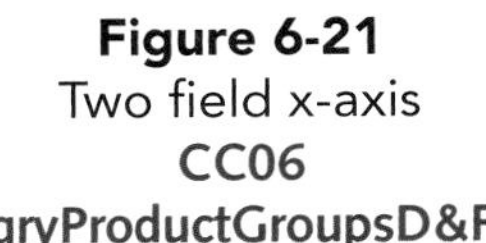

Figure 6-21
Two field x-axis
CC06
qryProductGroupsD&F

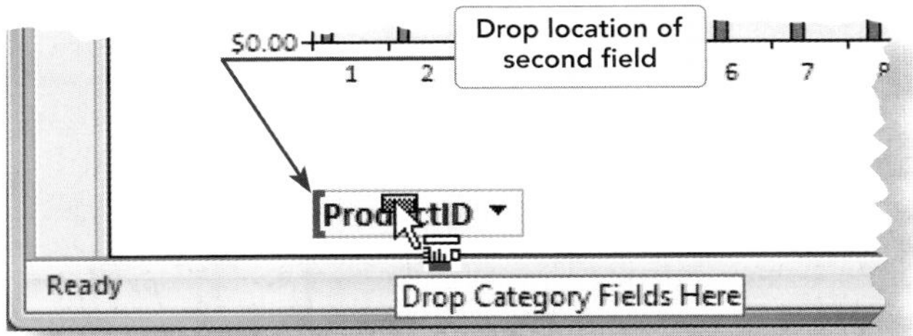

13. Click the drop-down arrow for **ProductGroup**. Deselect C, E, and T.

Figure 6-22
Product Groups D and F
CC06
qryProductGroupsD&F

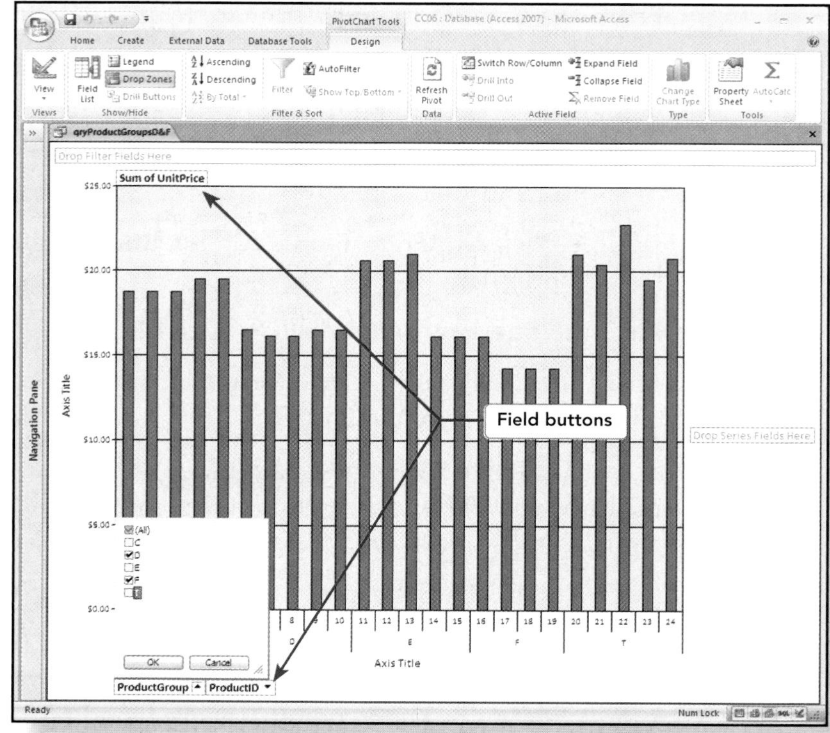

NOTE

When the drop-down arrow of a Field button turns blue, it means that not all choices are selected.

14. Click **OK**. Only the Product IDs for product groups D and F are now visible.

15. Right-click the **Axis Title** at the bottom of the chart. Choose **Properties**. Click the **Format** tab. Key **Product ID / Product Group** as the new **Caption**.

16. Click the **Axis Title** to the left of the chart. Clicking on a new object automatically switches the Property Sheet to that new object. Key **List Price** as the new **Caption**. Close the Properties Sheet.

17. From the **Design** tab, in the **Show/Hide** group, click the Drop Zones command to remove the unused drop zones.

18. Switch to Datasheet View. Notice that making changes to the query's PivotChart has no effect on the dynaset. The PivotChart View is just another way of viewing the data.

19. Save and close the query.

20. Compact and close the database.

Lesson 6 Summary

- Only a single filter can be saved per table, but multiple queries can be associated to a single table.
- A select query, the most common type of query, locates data from one or more tables and displays the results as a datasheet.
- The Query Design window has an upper and lower pane. The upper pane is the Field List pane in which you choose the data source from one or more Field Lists. The lower pane is the design grid in which you specify criteria.
- A dynaset is a dynamic recordset that automatically reflects changes to its underlying data source.
- In the design grid of a query, the check box in the **Show** row indicates that the field will display in the Datasheet View.
- When two or more tables are used in a query, the tables must be linked through a common field.
- In a query, more than one condition can be placed on multiple fields.
- An operator is a word or symbol that indicates a specific arithmetic or logical relationship between the elements of an expression.
- Operators can include arithmetic operators, comparison operators, logical operators, concatenation operators, and special operators.
- A function is a procedure used in an expression.
- An argument is a reference in a function assigned as a single variable.
- Criterion using text values include leading and closing quotation marks. Criterion using date values include leading and closing pound signs (#). Numbers and expressions do not require leading or closing symbols.
- When using a wildcard in the **Criteria** row of a query, the "Like" operator compares the criterion condition to each record.
- Only the keyword "Like" is automatically added to a criterion. All other keywords must be specified.
- Criterion expressions can be viewed in the Zoom box. You can open the Zoom box by pressing Shift+F2.
- An AND criterion exists when two conditions must occur simultaneously for the statement to be true.
- An OR criterion exists when one of two conditions must occur for the statement to be true.
- When using the Top Values property, Access displays records based upon the defined sort order.
- The Top Values property displays either a static number of records (such as the top five) or a percentage of all records in the dynaset (such as the top 5%).
- A calculated field is a field that uses an expression or formula as its data source.
- When a field does not have a name, Access assigns an alias name. The alias name for a calculated field displays as text followed by a colon.

- Calculated fields can be entered directly into the design grid or can be entered using the Expression Builder. The Expression Builder is an interface used to create a function, calculation, or expression.
- A Crosstab query displays information similar to a spreadsheet. Crosstab queries require that you have data suitable for summarizing. Many tables do not have fields appropriate to display as a crosstab.
- The Find Duplicates Query Wizard analyzes a table for duplicate data.
- The Find Unmatched Query Wizard finds unmatched, or orphaned, records.
- A PivotTable is an interactive table that combines and compares data in a summarized view.
- A PivotChart is an interactive graphical representation of data displayed in a PivotTable.

LESSON 6		Command Summary	
Feature	**Button**	**Menu**	**Keyboard**
	<=>	Match	
		Home, Records, Refresh All	
	>>	Add All	
		Create, Other, Query Wizard	
		Design, Query Setup, Builder	
		Create, Other, Query Design	
Rows, Delete		Design, Query Setup, Delete Rows	
Query, View		Design, Results, View	
Query, Run	!	Design, Results, Run	
Query Design, View		Create, Other, Query Design	
Query, Properties, View		Design, Show/Hide, Properties Sheet	

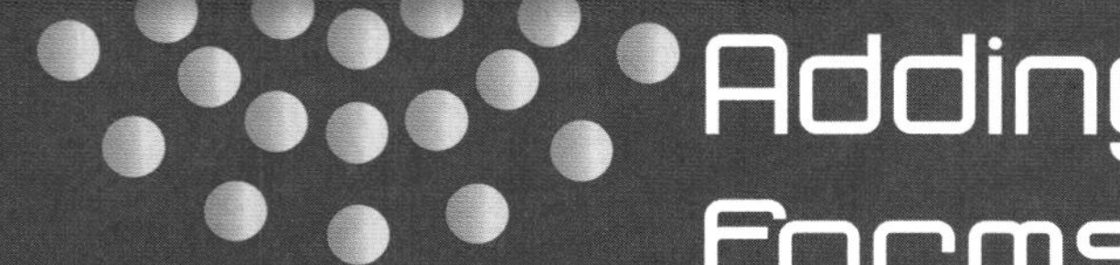

Lesson 7

Adding and Modifying Forms

OBJECTIVES

After completing this lesson, you will be able to:

1. Generate forms quickly.
2. Modify controls in Layout View.
3. Work with form sections.
4. Modify controls in Design View.
5. Add calculated controls to a form.
6. Print/Save forms.

MCAS OBJECTIVES

In this lesson:

AC07 70-605 2.5.2
AC07 70-605 2.5.3
AC07 70-605 2.5.4
AC07 70-605 2.5.7
AC07 70-605 2.5.8
AC07 70-605 2.7.1
AC07 70-605 2.7.2
AC07 70-605 2.7.3
AC07 70-605 2.7.4
AC07 70-605 2.7.5
AC07 70-605 2.7.7
AC07 70-605 5.5
AC07 70-605 5.6

Estimated Time: 2 hours

Although you can enter, edit, and delete data directly in the datasheet of a query or table, database operators usually use forms to perform these activities. When you use the datasheet view of a table or a query, the dynaset can display only in columns and rows. When each record of the dynaset contains numerous fields, the entire record cannot be seen at once.

The limitations of a datasheet emphasize the need for forms. A form can be designed to view an entire record on a single screen. Other advantages of forms include the following:

- You can arrange data in an attractive format that may include special fonts, colors, shading, and images.
- You can design a form to match a paper source document.
- You can include calculations, functions, and totals in the form.
- You can display data from more than one table.

Generating Forms Quickly

The quickest way to create a form is to use the Form Wizard or to use a form tool. When using the Form Wizard, select the source dynaset(s), fields, layout, and style. The fields may come from multiple tables or queries, as long as a relationship exists between the recordsets.

When using either of the first three Form tools, all fields from the source dynaset are automatically placed on the form. You can use the new form immediately, or you can modify the form in Layout View or Design View. Database designers often use either the Form Wizard or a Form tool to create a beginning form that they can later modify and enhance.

Exercise 7-1 CREATE A FORM WITH A WIZARD

The Form Wizard lets you select fields, a layout, and a style. The layout determines whether the records are arranged in columns, rows, or a hybrid of columns and rows. The style automatically determines colors, backgrounds, and fonts used for the form.

NOTE

A form is created from a recordset and does not have to include all the fields from the query or table.

1. Locate and open the **Lesson 07** folder.
2. Make a copy of **CC07**, and rename it *[your initials]*-CC07.
3. Open and enable content for ***[your initials]*-CC07**.
4. From the **Create** tab, in the **Forms** group, click **More Forms** and choose the Form Wizard command.

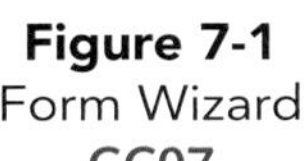

Figure 7-1
Form Wizard
CC07

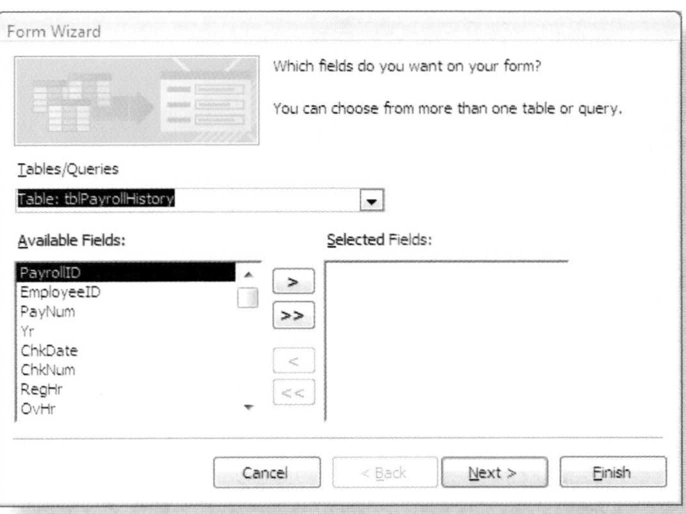

5. In the **Tables/Queries** drop-down box, choose **Table: tblPayrollHistory**.
6. The dialog box asks which fields to use in the form. Click the Add All button to choose all fields.

7. Click **PayrollID** in the **Selected Field** list. Click the Remove One button to move it back to the list on the left.
8. Click **Next**. The dialog box asks you to choose a layout. Click each layout to see a preview. Select **Tabular**.

9. Click **Next**. The next dialog box lists several styles. Click each style to see a preview. Select **Apex**.
10. Click **Next**. The dialog box asks for a title for the form. This title is used as both a title and the name of the form. Key **frmPayrollHistory**.
11. Select **Open the form to view or enter information**, and then click **Finish**.
12. Close the form.

Exercise 7-2 GENERATE A FORM WITH ONE CLICK

When using the Forms tool, you can create a Simple form, Split, or Multiple Items form by selecting the appropriate command button located in the **Forms** group. Each command uses all the fields in the source recordset to create a pre-determined form.

The Simple Form tool creates a form for entering one record at a time. The Split Form tool creates a form that shows a datasheet in the upper section and a form in the lower section. The Multiple Items tool creates a form that shows multiple items in a datasheet, with one record per row.

1. In the Navigation pane, select **tblPayrollHistory**.

2. From the **Create** tab, in the **Forms** group, click the Form command. The new form is now in Layout View and shows only one record.

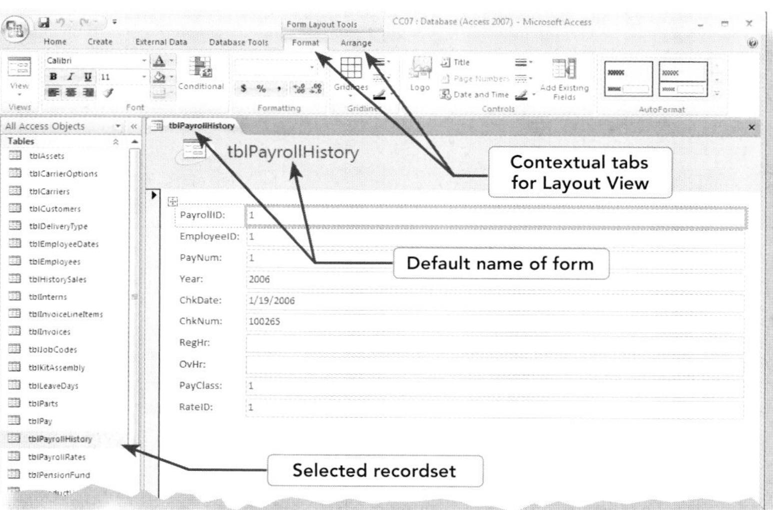

Figure 7-2
New form in Layout View
CC07
frmPayrollHistoryOne

REVIEW

When creating a new form, you should use the Leszynski Naming Convention. This means forms are preceded by the prefix "frm," and the first letter of main words are capitalized with no spaces between words.

3. Right-click the new form's document tab, and choose **Save**. The default name is the name of the recordset used to create the form.
4. In the **Save As** dialog box, key **frmPayHistoryOne** and click **OK**.
5. In the Navigation pane, select **tblPayrollHistory** again.

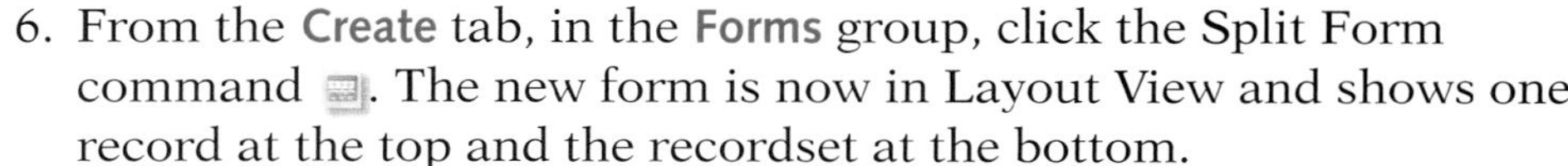

6. From the **Create** tab, in the **Forms** group, click the Split Form command. The new form is now in Layout View and shows one record at the top and the recordset at the bottom.

7. From the Quick Access toolbar, click the Save button to save the new form.
8. In the **Save As** dialog box, key **frmPayHistorySplit** and click **OK**.
9. In the Navigation Pane, select **tblPayrollHistory** again.

10. From the **Create** tab, in the **Forms** group, click the Multiple Items command. The new form is now in Layout View and shows all records.
11. Press Ctrl+S to save the new form.
12. In the **Save As** dialog box, key **frmPayHistoryList** and click **OK**.
13. In the Navigation Pane, select **tblPayrollHistory** again.

14. From the **Create** tab, in the **Forms** group, click **More Forms** and choose the Datasheet command. The new form is now in Datasheet View and shows all records.
15. Press Ctrl+S to save the new form.
16. In the **Save As** dialog box, key **frmPayHistoryData** and click **OK**.
17. Right-click any document tab and choose **Close All**.

Modifying Controls in Layout View

A *control* is a database object that displays data, performs actions, and lets you view and work with information that enhances the user interface, such as labels and images. Controls can be bound, unbound, or calculated.

A *bound control* is a control whose source of data is a field in a table or query. You use bound controls to display values from the dynaset. The values can be text, dates, numbers, Yes/No values, pictures, or graphs. An *unbound control* is a control without a source of data. You use unbound controls to display lines, rectangles, or pictures. A *calculated control* is a control whose source of data is an expression, rather than a field.

Exercise 7-3 MODIFY A CONTROL LAYOUT

A control layout assists you to horizontally and vertically align the controls within a form. A control layout is similar to a table in which each cell is a control. In addition to creating a control layout, you can switch a control layout between tabular and stacked, split one control layout into two, and change the padding or margins of the controls.

Control padding is the space between the gridline of the form and the control. A *control margin* is the specified location of information inside a control.

1. From the Navigation Pane, right-click **frmCustomers** and choose **Layout View**. The layout of the controls is known as Stacked.

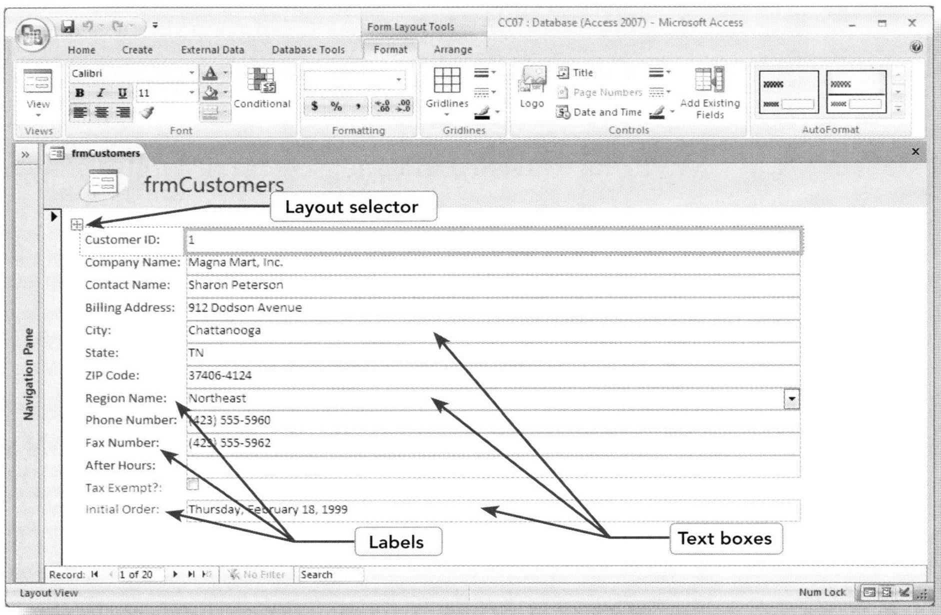

Figure 7-3
Form in Layout View
CC07
frmCustomers

2. Click the Layout Selector command. This selects the entire control layout.

3. From the **Arrange** tab, in the **Control Layout** group, click **Control Padding** and choose the Narrow command. Space has been added between all controls.

4. From the **Arrange** tab, in the **Control Layout** group, click **Control Margins** and choose the Medium command. Space has been added between the content of the controls and the outside edge of the controls.

Exercise 7-4 RESIZE AND MOVE CONTROL LAYOUTS

Layout View is an efficient means to resize and move controls within a form. While viewing the source data on the form, you can rearrange the controls and adjust their sizes to improve the form's appearance and functionality.

1. Click the first text box (contains 1). An orange box indicates the selected control.

NOTE

An attached label shows the field's caption property by default.

2. Place your mouse pointer on the right edge of the selected text box. When you see the resize pointer, drag it to the left to make the controls smaller, but make sure you still can see all the data.

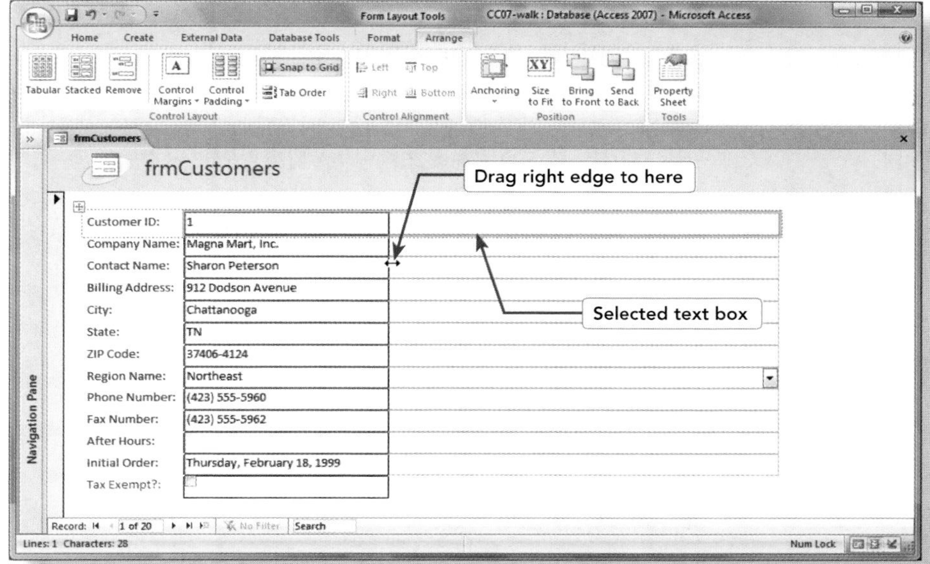

Figure 7-4
Resize a text box in Form Layout View
CC07
frmCustomers

3. Click the **Billing Address** text box.
4. While pressing Shift, click the text boxes for **City**, **State**, and **Zip Code**. This action selects the four controls.
5. From the **Arrange** tab, in the **Control Layout** group, click the Stacked command. The four controls have created their own control layout.
6. Drag the new control layout so that it is located to the right of the other control layout and the top margins are aligned.

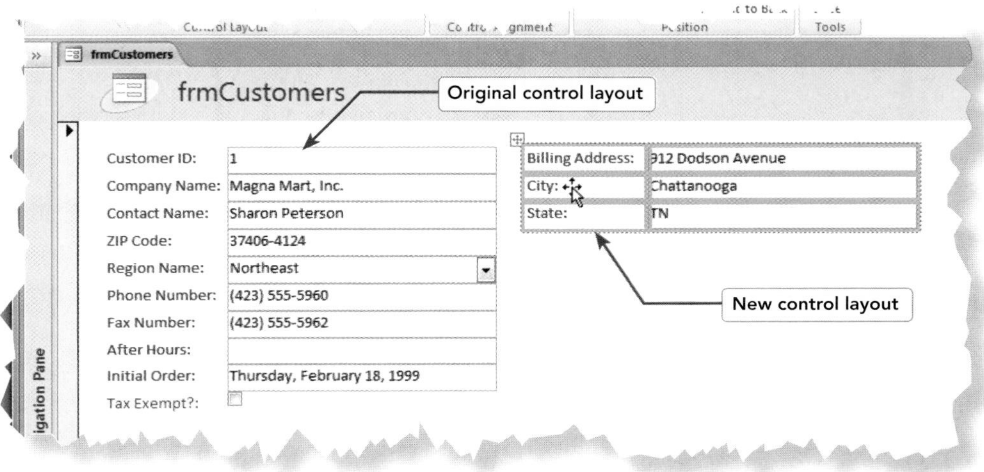

FIGURE 7-5
Moving a control layout
CC07
frmCustomers

7. Click the **Phone Number** text box.
8. Press Shift and click the text box for **Fax Number**.
9. From the **Arrange** tab, in the **Control Layout** group, click the Stacked command.

10. Align the newest control layout under the **Zip Code** control. Leave about 1/4 inch of space between the two control layouts.
11. Click the **After Hours** text box.
12. While pressing Shift, click the **Initial Order** text box and **Tax Exempt?** check box.
13. From the **Arrange** tab, in the **Control Layout** group, click the Stacked command.
14. Drag the newest control layout down about 1/4 inch below **Region Name**.
15. Save the form.

Exercise 7-5 ALIGN CONTROL LAYOUTS

When aligning selected controls, you change where the controls appear on the form. Selecting an alignment of "left" moves all controls so that the left edge of each control is aligned with the left edge of the control farthest to the left. Selecting "top" moves all controls so that the top edge of each control aligns with the top edge of the highest control. Aligning a control is different than aligning the text within a control. Aligning the text within a control does not change the placement of the control on the form, only the contents of the control.

Table 7-1 Alignment Options

Choose	To Do This
Left	Vertically align the left edges of the controls with the control that is the farthest to the left.
Right	Vertically align the right edges of the controls with the control that is the farthest to the right.
Top	Horizontally align the top edges of the controls with the control that is the highest.
Bottom	Horizontally align the bottom edges of the controls with the control that is the lowest.
To Grid	Align the uppermost corner of the selected control with the design grid.

1. Click the **Customer ID** text box. Click the layout selector for that control layout.
2. While pressing Shift, click the **Billing Address** text box. Now the layout selector is visible for the second control layout. While pressing Shift, click the layout selector for the second control layout. Both control layouts should now be selected.

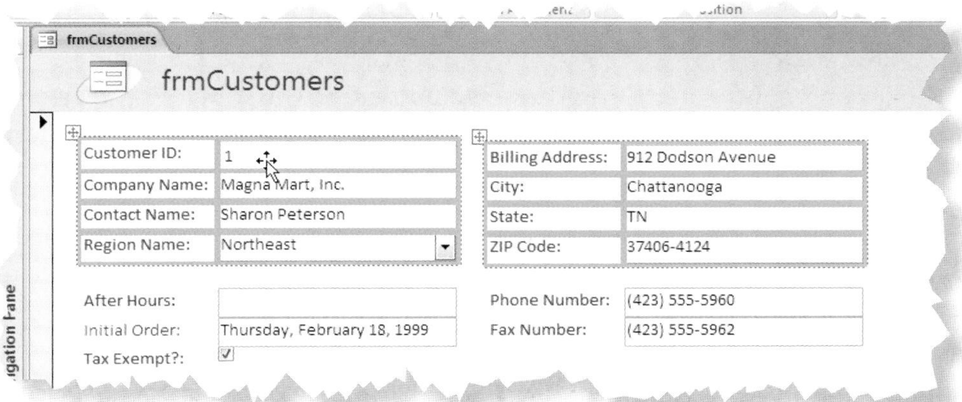

Figure 7-6
Aligning two control layouts
CC07
frmCustomers

3. From the **Arrange** tab, in the **Control Alignment** group, click the Top command.
4. While pressing Shift, click the **Billing Address** layout selector. This action removes that control layout from the selection.
5. While pressing Shift, click the **After Hours** text box. Now that the layout selector is visible for the second control layout, click it. Both control layouts should now be selected.
6. From the **Arrange** tab, in the **Control Alignment** group, click the Left command.
7. Click the **Billing Address** text box. Click the layout selector for this control layout.
8. While pressing Shift, click the **Phone Number** text box. Now that the layout selector is visible for the second control layout, click it. Both control layouts should now be selected.
9. From the **Arrange** tab, in the **Control Alignment** group, click the Left command.
10. Save the form.

Exercise 7-6 REMOVE AND ADD CONTROLS TO A CONTROL LAYOUT

A single form can have multiple control layouts. For example, you might use a tabular layout to create a row of data for each record, and then one or more stacked layouts underneath that contain more data from the same record.

In tabular control layouts, controls are arranged in rows and columns like a spreadsheet, with labels across the top. Tabular layouts always span two sections of a form; whichever section the controls are in, the labels are in the section above it.

In stacked layouts, controls are arranged vertically, like you might see on a paper form, with a label to the left of each control. Stacked layouts are always contained within a single form section.

1. Click the **After Hours** text box. Make certain that you do not click the control layout selector.
2. Drag the selected text box just below the **Fax Number** control. An insertion bar will appear to let you know where the control will be added.

Figure 7-7
Move a control to another control layout
CC07
frmCustomers

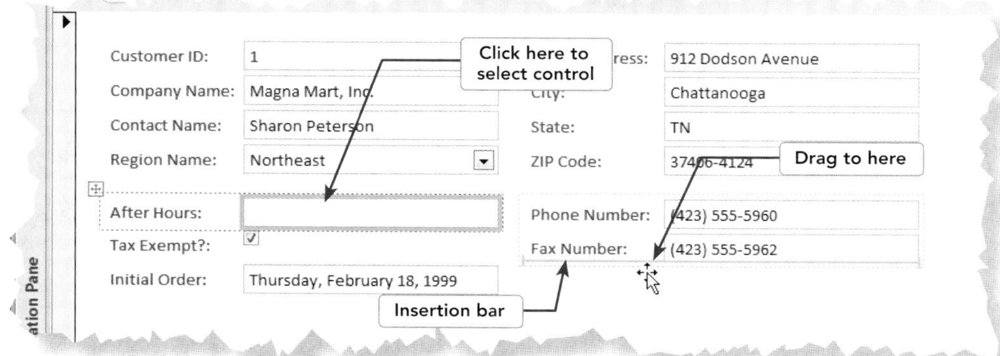

3. Select the layout selectors for the two bottom control layouts, and align them Top.
4. Click the **After Hours** text box, and press Delete. The field has been removed from the form.
5. From the **Format** tab, in the **Controls** group, click the Add Existing Fields command.

6. You can resize the Field List by dragging its left edge.
7. From the Field List, click **NightNum**. Drag **NightNum** just below the **Fax Number** control.

Figure 7-8
Use the Field List to add a field
CC07
frmCustomers

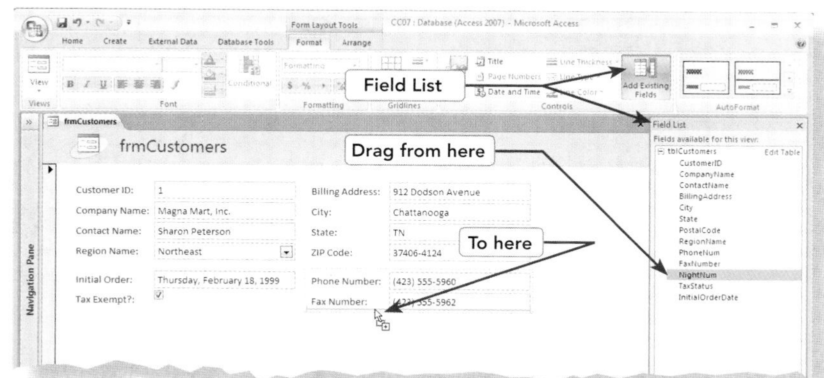

8. From the **Format** tab, in the **Controls** group, click the Add Existing Fields command to close the Field List.
9. From the **Format** tab, in the **Controls** group, click the Date and Time command.

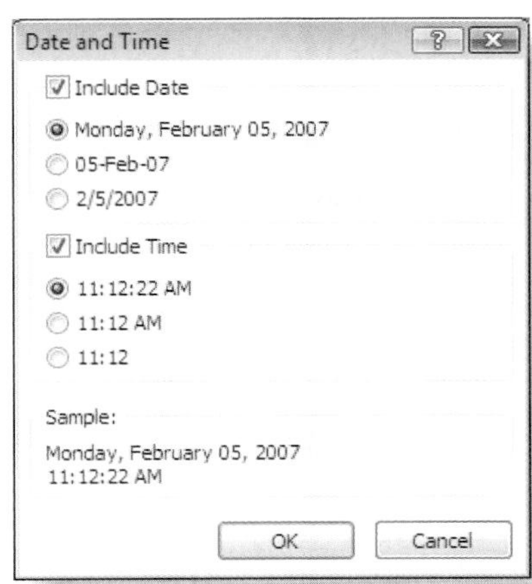

Figure 7-9 Adding a Date and Time control CC07 frmCustomers

10. Click **OK**.
11. Click the **Billing Address** text box. While pressing Shift, click the Date and Time text boxes that you just added to the form.
12. From the **Arrange** tab, in the **Control Alignment** group, click the Left command.
13. Save the form.

Exercise 7-7 SET TAB ORDER

Tab order is a form setting that determines the movement of the insertion point through a form. The tab order determines where the insertion point goes when you press Tab in Form View. The usual order is left-to-right, top-to-bottom. When you move controls in Design View, the tab order might be changed and might not be what you expect.

1. From the **Format** tab, in the **Views** group, click the **View** command to switch to Form View.
2. Press Tab to determine how the insertion point moves through the form.
3. Switch to Layout View.

4. From the **Arrange** tab, in the **Control Layout** group, click the Tab Order command.
5. Click **Auto Order**. Click and drag the field selectors for **PhoneNum** through **NightNum**. Drag the three fields above **InitialOrderDate**.

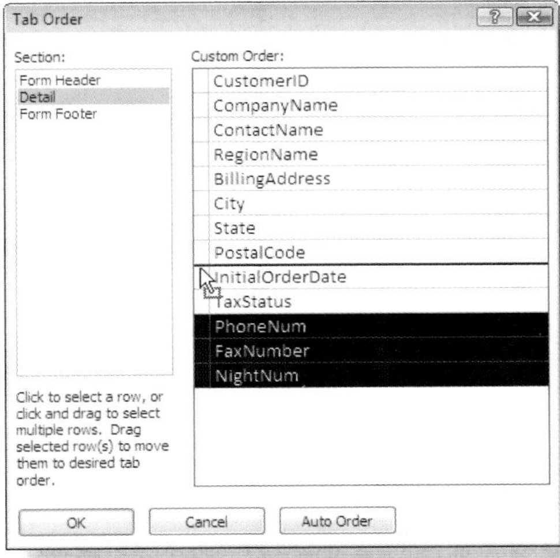

Figure 7-10 Tab Order dialog box CC07 frmCustomers

6. Click **OK**.
7. Switch to Form View.
8. Press Tab to move from text box to text box. Labels are not included in the Tab Order.
9. Save the form, and switch to Layout View.

Exercise 7-8 FORMAT A FORM IN LAYOUT VIEW

You can easily refine the placement and size of controls through Layout View. Layout View allows you to modify the properties of controls by viewing the source data in each control. In Layout View, you can navigate through the dynaset to determine the best layout for the controls. In Layout View, you can apply an AutoFormat. *AutoFormat* is a tool that applies a predefined format to a form or report.

1. From the **Format** tab, in the **Controls** group, click the Title command.
2. Key **Customer Information**. Press Enter.

3. From the **Arrange** tab, in the **Position** group, click the Size to Fit command. This tool only works on labels.
4. From the **Format** tab, in the **Font** group, click the Font Color command and choose **Automatic**.
5. Click in the blank area below all the controls.

6. From the **Format** tab, in the **Font** group, click the Fill/Back Color command.
7. From the **Access Theme Colors** section, choose **Access Theme 3** (third column, second row).

Figure 7-11
Pick a color
CC07
frmCustomers

8. Click to the right of the **Date** control.
9. From the **Format** tab, in the **Font** group, click the Fill/Back Color command.
10. From the **Access Theme Colors** section, choose **Dark Header Background** (seventh column, first row).
11. Save the form. It's a good idea to always save before using the AutoFormat command.

12. From the **Format** tab, in the **AutoFormat** group, click the More arrow.
13. Click on **Trek** (second column, fifth row). Each AutoFormat has different sized header graphics, so controls usually need to be moved.
14. Close the form without saving the changes.

Working with Form Sections

A basic form contains controls only in a single section. Advanced forms use multiple sections. Some sections display on every screen or on every printed page. Other sections display only at specific times. The five form sections are as follows:

- **Detail** section is part of a form or report that displays data once for every row in the record source. This section makes up the main body of the form or report.
- **Form Header** section is a section of a form that displays once at the beginning of a form. This section often is used to display objects that would appear on a cover page, such as a logo, title, or date.
- **Form Footer** section is a section of a form that appears once at the end of a form. This section often is used to display summary information such as totals.
- **Page Header** section is a section of a form that displays at the top of each printed page. This section often is used to display title information or page numbers to be repeated on each page.
- **Page Footer** section is a section of a form that displays at the bottom of each printed page. This section often is used to display title information or page numbers to be repeated on each page.

The **Page Header** and **Page Footer** sections can only be seen in Print Preview or when the form is printed. The sections that initially appear in a form depend on the type of form originally created.

Exercise 7-9 OPEN AND SIZE FORM SECTIONS

When you scroll through a form, the **Form Header** always displays at the top of the screen. The **Form Footer** always appears at the bottom of the screen.

1. From the Navigation Pane, right-click **frmCustomers** and choose **Design View**. This form has two sections opened, **Form Header** and **Detail**.
2. Place the mouse pointer on the top of the **Form Footer** section bars. When the pointer changes to a two-headed arrow, click and drag up to the 3-inch mark on the vertical ruler.
3. Place the mouse pointer on the bottom of the **Form Footer** section bars. When the pointer changes to a two-headed arrow, click and drag down 1/2 inch.

Figure 7-12
Form Design View
CC07
frmCustomers

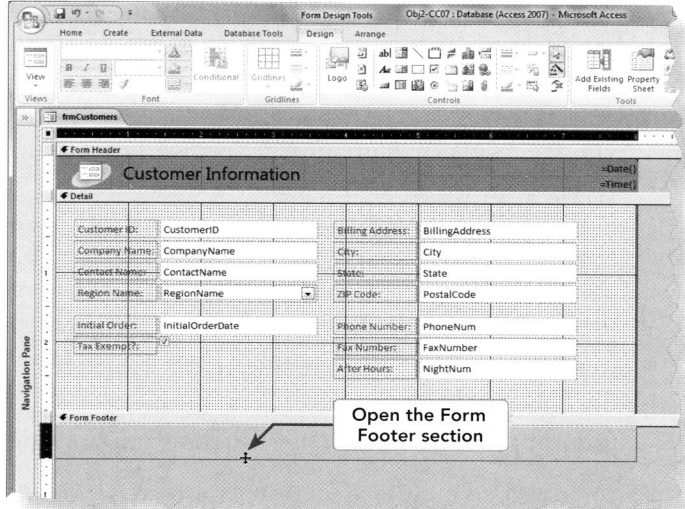

TIP

Each square of the design grid is 1 inch by 1 inch.

4. Drag the top border of the **Detail** section down to make the **Form Header** section about 1 inch tall.
5. From the **Arrange** tab, in the **Show/Hide** group, click the Page Header/Footer command.

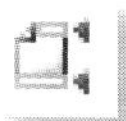

6. Drag the top border of the **Detail** section down to make the **Page Header** section about 1/2 inch tall.
7. Drag the top border of the **Form Footer** section down to make the **Page Footer** section about 1/2 inch tall.

Figure 7-13
All Form sections expanded
CC07
frmCustomers

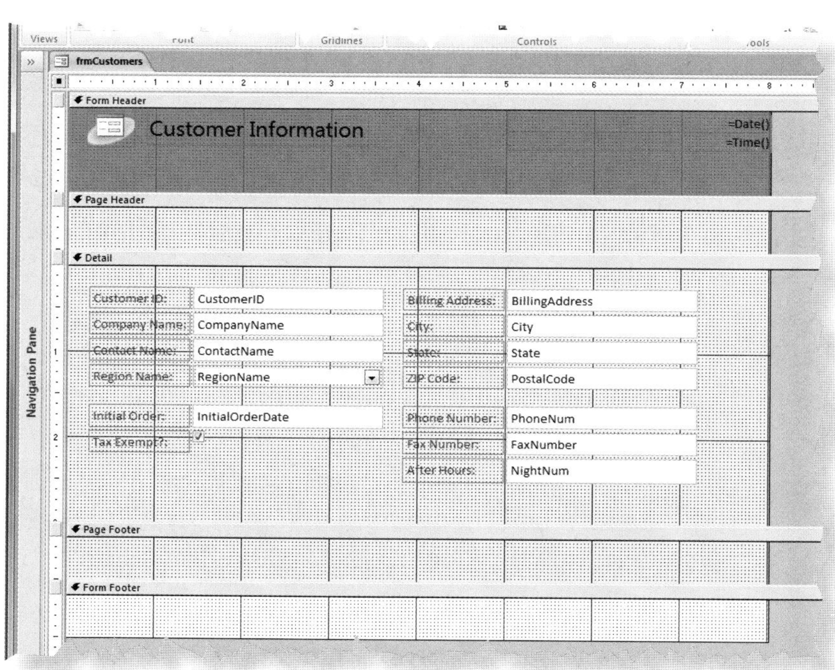

8. Save the form.

Exercise 7-10 ADD LABELS AND VIEW FORM SECTIONS

The Label tool in the Control command group is used to enter text or titles in a form. The text displayed in a label is independent of the recordset and does not change from record to record.

When you select a label or any other object, selection handles appear around the object. Selection handles are eight small black rectangles around an active object. The top left selection handle is known as the moving handle and is used to move the object without resizing it. The other seven handles are known as sizing handles. Sizing handles are any selection handles on a control except the top left one and are used to adjust the height and width of the object.

1. From the **Design** tab, in the **Controls** group, click the Label command. The pointer changes to a crosshair cursor with the letter A.

NOTE

Pressing Enter does not move the cursor to the next line in a label. It finishes the label and selects it.

2. Place the pointer in the **Form Header** section at the 4-inch mark, below the other controls. Click and drag down and to the right to draw a box about 2 inches wide and 5 dots tall. When you release the mouse button, you will see the box and a text insertion point.
3. Key **Form Header** and press Enter. The label box is selected and displays the eight selection handles around its edges.

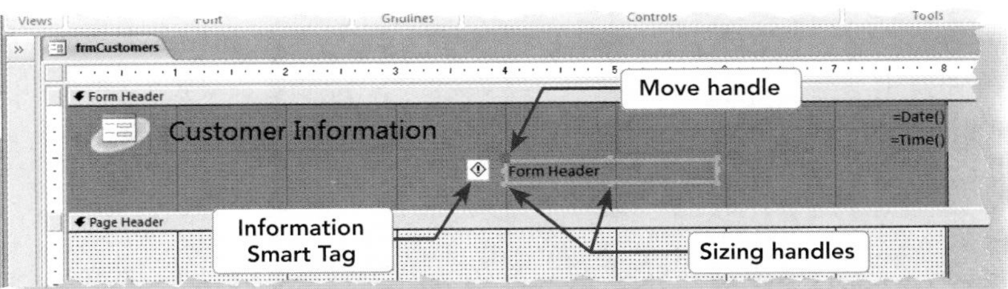

Figure 7-14
Adding a label to the Form Header
CC07
frmCustomers

4. Click the Smart Tag. This label is not associated with another control. This is our intention. Choose **Ignore Error**.
5. Double-click any of the sizing handles. The label adjusts its size to fit the text.
6. In the **Page Header** section, add a label that is the same size as the one in the **Form Header** section. Key **Page Header** in the label.
7. In the **Page Footer** section, add a label that is the same size as the one in the **Form Header** section. Key **Page Footer** in the label.
8. In the **Form Footer** section, add a label that is the same size as the one in the **Form Header** section. Key **Form Footer** in the label.
9. Switch to Form View. You can see both the **Form Header** and **Form Footer**.

10. Press PageDown to move to the next record. There is no change in the **Form Header** or **Form Footer**.

11. Press Ctrl+End to move to the last record. There is no sign of the **Page Header** or **Page Footer**.

12. Click the Office button. Point at the **Print** option, and click Print Preview. Click near the top of the preview to zoom in. You can see the **Form Header** and **Page Header** at the top of the first page.

13. Scroll down to see the **Page Footer**.

14. Click the Last Page button. After the last record, you can see the **Form Footer** appear.

15. From the **Print Preview** tab, in the **Zoom** group, click the More Pages command.

16. From the **Print Preview** tab, in the **Close Preview** group, click the Close Print Preview command.

17. Close the form and save the changes.

Modifying Controls in Design View

NOTE

A form inherits the field properties of the table. Changes to the form's properties do not affect the table's properties.

Certain actions cannot be completed in Layout View. To perform these tasks, you will need to switch to Design View. Design View provides a more detailed view of the form's structure. In Design View, you can view the **Header**, **Detail**, and **Footer** sections. Unlike Layout View, when the form is in Design View, the form does not display the underlying data while making design changes.

Exercise 7-11 FORMAT A FORM IN DESIGN VIEW

When using Design View to modify the format of a form, you can begin by selecting a predefined format using AutoFormat.

1. From the Navigation Pane, right-click **frmAnimals** and choose **Design View**.

2. Click the **ProductID** text box.

3. From the **Arrange** tab, in the **AutoFormat** group, click the AutoFormat command to expand the AutoFormat options.

4. Choose **Civic** (fifth column, first row). Because only the text box was selected, only it was formatted.

5. Click the Form selector.

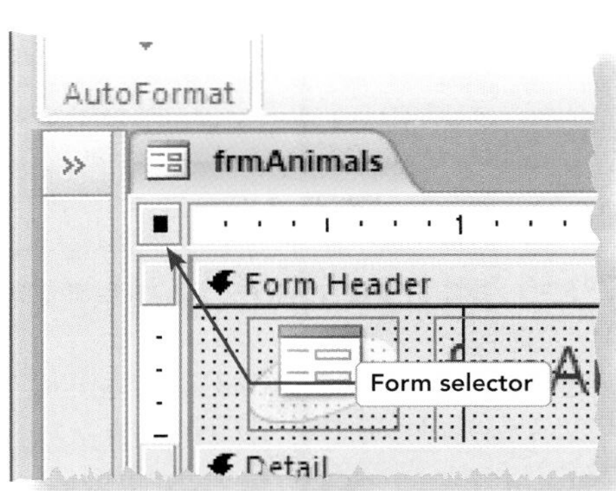

Figure 7-15
The Form selector
CC07
frmAnimals

6. Choose **Civic** (fifth column, first row). The whole form is now formatted.
7. Right-click the form's document tab, and choose **Form View**. To see how data look in the form, you must switch to either Layout or Form Views.
8. Switch to Design View.
9. Place your mouse pointer over the top edge of the **ProductID** text box. When a small, black, down arrow appears, click. All controls below the arrow are now selected.

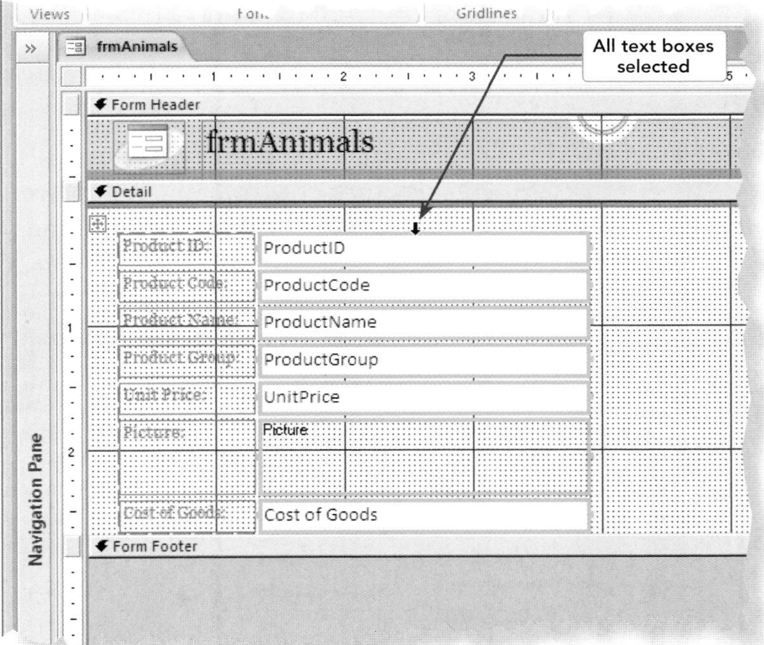

Figure 7-16
All text boxes selected
CC07
frmAnimals

10. While pressing Shift, click the **Picture** control to remove it from the selection.

11. From the **Design** tab, in the **Controls** group, click the drop-down arrow for the Special Effect command and choose **Special Effect: Shadowed**.
12. From the **Design** tab, in the **Controls** group, click the drop-down arrow for the Line Type command and choose **Solid** (second option on the list).
13. Click to the right of the selected controls to deselect them. You can now see your changes.
14. From the **Design** tab, in the **Controls** group, click the Title command and key **Product Information**.

15. From the **Arrange** tab, in the **Size** group, click the Size to Fit command.

16. Save the form.

Exercise 7-12 RESIZE AND MOVE CONTROLS

When resizing and moving controls, you can use the gridline marks in Design View. You can use the vertical and horizontal rulers to position the edges of each control.

1. Right-click the **ProductGroup** text box, and choose **Delete**.
2. Click the **Picture** control. From the **Arrange** tab, in the **Control Layout** group, click the Remove command.

3. Click the **Picture** control label, and press [Delete].

REVIEW

If you make an error deleting, sizing, or moving a control, click the Undo button and try again.

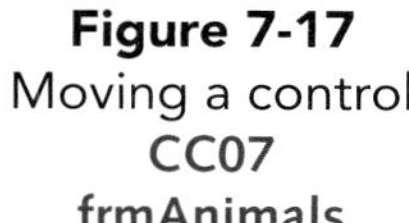

4. Drag the Picture control to the right of the **ProductID** control.
5. Place your pointer to the middle bottom of the Picture control. When you see the resize arrow, drag down the bottom to 2.5 inches on the vertical ruler.

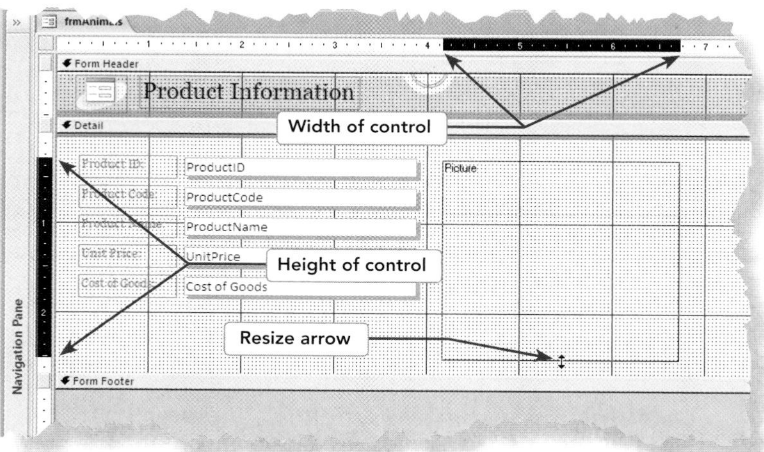

Figure 7-17
Moving a control
CC07
frmAnimals

6. Place your pointer in the vertical ruler to the left of the **ProductID** control. When you see a small, black, right arrow, click and drag until you are below the **Cost of Goods** control. This action selected all controls in the **Detail** section of the form.
7. From the **Arrange** tab, in the **Control Alignment** group, click the Top command to align the top of the control layout and the **Picture** control.
8. Click to the right of the **Picture** control to deselect the controls.

9. Place your pointer in the middle of the **Picture** control. With the move pointer, click and drag down 1/8th inch (one tick on the ruler).
10. Click the **UnitPrice** control. While pressing Shift, click **Cost of Goods**.
11. From the **Arrange** tab, in the **Control Layout** group, click the Stacked command.
12. Drag the new control layout down until its bottom is at 2.5 inches on the vertical ruler.
13. Place your pointer over the top of the **ProductID** text box. When you see the small down arrow, click.
14. From the **Design** tab, in the **Font** group, click the Align Text Right command.

15. Drag the right edge of the form to 7.5 inches on the horizontal ruler.
16. Deselect the controls.
17. Save the form.

Exercise 7-13 MODIFY PROPERTY SETTINGS

Every control has property settings. The property settings allow you to modify a control more precisely. For example, through the property settings, you can modify how an image will appear. The various Picture Size Mode settings for an image include the following:

- Clip Mode sizes an image to its original size.
- Stretch Mode sizes an image to fit the control without regard to the proportions of the original image.
- Zoom Mode sizes an image to fit the control while maintaining the proportions of the original image.

1. Double-click the **Picture** control to open the Property Sheet for this control.
2. On the **Format** tab, click the **Picture Size Mode**. Click the drop-down arrow and choose **Clip**. This mode shows the image at normal size.
3. Switch to Form View. The image does not fit the control.
4. Switch to Design View. Change the **Picture Size Mode** to **Zoom**.
5. Switch to Form View. This time the image fits the control.
6. Switch to Design View
7. In the Property Sheet for the **Picture** control, click the **Picture Alignment** property.
8. Click the drop-down arrow and choose **Center**.
9. Change the **Width** property to **3**.

10. In the **Height** property, key **3**.
11. In the **Border Style** property, choose **Solid**.
12. In the **Border Width** property, choose **2 pt**.
13. In the **Back Style** property, choose **Normal**.
14. Switch to Form View.

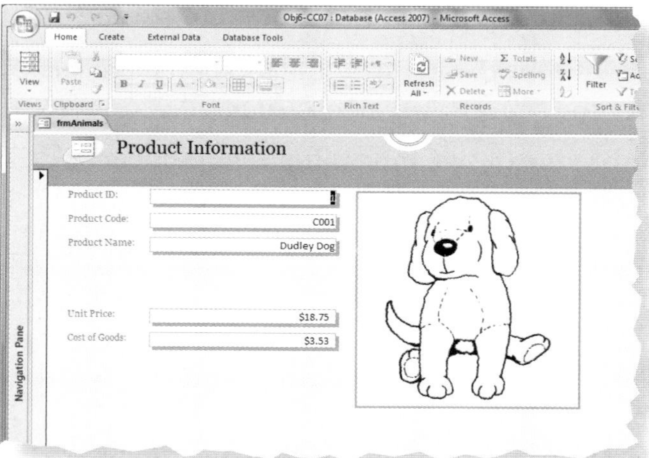

Figure 7-18
Form View
CC07
frmAnimals

15. Switch to Design View. Close the Property Sheet.
16. Save the form.

Exercise 7-14 ADD A LABEL

Adding a label to a form helps identify the entire form or aspects of the form. For example, you might add a label to identify the department for which the form was created or a date on which the form was last modified. A label is not associated with data stored in the record source. A label is only associated to the major object to which it is attached.

1. Drag the bottom of the **Form Footer** section down 1/2 inch.
2. From the **Design** tab, in the **Controls** group, click the Label command Aa.
3. Place the pointer in the **Form Footer** section at the left edge. Click and key **Prepared by:** *[your full name]*.
4. Save the form.

Adding Calculated Controls to a Form

A calculated control in a form allows you to display the results of a calculation based upon one or more values. You create a calculated control by adding an expression to the Source Control property of a control. An expression can be any combination of mathematical operators, logical operators, constants, and functions.

Exercise 7-15 ADD UNBOUND TEXT BOXES

Although any control that has a Control Source property can be used as a calculated control, an unbound text box is the easiest control to change to a calculated control. An unbound text box inherits the format of the control layout to which it is added.

1. From the **Design** tab, in the **Controls** group, click the Text Box command. The pointer changes to a crosshair cursor with the letters "ab."
2. Click below the **Cost of Goods** control. This adds an unbound text box with a label.
3. Drag the **Unbound** text box up until you see the insertion bar below the **Cost of Goods** control. The new text box inherits the format of the control layout.
4. Add a second text box to the form in the same manner as above.
5. Add the new text box to the same control layout as you did with the last text box.
6. Select the **UnitPrice** text box, and drag its right edge to the 3-inch mark on the horizontal ruler.

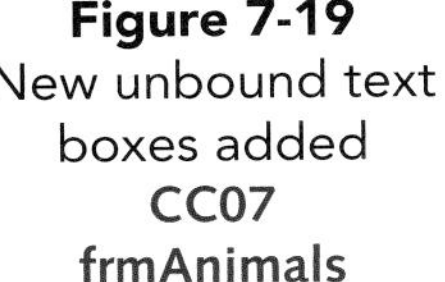

Figure 7-19
New unbound text boxes added
CC07
frmAnimals

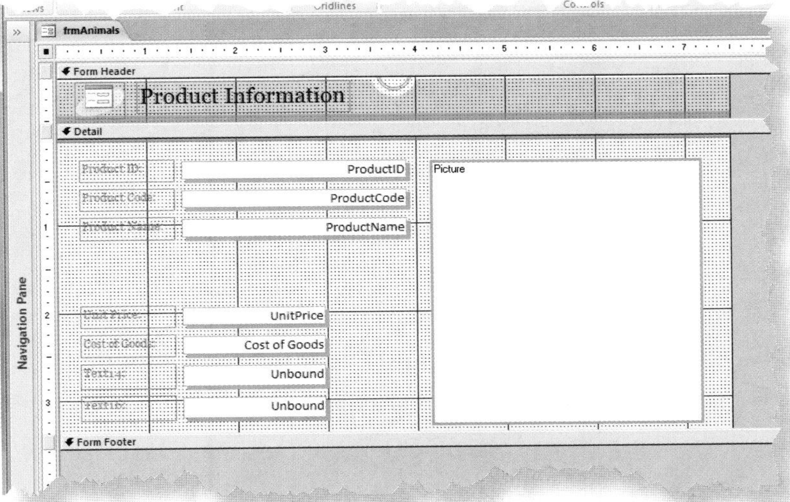

7. Save the form.

Exercise 7-16 ADD A CALCULATED CONTROL

You can use a calculated control to display the solution to a calculation. The calculation can be an expression or a function. For example, if you have a form displaying the number of items sold and the unit price for each item, you can add a calculated control to multiply the two fields and display a total price.

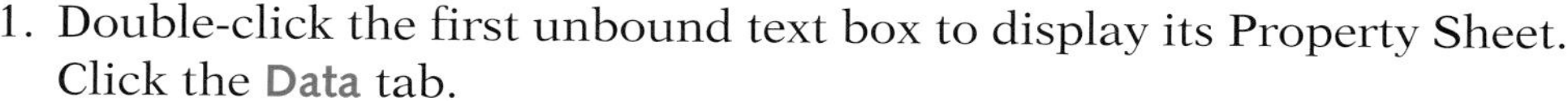

1. Double-click the first unbound text box to display its Property Sheet. Click the **Data** tab.

2. Click the **Control Source** property; read the status bar. Click the Build button to open the **Expression Builder** dialog box.
3. In the left panel, your **frmAnimals** form is shown as the current object at the top of the list.
4. In the middle panel, click **<Field List>**. The right panel shows the fields in the form.

NOTE

You can double-click the field names or select them and click the Paste button.

5. In the right panel, double-click **UnitPrice**. It is pasted into the preview area with square brackets.
6. Click the Division button / in the operator row.
7. In the right panel, double-click **Cost of Goods**.

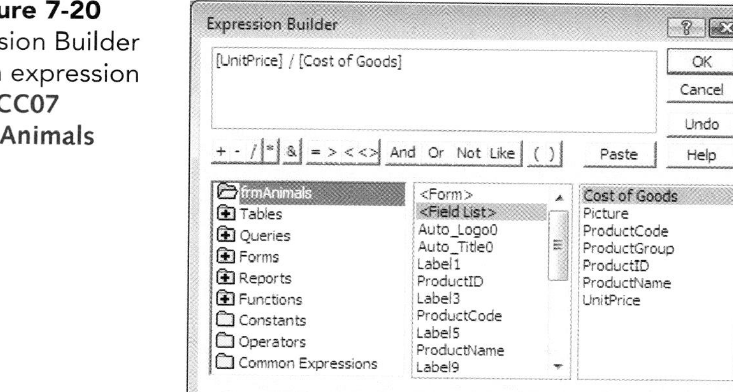

Figure 7-20
Expression Builder with an expression
CC07
frmAnimals

8. Click **OK** to close the **Expression Builder**. The equation appears in the unbound text box.

TIP

You must click the OK button to accept the changes in the Expression Builder.

9. Click the **Format** tab in the Property Sheet. Click the **Format** row and its drop-down arrow. Choose **Percent**.
10. Click the **Decimal Places** property, and choose **2**.
11. Click the label of the text box you just modified. In the Property Sheet, click the **Caption** property and key **Points:**. Press ↓ to see the changes.
12. Click the second unbound text box. In its Property Sheet, click the **Data** tab.
13. Click the **Control Source** property, and click the Build button.
14. In the **Expression Builder** dialog box, in the middle panel, click **<Field List>**.

15. In the right panel, double-click **UnitPrice**. Press [-].
16. In the right panel, double-click **Cost of Goods**. Click **OK**.
17. On the **Format** tab, click the **Format** property and choose **Currency**.
18. Click the label of the text box you just modified. In the Property Sheet, click the **Caption** property and key **Profit Margin:**.
19. Close the Property Sheet.
20. Switch to Form View. Press [PageDown] to view a few records.

Figure 7-21 Completed form CC07 frmAnimals

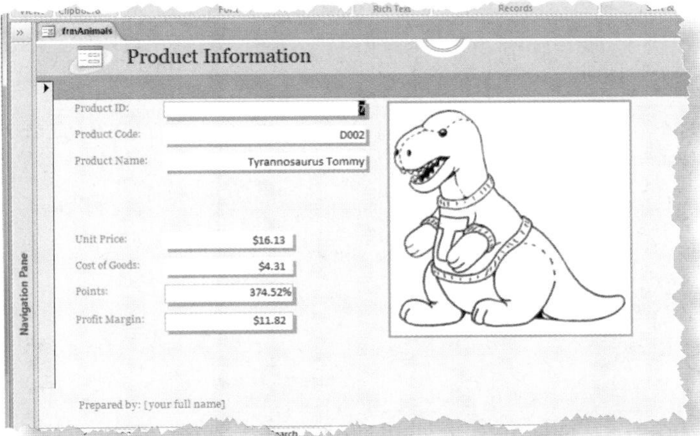

21. Close and save the form.

Printing/Saving Forms

Although forms are designed to view data on a screen, on occasion you may need to print a form. If you choose to print the entire form, all records will display. Each record may display on a single page, on multiple pages, or on a portion of a page, depending on the size of the form and the size of the paper on which you print.

When printing a form, the **Page Header** and **Page Footer** sections will appear on each printed page. If a form is wider than the paper width, a single page of the form may print on two or more pages of paper. You can change the width of the form and the margins of the page to optimize the print quality of a form.

Exercise 7-17 PRINT SPECIFIC PAGES

As with other Office applications such as Word, you can print a specific page or range of pages. When printing a specific range of pages, you must enter a single page number, or a page range including the first page through the last page.

1. From the Navigation Pane, double-click **frmEmployeesInfo**.
2. Click the Office Button. Point at the **Print** option and click Print Preview.

3. From the **Print Preview** tab, in the **Zoom** group, click the More Pages command and choose **Four Pages**. Notice that each record is too wide to fit on one page.
4. From the **Print Layout** group, click the Landscape command.
5. From the **Print Layout** group, click the **Margins** command, and choose the Normal command.
6. From the **Print Preview** tab, in the **Print** group, click the Print command. The report now fits on three pages.
7. In the **Print** dialog box, in the **Print Range** section, choose **Pages**.
8. In the **From** control, key **1**. The **To** control is now active.

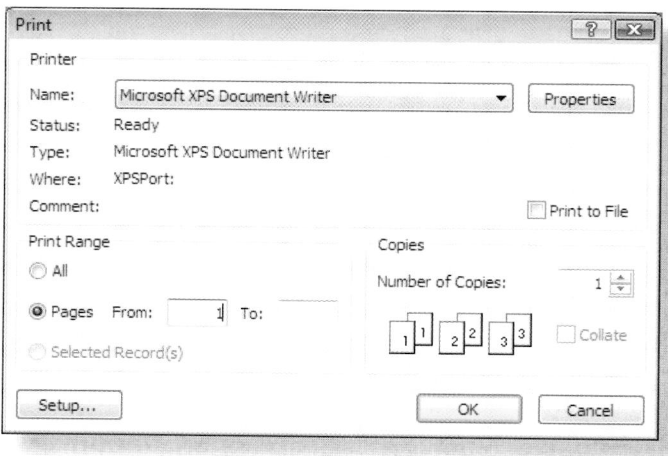

Figure 7-22
Print dialog box
CC07
frmEmployeesInfo

9. Click the **To** control and key **1**.
10. Based on your classroom procedure, you can either print the form or cancel the print process. To cancel, click **Cancel**. To print the form, click **OK**. If you are uncertain, ask your instructor.
11. From the **Print Preview** tab, in the **Close Preview** group, click the Close Print Preview command.

Exercise 7-18 PRINT ONE RECORD

When printing a single record, you must first select the record through the form. You cannot choose to print a single record through the Options in the Print or Print Preview commands.

1. In the Form View of **frmAnimals**, press PageDown until you reach the record for Barney Bulldog.
2. Click the record selector. The record selector is very tall in this form because the form is set to show only one record at one time.
3. Click the Office Button. Point at the **Print** option and click Print.

4. In the **Print** dialog box, in the **Print Range** section, choose **Selected Record(s)**.
5. Based on your classroom procedure, you can either print the form or cancel the print process. To cancel, click **Cancel**. To print the form, click **OK**. If you are uncertain, ask your instructor.

Exercise 7-19 PRINT MULTIPLE RECORDS

Similar to printing a single record, you can print a contiguous range of records. The order in which the multiple records will print depends on how the dynaset is sorted.

1. Open **frmEmployeesInfo** in Form View.
2. Click the record selector for **EmployeeID** "3."
3. Drag down to **EmployeeID** "23." These are all the employees whose last names start with "C".

Figure 7-23
Print dialog box
CC07
frmEmployeesInfo

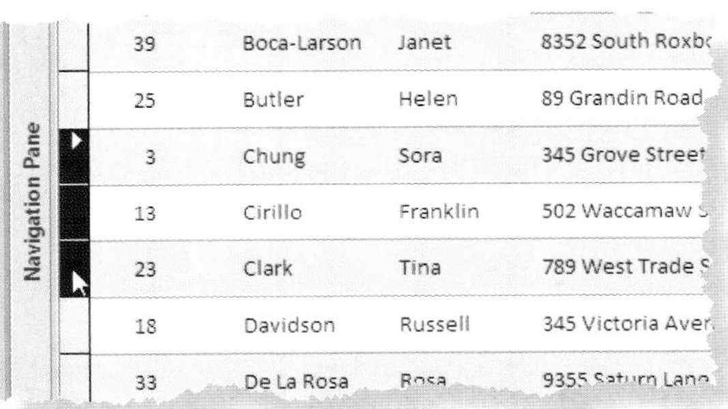

Navigation Pane
39 Boca-Larson Janet 8352 South Roxb
25 Butler Helen 89 Grandin Road
3 Chung Sora 345 Grove Street
13 Cirillo Franklin 502 Waccamaw
23 Clark Tina 789 West Trade
18 Davidson Russell 345 Victoria Ave
33 De La Rosa Rosa 9355 Saturn Lane

4. Click the Office Button. Point at the **Print** option and click Print.
5. In the **Print** dialog box, in the **Print Range** section, choose **Selected Record(s)**.
6. Based on your classroom procedure, you can either print the form or cancel the print process. To cancel, click **Cancel**. To print the form, click **OK**. If you are uncertain, ask your instructor.

Exercise 7-20 SAVE A RECORD

Just as with other major objects, a form can be saved as a PDF or XPS file. To save a single record or range of records through a form, the record or records first must be selected.

1. Click the document tab for the form **frmAnimals**.
2. Press PageDown until you reach the Barney Bulldog record.
3. Click the record selector on the left side of the form.

4. Click the Office Button. Point at the **Save As** option and click PDF or XPS.

5. In the **Publish as PDF or XPS** dialog box, click **Options**.
6. In the **Options** dialog box, in the **Range** section, click **Selected records** and click **OK**.
7. Change the location to where you will be storing your work.
8. Select either **PDF** or **XPS** as the file type.
9. Click **Publish**.
10. Close both forms.
11. Compact and close the database.

Lesson 7 Summary

- A form can be designed to view an entire record on a single screen.
- A form can include calculations, functions, and totals.
- The quickest way to create a form is to use the Query Wizard or a tool in the Forms group.
- The Form Wizard lets you select fields, a layout, and a style.
- When using the Forms tool, you can create a Simple Form, Split Form, or Multiple Items Form by selecting the appropriate command button located in the Forms group.
- A control is a database object that displays data, performs actions, or controls user interface information, such as labels and images. Controls can be bound, unbound, or calculated.
- A control layout assists you to horizontally and vertically align the controls within a form. A single form can have multiple control layouts.
- In Layout View of a form, you can rearrange and adjust the size of controls to improve the form's appearance and functionality.
- In Layout View, you can navigate through the dynaset to determine the best layout for the controls.
- Aligning a control is different than aligning the text within a control. Aligning the text within a control does not move the placement of the control on the form, but only the contents of the control.
- The five sections of a form include the **Detail**, **Form Header**, **Form Footer**, **Page Header**, and **Page Footer** sections.
- The **Page Header** and **Page Footer** sections can only be seen in Print Preview or when the form is printed.
- When you select a label or any other object, selection handles appear around the object.
- When resizing and moving controls, you can use the gridline marks, vertical ruler, and horizontal ruler to position the edges of each control.
- The property settings of a control allow you to modify a control more precisely.
- A **Picture Size Mode** can be set to **Clip Mode**, **Stretch Mode** or **Zoom Mode**.

- A label control is only associated with the major object to which it is attached.
- An unbound text box is the easiest control to change to a calculated control.
- A calculated control can contain an expression or a function.
- When printing a form, the **Page Header** and **Page Footer** sections will print on each vertical page.
- When printing a specific range of pages, you must enter a single page number, a list of page numbers separated by commas, or a page range including the first page through the last page.
- To print a single record, first you must select the record through the form. You cannot select to print a single record or range of records through the Options in the Print or Print Preview commands.
- The order in which multiple records will print depends on how the dynaset is sorted.

LESSON 7		Command Summary	
Feature	**Button**	**Path**	**Keyboard**
Controls, Add Existing Fields		Formatting, Controls, Add Existing Fields	
Controls, Align Text Right		Design, Font, Align Text Right	
Controls, Date and Time		Formatting, Controls, Date and Time	
Controls, Left		Arrange, Control Layout, Left	
Controls, Lines		Design, Controls, Line Type	
Controls, Margins		Arrange, Control Layout, Control Margins	
Controls, Padding		Arrange, Control Layout, Control Padding	
Controls, Remove		Arrange, Control Layout, Remove	
Controls, Right		Arrange, Control Layout, Right	
Controls, Special Effects		Design, Controls, Special Effects	
Controls, Stacked		Arrange, Control Layout, Stacked	
Controls, Tab Order		Arrange, Control Layout, Tab Order	

continues

LESSON 7		Command Summary *continued*	
Feature	**Button**	**Path**	**Keyboard**
Controls, Text Box, Add		Design, Controls, Text Box	
Controls, Top		Arrange, Control Layout, Top	
Fields, Choose All		Add All	Ctrl+A
Fields, Fill/Back Color		Formatting, Font, Fill/Back Color	
Fields, Font Color		Formatting, Font, Font Color	
Fields, Remove One		Remove One	
Fields, Size to Fit		Arrange, Position, Size to Fit	
Form, AutoFormat		Formatting, AutoFormat	
Form, Control Layout Selector		Layout Selector	
Form, Create, Datasheet Form		Create, Forms, More Forms, Datasheet Form	
Form, Create, Multiple Form		Create, Forms, Multiple Form	
Form, Create, Simple Form		Create, Forms, Form	
Form, Create, Split Form		Create, Forms, Split Form	
Form, Page Header/ Footer View		Arrange, Show/Hide, Page Header/Footer	
Form, Title		Formatting, Controls, Title	
Form, Wizard		Create, Forms, More Forms, Form Wizard	
Forms, AutoFormat		Arrange, AutoFormat, AutoFormat	
Label, Add		Design, Controls, Label	
Print Preview, More Pages		Print Preview, Zoom, More Pages	
View, Form View		Formatting, Views, View	

Lesson 8

Adding and Modifying Reports

OBJECTIVES

MCAS OBJECTIVES

In this lesson:
AC07 70-605 2.6.1
AC07 70-605 2.6.2
AC07 70-605 2.6.4
AC07 70-605 2.6.5
AC07 70-605 2.6.6
AC07 70-605 2.6.7
AC07 70-605 2.7.1
AC07 70-605 2.7.4
AC07 70-605 2.7.5
AC07 70-605 2.7.6
AC07 70-605 2.7.7

After completing this lesson, you will be able to:

1. Generate reports quickly.
2. Modify controls in Layout View.
3. Work with report sections.
4. Work with controls in a report.
5. Use Format Painter and Conditional Formatting.
6. Create a multicolumn report and labels.

Estimated Time: 2 hour

A well-designed report can present information more effectively than other major objects. In a report you can:

- Display data in an attractive format that may include variations in fonts, colors, shading, and borders.
- Display sorted, grouped, or summarized information.
- Display images, graphics, charts, and logos.
- Display fields from more than one table.
- Display titles and headings.

In this lesson, you will learn how to create and modify reports. You will work with the Report Wizard, Design View, and Layout View. With reports, your design concerns are different than those with forms because when working with reports, you must account for margins, page breaks, and page orientation.

Generating Reports Quickly

Access provides wizards and tools to create reports using standardized styles. Depending on the Report tool you select, the report may have header and footer sections in addition to the section containing the record source detail.

Stacked style reports are commonly used when the width of data is too wide to display properly in tabular layout.

Exercise 8-1 CREATE A REPORT WITH A WIZARD

The Report Wizard allows you to select a record source and the fields to include in the report. When selecting multiple tables or queries as the record source, the objects must have a valid relationship already created. You can group and sort the fields in a report.

1. Locate and open the **Lesson 08** folder.
2. Make a copy of **CC08,** and rename it *[your initials]*-CC08.
3. Open and enable content for ***[your initials]*-CC08**.
4. From the **Create** tab, in the **Reports** group, click the Report Wizard command.
5. In the **Tables/Queries** drop-down box, choose **Query: qryStuffedAnimals**.
6. The dialog box asks which fields to use on the form. Double-click the following fields to add them to the **Selected Fields** section:

   ProductID
   ProductCode
   ProductName
   UnitPrice
   Picture

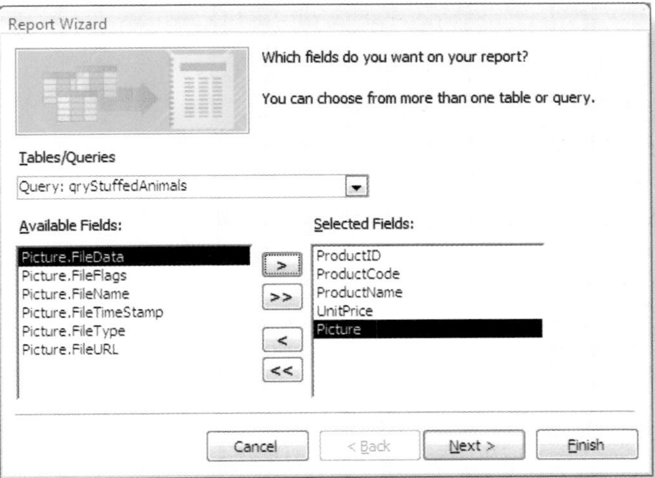

Figure 8-1
Report Wizard dialog box
CC08.accdb

7. Click **Next**. This part of the Wizard asks you to add groups. This skill will be covered later in this lesson. Click **Next**.
8. Click the first combo box drop-down arrow, and select **ProductName**. The report will be sorted by this field. Click **Next**.

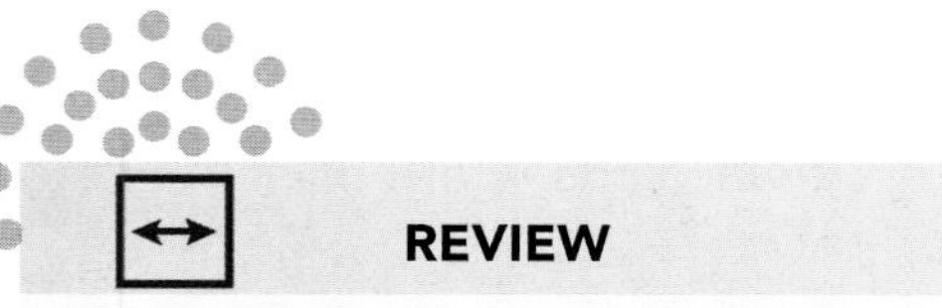

REVIEW

When creating a new report, you should use the Leszynski Naming Conventions. Therefore, forms are preceded by the prefix "rpt," and the first letter of main words are capitalized with no spaces between words.

TIP

The pointer toggles between the last zoom size and fit.

9. In the **Layout** section, select **Columnar** and in the **Orientation** section, select **Portrait**. Click **Next**.
10. Click each of the different styles to view a small preview. Select **Paper**.
11. Click **Next**. Modify the title to **rptStuffedAnimals**.
12. You can choose to preview the report or modify the design. Select **Preview the report** and click **Finish**.
13. The report opens in Print Preview.
14. From the **Print Preview** tab, in the **Zoom** group, click the More Pages command and choose **Twelve Pages**.
15. From the **Print Preview** tab, in the **Close Preview** group, click the Close Print Preview command.
16. Close the report.

Exercise 8-2 GENERATE A REPORT WITH ONE CLICK

The Report tool is the quickest method to create a basic report based on a selected table or query. The report displays all fields from the source table or query. You can create a basic report and later modify it using Design or Layout View. The last style used on the workstation will be the default style used by the Report tool.

1. In the Navigation Pane, select **qryStuffedAnimals**.
2. From the **Create** tab, in the **Reports** group, click the Report command. The new report is now in Layout View showing multiple records.

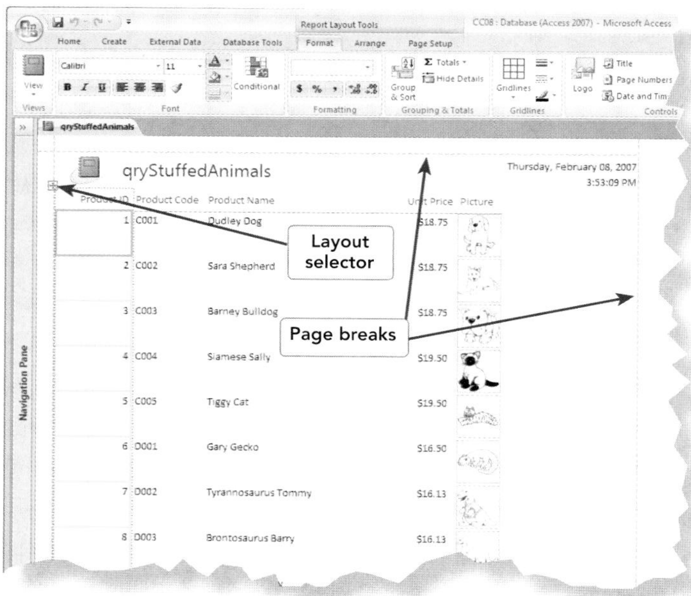

Figure 8-2
Report in Layout View
CC08.accdb
rptStuffedAnimalsList

3. From the Quick Access toolbar, click the Save button to save the new report.
4. In the **Save As** dialog box, key **rptStuffedAnimalsList** and click **OK**.

5. From the **Format** tab, in the **Views** group, click the Report View command.
6. Scroll down the report. Notice that there is only one page.
7. Right-click the report's document tab, and choose **Print Preview**.

8. From the **Print Preview** tab, in the **Zoom** group, click the Two Page command. Only one page will display in Report or Layout View.
9. From the **Print Preview** tab, in the **Close Preview** group, click the Close Print Preview command.
10. Switch to Report View.

Modifying Controls in Layout View

Layout View for a report is very similar to Layout View for a form. You use Layout View to resize controls, adjust column widths, move columns, and change labels while viewing the actual data in the report. You also can insert or remove controls and set the properties for the report or a control.

Exercise 8-3 FORMAT A REPORT IN LAYOUT VIEW

Any report, including a basic report, can be modified in Layout View. You may find it easier to start by applying an AutoFormat to the report and then modifying the design.

1. Switch to Layout View for **rptStuffedAnimalsList**.

2. From the **Format** tab, in the **AutoFormat** group, click the More arrow and choose **Origin** (4th column, 4th row).
3. Click the first record's **Product Code**.

4. From the **Format** tab, in the **Font** group, click the Center command.
5. Click the first record's **Picture**.
6. Drag the right edge to the right about 1/4 inch.
7. Click the column heading **Picture**.
8. From the **Format** tab, in the **Font** group, click the Center command.

Figure 8-3
Formatting a report in Layout View
CC08.accdb
rptStuffedAnimalsList

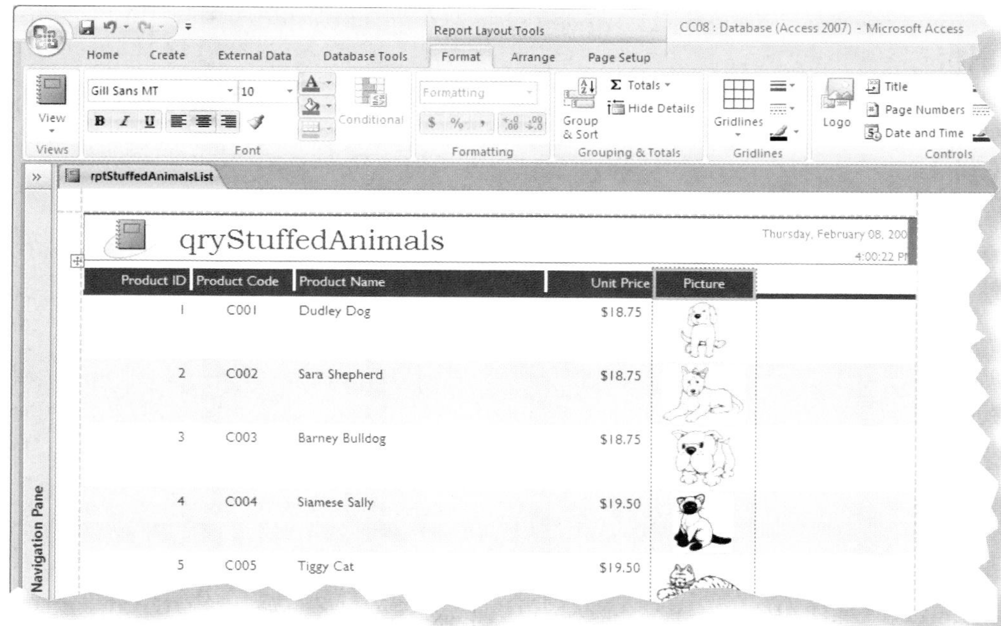

9. From the Quick Access toolbar, click the Save button.

Exercise 8-4 ADD AND REARRANGE CONTROLS IN A REPORT

When you add fields in Layout View, a Field List pane displays. The top part of pane displays fields available in the current record source. The middle part of the pane displays fields available in related tables. The bottom part of the pane displays fields available in other tables.

1. Click the column heading **Product ID**.
2. Press Delete. The other fields in the control layout have moved to the left.

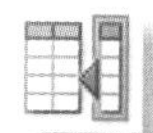

3. From the **Format** tab, in the **Controls** group, click the Add Existing Fields command. The Field List pane appears.
4. Click the toggle button at the bottom of the Field List to switch the display between **Show only fields in current record source** to **Show all tables**.

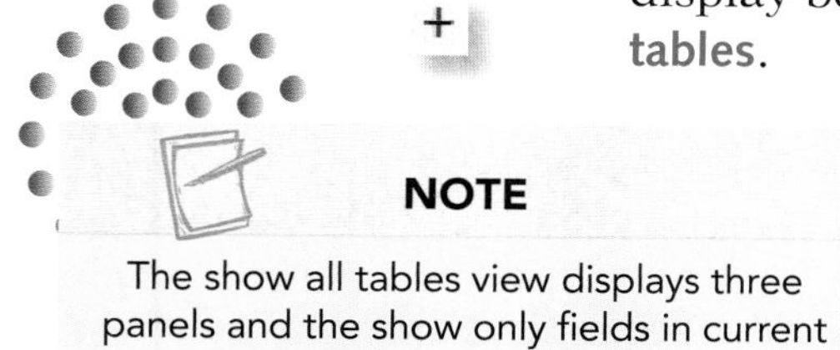

NOTE

The show all tables view displays three panels and the show only fields in current record source view displays only one panel.

5. From the Field List, in the **Fields available in related tables:** panel, click the Expand button + for **tblProductLines**.
6. From **tblProductLines**, drag the field **ProductLine** to the left of **Product Code** in the report.

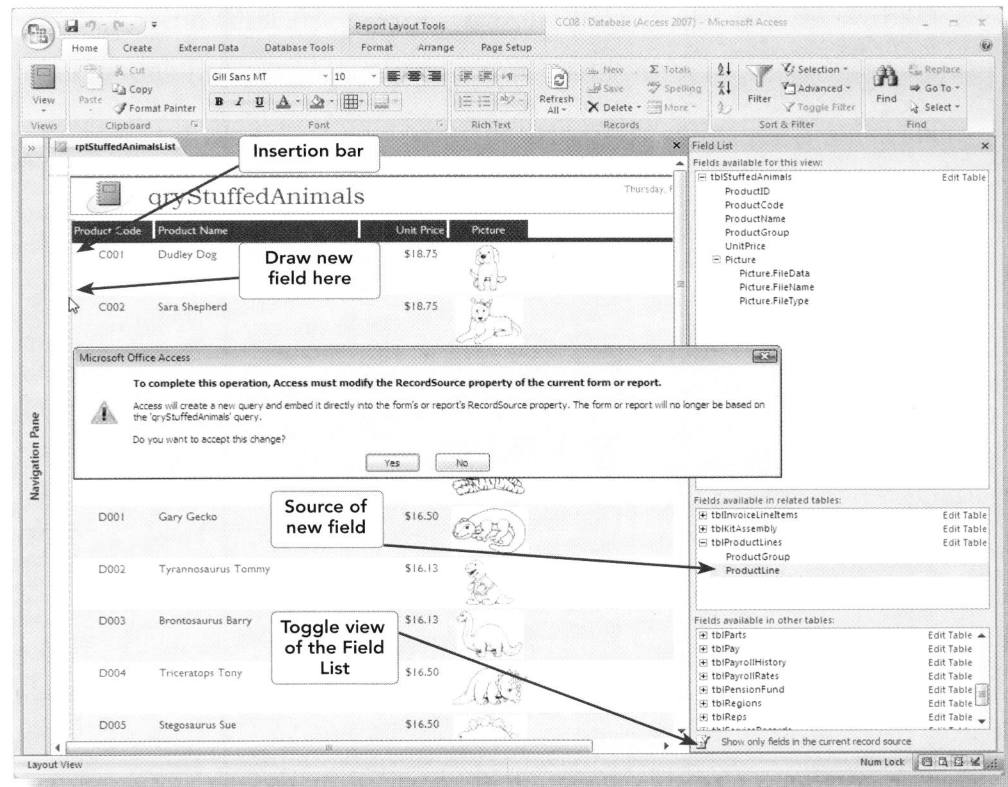

Figure 8-4 Adding a field to a report in Layout View CC08.accdb rptStuffedAnimalsList

7. The warning dialog box states that the recordset must be modified to include the table and field just added. Click **Yes**.
8. From the **Format** tab, in the **Controls** group, click the Add Existing Fields command to remove the **Field List**.
9. Press Ctrl+S to save the report.

Exercise 8-5 FORMAT A REPORT USING THE PROPERTY SHEET

You can modify the properties of a control through its Property Sheet. For each property, you can change the paddings and margins. A padding is the space between the gridline of the report and the control. A margin is the specified location of information inside the control.

1. From the **Arrange** tab, in the **Tools** group, click the Property Sheet command .
2. Click the column header **Name of Product Group**.
3. In the Property Sheet, click the **Format** tab. Click in the **Caption** property.
4. Delete "Name of" from the field's **Caption**. Press ↓.
5. Change the field's **Width** property to **1.2**.

6. In the **Text Align** property, click the drop-down arrow and choose **Center**.
7. In the first record, click the **Product Group** text box.
8. In the Property Sheet, on the **Format** tab, click in the **Hide Duplicates** property, click the drop-down arrow, and choose **Yes**.
9. Place your pointer over the left edge of the **Product Group** text box. When a small right arrow appears, click. This action selects the data part of the control layout.

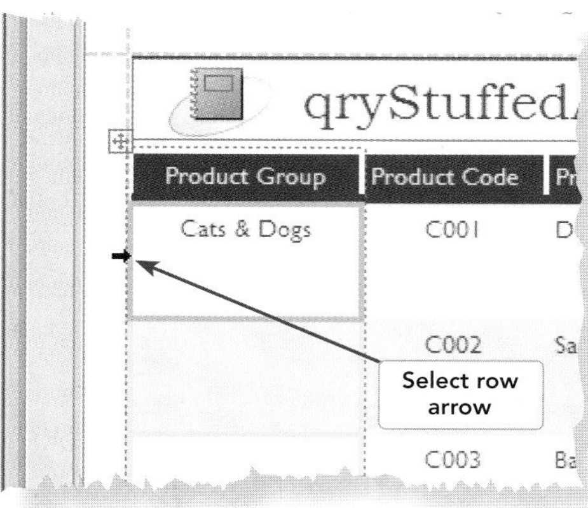

Figure 8-5
Select a row in Layout View
CC08.accdb
rptStuffedAnimalsList

10. In the first record, click the **Product Group** text box. While pressing [Shift], click the text boxes for **Product Code**, **Product Name**, and **Unit Price**.
11. In the Property Sheet, on the **Format** tab, change the **Top Padding** property to **.15**.
12. On the **Format** tab, change the **Top Margin** property to **.15**.
13. Press [↓]. The content of each control selected has moved down.

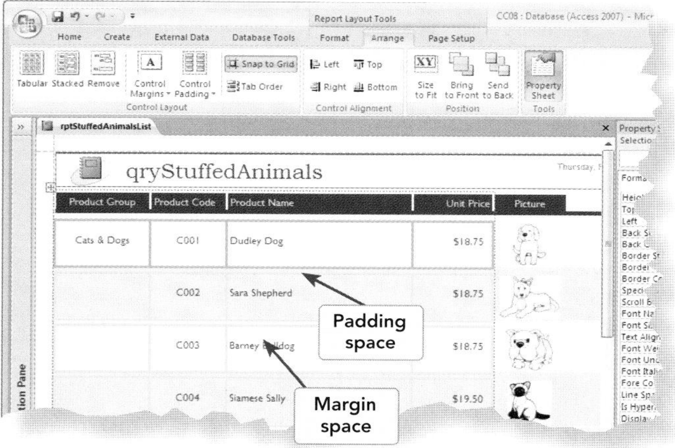

Figure 8-6
Setting the margin and padding properties
CC08.accdb
rptStuffedAnimalsList

14. From the Quick Access toolbar, click the Save button.
15. Close the report.

Working with Report Sections

Reports can have numerous sections. The Detail section displays data from the record source. The **Report Header** or **Report Footer** section prints once at the beginning or end of the report (first or last page). Headers and footers can contain main titles, summary calculations, design lines, or even images. The **Page Header** and **Page Footer** sections print at the top and bottom of every page and are often used for page numbers and the date.

Reports may also have one or more Group Header/Footer sections. A Group Header/Footer prints either before or after a defined group.

TABLE 8-1 Sections of a Report

Name of Section	Purpose
Detail Section	Prints data once for every row in the record source.
Report Header	Prints once at the top (first page) of the report.
Report Footer	Prints once at the bottom (last page) of the report.
Page Header	Prints once at the top of every printed page.
Page Footer	Prints once at the bottom of every printed page.
Group Header	Prints once at the start of each group.
Group Footer	Prints once at the end of each group.

Exercise 8-6 CREATE A GROUPED REPORT USING A WIZARD

The Report Wizard is the quickest method for creating a grouped report.

1. From the **Create** tab, in the **Reports** group, click the Report Wizard command.
2. In the **Tables/Queries** drop-down box, choose **Query: qrySalesSummary**.

3. Click the Add All button >>.

>

4. Click **Next**. Click **RegionName** and click the Add One button >. This action will group the report by **RegionName**.

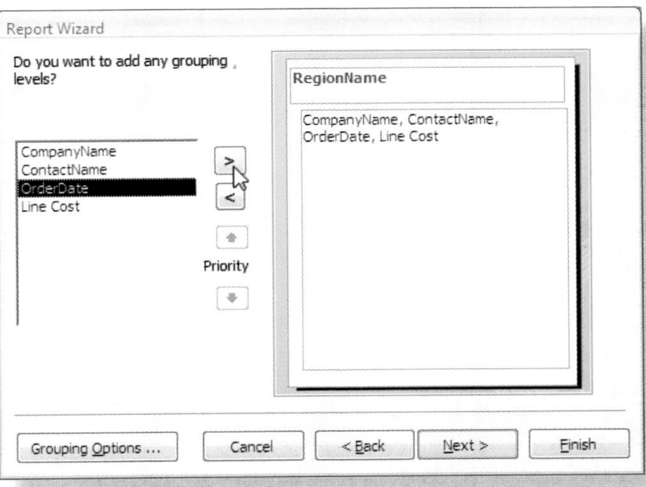

Figure 8-7
Grouping a report in the Report Wizard
CC08.accdb

5. Click **Next**. Click the first combo box drop-down arrow, and select **CompanyName**. The report will be sorted by this field.

6. Click **Summary Options**. You can pick what type of aggregate functions to add to the report.
7. Click the check boxes for **Sum**, and **Calculate percent of total for sums**. Click **OK**.
8. Click **Next**.
9. Your options in the **Layout** section are different because you have added a group to the report. In the **Layout** section, select **Stepped** and in the **Orientation** section, select **Portrait**. Click **Next**.
10. Select **Oriel** as the style. Click **Next**.
11. Modify the title to **rptSalesSummaryByRegion**.
12. Select **Preview the report**, and click **Finish**.
13. Scroll through the report. Notice the functions at the bottom of each **Region Name** grouping.
14. Close **Print Preview**.
15. The report opens in Design View. Notice that there are two new sections in the report: **RegionName Header** and **RegionName Footer**.

Exercise 8-7 ADD A GROUP SECTION IN DESIGN VIEW

A group organizes or categorizes a recordset by a particular field. Grouping allows you to separate records by displaying introductory and summary data. When using more than one group in a report, each subsequent group must be nested in the original group. You can group a report by up to 10 different fields.

1. From the **Design** tab, in the **Grouping & Totals** group, click the Group & Sort command. This action opens the **Group, Sort, and Total** pane.

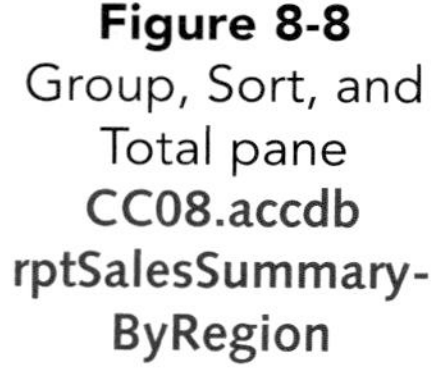

Figure 8-8 Group, Sort, and Total pane CC08.accdb rptSalesSummary-ByRegion

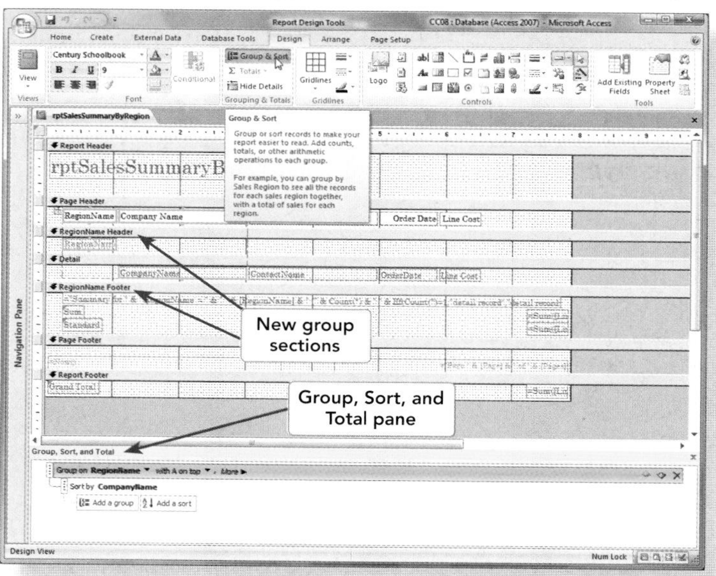

2. In the **Group, Sort, and Total** pane, click the **Sort by** level. Click the **CompanyName** drop-down arrow, and choose **RegionName**.
3. Click the **Add a group** button, and choose **CompanyName**. A new **CompanyName Header** section has been added above the **Detail** section but is empty.

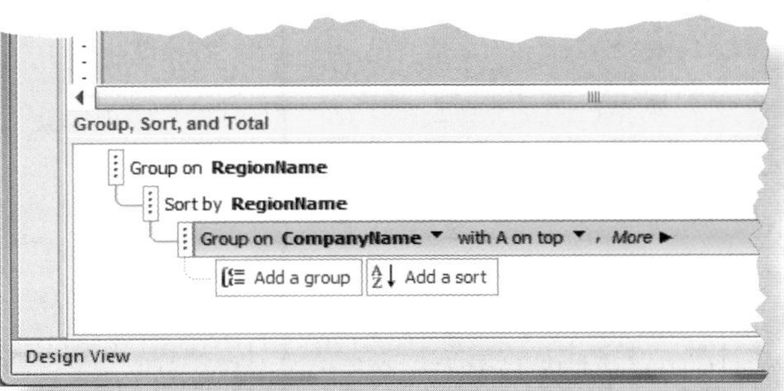

Figure 8-9
Adding a new group to the report
CC08.accdb
rptSalesSummary-ByRegion

4. In the **Detail** section, click **CompanyName**. Make sure that you select only the text box.
5. While pressing Shift, click **ContactName** text box.
6. Right-click the selected text boxes. From the menu, choose **Layout**, then **Move Up a Section**. This action moves the text boxes into the **CompanyName Header** section.
7. Switch to Report View. The first three fields no longer repeat for each record.
8. Press Ctrl+S to save the report.

Exercise 8-8 ADD A GROUP SECTION IN LAYOUT VIEW

You usually use a group header to display identifying labels. Group footers often display summary data such as totals or counts.

1. Switch to Layout View.
2. From the **Group, Sort, and Total** pane, click the **Add a group** button and choose **OrderDate**.
3. From the **Group, Sort, and Total** pane, in the **Group on OrderDate** level, click the **from oldest to newest** drop-down arrow and choose **from newest to oldest**.
4. From the **Group, Sort, and Total** pane, in the **Group on OrderDate** level, click the **by quarter** drop-down arrow and choose **by year**.

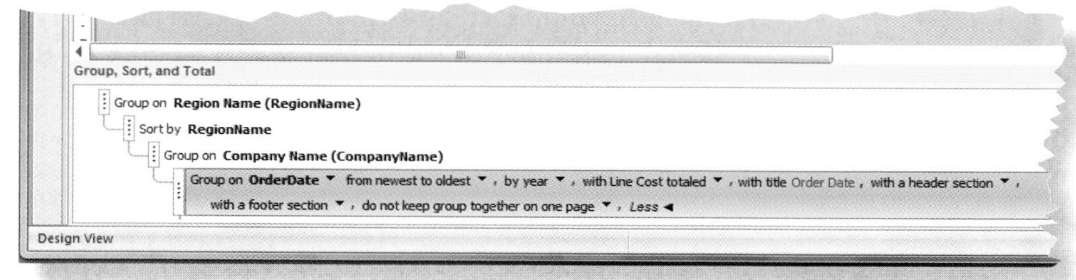

Figure 8-10 Group options for dates CC08.accdb rptSalesSummary-ByRegion

5. There are now two **Order Date** labels. Click the **Order Date** label next to the **Line Cost** label, press Delete.
6. Switch to Report View and review the report. The remaining **Order Date** control is now showing an error.
7. Switch to Design View and then return to Report View. The error is now gone.
8. Press Ctrl+S to save the report.

Exercise 8-9 MODIFY GROUP OPTIONS

The default page break for a report occurs when the text reaches the bottom margin. If you do not want to split a group between pages, you can choose to keep the records together.

1. Switch to Layout View.
2. From the **Group, Sort, and Total** pane, in the **Group on OrderDate** level, click **More**.
3. Click the **with no totals** drop-down arrow. Click the **Total On** drop-down arrow and choose **Line Cost**.

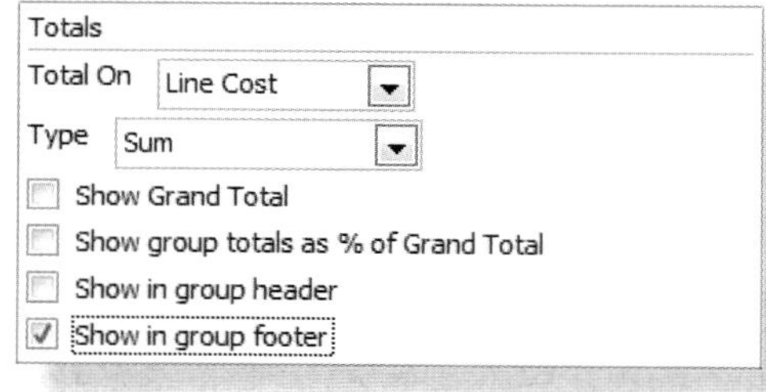

Figure 8-11 Add an aggregate function to a group CC08.accdb rptSalesSummary-ByRegion

4. Click the check box **Show in group footer**.
5. From the **Group, Sort, and Total** pane, in the **Group on RegionName** level, click **More**.
6. In the **with title RegionName** option, click **RegionName**.
7. In the **Zoom** dialog box, add a space between **Region** and **Name**. Click **OK**.
8. From the **Group, Sort, and Total** pane, in the **Group on RegionName** level, click the **do not keep group together on one page** drop-down arrow, and choose **keep header and first record together on one page**.

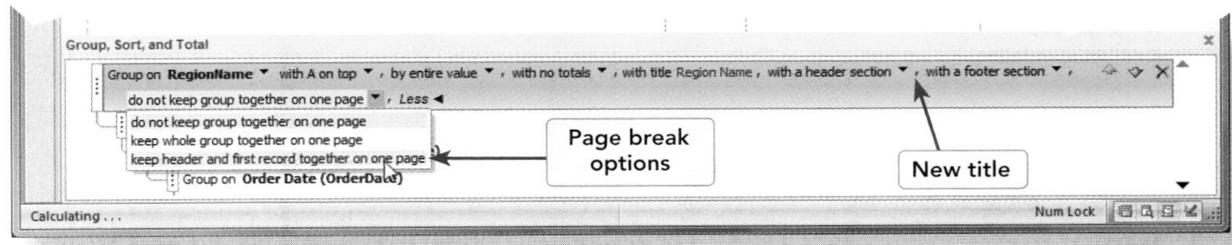

Figure 8-12
Page break options
CC08.accdb
rptSalesSummary-ByRegion

9. Right-click the **rptSalesSummaryByRegion** document tab and choose **Print Preview**. Scroll through the report.
10. Switch to Design View.
11. Press Ctrl+S to save the report.

Exercise 8-10 ADD A COMMON EXPRESSION CONTROL

When you place a summary expression, such as Count(*), in a group footer, the expression only will apply to the group. For example, assume that you create a report with a list of addresses grouped first by state and then by city. Placing the count function in the state group footer will count all records by state. Placing the count function in the city group footer will count all records by city.

1. From the **Design** tab, in the **Grouping & Totals** group, click the Group & Sort command to close the pane.
2. From the **Design** tab, in the **Controls** group, click the Text Box command. In the **Detail** section, click on the 7-inch mark on the horizontal ruler.

3. Drag the new text box to the left until you see the vertical insertion bar on the right side of the **Line Cost** text box. This adds the new control to the Control Layout.

Figure 8-13
Add a new text box
CC08.accdb
rptSalesSummary-ByRegion

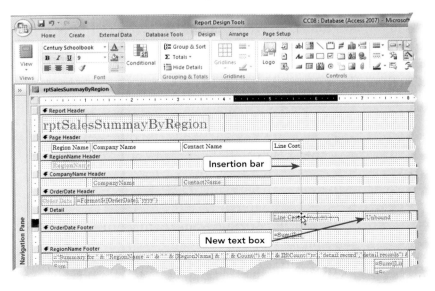

4. Click away from the new control to deselect it.
5. Right-click the new text box. From the menu, choose **Layout**, then **Move Down a Section**. This action moves the text boxes into the **OrderDate Footer** section.
6. From the **Design** tab, in the **Tools** group, click the Property Sheet command .

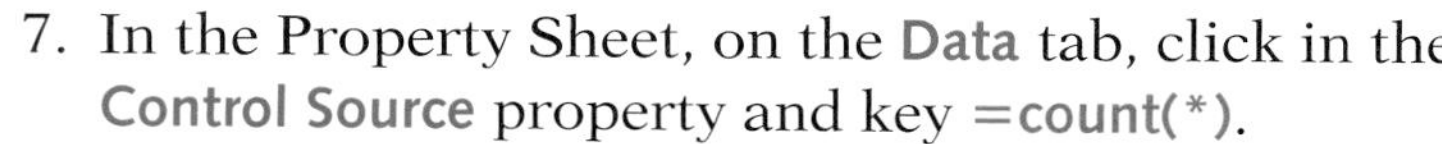

NOTE

The asterisk can be used in the Count function when you need to count just records and not the content of a field.

7. In the Property Sheet, on the **Data** tab, click in the **Control Source** property and key **=count(*)**.
8. Click the new text box's label.
9. In the Property Sheet, on the **Format** tab, click in the **Caption** property and key **Number of Orders**.
10. Close the Property Sheet.
11. Switch to Report View. There is now a Count function at the end of each **Order Date** section.
12. Press Ctrl+S to save the report.

Working with Controls in a Report

A report can contain bound controls, unbound controls, and calculated controls just like a form. In a report, you can move, resize, align, and format controls the same way you did in a form.

Exercise 8-11 MOVE AND RESIZE CONTROLS

Depending on the amount of changes you will need to make to a report, you may find that it will be easier for you to delete a control and then reinsert it rather than move it.

1. Switch to Layout View, and select the **Order Date** control layout.
2. From the **Arrange** tab, in the **Control Layout** group, click the Tabular command . This moves the **Order Date** text box to another section than its label.

3. Drag the **Order Date** control layout to the right and up to **Contact Name** until you see the vertical insertion bar on the right side of the **Contact Name** control.
4. Resize the **Company Name** control to best fit the company "Kadoodles Games and Toys."
5. Resize the **Contact Name** control to best fit the contact "Craig Aspinall Koikas."
6. Resize the **Order Date** control to best fit the label **Order Date**.

7. Resize the **Line Cost** control to best fit the largest number on the column.
8. Resize the **Number of Orders** to fit the label.
9. Switch to Design View.
10. In the **RegionName Footer** section, there is a very long text box with an expression. Drag its right edge to the 7-inch mark.
11. Place your pointer in the horizontal ruler at the 7½-inch mark. When you see a black down arrow, click. This selects four text boxes in the lower right corner of the report.

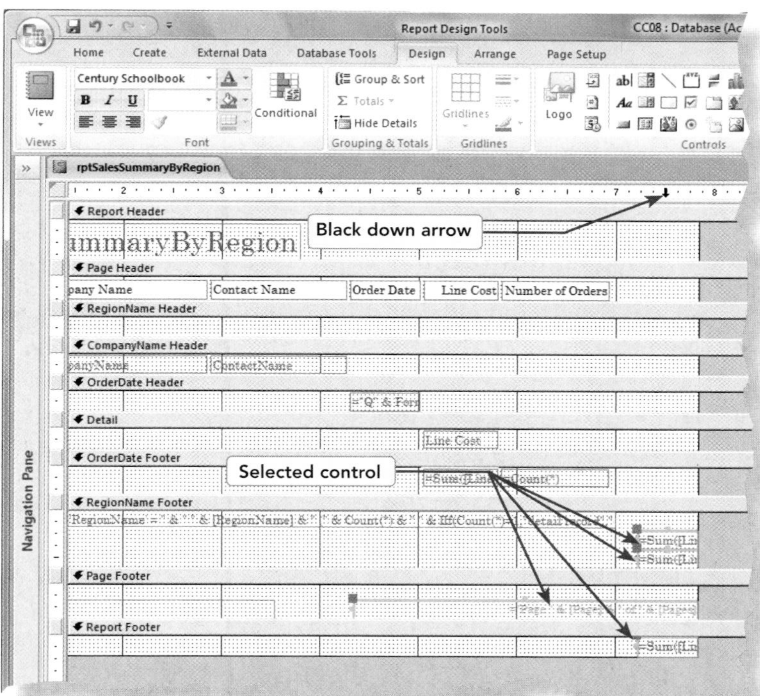

FIGURE 8-14 Selecting multiple controls CC08.accdb rptSalesSummaryByRegion

12. Drag the selected controls to the left until their right edges are at the 7-inch mark. Resize the report to the 7¼-inch mark.
13. Press Ctrl+S to save the report.

Exercise 8-12 ALIGN CONTROLS

When grouping fields in a report, the title of the field by default appears in the group header. When you move a control, such as a title, from one section to another, you will need to align the controls.

1. Switch to Layout View.
2. Click the first year under the **Order Date** label.

3. From the **Format** tab, in the **Font** group, click the Center command.

4. Click the **Line Cost** label.
5. From the **Format** tab, in the **Font** group, click the Center command.
6. Click the number under the **Number of Orders** label.
7. From the **Arrange** tab, in the **Tools** group, click the Property Sheet command.
8. In the Property Sheet, on the **Format** tab, click the **Right Margin** property and key **.5**. Close the Property Sheet.
9. Switch to Design View.
10. In the **RegionName Footer** section, there are three text boxes. Select the two small ones that start with "=Sum([Line..."
11. While pressing Shift, click the text box in the lower right corner of the **Report Footer** section.
12. Drag the left edge of the text boxes to the 6-inch mark.
13. Move the three text boxes to the left so that they are under the **Line Cost** column.
14. In the **Report Header** section, edit the label to **Sales Summary by Regions**.
15. Switch to Layout View.
16. From the **Format** tab, in the **Grouping & Totals** group, click the Hide Details command.

NOTE

To unhide the details, just click the Hide Details command again.

17. Right-click the first number under **Number of Orders**. From the menu, choose **Layout**, then **Move Up a Section**.
18. Switch to Print Preview.

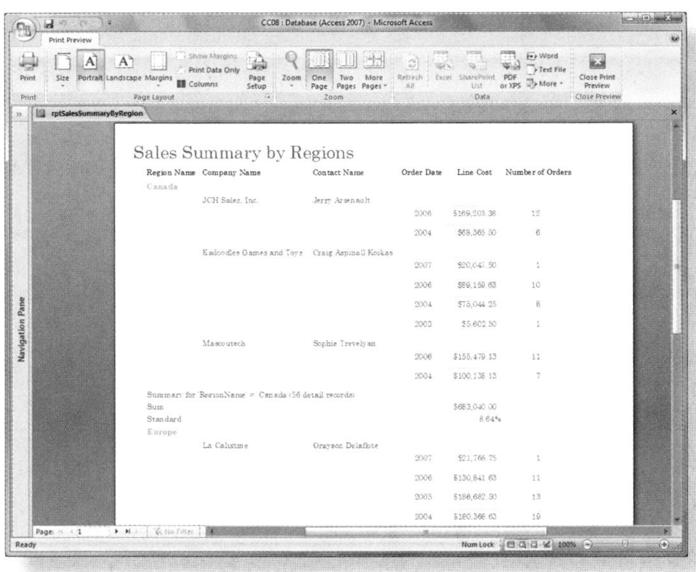

FIGURE 8-15
Report without Detail section hidden
CC08.accdb
rptSalesSummary-ByRegion

19. Press Ctrl+S to save the report.

Exercise 8-13 ADD LINES TO A REPORT

To make a report more visually appealing and distinguish information in each group, you can insert a horizontal line. Lines are added most often to the header sections of a report.

1. Switch to Design View.
2. Drag the top part of the **RegionName Header** section down 1/2 inch.
3. From the **Design** tab, in the **Controls** group, click the Line command.

4. Click under the left edge of the **Region Name** label and drag to the 7 1/4 -inch mark on the horizontal ruler.
5. From the **Design** tab, in the **Tools** group, click the Property Sheet command.
6. On the **Format** tab, click the **Height** property. If you dragged the line control across the page in a straight line, this number would be **0**. If needed, change this property to **0**.
7. Change the **Border Style** property to **Solid**.
8. Click the **Border Width** property, click the drop-down arrow, and choose **4 pt**.
9. Move the line control just below the labels.
10. Drag the top of the **RegionName Header** sections up to just below the line control.
11. Drag the top part of the **Page Footer** section down 1/2 inch.
12. From the **Design** tab, in the **Controls** group, click the Line command.
13. While pressing Shift, click under the left edge of the **Standard** label and drag to the 6-inch mark on the horizontal ruler.
14. In the Property Sheet, on the **Format** tab, set the following properties:

Height	0
Border Style	Dots
Border Width	2 pt

15. Move the line control so that there are two rows of dots below the **Standard** control.
16. Resize the **Page Footer** section so that there are two rows of dots below the line control.
17. Switch to Print Preview.

TIP

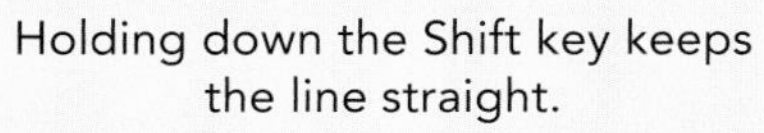

Holding down the Shift key keeps the line straight.

Access 2007

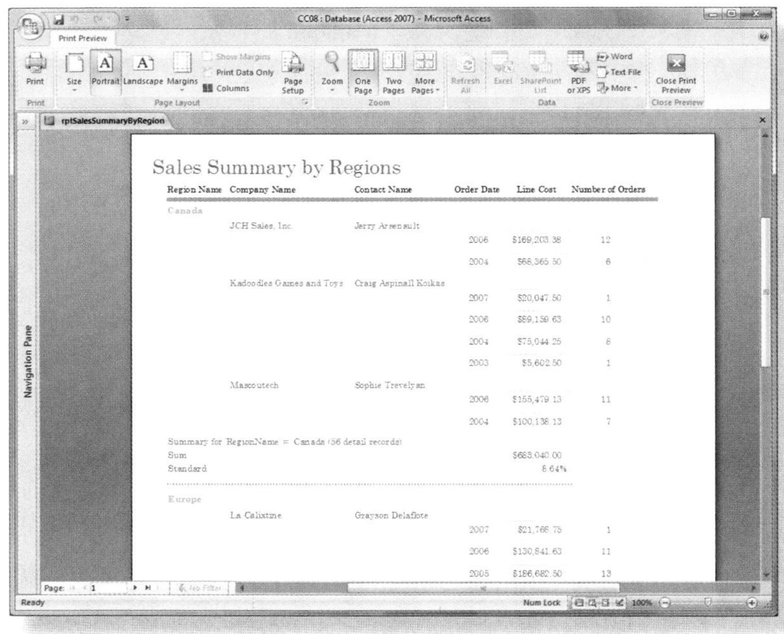

Figure 8-16
Report with lines added
CC08.accdb
rptSalesSummary-ByRegion

18. Press Ctrl+S to save the report.
19. Close Print Preview and switch to Design View.

Exercise 8-14 EDIT COMMON EXPRESSION CONTROLS

The Page Footer has two text boxes that use common expressions to display the date and page number. A common expression is a control with built-in commands to display dates, times, and page numbers.

1. In the **Page Footer** section, click the **=Now()** control. The Property Sheet shows that this is a text box.
2. In the Property Sheet, click the **Data** tab. The **Control Source** for this control is an Access common expression that displays the current date.

Property Sheet
Selection type: Text Box
Text18
Format | Data | Event | Other | All

Control Source	=Now()
Text Format	Plain Text
Running Sum	No
Input Mask	
Enabled	Yes
Smart Tags	

Figure 8-17
The =Now() Property Sheet
CC08.accdb
rptSalesSummary-ByRegion

3. Click the **Format** tab. Click the **Format** property drop-down arrow, and choose **Medium Date**.
4. In the **Page Footer** section, click the page number control.

5. In the Property Sheet, on the **Data** tab, click the **Control Source** property. Click the Build button. The **Expression Builder** shows the Access code for this control.
6. Close the **Expression Builder**, and click the **Format** tab. Change the **Width** property to **1.5**.
7. Close the Property Sheet.
8. Drag the page number control to the 7-inch mark.
9. Switch to Print Preview and review the report.
10. Press Ctrl+S to save the report.

Working with Format Painter and Conditional Formatting

Access has a **Format Painter** like Word and Excel. The *Format Painter* is a tool that copies the font, size, color, and alignment from one control to another. It saves you from having to set the individual properties for each control. To use the **Format Painter**, first select the control that has the desired formatting, click the **Format Painter** button, and then click the control to be changed.

You can also apply conditional formatting. Conditional formatting is formatting that displays in certain conditions, such as a style, color, or other setting. For example, you can set conditional formatting to show values over $15,000 in a different color, bolded, and underlined.

Exercise 8-15 USE THE FORMAT PAINTER

The calculated control should have the same format as the other controls in the **Detail** section. Use the **Format Painter** to match the control characteristics.

1. Switch to Layout View. Select the text box under the label **Region Name** that contains "Canada."
2. From the **Format** tab, in the **Font** group, change the **Font** to **Calibri**.
3. In the **Font** group, change the **Font Size** to **10**.
4. From the **Format** tab, in the **Font** group, double-click the Format Painter command. The pointer changes to an arrow with a paintbrush.
5. Click the first company under the **Company Name** label. The formats are copied.
6. Click the first contact under the **Contact Name** label. Press Esc to cancel the **Format Painter**.
7. Press Ctrl+S to save the report.

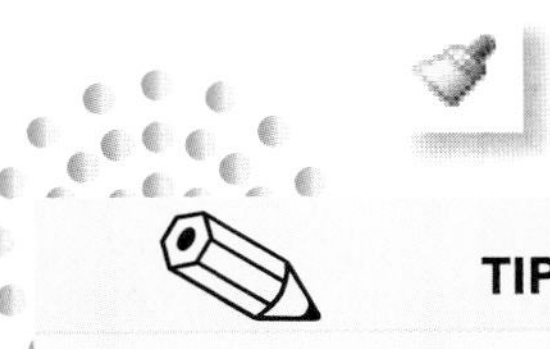

TIP

Clicking the Format Painter command will allow you to format only one other control. Double-clicking the Format Painter command will allow you to format many other controls.

Exercise 8-16 USE CONDITIONAL FORMATTING

Many database designers use conditional formatting to call attention to records that are outside a specified parameter. Often managers use reports to track sales, production, and inventory levels. Conditional formatting helps quickly identify actions that may need to be taken. You can define up to three conditions.

1. Click the first number under the **Line Cost** label.
2. From the **Format** tab, in the **Font** group, click the Conditional command.

3. Press Tab to move to the second combo box. Click the drop-down arrow, and choose **greater than or equal to**.
4. Press Tab and key **100000 (a one and 5 zeros.)**
5. In the bottom set of commands, click the Bold button and the Font Color button and choose the 7th row, 1st column.

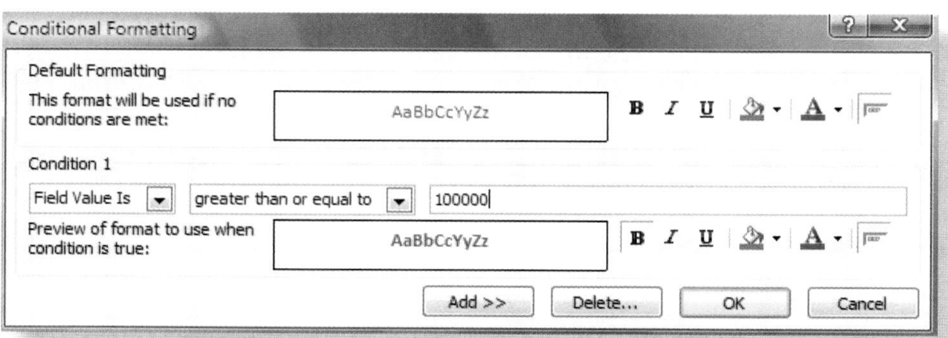

Figure 8-18 Conditional Formatting dialog box **CC08.accdb rptSalesSummary-ByRegion**

6. Click **OK**.
7. Values over $100,000 are now a different color.
8. Save and close the report.

Creating a Multicolumn Report and Labels

In addition to columnar and tabular reports, you can format a report to show the data in more than one column. You can use the Report Wizard or Design View to lay out the fields in a single column. Then use the **Page Setup** command to set the number and width of the printed columns.

You can also create labels using the Label Wizard, an option in the **New Report** dialog box. The Wizard lists common label brands and sizes, including mailing labels, package labels, CD labels, and more.

Exercise 8-17 CREATE A MULTICOLUMN REPORT

When creating a multicolumn report, you must define the number of columns, the number of rows, row spacing, column spacing, column width, and column height.

1. In the Navigation Pane, select **qryStuffedAnimals**.
2. From the **Create** tab, in the **Reports** group, click the Report command.
3. From the Quick Access toolbar, click the Save button. Key **rptMultiCol**.
4. Resize the **Product Code** control to just fit its label.
5. Resize the **Product ID** control to just fit its label.
6. Resize the **Product Name** controls to just fit the data.

NOTE

You can only see multiple columns in Print Preview.

7. Resize the **Unit Price** control to just fit its label.
8. Switch to Design View. In the **Detail** section, the **Picture** control's right edge, needs to be at 5 inches or less on the horizontal ruler.

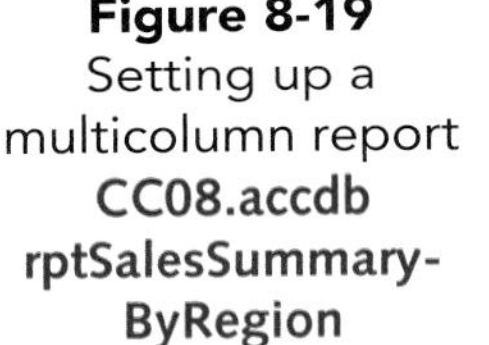

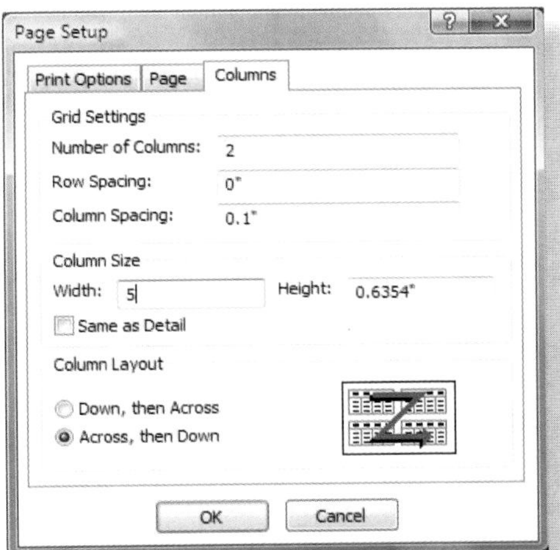

Figure 8-19 Setting up a multicolumn report **CC08.accdb rptSalesSummary-ByRegion**

9. From the **Page Setup** tab, in the **Page Layout** group, click the Landscape command.
10. From the **Page Setup** tab, in the **Page Layout** group, click the Columns command.
11. Set the **Number of Columns** to **2** and the **Column Spacing** to **.1**.
12. Set the **Column Size Width** to **5**.
13. Click **OK**. Switch to Print Preview and view both pages.
14. Close and save the report.

Exercise 8-18 CREATE PACKAGE LABELS

The Label Wizard assists you in creating package labels. After you select a label type and size, the Label Wizard asks which fields to place on the label, which font to use, and how to sort the labels.

1. In the Navigation Pane, select **tblStuffedAnimals**.

2. From the **Create** tab, in the **Reports** group, click the Labels command.

3. In the Label Wizard dialog box, in the Filter by manufacturer section, choose Avery.
4. In the Unit of Measure section, choose English. In the Label Type section, choose Sheet Feed.
5. In the top list box, choose the Product number "8164." Click Next.
6. Set the Font name to Times New Roman, the Font size to 14, the Font weight to Normal, and the Text color to black. Click Next.
7. Key Product ID: and press the spacebar twice.
8. In the Available fields section, double-click **ProductID** to place it in the Prototype label section.
9. Press Enter twice to leave a blank line in the Prototype label section.
10. Key Product Name, and press the spacebar twice. Double-click **ProductName**. Press Enter twice.
11. Key Product Group, and press the spacebar twice. Double-click **ProductGroup**.

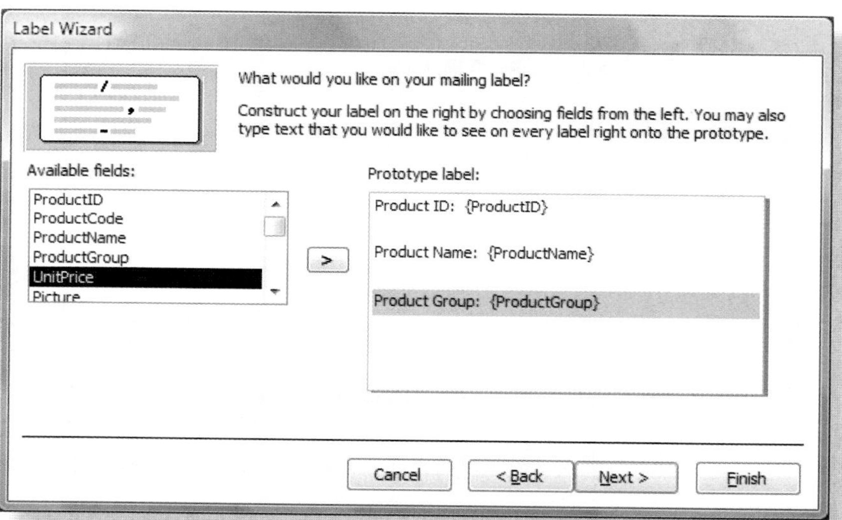

Figure 8-20
Prototype for large labels
CC08.accdb
rptAnimalLabels

12. Click Next. In the next dialog box, double-click **ProductID** to add it to the Sort by section. Click Next.
13. Edit the report name to rptAnimalLabels. Select the option Modify the label design. Click Finish.
14. Switch to Design View.

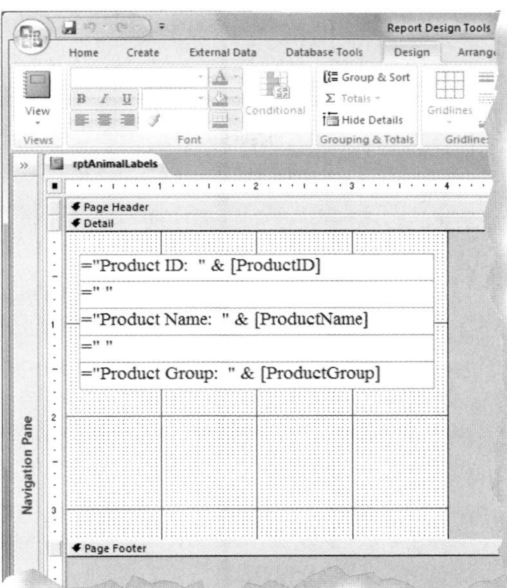

Figure 8-21
Design View for large labels
CC08.accdb
rptAnimalLabels

15. From the **Page Setup** tab, in the **Page Layout** group, click the Columns command. Notice the **Number of Columns** is set to 2. Click **OK**.
16. Right-click the **rptAnimalLabel** document's tab, and choose **Print Preview**.
17. If a warning message appears, just click **OK**.
18. View all four pages.
19. Close Print Preview. Close and save the report.
20. Compact and repair the database, and then close it.

Lesson 8 Summary

- A well-designed report can present information more effectively than other major objects can.
- Columnar style reports are most commonly used when the length of the data is too wide to display properly in tabular format.
- Depending on the report tool selected, the created report may have header and footer sections in addition to the detail section
- A Report tool is the quickest method to create a basic report.
- Before printing a report, it is good practice to view the report in Print Preview. In Print Preview, you can change the zoom size.
- When adding fields through Layout View, you will see a Field List pane.
- Padding specifies space between gridlines and controls. Margins specify the location of information in a control
- Reports can have numerous sections, including headers and footers.
- A group organizes or categorizes a recordset by a particular field. Groups can be nested up to 10 deep.
- The properties of controls can be modified.
- Simple reports can be created using the Report Wizard. A basic report can be created using the Report tool.
- Horizontal lines in a report can be created, moved, or resized, just like any other object.
- In a tabular report, each record displays on a separate line.
- Section properties can be viewed and modified in the Property Sheet.

- Group sections can organize and summarize information on the basis of categories.
- When adding or moving fields in a report, care should be given to aligning other controls in the header or footer to match the detail section.
- Controls should be sized and aligned to make the report easy to read.
- The date and page number are common controls created by the Report Wizard.
- The Property Sheet for each object in a report lists all the characteristics or attributes of that object.
- Calculated controls display the results of a numeric expression based on one or more fields in a record.
- Conditional formatting applies the property only when certain conditions are met.
- Records in a multicolumn report or label display in two or more columns.
- The Label Wizard can create non-standard labels.

LESSON 8		Command Summary	
Feature	**Button**	**Path**	**Keyboard**
Reports, Wizard		Create, Reports, Report Wizard	
Reports, Preview, Multiple Pages		Print Preview, Zoom, More Pages	
Reports, Create, Basic		Create, Reports, Report	
Reports, View, Report View		Formatting, Views, Report View	
Reports, Add Fields		Formatting, Controls, Add Existing Fields	
Control, Property Sheet		Arrange, Tools, Property Sheet	
Reports, Group and Sort		Design, Grouping & Totals, Group & Sort	
Reports, Grouping & Totals		Design, Grouping & Totals	
Line, Add		Design, Controls, Line	
Reports, Label		Create, Reports, Labels	

Word Index

D

E

F

G

H

I

J

K

L

Q

R

S

Excel Index

Symbols

A

B

C

G

H

I

PowerPoint Index

D

E

F

M

N

O

P

T

Access Index

G

H

I

J

K

L

M

N

O

P

Q

S

T

U

V

W

X

Y

Z